THEOLOGICAL DICTIONARY

OF THE

NEW TESTAMENT

EDITED BY

GERHARD FRIEDRICH

Translator and Editor

GEOFFREY W. BROMILEY, D. LITT., D. D.

Volume IX

Φ—Ω

WM. B. EERDMANS PUBLISHING COMPANY

GRAND RAPIDS, MICHIGAN

THEOLOGICAL DICTIONARY OF THE NEW TESTAMENT

Translated from
THEOLOGISCHES WÖRTERBUCH ZUM NEUEN TESTAMENT
Neunter Band: Φ-Ω, herausgegeben von Gerhard Friedrich

Published by
W. KOHLHAMMER VERLAG
Stuttgart, Germany

ISBN 0-8028-2322-X

First Printing, March 1974
Second Printing, February 1975

PHOTOLITHOPRINTED BY CUSHING - MALLOY, INC.
ANN ARBOR, MICHIGAN, UNITED STATES OF AMERICA

Preface

We are now pleased to present the final volume of the Theological Dictionary of the New Testament. When G. Kittel began work on the Dictionary in 1928 he projected two volumes and believed that with the help of fifteen colleagues it could be finished within the space of three years. He was just as wrong as J. Grimm was when he planned his dictionary in seven volumes and hoped that it would be completed in seven years. The Theological Dictionary of the New Testament has grown to nine volumes, publication has taken forty-five years, and instead of fifteen colleagues there have been one hundred and five contributors. Many who read the first sections as students began to ask rather anxiously through the years whether they would live to see the whole work. Of the extended circle of authors fifty have died during the period 1930-1973. When Kittel summoned me to his own deathbed in 1948, and committed the future of the Dictionary to me in spite of my resistance, he laid great stress on the fact that a younger New Testament scholar should take up the work in order that he might have a chance to complete it.

Now at last the end has come and the editor and his many co-workers can breathe more freely. During the last twenty-five years I have often been reminded of the truth of the saying *quem dii oderunt, lexicographum fecerunt,* and more than once I have had actual experience of it.

Those who compare the first volume of the Theological Dictionary with the later ones will see that the basic conception, namely, the arrangement of the material by stems, has been maintained, but that there has been considerable change in the execution of individual articles. Etymological discussion has been considerably reduced. The New Testament is no longer taken as a unity as it often was in the earlier articles. Greater distinction has been made between the Gospels and Epistles, within the Gospels between Mark, the Sayings Source, and Luke, and within the Epistles between Paul and the rest of the Pauline Corpus. Closer attention has also been paid to the context in which the words are used, which has added a great deal to the scope of the individual articles. Discussion of Gnosticism has also been given a bigger place in the post-New Testament sections than it was previously.

As editor, I must not fail in this final volume to thank my editorial assistants for their unselfish work. I mention G. Bertram, P. Boendermaker, E. Dammann, J. Denker, A. Dihle, G. Fohrer, E. P. O. Gooding, H. Hammerich, A. Hiller, G. Kelber, H. Krämer, T. H. Mahnke, C. F. D. Moule, E. Nestle, K. Reinhardt, K. H. Rengstorf, E. Risch, K. H. Schelkle, G. Schlichting, W. Schneemelcher, K. Staab and H. Traub.

God has called from their labours O. Bauernfeind, E. Nestle, G. von Rad and J. Schneider, who were closely associated with the Theological Dictionary from its earliest beginnings.

G. Friedrich

Kiel, March 6 1973.

Editor's Preface

This final volume of the Theological Dictionary is published in the hope that it will serve the church both by stimulating scholars and also by deepening and enriching the work of preachers and teachers.

Some peculiar problems have arisen in the closing stages of the volume due to catching up with the original. First proofs of the German have had to be used in the last hundred pages and breaks have been unavoidable in translation, printing, and proof-correcting. If readers find traces of the difficulties in the text, we beg their indulgence.

Through the years those who have used the Dictionary have brought to light not a few errors of greater or lesser consequence and notification of others will be welcomed and acted upon at the first opportunity.

The diligent labours of Professor F. F. Bruce with the proofs again call for a special word of thanks, the more so as he has combined this exacting work with many other notable contributions to New Testament scholarship.

At the end of so monumental a task it is perhaps permissible to pay tribute also to the printers, who wrestled manfully with difficult materials and manuscripts, and to the publishers, whose courage in undertaking the work has been equalled only by their patience in seeing it through.

G. W. Bromiley

Pasadena, California, Easter 1973.

Contents

Page

Contributors

Editor:

Gerhard Friedrich, Kiel.

Contributors:

Horst Balz, Kiel.
Georg Bertram, Giessen.
Otto Betz, Tübingen.
Georg Braumann, Waldeck.
Rudolf Bultmann, Marburg.
Hans Conzelmann, Göttingen.
Gerhard Delling, Halle.
Albert Dihle, Cologne.
Gottfried Fitzer, Vienna.
Walter Grundmann, Jena and Eisenach.
Günther Harder, Berlin-Zehlendorf.
Martin Hengel, Tübingen.
Franz Hesse, Münster.
Edmond Jacob, Strassburg.
Marinus de Jonge, Leiden.
Gerhard Kelber, Schweinfurt.
Helmut Köster, Harvard University, USA.
Eduard Lohse, Hanover.
Ulrich Luck, Bethel.
Dieter Lührmann, Heidelberg.
Christian Maurer, Bern.
Rudolf Meyer, Jena.
Otto Michel, Tübingen.
Bo Reicke, Basel.
Eduard Schweizer, Zürich.
Gustav Stählin, Mainz.
Karl-Wolfgang Tröger, Berlin.
Günther Wanke, Erlangen.
Konrad Weiss, Rostock.
Ulrich Wilckens, Hamburg.
Adam Simon van der Woude, Groningen.
Walther Zimmerli, Göttingen.

---

† φαίνω, † φανερός, φανερόω, † φανέρωσις,
† φαντάζω, † φάντασμα, † ἐμφανίζω,
† ἐπιφαίνω, † ἐπιφανής, † ἐπιφάνεια

---

† φαίνω.

1. The act. φαίνω [1] is found both in the trans. sense "to manifest," "to show" from Hom. Il., 2, 324; Od., 3, 173 etc. and also in the intr. sense "to shine," "to gleam," from Hom. Od., 7, 102; 19, 25; Plat. Tim., 39 b; Theocr., 2, 11 etc. From Hom., e.g., Il., 8, 556 one finds the mid./pass. deponent φαίνομαι for "to shine," "to gleam," esp. "to light up," "to arise and shine," of heavenly bodies, of persons "to become visible," "to show oneself," e.g., Aesch. Choeph., 143; cf. Hom. Il., 15, 275; Luc. Dial. Mortuorum, 23, 3, or "to appear as something," "to make a show," Xenoph. Cyrop., I, 4, 19, gen. "to appear," e.g., in a dream, Hdt., VII, 16γ, of strange phenomena, Hom. Hymn. Bacch., 2. In philosophy the ref. of φαίνομαι is to sense perception, Aristot. Phys., III, 5, p. 204b, 35; Cael., IV, 5, p. 312b, 30; the part denotes what is visible on earth as distinct from what is invisible, e.g., Plat. Resp., X, 596e, cf. Philo Rer. Div. Her., 270. In the Platonic dialogues φαίνεται is used for a weak form of affirmation, Plat. Prot., 332e; Resp., I, 333c etc., while in the koine it approximates to δοκέω (→ II, 232, 29 ff.), as in the use with the dat. of person, Pap. Cairo Zeno, I, 59044, 7, 16 (3rd cent. B.C.); [2] P. Oxy., IV, 811 (1 A.D.); Dion. Hal. Ant. Rom., 2, 14, 4.

2. In the NT the act. φαίνω occurs only intr. in the sense "to shine" of the sun in Rev. 1:16, the sun and moon in Rev. 21:23, [3] the lamp Jn. 5:35; 2 Pt. 1:19; Rev. 18:23 vl. [4] φαίνω can also be used of the day and even of the night as it is lit up by the moon and stars, Rev. 8:12. If it is always used here in the lit. sense, it is fig. or metaphorical at Jn. 1:5: τὸ φῶς ἐν τῇ σκοτίᾳ φαίνει (→ VII, 443, 17 ff.) and 1 Jn. 2:8: τὸ φῶς τὸ ἀληθινὸν ἤδη φαίνει. φαίνομαι is far more common. This, too, is often used lit. for "to shine," "to light up," "to rise and shine," e.g., the star in Mt. 2:7, stars in Phil. 2:15 (fig.), lightning Mt. 24:27; the light of the lamp Rev.

φ α ί ν ω κ τ λ.   Note: This group was originally assigned to R. Bultmann but D. Lührmann has expanded the MS and prepared it for publication.

Bibl. Liddell-Scott, Pr.-Bauer, s.v.

[1] The Gk. stem φαν- is obviously an ancient extension of φᾱ-, Indo-Eur. *bhā, which can mean both "to illumine" ("to make visible") and also "to speak" ("to make audible"), cf. Gk. φημί, lat. fārī. Cf. Pokorny, I, 105f. and also Boisacq, Hofmann, s.v. [Risch] → VI, 783f., n.7.

[2] Ed. C. C. Edgar, Zenon Pap., Cat. Général des Antiquités Egypt. du Musée du Caire, 79 (1925).

[3] Cf. πειθαρχεῖ σελήνη νυκτὶ φαίνειν κελεύοντι, Dg., 7, 2.

[4] One finds the same usage in the LXX at Ex. 25:37; 1 Macc. 4:50.

18:23 vl. But much more common is the gen. sense "to be visible, manifest" Jm. 4:14, [5] or quite unemphatically "to occur" in Mt. 9:33; 1 Pt. 4:18. Another common sense of φαίνομαι is "to become visible," "to show oneself"; in this case the distinction between manifestation for optical perception and for spiritual perception is fluid, cf. the former in Mt. 13:26 [6] and the latter in R. 7:13; 2 Cor. 13:7. [7] Eschatological manifestation is the point in Mt. 24:30 → VII, 236, 18 ff. [8] The ref. is to dream phenomena in Mt. 1:20; 2:13, 19, [9] to miraculous phenomena in Lk. 9:8, and esp. to the appearance of the Risen Lord in Mk. 16:9. [10] In a transf. use φαίνομαι can also mean "to appear," "to make the impression." [11] Impersonally it then means "to strike," "to look," [12] e.g., Mk. 14:64: τί ὑμῖν φαίνεται (vl. δοκεῖ). But in the sense of δοκέω, φαίνομαι can also mean "to look as though," [13] Mt. 23:27 f.; Lk. 24:11. [14] Related is the sense "to represent oneself," "to give the appearance," Mt. 6:16, 18, abs. 6:5. The only NT instance of the dualistic distinction between visible on earth and invisible is at Hb. 11:3. [15]

† φανερός.

1. The adj. is found from Pind. Olymp., 7, 56; 13, 98 etc. and cf. Hdt., II, 130, 1; 155, 3; 156, 1; III, 24, 3; 47, 3; IV, 30, 1. [1] The basic sense is "visible" φανερὸς ὄμμασιν ἐμοῖς, Eur. Ba., 501, "manifest," opp. ἀφανής "invisible," "hidden" ὑπὲρ τῶν ἀφανῶν τοῖς φανεροῖς μαρτυρίοις χράομαι, Aristot. Eth. Nic., II, 2, p. 1104a, 13; [2] of a person "outstanding," "distinguished," e.g., Hdt., II, 146, 1; Xenoph. Cyrop., VII, 5, 58. With verbs one finds φανερός εἰμι with part., Hdt., III, 26, 1; VII, 18, 4, and φανερὸς γίγνομαι, Xenoph. Cyrop., II, 2, 12. The neutr. τὸ φανερόν as noun "publicity" is found in the combination εἰς τὸ φανερὸν φέρω, Hyperides Or., 1, 13, 11 f. [3] The adv. φανερῶς means "visibly," "publicly," e.g., Hdt., IX, 71, 3; Plat. Symp., 182d.

2. In the NT φανερός always has the original sense and is not a theological term even though found in important theological connections. The primary reference is to what is visible to sensory perception, e.g., R. 2:28, where the ἐν τῷ φανερῷ Ἰουδαῖος and ἐν τῷ φανερῷ ἐν σαρκὶ περιτομή stand in juxtaposition to ἐν τῷ

---

[5] Cf. the same sense in ὃν τρόπον... τὸ σῶμα φαίνεται... ἡ ψυχὴ... δῆλος ἔστω, 2 Cl., 12, 4; also Ign. Tr., 4, 2; R., 3, 2; Herm. v., 3, 2, 6; s., 8, 2, 8; more emphatic Ign. Mg., 3, 1; Herm. s., 3, 2 f.

[6] Cf. Ign. Sm., 8, 2.

[7] Ign. Tr., 11, 2.

[8] Cf. also Did., 16, 6; 2 Cl., 16, 3; Ign. Eph., 15, 3.

[9] Cf. the same usage in the vision at Herm. v., 1, 4, 3.

[10] To the extent that Jesus' earthly manifestation is viewed as a miracle φαίνομαι can be used of this too, Barn., 14, 5; Ign. Mg., 6, 1; Dg., 11, 2-4, cf. ἐπιφάνεια (→ 10, 12 ff.). While first used of the future eschatological appearance of Jesus, it can be used of His earthly appearance as well.

[11] Of pers. Ign. Mg., 4; Tr., 2, 1; things Herm. v., 3, 2, 6; s., 8, 3, 1, cf. 9, 9, 7: ἐφαίνετο... ἐδόκει.

[12] Herm. v., 2, 3, 4; Ign. Mg., 7, 1; Sm., 11, 3.

[13] In this sense one finds it with antonym εἶναι, Aristoph. Ach., 441 and par. δοκέω, Eur. Hipp. 1071.

[14] Cf. Did., 16, 4.

[15] In this sense Ign. R., 3, 2 f.; Ign. Pol., 2, 2.

φ α ν ε ρ ό ς. [1] Pr.-Bauer, s.v.

[2] Cf. φανερά (sc. οὐσία) "landed property" with opp. ἀφανὴς οὐσία "personal property" Lys., 32, 4 and ἀργύριον φανερόν "money," Demosth. Or., 56, 1.

[3] Ed. C. Jensen (1917), 9.

κρυπτῷ Ἰουδαῖος and περιτομὴ καρδίας (→ VI, 82, 26 ff.), cf. the textus receptus of Mt. 6:4, 6, 18. In this sense of "visible," "manifest," φανερός, as in both Greek and the LXX, is often linked with εἰμί (R. 1:19; Gl. 5:19; 1 Tm. 4:15) or this must be supplied as in Ac. 4:16 (D reads φανερώτερόν ἐστιν). In such cases the reference is still to what can be perceived by the senses but in such a way that the perception involves understanding. While the transition is fluid, sensory perception no longer plays any part at 1 Jn. 3:10: ἐν τούτῳ φανερά ἐστιν τὰ τέκνα τοῦ θεοῦ καὶ τὰ τέκνα τοῦ διαβόλου. [4] If there is emphasis on what has not been seen thus far, or on what is hidden, φανερός takes on the nuance of "manifest," "revealed," as in the combinations εἰς φανερὸν ἔρχομαι (Mk. 4:22 and par.), φανερὸν ποιέω (Mk. 3:12 and par.) [5] and φανερὸς γίνομαι (Lk. 8:17a). φανερὸς γίνομαι also occurs in the sense "to come to light," "to become known" (Mk. 6:14; Ac. 7:13; 1 C. 11:19; 14:25; Phil. 1:13) [6] with no stress on sensory perception; this combination is particularly used for eschatological manifestation, 1 C. 3:13. [7]

The adv. φανερῶς occurs in the sense "publicly" so that people can see (Mk. 1:45; Jn. 7:10), [8] where the opp. is ἐν κρυπτῷ (→ V, 880, 14 ff.). It bears the sense of "plainly" at Ac. 10:3. [9]

† φανερόω.

A. Outside the New Testament.

The verb is probably a Hell. construct, for the only class. instance ἐφανερώθη ἐς τοὺς Ἕλληνας πάντας δαπάνῃσι μεγίστῃσι, Hdt., VI, 122, 1 occurs in only one part of the tradition. [1] Examples in Gk. before and outside the NT are not very numerous: Ἰερ. 40:6 for נגלה, [2] elsewhere transl. ἀποκαλύπτω (→ III, 576, 41 ff.); Dion. Hal. Ant. Rom., 10, 37; 1; Dio C., 59, 18, 2; 66, 16, 1 vl.; 77, 15, 1; Philo Leg. All., III, 47; Jos. Ant., 20, 76; Vit., 231; Corp. Herm., 4, 6; 5, 1 (twice). 9. 11; 11, 22; Joseph and Aseneth, 12. [3] As a denominative verb of φανερός (→ 2, 15 ff.) in -όω it has causative significance [4] "to make visible what is invisible," e.g., ὁ ποιήσας τὰ πάντα καὶ φανερώσας τὰ ἀφανῆ, Joseph and Aseneth (→ n. 3), 12 (p. 54, 24), cf. Corp. Herm., 5, 1. 9. 11, while the pass. means "to become visible," "to be revealed," e.g., καὶ τὰ μὲν τῇ βουλῇ δόξαντα ἄλλως ἐφανεροῦντο, Dio. C., 59, 18, 2, "to appear" (opp. "to be hidden,"

---

[4] Cf. the quotation of Mt. 12:33 in Ign. Eph., 14, 2, though here we find φανερόν (sc. ἐστιν) for γινώσκεται.

[5] Cf. φανεροποιέω in 1 Cl., 60, 1.

[6] Cf. ... ἐστὶν φανερά of the allegorical meaning of the OT, Barn., 8, 7.

[7] Cf. Herm. s., 9, 12, 3. The fut. of εἰμί can, of course, be used for γίνομαι, cf. Is. 64:1; Hem. m., 9, 10 and eschatologically s., 4, 3 f.

[8] Cf. Ign. Phld., 6, 3 with opp. λάθρα.

[9] Cf. Barn., 13, 4; Dg., 11, 2.

φ α ν ε ρ ό ω. R. Bultmann, "Der Begriff d. Offenbarung im NT," *Glauben u. Verstehen*, III (1960), 1-34; D. Lührmann, "Das Offenbarungsverständnis bei Pls. u. in paul. Gemeinden," *Wissenschaftliche Monographien zum AT u. NT*, 16 (1965); H. Schulte, "Der Begriff d. Offenbarung im NT," *Beiträge z. Evangel. Theol.*, 13 (1949).

[1] For another view cf. M. Pohlenz, *Herodot²* (1961), 47, n. 1.

[2] The ref. here is to revelation by God, whereas HT Jer. 33:6 speaks only of the opening of the wealth of perpetual salvation, cf. A. Weiser, *Die Ps., AT Deutsch* 14/15⁷ (1966), ad loc. [Bertram].

[3] Ed. P. Batiffol, *Studia Patristica* (1889/90), 52, 24.

[4] Cf. E. Fascher, "Deus invisibilis," *Festschr. R. Otto, Marburger Theol. Stud.*, 1 (1931), 72.

"to be invisible"), e.g., φανερῶν αὐτὸς οὐ φανεροῦται, Corp. Herm., 5, 1. The only instance of the reflexive is at Philo Leg. All., III, 47: πολλοῖς γὰρ οὐκ ἐφανέρωσεν ἑαυτόν (sc. θεός). [5]

B. In the New Testament.

As compared with the few examples before and outside NT Greek, it is striking how common the verb is in the NT and early Christian writings.

1. Mk. 4:22 has the sound of a proverbial saying, [6] cf. the Q version in Lk. 12:2 and par., which also influenced Lk. 8:17 (→ 3, 11). In the present context of Mk. 4, however, the statement has in view the hidden meaning of parables (cf. 4:11).

2. Paul uses φανερόω and ἀποκαλύπτω synonymously. [7] This may be seen especially in a comparison of R. 1:17 and 3:21. Only in 1 C. 4:5, an apocryphal quotation (→ VII, 442, 10 ff.), and R. 1:19 do we detect in the usage the sense "to make visible." In the other references the main point is revelation in the Gospel. The reflexive is never used; specific things are always revealed. R. 3:21 repeats 1:17, but with the perfect πεφανέρωται for the present ἀποκαλύπτεται. Yet this does not denote a specific time in the past; the reference is to a once and for all: the justification grounded in the Christ event (cf. R. 3:24-26; 1:3 f.) is now a reality for πίστις. The frequent use of φανερόω in 2 C. is surprising (9 times). It occurs in the polemical sections. Paul is perhaps adopting here a term of his opponents. [8] He uses it for revelation as this takes place in his preaching (2 C. 2:14; 11:6) [9] and indeed his very existence (4:10 f.). [10] In spite of the eschatological qualification (cf. 5:10) this revelation is definitive, 5:11.

3. Elsewhere in the Pauline corpus the situation is the same: ἀποκαλύπτω and φανερόω are used synonymously (cf. Eph. 3:5 with Col. 1:26), and we also find γνωρίζω (→ I, 718, 4 ff.). [11] Revelation takes place in proclamation (Col. 1:25 f.; 4:4; R. 16:25-27). But now the connection with light categories plays a bigger part (Eph. 5:13 f., cf. 3:9), and we also find the antithesis revelation/concealment (Col. 3:3 f.), especially in the form of the revelation schema. [12] This schema, which derives from pre-Pauline tradition [13] in which apocalyptic and Gnostic elements are intermingled, becomes the sustaining theologoumenon (Col. 1:26 f.; Eph. 3:4 f., 9 f.; R. 16:25-27). It speaks of the salvation-bringing mediation of proclamation by specific

---

[5] Schulte, 67-84 tries to prove that φανερόω is a special Gnostic term. But there is nothing specifically Gnostic about the instances before and outside the NT, which are in any case very few.

[6] Bultmann Trad., 84.

[7] Lührmann, 160.

[8] Schulte, 21; E. Güttgemanns, "Der leidende Apostel u. sein Herr," FRL, 90 (1966), 107, n. 75.

[9] τὴν γνῶσιν is to be supplied.

[10] Note the intensification from σῶμα to σάρξ.

[11] Cf. Eph. 3:5, 10; R. 9:22 f. ἀποκαλύπτω does not occur at all in Col.

[12] Cf. on this Bultmann Theol.[5], 107; N. A. Dahl, "Formgeschichtliche Beobachtungen zur Christusverkündigung in d. Gemeindepredigt," Festschr. R. Bultmann, ZNW Beih., 21[2] (1957),, 4 f.; Lührmann, 124-133.

[13] The only earlier instance in Paul is at 1 C. 2:6 ff., as against H. Conzelmann, "Pls. u. d. Weisheit," NTSt, 12 (1965/66), 239; otherwise the tensions in the text make no sense.

bearers of revelation. [14] In a free form we find it in the Pastorals (2 Tm. 1:10 → 10, 4 ff.; Tt. 1:2 f.) and also in 1 Jn. 1:2 → line 18 ff. The schema is understood christologically in 1 Pt. 1:18-20. With the hymn in 1 Tm. 3:16 this passage is the only one in the Pauline tradition in which φανερόω is applied to a past revelation that has taken place in Christ. [15]

4. In the Johannine writings ἀποκαλύπτω (→ III, 587, 36 ff.) does not occur until the OT quotation from Is. 53:1 in Jn. 12:38, but φανερόω is very common, and as in the later Pauline corpus (→ 4, 23 f.) γνωρίζω is a synon., cf. Jn. 17:6 with 17:26. [16] A difference from Paul (→ 4, 10 ff.) is that the derivation from φανερός is now more significant. There is a manifestation before all eyes (Jn. 7:4). Jesus discloses the divine reality, the name of God (17:6) and the works of God (3:21; 9:3). According to John all Jesus' work may be called revelation (cf. 2:11), as the Prologue shows already even though φανερόω is not used (but cf. φαίνω in 1:5 → 1, 23 f.). Indirectly the divine reality is also revealed in the witness, e.g., of John the Baptist, 1:31. In the supplementary chapter (21:1, 14) φανερόω refers to the appearances of the Risen Lord; the only other instance of this is in the secondary Marcan ending, 16:12, 14.

The work of Jesus is described as revelation in 1 Jn. 3:5, 8. It is the revelation of God's love in 4:9, cf. Jn. 3:16. If the goal is that we may have life (4:9), the whole revelation can also be summed up in ζωή, 1:2. It is also the content of the λόγος τῆς ζωῆς, 1:1. If the introduction to 1 Jn. clearly echoes the Prologue to the Gospel, λόγος here (→ IV, 127, 20 ff.) means — or at least includes — proclamation or the tradition [17] in which the revelation of the divine reality continues as a possibility of participation in it. Finally 1 Jn., in contrast to the Gospel, can also use the verb for a revelation which is yet to come, 2:28; 3:2. [18]

5. In Rev. the pass. of φανερόω occurs twice: "to become visible" with no theological significance at 3:18, and in a hymn: ὅτι τὰ δικαιώματά σου ἐφανερώθησαν at 15:4. [19]

C. The Post-Apostolic Fathers.

Ign. adopts the revelation schema in Eph., 19, 2 f.; for him it is fulfilled in Christ. [20] Revelation breaks the eternal silence, 19, 1; Mg., 8, 2, cf. Paul in R. 16:25 f. 2 Cl., 14, 2 f., adopting the ecclesiological concepts underlying Eph. 5:31 f., refers to the revelation of the heavenly and pneumatic ἐκκλησία that has taken place in the flesh of Christ. In the concluding doxology in 2 Cl., 20, 5 God is extolled as the One who through the σωτήρ καὶ ἀρχηγὸς τῆς ἀφθαρσίας has revealed the truth and heavenly life, i.e., made these possible. The phrase ἐφανερώθη ἐν σαρκί [21] runs through Barn., cf. 5, 6. 9; 6, 7. 9. 14;

---

[14] The schema is not meant christologically but refers to proclamation.
[15] So also Hb. 9:26.
[16] Cf. Bultmann J., 380, n. 2; 547, n. 2.
[17] Cf. also H. Conzelmann, "Was von Anfang war," Festschr. R. Bultmann, ZNW Beih. 21² (1957), 195 f.
[18] In view of the par. in 2:28 Christ is to be supplied as the subj. of φανερωθῇ in 3:2b, cf. 1 Pt. 5:14.
[19] Cf. Is. 56:1; Ps. 98:2; Damasc. 20:20 (9:44); 1 QH 14:16; 4 Esr. 8:36.
[20] Cf. H. Schlier, "Religionsgeschichtliche Untersuchungen zu d. Ignatiusbr.," ZNW Beih. 8 (1929), 5-32; H. W. Bartsch, Gnostisches Gut u. Gemeindetradition bei Ign. v. Antiochien (1940), 133-159.
[21] Schulte, 69.

12, 8. 10; 14, 5; 15, 9. This revelation is prophesied in advance by that in the OT, 2, 4; 6, 7; 7, 3. 7; 12, 8; 16, 5. In the Shepherd of Hermas φανερόω denotes the revelation of a vision ἵνα μοι φανερώσῃ τὴν ἀποκάλυψιν, v., 3, 1, 2 and also the appearance of the Shepherd, s., 2, 1. [22] In Dg., 7-10 we have the first *tractatus de revelatione*. [23] φανερόω is used for the revelation in Christ at 8, 11. It is the revelation of God's mercy and power after man's wickedness has been fully exposed, 9, 2.

† φανέρωσις.

1. The noun φανέρωσις "appearance," "revelation," is nomen agentis of φανερόω. There are very few examples, e.g., Corp. Herm., 11, 1: περὶ τοῦ παντὸς καὶ τοῦ θεοῦ. [1]

2. In primitive Christian literature φανέρωσις "revelation" is found only twice in Paul. In 1 C. 12:7: ἑκάστῳ δὲ δίδοται ἡ φανέρωσις τοῦ πνεύματος πρὸς τὸ συμφέρον, the gen. τοῦ πνεύματος is to be taken as a subj. gen., for only in 12:8 ff. are the different operations named and v. 11 expressly repeats that the Spirit is the subject at work (in different ways). Thus φανέρωσις is the revelation imparted by the Spirit and consisting in the charismata listed in vv. 8 ff., cf. R. 12:6. The revelation is not, then, theoretical instruction; it entails acts in which the Spirit manifests Himself. In 2 C. 4:2: ἀλλὰ τῇ φανερώσει τῆς ἀληθείας συνιστάνοντες ἑαυτοὺς πρὸς πᾶσαν συνείδησιν ἀνθρώπων ἐνώπιον τοῦ θεοῦ, Paul is describing true proclamation as a manifestation of the truth (→ I, 244, 15 ff.) in contrast to the craftiness of his adversaries, who falsify the Word of God.

† φαντάζω,   † φάντασμα.

1. The mid. or pass. of φαντάζω "to bring to manifestation" is often used in Gk. in the sense "to appear" for extraordinary or supernatural phenomena, thus the ὄνειρον: τετραμμένῳ γὰρ δὴ καὶ μετεγνωκότι ἐπιφοιτῶν ὄνειρον φαντάζεταί μοι, οὐδαμῶς συνέπαινον ἐὸν ποιέειν με ταῦτα, Hdt., VII, 15, 2, or strange events καὶ μυκαὶ σηκοῖς ἔνι φαντάζωνται, Apoll. Rhod., IV, 1285. In a spiritualised sense Wis. 6:16 ref. to the appearance of wisdom on the path of the worthy, while in Sir. 34:5 φαντάζομαι means "to invent," "to imagine," almost synon. with φαντασιοσκοπέω, "to see phantoms."

In primitive Chr. literature the word occurs only at Hb. 12:21 with reference to the phenomena at Sinai: οὕτω φοβερὸν ἦν τὸ φανταζόμενον.

2. The noun φάντασμα "phenomenon" is often used in Gk. for dream appearances or spirit appearances or apparitions, e.g., Aesch. Sept. c. Theb., 710; Plat. Phaed., 81d; Luc. Philops, 29, so also Wis. 17:14; but, spiritualised, it means a "deception" in Is. 28:7; Job 20:8, both times as a vl. for φάσμα, cf. also Philo Fug., 129, 143; Som., II, 162.

The only instance in primitive Chr. literature is for "ghost" at Mk. 6:49 and par.

---

[22] In s., 4, 2 (twice) and 4, 3 the text is uncertain.
[23] Lührmann, 19.

φανέρωσις. [1] Pr.-Bauer, *s.v.* gives instances from Aristot. De plantis, II, 1, p. 822a, 20 and II, 9, p. 828a, 41, but these are late translations back [Krämer].

† ἐμφανίζω.

1. ἐμφανίζω "to make visible" is used in Greek for "to demonstrate," "to set forth as," Xenoph. Ag., 1, 12; Aristot. Eth. Nic., X, 2, p. 1173b, 31, "to declare," "to proclaim," of a government, Wilcken Ptol., I, 42, 18 (c. 162 B.C.); βούλεσθαι γὰρ ἐμφανίσαι πρῶτον τὴν ἐπιβουλὴν τῷ βασιλεῖ, Diod. S., 14, 11, 2; cf. Est. 2:22; 2 Macc. 3:7; 11:29; Jos. Ant., 4, 43; 10, 166. In religious use it takes on in the act and mid. the sense "to manifest oneself," "to appear," Diog. L. prooem, 7, of God, Philo Leg. All., III, 101, cf. Ex. 33:13 to which Philo ref. here, and also Ex. 33:18 vl. If an outward revelation is at issue in these instances the ref. is to an inward revelation at Wis. 1:2; Philo Leg. All., III, 27.

2. In the NT the word is used for "to show" at Ac. 23:15, 22; 24:1; 25:2, 15, and also for non-official declaration not designed as such but contained indirectly in the words of the speaker at Hb. 11:14. The visible appearing of the dead raised from their graves is denoted by ἐμφανίζομαι at Mt. 27:53.[1] A characteristic of John's Gospel is the way in which play is made on the two possible ways of taking ἐμφανίζω. The promise of Jesus κἀγὼ ἀγαπήσω αὐτὸν καὶ ἐμφανίσω αὐτῷ ἐμαυτόν evokes the question of Judas καὶ τί γέγονεν ὅτι ἡμῖν μέλλεις ἐμφανίζειν σεαυτὸν καὶ οὐχὶ τῷ κόσμῳ; 14:21 f. Judas relates the promised revelation to the visible Easter appearance of the Risen Lord and thus misunderstands it, as v. 23 shows. The saying of Jesus is giving a new interpretation to the traditional view (→ 2, 7 f.; cf. ἐμφανῆ γενέσθαι of the Risen Lord in Ac. 10:40). The self-revelation of Jesus takes place when the Father and the Son take up residence in the believer, v. 23. A distinctive use is when Hb. 9:24 defines the meaning of Christ's exaltation as νῦν ἐμφανισθῆναι τῷ προσώπῳ τοῦ θεοῦ ὑπὲρ ἡμῶν. Possibly this is a priestly (→ VI, 767, 11 ff.; 777, 30 ff.) or legal expression.

† ἐπιφαίνω, † ἐπιφανής, † ἐπιφάνεια.

A. The Word Group in Classical and Hellenistic Greek.

1. The verb ἐπιφαίνω occurs in the act. trans. for "to show" from Theogn., 1, 359 and intr. "to show oneself," "to appear" esp. in LXX, e.g., Dt. 33:2.[1] The mid./pass. deponent "to show oneself" is more common from Hdt., II, 152, 3 etc., cf. Hom. Il., 17, 650. The adj. ἐπιφανής, "visible," "glorious," "magnificent," is found from Pind. Pyth., 7, 6 and Hdt., III, 27, 1 and is often in the superlative, e.g., Hdt., V, 6, 2; Polyb., 1, 78, 11; Diod. S., 1, 17. The noun ἐπιφάνεια "appearance" occurs from the pre-Socratics, e.g., Democr. Fr., 155 (Diels, II, 173); Emped. acc. to Stob. Ecl., I, 485, 11, but is rare in class. times as compared with its common use in Hell. The basic meaning governs the use in specific contexts.[2] As the "visible surface of a body" ἐπιφάνεια may be the

---

ἐμφανίζω. [1] Cf. also Herm. v., 3, 1, 2 and for the appearing of the ἐκκλησία v., 3, 10, 2.

ἐπιφαίνω κτλ. Liddell-Scott, Pr.-Bauer, s.v.; Steinleitner, passim; O. Casel, "Die Epiphanie im Lichte d. Religionsgeschichte," Benedikt. Monatsschr., 4 (1922), 13-20; E. Pfister, Art. "Epiphanie" in Pauly-W., Suppl. 4 (1924), 277-323; H. Schulte, "Der Begriff d. Offenbarung im NT," Beiträge z. Evangel. Theol., 13 (1949); Dib. Past.³, 77 f.; E. Pax, "ΕΠΙΦΑΝΕΙΑ. Ein religionsgeschichtlicher Beitrag z. bibl. Theol.," Münchener Theol. Stud., I, 10 (1955); C. Mohrmann, Études sur le latin des chrétiens (1958), 245-275; E. Pax, Art. "Epiphanie" in RAC, V, 832-909.
[1] In Liddell-Scott only Polyb., 5, 6, 6 apart from Lk. 1:79; Dt. 33:2.
[2] Cf. esp. Pax ΕΠΙΦΑΝΕΙΑ, 7-19.

"outward appearance" of a man or "the skin," Diod. S., 3, 29, 6; it is common in Galen., e.g., In Hippocratis praedictionum librum, I, 7 (Kühn, 16, 530), cf. also its use in mathematics and philosophy for a geometrical surface as distinct from a point σημεῖον (→ VII, 205, 13 ff.), line γραμμή, or body σῶμα (→ VII, 1031, 22 ff.). In military parlance ἐπιφαίνομαι and ἐπιφάνεια denote the sudden and unexpected appearance of the enemy with a view to forcing the issue of the battle, [3] e.g., ἐπιφάνεια in Aen. Tact., 31, 8; Polyb., 1, 54, 3, ἐπιφαίνομαι in Hdt., II, 152, 3. ἐπιφάνεια can also mean the "front" of the army, e.g., Polyb., 1, 22, 10. The adj. and noun can also denote the "renown," "fame" or "worth" of famous men, e.g., ἐπιφανής in Hdt., II, 89, 1; VII, 114, 2; VIII, 125, 1 and ἐπιφάνεια in Ps.-Plat. Alc., I, 124c.

The group acquires religious signification only in Hell. use, [4] in which it denotes the helpful intervention of the gods. The oldest instance is a Cos inscr. which ascribes the defeat of the Gauls before Delphi in 278 B.C. to an ἐπιφάνεια of Apollo: [5] ἐπειδὴ τῶν βαρβάρων στρατείαν ποιησαμένων ἐπὶ τοὺς Ἕλλανας καὶ ἐπὶ τὸ ἱερὸν τὸ ἐν Δελφοῖς, ἀναγγέλλεται τὸς μὲν ἐλθόντας ἐπὶ τὸ ἱερὸν τιμωρίας τετεύχεν ὑπὸ τοῦ θεοῦ καὶ ὑπὸ τῶν ἀνδρῶν τῶν ἐπιβοαθησάντων τῶι ἱερῶι ἐν τᾶι τῶν βαρβάρων ἐφόδωι, τὸ δὲ ἱερὸν διαπεφυλάχθαι τε καὶ ἐπικεκοσμῆσθαι τοῖς ὑπὸ τῶν ἐπιστρα- τευσάντων ὅπλοις, τῶν δὲ λοιπῶν τῶν στρατευσάντων τοὺς πλείστους ἀπολώλεν ἐν τοῖς γενομένοις ἀγῶσι ποτὶ τοὺς Ἕλλανας αὐτοῖς· ... ὅπως οὖν ὁ δᾶμος φανερὸς ἦι συναδόμενος ἐπὶ ταὶ γεγενημέναι νίκαι τοῖς Ἕλλασι καὶ τῶι θεῶι χαριστήρια ἀποδιδοὺς τάς τε ἐπιφανείας τὰς γεγενημένας ἕνεκεν ἐν τοῖς περὶ τὸ ἱερὸν κινδύνοις καὶ τᾶς τῶν Ἑλλάνων σωτηρίας, Ditt. Syll.[3], I, 398, 1-21 (278 B.C.). This use is related to the military use (→ lines 4 ff.); the ἐπιφάνεια of the god is a helpful intervention in the battle. [6] From the 3rd cent. on ἐπιφάνεια and ἐπιφανής are often found in this sense on inscr. esp. from Asia Minor. Ditt. Syll.[3], II, 557, 7; 558, 5; 559, 10; 560, 5; 561, 10; 562, 10 (all 207/206 B.C.); 867, 35 (c. 160 B.C.); Inscr. Perg., I, 247, 2, 3 (c. 135 B.C.); 248, 52 (134 B.C.), [7] and in literature Dion Hal. Ant. Rom., 2, 68, 1; Plut. Them., 30 (I, 127c), of Isis Diod. S., 1, 25, 4, of the Dioscuri Dion Hal. Ant. Rom., 6, 13, 4. [8] Important in all this is the consistent connection with datable events and with a cult. [9] Later ἐπιφάνεια is used more generally for divine assistance... μεγάλων δαιμόνων ἐπιφανείαις, αἵτινες ἐμοὶ καθηγεμόνες εὐτυχοῦς ἀρχῆς καὶ βασιλείαι πάσηι κοινῶν ἀγαθῶν αἴτιαι κατέστησαν, inscr. of Antiochus I of Commagene, Ditt. Or., I, 383, 85-88 (1st cent. B.C.), including that of Aesculapius in sickness. [10] The point now is the manifestation of the ἀρετή or δύναμις of the deity. [11]

---

[3] Ibid., 9 with many examples.

[4] The occasional use in Hdt., e.g., ἀπιγμένου δὲ Καμβύσεω ἐς Μέμφιν ἐφάνη Αἰγυπ- τίοισι ὁ Ἆπις ... ἐπιφανέος δὲ τούτου γενομένου ... in III, 27, 1 has no fuller sense than "visible."

[5] Cf. the account in Paus., 10, 23, which can hardly be distinguished from the description of the defeat of the Persians before Delphi, Hdt., VIII, 37 f.

[6] The group does not, then, cover the concept of epiphany, cf. Schulte, 62 for the NT, though this applies to Hell. in gen. Pax ΕΠΙΦΑΝΕΙΑ, 15 sees this and yet he uses the concept as the starting-point of both his investigations.

[7] For material on ἐπιφανής as a designation of the gods in this field cf. Steinleitner, 15-21.
[8] Cf. Pfister, 293 f.

[9] With the inscr. from Cos already quoted cf. esp. the temple chronicle of Lindos from 99 B.C. (ed. C. Blinkenburg, KIT, 131 [1915]): col. A 3 and 7 ref. to the ἐπιφάνεια τᾶς θεοῦ Athena, and in col. D under the heading ἐπιφάνειαι many such (dated) interventions are described. In D 34, 55 f., 58 ἐπιφάνεια is plainly distinguished from the ὄψις (D 17) which a defender of Lindos has in a dream; it corresponds rather to the βοάθεια of D 23, cf. also Inscr. Perg., I, 248, 51 (134 B.C.); Ditt. Syll.[3], II, 560, 8 (207/206 B.C.) etc. The cult may be celebrated on the day of the intervention or on the birthday of the god, when his ἐπιφάνειαι are declared.

[10] Cf. Pfister, 295.
[11] Ibid., 300.

Ptolemy V and his brother-in-law Antiochus IV adopted the title θεὸς ἐπιφανής. [12] The oldest instance is the Rosetta stone, Ditt. Or., I, 90 (196 B.C.); the full title runs here: ὁ αἰωνόβιος καὶ ἠγαπημένος ὑπὸ τοῦ ΦΘᾶ βασιλεὺς Πτολεμαῖος θεὸς Ἐπιφανὴς Εὐχάριστος, cf. line 49 and also Ditt. Or., I, 91, 1 f.; 92, 1 f.; 93, 1; 94, 1 f.; with Cleopatra θεοὶ ἐπιφανεῖς, 95, 1-5; 97, 1-6; 98; 99, 8 (all 2nd cent. B.C.). The title is esp. common among the Seleucids, but we find it in other dynasties too, e.g., Antiochus I Epiphanes of Commagene, Ditt. Or., I, 383, 1 f. (1st cent. B.C.). Ἐπιφάνεια in the sense of παρουσία (→ V, 859, 20 ff.) is found only from Caligula (37-41 A.D.). [13]

2. Findings in Jewish Hell. correspond to the frequent use of the term in Hell. lit. in gen. In LXX the verb (act. and dep.) occurs in the sense "to shine," "to rise" at Dt. 33:2 (for זרח); 2 Macc. 12:9 vl.; of lightning Ep. Jer. 60; the appearing of God, Gn. 35:7; the adj. has the meaning "magnificent," "splendid," at Est. 5:1a (cf. ἐπιφάνεια "splendour" in 5:1c); 2 Macc. 14:33; of hair 6:23. There is no true Hbr. equivalent, but ἐπιφαίνω τὸ πρόσωπον is often used for האר פנים Nu. 6:25; ψ 30:17; 66:2; 79:4, 8, 20; Da. 9:17 Θ; cf. ψ 117:27; the adj. ἐπιφανής is a transl. of נורא at Ju. 13:6 A (B φοβερόν); Jl. 2:11, 31; Hab. 1:7; Mal. 1:14; Zeph. 2:11 (vl. for ἐπιφανήσεται). The most common use of the group is for "mighty demonstrations of help," esp. in military connections in 2 and 3 Macc.: [14] ἐπιφάνεια in 2 Βασ. 7:23 (for נוראות); 2 Macc. 2:21; 3:24; 12:22; 14:15; 15:27; 3 Macc. 2:9; 5:8, 51, [15] ἐπιφανής in 1 Ch. 17:21 (HT נוראות); 2 Macc. 15:34; 3 Macc. 5:35, ἐπιφαίνομαι in Ez. 39:28 (diverging from HT); 2 Macc. 3:30; 3 Macc. 6:9, and ἐπιφαίνω in 3 Macc. 2:19; 6:4, 18, 39.

3. Josephus uses ἐπιφάνεια synon. with παρουσία (→ V, 864, 35 ff.), except in the sense of "fame" in Ant., 19, 328, for "helpful intervention," [16] Ant., 2, 339; 3, 310; 9, 60; 12, 136 (quoting Polyb.); 18, 286. [17] The verb has the sense "to appear," φάντασμα ἐπιφαίνεται, Ant., 5, 277, of God, 8, 240 and 268; for the adj. ἐπιφανής "splendid" cf. 4, 200.

Philo has ἐπιφάνεια for "external appearance" in Som., I, 21; Leg. Gaj., 357; Vit. Mos., II, 255; plur. Virt., 12, of man Poster. C., 118 (opp. τὰ ἐν αὐτοῖς σπλάγχνοις ἐγκεκρυμμένα); Leg. All., II, 38; Deus Imm., 35; Fug., 182; Vit. Mos., I, 108; Som., II, 144, for "renown," "splendour" etc. Spec. Leg., II, 149, plur. Leg. Gaj., 328; Vit. Mos., I, 3, for "geometrical surface" as opp. to point, line, or body (→ 8, 2 ff.) in connection with allegorising, Congr., 146 f.; Op. Mund., 49, 147; Vit. Mos., II, 96 and 115; Decal., 24-26, plur. Som., I, 187. The meaning "helpful intervention" does not occur in Philo. The adj. ἐπιφανής "outstanding," "splendid," "distinguished" occurs in Som., II, 44; Spec. Leg., II, 175; Fug., 30, of the temple, Leg. Gaj., 151 and 191, men, Omn. Prob. Lib., 10; Som., I, 155 and 226; Flacc., 185, of the emperors, Flacc., 81, God, Som., I, 112, cf. ἐπιφανέστατον αἶσχος, Migr. Abr., 161 and ἐπιφανὲς ὄνειδος, Jos., 172. The verb ἐπιφαίνομαι "to appear" occurs at Abr., 145; Jos., 106; Op. Mund., 83; Spec. Leg., I, 65, esp. for divine epiphanies, e.g., ὁ θεῖος λόγος at Som., I, 71, the angel, Abr., 142, the ὄψις of Abraham, 167, God in Jos., 255; Som., I, 228 and 232; Mut. Nom., 6 and 15.

---

12 The meaning of the title is "helping" rather than "visible," cf. the title Soter (→ VII, 1003, 29 ff.).

13 W. R. Paton and E. L. Hicks, *The Inscr. of Cos* (1891), 391.

14 2 Macc. 5:4 is the only place where one might render by "supernatural appearance," and even here the context is military.

15 Ἐπιφάνεια in Am. 5:22, ἐπιφανής in Prv. 25:14 and ἐπιφαίνομαι in Ἰερ. 36(29):14 are used in divergence from the HT.

16 In Ant., 1, 255, too, ἐπιφάνεια denotes God's intervention and not just a gen. appearing. In the case of the appearance of Anubis in 18, 75 there is doubt whether the meaning is theophany or, more probably, "magnificent external appearance."

17 Cf. Ep. Ar., 264. Aristobulus (in Eus. Praep. Ev., 8, 10, 3: λέγω δὲ τῶν κατὰ τὴν ἐπιφάνειαν) has the word in the sense of "outward appearance."

B. The Word Group in the New Testament.

1. As in the LXX the act. ἐπιφαίνω is used intr. [18] in the NT for "to show oneself," "to appear," e.g., externally of the stars in Ac. 27:20 or figuratively of the intervening of God to help in Lk. 1:79. [19] Here the subject of ἐπιφαίνω is the ἀνατολὴ ἐξ ὕψους (→ VIII, 605, 12 ff.) whose task it is ἐπιφᾶναι τοῖς ἐν σκότει καὶ σκιᾷ θανάτου καθημένοις. [20] Ἐπιφαίνομαι is rare in primitive Christian literature. [21] To the degree that Jesus' appearing on earth can be understood as an eschatological event it may be called an ἐπιφαίνεσθαι of the χάρις or χρηστότης and φιλανθρωπία of God, Tt. 2:11; 3:4.

2. Ἐπιφανής is not used as a divine attribute in the NT but only eschatologically, after the manner of Jl. 2:31, as a characteristic of the ἡμέρα κυρίου, Ac. 2:20.

3. Ἐπιφάνεια is used in the NT only as a religious term, mostly for the fut. eschatological appearing of Christ, 2 Th. 2:8; 1 Tm. 6:14; 2 Tm. 4:1, 8; [22] Tt. 2:13. [23] To the degree that Jesus' earthly appearing is seen as an eschatological event (→ lines 6 ff.) it, too, can be called an ἐπιφάνεια, as in 2 Tm. 1:9 f., which characterises the χάρις: δοθεῖσαν ἡμῖν ἐν Χριστῷ Ἰησοῦ πρὸ χρόνων αἰωνίων, φανερωθεῖσαν δὲ νῦν διὰ τῆς ἐπιφανείας τοῦ σωτῆρος ἡμῶν Χριστοῦ Ἰησοῦ. [24] Possibly 2 Tm. 4:8 is to be taken in the same sense.

Bultmann/Lührmann

---

[18] In the trans. sense "to show," "to cause to shine," the only act. use in early Chr. lit. is at 1 Cl., 60, 3 which adopts a liturgical expression from the OT (→ 9, 13 f.): ἐπίφανον τὸ πρόσωπόν σου ἐφ᾽ ἡμᾶς.

[19] So also Dt. 33:2; ψ 117:27.

[20] For the meaning of the text cf. the comm. and also P. Vielhauer, "Das Benedictus d. Zacharias," *Aufsätze z. NT, Theol. Bücherei*, 31 (1965), 28-46.

[21] God's appearance is besought as proof of His power to help τοῖς δεομένοις ἐπιφάνηθι, 1 Cl., 59, 4.

[22] On ἀγαπάω (τὴν ἐπιφάνειαν) cf. G. Bornkamm, "Zum Verständnis d. Gottesdienstes bei Pls.," *Das Ende d. Gesetzes*⁵ (1966), 124 f.

[23] Cf. the same usage in 2 Cl., 12, 1; 17, 4.

[24] Cf. also the vl. at R. 16:26.

<table>
<tr><td rowspan="6">Φαρισαῖος</td><td>καθαρός</td><td>(→ III, 413, 13 ff.)</td></tr>
<tr><td>κρύπτω</td><td>(→ III, 957, 16 ff.)</td></tr>
<tr><td>νόμος</td><td>(→ IV, 1022, 22 ff.)</td></tr>
<tr><td>προφήτης</td><td>(→ VI, 781, 2 ff.)</td></tr>
<tr><td>Σαμάρεια</td><td>(→ VII, 88, 12 ff.)</td></tr>
<tr><td>Σαδδουκαῖος</td><td>(→ VII, 35, 7 ff.)</td></tr>
</table>

Contents: A. Pharisaism in Judaism: I. Usage. II. Pharisaism from its Beginning to the Fall of the Hierarchy in Jerusalem: 1. The Origin of Pharisaism: a. The Chasidim; b. The Perushim; 2. The Pharisaic Societies: a. The Chabura; b. The Chaberim; c. The Chaberuth; 3. Pharisaic Wisdom and Learning: a. The Chakamim; b. The Soferim; 4. The Pharisees as a Party: a. Pharisees and Hasmoneans; b. Pharisaism from Herod to the Destruction of the Temple; c. Pharisees and Zealots; d. Pharisaism in the Light of Zadokite Criticism. III. The Triumph of Pharisaism: 1. Palestinian Judaism after the Fall of the Hierocracy; 2. The Reconstruction of Community Life: a. Religio-Social Change; b. Inner Reorganisation. IV. Summary. B. The Pharisees in the New Testament: I. The Pharisees in the Synoptic Tradition: 1. The Historical Problem; 2. The Pharisees and the Other Parties in Judaism; 3. The Opposition to Pharisaism as an Expression of Opposition to the Pharisaic Understanding of the Law. II. The Pharisees in John's Gospel. III. The Pharisees in Acts and in Paul. C. The Pharisees in Early Christian Writings outside the New Testament.

Φαρισαῖος. On A.: S. Abir, "Der Weg der Pharisäer," *Freiburger Rundschau*, 11 (1958/59), 29-34; M. Avi-Yonah," Gesch. d. Juden im Zeitalter d. Talmud in den Tagen v. Rom u. Byzanz," *Studia Jud.*, 2 (1962); B. W. Bacon, "Pharisees and Herodians," JBL, 39 (1920), 102-112; L. Baeck, *Die Pharisäer* (1934); W. Beilner, "Der Ursprung d. Pharisäismus," BZ, NF, 3 (1959), 235-251; E. Bikerman, "La chaîne de la tradition pharisienne," *Rev. Bibl.*, 59 (1952), 44-54; B. Z. Bokser, *Pharisaic Judaism in Transition. R. Eliezer the Great and Jewish Reconstruction after the War with Rome* (1935); I. Elbogen," Einige neue Theorien über den Ursprung d. Pharisäer u. Sadduzäer," *Jewish Stud. in Memory of I. Abrahams* (1927), 135-148; A. Finkel, "The Pharisees and the Teacher of Nazareth. A Study of their Background, their Halachic and Midrashic Teachings, the Similarities and Differences," *Arbeiten z. Gesch. d. Spätjudt. u. Urchr.*, 4 (1964); L. Finkelstein, "The Pharisees: Their Origin and their Philosophy," HThR, 22 (1929), 185-261; also *The Pharisees. The Sociological Background of their Faith*, I, II³ (1962); also "The Pharisees and the Men of the Great Synagogue," *Texts and Studies of the Jewish Theol. Seminary of America*, 15 (1950); also "The Ethics of Anonymity among the Pharisees," *Conservative Judaism*, 12 (1958), 1-12; W. Foerster, "Der Ursprung d. Pharisäismus," ZNW, 34 (1935), 35-51; also *Nt.liche Zeitgeschichte*, I³ (1959), 164-219; R. T. Herford, *Die Pharisäer. Mit einer Einleitung v. N. N. Glatzer* (1961); also *Judaism in the NT Period* (1928); M. Hengel, "Die Zeloten," *Arbeiten z. Gesch. d. Spätjudt. u. Urchr.*, 1 (1961); O. Holtzmann, "Der Prophet Mal. u. d. Ursprung d. Pharisäismus," ARW, 29 (1931), 1-21; M. D. Hussey, "The Origin of the Name Pharisee," JBL, 39 (1920), 66-69; G. Jeremias, "Der Lehrer d. Gerechtigkeit," *Stud. z. Umwelt d. NT*, 2 (1963); J. Jeremias, *Jerusalem z. Zt. Jesu*³ (1962), 279-303; J. Z. Lauterbach, "The Pharisees and their Teachings," HUCA, 6 (1929), 69-139; J. W. Lightley, *Jewish Sects and Parties in the Time of Jesus* (1925); G. W. Linhart, *The Pharisees* (Diss. Dallas, 1954); H. Loewe, "Pharisaism" in *Judaism and Christianity*, I (1937), 105-190; T. W. Manson, "Sadducee and Pharisee. The Origin and Significance of the Names," *Bulletin of the John Rylands Library*, 22 (1938), 144-159; R. Marcus, "Pharisaism in the Light of Modern Scholarship," *The Journal of Religion*, 32 (1952), 154-164; also "Pharisees, Essenes and Gnostics," JBL, 73 (1954), 155-161; J. C. Margot, "Les Pharisiens d'après quelques ouvrages récents," RevThPh, III, 6

A. Pharisaism in Judaism.

I. Usage.

The word Φαρισαῖος, which in the NT (→ 35, 30 f.) and Jos. [1] is more common in the plur. than the sing., is the Gk. transcription of an Aram. qatīl formation פְּרִישׁ, plur. פְּרִישַׁיָּא. This form is found in the Tg. and Rabb. lit. as an adj. in the sense "separated," "distinguished," [2] but it never has the meaning of the Gk. Φαρισαῖος, for which we find rather the Hbr. qatūl construct פָּרוּשׁ, plur. פְּרוּשִׁים and פְּרוּשִׁין. [3] This extraordinary fact can be explained only on the assumption that in the process of linguistic regularisation פְּרִישׁ or פְּרִישַׁיָּא in the sense of Φαρισαῖος was replaced with the Hbr. equivalent. At any rate, the fathers knew the Aram. original of Φαρισαῖος, for they regularly ref. to it when trying to explain the phenomenon of Pharisaism. Thus Orig. Comm. in J. Fr. 34 on 3:1 (p. 510, 5 ff.) says: *"Phares means among the Hebrews 'one who is set apart', for these men (sc. the Pharisees) separate themselves from the whole people of the Jews."* [4]

(1956), 294-302; R. Meyer, "Hellenistisches in d. rabb. Anthropologie," BWANT, IV, 22 (1937), Index, s.v. "Pharisäer"; also "Der 'Am ha-' Ares," *Judaica*, 3 (1947), 166-199; also "Die Bdtg. d. Pharisäismus für Gesch. u. Theol. d. Judt.," ThLZ, 77 (1952), 677-684; also "Tradition u. Neuschöpfung im antiken Judt. Dargestellt an d. Gesch. d. Pharisäismus. Mit einem Beitrag v. H. F. Weiss, Der Pharisäismus im Lichte d. Überlieferung d. NT," *Sitzungsberichte d. Sächsischen Akad. d. Wissenschaften zu Leipzig, philologisch-histor. Klasse*, 110, 2 (1965); G. F. Moore, "The Rise of Normative Judaism, I" HThR, 17 (1924), 307-373; II, *ibid.*, 18 (1925), 1-38; Moore, Index, s.v. "Pharisees"; J. Neusner, "The Fellowship (חבורה) in the Second Jewish Commonwealth," HThR, 53 (1960), 125-142; C. Rabin, *Qumran Studies* (1955), 53-70; also "Alexander Jannaeus and the Pharisees," *Journal of Jewish Stud.*, 7 (1956), 3-11; H. Rasp, "Flavius Josephus u. d. jüd. Religionsparteien," ZNW, 23 (1924), 27-47; C. Roth, "The Pharisees in the Jewish Revolution of 66-73," *Journ. of Semitic Stud.*, 7 (1962), 63-80; Schürer, II, 456-475 (Bibl. 447-9); F. Sieffert, Art. "Pharisäer u. Sadduzäer" in RE³, 15, 264-292; M. H. Segal, "Pharisees and Sadducees," *Exp.*, 8, 13 (1917), 81 ff.; M. Weber, "Die Pharisäer," *Gesammelte Aufs. z. Religionssoziologie*, III (1921), 401-442; J. Wellhausen, *Die Pharisäer u. Sadduzäer²* (1924). On B. and C.: I. Abrahams, *Stud. in Pharisaism and the Gospels*, I (1917), II (1924); W. Beilner, *Christus u. d. Pharisäer* (1959); B. H. Branscomb, *Jesus and the Law of Moses* (1930); F. C. Burkitt, "Jesus and the Pharisees," JThSt, 28 (1927), 392-7; T. F. Glasson, "Anti-Pharisaism in St. Matthew," JQR, 51 (1960/61), 316-320; L. Goppelt, "Christentum u. Judt. im ersten u. zweiten Jhdt.," BFTh, II, 55 (1954), 41-55; C. Gruber-Magitot, *Jésus et les Pharisiens* (1964); F. Heinrichs, *Die Komposition d. antipharisäischen u. antirabbinischen Wehe-Reden bei d. Synpt.*, Diss. Munich, 1957; R. Hummel, "Die Auseinandersetzung zwischen Kirche u. Judt. im Mt.," *Beiträge z. evangel. Theol.*, 33² (1966), 12-17; A. F. Klijn, "Scribes, Pharisees, Highpriests and Elders in the NT," Nov. Test., 3 (1959), 259-267; H. Merkel, "Jesus u. d. Pharisäer," *Katechetische Blätter*, 84 (1959), 433-440, 490-495; H. Odeberg, *Pharisaism and Christianity* (1964); J. van der Ploeg, "Jésus et les Pharisiens," *Mémorial Lagrange* (1940), 279-293; D. W. Riddle, *Jesus and the Pharisees* (1928); A. T. Robertson, *The Pharisees and Jesus* (1920); T. H. Robinson, "Jesus and the Pharisees," *Exp.T.*, 28 (1917), 550-554; P. Seidensticker, "Die Gemeinschaftsform d. religiösen Gruppen d. Spätjudt. u. d. Urkirche," *Studii Biblici Franciscani Liber Annuus*, 9 (1959), 94-108; P. B. Sellers, *The Doctrinal Basis of the Conflict of the Pharisees with Jesus*, Diss. South-western Baptist Seminary, 1950; M. Simon, "Les sectes juives d'après les témoignages patristiques," *Stud. Patristica*, I, TU, 63 (1957), 526-539; S. Umer, *Pharisaism and Jesus* (1962); S. Zeitlin, "The Pharisees and the Gospels," *Essays and Stud. in Memory of L. R. Miller* (1938), 235-286.

[1] Jos. Ant., 13, 171 f. 288-299. 401. 406. 408-415; 13, 3. 370; 17, 41. 44. 46; 18, 4. 11-15. 17. 23; Bell., 1, 110. 112. 571; 2, 119. 162. 166. 411; Vit., 10. 12. 21. 191. 197; for the chief instances cf. Schürer, II, 449-452.

[2] Cf. Levy Chald. Wört., Levy Wört., s.v. פְּרִישׁ.

[3] Cf. Schürer, II, 452-4; Kassovsky, 1489c-1490a; J. Kasowski, Thesaurus Thosephthae, V (1958), s.v. פָּרוּשׁ; L. Goldschmidt, *Concordance to the Babyl. Talmud*, s.v. פרוש; Str.-B., IV, 334-6.

[4] Cf. Comm. in Mt., 20 on 23:23 f. (GCS, 38, 35, 23 ff.).

Compared with the incidence of Φαρισαῖος in the NT and Jos. — thus far no non-Jewish or non-Chr. instances have been found — the Hbr. term פָּרוּשׁ in the sense of "Pharisee" is very rare. A pt. to note is that theologically the root prš, which in Middle Hbr. in the q and pi means not only "to separate" but "to separate oneself," can have both a positive and also a derogatory nuance. [5] Thus the root is used negatively in Ab., 2, 4b: "Do not separate thyself from the community," [6] cf. bPes., 70b, where פָּרוּשׁ occurs in the Aram. context and means "dissident": "R. Ashi had said: Should we expound a thing (sc. a verse of the Bible) according to the view of the dissidents?" [7] But the root can be used positively for separation from all cultic defilement (→ III, 418, 9 ff.) and also to express restraint, the verbal nouns פְּרִישׁוּת and פְּרִישָׁה ("separation") being employed in this connection. [8] Transf. the two terms can have ethical significance too. [9] פָּרוּשׁ in the sense of "abstemious" is attested in, e.g., T. Sota, 15, 11: "From the time of the destruction of the temple the abstemious increased in Israel; they ate no flesh and drank no wine." The complex usage shows that we cannot establish פָּרוּשׁ firmly for Φαρισαῖος and that it is not possible to explain all aspects of Pharisaism in terms of the root prš and derivates. Important here is the fact that the Pharisees did not gen. call themselves פְּרוּשִׁים or פְּרִישַׁיָּא but originally this title was ascribed to them by contemporaries in the derogatory sense of "separatists" or "sectarians." The influence of this may still be seen in the usage, for when the root prš and esp. פָּרוּשׁ are used positively it is seldom with express ref. to Pharisaism in its totality. It is thus necessary to consider a whole series of other terms like pious, fellow, wise man and scribe, since these express far more of the essence of the Pharisaic movement than the term Pharisee itself does.

II. Pharisaism from its Beginning to the Fall of the Hierarchy in Jerusalem.

1. The Origin of Pharisaism.

From the standpoint of sources the origins of Pharisaism are still obscure. Acc. to a floating anecdote in Jos. Ant., 13, 288-296 the Pharisees as a trend or party under John Hyrcanus I (135-104 B.C.) were already of older origin like the Sadducees (→ VII, 43, 20 ff.). In spite of the historical dubiety of the story, which is based on school rivalries, which Rabb. tradition in bQid., 66a relates to Alexander Jannaeus (103-76 B.C.) and in which the dispute between the priest-prince and the Pharisees is the issue, Jos. seems to be right to the degree that the beginnings of Pharisaism reach back into the 2nd cent. B.C. This is now confirmed by the fact that Damasc. and some Qumran Fr., while not using the term, are clearly aimed against the Pharisaic understanding of the Law → 28, 6 ff. Thus one may say very gen. that the Pharisaic movement arose in the 2nd cent. with its many crises. Essentially more difficult to answer is the question to which circle Pharisaism owed its origin.

---

[5] Cf. Levy Chald. Wört., Levy Wört., s.v. פָּרַשׁ.

[6] A saying of Hillel: אל תפרוש עצמך מן הצבור cf. jTer., 8, 2 (45d, 44) and bPes., 70b Bar.: יהודה בן דורתאי פירש הוא ודורתאי בנו והלך וישב לו בדרום. Jehuda b Dorotai (= Dorotheos) lived c. 20 B.C. and held against Shemaʿya and Abtalyon (c. 50 B.C.) the view that the feast-offering overrides the Sabbath. The tradition is important because it shows that at the time of the transition from B.C. to A.D. school rivalries were not confined to the Pharisaic trends linked with Hillel and Shammai.

[7] ואנן טעמא דפרושים ניקו ונפרוש with ref. to Jehuda b Dorotai and his son.

[8] Levy Chald. Wört., Levy Wört., s.v.

[9] Cf., e.g., Tg. J. I (ed. M. Ginsburger [1903]) on Nu. 6:3; Sota, 9, 15; Ab., 3, 13; Toh., 4, 12; Zabim, 5, 1.

a. The Chasidim.

When we look for possible precursors of the Pharisees in the 2nd cent. B.C., it is natural to think first of the ᾽Ασιδαῖοι (חֲסִידִים), the righteous, 1 Macc. 2:42; 7:13; 2 Macc. 14:6. One has to ask, of course, whether the Chasidim and the Pharisees are to be seen in a definite historical relation and also whether the Chasidim can be viewed as a homogeneous group or even perhaps a party. According to present sources, which are sparse and obscure, the Chasidim appear for the first time at the beginning of the religious persecution under Antiochus IV Epiphanes (167/166 B.C.). According to 1 Macc. 2:42 the Maccabees, after a severe defeat, were joined by "a company of Chasidim (συναγωγὴ ᾽Ασιδαίων), brave men of Israel, each of whom gave himself willingly for the law. And all who fled before the disaster joined them and strengthened them and brought together a great army." If the expression συναγωγὴ ᾽Ασιδαίων is debated, [10] the context favours the view that 1 Macc. distinguishes between the Maccabean movement under the local priest Mattathias on the one side and the Chasidim on the other. The latter are already an opposition movement long before the revolt. Their adversary is not Antiochus Epiphanes with his many Jewish collaborators but obviously a group in Jerusalem which determines the face of the hierocracy but which in the view of its critics has departed radically from the law of the fathers. It is true that the Chasidim make common against the Seleucid ruler, but they also maintain their independence of the Hasmoneans. This is clear from 1 Macc. 7:1-22. When the jurists establish the legitimacy of Alkimus the Aaronite, who was appointed by Demetrius, the Chasidim concede, since they are "the first among the Israelites" to ask for peace with the new and legally appointed high-priest and the Seleucid plenipotentiary, 1 Macc. 7:13. While we have only "a company of Chasidim" in 1 Macc. 2:42, the ref. in 7:13 is to "the Chasidim." Philology cannot solve the tension between the two references, but historical considerations can help. The suggestion (→ VII, 39, n. 27) that the concept Chasidim lives on indirectly in Aram. form in the term Essene [11] (᾽Εσσηνοί, ᾽Εσσαῖοι) is supported by Fr. 45, 6 of Murabbaʿāt (DJD, II, 163). Here a Jewish fugitive in the last year of the Ben Kosiba revolt (134/135 A.D.) mentions "the fortress of the Chasidim" (מצד חסידין), which in all likelihood is a ref. to the ruins of Qumran fortified as a centre of resistance. [12] The tension between the data in 1 Macc. 7:13 and the text found in Murabbaʿāt makes it clear for the first time that the term Chasidim could be used for people whose main concern was legitimacy within the Jerusalem hierocracy and the full validity of the Law as its basis, as well as for those who, insisting on strict observance of the Law, raised for themselves and their supporters an exclusive claim to legitimacy, and as the true Israel were opposed religiously and politically to the ruling system in Jerusalem. If we are to relate Pharisaism causally to one of the known Chasidic groups, it is thus best to think in terms of the Chasidim mentioned in 1 Macc. 7:13 → 14, 23 ff.

---

[10] The Hbr. equivalent of συναγωγὴ ᾽Ασιδαίων is probably עדת חסידים; as opposed to the thesis of Bousset-Gressm., 57 and 457 (cf. A. Kahana, הספרים החיצונים II [1959], 107: קהל חסידים) that the ref. is to the "synagogue of the Chasideans," συναγωγή in 1 Macc. has the basic sense of "company," "host," "assembly," like עֵדָה in Ps. 7:8; 68:30 (LXX συναγωγή).

[11] Cf. the main sources: Philo Omn. Prob. Lib., 12 f.; also Ὑπὲρ ᾽Ιουδαίων ἀναλογία in Eus. Praep. Ev., 8, 11; Jos. Bell., 2, 119-161; Ant., 13, 172; 15, 371-3; 18, 18-22; Plin. Hist. Nat., 5, 17, also Philo Vit. Cont., passim in relation to the Essene group of the Therapeutae. For discussion of the Essene problem cf. Bousset-Gressm., 456-468; F. M. Cross, The Ancient Library of Qumran and Modern Biblical Studies, The Haskell Lectures 1956-1957 (1958), 37-79; K. G. Kuhn, Art. "Essener" in RGG³, II, 701-3; S. Wagner, "Die Essener in d. wissenschaftlichen Diskussion," ZAW Beih., 79 (1960).

[12] As far as is known thus far we have in mesad hasidin a first Hbr. example of the naming of a specific opposition group as Chasidim. It is also likely that the name Qumran now attached to the ruined site is simply the Aram. equivalent of the Hbr. mesad, cf. on this R. Meyer, "Das Gebet des Nabonid," Sitzungsberichte d. Sächsischen Akad. d. Wissenschaften zu Leipzig, philosophisch-histor. Klasse, 107, 3 (1962), 9 f., n. 3.

b. The Perushim.

The thought of separation is also intrinsic to postexilic Judaism where universalist tendencies are dominant. Israel is separated from the nations by the Law (→ IV, 46, 9 ff.). From the Persian period, apart from a few years under Antiochus Epiphanes, the temple province of Judah enjoyed relative autonomy, and the Romans continued to recognise its special status even after the collapse of the Hasmonean state and the fall of the universal monarchy of Herod. It is separated from the world around. Yet this alone is not yet Pharisaism.[13] For in the first instance Pharisaism is not concerned about outer separation but inner separation, and it thus directs the understanding of God into a path unknown to Judaism in the Persian and Hell. period. The Law (Aram. דָּת) as the constitution of the Jerusalem hierocracy laid down in the Pent. is a priestly law.[14] This means that ultimately it does not refer to the people at large but only to the priests, and to the priests only when engaged in temple service.[15] Hence separation in the sense of sacral law is a primary quality of the priest, who during his spell of duty is to avoid all defilement (→ III, 418, 10 ff.) if his cultic acts are to be valid. Thus acc. to Yoma, 1, 1 the high-priest was to be separated from his family for seven days before the Day of Atonement and conducted into the "hall of the presidents of the Sanhedrin";[16] the isolation פְּרִישָׁה served as his sanctification acc. to bYoma, 8b. A seven-day separation was also imposed on the priest who had to prepare the red heifer; this again was designed to secure his "cleanness" (טָהֳרָה).[17] In analogy to this the Parush seeks by isolation (פְּרִישָׁה) to transfer into everyday life the cleanness (טָהֳרָה) and holiness (קְדוּשָׁה) which are proper to the priest during his period of temple ministry, thus applying in the broadest sense the vital forces which derive from the Law. This tendency of the Parush goes essentially much further than what is said about the Chasidic group mentioned in 1 Macc. 7:13 → 14, 23 ff. Hence one has to ask whether and how far that which is most distinctive of Pharisaism does not really derive from the priesthood. In fact the priestly concepts of separation, cleanness and holiness strongly support the view that there was once a priestly movement, probably a minority, which was enthused by the idea that the Law which they practised in the temple should be actualised in everyday life with the aim of sanctifying the people. In keeping is the fact that in their dogmatically controlled genealogy of the fathers the Rabb. alloted a key position to the priest-prince Simon II as the last outstanding representative of the sons of Zadok, Ab., 1, 2.[18] One might also adduce in favour of this view the fact that among the "fathers" R. Jose ben Jo'eser, scribe and priest of a lower priestly order, who

---

13 Cf. Wellhausen, 77; Schürer, II, 466.

14 Cf. on this E. Bickermann, Der Gott d. Makkabäer (1937), 50-58. One might describe the constitutional status of Jerusalem and related territory as either a theocracy or a hierocracy. The latter term is chosen in what follows, since it seems closest to the historical facts, cf. Meyer-Weiss, 19, n. 6.

15 Meyer-Weiss, 20, n. 1.

16 Cf. on this Str.-B., I, 999; Schürer, II, 254.

17 Cf. bYoma, 8b, 9b Bar. For the rest the rite of making a lustration out of the ashes of the red heifer does not seem to have been practised much. Acc. to Para, 3, 5, apart from Moses and Ezra, Simon the Just (c. 190 B.C.) and John Hyrcanus I (135-104 B.C.) and then the high-priests Elyeho'ehai b Kayyaf, Chanan'el the Egyptian (37-36 and 34 ff. B.C. → VII, 459, 18 ff.) and Yishma''el b Phiabi (59-61 A.D.) are supposed to have prepared a heifer. The atavistic custom was taken up into the halachic theory of the Rabb. and was defended against a non-Jew by R. Jochanan b Zakkai (c. 80 A.D.), cf. Pesikt., 4, 189-196 (Wünsche, 47) and Str.-B., I, 861.

18 For the Rabb. Simon II b Onias II (c. 190 B.C.), confused by Jos. with Simon I b Onias I, plays a part in their abbreviated chronology as a member of the fictional (cf. Neh. 8-10) "great congregation" and is thus stamped as one of themselves, Schürer, II, 419 f. In reality this priest-prince extolled in Sir. 50 (→ VII, 37, 19 ff.) was no Pharisee or Rabbi but as a son of Zadok the spiritual ancestor of the anti-pharisaic hierocracy of Qumran, cf. on this P. E. Kahle, Die Kairoer Genisa, Germ. ed., ed. R. Meyer (1962), 20 f.

must have lived. c. 150 B.C., [19] is depicted as a man who lived according to the Pharisaic ideal. [20] Similarly it may be pointed out that up to the destruction of the temple there were always priests who came under the category of Perushim. [21] In this light one may naturally assume that priestly thinking inaugurated a movement aiming at holiness, [22] although Pharisaic priests remained a minority both within the priesthood itself and also within the Pharisaic movement. The decisive factor for the future was that the idea of everyday sanctification by the Law fell on fruitful soil in lay circles, e.g., some of the Chasidim → 14, 30 ff. Although the evidence is incomplete, it is enough to show that the lead was taken by the laity from the very outset and that, in contrast to the Zadokidic Chasidim of Qumran, the priests did not enjoy any preeminence merely by right of birth. Lay dominance may be seen at once in the corporate structure of Pharisaism; this is obviously not based on a sacral model in the narrower sense but manifests a form which was possible anywhere and at any time, especially in the more numerous and spiritually predominant *diaspora*.

2. The Pharisaic Societies.

Societies and the formation of societies were of old standing in Israel. It is thus natural that the Perushim should form fellowships. These were not graded according to the hierocratic principle but formed rather from the standpoint of holiness, and both in the temple state and also in the *diaspora* they were more or less sharply differentiated from Judaism as a whole by definite rules. [23] Unfortunately we have virtually no data on Pharisaic societies in the pre-Chr. period and apart from the incomplete accounts of the 1st cent. A.D. the Rabb. tradition leaves many open questions even in relation to the 2nd cent. A.D. Yet polemical statements from Qumran (→ 28, 7 ff.) and some Rabb. traditions, as well as Jos., show that at the latest the Perushim must have begun to organise themselves firmly at the beginning of the 1st cent. B.C. The resolute resistance which Pharisaism put up to the Hasmonean Alexander Jannai (103-76 B.C.) would have been unthinkable without an organised union of some numerical strength, cf. Jos. Ant., 13, 372-6. Again T. Shab., 1, 15 presupposes that the existence of the Parush, who lives corporately acc. to specific rules, was already a natural and well-established factor at the commencement of our era: "The school of Shammai has said: A Parush must not eat with a 'Am ha-'Ares who has a discharge; but the school of Hillel permitted it." One may correctly assume from this that in gen. the relatively late Rabb. source material rests on older traditions, so that it is possible to sketch the character of Pharisaic societies at least in outline.

a. The Chabura.

Acc. to the sources available the Perushim banded together in "societies" חֲבוּרוֹת sing. חֲבוּרָה. The term "chabura" which is used here is in itself neutral. It tells us nothing about the nature of the society designated nor the form of union, and certainly one cannot detect any sacral ref. in it. Thus one might speak of a union of miscreants [24] or a society of the

---

[19] Cf. Schürer, II, 421 f. If there is a historical core to the story of Jose's martyrdom in Gn. r., 65, 22 on 27:27, which was fashioned by the spirit of a later age, then the tendency towards observing the perisha even outside the temple ministry proper must have been present already in the first half of the 2nd cent. B.C.

[20] Cf. Ab., 1, 4 and esp. Chag., 2, 7: "Josef b Jo'eser was a righteous man in the priesthood and his clothing [defiled by] impress (→ III, 418, 24 ff.) [only] in what is holy," i.e., be could keep his clothes so Levitically clean that he could eat the wave-offering in them and needed to change only before eating the sacrificial meat, cf. on him J. Jeremias, 266, 289, 292.

[21] J. Jeremias, 291 f.

[22] Cf. Schl. Gesch. Isr., 138; Meyer Pharisäismus, 680; J. Jeremias, 292.

[23] On what follows cf. esp. the full collection of material in Str.-B., II, 494-519.

[24] Gn. r., 87, 2 on 39:7: חבורה של רשעים.

righteous. [25] Chabura would have a purely gen. sense in such cases. A philanthropic society for ministry in the community would also be called a chabura. [26] There is nothing to show that such a society would have to be Pharisaic, and in view of the long history of Jewish benevolence this would indeed be most unlikely. [27] Furthermore a group of men meeting to sacrifice and eat the Passover together can be described as chabura. [28] In particular we may note that the term plays a role when in the sense of "college" chabura can denote a union of scholars or the society of a teacher and his pupils. [29] The chabura becomes a specific Pharisaic society only through the chaberuth (חֲבֵרוּת), i.e., the firm obligations accepted by the initiate, → lines 30 ff. [30] The apparently older nominal form חֶבֶר is to be distinguished from חֲבוּרָה. As distinct from this it occurs already in the canonical writings of the OT. [31] Cheber is used on Hasmonean coins for gerousia or senate and thus denotes the aristocratic union which as the nobility controlled the Jerusalem hierocracy along with the priest-prince. [32] Cheber is continually found in Rabb. works in the combination חֶבֶר הָעִיר "city-union." [33] Insofar as the few examples permit of an interrelating of cheber and chabura, it can only be along the lines that chabura and not cheber is always used when the ref. is to a Pharisaic society, which may suggest that the Pharisaic movement was originally private or individual by nature, or had more of the character of the conventicle. [34]

b. The Chaberim.

The member, or more precisely the full member (→ 18, 7 ff.), of a Pharisaic chabura is called חָבֵר. [35] The chaber in this sense is one who has accepted the society statutes or chaberuth. As such, unless he has done this as a priest, he is usually a layman in relation to the priesthood and the wise men and scribes. Probably from the very beginning, this does not preclude scribes or wise man (→ 20, 11 ff.) as well as priests from being members, esp. as the aim of good conduct demanded some material direction. Fundamentally, however, chaber and chakam or talmid-chakam are not identical, cf. the late tradition in Pesikt.r., 11 (42a): "Their (sc. the Israelites') chaberim are concerned to show benevolence ... their chaberim attach themselves to the wise." [36]

c. The Chaberuth.

The obligations accepted by the chaber are grouped under the master-concept חֲבֵרוּת. It is historically very likely — and the extant and often varying traditions support this —

---

[25] חבורה של צדיקים, loc. cit.

[26] bPes., 113b: חבורה של מצוה "benevolence society."

[27] Cf. Ab., 1, 2 (→ n. 18) and Str.-B., IV, 536-610.

[28] bPes., 89a b, where the members of such a society are בני חבורה.

[29] bBer., 9b: במעמד כל החבורה "in the presence of the full society of scribes"; jTer., 2, 3 (41c, 29 f.): When Rab lectured in his academy בחבורתיה, he taught acc. to the view of R. Meir; but in the congregation (בציבורא) acc. to that of R. Jochanan the sandal-maker."

[30] On the nominal construction in -ut cf. L. Gulkowitsch, *Die Bildung v. Abstraktbegriffen in d. hbr. Sprachgeschichte* (1931), 44.

[31] "Union," "fellowship" Hos. 6:9; בֵּית חֶבֶר "common house" Prv. 21:9; 25:24, cf. B. Gemser, *Sprüche Salomos, Hndbch. AT,* I, 16[2] (1963) on 21:9.

[32] Cf. Meyer-Weiss, 25 f.

[33] Cf. esp. S. Krauss, *Synagogale Altertümer* (1922), 19-23.

[34] Conversely חבורה can be used of the worshipping community, e.g., Cant. r., 8, 12 on 8:14 "At the hour when the Israelites read the Torah in (their) assemblies" בשעה שישראל (קורין בתורה בחבורות).

[35] On the everyday meaning of חָבֵר cf. Meyer-Weiss, 27.

[36] ... וחבריהם שלהם עוסקים בגמילות חסדים חבריהם דבוקים לחכמים, cf. Levy Wört., s.v., חָבֵר.

that the chaberuth underwent many shifts in the course of time and that the individual
schools within Pharisaism (→ 26, 39 ff.) lent different nuances to the societies influenced
by them. Nevertheless, the picture is uniform to the degree that there are always two
chief features in the chaberuth, namely, the obligation to pay tithes regularly and the
concern to carry the Law into everyday life in the form in which it applies to priestly
service in the temple. [37] From the 1st cent. A.D. we have certain traditions which show
that the Pharisaic organisation itself recognised gradations. A lower rank of הַמְעַשֵּׂר
"tithers" was distinguished from the true chaber who accepted the duty of ritual cleanness as well as the obligation to pay the temple tax, which reminds us of the concern for
legality in some 2nd cent. Chasidic circles (→ 14, 20 ff.). This inner differentiation may
be seen in Demai, 6, 6: "The school of Shammai has said: One should sell one's olives
only to a chaber; but the school of Hillel said: To a tither too." [38] Before acceptance
into the society, at least for the future chaber, there was a period of testing, different
schools using different criteria. In this period the candidates had to show whether they
knew how, e.g., to protect their fruits from unclean dew, water, wine, oil, blood and
honey, and also from unclean milk, or how to guard their clothes from contact with Levitically unclean persons. [39] The school of Hillel demanded 30 days in both cases, but followers
of Shammai asked for 30 days testing in the case of fluids and a full year in that of clothing,
so that we get two stages of chaber novitiate. [40] Teaching is also given concerning the
expulsion of a guilty chaber and eventual readmission. [41] At this date, however, we are
not told about the panel which decides whether to accept candidates or not. [42] In forming
structured societies, laying down basic statutes, and regulating admissions and expulsions,
the Pharisees are by no means original but simply stand in an older and broader tradition,
as may be seen from the account of the Essenes in Jos. Bell., 2, 137 f. and the rules of the
Zadokidic society of Qumran. [43]

The reconstruction of the Pharisaic societies acc. to sources after Hadrian seems to
have been along the same lines as the chabura and with the same thrust as the chaberuth.
Thus in the 2nd half of the 2nd cent. A.D. the one who has pledged to tithe himself is
called "accredited" or "reliable" נֶאֱמָן, jDemai, 2, 2 (22d, 41 ff.), and of the chaber the
fragmentary tradition in T Demai, 2, 2 says: "He who takes four things upon himself is
accepted as chaber, namely, that he will not give the priestly offering and tithes to any
'Am ha-'Ares (among the priests and Levites), [44] that he will not prepare his clean thing
alongside a 'Am ha-'Ares and that he will eat his profane food in cleanness . . . " [45] The
final obligation to be supplied is that of the law of cleanness, a basic provision being the
ritual washing of the hands before meals, T Demai, 2, 11. [46] At this later stage the future

---

[37] Cf. the def. of Nathan b Jechiel, Aruch completum, ed. A. Kohut (1878-1892), s.v.
פרוש: "Parush is the one who has separated himself from everything unclean, from unclean
food and from the 'Am ha-'Ares, who is not particular about food."

[38] Being soft, olives can easily become unclean, Str.-B., II, 504. On what follows in
T Demai, 6, 6: "The pious of the school of Hillel conformed to the school of Shammai," cf.
Meyer-Weiss, 28 and n. 2.

[39] Cf. Maksh, 6, 4 and Str.-B., II, 505.

[40] T Demai, 2, 12: When is the candidate accepted? The school of Shammai says: With
reference to fluids [after] 12 months. But the school of Hillel says: In this and the other [case
after] 30 days."

[41] bBek., 31a Bar. and par.; Str.-B., II, 506.

[42] Acc. to bBek., 30b Abba Sha'ul (c. 150 A.D.) was of the view that a talmid-chakam
as novice need not accept the chaberuth before a college of three chaberim. But one can
hardly agree with Str.-B., II, 506 in using this as a basis for the practice prior to 70 A.D.

[43] Cf. esp. 1 QSa and 1 QSb.

[44] After the fall of the hierocracy, then, priests and Levites had a claim to be admitted
only if they submitted to the Pharisaic rule, → 32, 1 ff.

[45] Cf. on this Nathan b Jechiel's def. of parush → n. 37.

[46] The practice of washing the hands, possibly taken over as a custom (מנהג) from
ordinary table manners and assimilated to the priestly rite of cleansing before offering, is a

chaber must still undergo a test before appearing before a college of three unless he has accepted the chaberuth for a longer period prior to his acceptance. [47] Since instruction of the new entrant is continued even after he is received into the society, one may suspect that as a rule the Rabb. have in mind the chaber who is not chakam or talmid-chakam and who has thus to be familiarised with the refinements of Pharisaic observance of the Law. [48] Thus the relatively late ref. from the 2nd cent. confirm the thesis advanced above (→ 17, 25 ff.) that a chaber does not have to be a representative of wisdom and scribal learning. The rules regarding the banishing and reinstatement of backsliders are the same now as earlier. This shows how little self-evident it was that a man should be a Pharisaic chaber in the true sense even after the official victory of Pharisaically orientated Rabbinism, → 31, 9 ff. R. Shim'on and R. Jehoshua (both c. 150 A.D.) with their ruling that backsliders can always be restored are normative for the halacha, TDemai, 2, 9; bBek., 31a Bar.

Just as the Zadokites of Qumran and their followers felt themselves to be the true Israel and marked themselves off in principle from the majority of the people as an opposing organisation, so the Pharisaic societies were comparatively small groups inspired by a similar claim to exclusiveness. Their statutes were aimed in like manner against the overwhelming majority of the people [49] and they saddled this non-Pharisaic majority with the uncomplimentary name of 'Am ha-'Ares. Irrespective of the later development of this term, it does not indicate here an uncultured person but a full Jew who is accustomed to thinking and living in the traditional framework and rejects the Pharisaic idea of the actualising of the priestly law in everyday life, → V, 589, 26 ff. Hence the judgment of the chaberim on the 'Am ha-'Ares does not relate to his social position — he may belong to the highest priestly nobility, or be a simple priest or Levite, or a normal pious Jew — nor to his general level of

---

typical example of the way in which "the wise" make a religious law out of a custom. Acc. to jShab., 1 (3d, 39) "Hillel and Shammai gave rulings about the cleanness of the hands הלל ושמאי גזרו על טהרת הידים. They could only establish a halacha for their chaburoth; they had no power beyond this. Ed., 5, 6, 7 tells us that the Tannaite Eli'ezer b Chanok was excommunicated because he opposed the gen. introduction of washing the hands. Unfortunately we do not know the exact date of the dispute, but it must be after the collapse of the hierocracy. For materials cf. Str.-B., I, 695-704; cf. also G. Lisowsky, Jadajim, Die Mischna, VI, 11 (1956), 5 f. and on Jad., 1, 1-24; on the minhag → 34, 18 ff.

[47] bBek., 30b Bar.: "He who would take upon him the rules of the chaberuth must accept them before three chaberim; the talmid-chakam too must accept them before three chaberim. But a senator [of the academy] and one who presides in the academy need not accept them before three chaberim since he has already been subject to them some time, since he took his seat [in the academy]." This Bar. is significant in that it shows that the primary point is accepting the religious law of Pharisaism, membership of the chabura being open. Cf. also bBek., 30b, Bar.: "If someone comes to take upon him the rules of the chaberuth, [and] he has been seen to follow them [already] in secret in his house, he is to be accepted [at once] and given further instruction. If [this is] not [so], he must be instructed [first] and then accepted. R. Shim'on b Jochai (c. 150 A.D.) says: Either way, he is to be accepted [at once in this case] and will then learn further"; the par. TDemai, 2, 10 f. is not so clear (cf. Str.-B., II, 508).

[48] Cf. bBer., 30b, Bar. and jDemai, 2, 3 (23a, 8 f.) Bar.: "A man is to be accepted in view of handwashing [observed by him] and then taught the laws of cleanness תני מקריבין לכנפים ואחר כך מלמדין לטהרות. Similarly the Amorean R. Yishaq b El'asar (I c. 280 A.D. or II c. 340 A.D.) gives the following sequence: washing the hands, lighter grades of uncleanness, true laws of cleanness and tithing.

[49] Acc. to Jos. Ant., 17, 42 there were under Herod over 6000 ὄντες ὑπὲρ ἑξακισχίλιοι Pharisees; Jos. probably bases this no. on Nicolaus of Damascus. In contrast there were about 4000 Essenes, cf. Ant., 18, 20. Only firmly organised Palestinian members are obviously counted here and not those of the diaspora or groups of sympathisers.

education nor to his economic status nor political rank; it refers solely and simply to his anti-Pharisaic attitude.

The trend of the chaberuth was to restrict the dealings of the chaberim with the 'Am ha-'Ares esp. in respect of fruits, which easily became Levitically unclean, and then in other matters → n. 37. The reality was often far different; apart from the bitter conflicts between the chaberim and the 'Am ha-'Ares of Galilee in the period after Hadrian, political, economic and social factors usually prevailed in the long run. [50]

3. Pharisaic Wisdom and Learning.

Pharisaism would soon have been consigned to the past if it had not been especially fruitful soil for wisdom and learning.

a. The Chakamim.

It may be accepted that the basically international and interreligious wisdom of the Ancient Orient had had a legitimate place in Israel from the days of Solomon → VII, 477, 16 ff. As an educational factor this probably played a much bigger role among the people than one might suspect from the canonical writings. The mark of the post-exilic age is that secular wisdom, which is concerned to give knowledge of the world and the orders of life, and seeks to make man a useful member of society, made a significant agreement with the sphere of faith in Yahweh, which originally stood alone and whose main themes are creation and revelation, salvation history and fulfilment. The process of fusion led men to see, or to think they saw, in the Law, not merely Yahweh's plan of creation and salvation but also the order of the world and life as something which God had originally designed and established. Thus the Law and wisdom could become different expressions for one and the same thing. A vivid picture of this new form of wisdom, which in contrast to the older sacral traditions or the prophetic traditions merits for the first time the predicate theology, is offered by Sir. 19:20: "All wisdom is fear of the Lord, and in all wisdom is [contained] the doing of the Law." The ref. is not just to the idea of the Law, but acc. to the hymn in Sir. 24:1-22 wisdom is visibly connected with the holy city, the temple and the Pent.: "All this is offered by the book of the covenant of God Most High, (namely) the law which Moses gave us as an inheritance for the congregations of Jacob," 24:23. The process at issue was essentially concluded already in the 3rd cent. B.C.; hence the close fusion of wisdom and the Law into an embracing theology is old-Jewish and pre-Pharisaic. The teacher of this wisdom, like his secular colleague, bears the title חָכָם. [51] The chakam as a man with a broad horizon and comprehensive education serves among the leading men of the state and comes before the ruler acc. to Sir. 39:4. He is an aristocrat of the spirit and has a constant and unbroken self-consciousness as such. For without him ordered government and law are inconceivable, as is also the education of the new generation. In the communal life of Qumran the wise man follows in rank the heads of the fathers of the community, directly after the hereditary sacerdotal and secular aristocracy, 1 QSa 2:11-22. [52] Given a fellowship in which leadership does not accrue necessarily to the native aristocracy but is dependent on specific educational advantages, it is natural that spiritual leadership at least should belong to the chakam in such a society. [53] This

---

[50] Cf. Meyer-Weiss, 32 f.

[51] Even after the fusion of wisdom and the Law we still find the idea of secular wisdom in the modern sense of science, cf., e.g., bBM, 85b-86a, which says critically of the renowned school-head of Neharde'a, Mar Shemu'el (d. 254 A.D.): "Shemu'el the astronomer is due the title of scholar (hakkim), [but] not that of Rabbi" (→ VI, 961, 9 ff.).

[52] Cf. Meyer-Weiss, 35, n. 1.

[53] On this cf. esp. J. Jeremias, 289.

explains why the wise man, if he found his way into the Pharisaic societies, should relatively quickly win a dominant influence in them. The chaburoth were democratic unions whose members were disturbed existentially by the problem of keeping God's will in everyday life. Only the chakam could give them a valid answer, since he placed his knowledge of wisdom and the Law at the service of Pharisaic conduct as well as instruction of the brethren.

With the increasing influence of the chakam, however, Pharisaism increasingly broke through traditional limits. From the 3rd cent. B.C., no doubt under the supreme influence of the *diaspora*, a new world of ideas forced its way into the complex of Jewish wisdom. The main effect of this influence is not so much in the concept of God as in anthropology, [54] soteriology, and eschatology (→ VII, 46, 15 ff.) to the degree that man began to be seen as not just in the world but rather as the member of two worlds. It is palpable that with the change in the concept of man ideas of salvation and the last things should be completely changed too, the result being a new dogmatic which was regarded as orthodox only because it carried the day and pushed into the background, if it did not entirely supplant, the older Jewish beliefs which were essentially identical with the statements of the canonical writings and which could thus be claimed as legitimate. [55] The bearers of these new religious ideas, which were originally alien to the thinking of Israel and older Judaism, were the chakamim to whom Pharisaism with its fundamental concern for the sanctification of the individual had recourse. This movement, then, became fruitful soil for the development of a partially new faith-world without which the theology of the New Testament would be inconceivable. Naturally there is no question here of a sudden breakthrough; what we have rather is a slow process over many generations, and yet a process which was persistent in its effects because it did not merely embrace the chaberim in the strict sense but also mastered and fructified popular faith and thought as well. In contrast, then, to the Sadducean colleges of older Jewish orthodoxy, the Pharisaic chakamim were the representatives of true progress and piety, and when at the end of the 1st cent. A.D. Judaism began to differentiate itself from the Hellenistic spirit in a comprehensive restriction enjoined by reconstruction, the central points of its anthropology and soteriology, which had their origin in the world of Hellenistic-Oriental belief, had already become constituent parts of Jewish faith (→ VI, 377, 32 ff.; 379, 13 ff.; 380, 25 ff.; VII, 46, 30 ff.).

But a tension also appears which the older Judaism represented by the Sadducees had never known and which finds expression in the fact that the traditional sacred text does not always agree with the theological ideas that had gradually developed in Pharisaism and finally become normative for Judaism as a whole. To unite the two, the old and the new, was the task of the scribes. We have thus to turn to the scribes or experts in the Law as the last of the groups of which Pharisaism is constituted.

b. The Soferim (→ I, 740, 22 ff.).

Even more than the term chakam the word סוֹפֵר has a broad range of meaning. On the one hand it simply stands for the "literate person" who could be of service to those unable to read or write for themselves. [56] Then it means the "elementary teacher" who

---

[54] Meyer Hellenistisches, *passim.*
[55] Cf. R. Meyer, Art. "Eschatologie, III" in RGG³, II, 662-5 (Bibl.).
[56] Cf. the natural way that "village scribes" κωμογραμματεῖς or κωμῶν γραμματεῖς are introduced in Jos. Bell., 1, 24; Ant., 16, 203.

taught writing acc. to exercise books and models found in Ugarit (c. 1500 B.C.) and also in the Wadi Murabbaʿāt (c. 130 A.D.). [57] In more educated circles the word sofer has the same sense as "secretary" in its wide modern range of meaning; we have examples from the adjutant of a commander [58] to the supreme office of the סֹפֵר הַמֶּלֶךְ "royal chancellor." [59] סוֹפֵר with its Aram. equivalent סָפְרָא takes on a special nuance in the post-exilic period. In place of the royal chancellor we now have the "secretary of state"; the Zadokite Ezra bears this title, not understood by a later age and changed into "scribe," acc. to Ezra 7:12, 21: סָפַר דָּתָא דִּי־אֱלָהּ שְׁמַיָּא "secretary for the law of the God of heaven." [60] Expressed in the phrase is Ezra's responsibility to the Persian emperor and also his authority as a government official over against the Jerusalem priesthood. But the term sofer, not this time at the level of imperial politics but in the narrower sphere of the temple province of Judah, can also have a special nuance in the form of the "temple scribe." The high-priest of Jerusalem was the authoritative interpreter of the Law for the temple province of Jerusalem-Judah in the narrower sense and then for the whole of Judaism in a broader sense. [61] To be able to discharge this function he needed a staff of experts which was not recruited primarily from the wise men as the representatives of general culture but from men devoted to the tradition of the text of the Law and also to its exposition, i.e., from the soferim. There is evidence of this group in a decree of Antiochus III in 200 B.C., in which the "temple scribes" γραμματεῖς τοῦ ἱεροῦ among others are excused from the poll tax. [62] In the first instance these scribes, like their secular colleagues, are men who can write. Their first task in the temple, then, is to provide more copies of the sacred text, esp. the Pent., and to correct and revise the copied MSS. But as earlier, so now this physical labour is not the main job of the soferim, no matter how skilful they are at it. [63] As a guardian of the sacred text the sofer of higher rank was also the man of legal understanding who could interpret the traditional Law and apply it validly to the present situation. Thus in 1 Macc. 7:12 it is the "scribes" γραμματεῖς who examine the Law (→ 14, 20 ff.) to establish the legitimacy of the Aaronite Alkimus. The scribes were also affected by the above-mentioned fusion (→ 20, 14 ff.) of the Law and wisdom, of interpretation of the Law and wisdom teaching, so that the two gradually came together and the terms sofer and chakam became more or less interchangeable, cf. already Sir. 38:24 - 39:11. Acc. to Sir. the task of the sofer [64] is to consider the Law of the Most High (39:1), to follow the wisdom of the fathers, to wrestle with prophecies, to see to the presentation of famous men (39:2), to exchange wise sayings, to unlock the secret meaning of parables (39:3) and to solve the riddles of proverbs.

Only the firm linking of wisdom and the Law or the chakam and sofer as their representatives yields the complex concept of the "scribe." Our express concern here, with ref. to the statements of the NT about the relation of the scribes to the Pharisees (→ 38, 16 ff.), is to emphasise that the scribe as such is not of Pharisaic origin, that long before Pharisaism ever existed there were scribes both in the Jerusalem temple and also throughout the dispersion, and that the scribes gave a religious and philosophical aspect to Judaism. [65] Nor should one overlook the fact that up to 70 A.D. there were always non-Pharisaic

---

[57] Cf. C. Virolleaud, "Le palais royal d'Ugarit II," Mission de Ras Shamra VII (1957), No. 184-9, Fr. 11 (DJD, II, 92) and ostraca, 73 (DJD, II, 175), 78-80 (II, 178 f.).

[58] E.g., 2 K. 25:19 (Jer. 52:25): סֹפֵר שַׂר הַצָּבָא.

[59] 2 K. 12:11 סֹפֵר הַמֶּלֶךְ; cf. further Ges.-Buhl and Köhler-Baumg., s.v. ספר.

[60] H. H. Schaeder, "Esra d. Schreiber," Beiträge z. hist. Theol., 5 (1930), passim; W. Rudolph, Esr. u. Neh., Hndbch. AT, I, 20 (1949), ad loc.

[61] Cf. Meyer-Weiss, 39.

[62] Cf. on this Bickermann, op. cit. (→ n. 14), 176 and n. 176 (Bibl.).

[63] Cf. F. M. Cross, "The Development of the Jewish Scripts" in G. E. Wright, The Bible and the Ancient Near East, Essays in Honor of W. F. Albright (1961), 131-202 (Bibl.).

[64] Cf. Sir. 38:24 where the Gk. text σοφία γραμματέως matches the Hbr. חכמת סופר.

[65] Cf. Jos. Ap., 1, 179 and Schl. Gesch. Isr., 395, n. 38.

scribes who united the Law and wisdom along the lines of Sir. [66] But as wisdom provided fertile soil for the development of sacral law on a broader basis, so did Pharisaism with its attempt to fulfil the Law in everyday life. For the Pharisee, even to the point of caricature, [67] studied the Law and its application in the individual situations of ordinary life. This meant, however, that the scribe in his capacity as a sofer, i.e., a guardian and interpreter of the Torah, was vitally necessary to the inner and outer life of the perushim or chaberim.

4. The Pharisees as a Party.

The foregoing sketch shows that originally Pharisaism was a trend or movement in Judaism which was open to all national groups and recognised no distinction between the small temple site as the heart of the Holy Land and the numerically far more imposing diaspora. Along these lines it always remained a trend or movement in the diaspora, finding its most significant expression in the individual chaburoth (→ 16, 35 ff.) or in the observance of the chaberuth (→ 17, 29 ff.) by individual Pharisees. The dispersion offered no basis for the formation of political groups. Things were very different, however, in Jerusalem and the related territory. Pharisaism, based on the idea of applying the Law in everyday life (→ 15, 26 ff.), had also a strong concern for legitimacy. Thus a corporate political will could easily be formed as the view arose among the chaberim that the hierocratic leadership was not legitimate or had made itself unworthy, or that the Law was not being fulfilled as they understood it. In this way the trend or movement developed into a party which, with the chaburoth as the core, had to maintain itself in the ebb and flow of domestic and foreign political events. In this derivative sense Pharisaism probably became a party within the Jerusalem hierocracy as early as the reign of Hyrcanus I.

a. Pharisees and Hasmoneans.

At the height of their power the Hasmoneans had bitter opponents, [68] as may be seen when John Hyrcanus I came to the throne in 134 B.C. They succeeded in coming to terms with the priestly nobility in Jerusalem (→ VII, 43, 34 ff.), but the Pharisees developed into an opposition party whose domestic programme was to replace what they regarded as an illegitimate dynasty with an Aaronite high-priestly family. Hyrcanus I was able to secure his government against all opposing groups, Jos. Ant., 13, 22. But this did not prevent the Pharisees from renewing the struggle as occasion offered, esp. as the demand for a legitimate priest-prince was regarded as the supreme expression of fulfilment of the Law. Under the second successor of Hyrcanus I, Alexander Jonathan-Jannai (103-76 B.C.), there was a civil war for 6 years (93-88 B.C.). [69] Towards the end of the conflict the Pharisees as the declared enemies of the king asked for the help of the Seleucid Demetrius III Eukairus. At Shechem the soldiers of Jannai were defeated by the Syrian mercenaries called in by the Pharisees. Jos. does not expressly say that it was the Pharisees who called

---

[66] This is rightly stressed by J. Jeremias, 263.

[67] Cf. jBer., 9 (13b, 38 ff.) and par., where the Pharisees are divided into five types, and only the "god-fearing Pharisee" פרוש יראה after the manner of Job and the "god-loving parush" פרוש אהבה after the manner of Abraham meet with approval.

[68] Cf. on this Meyer-Weiss, 44-50.

[69] Jos. Bell., 1, 86-106; Ant., 13, 324-344, 352-364, 372-383.

in the alien ruler in order that they might achieve their goal and the Rabb. tradition speaks only of the anti-Hasmonean position of the Pharisees under Jannai, [70] but the text 4 QpNa 1:2 on 2:12, although fragmentary, refers to a Demetrius who on the advice of the "exegetes of falsehood," i.e., the Pharisees (→ 30, 2 ff.), tried to enter Jerusalem. [71] This reference, which is probably to the war between Demetrius III and Jannai, is esp. valuable in that it explains the surprising turn in events. In spite of Jannai's defeat the opposition did not attain its end. Obviously when the Syrians threatened Jerusalem, some 6000 Jews ceased to support the policy of the Pharisees and went over from the opposition to Jannai. While Demetrius III deemed it prudent not to exploit his victory but to withdraw, Jannai, after a successful campaign, confined the rest of his opponents to a small and as yet unidentified locality in Judah [72] and at a feast to celebrate his victory had 800 of his leading opponents in Jerusalem crucified alive, an act of cruelty hitherto unknown in Israel, but noted in 4 QpNa 1:2 on 2:12 as well as Jos. [73] It is very probable that many and perhaps most of the victims were Pharisees. After this massacre there was a mass flight on the part of opponents, cf. Jos. Bell., 1, 98 and for a reflection of this from the Pharisaic standpoint cf. Ps. Sol. 17:15-19. Having broken the opposition in this way, Jannai did not need to fear it during the final years of his reign. But he in no way underestimated the spiritual power of Pharisaism. On the other hand the imposing procession at his funeral shows that his reputation had, surprisingly, been very little harmed by his violent suppression of the Pharisees and his cruelty, Jos. Ant., 13, 405 f.; Bell., 5, 304.

Things changed for the embattled Pharisees when Salome Alexandra came to power (76-67 B.C.). The queen, whom Jannai had advised to make peace with the Pharisees on his death-bed (Ant., 13, 399-404, cf. also bSota, 22b), clearly came under the influence of the Pharisees, who by all appearances controlled the council as a majority party. In spite of her successful foreign policy the dictum in Jos. Bell., 1, 112 applies in domestic affairs: "She had power over others, but the Pharisees had power over her." These again used their power brutally, murdering as they pleased among their aristocratic opponents, Bell., 1, 113. With the death of Salome Alexandra in 67 B.C. their rule came to an end, Bell., 1, 117-119. In the Rabb. tradition this short rule of the Pharisees is depicted as a prosperous period; thus acc. to S. Lv., 14, 1 on 26:4 the divine blessing of rain was so great on account of the sinlessness under Shim'on b Shatach and the queen that grains of wheat became as big as kidneys, grains of barley as big as olive kernels, and lentils as gold denarii, cf. Lv. r., 35, 10 on 26:4 and bBer., 48a. In fact, however, we know very little about the extent of the influence of the Pharisees in shaping external and internal life in Israel. The few extant school traditions relate merely to the cultic order in the temple and the festal calendar. [74] All the same, we do become acquainted for the first time with a leading Pharisee, Shim'on b Shatach, [75] even if he is presented for the most part as the hero of anecdotes and jokes [76] rather than a man who influenced the narrow circle of the

---

[70] Cf. bQid., 66a, where Jehuda b Gedidya condemns the priest-kingship of Jannai in the words: "King Jannai, content yourself with the kingly crown, leave the priestly crown to the successors of Aaron" ינאי המלך רב לך כתר מלכות הנח כתר כהנה לזרעו של אהרון. Rather later is a tradition in bYoma, 71b in which Shema'ya and Abtalyon reproach the Hasmonean high-priest for not doing the peaceful work of Aaron.

[71] (v 12 fin) פשרו על דמי]טרוס מלך יון אשר בקש לבוא לירושלים בעצת דורשי [ואין מחריד החלקות. J. M. Allegro, "Further Light on the History of the Qumran Sect," JBL, 76 (1956), 89 f.

[72] Jos. Ant., 13, 380: Βαιθομμει. Cf. the vl. and Jos. Bell., ed. and transl. O. Michel and O. Bauernfeind, I (1962), 408, n. 52.

[73] Cf. Jos. Ant., 13, 380 f.; Bell., 1, 97 f. with 4 QpNah 1:7 on 2:13: מות בדורשי החלקות אשר יתלה אנשים חיים; Allegro, op. cit., 91.

[74] Cf. Meyer-Weiss, 49.

[75] A brother-in-law of Jannai of non-priestly origin, cf. J. Jeremias, 176, n. 1.

[76] We must describe as humorous pranks the two anecdotes jBer., 7 (11b, 34-53) which tell how Shim'on by a halachic dodge tricked the king about 150 vows (→ n. 103) and how,

chaburoth. The later tradition which from the standpoint of an exclusive Pharisaic reading of history made him partly president נָשִׂיא and partly vice-president אַב בֵּית דִּין of the council [77] helps us to glimpse the claim to power which Pharisaism raised under Salome Alexandra and which is vividly depicted by Jos. Along with him there is mention of Juda b Tabbai; he, too, had to flee before Jannai. The two sayings preserved in Ab., 1, 8 f., which belong to the legal sphere, seem to suggest Pharisaic domination of the jurisdiction under the queen. [78] That the domestic policies of the Pharisees — they obviously left foreign affairs to the queen — were not generally liked may be seen from the great support for Aristobulus II, who in domestic matters followed the line of his father. The Pharisaic hegemony, then, was broken with the death of the queen, but a lasting gain for Pharisaism was that they were now constantly represented in the council, even if always as a minority (→ VII, 862, 20 ff.).

In the ensuing dynastic struggles the Pharisees took a position consistently hostile to the Hasmoneans. When Hyrcanus II and Aristobulus II brought their disagreement to Pompey in 64 B.C. not only the two brothers and their retinues came but acc. to Jos. Ant., 14, 41 the people also spoke as a third party which wanted nothing to do with the monarchy. It is easy to see that this embassy with its democratic tendencies came from the Pharisees even if they were not its leaders. Their objection to the royal house is new compared to their previous policy to the degree that they now call the Hasmonean prince-priesthood an innovation out of line with Jewish history. This involves a surrender of their previous insistence on a legitimate priest-prince in Jerusalem and its replacement with a complete rejection of the hierocracy. This initiated the policy which made it possible for Pharisaism both in the *diaspora* and also in the motherland to lead a national religious life without political dependence or even provincial autonomy. This new concept would soon come to political expression. When Sosius and Herod I besieged Jerusalem and Antigonus with his loyal supporters defended the holy city to the last, it was the Pharisee Pollion and his pupil Shema'ya who advised that the city should be surrendered to Herod I, Jos. Ant., 15, 3. 6. After Herod's victory in 37 B.C. they not only survived, in contrast to the Sadducean majority on the council (→ VII, 44, 20 ff.), but they were still respected, in contrast to Herod I. [79]

---

brought to the royal feast as chakam at the request of Jewish-Persian guests, he took a seat between the ruling couple and by an appropriate formulation of grace managed to get something set before him, but cf. Schl. Gesch. Isr., 154-7 who overlooks this aspect in the original stories. Among other anecdotes cf. the encounter with Onias in which the head of the Pharisaic school is depicted in the colours of an ethnarch (→ 32, 19 ff.) or patriarch of the period after 70 A.D., Jos. Ant., 14, 22-24; Taan., 3, 12, and also the execution of 50 women in Askalon, Sanh., 6, 8, probably told in view of the crucifixion of 800 Jews by his royal brother-in-law, Jos. Bell., 1, 96 and par. (→ 24, 11 ff.).

[77] Cf. Chag., 2, 2, where in relation to the five "pairs" the first, including Shim'on, is always נָשִׂיא and the second אַב בֵּית דִּין: הראשונים היו נשיאים ושניים להם אבות בית דין; cf. also jChag., 2, 2 (77d, 53 f.), where Shim'on is supposed to have said: "If I were Nasi, I would have killed the magicians": אין אנא מתעביר נשייא אנא מקטל חרשייא. But he can also be second, e.g., Ab., 1, 8 and cf. jChag., 2, 2 (77d, 18 ff.) where his place is debated.

[78] Nothing typical of Pharisaism may be inferred from this; cf. the careful legal judgments of the Zadokites acc. to Damasc. 9:16 - 10:3 (10:10-16).

[79] For the relation of Pollion and Samaias to Shema'ya and Abtalyon cf. Schürer, II, 422-4. It is unthinkable that the Samaias who supported Herod in 47 B.C. and is mentioned in Jos. Ant., 14, 172-6 should be the same as Shema'ya, who is always mentioned before Abtalyon in Rabb. lit., while Samaias, who comes 10 yrs. later and is expressly called a student of Pollion (= Abtalyon?), is more likely to be the school-head Shammai. If this is so, Jos. wrongly identified Shema'ya as Shammai, which is not surprising seeing the names are so similar (שמי ⟨ שמעיה), esp. as their basic positions were much the same too, cf. Strack Einleitung, 118.

b. Pharisaism from Herod to the Destruction of the Temple.

Herod I did not follow the Hasmonean principle of national particularism with a view to eschatological salvation. In both domestic and foreign affairs he adopted a pronounced universalistic line. He could essentially accept and even favour Pharisaism, for the main interest of the Pharisaic chakamim and soferim was in the religious community with their own chaburoth as its core, in the correct performance of the cultus, and in synagogal life according to their views. On this basis their concept of the high-priestly office was quite different from that of the Sadducees (→ VII, 44, 7 ff.). Since they rejected the prince-priesthood, the political position taken by the high-priest was a matter of indifference to them. The main point was whether he personally met canonical statutes. Herod I, although he made no alliance with the Pharisees and their adherents, did try from the very beginning of his reign not to wound their religious susceptibilities; thus he respected the principle behind their refusal to take an oath of allegiance to the ruler, Jos. Ant., 15, 370; 17, 42. [80] This benevolent neutrality or inclination of Herod towards the Pharisees may be seen finally in the fact that Pharisees were continually in and out the royal court and enmeshed in palace intrigues. [81] Consistently pursuing their anti-Hasmonean policy, the Pharisees throughout Herod's long reign were never champions of resistance along the lines of national particularism orientated to eschatological salvation. [82] Similarly Herod I never pursued a policy of hostility to the Pharisees as he did in relation to the Hasmoneans and the Sadducees who represented their spirit. [83]

Political developments after Herod's death in 4 B.C. were not favourable to the Pharisees, for with the banishment of Archelaus the older Sadducean opponents, who had been brutally suppressed under Herod (→ VII, 44, 22 ff.), regained the upper hand, [84] and one can hardly suppose that the new power structure representing older Jewish orthodoxy would adopt the same attitude of positive neutrality to the Pharisees as did Herod. Certainly the Pharisaic chaburoth and their leaders did not control the gerousia in the decades up to the revolt against Rome and even less did they control the political complexion of the hierocracy. An indirect ref. to this may be seen in the moving complaint of Jos. in Ant., 20, 179-181 at the increase of lawlessness after 50 A.D., for on his lips this simply means that the Pharisees no longer played a normative role in this period. On the other hand the political shift brought about by the banishment of Archelaus did not mean any loss of inner substance at the core of Pharisaism, for the upper stratum of the aristocracy did not attempt any forceful measures against the Pharisaic chaburoth and the Pharisaic scribes enjoyed great popularity, since on the basis of their view of the Law (→ 21, 3 ff.) they were always able to secure the favour of the masses by legalising popular customs and beliefs (→ 21, 8 ff.; VII, 50, 40 ff.).

c. Pharisees and Zealots (→ II, 884, 23 ff.).

We have only a few reliable historical traditions relating to the period in Pharisaic history between the death of Herod and the outbreak of the first revolt. Yet the traditions preserved show that Pharisaism did not constitute a unity in the individual chaburoth but

---

[80] Pollion and Samaias also refused the oath, a sign that the basis of the Pharisaic position was exclusively religious, not political.

[81] Cf. Schl. Gesch. Isr., 236; Meyer Prophet 57 f.; Meyer-Weiss, 51 f.

[82] If the two orators and teachers of the Law, Judas and Matthias, who acc. to Jos. Ant., 17, 149-163 incited their students to tear down the eagle Herod had put on the main gate of the temple and thus demonstrate the real or supposed lawlessness of the king, were actually Pharisees, then they belonged to a left wing from which the Zealots arose (→ 27, 12 ff.) and which was represented within Pharisaism by the Shammaites (→ 31. 30 ff.). Cf. on this H. Graetz, Gesch. d. Juden, III[5] (1905), 235-799; G. Hölscher, Art. "Jos." in Pauly-W., 9 (1916), 1974; W. O. E. Oesterley, A History of Israel, II (1932), 371; Hengel, 330 f.

[83] The massacre foreseen by Herod on his death does not relate to the Pharisees but to the upper stratum he had locked in the hippodrome at Jericho, Jos. Ant., 17, 174-181.

[84] Cf. Meyer-Weiss, 52 f.

that there were many different trends. The differences between Hillel, who came from the Bab. dispersion with a milder interpretation of the Law, and Shammai, whom tradition depicts as a rigorist, are gen. familiar. How far there might have been other Pharisaic schools in Palestine in the 1st cent. A.D. the very fragmentary sources do not permit us to say. We have knowledge of at least one independent group, which was not later put in the genealogy of the fathers, in the form of the Bene Bathyra, who were named after their place of origin, a Bab.-Jewish military colony in Batanaea established under Herod I, and who were highly regarded in Jerusalem prior to Hillel. [85]

The death of Herod I meant the beginning of a crisis for Pharisaism inasmuch as the older principle, which repudiated particularism and its eschatological salvation, was no longer retained in toto and different trends, sometimes sharply divided, established themselves in the movement. The inner disruption in Pharisaism finds historical expression for the first time with the founding of the Zealot party (→ lines 30 ff.; II, 884, 32 ff.) under Judas the Galilean [86] and a Pharisee named Sadoq, Jos. Ant., 18, 4 ff. In Ant., 18, 9 this party, which Jos. mentions alongside the Sadducees, Pharisees and Essenes, is called a "fourth philosophical school" τετάρτη φιλοσοφία. [87] It is to be pointed out that in this classification, as in that of the Pharisees (→ 13, 16 ff.), Jos., who is writing for a Hell. public, is at least not erroneously defining the character of the new movement. The new trend, which probably owes its name to others as the Sadducees, Pharisees and Essenes very likely did too, is in principle simply a radical or particularistic wing of the Pharisees. Thus Jos. Ant., 18, 23 says that Judas was the leader of this fourth philosophical school and that the movement was wholly in line with Pharisaism except for its invincible love of freedom and its acknowledgment of God alone as Ruler and Lord. The primarily Pharisaic character of the new movement is emphasised by Jos. when he mentions the Pharisee Sadoq as co-founder with Judas. There is no doubt that the party of the Zealots had a firmly religious and not, as often assumed, a predominantly political programme and that they had a consistent history which inevitably led them into the revolt under Vespasian. Jos. tells us that Judas had a great following and it may be assumed that this rapid growth was largely at the expense of the older Pharisaism, whether in terms of the chaburoth proper or the larger circle of Pharisaic sympathisers. The reason for this is plain to see. Herod I had brought discredit on the idea of a universal secular kingdom and Pharisaism suffered to some degree from this after his death. The result was opposition to the Pharisaic principle that a worldly form of government, other than the prince-priesthood, must be tolerated if it does not intervene in religious matters. But one part of the opposition, during the resultant inner conflict, left the Pharisaic fellowship while not abandoning the other basic ideas of the movement. Hence we are not merely to see in Sadoq a Pharisaic scribe; we are also to view Judas as a man who, far from being politically ambitious, united in his person politico-military ability and wisdom or scribal learning. Jos. describes him as ἡγεμών in Ant., 18, 23 and σοφιστής in Bell., 2, 118. If the political Messianic claim stands behind ἡγεμών, the title σοφιστής means "teacher" in Bell., 2, 118 and "scholar" in 2, 433 — in both the ref. is to Judas as the father of Menachem the Messianic heir-apparent; the Hbr. equivalent for the term is undoubtedly chakam → 20, 11 ff. The ref. in Jos., then, show that Judas is on the one side the Messianic heir-apparent and that on the other side he is a Pharisaically inclined chakam who fights, not for purely political autonomy, but to help the Law to victory and thus to establish eternal freedom in the form of God's rule. [88] The older Pharisaism tried to differentiate itself from the new daughter-party. [89] It failed to do so. In spite of the split of the more zealous, the Pharisaic

---

[85] On the ref. cf. J. Jeremias, 275, n. 6. It should be noted that the Tiber. Karaite Moshe b Asher regards the men of Bathyra as his spiritual ancestors in the 'Song of the Vine': "The perfect of the vine are the ancient of Bathyra, the heirs of the prophets, who had insight"; cf. on this Kahle, op. cit. (→ n. 18), 91-93.
[86] Cf. Meyer Prophet, 70-79, 160.
[87] Cf. on this Hengel, 79-150.
[88] Cf. Meyer-Weiss, 56 f.
[89] Hengel, 87, n. 5.

core which tried to cling to its basic universalism could not resist the obviously very strong Zealot spirit which enthused the Jews of Palestine.[90] Zealot trains of thought and aspirations remained alive even in strict Pharisaism. Thus it seems that the school of Shammai had a tendency this way,[91] and we can certainly ascribe an explicit Zealot position to Akiba (→ VI, 824, 11 ff.).

d. Pharisaism in the Light of Zadokite Criticism.

Apart from the anti-Pharisaic statements of the NT (→ 36, 2 ff.) there are even more instances from Qumran which show more plainly than the controversies in the Rabb. lit. and Jos.[92] that before its victory at the end of the 1st cent. A.D. Pharisaism was not uncontested but was in principle dogmatically opposed by the older Jewish orthodoxy and that in any case the opposition and rejection did not relate merely to individual rulings of the chaburoth but struck to the very heart of the Pharisaic understanding of the Law. Allusion has already been made to the fact that the translation of the priestly Law into terms of the everyday life of the laity was possible only as the wise man (→ 21, 2 ff.) or the scribe (→ 23, 1 ff.) of Pharisaic persuasion expounded the sacred text. There was, of course, an exposition of the Torah and a relating of the Law to the present day even amongst those in Judaism who were not inspired by the idea of a sanctifying of secular life. The distinctive feature of Pharisaism was that the detailed decisions of religious law not only became constituent statutes in the chaburoth but were also set alongside the Torah or set around it like a fence. Relatively early, then, there probably arose in the different schools collections of religious law which, clearly guarded very jealously by the various trends, took their place alongside the older priestly Law of the Pent. and as oral law claimed the same dogmatic validity as the written Torah. The class. example of oral law continually developed like a fence around the Torah is to be found thematically in Ab., 1, 1, where it is stressed on the one side that the Torah was received in twofold form by Moses on Sinai and it is demanded on the other that a "fence should be made for the written Torah."[93] Jos. is familiar with the same Pharisaic principle. Acc. to Ant., 13, 297 the Pharisees, on the basis of the tradition of the fathers, gave the people laws not contained in the Torah; acc. to the view of the Sadducees, however, the tradition of the fathers was not to be put on the same level as the Law (→ VII, 50, 4 ff.). The distinction between Sadducean-Zadokite and Pharisaic scholarship consists, then, in the fact that the Sadducee with his legal decisions is always subject to criticism, whereas the Pharisaic scribe is bound to a school-tradition which, handed down from teacher to student, is viewed as absolute, so that, as a bearer of the oral Torah and a guardian of the fence about the Law, he claims to be a final court of religious law.[94]

---

[90] Wellhausen, 110 (following Jos.) claims that in a spirit of realism the people brought the Pharisees out of the school, but this must be modified, for it was Zelotism, orientated to eschatological salvation, which brought active force to the Pharisees. Cf. the history of the Zealot movement, Hengel, 319-383.

[91] Cf. the tradition of the eighteen resolutions (Str.-B., Index s.v.) and the Shammaite "fast-scroll" (Megillath Taanith) in bShab., 13b; on this whole matter cf. Hengel, 204-211.

[92] Cf. the material in Str.-B., IV, 344-352.

[93] The demand עָשׂוּ סיג לתורה is traced back to the men of the so-called "great congregation." While it tells us nothing about the chronology, the prominent position of the statement at the beginning of Ab. shows that the Rabb. saw in the fence about the Law a long-standing mark of Pharisaism. But it is surprising that the two preceding statements: "Be careful in judgment," and "Produce many pupils," are more gen. and would fit any Jewish group of chakamim.

[94] It should be noted in this regard that prior to the victory of the Hillelites (→ 33, 1 ff.) this dogmatic claim did not basically go beyond the limits of current trends and the chaburoth who followed them, for Pharisees were able to impress laws from their tradition on the people only when a specific trend had established sole jurisdiction among them (→ 34, 5 ff.). Jos. is misleading here since he predates the relations obtaining after the destruction of the temple..

According to the statements of the Rabbis the legal fence in the form of tradition is designed to protect the faithful against transgressions which might make them guilty of mortal sin. [95] Thus the ideal, which was not attained prior to the destruction of the temple, consists in a nomistic order of life worked out down to the slightest detail and aiming at fellowship with God in all the changes and chances of life. In this light the Pharisees are the men of true piety and even in modern writings they are still regarded as the real orthodox who with their striving for a comprehensive fulfilment of the Law most consistently embody the essence of postexilic Judaism, and thus stand historically and logically at the climax of the development initiated by Ezra. [96] The more significant, then, is the criticism to which Pharisaism was subjected by the chasidim of Qumran under Zadokite leadership.

Damasc., which may now be definitively regarded as a Zadokite work and hence as hostile to Pharisaism, [97] attacks (4:19 [7:1]) with an allusion to Ez. 13:10 the principle of setting a fence around the Torah, the word "wall of partition" being used for fence. The opposing party is thus said to be made up of "builders of a wall of partition who run after a babbler" and thus transgress the Law themselves. Thus they are charged with licentiousness because contrary to Gn. 1:27; 2:7 they are not content with one wife but commit bigamy. [98] Acc. to 8:12 f., 16, 18 (9:21 f., 24, 26) these men are also guilty of laying God's hand heavily on the people: "But all this those who have built the wall of partition and daubed it with whitewash have not understood; for a windbag and lying prophet preached to them, so that God's wrath was kindled against His congregation... And this is the view of those who have turned in Israel: they have gone aside from the way of the people." The way the Zadokites describe their adversaries suggests a material distinction between the "builders of the wall of partition" on the one side and the "babbler" or "lying prophet" on the other. The first are obviously a society which exists long before and apart from the latter, while the latter plays or has played a leading role at a distinct point in the history of the fellowship, probably at the time when these polemical words were written. Apart from any such figure the same society is depicted as follows in Damasc. 1:18 - 2:1 (1:13-17): "Because they presented false expositions and preferred deceptions, because they spied out gaps,... made the wicked man righteous and the righteous man wicked... because they despised all who walked uprightly and persecuted them with the sword... God's wrath was kindled against the fellowship..." Apart from Damasc. we find in the Zadokite writings of Qumran the same polemic against those who claim that they are fulfilling the Law and encouraging its practice when from the Zadokite standpt. they simply weaken and dissolve the Law. [99] Now it is true that thus

---

[95] Cf. Ab., 3, 3: "R. Akiba (d. c. 135 A.D.) used to say: 'Tradition is a fence about the Torah.'"

[96] Cf. the historical picture which K. Schubert, *Die Religion d. nachbiblischen Judt.* (1955), 3-12 constructs from tradition alone.

[97] On Damasc. cf. O. Eissfeldt, *Einl. in d. AT*[3] (1964), 880-4 (Bibl.). The first editor S. Schechter has been completely vindicated now that Damasc. has been finally shown to be Zadokite, cf. his *Documents of Jewish Sectaries I: Fr. of a Zadokite Work* (1910), XXVIII. The thesis that Damasc. is of Pharisaic origin, strongly argued by J. Jeremias, *Jerusalem z. Zeit Jesu*, II B[2] (1958), 130-4, must now be abandoned, cf. Kahle, *op. cit.* (→ n. 18), 18-23 and J. Jeremias, 294-7.

[98] Damasc. 4:19-21 (7:1-3): בוני החיץ אשר הלכו אחרי צו הצו הוא מטיף אשר אמר הטף. The expression אחרי צו הלך is from Hos. 5:11 (LXX πορεύομαι ὀπίσω ματαίων) while מטיף and יטיפון הטף are based on Mi. 2:6, 11. In the context צו can only mean "lying" or "wicked" (cf. μάταιος), while מטיף is the lying prophet who leads others to make false prophecies (הטף יטיפון). יטיפון הם נתפשים בשתים בזנות לקחת שתי נשים בחייהם.

[99] J. Carmignac, "Les éléments histor. des Hymnes de Qumran," *Rev. de Qumran*, 2 (1959/60), 205-222.

far the idea of the Pharisaic fence as a wall of partition has not been found in the Scrolls, but Damasc. 1:18 (1:13) and, e.g., 1 QH 2:15, 32 are related, for we find דרש בחלקות in Damasc. and the corresponding part. plur. דורשי חלקות in 1 QH and also 4 QpNa and 4 QpIsᶜ;[100] the ref. is not so much to men who "seek smooth things" as to those who "give false expositions of Scripture."[101] Nor does Zadokite criticism confine itself to general charges of scribal misdirection. For all the indirectness of speech, it is easy to see what the concrete objections to Pharisaism are. Damasc. 1:18 f. (1:13) finds in its scribes men who try to spy out gaps in the Law which they exploit to their own advantage. 1 QH 2:34 describes them as men who "preach indolence." Their searching is aimed at evasion of the Law acc. to 1 QH 4:10.[102] The "lying," "deception," and "misdirection" of the Pharisaic scribes acc. to the Zadokite view consist in the fact that the fence about the Torah means its practical dissolution. In the eyes of the orthodox, of the Zadokites of older beliefs, the Pharisees are not men who keep the Law but men who destroy it. Damasc. 8:18 (9:26) are claims that these "men of laxity" have met the people in its lawlessness half-way when it says that "those who have turned in Israel have gone aside from the way of the people" → 29, 22 f. In these charges, which cannot be dismissed as the mere protest of a rigid priestly tradition, there may be seen at bottom a reflection of what Jos. Ant., 18, 12 presents positively when it says that the Pharisees saw it as their duty to follow at all costs what rational judgment has handed down as good or currently presents as such. If it is a fact that the "builders of the wall of partition" are the Pharisees, the question arises who among the Pharisaic leaders is in view when Damasc. in its Zadokite criticism speaks of "the babbler," "the windbag" and the "false prophet," 4:19 (7:1); 8:12 ff. (9:21 ff.) → 29, 15 ff. If we survey the history of the movement in the Hasmonean period (→ 23, 26 ff.), only the reign of Salome Alexandra fits Damasc. 1:20 f. (1:15 f.), where the men who offer "false expositions of Scripture" have the power to persecute "those who walk uprightly." In this period, however, Shimʿon b Shatach is the class. type who embodies the Pharisaic ideal even to the point of caricature and who by his very nature evokes opposition. Hence it is by no means impossible that he is the babbler of Zadokite criticism.[103] Shimʿon, of course, is not the only leading Pharisee to invite criticism. The same might be said of his younger contemporary Hillel. From the standpoint of the older Jewish orthodoxy an attack on the canonical law of money such as that of the prosbol championed by Hillel was quite impossible. The prosbol, Gk. προσβολή,[104] is a proviso whereby a creditor can prevent a loan given to a third party being included among the debts remitted in the sabbatical year. The creditor has to make a written declaration before at least two witnesses that the loan may be required at any time, even in the year of remission or afterwards.[105] Hillel is supposed to have introduced

---

[100] 1 QH 2:15 f., 32; cf. 4 QpNa 1:2 on 2:12 and 4 QpIsᶜ line 10, ed. J. M. Allegro, "More Is. Comm. from Qumran's Fourth Cave," JBL, 77 (1958), 215-221. On this and the equivalents cf. Carmignac, op. cit., 216 f.; on 4 QpNa 1:2 on 2:12 → n. 71.

[101] On the problem cf. Meyer-Weiss, 61 f.

[102] 1 QH 2:34: דורשי רמיה, in which רמיה can be transl. "deception" (Ges.-Buhl., Köhler-Baumg., s.v.); 4:9 f.: להמיר תורתכה . . . מליצי כזב וחוזי רמיה; cf. also 4:7 and J. Licht, The Thanksgiving Scroll (1957), 74, 92.

[103] Cf. jBer., 7 (11b, 34 ff.): Once when 300 men could not redeem their vows through poverty, Shimʿon asked the king to accept 150 vows while he would take over the rest. The king willingly agreed and paid his share; but the Pharisaic sage did not pay a penny, for he saw the gap or door by which one may escape without culpability in sacral law. The hero of the escapade is the clever Pharisee who made a fool of the priest-king, Meyer-Weiss, 63-66.

[104] On προσβολή cf. Preisigke Wört., s.v.; materially cf. D. Correns, Schebiit, Die Mischna, I, 5 (1960), 155 f. on Shebi., 10, 3.

[105] As may be seen from bGit., 36b, the Rabb. were not too happy about the prosbol at a later period; but it was taken up into the Rabb. halacha with the victory of Pharisaism and later embedded in the Mishna, although the sabbatical year and its stringent rules for Jews living on the soil of the Holy Land had lost all practical significance after the destruction of the Jerusalem hierocracy.

this acc. to Shebi., 10, 3 f. Now we can be sure that Hillel never could have set up such a rule, for as the head of a school he was simply a private person and had no official powers like the president of the Sanhedrin. But this supposed ordinance was probably counsel that he first gave his chaberim and that others gladly accepted since it was so convenient and relieved the conscience. Such a counsel, however, implies only the legitimate adoption into sacral law of a secular practice which is tantamount to an annulment of the law of remission in Dt. 15:2 and which thus represents precisely what the anti-Pharisaic criticism of the Zadokites calls a "deceitful exposition of the Torah."

III. The Victory of Pharisaism.

1. Palestinian Judaism After the Fall of the Hierocracy.

The history of Palestinian Judaism from Hyrcanus I (135-104 B.C.) is often depicted as if the Rabbis were uncrowned kings from 100 B.C. to 70 A.D., so that the inner and to a large extent the outer aspect of the period was essentially shaped by Pharisaism. In opposition to this view we must insist that apart from the few years of Salome Alexandra (→ 24, 21 ff.) and a more or less insignificant minority in the council between 67 B.C. and 70 A.D. Pharisaism did not shape Palestinian Judaism at any time in this period.

The great age of Pharisaism came only after the destruction of the temple and the smashing of the Jerusalem hierocracy. But around this period it gained a victory which was so comprehensive that even the catastrophe under Hadrian could not affect it.

The unhappy outcome of the first revolt meant externally the capture of Jerusalem and the ending of the temple ministry. It also meant internally the end of an idea, namely, that represented by Sadduceeism → VII, 43, 15 ff. Pharisaism on the basis of its inner presuppositions provided at once the direction needed for the reconstruction of Judaism under the new conditions. For Pharisaism was not primarily linked with a given status of religious and political autonomy. Its concern was for the safeguarding of community life in the synagogue. It was the Pharisees, then, who in a land devastated and occupied by the Romans gained the confidence of the authorities and took the initiative in reconstructing an orderly life. Certainly not all Pharisaic groups took part in this. For even true Pharisaism had not been able to avoid Zealot tendencies and it may be assumed that at the start of the revolt Pharisaic policy was directed by the school of Shammai with its strong Zealot leanings. It is patent that this type of movement could not provide the inner presuppositions for a peaceful reorganisation of relations, let alone secure the corresponding approval of the Romans. Hence among the Pharisaic leaders only those were left who followed Hillel and who had been opposed to, or had reservations about, the increasing radicalisation. In fact it was a Hillelite, Jochanan b Zakkai, who built up the community life of Judaism afresh from the smallest and most modest beginnings. [106] This is reflected in bGit., 56a. If the tradition found here, which has it that Jochanan, leaving besieged Jerusalem, came before Vespasian as a prophet and intercessor for his people, [107] is regarded as legendary, [108] it still rests on the fact that Jabne-Jamnia with its chakamim, who did not take part in the struggle, formed the centre for the reorganisation of Palestinian Judaism, and that Jochanan b Zakkai is to be regarded as the initiator.

---

[106] Meyer-Weiss, 70 f.
[107] Meyer Prophet, 56 f.
[108] In 68 A.D., before the siege of Jerusalem began, Jabne, with Lydda, was already designated a refuge by Jews who did not take part in the war against the Romans.

2. The Reconstruction of Community Life.

a. Religio-Social Change.

Now that the ancient Jewish bulwark had been overthrown by its own attempt at eschatological salvation, we see the Pharisaic chakamim becoming for the first time in the history of Judaism absolute rulers, and we also see quite obviously a full awareness of the fact, for now what had originally been purely theoretical conceptions began to be translated into deeds. [109] For the reconstruction of relations Pharisaism not only had its own concept but obviously it enjoyed also a good deal of support from the eastern *diaspora*; for a second time, and again for a new beginning, Bab. Judaism stood sponsor. [110] This strong and rich Jewish world differed in inner structure from Palestinian Judaism in the sense that the idea of the government of Israel reverting to a Davidic king had never been crowded out here by the concept of the priest-prince. It seems highly probable that Jochanan b Zakkai had the order of life in Bab. Judaism in view when he asked the emperor to release the family of Rabban Gamli'el. [111] Gamli'el was a great-grandson of Hillel who belonged to the Jewish *diaspora* and at least on his mother's side could trace his lineage to David. [112] The title of Gamli'el is נָשִׂיא in Hbr. (Ez. 44:3; 45:7; 48:21 f.) and the traditional transl. is "patriarch," though the Gk. equivalent might be ἐθνάρχης rather than πατριάρχης (cf. 1 Macc. 14:47; 15:11); [113] Origen, too, calls the leaders of Palestinian Judaism ethnarchs. [114] The ethnarch of Palestine, to whose royal appearance Rabb. lit. also ref., [115] correspond exactly to the exilarch [116] in Babylon. But in addition to the head there was also a supreme court over which the Nasi presided. The new Sanhedrin was essentially different, of course, from the sacerdotal-aristocratic senate which had been in existence up to the destruction of the temple. The time had now come when the final authority in the Senate was the scribe in the form of a chakam of Pharisaic-Hillelite persuasion. This produced the lasting Rabb. idea of the Sanhedrin, with the result that the older Jewish gerousia has often been anachronistically described along these lines. [117] With the new Sanhedrin under the ethnarch we find the יְשִׁיבָה, the academy of Jabne, which was supported both intellectually and practically by the pupils of Jochanan and of Ismael and Akiba. This means, however, that with the ethnarch there is now a new ruling caste which no longer derives its power from descent and family status but primarily from the religious and intellectual quality of the individual chakam who, after a long period of study and preparation, was at forty years of age officially proclaimed by semicha, "ordination," to be a qualified rabbi and therewith a follower in the spirit of the prophets. [118]

b. Inner Reorganisation.

The external reconstruction in Palestine, which conclusively put an end to older Judaism, provided the basis for a radical inner reform which was quickly adopted by the

---

[109] Meyer-Weiss, 71 f.

[110] On what follows, *ibid.*, 72-75.

[111] Cf. bGit., 56a.

[112] It is typical of Jochanan b Zakkai that he always thought of himself as the head of a school and obviously never claimed political leadership. Yet his plea for Gamli'el II is due to more than respect for Hillel. The stress on the descent of Hillel's house from David shows that in their opposition to the idea of the prince-priesthood Jochanan and his group deliberately espoused the ideology.

[113] This is stressed by Wellhausen, 41.

[114] Ep. ad Africanum, 14 (Orig. Opera Omnia, ed. C. Lommatzsch, 17 [1844], 44); cf. also M. Hengel, "Die Synagogeninschr. v. Stobi," ZNW, 57 (1966), 150-6.

[115] Cf. on this Avi-Yonah, 53-63.

[116] The original title runs רֵישׁ גָּלוּתָא: head of the company of exiles.

[117] Even Avi-Yonah, 54 does not escape the temptation to do this.

[118] Cf. the material in Str.-B., II, 647-661; cf. also E. Lohse, *Die Ordination im Spätjudt. u. im NT* (1951), 28-66.

diaspora too. [119] The first concern was to give the new community life a uniform basis in religious law. To this end the old debate between Hillel and Shammai was settled. Acc. to a tradition deriving from R. Jochanan b Nappacha it was decided at Jabne by a voice from heaven (→ VI, 818, 22 ff.), i.e., by way of divination, in favour of Hillel, jBer., 1, 7 (3b, 64 ff.). [120]

The result was the exclusion or excommunication of the other schools. Sadducean halacha and dogmatics were anathematised, and with such success that even now it is hard to grasp the full and sometimes tragic greatness of Sadduceeism as the older Jewish orthodoxy (→ VII, 46, 8 ff.). The final separation from the Samaritans probably took place at this period too (→ VII, 90, 13 ff.), and chasidic or Essene groups which did not find their way into the Hillelite dominated community either withdrew with Jewish Christianity or disappeared in other ways.

It was a tremendous achievement that the relatively small group at Jabne, supported by some like-minded heads of schools around, succeeded in giving a uniform stamp to Palestinian Judaism and also in influencing the *diaspora* along the same lines. From now on there was only the one leadership of Pharisaic Hillelites, and these gradually moulded the majority of the people. Their only rivals were the group called the 'Am ha-'Ares (→ V, 589, 26 ff.) and these, located primarily in Galilee, were not brought into subjection until the 2nd half of the 2nd cent. The achievement can be understood only if one realises that such a victory presupposes that those in control had great intellectual and religious power which did not lose its freshness with the years. [121] The reverse side of this influential historical fact, however, is that with the Hillelite triumph the older, complex Judaism was narrowed down to the synagogue.

The demarcation from all groups unacceptable to the Hillelite trend corresponded inwardly to the dogmatic demarcation from Sadduceeism (→ VII, 46, 8 ff.), the suppression of apocal. and mystical speculations, the fixing of the canon, the halacha and liturgical practice, and a standardising of speech and writing which put its stamp on Rabb. lit. in the centuries that followed. Neither the chakamim of the Jerusalem hierocracy, the Zadokites of Qumran, nor the Alexandrian theologians had been able to come up with a closed canon (→ III, 978, 9 ff.). [122] They had, of course, a practical concept of Scripture. The Pent. was *the* holy book. But in given cases there was no exact def. of what was canonical or what did not belong to the true canon. It is probable that the Pharisaic chakamim tried to solve this problem before the destruction of the temple (→ III, 981, 33 ff.). Only in conflict with the Sadducees, Jewish Christians, Samaritans, and Alexandrians, however, was the threefold Rabb. canon of law, prophets and writings firmly established (→ III, 982, 1 ff.). This fixing of the canon extended not merely to recognition of the individual books in gen. but also to a standardising of the consonantal text. There are some accounts of the history of the Hbr. text in the Rabb., but we have been able to get a full picture of the work the chakamim of Jabne did on the text only with the discovery of biblical fr. in Caves 4 and 11 of Qumran and the possibility of comparing these with the uniform text known from the caves of the Wadi Murabba'āt. [123] Here again there is evidence of the intellectual force of the chakamim of Palestine, for in a short time the normative, dogmatically establish-

---

[119] On what follows cf. Meyer-Weiss, 75-84.

[120] For the abs. dominance of the Hillelites in the ensuing period cf. the tables in Str.-B., VI (1961).

[121] This is shown by the fact that even after the great intellectual and material purge under Hadrian the Rabb., in spite of every difficulty, could still build successfully on the foundation laid by the men around Jochanan b Zakkai and Rabban Gamli'el II.

[122] Eissfeldt, *op. cit.* (→ n. 97), 756-773.

[123] On what follows cf. R. Meyer, Art. "Qumran III," RGG³, V, 742-4.

ed text replaced the LXX in the form of the Aquila transl., which corresponded fully to the exegetical principles of an Akiba. [124] The reverse side of this process of canonisation was the differentiation of all other edifying lit. as apocryphal, and in a few years much of this was forgotten.

The basic lines for future development were also laid down in respect of religious law. As already indicated (→ 33, 1 ff.), the Hillelites imposed their concept of oral law; in this regard they could link up with a school tradition already a hundred years old or so. This naturally does not mean that they refashioned the whole halacha on the basis of their own tradition. They took many parts of religious law, e.g., the halachoth, which were connected with temple worship and the related laws of purification, from the bankrupt estate of the hierocracy, and revised them in their own sense. Corresponding analogies from the Zadokite halacha of Qumran make it more than likely that in the systematisation of religious law the Hillelites did not appeal only to oral tradition. [125] The same applies in respect of the biblical tradition in so far as the ref. is to the Tg. and expository work, for here the men of Jabne had at their disposal a written tradition going back many generations and they had only to continue this in their own spirit without any basic need for creativity. Even when new decisions had to be taken, longstanding Jewish practice could be followed with an exclusive Hillelite interpretation. This relates esp. to the three principles by which halachoth become binding, namely, majority decision as the common rule, local custom, and the adoption of the decision of a normative authority. The proof from Scripture might be regarded as typically Pharisaic, but there were strict limits to this inasmuch as a halacha deduced from Scripture still needed official recognition. Thus older Jewish practice still had an influence in the critical attitude to proof from Scripture. [126] An explicit Pharisaic spirit may be seen where the Rabbis seek to establish the unity of the written and oral Torah by way of exegesis. [127] To this end many hermeneutical rules were used of which the seven middoth of Hillel go back at least in part to the 1st cent. B.C. [128] After the destruction of the temple they became the thirteen middoth of Ismael [129] and after Hadrian they then became the thirty-two middoth of Jose of Galilee. [130] Rather strangely these rules are not based on older Jewish tradition but in nature and form are borrowed from Hell. hermeneutics. [131] With the domination of the Hillelites their exegetical rules found general acceptance and thus a principle of exposition which was fundamentally alien to Judaism achieved supremacy, while the older and essentially simpler interpretation of Judaism, of which we now have impressive examples in the comm. of the Qumran Zadokites, was consigned to oblivion as heterodox along with the dogmatic complex of the Sadducees. [132] With the Rabb. as with the Qumran priests and the former Jerusalem

---

[124] On Aquila cf. Eissfeldt, 971 f.

[125] This should make it plain once and for all that the much quoted dogma of a prohibition of writing in respect of the halacha, haggadic materials and the related expository lit. is a legend; the Rabb. ref. adduced in favour of the prohibition do not have the cogency ascribed to them; on this problem cf. Strack Einl., 9-16.

[126] Cf. on this Meyer-Weiss, 79 f.

[127] Cf. E. L. Dietrich, Art. "Schriftauslegung II," RGG³, V, 1515-17 with bibl. Unfortunately the author does not go into the earlier history of the Rabb. rules nor does he do justice to the Qumran exposition when he speaks of the "sectarian" interest and character of this society under Zadokite leadership.

[128] T. Sanh., 7, 17 and par.; Strack Einl., 97-99.

[129] S. Lv. prooem, 1-4; Strack Einl., 99 f.

[130] Cf. b. Chul., 89a; on the form and textual transmission of the middoth cf. Strack Einl., 100-109.

[131] Cf. esp. S. Rosenblatt, *The Interpretation of the Bible in the Mishna* (1935). W. F. Albright, *From the Stone Age to Christianity* (1946), 274 has the pertinent remark: "Hillel's principles of interpretation have no more in common with the ancient Near East than they have with Mayan civilization but that are characteristically Hell. in concept and even in form."

[132] In contrast to Hillelite exegesis older Jewish exposition is more akin to Accad. and Egypt. Dietrich, *op. cit.* (→ n. 127) missed this.

priests whose temple went up in flames, we note that they did not merely hand down the religious law appertaining to the ruined sanctuary or the now desecrated and profaned Holy Land; they also revised it as though the old order still stood. As with the Qumran Zadokites and the former temple priests, a part is unquestionably played here by the eschatological concept that one must always be ready for the day when the temple and the Holy Land will be restored with the dawn of the kingdom of God. Thus a strong scholastic element was undoubtedly introduced for all time into halachic discusssion, [133] although on the other hand it should not be overlooked that the Rabb. with their practice of religious law were able to lay their impress so strongly on Jewish life that only modern research has succeeded in constructing, at least in general outline, a picture of Judaism prior to the fall of the Jerusalem hierocracy which in some degree at least is close to the historical reality.

IV. Summary.

Before the destruction of the temple Judaism was a multiform and variegated religious phenomenon. Within it there was room for older orthodox traditions, Alexandrian theology, and, under strong Hellenistic influence, the wisdom of the Pharisaic chakamim. After the destruction of the hierocracy, however, we see the triumph, not of Pharisaism as a whole, but of one movement within it. Even up to the outbreak of the first revolt and during the war, this movement was only a minority. But it was a minority of such religious force that in the period which followed it put its stamp on world-wide Judaism. Not until 700 years later did serious opposition arise to it in the form of the Karaites. Nor did this opposition enjoy any final success, for, although lasting credit is due to it in respect of the biblical text, [134] it could not decisively alter the totality of Rabbinic Judaism resting on a Pharisaic-Hillelite basis.

Meyer

B. The Pharisees in the New Testament.

In distinction from the Sadducees (→ VII, 35, 5 ff.) and other Jewish parties (→ I, 181, 25 ff.; 182, 18 ff.) [135] the Pharisees are mentioned very frequently in the NT. In all the word Φαρισαῖος, usually in the plur., occurs 98 or 101 times, [136] predominantly in the Synoptic Gospels. There are obvious historical reasons why this should be so. On the other hand, it should be noted that the presentation and assessment of Pharisaism in Ac. and Paul differs from what we find in the Synoptic Gospels. This raises the question in what sense the very polemical and hostile depiction of Pharisaism in these Gospels is to be regarded as a reliable source for Judaism in the days of Jesus.

---

133 Schl. Gesch. Isr., 346.

134 Cf. on this Kahle, *op. cit.* (→ n. 18), 17-29, 82-119.

135 On αἵρεσις in the sense of "trend," "school" and with ref. to the Pharisees cf. Jos. Ant., 13, 288; Bell., 2, 162; Vit., 10. 12. 191. 197; Ac. 15:5; 26:5 and Haench. Ag.14 on 26:5; P. Winter, *On the Trial of Jesus* (1961), 130.

136 Cf. the vl. in Mt. 7:29; 27:41; Lk. 11:44. We find secondary constructs like φαρισαϊκός and φαρισαΐζω "to live after Pharisaic style" only in the fathers: φαρισαϊκός or *pharisaicus* in Orig. Comm. in Joh., 6, 22, 121 on 1:24 f.; Bas. Hom. in Ps. 7:6 (MPG, 29 [1857], 241b); Theod. Mops. Fr., 80 on Mt. 15:13 f., ed. J. Reuss, "Mt.-Komment. aus d. griech. Kirche," TU, 61 (1957), 125; Thdrt., IV, 10, 4; Iren. Haer., IV, 12, 1; φαρισαΐζω in Sophronius of Jerusalem, Laudes in Cyrum et Joannem (MPG, 87, 3 [1865], 3384b).

I. The Pharisees in the Synoptic Tradition.

1. The Historical Problem.

In the Synoptic tradition the Pharisees appear already as opponents of John the Baptist, Mt. 3:7 ff.; Lk. 7:29 f. → V, 444, 32 ff. They are then esp. the opponents of Jesus. In the discussions they are almost always the contending party; they test Him (Mk. 10:1 ff.; 12:13 ff.; cf. also Jn. 7:53 - 8:11); at the very outset of His ministry they resolve on His death (Mk. 3:6); they also bear the main guilt for His crucifixion. The fundamentally hostile position of the Pharisees towards Jesus corresponds to His own anti-Pharisaic attitude (→ V, 428, 6 ff.) as this may be seen in the Synoptic controversies and esp. in the great anti-Pharisaic discourses in Mk. 7 and par. and Mt. 25. There are certain signs, however, that in this depiction of the relations between Jesus and the Pharisees we do not have a simple reflection of historical facts. Rather, there is perhaps a tendency in the Synoptic Gospels to present the Pharisees as typical representatives of a Judaism hostile to Christianity and opposing not only Jesus Himself but also at a later time the primitive Christian community. One may refer to the fact that the Pharisees are presented as a collective entity with no individual features. [137] We know, of course, that this was not so historically in the time of Jesus, for Pharisaism was not then a self-contained unity in every respect → 26, 39 ff. Furthermore, even in the Synoptic tradition the relation of Jesus to the Pharisees was not always or from the very outset negative. According to Lk. 7:36 (but cf. Mt. 26:6-13 and Mk. 14:3-9); 11:37; 14:1 Jesus enjoyed table-fellowship with the Pharisees and according to Lk. 13:31-33 the Pharisees could even warn Him of the plots of Herod. [138] There is no reason to suspect the authenticity of these references in Lk., the more so as they run contrary to the tendency observed elsewhere in the Synoptists. [139] Another fact pointing in the same direction is that in several discussions between Jesus and contemporary Judaism it seems to be only secondarily that an anti-Pharisaic interpretation has been given.

> An instructive example is the academic discussion in Mk. 12:28-34 and par. In the common Synoptic tradition of the question of the scribe (so Mk.; on Mt. and Lk. → IV, 1088, 20 ff.) as to the chief commandment Mt. and Lk. leave out the last and positive word of Jesus concerning the scribe as this is recorded in Mk. 12:34, so that the question is presented more as a testing of Jesus by him. [140] Mt. also makes the scribe of Mk. 12:28 into a Pharisaic scribe by connecting Mt. 22:34-40 with the preceding story of the question of the Sadducees in 22:23-33. In Mt. and Lk., then, the academic discussion of Mk. becomes more of a controversy. At this point Mk. seems to have the more original form of the tradition, which is then given a secondary anti-Pharisaic sense in Mt. and Lk.

Along these lines Mt. and Lk. express an understanding of the relation of Jesus to the Judaism of His day which represents a particular aspect of the actual historical data. [141] If we are to evaluate correctly the references to the Pharisees in the Synoptic

---

137 Cf. Winter, op. cit., 113; A. Jaubert, "Jésus et le Calendrier de Qumran," NTSt, 7 (1960/61), 11.

138 Cf. W. Grundmann, Das Ev. nach Lk., Handkomm. z. NT² (1963) on 7:36; 11:37; 14:1; G. Bornkamm, Jesus v. Nazareth⁷ (1965), 88 f.

139 Cf. on this Bultmann Trad., 38; Grundmann on 13:31; M. Goguel, Das Leben Jesu (1934), 219 and 223.

140 As regards historicity cf. Bultmann Trad., 57; in analysis of Mk. 12:28-34, ibid., 21.

141 On the priority of the Marcan version cf. E. Schweizer, "Matth. 5:17-20. Anmerkungen z. Gesetzesverständnis d. Mt.," Neotestamentica (1963), 402; S. Légasse, "Scribes et disciples de Jésus," Rev. Bibl., 68 (1961), 483, 486-9. On the relations of Mk. and Mt./Lk. cf. Kl. Mk., 127. On the anti-Pharisaic trend in the Synpt. cf. T. A. Burkill, "Anti-Semitism in St. Mark's Gospel," Nov. Test., 3 (1959), 34-53; Glasson, passim.

Gospels we shall have to take this anti-Pharisaic polemic into account, considering not only the attitude of Jesus to contemporary Pharisaism but also the impact of the controversy between the primitive Christian community and the Pharisaic-Rabbinic Judaism of the time. We must also remember that the Pharisees in Jesus' day did not enjoy the dominant role in Palestinian Judaism which one might sometimes think from the Synoptic records → 26, 21 ff. [142] This means concretely that they did not yet play a normative part in the Sanhedrin at Jerusalem; in the days of Jesus the Sadducees still exercised ultimate authority → VII, 53, 29 ff. [143] In keeping with this is the fact that according to the Synoptic tradition the Pharisees no longer play any significant part in the story of the passion. [144] This is obviously and indisputably an authentic and reliable reminiscence, especially in view of the general tendency of the Gospels to present the Pharisees as the chief adversaries of Jesus bearing much of the responsibility for His death. [145]

2. The Pharisees and the Other Parties in Judaism.

a. According to the Synoptic tradition, however, other parties as well as the Pharisees oppose Jesus, even if the distinction between the Jewish movements is not always too plain. It should be noted that the situation is clearest in Mark and Luke (→ 26, 1 ff.), while in Matthew there is a tendency to refer to the Pharisees as Jesus' adversaries even when they are not specifically mentioned in Mk. or Q. [146] Thus in the Baptist's preaching in Lk. 3:7 we simply have the crowds, but for the imprecise note in Lk. or Q Mt. substitutes a stock ref. to the Pharisees and Sadducees with no clear indication of the basic distinction between the two (→ VII, 52, 14 ff.). [147] The same may be said of Mt. 16:1, where Mk. 8:11 speaks only of the Pharisees, and again Mt. 16:6, where Mt. has the "leaven of the Pharisees and Sadducees," Mk. 8:15 the "leaven of the Pharisees and Herod," Lk. 12:1 the "leaven of the Pharisees." A particularly clear instance is Mt. 16:11 f., where it might appear

---

[142] Cf. Meyer-Weiss, 52-57, 95 f.

[143] Ac. 5:34 and 23:6-9 show beyond question that Pharisaic scribes were present in the Sanhedrin. On their influence there cf. Wellhausen, 30-43; A. Büchler, *Das Synedrium in Jerusalem* (1902), 99 f., 180; J. Blinzler, *Der Prozess Jesu*³ (1960), 154-163; also "Das Synedrium in Jerusalem u. d. Strafprozessordnung der Mischna," ZNW, 52 (1961), 54-65; J. S. Kennard, "The Jewish Provincial Assembly," ZNW, 53 (1962), 35-9, 41-3; cf. also J. Jeremias, 297 f.

[144] Apart from Mt. 27:62-66, though some do not accept this as original, cf. Bultmann Trad., 297. In the passion Jesus' opponents are the chief priests, elders and scribes. In Mk. 3:6 and par. the Pharisees with the Herodians decide on his death, in Mk. 11:18 the chief priests and scribes; cf. Loh. Mk., *ad loc.* and on 14:1; Bultmann Trad., 282; Winter, *op. cit.* (→ n. 135), 134. The predictions of the passion, apart from the indefinite Mk. 9:31, mention the elders, priests and scribes, Mk. 8:31 and par.; 10:33 and par., i.e., the Jewish representatives who actually enjoyed the most influence in the Sanhedrin in the days of Jesus; cf. Loh. Mk. on 8:31 and 10:32 f.; Grundm. Mk. on 8:31 and 10:33; Kl. Mk. on 10:33.

[145] From this standpoint one can hardly say that Jesus' condemnation was essentially the work of the Pharisees, so J. Jeremias, 299 appealing to Jn. (→ 43, 25 ff.). On the other hand, lack of ref. to the Pharisees in the passion narrative does not allow us to conclude that all the passages relating to them in the Gospels are secondary, so Winter, *op. cit.*, 124.

[146] Cf. G. Strecker, "Der Weg d. Gerechtigkeit," FRL, 89² (1966), 140 f.; Hummel, 12-14.

[147] Cf. Bultmann Trad., 55; Mt. 3:7 is treated as secondary by E. Lohmeyer, *Das Urchr.*, I (1932), 54; Loh. Mt. on 3:7; Grundmann, *op. cit.* (→ n. 138) on Lk. 3:7, but not K. H. Rengstorf, *Das Ev. nach Lk.*, NT Deutsch, 3¹² (1967) on 3:7 f.

that the Pharisees and Sadducees form a material unity even in respect of their teaching (διδαχή). Yet there is a differentiation between the two groups in the story of the question of the Sadducees (Mt. 22:34) which is common to the Synoptists. Since this belongs to the common tradition, however, it is hardly enough to dispel the suspicion that basically Mt. either did not have a clear view of the historical peculiarities of the groups or did not regard them as having any further significance.

b. The same applies to passages in which the Pharisees are mentioned along with the chief priests. At the end of the parable of the wicked husbandmen (Mk. 12:1-12 and par.) Mt. 21:45 refers to these two groups together. The problem here is that the incident takes place in the temple (21:23) and that at the beginning Mt. simply mentions the chief priests and the elders of the people, i.e., the groups which in the days of Jesus did in fact hold a dominant position in the hierocracy. Furthermore, when one compares the parallels to Mt. 21:45 in Mk. 12:12 (cf. also 11:27) and Lk. 20:19, it seems apparent that the reference to the Pharisees might be secondary in Mt. [148]

c. The situation is rather more complicated as regards the interrelating of the scribes and Pharisees, which is very common in Mt. In origin and current status the two should, of course, be distinguished → 20, 8 ff.; I, 741, 20 ff. [149] Nevertheless, it is a plain fact that a substantial number of the scribes belonged to the Pharisaic trend in Judaism. The tendency to identify the two groups is again very typical of Mt. In him the scribes and Pharisees seem to be a material and historical unity (cf. esp. Mt. 5:20; 12:38; 15:1 and Mt. 23). This might well be due to his writing at a time when all scribes were in fact Pharisees. In this regard Lk is again the closest to the historical situation in the time of Jesus. Thus in the parallel tradition to Mt. 23 in Lk. 11:37 - 12:1 (→ I, 741, 22 ff.) he expressly differentiates between Woes against the Pharisees (11:37-44) and Woes against the scribes (11:45 - 12:1). [150] Another reflection of the same situation is the reference to the "scribes of the Pharisees" in Mk. 2:16 (cf. Lk. 5:30) or the differentiation between "the Pharisees and some of the scribes" in Mk. 7:1. Thus we need not suppose that there is a simple equation of the two groups when, like Mt., Mk. and Lk. refer to the scribes and Pharisees together, Mk. 7:5; Lk. 5:21; 6:7; 11:23; 15:2, cf. also 7:30. These passages, esp. in Lk., are to be taken materially to have in view scribes of a Pharisaic persuasion. The difference is that Mt., for whom the Pharisees are the true enemies of Jesus, introduces the Pharisees into many contexts in which there is no ref. to them in Mk. or Q, cf. Mt. 12:24 with Mk. 3:22 par., Mt. 21:45 with Lk. 20:19 and Mt. 22:34 with Mk. 12:28 par. This is particularly clear in the common Synoptic pericope concerning the Son of David (Mk. 12:35-37 par.). It may be assumed that in the discussion of exegetical questions the scribes (Mk. 12:35 par.) rather than the Pharisees (Mt. 22:41) are the opponents of Jesus. Here, then, Mt. would seem to

---

[148] The chief priests and Pharisees are also mentioned together in Mt. 27:62-66; cf. Wellhausen Mt., ad loc.; Bultmann Trad., 297, 299, 305, 310; J. Schniewind, Das Ev. nach Mt., NT Deutsch, 2¹¹ (1964), ad loc. But in Mt. 28:11 f. we simply have the chief priests and elders, not the Pharisees.

[149] Cf. also Schürer, II, 380 f.; J. Jeremias, 286-291; on the question of Sadducean scribes ibid., 262 f.; Wellhausen, 8-11, 20; Meyer Ursprung, II, 284-6; Moore Rise, I, 258 f.

[150] Cf. also J. Jeremias, 288. Sometimes (cf. 11:45 f., 52 and 7:30; 10:25; 14:3) Lk. replaces γραμματεύς with νομικός, which a non-Jew would understand (→ IV, 1088, 20 ff.).

have introduced the Pharisees secondarily. [151] In all these passages the tendency in Mt. seems to be to diminish the historical distinction which, in respect of the actual relations at the time of Jesus, Mk. and Lk. portray in what they say about His adversaries, and in a simplification of the historical position to make the Pharisees the focal point of the opposition. [152]

d. A special feature in Mk. is the grouping of the Pharisees with the Herodians, who in Mk. 3:6; 12:13 (cf. also 8:15) almost seem to constitute a separate entity alongside or with them.

Except at Mt. 22:16, Mt. and Lk. substitute other Jewish groups for the Herodians of Mk. They obviously had no further interest in mentioning this group. It seems most likely that the Herodians were not just officials or servants of Herod but partisans, i.e., political followers. [153] Accepting the historicity of the incidents in Mk. in which the Herodians appear with the Pharisees, we can presume only that they were followers of Herod Antipas (4 B.C. to 39 A.D.). This does not seem so likely in Mk. 12:13, however, since here we find the Herodians at Jerusalem with the Pharisees, and Jerusalem did not fall within the jurisdiction of Herod Antipas, who was tetrarch of Galilee and Peraea. [154] All the same, one can see why a purely political group would be interested in the question of paying taxes. [155] Nothing is known elsewhere of any alliance between the Pharisees and the political followers of Herod Antipas. But the story about the healing on the Sabbath (Mk. 3:1-6), on the basis of which the Herodians and the Pharisees resolve to put Jesus to death, would seem to hint at some such material connection, along with common political interests. There is, of course, no evidence from the time of Herod Antipas to suggest that the Herodians took a similar line to that of the Pharisees on the matter of healing on the Sabbath. [156] Furthermore, for reasons we need not discuss here, Herod Agrippa I (41-44 A.D.) strongly favoured the Pharisees and even established close relations to Pharisaism. [157] If we relate the Herodians of Mk. to Herod Agrippa I, however, we are forced to assume that Mk. secondarily introduced the later relation into the story of Jesus. [158] Why he should do this is not clear. A possible reason might be found in Ac. 12:1 ff., where the royal Herodian house is regarded as hostile to Christianity in the primitive Christian churches, and similar opposition is thus seen in the story of Jesus Himself. On this view Lk. finally dropped all reference to the Herodians since their grouping with the Pharisees and the polemic against both groups would express not merely an anti-Herodian but also an anti-Roman attitude. [159]

---

[151] Cf. ad loc. J. Jeremias, 294, n. 3; M. Dibelius, Die Formgeschichte d. Ev.[5] (1966), 260 f.; on the authenticity of the incident cf. Bultmann Trad., 70, 145, but also C. G. Montefiore, The Synoptic Gospels, I (1927), 288 f.; Grundm. Mk., ad loc.

[152] Cf. also Winter, op. cit. (→ n. 135), 121-3, 126 f.; Bultmann Trad., 54-6; W. Trilling, "Das wahre Israel," Stud. z. AT u. NT, 10[8] (1964), 90 f.

[153] Cf. also Jos. Ant., 14, 450: οἱ τὰ Ἡρῴδου φρονοῦντες, 17, 41: οἱ τοῦ Ἡρῴδου. Cf. also Pr.-Bauer, s.v. Ἡρῳδιανοί, Kl. Mk., on 3:6; Goguel, op. cit., 220-222 and n. 587. There is no basis for the view that the Herodians were a Messianic-political movement.

[154] Cf. Loh. Mk., ad loc.

[155] On the political reasons for the interest of the Herodians in Jesus cf. Kl. Mk. on 3:7 and 12:13; Winter, op. cit., 128 f.

[156] Cf. Winter, 128 f.

[157] Cf. on this Jos. Ant., 19, 331; Ac. 12:1ff.; Schürer, I, 554-562; Zn. Ag. on 12:1; Haench. Ag.[14], 324-330; Hengel, 349. For Agrippa I in Rabb. lit. cf. Str.-B., II, 709 f. On the Pharisees and the Herod dynasty cf. G. Allon, "The Attitude of the Pharisees to the Roman Government and the House of Herod," Scripta Hierosolymitana, 7 (1961), 53-78; J. Jeremias, 298 f.

[158] Cf. Loh. Mk. on 3:6; 12:13 ff.; Winter, 128 f. wants to relate the Herodians of Mk. to Agrippa II, but this is unlikely, since Agrippa II does not seem to have had positive relations with the Pharisees, cf. Schürer, I, 590-592.

[159] On the Herodians in Mk. cf. also Bacon, passim; A. Loisy, Les Ev. synopt., I (1907), 518 f., 1001; II (1908), 333; Winter, 210, n. 27.

3. The Opposition to Pharisaism as an Expression of Opposition
to the Pharisaic Understanding of the Law.

The opposition of Jesus (and the primitive Christian community) to Pharisaism
in the Synoptic Gospels is in essentials the expression of opposition to their legal
piety. The whole Synoptic tradition of controversy with the legal piety of the
Pharisees certainly cannot be traced back to the Christian community alone. [160] At
this point the primitive community followed a tradition the core of which is finally
to be traced to Jesus Himself. [161]

a. The opposition of Jesus to the legal piety of the Pharisees and the resultant
practice of the law finds its basis in His critical attitude to the Mosaic Law itself
(→ IV, 1059, 38 ff.). Jesus did not, of course, abrogate the OT and Jewish Law
(Mt. 5:17; → II, 140, 6 ff.; VI, 293, 28 ff.). He subjected it to a sharper interpretation
(Mt. 5:21-48; → IV, 867, 32 ff.). [162] This inevitably meant opposition to the legal
piety of Pharisaism (→ IV, 1063, 17 ff.). [163] For now the criterion for fulfilment of
the Law (→ VI, 293, 28 ff.) is no longer the Law itself along with oral tradition,
which Pharisaism basically puts on an equal footing with the Law. It is love for
God and one's neighbour (Mt. 12:28-34 and par.). [164] The implication here, however, is that Jesus in proclaiming the will of God actually sets Himself above the
Law and its interpretation in Pharisaic Judaism. This more radical interpretation of
the Law necessarily goes hand in hand with a critical attitude to the oral tradition
of Pharisaic Judaism → II, 172, 10 ff.; VI, 661, 20 ff. The position of Jesus is
especially plain in His contrasting of the "tradition of the elders" (παράδοσις τῶν
πρεσβυτέρων) as a "tradition of men" (παράδοσις τῶν ἀνθρώπων) with the
ἐντολὴ θεοῦ, Mk. 7:8, 13 and par. → IV, 1063, 25 ff. Keeping the detailed statutes
and concretions of the OT Law contained in oral tradition is equivalent, in Jesus'
more radical understanding of the Law, to abrogation of the demand of God which
comes to expression in the OT Law → VIII, 324, 13 ff.; II, 549, 12 ff. [165] Since what
is essential is left undone, the legal practice of the Pharisees (→ VI, 480, 12 ff.)
is described as hypocrisy (Mt. 6:1 ff.; 23) → 43, 3 ff. [166]

b. The fundamental opposition of Jesus may be seen concretely in His opposition
to the Pharisaic observance whereby Pharisaism tries to represent the holy and pure
community of the true Israel, → 19, 13 ff.

---

[160] Even Winter, 119 and 134 f. allows that Jesus must have been at odds with some
Jewish tendencies in His day, although he thinks the controversy was primarily political, the
motive of religious hostility on the part of the Jews being introduced later, cf. 114 f.

[161] There is no basis for restricting Jesus' opposition to polemic against "zealous Pharisees,"
"the disciples of Shammai's academy" (Finkel, 134-143). Hengel, 385 is more cautious: "The
anti-Pharisaic polemic of Jesus was directed in part against the Zealots, the radical champions
of the left wing of the Pharisees."

[162] On authenticity cf. W. G. Kümmel, "Jesus u. der jüd. Traditionsgedanke," Heils-
geschehen u. Geschichte, Marburger Theol. Stud., 3 (1965), 31 f.; Bultmann Trad., 157 f.;
Trilling, op. cit. (→ n. 152), 207-211.

[163] On Jesus' attitude to the Law cf. also Kümmel, op. cit., 26-35; H. J. Schoeps, "Jesus
u. d. jüd. Gesetz," Aus frühchr. Zeit (1950), 212-220; Bornkamm, op. cit. (→ n. 138), 88-92.

[164] Cf. Loh. Mk., ad loc.

[165] Cf. also the material contrast, Mt. 23:23. Even if this saying with its Rabb. distinction
between "more weighty" and "lighter commandments" (cf. Str.-B., I, 901-5) was formulated
by Mt., it is an excellent reflection of the attitude of Jesus to oral tradition.

[166] Cf. Meyer-Weiss, 110 and n. 3 (Bibl.); Strecker, op. cit. (→ n. 146), 139 f.; R. L.
Rubenstein, "Scribes, Pharisees and the Hypocrites," Judaism, 12 (1963), 456-468.

This is true of the opposition of Jesus to the strict Sabbatarianism of Pharisaic Judaism as we see it esp. in Mk. 2:23-38 and par.; Mk. 3:1-6 and par., cf. also Lk. 13:10 ff.; 14:1 ff. → VII, 21, 20 ff. [167] It is also true of His attitude in some detailed questions of observance such as tithing, Lk. 18:12; Mt. 23:23 and par., [168] fasting, Lk. 18:12; Mk. 2:18 ff. and par. → IV, 931, 25 ff., [169] and esp. the attempt of Pharisaic and Rabb. Judaism to apply strictly to everyday secular life the rules of cleanness that were originally meant only for the priests → III, 418, 6 ff.; VIII, 320, 43 ff. The most important tradition in this regard is to be found in Mk. 7:1 ff. (Mt. 15:1 ff.). [170] Even if in its present form this shows signs of revision and interpretative application, [171] we must not overlook the fact that observance of the priestly rules of cleanness by the Pharisees in the form of external cleanness must have evoked the opposition of Jesus. Here again, then, the Pharisaic issue is a sharp one, and it comes to a head with the contrast between outer and inner purity. This thought is present in Mk. 7:15 and par. Here at least the attitude of Jesus finds expression even if, as some maintain, the verses which follows in 7:17 ff., and esp. the list of vices in 21 f., bear the marks of a secondary commentary in which what has been said is made relevant to Hell. readers who are no longer familiar with the Jewish laws of purification. [172] If, however, the saying in Mk. 7:15 and par. can be traced back to Jesus Himself, the same is basically true of the saying in Mt. 23:25 f. (Lk. 11:39 ff.). [173]

c. Materially related to the observance of the priestly rules of purification are the characteristic attempts of the Pharisees to separate themselves from the "people who knoweth not the law" (Jn. 7:49), i.e., the ʿAm ha-ʾAres → 19, 16 ff.; V, 589, 19 ff. [174] Incontestably one of the most important causes of the conflict between Jesus and Pharisaic Judaism lies in the attitude of Jesus to publicans and sinners. [175] The fact that Jesus Himself holds table-fellowship with the Pharisees

---

[167] On the authenticity of the various incidents cf. E. Lohse, "Jesu Worte über den Sabbat," Festschr. J. Jeremias, ZNW Beih., 26 (1960), 79-89; cf. also D. Daube, The NT and Rabbinic Judaism (1956), 67-71; Bultmann Trad., 40 f., 50 f.; H. Braun, Spätjüd.-här. u. frühchr. Radikalismus, Beitr. z. histor. Theol., 24 (1957), II, 70, n. 1 and 2.

[168] Cf. Str.-B., I, 933; Kl. Mt. on 23:23; Grundmann, op. cit. (→ n. 138) on Lk. 11:42.

[169] The fact that the failure of Jesus' disciples to fast is the starting-pt. in Mk. 2:18-22 and par. suggests that here a saying of Jesus is authoritatively adduced to settle a later question in the community, cf. Bultmann Trad., 17 f.; Dibelius, op. cit. (→ n. 151), 62 f.; also Die urchr. Überlieferung v. Johannes d. Täufer (1911), 40 f. Some think the Pharisees might have been brought in secondarily in Mk. 2:18 ff. and par., cf. Loh. Mk., ad loc.; Kl, Mk. on 2:18; J. Blinzler, "Qumran-Kalender u. Passionschronologie," ZNW, 49 (1958), 244 f.

[170] Cf. also Mt. 23:25 f. and Lk. 11:39-41; in analysis of Mk. 7:1-23 or Mt. 15:1-20 cf. Bultmann Trad., 15 f.; Dibelius, op. cit., 222 f.; Kümmel, op. cit., 28 f.; Montefiore, op. cit., I, 130-166.

[171] It is thus unlikely that the Pharisaic-Rabb. laws of cleanness applied to all Jews in the days of Jesus, Mk. 7:3; cf. A. Büchler, Der galiläische Am-ha-ʾares d. 2. Jhdt. (1906), 126; Montefiore, op. cit., I, 130 f.; II, 224-7; S. Zeitlin, "The Halaka in the Gospels and Its Relation to the Jewish Law at the Time of Jesus," HUCA, 1 (1924), 362-373; but cf. Kümmel, op. cit., 29. A surprising pt. here is that the attack is only on the disciples and not Jesus Himself, Mk. 7:5; cf. Bultmann Trad., 16 and 50 f.

[172] On the authenticity of Mk. 7:15 cf. Bultmann Trad., 15 and 158; Braun, op. cit. (→ n. 167), II, 62, n. 2; 65, n. 5; 72, n. 1; Montefiore, op. cit., I, 152-161. As regards the secondary character of Mk. 7:17-23, cf. Loh. Mk., ad loc.; Braun, II, 116 f., n. 2.

[173] Cf. Bultmann Trad., 139 and 158; Wellhausen Mt., ad loc. There seems to be a Gnostic interpretation of Mt. 23:25 f. (Lk. 11:39 ff.) in Ev. Thom. (ed. A. Guillaumont et al. [1959]), Logion 89 (96, 13-16).

[174] Cf. esp. Str.-B., II, 494-519 (on Jn. 7:49); J. Jeremias, 302 f.; Ps. Clem. Recg., VI, 11, 2 (ed. B. Rehm, GCS, 51 [1965]): Pharisees = a vulgo separati.

[175] Cf. W. Grundmann, Die Gesch. Jesu Christi (1960), 109, 132 f.

(Lk. 7:36; 11:37; 14:1) presupposes that He was not regarded by the Pharisees as a member of the lawless 'Am ha-'Ares. [176] For this reason His dealings with this lawless people, and His awareness of having a special mission to them, [177] were bound to run into severe Pharisaic criticism. Thus when Mk. 2:15 ff. and par. speak of Jesus (or His disciples, Lk. 5:30) eating with publicans and sinners (cf. also Mt. 11:19 or Lk. 7:34; 15:1 f.; 19:7), we are given a plain picture of the attitude of Jesus, which abrogated in fact the legal observance of the Pharisees. [178] This attitude is most clearly presented by way of contrast to the legal piety of the Pharisees in the typical story of the Pharisee and the publican which has come down to us in Lk. 18:9 ff. [179] Here the whole, subjectively honest [180] concern of Pharisaic Judaism to fulfil the Law correctly and thereby to contribute to the coming of God's kingdom is radically set aside in favour of the attitude of those who expect nothing of themselves and their works but everything from God → VIII, 16, 23 ff.

d. It should not be overlooked, of course, that this attitude of Jesus to the legal piety of Pharisaism was not always maintained by the primitive community with the same clarity. To be sure, the community adopted and even sharpened the critical position of Jesus towards Pharisaism. To some degree, however, there was a tendency to relapse in the form of a strict Jewish Christianity which in the last resort is still entangled in Pharisaic piety. This is most clearly reflected, perhaps, in Mt., and most of all in the Sermon on the Mount and the great anti-Pharisaic discourse in Mt. 23. [181] The infallible validity of the Law in its whole compass (→ II, 548, 32 ff.) is asserted in Mt. 5:18 f., which is regarded by some as a Jewish Christian addition wholly in keeping with Pharisaic-Rabbinic statements [182] and differing from the true attitude of Jesus. [183] But the real concern of the Evangelist is plainest in the discourse in Mt. 23 (cf. Lk. 11:37 ff.; Mk. 12:38 ff.). [184] Formally Mt. rejects

---

[176] But cf. Jn. 7:15 and J. Jeremias, 268.

[177] Cf. Mk. 2:17; Mt. 11:19 or Lk. 7:34; 19:10. Whether we have community theology here, esp. in ref. to Jesus having come, Mt. 11:19 and par. and Lk. 19:10, need not be discussed in this context; in any case the thought is to be found already in Mk. 2:17a. Cf. Bultmann Trad., 96, 164 f., 166; Grundmann, op. cit., on Lk. 7:34; Loh. Mk. on 2:15 ff.

[178] Since in the passages mentioned it is the Pharisees who criticise Jesus, there is no need to distinguish between sinners in the Pharisaic sense ('Am ha-'Ares) and sinners in the eyes of the people, and we may adopt the latter sense in these passages, J. Jeremias, "Zöllner u. Sünder," ZNW, 30 (1931), 293-5. The conflict between Jesus and the Pharisees is so sharp just because Jesus has dealings with those who are regarded as sinners even among the 'Am ha-' Ares.

[179] In analysis (Lk. 18:9 and 18:14b) cf. Bultmann Trad., 193; Dibelius op. cit., 254; Jeremias Gl.7, 99 and 141.

[180] It should be noted that the picture of the Pharisee here is no caricature. Cf. Montefiore, II, 556 f.; Rengstorf, op. cit. on 18:11.

[181] Cf. Strecker, op. cit., 137-143.

[182] Cf. Str.-B., I, 244-9.

[183] On Mt. 5:17-20 cf. Schweizer, op. cit., 399-406; Kümmel, op. cit., 33 f.; E. Stauffer, Die Botschaft Jesu (1959), 26-39; Braun, op. cit., II, 7, n. 2; 11, n. 2; 51, n. 1; 97, n. 2; Trilling, op. cit., 167-186, 203; Strecker, op. cit., 143-7. On the question of polemic against nomistic circles in the Hell. community (cf. Mt. 7:15 ff. and 24:11 ff. as well as 5:17 ff.) cf. G. Barth, "Das Gesetzesverständnis d. Evangelisten Mt." in G. Bornkamm, G. Barth and H. J. Held, Überlieferung u. Auslegung im Mt., Wissenschaftl. Monographien z. AT u. NT, 1⁴ (1965), 60-70, 149-154; but for another view cf. Strecker, op. cit., 137, n. 4.

[184] On Mt. 23 compared with Mk. 12:38-40 and Lk. 11:37-52 cf. Bultmann Trad., 118 f.; Kl. Mt., Wellh. Mt., ad loc.; T. W. Manson, The Sayings of Jesus³ (1954), 94-103, 227-240; E. Haenchen, "Matt. 23," Gott u. Mensch (1965), 29-54. In reconstruction cf. also Meyer Prophet, 14 f., 135. For Mk. as an abbreviation no ref. are available; cf. Schniewind, op. cit. on 23:1; Montefiore, op. cit., II, 290.

Pharisaic Judaism here and can even adopt elements from the Zadokite criticism of the Pharisees → 28, 6 ff. [185] Materially, however, one can detect a different nuance in Jesus' attitude to the legal piety of Pharisaism. The target is more the practice of the Pharisees rather than their legal piety or their understanding of the Law; the Pharisees do not practise what they preach, Mt. 23:3, 23. [186] In other words, the attack is not so much on the ideal set up by the Pharisees as on the fact that they do not reach it. In this respect the same position is adopted as that from which Pharisaic-Rabbinic Judaism itself could attack hypocrisy in its own ranks, → 19, 15 ff. [187] In themselves the directions in Mt. 23:2 f. do not free the Christian community from the teaching authority of the Pharisees. They leave the Law intact in its Pharisaic-Rabbinic interpretation. Christianity might well become a strictly observed Pharisaism, [188] as is especially plain from Mt. 23:2 f., which allows that the Pharisees and scribes sit in Moses' seat, i.e., have teaching authority. [189] The Christian community is expected to do and observe what the Pharisees and scribes say or teach. [190] Here and in Mt. 23:23 (→ III, 594, 3 ff.) [191] it is clear that Mt. is using older, authentic material in the discourse against the Pharisees but it is given a decidedly Jewish Christian sense (→ VI, 662, 14 ff.). We do not see the full radicalness of Jesus' judgment on the Pharisaic understanding of the Law as a whole (→ IV, 1064, 14 ff.). Mt. 23 reflects the polemic of the Jewish Christian community as well as that of Jesus. [192] This explains both its sharpness and also its in some sense simplified character whereby the Pharisees and scribes are a single and self-contained entity on which a collective rather than a differentiated judgment is passed. The Jewish Christian community has true Pharisaic legitimacy. It and not Judaism in its Pharisaic-Rabbinic form is the true Israel.

II. The Pharisees in John's Gospel.

In general the presentation of the relation between Jesus and the Pharisees in the Fourth Gospel agrees with what we find in the Synoptics. The Pharisees are already opponents of the Baptist (1:19, 24, cf. also 3. 25). [193] The main reason for the controversy between Jesus and the Pharisees is the supposed violation of the Sabbath commandment (→ VII, 26, 30 ff.) by Jesus, 5:1 ff., and cf. also the debate between Jesus and the Jews in 7:19 ff.; 9:1 ff. [194] Finally it is the Pharisees who resolve to put Jesus to death, 7:32; 11:46 ff. [195] Nevertheless, there are in John

---

185 Cf. the material agreement between Mt. 23:13 and par. and Damasc. 6:12 (8:11) ("closers of the door") and Mt. 23:14 and Damasc. 6:16 (8:13). The criticism of Pharisaism in Mt. is thus in the last analysis intra-Jewish criticism. On the anti-Pharisaic polemic of Qumran and its agreement with the anti-Pharisaic discourses in the Synoptics cf. J. Carmignac, "Les éléments histor. des 'Hymnes' de Qumran," *Revue de Qumran,* 2 (1960), 216-222.
186 Cf. esp. Mt. 23:3, 23, 28; *v.* Trilling, *op. cit.,* 198-202; Haenchen, *op. cit.,* 49.
187 Cf. Meyer-Weiss, 110 and n. 3.
188 Cf. Haenchen, *op. cit.,* 52; Barth, *op. cit.,* 80-83.
189 Cf. M. Ginsberger, "La chaire de Moise," REJ, 90 (1931), 161-5; Manson, *op. cit.,* 228.
190 Cf. Haenchen, 30 f.; Loh. Mt. on 23:2 f.; Braun, II, 13, n. 1.
191 Cf. Haenchen, 39 f.; Montefiore, *op. cit.,* II, 301 and 482.
192 On vv. 8-10 cf. Haenchen, 33-36; Légasse, *op. cit.,* 333-9. On v. 28 in relation to v. 27 and v. 33 (= Mt. 3:7) cf. Meyer Prophet, 14 f. and 135. On v. 34b as *vaticinium ex eventu* cf. Bultmann Trad., 118 f. and 134; Légasse, *op. cit.,* 323-333.
193 On Jn. 3:25 cf. Bultmann J., 122-5.
194 Cf. Lohse, *op. cit.,* 79 f., 89; on Jn. 7:22 f. → VIII, 327, 15 ff.; VI, 82, 6 ff.
195 Cf. J. Jeremias, 299.

many indications that the account of the conflict between Jesus and the Pharisees reflects the actual situation of the Evangelist as well as historical circumstances in the time of Jesus.

One may refer to the terminology. While there is in Synoptic usage some trace of differentiation between different Jewish trends, this is no longer so in Jn. Even "Pharisee" is less prominent compared to the comprehensive concept of "the Jews" (→ III. 377, 3 ff.), which in many passages does not denote the Jewish people as a whole, [196] but the intellectual and religious spokesmen of Judaism, esp. those who refuse to believe in Jesus → III, 378, 31 ff. One may also refer to the way the Pharisees are linked with the chief priests in Jn. at 7:32, 45; 11:47, 57; 18:3 → III, 271, 33 ff. [197] Now there were obviously some priests among the Pharisees → 15, 8 ff. [198] But in view of the fact that the Synoptic tradition with its close historical reflection of the situation in the days of Jesus does not originally relate the Pharisees and chief priests in this way → 38, 7 ff., one may ask whether the pertinent passages in Jn. are giving a precise historical portrayal of the situation. A specific point in this regard is that in these passages the Pharisees are in positions of power along with the chief priests. That is to say, they are members of the judicial authority, or the Sanhedrin (→ VII, 863, 24 ff.), before which the blind man cured by Jesus has to answer, cf. also Jn. 7:45, 47 f. and esp. in Jn. 11:47, 57; 12:42. [199] In all these verses one would expect a reference to the scribes rather than the Pharisees. If the Evangelist takes a different course, this seems to indicate that the original distinction between the Pharisees and the scribes is of no moment in this Gospel.

The hostility of the Pharisees or the Jews to Jesus is traced back in Jn., as in the Synoptics (→ 40, 1 ff.), to the critical attitude of Jesus to the Law (→ IV, 1082, 30 ff.). But from the whole complex of the relevant Synoptic tradition Jn. has preserved only two stories which tell of healings on the Sabbath, 5:1 ff.; 9:1 ff. These incidents are obviously taken to be a challenge to the Sabbath commandment by Jesus → VII, 26, 30 ff.; VIII, 290, 18 ff. [200] All the same, Jn. does express a fact which plays an essential role in the Synoptic Gospels too, namely, that in a special way Jesus turns to those whom the Pharisees call the "people who knoweth not the Law" (Jn. 7:49; → V, 589, 19 ff.). This may also be seen in Jn. 9:39 (cf. 12:40), for the Pharisees who reject the claim of Jesus are those who see and who yet are really blind, whereas those who do not see are the people of Jn. 7:49, who see by faith in Jesus (→ VIII, 291, 26 ff.). [201] The statement in Jn. 7:49 shows that the Evangelist is not unfamiliar with the relations in contemporary Judaism. In keeping is the fact that, while the Jews are severely judged → III, 378, 31 ff., he does not pronounce any collective sentence on the Pharisees themselves.

This is esp. plain not only when the reaction of the Pharisees to violation of the Sabbath commandment is shown to be radically rejected by Jesus in Jn. 9:16 (cf. also 8:30) but also when there is depicted in Nicodemus a Pharisee who in no sense opposes

---

[196] Cf. the distinction between the Jews and the people in Jn. 7:12, 20, 31, 49 and on this Bultmann J., 59; E. Grässer, "Die anti-jüd. Polemik im Joh.-Ev.," NTSt, 11 (1964/65), 74-90.
[197] But cf. in Jn. 1:19, 24 the distinction between the priests and Levites on the one side and the Pharisees on the other; on Jn. 1:24 cf. Bultmann J., 57 f.; on the linking of the Pharisees and chief priests cf. also Jn. 12:10, 19. The Pharisees occur with the scribes only in Jn. 7:53 - 8:11 at 8:6, where they test Jesus.
[198] Cf. J. Jeremias, 291 f.
[199] Cf. Bultmann J., 59, n. 5; 231, n. 7; 253.
[200] Cf. on Jn. 5:9b and 9:14 Lohse, op. cit., 79 f.; Bultmann Trad., 242.
[201] On the fig. usage cf. Bultmann J., 258, n. 6; materially cf. also Mt. 11:25.

Jesus from the very outset, Jn. 3:1 f., cf. also 7:47 ff. [202] In this regard one might also mention the passages in Jn. which tell how many of the leaders (ἄρχοντες) came to faith in Jesus, Jn. 12:42, cf. also 7:47 f. If it is also said that these believing rulers did not confess their faith for fear of the Pharisees "lest they should be put out of the synagogue" (Jn. 12:42, cf. also 9:42; 16:2 → VII, 848, 1 ff.), there is again reflected a situation in which Church and Synagogue were already confronting one another as hostile and separated forces. [203]

III. The Pharisees in Acts and in Paul.

1. There seems to be an obvious difference as between the Synoptic Gospels and Acts in the assessment of the Pharisees. The opposition between Jesus and the Pharisees no longer plays any part in Acts. The Jews in general rather than the Pharisees bear responsibility for the death of Jesus, Ac. 2:23, 36; 4:10; 3:15 ff.; 5:30; 7:52; 10:39; 13:27 f., cf. also 1 Th. 2:15. [204] Nor are the Pharisees the real opponents of the primitive community or Christianity. According to Luke's presentation the true foes are the Sadducees → VII, 52, 37 ff. It is true that Luke is familiar with the Pharisaic movement (αἵρεσις) and its special observance of the Law, Ac. 15:5; 23:9; cf. esp. 26:5: ἡ ἀκριβεστάτη αἵρεσις. [205] But essentially the only part played by the Pharisees is that some of them, like the teacher Gamli'el in Ac. 5:34, [206] belong to the Sanhedrin. [207] In this assembly they differ from the old-line Sadducees by confessing belief in the resurrection, angels and spirits, Ac. 23:6-9 → VII, 53, 37 ff. [208] As in the Gospel, so again in Acts Luke is well aware of the difference between the Pharisees and the scribes, Ac. 23:9. But the most outstanding difference from the general Synoptic portrayal of the Pharisees is that the attitude of Pharisaic representatives in the Sanhedrin is not depicted as one of hostility to Christianity. Thus Gamli'el in Ac. 5:34 ff. advocates a tolerant attitude towards Christians [209] and when Paul appears before the Sanhedrin in Ac. 23:6 ff. it is the Pharisees who for party reasons vouch for Paul's innocence. Along the same lines Luke can tell of Pharisees who became believers, Ac. 15:5; cf. also 21:20 f. [210]

2. Similarly there is no trace of a pronounced anti-Pharisaic attitude in Paul. The apostle can even speak with a certain pride of his pre-Christian Pharisaic

[202] The title ἄρχων (→ I, 489, 9 ff.) denotes here membership of the Sanhedrin, cf. Bultmann J., 94, n. 3; on Nicodemus cf. J. Jeremias, 269, 289; Légasse, op. cit. (→ n. 141), 321, n. 4.
[203] Grässer, op. cit., 86 thinks that the radical break of actual exclusion from the synagogue is a projection back into the life of Jesus.
[204] Cf. H. Conzelmann, "Die Mitte d. Zeit," Stud. z. Theol. d. Lukas, Beitr. z. histor. Theol., 17⁵ (1964), 136.
[205] Cf. on this Jos. Vit., 191: "... the school of the Pharisees who think that in regard to (following) the laws of the fathers they are distinguished from other Jews by scrupulosity (ἀκριβείᾳ)."
[206] On Gamli'el cf. Str.-B., II, 636-9; Schürer, II, 429-431.
[207] Cf. J. Jeremias, 261.
[208] Cf. Meyer Ursprung, II, 302 f.; on ἀμφότερα in Ac. 23:8 in the sense of "all" cf. Haench. Ag.¹⁴, ad loc. and also on 19:16.
[209] Cf. Haench. Ag.¹⁴, ad loc. and B. Reicke, "Glaube u. Leben d. Urgemeinde," AbhThANT, 32 (1957), 102-105.
[210] On the relation between the Church and Judaism in Luke cf. Conzelmann, op. cit., 135-8.

past. In the few relevant passages (Gl. 1:13 f.; Phil. 3:5 f.) [211] he claims that he corresponded in every way to the Pharisaic ideal: "As touching the law, a Pharisee... touching the righteousness which is in the law, blameless" (Phil. 3:5 f. → III, 390, 3 ff.). [212] In his zeal for the traditions of the fathers, i.e., for the specific legal tradition of the Pharisees, [213] he even surpassed his contemporaries according to Gl. 1:13 f. [214] Paul's own references may be supplemented biographically from the references in Acts. According to Ac. 23:6 he was the son of Pharisaically inclined parents. [215] From his youth up as a Pharisee in Jerusalem (Ac. 26:4 f.) he was even a student of Rabban Gamli'el (Ac. 5:34) according to Ac. 22:3. [216] There can certainly be no contesting the Pharisaic past of Paul in view of Gl. 1:13 f. and Phil. 3:5 f. (→ V, 619, 27 ff.; VI, 714, 19 ff.) even if the references in Acts are viewed cautiously. Thus it is questioned by some whether in the light of Gl. 1:22 Paul was quite so well known in Jerusalem as Ac. 22:3 and especially 26:4 suggest. [217] Again it has been asked whether, on Paul's appearance before the Sanhedrin in 23:6 ff., the Pharisees would have been likely to know so little of Paul that they would make alliance with the Christians merely because he appealed to his Pharisaic background. [218] A moot point is whether Paul was or was not an ordained scribe. [219] In fact, of course, Paul's Pharisaic past was no longer of any real significance for him. He was ready to count it but refuse for Christ's sake (Phil. 3:7 → II, 890, 22 ff.). This means ultimately that the historical opposition to Pharisaism which so largely shaped the history of Jesus according to the Gospel presentation is far less important in Paul than the theological conflict between Christ and the Law.

C. The Pharisees in Early Christian Writings outside the New Testament.

During the 2nd cent. and those which followed there was a sharp rift between the Church and Judaism. It is not to be expected, then, that early Chr. writings outside the NT will yield new insights on Pharisaism beyond what we have seen already. In the post-

---

[211] In keeping with the Pharisaic view is the argument in Gl. 5:3 that the circumcised are under obligation to keep the whole Law (cf. also R. 2:25), though cf. Schlier Gl.12, ad loc. It is less likely that the ἀφορίζειν of R. 1:1 and Gl. 1:15 echoes the Hbr. פרש in the sense of Pharisaic separation → V, 454, 8 ff.; Schlier Gl.12, ad loc. and esp. J. W. Doeve, "Paulus d. Pharisäer u. Gl. 1:13-15," Nov. Test., 6 (1963), 170-181.

[212] Cf. Loh. Phil.12, ad loc.; Paul is a Benjamite in R. 11:1 too; cf. J. Jeremias, 311.

[213] Cf. the tradition of the elders in Mk. 7:1 ff.; Schlier Gl.12, ad loc.; Kümmel, op. cit. (→ n. 162), 24 f.

[214] ζηλωτής denotes here the Pharisee with a special concern for the Law; cf. R. 10:2; Phil. 3:6; Ac. 21:20; 22:3; → II, 887, 7 ff.; Schlier Gl.12, ad loc.; Hengel, 181 f., 184 f.

[215] The "circumcised the eighth day" of Phil. 3:5 also suggests Pharisaic parents; for the construing of υἱὸς Φαρισαίων as student of a Pharisaic teacher or member of a Pharisaic society cf. J. Jeremias, 200, 286, n. 2 (cf. Mt. 12:27); M. Dibelius - W. G. Kümmel, Paulus³ (1964), 27; Zn. Ag. on 23:6. On the problem of diaspora Pharisaism cf. H. J. Schoeps, Paulus (1959), 12-16; H. F. Weiss, "Zur Frage d. histor. Voraussetzungen der Begegnung von Antike u. Christentum," Klio, 23-45 (1965), 318 f.

[216] In Ac. 22:3 we again find (cf. Gl. 1:13 f.) the term ζηλωτής (τοῦ θεοῦ), cf. the vl. τοῦ νόμου (cf. Ac. 21:20) and τῶν πατρικῶν μου παραδόσεων (cf. Gl. 1:14).

[217] Cf. Haench. Ag.14 on 22:3; R. Bultmann, Art. "Paulus," RGG², IV, 1020 f.; M. S. Enslin, "Paul and Gamaliel," The Journal of Religion, 7 (1927), 360-375 is esp. critical.

[218] Note that in Ac. 23:6 Paul claims that he is a Pharisee; cf. also 26:6: he is arraigned because he is a Pharisee; cf. Haench. Ag.14, ad loc.

[219] On the basis of Ac. 9:1 f.; 13:5; 22:5; 26:10, 12 ordination is favoured by J. Jeremias, 269, 288; also "War Paulus Witwer?" ZNW, 25 (1926), 310 f.; cf. also Dibelius-Kümmel, op. cit., 30 f., 33; on Ac. 26:10 cf. Haench. Ag.14, ad loc.

apost. fathers the Pharisees are not mentioned at all. [220] In other works we are simply told about the various Jewish parties [221] and attempts are made to explain the term Φαρισαῖος → 12, 10 ff. On what is at times the literal basis of the Synoptic tradition the Pharisees are presented as the adversaries of Jesus or the apostles. [222] In this respect they hardly differ from other Jewish movements. [223] Thus a Pharisaic high-priest (Φαρισαῖος τις ἀρχιερεύς) debates with Jesus about questions of cultic purification in an account recorded in an apocr. Gospel, P. Oxy., V, 840, 10 (4th cent. A.D.). [224] The hostility of early Christianity to Pharisaism is also reflected in Chr.-Gnostic texts such as the Apocr. of Joh. Cod. II, 1, 5-17, [225] where a Pharisee named Amanias or Arimanios calls Jesus a deceiver who has seduced his students from the traditions of their fathers. The Gnostic Ev. Thom. (→ n. 173) also attacks the Pharisees after the Synoptic manner: Logion 39 (88, 7 ff.) [226] has the saying of Jesus recorded in Lk. 11:52, cf. Mt. 23:13. Logion 102 (98, 2 ff.) has the same thought as Logion 39 but in fig. form: "Woe to them, the Pharisees, for they are like a dog lying on a trough for cattle; it will neither eat nor let the cattle eat" [227] (→ 50, 8 ff.). The stereotyped use of the combination "Pharisees and scribes" is also found in Just., e.g., in Jesus' prophecies of woe in Mk. 8:31 or Lk. 9:22, even though originally there was no ref. to the Pharisees, Just. Dial., 51, 2; 76, 7; 100, 3. [228] The only instances in early writings of a slightly different attitude to Pharisaism from that of the NT are in Iren. and the Ps. Cl. Acc. to Iren. Haer., IV, 12, 1 Jesus did not attack the Mosaic Law as such but only the lex pharisaica. On the basis of Mk. 7:1 ff. Jesus' opposition to the Pharisaic law is reduced to the formula: Non per Moysem datam legem dicens praecepta hominum, sed traditiones presbyterorum, quas finxerant. [229] In the

---

[220] Cf. Did., 8, 1 f. (cf. Mt. 6:16), which in connection with fasting calls the Jews "hypocrites," cf. Kn. Did., ad loc.; Blinzler, op. cit. (→ n. 169), 243 f.; H. Köster, "Synpt. Überlieferung bei d. Apost. Vät.," TU, 65 (1957), 202 f. On Ign. Phld., 6, 1 (cf. Mt. 23:27) cf. Köster, 36.

[221] For the Pharisees as αἵρεσις along with other Jewish parties cf. Just. Dial., 80, 4; Hipp. Ref., IX, 18, 2; Hegesipp. in Eus. Hist. Eccl., IV, 22, 7; Const. Ap., VI, 6, 1 ff.; Ps.-Tert. Adv. omnes Haer., 1 (CSEL, 47 [1906], 213); Filastrius Diversarum hereseon Liber 5-28, ed. V. Bulhart, CCh, 9 (1957); Ps. Cl. Recg. (→ n. 174), I, 54, 6 ff. Cf. also for the Jewish parties Hipp. Ref., IX, 28, 3 - 29, 4 (following Jos. Bell., 2, 162-6) and Epiph. Haer., 16. It is worth noting that Epiph. Haer., 15, 1 f. can still distinguish between the Pharisees and scribes δευτερωταὶ τοῦ νόμου.

[222] Only in Act. Joh. 93 (following Lk. 7:36; 14:1) does Jesus hold table-fellowship with the Pharisees.

[223] Cf. Ev. Pt. 8:28 (Hennecke³, I, 122) for scribes, Pharisees and elders; P. Oxy., X, 1224 Fr. 2 verso col. 2 (4th cent. A.D., Hennecke³, I, 73) scribes, Pharisees and priests; Syr. Gospel of Thomas (Hennecke³, I, 299) priests, scribes and Pharisees.

[224] Cf. J. Jeremias, Unbekannte Jesusworte³ (1963), 15 f., 50-60 (ἀρχιερεύς "chief priest"); Hennecke³, I, 57 f.; Bultmann Trad., 54 f.; J. Leipoldt, Jesu Verhältnis zu Griechen u. Juden (1941), 49 f. Cf. also Act. Phil. 13, where the chief priests, teachers of the law and Pharisees are the persecutors of Philip, and 96, 5 f.: Pharisees, Sadducees and chief priests.

[225] Ed. M. Krause and P. Labib, Die drei Versionen d. Apokr. d. Johannes (1962), 109 f.; cf. W. C. Till, "Die gnostischen Schriften d. kpt. Pap. Berolinensis 8502," TU, 60 (1955), 19, 6 - 20, 3; cf. Hennecke³, I, 235.

[226] P. Oxy., IV, 655, 41-9 (3rd cent. A.D.), cf. Hennecke³, I, 71 f.; Gospel of Thomas Logion 39 f. gives the different readings of Lk. 11:52 together (ἤρατε and ἐκρύψατε); on its dependence on Lk. 11:52 cf. E. Haenchen, Die Botschaft d. Thomasev. (1961), 66; G. Quispel, "The Gospel of Thomas and the NT," Vigiliae Christ., 11 (1957), 202 f.; on the text of Lk. 11:52 → III, 747, 14 ff.

[227] Cf. J. Bauer, "Echte Jesusworte?" Theol. Jbch. 1961 (1961), 214 and n. 80; cf. also 193 f. on Logion 39.

[228] There is a stereotyped use of "Pharisees and scribes" only in Just. Dial., 17, 4 (cf. Mt. 23:23); 102, 5; 103, 1.

[229] Cf. also Ep. Apostolorum, 30, 3 (ed. C. Schmidt, TU, 43 [1919]), 129. Acc. to Schmidt, 307 f. the pt. is that Christ has come down to cleanse the Law from Pharisaic distortions, Meyer-Weiss, 130 f.

Ps. Cl., on the other hand, conclusions are drawn from Mt. 23:2 f. and 23:13 or 23:23 which reflect the attitude of a Jewish Christianity that does not merely accept the binding nature of the Mosaic Law but also affirms basically the authority of the Pharisees and scribes sitting in Moses' seat. [230] The Pharisees and scribes have the key to the kingdom of heaven, i.e., they have the *verbum veritatis* ... *ex Moysei traditione,* even though they conceal it from the people (cf. Lk. 11:52), Ps. Cl. Recg. I, 54, 7. [231] Moses gave the Law and expositions ἐπιλύσεις to the elders, Ps. Cl. Hom., 2, 38, 1 cf. 3, 47, 1. The seat of Moses (Mt. 23:2) is honoured even though those who sit on it are sinners, 3, 70, 2, cf. 3, 18, 2. Reflected here is an attitude which is sharply critical of Pharisaic practice but finally leaves the authority of the Pharisees intact. Even though they do not exercise the office of the keys properly, they are still the ones who really know the Law, 3, 51, 1, cf. also 11, 28, 4. In this light one can readily see why Ps. Cl. Hom., 11, 29, 1 f. applies the Woes of Jesus to the hypocrites among the Pharisees rather than the Pharisees as such: "He spoke only to the hypocrites: Woe to you... (Mt. 23:25 f.)." [232] The distinction from Jesus' attitude to the Pharisees is plain, as is also the distinction from the attitude of Mt. to the Pharisaic-Rabbinic Judaism of his day. Acc. to the view of the Ps. Cl. the Jewish Chr. community is not just the true Israel; Jewish Christians are finally the true Pharisees. [233]

H. F. Weiss

---

[230] This does not mean that the Ps. Cl. give a clear picture of the relations in Jesus' day, for the Pharisees and scribes form a single group opposed to the Sadducees (Ps. Cl. Recg., I, 54); distinction is made between them, however, in I, 58 f.

[231] On Lk. 11:52 cf. also Ps. Cl. Hom., 3, 18, 2 f.; 18, 15, 7; Recg., II, 30, 1; 46, 3.

[232] Cf. also Ps. Cl. Recg., VI, 11, 2: *ad quosdam ergo ex ipsis, non ad omnes dicebat:* "*Vae vobis* ..." (Mt. 23:25 f.).

[233] On the idea of the true Israel cf. M. Simon, *Verus Israel. Les relations entre Juifs et Chrétiens sous l'empire romain*[2] (1964). On the understanding of the Jewish Law in the Ps. Cl. cf. C. Schmidt, "Stud. zu d. PsClem.," TU, 46, 1 (1929), 60 f., 203, 317 f.; G. Strecker, "Das Judenchristentum in d. PsClem.," TU, 70 (1958), 163-6; cf. also 237 f.; H. J. Schoeps, *Theol. u. Gesch. d. Judenchristentums* (1949), 143-6, 211-8, 316 f.; on relations between Mt. and Ps. Cl., *ibid.,* 64 f.

φάτνη

A. Greek Usage.

Φάτνη, more rarely πάθνη,[1] is found from Hom.[2] esp. in the sense of "manger," "feeding trough," Il., 5, 271; 24, 280; 6, 506 = 15, 263. In the Il. a φάτνη is set up exclusively for horses which acc. to 10, 568 are tied to it with thongs. But Od., 4, 535 = 11, 411 speaks of the slaying of a βοῦς ἐπὶ φάτνῃ, cf. Philostr. Imagines,[3] II, 10, 4; Phot. Bibliotheca,[4] 271 (p. 503a, 25). The meaning "manger" is still the main one in Eur. Ba., 510; Hipp., 1240; Alc., 496; El., 1136; Xenoph. Cyrop., III, 3, 27; Epict. Gnom. Stob., 15 (p. 481); Luc. Gallus, 29 and Aesopus Fab.,[5] 93, 1, 6; 200, 2; 238, 8; Libanius Fab. (→ n. 5), 2, 11 (p. 131). The same is true in the special field of animal husbandry, Xenoph. Eq., 4, 1. 4; 5, 1; Eq. Mag., 1, 16; Aristot. Hist. An., IX, 1, p. 609b, 20; Geoponica,[6]

φ ά τ ν η . Bibl.: Liddell-Scott, Pass., Pr.-Bauer, Thes. Steph., s.v.; M. Baily, The Crib and the Exegesis of Lk. 2:1-20," *The Irish Eccles. Record,* 100 (1963), 358-376; also "The Shepherds and the Sign of a Child in a Manger," *The Irish Theol. Quarterly,* 31 (1964), 1-23; K. Bornhäuser, "Die Geburts- u. Kindheitsgesch. Jesu," BFTh, II, 23 (1930), 101-7; H. J. Cadbury, "Lexical Notes on Luke-Acts. III: Luke's Interest in Lodging," JBL, 45 (1926), 317-9; "V: Luke and the Horse-Doctors," JBL, 52 (1933), 61 f.; Clemen, 197 f., 203-9; Dalman Orte, 41-9; Dalman Arbeit, VI, 276-287; M. Dibelius, "Jungfrauensohn u. Krippenkind," *Botschaft u. Gesch.,* I (1953), 57-61; G. Erdmann, "Die Vorgeschichten d. Lk.- u. Mt.-Evang.," FRL, 47 (1932), 42 f., 52 f.; H. Gressmann, *Das Weihnachtsev. auf Ursprung u. Gesch. untersucht* (1914); P. Haupt, "The Crib of Christ," *The Monist,* 30 (1920), 153-9; A. Hug, Art. "Praes(a)epe" in Pauly W., 22 (1954), 1561-3; M. Miguens, "In una mangiatoia, perché non c'era posto...,'" *Bibbia e Oriente,* 2 (1960), 193-9; K. H. Rengstorf, "Die Weihnachtserzählung d. Ev. Lk.," *Festschr. H. Lilje* (1959), 15-30; H. Sahlin, *Der Messias u. d. Gottesvolk* (1945), 207 f., 220-222, 234 f.; A. van Veldhuizen, "De Kribbe van Bethlehem," *Nieuwe Theol. Stud.,* 13 (1930), 175-8; D. Völter, *Die evangel. Erzählungen von d. Geburt u. Kindheit Jesu* (1911), 48-53, 55; P. Winter, "The Cultural Background of the Narrative in Lk. I and II," JQR, 45 (1954/55), 238-240; D. Yubero, "Una opinión original del 'Brocense' sobre Lk. 2:7," *Cultura Bibl.,* 11 (1954), 3-6.

1 Thes. Steph., s.v. πάθνη. Acc. to Eustath. Thessal. Comm. in Il. on 22, 93 (IV, 228, 28), cf. Comm. in Od. on 15, 373 (II, 103, 7 f.) and Moeris Atticista (ed. I. Bekker, *Harpocration et Moeris* [1833], p. 212, 9) φάτνη was Attic and πάθνη koine, orig. Ionic. Both are from *φαθνᾱ, Indo-Eur. *bhndhnā root *bhendh Germ. "binden," Engl. "bind," v. Boisacq and Hofmann, s.v. φάτνη is common in inscr. for "hollowed out coffers in the cieling," IG, II/III², 2, 1, No. 1487, 37 (4th/3rd cent. B.C.); IV², No. 109 III, 85 (3rd cent. B.C.); XI, 2, No. 161 A, 45 f. (3rd cent. B.C.); XI, 3, No. 504 A 4. 6. 13 (c. 280 B.C.), cf. perhaps P. Lips., 106, 9 (1st cent. A.D. for πάθνη. φάτνη or πάθνη was adopted in Latin as *patena,* Walde-Hoffmann, s.v., cf. A. A. Barb, "Krippe, Tisch u. Grab," *Festschr. T. Klauser* (1964), 24.
2 In Hom. and poetry cf. κάπη, Il., 8, 434; Od., 4, 40.
3 Ed. O. Benndorf - C. Schenkl (1893).
4 Ed. I. Bekker (1824 f.).
5 Ed. A. Hausrath, Corpus Fabul. Aesopicarum, I, 1 (1957); I, 2 (1956).
6 Ed. H. Beckh (1895).

16, 1, 11; 17, 13, 1 f.; 15, 4, 1 (πάθνη). Here in 18, 2, 2 we also read of mangers for sheep, cf. Varro Res rusticae, [7] II, 2, 19; Columella Res rustica, [8] VII, 3, 21; Verg. Georg., III, 416; [9] elsewhere they are only for cattle, donkeys and horses. The same sense predominates in veterinary writings. [10] Sometimes it can express power and wealth. Thus in Jos. Ant., 8, 41 Solomon had 40,000 mangers for his chariot-horses, cf. 1 K. 5:6; 10:26; 2 Ch. 9:25 (→ 52, 10 ff. with n. 30), and in Iberian Turdetania the Carthaginians captured silver troughs, Strabo, 3, 2, 14, while in the tent of Mardonius the Tegeans seized a trough of bronze which they dedicated to Athena Alea, Hdt., IX, 70, 3. Proverbially we read of ἡ ἐν φάτνη κύων which itself eats no fodder and does not let horses eat, Luc. Tim., 40, cf. Indoct., 30; Anth. Graec., 12, 236 (Strato of Sardis); Constantinus Manasse, [11] 6, 28 f. → 47, 14 ff. The extended sense of "stall" is less common; the meaning might be either "crib" or "stall" [12] in Plut. Lys., 20 (I, 445a); Ael. Nat. An., 16, 24: πλησίον τινὸς φάτνης, ἐν ἧι δύω ἵπποι ἐξεφατνίζοντο, Nicolaus of Damascus Fr., 3 (FGrHist., IIa, 330, 14 f.). In Diod. S., 17, 95, 2 the meaning seems to be "feeding-place" in connection with the soldiers' camp-site. In the pap. we twice find φάτνη for "manger," P. Lille, I, 17, 15 (3rd cent. B.C.); P. Oxy., XIV, 1734 Fr., 2 (2nd/3rd cent. A.D.) [13] and once for "stall." [14] The range becomes so broad, however, that the word can even express the excitement of horses, Aristoph. Nu., 13, τὴν ψυχὴν ἐν ταῖς φάτναις εἶχεν, Plut. Alex. Fort. Virt., 2, 1 (II, 334b); in an inscr. of the Saassanidian king Sapor [15] the man in charge of the horses is called ὁ ἐπὶ τῆς πάθνης. The transf. sense is based on the meaning "manger" or "feeding-trough." The organs of digestion are called φάτνη, Plat. Tim., 70e; Aristot. Part. An., II, 3, p. 650a, 19, and cf. Philo Spec. Leg., I, 148 in exposition of Dt. 18:3. The "trough" expresses a parasitic life, Eur. Fr., 378 (TGF, 476), 670 (570); Eubulus Fr., 129 (FAC, II, 140); Ael. Nat. An., 9, 7; Fr., 39 (II, 201, 14), 107 (239, 2); Plut. Quaest. Conv., II, 10, 1 (II, 643b), cf. Horat. Ep., I, 15, 28; Plaut. Curculio, 227 f. The "hollow" in the roof, usually φάτνωμα, is φάτνη in Diod. S., I, 66, 4 (→ n. 1) [16] and so a "cavity" in a tooth in Poll. Onom., II, 93, cf. Philo Spec. Leg., I, 164, also a "star-cluster" (nebula) in the sign of cancer between two stars called ὄνοι. [17] The firm connection with the idea of feeding may be seen in the fact that the later lexicographers can define φάτνη as τράπεζα, Suid., s.v.; cf. Hesych., s.v.: καὶ ἡ τράπεζα, καὶ ἡ τῶν κτηνῶν, καὶ εἴ τι τῶν τοιούτων. The derived verbs φατνεύω "to feed at the trough" or φατνι(ά)ζομαι "to be fed" show the same emphasis.

The word has no specific religious sense. A Phrygian inscr. is dedicated to Zeus as

---

[7] Ed. G. Goetz (1912).
[8] Ed. W. Lundström (1940).
[9] Cf. Hug, 1561 and E. Orth, Art. "Schaf," Pauly-W., 2a (1923), 386.
[10] Corpus Hippiatricorum Graecorum, ed. E. Oder - C. Hoppe, I (1924), p. 42, 2; 208, 20, cf. 209, 7; 290, 13; II (1927), p. 222, 14, uses the word for a trough up against the wall. The same is true, in spite of Cadbury Horse-Doctors, 61, in the heading II, 222, 24 f.: πρὸς τὸ μὴ λακτίζειν ζῷα ἀλλήλων ἐν τῇ φάτνη, since ἐν expressing proximity can be transl. "up against" or "by."
[11] Ed. R. Hercher, Erotici Scriptores Graeci, II (1859).
[12] Cf. Pr.-Bauer, s.v., who over-emphasises the meaning "stall."
[13] Cf. Preisigke Wört. and Moult-Mill., s.v.
[14] Pap. Cairo Zeno, V, 59840, 11 (ed. O. Guéraud and P. Jouguet, Publications de la Société Fouad, I, 1940): Request for the building of a stall; perhaps also P. Lips., 106, 9 (1st cent. A.D.; → n. 1).
[15] Ed. A. Maricq, "Res gestae divi Saporis," Syria, 35 (1958), 325 on 58. Cf. L. Robert, "Bulletin Épigraphique," Revue d. Études Grecques, 61 (1948), 200 [Robert].
[16] Derived from φατνόω "to hollow out," strictly "to make a trough," cf. Pass., s.v.
[17] Theophr. De signis tempestatum, 1, 23; 3, 43; 4, 51; Arat. Phaen., 892, 996; cf. Theocr. Idyll., 22, 21 f.: ὄνων τ' ἀνὰ μέσσον ἀμαυρὴ φάτνη σημαίνουσα τὰ πρὸς πλόον εὔδια πάντα. Eratosthenes Catasterismorum reliquiae, 11 (ed. C. Robert [1878], 90-93); Nechepso-Petosiris Fr., 12 (ed. E. Riess, Philol. Suppl., 6, 1 [1892], 352, 51). Cf. Roscher, VI, 953 f.

guardian of the manger: Εὐ... οἰκονόμος Διὶ Φατνίῳ κατὰ κέλευσιν. [18] Pind. Olymp., 13, 92 speaks of the mangers or stalls of Zeus which admit Pegasus, and in Plat. Phaedr., 247e the heavenly horses, after the ascent of the soul, are put πρὸς τὴν φάτνην by their driver, fed with ambrosia, and given nectar to drink. Magical practices could be used to protect cattle in the manger, Geoponica (→ n. 6), 17, 13, 2. [19]

B. The Old Testament and Rabbinic Judaism.

1. In the LXX φάτνη occurs 7 times, 3 being for Hbr. אֵבוּס "feeding-trough," Is. 1:3; Job 39:9; Prv. 14:4, [20] but Hab. 3:17 and perhaps Jl. 1:17 for רֶפֶת, [21] 2 Ch. 32:28 for אֻרָוֹה, [22] and Job 6:5 in a free rendering of עַל בְּלִילוֹ "over his mash": ἐπὶ φάτνης ἔχων τὰ βρώματα. At Jl. 1:17; Hab. 3:17; Job 6:5 and 39:9 the prep. ἐπί with gen. or dat. suggests the meaning "manger." "Crib" or "stall" is possible at Is. 1:3; Prv. 14:4, but the latter is likely only at 2 Ch. 32:28, which depicts the wealth of Hezekiah: καὶ φάτνας παντὸς κτήνους καὶ μάνδρας εἰς τὰ ποίμνια. The few and late ref. to "stalls" in the OT show that apart from the royal stables these were relatively uncommon in Palestine, since men and animals often lived in the same dwelling, 2 S. 12:3; Ps. 50:9 → 52, 15 ff. Only the LXX with ἔπαυλις introduces the idea of an enclosure or stall for cattle. [23] ἔπαυλη and φάτνη occur together in a description of the death of Job's wife at a manger: καὶ ἀπελθοῦσα εἰς τὴν πόλιν εἰσῆλθεν εἰς τὴν ἔπαυλην τῶν βοῶν αὐτῆς τῶν ἁρπασθέντων ὑπὸ τῶν ἀρχόντων οἷς ἐδούλευσεν· καὶ περί τινα φάτνην ἐκοιμήθη καὶ τετελεύτηκεν εὐθυμήσασα, Test. Jobi, 40:5 f. [24]

2. In the Rabb. use of אֵבוּס the stress is on the sense "manger," "feeding-trough." The ox is brought to (עַל) the manger, TBM, 8, 20 (389, 6), cf. bBQ, 107b; the manger is in front of (לְפָנֵי) the animal, TYom Tob, 3, 18 (206, 25); if there is no food in it, the ass brays, bTem., 16a. Distinction is made between the אבוס של קרקע which is fastened to the ground and the אבוס של כלי which is a portable container, bShab., 140b; a damaged trough can be used for the latter, and this may be fastened to the wall, Kelim, 20, 4. The measurements for a manger which was used as a drinking-trough to get round the Sabbath commandment [25] were 10 handsbreadth in height by 4 in breadth, bErub., 20b. The trough is important in relation to feeding on the Sabbath, bShab., 20, 3 == TShab., 16, 2 (135, 3); bShab., 113a == TShab., 12, 15 (128, 8), cf. bShab., 140b, 155b. A chip could be taken as a toothpick on the Sabbath מן האבוס של בהמה, bShab., 81a Bar., cf. TYom Tob, 3, 18 (206, 25). T. Kelim BM, 8, 6 (587, 24) and 5, 9 (584, 13) show that in a Palestinian farmhouse (→ 52, 15 ff.) men and animals lived in the one dwelling with beds and manger close by each other. Thus the more gen. sense of "stall" is less common, as in the case of

---

[18] Ed. J. Keil and A. Wilhelm, Monumenta Asiae Minores Antiqua, I (1928), 5, No. 7, cf. L. Robert, Hellenica, 10 (1955), 108 f.; cf. J. Schmidt, Art. "Phatnios," Pauly-W., 19 (1938), 1900 [Robert].

[19] Cf. bSanh., 63b: Idolators put idols near mangers.

[20] From this comes אבס "to feed," Köhler-Baumg. and Jastrow, s.v. אבס and אֵבוּס.

[21] Hapax legomenon acc. to Köhler-Baumg.: s.v.; "Gehege"; in Middle Hbr. "stall", BB, 2, 3; 6, 4, v. Jastrow, s.v. At Jl. 1:17 רֶפֶת is one of several conjectures, v. BHK, ad loc.

[22] Köhler-Baumg., s.v. "Stallplatz," cf. 1 K. 5:6; 2 Ch. 9:25 → 50, 4 f. אֻרְיָה is related to Aram. אוּרְיָה → n. 27.

[23] Cf. Hatch-Redp., s.v. Cf. Ἐπαύλεις προβάτων οἰκοδομήσωμεν at Nu. 32:16 and ἐπαύλεις τοῖς κτήνεσιν at v. 24, also v. 36 (HT גְּדֵרָה "enclosure," "stone fold"). Cf. also Ac. 1:20 quoting Ps. 69:26 and αὐλή Jn. 10:1.

[24] Ed. S. P. Brock, Pseudepigr. Veteris Test., 2 (1967), 49 f.

[25] On this cf. Str.-B., II, 455.

φάτνη. [26] It is more prominent in the rarer Aram. equivalent אּוּרְיָה. [27] The distinction between man and animal is marked by Adam's exclamation in view of Gn. 3:18: אּוּר נקשר לאבוס כבהמה, "Shall I be bound to the manger like an animal?" Gn. r., 20, 10 on 3:18, cf. AbRNat. A 1 (Schechter, 7, 4); bPes., 118a. Yet the trough from which day-labourers eat is called האבוס שלפני הפועלים, Ned., 4, 4, cf. jDemai, 3, 1 (23b, 28). In the exposition of Is. 1:3 "to know his master's crib" could be interpreted as knowing the Torah. [28] The v. was never understood Messianically. The supposed Rabb. loan word אפוטני [29] for Gk. φάτνη is not attested.

C. Archaeological and Palestinian Testimonies.

The first archaeological testimonies to feeding-troughs in Palestine are in the stables of Ahab at Megiddo; [30] stalls, however, were an exception in ancient Israel. [31] Ancient oriental representations of mangers are found in Egypt and Assyria. [32] In the Hell. period (200 B.C.) we have the cave-stalls of ʿarāq el-emīr and later in other places in Palestine and Syria there are mangers hewn out of the rock. [33] But such installations are limited to big estates. [34] In the small farmhouse the feeding place for cattle would often be in the room where the family lived, the family quarters being simply separated from the ground by the 60 cm high platform. Feeding-troughs would either be at the approach to the platform or by the wall, often in the form of niches. [35] There were, of course, other possibilities, e.g., stalls in the ground-floor of the house or in annexes, or feeding-troughs outside, e.g., in the farm-yard. [36] Sometimes there might not be a stall at all and in winter the cattle, esp. sheep, would be brought into a fold sheltered from the wind or into one

---

[26] "Stall" is probable at Neg., 12, 4; TNeg., 6, 5 (Zuckermandel, 625, 25) and S. Lv. מצורע 6, 11 on 14:39, which speaks of the defiling of the wall by "leprosy." Dalman Arbeit, VI, 287 ref. to "manger-walls" here. Cf. also M. Ex., 1, 14 on 12:40 (ed. J. Lauterbach, I [1949], 112). היתה עומדה באבוס in jShebu., 7, 1 (37d, 9) is transl. "when the animal stood in the feeding-stall" in Levy Wört., s.v. אבוס, but "at the manger" is just as good, cf., 8, 1.

[27] Jastrow, Levy Chald. Wört., s.v.; Tg. Pro. on 1 K. 5:6 and Is. 1:3; Tg. Job 39:9; Tg. Prv. 14:4 (ed. P. de Lagarde, Hagiographa Chald. [1873]), on the meaning "crib" cf. bSanh., 98b; Tg. II Est. 6:10; on "stall" or "shed" T. Maas., 2, 20 (Zuckermandel, 84, 9); bErub., 55b and bMQ, 10b.

[28] A Galilean before R. Chisda (end of the 3rd cent. A.D.) bMakk., 23a; cf. S. Nu., 119 on 18:20 (cf. Kuhn, 406): He who does not know the Torah is like wild and tame beasts which do not know their master; cf. also S. Dt., 306 on 32:1 and Lv. r., 27, 8 on 22:27.

[29] Krauss Lehnw., II, 100; Pr.-Bauer, s.v.

[30] BR, s.v. "Stall" and cf. Y. Yadin, "New Light on Solomon's Megiddo," The Bibl. Archaeologist, 23 (1960), 62-8 and Y. Yadin, "Megiddo," Israel Exploration Journal, 16 (1966), 279 f.

[31] BR, s.v. "Stall."

[32] H. Schäfer - W. Andrea, "Die Kunst d. alten Orients," Propyläen-Kunstgesch., 2 (no date), 354: troughs in the open for horses and donkeys, relief from the tomb of Haremheb; 504: Assyr. scene; 540: feeding-troughs for camels [Galling].

[33] H. Gressmann, "Durch d. Ostjordanland," PJB, 4 (1908), 128 f.; further examples in Dalman Arbeit, VI, 287; Orte, 43. Cf. G. Lafaye, Art. "Equile," Darembg. Saglio, II, 1, 744 f. with Ill. 2709-2711, incl. one from Pompeii.

[34] The Lat. writers on husbandry reflect conditions on the great Italian estates with more elaborate arrangements, Hug, 1562 f.

[35] On the sheltering of cattle Dalman Arbeit, VI, 276-287; on the Palestinian farmhouse VII, 112-170. For ill. of houses with a common dwelling (and troughs) separated by the platform, cf. VII, Ill., 31, 36-39, 44 f., 55 f., 61, 67.

[36] Cf. Dalman Arbeit, VII, 130, 150, 155, 160 f., 164 and Ill., 37, 62, 71-77: Houses with separate stall and troughs, 138 f., Ill., 43: Village inn with feeding-trough on the outside wall; 148, 150, 155, 166 f., Ill., 83: Farmhouses with feeding-troughs in the yard.

of the many caves. [37] Wood was not used much for building in Palestine, but mud and wattle or stone. Jerome says that in his day the manger in the grotto at Bethlehem was made of clay. [38] There is a description of a typical crib in Vegetius Mulomedicina, [39] I, 56, 3 f.: *Patena* (from φάτνη → n. 1) . . . , *hoc est alveus ad hordeum ministrandum, sit munda semper, ne sordes aliquae cibariis admisceantur et noceant; loculis praeterea vel marmore vel lapide vel ligno factis distinguenda est, ut singula iumenta hordeum suum ex integro nullo praeripiente consumant.*

D. The New Testament.

1. In the NT φάτνη occurs only 4 times in Lk. At Lk. 13:15 (→ VII, 25, 14 ff.) Jesus refers to a practice which contradicted a rigorist view of the Sabbath but was still sanctioned by the Pharisaic scribes because of practical necessity, [40] namely, that of loosing cattle from their stalls and leading them out to drink even on the Sabbath. There may be inferred from the saying a tacit conclusion a *minori ad maius;* what is legitimate for animals is surely legitimate for men. [41] Even if one attributes to the Palestinian community the actual composition of the debate about a Sabbath healing, [42] there is not the least doubt that the underlying situation of conflict is based on the attitude of Jesus Himself. Indeed, the later Palestinian community had a tendency to play down the Sabbath conflict initiated by Jesus. Hence the saying might very well come from a polemical speech of Jesus, cf. Mt. 12:11 f.; Lk. 14:5.

2. The other three instances of φάτνη are in the nativity story (Lk. 2:1-20) in the depiction of the birth (v. 7), the promise of the angel (v. 12 → VII, 231, 10 ff.) and the adoration of the shepherds (v. 16). This surprising emphasis shows that, possibly already in the pre-Lucan source, great importance was attached to the concept. But exposition is difficult, since the text of Lk. 2:7 is not wholly clear [43] and there are no real parallels in religious history. [44] It must be stated firmly that

---

[37] Dalman Arbeit, VI, 277-282, 285, cf. VII, 88. A farmhouse with lean-to stall and nearby fold with cave-stall is described in Dalman VII, 155 and Ill., 65a; cf. also 133, Ill., 40. Materially cf. also S. Krauss, *Talmudische Archäol.,* II (1911), 133, 521, n. 943 f.

[38] Dalman Orte, 43. Hier. Hom. de nativitate Domini, ed. G. Morin, Analecta Maredsolana, III, 2 (1897), 393: *Nunc nos . . . quasi pro honore tulimus luteum, et posuimus argenteum.* Early Chr. depictions of the nativity from the 4th cent. might also reflect the form of ancient cribs, cf. the square-walled boxes, which are fairly common along with plaited baskets, G. Ristow, *Die Geburt Christi in d. frühchr. u. byzantinisch-ostkirchl. Kunst* (1963), Ill. p. 7 f., 14 f., 26, 30, 39 f. etc. Cf. → n. 64.

[39] Ed. E. Lommatzsch (1903).

[40] Cf. the Essene rules Damasc. 10:14 - 12:1 (13:1 - 14:3), esp. 11:5 f. (13:14), which go back to the rigorous sanctifying of the Sabbath by the early chasidim, and which have an anti-Pharisaic character, with the Rabb. examples in Str.-B., II, 199 f. Loosing cattle from the manger was one of the 39 main activities forbidden on the Sabbath, Str.-B., I, 616. But the commandments could be limited by casuistic differentiation, cf. the discussion in bErub., 20a-21b → 51, 28 ff.

[41] W. Grundmann, *Das Ev. nach Lk., Theol. Handkomm. z. NT,* 3² (1961), ad loc.; cf. 1 C. 9:9.

[42] Bultmann Trad., 42, 49 f.

[43] Cadbury Interest, 317: "the uncertainty in this passage"; cf. Dibelius, 57: "the one obscure element in the story," cf. Dalman Orte, 44 f.; Sahlin, 207.

[44] Cf. the negative findings of Clemen, 203-9 in debate with Gressmann, 37. The Egypt. adoration of a virgin in childbed and an infant in a crib τιμῶσι παρθένον λοχοῦν καὶ βρέφος ἐν φάτνῃ τιθέντες προσκυνήσουσι, Vita Jeremiae, 83, 3 (ed. T. Schermann, TU, 31, 2 [1907]) is undoubtedly under Chr. influence.

the meaning of φάτνη here is "feeding-trough"; it cannot be translated "stall." [45] The contrast between the διότι οὐκ ἦν αὐτοῖς τόπος ἐν τῷ καταλύματι [46] and the ἀνέκλινεν αὐτὸν ἐν φάτνῃ [47] should not be ignored. According to Lk. the child lies outside the human dwelling in an unusual place where there are only animals. [48] From the text itself one cannot say in detail whether the manger was in a separate stall, an enclosure in the open. [49] or the traditional cave → 55, 4 ff.; → VI, 491, 12 ff. [50] The one clear point is that the location was Bethlehem, 2:11, 15. All attempts to reconstruct a pre-Lucan original, perhaps in Hebrew, are hypothetical. [51] The crib is undoubtedly closely bound up with the shepherd setting and with Bethlehem as the birthplace of the Davidic Messiah, and it is to be understood accordingly. The child in a manger wrapped in swaddling bands [52] is for the shepherds a sign (→ VII, 231, 10 ff.) that the Messiah is born. [53] One can rule out any connection with the rural life of Hellenism → VI, 490, 42 ff.). [54] A Jewish Christian midrash has been suggested [55] comparable to stories of the hidden birth of the Messiah at Bethlehem or the secret birth of Abraham in a cave. [56] For Luke the manger expresses the contrast between the world-ruler Augustus and the hidden and lowly birth of the world-redeemer (Lk. 2:1, 11, 14). Finally it points forward

---

[45] As against Pr.-Bauer, s.v. and also Cadbury Interest, 319, who thinks φάτνη is "a place in the open"; for a correct view cf. Veldhuizen, 175-8.

[46] Whether κατάλυμα here is a khan πανδοχεῖον (Lk. 10:34) or, as often assumed, a simple guest-room, cf. Lk. 22:11 par. Mk. 14:14, makes little difference. On inns in ancient Palestine v. E. Pax, "'Denn sie fanden keinen Raum in d. Herberge,'" Bibel u. Leben, 6 (1965), 285-298. Farmhouses with separate guest-rooms are described in Dalman Arbeit, VII, 127 f., 129, 142, 148, 162 f., Ill., 31, 60, 71. The loft could often be used for this, VII, 57, 85, cf. 1 K. 17:19, 23; 2 K. 4:10 f. Sys solves the problem by leaving out ἐν τῷ καταλύματι.

[47] Cf. bShab., 20:3: ‏ונתן בתוך האבוס‎.

[48] As against Dibelius, 59, who has in view the large living-room of the Palestinian farmhouse; Bornhäuser, 101-104 thinks a large basin might have been used as a cradle, cf. Yubero, 3-6; Miguens, 195 f. Dalman Orte, 46 rightly observes that the real difficulty was not finding a place to lay the child but an undisturbed place for the birth. Cf. Rengstorf, 20 f., who correctly notes the contrast with Lk. 1:24. Just. Dial., 78, 5 pertinently interprets Lk. 2:7: οὐκ εἶχεν ἐν τῇ κώμῃ ἐκείνῃ ποῦ καταλῦσαι.

[49] Völter, 49; cf. Winter, 240: "φάτνη described here a trough in the open field, probably a hollow stone used by shepherds for watering their flock"; he quotes Mi. 4:10: "Thou shalt go forth out of the city, and thou shalt dwell in the field."

[50] So most Roman Catholic exegetes, e.g., M. J. Lagrange, "Év. selon S. Luc," Études Bibl.8 (1948), 72; cf. also Dalman Orte, 35-48.

[51] As against Sahlin, 222. Cf. earlier A. Resch, "Das Kindheitsevangelium nach Lk. u. Mt.," TU, 10, 5 (1897), 46, 124 f., 203-226.

[52] Cf. Dalman Orte, 45. Cf. the motifs in Jewish legends about the hidden birth of the Messiah at Bethlehem and the birth of Abraham in a cave, jBer., 2, 4 (5a, 18 ff.) par. Midr. Lam., 1, 51 on 1:16 (cf. Wünsche, 88): The mother of Messiah receives a linen cloth for her son; A. Jellinek, Bet ha-Midrasch, I (1853), 26: The mother of Abraham after the birth clothes her child with a piece from her own garment, cf. also Ez. 16:4.

[53] Bultmann Trad., 324 as against Gressmann, 17-37.

[54] As against Bultmann Trad., 325; Dibelius, 73 f.; Erdmann, 43 f.; correctly W. Schmid, Art. "Bukolik," RAC, II (1954), 788.

[55] There may be a connection with the tradition of the "Shepherd tower" at Bethlehem from which the Messiah will be manifested acc. to Tg. J. I on Gn. 35:21 and Tg. Pro. on Mi. 4:8, cf. Dalman Orte, 53-5 and Winter, 238 f. Cf. also 1 S. 16 (Baily, passim); ψ 77:70-72; Mi. 4:7-10 and 5:1-5; R. Laurentin, Structure et Théol. de Luc I-II (1957), 86-88 (Bibl.). On the Davidic-Messianic character of the shepherd setting 11 QPsa 151 (DJD, IV, 54-64).

[56] → n. 52. For the par. cf. H. Gressmann, "Der Messias," FRL, 43 (1929) 449-452 and A. Wünsche, Aus Israels Lehrhallen, I (1907), 16 f., 36. Cf. also the nativity stories PREl, 48 and Tg. J. I on Ex. 24:10 in L. Ginzberg, "The Legends of the Jews, II, (1910), 372.

to the way of humility and suffering which is taken by the Son of God who "hath not where to lay his head," Lk. 9:58. [57]

E. Early Church History.

The manger tradition and the cave tradition are already combined for the Palestinian Justin of Neapolis, Dial., 78, 5. But Prot. Ev. Jm. 17-20 shows that they were originally separate, for here the birth at Bethlehem is in a cave and the φάτνη βοῶν occurs only in 22:2 as a hiding-place for the child Jesus from the plots of Herod. [58] Crib and cave are closely related in Orig. Cels., I, 51, where a definite location is presupposed δείκνυται... ἡ ἐν σπηλαίῳ φάτνη that was already known to Just. [59] Sib., 8, 497 (3rd cent. A.D.?) also mentions the manger. About 330 A.D., following the first pilgrimage of Helena, the Church of the Nativity was built at what is now the traditional site of the crib and the cave. [60] It was only marginally that the par. cave story came into the text of the Gospel tradition. [61] The late Ev. Ps.-Mt. [62] solves the problem of three rival sites by telling of the birth in a cave in 13:2, putting Mary in a stall, where she lays the child in a crib, three days later, and then telling of the entry into Bethlehem six days later, 15:1. The ox and ass came into the stall on the basis of Is. 1:3 and Hab. 3:2 LXX and patristic exegesis: *et bos et asinus adoraverunt eum.* [63] They occur even earlier in the first depictions of the birth from the middle of the 4th cent. [64]

Hengel

---

[57] Schl. Lk., 186; cf. Rengstorf, 20 f. Tert. De carne Christi, 2 (CSEL, 69 [1939], 191) notes this: *Aufer hinc... molestos semper Caesaris census et diuersoria angusta et sordidos pannos et dura praesepia.* Materially → 51, 16 ff.; 52, 1 ff. and Eur. Ba., 510. Later apocr. tradition corrects the "lowliness" of the birth of Jesus, W. Foerster, "Bemerkungen u. Fragen z. Stätte d. Geburt Jesu," ZDPV, 57 (1934), 3 f.

[58] Ed. E. de Strycker, "La forme la plus ancienne du Protév. de Jacques," *Subsidia hagiographica,* 33 (1961), 174, cf. 417 f.

[59] As against A. M. Schneider, Art. "Bethlehem," RAC, II (1954), 226. Justin's account is certainly not derived from Is. 33:16, cf. Dalman Orte, 47 f. and J. Jeremias → VI, 491, n. 59. The quoting of this v. in Barn., 11, 5 is also an allusion to the cave tradition.

[60] Schneider, *op. cit.,* 226.

[61] Min. 544 reads at Mt. 2:9: ἐπάνω τοῦ σπηλαίου, cf. the oldest Arm. Gospel MS acc. to E. Preuschen, "Jesu Geburt in einer Höhle," ZNW, 3 (1902), 359 f. On the variant of Cod D in Lk. 2:6 v. Foerster, *op. cit.,* 4 f.

[62] Ed. C. v. Tischendorf, Evang. Apocr.² (1876).

[63] On Ev. Ps.-Mt. cf. Hennecke³, I, 303 f.: 8/9th cent. On apocr. tradition in gen. outside the Gospels v. W. Bauer, *Das Leben Jesu im Zeitalter d. nt.lichen Apokr.* (1909), 61-8. On the animals J. Ziegler, "Ochs u. Esel an d. Krippe," *Münchener Theol. Zschr.,* 3 (1952), 385-402. Orig. Hom. in Lk., 13 (GCS, 49 [1959], 82) already related Is. 1:3 to the crib, cf. Ziegler, 391. On Jewish exegesis → n. 28.

[64] G. Wilpert, I Sarcofagi Christiani Antichi, I (1929), Plate, 92, 2; 127, 2; II (1932), Plate, 221, 6; W. F. Volbach, *Elfenbeinarbeiten d. Spätantike u. d. frühen MA²* (1952), No. 114, 118 f., 127, 131, 173 f., 199 etc. For a Syr. depiction with inscr. Is. 1:3 (6th cent.) cf. J. Nasrallah, "Bas-reliefs chr. inconnus de Syrie," *Syria,* 38 (1961), 36-44 (Bibl.). Cf. → n. 38.

| φέρω, ἀναφέρω, διαφέρω, τὰ διαφέροντα, |
| διάφορος (ἀδιάφορον), εἰσφέρω, προσφέρω, |
| προσφορά, συμφέρω, σύμφορος, φόρος, |
| φορέω, φορτίον, φορτίζω |

The Indo-Eur. root *bher*[1] means "to carry or bring from one place to another," then "to be laden," which explains the old sense of "carrying or bringing forth" the fruit of the body, e.g., Hom. Il., 6, 59. Both lit. and transf. the basic sense carries with it the possibility of denoting many processes and this is realised in the many meanings of φέρω and compounds in Gk. literature. It is unnecessary and indeed impossible to give anything like a full account of the data here. The root φερ- is used only in the pres. and impf. It is supplemented by the roots οἰ- (fut. οἴσω) and ἐνεκ- (aor. ἤνεγκον, -α etc.).

φέρω αἴρω → I, 185, 17 ff.

1. In Secular Literature.

In relation to NT use the following meanings may be noted: a. the basic sense "to bring," "to lead," "to drive" of men, Hom. Il., 2, 838, animals, 3, 120 and things, Od., 21, 362, intr. of a way, gate etc. "to lead," Hdt., II, 122, 3, act. in the intr. sense "to blow" of the wind, Xenoph. An., V, 7, 7 and (only pass.) "to go," "to press on" esp. of sailors, Hom. Od., 9, 82; Plat. Phaedr., 254a; b. "to bring forth," "to express," "to convey," e.g., μῦθον "a word," Hom. Il., 10, 288; 15, 202, ἀγγελίην, Hom. Il., 15, 175; Od., 1, 408, λόγον, Pind. Pyth., 8, 38, ἐπιστολήν, Xenoph. Ag., 8, 3, παραδείγματα, Isoc., Or., 7, 6, from which we have later the intr. use of the pass. in the phrase κραυγῆς φερομένης, Plut. De Sulla, 30 (I, 471e); c. as a tt. in law "to issue" a complaint," "accusation" etc., Demosth. Or., 58, 22; Polyb., 33, 11, 2; d. "to bring" presents, gifts, Hom. Od., 8, 428, with the special expression χάριν φέρω "to show a favour," Il., 5, 211; Od., 5, 307, though after Hom. this means "to express thanks," e.g., Pind. Olymp., 10, 17; e. "to bear" burdens, Hom. Il., 5, 303; f. "to bear, produce fruit," abs. Xenoph. Oec., 20, 4 and with the fruit in the acc. Hom. Od., 9, 110; g. transf. "to bear," "to endure" both physical (Xenoph. Cyrop., VIII, 2, 21) and spiritual afflictions (Hom. Od., 18, 135; h. later "to rule, govern" (i.e., "carry," "uphold") a city, Plut. Lucull., 6 (I, 495c).[2]

2. In the Septuagint.

In the LXX φέρω is mostly the transl. of בוא hi "to bring, present" with obj. of all kinds, persons and things, but esp. gifts brought as offerings or sacrifices to the temple, priests or altar. The real act of offering or dedication, the burning or waving of the gift by the priest, is differentiated from this, although sometimes φέρω can include or even directly denote it, in which case it is to be transl. "to sacrifice," cf. ἤνεγκεν in Gn. 4:3 f.

φ έ ρ ω . [1] Cf. Sanscr. *bhárati* "carries," Arm. *berem* "I carry"; *v.* Boisacq and Hofmann, *s.v.*

[2] For meanings e-g βαστάζω (→ I, 596, 1 ff.) increasingly replaced φέρω in popular post-class. usage [Dihle].

(HT וַיָּבֵא or הֵבִיא) for the offerings of Cain and Abel. In the attack on the priests in in Mal. 1:13: καὶ εἰσεφέρετε ἀρπάγματα... καὶ ἐὰν φέρητε τὴν θυσίαν[3] (both times וַהֲבֵאתֶם) the latter term expresses the actual offering. In the phrase ἠνέγκατε θυσίας (HT וְהָבִיאוּ וְזִבְחֵיכֶם) in Amos 4:4 there is no distinction between the presenting and the offering and the latter is in view, cf. also λίβανον... φέρετε (HT תָּבוֹא) in Jer. 6:20. When used for עלה hi φέρω unquestionably means "to sacrifice," Lv. 14:20; 2 Ch. 1:6;[4] 35:16; Am. 5:22, and as a rendering of נוף hi it denotes the symbolical sacrificial rite of waving the gift, Ex. 35:22; Lv. 23:12.

The next most common equivalent for LXX φέρω is נשׂא. The sense is "to bear" a burden or "to bring" a gift (→ 56, 23 ff.), also "to pay" tribute in 2 Βασ. 8:2, 6, "to bear" fruit in Jl. 2:22; Ez. 17:8,[5] and "to blow" of the wind in Is. 64:5. Passages having the transf. meaning "to bear," "to endure," "to suffer" are theologically important. Moses neither can nor will "bear" the burden of responsibility for the people any longer, Nu. 11:14, 17; Dt. 1:9, 12; Yahweh Himself can no longer tolerate Judah and Jerusalem because of their evil ways, Ἰερ. 51:22; Israel bears the ὀνειδισμὸς ἐθνῶν, Ez. 34:29; 36:6; the Ebed Yahweh bears our sins, Is. 53:4.

In comparison the occasional rendering of other Hbr. roots by φέρω is of subordinate significance. We find it in the sense "to bring" gifts, offerings in Zeph. 3:10 (HT יבל hi); Ju. 6:18 (יצא hi) and ψ 28:1f.; 95:7 f. (הָבוּ), cf. φέρετε... βουλήν 2 Βασ. 16:20 (הָבוּ... עֵצָה). φέρομαι is the transl. of עבר "to turn to dust" in Is. 29:5; Jer. 13:24, שׁטף in Is. 28:15, 18, סער "to flood, to storm" in Is. 29:6, and נדף ni "to flee" in Lv. 26:36.

3. Josephus.

In Jos. we find the following senses:[6] "to bring" τὸν δακτύλιον... Καίσαρι φέρειν ἐνετέλλετο, Bell., 1, 669; ἄρτον ἐνεγκεῖν ἐκέλευσε, Ant., 8, 321; intr. "to lead" φερούσης εἰς τὸ βασίλειον πύλης, Ant., 9, 146; θύραν φέρουσαν εἰς αἴθριον, 19, 90; mid. or pass. "to be moved or snatched away" διὰ τῆς πόλεως ἐφέρετο βοῶν, 11, 221; "to ride" ἐμπηδήσαντες τοῖς ἵπποις ἐφέροντο, 7, 176.[7]

4. In the New Testament.

There are no distinctive features in the NT use of φέρω as compared with what we find in profane literature and the LXX. The only special aspect lies in the particular persons and objects to which it refers. In this regard the following points may be made.

a. In the simple meaning "to carry," "to bring," "to lead," the term is used with reference to the sick and demon-possessed who are constantly "fetched" in great numbers to Jesus (Mk. 1:32; 2:3; 7:32; 8:22; 9:17, 19 f. and par.) and to Peter (Ac. 5:6) and are therewith brought to deliverance. The word has a more lofty sense in the declaration to Peter ἄλλος... σε... οἴσει ὅπου οὐ θέλεις (Jn. 21:18),

---

[3] מִנְחָה, here in the later sense of "meat offerings," cf. K. Elliger, Das Buch d. zwölf kleinen Propheten, II, AT Deutsch, 25⁵ (1964), ad loc.; R. Hentschke, Art. "Opfer," RGG³, IV, 1645.

[4] In both passages with vl. ἀναφέρω → 60, 12 ff.

[5] Hos. 9:16 for עשׂה.

[6] Acc. to the list in Schl. Lk., 705.

[7] For the "bringing" of a complaint (→ 56, 22 ff.) Jos. usually has ἐπιφέρω, e.g., Bell., 7, 33 and occasionally ἐμφέρω, Ant., 20, 47.

for in this proverbial expression [8] he is given the promise that to God's glory he will be led off to martyrdom → II, 463, 12 ff. The mid. is used intr. in the image of an "onrushing" wind to depict what took place at Pentecost (Ac. 2:2), while the passive denotes the "driving" of the ship and its passengers before the wind (Ac. 27:15, 17). In the transf. sense of moral and spiritual progress the element of movement in φέρω is denoted in the demand ἐπὶ τὴν τελειότητα φερώμεθα, "let us strive, press one," Hb. 6:1. The pass. is also used of the prophets who spoke as they were φερόμενοι "impelled" by the Holy Ghost, 2 Pt. 1:21.

b. The "bringing" or "presenting" of the Gospel message (→ II, 720, 6, 17 ff.) is expressed by διδαχὴν φέρω (→ II, 163, 32 ff.) only at 2 Jn. 10. Here, in the conflict against the infiltration of a docetic christology, the rejection is demanded of anyone who does not "bring" or "present" correct teaching about Christ. The pass. ἠνέχθη is used intr. in 2 Pt. 1:17 f. for the voice which "came" to Jesus on the Mount of Transfiguration and in 1:21 for prophecy, which never "came" by the will of man.

c. As a legal term φέρω is used in the accounts of the trials of Jesus and the apostle Paul. Pilate asks: τίνα κατηγορίαν φέρετε τοῦ ἀνθρώπου τούτου; (Jn. 18:29), and Festus says of the plaintiffs: οὐδεμίαν αἰτίαν (namely, in respect of any of the crimes of which he is suspected) ἔφερον (Ac. 25:18). 2 Pt. 2:11 has the mythological concept of a judgment scene before the throne of God in which angels, as distinct from the false teachers here opposed, do not dare βλάσφημον κρίσιν φέρειν against the accused δόξαι (→ II, 251, 35 ff.). [9] The issue in Hb. 9:16 is the validity and force of the new διαθήκη which is understood here as a testamentary disposition in the legal sense. Hence proof of the death of the testator must "be adduced" (φέρεσθαι) to bring it into effect. On the tension between this legal presentation and the point at issue → II, 131, 6 ff.

d. In the sense "to bring" a gift or present φέρω occurs in various connections. In 1 Pt. 1:13 χάρις φερομένη is the gift of grace which will be offered believers at the parousia of Christ and on which they can and should set their hope: deliverance in the judgment and the heavenly inheritance, cf. vv. 3-12. Then in Rev. 21:24 (quoting Is. 60:11) the kings of the earth will "bring" their δόξα (→ II, 237, 26 ff.) into the heavenly Jerusalem and thereby "offer" it to God and the Lamb. In the primitive Jerusalem community, however, the members "bring" the possessions they have sold and converted into money and lay them at the apostles' feet to be used for the common good, Ac. 4:34, 37; 5:2; these gifts, too, are offered to God Himself, Ac. 5:3 f.

e. In the sense of "taking up" and "carrying" a burden φέρω occurs only in the expression τὸν σταυρὸν φέρειν, Lk. 23:26. [10]

f. The term has the special sense of bearing fruit in the metaphors of the tree which bears good or bad fruit (Mt. 7:18), the field which bears varying degrees of

---

[8] Cf. Bultmann J., ad loc.

[9] Jd. 9, where Michael contends with Satan for the body of Moses, has ἐπενεγκεῖν → n. 7.

[10] The par. Mk. 15:21; Mt. 27:32 have αἴρω, Jn. 19:17 the popular βαστάζω (→ n. 2; I, 596, 1 ff.). The former also occurs at Mt. 16:24 par. and the latter at Lk. 14:27, where the expression has the transf. sense of "enduring" → 56, 27 f.; 59, 10 ff.

fruit (Mk. 4:8) [11] and the vine with branches that bear fruit (Jn. 15:2, 4). Materially the term denotes in Mt. and Jn. the following of the words and commandments of Jesus, abiding in fellowship with Him, and hence doing God's will in the life and work of the disciples, while in the parable of the sower (Mk. 4 and par.) the primary reference is to the power with which, in defiance of all resistance, the rule of God achieves fulfilment. [12] In Jn. 12:24 Jesus uses the image of the grain of wheat that falls into the ground, dies, and bears much fruit, to describe the fruit of His own death. What is meant is the winning of disciples out of the world and the gathering of the community.

g. In a transf. sense the carrying of burdens becomes "bearing," "enduring." Thus Hb. 12:20 says that the people cannot "endure" (οὐκ ἔφερον) the command that any beast which touches the mount of God should be stoned, the reason being that there is manifested here the annihilating holiness of the divine appearing. An enduring of special dignity and promise is the "acceptance" and "bearing" by the community of the shame of Christ, who suffered outside the gate. This is the readiness for martyrdom of the community that the world has rejected, [13] Hb. 13:13. Paul says of God Himself in R. 9:22 (building on Ex. 9:16): ἤνεγκεν... σκεύη ὀργῆς, [14] i.e., that with great long-suffering He bears, i.e., "sustains" as well as "tolerates," men who in and of themselves are the objects of His wrath (→ VII, 363, 3 ff., 19 ff.), whom He has destined for the active fulfilment of His anger, and who are indeed already ripe for destruction. This sustaining and tolerating is thus God's sovereign act which in no sense prevents Him from showing His wrath (→ IV, 382, 21 ff.; V, 425, 24 ff.) but which also makes known His glory to those whom He has called to glory. In both His power is displayed.

h. This leads us on already to the use of the word for "upholding" and "ruling" [15] as in the expression φέρων τε τὰ πάντα with reference to the Son of God, or more strictly His Word of power (Hb. 1:3). The confession of Christ as the mediator of creation (v. 2), which Hb. shares with the Prologue to Jn., Col. and Eph. (→ V, 894, 23 ff.), is thus supplemented, as in Col. 1:17 (→ VI, 687, 33 ff.), [16] by a confession of Christ as the One who upholds creation.

5. In the Post-Apostolic Fathers.

When Is. 1:13 is quoted in Barn., 2, 5 and Gn. 4:3 f. in 1 Cl., 4, 1 φέρω has the sense of offering sacrifices → 56, 31 ff., and in relation to Is. 53:3 f. in 1 Cl., 16, 3 f. the expression φέρειν μαλακίαν or ἁμαρτίας ... φέρει (→ 57, 15 ff.) is taken from the LXX. Elsewhere φέρω means "to bear fruit" in Herm. s., 2, 3 f. and 8 (→ 56, 26 f.; 57, 10 f.; 58, 38 ff.), to "bear" suffering in 1 Cl., 45, 5 (→ 56, 27 f.; 57, 11 ff.; 59, 10 ff.), pass.

---

[11] Mk. 4:28 uses καρποφορέω → III, 616, 8 ff.

[12] Cf. Jeremias Gl.[7], 149 f.; R. Otto, *Reich Gottes u. Menschensohn*[2] (1940), 82-86.

[13] So with Mi. Hb.[12] and the early exegetes listed there. For other interpretations of ἔξω τῆς παρεμβολῆς v. Mi. Hb.[12], ad loc. and F. Bleek, *Der Br. an d. Hebräer*, II, 2 (1840), 1015-1017.

[14] Cf. Mi. R., ad loc., ʼΙερ. 27:25: ἐξήνεγκεν τὰ σκεύη ὀργῆς αὐτοῦ has no material connection with this text.

[15] In addition to the instances of this sense → 56, 28 f.; 57, 12 f. cf. the rich materials in Bleek, op. cit., II, 1 (1836), 70-72.

[16] Cf. also οὗτός ἐστιν πάντων κύριος, Ac. 10:36: ὁ ὢν ἐπὶ πάντων, R. 9:5; ἐπάνω πάντων ἐστίν, Jn. 3:31.

"to be impelled" of moral or immoral striving, Herm. s., 6, 5, 7; Dg., 9, 1, and in the expressions κατάγνωσιν φέρουσιν (1 Cl., 51, 2 → 56, 22 ff.) and ὑποδείγματα φέρειν (55, 1 → 56, 21 f.). Without par. in primitive Chr. lit. is the expression τὸ βάπτισμα τὸ φέρον ἄφεσιν ἁμαρτιῶν in Barn., 11, 1.

† ἀναφέρω.

1. In Secular Literature.

On the basis of the two possible meanings of the prep. ἀνά, namely, 1. "up" and 2. "back," the different meanings of ἀναφέρω fall into two groups. As regards the NT interest focuses on the first group and esp. on the senses "to bring up," "to lift up" (Hom. Od., 11, 625) and "to take on oneself," "to bear" or "to endure" (Aesch. Choeph., 841; Thuc., III, 38, 3).[1]

2. In the Septuagaint.

If in the LXX φέρω is often used for sacrificial tt. (→ 56, 31 ff.), this is almost exclusively true of ἀναφέρω. With προσφέρω (→ 65, 3 ff.) it is the proper term for making an offering. But unlike φέρω, ἀναφέρω denotes the actual sacrifice and only seldom the bringing of offerings. Of the Hbr. originals עלה hi comes first; it is used in about four fifths of the instances. The meaning of ἀναφέρω in such cases, either abs. or with acc. obj. (usually ὁλοκαύτωμα, cf. also εἰς ὁλοκαύτωμα), is plainly "to sacrifice."[2] The same is true in most of the instances with the second Hbr. original קטר hi, which replaces עלה hi in Lv. and Ex. 29:18, 25; 30:20. Only rarely is ἀναφέρω used for other Hbr. sacrificial terms, so עשׂה זבחים in 3 Βασ. 12:27; חטא pi in Lv. 6:19; עבר hi in 'Ιερ. 39:35; נוף hi in Lv. 8:27; 23:11. ἀναφέρω means "to bring" (sacrificial) gifts in 2 Ch. 29:31 f. (both times HT בוא hi); Lv. 3:14 (HT קרב hi); Dt. 14:24 (נשׂא) and Is. 18:7[3] (יבל ho). Some of the roots mentioned can also be transl. by ἀναφέρω when the ref. is to profane processes such as the presenting of persons or things, e.g., Gn. 31:39 (HT בוא hi), the bringing of a matter before someone, Ex. 18:19, 22, 26 (בנא hi) or the bringing or conveying of something, 1 Βασ. 2:19 (עלה hi).

The word has a transf. sense at Nu. 14:33; Is. 53:12; Ez. 36:15 (HT in each case נשׂא) and Is. 53:11 (סבל), where it is used for the bearing or accepting of suffering and of the guilt of others, namely that of the fathers by the children, Nu. 14:33, or that of the whole body (ἁμαρτίαι πολλῶν) by the Ebed Yahweh in Is. 53:11 f. Here the word may contain such senses as "to do away," "to set aside," "to expiate," "to atone."

3. In the New Testament.

a. Lit. ἀναφέρω is used in Mt. 17:1 par. Mk. 9:2 for the "taking up" of the disciples to the Mount of Transfiguration by Jesus; pass. in the text of the Egypt. MS of Lk. 24:51:

ἀ ν α φ έ ρ ω. [1] The exact meaning of ἀναφέρω in the execration tablets of Cnidus is uncertain, Audollent Def. Tab., 2, 11; 3 Col. A, 10 f.; 6 Col. A, 6; Col. B, 5; 9, 6 (2nd-1st cent. B.C.), cf. C. Wachsmuth, "Inschr. aus Korkyra," *Rhein. Mus.,* NF, 18 (1863), 573 f. and the notes in Ditt. Syll.³, III on 1179.

[2] 2 Ch. 29:21 seems to be the only exception with its ref. to the bringing up of animals for sacrifice.

[3] In the LXX writings found only in Gk. ἀναφέρω is also sacrificial in 12 of the 21 instances. Almost all the sacrificial statements are in the legal or historical books. Only 3 are in the Ps., 4 in Is., 1 in Jer. Is. 57:6; 66:3; 'Ιερ. 39(32):35 criticise sacrifices, Is. 60:7; 66:20 have a transf. sense, and 18:7 speaks of gifts brought to the Lord. Is. 53:11, 12 must be construed in terms of the Hb. original which does not contain the thought of sacrifice [Bertram].

καὶ ἀναφέρετο εἰς τὸν οὐρανόν, it denotes the ascension, for which πορεύομαι (→ VI, 576, 10 ff.) is used in Ac. 1:10 f.; 1 Pt. 3:22.

b. The most important sense is based on the LXX and is "to offer sacrifices," "to sacrifice," Hb. 7:27; 13:15; Jm. 2:21, 1 Pt. 2:5. But there is no direct dependence on the LXX, for at Lv. 16:6, 15, to which Hb. 7:27 alludes, the LXX does not have ἀναφέρω but προσάγω (→ I, 131, 21 ff.) and εἰσφέρω → 64, 19 ff. The texts on which Hb. 13:15 rests have θύω (→ III, 181, 6 f.), ψ 49:14, cf. 49:23 (HT זבח), ἀνταποδίδωμι (→ II, 169, 5 ff.), Hos. 14:3 (HT שׁלם pi), προσφέρω (→ 65, 3 ff.), Lv. 7:12 (קרב hi), προσάγω, 2 Ch. 29:31 (נגשׁ q) and φέρω (→ 56, 12 ff.), loc. cit. (בוא hi). Gn. 22:9, which underlies Jm. 2:21, simply says: Ἀβραάμ... ἐπέθηκεν (HT וישׂם) αὐτὸν (sc. Isaac) ἐπὶ τὸ θυσιαστήριον. The only text with ἀναφέρω which might arise in ref. to Hb. 13:15 is 2 Ch. 29:31b (HT בוא hi). Nevertheless, it is incontestable that the LXX is the basis of this NT use.

Materially the ref. in Hb. 7:27 is to the abolition of the Levitical offerings [4] by the once-for-all self-offering of Christ, in Jm. 2:21 to the offering of Isaac as the work which perfects faith, in Hb. 13:15 (based on Hos. 14:3) to the offering of fig. sacrifices, i.e., the offering of praise which consists in the fruit of the lips, and in 1 Pt. 2:5 to spiritual offerings, i.e., those which the Spirit accomplishes in the believer (→ II, 68, 36 ff.), which consist in the offering of the whole person to God in a new life, and which are thus distinguished from the sacrificial ministry of the cultus (→ III, 185, 6 ff., 44 ff.; IV, 142, 9 ff.). [5]

A distinctive interpretation is given to Is. 53:12 LXX (→ 60, 27 ff.) by 1 Pt. 2:24. The addition of ἐν τῷ σώματι αὐτοῦ ἐπὶ τὸ ξύλον changes the original τὰς ἁμαρτίας ἀνήνεγκεν into a "carrying." Kinship with the typical LXX expression ἀναφέρω ἐπὶ τὸ θυσιαστήριον suggests that linguistically ἀνήνεγκεν is also to be construed as "to sacrifice." This would mean that we have two ideas, first, the doing away or setting aside of sins, which Christ has taken up with Him when He hangs in His body on the cross, [6] and secondly, the self-offering of Christ ἐν τῷ σώματι αὐτοῦ for our sins. [7] In Hb. 9 the combining of the two ideas is clearly expressed in the parallel formulations εἰς ἀθέτησιν τῆς ἁμαρτίας διὰ τῆς θυσίας αὐτοῦ (v. 26) and Χριστὸς ἅπαξ προσενεχθεὶς εἰς τὸ πολλῶν ἀνενεγκεῖν ἁμαρτίας (v. 28).

4. In the Post-Apostolic Fathers.

Wherever the word is used in the post-apost. fathers it has the sense of "bringing to God." This is true of the prayers presented to him, Barn., 12, 7; 2 Cl. 2, 2 (→ lines 16 ff.) and also of believers themselves, whom the cross and the Holy Spirit lift up like pulleys, faith co-operating as ἀναγωγεύς and love as ὁδὸς ἡ ἀναφέρουσα εἰς θεόν, Ign. Eph., 9, 1.

---

[4] Here obviously a combination of the daily tamid offering and the offering on the day of atonement, v. Mi. Hb.[12], ad loc.

[5] Cf. Wnd. Kath. Br., ad loc. and v. K. Weiss, "Pls., Priester d. chr. Kultgemeinde," ThLZ, 79 (1954), 360-362; H. Schürmann, Art. "Kult," LexThK[2], VI, 663 f.; H. D. Wendland, Art. "Opfer," RGG[3], IV, 1648 f.

[6] Wnd. Kath. Br., ad loc. sees also a ref. to the high-priest laying the sins of the people on the scapegoat (Lv. 16:21 f.) but this is unlikely, for 1 Pt. does not ascribe to Christ the function of the high-priest.

[7] On the combining of the two groups of ideas cf. Kn. Pt., ad loc.

† διαφέρω,   † τὰ διαφέροντα,   † διάφορος (ἀδιάφορον).

1. In Secular Literature.

a. Of the many meanings the verb διαφέρω can have when taken lit., only the following need be noted in relation to the NT: "to transmit," "to carry through," Thuc., VIII, 8, 3, "to spread" news κηρύγματα, Eur. Suppl., 382, ἀγγελίας, Luc. Dial. deorum, 24, 1, and later "to drive a ship back and forth," Philo Migr. Abr., 148; Luc. Hermot., 28. Intr. διαφέρω has the transf. sense "to differentiate oneself," Eur. Or., 251; Thuc., V, 86 etc. The difference may be either positive or negative, i.e., "to excel," "to stand out," "to be more," Thuc., II, 39, 1; Plat. Ap., 35a b or "to be less," "to fall behind," Xenoph. Vect., 4, 25. Similarly the impers. διαφέρει means "it makes a difference," "it matters," Hippocr. Aphorismi, 5, 22 (Littré, IV, 538) etc. and "it is important," Gal. Comm. on Hippocr. Acut., I, 2. 7 (CMG, V, 9, 1, p. 118, 12; 122, 15), both also with ref. to a specific person: "it matters (or does not matter) to me," Plat. Prot., 316b; La., 187d, "it is of interest to me," Eur. Tro., 1248; Thuc., III, 42, 2.

b. The part. as noun can also mean "difference," "mark of difference," Thuc., I, 70, 1; Plat. Phileb., 45d, and then "what is useful," Antiph. Fr., 31, "interests," Thuc., VI, 92, 5, [1] "what is important or significant" σφόδρα διαφέροντα, Plut. Adulat., 35 (II, 73a); cf. τὸ διαφέρον μέρος, P. Oxy., 1204, 11 (299 A.D.).

c. The same applies to the adj. διάφορος. It means "different," "unlike," Hdt., II, 83; IV, 81, 1; Plat. Leg., XII, 964a etc. and later "varied," "manifold," [2] but also negatively "unwelcome," "displeasing," Plat. Leg., VIII, 843c, and more often positively "outstanding," "distinguished," Antiph. Fr., 175, 3 and "useful," "advantageous," with μᾶλλον in Thuc., IV, 3, 3; πρὸς σωτηρίαν διάφορος, Plat. Leg., VI, 779b. τὸ διάφορον means "interest" in P. Oxy., VII, 1040, 10 (225 A.D.); 1041, 9 (381 A.D.); 1042, 28 (578 A.D.) etc.

d. The negated form of the adj. is of special significance in Aristotelian logic and Cynic-Stoic ethics. By ἀδιάφορον Aristot. means the unity and integrity of a substance as this may be seen in the outward form of a thing ἓν λέγεται τῷ τὸ ὑποκείμενον τῷ εἴδει εἶναι ἀδιάφορον. ἀδιάφορα δ' ὧν ἀδιαίρετον τὸ εἶδος κατὰ τὴν αἴσθησιν, Metaph., 5, 6, p. 1016a, 17 ff. and also the similarity of individuals belonging to a species (→ II, 373, 28 ff.): (ταὐτὸν) εἴδει ὅσα πλείω ὄντα ἀδιάφορα κατὰ τὸ εἶδός ἐστι, καθάπερ ἄνθρωπος ἀνθρώπῳ καὶ ἵππος ἵππῳ, Top., I, 7, p. 103a, 10 f.; cf. IV, 1, p. 121b, 15 ff. The Cynics and Stoics call ἀδιάφορον the middle sphere between virtue and vice and the related goods and evils. It is that which the philosopher cannot call good or bad but only ethically indifferent. Thus the Cynics: τὰ δὲ μεταξὺ ἀρετῆς καὶ κακίας ἀδιάφορα λέγουσιν ὁμοίως Ἀρίστωνι τῷ Χίῳ, Diog. L., VI, 9, 105, of whom we read: τέλος ἔφησεν εἶναι τὸ ἀδιαφόρως ἔχοντα ζῆν πρὸς τὰ μεταξὺ ἀρετῆς καὶ κακίας μηδ' ἡντινοῦν ἐν αὐτοῖς παραλλαγὴν ἀπολείποντα, ἀλλ' ἐπίσης ἐπὶ πάντων ἔχοντα, VII, 2, 160, and Zeno: ἀγαθὰ μὲν ... πᾶν ὅ ἐστιν ἀρετὴ ἢ μετέχον ἀρετῆς· κακὰ δὲ ... πᾶν ὅ ἐστι κακία ἢ μετέχον κακίας, ἀδιάφορα δὲ τὰ τοιαῦτα· ζωὴν θάνατον, δόξαν ἀδοξίαν, ἡδονὴν πόνον, πλοῦτον πενίαν, ὑγίειαν νόσον καὶ τὰ τούτοις ὅμοια, Stob. Ecl., II, 57, 20 ff.; Zeno censuit voluptatem esse indifferens, id est neutrum, neque bonum neque malum, quod ipse Graeco vocabulo ἀδιάφορον appellavit, Gellius Noctes Atticae, 9, 5, 5. [3]

διαφέρω κτλ. [1] P. Wendland, "Zu Theophrasts Charakteren," Philologus, 57 (1898), 115, has the def.: τὰ διαφέροντα or τὰ διάφορα means all that falls within a man's sphere of interest. The more precise sense is given by the context. Thus τὰ διαφέροντα are official concerns..., for the philosopher 'what is of moral interest to him' (ἀδιάφορα 'the morally indifferent')."

[2] Cf. Philodem. Philos., Περὶ σημείων καὶ σημειώσεων, 24, 1 (ed. T. Gomperz, Herkulanische Stud., I [1865]); P. Oxy., VII, 1033, 8 (392 A.D.).

[3] Ed. C. Hosius (1903).

2. In the Septuagint.

a. The verb διαφέρω is normally used in the LXX for שָׁנָה, in Da. for Aram. שְׁנָא, in 1 Βασ. 17:39 Cod A for סוּר hi. We also find it fairly often in the works extant only in Gk. Lit. it means "to transmit" in 1 Ἐσδρ. 5:53, "to take away" in 1 Βασ. 17:39 Cod A, "to scatter" by pillage, 2 Macc. 4:39, [4] pass. "to be divided, alienated," Wis. 18:2 and mid. "to spread abroad," Wis. 18:10. Transf. it means "to differentiate oneself" with gen. Prv. 20:2; 27:14, with παρά Δα. 7:3, 23, here with a stress on the difference *in malam partem* as made clear by the διοίσει κακοῖς ὑπέρ in v. 24. A change for the worse is also denoted by ἡ ἕξις μου διήνεγκεν ἐμοί (for שְׁנָא ithpa'al) in Δα. 7:28. The part. with dat. of object means "outstanding" in Ἐσθ. 3:13c; 2 Macc. 15:13; 3 Macc. 6:26. The pass. with dat. of person means "to be separated, estranged," 2 Macc. 3:4.

b. The adj. διάφορος is used in Lv. 19:19; Dt. 22:9 for כִּלְאָיִם "of two kinds." Hence διάφορα in 2 Ἐσδρ. 8:27 (HT שְׁנַיִם) might actually mean "two," which would make it unnecessary to conjecture [5] that the transl. read שֹׁנִים and that the word means here "self-differentiating," "different" in a positive sense, hence "outstanding," "splendid" (→ 62, 21 f.). In writings of the Hell. period τὸ διάφορον, τὰ διάφορα means "money," Sir. 27:1; 42:5; 2 Macc. 1:35; 3:6; 4:28.

c. The adv. διαφόρως occurs in Δα. 7:7 meaning "differently" *in malam partem*.

3. Josephus.

Jos. employs the verb pass. for "to be driven hither and thither," "to be scattered," Bell., 5, 93 and more often in the intr. act. for "to differentiate oneself," Ant., 4, 19; 20, 263; Ap., 2, 269. The adj. διάφορος means "different" in Bell. 3, 508.

4. In the New Testament.

a. In the NT the verb διαφέρω is used lit. for "to carry through" ... ἵνα τις διενέγκῃ σκεῦος διὰ τοῦ ἱεροῦ, Mk. 11:16; "to drift hither and thither" διαφερομένων ἡμῶν ἐν τῷ Ἀδρίᾳ, Ac. 27:27, and in the pass. intr. for the "spreading" of the λόγος κυρίου, Ac. 13:49. The transf. sense "to differentiate oneself" occurs in 1 C. 15:41 and as "to be better than, superior" in dominical sayings from Q: μᾶλλον διαφέρετε αὐτῶν, Mt. 6:26 and par., πολλῶν στρουθίων διαφέρετε ὑμεῖς Mt. 10:31 and par., and the argument πόσῳ οὖν διαφέρει ἄνθρωπος προβάτου, which is found only in Mt. 12:12. The impers. οὐδέν μοι διαφέρει "it is of no account to me" is used by Paul in Gl. 2:6 with ref. to the δοκοῦντες in Jerusalem (→ II, 233, 24 ff.) in order to stress that the authority of his apostolic commission and work does not derive from them.

b. The part as noun is used by Paul at R. 2:18 and Phil. 1:10 in the expression δοκιμάζω (→ II, 260, 1 ff.) τὰ διαφέροντα and denotes the ascertaining of what is essential for the Jew and the Christian, [6] whether in the Law and in conduct faithful thereto on the one side, or for walking in the love of Christ on the other. As R. 2:18 suggests, this term, which was current in ordinary Hell. speech, [7] had already

---

[4] Cf. διαφορέω for HT שָׁסַם Ἰερ. 37(30):16.

[5] BHK, *ad loc.*

[6] In R. 2:18 there is neither linguistic nor material basis for relating the expression to "the true distinction between Judaism and paganism," Mi. R.[13], *ad loc.*

[7] Cf. Ltzm.R. on 2:18 and Loh. Phil. on 1:10.

found its way into the Hell. synagogue, and meant there much the same as what the νομικός (Mt. 22:36) had in view in his question about the great commandment.

c. When Paul tells the Roman community (R. 12:6) that the χαρίσματα it possesses are διάφορα, the sense he has in mind is simply that of "manifold" and not of "outstanding" or "superior," for, as the preceding verses show, his concern here as in 1 C. 12 is to check any disparagement of members of the community endowed with less prominent charismata. The word has a distinctly pejorative sense in the expression διάφοροι βαπτισμοί (Hb. 9:10); this is used to describe the practices of the Levitical cult, which are ineffectual in all their multiplicity. But the very same book can use the rare comparative[8] of the word to express the superiority of Christ, to whom is ascribed an ὄνομα διαφορώτερον παρ' ἀγγέλους (1:4) and who in contrast to the ministry of the Levitical priesthood διαφορωτέρας τέτυχεν λειτουργίας (8:6).

5. In the Post-Apostolic Fathers.

In Herm. s., 9, 4, 1; 9, 15, 5 διαφέρω has the lit. sense "to carry through" with ref. to the stones carried through the gate of the tower, the Church. In Dg., 3, 5 it means "to differentiate oneself." In 1 Cl., 36, 2 we have a quotation of Hb. 1:4 with the rare comp. διαφορώτερος → line 9 f.

† εἰσφέρω.

1. The word is found in secular lit. for "to carry or bring in" either things ἐσθῆτα, Hom. Od., 7, 6, or persons, P. Amh., II, 77, 22 (139 A.D.). It is also used for the "conveying" of messages ἀγγελίας, Hdt., I, 114, 2, cf. λόγους ... εἰς ὦτα φέρει ... Ὀδυσσεύς, Soph. Ai., 149.

2. In the LXX εἰσφέρω is almost exclusively the rendering of בוא hi and ho and apart from secular ref. it can be used like φέρω (→ 56, 31 ff.), ἀναφέρω (→ 60, 13 ff.) and προσφέρω (→ 65, 15 ff.) for the bringing of wave-offerings and sacrifices into the sanctuary.

3. In the NT the literal sense is the most common with ref. to things: "We brought nothing into this world" (1 Tm. 6:7), persons: The sick man is "brought" into the house (Lk. 5:18 f.), the missionary disciples will be "haled" before the synagogue courts, rulers, and powers (Lk. 12:11), and the sacrificial ministry: The blood of beasts is "brought" into the temple by the high-priest as an offering for sin (Hb. 13:11 quoting Lv. 16:27), and cf. the expression εἰσφέρεις εἰς τὰς ἀκοὰς ἡμῶν (Ac. 17:20). In a transf. sense the word occurs in the Lord's Prayer: μὴ εἰσενέγκῃς ἡμᾶς εἰς πειρασμόν (Mt. 6:13 and par.). Here the idea of spatial movement and the active sense are retained:[1] "Bring us not into temptation," or, if as in the LXX (→ lines 24 f.) one assumes an underlying hiphil or aphel: "Do not cause that it happen."[2]

---

[8] It also occurs in Sext. Emp. Math., IX, 218. Hesych., s.v. elucidates it by κρεῖττον, ὑψηλότερον.

εἰσφέρω.   [1] E. Lohmeyer, Das Vater-unser[5] (1962), 136 f.
[2] The early Church version μὴ ἀφῇς ἡμᾶς εἰσενεχθῆναι (→ VI, 31, 1 ff. and n. 42; cf. Lohmeyer, op. cit., 134 f., 137) tries to avoid the problem of God actively tempting (cf. Jm. 1:13), but the meaning rules out this solution and one should turn rather to the proper interpretation of πειρασμός in this context → VI, 31, 5 ff.; cf. Lohmeyer, 143-6.

4. In Herm. s., 8, 6, 5 διδαχὰς ἑτέρας εἰσφέροντες corresponds to the simple form διδαχὴν ... φέρει in 2 Jn. 10 → 58, 9 ff.

προσφέρω   θύω κτλ.   →   III, 180, 18 ff.
               προσάγω   →   I, 131, 3 ff.

A. In Secular Literature.

In relation to the NT the following senses of προσφέρω found in secular writings may be mentioned: 1. "to bring to," "to apply," Hdt., VI, 18; Soph. Oed. Col., 481; Eur. Phoen., 488; 2. "to set before" or "give to" of food or medicine, Hippocr. Acut., 26 (Kühlewein, I, 122); Plat. Phaedr., 270b; Xenoph. Mem., III, 11, 13, mid. "to take," "to enjoy," Aristoxenus Fr., 18 (FHG, II, 278); Epic. Men., 131; 3. "to bring" news, Thuc., II, 70, 1; 4. "to present, offer" gifts. Thuc., II, 97, 3; Soph. El., 434; 5. pass. "to act," "to encounter" someone, Thuc., I, 140, 5; V, 111, 4.[1]

B. In Jewish Hellenistic Literature.

1. In the LXX προσφέρω is seldom used in the secular sense, e.g., "to lead in" at Lv. 8:6 (HT קרב hi); Prv. 19:24 (שוב hi) and "to bring," "to offer" objects or gifts at Ju. 3:17 f.; 5:25 (קרב hi); 2 Βασ. 17:29 (נגש hi); ψ 71:10 (שוב hi). It is used in most cases for קרב hi and like this it is a sacrificial term found predominantly in the legal and historical books.[2] It means "to bring" offerings, either in a gen. sense with no distinction of the specific acts, or in such a way that one act is meant, either the bringing of the offering to the priest, temple or altar by the one who is making the sacrifice, or the actual sacrifice, which is usually done by the priest. The meaning, then, is "bringing" to the altar, libation, waving, or burning, presenting or offering to the deity.[3] This is a common use even though differentiation is not always possible. As a less common equivalent of בוא hi προσφέρω, like ἀναφέρω (→ 60, 22 f.), means "to bring" offerings, and it can also have the more gen. sense "to sacrifice." In a few instances προσφέρω can also be the rendering of other sacrificial terms like עלה hi, זבח, קטר hi, רום hi, נשא hi, נגש hi and also עָשָׂה חַטָּאת; in such cases it denotes the corresponding act of sacrifice or offering.

2. Jos. has the word in the secular sense "to bring" presents or hospitable gifts, Ant., 6, 67; 13, 101, "to serve" drinks, 11, 188, and in the mid. "to take" food and drink, 2, 66; 4, 72; 6, 337; 20, 106 etc. The word is a sacrificial term in 3, 231; 8, 118 and 228 etc.

3. No cultic use of the word has been found in Philo, but one finds the secular sense "to bring," Spec. Leg., I, 47 and in the mid. "to act," ibid., II, 83 and 122 and "to take" food and drink, Sacr. AC, 98; Plant., 160 and 162; Ebr., 151.

C. In the New Testament.

1. Whereas Mk. has the simple form (→ 57, 33 ff.) for the "bringing" of the sick and demon-possessed to Jesus, Mt. in 4:24; 8:16; 9:2, 32; 12:22; 14:35; 17:16 prefers the compound προσφέρω. Pilate in Lk. 23:14 uses the word for the "handing over" of Jesus

---

προσφέρω. [1] Cf. also the examples in Moult.-Mill., s.v.

[2] Job 1:5 and 1 and 2 Macc. are historical in this regard. Prv. 21:27 speaks of the futile offering of the ungodly. Sir. 7:9 says the same of that of the guilty. Sir. 35:2 spiritualises the concept. Am. 5:25 criticises sacrifices. Mal. 1:13 attacks deception in offerings. Jer. 14:12 rejects sacrifices. Only the future Torah of Ez. 43-46 has rules of sacrifice after the manner of Lv. [Bertram].

[3] Cf. R. Hentschke, Art. "Opfer," RGG³, IV, 1645.

into his hands by the Sanhedrin. In the story of the children who are "brought" to Jesus in order that He might bless them, all three Evangelists (Mk. 10:13 and par.) have προσφέρω.

2. In the sense "to hand," "to offer" we find the word in money transactions at Mt. 22:19; 25:20; Ac. 8:18 and also with ref. to the vinegar handed to Jesus on the cross, Lk. 23:36; Jn. 19:29.

3. Hb. 12:7 speaks of God's προσφέρεσθαι "dealings" with those whom He instructs as sons through suffering.

4. More extended discussion is called for in regard to the use of the term for "to bring offerings," "to sacrifice." Since the NT community has no sacrificial cultus, the vocabulary of sacrifice is limited to the few passages which refer to the contemporary Jewish cultus, or to that of the OT, or to specific accounts of sacrifice in the OT, or to the life and death of Jesus as a sacrifice, or to the conduct and acts of Christians as sacrifices in a transf. sense.

a. In this regard we must turn first to the attitude of Jesus Himself to the Jewish sacrificial system (→ III, 184, 13 ff.; 264, 1 ff.) and to His statements about it. In Mk. 1:44 and par. he tells the man cured of leprosy to bring the offering for cleansing prescribed in Lv. 14. In Mt. 5:23 f. he demands that the offering be interrupted if the one who is making it comes to realise that his brother has something against him. Since in neither case is Jesus addressing a priest, the προσένεγκε (Mk. 1:44) and ἐὰν προσφέρῃς (Mt. 5:23) can only refer to the handing of the offering to the priest, as the demand ἄφες ἐκεῖ τὸ δῶρόν σου ἔμπροσθεν τοῦ θυσιαστηρίου also shows, 5:24.[4] Even if the character of witness which Jesus imparts to the offering for cleansing with the words εἰς μαρτύριον αὐτοῖς (Mk. 1:44 → IV, 503, 12 ff.) is not also grounded in His faithfulness to the Law,[5] the two verses make it plain that Jesus not only accepts the validity of the laws of sacrifice and contemporary practice, but that He also reinterprets them in terms of His own mission and message. The offering for cleansing becomes a divine and definitive[6] witness (→ IV, 502, 38 ff.) against those who contest the content of His preaching and sending, the coming of the kingdom of God in whose power the cleansing took place. In Mt. 5:24 f. the sacrificial system is given a norm in the twofold commandment of love. The relation between God and man that is sought in sacrifice presupposes purification of the relation to one's brother.

b. Paul in Ac. 21:26 accepts the charges of four Nazirites and announces in the temple the day for the προσηνέχθη ... ἡ προσφορά.[7] This might be regarded as a practical fulfilment of the norm laid down by Jesus. It is true that Paul is not offering for himself. Nevertheless, he is making possible the offering of the Nazirites by an act of loving concern, and he is also attempting thereby, even if unsuccessfully, to effect a reconciliation with his Jewish brethren in Jerusalem who have something against him. Very different is the mood regarding the sacrificial ministry of the OT in Stephen's speech (Ac. 7:42), where the μὴ σφάγια (→ VII, 934, n. 40) καὶ θυσίας

---

[4] Zn. Mt., ad loc.; cf. Kl. Mt., ad loc.: "without fully handing over the gift to the priest."
[5] Cf. Zn. Mt., 336 and Grundm. Mk., ad loc.
[6] Cf. Loh. Mk., ad loc.
[7] For details of the procedure cf. Haench. Ag.14, ad loc.

προσηνέγκατέ μοι; (Am. 5:25 LXX) catches up the prophetic criticism of the cultus. [8] In the saying directed against Jewish persecution of the community in Jn. 16:2: πᾶς ὁ ἀποκτείνας ὑμᾶς δόξη λατρείαν (→ IV, 65, 16 ff.) προσφέρειν[9] τῷ θεῷ, this attitude takes on a much sharper edge. The accusation that the killing of the disciples will be regarded as doing God service naturally carries with it a radical condemnation.

c. With an intensity unparalleled in the NT, Hb. makes use of the sacrificial theology and practice of the old covenant to develop the witness to Christ. This comes to expression in the frequent employment of the cultic term προσφέρω along with ἀναφέρω (→ 61, 3 ff.). In Hb. the word always means "to accomplish the sacrifice" and not just to bring the offerings to the altar or the priest. There are different nuances in the contrast between the Levitical offerings and the sacrifice of Christ. On the one side the antithesis is stressed. The προσφέρειν of the Levitical priests involves daily or yearly repetition εἰς τὸ διηνεκές (10:1); of Jesus it may be said: μίαν ὑπὲρ ἁμαρτιῶν προσενέγκας θυσίαν εἰς τὸ διηνεκές (10:12). The former offered the blood of bulls and goats (10:4, 9, 7, 13) and brought meat offerings and drink offerings (9:9 ff.); Jesus sacrifices His blood, His σῶμα (→ VII, 1058, 19 ff.), Himself (9:14, 10:10). The sacrifices of the former effect only δικαιώματα and καθαρότητα σαρκός (9:10, 13) and do not cleanse from sins (10:2 f.); the sacrifice of Jesus (→ III, 186, 4 ff.; 280, 22 ff.) sanctifies ἐφάπαξ (10:10) and purges the conscience (9:14; 10:22). The ministry of the former is based on an outdated and passing (8:13) covenant; that of Jesus on one which is new and better (8:6). In the words of Ps. 40:6 f. Hb. 10:5 ff. has Christ Himself state the antithesis in all its starkness: The sacrifice of the old covenant, O God, thou wouldest not. But I have come according to Scripture to do Thy will, i.e., to offer the one sacrifice which avails for ever and which sanctifies all men. On the other side, however, the two ministries are brought into positive relationship. Thus the old sacrificial law and ministry can be characterised as σκιά (→ VII, 398, 31 ff.) τῶν μελλόντων ἀγαθῶν (10:1) or τῶν ἐπουρανίων (8:5), i.e., as an adumbration of the ministry and sacrifice of Christ. For the τύπος (8:5; → VIII, 257, 32 ff.) and that which is to come are not opposed to the shadow which they project. Aaron and Christ can even be brought into direct comparison in 5:1 ff. The *tertium comparationis* is the divine calling of both to high-priestly ministry; in Christ's case the witness to this is found in Ps. 2:7 and 110:4. Even this comparison ends, of course, when the incomparable sacrifice of Christ is described, for He did not bring δῶρα καὶ θυσίας like Aaron (v. 1) but δεήσεις τε καὶ ἱκετηρίας ... προσενέγκας (v. 7) by His ὑπακοή became αἴτιος σωτηρίας αἰωνίου to all who obey Him, v. 8 f.

For all who in obedience to Him (5:9) come in the πληροφορία πίστεως (10:22) and experience the cleansing and saving effect of this sacrifice of Christ, the sacrifices of the old covenant have naturally been superseded once and for all. Sacrifice is replaced with the offering of praise by lips that confess His name (13:15; → 61, 16 ff.) and more generally with πίστις. One may see this in the evaluation of the sacrifice of Abel (11:4) and of Abraham (11:17): πίστει ...

---

[8] On the reinterpretation of Am. by Stephen cf. Haench. Ag.[14], *ad loc.*
[9] On the incorrectness of this combination and its significance cf. Bau. J., *ad loc.*

Άβελ... προσήνεγκεν and πίστει προσενήνοχεν Ἀβραάμ. Πίστει they have become models for the NT community.

D. In the Post-Apostolic Fathers.

Almost the only use of the word in the post-apost. fathers is for "to sacrifice," "to bring offerings," cf. esp. where OT texts are quoted or there is ref. to OT sacrifices related in some way to the NT message. 1 Cl. simply uses OT procedures as models or examples in his exhortations. Thus Abraham's obedience in offering Isaac illustrates Chr. ὑπακοή (10, 7), the sacrificial order in Jerusalem is an example for the Corinthians of perseverance in the ὡρισμένος τῆς λειτουργίας κανών (4, 1 f.), and the offerings of Cain and Abel are a warning against the fatal consequences of ζῆλος and φθόνος (4, 4. 7). Barn., on the other hand, finds in the sacrificial acts and statutes of the OT τύποι (→ VIII, 253, 19 ff.; 256, 10 ff.) which are fulfilled in Christ, of whom (or whose flesh) it is said: As σκεῦος τοῦ πνεύματος ὑπὲρ ἁμαρτιῶν ἔμελλεν προσφέρειν θυσίαν (7, 3. 5), or that after the τύπος of the red heifer as μόσχος He was offered by sinners as προσφέροντες ἐπὶ τὴν σφαγήν (8, 1 f.).

Whereas in typology of this kind we tend to have no more than the views of individual writers, the referring of the idea of sacrifice to the eucharist determines the self-understanding of the Chr. community in its full breadth. Did., 14 sees in the Sunday eucharist a fulfilment of Mal. 1:11: ἐν παντὶ τόπῳ καὶ χρόνῳ προσφέρειν μοι θυσίαν καθαράν. The function of bishops which 1 Cl., 44, 4 describes with προσενεγκόντας τὰ δῶρα also has in view, or at least includes, the celebration of the eucharist.

Dg., 3, 3 uses προσφέρω abs. and 2, 8 has it with τιμή as obj. to describe the sacrificial order of paganism and its irrationality.

† προσφορά.

1. This word has many meanings in class. lit. as a noun correlative to the meanings of the verb in the act., mid., or pass. (→ 65, 3 ff.), but none of these occurs in the NT. Here προσφορά always means "sacrifice (as gift or act)," a meaning first found in the LXX (ψ 39:7 for מִנְחָה; Da. 3:38), then in Sir., and finally in writings (esp. Chr.) influenced by the LXX. [1]

2. In the NT προσφορά is used both for the Levitical offerings (Hb. 10:5 quoting ψ 39:7; Hb. 10:18; Ac. 21:26; 24:17) and also for the sacrifice of Christ (Hb. 10:10, 14; Eph. 5:2; → 67, 11 ff.; VIII, 83, 12 ff.). It is also used in a transf. sense for the offering or sacrifice of pagans won by and for the Gospel, R. 15:16. [2]

3. Among the post-apost. fathers Barn. in 2, 4 ff. follows Is. 1:11 f. in rejecting θυσίαι, ὁλοκαυτώματα and προσφοραί because they are ἀνθρωποποίητόν τι and God does not need them. On the other hand, 1 Cl., 40, 2-4 applies the rules and ordinances for OT προσφοραί and λειτουργίαι to προσφοραί and λειτουργίαι in the Chr. community with ref. to the eucharist → lines 16 ff. Acc. to 1 Cl., 36, 1 Jesus Christ is ἀρχιερεὺς τῶν προσφορῶν in this regard. In the lit. sense of "animal sacrifice" or "offering" προσφορά is used of the martyr in Mart. Pol., 14,'1; he is decribed as a choice ram from the flock εἰς προσφοράν, ὁλοκαύτωμα δεκτὸν τῷ θεῷ ἡτοιμασμένον.

π ρ ο σ φ ο ρ ά . [1] E.g., Jos. Ant., 11, 77. Philo does not have the word in the sense of sacrifice.

[2] Cf. K. Weiss, "Pls., Priester d. chr. Kultgemeinde," ThLZ, 79 (1954), 357.

† συμφέρω,   † σύμφορος.

Contents: A. The Word Group in Greek; I. Meaning: 1. συμφέρω; 2. σύμφορος; 3. Synonyms. II. Philosophical Discussion: 1. The Pre-Socratics; 2. The Sophists; 3. Socrates; 4. Post-Socratic Philosophy. B. The Old Testament. C. Judaism. D. The Word Group in the New Testament: I. Usage. II. Meaning. E. The Profitable and Useful in the Post-Apostolic Fathers.

A. The Word Group in Greek.

I. Meaning.

1. συμφέρω.

συμφέρω, older Attic ξυμφέρω, is used trans. in the following lit. senses: "to gather," "to bring together," Hdt., III, 92, 2; Xenoph. An., VI, 4, 9, "to bring," Epicharmus Fr., 35, 8 (CGF, 96), "to bear together," Eur. Alc., 370; Xenoph. An., VII, 6, 20, then intr. "to be of use," with dat. of person, Hdt., IX, 37, 4; Aesch. Suppl., 753, or thing which something serves, Aristoph. Pl., 38, and with εἰς, Thuc., IV, 26, 5, or πρός, Xenoph. Mem., II, 2, 5, to describe the goal, and finally in the impers. συμφέρει "it is useful, advantageous," Plat. Phaedr., 230e; Leg., IX, 875a. The part. means "useful," "beneficial," Soph. Oed. Tyr., 875; Plat. Gorg., 527b; Demosth. Or., 18, 308. As a subst. sing. (Soph. Phil., 926) or plur. (131) it means "that which is of service," Thuc., IV, 60, 1; Plat. Polit., 296e; Xenoph. Symp., 4, 39, "advantage," Demosth. Or., 18, 28, "profit," Dinarch., 1, 99, with gen. (Plat. Resp., I, 338c) or dat. of the one who enjoys it, I, 341d; 342b. Other intr. meanings of συμφέρω are "to assist," Soph. Phil., 627, "to agree," Aristoph. Eq., 1233, "to yield," Soph. El., 1465, "to suit someone," Xenoph. Cyrop., VIII, 4, 21, "to happen" with acc. and inf., Hdt., I, 73, 4; III, 129, 1 etc. or ὥστε, I, 74, 2, "to turn" to the good or the bad, VIII, 88, 1. The pass. occurs for "to happen" in either a good sense (Heracl. Fr., 10, Diels, I, 153) or a bad (Hom. Il., 8, 400; Ps.-Hes. Scutum, 358 [ed. C. F. Russo, 1950]), "to unite," Luc. Hermot., 34, "to agree," Hdt., II, 80, 1, "to correspond," "to be like," Eur. El., 527, "to take place," Thuc., VIII, 84, 1, "to turn out" well or badly, ἐπὶ τὸ βέλτιον, Aristoph. Nu., 594. The impers. συμφέρεταί τινι means that "it happens to someone," Hdt., II, 111, 1 etc. As a tt. in grammar the pass. means "to be construed with," Apollon. Dyscol. Synt., III, 160 (p. 407, 6).

2. σύμφορος.

σύμφορος means "accompanying," "one who accompanies," Hes. Op., 302, and "suiting," "useful," 783; later it has only the latter sense. The expression σύμφορόν ἐστιν means the same as συμφέρει, and τὰ σύμφορα the same as τὰ συμφέροντα. The constructions correspond to those with συμφέρω → lines 9 ff.

3. Synonyms.

As compared with συμφέρω the distinctive elements in synon. like ὠφελέω, ὠφέλεια, τὸ ὄφελος is in the main that the "profit" or "advantage" they denote can often have the more concrete form of "help," "source of help," Thuc., II, 7, 1; VI, 17, 1; III, 82, 6; Plat. Lys., 217a, or "booty," Antiphon Or., 2, 1, 4; Ps.-Xenoph. Cyn., 6, 4; Plut. Aem., 29 (I, 270 f.); De Caesare, 12 (I, 713b); Cato Maior, 10 (I, 342a), etc. This does not apply to λυσιτελέω, τὸ λυσιτελοῦν, as one might expect from the basic etym. meaning "to render account." There is in this case no specific difference of sense as compared with συμφέρω "to be profitable."

II. Philosophical Discussion.

It may be presupposed that in philosophical discussion of the useful or profitable there is no discernible difference of sense between συμφέρω and its synon. (→ 69, 31 ff.). From the very first the groups are interchangeable and indeed they are directly stated to be synon.

1. The Pre-Socratics.

The fragmentary tradition of pre-Socratic philosophy does not provide any clear-cut delineation of the problem of the useful. This is not surprising in the thinkers of the era with their bent for natural philosophy. On the other hand the Pythagorean teaching handed down by Aristoxenus in Stob. Ecl., IV, 15, 19 ff., ὡς ἡ μὲν τάξις καὶ συμμετρία καλὰ καὶ σύμφορα, ἡ δὲ ἀταξία καὶ ἀσυμμετρία αἰσχρά τε καὶ ἀσύμφορα, corresponds to the world-view of the older Pythagoreans as determined by the harmony of numbers, and also to the style of life practised in the Pythagorean union. When Democrit. discusses the συμφέρον, he does not do so in any obvious connection with his philosophical system, although we find in him motifs basic for the later schools. The stupidity of belligerence is proved for him by the fact that it turns attention away from ἴδιον συμφέρον to what is βλαβερόν for one's foe, Fr., 237 (Diels, II, 193). On the other hand, he seems to regard the συμφέρον as κοινῇ συμφέρον (→ 71, 18 ff.) when he claims that in protection against aggressive animals the men of the first generation joined forces ὑπὸ τοῦ συμφέροντος διδασκόμενοι, Democr. acc. to Diod. S., 1, 8, 2 (Diels, II, 135, 36 f.) and when ξυμφωνεῖν περὶ τοῦ ξυμφέροντος is for him a test as to whom one should regard as a true friend, Fr., 107 (II, 164). Finally, one finds the hedonistic idea of the συμφέρον when he makes τέρψις and ἀτερπίη (desire and non-desire) the ὅρος συμφόρων καὶ ἀσυμφόρων, Fr., 188 (II, 183), cf. Fr., 4 (II, 133) and gives the advice ἡδὺ μηδὲν ἀποδέχεσθαι, ἢν μὴ συμφέρηι, Fr., 74 (II, 159). Nausiphanes, a disciple of Democrit. acc. to Diog. L., I, 15 and a teacher of Epicurus (→ 73, 7 ff.) (IX, 69, cf. X, 8), also relates the συμφέρον to the ἥδεσθαι καὶ μὴ ἀλγεῖν as man's συγγενικὸν τέλος, Fr., 2 (Diels, II, 249, 10-16).

2. The Sophists.

The problem comes to a head only with the ethical relativism of the Sophists, whether it be that Protagoras demonstrates the relativity as well as the incommensurability of the ἀγαθόν and the ὠφέλιμον (Plat. Prot., 333d-334b) or that Thrasymachus defines the δίκαιον as τὸ τοῦ κρείττονος συμφέρον (Resp., I, 338c, cf. Ps.-Plat. Alc., I, 113d). The stronger finds his "advantage" συμφέρον by following natural law, while the laws of the state curtail this to the profit of the weaker, Plat. Gorg., 483b-c; Antiphon Fr., 44 A, Col. 4, 1-8 (Diels, II, 349). The συμφέρον is thus brought within the relativity of the good, Plat. Resp., I, 343c, so that Antiphon can say: χρῶιτ' ἂν οὖν ἄνθρωπος μάλιστα ἑαυτῶι ξυμφερόντως δικαιοσύνηι, εἰ μετὰ μὲν μαρτύρων τοὺς νόμους (the laws of the state) μεγάλους ἄγοι, μονούμενος δὲ μαρτύρων τὰ τῆς φύσεως (the commands of nature), Fr., 44 A, Col. 1:12-23 [1] (Diels, II, 346), cf. also Anaxarchus Fr., 1 (II, 239 f.).

3. Socrates.

Socrates launches a broad attack on the Sophist position in the Platonic dialogues. He begins with etym. discussion [2] in Crat., 417a-b and gives as the meaning of συμφέρον,

---

συμφέρω. [1] Cf. the discussion of this text in v. Arnim, "Gerechtigkeit u. Nutzen in d. griech. Aufklärungs-Philosophie," *Frankfurter Universitätsreden*, 5 (1916), 5-10.
[2] For a discussion of the significance of this and Stoic (→ 72, 1 ff.) etymologies cf. H. Steinthal, *Gesch. d. Sprachwissenschaft bei d. Griechen u. Römern*², I (1890), 79-112, 319-357; I. Opelt, Art. "Etymologie," RAC, VI, 798-810, with bibl.

τὴν ἅμα φορὰν τῆς ψυχῆς τῶν πραγμάτων. It is thus illuminating, τὰ ὑπὸ τοῦ τοιούτου πραττόμενα συμφέροντά τε καὶ σύμφορα κεκλῆσθαι ἀπὸ τοῦ συμπεριφέρεσθαι ("to pursue things"). τὸ συμφέρον is thus in some sense τῆς ἐπιστήμης ἀδελφός. μάθησις, μελέτη and παιδεία are thus needed that τά τε ὠφέλιμα καὶ τὰ βλαβερὰ τῶν πραγμάτων διαγνώσεσθαι, Xenoph. Mem., IV, 1, 5, cf. III, 9, 1-3. Now ἀρετή in the Socratic sense rests on ἐπιστήμη, Aristot. Eth. Nic., VI, 13, p. 1144b, 28-30: Σωκράτης μὲν οὖν λόγους τὰς ἀρετὰς ᾤετο εἶναι, ἐπιστήμας γάρ εἶναι πάσας. Ignorance is moral weakness, wisdom is strength οὐδὲ τὸ ἥττω εἶναι αὑτοῦ (against oneself) ἄλλο τι τοῦτ' ἐστὶν ἢ ἀμαθία, οὐδὲ κρείττω ἑαυτοῦ ἄλλο τι ἢ σοφία, Plat. Prot., 358c. To be good and righteous is to be happy τὸν μὲν γὰρ καλὸν καὶ ἀγαθὸν ἄνδρα καὶ γυναῖκα εὐδαίμονα εἶναί φημι, τὸν δὲ ἄδικον καὶ πονηρὸν ἄθλιον, Plat. Gorg., 470e, ὁ μὲν δίκαιος ἄρα εὐδαίμων, ὁ δ' ἄδικος ἄθλιος... Ἀλλὰ μὴν ἄθλιόν γε εἶναι οὐ λυσιτελεῖ, εὐδαίμονα δέ, Resp., I, 354a. The good deed is the useful deed, τὸ καλὸν ἔργον ἀγαθόν τε καὶ ὠφέλιμον, Prot., 358b. Thus τὸ συμφέρον is the same as the ἀγαθόν and everything that achieves eudaemonia: δέον καὶ ὠφέλιμον καὶ λυσιτελοῦν καὶ κερδαλέον καὶ ἀγαθὸν καὶ συμφέρον καὶ εὔπορον τὸ αὐτὸ φαίνεται, ἑτέροις ὀνόμασι σημαῖνον τὸ διακοσμοῦν, Crat., 419a, cf. Ps.-Plat. Alc., I, 116b-d → III, 538, 1 ff. The final saying with its indication of order and right relations refers the useful to society, i.e., for the Greeks of this period to the πόλις. At any rate, τὸ συμφέρον always means τὸ κοινῇ συμφέρον, which includes the ἰδίᾳ συμφέρον, cf. Plat. Leg., IX, 875a-b. Only with the just ruler as such can τὸ ἑαυτῷ συμφέρον and τὸ τῷ ἀρχομένῳ be differentiated, cf. Resp., I, 342e. Apart from this ἀγαθόν and συμφέρον can be equated concretely with written and unwritten laws and their observance, Xenoph. Mem., IV, 4, 16 ff., esp. 18: ἐγὼ (sc. Σωκράτης) μὲν οὖν... τὸ αὐτὸ ἀποδείκνυμαι νόμιμόν τε καὶ δίκαιον εἶναι. If existence after death is considered, συμφέρον applies here too. In his discussion with the Sophists Callicles, Polos and Gorgias, the "three wisest of living Greeks," Socrates ends with the statement: οὐκ ἔχετε ἀποδεῖξαι ὡς δεῖ ἄλλον τινὰ βίον ζῆν ἢ τοῦτον, ὅσπερ καὶ ἐκεῖσε φαίνεται συμφέρων, Plat. Gorg., 527b, cf. also ὡς τούτῳ ταῦτα εἰς ἀγαθόν τι τελευτήσει ζῶντι ἢ καὶ ἀποθανόντι, Resp., X, 613a.

4. Post-Socratic Philosophy.

The Socratic approach to the συμφέρον, namely, establishing the right relation between συμφέρον, eudaemonia, the (κοινῇ) καλὸν κἀγαθόν and ἀρετή, remained determinative for Gk. thought in every school and every thinker. The various solutions thus depend on the definition of ἀγαθόν, the nature of ἀρετή, and the view of eudaemonia.

a. For Aristot., too, τὸ συμφέρον and τὸ ἀγαθόν are identical, Rhet., I, 6, p. 1362a, 20; Pol., I, 2, p. 1253a, 14-18. He grants the individual συμφέρον; it is ἀγαθόν but not καλόν. Only συμφέρον ἁπλῶς [3] is καλόν and only in this sense can one strive ὁμοίως τὸ καλόν and τὸ συμφέρον, Rhet., II, 13, p. 1389b, 35 - 1390a, 4. For man as ζῷον πολιτικόν the συμφέρον consists in κοινῇ συμφέρον, Pol., III, 6, p. 1278b, 19-24. νομοθέται and ἄρχοντες must strive after τὸ κοινὸν συμφέρον, III, 7, p. 1279a, 28-32; III, 13, p. 1283b, 40-42, for it is τὸ δίκαιον, Rhet., I, 6, p. 1362b, 26-29; Eth. Nic., V, 3, p. 1129b, 14-19; VIII, 11, p. 1160a, 8-23.

b. What is συμφέρον for a given *polis* is found in the historians and on inscr. (*laudationes* and *foederationes*) [4] with no further philosophical ref., cf. the laudation of the Iliensians for Malusius, Ditt. Syll. [3], I, 330, 12-14 (306 B.C.) when they extol his deeds as τὰ συμφέροντα τῇ θεῷ (sc. Ἀθηνᾷ τῇ Ἰλιάδι).

---

[3] On the relative nature of this distinction → III, 541, 35 ff. and n. 15.
[4] Examples in, e.g., Ditt. Syll. [3], IV, 2, *s.v.* συμφέρω c β.

c. In Stoicism, as the lingistic interests of the school would suggest, the etym. derivation of the word again plays a role (→ 70, 44 ff. and n. 2): συμφέρον, φέρειν γὰρ τοιαῦτα ἃ συντείνει πρὸς τὸ εὖ ζῆν, Stob. Ecl., II, 100, 22 f.; συμφέρον μὲν ὅτι φέρει [τὰ] τοιαῦτα ὧν συμβαινόντων ὠφελούμεθα, Diog. L., VII, 99; πρόσεστι ... τὸ τῷ ὅλῳ κόσμῳ συμφέρον, οὗ μέρος εἶ. παντὶ δὲ φύσεως μέρει ἀγαθόν, ὃ φέρει ἡ τοῦ ὅλου φύσις, M. Ant., II, 3, 2. Materially Stoicism is close to Socrates. Acc. to Cl. Al. Strom., II, 131, 3 Cleanthes appeals to Socrates' doctrine of the identity of the δίκαιος and εὐδαίμων ἀνήρ (→ 71, 10 ff.) and his curse on the ἀσεβὲς πρᾶγμα of the one who first sundered the δίκαιον and the συμφέρον, which applies to both the Sophists (→ 70, 29 ff.) and also the Epicureans (→ 73, 7 ff.). Cic. De legibus, I, 12, 33, agrees with this anathema, which in Off., III, 7, 34 he ascribes to Panaetius. *Quicquid honestum ..., id utile ..., nec utile quicquam, quod non honestum,* is, acc. to Off., III, 3, 11, the formulation in which the Stoics accept the teaching of Socrates. With rhetorical exaggeration: *Tanta vis est honesti, ut speciem utilitatis obscuret,* III, 47. Lists of identical terms like those of Socrates (→ 71, 15 ff.) are common in the Stoics, cf. Cl. Al. Prot., VI, 72, 2; Epict. Diss., I, 27, 14; II, 7, 4 ff.; 17, 10. [5] Acc. to Diog. L., VII, 103 they regard as the typical characteristics of the ἀγαθόν: τὸ ὠφελεῖν, οὐ τὸ βλάπτειν. They define: ἀγαθόν ἐστιν ὠφέλεια ἢ οὐχ ἕτερον ὠφελείας, Sext. Emp. Math., XI, 22, cf. Diog. L., VII, 94; Stob. Ecl., II, 69, 11. Chrysipp. equates κινεῖν ἢ ἴσχειν κατ' ἀρετήν with ὠφελεῖν, Diog. L., VII, 104, cf. Stob. Ecl., II, 95, 3-8; Plut. Comm. Not., 22 (II, 1069a). What is profitable, however, is what promotes eudaemonia: ἀγαθόν ἐστι τὸ συλλαμβανόμενον πρὸς εὐδαιμονίαν or τὸ συμπληρωτικὸν εὐδαιμονίας, Sext. Emp. Math., XI, 30. Pertinent here is the correct delimitation of the ἀγαθόν: *Bonum sincerum esse debet et ab omni parte innoxium. Non est id bonum, quod plus prodest, sed quod tantum prodest,* Sen. Ep., 87, 36. This pure good is defined acc. to the school's concept of τέλος, namely, τὸ ὁμολογουμένως τῇ φύσει ζῆν, ὅπερ ἐστὶ κατ' ἀρετὴν ζῆν Diog. L., VII, 87. Human φύσις, however, is rational, whereas πάθος is ἡ ἄλογος καὶ παρὰ φύσιν ψυχῆς κίνησις, VII, 110 (Hicks). Only on this view can the good in the abs. be called useful. Goods "close to the nature of the good" acc. to Stob. Ecl., II, 84, 18 ff., the so-called προηγμένα among the ἀδιάφορα (→ 62, 33 ff.), e.g., good intellectual and physical attributes, friends, fame, descent, and wealth, may be viewed as useful and pleasant, but not as profitable to eudaemonia, Cic. Fin., III, 69. They are so-called οὐ τῷ πρὸς εὐδαιμονίαν τινὰ συμβάλλεσθαι, Stob. Ecl., II, 85, 8 f. Since Stoicism views itself from the outset as a society, its concept of the profitable excludes on the one side what is just ἰδίᾳ συμφέρον while on the other it is not confined to the bounds of a political society. Since man is πολίτης τοῦ κόσμου, general and individual advantages coincide, Stob. Ecl., II, 101, 21-27. [6] This corresponds to the φύσις τοῦ λογικοῦ ζῴου, cf. Epict. Diss., II, 10, 3 f.; I, 19, 13 ff.; M. Ant., V, 16, 3; VI, 44, 5; XI, 13, 4. Thus it would also be wrong to exclude individual profit; this must be brought in too, Epict. Diss., I, 28, 6; Sen. Ben., VI, 12, 2; 13. Since failure to see these interrelations entangles man in meaningless conflicts and leads to wrong acts, teaching and education are needed, Epict. Diss., II, 24, 15. 21. 23; 26, 1 ff.; III, 7, 33 ff. For the representatives of later Stoicism just mentioned τὸ ἀγαθόν and τὸ συμφέρον naturally still go together and are equated, Epict. Diss., II, 7, 4; IV, 7, 8 f.; M. Ant., III, 6, 6. It belongs to the προλήψεις κοιναὶ πᾶσιν ἀνθρώποις ... ὅτι τὸ ἀγαθὸν συμφέρον ἐστί, Epict. Diss., I, 22, 1. But this applies only when the συμφέρον and therewith the ἀγαθόν are set in προαίρεσις, i.e., morally free self-determination: ἐὰν μὲν ἐν τούτοις μόνοις ἡγήσηται τὸ ἀγαθὸν τὸ αὐτοῦ καὶ συμφέρον, τοῖς ἀκωλύτοις καὶ ἐφ' ἑαυτῷ ("wherein he is unhampered and his own master"), ἐλεύθερον ἔσται (sc. τὸ λογικὸν ζῷον), εὔρουν, εὔδαιμον, ἀβλαβές,

---

[5] Cf. Joh. W. 1 K., 158, n. 1.

[6] M. Ant., VI, 44, 6: πόλις καὶ πατρὶς ὡς μὲν ᾿Αντωνίνῳ μοι ἡ ῾Ρώμη, ὡς δὲ ἀνθρώπῳ ὁ κόσμος. τὰ ταῖς πόλεσιν οὖν ταύταις ὠφέλιμα μόνα ἐστί μοι ἀγαθά, cf. also II, 3, 2; X, 6, 2 and the negative counterpart VI, 54: τὸ τῷ σμήνει ("swarm of bees") μὴ συμφέρον οὐδὲ τῇ μελίσσῃ συμφέρει.

μεγαλόφρον, εὐσεβές, χάριν ἔχον ὑπὲρ πάντων τῷ θεῷ, μηδαμοῦ μεμφόμενον μηδενὶ τῶν γενομένων, μηδενὶ ἐγκαλοῦν, Epict. Diss., IV, 7, 9. Acc. to M. Ant., III, 6, 1. 6 f. a life κατὰ τὸν λόγον τὸν ὀρθόν, i.e., esp. ἀρκεῖσθαι ἑαυτῇ τὴν διάνοιαν, is for man as λογικὸν ζῷον the συμφέρον and κρεῖττον. But definition of the κρεῖττον underlies the free judgment of the individual which is to be made only after careful examination.

d. Epicurus describes συμμέτρησις καὶ συμφερόντων καὶ ἀσυμφόρων as the right way to achieve eudaemonia, Men., 130. In emphatic distinction from φιλοσοφία, this is part of the activity of the φρόνησις. Epic. calls it τὸ μέγιστον ἀγαθόν. For all virtues spring from it and it leads to the realisation that ἡδέως ζῆν ἄνευ τοῦ φρονίμως καὶ καλῶς καὶ δικαίως (sc. ζῆν) and the reverse are not possible, 132. ἡδονή, however, is ἀρχὴ καὶ τέλος τοῦ μακαρίως ζῆν, cf. 128 f. It is not lowly sensual desire but τὸ μήτε ἀλγεῖν κατὰ σῶμα μήτε ταράττεσθαι κατὰ ψυχήν, 131. It is thus profitable to restrain, e.g., certain things that arouse desire, if greater sorrows can be avoided thereby, Fr., 442 (Usener, 289, 11 f.). Thus in συμμέτρησις συμφερόντων καὶ ἀσυμφόρων it is more a matter of the ποσόν than the ποιόν, ibid. (lines 13-27). The Epicureans teach concerning obscenae voluptates: omninoque genus hoc voluptatum... prodesse numquam, Cic. Tusc., V, 33, 94. The concept of the profitable is related here not to the ethical goal ἡδονή itself but to what serves its achievement. It is the criterion for striving towards it. Thus the δίκαιον is what prevents reciprocal hurt and the συμφέρον is what promotes fellowship, Epic. Sententiae selectae, 31 (Usener, 78). The same applies to moral goods in detail. Bravery springs from the λογισμὸς τοῦ συμφέροντος, Fr., 517 (Usener, 317, 7) and friendship is embraced διὰ τὰς χρείας, Fr., 540 (324, 12).

B. The Old Testament.

Hbr. equivalents for συμφέρω etc. are יעל hi (construed personally and impers.) and סכן q, but esp. the former, which is usually abs. In Is. 48:17 it denotes the profit from the teachings and directions that Yahweh gives Israel and we find it in the many claims that false gods or idols are useless, e.g., 1 S. 12:21; Is. 44:9 f.; Jer. 16:19; Hab. 2:18; with the acc. of the one concerned Is. 57:12. The relative clause without relative particle [7] (לֹא יוֹעִיל[וּ]) in Jer. 2:8, 11 to denote the gods has the force of a noun, e.g., "no-profit." That they do not profit is also said in Jer. 7:8 of lying speeches, in 23:32 (with לְעַם־הַזֶּה) of false prophets, in Is. 47:12 of the magicians of Babylon, and in Prv. 10:2 (cf. 11:4) of unlawful possessions. Conversely the wicked in Job 21:15 ask: "What profit should we have, if we pray unto him (God)?" In gen. the ref. is to individual or national profit in this world, but there is a glance at the day of wrath in Prv. 11:4. סכן q occurs in Job 15:3; 35:3 par. to יעל hi for the lack of profit in Job's words or righteousness, cf. 34:9. Eliphaz makes it clear in 22:2 f. that the מַשְׂכִּיל profits סכן himself, not God. Thus the religious life is uninhibitedly seen from the standpoint of what is profitable. The abs. standards set by divine revelation raise problems as to what is profitable which are not easily resolved, at any rate by the foolish and the wicked.

C. Judaism.

1. In the LXX סכן hi is transl. (οὐ) δεῖ at Job 15:3 and ἐπισκοπή at 34:9. It is omitted at 35:3. [8] The equivalent of יעל is almost always ὠφελέω, while συμφέρον and σύμφορον are used for various Hbr. terms, namely טוב "good," שָׁוֶה "appropriate," and

---

[7] Cf. Ges.-K. § 155n.
[8] Job 22:2 (סכן twice) is replaced with repetition of 21:22 (God teaches σύνεσις and ἐπιστήμη).

נָאוָה "suitable." The words denote "profit" or harm for God's people, Gentile kingdoms and kings, and also individuals, as a result of doing God's commands, Dt. 23:7; 4 Macc. 1:17; Bar. 4:3, avoiding idolatry, Sir. 30:19 and excess, Prv. 19:10; Sir. 37:27 f., the fulfilment of human plans or measures, Est. 3:8; 'Ιερ. 33:14; Prv. 31:19; 2 Macc. 4:5; 11:15, and also, acc. to the view of the enemy of God, ungodly philosophy, 4 Macc. 5:11. A formula like τὸ σύμφορον κοινῇ καὶ κατ' ἰδίαν in 2 Macc. 4:5 shows the influence of Stoic thought and expression → 72, 33 ff. This is chiefly found in books of the Hell. period but it also finds its way into the older books through linguistic change and additions. 9

2. Philo's usage falls within the sphere of Gk. philosophy, esp. Stoicism. καλὸς καὶ συμφέρων and ἀγαθὸς καὶ συμφέρων are expressions constantly used by him, cf. Abr., 18; Cher. 13; Congr., 137; Decal., 132 etc. or Abr., 256; Spec. Leg., I, 203; II, 62, cf. also ἡ ἀλήθεια καὶ τὸ συμφέρον in Jos., 77; τὰ δίκαια καὶ συμφέροντα, Spec. Leg., II, 236. We find the series τὸ καλόν, τὸ ἀγαθόν, τὸ δίκαιον, τὸ φρόνιμον, τὸ ἀνδρεῖον, τὸ εὐσεβές, τὸ ὅσιον, τὸ συμφέρον, τὸ ὠφέλιμον, Jos., 143 → 72, 14 ff. It is καλὸν καὶ συμφέρον, πειθαρχεῖν ἀρετῇ, Ebr., 16, cf. Virt., 181; Det. Pot. Ins., 53. But striving for ἡδονή takes place ἀγνοίᾳ τοῦ συμφέροντος, Som., II, 150, cf. also Leg. Gaj., 21; Deus Imm., 135. The συμφέρον is always to be preferred to the ἡδύ, Agric., 48; Jos., 62; Praem. Poen., 33; Som., II, 9. This is true so long as the νοῦς rules the ψυχή (Leg. All., III, 84), then ἐνδίκως ἄπαντα καὶ συμφερόντως ἐπιτελεῖται (Som., II, 153). Cleansing from ἐπιθυμία is συμφέρον, Spec. Leg., I, 206. Finally, of course, it is εὐσέβεια (Spec. Leg., I, 250), σὺν θεῷ (Abr., 18) or ἡ τοῦ θεοῦ φαντασία (Cher., 13) that lead to the καλὸν καὶ συμφέρον.

3. Joseph. uses συμφέρω both lit. "to bring together," χρήματα συμφέρω, Ant., 16, 45 and also in the sense "to profit." Abraham taught Sarah συμφέρειν αὐτοῖς when he pretended she was his sister in Egypt, Ant., 1, 162. The depiction of Ananus II as πρό τε τῶν ἰδίων λυσιτελῶν τὸ κοινῇ συμφέρον ἀεὶ τιθέμενος in Bell., 4, 320 is modelled on Onias in 2 Macc. 4:5 (→ lines 1 ff.). The advantage or profit is always secular. This is also the point in the expression τὰ ἑαυτοῖς συμφέροντα, cf. Vit., 370.

4. In the Dead Sea Scrolls ואתה אל צויתם להועיל להועיל מדרכיהם is the rendering of Is. 48:17 in 1 QH 6:20. Apart from this the roots corresponding to συμφέρω (→ 73, 25 ff.) have not been found thus far in Qumran.

5. In Test. XII the conduct of the righteous and what God gives them are both called profitable. Thus we read of intercession for others without envy: ἐστὶν ὑμῖν συμφέρον, Test. G. 7:1. God extends to all men τὰ καλὰ καὶ συμφέροντα, 7:2. Man's life and abiding ἐν σωφροσύνῃ are the basic presupposition on which God grants external circumstances, whether affliction or δόξα, according to His wisdom, and as is always profitable συμφέρει to the righteous, Jos. 9: 2 f.

6. In Rabb. texts יעל hi and the noun תּוֹעֶלֶת, sometimes also תּוֹחֶלֶת from יחל "to expect," "to wait steadfastly," denotes "profit," "advantage," "success" in business, bMeg., 6a, claims to property, bBB, 100a, "the effectiveness" or not of a bill of divorce, bGit., 17b; 65b, a petition, 57b, a mark to fix Sabbath ways, bErub., 24b, "the success" (or failure) of a falsification of the text in the Samaritan Pent., jSota, 7, 3 (21c, 35); bSanh., 90b. Strictly religious or philosophical considerations are not linked with the term. 10 On the other hand the Rabb. use Hbr. נוֹחַ לוֹ and Aram. טַב לֵיהּ when they discuss in various contexts what is "(more) profitable" for man, esp. which of two evils

---

9 E.g., the words τὸ παράπαν οὐκ ὠφελήσουσιν ὑμᾶς (no HT) at 'Ιερ. 7:4.
10 For further material cf. Levy Wört. and Jastrow, s.v. יעל, תּוֹעֶלֶת, תּוֹחֶלֶת.

is the lesser. This question is of decisive significance for man's religious destiny. Thus the schools of Shammai and Hillel debate whether "it is better for man" נוֹחַ לוֹ לְאָדָם to have been created or not, bErub., 13b Bar. That it "is better" not to have been born is said in jBer., 1, 4 (3b, 25 f.) of the man who does not act acc. to what he learns (sc. the Law); cf. Lv. r., 35, 7 on 26:3. "It were better" (נוֹחַ לָרְשָׁעִים) for the wicked if they were blind, for through their eyes (their covetous glances) they bring a curse into the world, Nu. r., 20, 2 on 22:2. The "profit" in view is always without doubt the avoidance of judgment and eternal punishments, to which the lesser evil is preferred, cf. expressly Tg. pal. on Gn. 38:26: [11] (Judah speaks) טב לי to be shamed in this world, or to be burned with fire that can be quenched than with future and consuming fire. R. Tarphon (c. 100) said: He whose hand touches his shame, his hand should be hewed off at the navel ... It is better טָב לֵיהּ that his belly should be cut open than that he should plunge into the pit of perdition, bNidda, 13b Bar.

D. The Word Group in the New Testament.

I. Usage.

1. The only instance of συμφέρω in the lit. sense "to bring together" is at Ac. 19:19. In the sense "to profit" it occurs in the following constr.: abs. 1 C. 6:12; 10:23; 2 C. 12:1, with dat. of pers. 2 C. 8:10, with ἵνα following Mt. 5:29 f.; 18:6; Jn. 11:50; 16:7, and with inf. Mt. 19:10; Jn. 18:14. [12] The part. as noun occurs in sing. and plur. abs. at Ac. 20:20; 1 C. 12:7; Hb. 12:10.

2. τὸ σύμφορον "profit," "advantage" with gen. of pers. is used in 1 C. 7:35; 10:33.

II. Meaning.

1. When in transmission of sayings of Jesus about what is profitable the Synoptic Gospels vary in the use of συμφέρει, καλόν ἐστι and λυσιτελεῖ, this does not mean that they have adopted the corresponding equations from Greek philosophy → 71, 14 ff. These are simply different translations of the Hbr. נוֹחַ לוֹ or Aram. טָב לֵיהּ (→ 74, 46 ff.), so that we remain within the biblical and Jewish sphere of thought and expression. In Mt. 5:29 f.; 18:8 f. and par. the maiming of the body by the cutting off of a member that incites to sin (→ VII, 351, 31 ff.) is demanded on the ground that it is more profitable (συμφέρει) or advantageous (καλόν... ἤ) than the alternative destruction of the whole body, i.e., the whole person (→ VII, 1058, 9 ff.) in eternal hell-fire. The profit that Jesus has in view in this demand is thus εἰσελθεῖν εἰς ζωήν. [13] The sharpest form of the question of what is profitable is when the issue is not one's own salvation, however, but that of one τῶν μικρῶν (→ IV, 650, 31 ff.) τούτων τῶν πιστευόντων εἰς ἐμέ. He who leads one such astray in faith and thus causes him to miss eternal salvation, for him it would be more profitable συμφέρει αὐτῷ (Mt. 18:6; cf. Mk. 9:42: καλόν ἐστιν αὐτῷ μᾶλλον, Lk. 17:2: λυσιτελεῖ αὐτῷ) if he were drowned in the depths of the sea with a mill-stone about his

---

[11] Ed. P. Kahle, "Masoreten d. Westens, II," BWANT, 50 (1930), 43 f., cf. 19.
[12] Bl.-Debr. § 393.
[13] Whether the οὐ συμφέρει γαμῆσαι of the disciples in Mt. 19:10 belongs here, i.e., whether in acc. with Jesus' saying about leaving wives in Lk. 18:29; 14:26 and Paul's discussion in 1 C. 7:35 (→ 76, 25 ff.) they have in view what is profitable for discipleship and the kingdom of God, is open to question. It may be that οὐ συμφέρει simply ref. to the difficulties of a marriage that is no longer wanted, cf. Zn. Mt., 592.

neck. [14] Since the reference is to the one who seduces rather than the one seduced, the attaining of eternal life and avoiding of eternal perdition must be seen as the profit which is purchased with the loss of earthly life → VII, 351, 23 ff.

2. John's Gospel speaks in two different connections of ways in which Jesus' death is of profit. In 11:50 the saying of Caiaphas: συμφέρει ὑμῖν, ἵνα εἷς ἄνθρωπος ἀποθάνῃ ὑπὲρ τοῦ λαοῦ, is taken to be an unwitting prophecy of the true profit of this death; the profit consists in the gathering together in one of the children of God scattered abroad in the world, v. 52. This is again the special effect of the self-sacrifice of Jesus acc. to 10:15 f.; 12:32 f. It is, of course, a process which reaches its goal only in the heavenly world and the future beyond the confines of this space and time, 14:3; 17:24. In contrast, the context of 16:7 ff. has in view the way in which Jesus' going to the Father is profitable for the present life of the community. The profit now is the sending of the Spirit, which according to 7:39, too, presupposes the entry of Jesus into the glory of the Father. It is unfolded in the twofold function of the Spirit, who outwardly represents the community and its message to the unbelieving world as its accuser and judge, and who inwardly instructs the community in divine secrets and future things as the Spirit of truth. [15]

3. Paul uses συμφέρει, συμφέρον and τὸ σύμφορον for what profits the spiritual life. There are two aspects here. In 1 C. 6:12 he uses the formula πάντα μοι ἔξεστιν (→ II, 570, 10 ff.; 575, 7 ff.), ἀλλ' οὐ πάντα συμφέρει, to introduce a discussion of the use of the σῶμα appropriate to a Christian (→ VII, 1062, 29 ff.). Since the Christian's body belongs to the Lord, and is a temple of Christ and of the Holy Spirit indwelling the Christian, any union with a harlot in fornication is excluded. Hence one may say of it: οὐ συμφέρει. The profit at issue here is individual spiritual existence, the union of each Christian with the Lord and of the Lord with him. Paul's interest is the same when he gives advice about marriage to the young people of Corinth. Their σύμφορον (1 C. 7:35) consists in their sanctifying καὶ τῷ σώματι καὶ τῷ πνεύματι (v. 34). If here again the profit Paul has in view is in the individual Christian life, in μεριμνᾶν τὰ τοῦ κυρίου and the expression which terminates the discussion: πρὸς τὸ εὔσχημον καὶ εὐπάρεδρον τῷ κυρίῳ ἀπερισπάστως (v. 35) his gaze seems to be on the profit which the ministry of young people can and should entail for the community and its mission. This is the other aspect which is much more prominent in Paul in determining what is profitable. συμφέρον is that which edifies the community. The profit of the individual is far less important than this. This ranks first for Paul himself and his apostolic ministry: μὴ ζητῶν τὸ ἐμαυτοῦ σύμφορον ἀλλὰ τὸ τῶν πολλῶν, ἵνα σωθῶσιν (1 C. 10:33). The reason he speaks only under compulsion of the ὀπτασίαι and ἀποκαλύψεις κυρίου imparted to him is that he regards them as οὐ συμφέρον in relation to those he must serve as an apostle (2 C. 12:1) → I, 440, 17 ff. What really builds up the community is

---

[14] Cf. the saying of Jesus about the one who delivers Him up into the hands of unbelieving Jews καλὸν ἦν αὐτῷ, εἰ οὐκ ἐγεννήθη ὁ ἄνθρωπος ἐκεῖνος, Mt. 26:24.

[15] Jn. 6:63 also speaks indirectly of what profit the Spirit brings by ref. in contrast to the σάρξ that profits ὠφελεῖ nothing. Again there is a relation between the death of Jesus and the giving of the Spirit, esp. as the ἀναβαίνειν of v. 62 seems to point to the cross, cf. Bultmann J. on 6:62; H. Strathmann, Das Ev. nach Joh., NT Deutsch, 4[10] (1963), ad loc. If so the train of thought, as in 16:7, is that only when My flesh, which profits nothing, is offered up in death, does the life-giving Spirit come to you. Another sense obtains if v. 63a b is construed in the light of 63c (→ VII, 140, 4 ff.), cf. Strathmann, ad loc.

love. It is with this assertion that he begins the long discussion of the eating (→ II, 694, 1 ff.) of meat offered to idols (1 C. 8:1), and he closes the discussion by equating what συμφέρει with what οἰκοδομεῖ (→ V, 141, 39 ff.), 10:23. Similarly the basic rule for the charismata granted to the whole community is: πρὸς τὸ συμφέρον, 1 C. 12:7. In the middle of the discussion (c. 12-14) of the different value and profit of these gifts stands love as καθ' ὑπερβολὴν ὁδός (12:31; 13). This is the power which Paul also mobilises for the collection — a work that serves to build up the fellowship consisting of both Jews and Gentiles. For this, says Paul, ὑμῖν συμφέρει, 2 C. 8:8-10. Lk. pertinently formulates the nature and intention of Paul's apostolic work in the saying uttered by Paul in his farewell address to the Asiatic communities: οὐδὲν ὑπεστειλάμην τῶν συμφερόντων τοῦ μὴ ἀναγγεῖλαι ὑμῖν καὶ διδάξαι ὑμᾶς δημοσίᾳ, καὶ κατ' οἴκους, Ac. 20:20.

This is the point where we can see most clearly the difference between what the NT regards as profitable and what the Greeks and Jews regard as profitable. The supreme conception of which Greek thought was capable was that of the submerging of one's own profit in that of the πόλις (→ 71, 18 ff.) and finally of the κόσμος (→ 72, 33 ff.). The guiding principle for the Jew was ultimately that of what is serviceable to the actualisation of a nationally determined and limited theocracy (→ 74, 1 ff.). But the πολίτευμα (→ VI, 535, 8 ff.) of Christians ἐν οὐρανοῖς ὑπάρχει, Phil. 3:20. [16] It is what Col. 3:1 ff. calls τὰ ἄνω where Christ is seated at the right hand of God, from whence Christians await Him, but where their life is already hidden with Him because they are risen with Him. Hence Paul directs their thinking and aspiration thither, and he knows for his own conduct and that of all Christians no other profit than that which serves to build up the ἐκκλησία τοῦ θεοῦ, a comprehensive community of the chosen of God which ignores all social, political and national boundaries, which embraces both this aeon and the future aeon (→ I, 207, 25 ff.), and which finds actualisation in the concretely defined ἐκκλησίαι in Rome, Corinth and elsewhere, [17] → III, 506, 2 ff. To what is profitable to this community he subordinates even to the point of self-sacrifice all other profit, including that of the individual.

4. In Hb. the sufferings and difficulties of the recipients of the letter, whom the author exhorts to patient and trusting endurance, are described as the παιδεία which God assigns to them as His sons ἐπὶ τὸ συμφέρον εἰς τὸ μεταλαβεῖν τῆς ἁγιότητος αὐτοῦ, 12:10. The question arises whether the reference is to moral perfecting in this life or to participation in the holiness of God in eternal life. If a real alternative is seen here, we must opt for the latter. [18]

---

[16] G. Delling, R. 13:1-7 innerhalb der Briefe d. NT[1] (1963), 32 f. does not think the πολίτευμα of Phil. 3:20 has any "political" sense since it has no political counterpart on earth. He also links Phil. 3:20 very closely with Col. 3:1 ff.

[17] Cf. K. L. Schmidt, "Die Polis in Kirche u. Welt," Baseler Rektoratsprogramm (1939), esp. 14-40, 108-110; W. Bieder, Ekklesia u. Polis im NT u. in der Alten Kirche (1941), 19-22, 78.

[18] The comm. usually find an exclusive or predominant ref. to moral perfecting in this life. This certainly finds support in the prospect of καρπὸς εἰρηνικός ... δικαιοσύνης (gen. appos.) in v. 11. But cf. C. Spicq, L'Ép. aux Hébreux, II, Études Bibl. (1953) on 12:11: "δικαιοσύνης ... peut désigner l'acquisition de la vertu, la rectitude morale et l'union à Dieu ..., mais plus sûrement la béatitude éternelle." The main argument for profit in heavenly perfection is the broader context. In c. 11 the martyrs and in c. 12 Jesus Himself are models of the παιδεία that Christians undergo. The former did not attain the promise in this life and Jesus came to share God's throne only after He had experienced the cross and shame rather

E. The Profitable and Useful in the Post-Apostolic Fathers.

Ign. uses συμφέρω for what can lead to eternal fellowship with Christ. It is the martyrdom to which he moves full of desire, R., 5, 3. To the heretics against whom he warns in Sm., 5 ff. ἀγαπᾶν would yield the profit συνέφερεν of making participant in the resurrection, 7, 1. [19] The context of Barn., 4, 10 shows that this, too, has the goal of eternal life in view when it calls for common deliberation περὶ τοῦ κοινῇ συμφέροντος. In 4, 12 συμφέρον itself is the moral and spiritual perfection of the Christian, his δικαιοσύνη, which will go before him in the judgment. Hermas commends as σύμφορον the words of the old lady about the glorious world which God prepares for the elect who keep his commandments (v., 1, 3, 3), a walk in the ἐντολαί [20] of the Shepherd (s., 6, 1, 3) and delight in good works (s., 6, 5, 7). All these things serve the attainment of life, although it is not clear whether the ref. is to the future life with God or ζῆν τῷ θεῷ (s., 6, 1, 4) in this world. [21] In the depiction of the crooked way of unrighteousness that is full of obstacles and thorns as contrasted with the straight and level way of righteousness (m., 6, 1, 3-5) we are told that the one is βλαβερά whereas to walk the other is συμφορώτερον. Here it is apparent that the profit is that which an upright life represents as such.

† φόρος.

A. φόρος outside the New Testament.

1. A verbal abstr. of φέρω, φόρος means strictly "carrying," "bringing." It then denotes the tribute to be paid by subject peoples, [1] Hdt., I, 6, 2; 27, 1; II, 182, 2, κατὰ φόρους ἐν ἔτεσι δέκα "tributes to be paid in ten yearly instalments," Polyb., 18, 44, 7, the "dues" to be paid into the common fund by members of the Athenian naval alliance, [2] Thuc., I, 56, 2, in money: [3] (φόρος) ὠνομάσθη τῶν χρημάτων ἡ φορά, I, 96, 2, cf. also Plat. Gorg., 519a, though the word can sometimes be used for more gen. levies, services, or payments, Plat. Polit., 298a; Plut. Anton., 24 (I, 926b), including those which

---

than joy in this life. The πρὸς ὀλίγας ἡμέρας applied to the παιδεία of the earthly father in v. 10 also prevents us from seeing a temporal restriction or earthly goal for the divine παιδεία, cf. H. v. Soden, Hebräerbr., Br. d. Petrus, Jak., Judas, Hand-Comm. z. NT, III, 2² (1893), ad loc. and F. Bleek, Der Br. an d. Hb., II, 2 (1840), 892, who lists those who have held the view represented here → V, 622, n. 172.

[19] Bau. Ign., ad loc. and Pr.-Bauer, s.v. ἀγαπάω, 2 construe ἀπαπᾶν as ἀγάπην ποιεῖν "to hold a love-feast," but this is unlikely, since the meal from which the heretics hold aloof is called εὐχαριστία in 7, 1 and there is no linguistic support for this meaning. In 6, 2 the heretics are accused of a complete lack of active love, so that it makes sense that this should be demanded as profitable for participation in the resurrection.

[20] Cf. on this Dib. Herm. on v., 5, 5.

[21] Ibid. on m., 1, 2.

φόρος. [1] The word also has this sense in the tax-policies of the Alexander states. It means here the tribute as a property tax which the Diadochi princes imposed along with many other royal taxes, v. M. Rostovtzeff, Gesellschafts- u. Wirtschaftsgesch. d. hell. Welt, I-III (1955), I, 107 f., 266, 343-8, 361-6, 414-6 etc.

[2] On the corresponding levies and payments of the allies to the headquarters in Sparta v. U. Kahrstedt, Gr. Staatsrecht, I (1922), 337-341; W. Schwahn, Art. "Τέλη," Pauly-W., 5a (1934), 260. Plut has φόροι for the taxes for the Delian alliance imposed by Aristides, De Aristide, 24 (I, 333e), ἀποφορά εἰς τὸν πόλεμον for the levies to be paid to Sparta in the Persian wars, 24 (I, 333c) and εἰσφοραί for the taxes to pay for the Peloponnesian war, De Cleomene, 27 (I, 817e).

[3] In gen. there is no distinction between payments in kind and in money.

strictly fall under the concept of τέλη (→ VIII, 51, 1 ff.; 53, 23) [4] τότε μὲν ἐγὼ φόρον ἀπέφερον τῷ δήμῳ, νῦν δὲ ἡ πόλις τέλος φέρουσα τρέφει με (sc. Charmides, who has meantime been brought to poverty), Xenoph. Symp., 4, 32, the "tax" the Lacedaemonians had to pay to their own king, Ps.-Plat. Alc., I, 123a. The word occurs in the following combinations: φόρον τάττω "to impose," Andoc., 4, 11, φόρον ἀπάγω, Aristoph. Vesp., 707, cf. φόρου ἀπαγωγή, Hdt., I, 6, 2, φόρον φέρω, Aristoph. Av., 191; Xenoph. An., V, 5, 7, φόρον (ὑπο)τελέω, Hdt., I, 171, 2, all in the sense "to pay," and cf. also φόροι ἥκουσιν ("flow in"), Aristoph. Ach., 505 f., cf. φόρος προσιών, Vesp., 657; φόρον δέχομαι "to collect," Thuc., I, 96, 2.

If one may credit the accounts transmitted in Harp., s.v., σύνταξις, then χαλεπῶς ἔφερον οἱ Ἕλληνες τὸ τῶν φόρων ὄνομα. So too, acc. to Plut. De Solone, 15 (I, 86c), the Athenians, as they gen. disguised unpleasant things ὀνόμασι χρηστοῖς καὶ φιλανθρώποις ἐπικαλύπτοντες ἀστείως, also called φόροι συντάξεις. [5] Acc. to Theopompus Fr., 98 (FGrHist., IIb, 557) Callistratus first introduced this designation.

In the pap. the word has in private life the meaning "lease," "rent," "hire," so for an oil-mill, P. Giess., I, 95, 4 (95 A.D.), pasture, P. Oxy., X, 1279, 19 (139 A.D.), land, XVII, 2141, 2 (208 A.D.?). The use of the plur. seems to increase with this shift of sense. P. Tebt., II, 377, 23. 27 (210 B.C.) makes a clear distinction between φόρος (in money) and ἐκφόριον (in kind).

2. Hbr. equivalents of the term are מְנָחָה, מִדָּה, Aram and new Hbr. מִנְדָּה, מֶכֶס and עֹנֶשׁ. Materially מִנְחָה "gift" gradually takes on the sense of "tribute," i.e., the gift to placate a menacing enemy, e.g., to Esau in Gn. 32:14 ff.; 33:10, to a powerful person whose favour is sought, Gn. 43:11 (Joseph), gifts to one's own ruler, 2 Ch. 17:5, or an alien king, 1 K. 5:1; 10:25 etc. and esp. payments made to a victorious enemy, Ju. 3:15 ff.; 2 K. 17:3 f. מִדָּה or מִנְדָּה is esp. used in Ezr. and Neh. for the "poll-tax" to be paid to the great king. In Nu. 31:28, 37-41 מֶכֶס is the "tribute of war-booty" to be paid to Yahweh to make expiation for the soldiers. In 2 K. 23:33 עֹנֶשׁ means a "war-contribution."

3. In the Rabb. there are many terms for fiscal levies, tributes, taxes etc. Some of them are taken as loan words from other languages and it is not always possible to define them precisely. From the list repeated in Ezr. 4:13, 20; 7:24 מִנְדָּה בְלוֹ וַהֲלָךְ are interpreted in Est. rabba Intr. 5 on 1:1 (1d, 24 f., cf. Wünsche, 4) as מִנְדָּה "land-tax," בְלוֹ "poll-tax" and הֲלָךְ "statute-labour" (?), while in bBB, 8a the first two are "the king's share of the harvest" and "the poll-tax" כסף גולגלתא, and in Gn. r., 91, 4 on 42:6 מִדָּה is the "gate-tax" of the sons of Jacob in Egypt. מֶכֶס is the "toll" which belongs to the king (bSukka, 30a) and which was levied by the Romans, bAZ, 2b. Acc. to RAbba (c. 290 A.D.) God protects the man who gives alms from פיסין "imposts," זימיות (ζημία) "fines," גולגוליות "poll-taxes" and ארנוניות (annona?) "taxes in kind," jPea, 1, 1 (15b, 53 f.). Lv. r., 33, 5 on 25:14 mentions with these מסין (from מַס → 80, 6 ff.), Pesikt., 2 (11b-12a, cf.

---

[4] The interfusion of the terms was perhaps furthered by the fact that not a few of the independent states that belonged to the Athenian alliance became Attic dependencies and were incorporated into the Attic federation. This meant that Athens — wholly so from 413 B.C. — collected their τέλη and esp. their "tolls," cf. W. Schwahn, Art. "Phoroi," Pauly-W., 20 (1941), 545-644. The tax on property raised by the citizens of Athens is called εἰσφορά, Thuc., III, 19, 1.

[5] The word first means "agreement," Polyb., 5, 3, 3, then "arrangement of payments," 5, 95, 1, and finally the "payments" themselves, Plut. Alex , 21 (I, 676c). Cf. W. Schwahn, Art. "Σύνταξις," Pauly-W., 4a (1932), 1453-6.

Wünsche, 11) and דימוסיא (from δημόσια). [6] This rich terminology reflects the foreign governments and the various taxes they entailed for the Jews.

4. The LXX uses φόρος predominantly for "tribute," e.g., in 2 Ch. 36:3 the "tribute" Necho imposed on the land of Judah after the deposition of Jehoahaz. [7] The threefold formula above (→ 79, 30 f.) is transl. in 2 Εσδρ. 4:13, 20 by φόροι, and in 7:24 φόρος The plur. occurs at 6:8; 15:4 for a simple מִדָּה → 79, 26 f. [8] φόρος is most often the transl. of מַס "statute-labour" in the expressions γίγνομαι εἰς φόρον (HT הָיָה לָמַס), "to be or to become liable to forced labour," Ju. 1:29 ff. etc., ποιεῖν εἰς φόρον (HT שׂוּם לָמַס), "to impose forced labour," Ju. 1:28, ἐπὶ τοῦ φόρου (HT עַל הַמַּס), "overseer over those who do forced labour," 2 S. 20:24, ἀναφέρω φόρον (HT הֶעֱלָה מַס), "to enlist forced labourers," 1 K. 5:27. But here too, if the context does not fix the meaning, the Gk. might mean "tribute" [9] esp. when the expression is an addition to the HT ἐγένοντο αὐτοῖς εἰς φόρον, Jos. 19:48a. The goods which flow into Solomon's treasury as dues are also called φόροι in 1 K. 10:15. [10]

5. Philo in Spec. Leg., I, 142 contrasts the taxes which the Law lays down for the priests with the φόροι paid to ἡγεμόνες, and he has in view the "tribute" which αἱ πόλεις τοῖς δυνάσταις εἰσφέρουσιν, usually once a year, IV, 212. The ἐκλογεὺς φόρων of which he tells in III, 159, however, is searching for fugitives from the census, so that the ref. is to a "poll-tax." The sense is not specified in the comparison καθάπερ δεσποίναις οἰκέται φόρον τελοῦντες καθ᾽ ἑκάστην ἡμέραν ἀναγκαῖον, Agric., 58.

6. Joseph. uses φόρος in the sing. and plur., always in the sense of "tribute" to a foreign ruler. He tells of φόροι which the Philistines exacted of the Israelites ἐλάμβανον in Ant., 5, 275, and which these paid to the Assyrians ἐτέλουν, 181, cf. 12, 182. Tribute was also paid to the Roman emperor, Bell., 2, 403, [11] and to Ptolemy Euergetes, Ant., 12, 158. Since it is said of David that he "took" (ἐδέχετο) φόρους ὑπέρ τε τῆς χώρας καὶ τῆς ἑκάστου κεφαλῆς from the conquered Idumaeans (Ant., 7, 109), Jos. could also include among φόροι the "poll-taxes" paid to the Seleucid rulers, of which he says: ἃ ὑπὲρ τῆς κεφαλῆς τελοῦσι, 12, 142, and ὑπὲρ κεφαλῆς ἑκάστης ὃ ἔδει… δίδοσθαι, 13, 50.

B. φόρος in the New Testament.

1. In the NT we find φόρος or φόροι alongside τέλος, R. 13:6 f. In Lk. 20:22;

---

[6] Further examples of all the words in Levy Wört., Levy Chald. Wört., s.v. and Str.-B., I, 770 f. Whether מַכְסָא, which is attested for Sassanid. Babylon, bGit., 58b; bBM, 73b; 110a, bBB, 54b belongs here is open to question, since the texts do not enable us to decide between "lease" and "royal land-tax," and it is also debatable whether the term and thing might not be earlier. Cf. Rostovtzeff, op. cit. (→ n. 1), I, 365.

[7] At the par. 2 K. 23:33 HT has עֹנֶשׁ, transl. ζημία in LXX.

[8] At the relevant passages we find δῶρα for מִנְחָה. At 2 K. 17:3 f. it is simply transcribed as μαναα (Cod. B μαναχ).

[9] This seems to be confirmed by the transl. of נֹגֵשׂ "overseer of forced labour" by φορολόγος "tax-collector" at Job 3:18; 39:7, even though the transl. does not fit too well in the latter instance. The view is also favoured by the transl. of מִנְחָה at 2 S. 8:2 Σ (8:1 is construed accordingly by Σ); 2 K. 17:3 Σ, and of מַס at Prv. 12:24 ᾽ΑΣ and Is. 31:8 ᾽ΑΣΘ by φόρος. The meaning of φόρος at Gn. 49:15 ᾽Α is doubtful ("statute-labour"?) [Bertram].

[10] On the basis of the Syr. transl. of the par. 2 Ch. 9:14 BHK proposes מֵאַנְשֵׁי for HT מֵעֹנְשֵׁי.

[11] Interchangeably here with εἰσφορά, Bell., 2, 404.

23:2 it is a substitute for the Latin loan word κῆνσος, [12] Mk. 12:14 and par. In agreement with contemporary usage φόρος/φόροι means in all the references "tribute" paid to a foreign ruler, whether as "land-tax" or "poll-tax." It differs from τέλη, [13] i.e., the "tolls," "use-taxes," "customs dues" and "business taxes" which either native authorities or an alien power, in this case the Roman emperor, might exact. The problem in the texts, then, is that of the relation of members of God's people, both Jews and Christians, to pagan government. After the census of Quirinius in 6 A.D. and the opposition stirred up against it by Judas the Galilean, [14] the imposing of the φόρος and the collection of τέλη for the emperor gave new pertinence to the question as to the right of an earthly ruler to tax the people that belongs to God alone. If the term φόρος carried with it the odium of bondage for the Greeks (→ 79, 10 ff.), it posed for the Jews the alternative of loyalty or treason to God as the one and only Lord.

It is against this general historical background that we are to consider the specific account in Mk. 12:13 ff. and par. of the action and motives of those who asked Jesus about paying tribute. [15] This incident simply serves to bring the problem into focus along with the dilemma for Jesus. Jesus' answer can hardly be regarded as a judgment in the historically posed alternative between Zealot rejection and Pharisaic acceptance of the obligation to pay taxes. One certainly cannot regard Jesus as a champion of the Pharisaic solution of the problem. [16] Rather His answer lifts the problem on to another plane. It abandons to the earthly ruler the restricted claim of God to possession of this specific land and people with its politico-legal consequences in the Jewish sense (→ II, 387, 32 ff.), but then it immediately raises it again in a non-restricted sense. This means in practice that Jesus' answer transcends the question of the imperial tax as such by alluding to the universality of God's claim to dominion. In its enigmatic brevity it offers no basis for answering the question how this claim is to be realised and how the φόρος problem will finally be solved. The fact that the answer is anchored in the eschatological fulfilment of the kingdom of God [17] and

---

[12] A census is first an assessing of taxable property in capital, land and slaves, then the list of this, the tax-register, then the taxable property itself, and finally the sum exacted as poll-tax or land-tax, v. W. Kubitschek, Art. "Census," Pauly-W., 3 (1899), 1914-1924. κῆνσος in Mt. 17:25; 22:17, 19 is used in the final sense, whereas Lk. transl. the term by ἀπογραφή (Lk. 2:2 and Ac. 5:37) in acc. with the first sense, v. F. X. Steinmetzer, Art. "Census," RAC, II, 969 f. The use of the loan word קְנָס in the Rabb. sheds no light on the meaning of κῆνσος in the NT. It means there the money payment for punishable acts, bBQ, 38b; 41b; bKet., 35b; 36a, esp. the raping of virgins, Ket., 3, 1. 3. 8; bKet., 29a b; 42a; 43a. Criminal cases are called דִּינֵי קְנָסוֹת, bSanh., 8a b; 31b. J. Klausner, Jesus of Nazareth (1929), 162 traces back this use of the word to the reaction of the Jews against the census of Quirinius.

[13] The φόρος - τέλος of R. 13:7 should be compared with τέλη ἢ κῆνσος for the taxes exacted from ἀλλότριοι by the βασιλεῖς τῆς γῆς, Mt. 17:25.

[14] Cf. Ac. 5:37; Jos. Bell., 7, 253 ff.; Ant., 18, 3 ff.; M. Hengel, "Die Zeloten," Arbeiten z. Gesch. d. Spätjudt. u. des Urchr., 1 (1961), 132-145; B. Reicke, Nt.liche Zeitgeschichte (1965), 101 f.; S. G. F. Brandon, Jesus and the Zealots (1967), 30-38.

[15] Cf. the comm.; E. Haenchen, Der Weg Jesu (1966), ad loc.; E. Schweizer, Das Ev. nach Mk., NT Deutsch, 1² (1968) ad loc.

[16] There is even less ground for the attempt to interpret Jesus' answer along Zealot lines, cf. R. Eisler, ΙΗΣΟΥΣ ΒΑΣΙΛΕΥΣ ΟΥ ΒΑΣΙΛΕΥΣΑΣ, II (1930), 201 and Brandon, op. cit., 347.

[17] Loh. Mk. ad loc. speaks of the "imminence of the eschatological kingdom of God which will smash even the colossus of Caesarian rule like an earthen and earthly vessel." Cf.

the decision of the individual Christian standing responsibly before God [18] means that more is involved than the specific content of the saying. In this regard it leaves the question open.

2. Luke in his version of the story is able to use the saying as part of his apologetic to the Roman authorities. The two incidents in Lk. 20:20 ff. and 23:1 ff. may be seen together. They seem to be intentionally interrelated by the author. [19] In 23:2 the hearing before Pilate begins with members of the Sanhedrin accusing Jesus of revolutionary agitation including incitement not to pay the φόρος. In the course of the hearing the charge is repeated but on three occasions Pilate answers it by saying that he finds no fault in Jesus. It is expressly exposed as a lie; hence an interpretation seems to be offered of the tribute question and Jesus' answer to it in 20:20 ff. As is specifically added in 20:20, the real point of the question was to incite Jesus to disloyal repudiation of the tribute and to make Him culpable thereby. But Jesus, as Luke understands His decision, does not violate His loyalty, and the preaching of the Gospel by the community is thus relieved of the stigma of disloyalty.

3. Whether Paul with his demand for the payment of φόρος and τέλος in R. 13:7 is following the Synoptic saying of Jesus we cannot say for certain, but it seems likely enough. [20] This does not mean, however, that we should overlook the difference in the setting and purpose of Paul's statement. Since the character of the Roman church at the time of the epistle is still open to debate, [21] there is no solid basis for the hypothesis that relates the warning to the ἀντιτασσόμενος and ἀνθεστηκότες in 13:2 to particular movements in the Roman community, whether these be Jewish-Zealot [22] on the one side or pneumatic-enthusiastic [23] on the other. Since there is no possibility, then, of referring the hortatory complex of c. 12-13 and its detailed admonitions to specific situations in the church at Rome, we must be content, as regards the attitude to the state taught in this section, simply to assume as the background and occasion the general likelihood that Christians adopted a latently or patently negative position vis-à-vis state power. [24] It is natural enough that this subject should be treated with special emphasis in a letter to the Roman community. [25] Finally, the Jewish difficulty that lies behind

---

Haenchen, op. cit. (→ n. 15) on 12:17: "For the other Synoptists this aeon is already more or less at an end."

[18] Cf. Schweizer, op. cit. (→ n. 15) on 12:17: "Thus Jesus does not anticipate man's answer in this practical decision but sets him before God, before whom alone he must find and return his Yes or No in a given case."

[19] Cf. H. Conzelmann, Die Mitte d. Zeit[5] (1964), 78 and 130.

[20] Mi. R.[13], ad loc.; O. Cullmann, Der Staat im NT[2] (1961), 43 (E.T. [1956], 55 ff.); G. Delling, R. 13:1-7 innerhalb d. Br. d. NT (1962), 16 f., 19; F. Neugebauer, "Zur Auslegung v. R. 13:1-7," Kerygma u. Dogma, 8 (1962), 165 etc.

[21] On the discussion cf. W. G. Kümmel, Einl. in d. NT[15] (1967), 221 f.

[22] Cf. the discussion of this thesis in Delling, op. cit. (→ n. 20), 18 f.; E. Käsemann, "R. 13:1-7 in unserer Generation," ZThK, 56 (1959), 318.

[23] Mi. R.[13], 314; Käsemann, op. cit. (→ n. 22), 376.

[24] Cf. the well-considered judgment of Schl. R., 350 on this issue.

[25] It is rather different if documented historical matters affecting the Roman church are adduced in explanation, cf. A. Strobel, "Furcht, wem Furcht gebührt," ZNW, 55 (1964), 58-62, who argues that the granting of "full jurisdiction in fiscal matters" to the imperial procurator by resolve of the Senate in 53 A.D. is the "immediate occasion of the writing of R. 13:1-7" and esp. of the demand for fear of the state. Yet even this is, of course, only a hypothesis.

the question of the tribute put to Jesus in the Synoptics may be explicitly ruled out in R. 13 if, as is generally agreed, [26] v. 6a is to be taken in the indicative. For in this case the payment of taxes is so self-evident for the Roman church that Paul can regard it as palpable proof that there is a duty of obedience to the government. To establish this interpretation he uses in v. 6b the argument that rulers constantly and energetically discharge their prescribed functions as ministers of God → IV, 231, 4 ff. The argument has concrete significance if one sees in it a tacit reference to the force they use in doing this. [27] This also explains why Paul then issues a very general exhortation to pay φόρος and τέλος (v. 7) even though he could presuppose the regular fulfilment of this in the previous v. (6).

Exegetes usually take it that the section on the attitude to the state ends in v. 7. This means that the demand for payment of taxes is the goal, that it has a disproportionate emphasis within the totality, and that the erroneous assumption arises that Paul was really dealing with the tribute question → 79, 4 ff. It is surely obvious, however, that v. 7 itself is part of the broader context of exhortation in c. 12-13. This is suggested not merely by the asyndetic character of the v. but also and esp. by the new motivation the duty to pay taxes is given by its incorporation in a series of obligations the Christian must discharge to all men. Thus v. 7 stands in direct relation to v. 8, which repeats the admonition in negative form. [28] A wrong overstressing of the duty to pay taxes within the total exhortation is thus avoided and a more precise definition of its place is given alongside the other and undoubtedly more important obligations of the Christian, namely, the showing of → φόβος, τιμή (→ VIII, 174, 18 ff.), and finally of ἀγάπη (→ I, 51, 11 ff.). Furthermore, there is no more need to restrict the πᾶσιν of v. 7, or the showing of φόβος and τιμή, to the ἐξουσίαι and ἄρχοντες, which has always caused difficulty through a wrong relating to v. 3 and comparison with 1 Pt. 2:17. [29] This interpretation of the text is not without importance when the character and origin of the attitude to the state in this whole section are under discussion, although we cannot go into this here. [30] The duty of obedience to the state takes its place quite naturally in the obligations of the Christian to all men, and finally in the duty of ἀλλήλους ἀγαπᾶν.

† φορέω.

1. As a frequentativum found from Hom. φορέω [1] replaces φέρω esp. when there is ref. to a lasting, continuing, repeated, or customary action. It is used of a steady wind or of raging waves that "carry something forward," Hom. Od., 5, 327 f.; 6, 171 — in the

---

[26] An exception is Zn. R., ad loc.

[27] Cf. Zn. R., ad loc.

[28] Even Mi. R.[13], 323 f., who regards 13:8-10 as an excursus and sees no close relation between it and 13:1-7, since the two passages "come from different traditions," can still observe that vv. 8 ff. are a continuation of 12:9-21 on the one side and clearly follow up v. 7 on the other.

[29] Cf. Strobel, op. cit. (→ n. 25), 58 f.

[30] → VIII, 27, Bibl., to which we might add the ref. in → n. 20, 25 and H. v. Campenhausen, "Zur Auslegung v. R. 13. Die dämonistische Deutung d. ἐξουσία-Begriffes," Aus d. Frühzeit d. Christentums (1963), 81-101; J. Kosnetter, "R. 13:1-7: Zeitbedingte Vorsichtsmassregel oder grundsätzliche Einstellung?" Studiorum Paulinorum Congressus Internat. Catholicus, 1961, Analecta Bibl., 17-18, I (1963), 347-355; V. Zsifkovits, "Der Staatsgedanke nach Pls. in R. 13:1-7," Wiener Beitr. z. Theol., 8 (1964); J. Kallas, "R. 13:1-7: An Interpolation," NTSt, 11 (1964/65), 365-374.

φ ο ρ έ ω . [1] The other tense-forms are class. φορήσω, ἐφόρησα etc. from Hom. Il., 19, 11. But in the koine, perhaps in analogy to ἐκόρεσα, ἐκάλεσα, ἐπόθεσα etc., and also ἐπόνεσα, Hippocr. Morb., I, 4 (Littré, VI, 146), we find instead φορέσω, ἐφόρεσα, so LXX at Prv. 16:23; Sir. 11:5, NT at 1 C. 15:49, pap.: Preisigke Sammelb., III, 7247, 33 (3rd/4th cent. A.D.) and modern Gk., v. Bl.-Debr. § 70, 1; Schwyzer, I, 753 [Risch].

pass. their own movement, Eur. Suppl., 689; swirling dust, Soph. El., 715 — of the chariot that usually carries the hero to the battle, Hom. Il., 10, 323, of the female slave who must constantly fetch water from the well, Il., 6, 457, of the cupbearer who keeps the cup full, Od., 9, 10, of the herd who daily brings food to the animals, 17, 224 and of one who usually brings news, Hdt., III, 34, 1. The most common use, however, is for wearing (or carrying) clothes, e.g., τιάρας "turbans," Hdt., III, 12, 4 ἐσθήματα, Soph. El., 269, στολάς, Oed. Col., 1357, ἱμάτια, P. Oxy., III, 531, 14 f. (2nd cent. A.D.), of ornaments, e.g., δακτύλιον, Aristoph. Pl., 883, στρόφιον, "head-band," Ditt. Syll.³, II, 736, 178 (92 B.C.), of weapons, e.g., θώρηξ, Hom. Il., 13, 371 f., λόγχαν, Ditt. Syll.³, III, 1168, 95 (c. 320 B.C.), of the sceptre, Hom. Il., 1, 238, and what belongs to the person, hence also height δέμας, Eur. Hel., 619, individual parts of the body, σκέλεα, Hdt., II, 76, 1, κεφαλάς, III, 12, 4, and transf. ὄνομα, Soph. Fr., 658 (Pearson), καλὸν στόμα "an eloquent tongue," Fr., 930, ἦθος, Soph. Ant., 705, ἀγλαῖαι, Hom. Od., 17, 244 f., and also ἀπόνοια, "madness," Pap. Grenfell, I, 53, 15 f. (4th cent. A.D.). 2 φορέω can also be used for the habitual "standing" (or not) of e.g., unmixed wine, Plut. Quaest. Conv., VI, 7, 1 (II, 692d) or the heat of the sun, Ps.-Oppian., I, 298. In a late example φορέω in the abs. means "to last," "to endure," P. Flor., III, 384, 54 (5th cent. A.D.).

2. The LXX seldom has the word. In addition to the senses mentioned it employs it fig. for the "carrying" of wisdom, the Law or mercy on the tongue, Prv. 3:16a. We also find it for the σκολιός (→ VII, 406, 1 ff.) who "bears" destruction in his mouth, Prv. 16:26. 3

3. Jos. has φορέω for wearing clothes, Ant., 3, 153 and 279; 10, 235, and with a special emphasis on what is customary, ἔθος, 20, 6.

4. In the NT φορέω occurs only a few times and usually for "carrying for a longer time or continually," e.g., the sword by the authorities in R. 13:4, clothes, Mt. 11:8; Jm. 2:3, the crown of thorns and the purple robe by Jesus, Jn.19:5, and in a transf. sense the bearing of the εἰκών (→ II, 388, 27 ff., 395, 5 ff.) of the earthly or heavenly man by the Christian, 1 C. 15:49.

5. In the post-apost. fathers 1 Cl., 5, 6 has φορέω for the "carrying" of fetters by Paul. Otherwise the word occurs only in Herm. s., 9, 13-17 passim. The ref. is to the bearing of the name of the Son of God and His power, and to the bearing of the names and garments of the virgins and their spirits representing Chr. virtues; this guarantees inclusion in the foundation of the (church-) tower. 15, 6 says expressly that this is a "permanent bearing uninterrupted up to death."

† φορτίον.

1. φορτίον, dimin. of φόρτος, 1 occurs in the sing. and plur. from Hes. lit. for "ship's lading," Op., 643; Jos. Ant., 14, 377, "wagon load," Hes. Op., 693, "lading," "freight," Ditt. Or., I, 132, 11 (130 B.C.); P. Oxy., VII, 1049, 3. 9 (2nd cent. A.D.), "burden" in gen., Xenoph. An., VII, 1, 37; Jos. Ant., 2, 110 and 124 (sacks with grain), hence also of a child in its mother's womb, Xenoph. Mem., II, 2, 5, and very gen. in the

---

2 Ed. B. P. Grenfell, An Alexandrian Erotic Fr. and Other Gk. Pap. Chiefly Ptolemaic (1896).
3 Possibly Prv. 16:23: ἐπὶ χείλεσιν φορέσει ἐπιγνωμοσύνην, is also to be understood thus, since it is by no means certain that LXX read the חכל hi of HT here.
φ ο ρ τ ί ο ν . 1 φόρτος, from Hom. Od., 8, 163; 14, 296 "ship's cargo," later "burden." On the formation cf. Schwyzer, I, 501 [Risch].

sense of "goods," BGU, IV, 1079, 17 (41 A.D.); 1118, 19 (23 B.C.); Jos. Ant., 2, 32.
In the sense of "burdening" with cares, duties, tasks, sickness, age etc. we find the term
in Demosth. Or., 11, 14; Antiph. Fr., 3 (II, 13); Epict. Diss., II, 9, 22; IV, 13, 16; P. Oxy.,
XVI, 1874, 7 (6th cent. A.D.).

2. In the OT the verbal abstr. מַשָּׂא occurs both in the strict sense of "bearing" (Nu.
4:15 ff. *passim*) and also in the sense of "load" (Ex. 23:5; Is. 46:1 f.; Neh. 13:15 etc.) or
"burden" in gen. Ps. 38:4. In the phrase מִנְחָה וְכֶסֶף מַשָּׂא in 2 Ch. 17:11 it takes on the
sense of "present," "tribute" (→ 81, 31 ff.). The transf. sense of "toil," "trouble" occurs
at Nu. 11:11, 17 etc.

3. The LXX uses φορτίον for מַשָּׂא, both lit. for "burden," Is. 46:1 and fig. for the
"burden of sin" ψ 37:5, the "burden" one person can become for another, 2 Βασ. 19:36;
Job 7:20 (for God), or a fool's talk can become for the listener, Sir. 21:16. An unusual
transl. is φορτίον ξύλων "load of wood" for שׂוֹבֶךְ עֵצִים "shrubbery" (?) at Ju. 9:48 f.

4. In Rabb. texts מַשָּׂא means "bearing," Kelim, 1, 1 ff., then "trade," "business,"
bQid., 35a; bShab., 120a and "occupation" with something, bQid., 30b; bYoma, 86a.
מַשּׂוֹי has the concrete sense of burden in bErub., 22a etc. or the transf. sense of "obligation," "duty," jBer., 3, 1 (5d, 53-56. 61).

5. In the NT φορτίον has the lit. sense of "ship's cargo" in the account of
the voyage in Ac. 27:10 with its special stylistic features. [2]
Jesus indignantly describes the rules the Pharisaic rabbis lay on the righteous
as φορτία βαρέα or δυσβάστακτα in the transf. sense of "heavy burdens that
cannot be borne," Mt. 23:4 and par. The over-heavy burden is not the Law itself
(→ II, 900, 3 ff.) nor is it the fact of its interpretation by the rabbis. [3] What Jesus
is criticising is on the one side the contradiction between the rabbis' own conduct
and the duties they impose on men, and on the other the perverted direction in
which their exposition of the Law leads. [4] The this-worldly goal becomes the
intolerable burden of an activity that leads away from God rather than to God. [5]
The real concerns of the Law, κρίσις (→ III, 941, 38 ff.) and ἔλεος (→ II, 482,
16 ff.), i.e., a relation to one neighbour shaped by the will of God, and πίστις,
a relation of faithfulness to God Himself, [6] are overwhelmed by casuistic and
ritualistic obligations, i.e., by these φορτία. This helps us to understand the
Saviour's call (→ V, 992, 40 ff.) in which Jesus promises refreshment to the
weary and heavy-laden if they accept His φορτίον, Mt. 11:28-30. The apparent
paradox is telling us that the promised relief from burdens depends on fellowship
with Jesus. The φορτίον, then, is practical discipleship. [7] The fact that this is
called the taking of His yoke or burden is to be explained formally from the
vocabulary with which wisdom in the Wisdom literature (→ VII, 516, 13 ff.),
and esp. Sir. 51:23 ff., commends itself to the unlearned (→ V, 992, n. 288 f.; VII,

---

[2] Cf. H. Conzelmann, *Die Ag., Hndbch. NT*, 7 (1963), Exc. on 27:44 (Bibl.).
[3] Cf. G. Bornkamm, "Enderwartung u. Kirche im Mt.," in G. Bornkamm - G. Barth - H. J.
Held, *Überlieferung u. Auslegung im Mt., Wissenschaftliche Monographien z. AT u. NT*, 1[5]
(1968), 21 f.
[4] Bornkamm, *op. cit.*, 22 and 28.
[5] Cf. the criticism of the this-worldly goal of Pharisaic piety in Mt. 6:1-18 and the warning
against care for the things of this life that hamper seeking the βασιλεία in 6:25-34.
[6] Cf. Bornkamm, *op. cit.*, 24.
[7] Cf. G. Barth, "Das Gesetzesverständnis d. Evangelisten Mt.," Bornkamm-Barth-Held,
op. cit., 96 and n. 1.

893, n. 44). Materially we again see the contrast between the φορτία βαρέα of rabbinic legal piety and the φορτίον of discipleship of Jesus, which is ἐλαφρόν and which, indeed, refreshes,[8] since it brings into unity with God's will instead of leading away from it.

What Paul means by φορτίον in the expression φορτίον βαστάζω in Gl. 6:5 has to be deduced from the context and similar Pauline ideas elsewhere.

In 2 C. 10:12 ff. Paul refuses to compare himself with others in order to show that he is better and hence to boast against them → III, 651, 10 ff. Instead one should compare the achievement, the ἔργον, with the task imposed by God. This ἔργον will always be one that is accomplished in the power of God, and this yields the true boasting in which one may legitimately engage. In 1 C. 3:10-15; 4:5 Paul develops the same thought with ref. to himself and his missionary colleagues, his point being that only the last judgment will make their work and its value manifest. The same train of thought is probably to be found in the future statement ἕκαστος γὰρ τὸ ἴδιον φορτίον βαστάσει in Gl. 6:5.

If so, φορτίον is the "achievement" or "work" that each will bring with him for evaluation in the judgment. The same idea is present non-fig. in the statement ἕκαστος ἡμῶν περὶ ἑαυτοῦ λόγον δώσει in R. 14:12. In the image of the burden that each must carry to the judgment the negative aspect seems to be stressed as compared with the other texts.[9]

φορτίζω

1. φορτίζω, denominative verb from φόρτος (→ 84, 37 and n. 1) or the derived φόρτις "freighter," Hom. Od., 5, 250; 9, 323, occurs first in the mid. in Hes. Op., 690 in the sense "to load on the ship," "to ship," then in a Macho-quotation in Athen., 13, 45 (582 f.) in the sense "to take away a burden," and in Philodem. Philos. Περὶ κακιῶν, Col. 18, 30 f.[1] in the transf. sense "to burden oneself with." Act. φορτίζω τινά τι "to load," "to burden with," is later; it occurs in the LXX, NT, and then Babrius Fabulae, 111, 3[2] (2nd cent. A.D). The pass. occurs in the NT and Luc. Navigium, 45.[3]

2. The LXX has φορτίζω for שחד "to present with" at Ez. 16:33. The idea seems to be that of loading the recipient with gifts.

3. In the NT φορτίζω means the burdening of men (Lk. 11:46) and their being burdened with loads in a transf. sense, the work of Jesus being to relieve them of these, Mt. 11:28. In the first passage, the Woes on the νομικοί, the ref. is obviously to the burdening of men with the legal demands of the rabbis without any directions or help in their observance. The call to the κοπιῶντες καὶ πεφορτισμένοι in Mt. 11:28 resembles Sir. 51:23 (→ 85, 35 ff.) except that there it is the ἀπαίδευτοι rather than the κοπιῶντες καὶ πεφορτισμένοι who are called. Liberation from physical and spiritual afflictions, troubles and burdens of all kinds is part of the eschatological message of Jesus and is the direct theme of His work.

---

[8] Cf. Barth, op. cit., 148.

[9] In this case καύχημα in Gl. 6:4 is not to be taken positively but neutrally as vox media (→ III, 651, 23 ff.), cf. 1 C. 5:6: οὐ καλὸν τὸ καύχημα ὑμῶν.

φ ο ρ τ ί ζ ω . [1] Ed. C. Jensen (1911).
[2] Ed. O. Crusius (1897).
[3] Jos. does not have the word but he has καταφορτίζω pass. of "laden beasts of burden," Ant., 7, 205, cf. Schl. Mt. on 11:28.

Hence the call embraces those who sigh under such loads. [4] It should be noted, however, that Jesus leaves us in no doubt but that following Him also imposes its own burdens. Hence the specific signification of the term πεφορτισμένος is to be gathered from the contrast with the φορτία imposed by the rabbis → 85, 20 ff. The ref. is to those who sigh under Rabbinic legal practice. [5] What follows in Mt. 12 is by way of illustration, for in this c. we have a collection of stories of men whom Jesus frees from burdens and troubles of all kinds in spite of the opposition of the rabbis on the basis of the Law.

K. Weiss

[4] Outside the NT there are no instances of this transf. use, though we find it for φόρτος (→ 84, 37 and n. 1), φορτίον (→ 85, 2 ff.) and φορτικός, P. Amh., II, 145, 7 (4th/5th cent. A.D.); P. Oxy., VI, 904, 9 (5th cent. A.D.).

[5] E. Norden, *Agnostos Theos* (1913), 308 also ref. to the battle of Jesus against scribal learning, Cf. Schl. Mt. on 11:29: "Only he who does not know the contemporary rabbinate nor understand the opposition in which Jesus found Himself thereto can think in terms of borrowing from Sir."; cf. further G. Barth, "Das Gesetzesverständnis d. Evangel. Mt.," G. Bornkamm - G. Barth - H. J. Held, *Überlieferung u. Auslegung im Mt., Wissensch. Monographien z. AT u. NT*, 1[5] (1968), 139, n. 1.

---

† φθάνω, προφθάνω

---

1. Usage in Profane Greek.

This common verb[1] means "to come first," "to do first," "to be first," "to over-take."[2] The person preceded is in the acc. φθάνει δέ τε καὶ τὸν ἄγοντα, "water overtakes the man digging a ditch," Hom. Il., 21, 262. In the abs. the word means "to come, do first," opp. ὑστερέω, ὑστερίζω "to come, be later": κἂν μὲν φθάσωμεν, ἔστι σοι σωτηρία· ἢν δ᾽ ὑστερήσῃς, οἰχόμεσθα, κατθανῇ, Eur. Phoen 975 f. Often we find a conj. part. with the finite verb[3] to denote the element of being first ἔφθησαν πολλῷ οἱ Σκύθαι τοὺς Πέρσας ἐπὶ τὴν γέφυραν ἀπικόμενοι, Hdt., IV, 136, 2.[4] The comparative element in preceding is strengthened by the use of ἤ or πρὶν ἤ. Another early strengthening is by means of the compound προφθάνω: προφθάσασα καρδία γλῶτταν, Aesch. Ag., 1028, παρακύψασα προὔφθης, Aristoph. Eccl., 884.[5] Instead of the part. the inf. can also be used to strengthen φθάνω even though it is rarer: μόλις φθάνει... μὴ χαμαὶ πεσεῖν, Eur. Med., 1169.[6] The comparat. element becomes less prominent quite early[7] and later it fades out, esp. in prep. expressions, e.g., with μέχρι, ἐπί. φθάνω acquires the sense "to reach," "to reach to" (πρόνοια) ... μέχρι γῆς φθάνει used par. to μέχρι γῆς ἰέναι, Plot., III, 2, 7, 33 ff.

2. Usage in Hellenistic Judaism.

a. φθάνω occurs 27 times in the LXX.[8] The participle is no longer used as a supple-ment, being replaced with the inf. → n. 6. The term is used for Hbr. אנש hitp "to show oneself ready," "to do something quickly," "to accomplish it," 3 Βασ. 12:18. In three instances at Wis. 4:7; 6:13; 16:28 the author shows a good knowledge of Gk. In the abs. φθάνω in the LXX does not mean "to come first" but "to come" in the sense "to arrive," "to get there," "to attain to." This is plainest when the word is combined with concepts

---

φ θ ά ν ω .   [1] The etym. is obscure, v. Schwyzer, I, 326, app. 6; 742, n. 4; Boisacq, Hof-mann, s.v. προφθάνω and καταφθάνω are attested as compounds, P. Oxy., XII, 1482, 10 (2nd cent. A.D.).

[2] Liddell-Scott, Pass., Preisigke Wört., Thes. Steph., s.v.; D. Dimitrakos, Μέγα λεξικὸν τῆς Ἑλληνικῆς γλώσσης, IX (1951), s.v.

[3] "Part. to supplement verbs of modified being and doing are less prominent in the NT," Bl.-Debr. § 414, cf. part. with λανθάνω and τυγχάνω, Schwyzer, II, 392. All these three verbs occur in a single sentence in Thuc., III, 112, 1: οἱ προαποσταλέντες ... ἔλαθόν τε καὶ ἔφθασαν προκαταλαβόντες, τὸν δ᾽ ἐλάσσω ἔτυχον οἱ Ἀμπρακιῶται προανα-βάντες.

[4] The part. of φθάνω is used as a conj. part. with the finite verb; it has independent significance which it loses with part. construction → n. 3, cf. ἀνέῳξάς με φθάσας, Aristoph. Pl., 1102, cf. Schwyzer, II, 392, n. 3; Bl.-Debr. § 414, 4.

[5] A noun was also formed later from προφθάνω: προφθασία "anticipation," a feast in the Ionian Leucas founded by the Clazomenii, Diod. S., 15, 18, 2-4, cf. M. van der Kolf, Art "Prophthasia," Pauly-W., 23 (1959), 817.

[6] Schwyzer, II, 396.

[7] The fading of the sense "to precede" may be noted esp. in Ionic and not purely Attic texts, cf. Hdt., Thuc., Xenoph. and sometimes the tragic poets [Dihle].

[8] Bl.-Debr. § 101.

of time καὶ ἔφθασεν ὁ μὴν ὁ ἕβδομος, 2 Εσδρ. 3:1; 17:73 for נגע "to touch," "to reach something." In 10 of 21 instances with Hbr. equivalent נגע q and hi is transl. It is synon. with ἔρχομαι: ἕως ὅτου μὴ ἔλθωσιν ἡμέραι τῆς κακίας καὶ φθάσωσιν ἔτη, ἐν οἷς ἐρεῖς ... Qoh. 12:1, cf. 8:14; Cant. 2:12. The sense "to reach" is also right — Vg *pervenio* — in most of the cases in which φθάνω is used with prep. expressions. It is used in Ju. 20:34 B for נגע q "to attain," Ju. 20:42 for דבק hi, A καταφθάνω having the same sense here. To denote the greatness of the event it occurs at 2 Ch. 28:9 for נגע hi: ἕως τῶν οὐρανῶν ἔφθακεν. At 2 Βασ. 20:13 the transl. confused יגה hi and נגע and hence used φθάνω, which makes no sense here. The use of φθάνω in 8 passages in Da. is worth noting inasmuch as only Θ, which has better Gk. than LXX, [9] employs the term, and only in combination with prepos. ref. to time or place (ἕως, εἰς, ἐπί) in the sense "to reach," "to attain to," "to come to": for נגע hi at 8:7; 12:2; for מטה, מטא ἔφθασεν ἕως τοῦ οὐρανοῦ, 4:11; cf. 4:20, 22, 24, 28; ... ὡς υἱὸς ἀνθρώπου ἐρχόμενος ἦν καὶ ἕως τοῦ παλαιοῦ τῶν ἡμερῶν ἔφθασεν, 7:13. [10] At Tob. 5:19 we find the dat. instead of the common prepos. phrase. Anxious about her son Tobit, who is to fetch back money from abroad, the mother says: ἀργύριον τῷ ἀργυρίῳ μὴ φθάσαι. It sounds like a proverb: Money comes to money, except that it is negated here in the simple desire that her son should return.

προφθάνω occurs in the LXX for קדם pi in the ψ esp. in the sense "to come before" at ψ 16:13; 118:148; Jon. 4:2, "to meet," Job 30:27, "to encounter," ψ 58:11, "to encounter with," "to offer," ψ 94:2.

b. Ep. Ar., 137 has the negative optative with part. in the class. manner. In Philo the main use of φθάνω is in the weaker sense "to attain to," usually with prepos. ἐπί or ἄχρι. In the introduction to the work on creation Philo says that he wants to set out ἐφ' ἃ τὴν ἀνθρωπίνην διάνοιαν φθάνειν εἰκὸς ἔρωτι καὶ πόθῳ σοφίας κατεσχημένην, Op. Mund., 5. Similarly it is said of Moses φιλοσοφίας ἐπ' αὐτὴν φθάσας ἀκρότητα, 8. Praise of the laws has gone tempestuously through the world ἄχρι καὶ τῶν τῆς γῆς τερμάτων ἔφθακεν, Vit. Mos., I, 2. Sometimes one finds the older sense of "coming before." Both senses occur in Leg., All., III, 215: After the quotation of Ex. 3:9 "the cry of the children of Israel has come to me," we read: πάνυ καλῶς τὸ φθάσαι μέχρι θεοῦ τὴν ἱκεσίαν, but it would not have "reached" Him ἔφθασεν if He had not been the gracious God. Yet He meets some men in advance προσαπαντᾷ. "Thou dost see here how great is the goodness of the Author who anticipates our plans ὅση τοῦ αἰτίου ἡ χάρις φθάνοντος τὴν ἡμετέραν μέλλησιν." In Jos. φθάνω usually means "to come before." Achimas gets to David before Chusis with the good side of the news τὸν Χοῦσιν φθάνει, Ant., 7, 247, and Jeroboam anticipates the purpose of Solomon φθάσας δὲ γνῶναι τοῦτο 'Ιεροβόαμος πρὸς "Ισακον φεύγει τὸν Αἰγυπτίων βασιλέα, 8, 210. Jos. Vit., 15 tells how he himself was saved at sea and pulled out with 80 of 600 φθάσαντες ἄλλους. [11] Three times in Test. XII φθάνω is used in the sense "to reach," "to attain to," of the watchers who seem to the women to reach to the sky, R. 5:7, of a ship that reaches land after a storm ἔφθασε τὸ σκάφος ἐπὶ τῆς γῆς, N. 6:9, and then in L. 6:11, the most important ref. for 1 Th. 2:16 → 90, 21, of the inhabitants of Shechem

[9] J. Ziegler, *Susanna. Daniel. Bel et Draco, Septuag. Gottingensis,* 16, 2 (1954), 28 f. 61. 65.
[10] Sometimes we find synon. ἐγγίζω Cant. 2:12 Σ; Ιερ. 28:9; Δα. 4:11, 22; Is. 30:4 'Α, πάρειμι, Δα. 7:13; ἥκω, Δα. 4:23 corresponding to φθάνω at 4:24 Θ. The same verbs also occur in the NT proclamation of the kingdom of God: ἐγγίζω, Mt. 3:2; Lk. 10:9, 11; 21:8; ἥκω, Mt. 24:14; πάρειμι, Jn. 7:6; cf. ἔρχομαι, Mt. 6:10; Mk. 11:10; Lk. 11:2; 17:20; 18:30; 22:18; Jn. 4:35, cf. E. Grässer, "Das Problem d. Parusieverzögerung in d. synpt. Ev. u. in d. Ag.," ZNW Beih. 22² (1960), 7, n. 2; 89 f. [Bertram].
[11] "ἔφθασεν carries the idea that the event was not foreseen but came as a surprise," Schl. Mt. on 12:28.

and sons of Emor, who, having done wrong, were destroyed when the wrath of God reached and smote them ἔφθασε δὲ (ἐπ') αὐτοὺς ἡ ὀργὴ τοῦ θεοῦ εἰς τέλος. [12]

3. Usage in the New Testament.

a. The original sense "to precede someone" occurs in the NT only once at 1 Th. 4:15: "We which are alive and remain unto the coming (→ V, 868, 14 ff.) of the Lord shall not precede them which are asleep." [13] Strengthening of the basic sense by the compound with acc. and part. occurs in Mt. 17:25, which is peculiar to Mt. In these passages both the simple and the compound follow ancient class. usage. [14]

b. In the other 5 NT ref. φθάνω is used with a prepos. phrase: with ἐπί in Mt. 12:28 and par.; 1 Th. 2:16, with εἰς in R. 9:31; Phil. 3:16, and with ἄχρι in 2 C. 10:14. The meaning is always "to arrive at," "to reach," "to come or attain to." [15] At 2 C. 10:13 f. φθάνω means the same as the NT hapax legomenon ἐφικνέομαι: Paul has reached them with the Gospel. [16] The use is the same in Phil. 3:16 but more profound. Paul employs the clause πλὴν εἰς ὃ ἐφθάσαμεν, [17] τῷ αὐτῷ στοιχεῖν (→ VII, 668, 20 f.) [18] to conclude a train of thought contrasting imperfection and perfection. Above as a fixed norm is the Gospel of righteousness by faith in Christ. They have "attained to" it. But it is also the regula ac norma of conduct. [19] The same word is used in the same sense to say the opposite about Israel in R. 9:31: Ἰσραὴλ δὲ διώκων νόμον δικαιοσύνης εἰς νόμον οὐκ ἔφθασεν. [20] 1 Th. 2:16 has been much contested: [21] ἔφθασεν [22] δ' ἐπ'

---

[12] Test. XII, Charles, ad loc., thinks with J. E. Grabe, Spicilegium SS Patrum, I² (1714), 138 that Paul took the saying from Test. L. 6:11. One may rule out the possibility that Test. L. 6:11 is a Chr. interpolation, cf. Dib. Th. on 1 Th. 2:16. The idea of God's wrath is a common eschatological and Rabb. concept, → V, 416, 9 ff.

[13] Dib. Th. and Dob. Th., ad loc. It is unlikely that we have here a dominical saying transmitted in writing, cf. B. Rigaux, Les ép. aux Thess., Études Bibl. (1956), 539 f.

[14] Bultmann Trad., 26 thinks that in outward form the passage is a biographical apophthegm but that in inner character it is a discussion, since it is solving a community problem by a saying of Jesus rather than presenting a general truth metaphorically, 35. B. H. Streeter, The Four Gospels (1930), 504 adopts the view of commentators that since the stater was the official equivalent of two drachmas only in Antioch and Damascus the final version of the Gospel must have been composed in Syria. Mediation through a disciple suggests the style of specific communities, cf. Jn. 13:24; 12:21 f.; Lk. 7:3.

[15] Bl.-Debr. § 101; Dob. Th., 115.

[16] Wnd. 2 K. on 10:14b tries with Orig. et al. to establish the sense of "being before" here, so that Paul's pt. is that he was the first and thus better qualified than those who came later. But Wnd. finally rejects this view in favour of the weaker "to reach."

[17] p¹⁶ saᵖᵗ have ἐφθάσατε but this is undoubtedly an emendation.

[18] Here again there is much emendation, esp. by adding κανόνι, 69 D³ al f vg.

[19] "The apparent difficulty of the statement is that the relative clause speaks of the point already attained whereas the main clause speaks of the law whereby it is reached," Loh. Phil., ad loc. Lohmeyer finds the solution in martyrdom as goal, turning, and way.

[20] Mi. R.¹³, ad loc.

[21] Rigaux, op. cit. (→ n. 13), 451-6. E. Bammel, "Judenverfolgung u. Naherwartung. Zur Eschatologie d. Ersten Thessalonicherbr.," ZThK, 56 (1959), 308, suggests that one may perhaps infer the final extermination of the Jewish people but this is unlikely, cf. R. 11:25 f. "As God responds to the act of the Jews He leads the world a step further towards the τέλος," Bammel, 309.

[22] ἔφθακεν B D* 330 2127 256. "La correction n'est pas nécessaire, mais l'aoriste montre un fait: la colère tombée sur eux — pour la fin," Rigaux, op. cit., 454.

αὐτοὺς ἡ ὀργή (→ V, 434, 18 ff.) εἰς τέλος.[23] The Jews are an obstacle to the conversion of the Gentiles "that they might fill up the measure of their sins everywhere." The wrath of God has come upon them totally → VIII, 56, 2 ff.[24]

The most important passage is the Q saying: εἰ δὲ ἐν πνεύματι θεοῦ (Lk. ἐν δακτύλῳ θεοῦ) ἐγὼ[25] ἐκβάλλω τὰ δαιμόνια, ἄρα ἔφθασεν ἐφ᾽ ὑμᾶς ἡ βασιλεία τοῦ θεοῦ → II, 19, 4 ff. This is part of the most ancient tradition, Mt. 12:28 and par.[26] Here as in the LXX (→ 88, 5 ff.) the meaning of φθάνω is "to attain to," "to come."[27] It makes little difference whether one translates "the kingdom of God has reached you" or "come to you." For the material understanding of the statement in which φθάνω occurs depends upon theological

---

[23] G. Stählin (→ V, 434, 18 ff.) takes εἰς τέλος to mean "for ever" in the sense of לָנֶצַח, Ps. 9:7, 19 etc., but Dob. Th., ad loc. thinks it is a current adv. expression meaning "fully," "completely" (πάντοτε). He ref. to לְכָלָה in 2 Ch. 12:12. Yet this means "to destruction" in both instances (2 Ch. 12:12 and Ez. 13:13). LXX has εἰς καταφθορὰν εἰς τέλος or εἰς συντέλειαν. The ref. in both cases is to the ὀργὴ θεοῦ. Obviously "to destruction" will not do here. Paul is not relating God's wrath to an actual historical event but to eschatological judgment, as suggested by words like νόμος, ἁμαρτία, θάνατος, σταυρὸς Χριστοῦ, ἀνάστασις, ἐσχάτη ἡμέρα, cf. Dib. Th., ad loc. and C. Masson, Les deux Ép. de S. Paul aux Thess., Comment. du NT, 11a (1957), ad loc. In the Qumran texts, too, the concepts of God's wrath and destruction often occur together. In the curse of the Levites against the men of the lot of Belial there is ref. to the "destruction" כָּלָה ordained by God, 1 QS 2:6. It is said against the apostate: "God's wrath and the zeal of His judgments will burn against him to eternal destruction," 1 QS 2:15. In the war scroll it is said of the trumpets of pursuit: "God has smitten all the sons of darkness. His wrath does not cease until they are destroyed" עַד כַּלּוֹתָם, 1 QM 3:9. For Paul, however, there can be no question of God's wrath on Israel "to destruction" or "for ever." G. Stählin (→ V, 434, 27 ff.) notes that R. 9-11 is against this. Hence one must assume that Paul here is simply drawing on the common stock of eschatology without giving it any specific content. Test. L. 6:11 (→ 89, 42 ff.) is not quoted directly. We simply have a reminiscence which is set here in very different relationships.

[24] Rigaux, op. cit., 456: "Paul a pu de lui-même reprendre un dicton juif appliqué originairement aux pécheurs ou aux ennemis d'Israël. Ses vues sur l' ὀργή (1 Th. 1:10) cadrent très bien avec la pensée exprimée dans l' ἀναπληρῶσαι qui précède."

[25] Some MSS omit the ἐγώ in Lk., p45 א* ΑΧΓΔΛΠ, but p75 D א 1 B C L R 33 69 124 346 have it. The personal pronoun is surely original. No deductions may be drawn from the omission. v. Schl. Mt., ad loc.

[26] Bultmann Trad., 11 and 174 regards Mt. 12:28 and v. 27 and par. as originally independent: 12:28 "can claim as much authenticity as can be ascribed to any saying of Jesus. It has the full throb of eschatological power the coming of Jesus must have carried with it." Mt. does not have his customary βασιλεία τῶν οὐρανῶν for βασιλεία τοῦ θεοῦ, but he does render freely the basic בְּאֶצְבַּע אֱלֹהִים (Ex. 8:15; 31:18) which Lk. transl. lit., cf. H. v. Baer, "Der hl. Geist in d. Lukasschr.," BWANT, 39 (1926), 115.

[27] On Mt. 12:28 and par. linguistically cf. Dalman WJ, I, 88: ἔφθασεν ἐφ᾽ ὑμᾶς is to be traced back to מְטָא עַל:מַטָא Da. 4:21 "to come upon someone," cf. Tg. Pro. on Ez. 7:2; cf. also Dalman, 119 and O. Schmoller, Die Lehre vom Reich Gottes (1891), 139-142, who notes an inner connection with Lk. 11:20. C. H. Dodd, The Parables of the Kingdom (1956) thinks the expression brings out very emphatically the fact "that the Kingdom of God has actually arrived," 43, n. 1. W. G. Kümmel, "Verheissung u. Erfüllung," AbhThANT, 6³ (1956), 98-101: "Hence one can say with assurance that ... the proper transl. is that the rule of God has come to you," 100. Cf. also J. M. Robertson, Kerygma u. historischer Jesus (1960), 163, who speaks of a dialectical understanding of presence. R. Morgenthaler, Kommendes Reich (1952), 36-45 thinks that lexically we have a border-line case of coming that is not full presence, 42; in effect, however, he stresses the event of demon-expulsion and the significance of the figure of Jesus. R. F. Berkey, "ΕΓΓΙΖΕΙΝ, ΦΘΑΝΕΙΝ and Realized Eschatology," JBL, 82 (1963), 177-187 shows that discussion has bogged down in the alternative of present and future and that this cannot be decided lexically. E. Jüngel, Pls. u. Jesus³ (1967), transcends this alternative → n. 28 f.

exegesis of the concept of the kingdom of God and upon exegesis of the conditional clause, namely, upon interpretation of the connection of expelling demons [28]
with the figure of Jesus and its significance for the lordship of God. The statement
also offers occasion to discuss more fully the question of the eschatological
orientation of the proclamation of the divine rule in the Synoptic tradition of
Jesus and the question of the so-called delay in the *parousia*. [29] At any rate, apart
from the ἄρα with its emphasis on the conclusion, the contribution that φθάνω
makes semasiologically and with the aorist form to the shaping of the saying is
perfectly clear.

4. Usage in the Post-Apostolic Fathers.

In early Chr. writings outside the NT the word occurs in compound form at 2 Cl. 8,
2: ἐὰν προφθάσῃ ... βαλεῖν; the meaning is "to do something before." [30]

Fitzer

---

[28] Cf. Str.-B., IV, 501-535, esp. 6d e; 7h: "There have always been men who have gained
mastery over demons by using the means indicated," 527. Exorcism is essentially healing,
cf. G. Fitzer, "Sakrament u. Wunder im NT," *In memoriam E. Lohmeyer* (1951), 174-183,
Jüngel, *op. cit.,* 185-8 continues the discussion with Dodd, Kümmel and Robinson and fixes
the present ref. of God's lordship more precisely in the work of Jesus.

[29] Grässer, *op. cit.,* 6. The *basileia* dawns now. "Yet it must be emphasised at once: not
in the sense that God's lordship is present already but only in the sense that it is dawning."
But the verb φθάνω does not mean "to be dawning." Jüngel, *op. cit.,* 180 does not think it
"appropriate to characterise Jesus' preaching as imminent expectation, for by material necessity
this is then followed by the idea of delay in the *parousia*."

[30] Cf. Bl.-Debr. § 414, 4; 396, 2 and Kn. Cl., *ad loc.* [Schneemelcher].

---

† φθείρω, † φθορά, † φθαρτός,
† ἄφθαρτος, † ἀφθαρσία, † ἀφθορία,
† διαφθείρω, † διαφθορά, † καταφθείρω

Contents: A. The Word Group in the Greek World: I. In Literary and Non-Literary Greek in General. II. In Philosophical Usage: 1. Older Philosophy; 2. Aristotle; 3. The Later Hellenistic Period. B. The Word Group in the Old Testament and Judaism: I. The Old Testament. II. Palestinian Judaism: 1. The Dead Sea Scrolls; 2. Talmudic and Midrashic Writings. III. Hellenistic Judaism: 1. The Greek Old Testament; 2. Josephus; 3. Philo; 4. Other Hellenistic Jewish Works. C. The Word Group in the New Testament: 1. Real Sense; 2. Moral and Religious Sense; 3. Ideal Sense: Corruptible-Incorruptible. D. The Word Group in the Early Church.

A. The Word Group in the Greek World.

I. In Literary and Non-Literary Greek in General.

1. φθείρω [1] means "to ruin," "to destroy," mid. and pass. "to perish," "to be destroyed." Obj. are, e.g., οἶκος, σῶμα and ψυχή, Xenoph. Mem., I, 5, 3, τὰ οἰκεῖα, Thuc., I, 141, 7 πόλιν καὶ νόμους, Plat. Leg., XII, 958c, ἐκ νεῶν φθαρέντες ἐχθροί, "the enemies deprived of their ships," Aesch. Pers., 450 f. One often finds the sense "to kill," "to be killed," "to perish," esp. in battle, so also διαφθείρω, Thuc., III, 66, 2; IV, 124, 3, but also through illness διεφθείροντο ... ὑπὸ τοῦ ἐντὸς καύματος, II, 49, 6, hunger, P. Lond., III, 982, 7 (4th cent. A.D.), cf. ἀσεβεῖς πάντας διέφθειρεν, Rosetta Stone, Ditt. Or., I, 90, 26 (196 B.C.). Petitioners in prison for debt often note: "We perish here καταφθαρῆναι," P. Petr., II, 19, Fr. 2, 9 (3rd cent. B.C.). Obj. of κατα- or διαφθείρω are ships, P. Greci e Lat., 13, 1304, Fr. B. 32 f. (2nd cent. A.D.), τὰ φορτία, Aristoph. Vesp., 1398, χρήματα, Aesch. Fr., 17, 35, [2] buildings which crumble with age τὸ π[ρ]οπύλα[ιον] χρόνῳ [διαφθαρέ]ν, P. Fay. Inscr., 4, 4 (p. 34, c. 180 A.D.). φθείρομαι means "to destroy oneself," Thuc., I, 2, 4, cf. διεφθαρμένος τὸ σῶμα, Luc. Dial. deorum, 13, 2. καταφθείρομαι is often used to describe economic ruin, P. Greci e Lat., 4, 377, 11 (250/49 B.C.); 330, 6 (258/57 B.C.). Thus we read in marriage contracts μηδὲ φθείρειν τὸν κοινὸν οἶκον, P. Oxy., III, 497, 4 (2nd cent. A.D.); οἰκοφθόρος means "spendthrift," Pap. Grenfell, I, 53, 19 (4th cent. A.D.). [3]

φθείρεσθε is used as a curse "be damned," "go to the devil," Hom. Il., 21, 128, also sing. φθείρου, Aristoph. Pl., 610, or as a demand to "be off," φθερεῖ τῆσδ' ὡς τάχιστ' ἀπὸ στέγης, Eur. Andr., 708, cf. 715. It can also mean "to ruin," without always totally destroying. Obj. are δῆμον and δίκας, Theogn., 1, 45, θεῶν νόμους, Soph. Ai., 1344, τὴν πόλιν, νόμους, Plat. Leg., XII, 9, 358c, τὴν δημοκρατίαν (opp. σῶσαι), Aristot.

φθείρω κτλ. [1] The stem is related to Sanskr. kṣárati "flows," "dissolves," v. Boisacq, Hofmann, s.v.

[2] Ed. H. J. Mette, Die Fr. d. Tragödien d. Aesch., Deutsche Akad. d. Wissenschaften zu Berlin. Schriften d. Sektion f. Altertumswissenschaft, 15 (1959).

[3] Ed. B. P. Grenfell, An Alexandrian Erotic Fr. and Other Gk. Pap. Chiefly Ptolemaic (1896).

Pol., V, 9, p.1309b, 36 f., cf. καταφθείρω, Ditt. Or., I, 194, 5 (c. 40 B.C.), τὰ διαφθείροντα what "destroys" the state, V, 8, p. 1308a, 25 f., τὸ ὕδωρ ... διέφθαρτο "became unpalatable," Thuc., VII, 84, 5. Often in contracts it is laid down that the nurse engaged should not "spoil" her milk, φθείρειν τὸ γάλα, BGU, IV, 1058, 29 (age of Augustus). Many pap. ref. to animals that have fallen, e.g., ἵππος διέφθαρται, Pap. Cairo Zeno, I, 59093, 5 (3rd cent. B.C.). [4] The group can also be used for loss of food, ibid., I, 59021, 3 (3rd cent. B.C.), fruits destroyed by grasshoppers: ἡ ἀκρὶς ἐμπεσοῦσα κατέφθειρεν, P. Tebt., III, 772, 2 (236 B.C.).

2. φθορά, then, means "destruction," "death," Sib., 2, 9, διαφθοραί "murders," Eur. Ion, 617, τῶν ἔργων διαφθορά, "destruction" of buildings, Polyb., 1, 48, 3. 8. φθορὰ ὕδασιν is used for a disaster by water, Plat. Tim., 23c, φθοραί "ship-wrecks," Eur. Hel., 766, φθορὰ τῶν καρπῶν, P. Mich., III, 182, 38 (182 B.C.). Again and again contracts have the formula ἀκίνδυνον καὶ ἀνυπόλογον πάσης φθορᾶς; thus the leaseholder is obliged to pay the rent "without counting damages or without regard to possible risks," [5] P. Tebt., I, 106, 16 f. (101 B.C.). Isis is invoked: φθορὰν οἷς θέλεις διδοῖς, τοῖς δὲ κατεφθαρμένοις αὔξησιν διδ(οῖς), P. Oxy., XI, 1380, Col. 8, 175-7 (2nd cent. A.D.) and in a love charm the god is called a θεὸς φθοροποιός, Preis. Zaub., II, 12, 455 (c. 100 B.C.).

3. A special moral sense is "to lead astray," "to ruin"; διεφθαρμένοι are those who have fallen into moral decay, Aristot. Eth. Nic., X, 5, p. 1176a, 24, and φθορεύς is a "seducer," Plut. Aud. Poet., 3 (II, 18c). In the moral field it can also mean "to bribe," διαφθείρειν τοὺς ἐπὶ τῶν πραγμάτων, Demosth. Or., 18, 247, κριτάς, 21, 5, "to seduce" γυναῖκα, 45, 79, παρθένους, Luc. Tyr., 26, esp. in adultery, Lys., 1, 4. 16, or gen. "to ruin" ἔθη τῶν ἀνθρώπων, Diod. S., 16, 54, 4. Causes of moral corruption are χρήματα, Demosth. Or., 19, 7; Lys., 2, 29, rapid entrusting with honorary offices, Aristot. Pol., V, 8, p. 1308b, 14, λύπη, Eur. Or., 398, ἡδονὴ ἢ λύπη, Aristot. Eth. Nic., VI, 5, p. 1140b, 16-19, both "corrupt" the faculty of moral judgment. The soul, too, can be the object of corruption, διέφθαρται τῇ ψυχῇ, Polyb., 12, 23, 2.

4. διαφθείρω has a special sense in the following combinations: βοήθειαν, "frustrate," Thuc., III, 113, 5 σπουδὴν διαφθείρειν τῶν ἐναντίων γέλωτι, τὸν δὲ γέλωτα σπουδῇ, Gorg. Fr., 12 (Diels, II, 303), γνώμην "to alter" an opinion, Aesch. Ag., 932, so φθορά as the "weakening" or "destruction" of the other party (opp. ἀνίσωσις "agreement"), Thuc., VIII, 87, 4.

II. In Philosophical Usage.

1. Older Philosophy.

Gk. philosophy continually sought to understand φθείρεσθαι in antithesis to γίγνεσθαι. Thus one reads in Plat. Phaed., 95e: δεῖ περὶ γενέσεως καὶ φθορᾶς τὴν αἰτίαν διαπραγματεύσασθαι, or Resp., VIII, 546a: γενομένῳ παντὶ φθορά ἐστιν. Anaxagoras, acc. to Aetius De placitis reliquiae, I, 3, 5, [6] tries to link the two with ὄν and μὴ ὄν: ἐκ τοῦ μὴ ὄντος ... γίνεσθαι ἢ φθείρεσθαι εἰς τὸ μὴ ὄν. [7] Aristot. Cael., III, 1,

---

[4] Ed. C. C. Edgar, Catalogue Général des Antiquités Égypt. du Musée du Caire, 79 (1925).

[5] On the formula v. Mitteis-Wilcken, II, 1, 198. The danger of personal injury etc. also falls on the leaseholder. Ἀνυπόλογος means there can be no deductions from the rent, no changing of the lease, no ex dispari causa. Nor can the leaseholder raise counter-claims.

[6] Ed. H. Diels, Doxographi Graeci (1879).

[7] One must remember that these texts are later ref. and not the originals. Nevertheless they give a picture of the movement of thought in earlier Gk. philosophy.

p. 298b, 15 f. tells of Parmenides and Melissus: οὐθὲν γὰρ οὔτε γίγνεσθαι... οὔτε φθείρεσθαι τῶν ὄντων, ἀλλὰ μόνον δοκεῖν ἡμῖν, cf. οὐκ ἄρα γινόμενόν ἐστι τὸ ὄν... οὔτε φθαρήσεται τὸ ὄν, Simpl. Comm. on Aristot. Phys., I, 3. [8] In older Gk. philosophy the term φθείρεσθαι is used in understanding not merely one's own existence and self-consciousness but also the cosmos. The question is that of what abides in contrast to that which changes, which has a fixed span, which undergoes alteration in the world μέρος ἐπιδέχεσθαι φθορὰν ἅπαξ, τὰ πάντα δὲ μένειν αἰωνίως, Theagenes acc. to Schol. on Hom. Il., 20, 67. [9] What abides is the all as such, while the parts are all subject to corruption. Diog. L., IX, 19 says of Xenophanes: πᾶν τὸ γινόμενον φθαρτόν. For Parm. acc. to Plut. Col., 13 (II, 1114d) the νοητόν, which can be perceived only intellectually, is ἀΐδιον and ἄφθαρτον. Emped. again finds that which endures in the στοιχεῖα: πάντα φθαρτὰ πλὴν τῶν στοιχείων, Aristot. Metaph., II, 4, p. 1000b, 19 f. Melissus acc. to Epiph. De fide, 9, 16 is concerned to try to establish everywhere in nature the phenomenon of corruptibility: πάντα εἶναι φθαρτά. For Heracl. movement is what endures κίνησιν δὲ ἀΐδιον μὲν τοῖς ἀιδίοις, φθαρτὴν δὲ τοῖς φθαρτοῖς, Aetius De placitis reliquiae (→ n. 6), I, 23, 7. For Anaximand. acc. to Plut. in Euseb. Praep. Ev., 1, 8, 2 the ἄπειρον is αἰτία of γένεσις and φθορά, and for Anaxag. acc. to Simpl. Comm. on Aristot. Phys. (→ n. 8), I, 2 (p. 27, 5 ff.) the ὁμοιομερῆ are what abides: πάντα τὰ ὁμοιομερῆ... ἄφθαρτα. These examples show that the concept of the φθαρτόν is always defined by that of what abides and is immutable in the cosmos. The main concern of older Gk. philosophy is to know this abiding element in the changing, rising and perishing forms of nature.

2. Aristotle.

There is rich material in Aristot. on the question of the φθαρτόν and γενητόν: ἅπαντα γὰρ τὰ γινόμενα καὶ φθειρόμενα φαίνεται, Cael., I, 10, p. 279b, 29 f. Aristot. relates γένεσις and φθορά to ὄν and μὴ ὄν: ἡ γὰρ γένεσις φθορὰ τοῦ μὴ ὄντος, ἡ δὲ φθορὰ γένεσις τοῦ μὴ ὄντος, Gen. Corr., I, 3, p. 319a, 28 f. The φθαρτόν and ἄφθαρτον are not accidental (ἡ δὲ κατὰ συμβεβηκός) but necessary (ἐξ ἀνάγκης) antitheses, Metaph., 9, 10, p. 1058b, 26 - 1059a, 10. They condition one another and one cannot speak of the one apart from the other. They are also in par. relation to the γενητόν and ἀγένητον, the former corresponding to the φθαρτόν and the latter to the ἄφθαρτον, Cael., I, 12, p. 282b, 5-9. On the other hand οὐσία "being," "essentiality," has no part in φθείρεσθαι and γίγνεσθαι, Metaph., 7, 3, p. 1043b, 15. Yet οὐσίαι share partly in ἀγένητα and ἄφθαρτα, of which we can know little, and partly in γένεσις and φθορά, Part. An., I, 5, p. 644b, 23 f. οὐσία αἰσθητή decays into ἀΐδιος and φθαρτή, Metaph., 11, 1, p. 1069a, 31. Aristot. raises the question whether the ἀρχαί (principles or elements) are ἄφθαρτοι or φθαρταί. Since everything φθείρεται εἰς ταῦτ' ἐξ ὧν ἔστιν, "decays into what it came from," there must have been prior ἀρχαί, ibid., 2, 4, p. 1000b, 25 f. Aristot. is concerned about finer distinction in the concepts of φθορά and μεταβολή "change." The difference is that in the former no αἰσθητόν remains as the ὑποκείμενον in μεταβολή; γένεσις and φθορά are μεταβολή of ὑποκείμενα, "substances." ὕλη esp. is ὑποκείμενον δεκτικόν "a basis (substance) that can be adopted" for γένεσις and φθορά, Gen. Corr., I, 14, p. 320a, 2; in contrast with ἡ... ἐξ ὑποκειμένου εἰς μὴ ὑποκείμενον φθορά is ἡ... οὐκ ἐξ ὑποκειμένου εἰς ὑποκείμενον... γένεσις, Metaph., 10, 11, p. 1067b, 21-24. Nothing is the cause of its own γένεσις and φθορά, Mot. An., 5, p. 700a, 35. In another passage φθείρω is par. to βλάπτω and in antithesis to ὠφελέω, Part. An., II, 5, p. 651b, 2. In Aristot.'s description of nature φθορά means "death," which comes about through θερμοῦ ἔκλειψις, "loss of warmth," De respiratione, 17, p. 478b, 27-33 or "lack of blood," ὀλιγαιμία, Part. An.,

---

[8] Ed. H. Diels, Comm. in Aristotelem Graeca, 9 (1882), 103, 19 f.
[9] Ed. W. Dindorf, Schol. in Hom. Graeca, IV (1877), 231, 21.

II, 5, p. 651b, 11. In this connection ἄφθαρτος means "long-lived," De longitudine et brevitate vitae, 4, p. 466a, 1. Thus φθείρω is also the opp. of μένω, Gen. An., II, 1, p. 734a, 7 or it is διάλυσις τῆς οὐσίας, Topica, VII, 3, p. 153b, 31. φθείρομαι can then mean "to come to a halt" as opp. to κινοῦμαι: φθείρεται δὲ καὶ μηδὲν κινούμενον, Phys., IV, 13, p. 222b, 24. Ethically φθείρω is the opp. of σῴζω, "to destroy" and "to uphold," Eth. Nic., VII, 9, p. 1151a, 15. Politically, too, φθοραί and σωτηρίαι are antonyms, Pol., IV, 2, p. 1289b, 24.

3. The Later Hellenistic Period.

It is characteristic of this epoch of thought that the pair φθαρτόν-ἄφθαρτον is increasingly taken in a religious sense rather than in relation to nature or being, i.e., in an ontological or physical sense. Corp. Herm. is typical here. Γένεσις and χρόνος as ἀμετάβλητοι and ἄφθαρτοι are in heaven, while on earth they are μετάβλητοι and φθαρτοί, Corp. Herm., 11, 4. Whereas older Gk. philosophy is monistically inclined, there is here a plain dualistic thrust contrasting God and the world or the divine world and the earthly. φθορά and ἀπώλεια cannot affect the deity as the ἄφθαρτον, 12, 16. φθορά stands in antithesis to ἀθανασία, 1, 28. In Plut. the obj. of statements about eternity change. ἀφθαρσία is proper to the θεῖον along with δύναμις and ἀρετή, Plut. De Aristide, 6 (I, 322a); he, too, calls the godhead a ζῷον μακάριον καὶ ἄφθαρτον, Stoic Rep., 38 (II, 1051f.). But he can also ascribe ἀφθαρσία to the ἄτομοι, thus forming a bridge with older Gk. philosophy, Plut. Col., 8 (II, 1111d). Then again he describes the πᾶν as ἄπειρον, ἀγένητον and ἄφθαρτον, Col., 13 (II, 1114a). He thus writes of ψυχαί that they are ἀνώλεθροι and ἄφθαρτοι, Suav. Viv. Epic., 31 (II, 1107b). For later philosophy the eternal and immutable does not lie in the cosmos, in its elements or principles or abiding relations, but in the incorruptibility of that which is outside and above the world. In keeping is the ref. to Stoic fr.: γενητὸν καὶ φθαρτὸν τὸν ἕνα κόσμον, Simpl. Comm. on Aristot. Phys., VIII, 1, p. 1121, 12, [10] and cf.: the κόσμος φθείρεται, since all its parts are φθαρτά, Philo Aet. Mund., 124. On the other hand, it is the nature of the μακάριον to be ἀπαθές and ἄφθαρτον, Plut. Def. Orac., 20 (II, 420e).

B. The Word Group in the Old Testament and Judaism.

I. The Old Testament.

The real Hbr. equivalent of φθείρω is שׁחת, [11] which occurs 162 times in the OT. It is found in the ni, where it can mean "to be corrupt," through decay, Jer. 13:7, "to be perverted, depraved," Gn. 6:11 f., "to be laid waste," Ex. 8:20, and also in the pi for "to destroy," e.g., a city, Jer. 48:18, men, 2 S. 1:14, or the covenant, Mal. 2:8. In the moral sense it can mean "to act badly, dissolutely," Ex. 32:7, or "to become depraved," Hos. 9:9. We also find it in the hi for "to destroy," a city in Gn. 18:28, men in 1 S. 26:15, or even things, e.g., the increase of harvest, Ju. 6:4, cf. Mal. 3:11; הַמַּלְאָךְ הַמַּשְׁחִית is the "destroying angel" or "destroyer" in 2 S. 24:16. In the hi it can also mean "to do what is evil" in the moral sense in Ps. 14:1; Dt. 4:16; Is. 1:4. The ho has the special sense "to be castrated" in Mal. 1:14. מַשְׁחִית is the "destroyer" in Is. 54:16; Jer. 51:1, but also "destruction" in Ez. 21:36. לְמַשְׁחִית means "for destruction" in Ex. 12:13. מַשְׁחֵת is "destruction" in Ez. 9:1. מָשְׁחָת means "what is ravaged," "disfigured" in Is. 52:14, and מָשְׁחָת "what is corrupt" with ref. to sacrifices in Lv. 22:25.

---

[10] Ed. H. Diels, Comm. in Aristotelem Graeca, 10 (1895).

[11] Other transl. of שׁחת like διαπίπτω, ἐξολεθρεύω, ἐκτρίβω, ἐκτυφλόω, ἐκχέω, ἐξαλείφω, κατασκάπτω and λυμαίνω are governed by the context and do not denote any shift of meaning in the word group.

Other equivalents of φθείρω κτλ. are חרב "to dry out" in Ju. 16:7 Cod. B, מות hi in 1 S. 2:25, נבל "to fade" in Is. 24:4, מקק ni in Lv. 26:39, בקק in Is. 24:1, 3, שָׁמֵם "devastated" in Is. 49:19, כלה pi in Ez. 16:52, [12] מלל "to fade" in Job 15:32, נוס in Dt. 34:7, פרץ "to tear a hole" in Ex. 19:22 Σ, ריק hi "to leave empty" in Is. 32:6 Cod. A, אֵיד "disaster," "destruction" in Job 21:17 Σ. [13]

II. The Word Group in Palestinian Judaism.

1. The Dead Sea Scrolls.

The Dead Sea Scrolls show that in the Hbr. world שחת was gen. understood as "to destroy" and we find it in various phrases: מוקשי שחת "the snares of destruction" in 1 QH 2:21; Damasc. 14:2 (16:12), משברי שחת "waves of destruction," 1 QH 3:12, חצי שחת "arrows of destruction," 3:16, דלתי שחת "gates of destruction," 3:18, פחי שחת "snares of destruction," 3:26, ותעזור משחת חיי "keep thy life from destruction," 5:6, הגיעו לשחת חיי "my life drew near to destruction," 8:29. In 1 QS, too, we find the word in the same sense: שחת עולמים "eternal destruction," 1 QS 4:12, אנשי השחת "men of destruction, i.e., marked for destruction," 9:16, 22; 10:19, cf. בני השחת in Damasc. 6:15 (8:12); 13:14 (16:7), משחת יחלק נפשי in 1 QS 11:13, cf. 1 QH 3:5. In these works the verb again means "to destroy," "to ruin," e.g., a land, 1 QpHab 4:13, or Satan, the evil one, עשיתה בליעל לשחת "thou hast created Belial to destroy him totally," 1 QM 13:11, cf. רזי אל לשחת רשעה "the mysteries of God (His hidden plans) to annihilate," 3:9, cf. also the hi form להשחית רבים in 1 QH 2:27. משחיתים are "destroyers," 1 QH 3:38, משחית is "destruction," 5:32 (quoting Da. 10:8). שחת ni occurs in a moral sense: לכל השב מדרכו הנשחתה "to every man who turns from his corrupt way," Damasc. 15:7 (19:7).

2. Talmudic and Midrashic Writings.

The two stems used with special frequency are שחת and חבל .

a. שחת pi means here "to ruin," e.g., the eye, bQid., 24b, "to mar," e.g., the hair, T. Nazir, 4, 7 (Zuckermann, 289), "to destroy," namely, oneself לנפשו, Ex. r., 8, 2 on 7:1, Adam (said of the angels), AbRNat A, 1 (Schechter, 8 f.). שחת hi is used in this sense too, the body in bShab., 140b, the end of the whiskers, Mak., 3, 5, furniture, bShab., 129a. בל תשחית (Dt. 20:19) is found along with בל תטמא "to take by force" and בל תקוף "to snatch to oneself," T. Bik., 2, 3 f. (Zuckermandel, 101). The part. משחית means "destroyer" and is the name of an angel in Dt. r., 3, 11 on 9:1 (Wünsche, 48).

The nouns of this stem are שחת "pit," cf. באר שחת "the deepest pit," Pesikt. r., 10 (41a), and שחתא "pit," Tg. [14] on Ps. 94:13 vl. [15] (HT שחת), from which comes שחית "defective," "blemished," of sacrifices, Tg. J. I on Lv. 22:24 (HT נָתוּק). שחיתא means "corruption," morally "the bad" (HT זְמוֹת or זִמָּה), Tg. on Ps. 17:3.

---

[12] Here LXX probably read פֶּלַלְתְּ (from פלל pi "to make atonement") as כֻּלֵּית.

[13] ἄφθορος "untouched" at Est. 2:2 is a free rendering of בְּתוּלוֹת. For מַדְחֵפוֹת "stroke on stroke" LXX has εἰς διαφθοράν (Cod. B καταφθοράν) at ψ 139:12 and Σ Ps. 31:4 probably related לְשַׁדֵּי to שׁוֹד "devastation" (LXX ταλαιπωρίαν), cf. G. Bertram, "Zur Prägung d. bibl. Gottesvorstellung in d. griech. Übers. d. AT. Die Wiedergabe v. schadad u. schaddaj im Griech.," *Die Welt d. Orients,* II (1959), 502-513.

[14] Ed. P. de Lagarde, Hagiographa chaldaice (1873).

[15] Cf. Jastrow, *s.v.* שַׁחְתָּא.

b. Far more common in Talmudic and Midrashic works is חבל . חבל q means "to wrong," "to injure," Shab., 14, 1; bShab., 106a; TBQ, 9, 29 (Zuckermandel, 365 f.), "to wound," jKet., 4, 1 (28b, 1. 8. 10 f.), בעצמו "oneself," bBQ, 91b. חבל pi means the same, also in a transf. sense, BQ, 8, 1. 2; bBQ, 87a b, בהלכה, i.e., in discussion of the halacha, bSanh., 24a. In the pi it can then mean "to destroy," e.g., on the lips of the angel of death, who says יש לי רשות לחבל "I have power to destroy, to slay," bBer., 51a. The part. of חבל ni means "the wounded," Shebu., 7, 1, as does the part. pass. חבול, 7. 3; it is also found in the sense "to be ruined" of vessels, Kelim, 14, 2. חבל ithpaʿal is used in the same way as the ni pass., e.g., for "to fall sick," bBM, 97a. It can also mean "to become wicked," Tg. O. on Gn. 6:11 f. (HT: שחת), "to perish," Tg. on Prv. 13:13 (HT יֶחָבֶל), of the soul, Tg. on Job 17:1 (HT חֻבָּלָה).

It should be noted throughout the Tg. that חבל replaces Hbr. שחת, cf. וחבילו בישראל Tg. Pro. on Ju. 20:21 (HT וַיַּשְׁחִיתוּ), מחבל Tg. O. on Gn. 38:9 (HT שחת), "to overthrow one's neighbour with the mouth," Tg. on Prv. 11:9 (HT יַשְׁחִית), מחבלא the "destroyer" as a military unit, Tg. Pro. on 1 S. 14:15; 13:17 (HT מַשְׁחִית). Thus we find חבל for "corrupt" in a moral or physical sense, Tg. O. on Gn. 6:12 (HT הִשְׁחִית), the walk, Tg. Pro. on Is. 1:14 (HT מַשְׁחִיתִים), acts, Tg. O. on Dt. 4:16, the soul, Tg. on Prv. 6:32 (HT מַשְׁחִית). מחבל means "mutilated," Tg. O. on Dt. 23:2 (HT כְּרוּת); Tg. Pro. on Mal. 1:14 (HT מָשְׁחָת).

Nouns of this stem remain in the same circle of meaning, e.g., חבלה "destruction," "injury," bSanh., 100b. The מלאך חבלה is "the angel that brings destruction," jShebu., 6, 6 (37a, 67); bBer., 51a. Sanh., 1, 1 deals with cases of חבלות "injuries." The noun חבל "damage," "destruction," occurs in Tg. on Job 5:21 f. (HT שׁוֹד). חיבול means self-inflicted injury, Tg. O. on Lv. 19:28 (HT שֶׂרֶט); on Lv. 21:5 (HT שָׂרֶטֶת). חיבולא can mean "wound," "bodily mutilation," "destruction," but also "what is shameful," cf. Tg. on Job 11:15 and on 31:7; in Tg. on Qoh. 7:28 זכאי בלא חיבולה is "a just man in whom is nothing shameful," elucidating Hbr. אֶחָד . חבלה also means "destruction," "corruption," Tg. Pro. on Jon. 2:7, and even "pit" (HT שַׁחַת), Tg. Pro. on Ez. 28:8. חבל means "destroyer," fem. חבלנית Mak., 1, 10; bMak., 7a, where it is used to denote a court which passed more than one death sentence in a seven year span. חבלא means "destruction," as in מלאך חבלא the "angel of death," Tg. J. I on Ex. 4:25 f. In the HT it is God Himself who meets Moses, but in the LXX it is an ἄγγελος κυρίου and then in the Tg. it is the angel of destruction or death. Finally we have חבל in the sense of "destruction upon thee" as a malediction, bSanh., 111a.

III. The Word Group in Hellenistic Judaism.

1. The Greek Old Testament.

The main original is שחת in various forms. φθείρω κτλ. etc. occur 91 times for this root, διαφθείρω being used 51 times; it ref. to the "killing" of men in 2 Βασ. 24:16; Ἰερ. 28(51):1; Dt. 10:10 ΑΣΘ (LXX: ἐξολεθρεῦσαι), cf. καταφθείρω, Gn. 6:13 [16] and διαφθορά (HT שְׁחִית) ψ 106:20. [17] φθαρτός is an animal for sacrifice which is blemished or defective, Lv. 22:25 (HT מָשְׁחָת), cf. θύω διεφθαρμένον, Mal. 1:14; ears of grain are ἀνεμόφθοροι (Ἀ ἐφθαρμένοι καύσωνι), Gn. 41:6 (HT שְׁדוּפֹת קָדִים). Obj. of διαφθείρω are seed in Gn. 38:9 ΑΣ (HT שחת pi), fruits in Ju. 6:4 Cod. A, κληρο-

---

[16] τὸ ὕδωρ τὸ καταφθειρόμενον 2 Βασ. 14:14 Cod. B (HT נגר ni "to flow") is a slip for καταφερόμενον.
[17] Cf. "to trim the beard," Lv. 19:27.

νομία, Rt. 4:6, ἰσχυροί, Da. 8:24 Θ, cf. διαφθείροντα τοῦ ἐκφθεῖραι (LXX εἰς ἀπώλειαν), [18] "the destroyer who destroys weapons," Is. 54:16 ᾿ΑΣΘ (HT מַשְׁחִית). For "wasting" a land etc. we find φθείρω at 1 Ch. 20:1; Ex. 8:20 Σ (LXX ἐξωλεθρεύθη), and διαφθείρω, e.g., τὴν πόλιν at 1 Βασ. 23:10, αὐτήν (sc. βασιλείαν) at Da. 11:17 Θ, γῆν at 4 Βασ. 18:25; Is. 36:10 ᾿ΑΣΘ (LXX πολεμῆσαι); Jer. 36(43):29 ᾿ΑΣ (LXX ἐξολεθρεύσει), cf. 1 Βασ. 6:5; διαφθείρων (Σ διαφθείροντες) of the spoilers, 1 Βασ. 13:17. Esp. common is the use of φθορά for the noun שַׁחַת "pit," which is obviously used together with the verbal stem שׁחת even though it comes from שׁוּחַ: [19] οὐδὲ δώσεις τὸν ὅσιόν σου ἰδεῖν διαφθοράν, ψ 15:10 (→ 103, 8 f.), τὸν λυτρούμενον ἐκ φθορᾶς τὴν ζωήν σου, ψ 102:4, cf. καταφθορά, ψ 48:10, διαφθορά, Prv. 26:27 ᾿ΑΣ (LXX βόθρον "pit"); Ps. 7:16 ᾿ΑΣ (LXX: εἰς βόθρον), εἰς φρέαρ διαφθορᾶς, ψ 54:24 (Σ εἰς λάκκον, "pit"), cf. Jer. 18:22 ᾿ΑΣ. [20] διαφθορά occurs also in Lam. 4:20 (HT שְׁחִיתָה); Ez. 19:4, 8; Job 33:30 Cod. A V; ψ 9:16; 34:7 (HT always שַׁחַת); Prv. 28:10 (HT שְׁחוּת); μὴ διαφθείρεσθαι (LXX ἀπόληται), Is. 38:17 Σ (HT מִשַּׁחַת), Jon. 2:7 is difficult, ᾿Α has the best rendering: ἐκ φθορᾶς ἡ ζωή μου (Σ ζωῆς μου); LXX has ἀναβήτω φθορὰ ζωῆς μου. [21] At Ez. 9:6 LXX links לְמַשְׁחִית with מְשׁ and transl. εἰς ἐξάλειψιν (᾿ΑΣΘ εἰς διαφθοράν). [22] Similarly for לְמַשְׁחַת at Ez. 28:8 ᾿ΑΣΘ have εἰς διαφθοράν (LXX εἰς ἀπώλειαν), for בַּשַּׁחַת at Job 9:31 ᾿Α has ἐν διαφθορᾷ (LXX ἐν ῥύπῳ), and for לַשַּׁחַת at Job 33:22 ᾿ΑΣΘ have εἰς διαφθοράν (LXX εἰς θάνατον). διαφθορά is used in Ez. 21:36 LXX (HT מַשְׁחִית) and Da. 10:8 Θ. [23] Worth noting is διέφθαρται πᾶσα ἡ ἐπιφυλλὶς αὐτῶν (HT עֲלִילוֹתָם כֹּל הִשְׁחִיתוּ, "they have corrupted all their doings") at Zeph. 3:7 LXX. [24] God's word of promise will not perish οὐ μὴ διαφθείρῃ, Sir. 47:22. Idols will be destroyed, 4 Βασ. 19:12. It is said of the people: διεφθείρατε τὴν διαθήκην (HT שׁחת pi) at Mal. 2:8, and of Edom: διέφθειρε σπλάγχνα αὐτοῦ, "he suppressed his pity," Am. 1:11 ᾿ΑΣ.

φθείρω has a moral sense at Hos. 9:9; Gn. 6:11. διαφθείρω means "to act in a morally corrupt way" at Dt. 9:12 ᾿Α; 31:29 ᾿Α (LXX both times ἀνομέω); Ez. 16:47 ᾿ΑΣΘ; Ju. 2:19; ψ 13:1; 52:2, [25] cf. also υἱοὶ διαφθείροντες, Is. 1:4 ᾿ΑΣΘ (LXX ἄνομοι), διεφθαρμένοι, Jer. 6:28, ἐπιτηδεύματα διεφθαρμένα, "corrupt walk," Ez. 20:44, cf. 23:11, διεφθάρη ἡ ἐπιστήμη, Ez. 28:17, ῥῆμα ψευδὲς καὶ διεφθαρμένον (Aram. כִדְבָה וּשְׁחִיתָה מִלָּה), Da. 2:9 Θ. καταφθείρω has the sense "to sin," "to corrupt (morally)" at Gn. 6:12. [26]

The word group stands for few Hbr. equivalents apart from שׁחת → 97, 1 ff. The most common is חבל or Aram. חֲבַל "to destroy," "to overthrow," φθείρω at Is. 54:16 (HT לְחַבֵּל); Δα. 2:44; 7:14 (both Aram. חֲבַל ithpa'al), διαφθείρω at Da. 2:44 Θ; 4:23 Θ;

---

[18] Here perhaps LXX read לְשַׁחֵית; in any case the transl. is free. v. 17 ref. to a perishable φθαρτός weapon in the hands of the enemies of Israel (HT יוּצַר "formed"). The sense is not altered by punctuating after φθεῖραι or φθαρτόν.

[19] Ges.-Buhl, s.v. שַׁחַת.

[20] Σ perhaps read שַׁחַת for שׁוּחָה in HT.

[21] LXX construed וַתַּעַל "thou causest to rise up" as 3rd pers. fem. or read וַיַּעַל, and מְשַׁחַת as מַשַּׁחַת.

[22] At ψ 106:39 Σ read וַיִּשָּׁחֲתוּ for וַיָּשֹׁחוּ "they decreased" and transl. κατεφθάρησαν (LXX ἐκακώθησαν).

[23] Δα. 10:8 reads: καὶ ἰδοὺ πνεῦμα ἐπεστράφη ἐπ᾿ ἐμὲ εἰς φθοράν. Probably רוּחַ was read for וְהוֹדִי "my radiant face"; εἰς φθοράν is for לְמַשְׁחִית.

[24] Probably LXX read עָלֵהֶם "all their foliage."

[25] διαφθείρω is used for "to ruin" at Prv. 11:9 ᾿ΑΣΘ.

[26] Whether "to do wrong" or "to corrupt" is the correct transl. at 2 Ch. 26:16; 27:2 is an open question.

6:27 Θ, cf. διαφθορά at Da. 3:92 Θ (Aram. חֲבַל "hurt" at Da. 3:25); 6:24 Θ; διαφθείρω means "to be dissuaded," Qoh. 5:5 (HT חבל pi), διαφθείροντας "lay waste," Cant. 1:15 Σ (HT מְחַבְּלִים); καταφθείρεται (Θ διαφθείρεται) ὁ ζυγός "the yoke is set aside," Is. 10:27, cf. 13:5. Similarly in Mi. 2:10 חֲבַל is transl. φθορά even though its meaning is doubtful in the context. [27] Some forms of נבל "to sink down," "to fade," "to lie exhausted," are also equivalents of the φθείρω group, e.g., καταφθείρω at Ex. 18:18, cf. ἐφθάρη ἡ οἰκουμένη, Is. 24:4.

2. Josephus.

Here, too, διαφθείρω means "to kill" and is common in military accounts, e.g., Ant., 15, 123; Bell., 1, 334. It also means "to drive off" τὸ σπαρέν, Ap., 2, 202. cf. διαφθείρω and καταφθείρω, which in the pass. means "to perish," Bell., 2, 549, cf. φθείρω at Bell., 6, 182 and 193. φθορά is "bloodshed," Bell., 2 223, "massacre," 2, 477. καταφθείρω can also mean "to harm" (politically), Ant., 16, 297, while φθείρω means "to perish," e.g., through sickness, Bell., 5, 383. In Jos. we find the form φθάρμα "destruction," of men φθάρματα ἔθνους, Bell., 5, 443. The less common φθόρος is used for φθορά to describe Antipater, a "nuisance," "a real pest," Bell., 1, 521. But φθόρος can also mean "catastrophe," Ant., 18, 10, or "destruction," e.g., of an earthquake, Ant., 15, 121; φθορά is an "annihilating defeat" in Bell., 2, 559. Rotting corpses pollute διέφθειρον the air, Bell., 3, 530. Thanksgiving for food can "grow dumb," διαφθείρομαι, Ant., 3, 34. διαφθείρω is common for military annihilation, Ant., 13, 120. Idols, too, can be destroyed, 7, 77. διαφθορά is the "destroying" or "damaging" of, e.g., τοῦ δικαίου, Ant., 4, 216. It means physical destruction through illness in 9, 101 and the destruction of politically important people in 18, 7. In the moral field Jos. follows normal usage. διαφθείρω can mean "to bribe" in Ant., 14, 327; Vit., 73, and φθείρω παρθένον, like φθορά, can be used for seducing, Ant., 4, 252; 17, 309 and also gen. for making wicked decisions or doing wicked acts, Ant., 10, 105; Ap., 2, 264, where, with ref. to Socrates, the expression νέων διαφθοραί is adopted from Gk. lit., Xenoph. Ap., 19. διαφθείρω in the pass. means gen. moral "corruption," Ant., 18, 176; Bell., 1, 359, and διαφθορά can also ref. specifically to adultery, Ant., 2, 55. Obviously the antithesis φθαρτός - ἄφθαρτος also plays a part in Jos. σώματα are φθαρτά, Bell., 2, 154, cf. καὶ ἐκ φθαρτῆς ὕλης, 3, 372, and v. also Ant., 8, 280. But the ψυχή is ἄφθαρτος, Bell., 2, 163. This is typically Hell. → 96, 8 ff. Equally typical is the rejection of the Epicureans, of whom Jos. writes: τὴν πρόνοιαν ἐκβάλλουσιν ... τὸν θεὸν οὐκ ἀξιοῦσιν ἐπιτροπεύειν τῶν πραγμάτων οὐδ' ὑπὸ τῆς μακαρίας καὶ ἀφθάρτου πρὸς διαμονὴν τῶν ὅλων οὐσίας κυβερνᾶσθαι τὰ σύμπαντα, Ant., 10, 278. God is introduced as a blessed and imperishable being (→ 96, 18) and His sustaining of the world is equated with Stoic πρόνοια. Like God, the divine voice is also ἄφθαρτος, Ant., 3, 88.

3. Philo.

In Philo, too, διαφθείρω means "to kill," "to do away with," Sacr. AC, 122, of mankind in the flood, Deus Imm., 73. φθορά is the "corruptibility" of the soul, Ebr., 23, πάθος, Som., II, 270; everything sick is φθορά "the destruction" of the healthy, Deus Imm., 124. With ἀταξία and ἀκοσμία, φθορά is also something whose cause does not

---

[27] T. H. Robinson, *Die Zwölf Kleinen Proph. Hosea bis Micha*, Hndbch. AT, I, 14² (1954), ad loc.; A. Weiser, *Das Buch d. Zwölf Kleinen Propheten*, AT Deutsch, 24, 1⁴ (1963), ad loc. The meaning "destruction" for חֲבַל is supported by מלאכי חבל "angel of destruction" in 1 QM 13:12; 1 QS 4:12; Damasc. 2:6 (2:4), v. J. Carmignac, *La Règle de la guerre des fils de Lumière contre les fils de ténèbres* (1958), 194 f., 206 f.

lie in God, Aet. Mund., 106; τὰ ἀΐδια φθορᾶς ἀνεπίδεκτα, "the eternal is not subject to corruptibility," *ibid.*, 53, while εἰς τὸ μὴ ὂν γίνεσθαι means τὴν φθορὰν παραδέχεσθαι, 82. The cause of φθορά is ἡ παρὰ φύσιν τάξις, 34, which has four forms, namely, πρόσθεσις, ἀφαίρεσις, μετάθεσις and ἀλλοίωσις, 113. Elsewhere the nine δυναστεῖαι, i.e., the four emotions and five senses, are described as φθαρταί τε καὶ φθορᾶς αἴτιαι, Abr., 244. φθοροποιός, "bringing or causing destruction," is used, e.g., of the δύναμις of water, which can also be ζωτική "life-bringing," Vit. Mos., I, 100.

Philo is familiar with the use of the group in the moral sphere. ἁμαρτήματα may be φθοροποιά for political order, Spec. Leg., III, 167. In a pure Hell. use it is said of the σάρξ (→ VII, 122, 1 ff.) that it is a τὴν αὑτῆς φθείρουσα ὁδόν, Deus Imm., 142. φθορεύς "seducer" appears in lists of vices, Spec. Leg., IV, 89; Decal., 168; Jos., 84. Conf. Ling., 48 has the stronger φθορεὺς ἀγαθῶν "corrupter of moral goods," contrasted with the νόμιμος ἀνήρ in Leg. All., III, 220. φθοραί are mentioned alongside μοιχεῖαι in Det. Pot. Ins., 102. Agric., 73 ref. to the οἰκοφθόρος who ruins his household. Philo expounds as follows κατέφθειρε πᾶσα σάρξ τὴν ὁδὸν αὐτοῦ in Gn. 6:12: κατέφθειρε πᾶσα σάρξ τὴν τοῦ αἰωνίου καὶ ἀφθάρτου τελείαν ὁδὸν τὴν πρὸς θεὸν ἄγουσαν, i.e., in terms of the way of moral perfection that leads to God and has a part in Him, Deus Imm., 142. Among perishable things which fall victim to φθείρεσθαι he reckons the κόσμος, Aet. Mund., 5, 79 etc. When τὸ ἄφθαρτον εἶδος arises in the soul, the θνητόν is destroyed, Deus Imm., 123.

Not surprisingly the antithesis φθαρτόν - ἄφθαρτον plays a special role in Philo. In Op. Mund., 119 the σῶμα is φθαρτόν, but for Philo, unlike Paul, the ψυχή is not the earthly and perishable life-force, but the locus of supraterrestrial possibilities and achievements. The cause of man's preservation διαμονή cannot be a corruptible thing but only God, Spec. Leg., II, 198. In him, too, we find the philosophical def.: οὗ πάντα τὰ μέρη φθείρεται φθαρτόν ἐστιν ἐκεῖνο, Aet. Mund., 143. As φθαρτόν we reckon φύσις, Leg. All., II, 89, ὕλη, I, 88, τροφή, Sobr., 3, τὰ σιτία, Rer. Div. Her., 311, τὰ ὄργανα, Decal., 34, the νοῦς, Leg. All., I, 32. 90, ὁ κόσμος, Aet. Mund., 7. 9. 78. 131, εἶδος, the "form" of things, Poster. C., 105, θνητῶν ἔργα, Aet. Mund., 44, τὰ γένη, Vit. Mos., II, 121; the gen. rule is: τὸ γενητὸν φθαρτὸν πᾶν, Aet. Mund., 73. But there is also γένη ἄφθαρτα, Poster C., 105, so that the soul has two kinds of γένη, τὸ μὲν θεῖον, τὸ δὲ φθαρτόν, Leg. All., II, 95. The γένεσις φθαρτή creates κακά and βέβηλα, while God is the ποιητής of ἀγαθά and ἅγια, Plant., 53. There is juxtaposition and coinherence of a natural world of becoming and perishing and an inner, supernatural and incorruptible world made by God, φθαρτά and ἄφθαρτα have nothing to do with one another, Abr., 243. Thus the ἄφθαρτος θεός cannot be φθαρτός as the χωνεύματα statues of false gods are, Leg. All., III, 36. Merely to think of God as φθαρτός is against θέμις, a sacrilege, II, 3. The soul filled with the vision of ἄφθαρτα ἀγαθά has found release from temporal and inauthentic things, Deus Imm., 151. Hence it can be said of such a soul that it "will never be profaned" οὐδέποτε ἐφθείρετο, Migr. Abr., 225. ὁ μὲν δὴ σοφὸς τεθνηκέναι δοκῶν τὸν φθαρτὸν βίον ζῇ τὸν ἄφθαρτον, Det. Pot. Ins., 49, cf. Virt., 67. Thus a γενική and ἄφθαρτος ἀρετή is contrasted with an εἰδική and φθαρτὴ ἀρετή, Cher., 7. If there is no ἐπιστήμη of ἄφθαρτα, φθαρτά are regarded as λαμπρά, Ebr., 209. The real wealth of the wise is not silver or gold, which are only οὐσίαι φθαρταί, Cher., 48; the ὀρθὸς λόγος, equated with the Law, is οὐ φθαρτός, Ebr., 142.

Naturally Philo also uses the Hell. concept of ἀφθαρσία → 96, 17 and 19. It is ascribed to the ἀγένητον, Aet. Mund., 27. There are virtues which are ἄφθαρτοι and ἀφθαρσίας ἄξιαι as such, Som., II, 258. Abraham enjoys ἀφθαρσία after death, Sacr. AC, 5. The ἄνθρωπος θεοῦ is also ἄφθαρτος, Conf. Ling., 41. The heights of the life of friends of virtue are also called ἄφθαρτοι, Cher., 6. The life βίος for which the wise man lives is ἄφθαρτος, Det. Pot. Ins., 49. That the world is ἄφθαρτος is deduced from the incorruptibility of πρόνοια, Aet. Mund., 51. ἡ καθόλου φρόνησις "insight in general," also called ἡ γενικὴ φρόνησις, Mut. Nom., 79, is ἄφθαρτος as compared with the individual insight, Leg. All., I, 78. The nature of the good is ἄφθαρτος, Plant.,

114, as is also the φύσις of ἀρεταί, Det. Pot. Ins., 77; Abr., 54. Hence the imperishable world can be summarised as τὰ ἄφθαρτα, Op. Mund., 82 etc. Heaven, however, is ἀφθάρτων τελειότατος, Praem. Poen., 1.

4. Other Hellenistic Jewish Works.

We find in other works the use of καταφθείρω for "to destroy," e.g., the temple, Test. A. 7:2. It is said of the πνεῦμα τοῦ φθόνου: ἀγριοῖ... τὴν ψυχὴν καὶ φθείρει τὸ σῶμα, S. 4:8. καταφθορά means "destruction," with θάνατος, Sir. 28:6. We find the παιδοφθόρος, who destroys children, in a list of vices, Test. L. 17:11. διαφθείρω can mean "to destroy," e.g., τὸ σπέρμα, Test. Jud. 10:5, and it can also be used in a moral sense: ἐν ἁμαρτίαις φθαρείς, 19:4, κακίᾳ διαφθειρόμενοι, A. 7:5, διαφθορά with πονηρία and κάκωσις, G. 8:2, τὰς πράξεις διαφθείρω, N. 3:1, ἐν πορνείᾳ φθαρήσονται, S. 5:4. In Hell. Judaism we find the antithesis φθαρτός - ἄφθαρτος familiar to us from Gk. philosophy → 96, 8 ff. Man as such is φθαρτός, 2 Macc. 7:16, as is also his body, Wis. 9:15, or life's goods, Test. B. 6:2. It is said of the idol: τὸ δὲ φθαρτὸν θεὸς ὠνομάσθη, Wis. 14:8. In contrast, God's Spirit, who dwells in all, is ἄφθαρτον, Wis. 12:1, and the light which consists in the Law and goes forth from it is τὸ ἄφθαρτον νόμου φῶς, 18:4. Typically Hell. is the concept of ἀφθαρσία → 96, 17 and 19. God has created man ἐπ' ἀφθαρσίᾳ, Wis. 2:23. To keep the commandments is βεβαίωσις ἀφθαρσίας "an assurance of immortality," which is already given herewith and which means closeness to God, 6:18 f. The martyr is changed into immortality, 4 Macc. 9:22; his victory is immortality, 17:12. [28]

C. The Word Group in the New Testament.

1. Real Sense.

Rev. 11:18 is the only instance of διαφθείρω being used in the NT for the destruction of men as a result of God's judgment. φθείρω is to be taken in this sense in 1 C. 3:17b [29] (cf. also Jd. 10). Rev. 8:9 follows Greek usage with its reference to the destruction of ships, and so, too, does Lk. 12:33 when it speaks of the destruction of clothes by moths → VII, 275, 17 ff.. The context of 2 C. 7:2 suggests that φθείρω means "to ruin economically" here → 93, 27 ff.; VI, 273, 14 ff.; in the light of exaggerated criticism it is meant ironically and not in a moral or religious sense. [30] Somewhat similar is φθείρω τὸν ναὸν τοῦ θεοῦ in 1 C. 3:17. Here we have a metaphor, and in terms of the metaphor the reference is to real destruction, the collapse of a house, [31] not leading astray, [32] esp. as there has not yet been any mention of express heresies in the Corinthian factions. In Col. 2:22 the point of εἰς φθοράν is that all kinds of foods are destined for destruction in their natural use. [33] The same applies to the expression ζῷα γεγεν-

---

[28] Changing into incorruptibility is the presupposition of immortality, G. Bertram, "The Problem of Death in Popular Judaeo-Hell. Piety," *Crozer Quart.*, 10 (1933), 257-287; A. Dupont-Sommer, *Le quatrième livre des Machabées* (1939), 44-48; H. Bückers, "Die Unsterblichkeitslehre d. Weisheitsbuches. Ihr Ursprung u. ihre Bedeutung," *At.liche Abh.*, 13, 4 (1938), 108.

[29] Heinr. 1 K., *ad loc.*: The death penalty that God will exact on those who destroy His temple. Cf. E. Käsemann, "Sätze hl. Rechtes im NT," *Exeget. Versuche u. Besinnungen*, II² (1965), 69-71.

[30] Wnd. 2 K., *ad loc.*, but cf. also Schl. K., *ad loc.*

[31] οἰκοφθόρος in Ign. Eph., 16, 1 means the same, cf. Pr.-Bauer, *s.v.*

[32] E.g., Heinr. 1 K., *ad loc.*

[33] Dib. Gefbr., *ad loc.*, cf. also T. K. Abbott, *A Crit. and Exeget. Comm. on the Epistles to the Eph. and Col.*, ICC (1897), *ad loc.*: "physical dissolution."

νημένα φυσικὰ εἰς ἅλωσιν καὶ φθοράν in 2 Pt. 2:12a; as those who have come into being they are destined to perish, to be destroyed. Much more difficult is the next saying in 2:12b with reference to the false teachers: ἐν τῇ φθορᾷ αὐτῶν καὶ φθαρήσονται. [34] One might paraphrase: They will perish in their conduct, which destroys faith and morality. [35] More illuminating, however, is the explanation that relates φθορὰ αὐτῶν to the beasts: In their destruction, i.e., as they perish, so the false teachers will perish too, as all things must perish in the Last Judgment apart from those who are rescued for a new world. [36] In the quotation from ψ 15 in Ac. 2:27, 31; 13:34-37 διαφθορά means "corruption," "decay" → 99, 8 f.

2. Moral and Religious Sense.

One may refer here to the quotation from Menander in 1 C. 15:33. In 2 C. 11:3 the νοήματα of the Corinthians are the object of possible perversion → 94, 19 ff. The allusion to Eve plainly indicates the meaning of φθείρω here. The expression φθείρω ἀπό is also assimilated to πλανάομαι ἀπό. [37] In 1 Tm. 6:5 and 2 Tm. 3:8 νοῦς is used in the same way as νόημα in 2 C. 11:3: διεφθαρμένοι or κατεφθαρμένοι τὸν νοῦν, "of corrupt mind." The παλαιὸς ἄνθρωπος becomes degenerate in or according to his desires, Eph. 4:22. [38] The διαφθείροντες τὴν γῆν of Rev. 11:18b are those who "corrupt" or "seduce" the earth, mankind, in morality and faith, as the whore of 19:2 does. The ἀφθορία mentioned in Tt. 2:7 also belongs to this sphere. [39] It is used with σεμνότης to describe the moral attitude of Titus, who will not let himself be led astray; it refers, then, to his conduct relative to teachers and teaching. [40] We are not to think in terms of the impregnability against false teaching that Titus is establishing in the churches, [41] nor in terms of doctrine safeguarded by the truth, [42] but rather of innocence in the sense of not being, or not able to be, corrupted. In other words, what is described is the disposition of Titus. [43]

3. Ideal Sense: Corruptible-Incorruptible.

The group is often used to denote the corruptibility of man, his subjection to death. Paul has in view the outward man who experiences death in himself (2 C. 4:16), not as a once-for-all event, but as an ongoing process, as the ἀνακαινοῦται ἡμέρᾳ καὶ ἡμέρᾳ shows. The fact that the body is given up to death and destruction is often stated in Greek and later Jewish writings (→ VII, 102, 13 ff.; 116,

---

[34] The vl. καταφθαρήσονται in the *koine* text might have arisen from the καί or it might be an attempt to show the difference between φθορά and φθαρήσονται, the latter being actual destruction as a punishment and the former moral corruption.

[35] Cf. Wbg. Pt., *ad loc.*

[36] So Kn. Pt., Wnd. Kath. Br.³, *ad loc.*

[37] Ltzm. K., *ad loc.* Wnd. 2 K., *ad loc.* ref. to Herm. v., 1, 3, 1, where καταφθείρω is used with ἀπό.

[38] Cf. Dib. Gefbr., Schlier Eph., *ad loc.*

[39] The *koine* text reads ἀδιαφθορία, cf. Pr.-Bauer, *s.v.*

[40] B. Weiss, *Krit. exeget. Hndbch. über d. Br. Pauli an Tm. u. Tt., Krit. exeget. Komm. über d. NT,* 11⁵ (1886), *ad loc.*

[41] Schl. Past., 192.

[42] Wbg. Past., *ad loc.*

[43] Cf. Dib. Past.⁴, *ad loc.*, who ref. to Just. Apol., 15, 6, where ἄφθορος means "chaste," and Dial., 100, 5, where it is used of Eve before the fall.

4 ff.). [44] Man is φθαρτός (R. 1:23) precisely in antithesis to the ἄφθαρτος θεός. But the wreath sought in worldly contests (→ I, 137, 24 ff.) is also φθαρτός as distinct from the eternal goal of the Christian life, 1 C. 9:25. τὸ φθαρτόν is man's existence in the world as this is controlled by the σάρξ. ἀφθαρσία, a new mode of being, must be imparted to him, 1 C. 15:53. Christians are not redeemed with φθαρτοῖς ("corruptible") means such as ἀργυρίῳ ἢ χρυσίῳ, but by the blood of Christ, which is indestructible, which is a divine means, and which is thus said to be τίμιος, 1 Pt. 1:18. [45] Opposed to the σπορὰ φθαρτή is the ἄφθαρτος λόγος by which Christians are begotten as new men, 1 Pt. 1:23. [46] In this connection φθορά (R. 8:21) means "corruptibility," and it elucidates the ματαιότης of v. 20. φθορᾶς is a gen. qualitatis, not obj., in relation to δουλεία, so that we have a counterpart of ἐλευθερία τῆς δόξης. [47] φθορά is the "corruptibility" which must pass away, as flesh and blood must also pass away, 1 C. 15:50. Yet the concept is not merely that of decay and subjection to it. [48] As ζωή corresponds to πνεῦμα, so φθορά does to σάρξ, and in Gl. 1:8 this means "eternal destruction" (→ I, 396, 18 ff.) and undoubtedly much more than mere decay. [49] Both φθορά and ζωή are to be understood eschatologically, [50] so that only the *parousia* brings the corruptible to light as such. φθορά is displayed in its quality as corruptibility only with the manifestation of the incorruptible and not in the daily experience of the natural man. In both the instances in 2 Pt. (1:4; 2:19) φθορά again means "corruptibility" and not moral corruption. [51] What is meant seems to be the world of the φθαρτόν, in the late Hell. sense → 96, 8 ff. Moral failure consists in succumbing ἐν ἐπιθυμίᾳ (1:4) to corruptibility as though this were the one essential thing: δοῦλοι ὑπάρχοντες τῆς φθορᾶς, 2:19.

The dead will rise again as ἄφθαρτοι, changed and belonging to a new world, 1 C. 15:52. [52] In the later epistles of the Pauline corpus there is increasing reference to the ἄφθαρτον and ἀφθαρσία under developing Hell. influence. God is lauded here as the ἄφθαρτος (→ 96, 15 ff.), 1 Tm. 1:17 [53] → III, 112, 9 ff.; cf. R. 1:23. Also ἄφθαρτος is the κληρονομία into which Christians will one day enter. The adjectives ἀμίαντος, ἀμάραντος and ἄφθαρτος show that this belongs to God, 1 Pt.

---

[44] Wnd. 2 K., *ad loc.* ref. to Ps.-Plat. Alc., I, 135a: διαφθαρῆναι of the body of the irrational sick. Schl. K., *ad loc.*: "Paul uses εἰ καὶ φθείρεται to describe the corruption of his outward man as something that is actually taking place."

[45] Kn. Pt., 71 and 74.

[46] Kn. Pt., *ad loc.* stresses that elsewhere the new birth of the Christian is by baptism or the πνεῦμα, Jn. 3:5; Tt. 3:5, cf. Herm. s., 9, 16, 2 ff., and that only here is it by the λόγος.

[47] But cf., e.g., Mi. R.[13], *ad loc.*, who thinks φθορᾶς is a subj. gen., and R. A. Lipsius, *Die Briefe an d. Galater, Römer, Philipper, Hand-Comm. z. NT*, 2, 2² (1892), *ad loc.*: Corruption... is seen as a ruling power. Acc. to Mi. R.,[13], *ad loc.* the background is apocalyptic.

[48] So Heinr. 1 K., *ad loc.*

[49] Lipsius, *op. cit., ad loc.*

[50] Schlier Gl., *ad loc.*

[51] So C. Bigg, *A Crit. and Exeget. Comm. on the Ep. of St. Peter and St. Jude*, ICC² (1902), on 2 Pt. 2:19: "moral corruption." For corruptibility *v.* Wnd. Kath. Br. on 2 Pt. 2:19; Kn. Pt. on 2 Pt. 1:4 and esp. 2:19: "In no sense is φθορά moral corruption here." Wbg. Pt. on 2:19: "The visibility achieved by sin with the seeds of corruption and death." K. H. Schelkle, *Die Petrusbr. Der Judasbr., Herders Theol. Komm. z. NT*, 13, 2² (1964) on 2 Pt. 2:19: "The destruction which overtakes the sinner in the judgment."

[52] Ltzm. K., *ad loc.*

[53] Dib. Past.⁴, *ad loc.* ref. to Epic. Men., 123 (Usener, 59): πρῶτον μὲν τὸν θεὸν ζῷον ἄφθαρτον καὶ μακάριον νομίζων, cf. Plut. Stoic. Rep., 38 (II, 1051 f.) → 96, 18 f.

1:4. [54] The ἄφθαρτον can be more precisely defined in terms of πνεῦμα: ἐν τῷ ἀφθάρτῳ [55] τοῦ πραέος καὶ ἡσυχίου πνεύματος, 1 Pt. 3:4. Here again τὸ ἄφθαρτον denotes the sphere, environment and mode of being in which man moves with a meek and quiet spirit [56] in contrast to that governed by the φθαρτόν. ἀφθαρσία as well as ἄφθαρτον stands in antithesis to the φθαρτόν. Eph. 6:24 is difficult to expound (→ VII, 778, 16 ff.): ἡ χάρις μετὰ πάντων τῶν ἀγαπώντων τὸν κύριον ἡμῶν ᾽Ιησοῦν Χριστὸν ἐν ἀφθαρσίᾳ. If one takes ἐν ἀφθαρσίᾳ with χάρις, [57] the meaning is: "with incorruptibility," and both ἀφθαρσία and χάρις characterise the mode of being in supraterrestrial life. But there is not much to commend this. If instead one takes it with Χριστός or ἀγαπῶντες, then it denotes the new and heavenly mode of existence of Christ or Christians. [58] If one does not relate it to Χριστόν as the nearest word, and there is much to be said for this, then the whole verse must be understood as a concluding liturgical salutation. In this case ἐν ἀφθαρσίᾳ amounts to much the same as "in eternity" and shows that the wish is one that is to be fulfilled in eternity: "Grace be in incorruptibility, unceasingly, with those who love Jesus Christ." With ζωή, ἀφθαρσία is the "future eternal life" which Christ has brought as a light into the dark, corruptible world, 2 Tm. 1:10. Mostly for Paul ἀφθαρσία is a strictly future blessing of salvation which is understood in exclusively eschatological terms → 104, 16 ff.. It will be manifested only with the parousia, 1 C. 15:42, 50, 53 f. Like the divine δόξα and τιμή, it is still to be sought after here on earth and it always remains hidden (R. 2:7). There is similarity here to the way in which apocalyptic speaks of the incorruptibility we are to wait for. [59]

D. The Word Group in the Early Church.

Under growing Hell. influence the antithesis φθαρτός - ἄφθαρτος plays a big part in the post-apost. fathers. The fact that the corruptible (τὰ φθειρόμενα) is called θεοί is the subject of polemic in Dg., 2, 4 f. Man is φθαρτός in Herm. s., 9, 23, 4, and all men are φθαρτοί as opposed to Christ, who is ἄφθαρτος, in Dg., 9, 2; τὰ ἐνθάδε "things here" are φθαρτά, 2 Cl., 6, 6, while, as in 1 C. 9:24 ff., the ἀγών is φθαρτός in contrast to the τῆς ἀφθαρσίας ἀγών, 2 Cl., 7, 4 f., cf. 7, 3; the same is true of the heart of the natural man, which as Chr. is a temple of God, Barn., 16, 7. There is polemic against the genuinely Gk. idea that the σάρξ is φθαρτή and that one can stain it for this reason, Herm. s., 5, 7, 2. ὕλη is φθαρτή, Dg., 2, 3, τὰ φθαρτά are corruptible goods as distinct from the ἄφθαρτον which one is to share with the fellow-Christian, Barn., 19, 8. τὰ φθαρτά can also be the perishable dwelling in Dg., 6, 8; perhaps σκηνώματα is to be supplied. Similarly φθορά means "corruptibility," so τροφή in Ign. R., 7, 3. Among imperishable things, however, is Christ, Dg., 9, 2, the true temple, Barn., 16, 9, the ἀγάπη "love-feast," Ign. R., 7, 3, καρπός, Ign. Trall., 11, 2. ἀφθαρσία is also found here for "immortality" and "incorruptibility." The Chr. ἀγών has this as its goal and it is thus the ἀγὼν τῆς ἀφθαρσίας, 2 Cl., 7, 5; similarly the crown of victory is ὁ τῆς ἀφθαρσίας στέφανος, Mart. Pol., 17, 1; 19, 2. ἀφθαρσία occurs with ζωή, 2 Cl., 14, 5. Christ is called the ἀρχηγός [60] τῆς ἀφθαρσίας "the One who leads to immortality," 2 Cl., 20, 5.

---

54 Wnd. Kath. Br., ad loc.: "transcendence." Kn. Pt., ad loc. thinks the adj. describe the characteristics of the heavenly garden of God. Cf. also Schelkle, op. cit., ad loc.

55 Wnd. Kath. Br., ad loc. thinks κόσμῳ is to be supplied.

56 Kn. Pt., ad loc. is strongly in favour of taking ἄφθαρτον as a noun.

57 Schlier Eph., Ew. Gefbr., ad loc.

58 Dib. Gefbr., ad loc. Abbott, op. cit. (→ n. 33), ad loc. takes ἀφθαρσία to be "an attribute of love."

59 Cf. 4 Esr. 7:95 f. and the ref. in Mi. R.¹³, ad loc.

60 Like ἀφθαρσία, ἀρχηγός is a Hell. concept, cf. ἀρχηγὸς τῆς ζωῆς in Ac. 3:15.

ἀφθαρσία is a present blessing granted to the community of Christ, a power of life at
the heart of this world of death: ἵνα (sc. Christ) πνέῃ τῇ ἐκκλησίᾳ ἀφθαρσίαν, Ign.
Eph., 17, 1. Thus the εὐαγγέλιον can be called the ἀπάρτισμα... ἀφθαρσίας "the
prepared dimension of immortality," Ign. Phld., 9, 2. It is a spiritual gift ἐν ἀφθαρσίᾳ
πνεύματος ἁγίου, Mart. Pol., 14, 2 and is the theme of expectation, Dg., 6, 8 and sound
doctrine, Ign. Mgn., 6, 2.

Harder

φιλάγαθος → I, 18, 11 ff.
φιλαδελφία, φιλάδελφος → I, 146, 14 ff.

| † φιλανθρωπία, † φιλανθρώπως | φιλοξενία, φιλόξενος → V, 1, 1 ff. |

Contents: A. The Word Group in the Greek World: 1. Occurrence and Meaning; 2. φιλανθρωπία in the Greek-Hellenistic World. B. The Word Group in the Septuagint and Hellenistic Judaism. C. The New Testament. D. The Early Church.

A. The Word Group in the Greek World.

1. Occurrence and Meaning.

The group, which comes from φιλανθρωπ-,[1] is found from the 5th cent. B.C. and hence does not occur in Hom. and other epic poets.[2] Originally it has the comprehensive sense of a friendly relation.[3] If in the first instance it is used for the approach or help of the gods to men, Aristoph. Pax, 392 f., it can also be extended to the relation of kings and other outstanding persons to those beneath them, Isoc. Or., 9, 43. Finally it spans the whole field of relations between men, with a continuing sense of benevolent condescension. It is hard to give either an exact def.[4] or a satisfactory equivalent, cf. already Gellius Noctes Atticae, 13, 17, 1.[5] The meaning ranges from "hospitality" in Polyb., 33, 18, 2 (cf. Diod. S., 13, 83, 1) to "mildness" in punishment and "help" in time of need, Jul. Ep., 89b, 289a-c. Related to institutions, things and animals it means what is "useful" to man: the φιλανθρωπία of husbandry is its "usefulness," Xenoph. Oec., 15, 4, cf. 19, 17.[6] In this

---

φ ι λ α ν θ ρ ω π ί α, φ ι λ α ν θ ρ ώ π ω ς. Cr.-Kö., Liddell-Scott, Pr.-Bauer, Thes. Steph., s.v.; M. Schneidewin, Die antike Humanität (1897); R. Reitzenstein, Werden u. Wesen d. Humanität im Altertum (1907); S. Lorenz, De progressu notionis ΦΙΛΑΝΘΡΩΠΙΑΣ Diss. Leipzig (1914), rev. W. Nestle, Philol. Wochenschr., 36 (1916), 878-880; S. Tromp de Ruiter, "De vocis quae est φιλανθρωπία significatione atque usu," Mnemosyne, 59 (1932), 271-306; A. Vögtle, "Die Tugend- u. Lasterkataloge im NT," NTAbh, 16, 4/5 (1936), esp. 142-4; H. Bolkestein, Wohltätigkeit u. Armenpflege im vorchr. Altertum (1939), Index, s.v. φιλανθρωπία; F. Wehrli, Vom antiken Humanitätsbegriff (1939); H. Merki, "Ὁμοίωσις θεῷ," Paradosis, 7 (1952); F. Normann, Die von d. Wurzel φιλ- gebildeten Wörter u. Vorstellungen von d. Liebe im Griechischen, Diss. Münster (1952); M. T. Lenger, "La notion de bienfait (φιλανθρωπον) royal et les ordonnances des rois Lagides," Studi in onore di V. Arangio-Ruiz, I (1953), 483-499; G. Downey, "Philanthropia in Religion and Statecraft in the Fourth Century After Christ," Historia, 4 (1955), 199-208; C. Spicq, "La philanthropie hell., vertu divine et royale," Stud. Theol., 12 (1958), 169-191; J. Kabiersch, "Untersuchungen z. Begriff der Philanthropie bei d. Kaiser Julian," Klass.Philol. Stud., 21 (1960); H. Hunger, "Φιλανθρωπία. Eine gr. Wortprägung auf ihrem Wege v. Aischylos bis Theodoros Metochites," Anzeiger d. Österreichischen Akad. d. Wissensch., Philosophisch-Hist. Klasse, 100 (1963), 1-20; R. le Déaut, "φιλανθρωπία dans la littér. grecque jusqu'au NT (Tt. 3:4)," Festschr. E. Tisserant, I (1964), 255-294; Dib. Past.[4], 108-110.

[1] Gram. a dep. verbal comp. cf. Schwyzer, I, 442. The φιλάνθρωπος is he who loves men, Hunger, 1. The denominatives φιλανθρωπέω, φιλανθρωπεύομαι do not occur in the NT.

[2] Tromp de Ruiter, 272. Hom. Il., 6, 14 f. says of Axylos: φίλος δ' ἦν ἀνθρώποισι· πάντας γὰρ φιλέεσκεν ὁδῷ ἔπι οἰκία ναίων.

[3] B. Snell, Die Entdeckung d. Geistes (1955), 340.

[4] For def. cf. Ps.-Plat. Def., 412e and Diog. L., III, 98 → n. 12, 16. Acc. to Diog. L. φιλανθρωπία shows itself in three ways: 1. friendly greetings; 2. readiness to help anyone in need; 3. hospitality.

[5] Ed. C. Hosius (1903).

[6] On φιλανθρωπία in relation to things cf. Tromp de Ruiter, 281; W. Schubart, "Das hell. Königsideal nach Inschr. u. Pap.," APF, 12 (1937), 10.

sense animals can be φιλάνθρωποι, Xenoph. Eq., 2, 3; Aristot. Hist. An., X, 26, p. 617b, 26.[7] τὰ φιλάνθρωπα are royal decrees (→ 109, 37) or the rights and privileges conferred by them, Xenoph. Vect., 3, 6; Ditt. Syll.[3], II, 563, 7 f. (c. 205 B.C.).[8] A weak sense is that of "tip" or "present."[9]

2. φιλανθρωπία in the Greek-Hellenistic World.

In the oldest instances gods are called φιλάνθρωποι. Aesch. extols the theft of fire by Prometheus as friendly to man, though Prometheus must do penance for it in order to learn to acknowledge Zeus' dominion, φιλανθρώπου δὲ παύεσθαι τρόπου, Aesch. Prom., 10 f., 28. Hermes is addressed: ὦ φιλανθρωπότατε καὶ μεγαλοδωρότατε δαιμόνων, Aristoph. Pax, 392 f.: φιλανθρωπία and generosity go together here. In Plat. Symp. Aristophanes says: ἔστι γὰρ θεῶν φιλανθρωπότατος, ἐπίκουρός τε ὢν τῶν ἀνθρώπων καὶ ἰατρὸς τούτων ὧν ἰαθέντων μεγίστη εὐδαιμονία ἂν τῷ ἀνθρωπείῳ γένει εἴη. The god is called φιλάνθρωπος because he gave the men of the story super-natural beings to rule over them, Plat. Leg., IV, 713d. φιλάνθρωπος can also be a title of revealed deity; thus Aesculapius bears the name in his healing and saving work, CIG, III, 6813, 3 (2nd cent. A.D.); Ael. Nat. An., 9, 33.[10] But Plato can also ref. already to the φιλανθρωπία of a man; Socrates seems to have shared his knowledge with anyone ὑπὸ φιλανθρωπίας Plat. Euthyphr., 3d.[11] At first, however, we read of the φιλανθρωπία only of extraordinary men. Xenoph. sees in φιλανθρωπία a virtue of Cyrus as ruler. He describes him as follows: εἶδος μὲν κάλλιστος, ψυχὴν δὲ φιλανθρωπότατος καὶ φιλομαθέστατος καὶ φιλοτιμότατος, Cyrop., I, 2, 1, cf. 4, 1; VIII, 2, 1. His φιλανθρωπία finds expression in his hospitable nature and hospitality in relation to his subjects, VIII, 4, 7 f., or in his clemency towards the vanquished in victory, VII, 5, 73.[12] Xenoph. portrays King Agesilaus similarly. He took by φιλανθρωπία cities that he could not conquer by force. Xenoph. Ag., 1, 22.[13] Acc. to Isoc. the king should rule θεοφιλῶς καὶ φιλανθρώπως, Or., 9, 43.[14] Here, however, φιλανθρωπία is not just a royal virtue; it should characterise every man, esp. the Athenian, 4, 29.[15]

In philosophical ethics the group finds no entry into Plat. or Aristot. or indeed the older Stoics and Epicureans.[16] As may be seen in Isoc., the rhetoricians were following

---

[7] Lorenz, 11.

[8] Further examples in H. Kortenbeutel, Art. "Philanthropon," Pauly-W. Suppl., VII (1940), 1032-4; Lenger, 483-499.

[9] Preisigke Wört., s.v. φιλάνθρωπον. Snell, op. cit., 340 explains the development of φιλάνθρωπον as "tip" by saying that for the Greeks there was always "something dubious and pitiable" about man.

[10] Cf. O. Weinreich, "De dis ignotis quaestiones selectae," ARW, 18 (1915), 25. 50 f. J. Schmidt, Art. "Philanthropos," Pauly-W., 19a (1938), 2125 gives further examples of the use of the term as a divine name. On Aesculapius cf. R. Herzog, Art. "Asklepios," RAC, I, 795-9 (Bibl.); Ant. Christ., 6 (1950), 241-272.

[11] Acc. to Lorenz, 15 Socrates ascribes the term to himself per iocum as to a god.

[12] Cf. E. Scharr, Xenophons Staats- u. Gesellschaftsideal u. seine Zeit (1919), 182. Acc. to Tromp de Ruiter, 280 φιλανθρωπία in Xenoph. Cyrop. corresponds to the def. in Diog. L., III, 98 → n. 4.

[13] πρᾶος and φιλάνθρωπος often occur together, e.g., Xenoph. Eq., 2, 3.

[14] Cf. also Isoc. Or., 2, 15; Hunger, 4. φιλανθρωπία is often the virtue of a ruler in decrees and documents, Ditt. Or., I, 90, 12 (196 B.C.); 139, 20 (2nd cent. B.C.), cf. 168, 12. 46 (115 B.C.); Ditt. Syll.[3], II, 888, 101 (238 A.D.). For more examples cf Wendland Hell. Kult., 406 f.; Vögtle, 74-78, 80 f., 84.

[15] Cf. also Aristot. Eth. Nic., VIII, 1, p. 1155a, 20. Elsewhere the word group is of no special significance in Aristot.

[16] Plat. uses the group non-philosophically in Symp., 189d; Leg., IV, 713d. The def. in Diog. L., III, 98 and Ps.-Plat. Def., 412e (→ n. 4, 12) have been incorrectly attributed to Plat. On Aristot. → n. 15.

polite popular ethics when they lauded the virtue of φιλανθρωπία, e.g., Demosth. Or., 20, 165; 21, 43 and 48; 25, 81 and 18, 112. φιλανθρωπία should be displayed esp. in the courts, Or., 13, 17; 25, 81.[17] In the long run this meaning in popular ethics was not without influence on philosophical ethics. Middle Platonism, e.g., Ps.-Plat. Def., 412e, and Stoicism under the empire, e.g., Epict. Diss., III, 24, 64; IV, 8, 32 find in φιλανθρωπία an outstanding virtue. The high evaluation of it is reflected in Plut.[18] It is even extended to enemies, Plut. Praec. Ger. Reip., 3 (II, 799c). In Plut. it is still very largely an attribute of the gods οὐ γὰρ ἀθάνατον καὶ μακάριον μόνον, ἀλλὰ καὶ φιλάνθρωπον καὶ κηδεμονικὸν καὶ ὠφέλιμον προλαμβάνεσθαι καὶ νοεῖσθαι τὸν θεόν, Plut. Comm. Not., 32 (II, 1075e), cf. Gen. Socr., 24 (II, 593a), The gods are εὐεργετικοὶ καὶ φιλάνθρωποι, Plut. Stoic. Rep., 38 (II, 1051e). Their φιλανθρωπία is their gracious work for man, cf. Muson. Fr., 17 (p. 90, 12) and esp. Ar. Did. Fr., 29, 5. Under the empire Stoicism transferred to nature these statements about God's goodness to man, cf. Cic. Nat. Deor., II, 131, but also Xenoph. Mem., IV, 3, 10.[19] Within a doctrine of twofold virtue that distinguishes between right conduct to the gods and to men, the φιλανθρωπία of men is imitation of the goodness of God. This idea may be traced back in different forms in ethical philosophy to Plato.[20] It becomes highly significant under the empire to the degree that the emperor must practise φιλανθρωπία in imitation of God.[21] For him this is the first of all virtues, Themist. Or., 1, 8c, cf. Dio C., 77, 19, 4.

For the emperor Julian φιλανθρωπία stands at the heart of thought and action.[22] He sees in it the typical quality of the Hellenes and Romans, Jul. Gal. Fr., 116a (p. 180, 9 f.). But for him it is in the first instance the real virtue of the ruler, Jul. Or., 2, 12b, cf. 1, 7b; 16b; 20d; 26d; 41b; 48c; 3, 99d. He declares it in his decrees, Ep., 75, 398b, and he requires it of his officials and the pagan clergy as a criterion in the exercise of government, 89b, 289a. His def. runs as follows: ἡ δὲ φιλανθρωπία πολλὴ καὶ παντοία· καὶ τὸ πεφεισμένως κολάζειν τοὺς ἀνθρώπους ἐπὶ τῷ βελτίονι τῶν κολαζομένων, ὥσπερ οἱ διδάσκαλοι τὰ παιδία, καὶ τὸ τὰς χρείας αὐτῶν ἐπανορθοῦν, ὥσπερ οἱ θεοὶ τὰς ἡμετέρας, 89b, 289b c. Clemency in punishment and aid in distress should be the marks of a political and economic order governed by philanthropy. The laws should also be controlled by this principle, Jul. Or., 2, 115a; Gal. Fr., 131b c (p. 180, 17 ff.), 202a (p. 198, 13 ff.).[23] Julian is indubitably influenced here by insurgent Christianity, to whose practice of love he repeatedly appeals as an example.[24]

B. The Word Group in the Septuagint and Hellenistic Judaism.

1. In the LXX the word φιλανθρωπία occurs in apocr. works. The understanding of it is fundamentally the same as in the Greek-Hell. tradition. Alien kings ruling over the Jewish people, the Seleucids and Ptolemies, stress their φιλανθρωπία in their decrees, i.e., their kindness and clemency to the peoples over whom they rule, 3 Macc. 3:15, cf.

---

[17] Tromp de Ruiter, 285; Lorenz, 20.
[18] Tromp de Ruiter, 296; Lorenz, 46. R. Hirzel, *Plutarch* (1912), 25 calls Plut. an "apostle of philanthropy."
[19] On the relations of Cic. Nat. Deor., II, 131 and Xenoph. Mem., IV, 3 cf. M. Pohlenz, *Die Stoa*, II³ (1964), 56; also Art. "Panaitios," Pauly-W., 18 (1949), 429-432.
[20] Merki, 8-10 and 30-32.
[21] This does not exclude its being a καλὸν κτῆμα for the private individual, Themist. Or., 11, 146c d.
[22] H. Raeder, "Kaiser Julian als Philosoph u. religiöser Reformator," *Classica et Mediaevalia*, 6 (1944), 179-193.
[23] φιλανθρωπία has here the concrete sense of *clementia*, cf. also Jul. Conv., 321d and 332a: Caesar's *clementia* as φιλανθρωπία. The same equation may be found also in Hier. Ep., 55, 3, 4.
[24] Kabiersch, 3.

v. 20; 2 Macc. 9:27; this virtue of rulers is also ascribed to them, 2 Macc. 14:9. 25 It can also be deduced from this reference to the φιλανθρωπία of foreign princes that the Jews should show themselves worthy of kindness and clemency by their obedience, i.e., by renunciation of their faith, 2 Macc. 6:22, cf. 4 Macc. 5:12. In Wis. the right conduct of the righteous can be described as φιλανθρωπία: δεῖ τὸν δίκαιον εἶναι φιλάνθρωπον, 12:19. Indeed, wisdom itself is a φιλάνθρωπον πνεῦμα, 1:6; 7:23. This means on the one side that it is addressed to man, that man lives by it, 1:6, 26 and on the other that it comes to expression in the φιλανθρωπία required of man, 12:19.

2. Ep. Ar., however, shows that this virtue of rulers can be properly practised only in obedience to God. The king asks the Jewish sages how he may be φιλάνθρωπος, 208. 27 Even for the king God in His mildness and pity sets an example of conduct acc. to the norm of φιλανθρωπία.

3. The same holds good in Joseph. φιλανθρωπία is the generous and clement conduct of the Romans, Ant., 12, 124; Bell., 2, 399, or of Herod in pardoning the Syr. garrison, Ant., 14, 298. But Jos. also speaks of God's μεγαλειότης καὶ φιλανθρωπία, Ant., 1, 24. He thus depicts God in His transcendent majesty and yet also in His condescension to the world and to Israel. This condescension of God implies that the Torah and Jewish customs cannot be alien or hostile to humanity, Ap., 2, 291; Ant., 16, 42. 28

4. Philo too, belongs to the Greek-Hell. tradition in his understanding and use of the word group. 29 But it is quite plain that he integrates this virtue into his own thinking. In Virt., 51 φιλανθρωπία is def. as τὴν ... εὐσεβείας συγγενεστάτην καὶ ἀδελφὴν καὶ δίδυμον ὄντως and called ὁδὸν ... οἷα λεωφόρον ἄγουσαν ἐφ᾽ ὁσιότητα. Perfect virtue is possible only as there is both love of God and love of man, Abr., 107-118. 30 The friend of God must also be a φιλάνθρωπος, Decal., 110; in the pious, then, one will actually find justice towards other men as well, Abr., 208. The Law consists of two parts, duties towards God and duties towards other men, Decal., 110. In Philo φιλανθρωπία is to be shown not only towards the ἀδελφός, Virt., 82, but also towards πολέμιοι, 109-115, and ἐχθροί, 116-118. It embraces slaves, 121-124, animals, 125-147, and even plants, 148-160. 31 All legislation is filled with precepts on the exercise of ἔλεος and φιλανθρωπία, Spec. Leg., IV, 72. God Himself in His acts by and to man is determined by ἡμερότης and φιλανθρωπία, Virt., 77 and 188; Abr., 79; Cher., 99. This may be seen both in creation, Op. Mund., 81, and also in the history of Israel, Vit. Mos., I, 198. 32

---

25 In 2 Macc. 4:11 the privileges of Judaism are called τὰ φιλάνθρωπα βασιλικά → n. 8.
26 H. Bois, *Essai sur les origines de la philosophie judéo-alexandrine* (1890), 379 suggests on good grounds that 1:6 should come between 1:13 and 1:14.
27 In Ep. Ar., 207 the Jewish sage commends the golden rule to the seeking king as the doctrine of wisdom which he should follow even in dealings with his subjects. The basis is that God deals clemently with men. Thus Ep. Ar., 207 and 208 are inwardly related. On the golden rule cf. A. Dihle, "Die Goldene Regel. Eine Einführung in d. Gesch. d. antiken u. frühchr. Vulgärethik," *Studienhefte zur Altertumswissenschaft, 7* (1962).
28 Cf. Schl. Theol. d. Judt., 29.
29 Cf. the virtues in Virt. and Leisegang, II, *s.v.*; Vögtle, 110-112.
30 Abr., 208 stresses the natural link between piety and philanthropy, cf. F. Geiger, *Philon v. Alex. als sozialer Denker* (1932), 7-10.
31 Cf. Kabiersch, 41; he thinks the depiction of Moses in Virt., 52-57 draws on the concept of the ruler in Hellenism.
32 On the influence of περὶ φιλανθρωπίας, Virt., 51-174 on Cl. Al. cf. P. Heinisch, *Der Einfluss Philos auf die älteste chr. Exegese* (1908), 280.

C. The New Testament.

The word group is much less prominent in the NT writings. Faith even in orientation to the neighbour is not expounded as φιλανθρωπία, as in Hellenistic Judaism, → 110, 4 ff., 22 ff. [33] Only marginally even in Acts do we find the use customary in Greek and Hellenistic literature. It is said of the centurion of the imperial cohort who escorted Paul and other prisoners on the journey to Rome that he acted φιλανθρώπως when he allowed Paul to visit friends in Sidon, Ac. 27:3. Then when Paul's ship was wrecked on Malta it is said of the inhabitants of the island that they showed φιλανθρωπία, in this case "aid" and "hospitality" (→ 107, 14 f.), Ac. 28:2. [34]

Only Tt. 3:4 is theologically significant: ὅτε δὲ ἡ χρηστότης καὶ ἡ φιλανθρωπία ἐπεφάνη. Here the Christ event is portrayed as an epiphany of God's φιλανθρωπία. [35] The phraseology is influenced by the worship of manifested gods as seen especially in emperor worship → 108, 14 ff. [36] This favour of God to man takes place through baptism as λουτρὸν παλιγγενεσίας, in which there is also renewal by the Holy Spirit. Inasmuch as God has condescended to the world in His φιλανθρωπία, He is not a remote or alien God, and life in this world under concrete obedience to this God becomes a constant duty. God's saving work on man also demands here man's right conduct in the world. [37]

D. The Early Church.

In early writings apart from and after the NT there is, as in the NT itself, a remarkable hesitation to describe the conduct of Christians as φιλανθρωπία even though other terms for virtues are now being used. The only NT use to be continued is that of Tt. 3:4 in which God's work is the content, cf. Just. Dial., 47, 5: ἡ γὰρ χρηστότης καὶ ἡ φιλανθρωπία τοῦ θεοῦ καὶ τὸ ἄμετρον τοῦ πλούτου αὐτοῦ κτλ. Another instance is Dg., 9, 2: ἦλθε δὲ ὁ καιρός, ὃν θεὸς προέθετο λοιπὸν φανερῶσαι τὴν ἑαυτοῦ χρηστότητα καὶ δύναμιν (ὦ τῆς ὑπερβαλλούσης θιλανθρωπίας καὶ ἀγάπης τοῦ θεοῦ), cf. 8, 7 and Act. Thom., 123 and 156. Act. Thom., 170 calls Jesus the Messiah

---

[33] On φιλανθρωπία in the NT cf. Tromp de Ruiter, 301 f.; Kabiersch, 42 f.; Hunger, 7. In the works of older philologists on φιλανθρωπία there is a tendency to treat the twofold command of love for God and neighbour as a Chr. form of philanthropy, Kabiersch, 42 f. But it should not be overlooked that the group is not adopted in the NT, not even in the lists of virtues in the Past.. although φιλανθρωπία was highly extolled at this time in the Hell. Roman world. Mak. Hom., 37, 1 (MPG, 34 [1861] 749d) has an apocr. dominical saying: ἐπιμελεῖσθε πίστεως καὶ ἐλπίδος δι᾽ ὧν γεννᾶται ἡ φιλόθεος καὶ φιλάνθρωπος ἀγάπη, ἡ τὴν αἰώνιον ζωὴν παρέχουσα. Cf. A. Resch, "Agrapha. Aussercanon. Schriftfr.," TU. NF, 15, 3/4² (1906), 153-161. Cf. also P. de Labriolle, "Pour l'histoire du mot Humanité," Les Humanités (1932), 483.

[34] On Ac. 27:3 cf. H. J. Cadbury, "Lexical Notes on Luke-Acts, II: Recent Arguments for Medical Language," JBL, 45 (1926), 202 and H. Conzelmann, Die Apostelgeschichte, Hndbch. NT, 13 (1963), ad loc.

[35] Terminologically Tt. 3:4-8 goes with 2:11-14, cf. Dib. Past.⁴, 108-110. φιλανθρωπία is a divine quality, Muson. Fr., 17 (p. 90, 12); Philo Virt., 77. χρηστότης and φιλανθρωπία are also commonly used together for human virtues, Philo Jos., 176; Leg. Gaj., 73; Jos. Ant., 10, 163, cf. Spicq, 176.

[36] Wendland Hell. Kult., 221, 409 f.; Deissmann LO, 311 f.

[37] Although the connection between God's acts and man's conduct is plain here, one cannot speak of imitating God → n. 20. God's φιλανθρωπία is also saving grace (Tt. 2:11) which gives new life and hence righteousness through baptism.

φιλάνθρωπος. Only in Cl. Al. and Orig. does the reluctance to use the group evaporate. It is now referred to God and His work, to Jesus Christ, and to the conduct of Christians. [38] Christ had to die for us διὰ φιλανθρωπίαν, Orig. Comm. in Joh., II, 26 on 1:5 (p. 83, 26), cf. I, 20 on 1:1 (25, 6) etc. [39]

Luck

---

[38] Cf. Cl. Al. (GCS, 39), Index, *s.v.* and Index on Orig. (GCS, 3. 6. 10. 35. 41, 2; 49), *s.v.* φιλανθρωπία, φιλάνθρωπος. Cf. also → n. 32; Kabiersch, 43; A Miura-Stange, "Celsus u. Orig.," ZNW Beih. 4 (1926), 45, 47-50.
[39] For further development in Chr. antiquity cf. the sketches in Hunger, 8-20; Kabiersch, 42-9.

φιλέω, καταφιλέω, φίλημα, φίλος, φίλη, φιλία	ἀγαπάω → I, 21, 23 ff.
	ἀδελφός → I, 144, 1 ff.
	ἀσπάζομαι → I, 496, 9 ff.
	ἑταῖρος → II, 699, 31 ff.
	ξένος → V, 17, 1 ff.
	πλησίον → VI, 311, 22 ff.
	προσκυνέω → VI, 758, 11 ff.
	συγγενής → VII, 736, 19 ff.

The etym. of the stem φιλ- is still uncertain. [1] The two most important attempts to give it an Indo-Eur. derivation are not convincing. 1. This relates it to Celtic bil "good" and Germanic bila "kind" [2] (cf. billig, Unbill, Unbilden) and pts. out esp. that this stem is often found, like φιλ-, in proper names, [3] e.g., Bilhildis, Biligrim, Billo; cf. Φιλήμων

φιλέω κτλ. Bibl. On A.: C. F. Hogg, "Note on ἀγαπάω and φιλέω," Exp. T., 38 (1926/27), 379 f.; M. Landfester, "Das gr. Nomen 'Philos' u. seine Ableitungen," Spudasmata, 11 (1966); F. Normann, Die von d. Wurzel φιλ- gebildeten Wörter u. die Vorstellung d. Liebe im Griechentum, Diss. Münster (1952); C. Spicq, "Agapè, Prolégomènes à une étude de théol. néo-test.," Studia Hellenistica, 10 (1955); also "Le lexique de l'amour dans les pap. et dans quelques inscr. de l'époque hell.," Mnemosyne, IV, 8 (1955), 25-33; also "Le verbe ἀγαπάω et ses dérivés dans le grec class.," Rev. Bibl., 60 (1953), 372-397; J. E. Steinmüller, "'Ἐρᾶν, φιλεῖν, ἀγαπᾶν in Extra-Bibl. and Bibl. Sources," Miscellanea Bibl. et Orientalia, Festschr. A. Miller (1951), 404-423. On A. 4: A. Delatte, "Le baiser, l'agenouillement et le prosternement de l'adoration (προσκύνησις) chez les Grecs," Acad. royale de Belgique. Bulletins de la Classe des lettres et des sciences morales et politiques, V, 37 (1951), 423-450, here 425 older bibl.; E. W. Hopkins, "The Sniff-kiss in Ancient India," Journ. of the Amer. Oriental Society, 28 (1907), 120-134; A. Hug, Art. "Salutatio," Pauly-W., 1a (1920), 2063 f., 2070-2072; B. Karle, Art. "Kuss," Handwörterb. d. Deutschen Aberglaubens, V (1932/33), 841-863; W. Kroll, Art. "Kuss" in Pauly-W. Suppl., V (1931), 511-520; B. Meissner, "Der Kuss im Alten Orient," SAB, 1934, 28 (1934), 914-930; E. Pfister, Art. "Kultus," Pauly-W., 11 (1922), 2158 f.; C. Sittl, Die Gebärden d. Griech. u. Römer (1890), Index, s.v. "Küssen," "Liebe," φιλεῖν. On B.: I. Löw, "Der Kuss," MGWJ, 29 (1921), 253-276, 323-349; M. Paeslack, "Zur Bedeutungsgesch. d. Wörter φιλεῖν 'lieben,' φιλία 'Liebe,' 'Freundschaft,' φίλος 'Freund' in d. Septuag. u. im NT," Theol. Viat., 5 (1953/54), 51-142; A. Wünsche, Der Kuss in Bibel, Talmud u. Midr. (1911). On C. I: C. R. Bowen, "Love in the Fourth Gospel," Journ. of Religion, 13 (1933), 39-49; E. Buonaiuti, "I vocaboli d'amore nel NT," Rivista Storico-Critica delle Science Teol., 5 (1909), 257-264; J. Moffatt, Love in the NT (1930); H. Pétré, Caritas. Étude sur le vocabulaire latin de la Charité chr. (1948); S. N. Roach, "Love in Its Relation to Service. A Study of Φιλεῖν and Ἀγαπᾶν in the NT," The Review and Expositor, 10 (1913), 531-553; C. Spicq, Agapè dans le NT, I-III (1958/59); also "Notes d'exégèse johannique: La charité est amour manifeste," Rev. Bibl., 65 (1958), 358-370; B. B. Warfield, "The Terminology of Love in the NT," The Princeton Theol. Rev., 16 (1918), 1-45, 153-203. On C. II: G. Bornkamm, "Zum Verständnis d. Gottesdienstes bei Pls.," Das Ende d. Gesetzes[5] (1966), 123-132; F. Cabrol, Art. "Baiser," DACL, II (1925), 117-130; A. E. Crawley, Art. "Kissing," ERE, VII (1914), 739-744; Ant. Christ., I, 186-196; II, 156-160, 190-221; K. M. Hofmann, "Philema hagion," BFTh, II, 38 (1938); A. Schimmel, Art. "Kuss," RGG³, IV, 189 f.; V. Schultze, Art. "Friedenskuss," RE³ 6 (1899), 274 f.; R. Seeberg, "Kuss u. Kanon," Aus Religion u. Gesch., I (1906), 118-122; Str.-B., I, 995 f.; Wnd. 2 K. on 13:12.
1 [Frisk]. Cf. Landfester, 34-41; Boisacq, s.v.; Hofmann, s.v.
2 A. Fick, Vergleichendes Wörterb. d. idg. Sprachen, II⁴ (1894), 174; also Review of Prellwitz Etym. Wört.¹ (1892), GGA, 1894, I (1894), 247, adopted Prellwitz Etym. Wört., s.v.; Walde-Pok., II, 185 ("conjecturally"); J. Pokorny, Idg. etym. Wörterb., I (1959), 153 f.; W. Havers, Neuere Lit. z. Sprach-Tabu (1946), 57, n. 2.
3 It is of separate significance that Φίλα, Φίλη itself is a common girl's name (→ 149, 8 ff.), esp. in Athens and Macedonia, cf. A. Fick, "Zum macedonischen Dialecte," ZvglSpr, 22 (1874), 193-235. It is common among hetaerae, v. K. Schneider, Art. "Hetairai," Pauly-W., 8 (1913), 1369, cf. Φιλημάτιον, "Little Kiss," Φιλουμένη etc. Examples in W. Pape - G. E. Benseler, Wörterb. d. griech. Eigennamen³ (1884), s.v.

Phlm. 1, Φίλητος 2 Tm. 2:17, Φίλιππος Mk. 3:18 and par., Macedonian Βίλιππος, Φιλόλογος R. 16:15 etc. Morphologically this derivation is sound enough but it is semantically questionable. [4] 2. Others see in φιλ- a development from the pronominal stem (σ)φ(ιν)-. [5] The original meaning and use of φίλος (→ lines 8 ff.; 146, 21 ff.) support this but morphologically it arouses suspicions. Seeing it is so hard to find a convincing Indo-Eur. link, there is much to be said for relating a pre-Greek φιλ- to a Lydian pronominal possessive adj. bilis. [6]

While the two latter attempts are quite different, they yield the same basic sense "(to be) proper to, related." [7] They also imply priority of the adj. φίλος, not found in the NT, over the noun. φίλος is primarily a reflexive possessive pronoun. [8] In fact Hom. often uses the adj. φίλος in this sense, esp. for parts of one's own body, e.g., Il., 1, 569: [9] φίλον κῆρ, and cf. Hes. Theog., 163: φίλον τετιημένη ἦτορ. [10] φίλος also occurs as a noun for "one's kin," "nearest relatives," Hom. Il., 14, 256; Od., 2, 333; Eur. Med., 84. [11] φίλος is thus very close to ἴδιος. In the NT, too, οἱ ἴδιοι and οἱ φίλοι are more or less synon., [12] cf. Jn. 13:1 with 15:13 → 166, 4 ff. and Ac. 24:33 with 27:3 → 161, 13 ff. The correlation of φίλος, φιλέω and ἴδιος finds expression in Jn. 15:19: ὁ κόσμος ἂν τὸ ἴδιον ἐφίλει → 129, 23 ff. [13]

† φιλέω,   † καταφιλέω,   † φίλημα.

Contents: A. Common Greek Usage: 1. φιλέω with Personal Object; 2. φιλέω with Neuter Object; 3. φιλέω with Infinitive; 4. φιλέω "to kiss," καταφιλέω, φίλημα: a. Usage; b. The Kiss in Antiquity outside the Bible. B. Use in the Septuagint: I. Usage; II. The Kiss

---

[4] A. Fick, "Allerlei," ZvglSpr, 18 (1869), 415 attempts derivation from Sanskr. bhu: bhavila, "favourable," related to "Buhle," "the beloved." But cf. S. Bugge, "Zur etym. Wortforschung," ZvglSpr, 20 (1872), 41 f. For further suggestions cf. Hofmann, 1 f.; R. Loewe, "Die idg. Vokativbetonung," ZvglSpr, 51 (1923), 187-189.

[5] Bugge, op. cit., 42-50; A. Vaniček, Griech.-lat. etym. Wörterb., II (1877), 1035; K. F. Johansson, "Sanskr. Etymologien," Idg. Forsch., 2 (1893), 7; cf. Pfister, 2128. T. Birt, "Perses u. d. βασιλῆες bei Hes.," Philol. Wochenschr., 48 (1928), 191 f. favours this view, expressly preferring it to that under → n. 6, and suggesting analogies for the "good Greek" -ίλος, e.g., ὀργίλος from ὀργή, ναυτίλος from ναύτης.

[6] P. Kretschmer, "Griech. φίλος," Idg. Forsch., 45 (1927), 267-271.

[7] So already Vaniček, op. cit., 1035, cf. G. Heine, Synonymik d. Nt.lichen Griech. (1898), 154: "proper," "to which one is accustomed, or attached."

[8] Landfester, 1. 16.

[9] Cf. Schol., ad loc. (ed. I. Bekker 1825): φίλον δὲ τὸ ἴδιον.

[10] Further examples in Liddell-Scott, s.v. φίλος and J. P. A. Eernstmann, οἰκεῖος, ἑταῖρος, ἐπιτήδειος, φίλος, Diss. Utrecht (1932), 77-81; Normann, 36 f., 74. On the attempt of H. B. Rosén, "Die Ausdrucksformen fur 'veräusserlichen' u. 'unveräusserlichen' Besitz im Frühgriech. (Das Funktionsfeld v. homerisch φίλος)," Lingua, 8 (1959), 264-293 to limit φίλος in the sense of the poss. pronoun in Hom. to inalienable possessions (parts of the body, relatives, articles of clothing, furnishings), cf. Landfester, 9-13. Only with Eur. Med., 1071; Hipp., 856; Tro., 1180 does φίλος come to mean "dear" for the members of others too. All conclusions from the attributive Homer. use of φίλος when taken in the sense of "dear" are misleading, Landfester, 3 f., though perhaps one does not have to distinguish as sharply as he does between the attributive and predicative φίλος.

[11] Cf. also the tragedians, Normann, 76 f.

[12] Acc. to Vaniček, op. cit., 1035 ἴδιος and φίλος are even from the same stem, and also ἑταῖρος → 148, 2 ff.; 159, n. 113. The two can also be used synon. inasmuch as they have an unemphatic use for a poss. pronoun. On ἴδιος cf. Pr.-Bauer, s.v.; Deissmann B., 120 f., on φίλος E. Curtius, "Die Freundschaft im Alterthume," Alterthum u. Gegenwart (1875), 187: "φίλος is mostly a less rigid term for poss. pronouns," e.g., Ael. Nat. An., 2, 38: (black ibises) τῆς γῆς τῆς φίλης (sc. Egypt) προπολεμοῦσαι.

[13] There is a related thought in Plat. Lys., 221e, 222a: Loving (not just φιλεῖν but also ἐρᾶν and ἐπιθυμεῖν) is always orientated to an οἰκεῖον.

in the Old Testament and Judaism. C. Use in the New Testament: I. "To Love": 1. φιλέω with Neuter Object and with Infinitive; 2. φιλέω with Personal Objects: a. In the Synoptists; b. In John; c. In the Rest of the New Testament; II. The Kiss in the New Testament; 1. Manner and Occasion of Kissing; 2. The Kiss of Judas. D. The Kiss in the Post-New Testament Period; I. The Early Church; II. Gnosticism.

A. Common Greek Usage.

1. φιλέω with Personal Object.

a. If the most likely basic sense of the stem φιλέω is "proper to," "belonging to," the original sense of the verb φιλέω is "to regard and treat somebody as one of one's own people."[14] It thus denotes natural attraction to those who belong, love for close relatives → I, 36, 24 ff., e.g., ὃν δὲ χρῆν φιλεῖν (sc. spouse and son) στυγεῖς, Aesch. Choeph., 907. The word is thus used for the love of parents for children, Eur. Herc. Fur., 634[15] (→ 126, 3 ff.), of spouses for one another, Anth. Graec., 7, 378, 2; cf. 475, 7, of masters for servants, Hom. Od., 14, 146; 15, 370, for love of one's nation, IG, I², 15, 36 (5th cent. B.C.?), or city, P. Oxy., I, 41, 30 (3rd/4th cent. A.D.).[16] In a further development, however, φιλεῖν then shifts from that which belongs to that which is chosen → I, 48, 1 ff., cf. φιλεῖν τό τε ἴδιον καὶ τὸ ἀγαπητόν, Aristot. Pol., II, 4, p. 1262b, 23. We thus find it for the love of the gods for men, Hom. Il., 2, 197; 16, 94; Od., 15, 245 f. (→ 134, 2 f.)[17] with its element of preference or favour → 116, n. 23,[18] but not vice versa, → 134, n. 191.[19] It is then used esp. for the love of friends, which like that of married couples is based on reciprocity.[20] b. φιλέω can often take on in this regard the concrete sense

14 Vaniček, op. cit., 1036. It is still in accord with the basic sense when φιλέω is used for self-love, e.g., ἄρτι γινώσκεις τόδε, ὡς πᾶς τις αὐτὸν τοῦ πέλας μᾶλλον φιλεῖ, Eur. Med., 85 f.; ἀπορεῖται δὲ καὶ πότερον δεῖ φιλεῖν ἑαυτὸν μάλιστα ἢ ἄλλον τινά· ἐπιτιμῶσι γὰρ τοῖς ἑαυτοὺς μάλιστα ἀγαπῶσι, Aristot. Eth. Nic., IX, 8, p. 1168a, 28-30, cf. IX, 7, p. 1168a, 1-8, p. 1169b, 2 and on this F. Dirlmeier, Aristot. Nik. Ethik⁵ (1969), 550-4. Aristot. understands self-love in a sublimer sense in Eth. Nic., IX, 4, p. 1166a, 1-b, 29, cf. also Eth. Eud., VII, 6, p. 1240a, 8-11 and Normann, 142-4. On the NT expression for "to love oneself" → 130, 10 ff.
15 πάντα τἀνθρώπων ἴσα· φιλοῦσι παῖδας οἵ τ' ἀμείνονες βροτῶν οἵ τ' οὐδὲν ὄντες... πᾶν δὲ φιλότεκνον γένος, Eur. Herc. Fur., 633-6.
16 ἴς ὥρας πᾶσι τοῖς τὴν πόλιν φιλοῦσιν, "Hail to all who love our city," cf. Ps. 122:6 and the inscr. in B. Lifshitz - J. Schiby, "Une synagogue Samaritaine à Thessalonique," Rev. Bibl., 65 (1968), 369 (4th cent. A.D.; αὐτὴν is to be supplied in line 20); cf. 1 C. 16:22 → 136, 14 ff. and Tt. 3:15 → 137, 1 ff.
17 Cf. Menand. Fr., 111 (Körte): ὃν οἱ θεοὶ φιλοῦσιν ἀποθνῄσκει νέος, Ditt. Syll.³, III, 985, 46-48 (1st cent. B.C.): οἱ θεοί... δώσουσιν αὐτο[ῖς ἀεὶ πάντα τἀγα]θά, ὅσα θεοὶ ἀνθρώποις, οὓς φιλοῦσιν, [διδόασιν], P. Mich., VIII, 482, 17 (133 A.D.): ὡς φειλῶ σοι (= φιλῶ σε) ὁ θεὸς ἐμὲ φειλήσει, P. Oxy., III, 528, 4 ff. (2nd cent. A.D.): "Each morning and evening I do devotion for thee before Thoeris (protector of pregnant women), who loves thee" τῇ σε φιλούσῃ.
18 Cf. the fixed formula ὃν Ἥλιος (or Ἄμμων) φιλεῖ (or ἀγαπᾷ) or ὑπὸ Ἡλίου φιλούμενος in the 13th cent. (B.C.) inscr. given in Gk. in Amm. Marc., 17, 4, 18-23, cf. E. Norden, Agnostos Theos (1913), 225 and Ditt. Or., I, 90, 1, 8 f. 37. 49 (196 B.C.).
19 Aristot. denies not only φιλία πρὸς θεόν, but φιλεῖν and ἀντιφιλεῖν between God and man in gen., so Eth. M., II, 11, p. 1208b, 27 ff.; Eth. Eud., VII, 3, p. 1238b, 27 ff., cf. Cr.-Kö., 15; Warfield, 20-23, for to Gk. sensibility φιλέω has a specific intra-human element that is not fitting in relation to the gods. Philo never has φιλέω for love of God (and ἀγαπάω only once, Abr., 50), cf. H. Neumark, Die Verwendung griech. u. jüd. Motive in d. Gedanken Philons über d. Stellung Gottes zu seinen Freunden, Diss. Würzburg (1937), 60 f. → n. 191.
20 Examples: Democr. Fr., 103 (Diels, II, 163): οὐδ' ὑφ' ἑνὸς φιλέεσθαι δοκέει μοι ὁ φιλέων μηδένα, Pind. Pyth., 10, 66: φιλέων φιλέοντ'(α), Anth. Graec., 12, 103: οἶδα φιλεῖν φιλέοντας, Moschus Fr., 2, 8 (ed. U. v. Wilamowitz-Moellendorff, Bucolici Graeci [1905], 138): στέργετε τὼς φιλέοντας, ἵν' ἢν φιλέητε φιλῆσθε. The basic passage for

"to help," "to assist," cf. the gods and their human friends, Hom. Il., 5, 423, often with παρίσταμαι, 5, 117; 10, 280; Od., 3, 221, or "to care for" (→ I, 36, 25), so esp. with κήδομαι, Hom. Od., 3, 223; 14, 146; Il., 1, 196; Aristot. Pol., II, 4, p. 1262b, 22 f. or τρέφω, Hom. Od., 1, 435; 5, 135. It then means "to treat as a guest," "to entertain," Hom. Il. 6, 15, now with ξεινίζω, 3, 207; Od., 14, 322, δέχομαι, 14, 128, ἀγαπάζομαι, 7, 33. c. φιλέω can also denote "sensual love," love between the sexes (→ 125, 1 f.), Hom. Il., 9, 340-343, 450; Od., 8, 309-316; 18, 325; Aesch. Choeph., 894, 906; Soph. Trach. 463, cf. Hdt., IV, 176: αὕτη ἀρίστη δέδοκται εἶναι ὡς ὑπὸ πλείστων ἀνδρῶν φιληθεῖσα, in an incantation in a love charm: ἵνα με φιλῇ καὶ ὃ ἐὰν αὐτὴν αἰτῶ, ἐπήκοός μοι ᾖ [ν], Preisigke Sammelb., I, 4947, 5 f. (3rd cent. A.D.), or love for the same sex, Theogn., 2, 1255, 1345; Plat. Lys., 212a-213c. [21] Here φιλέω is close to ἐράω, which does not occur in the NT → I, 35, 5 ff., cf. οὐκ ἔστ' ἐραστὴς ὅστις οὐκ ἀεὶ φιλεῖ, Eur. Tro., 1051 and οὐκ ἂν ἐπεθύμει οὐδὲ ᾕρα οὐδὲ ἐφίλει, Plat. Lys., 222a → 125, n. 120. [22]

d. In relation to the NT it is important to note that φιλέω often approximates to ἀγαπάω (→ I, 21, 23 ff.) in meaning and use. [23] In the non-biblical sphere it is, however, more common than ἀγαπάω; the reverse is true in the LXX and NT. [24] One may also note that the Greeks sense a distinction between φιλέω and ἀγαπάω similar to the distinction between "to like" and, with strong feeling, inwardness, devotion, and even passion, "to love."

---

the principle of reciprocity in antiquity is Hes. Op., 353: τὸν φιλέοντα φιλεῖν as a rule of life. For the same principle cf. Prv. 8:17: ἐγὼ τοὺς ἐμὲ φιλοῦντας ἀγαπῶ, but in criticism Jesus in Mt. 5:46 and par.: ἐὰν γὰρ ἀγαπήσητε τοὺς ἀγαπῶντας ὑμᾶς, τίνα μισθὸν ἔχετε; cf. also Lk. 14:2 and as a counterpart Hes. Op., 342 f. All the worldly wisdom of Hes. and his followers focuses on the advantages of mutual love, which Jesus teaches us to forego, although cf. the reciprocity in Jn. (→ 130, 1 ff. with n. 162) at Jn. 13:34; 16:27 (→ 133, 25 ff.).

[21] Cf. Normann, 48 f., 25 f., 65-67.

[22] φιλέω and (ἀντ-)ἐράω are often nearly or wholly synon., cf. Bion Fr. 8, 1 (Bucolici Graeci [→ n. 20], 142); Aristoph. Eq., 1341 f., where ἐραστής εἰμι, like φιλέω elsewhere, means "to be fond of," "to cherish" → 117, 17 ff. But various distinctions can be made, cf. τούτους μάλιστά φασιν φιλεῖν ὧν ἂν ἐρῶσιν, Plat. Phaedr., 231c; (εἰκός) ... τὸ φιλεῖν τοὺς ἐρωμένους, Aristot. An. Pri., II, 27, p. 70a, 6 f. Esp. instructive is Plut. De Bruto, 29 (I, 997c): Βροῦτον δὲ λέγουσι δι' ἀρετὴν φιλεῖσθαι μὲν ὑπὸ τῶν πολλῶν, ἐρᾶσθαι δ' ὑπὸ τῶν φίλων, and cf. Dio Chrys. Or., 1, 20; Xenoph. Hier., 11, 11, where ἐράω does not have the element of sensuality but denotes a stronger and warmer degree of love than φιλέω, Warfield, 12 f., 17.

[23] ἀγαπάω can also be used for parental love, Plat. Resp., I, 330c, or the love of the gods, (Ps.-)Demosth. Or., 61, 9; Ditt. Or., I, 90, 4 (196 B.C.), or the love that selects and prefers → I, 36, 37 ff.; 48, 1 ff., Demosth. Or., 18, 109 and often in Aristot., e.g., Eth. Nic., IV, 2, p. 1120b, 13 in the phrase μᾶλλον ἀγαπάω, or the love for a guest → lines 4 ff.; 148, 31 ff.; or esp. sensual love, Anaxilas Fr., 22, 1 (CAF, II, 270); Luc. Jup. Trag., 2 and the epigram ἠράσθην, ἐφίλουν, ἔτυχον, κατέπραξ', ἀγαπῶμαι. τίς δὲ καὶ ἧς καὶ πῶς, ἡ θεὸς οἶδε μόνη, Anth. Graec., 5, 51, in which ἐράω, φιλέω and ἀγαπάω all denote sensual love. ἀγάπη itself also has a sensual and even sexual sense in some Gnostics, cf. the cultic call of the man to the woman: ἀνάστα, ποίησον τὴν ἀγάπην μετὰ τοῦ ἀδελφοῦ, Epiph. Haer., 26, 4, 4, cf. Hipp. Ref., VI, 19, 5 of the Simonians: ταύτην (sc. promiscuity) εἶναι λέγοντες τὴν τελείαν ἀγάπην, and Cl. Al. Strom., III, 10, 1 of the Carpocratians. At Jd. 12 and esp. 2 Pt. 2:13 vl. one is reminded of this misuse of ἀγάπη. Materially cf. L. Fendt, Gnostische Mysterien (1922), 3-14, cf. also the Gnostic Fr. "The Questions of Mary" in Epiph. Haer., 26, 8, 2 f. and on this H. C. Puech in Hennecke³, I, 250. Finally ἀγαπάω and φιλέω are used in the same sense with neut. obj., cf. Lk. 11:43 with 20:46 → 129, 1 ff.

[24] Normann, 164 thinks that in the NT φιλέω and φιλία are replaced by ἀγαπάω and ἀγάπη as φίλος is by ἀδελφός. But the decisive reason for this is on the one side the preference for ἀγαπάω in the LXX (→ 124, 8 ff.) and on the other the fact that the category of friendship is not so suitable as that of the family for the relations between Jesus and the disciples and the disciples themselves, cf. on Jn. 15:14 → 165, 19 ff. φίλος comes into use as a Chr. self-designation only secondarily in early Christian works → 162, 16 ff.; 166, 16 ff.

One can catch this in, [25] e.g., the statements ὁ δὲ μή του δεόμενος οὐδέ τι ἀγαπῴη ἄν· ... ὁ δὲ μὴ ἀγαπῴη, οὐδ᾽ ἄν φιλοῖ, Plat. Lys., 215a b; ἐφιλήσατε αὐτὸν (sc. Caesar) ὡς πατέρα καὶ ἠγαπήσατε ὡς εὐεργέτην, Dio C., 44, 48, 1. The distinction is rather different in Aristot. Rhet., I, 11, p. 1371a, 21: τὸ δὲ φιλεῖσθαι ἀγαπᾶσθαί ἐστιν αὐτὸν δι᾽ αὐτόν "to be loved as a friend is to be loved for one's own sake." [26] One has also to take into account the different nuances of φιλέω and ἀγαπάω when the two are combined, e.g., Plat. Lys., 220d; Aristot. Eth. Nic., IX, 7, p. 1167b, 32 or used as par., e.g., Philo Rer. Div. Her., 44: ἀγάπησον οὖν ἀρετὰς ... καὶ φίλησον ὄντως → I, 498, 15 ff. Yet already in class. Gk. the verbs are often interchangeable, cf. Xenoph. Mem., II, 7, 9: σὺ μὲν ἐκείνας φιλήσεις ... ἐκεῖναι δὲ σὲ ἀγαπήσουσιν, and II, 7, 12 [27] (→ I, 37, n. 83): Aristot. Eth. Nic., IX, 8, p. 1168a, 28-30; Ael. Var. Hist., 9, 1. [28] This applies esp. to the *koine* of the NT even though one has still to reckon with a feeling for the original distinctions → 134, 2 ff. with n. 191 f. [29] But the relationship of mood and content has shifted from what it was earlier (→ 116, 18 ff.); far from being less warm than φιλέω, ἀγαπάω is now deeper and more inward → 134, n. 195.

2. φιλέω with Neuter Object.

In the sense "to like," "to value," φιλέω, like ἀγαπάω (→ 128, 26 f.) and ἀσπάζομαι (→ I, 497, 31 ff.), goes with a neut. obj. cf. οὐ μὲν σχέτλια ἔργα θεοὶ μάκαρες φιλέουσιν in Hom. Od., 14, 83, φιλῶ γε πράμνιον ("strong") οἶνον Λέσβιον in Ephippus Fr., 28 (CAF, II, 264), cf. Prv. 21:17 → 125, 4.

3. φιλέω with Infinitive.

a. In the sense "to like doing," [30] found from Hdt., VII, 10, 5 and an equivalent of the adv. "gladly," [31] one may see the orig. sense of the stem (→ 114, 8 ff.): "to do what is proper to the φιλῶν," "what is natural for him," not what he might just as well do otherwise, [32] cf. φύσις ... κρύπτεσθαι φιλεῖ, Heracl. Fr., 123 (Diels, I, 178); μεγάλων δ᾽ ἀέθλων Μοῖσα μεμνᾶσθαι φιλεῖ, Pind. Nem., 1, 11 f.; [33] b. "to be accustomed to doing something," common in non-bibl. Gk., Hdt., II, 27; Xenoph. Eq., Mag., 7, 9; Mitteis-Wilcken, II, 2, No. 372, Col. 6, 14 f. (1st cent. A.D.). Often either transl. is possible, cf. φιλεῖ δὲ τίκτειν Ὕβρις μὲν παλαιὰ νεάζουσαν ... Ὕβριν, Aesch. Ag., 763-6; ὅπερ φιλεῖ ὅμιλος ποιεῖν. "as the crowd likes" or "usually does," Thuc., II, 65, 4, cf. also VIII, 1, 4. [34]

[25] There is originally the same distinction between *diligo* and *amo*, cf.: *ut scires eum a me non diligi solum verum etiam amari*, Cic. Fam., 13, 47.

[26] Warfield, 32-34, though he undoubtedly makes too much of the distinction and his differentiation: φιλεῖν "is taking pleasure in" and ἀγαπᾶν "is ascribing value to," is pressed much too far.

[27] But cf. Warfield, 35-37 with bibl. n. 109. The mere fact that Xenoph. Mem., II has φιλέω for Aristarchus at 7, 9 and ἀγαπάω for the female relatives at 7, 12, but uses the two verbs conversely and with the same explanation, shows that they are synon.

[28] Further examples are Plat. Phaedr., 241c, cf. Spicq Le verbe 382 with n. 5; 392 with n. 6 → I, 37, 17 ff.

[29] Cf. Trench, 29-33; Moult.-Mill., *s.v.* ἀγαπάω, Cr.-Kö., 10 f. On the distinctions between φιλέω, στέργω, ἐράω, ἀγαπάω cf. also Spicq Le verbe, 393 f.; E. M. Cope, *The Rhetoric of Aristot.*, I (1877), 292-6; F. Höhne, "Zum nt.lichen Sprachgebrauch, I. ἀγαπᾶν, φιλεῖν, σπλαγχνίζεσθαι," ZWL, 3 (1882), 6-19.

[30] On the transition from "to like" to "to like doing" cf. οὐκ ἐξ ἅπαντος δεῖ τὸ κερδαίνειν φιλεῖν, Soph. Ant., 312.

[31] Winer⁷, 435; Bl.-Debr. § 392, 2; 435.

[32] Normann, 7 f.

[33] Further examples Liddell-Scott, *s.v.* The only NT instances of φιλέω in this sense are Mt. 6:5; 23:6 f. → 128, 15 ff.

[34] Hom. often has φίλον τινί ἐστι for φιλέω "to be used to," with a preceding ἀεί to stress the element of duration native to φιλέω and φίλος, e.g., Hom. Il., 1, 107, 177, 541.

4. φιλέω "To Kiss," καταφιλέω, φίλημα.

a. Usage.

As the use for sensual love shows (→ 116, 6 ff.), φιλέω, like ἀγαπάω (→ I, 36, 32 ff.; 37, 11 ff.), can have positive and palpable acts of love as its content, e.g., caressing, fondling,[35] and esp. kissing. ἀγαπάω[36] is hardly ever used for this, but from[37] Theogn.[38] φιλέω[39] is, and then, since its meaning is not clear,[40] from Xenoph.[41] and

---

[35] φιλέω as vl. with καταφιλέω, Plut. Anton., 70 (I, 948e): 'Αλκιβιάδην... ἠσπάζετο καὶ καταφίλει, "he kissed and cuddled." Cf. ἀγαπάω for stroking young animals, Plut. Pericl., 1 (I, 152c).

[36] T. Zahn, Ign. v. Antiochien (1873), 415 et al. transl. τὰ δεσμά μου ἃ ἠγάπησας at Ign. Pol., 2, 3 by "to kiss the bonds." G. Krüger, who follows this transl. in Hennecke[1], 131, changes it to "the bonds thou hast grown fond of" in Hennecke[2], 534. Bau. Ign., ad loc.; J. A. Fischer, Die Apost. Väter, Schr. d. Urchr., I (1956), 219, have a similar rendering. Yet it should be remembered that Tert. Ad uxorem, II, 4 (CSEL, 70 [1942], 117) can already speak of kissing the vincula martyris and that we read in Act. Pl. et Thecl. 18 of Thecla: καταφιλούσης τὰ δεσμὰ αὐτοῦ (sc. Paul's); cf. also Prud. Peristephanon (CCh, 126 [1966]), 5, 337 f. and on this Ant. Christ., II, 211 with n. 69. "He kissed him" has been conjectured for ἠγάπησεν αὐτόν in Mk. 10:21, cf. the anon. Lat. transl. of Orig. Comm. in Mt., 15, 14 on 19:20 (GCS, 40 [1935], 386, 26): "dilexit eum" vel "osculatus est eum," and F. Field, Notes on the Transl. of the NT[2] (1899), 34; cf. Moult.-Mill., s.v. ἀγαπάω. An argument for this is that the ἠγάπησεν πολύ in Lk. 7:47 ref. back to the καταφιλεῖν of v. 38 and 45 → 138, 23 ff. But this is all very unlikely in view of the preponderant use of ἀγαπάω elsewhere in the NT, as distinct from the LXX → 125, 1 ff. with n. 118. In gen. there is no certain instance of ἀγαπάω for "to kiss," cf. Pr.-Bauer, s.v.; Bau. Ign. on Pol., 2, 3; Warfield, 26 f.

[37] The oldest Gk. word for "to kiss" is κυνέω, e.g., Hom. Od., 17, 35 and 39 (→ VI, 758, 16 ff.). It is perhaps of the same onomatopoeic origin as the Engl. and Germ., Meissner, 930. It is still found later, e.g., Aristoph. Nu., 81; Thes., 915; Lys., 923, with φιλέω, Lys., 890, even in Luc. Alex., 41 in stylistic alternation with καταφιλέω. But it is then replaced not only by (κατα)φιλέω but also ἀσπάζομαι, perhaps already Plat. Symp., 209b, certainly Appian. Bell. Civ., III, 84; Lib. Or., 18, 156; Ἐσθ. 5:2; Ps.-Dionys. Areop., De ecclesiast. hierarchia, 3, 8 (MPG, 3 [1857], 437) etc. (→ 143, 15 ff.; 144, 17 ff., cf. 138, 23 f. → I, 496, 13 ff.) and sometimes προσκυνέω, Delatte, 426 (→ 138, n. 229; 143, 16 f., cf. 123, n. 103) and poetic periphrases like προσπτύσσομαι στόμα, Eur. Phoen., 1671, ἀμφιπίπτω στόμασι, Soph. Trach., 938 etc., cf. Sittl, 37. In distinction from Lat. words like osculum, basium, suavium, cf. Sittl, 43, n. 1, the Gk. authors do not systematise terms for "kiss."

[38] ἔνθα μέσην περὶ παῖδα βαλὼν ἀγκῶν' ἐφίλησα δειρήν ("neck"), Theogn., I, 265 f.

[39] E.g., περὶ χεῖρε βαλοῦσα φιλήσει, Aesch. Ag., 1559; ὡς ψαύσω φιλήσω τ', εἰ θέμις, τὸ σὸν κάρα, Soph. Oed. Col., 1130 f., cf. Hdt., I, 134, 1; Aristot. Probl., 30, 1, p. 953b, 16. φιλέω is esp. common for "to kiss" in the Hell. novel, e.g. Xenoph. Ephes., I, 9, 6 f.; Heliodor. Aeth., I, 2, 6 f., cf. K. Kerényi, Die gr.-oriental. Romanliteratur in religionsgeschichtlicher Beleuchtung[2] (1962), 42 f. For reflections on the meanings "to love" and "to kiss" cf. the interpolated Xenoph. Symp., 4, 26: ἴσως δὲ καὶ διὰ τὸ μόνον πάντων ἔργων τὸ τοῖς στόμασι (conjecture) συμψαύειν ὁμώνυμον εἶναι τῷ ταῖς ψυχαῖς φιλεῖσθαι ἐντιμότερόν ἐστιν. For word play on the two senses cf. Antipater Thessalonicensis: πρὸς Διός, εἴ με φιλεῖς, Πάμφιλε, μή με φίλει, Anth. Graec., 11, 219, 2 and Cl. Al. Paed., III, 81, 2: οἱ δὲ οὐδὲν ἀλλ' ἢ φιλήματι καταψοφοῦσι τὰς ἐκκλησίας, τὸ φιλοῦν ἔνδον οὐκ ἔχοντες αὐτό "but they (sc. nominal Christians) cause the churches to resound with their kisses and yet they do not have true love in them."

[40] Not even in the NT, cf. on 1 C. 16:22 → 136, n. 211. To clarify the sense "to kiss," (τῷ) στόματι was often added, e.g., Hdt., II, 41, 3; Aristot. Probl., 30, 1, p. 953b, 16 → 120, n. 65; Plut. Quaest. Rom., 6 (II, 265b). In modern Gk. φιλῶ means only "to kiss."

[41] Cf. ἔπειτα δὲ Κύρου κατεφίλουν καὶ χεῖρας καὶ πόδας, Xenoph. Cyrop., VII, 5, 32, cf. VI, 4, 10.

increasingly we find καταφιλέω. [42] From Aesch. [43] to the NT [44] the noun for "kiss" is always φίλημα. [45]

b. The Kiss in Antiquity outside the Bible. [46]

(a) The origin of kissing is probably to be sought in animistic ideas. Both the kiss on the mouth and the equally widespread nose-kiss serve orig. to convey the soul, → 125, 17 ff. [47] Later the essence of kissing was often found in this transfer of breath, the "soul," inward living fellowship being set up by the transferring and intermingling of ψυχαί. [48] But another derivation finds the origin in the indrawing of breath with the twofold aim of 1. knowing the related person by scent and 2. the resultant pleasure, [49] for in the Vedic writings there is no word for kiss but there is ref. to "sniffing" and "scent." [50]

(b) Kisses are for relatives, rulers, and those we love. It is secondary that the kiss expresses erotic inclination, [51] as one may see in relation to the Gk. world from the fact that Hom. does not mention the lovers' kiss and it is of no gt. importance in class. lit. [52] At first we find only kissing by close relatives. Children are kissed by their parents, Hom. Il., 6, 474; Aristoph. Lys., 890, and parents, Eur. Andr., 416; Aristoph. Nu., 81 and grandparents, Xenoph. Cyrop., I, 3, 9 are kissed by children and grandchildren. Similarly brothers and sisters kiss, Eur. Phoen., 1671, friends [53] and hosts and guests, Apul. Met., IV, 1, 1; Ps.-Luc. Asin., 17, [54] and in Hom. at least servants and maids kiss their masters,

---

[42] E.g., λαμβάνων μου κατεφίλει τὰς χεῖρας, Menand. Epit., 97 f., only rarely in later pap.: P. Lond., V, 1787, 18 (6th cent. A.D.); Preisigke Sammelb., I, 4323, 5 (Byzantine period): καταφιλῆσαι τοὺς τιμίους αὐτοῦ πόδας. On the distinction between φιλέω and καταφιλέω cf. Xenoph. Mem., II, 6, 33 and Philo Rer. Div. Her., 40-44. In modern works, Sittl, 41: καταφιλεῖν (deosculari) kissing off various parts of the body → 122, n. 80, but cf. Heine, op. cit., 153: plus quam semel osculari; multum et impense osculor, cf. also → n. 240 on Mk. 14:44 f. But since the words are used interchangeably → 125, 12 ff. these distinctions seem groundless.

[43] No noun for "kiss" is attested before Aesch. Fr., 135.

[44] E.g., ἑταιρικὰ φιλήματα, Cl. Al. Paed., II, 98, 1 → 142, 9 ff.

[45] E.g., ὡς δεινήν τινα λέγεις δύναμιν τοῦ φιλήματος εἶναι, Xenoph. Mem., I, 3, 12, cf. Eur. Iph., 679 and 1238: Suppl., 1154: kisses as rewards in games, Plato Comicus Fr., 46, 5 (CAF, I, 612) → 122, 19 ff., cf. also Eubulus Comicus Fr., 3, 4 (II, 165), as a finder's reward in Moschus, 1, 4 (Bucolici Graeci [→ n. 20], 120). φίλημα is esp. common in comedies and novels, in bucolic lit. and epigrammatic lyrics, e.g., Anth. Graec., 12, 183, 1; 200, 1; cf. 203, 1. The fig. etym. φίλημα φιλέω occurs, Moschus, 3, 68 f. (p. 93), cf. also Cant. 1:2 LXX: φιλησάτω με ἀπὸ φιλημάτων στόματος αὐτοῦ. Lk. 7:45 has φίλημα δίδωμι for this, cf. already Eur. Iph. Aul., 679, 1238; Nicopho Comicus Fr., 8 (CAF, I, 776); Kroll, 512. The plur. φιλήματα can sometimes mean "cosmetics," cf. Liddell-Scott, s.v.

[46] Cf. Sittl, 36-43, older bibl. 36, n. 2; Kroll, 511-8.

[47] Cf. Schimmel, 189 f.

[48] As an esp. fine example cf. Plat. Epigr., 1 (Diehl³, I, 102): "When I kissed Agathon I held the soul on the lips. Boldly it seemed on the point of passing over into him." Cf. Aristaenetus Ep., II, 19 (Epistolographi, 170); Petronius Satyricon (ed. K. Müller [1961]), 79, 8; 132, 1, and cf. Anth. Graec., 12, 133, 5 f. For further examples v. Kroll, 512, 39-48 and materially cf. A. Bertholet, Art. "Atem" in RGG², I, 600 f.; W. Wundt, Völkerpsychologie, IV, 1⁴ (1926), 136 f.

[49] Cf. Hopkins, 131: O. Schrader - A. Nehring, Art. "Kuss," Real-Lex. d. idg. Altertumskunde, I² (1917), 668.

[50] Hopkins, 130.

[51] In contrast the tongue kiss καταγλώττισμα, Aristoph. Nu., 51 and bite kiss, Catullus (ed. W. Kroll³ [1959]), 8:18: quem basiabis? cui labella mordebis?, already common in Indian lit., are orig. erotic, cf. Plaut. Asinaria, 695; Kroll, 513, 7-20.

[52] Cf. Kroll, 511 f., who thinks the reason is that the kiss was too realistic a subject and too close to greater delights.

[53] Cf. also Hopkins, 131, who ref. to the sniff-kiss (→ line 9 f.) among friends in India.

[54] Further examples in Hug, 2063.

Od., 16, 15. 21; 17, 35; 21, 224; 22, 499. In all these instances the kiss expresses close relationship [55] and the corresponding love. [56]

In many cases the element of respect is present as well as love. This is predominant in a practice which comes from the East and which was orig. meant to honour the one kissed but then came to be regarded as an honour for the one who kisses, namely, the privilege of kissing the king, which was granted to those closest to him, not merely his relatives, but also the "friends of the king" (→ 147, 14 ff.). This custom was adopted by Alexander the Gt., and on those elevated to be his "relatives," Arrian. Alexandri Anabasis, [57] VII, 11, 1, 6 f., [58] as well as his Macedonian "friends," it was conferred as a right, although only together with obeisance (→ VI, 758, 15 ff.), cf. Plut. Alex., 54 (I, 696a). Then by way of the Seleucid and Ptolemaic empires it was introduced to Rome by Augustus, cf. Suet. Caes., III, 10, 2; Sen. De ira, II, 24, 1, abolished again as a daily custom by Tiberius, Suet. Caes., III, 34, 2, and then re-adopted. [59] The Younger Pliny in Panegyricus, 23, 1 lauds Trajan for granting the senate the right of kissing at the beginning and end of sessions. The kiss conferred by the emperor was regarded as a high honour, cf. Amm. Marc., 22, 9, 13 and also 29, 5, 16. but that demanded by the emperor was often a burdensome duty, cf. Thdrt., V, 16, 3. Many hoped to share the imperial power of healing through the kiss, cf. Script. Hist. Aug., 1, 25, 1 (→ 123, 6 f. with n. 94). [60] Like the emperors, Roman patrons allowed themselves to be kissed by their clients, cf. Mart., 8, 44, 5; 12, 26, 4; 59, 2-10.

Attestation of the erotic kiss is relatively late; [61] it occurs in the Graeco-Roman world along with the kiss of love for the opposite sex, e.g., Theogn., 1, 265; Aristoph. Lys., 923; Av., 671 and 674, and is esp. common in bucolic poetry, e.g., Theocr. Idyll., 2, 126; 23, 9, in the elegy of love, e.g., Prop., I, 3, 16, [62] and the novel, e.g., Heliodor. Aeth., I, 2, 6, but almost as common is the kiss of homosexual love, e.g., Plat. Resp., V, 468b; Ael. Var. Hist., 13, 4; Catullus (→ n. 51), 99; Petronius Satyricon (→ n. 48), 74, 8; 75, 4. [63]

(c) Kisses are on the mouth, hands and feet, along with substitute kisses. As the erotic kiss is secondary compared to kissing close relatives, so is the kiss on the mouth, at least in India and Greece. [64] It does not occur at all in Hom., [65] but we find kissing on the

---

[55] Plut. Quaest. Rom., 6 (II, 265d) calls it a σύμβολον καὶ κοινώνημα τῆς συγγενείας.

[56] On the kissing of relatives in the Rom. period cf. Athen., 10, 56: This is required of a woman (δεῖ), daily, at the first meeting; cf. Plin. Hist. Nat., 14, 13, 90; Plut. Quaest. Rom., 6 (II, 265b-d); Gellius Noctes Atticae (ed. C. Hosius [1903]), 10, 23, 1, and on this E. Schwyzer, "Zum röm. Verwandtenkuss," Rhein. Mus., 77 (1928), 108-111. Soon of course, such kisses became purely formal, Meissner, 921. Later συγγενής, φίλος and other terms of personal relation were made titles (→ lines 27 ff.; 147, 14 ff.; 148, 15 ff.) and the kiss increasingly lost its significance, cf. Valerius Maximus (ed. C. Kempf² [1888]), II, 6, 17.

[57] Ed. A. G. Roos² (1967).

[58] One should not conclude from this that the Macedonian kings, like the Numidian, originally denied the kiss to mortals, Valerius Maximus, op. cit., II, 6, 17; the innovation was the granting of the title "relatives," and therefore the right of the kiss, to the king's confidants, Meissner, 914, n. 2.

[59] Cf. E. Meyer, "Alex. d. Grosse u. d. abs. Monarchie," Kleine Schr., I² (1924), 308; Hug, 2070 f.; L. Friedländer, Darstellungen aus d. Sittengeschichte Roms in d. Zeit v. August bis zum Ausgang der Antonine, I⁹ (1919), 93 f.

[60] Cf. Hofmann, 88 f.; Sittl, 79 f.

[61] Cf. Meissner, 920 f.

[62] Carmina 5 and 7 of Catullus, op. cit. (→ n. 51) are real kiss poems; the kiss is naturally important in the whole genre of the ars amatoria, cf. W. Kraus, Art. "Ovidius," Pauly-W., 18 (1942), 1920-1937.

[63] Cf. Kroll, 512 f.

[64] Kissing on the lips is attested among the Sumerians, Meissner, 917.

[65] Kroll, 513 and 515. It is said to be an orient. custom: ... τοὺς συγγενεῖς (sc. of Cyrus) φιλοῦντας τῷ στόματι ἀποπέμπεσθαι αὐτὸν νόμῳ Περσικῷ, Xenoph. Cyrop., I, 4, 27, cf. Hdt., I, 134, 1; Xenoph. Ag., 4, 5 f. In India, too, the kiss on the lips is usual only among lovers of different sexes, Hopkins, 124.

cheeks, the forehead, [66] the eyes, Od., 16, 15; 17, 39, [67] the shoulders, 17, 35; 21, 224; 22, 499, [68] and the hands, 16, 15; 21, 225; 24, 398. [69] As the erotic kiss develops, the kiss on the mouth becomes predominant as the true kiss. But where the kiss is a mark of honour, it is usually on the hands, [70] Hom. Il., 24, 478; Menand. Epit., 97 f. (→ 119, n. 42), or the breast, Luc. Nec., 12; Nigrinus, 21; Petronius Satyricon, 91, 9, [71] or the knee, as already in Egypt, cf. Hom. Od., 14, 279, and also the Gks., cf. Hom. Il., 8, 371, [72] or the feet. [73] With direct kisses on some part of the body of those honoured or loved, we find various substitute kisses on things [74] connected with the ones who should really be kissed, e.g., when they are physically out of reach, Xenoph. Cyrop., VI, 4, 10, [75] or too exalted. [76] In the latter case the earth before their feet is kissed [77] or a hand kiss is blown towards them, Juv., 4, 118. [78]

(d) Occasions of kissing are greeting, parting, making contracts, reconciliation, games etc. Kissing at meeting and salutation seems to have been general throughout the Orient. [79]

---

[66] Cf. Hom. Od., 16, 15; 17, 35. 39; 21, 224 f.; 22, 499; 23, 208 and the Rabb., e.g., RH, 2, 9d in Str.-B., I, 995.

[67] Cf. Epict. Diss., I, 19, 24; Apul. Met., III, 14, 3; Plaut. Casina, 136; Plin. Hist Nat., 11, 146.

[68] Later erotic too, Ovid Ars amatoria, III, 310.

[69] For many further examples cf. Sittl, 166-9; Kroll, 516; also a slaves' kiss, e.g., Epict. Diss., I, 19, 24; on the whole subj. cf. Sittl, 40 f.

[70] Mentioned as an old Median practice in bBer., 8b, cf. Str.-B., I, 995.

[71] Cf. Sittl, 166.

[72] Ibid., 169; cf. also Aesculapius' kiss on the knees of the sleeping Proclus, Marin. Vit. Procl., 31: οὐδὲ τὰ γόνατα διὰ φιλανθρωπίαν ἀπαρνησάμενον φιλεῖν.

[73] In the East the kiss on the feet is the most widespread form of honour; for India, Hopkins, 130; Egypt, A. Erman, Ägypten u. ägypt. Leben im Altertum (1885), 109, rev. H. Ranke² (1923), 82; H. Kees, Kulturgesch. d. alten Orients, I. Ägypten (1933), 183. In Babylonia kissing the foot is part of the coronation ritual, and then it is a gen. honouring of the king, being also part of the rite of victory. "To kiss the feet" in the sense "to do homage" is a common expression in Assyr. inscr. (Wünsche, 29, n. 1) but it then becomes an epistolary flourish like "kiss the hand" in Austria. Cf. Meissner, 923-6; Hofmann, 61 f. Kissing the feet was adopted by the Persians, Xenoph. Cyrop., VII, 5, 32, and the Carthaginians, Polyb., 15, 1. 7. It is rare in the Gk. sphere, e.g., Preisigke Sammelb., I, 4323, 5 → 119, n. 42. In Rome it involves humiliation, Dio C., 59, 29, 5, esp. when Caligula has himself kissed on the left foot, Sen. Ben., II, 12, 1 f. A loved one might be kissed on the feet, Ovid Ars amatoria, II, 534; Epict. Diss., IV, 1, 17. The Church took over kissing on the foot from state ceremonial, for bishops, and esp. the pope, though naturally in reverentia Salvatoris, cf. Sittl, 169 f.; L. Zscharnack, Art. "Fusskuss," RGG², II, 841; E. Hertzsch, Art. "Fusskuss," RGG³, II, 1182. For the NT → 139, 7 f.

[74] Even when not as substitutes things are kissed in antiquity, e.g., letters, Sittl, 42 with n. 1; 172 with n. 4; so are animals, Longus, I, 18, 1; Hofmann, 67 with n. 3.

[75] A favourite theme in love lyrics is kissing the post of the door closed by the beloved, Callim. Epigr., 42, 5 f.; Theocr. Idyll., 23, 18; Lucretius De rerum natura (ed. H. Diels [1923]), IV, 1179; Plaut. Curculio, 94; Prop., I, 16, 42.

[76] Caligula in his imperial mania instituted a kind of substitute kiss when he had his slippers kissed instead of his feet, Sen. Ben., II, 12, 1. In the later Empire it was ordered officially that the tip of the purple imperial robe should be kissed, cf. Cod. Theodosianus (ed. T. Mommsen [1954]), 6, 24, 4; 8, 7, 16; O. Seeck, Art. "Adoratio," Pauly-W., 1 (1894), 400 f.

[77] For Egypt cf. Kees, op. cit. (→ n. 73), 183; Erman-Ranke, op. cit., 82. In the Old Kingdom it was a special honour if a noble was allowed to kiss the king's feet and not the earth. In the New Kingdom only servants still kissed the earth before the king. For Mesopotamia cf. Meissner, 926. This practice came into the later Roman period from the East, Sittl, 171, n. 1.

[78] Further examples in Sittl, 171 f. Cf. also the kissing of graves (→ n. 82) and of portraits of the dead, Suet. Caes., IV, 7 → 124, n. 113.

[79] The idea that the Gks. took over the kiss of greeting only from the Persians (Meissner, 930) contradicts Homer (→ 122, 1 f.) though it is supported by the accounts of differences between Persian and Gk. customs in Hdt. and Xenoph. → n. 80.

We find it in Persia, [80] and there are many ref. to it among the Gks. and Romans, cf. Hom. Od., 16, 15. 21; 17, 35 etc., then much later (→ 126, 26 f.; 138, 17 ff.), e.g., Apul. Met., IV, 1, 1; Luc. Lucius, 17; Chrys. Hom. in 2 C., 30, 1 on 13:12 (MPG, 61 [1862], 606). The *suprema oscula* in Tac. Hist., IV, 46 is an instance of the kiss at parting. The kissing of the dying or dead might also be mentioned in this connection, Soph. Trach., 938; Statius Silvae, [81] II, 1, 172 f.; Prop., II, 13, 29; Suet. Caes., II, 99; Theocr. Idyll., 23, 40 f. [82] → 144, 23 ff. The kiss is a seal of fidelity when a pact of friendship is made, Aristoph. Ra., 755, or a contract, e.g., δεξιάς τέ σφισιν ἔδοσαν καί ἐφίλησαν ἀλλήλους, [83] Dio C., 48, 37, 1. On reception into a closed circle the kiss is a sign of brotherhood; thus the newly elected chief of a robber band kisses each member, Apul. Met., VII, 9, 1. [84] Those received into a religious fraternity by a kiss are called οἱ ἐντός τοῦ φιλήματος. [85] The kiss is also a sign and pledge of reconciliation, e.g., in the ancient eastern myth of Nergal and Ereshkigal, [86] then among the Gks. and Romans, cf. διαλλάξεις με φιλάσας, Theocr. Idyll., 23, 42; ὁ δὲ πένης ἱλάσατο τὸν θεὸν φιλήσας μόνον τὴν αὐτοῦ δεξιάν, De sacrificiis, 12; cf. Plaut. Poenulus, 404; Petronius Satyricon, 91, 9; 99, 4 → 139, 16 f.; on the conclusion of a treaty of peace, 109, 4. [87] In the mysteries the initiate kisses the mystagogue, Apul. Met., XI, 25, 7, linked here with the plea for pardon, cf. Lk. 7:38 → 139, 9 ff. Finally kissing is common in games; there are contests in kissing in which the one "who kisses the sweetest" carries off the prize, [88] and there are games, esp. the cottabos, [89] in which kisses are the prizes. [90]

---

[80] Cf. Hdt., I, 134, 1 and also Strabo, 15, 3, 20: Equals kiss on the mouth. With the slightly inferior one kisses on the cheeks, Hdt., I, 134, 1, or offers the cheek to be kissed, Strabo, 15, 3, 20. The very lowly do obeisance instead of kissing. That relatives kiss in greeting and parting is mentioned as a Persian custom, Xenoph. Cyrop., I, 4, 27 f. We also find in Persia the Egypt. story "The Bewitched Prince" (A. Erman, *Die Lt. d. Ägypter* [1923], 209-214) in which the foreign king's son is kissed on all his members in greeting, cf. the πάντα κύσεν περιφύς of Telemachus by Eumaeus, Hom. Od., 16, 21.

[81] Ed. A. Klotz (1911).

[82] Cf. Petronius Satyricon (→ n. 48), 74, 17: *nolo me mortuum basiet*. Originally the idea was to catch the departing soul with the mouth by kissing the dying → 127, 16 ff. On kissing the dead cf. Meissner, 922 f. and 923, n. 1; Hopkins, 131; Löw, 275; Sittl, 82 with examples in n. 9, 10; Kroll, 517; Hofmann, 72 f.; Karle, 854 f. In love and respect for the dead the Jews, cf. Löw, 275 f., and also Gentiles, Ant. Christ., II, 210, kiss the coffin and burial mound as well, and Gentiles the urns for ashes → 124, n. 107. Kissing the dead also has a part in the interpretation of dreams in antiquity, cf. Artemid. Onirocr., II, 2.

[83] The kiss and the handshake are also associated in Eur. Iph. Aul., 679.

[84] Cf. Ant. Christ., I, 194-6. Dölger thinks the kisses in Petronius Satyricon, 41, 8 are an act by which freedmen are welcomed into the circle of the free.

[85] F. J. Dölger, Ant. Christ., III, 79 f. correctly interprets thus the expression in Luc. Alex., 41, cf. H. D. Betz, "Lukian v. Samosata u. d. NT," TU, 76 (1961), 115 with n. 1. The sense is different in Plut. Ages, 11 (I, 602b). In the early Church kissing at baptism and ordination (priests and monks) is connected with this practice of pagan antiquity, cf. Ant. Christ., I, 193 f. → 144, 1 ff. For later examples cf. Hofmann, 130, n. 3.

[86] Cf. AOT, 212. For other examples of the kiss of reconciliation in the ancient Orient cf. KAT, 583 f. *et al.*

[87] The dream-books of late antiquity also presuppose this significance of kissing, Artemid. Onirocr., II, 2; Achmes Oneirocriticon, 136 (ed. F. Drexl [1925], 90).

[88] We find the kissing contest at the Diocleia in Megara, cf. Theocr. Idyll., 12, 30 and on this M. P. Nilsson, *Gr. Feste v. religiöser Bdtg.* (1906), 459, who thinks that orig. the grave stele of the cult hero Diocles was kissed in repetition of the parting kiss.

[89] Cf. Pass., *s.v.* κότταβος, K. Schneider, Art. "Kottabos," Pauly-W., 11 (1922), 1528-1541.

[90] E.g., Callim Fr., 227, 6 ff. (I, 217), with further examples; Plato Comicus Fr., 46, 5 (CAF, I, 612 → 119, n. 45).

(e) The effects of kisses (→ 119, n. 45) [91] and their value were estimated very differently. With uninhibited pleasure in them we find serious warnings, [92] esp. against the homo-erotic kiss, Xenoph. Mem., I, 3, 8-13, [93] but also against excess, Mart., 12, 59; Cl. Al. Paed., III, 81, 3. We even find prohibition on the ground that kisses can be the vehicle of demonic infection or cultic defilement, Hdt., II, 41, 3 → 127, 10 ff. with n. 137.

(f) Cultic kisses play a gt. part in antiquity and they are not just signs of religious reverence (→ 122, 16 f.) but also means to attain supernatural strength. [94] Images are kissed, [95] esp. the mouth, chin, [96] hands, [97] and feet. [98] A direct continuation of this pagan custom is kissing statues of the saints both in the West, cf. kissing the foot of the statue of Peter in Rome, and esp. too in the East. [99] The kisses that gods and heroes have themselves given (or give) when they appear to their favourites are a counterpart, e.g., Philostr. Heroic., 290 (II, 142, 22 f.). In the common practice of cultic incubation [100] these kisses of the gods are a means of healing, as in the temples of Aesculapius. [101] In the cultic sphere, too, we find many substitute kisses; indeed, these are almost the rule, esp. kissing the earth at shrines (→ VI, 759, 15 ff.), or in front of idols, which is probably older than kissing the idols themselves, [102] or altars (→ VI, 759, n. 13), [103] temple thresholds, [104] sacred trees, [105]

---

[91] Cf. Xenoph. Symp., 4, 25: οὖ, i.e., in comparison with the kiss (πεφιληκέναι) ἔρωτος οὐδέν ἐστι δεινότερον ὑπέκκαυμα, with Theocr. Idyll., 23, 9: The shy beloved grants nothing, οὐχὶ φίλαμα, τὸ κουφίζει τὸν ἔρωτα.

[92] The warning against the kisses of Eros in Moschus, 1, 26 f. (Bucolici Graeci [→ n. 20], 121) is in jest: ἢν ἐθέληι σε φιλᾶσαι, φεῦγε· κακὸν τὸ φίλαμα, τὰ χείλεα φάρμακον ἐντί.

[93] The comparison with the biting of spiders which Socrates offered as a warning acc. to Xenoph. Mem., I, 3, 12 f. is often repeated, cf. Cl. Al. Strom., II, 120, 5; Paed., III, 81, 4; Thdrt. Graecarum affectionum curatio (ed. J. Raeder [1904]), 12, 57. Instructive for critical views of the homo-erotic kiss even among the Gks. is Plut. Ages., 11, (I, 602b).

[94] Cf. Hofmann, 74-83 with rich materials, though the motif is often sought artificially.

[95] In the OT cf. Hos. 13:2 HT and 'A and on this H. W. Wolff, Dodekapropheton, I. Hosea, Bibl. Komm. AT, 14, I² (1965), ad loc.; 1 K. 19:18 (→ 124, n. 112) 'A: δ οὐ κατε-φίλησεν αὐτόν (sc. Baal); for the broader Semitic world cf. Meissner, 928, though cf., e.g., Sanh., 7, 6; Ambr. De Abrahamo, II, 11, 81 (CSEL, 32 [1897], 633); for the Gk. world, e.g., Hipponax. Fr., 37 (Diehl³ III, 91). Cf. also Ps.-Melito, Orat. ad Antoninum Caesarem, 9 (Corpus Apologetarum, 9 [1872] 429), where the stones that are kissed are idols. Cf. also F. J. Dölger, "Sol Salutis," Liturgiegeschichtliche Forschungen, 4/5 (1920), 8-14.

[96] E.g., Cic. Verr., II, 4, 94: The mouth and chin of the bronze statue of Hercules in the temple in Agrigentum are "somewhat worn" by kissing.

[97] Lucretius De rerum natura, I, 316-8: The right hands of bronze statues of the gods are slimmer through the touches (kisses) of worshippers.

[98] Kissing the feet of the gods is common too (→ n. 73), first in the ancient Orient, cf. Meissner, 928; Hofmann, 61, and then in the Hell. world, e.g., Charito, I, 1, 7 (ed. W. E. Blake [1938]); Apul. Met., XI, 17, 3; Sittl, 181 with n. 2, 3.

[99] Cf. Karle, 846 f.

[100] C. J. Classen, Art. "Inkubation," Lex. d. Alten Welt, ed. C. Andresen, H. Erbse et al. (1965), 1383 f.; J. Pley, Art. "Incubatio," Pauly-W., 9 (1926), 1256-1262; E. Stemplinger, Antike u. moderne Volksmedizin (1925), 28-34; E. and L. Edelstein, Asclepius (1945), I, Testimonia, 414-442, cf. II, 139-180.

[101] Cf. Meissner, 915 f., 919 f.; R. Herzog, "Die Wunderheilungen v. Epidauros," Philol. Suppl., 22, 3 (1931), 139-160; Stemplinger, op. cit., 29; Edelstein, op. cit., I, Testimonia, 423, 41; 446 (= Marin. Vit. Procl., 31). Elsewhere, too, kisses play a big part in the interpretation of dreams, e.g., Achmes Oneirocr., 135 (p. 90 f.), and the practice of superstition, cf. Stemplinger, op. cit., 67; Karle, 853-861.

[102] Cf. A. Erman, D. Religion d. Ägypter (1934), 175; Meissner, 928 f.; Sittl, 42; Hofmann, 55; examples: καὶ τὰ δάπεδα κατεφίλουν, Dio C., 41, 9, 2; Ovid. Metam., 7, 631 f.: oscula terrae roboribusque dedi.

[103] Haec (the knee of the one whose help is sought) ut aras adorant, Plin. Hist. Nat., 11, 250, adorare meaning "to kiss" here. Cf. also the practice of kissing the table as a house-

amulets, [106] and urns of the dead. [107] Basically important here is that all these *sacra* share the sanctity and *mana* of the deities with which one is thus brought into direct contact. [108] One of these substitute kisses is the blown kiss (→ VI, 759, 8 ff.), [109] esp. for stellar deities which cannot be reached, [110] but also as a hasty sign of reverence for other gods, [111] e.g., when passing sanctuaries [112] and graves. [113]

B. Use in the Septuagint.

I. Usage.

1. In the LXX φιλέω as "to love" is mostly [114] used for אהב (→ I, 22, 1 ff.), though as in the NT it is far less common than ἀγαπάω: φιλέω 15 times, ἀγαπάω 266 times. [115] In meaning, as in non-bibl. Gk. (→ 116, n. 23; 117, 9 ff.) and Jn. (→ 128, n. 150; 131, n. 167; 135, 1 ff.), there is often no discernible distinction between the two verbs in the LXX, cf. Gn. 37:4 with 3; [116] Lam. 1:2, where it is hard to see any difference between οἱ ἀγαπῶντες and οἱ φιλοῦντες (sc. Jerusalem); and Tob. 6:19, where the tradition vacillates between ἐφίλησεν (Cod. AB) and ἠγάπησεν (Cod. S) αὐτήν. [117] In particular

altar after a meal, Petronius Satyricon, 64. Cf. K. Müller, *Petronii Arbitri Satyricon* (1961), *ad loc.*; Ant. Christ., II, 218-220, 213-6; Hofmann, 77-9.

[104] Cf. *non ego . . . dubitem procumbere templis et dare sacratis oscula liminibus,* Tib., I, 2, 85 f., cf. Arnobius Adversus nationes, I, 49 (CSEL, 4 [1875]); further examples Ant. Christ., II, 158; Hofmann, 76 f. Christians were later to kiss the thresholds of churches in just the same way, Cabrol, 129 → 145, 9 ff., cf. → n. 108.

[105] Ovid. Metam., 7, 631 f. → n. 102; the ref. is to a sacred oak on Aegina, offshoot of the oaks of Dodona, 7, 623.

[106] Plut. De Sulla, 29 (I, 471b): Sulla kisses his ἀγαλμάτιον in dangerous situations to get power from it → 123, 7 f.; cf. bSanh., 63b on Hos. 13:2; Preis. Zaub., I, 4, 656 ff. (4th cent. A.D.); Mithr. Liturg., 12, 15; 14, 23.

[107] Cf. Ant. Christ., II, 209 f.; Pfister, 2158 f.; Sittl, 41 with n. 7, 183 f.

[108] For the sanctity of the threshold cf. E. Norden, *Aus altröm. Priesterbüchern* (1939), 152, 171 f. Another bearer of otherworldly power is the letter from the heavenly home kissed by the king's son in the Pearl Song, Act. Thom., 111, cf. → 121, n. 74.

[109] Sittl, 181-3; Hofmann, 81-3; Delatte, 425, 430-432.

[110] Cf. Job 31:27 and A. Weiser, *Das Buch Hiob, AT Deutsch,* 13⁴ (1963), *ad loc.;* Luc. Salt., 17; Macrob. Sat., I, 17, 49, cf. K. Wernicke, Art. "Apollon," Pauly-W., 2 (1896), 72.

[111] We may leave open whether there is any sharp distinction between kissing one's own hand as a mark of respect, Luc. De Sacrificiis, 12; Apul. Met., IV, 28, 4; Hier. Apolog. adv. libros Rufini, I, 19 (MPL, 23 [1883], 432) and a kiss blown to the deity, cf. Delatte, 431 f.

[112] Apul. Apologia, 56, 4; Minucius Felix Octavius (ed. J. Beaujeu [1964]), 2, 4; *in adorando dextram ad osculum referimus,* Plin. Hist. Nat., 28, 5, 25. Vg obviously has something similar in view in transl. 1 K. 19:18: *omne os, quod non adoravit eum* (Baal) *osculans manus* (LXX προσεκύνησεν αὐτῷ). In Rome the cultic kiss is also secularised, cf. Sittl, 171; Hofmann, 83. Thus Dio C., 64, 8, 1 reports of the emperor Otto: φιλήματα . . . διὰ τῶν δακτύλων ἔπεμπε.

[113] Hence a gesture in the cult of the dead, cf. Rohde, 346 and n. 3.

[114] At Lam. 1:2 φιλέω is used for רֵעַ → 154, 8 f. with n. 70.

[115] Buonaiuti, 260 has 268 ref. A reason for preferring ἀγαπάω is the kinship in sound to אהב, cf. W. Michaelis, "Zelt u. Hütte im bibl. Denken," *Ev. Theol.,* 14 (1954) 45 → VII, 371, 31 ff.; 341, 25 ff. It is worth noting that the Tg. has רחם and derivates with חבב and derivates instead of אהב for erotic love, cf. Tg. O. on Dt. 21:15 f.; Tg. Pro. on 1 S. 18:20; 2 S. 13:15; Ez. 23:17.

[116] Hogg, 380 tries to prove that the transl. is psychologically correct, for v. 3: ἠγάπα τὸν Ἰωσὴφ παρὰ πάντας τοὺς υἱούς, describes the preference of Jacob on the basis of Joseph's character and what is ordained in salvation history, while v. 4: αὐτὸν ὁ πατὴρ φιλεῖ ἐκ πάντων τῶν υἱῶν αὐτοῦ, is formulated from the standpt. of the brothers; their father unfairly favours the younger brother. But this is not very convincing.

[117] Cf. also Prv. 8:17: ἐγὼ τοὺς ἐμὲ φιλοῦντας ἀγαπῶ, and 21:17, where ἀγαπάω εὐφροσύνην is par. to φιλέω οἶνον καὶ ἔλαιον.

these examples show that both words (→ 116, n. 23) can denote sensual love → lines 10 ff.; 128, 11 ff. [118]

In 6 passages φιλέω means "to like" a neuter obj. → 117, 16 ff.; 128, 14 ff.: ἐδέσματα ὡς φιλῶ ἐγώ, Gn. 27:4, cf. v. 9, 14, φιλοῦσιν μέμματα μετὰ σταφίδων (raisin cakes), Hos. 3:1, φιλῶν οἶνον καὶ ἔλαιον (anointing oil), Prv. 21:17, ἀνδρὸς φιλοῦντος σοφίαν εὐφραίνεται πατὴρ αὐτοῦ, 29:3. [119] In the sense "to like to do" with inf. (→ 117, 21 ff.; 128, 20 ff.) φιλέω occurs only once: The watchers of the people φιλοῦντες νυστάξαι "love to sleep," Is. 56:10. Mostly φιλέω is linked to a pers. obj. As already in extra-bibl. Gk. (→ 115, 15 ff.) and then in the NT sphere (→ 131, 7 ff.) it can also have sometimes the sense "to love particularly," "to prefer," Gn. 37:4. It is used 5 times for sensual love (→ 116, 6 ff.): Tob. 6:15, 19 Cod. AB; Ἰερ. 22:22; Wis. 8:2; Lam. 1:2. [120]

2. In the sense "to kiss" φιλέω, like καταφιλέω, which is used more or less as often, [121] is the equivalent of נשׁק q, pi, hi [122] with acc. or לְ. The noun φίλημα occurs twice for OT נְשִׁיקָה. The ref. is to the "kiss" of the beloved in Cant. 1:2 and the treacherous "kiss" of the enemy (→ 141, n. 243) in Prv. 27:6.

II. The Kiss in the Old Testament and Judaism.

1. In some OT passages we may see traces of the animistic origin of the kiss (→ 119, 4 ff.), esp. Gn. 2:7: God breathes the breath of life into the nostrils of lifeless man, [123] cf. also Ez. 37:9 f. and Jn. 20:22, and also 4 Βασ. 4:34: "He (sc. Elisha) put his mouth upon his mouth" (sc. the dead boy at Shunem) to convey life to him. [124] One may see clearly here the idea of transmitting the soul-breath by the lifegiving contact of the nose

---

[118] On ἀγαπάω cf. also 2 Βασ. 13:1, 15; Hos. 3:1; 9:10; Is. 57:8; Ἰερ. 2:25; Ez. 16:37, always for אהב q; the LXX favours ἐραστής for the pi, e.g., Hos. 2:7; Ez. 16:33, 36 f. In the same sense we find ἀγάπη, e.g., 2 Βασ. 13:15; Cant. 2:4 f., 7 etc. (→ I, 23, 25 ff.) and ἀγάπησις, Ἰερ. 2:33; 2 Βασ. 1:26 (vl. ἀγάπη). This use is esp. common in Cant. (ἀγαπάω 8 times, ἀγάπη 11). But it does not occur in Sir. or the post-canonical Gk. Test. XII (except at Jos. 8:6), Ep. Ar., Ps. Sol., Philo or Joseph. On this cf. M. Moroff, Die Stellung d. lukanischen Christus zur Frau u. zur Ehe, Diss. Erlangen (1966), 110-116 who sees the influence of "spiritualising" and even "devitalising" tendencies in priestly theology, 113.

[119] In the Dead Sea Scrolls, too, we often find אהב with a neut. obj., e.g., "discipline" in 1 QH 2:14, "what I have commanded them" in 1 Q Dires de Moise, Col. 1:5 f. (DJD, I, 92) etc. But cf. Damasc. 2:3 (2:2): "God loves the knowledge of wisdom," where we have personification.

[120] As in non-bibl. Gk. (→ 116, 6 ff.) φιλέω has here the sense of ἐράω: οἱ φιλοῦντές σε in Ἰερ. 22:22 are the same as οἱ ἐρασταί σου, "thy paramours," cf. A. Weiser, Das Buch d. Propheten Jeremia, AT Deutsch, 20⁵ (1966), ad loc. Similarly φιλία in Prv. 7:18 has the same meaning as ἔρως. Again, in Wis. 8:2 φιλέω means the same as ἐραστὴς ἐγενόμην, bridal love being here a fig. for love of wisdom.

[121] In distinction from the LXX Test. XII clearly prefer καταφιλέω because it is clearer → 118, 6 ff., cf. Test. R. 1:5; S. 1:2; D. 7:1; N. 1:7; B. 1:2; 3:7. φιλέω for "to kiss" occurs only once as vl. at Test. B. 1:2. Much the same may be said of the NT → 140, n. 240.

[122] נשׁק ni means "to kiss one another," cf. Ps. 85:10 → 126, n. 135.

[123] The opp. of this kiss is God's kiss of death which takes the life of Moses → 127, 12 ff. The opp. of lifegiving breathing is God's fiery breath which slays, Is. 11:4; 40:24; Job 4:9, cf. 2 Th. 2:8.

[124] This kind of creative kiss of God will also bring about the eschatological awakening of the dead, Seder Eliyyahu Rabba, 17 (ed. M. Friedmann² [1960], 86) in Str.-B., III, 847: God will "embrace them (sc. the Israelites) and kiss them and bring them into the life of the world to come."

or mouth. The theme of conveying powers of soul by the kiss also plays a part in the consecration of the king, where we find a kiss along with the anointing, 1 Βασ. 10:1. [125]

2. The OT also tells us that parents and grandparents (→ 119, 14 ff.) kiss their children, Gn. 31:28; 32:1; 2 Βασ. 14:33; Tob. 10:12 Cod. AB, or grandchildren, Gn. 31:28; 32:1; 48:10. Even more frequently the OT ref. to children kissing their parents, Gn. 27:26 f.; 50:1; 3 Βασ. 19:20; Tob. 5:17 Cod. S. We also find brothers and sisters kissing one another, Gn. 33:4; 45:15; Ex. 4:27, cf. Cant. 8:1, and other close relatives kiss, Gn. 29:11, 13, as do parents-in-law and children-in-law, Ex. 18:7; Rt. 1:9, 14; Tob. 7:6; Joseph and Aseneth (→ n. 125), and also friends, 1 Βασ. 20:41 → 120, 7 ff. [126] Along with the kiss of relationship and friendship we find the kiss of respect in the OT, as when the king kisses an old and well-deserving subject, 2 Βασ. 19:40. In particular the kiss of respect plays no small role in later Judaism. [127]

3. As outside the Bible the kiss on the lips in the service of Eros becomes the true kiss, so it is in the OT world. This may be seen clearly in Prv. 24:26: "As a kiss on the lips, so is a good answer." Again it is mostly presupposed even when not expressly mentioned, cf. Gn. r., 70, 12 on 29:11. But when the ref. is to the kiss of honour → 121, 3 ff., in the OT too the hands are kissed, e.g., Sir. 29:5, [128] the knees, [129] and esp. the feet. In the first instance, however, the kissing of the feet, like the humiliating kissing of the earth, [130] is ascribed in the OT to the nations, cf. Ps. 2:12, [131] but forbidden to the Israelites, since it cannot be separated from proskynesis, [132] cf. Mordecai in relation to Haman in 'Εσθ. 4:17d. In the course of further development, however, kissing the feet comes to be practised by the Jews too as mark of grateful respect, bKet., 63a; bSanh., 27b; jPea, 1, 1 (15d, 28). [133] The Rabb. also mention many substitute kisses (→ 121, 7 ff.; 123, 13 ff.) apart from kissing the earth. [134]

4. Firmly rooted in custom, and hence not contested by the Rabb., was the kiss of greeting and salutation and also of parting. The early stories of the OT have many instances of the kiss of greeting, Gn. 29:11, 13; 33:4; Ex. 4:27; 18:7; 2 Βασ. 20:9 — 141, n. 243, [135] and also the kiss of parting, Gn. 31:28; 32:1; 2 Βασ. 19:40; 3 Βασ. 19:20;

---

[125] H. W. Hertzberg, *Die Samuelbücher, AT Deutsch*, 10³ (1965), ad loc. suggests that Samuel's kiss here is not a constituent part of the royal consecration but is based on his personal relation to Saul. But in the light of ancient thought it seems likely that anointing and kissing are to be viewed as the double act of transferring charisma from one charismatic to another. Cf. the three kisses with which Joseph conveys the spirits of life, wisdom and truth to Aseneth, Jos. and Aseneth, 19, 3 vl. (ed. M. Philonenko [1968]); Hofmann, 70-72.

[126] The kiss of Gn. 29:13 is probably that of hospitality → 119, 17 f., cf. Lk. 7:45 → 139, 4 ff.

[127] Rabb. examples in Str.-B., I, 995 and cf. T. Nidda, 5, 15 (Zuckermandel, 646) in Str.-B., II, 151. The only legitimate kisses for the Rabb. were the kiss of respect and kisses on seeing again and parting, all others being derided as "folly," Gn. r., 70, 12 on 29:11 in Str.-B., I, 995; cf. Wünsche, 29, n. 1; Löw, 256.

[128] For other examples from Judaism cf. Str.-B., I, 995 f.

[129] Cf. Rashi, AZ, 17a in Str.-B., I, 996.

[130] Probably the phrase "to lick the dust" in Ps. 72:9; Is. 49:23; Mi. 7:17 has this form of honouring in view.

[131] BHK, ad loc. 'Α conjectures καταφιλήσατε. Perhaps LXX δράξασθε παιδείας is a free transl. of the same thought: "Practise the good custom (sc. of subjection by kissing the foot)," cf. πεπαίδευνται καταφιλεῖν in Philo Rer. Div. Her., 42 [Bertram].

[132] Nevertheless Mordecai says in his prayer: ηὐδόκουν φιλεῖν πέλματα ποδῶν αὐτοῦ πρὸς σωτηρίαν Ἰσραήλ, "if I could save Israel thereby, I would be ready (even) to kiss the soles of his feet," 'Εσθ. 4:17d.

[133] In Str.-B., I, 996, cf. also the strange story of a foot-kiss of Satan, bBB, 16a.

[134] bSukka, 53a: RSimon bGamliel kisses the paving of the temple court. Kissing coffins and graves also belongs to this category.

[135] Cf. also Ps. 85:10b, since in the parallelism "kissing each other" (→ n. 122) corresponds to "meeting each other" in v. 10a.

Rt. 1:9, 14; Tob. 5:17; 10:12; 3 Macc. 5:49, and in the Rabb., e.g., bGit., 57b. In particular circumstances the kiss may also be in the OT a sign and proof of reconciliation, Gn. 33:4; 45:15; 2 Βασ. 14:33. [136] It may ratify an adoption, Gn. 48:10, or be given in blessing, e.g., Gn. 27:26 f., and cf. Jos. and Aseneth, 22, 5, mutual here, cf. 20, 4 and 21, 5.

5. Apart from the circumstances mentioned, the kiss is judged critically and rejected, partly so in the OT and totally in Judaism. This applies not merely to the harlot's kiss, Prv. 7:13, [137] but to the kiss of Eros in gen. [138] Cant. sings this kiss; it begins: "Let him kiss me with the kisses of his mouth," 1:2, cf. also 8:1. In the gen. view of the Rabb., however, Cant. was acceptable, and could have a place in the Canon, only on the basis of thoroughgoing allegorical interpretation. Similarly, for fear of demonic defilement, the kisses of impure Gentiles were avoided in Judaism, cf. Jos. and Aseneth, 8, 5-7.

6. The OT has nothing comparable to the cultic kissing of paganism mentioned earlier. In Jewish legend, however, we find the counterpart to one specific form of the cultic kiss, i.e., that which a god gives his worshippers → 123, 12 ff. This is the kiss of God. But in contrast to the positive nature of such kisses in paganism, Judaism, surprisingly, attributes to it for the most part [139] the very opposite effect; it kills. It might be that another widespread animistic idea lies behind this, namely, that one can catch with the mouth the soul of a dying man as he breathes his last → 122, n. 82. [140] Acc. to the Jewish Haggada God kissed Moses on the lonely mount "and took his soul with the kiss of the mouth," Dt. r., 11, 10 on 31:14 (Wünsche, 117). [141] This legend rested on a misunderstanding or more probably a deliberate reinterpretation of (עַל־פִּי־יְהוָה) in Dt. 34:5: "on the mouth" for "acc. to the word" of Yahweh. [142] Acc. to bBB, 17a Bar. [143] Aaron and Miriam [144] also died through God's kiss. Other legends say the same of Abraham, [145] Isaac and Jacob, [146] bBB, 17a. Indeed, acc. to Rabb. expectation all the righteous of the Torah are made worthy of death through God's kiss. [147] For the Rabb. this kiss is the easiest of the 903 forms of death [148] that they distinguish, bBer., 8a. [149]

---

[136] Philo Quaest. in Ex., II, 78 on 25:37a and II, 118 on 28:32 are also examples, although osculum concordantiae and osculum pacis are used in a transf. sense here. For Rabb. Judaism cf. Wünsche, 33.

[137] Probably one should compare Lk. 7:38 with this, for behind the judgment of the Pharisee there possibly stands the idea of defilement through contact with a harlot.

[138] There is no ref. to the homo-erotic kiss in the Bible.

[139] But cf. Löw, 334-6.

[140] Cf. Hofmann, 72 f.

[141] Str.-B., II, 136.

[142] Cf. M. Abraham, Légendes juives apocr. sur la vie de Moïse (1925), 30, n. 4; A. Rosmarin, Moses im Licht d. Agada, Diss. Würzburg, 1930 (New York, 1932), 146 f. with n. 615 (many Rabb. examples here); Wünsche, 48 f.; Löw, 337 f. and, for further Jewish sayings about God's kiss, 335 f., 339-342.

[143] Str.-B., I, 755.

[144] On Miriam's death cf. bMQ, 28a as well as bBB, 17a.

[145] B. Beer, Leben Abraham's nach Auffassung d. jüd. Sage (1859), 84: A divine kiss took away his breath, the angel of death did not touch him; cf. also G. Beer, Art. "Abraham-Testament," RGG² I, 69.

[146] bBB, 17a; cf. Beer, op. cit., 201, n. 924; Wünsche, 49 f.

[147] Wünsche, 50; on the kisses of angels, 51 f.

[148] Ibid., 46 f. with n. 13.

[149] On the kiss of death in fairy-stories cf. Hopkins, 122. The poet F. v. Schiller also sheds an illuminating light on this kiss in Die Götter Griechenlands, 66 f. (ed. C. Höfer, Schillers sämtliche Werke, 10 [1913], 3): "A kiss took the last bit of life from the lips." The poet does not say, of course, who put the kiss on the lips of the dying person. But since personified death precedes and genius follows with dipped torch, the kiss is obviously not that of a human being.

C. Use in the New Testament.

I. "To Love."

The far less frequent use of φιλέω is due in the NT, as in the LXX (→ 124, 8 ff.), to the preference for ἀγαπάω. In the sense "to love" φιλέω occurs in the NT, apart from Jn.'s Gospel, almost always in what are obviously stereotyped expressions, 1 C. 16:22 (→ 136, 14 ff.); Tt. 3:15 (→ 137, 1 ff.) or with neut. obj. or infin. (→ 117, 16 ff., 21 ff.); the only exceptions (on Rev. 22:15 → 138, 1 ff.) are Mt. 10:37 (→ 129, 8 ff.) and Rev. 3:19 (but → 136, 10 ff.). Only Jn.'s Gospel with 13 of the total of 25 NT instances makes a more significant theol. use of φιλέω along with the largely synon. [150] ἀγαπάω → 116, 15 ff. Nor is φιλέω merely less prominent quantitatively; it is also subjected to qualitative restiction. In the NT φιλέω is never used for love of God (→ 115, 19 f.), nor, and the same applies to ἀγαπάω even in Lk. 7:47 (→ n. 118), for erotic love → 116, 6 ff.; 131, n. 173.

1. φιλέω with Neuter Object and with Infinitive.

Neuter objects in the strict sense are found with φιλέω only in the saying against the Pharisees in Mt. 23:6 f. and par. (→ I, 498, 23 ff.; VI, 870, 12 ff.). In both forms of this φιλέω is linked with a series [151] of three similarly constructed objects: φιλοῦσιν δὲ τὴν πρωτοκλισίαν ἐν τοῖς δείπνοις καὶ τὰς πρωτοκαθεδρίας ἐν ταῖς συναγωγαῖς καὶ τοὺς ἀσπασμοὺς ἐν ταῖς ἀγοραῖς.

Mt. also adds an infin.: καὶ καλεῖσθαι ὑπὸ τῶν ἀνθρώπων ῥαββί. This constr. of φιλέω with the infin. (→ 117, 21 ff.), which in the NT is found only in Mt., is used in a similar anti-Pharisaic passage at Mt. 6:5: οἱ ὑποκριταὶ ... φιλοῦσιν ἐν ταῖς συναγωγαῖς ... ἑστῶτες προσεύχεσθαι "they like to show themselves (publicly) to pray." Mk. 12:38 f. has a similar constr. but with θέλω. [152] Lk. avoids the constr.; [153] he links the infin. to the θέλω "to like to do" (→ III, 45, 1 ff., 9 ff.) of Mk. and the three acc. obj. to the φιλέω of Mt. In the doublet [154] of the saying at Lk. 11:43 ἀγαπάω is used for φιλέω but in the same sense. [155]

---

[150] So, e.g., M. Dibelius, "Joh. 15:13," *Botschaft u. Geschichte*, I (1953), 208 with n. 6; C. K. Barrett, *The Gospel acc. to St. John* (1955) on 5:20; 21:15. In proof cf. Jn. 3:35 with 5:20 (→ 134, 3 ff.), 13:23 with 20:2 (→ 131, 5 ff.), 14:23 with 16:27 (→ 133, 21 ff.), 11:5 with 11:3, 36 (→ 131, 3 ff.), and also Rev. 12:11 with Jn. 12:25 (→ 130, 4 ff.). To be sure, distinction is often argued in Jn. 21:15 f. (→ 134, n. 195; → I, 36, 30 ff.). Earlier there might be a distinction in Jn. 11:3, 5 (→ 131, n. 167); the Western text, however, has ἐφίλει in v. 5 (as well as v. 3) for ἠγάπα.
[151] Cf. R. Morgenthaler, *Die lk. Geschichtsschreibung als Zeugnis*, I, AbhThANT, 14 (1949), 56 and on this whole problem the fine collection of material in E. v. Dobschütz, "Zwei- u. dreigliedrige Formeln," JBL, 50 (1931), 117-147.
[152] There is another double constr. of φιλέω with infin. and ἵνα at 1 C. 14:5.
[153] The same double constr. of φιλέω probably occurs already in Hes. Op., 788 f.: φιλέοι δ' ὅ γε κέρτομα βάζειν ψεύδεά θ' αἱμυλίους τε λόγους κρυφίους τ' ὀαρισμούς, "This (boy) loves to speak mockingly, lying, flattering words and secret whispering." The last three nouns could be taken par. to κέρτομα as obj. of βάζειν, but cf., e.g., R. Peppmüller, *Hesiodos* (1896), 242, who transl. φιλέω three times here.
[154] Cf. H. Schürmann, "Die Dubletten im Lk.-Ev.," *Traditionsgeschichtliche Untersuchungen zu d. synopt. Ev.* (1968), 274 f., 277.
[155] Comparison shows that Mt. has fused Q and Mk. while Lk. has kept the two with minor alterations.

φιλέω with its synon. ἀγαπάω (Lk. 11:43) and θέλω (Mk. 12:38 f.) serves in this complex of passages to denote Jewish complacency and ambition (cf. Lk. 14:7), esp. among the scribes (20:46) and Pharisees (11:43). [156]

Only formally do Jn. 12:25; 15:19; Rev. 22:15 belong to this category, since it is only improperly that the obj. of φιλέω are neut. here → lines 23 ff.; 130, 4 f.; 138, 1 ff.

2. φιλέω with Personal Object.

a. In the Synoptists.

With a personal obj. φιλέω "to love" occurs only at Mt. 10:37: ὁ φιλῶν πατέρα ἢ μητέρα ὑπὲρ ἐμὲ οὐκ ἔστιν μου ἄξιος. καὶ ὁ φιλῶν υἱὸν ἢ θυγατέρα ὑπὲρ ἐμὲ οὐκ ἔστιν μου ἄξιος. φιλέω ὑπέρ has the same sense as ἀγαπάω μᾶλλον (→ 116, n. 23), φιλέω ἐκ πάντων (Gn. 37:4 → 124, n. 116): "to prefer," "to place above." This form of the saying in Mt. safeguards love for Jesus against any restriction by love for relatives. In contrast the Lukan form (14:26) radically limits the most basic love, that for those nearest to us (→ 115, 10 ff.), in favour of following Jesus (→ IV, 690, 28 ff.): εἴ τις ἔρχεται πρός με καὶ οὐ μισεῖ [157] τὸν πατέρα αὐτοῦ ... καὶ τὴν γυναῖκα ... ἔτι τε καὶ τὴν ψυχὴν ἑαυτοῦ, οὐ δύναται εἶναί μου μαθητής. Jesus does not claim for Himself the same measure of love as that given to neighbours but the superabundance of love due to God, cf. Mk. 12:30 f. and par. [158] If the saying in all its radicalness [159] is regarded as authentic, then it is one of the strongest expression of Jesus' self-understanding. Because He is and speaks and acts like God, He wants to be loved like God. [160]

b. In John.

(a) In Jn. 15:19 the original meaning of φιλέω "to love what belongs or is one's own" (→ 115, 8 ff.; IV, 173, 43 ff.) is quite plain: εἰ ἐκ τοῦ κόσμου ἦτε, ὁ κόσμος ἂν τὸ ἴδιον ἐφίλει. The subordinate clause shows that τὸ ἴδιον means men ἐκ τοῦ κόσμου, [161] cf. Jn. 17:14; 8:23; 1 Jn. 4:5. Jesus and His ἴδιοι are the counterpart;

---

[156] Str.-B., I, 914-9 shows that the depiction is right: the Rabb. themselves, of course, were aware of the danger, cf. Ab., 1, 10 → I, 45, n. 126.

[157] Like its Hbr. original שָׂנֵא, μισέω in the LXX often means "to neglect," "to disregard," cf. Gn. 29:31, 33; Dt. 21:15-17; Is. 60:15; Prv. 20:23 (→ IV, 685, 19 ff.). But the element of will is stronger in μισέω at Lk. 14:26: "to negate, renounce love for one's neighbour and oneself" (→ 119, 14 ff.; IV, 690, n. 24; 691, n. 27). Normann suggests it means "to avoid," "to give up dealings with," and he quotes Hes. Op., 299 f. But his interpretation is based on a rather artificial attempt to see the element of "loving intercourse" in φιλέω.

[158] The development from the Mt. form to the Lk. form corresponds to that from Mk. 9:40 and par. to Lk. 11:23 and par.

[159] It has no par. in Judaism, cf. H. Braun, Spätjüd.-häret. u. frühchr. Radikalismus, Beiträge z. histor. Theol., 24² (1969), II, 107, n. 3.

[160] Here and in Mk. 1:16-20 and par.; Lk. 9:57-62 and par.; 17:33 and par. this is the basis of the radicalism of Jesus. Cf. Braun, op. cit. (→ n. 159), II, 10 f., n. 2. Comparable, though not the same, is the putting of the love of friends over love for blood-relations among the Gks., cf. Plat. Ep., 7, 334b.

[161] The pers. use of the neut. sing. or plur, is common in Jn. 3:6 (cf. v. 7); 6:37 (ὁ ἐρχόμενος πρός με in v. 37b catches up πᾶν ... πρὸς ἐμὲ ἥξει in v. 37a); 6:39 (cf. v. 40); 17:2, 24 (in both vv. ὅ is at once caught up in αὐτοί or κἀκεῖνοι), and also 1 Jn. 5:1 vl.; the closest par. to τὸ ἴδιον is τὰ ἐμά in Jn. 10:14 even if here too a supplementary πρόβατα hovers in the background. We find something of the same elsewhere in the NT, e.g., at Rev. 21:27,

His love for the ἴδιοι (13:1: ἀγαπήσας τοὺς ἰδίους) corresponds to the love of the world for its ἴδιον. It is of the nature of this love for one's own, for what belongs, to be reciprocal (→ 115, n. 20); this is a secular phenomenon, cf. Lk. 6:32 and par. [162]

The Johannine Jesus, like the Synoptic Jesus (Mt. 10:37 and par. → 129, 8 ff.), demands the unconditional love of His disciples with a readiness for total commitment, cf. Jn. 14:15, 21, 23; 15:9 f. He thus demands an uncompromising renunciation of self-love: ὁ φιλῶν τὴν ψυχὴν αὐτοῦ ἀπολλύει (→ I, 395, 5 ff.) αὐτήν, καὶ ὁ μισῶν τὴν ψυχὴν αὐτοῦ ἐν τῷ κόσμῳ τούτῳ εἰς ζωὴν αἰώνιον φυλάξει αὐτήν, Jn. 12:25.

The expressions φιλεῖν τὴν ψυχὴν αὐτοῦ [163] and μισεῖν τὴν ψυχὴν αὐτοῦ [164] (→ 129, n. 157) correspond to the Synoptic expression θέλειν τὴν ψυχὴν αὐτοῦ σῶσαι (Mk. 8:35 and par.), ζητεῖν τὴν ψυχὴν αὐτοῦ περιποιεῖσθαι (Lk. 17:33) and εὑρίσκειν τὴν ψυχὴν αὐτοῦ (Mt. 10:39) or ἀπολλύναι τὴν ψυχήν, Mk. 8:35 and par.; Lk. 17:33; Mt. 10:39 → ψυχή. As Mk. 8:34 f. and par. show, however, to love one's life is above all the counterpart of (ἀπ-)ἀρνεῖσθαι ἑαυτόν. It thus means "to love oneself" (→ 115, n. 14) and is synon. with ἀγαπᾶν ἑαυτόν, Lv. 19:18, quoted in Mk. 12:31 and par., 33; Mt. 19:19; R. 13:9; Gl. 5:14; Jm. 2:8. To be sure, a different assessement of self-love is to be found in these quotations of Lv. 19:18. It is now a simple fact (cf. also Eph. 5:28 f.) which serves as a criterion for love of one's neighbour. In Jn. 12:25, however, renunciation of self-love, or self-abnegation, is, like the renunciation of self-assertion (cf. Mt. 5:39-42 etc.) or self-justification (cf. Lk. 18:13 f. etc.), a presupposition of salvation. Self-denial, however, can mean the forfeiture of life. This Synoptic-sounding saying [165] comes in Jn. after the image of the grain of wheat that must die, v. 24. It thus makes the self-abnegation of the disciple parallel to Jesus' own self-sacrifice in death.

Only in Jn. 11:3 and 36 is φιλέω used for the love of friends → 151, 13 ff.; 156, 13 ff. It occurs here in explanation of the relation between Jesus and Lazarus. But this is only the surface meaning, for here φιλέω is at very least one of the ambivalent expressions in Jn. [166] What the Evangelist has esp. in mind here is the love of Jesus

---

cf. the continuation and the quotation of Is. 52:1 LXX: ἀπερίτμητος καὶ ἀκάθαρτος and cf. also Soph. El., 972: φιλεῖ γὰρ πρὸς τὰ χρηστὰ πᾶς ὁρᾶν, "everyone is glad to look at the brave." Most significant, however, is the use of the neut. in the Dead Sea Scrolls, which is an exact par. of the Johannine use and which follows Deuteronomistic use, cf. C. Westermann, Das Buch Jesaja Kp. 40-66, AT Deutsch, 19 (1966) on 65:12, e.g., Damasc. 2:15 (3:1); 1 QS 1:3 f.; 1 QH 14:10 f.: "What God loves chooses what pleases Him" ref. to "the sons of light" and "what He hates, what He has rejected" to "the sons of darkness," cf. 1 QS 1:9 f., and cf. also J. Maier, Die Texte vom Toten Meer, II (1960), 12 on 1 QS 1:3 f., though also P. Wernberg-Møller, The Manual of Discipline (1957), 45, n. 7.

[162] One can hardly avoid the view that unrestricted love for the neighbour (cf. Lk. 6:27-36 and par.) is denied in Jn. to the degree that, as at Qumran, it is limited to reciprocal love in the community, cf. E. Käsemann, "Ketzer u. Zeuge," Exeget. Versuche u. Besinnungen, I⁴ (1965), 179, n. 38; O. Böcher, Der johann. Dualismus im Zshg. d. nachbibl. Judt. (1965), 142-7. Paul, too, speaks of love within the community but only in connection with love for all men, → V, 134, 26 ff.

[163] We find the same expression with ἀγαπάω in Rev. 12:11. Closely akin are φιλόψυχος in Eur. Hec., 348 and φιλοψυχέω, 315.

[164] This expression occurs also at Lk. 14:26; it is one of many linguistic and material similarities between Lk. and Jn. → 165, 7 ff.

[165] Cf. C. H. Dodd, "Some Johann. 'Herrnworte' with Par. in the Synopt. Gospels," NTSt, 2 (1955/56), 78-81. Dodd traces the variations back to oral tradition and thinks the Johann. form might be closest to the underlying original.

[166] Cf. F. W. Gingrich, "Ambiguity of Word Meaning in John's Gospel," Class. Weekly, 37 (1943/44), 77; O. Cullmann, "Der Joh. Gebrauch doppeldeutiger Ausdrücke als Schlüssel z. Verständnis d. 4. Ev.," Vorträge u. Aufsätze, 1925-1962 (1966), 176-186.

for the φίλοι chosen by Him, 15:14-16; → 165, 19 ff. [167] Hence Lazarus is called in 11:11 (→ 165, 13 ff.) ὁ φίλος ἡμῶν, not ὁ φίλος μου. [168]

(b) A special form of friendship which distinguishes the one thus loved from the general Johannine circle of friends of Jesus is the love of Jesus for the so-called beloved disciple. [169] Only once in fact is this disciple called the μαθητής, ὃν ἐφίλει ὁ Ἰσοῦς (Jn. 20:2); elsewhere he is always the one ὃν ἠγάπα ὁ Ἰησοῦς, [170] 13:23; 19:26; 21:7, 10. [171] This is the most striking instance of the use of φιλέω for a love which chooses and prefers → 115, 15 ff. [172]

The privilege of lying at table ἐν τῷ κόλπῳ or ἐπὶ τὸ στῆθος of Jesus (Jn. 13:23, 25; 21:20) expresses the intimacy of a unique relationship of trust, cf. 13:26. [173] It is

---

[167] φιλέω, which on the lips of the sisters in v. 3 and the Jews in v. 36 has a different nuance from ἀγαπάω, is thus synon. with ἀγαπάω in the mind of the Evangelist, cf. v. 5, and on this, as on the family at Bethany in gen., J. N. Sanders, "Those whom Jesus loved (Jn. 11:5)," NTSt, 1 (1954/55), 29-41.

[168] It is thus a mistake to equate Lazarus and the beloved disciple (→ 132, 25 f.), cf. Barrett, op. cit., 324; A. Kragerud, Der Lieblingsjünger im Joh.-Ev. (1959), 45 with n. 15.

[169] B. W. Bacon, The Fourth Gospel in Research and Debate (1910), 301-331; Bau. J., Exc. on Jn. 13:23; Bultmann J., 369 f.; A. Dauer, "Das Wort d. Gekreuzigten an seine Mutter u. den 'Jünger, den er liebte,'" BZ, 11 (1967), 222-239; 12 (1968), 80-93; C. Erbes, "Der Apostel Joh. u. d. Jünger, welcher an der Brust d. Herrn lag," ZKG, 33 (1912), 159-239; F. V. Filson, "Who was the Beloved Disciple?" JBL, 68 (1949), 83-8; also "The Gospel of Life," Festschr. O. A. Piper (1962), 119-123; W. Heitmüller, "Zur Joh. Tradition," ZNW, 15 (1914), 205 f.; Käsemann, op. cit. (→ n. 162), 180 f.; Kragerud, op. cit.; W. F. Lofthouse, The Disciple whom Jesus Loved (1936); J. A. Maynard, "Who was the Beloved Disciple?" Journ. of the Society of Orient. Research, 13 (1929), 155-9; E. Schwartz, "Aporien im vierten Ev., I," NGG, 1907 (1907), 342 f., 349, 361 f.; T. D. Woolsey, "The Disciple whom Jesus Loved," The Andover Review, 4 (1885), 163-185; Zahn Einl., II, 478-484, also P. Feine-J. Behm - W. G. Kümmel, Einl. in d. NT16 (1969), 161-5; W. Michaelis, Einl. in d. NT2 (1954), 97-101; J. Roloff, "Der joh. 'Lieblingsjünger' u. d. Lehrer d. Gerechtigkeit," NTSt, 15 (1968/69), 129-151.

[170] It has naturally been asked why φιλέω is used of the beloved disciple in Jn. 20:2, e.g., by E. A. Abbott, Johann. Vocabulary (1905), 241, who thinks the disciple had meantime lost his faith and hence was not worthy of the higher love of ἀγαπᾶν. Cf. Warfield, 191-4, who relates φιλέω in Jn. 20:2 to Peter: The other disciple whom Jesus (also) loved.

[171] Perhaps the disciple is also mentioned in 18:15 f.; 19:35; 21:24, and he may be the anon. companion of Andrew in 1:35, though the characteristic phrase is not used in these passages.

[172] Cf. Bultmann J. on 13:23.

[173] It gives rise to erroneous ideas if on the basis of this privilege the disciple is called Jesus' "bosom friend" as in Act. Joh. 89 f., cf. G. Fuchs, Die Aussagen über die Freundschaft im NT, verglichen mit denen d. Aristot. (Eth. Nic., 8. 9), Diss. Leipzig (1914), 16. It is even more misleading if on the basis of the meal in Jn. 13:2 ff. Jesus and the beloved disciple are viewed as a "couple" in the sense found in class. Symposium lit. from Plato on, J. Martin, Symposion, Stud. z. Gesch. u. Kultur des Altertums, 17, 1/2 (1931), 317: "John in his last supper composed a complete literary symposium"; 316: "Jesus and John are firmly anchored in the last supper by the stereotyped topos of the two who love one another." In spite of Jn. 21:20 the background of the meal is by no means essential to the relation of love between Jesus and the disciple. Furthermore, integration into the symposium lit. gives the relation a quite inappropriate erotic undertone, cf. Bultmann J. on 13:25. Only in the apocr. Act. Joh., esp. 89 f., do we find this kind of erotic tinging of the relations between Jesus and the beloved disciple John. The same applies to the par. love for Mary Magdalene in the Gnostic Gospel acc. to Mary (ed. W. C. Till, "D. gnost. Schr. d. kpt. Pap. Berolinensis, 8502," TU, 60 [1955]), where He not only loves her more than other women. 10, 2 f. (cf. Hennecke3, I, 253, also Ev. Philip., 112, 1 f. ed. W. C. Till, Patristische Texte u. Stud., 2 [1963], 28 f.) but also more than the disciples, 111, 34, cf. Ev. acc. to Mary, 17, 22; 18, 14, cf. Hennecke3, I, 254.

probable that the Evangelist brought this feature into conscious relation with 1:18.[174] This close friend of Jesus is the disciple κατ᾽ ἐξοχήν as Jesus Himself is the Son κατ᾽ ἐξοχήν and to this extent both are primary witnesses, the One for God and the other for Jesus. This is the most important function of the beloved disciple in the Fourth Gospel, cf. esp. 19:35; 21:24; for this disciple knows Jesus best, 21:7. In particular he is found at the foot of the cross, when Peter, who usually accompanies him, has fled, so that he is the only witness of what is in John's mind the decisive event (19:35) and therewith of the basic message of salvation and the two Johannine sacraments, cf. 1 Jn. 5:6-8. Indeed, in virtue of his special closeness to Jesus, the beloved disciple can even exercise a kind of mediatorship, cf. 13:24 f.; 21:7; and also 18:16. As the friend κατ᾽ ἐξοχήν he is also made by Jesus the brother κατ᾽ ἐξοχήν, cf. Jn. 20:17, to whom He entrusts His own mother, 19:26. Finally his unique significance is brought to light in the fact that on the basis of his special relation to Jesus he is the first to come to Easter faith even prior to the resurrection appearances. At this pt., too, he is above Peter (cf. 20:4, 8), relating the ambivalent fact of the empty tomb to Scripture (20:8 f.), for this rather than logical deduction is the meaning of ἐπίστευσεν.[175]

Since this disciple ὃν ἐφίλει ὁ Ἰησοῦς is never mentioned by name, from the days of the early Church there has been much conjecture as to his identity.[176] The author of the appendix in c. 21 identifies him in v. 24 as the author of chapters 1-20.[177] Since rather oddly the Fourth Gospel does not mention the sons of Zebedee by name, and James can be dismissed in view of his early death (Ac. 12:2), tradition from Polycrates of Ephesus to Eus. Hist. Eccl., V, 24, 3 (cf. Iren. Haer., III, 1, 2 and Orig. Comm. in Joh., 32, 260 f. on 13:23 ff.)[178] has seen in John, the son of Zebedee, the beloved disciple, and hence also the author of the Gospel. But in the Gospel itself it would seem that the question is deliberately left an open one,[179] and so other interpretations were suggested later. On the one hand we find attempts to equate the beloved disciple with someone else, e.g., Lazarus in view of Jn. 11:3: ἴδε ὃν φιλεῖς ἀσθενεῖ,[180] or the rich young ruler in view of Mk. 10:21: Ἰησους... ἠγάπησεν αὐτόν,[181] or the timid young disciple of Mk. 14:51 f., who belonged to the priestly caste in Jerusalem, cf. Jn. 18:15 f.,[182] and lived near Gethsemane, or Paul,[183] or even the "elder John" when it is thought that he wrote the Fourth Gospel.[184]

---

[174] Kragerud, op. cit., 73 f.; cf. → n. 185.

[175] So O. Michel, "Ein joh. Osterbericht," Festschr. E. Klostermann, TU, 77 (1961), 36 f., 42; also "Jüd. Bestattung u. urchr. Ostergeschichte," Judaica, 16 (1960), 1-5.

[176] Cf. Kragerud, op. cit., 42-6 et al.

[177] The question arises whether καὶ ὁ γράψας ταῦτα is not secondary, cf. A. v. Harnack, "Das 'Wir' in d. joh. Schr.," SAB, 1923, 17 (1923), 109; yet there is hardly a solid enough basis for this view.

[178] For further examples cf. Zahn Einl., II, 488, n. 11.

[179] Even in Jn. 21:2, which ref. to the sons of Zebedee, and in 21:7, there is no clear identification as John; the beloved disciple might just as well be one of the two others in v. 2 whose names are not given, Kragerud, 44.

[180] So J. Kreyenbühl, Das Ev. d. Wahrheit, I (1900), 157-162; R. Eisler, "Dat Rätsel d. Joh.-Ev.," Eranos-Jbch., 1935² (1936), 371-390; Filson, op. cit., 83-8 and 120; Sanders, op. cit., 33 f.; K. A. Eckhardt, Der Tod d. Joh. als Schlüssel z. Verständnis d. joh. Schr. (1961), 17-45, who theorises that the beloved disciple, whom with Zahn Einl., II, 474-484 etc. he identifies as the son of Zebedee, was the "friend of Jesus" raised from the dead in c. 11, who only later and not consistently was called Lazarus, cf. 11:3.

[181] Eisler, op. cit., 374 f.

[182] Erbes, op. cit. (→ n. 169), 169-181; cf. Maynard, op. cit (→ n. 169), 155-9, who solves the difficulty of a disciple who was not one of the twelve occupying the place of honour by suggesting that the Last Supper was held in his house, whereas Erbes, 172 thinks the historical "place" of the ἀναπίπτειν ἐπὶ τὸ στῆθος in Jn. 13:25; 21:20, was on the way to Gethsemane (Mk. 14:51), where the νεανίσκος not named by Mk. or Jn. "threw himself with sorrowful love on Jesus' breast," and this was later equated by Jn. with the ἀνακεῖσθαι ἐν τῷ κόλπῳ in Jn. 13:23, so that the incident came to be part of the Last Supper.

[183] Cf. Bacon, op. cit. (→ n. 169), 326; Bultmann, J., 370 n.

[184] Cf. Zahn Einl., II, 490, n. 17.

On the other hand, in terms of John's evident symbolism, the beloved disciple has been regarded as a symbolical or ideal figure. Thus he has been called the model of every believer "lying close to the breast of his Lord," [185] or the embodiment of the ideal witness, or a projection of the author and his community into the history of Jesus. [186] Others again see him as embodying Gentile Christianity over against Peter (and Mary) as Jewish Christianity [187] or as the representative of prophetic ministry over against Peter as the representative of pastoral ministry. [188] It may well be that the beloved disciple is an example of Christian witness acc. to the intent of the Fourth Evangelist → 132, 2 ff. Nevertheless, he undoubtedly had a specific disciple in view, and this disciple was one of the twelve and stood in a relation to Peter which was close even if full of tension, and which we can no longer unravel → 136, 2 ff. The circumlocutions, however, intentionally conceal this disciple so that he can no longer be identified. By introducing him into the accounts of the passion and resurrection the author is telling us that this disciple, who vouches for the message (19:35; 21:24), understood Jesus better than all the other disciples, especially Peter, even though Peter is recognised to be a confessor (cf. Jn. 6:69) and the leader of the first community (cf. 21:15 ff.). In the figure of the beloved disciple the author and his circle advance the claim that their presentation of the story of Christ, and especially of the decisive events of His death and resurrection, is the abiding form of the Gospel validated by Jesus Himself, and that the Johannine community which the Gospel accredits and champions in this form is closest to Jesus. [189]

(c) According to Jn. 16:27 the disciples fully and completely met Jesus' claim that they should love Him: ὑμεῖς ἐμὲ πεφιλήκατε, and they did this by completely fulfilling His demand for faith. To believe in Jesus as the One who comes from God and acts and speaks in His name, to receive in Him the love of God (3:16), is to love Him. To this love of the disciples for Jesus corresponds the reciprocal love [190] of God for the disciples: αὐτὸς γὰρ ὁ πατὴρ φιλεῖ ὑμᾶς, which is obviously different from His love for the world, cf. 3:16: ἠγάπησεν ὁ θεὸς τὸν κόσμον. Yet one cannot say that φιλέω is used for God's special love for the disciples and

---

[185] E. Schweizer, "The Service of Worship," *Neotestamentica* (1963), 342, n. 30; cf. already Dibelius, *op. cit.* (→ n. 150), 214: "the type of discipleship, the man of faith, the witness of the mystery of the cross," and E. C. Hoskyns, *The Fourth Gospel*[2] (1947), 443: "The concrete position of the disciple (sc. in the bosom of the Son) marks the verity that the true disciples are in Jesus as Jesus is in the Father"; the beloved disciple is also called "the ideal Christian convert," 530, and cf. also Bultmann J., 369, n. 6. On Johannine symbolism cf. Bultmann J., *passim, v.* Index, II, *s.v.* "Symbolik."

[186] Käsemann, *op. cit.*, 180, cf. also 187: The elder (author of the Gospel) is a manifestation of the beloved disciple.

[187] Bultmann J., 369 f. and earlier A. Loisy, *Le quatrième Ev.* (1903); Bultmann is close to Dibelius, *op. cit.*, 214; Käsemann, *op. cit.*, 180 f.; Schweizer, *op. cit.*, 342, n. 30 *et al.* to the degree that he sees in Gentile Christianity the real Christianity that has attained to self-understanding.

[188] Kragerud, *op. cit.*, 84-92, 113-148, and cf. the review by W. Michaelis, ThLZ, 85 (1960), 667-9.

[189] E. Hirsch, *Das vierte Ev. in seiner urspr. Gestalt* (1936), 340 thinks the phrase "whom Jesus loved" was added editorially and is thus "an ideal construct ... just good enough to fool theologians," 342; cf. also his *Stud. z. vierten Ev.* (1936), 102 on Jn. 13:23, where the supposed interpolation is based on the remote and ambiguous ὅν; but this is Johannine style, cf. 19:26.

[190] The ὅτι in this saying of the Johannine Jesus is not to be misunderstood as though God's love for the disciples were dependent on their love and faith in Jesus, as a reward for this. Their love is a response to the love of Him who has come into the world and of Him that sent Him, cf. Barrett, *op. cit.*, 414. God's love is first (1 Jn. 4:19) and it embraces the circle of love around Jesus, replying to the love of the disciples with which they are drawn into this circle. Soph. Phil., 390 is in some sense a par. to Jn. 16:27. He who is φίλος to him (sc. Neoptolemos) is for this reason φίλος to the gods too, Normann, 86.

ἀγαπάω for His general love for the world, for in 14:21, 23 the idea of 16:27 is expressed by ἀγαπάω. Jn. 16:27 is the only verse in the NT in which φιλέω is used for God's love for man. [191] But there is full par. in the ὁ γὰρ πατὴρ φιλεῖ τὸν υἱόν of 5:20, another unique use of φιλέω, since elsewhere ἀγαπάω is used to denote the love of the Father for the Son, cf. Jn. 3:35; 10:17; 15:9; 17:23 f. → I, 52, 39 ff. [192] Thus in the mutual relations of love which in Jn. sustain the circle of love between God, Christ and the disciples (→ n. 190; I, 53, 14 ff.), it is only occasionally that φιλέω is used to denote the love of God for the Son (5:20), the love of God for the disciples (16:27) and the love of the disciples for Jesus (16:27), whereas ἀγαπάω is always used to denote the love of Jesus for the disciples (13:1, 34; 14:21; 15:9, 12; cf. 11:5), the love of the disciples for one another (13:34; 15:12, 17), and esp. the love of Jesus for the Father (14:31). Neither φιλέω nor ἀγαπάω occurs to describe the love of the disciples for God (in contrast cf. Mk. 12:30 and par. → n. 19, 191), for John speaks instead only of their love for Jesus. [193]

(d) We have a special instance of the love of the disciples when φιλέω occurs in the conversation between Jesus and Peter in Jn. 21:15-17. [194] Worth noting here is the alternation of ἀγαπάω and φιλέω, not merely in the distribution to question ἀγαπᾷς με; and answer φιλῶ σε in the first two rounds of the dialogue but also in the switching from ἀγαπᾷς με; to φιλεῖς με; in the third round. Many exegetes [195]

---

[191] φιλέω is never used in the NT for the love of man for God (though cf. φιλόθεος in 2 Tm. 3:4), but it is used for love of Jesus, cf. Jn. 21:15-17 and 1 C. 16:22 as well as Jn. 16:27. In the NT, as in the LXX, ἀγαπάω can be used in either direction, cf. Dt. 4:37; Jn. 14:21, 23 with Ex. 20:6; Dt. 6:5; 11:1; Mk. 12:30 par., 33; R. 8:28. The same applies later to στέργω (στοργή), cf. Constantinus Ad Coetum Sanctorum, 2 (ed. I. A. Heikel, *Eusebius' Werke*, GCS [1902], 155, 29 f.).

[192] Perhaps the reason for the exception is that the love of the Father is viewed here as an unequal relation of friendship. The friend in full confidence gives the other a share in everything, → 165, 25 ff. Hogg, 380, however, explains the difference between Jn. 3:35 and 5:20 in terms of "the unchanging love of approbation" on the one side and "the tender intimacy of affection" on the other.

[193] Qumran offers the nearest par. to the close connection between love of God and love of the brethren (→ I, 52, 35 ff.) as developed in the Epistles of Jn. Members of the sect are also bound together by a bond of exclusive love, cf. Damasc. 6:20 (8:17): "... each to love his brother (i.e., members of the community; on this interpretation of Lv. 19:18 → V, 13, 34 ff.; VI, 314, 31 ff. with n. 30) as himself"; cf. also 1 QS 1:9 f.: "... to love all the sons of light, each acc. to his lot (rank) in the assembly of God." We have the same exclusive sense when Jos. Bell., 2, 119 calls the Essenes φιλάλληλοι. אַהֲבַת חֶסֶד often occurs as a tt. for this inner community love: "loving relation," "heartfelt love," 1 QS 2:24; 5:4; 8:2; 10:26; Damasc. 13:18 (16:8). In 1 QS 5:25 this is even recommended as the right attitude in correcting tested members, cf. J. P. Hyatt, "On the Meaning and Origin of Micah 6:8," *Anglican Theol. Review*, 34 (1952), 232-9; B. Otzen, "Die neugefundenen hbr. Sektenschr. u. d. Test. XII," *Stud. Theol.*, 7 (1953/54), 131-3.

[194] This conversation, which is carefully constructed in par. three-membered rounds (Jesus' question, Peter's answer, Jesus' commission), has the ring of a liturgical form and might well echo an ordination interrogatory just as Ac. 8:37 seems to echo the baptismal examination. Another possible influence, of course, is the oriental model of a formula uttered solemnly three times before witnesses and establishing law, cf. P. Gaechter, "Das dreifache 'Weide meine Lämmer,'" *Zschr. f. kathol. Theol.*, 69 (1947), 334-344.

[195] Zn. J., 635; cf. also K. Horn, *Abfassungszeit, Geschichtlichkeit und Zweck v. Ev. Joh. Kp. 21* (1904), 167-171: ἀγαπάω is determined by the will and decision whereas φιλέω denotes the love of natural affection, which is as unstable as the human heart; cf. also R. H. Strachan, "The Appendix to the Fourth Gospel," *Exp.*, 40 (1914), 263-7; cf. Roach, 533: "Agapan ... carries with it invariably the idea of ... the good of the object sought at the cost of the subject, while philein as uniformly suggests the pleasure of the subject associated

have seen a fine distinction here, Peter being troubled because the third time Jesus said to him: φιλεῖς με; "dost thou care for me," instead of ἀγαπᾷς με; as before. But it is more like that in c. 21 as throughout the Gospel (→ n. 167) ἀγαπάω and φιλέω are synon., [196] for the strict parallelism in the three rounds of conversation is relaxed a little by the use of other synonyms: βόσκω - ποιμαίνω, ἀρνίον - προβάτιον, σὺ οἶδας (v. 15 f.) — σὺ γινώσκεις. [197] Furthermore the little clause λέγει αὐτῷ τὸ τρίτον supports a parallel meaning, since it denotes "for the third time," not "the third time." The threefold questioning (→ VIII, 222, 22 ff.) of love, [198] and its threefold affirmation, are elucidated by the threefold commission. A strong and incontestable love of the Lord is indispensable in him who is to represent Jesus in the pastoral ministry. This is why Peter must love Jesus πλέον τούτων (21:15), these being other disciples, not as those who also bear a special commission, [199] but as the company of disciples. [200] The shepherd of the community must stand in a uniquely close relation of love with his Lord and theirs. The threefold questioning of the love of Peter for Jesus is certainly to be related, too, to the threefold denial of Peter, cf. Jn. 13:38; 18:17, 25-27. [201] By threefold installation in the pastoral office Jesus proclaims to him forgiveness for his betrayal. [202] On this forgiveness

---

with and derived from the object," on this Warfield, 194-7; cf. Hogg, 380: "ἀγαπάω: the love that faces the issue and ..., at whatever cost, denies itself; φιλέω: the personal affection that comes from intimate association" (→ n. 192), but cf. H. Highfield, "ἀπαπάω and φιλέω. A Rejoinder," Exp. T., 38 (1926/27), 525; Moult.-Mill., s.v. ἀγαπάω and φιλέω; A. Šuštar, "De caritate apud Sanctum Joannem," Verbum Domini, 28 (1950), 116-9; Spicq Agapè NT, III, 230-237.

[196] So also Barrett, op. cit.; Bau. J. on 21:15; J. H. Bernard, A Crit. and Exeg. Comm. on the Gospel acc to St. John, ICC (1928), II, Exc. on 21:15; Bultmann J., 551, n. 2, 6 with Suppl., 48 etc., cf. also esp. Gaechter, op. cit. (→ n. 194), 328 f.; also his Petrus u. seine Zeit (1958), 12 f. J. A. Scott, "The Words for 'Love' in Jn. 21:15 ff.," Class. Weekly, 39 (1945/46), 71 f.; 40 (1946/47), 60 f.; cf. Spicq Agapè NT, III, 232, n. 2 (with bibl.).

[197] Cf. Gaechter, op. cit. (→ n. 196), 13-15. Apart from Gk. linguistic sense as distinct from Semitic, cf. Gaechter, op. cit. (→ n. 194), 330 f., there might be liturgical reasons for the alternation, cf. the Agnus Dei and the common extension of the third invocation in the Kyrie; cf. E. Jammers, Art. "Agnus Dei," RGG³, I, 176 and also Art. "Kyrie eleison," ibid., IV, 192; E. Stommel, "Stud. z. Epiklese d. röm. Taufwasserweihe," Theophaneia, 5 (1950), 38-43, esp. 40 f.; R. Mehrlein, Art. "Drei," RAC, IV (1959), 307.

[198] Cf. on this Bultmann J., 551 with n. 5; Gaechter, op. cit. (→ n. 196), 19-30. The threefold repetition of the question might also have a liturgical root, cf. the Kyrie, Agnus Dei, and already the Trishagion in Rev. 4:8 along with the Aaronic and apostolic benediction. We find similar repetitions and triplications elsewhere, e.g., in Babyl. magic; cf. G. Meloni, "Petre, amas me? (Jn. 21:15 ff.). Della ripetizione nello stilo semitico," Rivista Storico-Critica delle Scienze Teol., 5 (1909), 465-475. For other examples cf. O. Weinreich, "Trigeminatiòn als sakrale Stilform," Studi e materiali di storia della religioni, 4 (1928), 198-206; E. Norden, Aus altröm. Priesterbüchern (1939), 238-244; Mehrlein, op. cit., 282-291, 298 f., 306 f.; Stommel, op. cit., 35-43.

[199] As is well-known, neither the concept nor the special position of the apostles is ref. to in Jn. → I, 421, 27 ff.; 434, 17 ff.; 435, 7 ff.

[200] In Jn. 20:21-23 the ten again represent all the disciples, as the twelve do in c. 13-16, cf. Bultmann J., 349, 537; H. v. Campenhausen, Kirchliches Amt u. geistliche Vollmacht in d. ersten drei Jhdt. (1953), 151-4; E. Schweizer, Gemeinde u. Gemeindeordnung im NT (1959), 112; Kragerud, op. cit., 54.

[201] So already Greg. Naz. Or., 39, 18 (MPG, 36 [1858], 358a), and esp. Aug. In Joh. Ev. Tract., 123, 5 on 21:15-19: redditur negationi trinae trina confessio. Further examples in Stommel, op. cit., 41, n. 1. It is an open question whether the author intended a par. with the meal in 13:2 ff., 38; 21:13 and fire in 18:18; 21:9, so Gaechter, op. cit. (→ n. 194), 332.

[202] The double experience of deepest humiliation and supreme exaltation (as commissioning), which is also to Peter an attestation of the Lord's forgiveness, corresponds exactly to Paul's experience, 1 C. 15:9 f.; cf. 1 Tm. 1:15 f., v. also G. Stählin, Die Apostelgesch., NT Deutsch, 5² (1966) on 9:9.

and the special love of Peter for Jesus thereby required Jesus bases the twofold discipleship of Peter in his pastoral office and his death. Plainly the author wants this solemnly confirmed, exceptional love of Peter for Jesus to be regarded as a counterpart to the exceptional love of Jesus for the beloved disciple. In this way it would appear that he wants to relate the two disciples in a special manner, though one that we can no longer understand to-day, cf. Jn. 21:20-23. [203]

c. In the Rest of the New Testament.

Outside the Gospels φιλέω "to love" occurs only twice in the Pauline Corpus in stereotyped formulae at 1 C. 16:22 and Tt. 3:15 and then twice in Rev., the first time in a quotation at 3:19 and the second in a formula in the list of vices at 22:15, cf. the use of φιλία in Jm. 4:4 → 167, 8 ff. The impression one gets already from the Synoptic use is even stronger now, namely, that outside Jn. there is no special liking for φιλέω → 128, 4 ff.

(a) At 1 C. 16:22 one reads: εἴ τις οὐ φιλεῖ τὸν κύριον, ἤτω ἀνάθεμα. It is probable that here, as with the directly related Maranatha (→ IV, 470, 6 ff.), Paul is simply adopting fixed formulae [204, 205] that had developed liturgically. [206] Perhaps one can define their liturgical character even more precisely by saying that they come from the liturgy of the Lord's Supper. [207] The apostle is using the exclusive formula of the eucharistic meal: [208] Only those who love the Lord are invited to the Supper. We thus have a principle of sacral law: [209] He who denies or rejects [210] the Lord (cf. 1 C. 12:3), let him be accursed! Only to him who confesses his love for Christ [211] by word and deed (→ V, 212, n. 39) does the grace of the Lord apply. [212] Here φιλέω is a comprehensive term for an attitude of faith which is

---

[203] On the problem of the relation between the beloved disciple and Peter cf. → 132, 12 ff.; 133, 9 ff.

[204] A point in favour of this is that Paul prefers ἀγαπάω to φιλέω in similar passages in 1 C. 2:9; 8:3; R. 8:28, cf. also Eph. 6:24; 2 Tm. 4:8, and cf. the observation of E. Peterson, "Εἷς Θεός," FRL, 41 (1926), 130 that the saying begins with εἴ τις like the invitations to communion in Did., 10, 6 and Const. Ap., VII, 26, 6.

[205] Only few commentators think the formulations are the apostle's own, cf. Schl. K. and Bchm. 1 K., ad loc.

[206] Cf. Peterson, op. cit., 130 f.; Bornkamm, 123-132; J. A. T. Robinson, "The Earliest Chr. Liturgical Sequence?" Twelve NT Studies (1962), 154-7; O. Cullmann, Die Christologie d. NT⁴ (1966), 216-8 (→ n. 194, 197 f.).

[207] It is possible, as Paul himself hints in v. 20b (→ 139, 23 ff.), 22 f., that when the letters of the apostle were read at the gathering of the community the administration of the Lord's Supper followed, cf. H. Lietzmann, Messe u. Herrenmahl (1926), 229; Bornkamm, 123. The same might well apply to Rev., cf. Bornkamm, 126 f.

[208] Cf. Bornkamm, 124 with n. 4. The positive counterpart was the probably related invitation formula εἴ τις φιλεῖ τὸν κύριον, ibid., 125.

[209] Cf. E. Käsemann, "Sätze hl. Rechtes im NT," Exeget. Versuche u. Besinnungen, II² (1965), 72.

[210] C. Spicq, "Comment compendre φιλεῖν dans 1 C. 16:22?" Nov. Test., 1 (1956), 204, stresses that in οὐ φιλεῖ the litotes has much the same force as in οὐκ οἶδα ὑμᾶς at Mt. 25:12; Lk. 13:27 vl. and οὐκ ἐδέξαντο at 2 Th. 2:10; cf. Spicq Agapè NT, III, 81-85.

[211] Earlier attempts to relate the φιλεῖ of v. 22 to the φίλημα of v. 20, cf. Bengel, ad loc., or to construe ἀθά as "sign" אות, E. Hommel, "Maranatha," ZNW, 15 (1914), 317-322, have been more or less abandoned to-day. A. Klostermann, Probleme im Aposteltexte, neu erörtert (1883), 224 related the two interpretations: "If any man will not kiss the Lord," i.e., if he refuses the fraternal kiss, v. 20, "this is the sign"; cf. Dölger, op. cit., 201, 203.

[212] Cf. the closely related formula of blessing at the end of Eph. 6:24.

completely orientated to Christ.[213] At Tt. 3:15: ἄσπασαι (→ I, 496, 9 ff.) τοὺς φιλοῦντας ἡμᾶς ἐν πίστει, the author again make use of a fixed formula, though this time it is epistolary rather than liturgical.[214] A conventional formula[215] is obviously given a Christian sense by the addition of ἐν πίστει.[216] φιλέω ἐν πίστει corresponds materially to ἀγαπάω ἐν θεῷ, Jd. 1; cf. also 2 Jn. 1; 3 Jn. 1. This love is strictly the mark of all Christians, but by the addition of the apostle's ἡμᾶς[217] it is given a similar exclusive sense (→ I, 501, 23 ff.) to οἱ φίλοι, 3 Jn. 15 (→ 166, 16 ff.). Love for the apostle is the bond which unites in a special way the churches of the Pastorals and which at the same time differentiates them from those outside.

(b) There is similar adoption of prior formulae in Rev. 3:19: ἐγὼ (→ II, 351, 8 ff.) ὅσους ἐὰν φιλῶ ἐλέγχω καὶ παιδεύω, for here the author is citing a familiar saying[218] based on Prv. 3:12 LXX (→ V, 622, 4 ff.).[219] It is one of the many cases in which the exalted Kurios quotes an OT saying about God with reference to Himself;[220] His chastising love (cf. 1 C. 11:32) for the threatened communities is no other than God's own love. The suggestion has been made[221] that behind this φιλῶ, as behind Jn. 15:14 f. (→ 165, 23 ff.), there stands the idea of the φίλος θεοῦ (→ 167, 12 f.), a close connection with v. 20 being assumed: The common meal is the most intimate proof of friendship and grants fulfilment of the burning desire for union with the heavenly Friend. But the place from which the quotation is taken and the par. use in Hb. 12:6 suggest a different complex of images as the true background — a complex which is more in keeping with the context of the letter to Laodicea than the metaphor of the friend, namely, the strict love of the father which manifests itself to the erring child in chastisements (→ V, 623, 9 ff.) so that he will

---

213 Cf. 1 Jn. 4:20; 1 Cl., 15, 4 and Bornkamm, 124 f. with n. 7.

214 Non-bibl. instances of οἱ φιλοῦντες ἡμᾶς "our friends" are BGU, II, 625 (2nd/3rd cent. A.D.); III, 814, 38 (3rd cent. A.D.); ἀσπάζου 'Επαγαθὸν καὶ τοὺς φιλοῦντες [sic] ἡμᾶς πρὸς ἀλήθιαν, P. Fay., 119, 25-27 (c. 100 A.D.); Preisigke Sammelb., V, 7992, 26 f. (2nd/3rd cent. A.D.). More common than οἱ φιλοῦντες ἡμᾶς is the greeting οἱ φιλοῦντές σε attested from the end of the 1st cent. A.D. (→ I, 496, 10 ff.; cf. U. Wilcken, "Pap.-Urkunden," APF, 6 [1920], 379, n. 2) in the sense of οἱ φίλοι σου, e.g., ἀσπάζου τοὺς φιλοῦντές σε πάντες [sic] πρὸς ἀλήθιαν, P. Fay., 118, 25 f. (110 A.D.). The formula φιλέω πρὸς ἀλήθειαν, unlike 2 Jn. 1; 3 Jn. 1 (→ line 5 f.), shows how formal and devalued the use of "to love" now was (→ 150, 11 ff. with n. 30), cf. also P. Oxy., III, 529, 11-15 (2nd cent. A.D.), ἀσπάσασθαί σε καὶ πάντας τοὺς φιλοῦντάς σε, P. Ryl., II, 235, 4 f. (2nd cent. A.D.), cf. P. Greci e Latini, 1, 94, 10-12 (2nd cent. A.D.). Further examples in F. X. J. Exler, *The Form of the Ancient Greek Letter*, Diss. Washington (1923), 114 f.; P. Giess., I, 12, 8 f.; P. Oxy., XIV, 1757, 26 f. (2nd cent. A.D.), and F. Ziemann, *De epistularum Graec. formulis sollemnibus quaestiones selectae*, Diss. Halle (1911), 329 f.; Preisigke Wört., *s.v.* φιλέω; Spicq Le lexique, 27, n. 4; Spicq Agapè NT, III, 85 f.; Dib. Past., *ad loc.*; H. Koskenniemi, *Stud. z. Idee u. Phraseologie d. griech. Briefes* (1956), 115 f.

215 τὸ προσκύνημα τῶν τέκνων μου καὶ τῶν φιλούντων με, Ditt. Or., I, 184, 8-10 (74 B.C.), cf. Preisigke Sammelb., V, 7942, 5 f.; 8401, 5 f. (73 B.C.).

216 Dib. Past.⁴, *ad loc.*; cf. Ziemann, *op. cit.* (→ n. 214), 330.

217 Cf. E. v. Dobschütz, "Wir u. Ich bei Pls.," ZSTh, 10 (1933), 251-277; W. F. Lofthouse, "'I' and 'We' in the Paul. Letters," Exp. T., 64 (1952/53), 241-5.

218 Cf. H. Ringgren and W. Zimmerli, *Sprüche, Prediger, AT Deutsch*, 16, 1 (1962) on Prv. 3:12.

219 LXX and Hb. 12:6 have ἀγαπάω, but the alternation is no more important than that between Rev. 3:9: ἐγὼ ἠγάπησά σε and 3:19. Bengel on 3:19 again sees a fine distinction here: Philadelphiensem ἠγάπησε; Laodicensem φιλεῖ.

220 Cf. G. Stählin, "Siehe, ich mache alles neu," Ökumen. Rundschau, 16 (1967), 240 f.

221 Cf. Loh. Apk. and J. Behm, *Die Offenbarung d. Joh.*, NT Deutsch, 11⁷ (1956), *ad loc.*

not be lost but will be led to repentance. [222] In the case of Rev. 22:15 there is again good reason to suspect that we have a current formulation, for πᾶς φιλῶν καὶ ποιῶν ψεῦδος forms the conclusion to a list of vices, and like the opening οἱ κύνες (→ III, 1103, 35 ff.) it characterises comprehensively the intervening concepts. φιλῶ καὶ ποιῶ [223] ψεῦδος "to give oneself with active love to the lie, the primal liar," is synon. with ἀγαπῶ τὸ σκότος in Jn. 3:19 and closely akin to ἀγαπῶ τὸν κόσμον in 1 Jn. 2:15, to φιλία τοῦ κόσμου (→ III, 895, 24 ff.), and hence to φίλος εἰμὶ τοῦ κόσμου in Jm. 4:4 (→ 167, 8 ff.; II, 920, 23 ff.). To this extent it is the absolute antithesis of ἀγάπη τοῦ θεοῦ.

II. The Kiss in the New Testament.

In the NT the kiss naturally plays a subordinate role. Its occurrence in some passages is thus of theological significance.

1. Manner and Occasion of Kissing.

Among the types of kisses mentioned we do not find the erotic kiss (→ 120, 21 ff.), just as we do not find φιλέω used for "to love" in the erotic sense (→ 128, 11 ff.; → n. 22). Nor do we find the kiss between close relatives (except at Lk. 15:20 → 139, 16 f.). On the other hand Lk. 7:45 presupposes the custom [224] of a greeting kiss [225] (→ 121, 12 ff.; 126, 25 ff.) and the father's kiss in Lk. 15:20 [226] (but cf. → 139, 16 f.) and Judas' kiss in Lk. 22:47 (→ 140, 15 f.) might well be put in this category. [227] There is only one emphatic ref. to the parting kiss, Ac. 20:37 → 139, 17 ff. In many cases where one might expect greeting or parting kisses to be mentioned, they are perhaps implied in other words like ἀσπάζομαι (→ I, 496, 10 ff. cf. Ac. 21:5 f. with 20:36 f.; R. 16:16 → 139, 21 ff.), [228] → n. 37. [229] The kisses of

---

[222] Cf. Warfield, 189 et al. (cf. Dt. 8:5).

[223] Perhaps with ℵ and Tisch. NT one should reverse the order to ποιῶν καὶ φιλῶν, since φιλέω (like συνευδοκέω in R. 1:32) goes beyond ποιέω, so Warfield, 188 f. ποιέω is used similarly in Jn. 3:21: ὁ ποιῶν τὴν ἀλήθειαν, and esp. in 1 Jn. 1:6: ψευδόμεθα καὶ οὐ ποιοῦμεν τὴν ἀλήθειαν, cf. also Rev. 22:11.

[224] Possibly Lk. has in view the Gk. practice of greeting guests on their arrival with a kiss, cf. Hug, 2063 → 119, 17 f.

[225] Some later witnesses read φίλημά μοι ἀγάπης οὐκ ἔδωκας here. This is perhaps to date back the primitive Chr. "holy kiss" (cf. 1 Pt. 5:14 → 139, 23 ff.) to the lifetime of Jesus prior to the institution of the Supper.

[226] This is construed as a kiss of greeting after long parting when it is viewed as a prototype of the kiss at baptism: διὰ τοῦτο καὶ ἐξ ἀποδημίας ἐπανιόντες ἀλλήλους φιλοῦμεν, τῶν ψυχῶν ἐπιγινομένων εἰς τὴν πρὸς ἀλλήλους συνουσίαν, Chrys. Hom. in 2 C., 30, 1 on 13:12 (MPG, 61 [1862], 606).

[227] To be sure, this view of Judas' kiss is improbable, since the Jews allowed greeting kisses only after longer parting, cf. Gn. r., 70, 12 on 29:11 in Str.-B., I, 995, whereas Judas had been with Jesus just before at the Last Supper. As distinct from Jn. 13:30 the Synoptists do not even say that Judas had left the group prior to going to Gethsemane, → n. 244.

[228] As a rule ἀσπάζομαι needs an explanatory addition, e.g., ἐν φιλήματι ἁγίῳ 1 Th. 5:26 etc. (→ 139, 23 ff.), cf. Plut. Pericl., 24 (I, 165d): καὶ γὰρ ἐξιὼν (sc. Pericles) ... καὶ εἰσιὼν ἀπ' ἀγορᾶς ἠσπάζετο καθ' ἡμέραν αὐτὴν (his wife) μετὰ τοῦ καταφιλεῖν, so also Quaest. Rom., 6 (II, 265c).

[229] The same applies to ἐναγκαλίζομαι, Mk. 9:36; 10:16, which includes the tender kiss for small children, and προσκυνέω (→ VI, 758, 15 ff.), e.g., Mt. 28:9; Ac. 10:25, which can mean "to hug with a kiss on the foot"; cf. Loh. Mt. on 28:9; Str.-B., I, 1054; also I. Benzinger, Hbr. Archäol.[2] (1907), 133.

Lk. 22:47 f.; 7:38, 45 might be meant as marks of honour → 120, 3 ff.; 126, 16 f. If it was customary for a disciple to honour his master with a kiss when seeing him again or parting, the kiss of Judas (→ 140, 8 ff.) might have seemed completely natural to those present. Again the kiss which Jesus did not get from His host in Lk. 7:45, while it might have been the customary kiss at greeting (→ VII, 232, n. 219), was more likely the sign of special respect such as one finds among teachers, → n. 127; → 126, 21 ff. [230] In any case kissing the feet of Jesus was a mark of unusual reverence, Lk. 7:38, 45.

The many kisses of the woman who sinned much are, of course, far more; they are signs of repentance. In the antithetical list [231] (Lk. 7:44-46) in which Jesus contrasts the lack of love and respect on the part of His Pharisaic host with the superabounding love and respect of the sinful woman, the kiss is the decisive embodiment of ἀγάπη, which for its part is the sign of accepted forgiveness, v. 47. If the woman cannot do enough in her repeated kissing of the feet (v. 45) — the imperfect κατεφίλει in v. 38 is already to the same effect — the significance of the whole event is here gathered up in the kiss. The kiss of the father in Lk. 15:20 is to be regarded as supremely a sign of reconciliation → 122, 12 ff. The parting kiss of the Ephesian elders in Ac. 20:37 [232] is also an expression of their gratitude (→ 126, 21 ff.) for all that Paul had done for his churches. This kiss might also have a liturgical character, since it stands in direct relation to a common prayer, v. 36. We find the liturgical kiss [233] five times. Four Pauline epistles (1 Th. 5:26; 1 C. 16:20; 2 C. 13:12; R. 16:16) [234] close by asking the recipients to kiss one another, and cf. also 1 Pt. 5:14. The greeting demanded of the churches (→ I, 501, 14 ff.) with the φίλημα ἅγιον [235] (→ I, 108, 28 ff.) or ἀγάπης (1 Pt. 5:14), along with the accompanying formulae Anathema and Maranatha (1 C. 16:22), might well be the introduction to the Supper that follows, → 136, 14 ff. [236] The mutual kiss (→ 119,

---

[230] Cf. Str.-B., I, 995.

[231] The element of crescendo in the antithesis finds expression in the fact that the marks of respect not shown by the host move up from the feet (v. 44) to the cheeks (v. 45) and the head (v. 46), whereas the humble respect shown by the woman focuses solely on the feet of Jesus; on the anointing cf. Jn. 12:3 as distinct from Mk. 14:3 and Mt. 26:7; on the footwashing → V, 25, n. 177. There is a striking similarity between the depicted acts of the woman and the description in Heliodor. Aeth., I, 2, 6: "The girl embraced him (the mortally wounded youth) in her arms, wept, kissed him, and dried him," except that here the feet are not obj. of the kisses and the other demonstrations of love, since these are erotic kisses.

[232] The motif of parting is esp. important here because the parting is final, v. 38, 25. To this extent it is par. to the parting kiss for martyrs in both Judaism, 3 Macc. 5:49, and early Christianity (→ 144, 33 ff.), and also for the dying in gen. → 122, 4 ff.

[233] On pre-Chr. liturgical kisses → 123, 6 ff. The conjecture of F. L. Conybeare, "The Kiss of Peace," Exp., IV, 9 (1894), 460-2, that Paul was following a synagogue custom with the cultic kiss cannot be based at any rate on Philo Quaest. in Ex., II, 78 on 25:37a; II, 118 on 28:32, since the ref. here is to something different, namely, the harmony of the elements → n. 136.

[234] There is no brotherly kiss in Gl., but one might say that the wishing of εἰρήνη for the Israel of God in 6:16 takes its place. Later the "peace" was often associated with the kiss, → 143, 8 ff.

[235] ἅγιος here means more than "Christian" or "liturgical," cf. Dob. Th. on 5:26; it denotes the kiss proper to and seemly for the ἅγιοι; Hofmann, 91; R. Asting, Die Heiligkeit im Urchr. (1930), 148. Cf. also Cl. Al. Paed., III, 81, 4, who contrasts the φίλημα ἅγιον and the φίλημα ἄναγνον.

[236] Cf. Seeberg, 120 f.; Wnd. 2 K. on 13:12; Lietzmann, op. cit. (→ n. 207), 229; Hofmann, 23-26, 94-121; Bornkamm, 123 f. et al. This is how the early Church always understood the φίλημα ἅγιον, putting it into the eucharistic liturgy at various pts., e.g., Const. Ap., VIII, 11, 7-9 → 142, 9 ff.

14 ff.), found only here in the NT, is a sign and seal of the forgiveness granted to and gratefully received by the brother, this being the presupposition of proper observance of the Supper. Like the Supper itself, on each occasion it confirms and actualises the unity of the community as a brotherhood (→ 122, 9 ff.), i.e., as the eschatological family of God. [237] The kiss and the Supper point forward to the eschatological consummation of salvation, to the future fellowship of the perfected. [238]

2. The Kiss of Judas.

The kiss of Judas is a problem on its own. [239] It formed a difficult problem for early Christianity from the very outset, as is shown by the variations in the Synoptic accounts and its omission from the Fourth Gospel. In Mk. 14:44 f. the kiss has plainly a pragmatic meaning; it is the agreed sign of recognition leading on at once to the arrest. [240] Mt. 26:50 puts before it the enigmatic saying of Jesus: ἑταῖρε, ἐφ' ὃ πάρει, probably: "Friend, for this then thou hast come!" or: "Friend, why thou hast come (I know)" — a kind of aposiopesis. [241] In Lk. 22:47 f. it is an open question whether the kiss is actually given.

---

[237] Hofmann, 99 f. thinks that even in the NT the φίλημα ἅγιον implies the transmission of forces and spiritual qualities → n. 94. But in the NT such animistic, dynamistic and even demonistic ideas originally associated with the kiss are in fact transcended by concepts rooted completely in the christology, soteriology and eschatology of the Gospel. For the post-NT period → 142, 17 ff.

[238] Cf. the kiss of greeting for martyrs on entering eternal bliss, Cyprian Ep., 37, 3 (CSEL, 3, 2 [1871], 578); Pass. Perp. et Fel., 10. 12, cf. Ant. Christ., II, 207 f.

[239] Cf. F. W. Belcher, "A Comment on Mk. 14:45," Exp. T., 64 (1952/53), 240; M. Dibelius, "Judas u. d. Judaskuss," Botschaft u. Gesch., I (1953), 272-7.

[240] Naturally the change from φιλέω in v. 44 to καταφιλέω in v. 45, cf. Mt. 26:48 f., has attracted attention and given rise to the suggestion there might be some change of meaning, e.g., φιλέω "to embrace" and καταφιλέω "to kiss," so Spicq Agapè NT, I, 176; cf. also Belcher, op. cit., 240: "καταφιλέω has a sense of intense emotion, while the latter (sc. φιλέω) lacks this quality"; cf. also Loh. Mk., ad loc.: "the compound . . ., which in the NT always denotes the intense and ardent kiss (Lk. 7:38)." But the reason for the change might well be just stylistic, cf. → n. 42.

[241] The meaning of this saying is not unequivocal and has always been debated. Since the passage is not discussed in → II, 701, n. 12 or → V, 859, 13 f., the most important possibilities might be mentioned here: 1. "Friend, why hast thou come?" so Vg.: amice, ad quid (quod) venisti?, Luther, and most older transl., also Deissmann LO, 100-105 et al., v. Pr.-Bauer, s.v. ὅς I, 9b. But this hardly does justice to the relative pronoun ὅ. 2. "Friend, hast thou come for this?" corresponding in sense and tone to Lk. 22:48, so F. Rehkopf, "Ἑταῖρε, ἐφ' ὃ πάρει (Mt. 26:50)," ZNW, 52 (1961), 114, cf. O. Karrer, Neues Testament² (1959), ad loc.: "Friend, for this then thou hast come!" Others take the saying as an aposiopesis: 3. "Friend, do what thou hast come for," cf. Jn. 13:27, so the Book of Armagh, an Irish MS of the Vg (amice, fac ad quod venisti), cf. Deissmann LO, 102; W. Eltester, "'Freund, wozu du gekommen bist' (Mt. 26:50)," Festschr. O. Cullmann (1962), 73, with n. 4, 90 f., and some Coptic MSS, cf. W. Spiegelberg, "Der Sinn von ἐφ' ὃ πάρει Mt. 26:50." ZNW, 28 (1929), 343, n. 1, and various English transl.: R.V. (1881), N.E.B. (1961); J. Moffatt, The New Test. A New Transl. (1935): "My man, do your errand"; cf. also H. J. Holtzmann, Hand-Comm. z. NT, I, 1³ (1901), ad loc.; M. Dibelius, Die Formgeschichte d. Ev.⁵ (1966), 198 with n. 1 et al., v. Pr.-Bauer, s.v. ὅς, I, 2bβ. In this way Jesus would actively bring on His passion in Mt. as He does in Jn. 4. "Friend, let that be done for which thou hast come!" corresponding to the prayer in Gethsemane, Mt. 26:42, so Eltester, 70-91, who rightly conjectures (88) that in the whole incident and esp. the address (→ 159, n. 113) ἑταῖρε as well as the phrase added in v. 38 to the quotation from Ps. 42:6 (ἕως θανάτου), Sir. 37:2 (→ 156, 31 ff.), is in the background, cf. also Spicq Agapè NT, I, 177, n. 6. 5. Also possible is: "Friend, why thou hast come I know." For other attempts to supplement cf. Radermacher, 78; Bl.-Debr. § 300, 2; Pr.-Bauer, s.v. ὅς I, 2a. In any case this final saying to Judas in Mt. and the corresponding Lk. 22:48 seem to indicate that Jesus knew in advance not only the fact of the betrayal and the identity of the traitor, Mt. 26:21-25 and par., but also that the betrayal or handing over would be accomplished with a kiss, cf. Loh. Mt. on 24:48-50.

What the Synoptic Judas aims to do is done by Jesus Himself in Jn. 18:5 f. with His ἐγώ εἰμι. [242] The betrayal of the Master by a kiss [243] of one of the Twelve, cf. Mk. 14:10 and par., 20, 43 and par.; Jn. 6:71 became an increasing offence that was hard to overcome. The difficulty was resolved by the proof from prophecy, cf. Jn. 13:18; 17:12, intimated already in Mk. 14:18, and by the prediction of the betrayal by Jesus Himself, cf. Jn. 6:70 f.; 13:18 f., 21, 26 f.

Not too easy to answer is what practice lies behind the kiss of Judas. Was it a routine kiss that would not surprise the other disciples who were with Jesus? Was it simply a kiss of greeting [244] (→ 138, 19 f. with n. 227)? This is not likely after so short a time, cf. Mk. 14:17 ff. Was it usual for the disciples to kiss their Master as the pupils of the rabbis did [245] → 139, 3 ff.? Or was the band of disciples, as the family of God gathered around Jesus cf. Mk. 3:34 f., already practising the kiss of brotherhood as the Pauline churches were very soon to do, cf. 1 Th. 5:26 → 139, 21 ff.; Ac. 20:37 → 139, 17 ff.? [246] Since, however, there are no other examples of the disciples kissing Jesus, it might also be that this was an unusual act undertaken ad hoc. It was thus, as a sign of feigned love and reverence, that early Christianity always interpreted the kiss of Judas, [247] and it condemned as the shabbiest part of this betrayal this misuse of the sign of love as a "sign" (Mk. 14:44; Mt. 26:48) of παραδιδόναι. [248]

---

[242] This is one of many features in Jn. which show Jesus Himself acting with sovereign power, cf. esp. 13:27b; 10:17 f. From first to last His passion is His action, → n. 241 under 3. In contrast, Judas, the embodiment of ungodly power in Jn. cf. 6:70; 13:27a, is passive here as distinct from the Synoptics. Hence there is no kiss, cf. K. Lüthi, "Das Problem d. Judas Iskariot — neu untersucht," Ev. Theol., 16 (1956), 112; also Judas Iskarioth (1955), Index, s.v. "Joh. Fragen."

[243] In the OT we find the false kiss of the deceiver, Gn. 27:26 f., of the political seducer, 2 S. 15:5, of the temptress, Prv. 7:13, of the flatterer for whom the kiss is the means to an end, Sir. 29:5, of the enemy who wants to move in safety, Prv. 27:6, and esp. of the murderer, 2 S. 20:9. The kiss of Joab and his hypocritical greeting: "Art thou in health, my brother?" which accompany his vile act of assassination, are an ancient prototype of greeting, esp. in the form χαῖρε, ῥαββί (Mt. 26:49) and the kiss with which Judas delivers up His Master to those who slay Him. There are many instances of such hypocritical kisses outside the Bible too, cf. Philo Rer. Div. Her., 40-44, 51. Cf. also the interpretation of kisses in dream-books, e.g.: He who kisses an ape in a dream ἐχθρὸν πολύτροπον ἀδύνατον γνωρίσει δόλῳ φιλοῦντα αὐτόν, Achmes Oneirocriticon (→ n. 87), 136 (p. 90 f.), cf. 135 f. (p. 90 f.) for further instances of the interpretation of dream-kisses from Indian, Persian and Egypt. sources; cf. also Artemid. Onirocr., II, 2. Galba and Otho are a counterpart to Jesus and Judas: Galba unsuspectingly greets his murderer Otho with the usual eastern kiss: (Otho) mane Galbam salutavit, utque consueverat osculo exceptus; etiam sacrificanti interfuit . . . , Suet. Caes., VII Otho, 6, 2 f.

[244] Orig. Comm. in Mt., Fr. 533 (GCS, 41 [1941], 218) maintains: εἰώθει δὲ ἀσπάζεσθαι ὁ προδότης τὸν διδάσκαλον ὡς πάντες οἱ μαθηταί, ὅτε μακρόθεν ἤρχοντο.

[245] So Dibelius, op. cit., 275 f. Jesus, of course, was not a rabbi, cf. M. Hengel, "Nachfolge u. Charisma," ZNW Beih. 34 (1968), 2 and 46-63.

[246] Thus it might have been one of the practices early Christianity took over from the first community and then developed, like giving up property and the common chest, cf. Stählin, op. cit. (→ n. 202), 80; cf. also the sending out of evangelists in pairs.

[247] Cf. Orig. Cels., II, 11 (GCS, 2 [1899], 138 f.); Comm. in Mt., 100 on 26:48-50 (GCS, 38 [1933], 219 f.); cf. Hier. Comm. in Mt., IV on 26:49 (MPL, 26 [1884], 207d).

[248] Orig. Comm. in Mt., 100 on 26:48-50 (GCS, 38 [1933], 218 f., 219 f.) etc., e.g., Hier. Comm. in Mt., IV on 26:49 (MPL, 26 [1884], 207d), suggest that with the motif of reverence there is another remarkable one that Orig. owes to a tradition, namely, that with a kiss Judas could lull Jesus into security and could also prevent Him from disguising Himself from those who were after Him; but cf. Orig. Cels., II, 64 (GCS, 2 [1899], 186). The Proteus motif, cf. H. Herter Art. "Proteus, 1" in Pauly-W., 23 (1957), 965-971, is thus transferred to Jesus, cf. also Act. Joh., 91. 82; Act. Andr. et Matth., 17 (p. 84, 4 ff.) etc., as to many pagan deities, e.g., Demeter, cf. Hom. Hymn. Cer., 94-97, and esp. 111, 275-291, and Dionysus, cf. Eur. Ba., 4 and 1017-1019 → IV, 746, 16 ff.

D. The Kiss in the Post-New Testament Period.

I. The Early Church.

1. In spite of growing ascetic tendencies in the early Church the kiss is still used a good deal among post-NT Christians. The kissing of relatives [249] and married couples is taken for granted except that a husband should not kiss his wife in front of slaves, Cl. Al. Paed., III, 12, 84, 1. The erotic kiss plays a special part in a similitude in Herm. s., 9, 11, 4. In the love game (παίζειν) that the twelve virtues play with the seer in 9, 15, 2 [250] one after the other embraces and kisses him καταφιλεῖν καὶ περιπλέκεσθαι.

2. Most important, however, is the continuation and development [251] of the φίλημα ἅγιον → 139, 23 ff. The cultic kiss is carried much further than in its early beginings in the NT, although with certain restrictions too. Because in the kiss *plenae caritatis fidelis exprimitur affectus*, and because it can thus be regarded as *pietatis et caritatis ... signum*, the kiss itself shares the high estimation of these supreme virtues, Ambr. Exameron, VI, 9, 68 (CSEL, 32 [1896], 256).

a. In the post-NT age the eucharistic kiss is rather oddly not mentioned in the post-apost. fathers but we find it in Just.: ἀλλήλους φιλήματι ἀσπαζόμεθα παυσάμενοι τῶν εὐχῶν, Apol., 65, 2. Because the place of the kiss in worship at the time came after the common prayer and before the eucharist, [252] Tert. De oratione, 18 (MPL, 1 [1879], 1280 f.) calls it a *signaculum* ("sealing") *orationis*. Tert. is a strong champion of the *osculum pacis* even in times of private fasting apart from the pre-Easter fast, when all Christians should desist from the kiss of peace. [253] Its gt. significance for the community is that is underscores the need for reconciliation before receiving the holy Supper → 139, 26 ff. [254] That the kiss of peace τὸ ... πρὸς ἀλλήλους ἡνῶσθαι ... δηλοῖ and leads on to τὴν πρὸς τὸν ἀδελφόν ... σύμπνοιαν is also stressed by Ps.-Dionysius the Areopagite De ecclesiast. hier. (Paraphrasis Pachymerae), 3, 3, 8 (MPG, 3 [1857], 464b), where between the creed and the presentation of the (still covered) elements. [255] on the one side, and the reading of the diptycha, the lists of dead and living members of the community remembered at the mass. and the washing of the priests' hands on the other, [256] ὁ θειότατος ἀσπασμὸς ἱερουργεῖται, 3, 3, 8 (p. 437a). Similarly Cyr.

---

[249] But pagan relatives are not to be kissed. Greg. Naz. Or., 18, 10 (MPG, 35 [1857], 996c) praises his mother Nonna because she would never offer a pagan woman a hand or a kiss, however high in rank or closely related, lest she should be defiled with pagan hands and lips → 127, 10 ff., cf. Hofmann, 131 f., who gives another example from the Passio Georgii.

[250] Acc. to Dib. Herm., 618 f. this is an erotic but chaste fellowship portraying the syzygy between the seer and the virtues, cf. also s., 9, 6, 2.

[251] Cf. Schultze, 274 f.; Hofmann, 94-121. The φίλημα ἅγιον used by Paul at the end of his epistles also occurs later, e.g., Cyril of Alex. Ep., 19 (MPG, 77 [1859], 128c).

[252] Cf. Hipp. Ch. Order, 46, 8 (Hennecke², 580); cf. Orig. Comm. in Ep. ad Romanos, X, 33 on 16:16 (MPG, 14 [1862], 1282 f.): *mos Ecclesiis traditus est ut post orationes osculo se invicem suscipiant fratres*, and cf. many eastern liturgies, esp. Const. Ap., VIII → n. 236. On the different placings of the kiss in eastern liturgies cf. R. Storf, *Gr. Liturgien, Bibliothek d. Kirchenväter*, 5 (1912), 300; in the Liturgy of James (ed. F. E. Brightman, *Liturgies Eastern and Western*, I [1896], 43, cf. Storf, 170 f.) it comes after the creed, in that of Mark (Brightman, 123; Storf, 170 f.) and Chrys. Liturg. (Brightman, 382, cf. Storf, 243 f.) before the creed. Cf. also A. Seeberg, "Vaterunser u. Abendmahl," *Festschr. G. Heinrici* (1914), 110; Hofmann, 106 f.

[253] J. Schümmer, *Die altchr. Fastenpraxis* (1933), 77, cf. also the Jewish custom of omitting the greeting in public fasting, Str.-B., IV, 84 with n. 2; 89. 105.

[254] As a Scripture ref. Mt. 5:23 f. is often quoted, e.g., Cyr. Cat. Myst., 5, 3 and cf. Chrys. Ad Demetrium, I, 3 (MPG, 47 [1863], 398), where the cultic kiss is called an empty show σκηνή τις and τὸ ἀπὸ τῆς ψυχῆς φίλημα καὶ τὸν ἀπὸ τῆς καρδίας ἀσπασμόν is contrasted with it. Cf. also Hofmann, 123-8.

[255] At this pt. too in Testamentum Domini Nostri Jesu Christi (ed. J. E. Rahmani [1899], 37, cf. 181 f.); Hofmann, 100.

[256] Acc. to W. Tritsch, *Dionysius Areop., Die Hier. d. Engel u. d. Kirche* (1955), 272, n. 10, this was the customary place in the Syrian liturgy.

Cat. Myst., 5, 3 calls the φίλημα a σημεῖον τοῦ ἀνακραθῆναι τὰς ψυχάς and Chrys. Hom. de proditione Judae, 2, 6 (MPG, 49 [1862], 391) calls it a φρικωδέστατος ἀσπασμός, a greeting woven around him who sees the *mysterium tremendum,* binding together senses and souls, and thus making all into one σῶμα. [257]

In the West, where the original place of the kiss of peace seems to have been between the prayers and the offertory, it comes to be put immediately before communion in connection with the development of sacrificial theory and esp. with regard to Mt. 5:23 f., [258] cf. Aug. Serm., 227 (MPL, 38 [1865], 1101). Terms used for the liturgical kiss alternate. It is often simply called εἰρήνη as well as φίλημα εἰρήνης in the East, e.g., Ps.-Dion. De eccles. hier., 3, 3, 8 f. (MPG, 3 [1857], 437a-c), while in the West it is the *osculum pacis* in, e.g., Tert. De oratione, 18 (MPL, 1 [1879], 1280 f.), Aug. [259] Contra litteras Petiliani Donatistae, II, 23, 53 (MPL, 43 [1865], 277), but also the *pax,* e.g., several times in Tert. De oratione, 18 (p. 1281); 26 (p. 1301). The shorter designation is based on the close connection between the liturgical kiss and the greeting εἰρήνη σοι *pax tibi.* [260] For the same reason ἀσπασμός is often used for the eucharistic kiss, e.g., Ps.-Dion. De eccles. hier., 3, 3, 8 (p. 437a). Because of a possible misunderstanding Athenag. Suppl., 32 can even prefer προσκύνημα to φίλημα. [261]

Quite early we find objections to unrestricted use of the kiss in the cultus, partly by reason of the suspicions of non-Christians and partly by reason of the dangers of erotic perversions. Along these lines Athenag. Suppl., 32 quotes an agraphon (?) [262] against repetition of the kiss: ἐάν τις... ἐκ δευτέρου καταφιλήσῃ, ὅτι ἤρεσεν αὐτῷ, and he himself adds: [263] οὕτως οὖν ἀκριβώσασθαι τὸ φίλημα... δεῖ, "because it would mean our exclusion from eternal life if it (the kiss) were even a little to defile our mind." Related is the discussion in Cl. Al. Paed., III, 81, 2-4, where Cl. scourges the emptiness of the cultic kiss and condemns those who οὐδὲν ἀλλ' ἢ φιλήματι καταψοφοῦσι τὰς ἐκκλησίας, τὸ φιλοῦν ἔνδον οὐκ ἔχοντες αὐτό (→ n. 39) because they arouse shameful suspicions and evil gossip with this undisciplined kissing. He thus demands the φίλημα μυστικόν in which, as he says with a play on words, the mouth remains closed. The prayers linked to the kiss of peace also show traces of these dangers and anxieties, e.g., the Liturgy of Mark (Brightman, 123, cf. Storf, 170 f.). On these grounds from the 3rd cent. [264] at the latest the sexes were separated for the kiss of peace, Const. Ap., II, 57, 17; Const. Ecclesiae Aegypt., 13, 4, [265] and then the clergy and laity were separated, Const. Ap., VIII, 11, 9.

---

[257] Obviously Platonic ideas (→ 119, 6 ff. with n. 48) are interwoven with Pauline thoughts here, Ant. Christ., II, 315 f.

[258] Schultze, 274; Hofmann, 113-6.

[259] Aug. in Joh. Ev. Tract., 6, 4 on 1:32 f. sees in the kissing of doves a symbol of the kiss of peace and therefore of peace in gen., cf. Cabrol, 117-130; Pétré, 309-311.

[260] Pétré, 310, n. 1.

[261] Cf. also Const. Ap., II, 57, 17; VIII, 5, 10: τὸ ἐν κυρίῳ φίλημα, cf. Crawley, 742a, n. 12.

[262] Cf. A. Resch, *Agrapha²* (1906), 177 f.

[263] So J. Geffcken, *Zwei gr. Apologeten* (1907), 232 with E. Schwartz; others like Resch, *op. cit.,* 177 f. and A. Eberhard, *Frühchr. Apologeten u. Märtyrerakten, I, Bibl. d. Kirchenväter,* 12 (1913), 321 think the agr. is continued.

[264] There does not seem to have been any separation in Tert.'s day, for in Ad uxorem, II, 4 (CSEL, 70 [1942], 117) he uses the kiss of peace as an argument against a Christian woman remarrying a pagan: What pagan husband will let his Chr. wife *alicui fratrum ad osculum convenire?* — as against Schultze, 275 with Hofmann, 111.

[265] Ed. F. X. Funk, *Didasc. et Const. Apostolorum,* II (1905), 108. Here are new rules for the kiss of peace: *virum autem ne sinas mulierem osculari;* cf. F. Haase, *Die kpt. Quellen zum Konzil v. Nicäa* (1920), 43. Women catechumens are gen. excluded from the kiss, and for the same reason that the kiss was denied to pagans by both Jews (→ 127, 10 ff.) and Christians (→ n. 249): *nondum enim earum osculum mundum fiebat,* Hipp. Ch. Order, 43, 4 (Hennecke², 578).

b. The liturgical kiss occurs in many other parts of the liturgy apart from the eucharist. It comes twice in baptism. [266] There is first the kissing of the candidates by the bishop Hipp. Church Order, 46, 7 (Hennecke[2], 580); Const. Eccles Aegypt., 16, 20, whereby he pronounces their reconciliation with God and their acceptance into the community. [267] This is compared to the kiss of greeting after a long absence abroad, Chrys. Hom. de utilitate lectionis scripturarum, 6 (MPG, 51 [1862], 98) and Hom. in 2 C., 30, 1 on 13:12 → n. 226. [268] Then there is the kiss the baptised give their new brothers and sisters, Hipp. Church Order, 46, 8 (Hennecke[2], 580) in order to impart to them a share in the newly granted grace and power of peace. [269]

c. On the consecration of a bishop ἱεράρχης the kiss of peace has a firm place in many liturgies. [270] Acc. to Const. Ap., VIII, 5, 9 f. the other bishops give the one newly consecrated a kiss in the Lord, cf. Canones Hipp., [271] 3, 19; Hipp. Church Order, 31, 6 (Hennecke[2], 575). The Didascalia Arabica, 36, 23 [272] ref. to two kisses at episcopal consecration, the one by the consecrating bishops and the other by the whole congregation. Acc. to Ps.-Dion. De eccles. hier., 5, 2; 5, 3, 1 (MPG, 3 [1857], 509) the τελειωτικὸς ἀσπασμός was also given on the ordination of the priest ἱερεύς and deacon λειτουργός, both by the ordaining bishop and also by all the presbyters present. At the consecration of monks, the highest of the three ranks, the kiss of peace is again given, acc. to Ps.-Dion. 6, 2 (p. 533b) and 6, 3, 4 (p. 536b), by the consecrating priests and by all the believers present; it comes at the end of the ceremony after clothing with the monastic habit and before the attached eucharist.

d. The kiss at the burial of the dead occurs in Ps.-Dion. De eccles. hier., 7, 2 (MPG, 3 [1857], 556d); 7, 3, 4 (p. 560a), 8 (p. 565a): the bishop and all the believers present kiss the dead person after prayers for him. This kiss, [273] along with the giving of the eucharist to the deceased, was soon after forbidden, first by the Synod of Autissiodorum/ Auxerre in 585 (?), Can. 12: [274] non licet mortuis, nec eucharistiam, nec osculum tradi.

e. The kiss is also found in the early venerating of martyrs. [275] The habit was to visit martyrs in prison and to kiss them, Eus. De martyribus Palaestinae, 11, 20 (GCS, 9, 2 [1908], 942), and esp. their wounds, Prud. Peristephanon, 5, 337-340 (CCh, 126 [1966], 305) and their chains, Tert. Ad uxorem, II, 4 (CSEL 70 [1942], 117). Bold spirits like Origen kiss martyrs on their way to the place of judgment, Eur. Hist. Eccl., VI, 3, 4, and also the corpses (→ 122, 4 ff. with n. 82) of those executed, Eus. De martyr. Palaest., 11, 25 (GCS, 9, 2 [1908], 944). Martyrs themselves kiss one another just before execution, as the Jewish martyrs did in 3 Macc. 5:49, ut martyrium per sollemnia pacis consummarent,

---

[266] Cf. Schultze, 275; Hofmann, 99; Ant. Christ., I, 186-196; II, 159 f.

[267] The baptismal kiss corresponds formally to the kiss of Apul. Met., VII, 9, 1 (→ 122, 9 ff.), which also represents reception into a brotherhood; in both cases, too, there is a new robe and a common meal, cf. Lk. 15:20, 22 f. → 139, 23 ff.

[268] Cf. Ant. Christ., I, 193.

[269] A par. to the idea that the first kiss of peace of the newly baptised carries special powers is the view that the kiss of those who fast gives a share in their special spiritual power, Tert. De oratione, 18 (MPL, 1 [1879], 1281), cf. Tertullian, ed. F. Oehler, I (1853), 569, n. a; Hofmann, 133 f. This does not arise, of course, in infant baptism, where there can only be the first kiss, but Cyprian argues strongly in Ep., 64, 4 (ed. G. Hartel, CSEL, 3, 2 [1871], 719) for the baptismal kiss of the new-born, cf. Aug. Contra duas epist. Pelagianorum, IV, 8, 24 (MPL, 44 [1865], 626).

[270] Cf. W. Riedel, Die Kirchenrechtsquellen d. Patriarchats Alexandrien (1900), 202; Hofmann, 96 and 98 f.

[271] Transl. Riedel, op. cit.

[272] Transl. Funk, op. cit. (→ n. 265), 129, 23. 25.

[273] Dölger, op. cit. (→ n. 95), 254, n. 5; Sittl, 72 with n. 8.

[274] Ed. J. D. Mansi, Sacrorum Conciliorum nova et amplissima collectio, 9 (1960), 913.

[275] Cf. Ant. Christ., II, 210-212; Hofmann, 137-143 → n. 232.

Pass. Perp. et Fel., 21; Pass. Montani et Lucii, 23, [276] and also in anticipation of the kiss of greeting in heaven → n. 238. Cultic veneration of martyrs in the strict sense focuses on their tombs, relics, and memorial churches. Kissing their graves (→ n. 82, 134) is mentioned, Prud. Peristephanon, 11 193 f. (CCh, 126 [1966], 376), cf. Greg. Nyss. Vita Macrinae, 996, [277] also of relics, Paulinus of Nola Carmen, 18, 125-129 (CSEL, 30 [1894], 103), of relic containers, Hier. Contra Vigilantium 4 (MPL, 23 [1883], 375b), and of the thresholds of the churches of the martyrs (→ n. 104), Prud. Peristephanon, 2, 517-520 (CCh, 126 [1966], 275).

f. There are various substitute kisses in the early Church → 121, 7 ff. Here it seems in many details to inherit pagan practices → 123, 8 ff., as in the kissing of doorposts and thresholds in churches, [278] e.g., Paulinus of Nola Carmen, 18, 249 (CSEL, 30 [1894], 108); Chrys. Hom. in 2 C., 30, 2 on 13:12 (MPG, 61 [1862], 606 f.) and also of altars, [279] e.g., Ambr. Ep., I, 20, 26 (MPL, 16 [1880], 1044b): *milites, irruentes in altaria, osculis significare pacis insigne;* Prud. Peristeph., 9, 99 f. (CCh, 126 [1966], 329). Kissing the altar has a central place in the liturgy since the altar points to Christ. Hence the kiss of peace given just after derives its force from Christ and takes on sacramental significance. [280] Something of the same idea may be seen in the eastern practice (still in force) of kissing icons and achiropoiita, [281] since the power of the heavenly original attaches to icons, which through the centuries have been faithful copies even in matters of detail. We find many other liturgical kisses in eastern liturgies, e.g., Chrys. Liturg., 355, 12. 37; 356, 1; 362, 1; 382, 26 f.; 385, 14 f.: the Gospel book, discos, cup, signs of the cross on the orarion (stola) etc. [282] These were adopted in the West [283] along with the medieval *osculatorium,* the kissing tablet of precious metal, ivory, wood or marble which the priest hands communicants to kiss — a prime example of the substitute kiss. [284] Originally common to all these liturgical kisses is their desire to give a share in the sacred force of that which is kissed.

II. Gnosticism.

In Gnostic mysticism the kiss is a favourite symbol for union with the redeemer and the reception of immortal life mediated thereby. Good examples may be found in O. Sol. in which the sacrament of the bridal chamber and the soul's marriage with the Lord are described as the present eschaton, [285] cf. 3:2: "His body is by me; I cling to him and he kisses me"; 3:5: "I kiss the beloved and I am loved by him"; 28:6: "Immortal life caressed and kissed me." [286] Acc. to Ev. Phil. (→ n. 173), 117, 14-28 the sacrament of the bridal chamber is for Gnostics the supreme sacrament, more highly regarded than baptism and

[276] Ed. R. Knopf - G. Krüger, *Ausgewählte Märtyrerakten³* (1929), 82; cf. Pétré, 310, n. 5.
[277] Ed. V. W. Callahan - W. Jaeger, VIII, 1 (1952), 410, 5.
[278] Cf. Ant. Christ, II, 156-8.
[279] *Ibid.,* 190-221; J. A. Jungmann, *Missarum Sollemnia,* I⁴ (1958), 406-9.
[280] Cf. the phrase *sollemnia pacis* in Pass. Perp. et Fel., 21. Cf. Ant. Christ., II, 205-7; Hofmann, 135-7; also E. S. Drower, *The Mandaeans of Iraq and Iran²* (1962), 238.
[281] Cf. Schimmel, 190; H. Paulus, Art. "Heiligenbilder, I" in RGG³, III, 165; Hofmann, 106 with n. 1. The kissing of Mary's statue esp. has a firm place in the liturgy, so Chrys. Liturg. (Brightman, 354, 22, cf. Storf, *op. cit.,* 207).
[282] Cf. Hofmann, 105. We sometimes find kissing the eucharistic bread in both East and West, cf. Ant. Christ., IV, 231; Storf, *op. cit.,* 244 with n. 1.
[283] Cf. Schultze, 275; Hofmann, 117 f.; Jungmann, *op. cit.,* II⁴ (1958), 638, *s.v.* "Kuss."
[284] Schultze, 275; Hofmann, 116 f.; J. Braun, *Das chr. Altargerät* (1932), 557-572, with various names for the kiss-of-peace tablet, 560-562.
[285] Cf. H. Gressmann on O. Sol. 3, Hennecke², 438; Mithr. Liturg., 121-134; Hofmann, 86 f.
[286] Cf. H. Gressmann, Hennecke², 438, 462, who gives Ode 28 the title "Kiss of Life"; W. Bauer also transl. "to kiss" at 28:6: "He embraced me in life without death and kissed me," but he has "to burn" or "to glow" at 3:2, 5. At all events there is a strongly erotic Christ mysticism here. The love of the singer for Christ is ardent eros, and the Lord's love is viewed similarly, cf. also R. Abramowski, "Der Christus d. Salomooden," ZNW, 35 (1936), 53.

the Lord's Supper. Here the mutual kiss is the means of mystic conception, [287] 107, 2-6. The model of this Gnostic mysticism is the spiritual marriage, κοινωνία, between Jesus and Mary Magdalene (→ n. 173). Jesus kissed Mary, His κοινωνός, 107, 8 f.; 111, 32-34, often on the lips, naturally in an undefiled fellowship → n. 250. [288] Another kiss of Jesus plays an important part in the Gnostic legend of Pist. Soph.; by it the earthly Jesus is united with His heavenly twin. Mary tells how "He (the twin-redeemer) embraced thee and kissed thee, and thou didst kiss Him and you were one," Pist. Soph., 61 (GCS, 13, 78). [289] Finally a kiss is mentioned in the Manichaean myth of Mani's entry into the realm of light; [290] this reminds us of the kiss of greeting on the entry of martyrs into the heavenly world → n. 238. [291]

† φίλος,   † φίλη,   † φιλία.

Contents: A. In Non-Biblical Antiquity: I. Meaning of the Words: 1. φίλος; 2. φίλη; 3. φιλία; II. Friendship in Antiquity. B. φίλος, φιλία (φιλιάζω) in the Old Testament and Judaism: I. Usage: 1. φίλος; 2. φιλία; II. Friendship in the Old Testament and Judaism. C. φίλος, φίλη, φιλία in the New Testament: I. Usage; 2. φίλος (and φίλη) in Luke's Writings; 3. φίλος in John's Writings. 4. φίλος and φιλία in James. D. φίλος and φιλία in the Post-New Testament Period: I. The Early Church; II. Gnosticism.

A. In Non-Biblical Antiquity.

I. Meaning of the Words.

1. φίλος.

a. In the light of → 115, 8 f. the meaning of the adj. φίλος is "intrinsic, belonging, proper to," (→ 114, 8 ff.), "beloved," "dear," e.g., Hom. Il., 20, 347 f.: Αἰνείας φίλος

---

[287] Cf. A. Bertholet, Art. "Atem," RGG², I, 600 f. with Ill.
[288] Cf. Moroff, op. cit. (→ n. 118), 229 f.
[289] Cf. H. Leisegang, "Der Bruder d. Erlösers," Angelos, 1 (1925), 24-33.
[290] Manich. Homilien, ed. H. J. Polotsky (1934), 86, 34; 87. 2.
[291] On the kiss in the Mandaeans cf. K. Rudolph, Die Mandäer, II (1961), 207-9.

φίλος κτλ. Bibl. On A. I: F. Dirlmeier, Φίλος u. φιλία im vorhellen. Griechentum, Diss. Munich (1931); J. P. A. Eernstman, Οἰκεῖος, ἑταῖρος, ἐπιτήδειος, φίλος, Diss. Utrecht (1932); M. Landfester, "Das gr. Nomen 'philos' u. seine Ableitungen," Spudasmata, II (1966); F. Normann, Die von d. Wurzel φιλ- gebildeten Wörter u. d. Vorstellung der Liebe im Griechentum, Diss. Münster (1952); H. B. Rosén, "Die Ausdrucksform f. 'veräusserlichen' u. 'unveräusserlichen Besitz' im Frühgriech. (Das Funktionsfeld von homerisch φίλος)," Lingua, 8 (1959), 264-293. On A. II: E. Bickel, "Peter von Blois und Pseudocassiodor de amicitia," Neues Archiv d. Gesellschaft f. ältere deutsche Geschichtskunde, 45 (1957), 223-234; G. Bohnenblust, Beiträge z. Topos περὶ φιλίας, Diss. Bern (1905); A. Bonhöffer, "Epiktet u. d. NT," RVV, 10 (1911), 165 f.; also Die Ethik d. Stoikers Epict. (1894), 106-9, 121; E. Curtius, "Die Freundschaft im Alterthume," Alterthum u. Gegenwart (1875), 183-202; L. Dugas, L'amitié antique d'après les moeurs populaires et les théories des philosophes² (1914); R. Eglinger, Der Begriff d. Freundschaft in d. Philosophie, Diss. Basel (1916); R. Eucken, "Aristoteles' Anschauung v. Freundschaft u. v. Lebensgütern," Sammlung gemeinverständlicher wissenschaftl. Vorträge, 19, 452 (1884), 733-6; F. Hauck, "D. Freundschaft bei d. Griechen u. im NT," Festschr. T. Zahn (1928), 211-228; G. Heylbut, De Theophrasti libello περὶ φιλίας, Diss. Bonn (1876); H. J. Kakridis, La notion de l'amitié et de l'hospitalité chez Homère, Diss. Paris (Thessalonica, 1963); H. Kortenbeutel, Art. "Philos," Pauly-W., 20 (1941), 95-103; W. Kroll, Freundschaft u. Knabenliebe (1924); R. Löhrer, Freundschaft in d. Antike (1949); C. Märklin, "Über die Stellung u. Bdtg. d. Freundschaft im Alterthum u. in d. neuen Zeit," Programm Heilbronn (1842); L. Robin, La théorie platonicienne de l'amour, Diss. Paris (1908); E. J. Schächer, Stud. z. d. Ethiken d. corpus Aristot., II (1940); M. Schneidewin, Die antike Humanität (1897), 126-159; K. Treu, Art. "Freundschaft," RAC; W. Ziebis, Der Begriff d. φιλία bei Plato, Diss. Breslau (1927). On B. II: B. Hartmann, Art.

ἀθανάτοισι θεοῖσιν ἦεν (→ n. 182),[1] and for the noun φίλος "friend" in various nuances acc. to the relation, "personal friend," e.g., Soph. Phil., 421: ὁ παλαιὸς κἀγαθὸς φίλος τ'ἐμός, Aristot. Eth. Nic., IX, 11, p. 1171b, 2: παραμυθητικὸν γὰρ ὁ φίλος καὶ τῇ ὄψει καὶ τῷ λόγῳ, the "loved one" in a homo-erotic sense, e.g., Xenoph. Resp. Lac., 2, 13, "the lover" e.g., Plat. Phaedr., 255b: ὁ ἔνθεος φίλος, "the lover inspired by eros"; the "favourite,"[2] esp. of the gods, e.g., Aesch. Prom., 304: τὸν Διὸς φίλον (→ n. 1); the "ally," e.g., Xenoph. Hist. Graec., VI, 5, 48: ... πολλάκις καὶ φίλοι καὶ πολέμιοι γενόμενοι Λακεδαιμονίοις, usually plur.: the "followers" of a political leader, e.g., Plut. Apophth. Pisistratus, 1 (II, 189b), "friends" ("clients") who cluster around a prominent and wealthy man; in contrast to the equal relation in personal friendship (but → 153, 5 ff.) the relation is now unequal (→ 153, 17 ff.), friendship embracing parasites, cf. Lux. Toxaris, 16, advisers (→ 148, 25 ff.), legal assistants and political supporters, cf. Velleius Paterculus Hist. Romana,[3] II, 7, 3: amici clientesque Gracchorum. The most characteristic development of this use is in φίλοι τοῦ βασιλέως, e.g., Ditt. Or., I, 100, 1 f. (c. 200 B.C.),[4] and φίλοι (τοῦ) Καίσαρος, e.g., Epict. Diss., IV, 1, 95 (→ 166, 29 ff.); Philo Flacc., 40. Usually in the plur. φίλος is a (self-)designation for a philosophical or religious fellowship, e.g., the Pythagoreans, cf. Iambl. Vit. Pyth., 33, 237,[5] and the Epicureans.[6] There was a similar circle around Plato: φίλων βεβαίων τε καὶ ἦθος ἐχόντων ὑγιές, Ep., 6, 322d; μία φιλίας συμπλοκή, 332b.[7] Sometimes φίλος occurs in a transf. sense with abstract concepts (gen.), e.g., Aristot. Rhet., I, 11, p. 1371a, 17: ὁ φίλος τῶν ἡδέων → 148, 28 ff.; 157, 16 ff.

"Freund," Bibl.-Historisches Handwörterb., I (1962), 499 f.; J. de Vries, Art. "Freundschaft," RGG³ II, 1128. On C.: I. Abrahams, Studies in Pharisaism and the Gospels, II (1924), 213; M. Dibelius, "Johannes 15:13," Botschaft u. Gesch., I (1953), 204-220; G. Fuchs, Die Aussagen über d. Freundschaft im NT, verglichen mit denen d. Aristot. (Eth. Nic., 8/9), Diss. Leipzig (1914); W. Grundmann, "Das Wort von Jesu Freunden (J. 15:13-16) u. d. Herrenmahl," Nov. Test., 3 (1959), 62-9; L. Lemme, Art. "Freundschaft," RE³, 6 (1899), 267-9; W. Michaelis, "Die 'Gefreundeten' d. Ap. Pls.," Der Kirchenfreund, 67 (1933), 310-313; 328-334; H. van Oyen, Art. "Freundschaft," RGG³, II, 1130-2; O. Rühle, Art. "Freundschaft," RGG², II, 778 f. On D.: P. Fabre, S. Paulin de Nole et l'amitié chr. (1949); Harnack Miss., I, 433-6; A. v. Harnack, "D. Terminologie d. Wiedergeburt u. verwandter Erlebnisse in d. ältesten Kirche," TU, 42, 3 (1918), 104-6; M. A. McNamara, Friendship in St. Augustine (1958); V. Nolte, Augustins Freundschaftsideale in seinen Br. (1939); K. Treu, "Φιλία u. ἀγάπη. Z. Terminologie d. Freundschaft bei Basilius u. Greg. v. Nazianz," Studii Clasice, 3 (1961), 421-7; L. Vischer, "Das Problem d. Freundschaft bei d. Kirchenvätern," ThZ, 9 (1953), 171-200. Cf. also → 113, Bibl.

[1] Hom. always construes φίλος with the dat., but cf. Od., 6, 203; Il., 1, 381. The use with the gen. and as a noun are post-Homeric, but predominate in tragedy, e.g., Aesch. Prom., 304: τὸν Διὸς φίλον. Both occur together, Max. Tyr., 14, 6 f. (Hobein, 178), cf. Philo (→ n. 109) and Chr. inscr. before Constantine in Harnack Miss., 779, n. 1.

[2] In the senses → lines 4 ff. φίλος can be both act. and, more often, Normann, 17. 111, pass. Cf. Plat. Lys., 212a b: ἐπειδάν τίς τινα φιλῇ, πότερος ποτέρου φίλος γίγνεται, ὁ φιλῶν τοῦ φιλουμένου ἢ ὁ φιλούμενος τοῦ φιλοῦντος, cf. 212c, and the answer in 213a: ... οὐκ ἄρα ὁ φιλῶν φίλος ..., ἀλλ' ὁ φιλούμενος, cf. 213b. But finally the discussion ends with the problem: neither οἱ φιλοῦντες φίλοι ἔσονται, nor οἱ φιλούμενοι, nor οἱ φιλοῦντές τε καὶ φιλούμενοι, 213c.

[3] Ed. C. Halm (1876).

[4] Cf. Stob Florilegium Monacense, 73 (ed. A. Meineke, IV, [1857], 272). Acc. to Themist. Or., 16, 203b c Alexander answered the question where he kept his treasures by "in these" δείξας τοὺς φίλους, cf. the use of the saying by St. Lawrence in Ambr. De officiis ministrorum, II, 26, 140 (MPL, 16 [1845], 141b); Aug. Serm., 303, 1 (MPL, 38 [1842], 1394).

[5] Acc. to Diod. S., 10, 4, 3-6 Damon and Phintias were Pythagoreans; their loyalty in sacrificial friendship is thus an example of this among the Pythagoreans. Acc. to Simpl. In Epict., 30 (Dübner, 89, 14 ff.) φιλία is for the Pythagoreans σύνδεσμος ... πασῶν τῶν ἀρετῶν.

[6] Cf. Harnack Miss., 435.

[7] Plat. was a master at ἀνθρώπους νέους ... εἰς φιλίαν τε καὶ ἑταιρίαν ἀλλήλοις καθιστάναι ἑκάστοτε, Ep., 7, 328d.

b. The multiplicity of meanings corresponds to that of the terms used as synon. or correlative concepts. Closest is ἑταῖρος (→ II, 699, 31 ff.). In Plat. Lys the two words are used more or less interchangeably,[8] cf. esp. 211e, 212a and also 206d with 207e. ἑταῖρος τοῦ Καίσαρος occurs with φίλος τοῦ Καίσαρος, e.g., Epict. Diss., IV, 1, 95 → n. 74. But some distinction must have been felt when the two words were paired, as often in Plat., e.g., La., 180e: ἑταίρῳ τε καὶ φίλῳ, cf. Leg., V, 729c; Aristot. Eth. Nic., VIII, 14, p. 1162a, 31-33.

c. Of terms which are synon. or almost synon. with φίλος, but may also be used along with it, we should note, too, ἴδιος → 114, 14 ff. with n. 12, e.g., Vett. Val., II, 16 (p. 70, 5); cf. → 129, 23 ff., οἰκεῖος, Plat. Resp., I, 328d; Tim., 20e; Ditt. Syll.[3], II, 591, 59 (195 B.C.), γνώριμος, Philo Abr., 273, and γνωστός, ψ 87:19 → n. 74; → 155, 8 f.

d. Closely connected with φίλος from an early time is συγγενής (→ VII, 736, 19 ff.), since relatives and friends form the closest living circle, e.g., Jos. Ant., 18, 23. οἱ συγγενεῖς may be identical with φίλοι to the degree that there is agreement of interests, Democr. Fr., 107 (Diels, II, 164). In the Hell. Roman sphere the linking of the two has a twofold political significance, as an honorary title at Hell. courts[9] (the συγγενεῖς are the top group and the φίλοι next to the top),[10] and then for an allied people, Ditt. Syll.[3], II, 591, 18 f. (195 B.C.). The two words can also be related in a transf. sense, Plat. Resp., VI, 487a: φίλος τε καὶ συγγενὴς ἀληθείας, δικαιοσύνης, ἀνδρείας, σωφροσύνης. While the combination with συγγενής occurs at the highest social level, popular usage prefers to link φίλος with individual degrees of close relationship, parents and brethren, e.g., Preisigke Sammelb., I, 4086, 4 f. (4 A.D.), cf. also 4324, 4 f.; Epigr. Graec., 35, 7 f. (4th cent. A.D.).[11] In Xenoph. An., VII, 2, 25 we find φίλος with ἀδελφός (not lit. → I, 146, 6 f.) in the hendiadys "brotherly friend."

e. The orig. oriental, then widespread Hell. idea of "friends of the king" (→ 147, 14 ff.), who acted as counsellors etc.,[12] brought about a close connection with σύμβουλος or συμβουλευτής → 154, 23 ff.

f. φίλος has a pronounced political character when used with σύμμαχος, so Demosth. Or., 9, 12, esp. as the Romans made this pair an honorary title for nations in alliance with or belonging to the Empire → 155, 2 ff.

g. The whole φιλ-group can be used for "hospitality";[13] φιλέω "to entertain," e.g., Hom. Il., 6, 15 → 116, 4 ff.; in 6, 14 one might transl. φίλος δ' ἦν ἀνθρώποισιν by "Axylos was hospitable to men,"[14] and φιλότης can mean "hospitality" in Hom. Od., 15, 55 and 196 f.[15] Often we find φίλος and ξένος (→ V, 1, 1 ff.) together, e.g., Διονυσίου φίλου ὄντος καὶ ξένου, Lys., 19, 19; cf. Luc. Toxaris, 63; Ps.-Luc. Asinus, 5, or φίλος and σύσσιτος, Isaeus Or., 4, 18.

---

[8] But cf. the distinction between φίλε and ἑταῖρε in the NT, → n. 113.

[9] E.g., Caes. De bello civili (ed. P. Fabre [1947]), III, 103, 2: propinqui atque amici = συγγενεῖς καὶ φίλοι.

[10] Cf. Ditt. Or., I, 104, 2 (2nd cent. B.C.) with n. 2; M. L. Strack, "Griech. Titel im Ptolemäerreich," Rhein. Mus., 55 (1900), 161-190; H. Willrich, "Zum hell. Titel- u. Ordenswesen," Klio, 9 (1909), 416-421; E. Bickermann, Art. "Συγγενής," Pauly-W., 4a (1932), 1368 f.; Preisigke Wört., III, 200, s.v. συγγενής → VII, 737, 2 ff. with n. 4; 738, 15 ff.

[11] Cf. W. Peek, Griech. Grabgedichte (1960), 441, 7 f.

[12] E.g., Diod. S., 22, 3, 1: τῶν γὰρ φίλων αὐτῷ (Ptolemaeus Ceraunus) συμβουλευόντων... The same then applies to the φίλοι Καίσαρος, cf. J. Crook, Consilium Principis (1955), 105 → 166, 28 ff. with n. 171.

[13] Normann, 26-28.

[14] "He was loved among men" is, of course, more likely.

[15] Normann, 42.

2. φίλη.

φίλη first means "dearest," "love," "beloved" (fem.) with no erotic suggestion, e.g., mother in Aesch. Pers., 832 and wife in Hom. Il., 9, 146 and 288. But then it acquires on the one side an erotic sense, Xenoph. Mem., III, 11, 16, perhaps also II, 1, 23, cf. Preisigke Sammelb., I, 4559, 5: τῆς φίλης αὐτοῦ, and on the other hand and esp. it is used for "friend" (fem.) of women. [16] Thus Antigone says: λόγοις δ' ἐγὼ φιλοῦσαν οὐ στέργω φίλην, Soph. Ant., 543; cf. Luc. Dialogi Meretricii, 12, 1; Jos. Ant., 9, 65 → n. 115; P. Tebt., II, 413, 18 (2nd/3rd cent. A.D.). [17] As various motifs come together in the use of φίλη, so it is with the name Φίλη → 113, n. 3. We find it for Aphrodite, Athen, 6, 255c, for hetaerae, [18] and also for honorable women, Isaeus Or., 3, 2 etc. Finally φίλη is a political title → 147, 13 ff., though φίλη βασιλέως appears in a dubious light when used for the town of Tiberias in Jos. Vit., 384. [19] In a transf. and disparaging sense φίλη occurs with ἑταίρα, as in Plat. Resp., X, 603b of μιμητική, the "art of mimicry": ἑταίρα καὶ φίλη ἐστὶν ἐπ' οὐδενί ὑγιεῖ οὐδ' ἀληθεῖ.

3. φιλία.

a. φιλία "love," "friendship," has the same broad and varied range of meaning as φίλος → 147, 1 ff. [20] As the stem φιλ- suggests (→ 114, 8 ff.; 115, 10 ff.) it is first of all love for οἰκειότατοι, Luc. Toxaris, 8; this φιλία, then, is naturally κοινωνία βίου, Chrysipp. Fr., 112 (v. Arnim, III, 27). Primarily φιλία is thus φιλία συγγενική, loc. cit. → n. 27; Aristot. Eth. Nic., VIII, 14, p. 1161b, 12. [21] Love for one's mother, Epigr. Graec., 69, 4 f. (4th cent. B.C.), [22] spouse and children, Eur. Alc., 279, and brothers and sisters, Epigr. Graec., 81, 2; 35, 7 (4th cent. B.C.), [23] spouse μυρόμενος φιλίην τερπνοτάτην ἀλόχου, ibid., 550, 2 (2nd/3rd cent. A.D.) [24] are the strongest ties of love, cf. Xenoph. Hier., 3, 7: βεβαιόταται μὲν γὰρ δήπου δοκοῦσι φιλίαι εἶναι γονεῦσι πρὸς παῖδας καὶ παισὶ πρὸς γονέας καὶ ἀδελφοῖς πρὸς ἀδελφοὺς καὶ γυναικὶ πρὸς ἄνδρας καὶ ἑταίροις πρὸς ἑταίρους. [25]

b. Connected with φιλία συγγενική in true marriage, [26] and often in Gk. friendship too, is φιλία ἐρωτική, [27] whether between the sexes, cf. Anth. Graec., 5, 52, 2 (Beckby), [28]

---

[16] There were friendships only between φίλαι, not φίλος and φίλη. Socrates and Diotima and Synesius and Hypatia were exceptions.

[17] Cf. also Ev. Pt. 12:51 → n. 135. There was a group of φίλαι around Sappho like the φίλοι around Pythagoras, Socrates and Epicurus → 147, 15 ff.; cf. W. Aly, Art. "Sappho," Pauly-W., 1a (1920), 2377 f.

[18] Cf. K. Schneider, Art. "Hetairai," Pauly-W., 8 (1913), 1369.

[19] It might well have been formed ad hoc, cf. σύμμαχος καὶ φίλη of the Galilean town of Gabara in Jos. Vit., 235.

[20] There are accounts of various sorts of φιλία in Chrysipp. Fr., 98 (v. Arnim, III, 24), 723 (III, 181) and with special depictions of the three kinds of φιλία for the sake of χρήσιμον, ἡδονή and ἀγαθόν in Aristot. Eth. Nic., VIII, 3-11, p. 1156a, 6-1160a, 30.

[21] Cf. F. Dirlmeier, Aristot. Nik. Ethik⁵ (1969), 529 on 187, n. 2.

[22] Cf. Peek, op. cit. (→ n. 11), 86, 4 f.

[23] Ibid., 468, 2; 441, 7 f.

[24] Ibid., 466, 2 and cf. esp. Plut. Fr., 18, 10 (ed. G. N. Bernardakis, VII [1896]): true marriage is φιλίας διττῆς κρᾶσις.

[25] Is there meant to be an anticlimax here?

[26] Plut. Amat., 6 (II, 752c) calls a marriage, ἀνέραστος καὶ ἄμοιρος ἐνθέου φιλίας κοινωνία, "living together with no mutual desire or loving fellowship winged by Eros," a farce.

[27] Chrysipp. Fr., 112 (v. Arnim, III, 27): εἶναι δὲ καὶ συγγενικήν τινα φιλίαν ἐκ συγγενῶν· καὶ ἐρωτικὴν ἐξ ἔρωτος. Aristot. similarly distinguishes various forms of ἑταιρικὴ φιλία, Eth. Nic., IX, 10, p. 1171a, 14 f. is closely related to συγγενική or ἀδελφική, VIII, 14, p. 1161b, 12; cf. 1161b, 35 f.; 1162a, 9 f., also VIII, 13, p. 1161a, 25 f.

[28] Peek, op. cit., 402, 2 (2nd/3rd cent. A.D.): χαίρετε καὶ φιλίης μεμνημένοι ἄνδρες ἄριστοι.

or homo-erotic: αἱ τῶν παίδων φιλίαι, Plat. Clit., 409d, ἡ παρ' ἐραστοῦ φιλία, Phaedr., 256e. ἡ κατὰ τελείαν φιλία is possible only with one friend as in the case of the related sensual love ἐρᾶν, Aristot. Eth. Nic., VII, 7, p. 1158a, 10-13; cf. also IX, 10, p. 1171a, 10-12.

c. The third and typically Gk. form is φιλία ἑταιρική, "friendship" in the strict sense, pure φιλία for the Gks. This is the first form to bear the name φιλία in Gk. lit. in Theogn., 1, 306. 600; 2, 1278b. [29] φιλότης is used instead in Hom. and Hes. Nor is φιλία used in Aesch. or Soph. But we find it in Hdt. (→ line 18) and Eur. (→ 149, 21 f.), cf. Cyc., 81: σᾶς χωρὶς φιλίας, the bond of love between Dionysus and the satyrs. It is common in Plat. and Aristot. The plur. is common too, e.g., φιλίαι ἐθνικαί, "friendships with pagans," Herm. m., 10, 1, 4. Finally the usage becomes so gen. that φιλία denotes little more than a "pleasant relation" between two people, cf. P. Fay., 135, 9-11 (4th cent. A.D.), where a son asks his father to repay a debt: σπούδασον πληρῶσαι ("to pay") ἵνα ἡ φιλία διαμίνη μετ' ἀλλήλων. [30] As with φίλος (→ 154, 14 f.) there are friendships across the generations; φιλία thus denotes "family friendship," which usually carries the idea of "hospitality" too, so P. Tebt., I, 59, 6-8 (99 B.C.): ... ἥν ἔχετε πρὸς ἡμᾶς ἄνωθεν πατρικὴν φιλίαν.

d. Like φίλος and φίλη, φιλία has a place in politics too; [31] in Hdt., VII, 151 f. it is already an "alliance." There is frequent ref. to the renewal of such a φιλία between states or rulers, P. Oxy., IV, 705, 31 f. (200 A.D.): ἡ πρὸς Ῥωμαίους εὔνοιά τε καὶ πίστις καὶ φιλία, Ditt. Syll.³, II, 674, 19. 43 (c. 150 B.C.): φιλίαν συμμαχίαν τε ἀνενεώσαντο → 151, 9 ff. Here and in many other passages we find the fixed combination φιλία καὶ συμμαχία, cf. φίλος καὶ σύμμαχος → 148, 28 ff.; examples are Thuc., VI, 34, 1; Polyb., 31, 1, 1 and 3.

e. In a transf. sense Emped. uses φιλία for one of the basic principles of all being, "harmony" as a principle of union in contrast to νεῖκος, that of separation. But usually, or always, [32] he has φιλότης instead like Hom. and Hes. (→ line 7), Emped. Fr., 17, 7. 20 (Diels, I, 316 f.); [33] 20, 2 (318); 21, 8 (320) etc. On the other hand the writers who quote him mostly use φιλία, e.g., Plut. De amicorum multitudine, 5 (II, 95b); Simpl. Comm. on Aristot. Phys., VIII, 1; [34] Athenag. Suppl., 22, 1 f.; [35] Hipp. Ref., VII, 29, 9 f. 13.

f. Already in Emped. Fr., 59, 1 f. (Diels, I, 333) φιλία and νεῖκος are to some extent personified. In a different way we find the same in, e.g., the elegy of Aristot. Fr., 1, 2 (Diehl, I, 115). [36] Φιλία is also one of the many names of Isis (→ I, 38, 6 f.), P. Oxy.,

[29] The genuineness of the v. is, of course, in doubt.
[30] Grenfell-Hunt, ad loc.: "In order that we may remain on good terms with each other."
[31] Platonic φιλία also has a political side (cf. Plat. Ep., 7, 323d-352a) to the degree that it is a condition of harmony politically as well as ethically; the need for a φιλία or circle of friends for real political action is also stressed, 325d. Plat. thinks Darius and his sworn κοινωνοί are a model of this political friendship underlying statecraft, 332a b. Of Dionysius the Elder as a counterpart he says πένης γὰρ ἦν ἀνδρῶν φίλων καὶ πιστῶν, 332c.
[32] Plut. Is. et Os., 48 (II, 370d) maintains that Emped. used φιλία as well as φιλότης.
[33] It is worth noting that Plut. Amat., 13 (II, 756d) calls φιλότης ἔρως here but Cl. Al. Strom., V, 2, 15, 4 calls it ἀγάπη.
[34] Ed. H. Diels, Comment. in Aristot. Graeca, 10 (1895), 1124, 10.
[35] Athenag. here cites Emped. Fr., 17, 18-20 (Diels, I, 316 f.) when of the four elements καὶ φιλίη μετὰ τοῖσιν he says: ἃ χωρὶς τῆς φιλίας οὐ δύναται μένειν ὑπὸ τοῦ νείκους συγχεόμενα... ἀρχικὸν ἡ φιλία κατὰ τὸν Ἐμπεδοκλέα... τὸ δὲ ἀρχικὸν κύριον ("the absolute").
[36] Cf. C. J. Classen, Art. "Philia," Lex. der alten Welt (1965), 2291.

XI, 1380, 94 [37] (1st cent. A.D.); one might regard it as the fem. of (Ζεὺς) Φίλιος, [38] but since line 28 has ἀγάπη we have here personified φιλία. [39]

g. Some special uses might be mentioned. The word can denote friendships with animals, sometimes with a positive [40] and sometimes with a negative nuance, so Plat. Clit., 409d. The kiss as a sign of loving fellowship can also be meant, as among Christians at baptism, Chrys. Hom. de utilitate lectionis scripturarum, 6 (MPG, 51 [1862] 98): ἀσπασμοὶ καὶ φιλίαι. [41] In the baroque style of the Byzantine age (6th-7th cent. A.D.) φιλία can also be a formal address or title. [42] Other words can also be paired with it (→ 148, 1 ff.), e.g., ξενία: ...ἀνανεούμενος τὴν φιλίαν καὶ ξενίαν τὴν πρότερον ὑπάρχουσαν, Isoc. Ep., 7, 13, ἔρως, [43] e.g., Philo Fug., 58, also plur. Abr., 194, [44] and συμμαχία → 150, 21 ff.

II. Friendship in Antiquity.

1. Through the centuries a whole library has grown up around the theme of friendship among the Gks. and Romans. Here only a few aspects and facts can be discussed. Antiquity itself wrote a great deal on friendship. We have separate treatises, the most important and best known being Cic. Laelius sive de amicitia, Luc. Toxaris sive de amicitia and Plut. Quomodo adulator ab amico internoscatur, De amicorum multitudine, and a letter de amicitia. [45] We also have remnants of Chrysipp. Περὶ φιλίας (v. Arnim, III, 182), of Seneca's Dialogue on friendship et al. There are ref. to lost works by Xenophanes in Diog. L., IV, 12; Theophr., ibid., V, 45; Gellius Noctes Atticae, [46] 1, 3, 10-12, 21-29; Cleanthes in Diog. L., VII, 175. Individual sections of larger works also deal with the subject. The most significant discussions, apart from Cic. Lael, are in Plat. Symp., Phaedr. and Lys., [47] in Aristot. [48] Eth. Nic., VIII, 1, p. 1155a-IX, 12, p. 1172a; Eth. Eud., VII, 1-13, p.1234b, 18-1246b, 36; Eth. M., II, 11-17, p. 1208b-1213b, in Xenoph. Mem., II, 4-6, in Isoc. Or., 1, 24-26, in Epict. Diss., II, 22, in Gellius, Noctes Atticae (→ n. 46), 1, 3; cf. 17, 5, in Valerius Maximus, [49] IV, 7, and in Themist. Or., 22. [50]

2. Antiquity's views on friendship find very typical expression in a series of maxims and proverbs which in part are significant for the NT too → n. 52. Aristot. Eth. Nic., IX, 8, p. 1168b, 6-8 [51] offers three of the most important: καὶ αἱ παιροιμίαι δὲ πᾶσαι

---

[37] Cf. also Deissmann LO, 59, n. 3.

[38] Cf. Liddell-Scott, s.v. φίλιος (→ n. 60).

[39] There is a similar personification of amor in Suet. Caes. Titus, 1, 1: Titus is called amor ... generis humani as the opp. of odium generis humani.

[40] Cf. Peek, op. cit., 474, 5 (2nd/3rd. cent. A.D.).

[41] Cf. Ant. Christ., I, 193.

[42] Examples in Preisigke Wört., III, 202; Moult.-Mill., s.v.

[43] Antiquity often discusses the relation between φιλία and ἔρως, cf. esp. Plat. Lys., Phaedr. and Symp.

[44] Philo also has εὔνοια, συγγένεια, κοινωνία, ὁμόνοια and οἰκειότης with φιλία, v. Leisegang, s.v. φιλία.

[45] Plut. Fr., 159-171 (ed. F. H. Sandbach [1967]), cf. Fr., 18 (ed. G. N. Bernardakis, VII [1896]), 115-118.

[46] Ed. C. Hosius (1903).

[47] Not Lysias (H. van Oyen, Art. "Freundschaft," RGG³ II, 1131 Bibl.) but Lysis. Cf. materially Normann, 100-110.

[48] Normann, 129-155.

[49] Ed. C. Kempf (1888), 201-210. In many of these works there is palpable dependence on earlier authors, e.g., Valerius Maximus on Cicero etc., Bickel, 224.

[50] Friendship is also a common theme in the fathers, e.g., Ambr. De offic. ministrorum, 3, 125-130; Ps.-Aug. De amicitia (MPL, 40 [1887], 831 f.), and then well on into the Middle Ages, e.g., Petrus Blesensis De amicitia christ. et de caritate Dei et proximi tractatus duplex (MPL, 207 [1855], 871-958), cf. Bickel, 223.

[51] Cf. also Eth. M., II, 11, p. 1211a, 32 f.; Eth. Eud., VII, 6, p. 1240b, 9.

όμογνωμονοῦσιν, οἷον τὸ "μία ψυχή" καὶ "κοινὰ τὰ φίλων" καὶ "ἰσότης φιλότης."
Acc. to Diog. L., VIII, 10 and Porphyr. Vit. Pyth., 33 the last two go back to Pythagoras. [52]
The motif of κοινωνία esp. recurs with considerable monotony, [53] from Eur. Or., 735;
Andr., 376 f. and Plat. Lys., 207c; Phaedr., 279c; Leg., V, 739c; Resp., V, 449c; IV, 424a
by way of Aristot. Eth. Nic., IX, 11, p. 1159b, 31 f.; Eth. Eud., VII, 2, p. 1237b, 32 f.;
1238a, 16; Pol., II, 5, p. 1263a, 30 to the later period, Diog. L., VI, 37 and 72; Philo Vit.
Mos., I, 156; Muson. Fr., 13 (p. 67). The thought of the "one soul" is also attributed to
Aristot.: ἐρωτηθεὶς τί ἐστι φίλος, ἔφη· μία ψυχὴ δύο σώμασιν ἐνοικοῦσα, Diog. L.,
V, 20, cf. Plut. De amicorum multitudine, 8 (II, 96 f.). The third saying ἰσότης φιλότης
is very often quoted. Plat. Leg., VI, 757a adduces it as a word of ancient wisdom, ὡς
ἰσότης φιλότητα ἀπεργάζεται. Aristot., apart from passages already quoted → 151,
28 ff., has it several times, e.g., Eth. Nic., VIII, 7, p. 1157b, 34-36; Eth. Eud., VII, 6,
p. 1240b, 1 f. [54] A fourth saying is also said to be important: The friend is the *alter ego*
of the friend. [55] Diog. L., VII, 23 says of Zeno: ἐρωτηθεὶς τίς ἐστι φίλος, ἄλλος,
ἔφη, ἐγώ, cf. VII, 124. Aristot. expressly calls it a proverb: ὁ ... φίλος βούλεται
εἶναι, ὥσπερ ἡ παροιμία φησίν, ἄλλος Ἡρακλῆς, ἄλλος οὗτος, Eth. Eud., VII,
12, p. 1245a, 29 f., [56] cf. ἔστι γὰρ ὁ φίλος ἄλλος αὐτός, Eth. Nic., IX, 4, p. 1166a,
31 f.; ἕτερος γὰρ αὐτὸς ὁ φίλος ἐστίν, IX, 9, p. 1170b, 6 f., and Plut. De amicorum
multitudine, 2 (II, 93e): ... καὶ τὸ ἄλλον αὐτὸν ἡγεῖσθαι τὸν φίλον. [57]

3. In spite of the importance of various groups of friends (→ 147, 8 ff.; 147, 14 ff.)
personal friendship is still the heart of the matter for the Gks. and it is often emphasised
that real friendship is possible only with a few, e.g., Aristot. Eth. Nic., IX, 10, p. 1170b,
20-1171a, 20; cf. Eth. Eud., VII, 12, p. 1245b, 20 f.: οὐθεὶς φίλος ᾧ πολλοὶ φίλοι. In
Luc. Toxaris, 37 the πολύφιλος is even compared to a harlot and Plut. devoted a whole
tractate to the theme, Περὶ πολυφιλίας (II, 93a-97b). But the Stoics took a different
view; acc. to Chrysipp. Fr., 631 (v Arnim, III, 161) πολυφιλία is a good, cf. also Diog.
L., VII, 124. Sometimes close personal friendship is contrasted with wider groups of
friends who form the forces sustaining the *polis* → n. 31.

---

[52] Lk. combines the first two in a summary of the main theme of primitive Chr. life in
Ac. 4:32: ἦν καρδία καὶ ψυχὴ μία... ἦν αὐτοῖς πάντα κοινά → 163, 2 ff. This is
typical of Lk. He links the bibl. pair heart and soul, cf. Mk. 12:30 and also 1 QS 5:8 f. with
the proverbial Gk. μία ψυχή. In relation to the Gk. πάντα κοινὰ φίλοις we also find in Gk.
lit. the elucidation οὐδὲ εἷς τι ... ἔλεγεν ἴδιον εἶναι, cf. Eur. Andr., 376; Muson. Fr., 13a
(p. 67).
[53] The thought can, of course, be stated and developed differently, cf. Xenoph. Mem.,
II, 6, 23 on true friends: τὰ μὲν ἑαυτῶν ἀγαθὰ τοῖς φίλοις οἰκεῖα παρέχοντες, τὰ δὲ
τῶν φίλων ἑαυτῶν νομίζοντες.
[54] Cf. Dt. 13:7: ὁ φίλος ὁ ἴσος τῆς ψυχῆς σου, and the comment of Philo Rer. Div.
Her., 83: οὕτως ὁ φίλος ἐγγύς ἐστιν, ὥστε ἀδιαφορεῖ ψυχῆς. ὁμοιότης is often used
for ἰσότης, so Plat. Leg., IV, 716c; Aristot. Eth. Nic., VIII, 2, p. 1155a, 32; the two are
combined in VIII, 10, p. 1159b, 2-4: ἡ δ' ἰσότης καὶ ὁμοιότης φιλότης, καὶ μάλιστα μὲν
ἡ τῶν κατ' ἀρετὴν ὁμοιότης, cf. also Cl. Al. Strom., VII, 11, 68, 2: ἥ τε φιλία δι'
ὁμοιότητος περαίνεται. What gave the preference to ὁμοιότης was the saying: τὸ ὅμοιον
τῷ ὁμοίῳ φίλον, or φίλον ἀεὶ παντὶ τὸ ὅμοιον, "like gladly associates with like," e.g.,
Aristot. Eth. Nic., IX, 3, p. 1165b, 16 f.; Plat. Lys., 214b; Plat. Gorg., 510b, also Symp., 195b;
Jos. Ap., 2, 193. But the correctness of the principle that likeness means friendship was much
discussed, e.g., Plat. Lys., 214b-216d. Here too (→ n. 2) Plat. ends with a problem: οὔτε
ἄρα τὸ ὅμοιον τῷ ὁμοίῳ οὔτε τὸ ἐναντίον τῷ ἐναντίῳ φίλον, 216b, cf. also Aristot.
Eth. Nic., VIII, 2, p. 1155a, 32 - b, 16. Cf. Dirlmeier, *op. cit.* (→ n. 21), 511 on 171, A 5;
M. Dibelius, "Die Christianisierung einer hell. Formel," *Botschaft u. Gesch.*, II (1956), 25 f.
with n. 23 f. (→ n. 145).
[55] Hauck, 213.
[56] One should read αὐτός. "A second Heracles" occurs also at Eth. M., II, 15, p. 1213a,
12 f. with ἄλλος φίλος ἐγώ. Cf. on this Liddell-Scott, *s.v.* Ἡρακλῆς and F. Dirlmeier,
*Aristot. Magna Moralia*² (1966), 470 f. on 88, 6.
[57] This proverb probably lies behind the Syr. transl. of Sir. 37:2: "The true friend will
be to thee (just) as thyself," cf. V. Ryssel in Kautzsch Apkr. u. Pseudepigr., I, 411 n. k.

The true ideal, however, is the pair of friends. Early examples of such pairs are extolled in epic and drama. In the "much sung friendships of the past the ref. is always to pairs," Aristot. Eth. Nic., IX, 10, p. 1171a, 15. [58] We often have lists of pairs, e.g., Plut. De amic. multit., 2 (II, 93e); Luc. Toxaris, 10; Cic. Lael., 15; Fin., I, 65. Achilles and Patroclus usually come first. [59] Inequality is already found here, since Patroclus is simply Achilles' follower, the φίλος ἑταῖρος, Hom. Il., 1, 345; 11, 616. Yet acc. to Athen., 13, 601a this φιλία is construed as eros by Aesch., and rather differently Plat. Symp., 179e-180b, although Xenoph. Symp., 8, 31 rejects this interpretation. Orestes and Pylades are also revered, esp. by the Scythians (acc. to Luc. Toxaris, 7), who worshipped them as φίλιοι δαίμονες, [60] cf. also Eur. Iph. Taur., 498. We also hear of Theseus and Peirithoos, Damon and Phintias, Epaminondas and Pelopidas, whose friendship was thought to be the germ of the political renaissance of Thebes. [61] Many friendships were also invented, since those who were akin in spirit could be depicted only as friends, e.g., Homer and Lycurgus, Numa and Pythagoras → IV, 416, 35 ff. There are also partly historical and partly fictional accounts of pairs of friends that were passed down from mouth to mouth, cf. the five stories recounted by the Greek and the Scythian in the discussion in Luc. Toxaris. Here one of the two is always the more active and the other more or less passive. [62] The friendships between older and younger men practised and·lauded by Socrates correspond in the main to the relation between teacher and student, so that friendship is the start of instruction, → 157, 20 ff.; 163, 24 ff. [63]

In many variations the supreme duty of a friend is to sacrifice himself for his friend even to the pt. of death. Thus Aristot. Eth. Nic., IX, 8, p. 1169a, 18-20 says: "To a noble man there applies the true saying that he does all things for the sake of his friends... and, if need be, he gives his life for them," cf. also line 25 f. Epicurus acc. to Diog. L., X, 121 [64] was also of the opinion that the wise man must in some circumstances die for his friend. The Epicurean Philonides followed this saying of the master, for it is said of him [65] that "for the one he loved most (ἀγαπωμένου) among those close to him or friends (φίλων) he was ready to offer his neck." Epict. Ench., 32, 3 attributes to Socrates the thesis that συγκινδυνεῦσαι φίλῳ ἢ πατρίδι is so self-evident that one need not consult the oracle about this duty, and he concludes: Follow then the great seer, Apollo himself, who chased a man out of his temple who did not come to the aid of his friend when in mortal danger (ἀναιρουμένῳ τῷ φίλῳ), cf. Sen. Ep., 1, 9, 10: in quid amicum paro? ut habeam pro quo mori possim etc. Apollonius of Tyana acc. to Philostr. Vit. Ap., VII, 14 (p. 265) can even say that it is a command of φύσις to die for relatives or friends or beloved boys, cf. VII, 11 (p. 262): φιλοσοφίᾳ... προσήκει... ἀποθανεῖν... ὑπὲρ φίλων ἀγωνιζόμενον. Hence examples of dying for friends are always highly extolled, esp. that of Damon,[66] e.g., Diod. S., X, 4, 3-6; Valerius Maximus, IV, 7 ext. 1 (p.207 f.); Iambl. Vit. Pyth., 33, 234-6. Luc. Toxaris, 6 describes Scythian pictures of Orestes and Pylades which show each of the two παρ' οὐδὲν τιθέμενον, εἰ ἀποθανεῖται σώσας τὸν φίλον, while in 36 the Scythian speaker says: ἐγὼ δέ σοι διηγήσομαι... θανάτους ὑπὲρ τῶν φίλων, and in 37 he mentions the solemn pact of friendship (ὅρκος ὁ μέγισ-

---

[58] Cf. Dirlmeier, op. cit. (→ n. 21), 529 on 187 A 2; 558 f. on 213 A 2.

[59] Normann, 24-26.

[60] Zeus' title ὁ φίλιος "the refuge of friendship," Lux. Toxaris, 12 or ὁ Φίλιος "the God of friendship," 11 is obviously the basis of the term.

[61] Curtius, 197.

[62] A counterpart running across the centuries is the motif of close friends who in a supreme culmination of the principle ἰσότης φιλότης (→ 152, 9 ff.) are fully alike in form and disposition, cf. the mediaeval tale of Amicus and Amelius, W. Bauerfeld, Die Sage v. Amis u. Amiles, Diss. Halle (1941).

[63] Curtius, 194. On tests that prove friendship, cf. Bauerfeld, op. cit., passim.

[64] Cf. H. Usener, Epicurea (1887), XXX.

[65] Vita Philonidis, 22, ed. W. Crönert, SAB, 1900, 2 (1900), 951 in Deissmann LO, 94 f.

[66] Cf. E. Wellmann, Art. "Damon," Pauly-W., 4 (1901), 2074.

τος) among the Scythians: ἦ μὴν καὶ βιώσεσθαι μετ' ἀλλήλων καὶ ἀποθανεῖσθαι, ἢν δέῃ, ὑπὲρ τοῦ ἑτέρου τὸν ἕτερον.

B. φίλος, φιλία (φιλιάζω) in the Old Testament and Judaism.

I. Usage.

1. φίλος.

a. It is obvious from even a cursory glance at LXX usage that only in a minority of instances do φίλος and φιλία [67] render Hbr. words, φίλος in 70 out of some 180 cases and φιλία only 7 times out of 38. [68] In more than 30 instances the original of φίλος is רֵעַ (→ VI, 312, 19 ff.; V, 14, 8 ff.), [69] although mostly, some 112 times, this is transl. ὁ πλησίον (→ VI, 312, 17 ff.). [70] In 27 instances [71] it stands for אֹהֵב [72] q and pi, in 4 for מֵרֵעַ (→ VI, 313, n. 13): Ju. 14:20; 15:2, 6; Prv. 12:26, and in 2 each for אַלּוּף "friend," "confidant," Prv. 16:28; 17:9, and חָבֵר, Sir. 7:12; 37:6. Aram. חֲבַר, Hb. חָבֵר, is also transl. φίλος in Da. 2:13, 17 f. Θ. [73] In LXX usage, as in common Gk. usage (→ 147, 1 ff.), we have a scale of nuances: the very close "personal friend" ὁ φίλος ὁ ἴσος τῆς ψυχῆς σου, Dt. 13:7 (→ n. 54), the "friend of the house" φίλος πατρῷος, Prv. 27:10 (→ 150, 14 ff.), the "friend of the bridegroom," the "best man," 1 Macc. 9:39 (→ 165, 1 ff.), the "client" or "political supporter" of someone in high position, Est. 6:13, as a title "friend of the king," φίλος τοῦ βασιλέως, 1 Ch. 27:33 [74] (→ 147, 14 ff. with n. 4; VI, 313, 1 with n. 10), cf. Est. 6:9; Δα. 3:94; 1 Macc. 10:20.

In the LXX φίλος is used with many related terms in combination or parallelism, e.g., ἀδελφός Prv. 17:17, [75] ἑταῖρος Sir. 37:2 (→ 148, 2 ff.), [76] ὁ πλησίον ψ 37:12, ψ 87:19 where οἱ γνωστοί is a third synon., οἰκεῖος (→ 148, 10 f.) Prv. 17:9, γείτων 3 Macc. 3:10 [77] (→ 159, 34 ff.). Gen. Hell. is the thinking of φίλος with σύμβουλος (→ 148, 25 ff.) or συμβουλευτής, since the friends of the king and of leading men were also their advisers. [78] Thus the φίλοι of King Artaxerxes in 1 Εσδρ. 8:13 are obviously οἱ

---

[67] φίλη does not occur in the LXX.

[68] The no. is relatively large compared to ἀγάπη (20), ἀγάπησις (10), στοργή (4, only 3 and 4 Macc.), ἔρως (2, only Prv.). Most remarkable is comparison with the NT, which does not have ἔρως, στοργή or ἀγάπησις at all, and φιλία only once at Jm. 4:4; ἀγάπη sweeps the field. How ἀγάπη replaces φιλία may be seen if we compare Prv. 10:12 and Jm. 5:20; 1 Pt. 4:8.

[69] Cf. on this J. B. Souček, "Der Bruder u. d. Nächste," *Festschr. E. Wolf* (1962), 362-371.

[70] For other transl. of רֵעַ → VI, 312, n. 7. Of the 6 instances of ἕτερος we may say that at Qoh. 4:4; Prv. 27:17 it is a simple slip for ἑταῖρος, cf. the reading τοῖς ἑτέροις alongside τοῖς ἑταίροις at Mt. 11:16, though in this case we have a different understanding of the parable of the children at play, Jeremias Gl.⁷, 161.

[71] 17 of these in Sir.

[72] Cf. D. W. Thomas, "The Root אָהֵב 'love' in Hebrew," ZAW, 57 (1939), 57-64.

[73] LXX transl. Da. 2:13, 18: οἱ μετ' αὐτοῦ, 2:17: οἱ συνέταιροι.

[74] In the same sense ἑταῖρος τοῦ βασιλέως, 3 Βασ. 4:5 (also Philo Omn. Prob. Lib., 42, both together Plut. Demetr., 49 [I, 913c-f]) and obviously too οἱ γνωστοὶ αὐτοῦ (sc. of Ahab), 4 Βασ. 10:11.

[75] Cf. Ps. 122:8. In the OT ἀδελφός is often the most intimate term for friend, cf. Ges.-Buhl, s.v. אהב, אָח.

[76] The textual tradition shows that φίλος and ἑταῖρος are synon., cf. Ju. 14:20 and 15:2 LXX: Cod. A has ἑταῖρος or συνέταιρος, Cod. B φίλος.

[77] Cf. Jos. Ant., 18, 376, and in 18, 23 the typically Hell. combination with συγγενής (→ 148, 12 ff.).

[78] E.g., Est. 5:14; 6:13.

ἑπτὰ φίλοι συμβουλευταί in v. 11 and οἱ ἑπτὰ σύμβουλοι in 2 Εσδρ. 7:14. [79] But the two groups are found side by side in 1 Εσδρ. 8:26. [80] Finally the combination of φίλος and σύμμαχος (→ 148, 28 ff.) has a political character in 1 Macc. 14:40: φίλοι καὶ σύμμαχοι καὶ ἀδελφοί (an honorary Roman title for the Jews).

b. Much the same may be said about the usage in Philo. He often has φίλος as an adj., e.g., Poster. C., 172 and he links it, esp. as a noun, with many related terms: συγγενής Leg. All., III, 71 and 205; Flacc., 72, ἀδελφός Leg. All., III, 71, ἑταῖρος Vit. Cont., 13; Omn Prob. Lib., 44; Flacc., 32, οἰκεῖος Leg. Gaj., 343; Leg. All., III, 205, γνώριμος Abr., 273, σύμβουλος Agric., 95 (the serpent as φίλος καὶ σύμβουλος... of Eve!), σύμμαχος Spec. Leg., IV, 219, ἔνσπονδος Spec. Leg., IV, 224, cf. Migr. Abr., 202.

2. φιλία.

φιλία is used 6 times for אַהֲבָה or אָהַב Prv. 5:19 (twice); 10:12; 15:17; 17:9; 27:5 and once for דּוֹד "sensual love," Prv. 7:18. Thus there are Hbr. equivalents only in Prv., where we also find it without original at 5:19 vl.; 25:10a. Apart from that it occurs only in Wis., Sir. and Maccabees. This is just as noteworthy as that φίλος is not as common in any other OT book [81] as in Prv., Sir. and Macc. → 154, 20 ff.

In the LXX there are two main kinds of φιλία, ἐρωτική (→ 149, 27 ff.) whether with respect to the wife in Prv. 5:19 or the harlot in 7:18, and political, [82] esp. in Macc., e.g., 1 Macc. 8:1, 11, esp. with συμμαχία, 8:17; 2 Macc. 4:11, [83] and sometimes with ἀδελφότης, 1 Macc. 12:10. The vocabulary of politics has some established tt: φιλίαν ἵστημι at 1 Macc. 8:1, 17; 10:54; 12:1, φιλίαν ἀνανεοῦμαι (→ 150, 19 ff.), 12:1, 3, 10; 14:28, 22; 15:17, φιλίαν συντηρέω, 8:11; 10:20, cf. v. 26. With this collective political friendship, as with φίλος (→ 147, 13 ff.), there is also an individual political use, cf. 4 Macc. 8:5: ἡ ἐμὴ φιλία, which, said of a king, describes the position of a φίλος τοῦ βασιλέως → 154, 17 f.

The LXX use of the stem φιλ- includes the verb φιλέω, which in the sense "to love" relates to φιλία as "love," and also φιλιάζω, which is derived from φιλία as "friend-ship" and can thus be closely related to φίλος "friend," as in the expression φιλιάζω φίλοις at Ju. 5:30 Cod. A; 1 Εσδρ. 3:22. Elsewhere, too, it mostly takes the dat., so 2 Ch. 19:2; 20:37; Prv. 22:24 Σ; Ps. 59:10 Θ; [84] but abs. Sir. 37:1. [85] It means "to be a

---

[79] On this group of seven cf. Est. 1:10: οἱ ἑπτὰ εὐνοῦχοι οἱ διάκονοι τοῦ βασιλέως Ἀρταξέρξου, also Est. 1:14 (HT): the seven princes of the Medes and Persians who had access to the king and precedence in the empire. Comparable and perhaps conceptually related are the seven spirits before God's throne, Rev. 1:4; 4:5, though there may well be older religious ideas here, cf. Bss. Apk. and E. Lohse, *Die Offenbarung d. Joh.*, NT Deutsch, 11⁹ (1966) on 1:4.

[80] Cf. also Sir. 37:1-6 with 7-12. φίλος and σύμβουλος are also equated and combined in Herm., where the angels as the Lord's φίλοι and σύμβουλοι are depicted as a kind of oriental court; cf. on the one side προσκαλεσάμενος... τοὺς φίλους, οὓς εἶχε συμβούλους, s., 5, 2, 6; ἐδεήθην αὐτὸν πολλά, ἵνα μοι δηλώσῃ τὴν παραβολήν... τῶν φίλων τῶν συμβούλων, s., 5, 4, 1 and on the other side οἱ... φίλοι καὶ σύμβουλοι, s., 5, 5, 3.

[81] The frequent use in Job is due to the special role of Job's three φίλοι.

[82] B. B. Warfield, "The Terminology of Love in the NT," *Princeton Theol. Review*, 16 (1918), 167 with n. 16.

[83] Cf. also Const. Ap., VI, 18, 7.

[84] Cf. BGU, IV, 1141, 23 (1st cent. B.C.).

[85] So also in the title of a mime Φιλιάζουσαι ("women friends in intimate conversation"), Herond. Mim., 6.

friend," "to act as a friend" at Sir. 37:1; Ju. 5:30 Cod. A; 1 Εσδρ. 3:22, "to become a friend," "to make friends" at Ju. 14:20 Cod. B; Prv. 22:24 Σ. [86]

II. Friendship in the Old Testament [87] and Judaism.

1. The very fact that φίλος and φιλία occur predominantly in the originally Gk. texts of the LXX shows that we have here a concept which is fundamentally alien to the OT world. רֵעַ is something quite different (→ VI, 312, 24 ff.). Its far more common rendering by (ὁ) πλησίον (→ VI, 312, 13 ff.) is to the point, for translation by φίλος is strictly a μετάβασις εἰς ἄλλο γένος, at least when one has in view typically Gk. ideas of friendship. But the Alexandrian translators, who naturally thought of friendship in Hellenistic categories, arbitrarily introduced φίλος for רֵעַ at many points (→ 154, 8 f.) and the authors of works originating in the world of Hellenism used φίλος and φιλία in the current sense.

2. It is to be noted, however, that the OT contains one of the finest instances of friendship. In the final strophe of David's lament for Saul and Jonathan we read: "I am distressed for thee, my brother Jonathan: very pleasant hast thou been unto me: thy love to me was wonderful, passing the love of women," 2 S. 1:26. The final thought is common to antiquity and David and Jonathan are also worthy to rank with the other pairs of friends extolled in ancient lit. → 153, 1 ff. The story that ends with the lament is itself a song in praise of friendship. It is said of the two friends in 1 S. 18:1, 3, cf. 19:1; 20:17 that they loved one another as their own life, the supreme stage of human fellowship, cf. Dt. 13:7 → n. 54. It is also characteristic of antiquity that the friendship should be sealed with a solemn pact and thus made unbreakable, 1 S. 18:3 f. The decisive symbolical act is the handing over of cloak and weapons by the king's son and heir to David, so that he is made the *alter ego* of his friend. [88] Probably this ceremony itself involved an oath before Yahweh. Certainly such an oath is expressly mentioned in 1 S. 20:16 f., and it applies to their children too even after death, 2 S. 21:7. [89] On the other hand, this classic instance of friendship in the OT shows that there is no tt. for it, cf. the circumlocutions in 2 S. 1:26, where even LXX twice has ἀγάπησις and does not use φιλία.

3. In contrast there are many friendship sayings in OT Wisdom lit., esp. Prv. and Sir. [90] Sir. 6:5-17 even offers a small connected section comparable to similar passages in Gk. and Hell. lit. → 151, 13 ff. Sir. 6:8-13 deals mainly with dubious friends; indeed, scepticism and warning are gen. more common in Wisdom writings than is the praise of friendship, cf. esp. Sir. 37:2 οὐχὶ λύπη ἔνι ἕως θανάτου ἑταῖρος καὶ φίλος τρεπόμενος εἰς ἔχθραν; and cf. Lk. 21:16 → 163, 7 ff. The reason for this is often the misfortune of a friend. Warning to this effect is a common theme in Wisdom exhortation,

---

[86] Cf. Achmes Oneirocriticon, 13 (ed. F. Drexl [1925], 10): "He will win the friendship of another king and gain (φιλιάσει) his love (ἀγάπην)." After the manner of the political use of φίλος (→ 147, 7 f.; 154, 23 ff.) and φιλία (→ 155, 20 ff.; 150, 18 ff.) φιλιάζω here might also mean "to ally oneself with," cf. 2 Ch. 19:2; 20:37 and perhaps Ps. 59:10 Θ.

[87] Cf. A. Bertholet, *Kulturgeschichte Israels* (1919), 168; Treu Freundschaft, A. IV etc.

[88] Cf. H. W. Hertzberg, *Die Samuelbücher, AT Deutsch*, 10³ (1965) on 1 S. 18:1-4; also R. Kittel, *Gesch. Isr.*, II⁴ (1922), 111, n. 2; cf. the exchange of clothes between Diomedes and Glaucos in Hom. Il., 6, 230 f.

[89] Cf. Hertzberg, *op. cit.* on 1 S. 20:14-17. The friendship between David and Jonathan seems to be isolated in the OT but it finds par. in ancient oriental lit., esp. in the witness to the friendship between Gilgamesh and Enkidu at the end: "Then he covered his (dead) friend as a bride" (Gilgamesh Epic, Tablet 8, 19 [AOT, 167], cf. 7-10 [166-174]) and the repeated lament.

[90] Cf. the collection in P. Volz, *Hiob u. Weisheit, Schr. AT*, III, 2 (1921), 206-8 with 208, n. 2.

e.g., Sir. 5:15: ἀντὶ φίλου μὴ γίνου ἐχθρός. Many statements and teachings remind us vividly of Gk. wisdom and esp. of Theogn. (→ 150, 6 f.; → n. 95), who seems to have had esp. bad experiences with unreliable friends. [91] In both cases we get the same thought that there are very few real friends. Most friends are egoists; [92] hence only the fortunate, [93] esp. the rich, [94] have many friends. But many only protest friendship; [95] the true friend will not be known in times of prosperity. [96] Friends can even be a gt. danger. [97] Since finally Jewish Wisdom could agree with ancient popular wisdom that a man's best friend is himself, [98] it is the more significant that like the Gks., who could regard only the good as capable of friendship, [99] it advanced the principle of Sir. 6:16 f.: Only those who fear God are capable of true friendship and they alone find true friends. Relatively early in the OT one finds political friendship, e.g., that between David and the Philistine king Achish, [100] or that between Jehoshaphat and Ahab, cf. 2 Ch. 19:2, and later Ahaziah, 2 Ch. 20:37. Ch. also records the appointment of the πρῶτος φίλος τοῦ βασιλέως (→ 154, 17 f.) in the time of David, 1 Ch. 27:33, and a ἑταῖρος τοῦ βασιλέως (of Solomon) is mentioned in 3 Βασ. 4:5 → n. 74.

In a transf. sense (→ 150, 5 ff.; 147, 19 ff.; 148, 18 ff.) the Wisdom lit. can speak of friendship with wisdom, cf. Wis. 8:18: ἐν φιλίᾳ αὐτῆς τέρψις ἀγαθή. Test. L. 13:8 says of the σοφία achieved in the fear of the Lord: καὶ ἐν μέσῳ ἐχθρῶν εὑρεθήσεται φίλος.

4. In Palestinian Judaism we find certain forms of friendship, but these are all different from Gk. friendship. In Rabb. Judaism the concept is applied to the relation between students and teachers of the Law. [101] Probably Test. L. 13:4 already has students in view when it speaks of those who know the Law: πολλοὺς φίλους ... κτήσεται. The ref. is to colleges for the study of the Torah when we read of friends whose honour should stand as high as reverence for God, Ab., 4, 12. The close friendship between those studying the Law comes to light in the sorrow of R. Jochanan for Resh Laqish, bBM, 84a. [102] It is worth noting that bAZ, 10b ref. to a very one-sided friendship between RJehuda Hanasi and the Emperor Antoninus (Marcus Aurelius or Septimius Severus) [103]

---

91 Theogn., 1, 575 and 813 even says twice: "My friends have betrayed me." Cf. Ps. 41:9 → 141, 3 f.

92 Cf. Luc. Toxaris, 16. Similarly in Ab. 2, 3 the authorities are compared to friends who are this only so long as one is useful to them.

93 Cf. Sir. 12:9: ἐν τοῖς κακοῖς αὐτοῦ (man's) καὶ ὁ φίλος διαχωρισθήσεται with Theogn., 1, 697 f.: εὖ μὲν ἔχοντος ἐμοῦ πολλοὶ φίλοι· ἢν δέ τι δεινὸν συγκύρσῃ, παῦροι πιστὸν ἔχουσι νόον, and also 1, 209. 299.

94 Cf. Prv. 14:20: φίλοι μισήσουσιν φίλους πτωχούς, φίλοι δὲ πλουσίων πολλοί, and 19:4; Sir. 6:10; 13:21; cf. Democr. Fr., 101 (Diels, II, 163): ἐκτρέπονται πολλοὶ τοὺς φίλους, ἐπὴν ἐξ εὐπορίης εἰς πενίην μεταπέσωσιν, and Fr. 106 (p. 163).

95 Cf. Theogn., 1, 979: μή μοι ἀνὴρ εἴη γλώσσῃ φίλος, ἀλλὰ καὶ ἔργῳ, also 1, 63 and 95 f. and cf. 1 Jn. 3:18. Gk. ethics distinguishes more clearly than Jewish Wisdom between the friend and the flatterer, cf. φαινόμενος φίλος ὁ κόλαξ, Aristot. Rhet., I, 11, p. 1371a, 24 and Antiphon. Fr., 65 (Diels, II, 366): Many do not know the φίλοι they have, ἀλλ' ἑταίρους ποιοῦνται θῶπας πλούτου καὶ τύχης κόλακας, and Anth. Graec., 10, 125.

96 Cf. Sir. 12:8 and Luc. Toxaris, 12-18. Hence Sir. 6:7 advises: "Take no man as a friend until thou hast known him in adversity, and even then do not trust him too soon."

97 Hence καὶ ἀπὸ τῶν φίλων σου πρόσεχε, Sir. 6:13, esp. against guaranteeing a friend, Prv. 6:1-5.

98 Cf. Bultmann Trad., 104 f. with n. 2 on Sir. 37:10-15.

99 Cf. e.g., Plat. Lys., 214d: ὁ ἀγαθὸς τῷ ἀγαθῷ μόνος μόνῳ φίλος.

100 1 S. 27, esp. v. 12; cf. Kittel, op. cit. (→ n. 88), 121. David, of course, is more a vassal here.

101 Cf. M. D. G. Langer, Liebesmystik d. Kabbala (1956), 52-4, and for the later period 54-64.

102 Sorrow for a dead friend is common in Gk. burial inscr., e.g., Preisigke Sammelb., I, 5198, 5 (Roman period); Peek, op. cit. (→ n. 11), 342, 7 (2nd. cent. A.D.); cf. 402, 2 (2nd/3rd cent. A.D.).

103 Cf. Strack Einl., 133.

and even to a pact of friendship between the two, 10b, 11a. Similarly in AbRNat, 6 and 19 [104] Jochanan bZakkai is called a "friend of the king" (the emperor). [105]

The most significant example of close and comprehensive fellowship in the Judaism of NT days is to be found in the יחד of Qumran. As the name indicates, κοινωνία, Philo Omn. Prob. Lib., 84 and 91 (→ III, 803, 23 f. with n. 46), τὸ κοινωνικόν, Jos. Bell., 2, 122, is the chief mark of the sect. But is this really a fellowship of friends? Jos. Bell., 2, 119 certainly says of the Essenes that they display more mutual friendship than other groups in Judaism, φιλάλληλοι τῶν ἄλλων πλέον, and one of the proverbial sayings with which the ancients described the essence of friendship, φίλοις πάντα κοινά (→ 151, 28 ff.) is certainly carried out as fully at Qumran as anywhere in antiquity, for the πάντα really does apply to every aspect of life apart from marriage. [106] In no other fellowship do we find to a higher degree a genuine sharing of lodging, mode of life, or table, Philo Omn. Prob. Lib., 86. [107] Knowledge, talents, abilities and work all belong to the πάντα κοινά, cf. 1 QS 1:11 f. Philo Omn. Prob. Lib., 84 also lauds the ἰσότης of the Essenes, another mark of friendship, → 152, 9 ff. But this is offset by the pedantically strict ranking, cf. 1 QS 2:22 f., and the sharp separation between members and novices, cf. Jos. Bell., 2, 150; 1 QS 5:13-18. Hence it is hardly correct to apply the concept of friendship to the Qumran community. [108]

5. In distinction from the statements of Palestinian Judaism, Philo the Hellenist, while developing OT ideas (→ 167, 12 ff. with n. 180 f.), esp. those of Wisdom (→ 157, 16 ff.; n. 181), can speak of a mutual friendship between God and His human friends, Fug., 58; Plant., 90. The boldness with which Moses speaks to God, Ex. 32:32; Nu. 11:12 f., 22; Ex. 5:22 f., is a mark of his friendly relation φιλία to God: παρρησία φιλίας συγγενές, Rer. Div. Her., 21. His φιλία is mediated to the Therapeutae through the ἀρετή which commends them to God, Vit. Cont., 90. For Philo the "friends of God" [109] are first Abraham, Sobr., 56, cf. Abr., 273 (→ n. 184), and the two other patriarchs, cf. Abr., 50, then Moses, Sacr. AC, 130; Migr. Abr., 45; Vit. Mos., I, 156; cf. Rer. Div. Her., 21; Ebr., 94. Acc. to Philo's understanding these are all examples of σοφοί, cf. οἱ σοφοὶ πάντες φίλοι θεοῦ, Rer. Div. Her., 21; cf. Leg. All., III, 1 → n. 182. From these and other passages, e.g., Fug., 58; Ebr., 94, one may infer that in Philo's sense all the righteous may be called "friends of God." τὸ τῶν φίλων συνέδριον in Som., I, 193, cf. ὁ φιλικὸς θίασος in 196, may be taken the same way, though the context shows that in Rer. Div. Her., 265 the ref. is to τὸ προφητικὸν γένος to which special revelations are given in ecstasy. The title οἱ φίλοι is here used in the abs. as in the philosophical schools (→ 147, 16 ff.), perhaps in the mystery cults too (→ n. 137), and then among Christians (→ 162, 16 ff.; 166, 16 ff.). Yet what may or may not apply there definitely applies in Philo, namely, that τοῦ θεοῦ is to be supplied; for φίλος ... ὁ προφήτης ἀνείρηται θεοῦ, Vit. Mos., I, 156 [110] (cf. → n. 181).

---

[104] Cf. Schl. Mt., 373.

[105] Cf. the use of βασιλεύς in Ac. 17:7 (on this G. Stählin, Die Ag., NT Deutsch, 5² [1966], ad loc.); Jn, 19:15 and many examples from profane lit. in Pr.-Bauer, s.v. βασιλεύς → I, 577, 4 ff.

[106] Acc. to Jos. Bell., 2, 160 f.; Damasc. 7:6-9 (9:1 f.); 12:1 (14:4) etc.; 1 QSa 1:4, 9 f. some of the Essenes were married. But acc. to Jos. Bell., 2, 120; Ant., 18, 21; Philo Apol. pro Iudaeis in Eus. Praep. Ev., 8, 11, 14 and 1 QS others practised celibacy, cf. H. Braun, Spätjüd.-häret. u. frühchr. Radikalismus, I² (1969), 84 f. 40 with n. 1 on 1 QS; 131-3 on Damasc.

[107] Cf. also Philo's depiction in Eus. Praep. Ev., 8, 11, 4 f. 10-12. On communion of goods in Qumran cf. Braun, op. cit., I, 35 f. 77 f., on the common meal, I, 73, n. 5.

[108] Jos. Bell., 2, 122 once calls the Essenes a family since they all share their possessions like brothers. But in relation to the Essenes this metaphor is to be taken with a pinch of salt.

[109] In Philo, too, φίλος is construed with the dat. and gen. in this topos, cf. Sobr., 55 f. → n. 1.

[110] Cf. S. Sandmel, Philo's Place in Judaism. A Study of the Conceptions of Abraham in Jewish Literature (1956), 177, n. 347. On the abs. use of φίλος for friend of God cf. also Jub. 30:20 f.; 1 Cl., 10, 1; Ps.-Clem., 18, 13, 6.

In keeping with his Hell. tradition we also and esp. find in Philo statements about the friendship between men. [111] Thus he sees in Moses and Joshua a gt. pair of friends (→ 156, 16 ff.), Virt., 55 and 60, and with honouring parents, mercy to the poor, and sacrifice in defence of one's country, he calls φίλους εὐεργετέω an act pleasing to both God and men, Mut. Nom., 40. For οὔτε φιλικῶν ἀμελὴς δικαίων θεὸς ἑταιρεῖος (not φίλιος → n. 60) ὤν, "God, the refuge of friendship, does not despise the rights of friendship" and has regard to the rules obtaining among comrades, Omn. Prob. Lib., 44. An odd statement is that God is His own συγγενής, οἰκεῖος, φίλος, Leg. All., III, 205. Like Aristot. and others (→ 147, 19 ff.), Philo can also use φίλος variously in a transf. sense, e.g., Deus Imm., 55: τῶν... ἀνθρώπων οἱ μὲν ψυχῆς, οἱ δὲ σώματος γεγόνασι φίλοι.

C. φίλος, φίλη, φιλία in the New Testament.

1. Usage.

φίλος occurs 29 times in the NT, φίλη and φιλία only once each. As in the OT φίλος and φιλία (→ 155, 14 ff.) are used only in books under strong Hell. influence, so in the NT the group is almost entirely confined to the Lucan [112] and Johannine writings. Only once does φίλος occur in Q at Mt. 11:19 and par. and we find it twice in Jm. at 2:23; 4:4, the only instance of φιλία being also in Jm. 4:4. In the meaning and use of φίλος Jm. differs from Lk. and Jn. → 167, 6 ff.

2. φίλος (and φίλη) in Luke's Writings.

a. Of the 29 NT instances of φίλος, 17 are in Lk., and so, too, is the one example of φίλη. At various pts. Lk. has φίλοι where the par. tradition has not, cf. Lk. 7:6 with Mt. 8:8; Lk. 12:4 with Mt. 10:28; Lk. 15:6 with Mt. 18:13; Lk. 21:16 with Mk. 13:12 and par. Yet Lk. the Hellenist shows restraint in that he never calls Jesus φίλος except in the taunt in 7:34 which he takes from Q → 161, 8 ff. Almost always the use in Lk. falls into the common categories of profane speech. Only three times at Lk. 12:4; 16:9; Ac. 27:3 can one speak of special NT usage → 163, 16 ff.; 164, 10 ff.; 162, 16 ff.), though most of the other passages have some theological significance. In the first instance φίλος is the "friend" as "one who is close or well-known," cf. συγγενής (→ VII, 740, n. 19); it is usually in the plur., so Lk. 14:12; 15:6, 29; 21:16 and Ac. 19:31, where the Asiarchs are well-known to Paul. The "boon-companion" of Lk. 7:34 and par. is a special form of this general use, and cf. 15:29, though here more in the sense of "friend of youth." The Hell. Luke can also employ the term for "close personal friend," Lk. 11:5, 8; 23:12, [113] "guest," Lk. 11:6 and member of a circle of friends gathered around a leader (→ 147, 9 ff.; 154, 16 f.), Lk. 7:6; Ac. 10:24 and also 16:39 Cod. D. Lk. alone in the NT combines φίλος with two related terms often found with it elsewhere, συγγενής (→ n. 112) and γείτων, so Ac. 10:24: συγκαλεσάμενος τοὺς συγγενεῖς (→ VII, 740, 26 ff.) αὐτοῦ

---

[111] Cf. Treu Freundschaft, A. IV.

[112] συγγενής (συγγενίς, συγγένεια), which esp. outside the NT is so often found with φίλος (→ 148, 12 ff.; 155, 6 f.), also occurs only in Lk. apart from a special use in Romans → VII, 741, 3 ff.

[113] The vocative φίλε, used of a personal friend in Lk. 11:5, is merely friendly address to an acquaintance in 14:10 (but → n. 148). Since φίλε has this friendly ring, it is left out of the friend's answer in Lk. 11:7, cf. v. 5, and also in the summons of the host in 14:9, cf. v. 10. Obviously the vocative ἑταῖρε has a different note, for in all instances (Mt. 20:13; 22:12; 26:50 → 140, n. 241) it is clearly negative → II, 701, 1 ff., though cf. Jeremias Gl.⁷, 137; Orig senses this already in Comm. in Mt., 100 (GCS, 38, p. 220, 14-24). In the NT as distinct from other usage (→ 148, 2 ff.) there is no connection between φίλος and ἑταῖρος. On the development of the vocative forms of φίλος (adj. φίλε and noun φίλος) cf. R. Loewe, "Die idg. Vokativbetonung," ZvglSpr., 59 (1923), 189-192.

καὶ τοὺς ἀναγκαίους [114] φίλους, Lk. 15:6: συγκαλεῖ τοὺς φίλους καὶ τοὺς γείτονας, and cf. φίλη in v. 9: συγκαλεῖ τὰς φίλας καὶ γείτονας. [115] Furthermore, Luke with his stylistic liking for groups of four puts φίλος in such groups in Lk. 14:12; 21:16 → VII, 740, 19 ff. [116]

b. The rule of Lk. 14:12: "When thou makest a dinner or a supper, call not thy friends, nor thy brethren, neither thy kinsmen, nor thy rich neighbours," stands in open antithesis to the conventions of antiquity. [117] Here everything is based on the principle of reciprocity, [118] whereas Jesus expressly excludes this: μήποτε καὶ αὐτοὶ ἀντικαλέσωσίν σε καὶ γένηται ἀνταπόδομά σοι. [119] The sayings in Mt. 5:46 f. and par. correspond exactly to the rule of Lk. 14:12. Some witnesses (W Θ and koine text) read ἐὰν ἀσπάσησθε (→ I, 499, 1 ff.) τοὺς φίλους (for ἀδελφοὺς) ὑμῶν, 5:47. Acc. to the parallelism οἱ φίλοι ὑμῶν corresponds [120] to ἀγαπῶντες ὑμᾶς (v. 46), and, as the first and second ἀγαπᾶν correspond to one another in v. 46, so do φίλον εἶναι and ἀσπάζεσθαι in v. 47. [121] The wall of the exclusiveness of fellowship and love which is at issue here, and of which all groups at all times have been guilty, is what Jesus is trying to break down in His community, cf. along

---

[114] ἀναγκαῖος φίλος, cf. P. Flor., II, 142, 3 (264 A.D.), is, like homo necessarius, C. Matius in Cic. Fam., 11, 28, 2, a "close friend," cf. Pr.-Bauer and Moult.-Mill., s.v. ἀναγκαῖος. Very instructive, too, is the section in Plat. Resp., IX, 574b c on the conduct of the one under the tyranny of Eros to his νεωστὶ φίλη καὶ οὐκ ἀναγκαία ἑταίρα γεγονυῖα as compared with his πάλαι φίλη καὶ ἀναγκαία μήτηρ and his νεωστὶ φίλος γεγονὼς οὐκ ἀναγκαῖος as compared with his ἄωρός τε καὶ ἀναγκαῖος πρεσβύτης πατὴρ καὶ τῶν φίλων ἀρχαιότατος.
[115] Cf. Jos. Ant., 9, 65: μετὰ ... γυναικὸς γειτνιώσης καὶ φίλης αὐτῇ τυγχανούσης.
[116] Cf. R. Morgenthaler, Die lk. Geschichtsschreibung als Zeugnis, I (1949), 39 f.
[117] As a pure hypothesis one finds in Socratic dialectic the idea that it might be better to invite to festivities beggars and those in need rather than friends. This sounds like the rule of Jesus but the reason is the very opposite of His; these will yield more profit, for they will not be sparing in their thanks and they will wish the very best of fortune. Furthermore, Socrates himself chooses the opposite course, since it is unseemly that gratitude should be imposed on the needy and not rather on those who are in a position to repay and can also be friends for life, Plat. Phaedr., 233d-234a. Here we have the same do-ut-des thinking as in Hes. Op., 342 f.: "Invite thy friend to a meal and not thine enemy. Invite first the man most closely related to thee." For neighbours and friends are the first to help in time of need, 345. Very different is the rule of Jose bJochanan (c. 140 B.C.): "Let thine house be wide open; let the poor be members of it," Ab., 1, 5. Cf. the elucidation by the examples of Job and Abraham in AbRNat, 7, and also bTaan., 20b on the open house of Rab Huna, Str.-B., II, 206 f. Nevertheless, the poor are not to be invited in place of friends.
[118] Cf. also Hes. Op., 353-5 and → 115, n. 20; cf. also, e.g., Xenoph. Mem., II, 6, 28. "My one aim is to be loved by those whom I love and to kindle longing for me in those for whom I long."
[119] Jesus, too, does have a reward in view, as shown by the μήποτε κτλ.: the ἀνταπόδομα of the recipients must be avoided, since everything depends on attaining ἀνταπόδομα at the raising again of the just, v. 14. The argument is the same in v. 10, the goal being the eschatological δόξα that God will give the humble, v. 11: ὑψωθήσεται. The eschatological conclusion of vv. 12-14 is in keeping with the integrating of rules of hospitality into eschatological exhortation; the pass. of v. 11 and v. 14 are to be taken as pass. divina, cf. M. Dibelius, Die Formgeschichte d. Ev.[5] (1966), 248 f.; Bultmann Trad., 108 with App.; Jeremias Gl.[7], 191 f.
[120] Athenag. Suppl., 12, 3 has στέργω τοὺς φίλους for ἀγαπάω τοὺς ἀγαπῶντας. This interpretation of the Hell. philosopher Athenagoras supports the view that the reading φίλους in Mt. 5:47 is a later Hell. alteration.
[121] This also results from the parallelism in Test. L. Aram. Fr., 92 (Riessler, 1177): "Many are his (Joseph's) friends, and those who greet him are the great," cf. R. H. Charles, The Apocr. and Pseudepigr. of the OT, II (1913), 367.

with Mt. 5:42-48 and par. and Lk. 14:12-14 such passages as Lk. 14:21-23 and esp. 10:27-37.

Lk. 14:12 also shows that friendship and table fellowship are correlative. [122] Thus when the elder brother hears of the feast given for the returning prodigal he at once thinks of his friends, Lk. 15:29. The feasts he has not held for them [123] (→ VII, 794, 19 ff.), even though he wanted to, are a secular counterpart to the father's feast of friendship and reconciliation. When the fortunate finders of Lk. 15:6, 9 summon their friends, it is again to a feast. [124] We find the same connection and thinking, although now given a sinister connotation, in Lk. 7:34 and par.: ἰδοὺ ἄνθρωπος φάγος καὶ οἰνοπότης, φίλος τελωνῶν (→ VIII, 104, 29 ff.) καὶ ἁμαρτωλῶν (→ I, 303, 31 ff.). The fact that Jesus sits at table with notorious sinners is the specific basis of the charge that He is a "boon-companion of publicans and sinners." The *kerygma* of Jesus takes up the charge in a positive way. φίλος is both active and passive. Jesus loves sinners and is loved by them in return, as shown in Lk. 7:37-50 by the washing of His feet (→ V, 25, n. 177), the kiss (→ 139, 10 ff.) and the anointing with costly ointment (→ IV, 801, 6 ff. with n. 9), which are manifestations of grateful love → II, 472, 10 ff. The close relation between friendship and table fellowship [125] found very early expression in hospitality → 148, 31 ff. This is the basis of the parable in Lk. 11:5-8. φίλος occurs here 4 times, three times almost in the sense of "good neighbour" (v. 5, 8) and once (v. 6) in that of "guest" [126] with a close approximation to the idea of hospitality, cf. φιλέω "to entertain" → 116, 4 ff. [127] The two relations of neighbourliness and hospitality carry with them a sacred duty. The friend as a neighbour and host must be available for a friend. These relations are decisive in relation to the application, namely, that the friend may ask and the friend wants to be asked [128] (→ 164, 2 ff.), for the parable stands in the Lucan Prayer Catechism, [129] Lk. 11:1-13.

c. Friendship and joy are closely related. Friends are invited for merry-making (→ 165, 7 ff.), Lk. 15:6, 9, 29. Yet the opposite relation is even more important and characteristic, namely, that of sharing in the lot of a friend, especially when it is hard: λέγω δὲ ὑμῖν τοῖς φίλοις μου, μὴ φοβηθῆτε ἀπὸ τῶν ἀποκτεννόντων τὸ σῶμα, Lk. 12:4. Friendship means service, concern, and sacrifice even to the point of life itself → 153, 21 ff. The parable of the friend who asks and is asked in Lk. 11:5-8 makes this clear. Whether in terms of hospitality or of neighbourliness, the friend can expect help from his friend even when it is inconvenient. The

---

[122] This thought, too, is old; the φίλος of the king is as such his σύσσιτος and σύμβουλος, Hdt., V, 24, 3 f. In the Gk. world again the locus of friendship is the symposium. ξενίζειν "entertaining" is a chief means of building up friendship, Plat. Ep., 7, 333e → n. 160.

[123] Cf. ἵνα μετὰ τῶν φίλων μου εὐφρανθῶ. Cod. D only has ἀριστήσω, here as in 3 Βασ. 13:7; Lk. 11:37 not specifically "breakfast" but in the sense of "holding a meal." On the use of μετά (not σύν) in expressions of fellowship cf. Bl.-Debr. § 227, 2.

[124] Cf. Jeremias Gl.[7] 134.

[125] The relation between friendship and table fellowship also seems to lie behind some Johannine texts, cf. Jn. 11:11 with 12:2 and also 3:29: The friend of the bridegroom with the bridegroom accompanies the bridal procession to the marriage feast, cf. the full survey in Str.-B., I, 505.

[126] Cf. Jeremias Gl.[7], 157; W. Grundmann, *Das Ev. nach Lk.*, Theol. Handkomm. z. NT, 3[4] (1966) on 11:16.

[127] Here, then, the two terms "neighbour" and "host," which are often linked with "friend" → 159, 34 ff.; 148, 34 ff., are combined in the use of φίλος itself.

[128] Cf. Jeremias Gl.[7], 158 f.: "The parable of the friend who is asked for help at night."

[129] *Ibid.*, 158.

friends of the centurion of Capernaum are obviously at his service, Lk. 7:6. Conversely the centurion Cornelius wants to give his acquaintances and close friends a share in the greatest experience of his life as this was brought to him by God's messenger, Ac. 10:24. In Ephesus the asiarchs, who according to Luke's remarkable note were friends of Paul, [130] even though they were probably the chief pagan priests of the province of Asia, intervened to save the life of their friend, Ac. 19:31.

Only here and perhaps in Ac. 27:3 (though → lines 13 ff.) do we hear of friends of Paul. Once Lk. ref. to μαθηταί of Paul at Ac. 9:25; these were probably (young) friends, since nowhere else do we read of these disciples → IV, 459, 20 ff. Paul himself never uses the terms φίλος and μαθητής (→ VII, 742, 13 ff.); he has ἀδελφός and τέκνον instead. It seems from Lk. that Paul was the head of a large circle of friends that had gathered around him. [131]

In Ac. 27:3 there is again an obvious co-ordination of the word φίλος with solicitude [132] for the friend. The φίλοι are neither Paul's hosts in Sidon nor, as Lk.'s terminology might seem to indicate, personal friends of the apostle to whose friendly care he was committed during his stay in Sidon. Rather the φίλοι are Christians whose care for the apostle is continually mentioned by Luke [133] and Paul (e.g., 2 C. 11:9; Phil. 4:10, 16, 18).

The question arises whether Luke with his class. education himself chose the term οἱ φίλοι for Christians. [134] A point against this is that John knows the designation and himself has it in 3 Jn. 15, → 166, 16 ff. [135] But if Luke takes over the term, the further question arises: What is the derivation of this description which in both Lk. and Jn. is far less prominent than other terms like οἱ ἀδελφοί (→ I, 145, 10 ff.)? [136] It is conceivable that in native Hell. churches there was borrowing from the terms which other Hell. groups used for themselves. [137] But it is much more likely that the primitive Chr. communities took over traditions from the disciples' band. It is precisely Lk. (12:4) and Jn. (15:13 ff. → 165, 19 ff.; Jn. 11:11 → 165, 16 ff.) and they alone who tell us that Jesus called His disciples φίλοι. But behind this, esp. in Jn. 15, lies the thought that Christians, as friends of Jesus and also φίλοι among themselves, [138] are at the same time the new friends of

---

[130] On the construction ὄντες αὐτῷ φίλοι cf. Bl.-Debr. § 190.

[131] Cf. Michaelis, 310-3, 328-334. Fuchs, 23-8 undoubtedly goes too far in using the category of friendship for the relation of the Pauline churches and of many individuals like Philemon to Paul. A false note is introduced into NT sayings by the orientation of his understanding of friendship to Aristot.

[132] For examples of friendly concern for the well-being of a friend drawn from non-biblical antiquity cf. Schneidewin, 141-4. Linguistically related is Xenoph. Symp., 4, 46: ... ἐπιδεικνύναι ὡς ... σοῦ ἐπιμέλονται, sc. οἱ φίλοι, and also the description of a friend in Luc. Toxaris, 31.

[133] Cf. Stählin, op. cit. (→ n. 105) on 16:15; 21:16 etc.

[134] Harnack Miss., 435.

[135] Perhaps this self-designation of Christians finds an echo in Ev. Pt. 12:51: (Mary Magdalene on Easter morn) λαβοῦσα μεθ' ἑαυτῆς τὰς φίλας.

[136] Closely akin are οἱ ἴδιοι, Ac. 4:23; 24:23, and οἱ οἰκεῖοι θεοῦ, Eph. 2:19.

[137] Harnack Miss., 435 ref. to the Epicureans, who called themselves "the friends" → 147, 15 ff. If the Aberkios inscr. is from the Isis cult, it contains in line 17 an example of φίλοι for the members of the Attic cult, cf. H. Strathmann - T. Klauser, Art. "Aberkios," RAC, I, 13.

[138] One cannot like Fuchs, 28-33 explain many NT themes in community ethics as elements of reciprocal friendship, e.g., 1 C. 13:5, 7. Primitive Chr. ἀγάπη is rooted in the ἀγάπη θεοῦ and actualises itself in the brotherhood or family of God united by this ἀγάπη. Hence Fuchs, 32 strikes a false note when he says that Chr. brotherhood has the stamp of an exclusive, aristocratic friendship.

God (→ 164, 7 ff.), and that they are this as members of the *familia Dei*, as οἰκεῖοι (→ V, 134, 29 ff.) τοῦ θεοῦ, Eph. 2:19. Even when the term φίλοι does not occur, many features in the picture of the primitive community are to be regarded as outworkings of this φιλία, esp. in Ac. 2:44-46; 4:32 → n. 52. The name φίλοι seems not to have found any further use in the main body of the Church, but is was possibly employed in Gnostic groups. [139]

d. In contrast to the varied positive aspects of friendship in Lk. there is also a negative side. Among the motifs of the Messianic Woes in Lk. we find not only the reversal of love for parents, children and brothers into hate (cf. Mk. 13:12 and Mt. 10:21 → IV, 690, 23 ff.) but also the changing of friends into enemies: παραδοθήσεσθε δὲ καὶ ὑπὸ γονέων καὶ ἀδελφῶν καὶ συγγενῶν καὶ φίλων... καὶ ἔσεσθε μισούμενοι ὑπὸ πάντων, Lk. 21:16 f. The motif of reversal is not in itself eschatological, for it is part of the common experience of life. This is why we find both in the paganism of the time (→ 157, 1 ff.) and also in Judaism (→ 156, 30 ff.) concern and warning and complaint about the unreliability of friends.

e. Jesus calls His disciples φίλοι, [140] Lk. 12:4. This does not have to be a Lukan (→ 162, 19 ff.) addition to the picture of the relation between master and disciples; [141] the parallels in John (→ 165, 18 ff.) are an argument against this. [142] It is possible, of course, that both Luke and John had Hellenistic court style in view when using this designation (→ 148, 25 ff.). [143] But there are other possibilities. In the last resort the term φίλοι is part of the imagery of the family of God. This connection is supported especially by the fact that in almost the same sense (cf. Jn. 15:15 with 20:17) Jesus also calls the disciples ἀδελφοί (→ I, 145, 26 ff.). [144] As distinct from Gk. φιλία (→ 152, 9 ff.), this is not a friendship of equals. [145] It is the Master and Teacher who is calling His disciples and pupils φίλοι, → 153, 18 ff. To this extent it is worth noting that in Luke and John Jesus uses the designation φίλοι when He is teaching the disciples about their future tasks and destiny, cf. Lk. 12:4 f.; Jn. 14:26.

---

[139] If the Aberkios inscr. is of Chr. derivation, line 15: καὶ τοῦτον (sc. ἰχθύν) ἐπέδωκε φίλοις ἔσθειν διὰ παντός, attests to the use of φίλοι as a self-designation of Christians in the 2nd cent., cf. Strathmann, *op. cit.*, 16; F. J. Dölger, ΙΧΘΥΣ, Ι² (1928), 134 f. But if a Gnosticising group is behind it, Harnack Miss., 436, we have here Gnostic usage, cf. Valentinian's homily περὶ φίλων ref. to in Cl. Al. Strom., VI, 6, 52, 3 f. In the passage quoted from this the description of a Gnostic society as ὁ λαὸς ὁ τοῦ ἠγαπημένου (sc. Christ, cf. Cl. Al. Strom., III, 4, 29, 2), ὁ φιλούμενος καὶ φιλῶν αὐτόν might be regarded as an interpretation of the title φίλοι, cf. A. Hilgenfeld, *Die Ketzergesch. d. Urchr.* (1884), 301 f.; Harnack Miss., 433-6; Jackson-Lake, I, 4, 326 on Ac. 27:3; H. J. Cadbury, "Names for Christians and Christianity," *ibid.*, I, 5, 379 f.; Stählin, *op. cit.* (→ n. 105) on 27:3.
[140] Apollonius of Tyana, whose manifestation offers so many par. to the NT, called his disciples ἑταῖροι rather than φίλοι, e.g., Philostr. Vit. Ap., IV, 29. 34; V, 21, and sometimes γνώριμοι, e.g., IV, 47.
[141] Thus, e.g., Hauck, 226 ascribes the introduction to the Q saying in Lk. 12:4 to the author.
[142] In an agr. in Cl. Al. Quis Div. Salv., 33, 1 φίλοι as a term Jesus uses for the disciples is linked with the same word for the mutual relationship of Christians: δώσω γὰρ οὐ μόνον τοῖς φίλοις, ἀλλὰ καὶ τοῖς φίλοις τῶν φίλων, cf. Jn. 17:20.
[143] Deissmann LO, 324, → V, 840, n. 11.
[144] One may ask why Jesus in Jn. as distinct from the Synoptists calls His disciples φίλοι but not ἀδελφοί prior to Easter. John wanted to keep the lofty title ἀδελφός for the post-Easter period, cf. Jn. 20:17.
[145] Nor can one compare the Gk. friendships between non-equals, e.g., the man and boy or the king and his φίλοι cf. also → 147, 8 ff.; 153, 5 ff., 17 ff.

f. In some parables and comparisons the thought is implied that God is the Friend of men and esp. of the disciples. Although we have in Lk. 11:5-8 (→ 161, 19 ff.) a comparison with a conclusion *a minori ad maius* — if even a true friend does not hesitate for a moment to meet the requests of his friend, how much more prompt will God be! [146] — there still lies in the background the idea that God is the best friend who grants the requests of His friend and who indeed wants to be asked. Hence we have the corresponding thought that the disciples are God's friends → 167, 12 ff. [147] The same idea may be seen in the implication of the parable in Lk. 14:11; God is both the Lord and also the Host at the eschatological banquet who elevates His friend, v. 10. [148] Possibly the saying at Lk. 16:9: ἑαυτοῖς ποιήσατε φίλους ἐκ τοῦ μαμωνᾶ (→ IV, 390, 2 ff.) τῆς ἀδικίας (→ I, 152, 30 ff.), ἵνα ὅταν ἐκλίπῃ δέξωνται ὑμᾶς εἰς τὰς αἰωνίους σκηνάς, also has in view God as Friend. We should use as ἀγάπη to God and men all that life offers us in this wicked world so that we may win God as our Friend. [149] The plur. φίλοι might seem to be against this interpretation but it is determined by the two examples in vv. 5-7 and it also makes possible the understanding of δέξωνται in v. 9 as a circumlocution for the name of God [150] → 168, 7 ff. [151] The primitive community saw concealed in the reviling of Jesus in Mt. 11:19 and par. the insight that His love for sinners is an enacted parable expressing His message that God makes Himself the Friend [152] of sinners. [153]

---

[146] Cf. Jeremias Gl.[7], 158 f.

[147] Cf. Grundmann, *op. cit.* (→ n. 126) on 11:8. It is no accident that the parable in Lk. 11:5-8 comes immediately after the Lord's Prayer.

[148] Behind the address φίλε found in both παραβολαί there stands in Lk. 11:5 God as the One to whom man speak as to a friend and in Lk. 14:10 the humble man who is worthy to be so addressed by God, cf. ἑταῖρε in eschatological parables, Mt. 22:12; 20:13 → n. 113.

[149] Cf. W. Michaelis, *Die Gleichnisse Jesu*[3] (1956), 256, n. 163.

[150] Cf. Grundmann, *op. cit.* (→ n. 126), *ad loc.;* Str.-B., II, 221 with Jewish par. for this way of expressing God's name; cf. also Lk. 6:38; 12:20.

[151] Often, of course, these φίλοι are interpreted differently, cf. Grundmann, *op. cit.* on 16:9. Cl. Al. Quis Div. Salv., 31, 9-33, 3 thinks they are needy men on whose behalf we are to use our goods and who as friends of God will come forward as advocates at the judgment. Jeremias Gl.[7], 43, n. 3 prefers interpretation in terms of almsgiving and other good works which acc. to Jewish expectation will one day intercede with God for us, cf. Ab., 4, 11 and Str.-B., II, 561 f. The φίλοι of Lk. 16:9 might also be the angels which play a big part in connection with the Last Judgment elsewhere in the NT too, cf. Mt. 13:41, 49; Lk. 12:8 f.; Rev. 3:5; 14:10. In Judaism also the angels are often intercessors, cf. H. M. Hughes, "The Gk. Apoc. of Baruch" in Charles, *op. cit.* (→ n. 121), 531 f.; Str.-B., II, 560 f.; N. Johansson, *Parakletoi* (1940), 75-178; O. Betz, "Der Paraklet," *Arbeiten z. Gesch. d. Spätjudt. u. des Urchr.*, 2 (1963), 60-64, and they are esp. depicted as friends of the righteous, Gr. Bar. 15. The angels also have an eschatological function in Lk. 15:10, and perhaps in the interpretation of the par. parable in v. 7 if "in heaven" is to be understood here as in Mt. 6:10, i.e., "by or with the angels." But "heaven" may stand for "God," as often elsewhere, e.g., Jn. 3:27. Since the angels simply come to represent God in Judaism as a result of the increasing stress on the divine transcendence, it makes no essential difference in either Lk. 16:9 or 15:7 whether we see in the friends or heaven a ref. to the angels or to God.

[152] Often in Gk. antiquity the gods are friends of men, e.g., Xenoph. Symp., 4, 48 f.; on the two-sidedness of friendship between the gods and the wise cf. Diog. L., VI, 37 with 72. In the OT we find the bold theologoumenon that God is the Friend of the righteous in Job 16:21 (→ VI, 313, n. 13), and this is echoed in Judaism, e.g., bTaan., 24a. The friendship between God and Abraham is again two-way, cf. Gn. r., 41, 8 on 12:17 in Str.-B., III, 755 (→ 169, 5 ff.). On Israel as friend cf. Lv. r., 6, 1 on 5:1 in Str.-B., II, 138 (→ n. 184; V, 811, 17 ff.). The thought is common in the early Church, Const. Ap., VIII, 39, 3; Cl. Al. Prot. 12, 122, 3 → 170, 1 ff.

[153] Cf. J. Schniewind, *Das Ev. nach Mt., NT Deutsch,* 2[11] (1964) on 11:19a.

3. φίλος in John's Writings.

John alone in the NT uses φίλος in the specific sense of the (special) "friend of the bridegroom," the "best man," Jn. 3:29 → 154, 16; IV, 1102, 2 ff. As a metaphor for John the Baptist this brings out both his close relationship and also his unselfish subordination to Jesus, [154] for the tasks of the best man presuppose most unselfish friendship, but cf. Ju. 14:20; 15:2, 6.

As in many other areas, [155] Jn. has striking similarities to Luke in his concept of the friend; the correlation of friendship and joy (→ 161, 27 f.) comes out particularly well in the similitude of the friend of the bridegroom: ὁ ... φίλος τοῦ νυμφίου, ὁ ἑστηκὼς καὶ ἀκούων αὐτοῦ, χαρᾷ χαίρει [156] διὰ τὴν φωνὴν τοῦ νυμφίου, Jn. 3:29. The connection between friendship and table fellowship (→ 161, 11 ff.) also finds clear expression in the Bethany family, Lk. 10:38-42; Jn. 12:1-8. Luke never calls the brother and sisters φίλοι of Jesus, but John often expresses the close relation of friendship between them and Jesus, Jn. 11:3, 5, 11, 36. While this is shown to be personal friendship by the use of the verb φιλέω (11:3, Cod. D and v. 36), Λάζαρος ὁ φίλος ἡμῶν in 11:11 makes it plain that discipleship is involved too → 130, 25 ff. [157]

Jn. 11:11 is an indication that the Johannine Jesus called His disciples "friends." Their position as friends of Jesus (15:13-16) dates from the day of His selection. [158] This was the free choice of the κύριος by which He raised His δοῦλοι [159] to the status of φίλοι → II, 276, 15 ff. As God chose His friends in the OT (→ n. 184; → 169, 8 f.), so Jesus chooses His friends. [160] Their obedience to His ἐντέλλεσθαι (v. 14) brings out very sharply the fact that this is not at all a friendship between equals (→ 163, 23 ff. with n. 145). He remains the κύριος. But His ἐντολή is defined as the command of love (v. 17) which He Himself fulfils perfectly, cf. v. 10. He thus makes Himself like them. This is the point of v. 15b: πάντα ἃ ἤκουσα παρὰ

---

154 This is very important in the depiction of the Jesus-Baptist relation in Jn. The Bridegroom is to the best man as φῶς in Jn. 1:4 f., 8 to λύχνος in 5:35, or λόγος in 1:1 to φωνή in 1:23, or μονογενὴς θεός in 1:18 to ἄνθρωπος in 1:6; cf. Bau. J., 15 f.

155 Cf. Grundmann, op. cit. (→ n. 126), 17-22; Schl. Lk.², 466-9; P. Parker, "Luke and the Fourth Evangelist," NTSt, 9 (1962/63), 317-336; J. A. Bailey, The Traditions Common to the Gospels of Luke and John (1963).

156 On the dat. etym. fig. cf. Bl.-Debr. § 198, 6; Bultmann J., ad loc.

157 φίλος ἡμῶν might also mean "our host," cf. Jn. 12:2 → 161, 20 f. But neither here nor in Lk. does Lazarus appear as host; in the house at Bethany Martha seems to play this role, Lk. 10:38.

158 ἐξελεξάμην in Jn. 15:16 is to be taken as a past ref., cf. Ac. 1:2. Hence ὑμᾶς ... εἴρηκα φίλους in v. 15 pts. back to a fact posited from the outset.

159 οὐκέτι in Jn. 15:15 does not imply that only now do the Parting Discourses establish a new relation between Jesus and His disciples, though cf. 16:29. It rather ref. back to a time before the period denoted by εἴρηκα and ἐγνώρισα.

160 Non-biblical antiquity also speaks of the choice of friends, e.g., Chrysipp. Fr., 112 (v. Arnim, III, 27): φιλία καθ' αἵρεσιν. Luc. Toxaris, 37 discusses the principles of choice among the Scythians. Elsewhere much thought is given to how friendship originates, Plat. Lys., 212a, and many answers are given to this question, cf. esp. Cic. Fam., 3, 10, 9; 5, 15, 2. True friends are φύσει φίλοι, Plat. Lys., 221e; Phaedr., 255a; ἡ ἐπιθυμία τῆς φιλίας αἰτία, Lys., 221d. Similarity of age causes friendship, Phaedr., 240c, for many friendships go back to early youth, e.g., Luc. Toxaris, 12. Plat. Ep., 7, 333e compares two very different origins of friendship: ἐκ φιλοσοφίας and ἐκ τοῦ ξενίζειν τε καὶ μυεῖν καὶ ἐποπτεύειν, common meals and initiations. These words suggest that a frequent basis of friendship was common adherence to a cult and membership of a cultic society in which common meals figured prominently. The poets, however, τὸν θεὸν αὐτόν φασιν ποιεῖν φίλους αὐτούς, ἄγοντα παρ' ἀλλήλους, Lys., 214a. This sentence sounds like Jn. 15:16 but here it is Eros who brings those who are alike together.

τοῦ πατρός μου ἐγνώρισα ὑμῖν. Elsewhere, too, unrestricted self-impartation is a mark of genuine friendship, → n. 180. But the disciples must do the same, esp. in the love (v. 10) which is even ready for the laying down of life, v. 13, cf. 1 Jn. 3:16. In the statement μείζονα ταύτης ἀγάπην οὐδεὶς ἔχει, ἵνα τις τὴν ψυχὴν αὐτοῦ θῇ (→ VIII, 155, 30 ff.) ὑπὲρ τῶν φίλων αὐτοῦ (Jn. 15:13) John is probably clothing an ancient rule of friendship [161] in biblical speech in order to apply it to the relation of Jesus to His disciples and also to that of the disciples with one another. [162] Here, then, the rule of friendship is made to serve the NT thought of substitution which John applies not merely to Christ Himself but also to Christians, 1 Jn. 3:16. The demand that the disciples should give their lives for their friends (or brothers) as Jesus did is basically contained already in Jn. 15:12: They will show themselves to be Jesus' friends, who love as He did, by their laying down their lives for one another. [163] Hence the saying about supreme love (v. 13) applies to the disciples as [164] it does to Jesus. The friend-saying has twofold significance; it is first soteriological [165] and then hortatory. [166]

Like Luke (→ 162, 13 ff.) John is acquainted with the use of φίλοι as a self-designation for Christians. 3 Jn. closes with the mutual salutations of friends: ἀσπά-ζονταί σε οἱ φίλοι. ἀσπάζου τοὺς φίλους κατ᾽ ὄνομα (v. 15). Undoubtedly the term φίλοι in this connection with the salutations (→ 160, 9 ff.) has a share in the exclusiveness of the Johannine communities [167] (→ 130, n. 162). Nevertheless the translation "partisans" [168] or "party members" [169] misses the real point which it at issue here too, namely, that they have become friends by relationship to Jesus, that they are "fellow-believers." The author of 3 Jn. is undoubtedly adopting a common formula (→ 137, 1 ff. with n. 214). But in this letter as distinct from secular letters it is fully stamped with the character of the Johannine communities (though → I, 501, 24 f.). It is fellow-believers who send and receive the greetings; the same exclusiveness attaches to this ἀσπάζεσθαι as in Mt. 5:47 → 160, 12 ff.

Once in John — the only instance in the NT [170] — φίλος is used as a political term. When Pilate is hesitating to condemn Jesus, the Jews cry out to him: ἐὰν

---

[161] Cf. Mi. R.[13] 134, n. 1; Grundmann, 62-9 and → 153, 21 ff.

[162] The decisive expression τίθημι τὴν ψυχὴν ὑπέρ τινος (cf. also Jn. 10:11, 15, 17 f.; 1 Jn. 3:16) is probably an alternative transl. of the παραδιδόναι formula (→ V, 710, 18 ff.) from Is. 53:12 LXX, cf. W. Popkes, "Christus traditus," AbhThANT, 49 (1967), 190-193. It can mean either "to hazard one's life" or "to give one's life" (cf. ὑποτίθημι τὸν τράχηλον in R. 16:4 and παραβολεύομαι τῇ ψυχῇ in Phil. 2:20); its probable derivation from Is. 53:12 favours the latter sense.

[163] The synoptic counterpart of Jn. 15:13 is Mk. 8:35 par.: the giving of life for Jesus; the only difference is that we have here ἔνεκεν ἐμοῦ rather than ὑπέρ, which only Paul dare apply to himself, e.g., Col. 1:24 (→ VIII, 508, 24 ff.) and cf. 1 C. 4:13 → VI, 91, 23 ff.

[164] This "as" is impressively worked out as typical of John by G. P. Wetter, "Der Sohn Gottes'" FRL, 26 (1916), 62 f.; cf. Bultmann J., 417, n. 7.

[165] Cf. Dibelius, 215-7; E. Lohse, Märtyrer u. Gottesknecht² (1963), 134; Grundmann, 63-9.

[166] In this light the assurances of Peter in Jn. 13:37 and Thomas in 11:16 that they are ready to die for Jesus are for Jn. protestations of friendship for Him. The conduct of Aquila and Prisca in R. 16:4 and of Epaphroditus in Phil. 2:30 may also be regarded as demonstrations of the mutual friendship of Christians (→ n. 4; → 153, 21 ff.).

[167] Cf. E. Käsemann, "Ketzer u. Zeuge," Exeget. Versuche u. Besinnungen, I⁴ (1965), 178 f. with n. 38.

[168] So F. Hauck, Die Kirchenbriefe, NT Deutsch, 10⁶ (1953), ad loc.; cf. J. Schneider, Die Br. d. Jk., Pt., Jd. u. Joh., NT Deutsch, 10² (1967), ad loc.

[169] So Bü J., ad loc.

[170] One might also regard as a political friendship the friendship between Herod Antipas and Pilate, which is reported only in Lk. 23:12.

τοῦτον ἀπολύσῃς, οὐκ εἶ φίλος τοῦ Καίσαρος (Jn. 19:12). Whether the title is used in a technical sense here [171] (→ 147, 13 ff.) is open to question, for the Jews can hardly take the title away from Pilate; they are rather delivering a judgment on the relation between Pilate and the emperor. But the word is, of course, associated with the common court title → 148, 15 ff. [172]

4. φίλος and φιλία in James.

The two places where φίλος occurs in Jm. (2:23; 4:4, where we also find φιλία) centre in different ways on friendship with God. In 4:4 ἐχθρὸς τοῦ θεοῦ presupposes φίλος τοῦ θεοῦ as its opposite, and similarly φιλία τοῦ κόσμου presupposes φιλία τοῦ θεοῦ. [173] He who seeks friendship with the world necessarily becomes [174] an enemy of God. The basis of this thesis is a dualism similar to that of John [175] as this comes to expression especially in 1 Jn. 2:15. [176] Jm. 2:23 is the only v. in the NT which has the title [177] "friend of God": [178] ἐπληρώθη ἡ γραφὴ ἡ λέγουσα· ἐπίστευσεν δὲ Ἀβραάμ (→ I, 8, 17 ff.) τῷ θεῷ καὶ ἐλογίσθη αὐτῷ εἰς δικαιοσύνην, καὶ φίλος θεοῦ ἐκλήθη. [179] Whether the third statement is seen as part of the

---

[171] Cf. K. C. Atkinson, "Some Observations on Ptolemaic Ranks and Titles," *Aegyptus*, 32 (1952), 204-214; E. Bammel: "Φίλος τοῦ Καίσαρος," ThLZ, 77 (1952), 205-210; M. Bang, "Die Freunde u. Begleiter d. Kaiser," L. Friedländer - G. Wissowa, *Darstellungen aus d. Sittengesch. Roms in d. Zeit v. August bis zum Ausgang der Antonine*[9-10], IV (1921), 56-76; E. Bikerman, *Institutions des Séleucides* (1938), 36-50; J. Crook, *Consilium Principis, Imperial Councils and Counsellors from Augustus to Diocletian* (1955), 21-30; Deissmann B, 159 f.; F. Dölger, "Die 'Familie der Könige' im Mittelalter," *Byzanz u. d. europäische Staatenwelt* (1953), 34-69; H. Donner, "Der 'Freund d. Königs,'" ZAW, 73 (1961), 269-277; A. Momigliano, "Honorati Amici," *Athenaeum*, NS, 11 (1933), 136-141; K. J. Neumann, Art. "Amicus," Pauly-W., 1 (1894), 1832 f.; J. Oehler, Art. "Amicus," Pauly-W., 1 (1894), 1831 f.; H. H. Schmidt, Art. "Philoi," *Lex. d. Alten Welt*, (1965), 2299 f.; M. L. Strack, "Griech. Titel im Ptolemäerreich," *Rhein. Mus.*, 55 (1900), 161-190; M. Trindl, *Ehrentitel im Ptolemäerreich*, Diss. Munich 1937 (1942), 35-40, cf. 9-73; H. Willrich, "Zum hell. Titel- u. Ordenswesen," *Klio*, 9 (1909), 416-421. On the continued use of the title φίλος in the M. Ages, esp. in the Byzantine Empire, cf. Dölger, 39 with n. 8; 47, 51, 65 with n. 74.

[172] That the Jews touched a nerve here may be seen from the gt. importance of one's ranking in the list of *amici Caesaris*; only those in the first class were strictly given a place at court, cf. T. Mommsen, *Röm. Staatsrecht*, III, 1 (1887), 556. For as already at the court of the Diadochi (cf. esp. Trindl, *op. cit.*, 23-26, 50-64) there were in Rome, too, distinctions between the various classes of imperial or royal friends.

[173] The idea that two friendships may be mutually exclusive occurs already in Hom. Il., 9, 613 f.; cf. Plut. De amicorum multitudine, 6 (II, 96a); Fr., 4 (→ n. 24); Normann, 20, 80-99.

[174] As in R. 5:19 καθίσταμαι means "to become" or "to show oneself."

[175] Cf. O. Böcher, *Der joh. Dualismus im Zshg. d. nachbiblischen Judt.* (1965), 72-74, 142-145.

[176] Cf. J. Moffatt, *Love in the NT* (1930), 272-5.

[177] This is in the background in at least some of the sayings and parables of Jesus, cf. Lk. 12:4; 11:8; 14:10 → 164, 1 ff.

[178] Cf. E. Barnikol, Art. "Gottesfreund," RGG³, II, 1789 f.; F. Dirlmeier, "θεοφιλία-φιλόθεια," *Philol.*, 90 (1935), 57-77, 176-193; R. Egenter, *Gottesfreundschaft. Die Lehre v. d. Gottesfreundschaft in der Scholastik u. Mystik d. 12. u. 13. Jhdt.* (1928); G. van der Leeuw, *Phänomenologie der Religion*² (1956), 542-4; H. Neumark, *Die Verwendung gr. u. jüd. Motive in den Gedanken Philons über die Stellung Gottes zu seinen Freunden*, Diss. Würzburg (1937); E. Peterson, "Der Gottesfreund," ZKG, 42 (1923), 161-202; F. Pfister, Art. "Kultus," Pauly-W., 11 (1922), 2128; H. Speyer, *Die bibl. Erzählungen im Qoran* (1961), 173; M. Vidal, "La Theophilia dans la penseé religieuse des Grecs," *Recherches de Science Religieuse*, 47 (1959), 161-184.

[179] Cf. Dib. Jk.¹¹, ad loc., esp. 161 f. and 212 f.; Hck. Jk., ad loc.; Kn. Cl. on 1 Cl., 10, 1; E. Hennecke, *Altchr. Malerei u. altchr. Lit.* (1896), 212 with n. 6; E. Fascher, "Abraham Φυσιολόγος u. Φίλος θεοῦ," *Festschr. T. Klauser* (1964), 111-124.

quotation along with the first two is not quite certain but very likely. There is probably allusion to verses like Is. 41:8 and 2 Ch. 20:7 [180] and we are to seek the origin of the idea of the friend of God in the OT [181] and not in Greek [182] or Egyptian usage. [183] Abraham is the only one to whom the NT grants the honorary title of φίλος θεοῦ → n. 177, just as he is the one who is most commonly called this in the whole sphere of Judaism. [184] Due to the link with Gn. 15:6 the meaning of φίλος θεοῦ is very close to "he who is just through faith." The ἐκλήθη added to the title

---

[180] Abraham is called אֹהֵב, corresponding to the title "friend of God," when Israel in Is. 41:8; 2 Ch. 20:7 is called "shoot, descendant of Abraham" אֹהֲבִי (or אֹהַבְךָ). One can render this by "my" or "thy (i.e., God's) friend," cf. Is. 41:8 Σ Vg; 2 Ch. 20:7 Vg, cf. also Jdt. 8:22 Vg. Esp. important is Gn. 18:17 (though the corresponding term is not in the original): A true friend has no secrets from his friend; hence God says: "Shall I hide from Abraham that thing which I do?" Cf. Philo Sobr., 56, where Gn. 18:17 as against HT and LXX is quoted in the form μὴ ἀποκαλύψω ἐγὼ ἀπὸ Ἀβραὰμ τοῦ φίλου μου; Tg.J.II (ed. M. Ginsburger [1899]) on Gn. 18:17; cf. Sandmel, op. cit. (→ n. 110), 44, n. 130.

[181] The full expression "friend of God" does not occur in the HT but there are approaches to it, cf. → n. 180, also Ex. 33:11: Yahweh speaks to Moses face to face as a man speaks to his friend. In Wis. 7:27 the friends of God, like the prophets, are a work of the divine wisdom indwelling them. Possibly the φίλοι θεοῦ are equated here with the prophets and the latter are thus given the title "friends of God." In 2 Ch. 20:7 LXX: σπέρματι Αβρααμ τῷ ἠγαπημένῳ σου, ἠγαπημένος is treated as a noun synon. with φίλος and thus takes the gen. instead of ὑπό.

[182] On the title "friend of God" (→ n. 152) in the Gk. world cf. Normann, 28-30; Peterson, op. cit. (→ n. 178), 165-172; Reitzenstein Hell. Myst., 185. As friends of the gods we find esp. heroes, Hom. Il., 20, 347, cf. Od., 6, 203, heralds, Il., 8, 517, priests, Il., 1, 381, poets, Od., 8, 480 f.; Hes. Theog., 96 f. men of the golden age, Hes. Op., 120, οἱ ἀγαθοὶ ἄνδρες, Plat. acc. to Cl. Al. Strom., V, 14, 96, 1, the Stoics, Ps.-Plut. Vit. Poes. Hom., 143, the pious, Max. Tyr., 14, 6 f. (Hobein), the wise, Plat. Leg., IV, 716d; Aristot. Eth. Nic., X, 9, p. 1179a, 22-30 (but cf. VIII, 9, p. 1158b, 35 ff.; Dirlmeier, op. cit. [→ n. 21], 520 f. on 180 A, 3 f.); Diogenes acc. to Diog. L., VI, 37, cf. 72; Philo Vit. Mos., I, 156; Rer. Div. Her., 21 → 158, 29 f., v. Joh. W. 1 K. on 3:21-23; Dib. Jk.[11], 212 with n. 3 Individuals called "friend of God or the gods" are, e.g., Epictetus, cf. his supposed funerary inscr., Anth. Pal., 7, 676, Apollonius of Tyana, Philostr. Vit. Ap., I, 12; Apollonius Ep., 11 (ed. C. L. Kayser, Flavii Philostrati Op., I [1870], 348); Flavius Vopiscus, Divus Aurelianus, 24, 3 (ed. E. Hohl, Scriptores Historiae Augustae, II [1927], 167). Finally the beloved dead can also be called "friends of the gods," Epigr. Graec., 460, 1; 569, 9 (2nd/3rd cent. A.D.); 650, 2 (3rd cent. A.D.) (→ V, 494, 14); Juncus in Stob. Ecl., V, 1109, 14 f., and also stars and astral spirits, Max. Tyr., 11, 12a (Hobein). Cf. also proper names like Diphilos, Menophilos, Theophilos.

[183] Already in ancient Egypt "Friend of a God" was a title of the kings cf. E. Lehmann-H. Haas, Textbuch z. Religionsgesch. (1922), 332; A. Ermann - H. Ranke, Ägypten u. ägypt. Leben im Altertum² (1923), cf. also the priest, A. Ermann, Die Lit. d. Ägypter (1923), 88.

[184] The title is fully developed in Jewish lit. not included in the LXX, e.g., Jub. 19:9; Apc. Abr. 9:6; 10:6; Test. Abr. 13 (p. 117, 18 f.). Other bibl. figures were also called friends of God in this period, Levi in Jub. 30:20, Jacob in Jos. and Aseneth (ed. M. Philonenko [1968]) 23:10, Moses in Sib., 2, 245. We find a collective and abs. use in Jub. 30:21, cf. also v. 20. In Rabb. lit. the title is preferably conferred on the whole people, Str.-B., II, 138; III, 755, cf. also II, 564; III, 682; not so commonly it is accorded to the patriarch Abraham, Str.-B., III, 755, cf. also II, 138. In the same sense Abraham is "God's beloved" or "the beloved" (יָדִיד) on the basis of Jer. 11:15, bMen., 53b; in 53a b this applies to Solomon (2 S. 12:25), Benjamin (Dt. 33:12) and Israel (Jer. 12:7) as well. Moses, too, is the "friend of God," Str.-B., III, 683 → n. 181. In Ab., 6, 1 the man who studies the Torah for its own sake is called רֵעַ and אָהוּב sc. of God. At Qumran Abraham is God's friend in Damasc. 3:2 (4:2), cf. Str.-B., II, 565; III, 755, and the same title is given to Isaac and Jacob in Damasc. 3:3 f. (4:3). Philo (→ 158, 19 ff.) honours Abraham, Isaac and Jacob as God's friends, Abr., 50, and Moses too, Vit. Mos., I, 156; Rer. Div. Her., 21. From this passage (οἱ σοφοὶ πάντες φίλοι θεοῦ) and Fug., 58 one may conclude that all the righteous acc. to Philo's ideal deserve the title → 158, 28 ff.

adopted from the OT is to be construed as a pass. divinum, like ἐλογίσθη. That is, God Himself has given Abraham the title "friend of God" cf. Jn. 15:15: ὑμᾶς εἴρηκα φίλους, → 165, 19 ff. The aorist suggests that we are to relate it to a specific event in Abraham's life. [185] According to the context the works of faith done by Abraham are the reason why God conferred this title on him. [186] If the title "friend of God" carries with it the thought of Abraham's love for God (→ n. 186), the passive element is still predominant in contrast to φιλία and φίλος in Jm. 4:4 and φιλόθεος in 2 Tm. 3:4 → n. 2. The same applies to the pass. ἐκλήθη; Abraham is the man who is loved and chosen by God.

D. φίλος and φιλία in the Post-New Testament Period.

I. In the Early Church.

1. In the main there is only a slender use of the group in post-NT lit. [187] It is much less prominent than ἀγάπη-ἀγαπάω [188] and ἔρως-ἐράω. Yet words of the stem φιλ- occurs sometimes in NT quotations when the NT employs other terms; thus ἀγαπᾶτε in Mt. 5:44 and par. is replaced with φιλεῖτε in Did., 1, 3 → n. 120. In many cases such linguistic changes are accompanied by more important changes in the NT statements. Thus in Ign. Pol., 2, 1 Lk. 6:32 (cf. Mt. 5:46) occurs in the form: καλοὺς μαθητὰς ἐὰν φιλῇς, χάρις σοι οὐκ ἔστιν. The gen. rule of Jesus is reapplied to the bishop who is to be concerned about the λοιμότεροι in his congregations rather than being friendly only to good Christians. 2 Cl., 6, 5 changes the saying about the two masters in Mt. 6:24 and par. into a saying about the two aeons: οὐ δυνάμεθα ... τῶν δύο (sc. αἰώνων) φίλοι εἶναι· δεῖ δὲ ἡμᾶς τούτῳ ἀποταξαμένους ἐκείνῳ χρᾶσθαι → 170, 29 ff.; n. 173. Const. Ap., IV, 13, 2 seems to be a variant of the thought of R. 13:8: μηδενί τι χρεωσ-τεῖν εἰ μὴ τῆς φιλίας σύμβολον, ὃ ὁ θεὸς διετάξατο διὰ Χριστοῦ. [189] Another alteration of a NT saying is to be found in Ev. Pt. 2:3. [190] Here Joseph of Arimathea, who certainly belonged to the wider circle of disciples acc. to Mt. 27:57 and Jn. 19:38, but can hardly have known Pilate previously (cf. τολμήσας, Mk. 15:43), is presented not merely as a friend of Jesus [191] but also as a friend of Pilate. Thus two very different friendships are brought under the one term "friend," which is admittedly a fairly broad master-concept in all languages.

---

185 E.g., Gn. 15:1-6 (Jub. 19:9), or Gn. 22:9 f., cf. Jm. 2:21. Other ref. to the title relate to other events: Gn. 15:7-21 (cf. 13:16; 22:17) in 4 Esr. 3:14; Apc. Abr. 9:6, Gn. 12:1 ff. in 1 Cl., 10, 1 f. and Gn. 18:1-8 in Cl. Al. Strom., IV, 17, 105, 3.

186 Elsewhere related but different reasons are given, e.g., because Abraham trusted God and proved himself in all temptations, Jub. 19:9, because he sought God, Apc. Abr. 9:6, because he kept God's commandments, Damasc. 3:2 (4:2), because he obeyed God, 1 Cl., 10, 1, cf. Bas. Contra Eunomium, V (MPG, 29 [1857], 752c), in virtue of his faith and hospitality, Cl. Al. Strom., IV, 17, 105, 3 in free quotation of 1 Cl., 10, 1. Others, too, regard Abraham's hospitality (Gn. 18:1-8) as the reason he was given the title, cf. Peterson, op. cit. (→ n. 178), 173 so that "friend of God" seems almost to be "host of God," cf. Plat. Leg., IV, 716d; Hom. Il., 1, 381; 22, 168 f. For the post-NT period → 170, 1 ff.

187 Cf. Moffatt, op. cit. (→ n. 176), 47.

188 This corresponds to the statistical profile in the LXX and NT → 124, 6 ff.; 128, 1 ff.

189 This singular σύμβολον φιλίας might mean many things, e.g., the true celebration of the agape or Lord's Supper, or the practical achievement of κοινωνία in the sense of Ac. 2:42, or the φίλημα τῆς ἀγάπης → 139, 23 ff., or the use of the address "friend" or "brother" and the corresponding life, or the laying down of life for friends (Jn. 15:13 → 166, 4 ff.), or even foot-washing.

190 Hennecke[3] I, 121.

191 Cf. the use of φίλος for the broader circle around Jesus in Jn. 11:11 → 165, 16 ff.

2. The divine friendship of Abraham (→ 167, 12 ff.) is often ref. to in the post-NT period, cf. 1 Cl., 10, 1; 17, 2; Ps.-Cl. Hom., 18, 13; Tert. Adv. Judaeos, 2 (CSEL, 70 [1942], 256). Acc. to Alexander Polyhist. in Eus. Praep. Ev., 9, 19, 2 (Apollonius) Molon. took the name Abraham to mean πατρὸς φίλος and he equated this with θεοῦ φίλος. [192] Moses, too, was sometimes called God's friend; thus Greg. Nyss. thinks friendship with God was the goal and climax of his ascent. [193, 194] More common is the collective use of the title, → 158, 24 ff.; n. 182. Thus Aphrahat in Hom., 17, 3 [195] says that God describes the men in whom He is well-pleased, like Moses, as "my children and friends." [196] Cl. Al. Prot., 12, 122, 3 can even apply the syllogism of Diogenes in Diog. L., VI, 37 to man in gen., so that man is the friend of God. [197] Cl. Al. Strom., VII, 68, 1. 3 calls true Gnostics "friends of God," while Tert. De poenitentia, 9 and Cyprian Ad Demetrianum, [198] 12 use the term for martyrs, and Aug. Conf., 8, 6, 15 (CSEL, 33 [1896], 182 f.) thinks in terms of ascetics. ὁ θεοῦ φίλος is the title of a bishop in a 3rd cent. inscr. from Isaura Nova in Asia Minor. [199]

3. The name of friend which Jesus conferred on His more immediate disciples acc. to Lk. 12:4 and Jn. 15:14 f. (→ 163, 16 ff.; 165, 18 ff.) undergoes extension and alteration to the degree that in the apocr. apostolic writings it acquires in part a mystico-gnostic and in part an erotic nuance. Mart. Pt., 10 in its seven-membered list of Christ-predicates is trying to characterise the close relation of the disciple to his Master from every possible standpt.: σύ μοι πατήρ, σύ μοι μήτηρ, σύ μοι ἀδελφός, σὺ φίλος, σὺ δοῦλος, σὺ οἰκονόμος· σὺ τὸ πᾶν καὶ τὸ πᾶν ἐν σοί → n. 207. In Act. Jn., 113 Jn. in his dying prayer claims for himself a φιλία ἄσπιλος with Jesus. In some preceding depictions of this φιλία, esp. 89 f., it has an almost homosexual colouring (→ n. 173), appealing to the physical proximity which Jesus allowed in the case of the beloved disciple, Jn. 13:23, cf. 20:2 → 131, 9 ff.

4. A special problem was posed for Christians by φιλίαι ἐθνικαί, i.e., friendships with non-Christians contracted either in pre-Chr. days or later. These often seemed to be incompatible with the principles of the Chr. life and carried with them dangers to the maintaining of a Chr. ethos. Hence Herm. m., 10, 1, 4 groups such φιλίαι ἐθνικαί with πλοῦτος etc. among the πραγματεῖαι τοῦ αἰῶνος τούτου (cf. 2 Tm. 2:4) which burden an incomplete Chr. state and should thus be avoided by the advanced. This is why, e.g., Paulinus of Nola broke all ties with non-Chr. friends, esp. Ausonius, after his conversion. [200]

---

[192] Cf. E. H. Gifford, Eusebii Pamphili Evang. Praep., IV (1903), 303; H. Rönsch, "Abraham der Freund Gottes," ZwTh, 16 (1873), 587-590, cf. 583-6.

[193] Greg. Nyss. De vita Moysis, II (ed. H. Musurillo - W. Jaeger, VII, 1 [1964], 144 f.).

[194] Cf. Plat. Resp., X, 621c, where the supreme goal is ἵνα καὶ ἡμῖν αὐτοῖς φίλοι ὦμεν καὶ τοῖς θεοῖς.

[195] Cf. G. Bert, TU, 3 3/4 (1888), 280.

[196] Aphrahat (→ n. 195) Hom., 17, 8 (p. 288 f.) expressly relates these OT par. to the saying of Jesus to His disciples in Jn. 15:15: "I have called you friends."

[197] Cf. Harnack Miss., 433, n. 6.

[198] Ed. W. Hartel, CSEL, 3, 1 (1868), 360.

[199] Cf. Harnack Miss., 433, n. 6; 779, n. 1, where the background is sought in a use in the pagan priesthood. The history of the idea of divine friendship continues through the M. Ages to the present, cf. Egenter, op. cit. (→ n. 178); F. X. Kessel, Art. "Gottesfreunde," Kirchenlex., V² (1888), 893-900. In the Koran, e.g., Sura 4, 124, el-Chalil "friend" (sc. of God) is constantly used of Ibrahim (Abraham), cf. Speyer, op. cit. (→ n. 178), 172 f. with further examples. Even to-day the Arabs call Hebron (which is close to Mamre, Gn. 13:18; 23:19), el-Chalil.

[200] A. Boulanger, "Saint Paulin de Nole et l'amitié chrét.," Vigiliae Christ., 1 (1947), 184; cf. also the attitude of Nonna, mother of Greg. Naz., to her pagan relatives and friends → 142, n. 249. There are similar warnings in the Koran, Sura, 9, 23, cf. 5, 56. 62. 83; 60, 9. 13 etc.

The friendships suitable for Christians are of a new kind [201] quite different from pagan friendships with their dangerous religious and moral implications. [202] True friendship between Christians is based on two-sided communion with Christ. Hence Paulinus of Nola writes to his friend Sulpicius Severus: *totus es meus in Christo domino, per quem sum invicem tuus.* [203] Paulinus had a singular and very close friendship with St. Felix, who was interred at Nola, cf. the Carmina Natalicia (thirteen poems on the feast of the saint) → n. 20.

5. The heavenly original of a circle of friends is depicted in Herm. s., 5, 2, 6 - 5, 3 in one of his incomplete [204] similitudes. It is obviously modelled on the rulers and nobles of the Hell.-Roman world around which larger groups of friends clustered who were also their advisers → 147, 13 ff.; 154, 22 ff. Here too, then, the δεσπότης (sc. God), is surrounded by φίλοι who at all times can be summoned as His σύμβουλοι, s., 5, 2, 6. 11. In answer to the question of the seer in s., 5, 4, 1 it is then explained that these φίλοι are οἱ ἅγιοι ἄγγελοι οἱ πρῶτοι κτισθέντες, 5, 5, 3, the ref. being (v., 3, 4, 1) to the archangels to whom the whole creation is committed and who will perfect the Church.

II. Gnosticism. [205]

A special Gnostic vocabulary of friendship is reflected in the many conversations between the Redeemer and the redeemed. Thus in the Manichaean member-hymns [206] the Redeemer says: Thou art my beloved, the love in my members. Man also calls the Redeemer "friend" [207] in the sense of "friend of lights, i.e., beings of light." [208] This two-sided address expresses the reciprocity → 115, n. 20; 133, 25 ff.) of love and friendship [209] in the sense of the Gnostic *unio mystica* between the Gnostic and his Redeemer.

Stählin

---

[201] Hence Paulinus seems to think that *amicitia* is not a suitable word for Christians; he prefers *dilectio, caritas* or *pietas*, cf. Boulanger, *op. cit.*, 184.

[202] On the problem of friendship in the fathers → Vischer, 173-200 and monographs on the ideals of friendship of individual fathers, e.g., Fabre, 137-154; Treu Freundschaft; Treu Φιλία, 421-7. Teixeira de Pascoaes, *Hieronymus der Dichter d. Freundschaft* (1941) deals more poetically with Jerome's friendships with Bonosus, Rafinus, Heliodorus etc.

[203] In Boulanger, *op. cit.*, 185; cf. Fabre, 217-228.

[204] Cf. the fact that a little later in s., 5, 5, 3 the χάρακες "posts" and φίλοι are taken to be the angels.

[205] Cf. C. Colpe, "Die religionsgeschichtliche Schule," FRL, 78 (1961), 70 f., 83 f. 94 f., 97; Wetter, *op. cit.* (→ n. 164), 63, n. 2; Bultmann J., 419, n. 3.

[206] In Colpe, *op. cit.* (→ n. 205), 83 f., 94.

[207] There may well be Gnostic influence when Christ is called σὺ φίλος by Peter in Mart. Pt. 10 (→ 170, 18 ff.), cf. E. Käsemann, "Das wandernde Gottesvolk," FRL, 55² (1957), 97, with n. 4.

[208] Colpe, *op. cit.* (→ n. 205), 83 and 70 f.

[209] *Ibid.*, 94.

φιλήδονος   → II, 909, 24 ff.
φιλοξενία, φιλόξενος   → V, 1, 1 ff.

---

† φιλοσοφία, † φιλόσοφος

Contents: A. Greek Usage outside the Bible: 1. From the Beginnings to Sophism; 2. Plato and Aristotle; 3. The Schools of the Hellenistic Period; 4. The Use of the φιλοσοφ- Group in Relation to Oriental Wisdom and the Religious Sphere. B. Hellenistic Judaism: 1. Septuagint; 2. Epistle of Aristeas; 3. Philo; 4. Josephus. C. Rabbinic Judaism. D. New Testament. E. Gnosticism. F. Apologists.

A. Greek Usage outside the Bible.

1. From the Beginnings to Sophism.

The nominal compound φιλόσοφος and the related words φιλοσοφέω and φιλοσοφία are comparatively late constructs attested in the Ionic field from the 5th cent.[1] The dominant first member φιλο- is to be taken verbally as in compounds of the stem μισο-.[2]

φ ι λ ο σ ο φ ί α. Bibl.: A.: A. Bonhöffer, *Epictet u. d. Stoa* (1890), 1-28; W. Burkert, "Platon oder Pythagoras? Zum Ursprung d. Wortes 'Philosophie,'" *Hermes,* 88 (1960), 159-177; T. Hopfner, "Orient u. griech. Philosophie," Beih. z. AO, 4 (1925); W. Jaeger, *Paideia. Die Formung d. griech. Menschen,* I⁴ (1959); II³ (1959); III³ (1959); also *Aristoteles²* (1955); also "Platos Stellung im Aufbau d. griech. Bildung," *Humanistische Reden u. Vorträge²* (1960), 117-157; also "Über Ursprung u. Kreislauf d. philosophischen Lebensideals," *Scripta minora,* I (1960), 347-393; A. M. Malingrey, "'Philosophia.' Étude d'un groupe de mots dans la littérature grecque, des Présocratiques au IVe siècle après Chr.," *Études et commentaires,* 40 (1961); W. Nestle, "Spuren d. Sophistik bei Isoc.," *Griech. Stud.* (1948), 451-501; M. Pohlenz, *Die Stoa. Geschichte einer geistigen Bewegung,* I³ (1964); II³ (1964); K. Reinhardt, Art. "Poseidonios," Pauly-W., 22 (1953), 558-826; Reitzenstein Hell. Myst., 236-240; E. Schwartz, *Ethik d. Griechen* (1951), 119 f., 214 f.; F. Überweg, *Grundriss d. Gesch. d. Philosophie, I: Das Altertum,* ed. K. Praechter¹² (1926), Index, *s.v.* "Philosophie"; Wendland Hell. Kult., Index, *s.v.* "Philosophie"; E. Zeller, *Die Philosophie d. Griechen,* I⁷ (1923); II, 1⁵ (1922); II, 2⁴ (1921); III, 1⁵ (1923); III, 2⁵ (1923). B.: E. Bréhier, *Les idées philosoph. et relig. de Philon d' Alexandrie³* (1950); P. Dalbert, "Die Theol. d. hell.-jüd. Missionsliteratur," *Theol. Forschung,* 4 (1954); I. Heinemann, *Philons gr. u. jüd. Bildung* (1932); R. Marcus, "Hell. Jewish Lit.," *The Jews, Their History, Culture and Religion,* ed. L. Finkelstein, II² (1955), 1100-1114; J. Pascher, Η ΒΑΣΙΛΙΚΗ ΟΔΟΣ. Der Königsweg zu Wiedergeburt u. Vergottung bei Philon v. Alex.," *Stud. z. Gesch. u. Kultur d. Altertums,* 17, 3/4 (1931), 29 ff., 88 ff.; Schl. Theol. d. Judt., 233 f.; H. A. Wolfson, *Philo,* I-II³ (1962), Index, *s.v.* "Philosophy." C.: J. Guttmann, *Die Philosophie d. Judt.* (1933); S. Liebermann, *Hellenism in Jewish Palestine* (1950), 100 ff. and 180 ff. D.: G. Bornkamm, "Die Offenbarung d. Zornes Gottes," *Das Ende des Gesetzes⁵* (1966), 18 f.; also "Die Häresie d. Kol." *ibid.,* 139-156; W. D. Davies, "Paul and the Dead Sea Scrolls: Flesh and Spirit," *Christian Origins and Judaism* (1962), 145-177; also "Reflexions on Tradition: The Aboth Revisited," *Festschr. J. Knox* (1967), 127-159; M. Dibelius, "Pls. auf dem Areopag," *Aufsätze z. Ag.,* FRL, 42³ (1957), 29-70; W. Eltester, "Gott u. d. Natur in d. Areopagrede," *Festschr. R. Bultmann,* ZNW Beih., 21² (1957), 202-227; also "Schöpfungsoffenbarung u. natürliche Theologie im frühen Christentum," NTSt, 3 (1956/57), 93-114; B. Gärtner, "The Areopagus Speech and Natural Revelation," *Acta Seminarii Neotest. Upsaliensis,* 21 (1955); Haench. Ag. on 17:16-34; H. Hommel, "Platonisches bei Lk.," ZNW, 42 (1949), 70-81. E.: H. A. Wolfson, *The Philosophy of the Church Fathers* (1956), 559-574. F.: W. Jaeger, *Das frühe Christentum u. d. griech Bildung* (1963), 20-26.

[1] Malingrey, 38; Thes. Steph., VIII, Pass., Pape, Herwerden, Liddell-Scott, Δ.Δημητράκος, Μέγα Λέξικον τῆς Ἑλληνικῆς γλώσσης, 9 (1953), Pr.-Bauer, *s.v.*
[2] Schwyzer, I, 442 with n. 3.

It occurs already with a noun in Hom., Hes. and Pind. and can also be used with an adj. [3] It denotes willing intercourse with people, zealous handling of things, [4] and striving towards a worthwhile goal. [5] From the 6th cent. B.C. onwards there arose in Ionia, in competition with mythological cosmogonies, the question of the ἀρχή (→ I, 480, 1 ff.), of a being underlying the multiplicity of things. Aristot. sees here the start of philosophy, Metaph., 1, 3, p. 983b, 6 - 984a, 18. The first instance of the word φιλόσοφος is in Heracl. Fr., 35 (Diels, I, 159): χρὴ γὰρ εὖ μάλα πολλῶν ἵστορας φιλοσόφους ἄνδρας εἶναι. It is said in a fr. that variety of personal experience is necessary for "men who strive for knowledge." [6] Practical political experience is won by "observation" θεωρία of foreign lands and peoples, Hdt., I, 30, 1 f. In both cases φιλοσοφέω is used in the sense of ἱστορέω (→ III, 391, 12 ff.). [7] In Hippocr. Vet. Med., 20 (CMG, I, 1, p. 51) [8] there is ref. to a medical school that does not build its medicine on the collection of empirical data alone but makes it dependent on knowledge of the whole man. [9] In all cases the worthwhile goal is a specific and comprehensive whole.

In the Sophist enlightenment man's action is considered critically. Pedagogy, ethics and politics are now the main themes of worthwhile knowledge. In a written copy of Sophist lectures dating from c. 400 B.C. [10] φιλοσοφέω is used in the sense of methodical reflection and investigation in relation to ethical knowledge, Δισσοὶ λόγοι, 1, 1 (Diels, II, 405). [11] That φιλοσοφία and φιλοσοφέω were current terms in the cultural life of Athens may be seen esp. from the orations of Isoc. [12] On a Sophist basis he denies to man the capacity for genuine knowledge ἐπιστήμη, Or., 15, 271. What a thing is, is not important; everything depends on what it appears to be δόξα. [13] The wise man can reach a successful decision on the basis of outward appearance, 12, 30. The φιλόσοφος is the man who studies things which will give him this practical insight, 15, 271 f. Since success depends on the ability to present a thing practically, φιλοσοφία consists primarily in learning rhetoric, 4, 10. [14] In Sophism a great part was played by disputations φιλοσόφων λόγων ἅμιλλαι in which the aim was to present something as either true or false on the basis of etym. and logical factors. [15]

---

[3] Important in this connection is the group φιλόκαλος, Gorg. Fr., 6 (Diels, II, 286, 12); Xenoph. Cyrop., I, 3, 3; II, 1, 22; Plat. Phaedr., 248d, φιλοκαλέω, Thuc., II, 40, 1 and φιλοκαλία, Aristoxenus Fr., 40 (ed. F. Wehrli, Die Schule d. Aristot.: Aristoxenus [1945]. 20). Cf. also φιλάγλαος, Pind. Pyth., 12, 1; Bacchyl., 18, 60.

[4] The Trojans regard themselves as φιλοπτόλεμος for battle, Hom. Il., 16, 90; the Phaeacians are active in sailing φιλήρετμος, Hom. Od., 5, 386.

[5] Civilised peoples practise hospitality φιλόξεινος, Hom. Od., 6, 121. Striving for possessions φιλοκτέανος, Hom. Il., 1, 122, gain φιλοκερδής, Theogn., 1, 199; Pind. Isthm., 2, 6, victory φιλόνικος, Pind. Olymp., 6, 19; Xenoph. Mem., II, 6, 5, and honour, ibid., II, 3, 16; Aristot. Eth. Nic., IV, 10, p. 1125b, 9 can be expressed by compounds with φιλο-, Burkert, 172, n. 2.

[6] On σοφός and σοφία (→ VII, 467, 14 ff.) before Plato cf. B. Snell, "Die Ausdrücke f. den Begriff des Wissens in d. vorplat. Philosophie," PhU, 29 (1924), 1-19; W. Nestle, Vom Mythos zum Logos (1940), 14-17.

[7] Cf. Nestle, op. cit., 507; Malingrey, 38.

[8] This tractate shows the influence of Protagoras and probably belongs to the second half of the 5th cent., cf. W. Nestle, Griech. Geistesgesch. (1944), 146.

[9] The representatives of this school are called ἰητροὶ καὶ σοφισταί in Hippocr. Vet. Med., 20 (CMG, I, 1, p. 51).

[10] Cf. Diels, II, 405, n. 1.

[11] The ref. is to investigations of the principles of ethics. Cf. also Δισσοὶ λόγοι, 9, 1 (Diels, II, 416).

[12] While the body is developed by physical education, παιδοτριβική, the aim of φιλοσοφία is to make the soul wise, φρόνιμος, Isoc. Or., 15, 181, cf. E. Mikkola, Isokrates (1954), 202 f.; E. Buchner, Der Panegyrikos d. Isokrates, Historia, Einzelschr., 2 (1958), 54 f.

[13] Nestle, 455.

[14] φιλοσοφία does not itself denote rhetoric; we must supplement it ἡ περὶ τοὺς λόγους φιλοσοφία. Isoc. ranks this with other skills, τέχναι, Or., 4, 10.

[15] In Plat. Euthyd., 304a b eristics is mentioned as an area of Sophist training, cf. Nestle, 461 f.; Burkert, 173.

2. Plato and Aristotle.

a. Plato's starting-point in the idealistic period is an interpretation of Socrates' criticism of all supposed knowledge in virtue of "divine ignorance," Ap., 21a c d; 22d; 29c d; 30a. [16] In his depiction the figure of Socrates and Eros fuse with the φιλόσοφος, Symp., 203a b; 204a b, cf. also ὄρεξις and φιλοσοφία, Ps.-Plat. Def., 414b. To express the way that man is part of the ideal and immutable being of ideas Plato adopts the oriental motif of the transmigration of souls as this had been handed down in the Orphic mysteries, Pythagoras and Emped. In the process the group φιλοσοφ- comes to denote a fundamental possibility of life. Resort to λόγοι, "rational speeches," Phaed., 99e, in διαλέγεσθαι (→ II, 93, 36 ff.), in dialogical-dialectical thought, Resp., VI, 510e-511c; VII, 532a-d, changes man in his totality. [17] This takes place in concrete encounter with a philosophical man who is capable of instruction; παιδεία is περιαγωγή, the "reorientation" of existence, Resp., VII, 518b-519a. [18] It is in keeping that the Platonic school, as the dialogues of Plato show, took on the character of a living fellowship and was as such a model for the later philosophical schools. Plato criticises the purely theoretical attitude of Socrates and of his own idealism and makes practical actualisation a criterion of properly understood philosophical speculation, Resp., VII, 519d-520c; 540a. The connection between striving for truth and educational and political action constitutes the heart of φιλοσοφία as Plat. understood it here.

b. Aristot. uses the verb φιλοσοφέω for methodical attempts to understand the world around man εἰς ἐπίσκεψιν τῶν ὄντων ἐλθόντας καὶ φιλοσοφήσαντας περὶ τῆς ἀληθείας, Metaph., 1, 3, p. 983b, 2. It denotes esp. knowledge of the sensorily perceptible reality of the κόσμος. The goal of the epistemological process, which progresses from the near to the distant, is the reduction of phenomena to basic principles, 1, 3, p. 983a, 24 ff. Although reality in its total compass is the object of investigation φιλοσοφία, [19] the knowledge of eternal and unmoved or general being has priority, 5, 1, p. 1026a, 19-23. [20] This is expressed in statements on systematising arrangement within the totality of knowledge. φιλοσοφία means on the one side knowledge as a whole καὶ τοσαῦτα μέρη φιλοσοφίας ἐστὶν ὅσαιπερ αἱ οὐσίαι, 3, 2, p. 1004a, 3 and on the other side the individual discipline, 5, 1, p. 1026a, 18 f. and it can be used interchangeably with ἐπιστήμη, ibid., 22. [21] πρώτη φιλοσοφία or ἐπιστήμη is the name of the science devoted to the unmoved mover, ibid., 29 f. It can be called θεολογικὴ ἐπιστήμη, ibid., 19 and 10, 9, p. 1064b, 3. [22] In distinction from the πρώτη φιλοσοφία, physics as the δευτέρα φιλοσοφία investigates the reality that may be perceived with the senses, 6, 11, p. 1037a, 14-16, or moved being, 5, 1, p. 1025b, 26 f.; 1026a, 12; 10, 3, p. 1061b, 6 f.; 11, 1, p. 1069a, 36 f. [23] Over against the two theoretical disciplines of

---

[16] In contrast to Sophist pragmatism on the basis of appearance Socrates tries to establish true criteria for moral action in the *polis* and shows the worthlessness of the false standards of his fellow-citizens. This task, imposed on him by the Delphic deity, Plat. Ap., 30a, is repeatedly called φιλοσοφέω; on each occasion a description is added to stress the critical aspect.

[17] Cf. on this K. Gaiser, *Platons ungeschriebene Lehre* (1963), 1-38.

[18] Following M. Heidegger, R. Schaeffler, *Die Struktur der Geschichtszeit* (1963), 49-67 works out in detail the existential character of Plato's philosophy.

[19] Jaeger Ursprung, 398: "(Aristotle) extended the Platonic doctrine of ideas into a universal empirical science of being."

[20] The science of being as such is, without addition, the science of the philosopher, Metaph., 3, 2, p. 1004b, 15 f., cf. 21 f.; 10, 3, p. 1060b, 31-34. On the interrelation of the sciences in Aristot. v. Zeller, II, 2, 177-185.

[21] In Metaph., 10, 3, p. 1061b, 5 φιλοσοφία and ἐπιστήμη are mentioned together in the sense of "scientific discipline," cf. also 11, 8, p. 1073b, 4.

[22] Jaeger Aristoteles, 225 f.

[23] If there were no unmoved being, physics, which investigates individual things, would be the only theoretical discipline, Metaph., 5, 1, p. 1026a, 28 f.

metaphysics and physics [24] are the disciplines that teach the shaping of reality ἐπιστῆμαι ποιητικαί and perfect action ἐπιστῆμαι πρακτικαί. [25] There is in Aristot. no comprehensive system assigning a given place to each branch of knowledge. By redefining πρώτη φιλοσοφία as the ontological doctrine of God and by the concept of ἔνυλον εἶδος he laid a systematic foundation on which Hell. metaphysics could on the one side seek a concept for the unity of the world and on the other side bring all reality into the range of its enquiry, using both phenomenological and morphological investigations. [26]

3. The Schools of the Hellenistic Period.

The philosophical schools each had leaders and a specific dogmatics, Diog. L., I, 13-16, 20. This often led to sharp debates between the individual representatives. [27] From this time on the philosophers were the educated section of a people or state and they formed a separate stratum in politics. Thus Polyb., 33, 2 tells of an Athenian embassy to Rome made up of representatives of the most important philosophical schools. The development of systems meant that the individual schools, esp. the Epicureans, could take on esoteric features. At the same time the self-awareness of the philosophers expressed itself in the fact that at all costs they had to be different from the common herd, Dio Chrys. Or., 70, 7 f. In many cases a man would pretend to be a philosopher in order to boast of it and to take people in, ibid., 70, 10. Hence there was constant friction between classical philosophers with an honourable tradition and so-called philosophers without a name, ibid., 72, 2-16. The resultant polemical vocabulary was secondarily adopted by the schools. With the older Academicians and Peripatetics the Epicureans and Stoics represented the most important philosophical schools in the Hell. period. [28]

a. For Epicurus sensory perception is the measure of knowledge, Diog. L., X, 52. An atomistic physics corresponds to this theory of knowledge, ibid., 41. Epistemology and ontology serve esp. to free man from superstitious fear of the gods and of divine punishment, ibid., 76 ff.; Cic. Nat. Deor., I, 25, 69 ff., and to prepare the way for an ethics based on Cyrenaic hedonism. The goal of human culture is passionless ἡδονή, Diog. L., X, 131 (→ II, 914, 7 ff.). ἡδονή is achieved in the fellowship of the school united in φιλία, Gnomologium Vaticanum, 28. 52. 78. [29] φιλία is the determinative life-form of the Epicureans. φιλοσοφέω, the more pregnant συμφιλοσοφέω, and the combination φιλοσοφέω μετά, Epic. Fr., 217 (Usener, 165 f.) take on this sense. If the Epicureans spiritualised the concept of deity in terms of their hedonistic ethics, they still clung to the cultus. A later member of the school, Philodem. Philos., De Epicuro Fr., 8, Col. 1, 3 ff., [30] expressly pts. out how exemplary it is that the gods were invited to the common meal of the group. The educational ideal of the Epicureans is of practical significance for public life to the extent that men are urged to avoid any excessive emotion that might bring about other disorders, Diog. L., X, 139. To keep the mind calm it would seem that Epic. himself

---

[24] Along with theology and physics mathematics is sometimes called a theoretical discipline, Metaph., 5, 1, p. 1026a, 19; 10, 9, p. 1064b, 2 f. In some sense it is between metaphysics and physics since its object is constant but not self-existing, 10, 9, p. 1064a, 32 f.; 5, 1, p. 1026a, 7 f. Cf. Jaeger Aristoteles, 225.

[25] Aristot. detaches ethics from metaphysics. Right action is not governed by the idea of the good but by observation of empirical data, Jaeger Aristoteles, 84-90, 241-270; Jaeger Ursprung, 361-5. The most important ἐπιστήμη πρακτική is politics which relates to the individual citizen as well as the state, Eth. Nic., I, 1, p. 1094a, 27-b, 2. Cf. F. Dirlmeier, Aristoteles, Nikomach. Ethik⁵ (1969), 269 f.

[26] Jaeger Aristoteles, 428-434.

[27] Diog. L., VII, 162 f. tells of conflicts between Aristo, who went over to the Academy, Persaeus, a follower of Zeno, and the Peripatetic Arcesilaus. The Stoic Diotimus, foe of Epicurus, published 50 licentious books which he made out to be Epicurean, cf. Diog. L., X, 3-8.

[28] Schwartz, 149.

[29] Ed. G. Arrighetti, Epicuro opere, Class. della filosofia, 4 (1960), 145. 151. 157.

[30] Ed. A. Vogliano, Epicuri et Epicuraeorum Scripta (1928), 70, cf. 126 f.

advised that entanglement in public life should be avoided if possible: λάθε βιώσας, Fr., 551 (Usener, 326).

b. Early Stoicism was established by Zeno in Athens c. 301 B.C. It explains all becoming by the action of a fashioning principle, φύσις or λόγος, on a passive one, matter. [31] φιλοσοφία takes shape in a strictly integrated system in which Stoicism tries to grasp and master all reality. [32] As in the Academy three μέρη are distinguished: φυσικόν, ἠθικόν, λογικόν, which represent an organic unity, Sext. Emp. Math., VII, 16; Diog. L., VII, 39. Logic is the fence, physics the trees and ethics the fruits, Sext. Emp. Math., VII, 16 f.; Diog. L., VII, 40. [33] With the living out of ethics Stoic teaching reaches its goal. [34] The man who has a concern for right conduct, and who in particular is open to Stoic teaching, is the προκόπτων (→ VI, 706, 10 ff.), a man engaged in moral progress, Chrysipp. in Stob. Leg., V, 906, 18 ff. [35] Placed between the φαῦλος and the σοφός, the προκόπτων reminds us of the Platonic φιλόσοφος (→ 174, 8 ff.). The central significance of moral progress is perhaps the reason why the group φιλοσοφ-, which denotes a theoretical attitude, is rare in early Stoicism. φιλόσοφος is used for a man who works in the three spheres of philosophy, Stob. Ecl., II, 8, 13, cf. Plut. Stoic. Rep., 2 (II, 1033d). [36] Zeno can also use it for the ideal Stoic sage, Plut. Phoc., 5 (I, 743e). [37]

c. While early Stoicism handled the problem of causality with ref. to the doctrine of fate and the possibility of ethical decision, Posidonius gave philosophy the task of probing the basic causes of things in examination of both the microcosm and the macrocosm. The def. of σοφία is broadened accordingly. It is ἐπιστήμη θείων καὶ ἀνθρωπίνων καὶ τῶν τούτων αἰτίων, Philo Congr., 79. [38] This broadening out carries with it a redefining of the relation between individual disciplines and philosophy; the former describe reality and the latter seeks the formal nexus in being. Physics and the sciences deal with the same subjects but from different angles. [39] The individual disciplines, including mathematics, have their own methods of enquiry but build on foundations laid for them by philosophy. Philosophy utilises the results of the sciences but itself works out their principles, Sen. Ep., 13, 88, 24 ff. [40] To express the unity of the three spheres of philosophy, Pos. presented philosophy as a living creature ζῷον, physics being the flesh and blood, logic the bones and sinews, and ethics the soul, Sext. Emp. Math., VII, 19. [41] This grouping of philosophy with the σώματα ἡνωμένα καὶ συμφυᾶ, Plut. Praec. Coniug., 34 (II, 142 f.), results from his doctrine of the organic sympathetic unity of the cosmos. [42]

---

[31] Logos and matter are the two sides of the one being, οὐσία, Pohlenz, I, 68.

[32] Cf. U. Wilckens, "Weisheit u. Torheit," Beiträge z. hist. Theol., 26 (1959), 225 f.

[33] Here, too, we find the comparison with the egg, Sext. Emp. Math., VII, 18, but cf. Diog. L., VII, 40, cf. Bonhöffer, 16 f.; Pohlenz, I, 33; II, 19.

[34] The sequence of the individual parts of philosophy in the course of instruction displays no arrangement in terms of values, Bonhöffer, 17-19.

[35] On προκοπή cf. Pohlenz, I, 154.

[36] Among Chrysipp.'s writings on logic we find (Diog. L., VII, 189) one with the title τὰ τοῦ φιλοσόφου σκέμματα.

[37] Acc. to Cic. Tusc., I, 32, 79 Panaetius spoke of Plato as divine and all-wise, the Homer of philosophers.

[38] Cf. also Quaest. in Gn., I, 6; III, 43; Sen. Ep., 14, 89, 5, and J. Heinemann. Poseidonios' metaphys. Schr., I (1921), 130 f.; K. Reinhardt, Poseidonios (1921), 58; Reinhardt, 641 f.

[39] Pos. thought of himself basically as a philosopher but had a broad grasp of many disciplines. In a special monograph he defended against the Epicurean Zeno the logical character of mathematical proof, Proclus Comm. on Euclid's Propositiones, I, prooem. (ed. G. Friedlein [1873], 199 f.), cf. Pohlenz, I, 214; II, 105 f.

[40] Cf. also Strabo, 2, 5, 2; Geminus in Simpl. Comm. on Aristot. Phys., II, 2 (ed. H. Diels, Comment. in Aristot. Graeca, 9 [1882], 291, 23 ff.); Philo Congr., 144-150, cf. Reinhardt, op. cit. (→ n. 38), 43-58, 222-4; Reinhardt, 644-6; Pohlenz, I, 214; II, 105 f.

[41] Cf. Bonhöffer, 17.

[42] Cf. K. Reinhardt, Kosmos u. Sympathie (1926), 34-54; Reinhardt, 647-657.

For him life in the cosmos shares in the divine spirit which fills, shapes and permeates it. [43] Even animals and plants feel in a sense the universal divine spirit but clear knowledge of God is a privilege reserved for rational man, Dio Chrys. Or., 12, 32 and 35. At the beginning of his development man was fused with the divine συμπεφυκώς, absorbing it with the senses αἰσθήσεις, with primal nourishment τροφή, or the air πανταχόθεν ἐμπιμπλάμενοι τῆς θείας φύσεως. He thus received insight into and understanding of the divine, ibid., 12, 28-30. [44] From this union arose without the mediation of any teacher or mystagogue a "native" ἔμφυτος primal religion common to both Gks. and barbarians, ibid., 12, 27 and 39. As the union dissolved with the lapse of time, "acquired" ἐπίκτητα religions developed in different ages and places, though these owe their force to the primal religion, ibid., 12, 39 f. [45] They are taught by poets, law-givers and artists, but the best prophet and interpreter of immortal nature is the philosopher φιλόσοφος ἀνήρ, ibid., 12, 45 f. [46]

　　d. With the rise of the empire the capital city of Rome became so important culturally that representatives of the various philosophical schools came to teach there. [47] Above all the Epicureans and the later Stoics claimed that they could pass on to a wider public a philosophical basis of culture that would lead to personal salvation. [48] For later Stoicism the work of Chrysipp. is the indispensable foundation of all philosophical reflection. [49] In express opposition to Pos. [50] Sen. denies that the arts and crafts which bring about man's cultural development are the product of philosophy. Ep., 14, 90, 7. Wisdom does not instruct the hands but the spirit magistra animorum, 14, 90, 26. The true object of philosophy is knowledge of the good and the bad, 13, 88, 28, and other disciplines are no help here, 88, 3-17, 29-31. In later Stoicism far more than earlier Stoicism the centre and goal are located in the practical part, in ethics. The orientation of philosophy to life-style finds expression in the corresponding def. [51] Philosophy is the "right way of living," recta vivendi ratio, [52] the law of life, Sen. Ep., 15, 94, 39, concern for rectitude, Muson. Fr., 8 (p. 38, 15f.), cf. Fr., 3 (p. 9, 13-15). Under the empire the special focus of the Stoics was on the process of moral perfection in which philosophical insights are actualised. In the Platonic tradition Stoic instruction is depicted as a process of healing (→ 174, 9 ff.) and philosophy is a message or means of salvation for the soul, Sen. Ep., 9, 72, 6; Muson. Fr., 3 (p. 12, 15-19). [53] The doctrine of εἱμαρμένη explains the interest of the Stoics in

---

[43] Cf. Pohlenz, I, 234 f.; Reinhardt, 808-814.

[44] Iambl. Myst., I, 3 (p. 7, 14; 9, 11) speaks as Pos. does of a native knowledge of the gods, cf. Cic. Nat. Deor., I, 36, 100; Sen. Ep., 13, 90, 44 (viros ... a dis recentes); Dio Chrys. Or., 12, 32; Reinhardt, 810 f.; Pohlenz, I, 227 f. 234; II, 119.

[45] Cf. Reinhardt, 810; Reinhardt, op. cit. (→ n. 38), 412 f.

[46] Cf. Reinhardt, 807.

[47] Schools still continued, of course, in Athens, Pohlenz, I, 280 and 288.

[48] The Stoics emphasise that social status does not exclude anyone from philosophy, Sen. Ep., 2, 17, 6; 5, 44, 1 ff.; Muson. Fr., 8 (p. 39, 14-18). Women can pursue it as well as men, Muson. Fr., 3 (p. 9, 1-13); Fr., 4 (p. 14, 13-19).

[49] Cf. Pohlenz, I, 291 f.

[50] In spite of occasional criticism Sen. neither could nor would escape the influence of Pos., cf. Sen. Ep., 14, 90, 20.

[51] Sen. Ep., 14, 89, 4-6 distinguishes between philosophia and sapientia, the one being "love and striving for wisdom" sapientia amor et adfectatio, the other the perfect good of the human spirit, perfectum bonum mentis humanae, cf. also 19, 117, 12.

[52] Philosophia, inquit, nihil aliut est quam recta ratio vivendi vel honeste vivendi scientia vel ars rectae vitae agendae. Non errabimus, si dixerimus philosophiam esse legem bene honesteque vivendi, Sen. in Lact. Inst., III, 15, 1.

[53] The par. between medicine and wisdom is old, cf. Democr. Fr., 31 (Diels, II, 152); Diog. L., VI, 6. It seems to be a favourite one in Stoicism, Sen. Ep., 5, 50, 9; 9, 72, 6; 15, 94, 24; 19, 117, 33; Muson. Fr., 6 (p. 22, 9) etc.; Epict. Diss., III, 22, 73; III, 23, 30, cf. Bonhöffer, 4 f.; Wendland Hell. Kult., 82, n. 2; J. H. Waszink, Quinti Septimi Florentis Tert. De Anima, ed. with Intro. and Comm. (1947), 111 f. on 2, 6.

popular religion. They borrow the idea of the δαιμόνιον from Socrates and Plato. Diog. L., VII, 151 emphasises: φασὶ δὲ εἶναι καί τινας δαίμονας ἀνθρώπων. συμπάθειαν ἔχοντας. Panaetius had a special understanding of the polytheism of popular religions which sensed and tried to express the operation of the universal logos in natural forces. [54] For Pos. demons were intermediate beings between matter and logos and as such they were manifestations of universal cosmic life, Plut. Gen. Socr., 20 (II, 589b d). In later Stoicism, too, the daimonion plays a role in the gen. sense of the "divine" and it ref. esp. to personal destiny, Epict. Diss., III, 1, 37; IV, 4, 39 and Fr., 11. The Epicureans and Stoics were at one in their concern that education in the art of living should lead to liberation from the stresses of the world; they were so akin at this pt. that they became the bitterest rivals. In particular the Stoics tried to deny any παιδεία to Epic., Dio Chrys. Or., 12, 36; Diog. L., X, 3-8, and to point out to his followers the contradiction between the postulate of personal ἡδονή and the practical human need of communication. In this way they hoped to show the superiority of their own principle of a κοινωνία understood as natural law, Epict. Diss., II, 20, 6-20.

e. Middle Platonism used eclectically elements from the teaching of the Peripatetics, the Stoics and the Neo-Pythagoreans. [55] Acc. to Ar. Did. in Stob. Ecl., II, 49, 8-14 Pythagoras, Socrates and Plato agree in the basic principle that the goal of philosophy is ὁμοίωσις to the divine. Becoming like God is crucially related to man's moral action. [56] With the principle of ὁμοίωσις we find among the Platonists a second def. of philosophy which derives from Plat. Phaed., 64a, 80e, 81a and hence from an Orphic motif. Philosophy is a "practising of death" μελέτη θανάτου. We find this phrase of Plato in Plut. Suav. Viv. Epic., 28 f. (II, 1105c-1106c).

4. The Use of the φιλοσοφ-Group in Relation to Oriental Wisdom and the Religious Sphere.

Alexander's campaign created the external presuppositions for an encounter between Gk. and oriental wisdom. [57] In this period the Gks. discovered in the castes of the Brahmans and Garmans that stratum of the Indian people whose life-style and intellectual work reminded them of Gk. philosophy, Megasthenes Fr., 33 (FGrHist, IIIc, 636-8); Fr., 3 (IIIc, 605). [58] Pos., who through his extended travels came to know several barbarian peoples at first hand, [59] found in their customs and religious practices features which proved to him that among them, too, violent "impulse" θυμός was subject to wisdom. He could speak of philosophical Druids, Fr., 116 (FGrHist, IIa, 305). [60] Perhaps the

---

[54] Pohlenz, I, 197 f.

[55] Eclecticism had its basis in the thesis worked out by Antiochus of Ascalon that the Academy, the Peripatetics and the Stoics agreed in all essential pts., Überweg-Praechter, 465 and 470.

[56] Cf. Überweg-Praechter, 543. For a more precise elucidation cf. Albinus, Didascalicus, 28 (ed. P. Louis, Albinos Epitome [1945]), where the relevant passages in Plato are given.

[57] Cf. O. Stein, Art. "Megasthenes," Pauly-W., 29 (1931), 234; J. Kerschensteiner, Plato u. d. Orient (1945), 1; F. Wehrli, Die Schule d. Aristot.: Klearchos (1948), 50 on Clearchus Fr., 13.

[58] An Indian conversing with Socrates, answering the question in what philosophy consists, says that we cannot know human things if we are uncertain as to divine things, Aristoxenus Fr., 53 (Wehrli, op. cit., 24). The anecdote puts man's integration into the cosmos, which goes beyond what we find in Socrates, under the authority of the wisdom of the East.

[59] Cf. Pohlenz, I, 209 f.

[60] The Druids are described along with singers ποιηταὶ μελῶν and seers. They are philosophers and theologians, Diod. S., 5, 31, 2. They investigate nature and study ethics πρὸς τῇ φυσιολογίᾳ καὶ τὴν ἠθικὴν φιλοσοφίαν ἀσκοῦσιν, Strabo, 4, 4. No sacrifice can be brought without a Druid who as a φιλόσοφος knows the divine nature, Diod. S., 5, 31, 4 f. cf. Pohlenz, I, 210; II, 103; Reinhardt, 823; A. Dihle, "Zur hell. Ethnographie," Grecs et Barbares, Entretiens sur l'Antiquité Class., 8 (1961), 221, n. 1.

substance of the section on the Chaldeans in Diod. S., 2, 29, 2 also goes back to him.[61] These are set apart for the veneration of the gods and they bring their whole lives into relation with wisdom πάντα τὸν τοῦ ζῆν χρόνον φιλοσοφοῦσιν. Similarly Clearchus sees in the Jews the φιλόσοφοι, the philosophical class of the Syrians, which he derived from Indian philosophy ἀπόγονοι τῶν ἐν Ἰνδοῖς φιλοσόφων, Fr., 6,[62] which for its part is connected with the Magi, Fr., 13.[63]

The Herm. writings contain a fusion of elements of Gk. (esp. Platonic and Stoic) philosophy with items of oriental wisdom and mythology. Man's salvation is very closely linked to knowledge μαθεῖν θέλω τὰ ὄντα καὶ νοῆσαι τὴν τούτων φύσιν καὶ γνῶναι τὸν θεόν, Corp. Herm., 1, 3, cf. 1, 26.[64] It is mediated, not by methodical ʾobservation and thought, but by revelation, Hermes Trismeg. Fr., 23, 29 in Stob. Ecl., I, 393, 26 ff.[65] Hermes writes down his revelations out of love for men[66] and piety towards God.[67] They consist primarily in the fact that insight is received into true being and thanks are given to the Creator for this. Reception of the insight mediated through revelation is called φιλοσοφία, Fr., 2b, 1-3 in Stob. Ecl., I, 273, 5-24.[68] The task and nature of philosophy are described similarly in the instruction of Ascl. by Herm. Trismeg., Ascl. Fr., 12 f. (Nock-Fest., II, 311 f.); it is defined as continuing contemplation and holy piety orientated to the knowledge of God *quae sola est in cognoscenda divinitate frequens obtutus et sancta religio*. True philosophy consists, not in investigion with a view to scientific knowledge, but in grateful veneraton of deity, Ascl., 12-14 (II, 311-3).[69] The words φιλόσοφος and φιλοσοφία are fairly common in alchemy.[70] The philosopher, who has insight into the secrets of nature and recognises physical interrelations, can bring about changes and control the corresponding processes of transmutation.[71] In this regard he is not just an expert acquainted with certain processes; he shapes his own life in a manner appropriate to his exalted position.[72]

B. Hellenistic Judaism.

1. Septuagint.

In the LXX the group φιλοσοφ- is confined to Da. and 4 Macc.[73] It does not occur in Wis. At Δα. 1:20 the Hbr. הַחַרְטֻמִּים הָאַשָּׁפִים which is used for the magicians and sorcerer-

---

[61] Cf. Reinhardt, 823 f.

[62] Wehrli, *op. cit.*, 11.

[63] *Ibid.*, 13 with Comm., 50.

[64] The knowledge of God is put emphatically at the end as a climax, cf. Nock-Fest., III. p. XVII.

[65] Cf. F. Cumont, *Afterlife in Roman Paganism* (1923), 121.

[66] Cf. Nock-Fest., III, p. XIX, n. 2.

[67] The written transmission of ancient wisdom enhances its authority, cf. also Herm. Trism. Fr., 23, 66 f. in Stob. Ecl., I, 406, 11-25; Iambl. Myst., I, 2; Hopfner, 79 f.; Reitzenstein Hell. Myst., 129.

[68] φιλοσοφία is the force the soul must master to free itself from the σῶμα, Herm. Trism. Fr., 2b, 1-8 in Stob. Ecl., I, 273, 5 - 274, 20.

[69] Cf. also Herm. Trism. Fr., 23, 43-46 in Stob. Ecl., I, 399, 17 - 401, 9; A. Wlosok, "Laktanz u. d. philosophische Gnosis," AAHdbg, 1960, 2 (1960), 135 f.

[70] Cf., e.g., Zosimus Fr., 6, 5 (Berthelot, II, 121, 8); 6, 7 (123, 1); 6, 8 (124, 2); 6, 9 (126, 2); 6, 15 (130, 19); cf. W. Gundel, Art. "Alchemie," RAC, I, 239-260; E. Strunz-C. M. Edsman, Art. "Alchemie," RGG³, I, 219-223.

[71] Cf. Zosimus Fr., 6, 17 (Berthelot, II, 131, 17); 6, 19 (133, 8). Basic to alchemy is the Hell. doctrine of the constant shifting of forces in the cosmos, cf. Gundel, *op. cit.*, 255; Strunz-Edsman, *op. cit.*, 220.

[72] Attributes are here ascribed to him which distinguish him from other men, cf. Gundel, *op. cit.*, 246 f., 252. Alchemy takes over forms from the mystery religions. Acc. to a work ed. by R. Reitzenstein, "Zur Gesch. d. Alchemie u. d. Mystizismus," NGG, 1919 (1919), 24, 13 ff., the philosopher Comarios introduces Cleopatra into mystical philosophy, cf. also Reitzenstein Hell. Myst., 129.

[73] On its significance in 4 Macc. cf. Malingrey, 93-98.

priests at the court of the king of Babylon, [74] is transl. σοφισταὶ καὶ φιλόσοφοι in the LXX, while Θ has the historically less ambiguous rendering ἐπαοιδοὶ καὶ μάγοι. [75] In 4 Macc. exposition of the Stoic principle that reason is mistress over impulse, 1:1, 7, 13, 30; 2:9; 7:16, [76] is linked to a martyr tradition, 1:10-12, which extols obedience unto death in fulfilment of the Law as a model for Judaism, 7:8-15; 9:6; 13:9; 17:16, cf. 6:20-22, and which teaches that martyrdom is to be understood as an expiation for Israel, 6:28 f.; 17:21 f. In the depiction of the struggle between Antiochus and the martyrs the question arises whether the Jewish worship of God ἡ 'Ιουδαίων θρησκεία (5:7) with all that it entails can be regarded as a rational and natural mode of life in the Hell. sense, i.e., as φιλοσοφεῖν, 5:7-11, cf. μετὰ εὐλογιστίας βιοῦντες, 5:22. [77] The philosophical character of the Jewish religion ἡμῶν ἡ φιλοσοφία (5:22) may be seen from the fact that it practises the three cardinal virtues σωφροσύνη, ἀνδρεία and δικαιοσύνη and teaches εὐσέβεια, thus bringing it about that the true God τὸν ὄντα θεόν alone is glorified, 5:23 f. [78] The authenticity of Jewish philosophy is proved by the death of Eleazar, which shows that he is king over the impulses, 7:9 f. Examples from biblical history and esp. the martyr tradition prove the truth of the Stoic principle that reason rules over the impulses in concrete decision. They also make it plain that the principle finally reaches its true goal only on Jewish soil, 7:18, cf. 9:18. [79]

2. Epistle of Aristeas.

In a symposium in Ep. Ar., 187-300 [80] there is repeated stress on the unqualified recognition of Jewish wisdom and culture by the philosophers of the museum as the leading representatives of Hell. learning, [81] 200 f., 235, 295 f. For their part the replies of the Jewish envoys reflect philosophical insights and esp. the rules of wisdom and experience

---

[74] Cf. Da. 2:2. In Gn. 41:8, 24; Ex. 7:11, 22; 8:3, 14 f.; 9:11 the scholars and magicians at Pharaoh's court are called חֲרְטֻמִּים and for this LXX has ἐξηγηταί at Gn. 41:8, 24 (Θ σοφισταί at 41:24), ἐπαοιδοί at Ex. 7:11, 22; 8:3, 14 f. and φαρμακοί at Ex. 9:11. In Ex. 7:11 חָכָם is transl. σοφιστής. On the meaning of חַרְטֹם cf. Ges.-Buhl, Köhler-Baumg., s.v.; A. Bentzen, Daniel, Hndbch. AT, I, 19² (1952), 18; B. H. Stricker, Oudheidkundige Mededeelingen (1943), 30-34.

[75] Possibly LXX means by σοφιστής and φιλόσοφος the same as Θ, i.e., "soothsayer" and "magician." But there is material Hellenisation in Δα. 1:20 so that σοφισταί and φιλόσοφοι might mean "teachers and investigators" as in the cultural tradition of Hellenism.

[76] On the literary form of 4 Macc. cf. A. Deissmann in Kautzsch Apkr. u. Pseudepigr., 150 f.; I. Heinemann, Art. "Makkabäerbücher," Pauly-W., 27 (1928), 801 f. Some features remind us of Pos., e.g., the def. of σοφία in 4 Macc. 1:16, cf. J. Freudenthal, Die Flavius Joseph. beigelegte Schr. "Über d. Herrschaft d. Vernunft" (1889), passim; Heinemann, op. cit. (→ n. 38), 154-9; also Makkabäerbücher, 803 f.

[77] The tyrant argues with the philosophical-sounding statement that it is wrong to despise the gifts of nature, 4 Macc. 5:8 ff. But the verb φιλοσοφέω has a dubious sound on his lips when he orders Eleazar to philosophise on the truth which is of some use, 4 Macc. 5:11.

[78] The reproach of Antiochus in 4 Macc. 5:8 ff. is refuted by the thesis that the Creator of the world in His natural sympathy allowed the Jews to eat only what is suitable to their nature, 5:25.

[79] ἀλλ' ὅσοι τῆς εὐσεβείας προνοοῦσιν ἐξ ὅλης καρδίας οὗτοι μόνοι δύνανται κρατεῖν τῶν τῆς σαρκὸς παθῶν, 4 Macc. 7:18.

[80] Cf. E. R. Goodenough, The Political Philosophy of Hell. Kingship, Yale Class. Studies, 1 (1928), 52-102; W. W. Tarn, The Greeks in Bactria and India (1938), 425-436; A. Pelletier, La Lettre d'Aristée à Philocrate (1962), 47 f.

[81] Philosophy and rhetoric were pursued at the museum in Alexandria as well as the natural sciences and philology. Thus φιλόσοφοι are mentioned in P. Ryl., II, 143, 3 (38 A.D.); Ditt. Or., II, 714, 4 f. (2nd cent. A.D.); Dio C., 77, 7, 3; cf. Ditt. Or., II, p. 453a, 4. That the king takes part in a disputation is also presupposed in Athen., 11, 85 (493e-494b), cf. E. Müller-Graupa, Art. "Museion," Pauly-W., 16 (1935), 809-811; Pelletier, op. cit. (→ n. 80), 48.

common in Hellenism. [82] The question: "What does wisdom teach?" τί ἐστι σοφίας διδαχή, is answered with the positive form of the Golden Rule widespread in both Hellenism and Judaism, 207. [83] φιλοσοφία thus seems to be orientated to practical living; it consists in properly evaluating and mastering all that happens and doing aright what each situation demands in accordance with the peripatetic requirement of the mean μετριοπαθής, 256. [84] Naturally these rules of Hellenistic living are very closely related to the will of God. Only he who worships God can know and do them, 256, cf. 226 f., 237 f., 251. [85] The Jewish Law should be put in the library at Alexandria as a place where the wisdom of Hell. and the barbarian peoples is collected. [86] In content it accords with criteria that the Hellenist uses to assess and commend barbarian traditions φιλοσοφωτέρα νομοθεσία, 30 f. The attributes ἀκέραιος and θεῖος, which establish and exceed the preceding φιλοσοφώτερος, can be understood in terms of Hell. presuppositions, but to the degree that one can expect on the lips of the supposedly pagan writer they point to the uniqueness of the revelation of God in Israel. [87]

3. Philo.

There is a singular blend of Gk. philosophy and biblical tradition in Philo's works. [88] Philosophical knowledge and biblical wisdom can be compared and related to a great extent. Finally the biblical tradition is hermeneutically elucidated by philosophical exegesis. Thus the Gk. philosophers οἱ παρὰ ῞Ελλησιν φιλοσοφοῦντες teach that the wise were the first to name things, cf. Plat. Crat., 401a b, but Moses says more accurately that names do not go back to several wise men but to only one, the first man to be created, Philo Leg. All., II, 15. [89] What the philosophers say is corrected by biblical wisdom. [90] Biblical teaching and Jewish piety, however, can be understood as a particular form of philosophy, cf. Vit. Cont., 25-28; Mut. Nom., 223; Leg. Gaj., 245; Vit. Mos., II, 211-216. [91] To the educational question much debated in antiquity Philo devotes the work Congr., an exposition of Gn. 16:1-6 in which he tries to explain the relation between

---

[82] Cf. H. Jaeger, "La doctrine bibl. et patrist. sur la royauté face aux institutions monarchiques hellén. et romaines," *Recueils de la société Jean Bodin*, 20.

[83] On the Golden Rule cf. H. J. Hein - J. Jeremias, Art. "Goldene Regel," RGG³, II, 1687-9; A. Dihle, "Die Goldene Regel," *Studienhefte z. Altertumswissensch.*, 7 (1962).

[84] Cf. also Ep. Ar., 285: By exercising restraint in every way the king practises philosophy in his acts and is thus honoured for his good life.

[85] Every answer of the Jewish envoys contains a ref. to God, who is a model for the king, Ep. Ar., 188, 190, 192, 207, 209, 211 and finally determines the course of history, 195, 197, 224, 239. This ref. to God is recognised by the king and the philosophers to be the true strength of their statements, cf. O. Michel, "Wie spricht der Aristeasbr. über Gott," ThStKr, 102 (1930), 302-6. On the historical aspect cf. A. Tscherikover, "The Ideology of the Letter of Aristeas," HThR, 51 (1958), 59-89.

[86] Cf. Pelletier, *op. cit.*, 66-8. On the Alexandrian library cf. E. A. Pearsons, *The Alexandrian Library* (1952).

[87] The sacredness of the Law prevented its being mentioned by authors, poets and historians, Ep. Ar., 31 cf. also 312-6.

[88] Philo came to know Gk. culture in his youth, Congr., 74-6; Spec. Leg., III, 4, but seems to have acquired a more exact knowledge of Jewish traditions only later. Cf. H. Leisegang, Art. "Philon aus Alex.," Pauly-W., 20 (1941), 3-6; Pohlenz, I, 369 f.; Heinemann, 511-574; Wolfson Philo, I, 3-27. Wolfson works in terms of historical tradition and also tries to show the basic significance of Philo's acceptance of the philosophical tradition for a theological hermeneutics.

[89] Moses as πάνσοφος surpasses other philosophers but the attribute ἄλλοι shows that he can be regarded fundamentally as a φιλόσοφος, Philo Abr., 13, cf. Som., I, 141.

[90] Philo's main work is an ongoing comm. on the Pent. to which many of his surviving pieces belong.

[91] Philo can integrate the acknowledged supremacy of the Egypt. people into his argument, Spec. Leg., I, 2. True wisdom is found among both barbarians and Gks., cf. Vit. Cont., 21.

encyclical education and philosophy. [92] With some Stoics [93] he thinks general culture is a prerequisite for acquiring virtue, Congr., 24. [94] The study of encyclical subjects is restricted to a specific age, Agric., 9 and 18. It is not to be done for its own sake, Congr., 77-79. ἐγκύκλιος παιδεία must serve ἀρετή, Congr., 12, 14-19, 128 and this must serve σοφία, Congr., 9. φιλοσοφία can be used for σοφία, Congr., 74-78. This is the true consort, Congr., 152 f., cf. Gn. 16:5, the most perfect study, Ebr., 48-51, the supreme good, Op. Mund., 53 f., cf. Plat. Tim., 47b, the source of goods and virtue, Philo Spec. Leg., III, 186, cf. 192. But Philo can give philosophy a limited position when he subjects it to σοφία; as ἐγκύκλιος μουσική is the handmaid of φιλοσοφία, so is φιλοσοφία the handmaid of σοφία, Congr., 79 f., cf. Mut. Nom., 66-71. [95] While philosophy gives directions as though they were worthwhile for their own sake, the goal of wisdom is that God be glorified, Congr., 79 f., cf. Quaest. in Gn., III, 21. If wisdom is the knowledge of divine and human things and their causes, for Philo knowledge begins with sensory perceptions and leads by way of contemplation of the cosmos to the knowledge and worship of the Creator, Spec. Leg., III, 189, cf. Abr., 163 f. Those who serve being rise up under Moses' leadership to ethereal heights and see the visible place where the unmoved and immutable God stands, Conf. Ling., 96. [96] The relation of σοφία to φιλοσοφία in the hierarchy of knowledge is thus a genuine problem; philosophy becomes the royal way to σοφία. In this differentiation between σοφία and φιλοσοφία Philo is unique in Hell. Judaism. As stages of knowledge the two cannot be separated. σοφία, which reminds us of *sapientia*, is the link between the tradition of Hell. philosophy and that of Judaism. The subordinate function of the fields of philosophy shows that Philo seeks primarily to win through to the truth of the Jewish tradition in his time. He thus separates the goal from the philosophical process of knowledge. Man does not reach the final stage of knowledge unaided. It must be disclosed to him by divine revelation. Moses presses on to the pinnacle of philosophy and is instructed concerning the cosmos by divine declarations, Op. Mund., 8.

4. Josephus.

Jos. makes no gt. use of the group φιλοσοφ-. But the actual instances show that an author had to have philosophical concepts at his disposal if in Rome during the second half of the 1st cent. he wanted to focus the attention of educated readers on Judaism and

---

[92] Cf. Malingrey, 79; Leisegang, *op. cit.* (→ n. 88), 34. Abraham is a student of virtue, Hagar, the Egypt. maid, represents encyclical education, and Sarah virtue itself, Congr., 1-23, cf. 72, 154; Poster. C., 130; Leg. All., III, 244. The exposition reminds us of the favourite comparison (ascribed to Aristo of Chius) of the students of encyclical wisdom with Penelope's suitors, Stob. Ecl., III, 246, 1 ff.

[93] Cf. in Wolfson Philo, II, 529, Index, *s.v.* "Stoics," the sections in which the author discusses Philo's relation to the Stoics.

[94] The relation between προπαιδεύματα and ἀρετή is illustrated by many comparisons from the biblical tradition, Congr., 10; Fug., 183 f.; Agric., 9 and 18. The bibl. passages adduced offer the true reason why one should open oneself to προπαιδεύματα.

[95] On the one side σοφία, as in Wis., is the universal manifestation of the Creator, Fug., 109, embodied in the Mosaic laws, Praem. Poen., 81-84, while on the other, by union with philosophical ontology in its distinction between corporeal and non-corporeal being, Fug., 196, it is related to the philosopher's process of knowledge, cf. Wolfson Philo, I, 255. The historicity of σοφία leads to a vital and indissoluble tension between the concrete and the universal element in φιλοσοφ-. φιλοσοφέω is on the one side allegorical exposition of the Jewish tradition ἐντυγχάνοντες γὰρ τοῖς ἱεροῖς γράμμασι φιλοσοφοῦσι τὴν πάτριον φιλοσοφίαν ἀλληγοροῦντες, Vit. Cont., 28 and on the other side it is speculative consideration of the cosmos ἦν ποτε χρόνος, ὅτε φιλοσοφία σχολάζων καὶ θεωρίᾳ τοῦ κόσμου καὶ τῶν ἐν αὐτῷ, Spec. Leg., III, 1. Cf. Malingrey, 81-91 on this whole matter.

[96] Cf. also Som., I, 62 f. and E. Stein, *Die Werke Philos v. Alex.*, VI, ed. I. Heinemann (1938), *ad loc.*

its history. Jos. occasionally quotes Gk. philosophers as well as poets and historians. [97] In accordance with Hell. usage he employs φιλοσοφέω and φιλοσοφία for the work of the pre-Socratics and barbarian sages and priests, Ap. 1, 14. [98] In his defence of Judaism Jos. adopts the thesis that early Gk. sages were dependent on barbarian wisdom and thus in many respects the Gks. were pupils of the Jews, 1, 162-5; 2, 168. 257. 281 f. [99] Moses, who surpasses all other law-givers in antiquity ἀρχαιότης, set forth the basic insights ἀρχαί for knowledge of God, so that these could be accepted by the wisest of the Gks., 2, 154. But while the Gks. passed on their teaching to only small groups πρὸς ὀλίγους φιλοσοφοῦντες the Jewish law-giver saw to it that all Jews without distinction could have faith in God, 2, 169, cf. 2, 170-5. Sometimes Jos. can use the φιλοσοφ-group for Jewish instruction. [100] When he tries to prove the pointlessness of suicide with philosophical and theological arguments, he calls his discussion φιλοσοφεῖν, Bell., 3, 161, cf. 362 and 382. The one who wants to consider reasons for the statements and rulings of the Law becomes engaged in extensive investigation πολλὴ γένοιτ᾽ ἂν ἡ θεωρία καὶ λίαν φιλόσοφος, Ant., 1, 25. As a priest Jos. knows the teachings on divine and human things contained in Holy Scripture μετεσχηκὼς τῆς φιλοσοφίας τῆς ἐν ἐκείνοις τοῖς γράμμασσιν, Ap., 1, 54. [101] If acc. to Ap. 2, 47 Ptolemy Philadelphus [102] wanted to know the laws and philosophy of the Jews as practised and transmitted by the fathers, this includes the doctrines of God and the origin of the world and also the cultic and social decisions and institutions presented in the Pent. Jos. presupposes a concept of the wise σοφίαν μαρτυροῦντες bound up with the exposition of Scripture, Ant., 20, 264, and showing signs of contact with chokmatism. This exegetical tradition can become a kind of sophistry which detaches itself rhetorically from the object and can be a temptation. Teachers close to Zealotism are often called sophists, Bell., 1, 648. 650; 2. 118. 443. 445. Three motifs are thus to be distinguished: a. chokmatism as a hermeneutical-exegetical understanding of Judaism; b. academic argumentation, which is a basic part of education; c. the academic outworking of Hell. philosophy into which fundamental Jewish convictions can also be integrated. [103] In distinction from Philo the political and institutional element is stronger here. Thus Jos. describes as philosophical schools the religio-political groupings of the Jewish people which constituted its historical strength from the 2nd cent. B.C. [104] He calls them αἱρέσεις in Bell., 2, 118. 137. 162; Ant., 13, 171; Vit., 10, 12, cf. αἱρετισταί,

---

[97] Cf., e.g., Ap., 1, 163-7, 176-182. In Ap., 1, 183-204 Jos. has excerpts from Hecataeus of Abdera, whom he calls a man of thought and action, ἀνὴρ φιλόσοφος ἅμα καὶ περὶ τὰς πράξεις ἱκανώτατος, Ap., 1, 183.

[98] Cf. Ap., 1, 162, which says of Pythagoras that he belongs to the early period and is generally thought to have surpassed all who philosophised in wisdom and piety.

[99] Acc. to Ant., 1, 168 Abraham brings to the Egypt. the arithmetic and astronomy which then pass from Egypt to the Gks.

[100] Jos. has a quotation from the Peripatetic Clearchus in which the philosophy of a Jew is lauded by Aristot., Ap., 1, 176-9.

[101] Many transl. see a ref. to Rabb. exposition of the Torah. C. A. v. Gutschmidt, Kleine Schr., 4 (1893), 411; H. St. J. Thackeray, Josephus, I: The Life. Against Apion (1926), 185; T. Reinach - L. Blum, Flavius Josèphe, Contre Apion (1930), 114. What the Law says about the power of destiny and human responsibility is a λόγος, Ant., 16, 398, cf. Schl. Theol. d. Judt., 33.

[102] In Ant., 12, 99 Jos. sums up the conversation between the king and the envoys in Ep. Ar., 187-300: The king began to philosophise and to ask them about problems of natural philosophy. On the meaning of φυσικός cf. R. Marcus, Josephus, VII (1943), ad loc.

[103] In Ant., 18, 11 it is said that the three schools of the Essenes, Sadducees and Pharisees arose very early among the Jews, Ἰουδαίοις φιλοσοφίαι τρεῖς ἦσαν ἐκ τοῦ πάνυ ἀρχαίου τῶν πατρίων. This strong statement is obviously meant to disqualify the Zealot party as new, cf. Ant., 18, 9 and on this M. Hengel, "Die Zeloten," Arbeiten z. Gesch. d. Spätjudt. u. d. Urchr., 1 (1961), 83 f.

[104] Cf. Schürer, II, 447-475; 579-680.

Bell., 2, 119, [105] or φιλοσοφίαι, Ant., 18, 9. 11. 23. The Essenes are compared to the Pythagoreans in Ant., 15, 371 and the Pharisees to the Stoics in Vit., 12. Jos. wants to show in this way that Judaism is a form of life that does not conflict with the basic forms of divine worship and human society developed in Hellenism.

C. Rabbinic Judaism.

To understand Rabb. Judaism the influence of popular Hell. philosophy and its forms of thought and speech is important on the one side, but equally important on the other is the rejection of motifs hostile to the Rabb. system of instruction and the process of assimilation, esp. in Haggadic materials. Among the gt. no. of Gk. and Lat. loan words used in the vocabulary of the Talmud and Midrash we find the noun פילוסופוס φιλό-σοφος, [106] plur. פילוסופין, TAZ, 6, 7; Gn. r., 61, 7 on 25:6; Eka r. prooem., 2; Tanch. [107] Bereshith, 7 (p. 8b); Shophtim, 12 (p. 113b); פילוספא Aram., bShab., 116b, which occurs in the Tannaitic material but not the Mishna, and then פילוסופיה = φιλοσοφία and the verb התפלסף, which come into Hbr. only in the post-Tannaitic period. The term "philosopher" is employed for representatives of the philosophical schools and also for accomplished orators and royal advisers distinguished for their counsel and wisdom. At points insights from popular Gk. philosophy may be found in the Rabb. writings. Thus we see acquaintance with Platonic thought when the Talmud gives the same example for God's invisibility as does Plat. Phaed., 76d: Even the radiance of the sun cannot be borne by the eye of man, bNid., 30b. Of Stoic derivation, too, is the comparison between God and the soul, which gives life to the body as God fills the world and sees it without being seen, bBer., 10a, cf. Sen. Ep., 7, 65, 23. Here Hell. material known through the scholastic tradition is incorporated into the teaching. [108] The superiority of Jewish instruction to Hell. philosophy is expressed in the many dialogues between Hell. philosophers and Rabb. scholars. Here one sees the influence of a specific style of argumentation. In the apophthegmatic tradition the philosopher is a typical figure like the emperor, bSanh., 39a, 90b, 91a, the governor, bBB, 10a, the heretic, bYoma, 56b-57a; bSanh., 39a, 91a; Gn. r., 14, 7 on 2:7, the Samaritan, Qoh. r., 5, 7 on 5:10 (cf. Wünsche, 76), the proselyte, bChag., 9b and other representatives of the non-Jewish world. [109] He usually challenges the faith or obedience of Israel by a polemical question or thesis. [110] But the attack is repuls-

---

[105] In the earlier account in Bell., 2, 117-166 Jos. does not use φιλοσοφία for the schools but αἵρεσις and εἶδος, which is not very common in this sense, Bell., 2, 119, Thackeray Lex. Jos., s.v. εἶδος. αἵρεσις seems then to have been used for the splitting of the people into groups; the αἵρεσις-αἱρετισταί word group has no negative connotations in this sense, cf. Schl. Theol. d. Judt., 196. The member of a party philosophises, Bell., 2, 116. 119; Ant., 18, 11. 23. The founder of the fourth philosophical school is called σοφιστής, Bell., 2, 118. Jos. is probably criticising hereby its theol. and exegetical position.

[106] Along with פילוסופוס, jJom tob, 2, 5 (61c, 37); Derek 'erez, 4 (Machsor Vitry, 729); S. Dt., 307 on 32:4; Gn. r., 1, 9 on 1:1; 11, 6 on 2:3; 20, 4 on 3:14 we find some variants: פלוסופוס, M. Ex. Bachodesh, 6 on 20:5 (ed. J. Lauterbach, II [1933], 244 f.); פלספוס, bAZ, 55a; פילוסופיס, Midr. Ps. 10:8; פלוסופיוס, jShab., 3 (6a, 62); פילוסוף, Yalqut Shimoni Zeph., 566 (ed. A. Eboli, II [1951], 866b, 15); Mal., 587 (II, p. 873b, 9); פולוסיפות, TShebu., 3, 6 (Zuckermandel, 450); פוליפוס, Midr. Ps. 9:9; 117, 1; פלוסלוס, jAZ, 3, 4 (42d, 48). The last may also be taken as a proper name.

[107] Ed. M. Sundel (1947).

[108] Cf. Guttmann, 51.

[109] Cf. Str.-B., III, 102-104; Bultmann Trad., 42-48.

[110] The most common form of introduction in dialogues is: "A philosopher asked the rabbi," bAZ, 55a, cf. M. Ex. Bachodesh, 6 on 20, 5 (ed. J. Lauterbach, II [1933], 244 f.), etc. An impressive structure was developed: question, answer in the form of a thesis, illustration (appended), climax of the illustration in the form of a divine saying, or in bAZ, 54b-55a

ed by a wisdom-type answer, sometimes in the manner of exegetical argument. [111]

In Rabbinism as in the Gk. schools tradition and succession are built up and nurtured, cf. the similar influence on Pharisaism and the tractate Abot. Gk. philosophical influence may be discerned in Elisha bAbuya, bChag., 15b.

D. New Testament.

1. With the transition from Aram.-Hbr. to Greek and the acceptance of the LXX as Holy Scripture, primitive Christianity had more opportunity to use and develop teachings from the world of philosophy. Concepts and ideas that had had a definite history in philosophical physics and ethics are repeatedly found in the NT, although one cannot say precisely in a given instance how far the NT authors knew the derivation and philosophical significance. The main sources are the language of Hell., enriched with many different cultural elements, [112] certain forms of syncretistic religion and revelation wisdom, and the theology and apologetics of Jewish Hell. as influenced by Platonic-Stoic physics and Stoic ethics. The terminology and thought-forms related to physics are employed esp. in the doctrines of God and creation and in the christology which goes with the latter and which has connections with some wisdom traditions, cf. Jn. 1:1-3; Col. 1:15-17; Hb. 1:3. Expressions and notions familiar from philosophical anthropology and ethics are found in missionary preaching when it is interwoven into accusation and the intimation of judgment, e.g., R. 1:20, 28; 2:15. [113] We also find them in exhortation, e.g., 1 C. 9:24; 11:13-15; Jm. 3:3-5; 2 Pt. 1:5-7. Yet adoption of philosophical terms does not mean unqualified acceptance of their content. Primitive Christianity uses the thought-forms and expressions of philosophy only to the degree that they can contribute to the presentation, elucidation, and establishment of the Gospel. The central theme of the NT message, the declaration of God's eschatological action which brings the history of Israel and the nations of the world to its divinely determined goal, is neither related to philosophy nor dependent on it. [114] On the contrary, it radically calls in question philosophy's own goal of helping to master being with the tools of human thought and contradicts fundamental philosophical ideas by Semitic thought-forms which to a certain extent are an irrevocable part of the message. [115]

2. Col. 2:8 offers the only NT instance of the noun φιλοσοφία. A warning is issued here against false teachers who ensnare the community "by philosophy and

---

(cf. the NT): Philosopher's attack on the basis of a biblical saying, answer by illustrations, conclusion with a text. The development of this kind of argumentation shows that a biblical starting-point may be rationally misunderstood but may still lead to the triumph of a Rabb. view through the assembling of arguments.

[111] Only from case to case can one say whether a genuine discussion is recorded or whether teaching important to the Jewish position is given the garb of a dialogue.

[112] In this regard one may speak of a "Hell. cultural milieu" (H. J. Schoeps, *Paulus* [1959], 23) from which Paul took his philosophical terms either in the early period or during the later mission.

[113] Cf. M. Pohlenz, "Paulus u. d. Stoa," ZNW, 42 (1949), 70-81; Bornkamm Offenbarung, 18 f.; Mi. R.[13], 60, 64, 71 f., 77-84.

[114] The attempt of radical 19th cent. criticism to derive Christianity from the development of secular philosophy and ethics does justice neither to its theology nor to its Jewish Palestinian origin. This idea had now been abandoned and philosophical thought-forms are seen as the hermeneutical horizon against which the NT tradition is expounded. The danger in this method is that of equating the tradition and the horizon. On this whole subject cf. W. G. Kümmel, *Das NT, Gesch. der Erforschung seiner Probleme* (1958), *passim*.

[115] Older research related the sharp statements on wisdom in 1 C. 1-3 to a rhetorical or philosophical penetration of the Chr. message. To-day, however, an attempt is being made to explain them in terms of conflict with a Gnostic christology related to the Jewish sophia myth. Cf. W. Schmithals, "Die Gnosis in Korinth," FRL, 66[2] (1965), *passim;* Wilckens, *op. cit.* (→ n. 32), 205-212; → VII, 519, 1 ff.

vain deceit, after the tradition of men, after the elements (→ VII, 685, 17 ff.) of the
world, and not after Christ." A first point that is clear is that the word φιλοσοφία
must refer to the false teachers whom Col. partly attacks explicitly (2:6-8, 13-23)
and partly tries to meet indirectly by the corresponding positive statements (1:9 -
2:5, 9-15; 3:1-4). [116] Paul is neither thinking generally of Greek philosophy as a
phenomenon of intellectual history nor is he thinking of the classical schools. He
has in mind a specific syncretistic-religious group quite separate from the Colossian
community as a whole [117] and having a dangerous power of attraction for the
community, 2:8, 16, 21. [118] In content the Colossian heresy raises the claim that it
enjoys a special insight into the relation between God, Christ, the angels or astral
powers, and creation. [119] Perhaps in so doing it was not radically rejecting the
proclamation of Christ but supposedly integrating it into a special understanding
of the visible and invisible, and thus establishing a necessary foundation and supplementation for it. [120] The Colossian heresy also imposed a set of rules to control the
lives of those who had received or should receive the knowledge of salvation
imparted thereby. [121] The attack on the παράδοσις τῶν ἀνθρώπων in 2:8, cf. 2:22,
might also suggest that the heretics appealed to a specific way of transmitting their
teaching and were claiming an authority of some importance in the later Hell. period,
namely, that of age and the esoteric. [122] The three characteristics cited, i.e., separa-

---

[116] Cf. Loh. Kol. on 2:8; Bornkamm Häresie, 143; Davies Paul, 145-177.

[117] Basic here is J. B. Lightfoot, *Saint Paul's Ep. to the Col. and to Philemon*[9] (1890),
71-111, 176-178, who tries to connect the Colossian heresy and Essenism. In his view the
warning against philosophy in Col. 2:8 corresponds to the ψευδώνυμος γνῶσις of 1 Tm.
6:20. Lightfoot recognises that the term comes from the false teachers. Whereas Loh. Kol.
on 2:8 simply equates philosophy with familiar Jewish Hell. material, Bornkamm Häresie,
143, building on the materials collected in Reitzenstein Hell. Myst., defines philosophy in
2:8 as "doctrine of revelation and magic." Davies Paul, 158 tries to link the דעה of Qumran
(1 QS 3:13 ff.) with the content of Col. 2:8: The ref. is not just to keeping feasts, sabbaths
etc., but to a new understanding of the world as in Col. 2:8. If Col. 2:8 is to be understood
in terms of Hell. Judaism we should think esp. of Philo's description of the Therapeutae (Vit.
Cont.), who are expressly called φιλόσοφοι, Vit. Cont., 2, and who derive their veneration
of the cosmos from a master-builder δημιουργός. Philo explicitly differentiates this from
pagan στοιχεῖα teaching, Vit. Cont., 3 ff. Cf. "principles of wisdom" τὰ σοφίας δόγματα
in 68. The polemic in Col. has some similarities to Philo's account in Vit. Cont.

[118] The dangerous character of φιλοσοφία is strongly emphasised by συλαγωγέω "to
carry off as booty" (cf. αἰχμαλωτίζω in 2 Tm. 3:6) and κενὴ ἀπάτη "empty deceit";
κενὴ ἀπάτη (without art.) qualifies φιλοσοφία.

[119] Bornkamm Häresie, 143-5 ref. to the mystery texts assembled in Reitzenstein Hell.
Myst. and A. Dieterich, *Mithr. Liturg.*, and assumes a kind of regeneration with invocation
of the elements. Rather different are the mystery-like views and assemblies of the Therapeutae
acc. to Philo Vit. Cont., 25 ff.; their concern was with exegesis and hymns. There is a basic
difference between what Philo thinks and what he presents. He has no thought of divinisation.

[120] As the discussion now stands, the heresy fully accepts the "body of Christ," which
consists of the cosmic elements τὰ στοιχεῖα τοῦ κόσμου and represents the fulness of deity,
cf. Bornkamm Häresie, 141. For the error, equation of the powers of Col. 1:16 with the cosmic
elements (understood as forces and attributes of God) is a necessary presupposition for an
understanding of Chr. teaching. For Paul, however, missionary preaching or baptismal teaching is a necessary presupposition for the doctrine of creation on the basis of the baptismal
event. The structure of theology is thus at issue as well as rejection of syncretism.

[121] Bornkamm Häresie, 147-9 understands the commandments and ascetic rules of the
false teachers (Col. 2:21 ff.) in terms of the syncretism of Judaism. Acc. to Philo Vit. Cont.,
34 ff. philosophising is reserved for the day and taking nourishment for the night.

[122] The phrase ἡ παράδοσις τῶν ἀνθρώπων is directed against a tradition which is
not validated but can be traced back to authorities, Mk. 7:8; Gl. 1:12. Philo Vit. Cont., 26 ref.
expressly to δόγματα τῆς ἱερᾶς φιλοσοφίας and has in view emphatic teachings reached
by exegesis.

tion, theoretical and practical insight into the cosmos, and tradition, show that the error has the features of a religious fellowship to which late Hellenism and Hellenistic Judaism could accord the predicate φιλοσοφία. For this reason we must assume that the word φιλοσοφία in 2:8 is not introduced disparagingly by Paul with reference to the heresy but that the apostle is adopting a designation which his opponents used with a claim to weighty authority [123] and that he sets it aside with the polemical addition καὶ κενῆς ἀπάτης. [124] His decisive contention is that primitive Christianity, in contrast to Philo and Josephus and syncretistic movements like the Hermetica or the so-called Colossian heresy, but in agreement with apocalyptic, never makes the claim that it should be regarded as a φιλοσοφία, although it can present itself as a distinctive form of sophia → VII, 519, 12 ff., cf. 1 C. 2:6.

3. Ac. 17:18 tells of an encounter in Athens between the primitive Christian message and the Epicureans and Stoics, the two most influential philosophical schools of the day. The expression τινές . . . τῶν Ἐπικουρείων καὶ Στωϊκῶν φιλοσόφων, a type of phrase also found quite often outside the NT, denotes philosophers who belonged to the Epicurean and Stoic schools and espoused the teachings of the schools at essential points. [125] The wording of the text suggests that the reactions to Paul's speech as described in v. 18b are the different reactions of the two groups. [126] Whereas the Epicureans reply with disparagement, [127] the Stoics show interest. [128] The juxtaposition of a hostile and a neutral or friendly party among the listeners in a mission or judgment scene is in keeping with one of Luke's rules of composition, Ac. 2:12 f.; 14:4; 23:6; 28:24. But it is also in agreement with the actual difference between the Epicureans and the Stoics. σπερμολόγος (→ III, 604, 33 ff.; IV, 845, 23 ff.) does not simply denote a "mouther of shibboleths" [129] but a "pseudo-philosopher" [130] and it thus carries a ref. to the self-conscious claim of the Greek-Hellenistic schools of philosophy that they were the mediators of true παιδεία → V, 597, 1 ff. [131] It was a principle of later Stoicism to practise fellowship with all men and to honour the gods. To this extent the Stoics were open to Paul and his religious preaching. [132] They grouped him with the wandering preachers who brought oriental deities and cults to Greece. [133] In an argument that fuses biblical and Stoic thought-forms into a unity which is difficult

---

[123] So already Lightfoot, op. cit., ad loc. with a ref. to Jewish Hell. usage.

[124] Cl. Al. Strom., VI, 8, 62, 1 notes already that Paul is not against philosophy in gen. here.

[125] In the MSS we find the variant forms Ἐπικουρίων and Ἐπικουρείων, Στοϊκῶν and Στωϊκῶν, cf. Bl.-Debr. § 35, 1. The plur. οἱ Στωϊκοὶ φιλόσοφοι is less common, but we often find the sing. with a proper name after it. Periphrases occur in the plur., e.g., οἱ ἀπὸ τῆς Στοᾶς, Plut. Plac. Phil., I, 5 (II, 879a), cf. R. Hobein, Art. "Stoa," Pauly-W., 4a (1931), 40-42.

[126] Cf. Haench. Ag.15, ad loc.; G. Stählin, Die Apostelgesch., NT Deutsch, 53 (1968), ad loc.

[127] Cf. Gärtner, 49.

[128] Cf. Haench. Ag.15, ad loc.; Stählin, op. cit., ad loc.

[129] Dibelius, 62 pts. out the difficulties involved in this interpretation.

[130] Cf. Dio Chrys. Or., 32, 9.

[131] Dion. Hal. uses the adj. σπερμολόγος to describe a barbarian who cannot distinguish between the sacred and profane, Ant. Rom., 19, 4, 2; 5, 2.

[132] On the openness of philosophy to religious matters → II, 3, 20 ff.

[133] The expression ξένα δαιμόνια reminds us of the charge against Socrates καινὰ δαιμόνια εἰσφέρων, Xenoph. Mem., I, 1, 1. Cf. also Jos. Ap., 2, 267.

to analyse and which had probably been anticipated in Jewish Hellenism, [134] Ac. 17:22-31 shows that pagan veneration of the gods in the form of temple and image worship was out of keeping with the nature and works of the one true God not as yet known to the Athenians. [135]

The address has the form of an accusation with an appended call for repentance and intimation of judgment, Ac. 17:30 f. There is no debate with Gk. philosophy but rather a criticism of pagan worship which in part uses arguments forged by philosophy itself.

E. Gnosticism.

In later Gnostic thought the word group plays no further part. In the Gk. text of Act. Thom. φιλοσοφία is mentioned twice as a Chr. cardinal virtue, and as love for God's wisdom it stands in contrast to the wisdom of men, 139 (p. 246, 12. 27). [136]

F. Apologists.

As in Hell. Judaism the φιλοσοφ-group is used by the Chr. Apologists to assert the truth-claim of their religion in educated circles. Along these lines their special interest is in the question of the true philosopher, which was much debated in the philosophical schools, Dio Chrys. Or., 49, 8. 9; 32, 9, and their concern is to point to the wisdom of God as contrasted with the "babblings of foolish philosophers," Theophil. Autol., II, 15, 43-48. The task of φιλοσοφία is ἐξετάζειν περὶ τοῦ θείου, Just. Dial., 1, 53. The method of dialectical discussion is helpful in pursuing this task. Without philosophy and proper debate which listens to the arguments of others no one has understanding, Just. Dial., 2, 3. The normative character of the Logos that embraces the world is constantly asserted, Just. Apol., 2, 1-4. If one follows the Logos one attains to acknowledgment of Christ who is the Logos, 46, 2-4. Because Christians let themselves be totally governed by the Logos μετὰ λόγου βιοῦντες, they are the true philosophers, 46, cf. 21 f. [137] Thus the element of presuppositionless critical thought is less prominent in the φιλοσοφ-group, and it becomes an apt basis for mediating the Chr. message.

Michel

---

[134] Cf. H. Conzelmann, *Die Apostelgesch., Hndbch. NT,* 7 (1963), Exc. on 17:32 (with bibl.).

[135] ἄγνωστος does not ref. to the Unknown of Gnosticism, so E. Norden, *Agnostos Theos* (1913), 56-73; along the lines of the Jewish-Hell. understanding, it simply means that pagans do not know God, Wis. 14:22; Philo Decal., 8; Jos. Ant., 10, 143 etc., cf. → I, 119, 26 ff.

[136] Gnosticism obviously avoided the φιλοσοφ-group so as to express its absoluteness over against all philosophical movements and apostolic Christianity. Iren. Haer., I, 20, 4 says: *gnosticos se autem vocant.* Hence the group φιλοσοφ- could be used in an anti-Gnostic sense to ref. to the non-speculative and humble attitude of apostolic Christians. On the relation of Gnosticism to philosophy cf. Wolfson Philosophy, 559-574.

[137] On the use of the group φιλοσοφ- in the Apologists cf. Malingrey, 107-128.

```
┌─────────────────────────────┐
│  † φοβέω,  † φοβέομαι        │
│  † φόβος,  † δέος            │
└─────────────────────────────┘
```

Contents: A. The Word Group Among the Greeks: 1. Derivation, Meaning and History of the Group; 2. General Usage; 3. The God Φόβος; 4. The Evaluation of Fear: a. Fear in Ordinary Speech; b. Fear in Philosophy. B. φόβος and φοβέομαι in the Old Testament: I. Occurrence and Hebrew Equivalents. II. The Stem ירא in the Old Testament: 1. Meaning; 2. Fear in the Human and Earthly Sphere; 3. Fear of God; 4. The Formula אַל־תִּירָא. III. The Stem פחד in the Old Testament: 1. Linguistic Aspects; 2. Material Aspects. IV. Fear in the Old Testament Apocrypha. C. Fear in Palestinian and Hellenistic Judaism: 1. The Pseudepigrapha; 2. Qumran; 3. Rabbinic Writings; 4. Philo and Josephus. D. The Word Group in the New Testament: 1. General Usage; 2. The Epiphany of God's Kingdom and Fear; 3. The Fear of God in Formulae; 4. Faith and Fear; 5. Fear in Exhortation. E. Fear in the Early Church and Gnosticism: 1. The Early Church; 2. Gnosticism.

A. The Word Group Among the Greeks.

1. Derivation, Meaning and History of the Group.

Basic to the group is the primary verb φέβομαι "to flee," which is hardly ever used except in Hom., e.g., Il., 15, 345; Od., 22, 299, and which with the Lithuanian bēgu, bēgti "to run" and Slavic cognates goes back to the Indo-Eur. bheg^u "to run from." [1] From this comes the verbal noun φόβος and then the secondary verb φοβέω, φοβέομαι, which both remain intact and are always felt to be related. At the latest from Hom. on φόβος was regarded as a verbal noun of φοβέω, φοβέομαι. [2] From the original sense of "being

---

φ ο β έ ω κ τ λ. Bibl.: W. Lütgert, "Die Furcht Gottes," Festschr. M. Kähler (1905), 163-186; B. Bamberger, "Fear and Love of God," HUCA, 6 (1929), 39-53; Bü. J., 75-78, Exc. 10: "Furcht u. Liebe"; R. Sander, "Furcht u. Liebe im paläst. Judt.," BWANT, 68 (1935); E. Bernert, Art. "Phobos," Pauly-W., 20 (1950), 309-317; W. Schadewaldt, "Furcht u. Mitleid? Zur Deutung d. Aristotel. Tragödiensatzes," Hermes, 83 (1955), 129-171; C. H. Ratschow et al., Art. "Gottesfurcht," RGG³, II, 1791-8; J. Gruber, Über einige abstrakte Begriffe d. frühen Griech. (1963), 15-39; S. Plath, "Furcht Gottes. Der Begriff ירא im AT," Arbeiten z. Theol., II, 2 (1963); K. Romaniuk, "La crainte de Dieu à Qumran et dans le NT," Revue de Qumran, 13 (1963), 29-38; also "Die 'Gottesfürchtigen' im NT. Beitrag z. nt.lichen Theol. der Gottesfurcht," Aegyptus, 44 (1964), 66-91; J. Becker, "Gottesfurcht im AT," Analecta Biblica, 25 (1965); J. Haspecker, "Gottesfurcht bei Jesus Sirach," Analecta Biblica, 30 (1967), K. Romaniuk, Il timore di Dio nella teologia di San Paolo (1967).

[1] Cf. Schwyzer, I, 717 f.; II, 228 f.; W. Porzig, Die Namen f. Satzinhalte im Griech. u. im Idg. (1942), 35 and 130 f.; Hofmann, Frisk, s.v. σέβομαι; Pokorny, I, 116. [186, 20 - 187, 6 acc. to Risch].

[2] The relation between φόβος and φόβη "mane," cf. Soph. El., 449, is not clear. E. Kapp in B. Snell, Die Entdeckung d. Geistes³ (1955), 303, n. 1 suggests "hair-raising" as the orig. meaning of φόβος, cf. ὀρθαὶ αἱ τρίχες ἵστανται ὑπὸ φόβου, Plat. Ion, 535c; Schadewaldt, 130, n. 3 agrees. A similar development in sense may be seen in the related σέβομαι (→ VII, 169, 8 ff.), where we have an intensive σοβέω "to chase off" and a form σόβη "horse-tail," cf. Frisk, s.v. σέβομαι and σοβέω. On the physiological connection between numinous terror and the raising of the hair cf. K. Lorenz, Das sog. Böse. Zur Naturgesch. d. Aggression³ (1964), 386 f. But the linguistic relation is dubious, since Indo-Eur. has a root for the raising of the hair, Gruber, 15 with n. 3.

startled" and "running away" there developed acc. to the familiar rule, whereby many terms for emotions derive from orig. plastic words for their physical accompaniments, the sense of "fear" or "to make afraid," "to fear."³ If φόβος can still mean "flight" in the poets, e.g., Bacchyl., 13, 145, this is a Homeric archaism. The older word for "to fear," "fear," is the Homeric δείδω, Attic δέδοικα with neut. δέος. This group includes θεουδής "godfearing," Hom. Od., 6, 121 and δειλός, "fearful."⁴ It is worth noting that even later the δέος group denotes "fear," "apprehension," while φόβος is used for "sudden and violent fear," "fright," "panic."⁵

2. General Usage.

The word group carries the following nuances: a. "flight," "terror," Hom. Il., 8, 139; 11, 71; 17, 597, cf. esp. φύζα, φόβου κρυόεντος ἑταίρη, "headlong flight, comrade in terror-stricken flight," Il., 9, 2; ἑστάμεναι κρατερῶς, μηδὲ τρωπᾶσθε φόβονδε (= φύγαδε), 15, 666. "Fear" is already the meaning, it would seem, in 11, 544; 12, 46; 21, 575.⁶ φοβέω means "to put to flight," "to terrify," Il., 16, 689, φοβέομαι "to flee," "to be frightened," 8, 149; 11, 172 etc. φόβος can be personified as "might" which puts to flight, 13, 299 → 191, 16ff.⁷ b. In the post-Homeric period we still find the senses "to frighten," "to be afraid" and "to fear," cf. μὴ φίλους φόβει, Aesch. Sept. c. Theb., 262; of camels ἐφόβουν... τοὺς ἵππους, Xenoph. Cyrop., VII, 1, 48; δουλεύειν καὶ τεθνάναι τῷ φόβῳ Θηβαίους, Demosth. Or., 19, 81; οἱ δὲ σύμμαχοι τεθνᾶσι τῷ δέει τοὺς τοιούτους ἀποστόλους, 4, 45. A god can cause sudden fear to strike an army, Hdt., VII, 10e, cf. τῶν Ἑλλήνων εἰς τοὺς βαρβάρους φόβος, Xenoph. An., I, 2, 18; III, 1, 18; Cyrop., III, 3, 53. φόβος can be the inner obj. of φοβέομαι: οἱ ἀνδρεῖοι οὐκ αἰσχροὺς φόβους φοβοῦνται, Plat. Prot., 360b but also the cause of fear: φόβος γάρ ἐς τὸ δεῖμα... μ' ἄγει, Eur. Hel., 312; φόβος μ' ἔχει, Aesch. Ag., 1243. ἄφοβοι θῆρες in Soph. Ai., 366 are fearless wild beasts that cause no fear.⁸ c. The sense "to fear," "to be apprehensive," is usually found with μή, e.g., φοβούμενοι, μὴ ληφθέντες ἀποθάνωσιν, Xenoph. Cyrop., III, 1, 25, cf. P. Magd., 9, 3 (3rd cent. B.C.); φοβεῖσθαι μὴ τῷ λιμῷ ἀποθάνοι, Teles Fr., 4a (p. 40, 6); φοβούμενος μὴ χειμών[ος τῆς τροφῆς ἐνδέ]ωσιν, Theopompus Fr., P. Oxy., V, 842, Col. 21, 6 f. For constr. with inf. cf. ἐγώ... φοβοῦμαι σοφιστὰς φάναι, "I have scruples in calling them sophists," Plat. Soph. 230e. d. Usually the group denotes the physical emotion of fear or anxiety, e.g., φόβῳ διόλλυται, Plat. Phaedr., 254e; τὸ πάσχειν φοβούμενοι, Resp., I, 344c; Ζεύς μοι σύμμαχος, οὐ φοβοῦμαι, Eur. Heracl., 766. This anxiety is viewed negatively → 192, 16 ff., cf. Aristot. Pol., V, 5, p. 1304b, 23 f. or the proper name Ἄφοβος, Demosth. Or., 27-29. φόβος leads to ἔκπληξις "confusion," Eur. Fr., 67 (TGF, 381) and often comes to expression in fear of death τὸ ἀποθνήσκειν φοβεῖται, Plat. Gorg., 522e. For philosophical teaching on the emotions → 195, 33 ff. Considered speech deals with the relation between φόβος and δέος → 196, 30 f.; n. 5. Socrates can reject the distinction

---

³ M. Leumann, "Homerische Wörter," *Schweizerische Beiträge z. Altertumswissenschaft,* 3 (1950), 13 f.; Gruber, 19-30.

⁴ Cf. Frisk, *s.v.*

⁵ Ammonius (1st/2nd cent. A.D.) stresses the distinction between the sudden and the long drawn-out in his lex. of synon. De adfinium vocabulorum differentia (ed. K. Nickau [1966]), 128: δέος καὶ φόβος διαφέρει. δέος μὲν γάρ ἐστι πολυχρόνιος κακοῦ ὑπόνοια, φόβος δὲ παραυτίκα πτόησις. The basis of this is not the difference between the god Φόβος and his brother Δεῖμος, as Bernert, 309 thinks, for there is no clear distinction in mythology, → 191, 15 ff. Further def. → lines 37 ff.

⁶ Cf. Leumann, *op. cit.,* 14; Gruber, 22-25.

⁷ Acc. to Porzig, *op. cit.,* 35 Hom. can put fright or putting to flight close to the name of the one who causes headlong flight, Il., 15, 326 f.; 16, 290 f., so that here the noun has content but is also a proper name.

⁸ We have here a preciosity playing on the compound against the background of the normal sense of "fearless" [Dihle].

which Prodicos made between the two: προσδοκίαν τινὰ λέγω κακοῦ τοῦτο, εἴτε φόβον εἴτε δέος καλεῖτε... οὐδὲν διαφέρει, Plat. Prot., 358d e, cf. Leg., VII, 798b, and Aristot. can sometimes define φόβος in the same way as he does δέος elsewhere: διὸ καὶ τὸν φόβον ὁρίζονται προσδοκίαν κακοῦ, Eth. Nic., III, 9, p. 1115a, 9, cf. Plat. La., 198b. But Aristot. also emphasises in φόβος the element of λύπη and ταραχὴ ἐκ φαντασίας μέλλοντος κακοῦ φθαρτικοῦ ἢ λυπηροῦ, for he believes: οὐ γὰρ πάντα τὰ κακὰ φοβοῦνται, οἷον εἰ ἔσται ἄδικος ἢ βραδύς, ἀλλ' ὅσα λύπας μεγάλας ἢ φθορὰς δύναται, καὶ ταῦτ' ἐὰν μὴ πόρρω ἀλλὰ σύνεγγυς φαίνηται ὥστε μέλλειν, Rhet., II, 5, p. 1382a, 21 ff. Hence only the closeness of what impends and the greatness of the evil constitute φόβος. In gen. usage, however, we do not find these distinctions. e. Sometimes the group can mean "respect," "awe," "reverence," esp. in relation to the gods or the mighty, e.g., veneration for the gods, Plat. Leg., XI, 927a b → 194, 23 ff.; 196, 24 ff.: "respect" for judgment → 194, 11 ff., P. Lips., 36, 6 (4th cent. A.D.), cf. also Aesch. Suppl., 893; Eur. Med., 1202.

3. The God Φόβος.

In Gk. superstition Φόβος is from primitive times a real and powerful deity. [9] Already in Hom. Il., 13, 298-300 he is given a place in the mythological system as the son of Ares, [10] and he is depicted as a typical war-god, cf. Hes. Theog., 933-6, where he is mentioned with Δεῖμος. [11] Cultic ref. show that this is not just a poetic personification of the one who causes terror. In a votive inscr. from Selinus (5th cent. B.C.) Φόβος is put just after Zeus and before all the other gods: δι]ὰ τὸν Δία νικῶμες καὶ διὰ τὸν Φόβον, IG, 14, 268, 2. [12] We are told that Alexander and Theseus both sacrificed to Φόβος, Plut. Alex., 31 (I, 683b); Thes., 27 (I, 12 f.), cf. also Appian. Rom. Hist., 8, 21, 85 (p. 199), 15); Aesch. Sept. c. Theb., 42 ff. In warlike Sparta there was a temple to Φόβος, Plut. De Cleomene, 8 f. (I, 808b-e). [13] In an anon. later comedy Φόβος takes the stage with the words: ἀμορφότατος τὴν ὄψιν· εἰμὶ γὰρ Φόβος πάντων ἐλάχιστον τοῦ καλοῦ μετέχων θεός, Sext. Emp. Math., IX, 188. [14] Later Φόβος is a less substantial figure. [15] On a black amulet we find the inscr. πρὸς δέμονα[ς] κὲ φόβους, IG, 14, 2413, 8, cf. φόβους... νυχαυγεῖς "shining by night," Orph. Hymn. (Quandt), 3, 14; φόβων ἔκπαγλε βροτείων, 11, 7; φόβων... δεινῶν, 39, 3. [16] Similarly at an earlier time

---

[9] Cf. on this Bernert, 309; A. Dieterich, "Abraxas. Stud. z. Religionsgesch. d. spätern Altertums," Festschr. H. Usener (1891), 86-93; H. Usener, Götternamen. Versuch einer Lehre von d. religiösen Begriffsbildung (1896), 364-375; O. Höfer, Art. "Phobos," Roscher, III, 2386-2395; H. Lietzmann, Gesch. d. Alten Kirche, I⁴ (1961), 285-9; U. v. Wilamowitz-Moellendorff, Der Glaube d. Hellenen, I (1956), 268 f.; Gruber, 15 f., 32-36.

[10] Φόβος and Δεῖμος are not always called the sons of Ares, cf. Hom. Il., 15, 119 f.; 4, 439 f.; 11, 37: Nonnus Dionys., 32, 178 f.; Artemid. Onirocr., II, 34 (p. 131); Bernert, 310 and 312. Athene can also be called Φοβερά "terrifying enemies," cf. Roscher, III, 2385 f.

[11] Terror et Metus accompany Minerva, Apul. Met., X, 32, 4.

[12] Cf. Bernert, 310; Dieterich, op. cit., 92. Φοῖβος with Apollo has nothing to do with Φόβος but indicates the radiant god, cf. Roscher, III, 2398; Gruber, 33 f.

[13] Φόβος is no longer a god of war for Plut. in De Cleomene, 9 (I, 808c-e), but an apparition. Wilamowitz-Moellendorff, op. cit., 274 f. stresses the basic apotropaic sense of Φόβος, cf. Höfer, op. cit. (→ n. 9), 2386; Bernert, 312; Dieterich, op. cit., 91. For further ref. to Φόβος as a god cf. Plut. Amat., 18 (II, 763c); Mulierum virtutes, 18 (II, 255a); Philodem. Philos. De pietate (ed. T. Gomperz, Herkulanische Stud., II [1886]), p. 35, 21.

[14] Cf. Fr. adespotum, 154 (CAF, III, 439).

[15] Bernert, 313 f.

[16] Dieterich, op. cit., 89 f. shows through comparison with similar statements about κῆρες (apparitions) that the φόβοι in the Orphic hymns are not just phantoms but ghostly phenomena, cf. also Nonnus Dionys., 14, 81, where Φόβος is one of the 12 Pans, a magic text in which the φόβοι are mentioned alongside the ἐχθροί, κατήγοροι, λησταί and φαντασμοὶ ὀνείρων, Preis. Zaub., II, 10, 24 ff. (4th/5th cent. A.D.) and Paus., II, 7, 7, where a place is called Φόβος after a phantom → 218, 42 ff.

Φόβος is depicted as an apotropaion in fear-inspiring form, mostly as a device on shields, Paus., V, 19, 4 (lion); Hom. Il., 5, 738-742; Ps.-Hes., Scutum, 144 (snake). [17] With grotesque figures and Gorgons we also find mixed forms. [18] The portrayal of Φόβος as a grotesque creature is a secondary actualisation of Homer's god of terror. [19] Thus at the beginning and at the end of what is said about Φόβος as a martial god we find the phenomenon of terror at the sinister one who causes fear. [20] In later syncretistic religion Φόβος again figures as a god, → 218, 42 ff.

4. The Evaluation of Fear.

Expressions containing words of the φόβος group always describe a reaction to man's encounter with force. The scale of reactions ranges from spontaneous terror and anxiety to honour and respect, which already presupposes mastery of the experience through reflection. Hence evaluation of the reaction of fear is closely bound up with the understanding of one's own existence. It also offers access to the religious self-understanding of specific individuals and groups.

a. Fear in Ordinary Speech.

The nature of the fear that oppresses man and causes him anxiety means that the absence of fear is regarded as an objective worth seeking. Proverbial and popular sayings make this clear. Thus one should not boast but show respect: ὅπως σε αἰσχύνωνται μᾶλλον ἢ φόβωνται, Stob. Ecl., III, 117, 2; cf. δόλον φοβοῦ, III, 126, 3. Riches do not free from fear φόβου ἀπαλλάττει, ἀλλὰ λογισμός, III, 101, 4 f. The epitome of the proverbs περὶ δειλίας assembled in Stob. Ecl., III, 340, 9 - 346, 11 lies in the statement ἅπαντα γάρ τοι τῷ φοβουμένῳ ψοφεῖ "makes a (terrifying) noise," III, 341, 1. Only δοῦλοι do the right διὰ φόβου, the free δι' αἰδῶ καὶ τὸ καλόν, Zaleucus in Stob. Ecl., IV, 127, 8 ff., cf. 124, 13 f. Eur. Andr., 142 is to the same effect: φόβῳ δ' ἡσυχίαν ἄγομεν, "fear immobilises us." The englightened exhortations of Isocrates try to ignore fear in the sense of anxiety, though → 193, 21 ff. Rule over others μετὰ φόβων καὶ κινδύνων καὶ κακίας is rejected, Or., 2, 26. Avoidance of φόβοι should govern action, 3, 52. One should spare citizens τοὺς πολλοὺς φόβους, 2, 23, while true ἀρετή cheerfully accepts what appears τῷ πλήθει φοβερά, 1, 7. For the σπουδαῖοι to fear is finally only ἡ ἐν τῷ ζῆν ἀδοξία, 1, 43. Philosophical interests, of course, play some part in Isoc. → 195, 8 ff.

There is a different understanding of fear in Gk. tragedy. Here the characters are filled with dread of the unknown future or the awfulness of fate: ἀμηχανῶ δὲ καὶ φόβος μ' ἔχει φρένας, Aesch. Suppl., 379; κραδία δὲ φόβῳ φρένα λακτίζει, Prom., 883, cf. 695 f. and Suppl., 223 f., 348-353 (without φόβος); Sept. c. Theb., 288-294. The terror of a helpless animal is a common metaphor. This kind of tension is not unknown in Homer. The only escape is in complaint and prayer to the god, who alone is perfect. [21]

---

[17] On the difficult question of plastic depiction cf. Bernert, 315-7; Höfer, op. cit., 2390-2392. The male Gorgon mask represents Phobos, the female is the Γοργείη κεφαλή, 2394.

[18] Cf. the discussion in P. Wolters, "Ein Apotropaion aus Baaden im Aargau," *Bonner Jahrbücher*, 118 (1909), 257-274, esp. 269-272; Bernert, 316 f.; Dieterich, op. cit., 88, n. 4; L. Deubner, "Phobos," *Ath. Mitt.*, 27 (1902), 253-264, 447; for ill. cf. Höfer, 2389-2394; Wolters; Deubner.

[19] Cf. A. Furtwängler, Art. "Gorgones u. Gorgo," Roscher, I, 1695-1727.

[20] Even the abstract concept reflects concrete fear in expressions like εἰσῆλθεν, ἐνέπεσε φόβος, cf. Usener, op. cit., 375.

[21] B. Snell, "Aischylos u. das Handeln im Drama," *Philol. Suppl.*, 20, 1 (1928), 43-51; cf. G. Nebel, *Weltangst u. Götterzorn. Eine Deutung d. griech. Tragödie* (1951), 22 f., 34 etc.; K. v. Fritz, *Antike u. moderne Tragödie. Neun Abhandl.* (1962), 2 f., 25 f., 30 f. etc.; G. Bornkamm, "Mensch u. Gott in d. griech. Trag. u. in d. urchr. Botschaft," *Das Ende d. Gesetzes*⁵ (1966), 173-195.

This fear can be expressed in the choral songs, [22] and the spectators themselves are sucked into the action. [23] Shaken by the suffering of others, they should consider their own destiny with fear in order that they might find therein sympathy with the fate of others. Aristot. popularises this aspect in his famous def. of tragedy: δι' ἐλέου καὶ φόβου περαίνουσα τὴν τῶν τοιούτων παθημάτων κάθαρσιν, Poet., 6, p. 1449b, 27 f., cf. 14, p. 1453b, 1 and 5, where φοβερόν is close to φρίττω. [24] That tragedy is simply imitation φοβερῶν καὶ ἐλεεινῶν (sc. πραγμάτων), Aristot. Poet., 9, p. 1452a, 2 f. is a popular def. that goes back at least to the age of the Sophists of the 5th cent., Gorg. Hel., 8 f. (Diels, II, 290). [25] If, however, the philosopher sees a purging of the emotions → 195, 13 ff., the poets were concerned about the ineluctability of human destiny which offers no way of escape precisely to the man of insight and knowledge. The anon. quotation from tragedy in Adespota, 356 (TGF, 906): φόβος τὰ θεῖα τοῖσι σώφροσι βροτῶν, admirably expresses this estimate of fear.

If man's uncertain future demands fear, authorities in education and social life also claim fear as the proper reaction. Thus the strong motif of φόβος is an unavoidable imperative in exhortation. For example, in the tradition of the seven wise men found on a stone which serves an educational purpose in Delphi (3rd cent. B.C.) we find the admonition: τὸ κρατοῦμ φοβοῦ → 196, 24 ff. Ditt. Syll.[3], III, 1268, Col. 2, 17. Traditional material of this kind is usually very old and is very persistent, as plainly shown by the adoption of the tradition of the seven wise men in Stob. Ecl., III, 127, 7 [26] and later echoes of the motif of fear in the language of officialdom → 194, 11 ff. Bias (Stob. Ecl., III, 123, 3-5) can even see in unavoidable fear the basis of respect: ἕξεις ... φόβῳ εὐσέβειαν, and the school of Isoc. shows that the fear exacted by earthly powers corresponds to that demanded by the gods: τοὺς μὲν θεοὺς φοβοῦ, τοὺς δὲ γονεῖς τίμα, τοὺς δὲ φίλους αἰσχύνου, τοῖς δὲ νόμοις πείθου, Ps.-Isoc. Or., 1, 16, [27] cf. διὰ τὸ ἄνωθεν φοβεῖσθαι καὶ σέβεσθαι τὸ ἱερόν, P. Tebt., I, 59, 10 (99 B.C.). φοβέομαι as a par. of αἰσχύνομαι means respect for one's father, Timocles Fr., 34 (CAF, II, 465) in Stob. Ecl., IV, 622, 20; the father who threatens his children acts wrongly: οὐκ ἔχει μέγαν φόβον, Menand. Fr., 388 (Körte). Only he who has the φόβος of man produced by law as well as ἐπιθυμία for the λόγος and αἰδώς attains to ἀρετή, Ps.-Hippodamus in Stob. Ecl., IV, 32, 6 ff.; φόβος τῶν νόμων, αἰσχύνη τῶν θεῶν and ἐπιθυμίαι τῶν λόγων help to resist ἀδικία, Ps.-Clinias in Stob. Ecl., III, 32, 1 ff., cf. φοβοῦνται τὸν νόμον in Plut. Sept. Sap. Conv., 11 (II, 154e). Indeed, to the question what law is, Solon is supposed to have given the reply: τῶν μὲν δειλῶν φόβος, τῶν δὲ τολμηρῶν κόλασις, Gnomologium Vaticanum, No. 507. [28] To repudiate fear is to

---

22 Snell, op. cit., 35 f., 41, 51; Snell, op. cit. (→ n. 2), 148. The spectators often break into tears, Hdt., VI, 21, 2.

23 Cf. W. H. Friedrich, Vorbild u. Neugestaltung (1967), 194; cf. gen. J. de Romilly, La crainte et l'angoisse dans le théatre d'Eschyle (1958).

24 On Aristot. cf. Schadewaldt, 129-131; Friedrich, op. cit., 198-205; cf. U. v. Wilamowitz-Moellendorff, Griech. Tragödien übers., 14: "Die griech. Trag. u. ihre drei Dichter" (1923), 61 f. Plat. Phileb., 50b-d speaks of a mixture of φόβος, ἔρως, ζῆλος, φθόνος etc.

25 Cf. M. Pohlenz, "Die Anfänge d. griech. Poetik," NGG, 1920 (1920), 167-178; Schadewaldt, 143-5; Friedrich, op. cit. (→ n. 23), 198-203 with n. 32.

26 This tradition recurs in several gnomologies esp. in the Byzantine period, cf. Ditt. Syll.[3], III, p. 392 f.; K. Horna, Art. "Gnome, Gnomendichtung, Gnomologien," Pauly-W. Suppl., VI (1935), 74-87.

27 Cf. P. Wendland, Anaximenes v. Lampsakos. Stud. z. ältesten Gesch. d. Rhetorik (1905), 86.

28 Ed. L. Sternbach, Texte u. Komm., 2 (1963), 187; similar sayings in Comparatio Menandri et Philistionis (ed. S. Jaekel [1964]), I, 140, 144, cf. Νόμον φοβηθεὶς οὐ ταραχθήσει νόμῳ, II, 146; τιμῶσι δὲ τὸν Φόβον οὐχ ὥσπερ οὓς ἀποτρέπονται δαίμονας ἡγούμενοι βλαβερόν, ἀλλὰ τὴν πολιτείαν μάλιστα συνέχεσθαι φόβῳ νομίζοντες, Plut. De Cleomene, 9 (I, 808c d) of the Spartans who "believe that the state is best held together by fear."

promote anarchy, Ps.-Hippodamus in Stob. Ecl., IV, 35, 8 f., cf. also Lys. Or., 9, 17; 32, 17; Aesch. Eum., 696. Soph. Ai., 1073 ff. already demands δέος for the νόμος and φόβος and αἰδώς for the clever leading of the army. A florilegium offers a list of 24 proverbs arranged alphabetically and all beginning with φοβοῦ. There is fear for ἄνδρας ἐν κρίσει τοὺς ξιφηφόρους, "bearing the sword," line 1, for δυνάστας καὶ βιαίους ἐν πόλει, 2, cf. Diog. L., VI, 2, 68, ζηλοτύπους καὶ πονηροὺς γείτονας, 6, wine, 16, harlots, 17, the θυμός τυράννου, 8 and, of course, laws: φοβοῦ νόμον, βέλτιστε, μὴ πάθης κακῶς, 14, φοβοῦ ἐάν τι πράξης τῶν νόμων ἐναντίον, 5. The good citizen is not just to fear avarice, garrulity and unsociability but also ὡροσκοπῆσαι and μαντικὰς ἐπαοιδίας, 24. [29]

That fear of the state authorities is an inescapable demand for citizens is shown clearly by the formulae of command and devotion in later official jargon, cf. τὰ φοβερώτατα ἤδικτα (of the emperor), P. Masp., III, 67295, Col. 2, 19 (6th cent. A.D.); διὰ προσταγμάτων φοβερῶν τοῦ δικαστηρίου, P. Masp., I, 67009, Col. 3, 7 (6th cent. A.D.), cf. P. Lips., 36, 6 (4th cent. A.D.), with ref. to God: ὄνομα (τοῦ θεοῦ) φοβερὸν τοῖς ὑπεναντίοις, P. Masp., III, 67294, 13, cf. P. Lond., II, 418, 4 (4th cent. A.D.); P. Greci e Lat., 1, 65, 6 (6th cent. A.D.); P. Oxy., XIV, 1642, 17 (3rd cent. A.D.), also VIII, 1151, 55 (5th cent. A.D.) on a Chr. amulet. φόβος can also mean "care," e.g., εἰδὼς φόβον τέκνου "for a child," BGU, II, 380, 19 (3rd cent. A.D.), "regard," for a command μετὰ παντὸς φόβου σπουδάσατε, P. Flor., III, 292, 4 (6th cent. A.D.) or "anxiety," e.g., φόβος τῶν προγραφῶν "warrants," BGU, II, 372, 8 (2nd cent. A.D.); τὸ κρίμα τοῦ θεοῦ φοβηθείς, P. Masp., I, 67089, 31 (6th cent. A.D.). [30]

Connected with this fear of powers and authorities is the fact that epiphanies of divine power in extraordinary and marvelous events often evoke fear and terror which in many cases are dispersed by a calming self-declaration of the deity concerned. The theme of epiphany fear is old, cf. Hom. Il., 20, 130 f.; Od., 1, 323; 16, 178 ff.; Eur. Ion, 1549 ff., and is very common in the Hell. period, e.g., (ἀπο-)θαυμάζω (→ III, 27, 30 ff.), P. Oxy., X, 1242, 53 (3rd cent. A.D.); Luc. Demon., 5. 11; Icaromenipp., 1; Philops., 12; cf. Apul. Met, XI, 13, 4, θαμβέω (→ III, 4, 1 ff), IG, XI, 1299, 30. 60. 91 (3rd cent. B.C.); Luc. De Amore, 14, ἐκπλήττομαι, Luc. Alex., 26; Pergr. Mort., 20. With these terms one finds φοβέομαι κτλ., Luc. Philops., 22; Jup. Trag., 30; Alex., 8. 25; Demon., 20; cf. *membra timore horruerant,* Ovid. Metam., 7, 630 f. In magical texts the deity in its power is "dreadful," e.g., ὄνομα τοῦ φοβεροῦ καὶ τρομεροῦ, Preis. Zaub., I, 4, 367 (4th cent. A.D.), cf. 369, and the epithet φοβεροδιακράτορας, 1357 f. [31] This reaction is evoked by outstanding personages as well as miracles. Even philosophers can be called φοβεροὶ τὴν πρόσοψιν, Luc. Philops., 6. This reaction of fear is a typical stylistic trait in Hell. aretalogy which is reflected in the miracle stories of the NT (→ 209, 5 ff.), though one can hardly call it a stock element.

---

[29] Ed. H. Schenkl, "Das Florilegium Ἄριστον καὶ πρῶτον μάθημα Anhang," *Wiener Stud.,* 11 (1889), 40-42; cf. J. F. Boissonade, Anecdota Graeca, III (1831), 473. I owe the gnomic material to G. Kelber.

[30] A constant phrase in contracts is δίχα παντὸς δόλου καὶ φόβου καὶ βίας καὶ ἀπάτης..., BGU, I, 317, 3; 319, 8 (6th/7th cent. A.D.) etc., cf. Preisigke Wört., *s.v.* βία.

[31] The goddess Isis causes gt. fear of the oath Δει[ν]ὸ[ν δ'] ἐ[π]άγω [φ]όβον ὅρκωι, Isis Hymn of Andros, 116 (1st cent. B.C., ed. W. Peek [1930], 20), cf. the Isis aretalogy of Ios, 33 (2nd-3rd cent.; Peek, 124); on this D. Müller, "Ägypten u. d. griech. Isis-Aretalogien," *Abh. d. Sächsischen Akad. d. Wissensch. zu Leipzig, Philologisch-hist. Klasse,* 53, 1 (1961), 59 f. On fear in epiphanies cf. O. Weinreich, "Antike Heilungswunder," RVV, 8, 1 (1909), *passim;* E. Peterson, "ΕΙΣ ΘΕΟΣ. Epigraphische, formgeschichtliche u. religionsgeschichtliche Untersuchungen," FRL, 41 (1926), 193-5; Bultmann Trad., 241; E. Pax, "ΕΠΙΦΑΝΕΙΑ. Ein religionsgeschichtlicher Beitrag zur bibl. Theol.," *Münchener Theol. Stud.,* I, 10 (1955), 33 f., 136, 189 f.; G. Naumann, *Die Wertschätzung d. Wunders im NT* (1903), 6, 78-85; H. D. Betz, "Lukian v. Samosata u. d. NT. Religionsgesch. u. paränetische Parallelen," TU, 76 (1961), 116, 159 f.

In the spheres of ordinary usage mentioned the group φόβος can often be used, then, either interchangeably with, or as a substitute for, other less emotional terms for fear and terror. The evaluation of fear ranges from its radical rejection to acceptance of its inescapability in face of certain structures of dependence and force. The meaning vacillates between "anxiety," "fear," and "respect." For a more differentiated picture we must turn to philosophical usage.

b. Fear in Philosophy.

From its first beginnings Gk. philosophy discussed the forms of fear. Representatives of predominantly individual and rational trends sharply rejected the φόβος group as an expression of a genuine attitude of fear or respect, while schools which took the irrational into account used the emotional vocabulary of φόβος for the fear necessarily demanded of man.

The rationalism of the pre-Socratics may be seen in their sharp criticism of emotional fear. It is for those who babble about the state after death to labour their whole lives in ταραχαῖς καὶ φόβοις, Democr. Fr., 297 (Diels, II, 207). The ideal of εὐθυμία presupposes that the ψυχή remains calm ὑπὸ μηδενὸς ταραττομένη φόβου ἢ δεισιδαιμονίας ἢ ἄλλου τινὸς πάθους (→ lines 33 ff.), Democr. in Diog. L., IX, 45 (Diels, II, 84, 21 f.). All talk about "fear of God" is invented to scare men: (θεῶν) δέος, Critias Fr., 25 (Diels, II, 387, 7, cf. 388, 7. 15), cf. also Gorg. Hel., 8 f. (II, 290). In practical life φόβος does not lead to εὔνοια but to κολακεία "servility," Democr. Fr., 268 (II, 200).

In the exact def. of Aristot. it is plain what distinguishes this negatively evaluated φόβος from. gen. terms for awe and reverence. It belongs to the πάθη (→ lines 33 ff.) and to λύπη, An., I, 1, p. 403a, 16 f.; Probl., 27, 9, p. 948b, 20, from which the σῶμα suffers, An. I, 1, p. 403a, 18 f. Physiologically this kind of fear involves cooling of the body [32] through lack of blood, so that cramps, trembling, pain and agony are caused, Probl., 27, 1, p. 947b, 12 ff., cf. on trembling, 27, 6, p. 948a, 35; 27, 7, p. 948b, 6, and on other accompanying phenomena of shock 27, 9, p. 948b, 20 ff.; 27, 10, p. 948b, 35 ff.; cf. Part. An., IV, 11, p. 692a, 23 f. [33] As in Socrates and Plato (→ 196, 24 ff.) φόβος is caused by the threat to existence, i.e., by malign fate, which also causes pity when it is that of others: ὡς δ' ἁπλῶς εἰπεῖν, φοβερά ἐστιν ὅσα ἐφ' ἑτέρων γιγνόμενα... ἐλεεινά ἐστιν, Rhet., II, 5, p. 1382b, 26 f.

The achievement of Stoic philosophy is to define this φόβος in sound psychological fashion as an irrational emotion which is to be repudiated. It is one of the four basic emotions [34] λύπη, φόβος, ἐπιθυμία and ἡδονή, and consists in προσδοκία κακοῦ (→ 190, 38 ff.), Diog. L., VII, 110. 112 f., cf. Stob. Ecl., II, 88, 14 f.; Chrysipp. in v. Arnim, III, 101, 29 f.; cf. also Plat. La., 191d and Prot., 352b; Phaed., 83b; Symp., 207e; Theaet., 156b; Resp., IV, 429c. 430a (→ 196, 26 ff.) and Aristot. (→ lines 22 ff.). φόβος, then, is distinguished from other emotional impulses like αἰδώς and αἰσχύνη, v. Arnim, III, 101, 34 ff.; even φόβος ἀπὸ θεῶν does not keep from ἀδικία, Plut. Stoic. Rep., 15 (II, 1040b). Fear is a κίνησις παρὰ φύσιν, Chrysipp. in v. Arnim, III, 126, 25 f., some-

---

[32] There is a striking closeness to similar statements about sleep (→ VIII, 547, 1 ff.).

[33] Medical wisdom is familiar with such notions. Thus φόβος, λύπη, ἀσθένεια etc. prevent pregnancy, Aetius De Placitis reliquiae, V, 6, 1 (ed. H. Diels, Doxographi Graeci [1874], 419). φόβοι are states of sleeplessness or other bodily disturbances in children, Hippocr. Aphorismi, 24 (Littré, IV, 496). They are a bad sign in fevered sleep, 67 (IV, 526). They can come at night even through hearing a flute, Epid., V, 81 (Littré, V, 250). Fear comes with melancholia, VII, 45 (V, 414) and is finally typical of schizophrenia, Περὶ παρθενίων, 1 (VIII, 466).

[34] On the tradition of four emotions cf. A. Vögtle, "Die Tugend- u. Lasterkataloge im NT," NT Abh., 16, 4-5 (1936), 61 f.

thing harmful, Chrysipp. in Plut. Comm. Not., 25 (II, 1070e). It is found only in
φαῦλοι but not in children, v. Arnim, III, 128, 10 f. and like other πάθη it must be
treated by asceticism, Ariston in Cl. Al. Strom., II, 20, 108, 1. [35] Epictetus demands of
the thinking man: ἄφοβος ... ἔσει καὶ ἀτάραχος, Diss., IV, 1, 84, cf. the triad
ἀταραξία, ἀφοβία, ἐλευθερία, II, 1, 22, cf. II, 5, 12; 10, 18 (→ 195, 14 ff.); οὐ γὰρ
θάνατος ἢ πόνος φοβερόν, ἀλλὰ τὸ φοβεῖσθαι πόνον ἢ θάνατον, Diss., I, 1, 13,
cf. 16, 19; Teles Fr., 2 (p. 11, 9); Epict. Ench., 5; Aeschin. in Stob. Ecl., V, 1072, 2 f.
(→ n. 40). From emotional fear of God, cf. Epict. Diss., II, 20, 23 (→ 194, 23 ff.) the truly
pious are freed by their relation to God as ποιητής and πατήρ, I, 9, 7, cf. 9, 26, while
non-emotional reverence is positively espoused in the terms αἰδώς, ἀπάθεια, ἀλυπία
and ἀφοβία. [36] Fear of tyrants is also nonsensical, Diss., IV, 7, 1-41, [37] for the only
evil man has to fear is that he does to himself, II, 1, 13; 8, 24. [38] We read similarly in
M. Ant. that fear of death is childish, II, 12, 3, cf. VIII, 58, 1 and that the true work of
the gods is διδόναι τὸ μήτε φοβεῖσθαι, IX, 40, 2; for all emotions are οὐδὲν ἄλλο ...
ἢ ἀφισταμένου τῆς φύσεως, XI, 20, 5, cf. similarly VII, 16, 2; 18, 1.

The sharpest rejection of fear is in the Epicurean message. Since Epic. can think of
eudaemonia only as freedom from pains of the body and upsets of soul, Diog. L., X, 131,
he radically condemns fear of the future, Epic. Fr., 116 (p. 60), [39] and of death, Fr., 102.
104 (p. 58 f.); for God is the ἄφοβον, Fr., 14 (p. 22) and he who would be freed from
fear regarding the most important questions of life needs knowledge of the τοῦ σύμπαντος
φύσις, Diog. L., X, 143; the simple life makes men πρὸς τὴν τύχην ἀφόβους, Epic.
Ratae sententiae, 10 (p. 14). [40] Lucretius borrows from Epic. when he repudiates every
timor, De rer. nat., I, 106; II, 55 f.; III, 982 f.; V, 1180 etc. [41]

If in these schools fear and anxiety before gods and men are suppressed or banished
by enlightenment and instruction, in some thinkers of the Academy and the Peripatetic
movement they still have meaning in some situations. If Plato rejects fear of death he
teaches fear of wrongdoing τὸ ἀδικεῖν φοβεῖται, Gorg., 522e. Fear of a divine name
is wrong, Crat., 404e, yet fear of God is natural in education: κατὰ φύσιν ... πρῶτον
μὲν τοὺς ἄνω θεοὺς φοβείσθων, Leg., IX, 927a b, while fear of evil events is to be
condemned: φοβούμεθα ... τὰ κακά, προσδοκῶντες γενήσεσθαι, Leg., I, 646e, the
antithesis being ἐλπίς as προσδοκία ἀγαθοῦ (→ II, 518, n. 6), cf. Leg., I, 644c, φόβος
can also be used in the sense of αἰσχύνη and αἰδώς, cf. the explicit dialogue on fear,

---

[35] Cf. also K. Reinhardt, *Poseidonios* (1921), 263-336. All emotions are basically alogical
or irrational; they change the soul for the bad, while only *ratio* can turn it to the good,
Sen. De ira, I, 8, 3; they have no positive significance for him who seeks ὁμολογουμένως
τῇ φύσει ζῆν, Zeno in Stob. Ecl., II, 76, 5 f.; Diog. L., VII, 87, cf. on this whole matter
M. Pohlenz, *Die Stoa. Gesch. einer geistigen Bewegung*, I² (1959), 141-153; II³ (1964),
77-83; also "Poseidonios' Affektenlehre u. Psychologie," NGG, 1921 (1921), 181-4.
[36] Cf. A. Bonhöffer, *Epict. u. d. Stoa. Untersuchungen z. stoischen Philosophie* (1890),
304 f. The feelings mentioned above are between the πάθη and the εὐπάθειαι. The wise
man fears the power neither of the gods nor of death, for the gods cannot hurt him: *errat si
quis illos putat nocere nolle: non possunt,* Sen. Ep., 15, 95, 49, cf. 9, 75, 17; Ben., IV, 19, 1;
De Providentia, 1, 5; 2, 7; Pohlenz Stoa, I, 321. Love characterises God; He loves men, i.e.,
the good [Hengel].
[37] Cf. A. Bonhöffer, *Die Ethik d. Stoikers Epict.* (1894), 46-9 on apathia; also Epict.,
op. cit. (→ n. 36), 282: The πάθη vanish with instruction in true insight, cf. also the question:
ἄλυπος καὶ ἄφοβος ⟨ὁ⟩ ἐκτὸς λύπης καὶ φόβου; Teles Fr., 7 (p. 56, 2 f.). Theoph.
thinks the πάθη, and esp. φόβοι, are cured by music rather than by reason, Fr., 88 (III,
185).
[38] A. Bonhöffer, "Epiktet u. d. NT," RVV, 10 (1911), 360 f.
[39] Ed. C. Diano (1946).
[40] On Epic. cf. E. Schwartz, *Ethik d. Griechen* (1951), 183-6. Cf. Aristoph.: τὸ γὰρ
φοβεῖσθαι τὸν θάνατον λῆρος πολύς· πᾶσιν γὰρ ἡμῖν τοῦτ' ὀφείλεται παθεῖν, Fr., 452
(CAF, I, 508).
[41] Ed. C. Bailey, I (1947).

Leg., I, 646e-650b [42] and the juxtaposition of δέος and αἰδώς, Euthyphr., 12a b. This does not change the fact, however, that the issue is νικᾶν τὰ προσπίπτονθ' ἡμῖν δείματα τε καὶ φόβους, Leg., VII, 790e - 791c.

Plut. adopts this not so negative view of φόβος when he charges the Stoics with seeing in φόβος only an irrational emotion; they should rather call τὸ ἥδεσθαι χαίρειν καὶ τοὺς φόβους εὐλαβείας (→ n. 46), De virtute morali, 9 (II, 449a). One cannot avoid fear of God, Superst., 4 (II, 166d) nor fear of death ὁ τοῦ θανάτου φόβος, since even Epic. admits that death means pain for most men, Suav. Viv. Epic., 30 (II, 1107a), cf. Cons. ad Apoll., 29 (II, 116e). The atheism of μὴ νομίζειν θεούς ends in μὴ φοβεῖσθαι and thus leads to a false δέος and even to δεισιδαιμονία (→ II, 20, 5 ff.) as a bad πάθος, Superst., 2 (II, 165b c), cf. 11 (II, 270e). But this anti-Stoic understanding of φόβος does not go so far that the understanding of fear in tragedy (→ 192, 32 ff.) can be naively adopted, for θεῖα bring about φόβος only in the irrational, while in the rational they stir up courage θάρσος, Aud. Poet., 12 (II, 34a), cf. also what is said about ἀφοβία and ἀπάθεια as ἕξις καθ' ἣν ἀνέμπτωτοί ἐσμεν εἰς φόβους, Ps.-Plat. Def., 413a, cf. 415e. In some Peripatetics [43] the educational significance of φόβος is recognised, cf. Theophr. in Sen. De ira, I, 12, 3; Critolaus in Cl. Al. Strom., II, 7, 32, 3; [44] for neo-Pythagorean statements → 193, 29 ff.

The φόβος statements of Greek philosophy are not uniform. Materially rejection of emotional fear is common to all schools. But this material rejection of fear is not co-extensive with the semantic use of φόβος κτλ. Sometimes the group can be employed for feelings akin to awe and reverence [45] which are regarded as imperative and unavoidable reactions to the claim of authorities and especially of the gods. [46]

Balz

B. φόβος and φοβέομαι in the Old Testament.

I. Occurrence and Hebrew Equivalents.

1. In almost five sixths of the occurrences of φοβέομαι in the canonical books of the Hbr. OT it is a transl. of the stem ירא "to fear," "to be afraid," "to have in honour"; it does not occur in Hos., Na., Cant. and Ἔσδρ. In the other instances it is used for various Hbr. and Aram. words, on seven occasions for פחד q "to quake," Dt. 28:66 f.;

---

[42] The dialogue focuses on the suggestion that it might be best for the state to induce φόβος as αἰσχύνη through a φάρμακον so that the citizens might grow in true fearlessness, while wine as a primitive means of freeing from naive fear might show who loses genuine φόβος through superficial boldness θρασύτης. For similar ideas cf. Artemid. Onirocr., III, 42 f.

[43] In the Peripatetics, too, we find Stoic elements, cf. the def. in Ps.-Andronicus Περὶ παθῶν (ed. F. G. A. Mullach, Fragmenta Philosophorum Graec., III [1881]): φόβος δ' ἔστιν ἄλογος ἔκκλισις· ἢ φυγὴ ἀπὸ προσδοκωμένου δεινοῦ, p. 570; cf.: Φόβου εἴδη... Αἰσχύνη δὲ φόβος ἀδοξίας. Δέος δὲ φόβος συνεστώς. Δεισιδαιμονία δὲ φόβος τοῦ δαίμονος, ἢ ὑπερέκπτωσις τῆς πρὸς θεοὺς τιμῆς etc., p. 571.

[44] Cf. on this F. Wehrli, Die Schule d. Aristot. Texte u. Komm. Hieronymus v. Rhodos, Kritolaos (1959), 53 and 69.

[45] The important statistical analyses agree that words in σεβ-, which are widely used in non-bibl. Gk. for veneration of the gods (→ VII, 168, 25 ff.), can be replaced with words of the φόβος group in popular usage and, remarkably enough, the LXX (→ 199, 4 ff.). In later NT works the stem σεβ- again comes to the fore (Ac. 16 times, Past. 15, 2 Pt. and Jd. 9). This reflects a replacing of LXX Gk. with Hell. usage.

[46] The dilemma posed by this non-uniform usage for the Chr. theologian with his positive biblical understanding of φόβος is finely noted by Cl. Al.: οὐ τοίνυν ἄλογος ὁ φόβος, λογικὸς μὲν οὖν... ἀλλ' εἰ σοφίζονται τὰ ὀνόματα εὐλάβειαν καλούντων οἱ φιλόσοφοι τὸν τοῦ νόμου φόβον εὔλογον οὖσαν ἔκκλισιν, Strom., II, 7, 32, 4.

Job 3:25; ψ 52(53):6; Is. 12:2; 19:17; 'Ιερ. 40(33):9 and once pi, Is. 51:13. [47] In Hbr. Sir. we find φοβέομαι 10 times for ירא|, 6:16 f.; 10:19 f., 24; 15:1, 13; 26:3; 32:16; 33:1. [48] There are 9 instances in Jdt. with no Hbr. original, 14 in Tob., 9 in 1 Macc. (also 1 Macc. 12:40 ℒ'), 1 each in 2 and 3 Macc., 7 in 4 Macc., 3 in Wis., 16 in Sir. 9 in Ps. Sol., 5 in Ep. Jer., and 1 in Sus. The word also occurs in many passages in which the LXX adds to or deviates from the Hbr. OT: Gn. 28:13; 3 Βασ. 2:29; 12:24c; 2 Ch. 5:6; 'Εσθ. 1:1h; 2:20; Prv. 7:1a; 29:25; Is. 33:7; 60:5; 'Ιερ. 2:30.

2. φόβος in about a third of the instances is used for nouns of the stem ירא, i.e., יִרְאָה "fear," "respect" 33 times (8 in Sir.) and מוֹרָא "fear," "terror" 5 times (Sir. once). In another third it is the transl. of פַּחַד "quaking," "horror," 35 times (Sir. twice); it represents יִרְאָה esp. in Prv., Ps. and Job and פַּחַד esp. in Ps., Job, Is. and Jer. In the final third φόβος is used for various Hbr. and Aram. terms. [49] With no Hbr. equivalent it occurs in Sir. 16 times, Jdt. 3, Wis. 5, Ep. Jer. 2, Bar. 1, Ps. Sol. 7, 1 Macc. 4, 2 Macc. 3, 3 Macc. 4, 4 Macc. 6, and cf. also Is. 8:13; 10:27; 26:17; 33:7 f.; Ez. 20:13 Cod. A; Δα. 4:37; 5:6; 11:31; ψ 13:3; Job 39:3; 41:17; 2 'Εσδρ. 16:16; 'Εσθ. 4:17z; 5:1b, 2a.

φοβερός (-ῶς) "terrible" is mostly used for ירא ni part. "feared," "terrible" (23 times and twice in Sir.). In combinations we also find ἐκφοβέω "to be very frightened" 7 times for חרד hi "to be startled," always in the formula וְאֵין מַחֲרִיד "and there is none there that makes afraid," Lv. 26:6; Dt. 28:26 Cod. B; Mi. 4:4; Na. 2:12; Zeph. 3:13; Ez. 34:28; 39:26, also for חִתִּית "terror," Ez. 32:27, חתת pi "to be frightened," Job 7:14, [50] and with no Hbr. original 6 times in Jdt. 16:25; Wis. 11:19; 17:9; Cod. A; 17:18; 1 Macc. 14:12; [51] 4 Macc. 9:5. We also find ἔκφοβος, Dt. 9:19; 1 Macc. 13:2 (par. ἔντρομος), φοβερίζω "to be startled," 2 'Εσδρ. 16:9, 14, 19; Da. 4:5 Θ; 2 'Εσδρ. 10:3, φοβερισμός "terror," ψ 87(88):17, φόβητρον "apparition," Is. 19:17, ὑπέρφοβος, Da. 7:19; ἄφοβος (-ως),

---

[47] φοβέομαι is also used for חתת ni "to be struck down," "terrified," Jos. 1:9; 'Ιερ. 1:17; 10:2 (twice), גור "to fear," Nu. 22:3; ψ 21(22):24; Prv. 30:1 with Agur, חרד (verb and adj.) "anxious," "to shake," Ju. 7:3; Ez. 26:16, 18, דחל q "to fear," Da. 5:19 Θ; 6:27 Θ, חיל "to move in circles," "to quake," ψ 76:17; 1 Ch. 16:30, רעש "to shudder," 'Ιερ. 30:15 (49:21) Cod. BS; Ez. 27:28, יגור "to be afraid" 'Ιερ. 46(39):17, ערץ hi "to be frightened," Is. 29:23, פלח "to serve (God)," Da. 3:17 (Θ λατρεύω), דאג "to be careful," 'Ιερ. 17:8, רגז "to shudder," Ex. 15:14 Cod. A, שׂים מָאַם עַל "to have regard for," Δα. 3:12 (Θ ὑπακούω), קוץ "to feel horror," Is. 7:16; in free transl. one finds φοβέομαι for עֶבֶד at Is. 66:14 Cod. B etc. (A etc. σέβομαι). In mistransl. or free transl. Ju. 6:34 Cod. B has φοβέομαι for זעק "to summon the levy" (A βοάω). When LXX uses φοβέομαι for the root ראה "to see" one should usually emend HT accordingly, so 1 K. 19:3; Mi. 6:9; Ex. 20:18; Ez. 18:14 and perhaps Ju. 14:11 Cod. A (B εἶδον); Neh. 6:16.

[48] In free transl. one also finds φοβέομαι (τὸν κύριον) for (יהוה) כבד "to reverence," Sir. 7:31 and (יהוה) דרש "to turn to," 32:14. At Sir. 15:19 LXX presupposes Hbr. יִרְאוּ.

[49] Nouns of the stem חתת "to be filled with terror" 8 times: חַת "terror," Gn. 9:2, חִתָּה "terror," Gn. 35:5, חִתִּית "terror," Ez. 26:17; 32 (5 times); אֵימָה "terror" 11 times (Sir. twice; 4:17?), חרד "to tremble," Is. 19:16, cf. 10:29 (LXX φόβος λαμβάνει), חֲרָדָה "trembling," "anxiety," Is. 21:4; 'Ιερ. 37(30):5; Δα. 10:7 (Θ ἔκστασις) and דחל pa'el "to frighten," Δα. 4:2(5): φόβος ἐπιπίπτει. In one series we have very free transl., Job 3:24; 38:17; Is. 33:3; Δα. 7:7; Est. 1:22; Sir. 45:23; esp. Job 4:13; 33:15, where (δεινός) φόβος is used for תַּרְדֵּמָה "deep sleep," "stupefaction," and Prv. 10:29, which has φόβος κυρίου for דֶּרֶךְ יהוה. One should emend 2 Ch. 26:5 acc. to LXX. In Ez. 38:21; Job 33:16; 36:19 the HT is difficult.

[50] At Job 33:16 one should emend HT acc. to the LXX.

[51] The Hbr. original here was probably וְאֵין מַחֲרִיד → line 18 f.

Prv. 1:33; 3:24; Wis. 17:4, in the sense of "carefree," Sir. 5:5, [52] and φοβεροειδής, 3 Macc. 6:18.

3. δέος occurs only in 2 Macc. 3:17, 30; 12:22; 13:16; 15:23.

4. As words of the stem φοβ- in the LXX are essentially used for the stems ירא (some 70%) and פחד (10%), so the latter words are predominantly (ירא some 85% and פחד some 60%) transl. by φόβος etc. ירא q and the adj. יָרֵא are transl. some 310 times by φοβέομαι as compared with only 25 times by other words, (θεο)σεβής 5 times, σέβομαι, εὐλαβέομαι, εὐλογέω, θαρσέω with negation 10 times. In the ni we find φοβερός (-ῶς) 23 times as compared with 23 alternatives, ἐπιφανής 8 times and θαυμασ- τός (-ῶς) 7 times. In the pi φοβερίζω occurs 3 times and φοβέομαι once. The noun יִרְאָה is transl. by φόβος 36 times and twice φοβέομαι as compared with 7 instances of εὐσέβεια, θεοσέβεια, σέβομαι and ἐπισκοπή, while the noun מוֹרָא is 4 times rendered φόβος and once φοβερός compared with 5 cases of ὅραμα, τρόμος and θαυμάσιος.

The verb פחד in the q is transl. 7 times by φοβέομαι and once (in the negative) by ἄφοβος as compared with 12 alternatives, including εὐλαβέομαι. In the pi we find φοβέομαι, εὐσεβής (Sir.) and καταπτήσσω once each and in the hi διασείω (vl. συσσείω). For the noun פַּחַד there are 32 instances of φόβος and 13 instances of other terms, ἔκστασις, θάμβος, θόρυβος, ὄλεθρος, πτόησις and τρόμος. There is no precise Hbr. equivalent for the formula φόβος καὶ τρόμος. Instead we always find a combination of two of the following words, רַעַד ,יִרְאָה ,אֵימָה ,פַּחַד and חֲרֵד, which would best be transl. by "dread," since in almost all cases Ex. 15:16; Dt. 2:25; 11:25; Ps. 55:5; Is. 19:16 (Jdt. 2:28; 15:2; 4 Macc. 4:10) it describes a state due to confrontation with a sudden, un- avoidable or already present threat which may be posed by Yahweh Himself or by a nation and its overwhelming military power. An exception is Gn. 9:2 (P), where φόβος καὶ τρόμος denotes the new relation of dominion between man and animal.

II. The Stem ירא in the Old Testament.

1. Meaning.

a. The verb ירא orig. meant "to tremble," "to quake," but in the whole of the OT and in Ugaritic it is used exclusively for the sphere of "fear" in the broader sense. [53] ירא q means abs. "to fear." With the acc. it usually has the weaker sense "to feel rever- ence," "to hold in respect," Lv. 19:3; 2 K. 17:7; with the prep. מִן ,מִפְּנֵי and מִלְפְנֵי it usually expresses real fear, Dt. 1:29; 1 S. 21:13. The part. as a verbal adj. means "fearful," cf. Mal. 3:16; Ju. 7:3. In the ni, apart from Ps. 130:4, one finds only the part. נוֹרָא which is used exclusively as an adj. in the sense of "terrible," Jl. 2:11; Ps. 99:3. ירא pi [54] expresses a lasting intention and means "to want to make afraid," 2 S. 14:15; Neh. 6:9.

b. The noun יִרְאָה is in form an inf. as noun and it occurs mostly in combination with אֱלֹהִים ,יְהוָה or the corresponding suffixes, Is. 11:2; Jer. 32:40. It means "fear" in Jon. 1:10, 16 but mostly in the weaker sense of "respect," Ps. 19:9; Job 6:14. The noun מוֹרָא, which is formed after the analogy of maqtal constructs, is closer to the original sense of the stem; except at Mal. 2:5 it always denotes "fear" as "terror."

---

[52] At Prv. 15:16; 19:23 ἀφοβία or ἄφοβος is the opp. of φόβος κυρίου (HT different).
[53] It is hard to find instances of the root yr' in this sense in other Semitic languages, Becker, 1 f.
[54] E. Jenni, *Das hebräische Piel* (1968), 83.

2. Fear in the Human and Earthly Sphere.

The subj. of fear in the OT is almost always man. [55] The OT tells of the fear both of individuals, e.g., Isaac in Gn. 26:7, Jacob in Gn. 32:8, 12, Moses in Ex. 2:14, David in 1 S. 21:13, Nehemiah in Neh. 2:2 etc., and also of groups and nations, e.g., the clan of Esau in Dt. 2:4, the Aramaeans in 2 S. 10:19, and often Israel itself.

Essential to the characterisation of fear is not only a ref. to its obj. but also a definition of the reason for it, although it is often hard to state this precisely. We often read of fear in relation to war, although it is not clear whether this is only fear of the enemy or defeat and not rather fear of death, [56] subjection, or slavery, Ex. 14:10; Dt. 2:4; 7:18; 28:10; Jos. 9:24 etc. More exact information is to hand in texts which by nature are more interested in individuals and their attitudes, e.g., in stories and psalms of various kinds. Here fear is fear of death, Gn. 26:7; Neh. 6:10-13, fear of enslavement, Gn. 43:18, fear of the loss of wife, Gn. 31:31, or child, 2 S. 14:15, fear of disaster, Zeph. 3:15; Ps. 23:4, or sudden terror, Prv. 3:25, fear of being smitten by misfortune, Job 6:21, [57] or fear of sinister events, Gn. 42:35, places, Dt. 1:19, and times, Ps. 91:5 f. In later texts one may sometimes discern a weakening of the content of ירא in the profane sphere, so that the ref. may be to the old man's fear of a hill that shows up his weakness, Qoh. 12:5, or the anxiety of a prudent housewife in face of inclement weather, Prv. 31:21, or the respect of youth for age, Job 32:6, or of children for parents, Lv. 19:3. The starting-pt. of fear, then, is esp. a threat to life, living space, and all the spheres that give life meaning. Fear can be caused by specific men such as Laban, Gn. 31:31, Goliath, 1 S. 17:11, 24, Jehu, 2 K. 10:4 etc., or by peoples like the Egyptians, Ex. 14:10 and Israelites, Dt.11:25, or by hostile nature, e.g., the raging sea in Jon. 1:5, the wild beasts in Job 5:21 f., the lion in Am. 3:8, or the desert, which the OT can call נוֹרָא, Dt. 1:19; 8:15 on account of snakes, scorpions and lack of water. One also "fears" ירא acts whose consequences cannot be foreseen and which may work negatively, e.g., an oath, 1 S. 14:26; Qoh. 9:2, imparting bad news, 1 S. 3:15; 2 S. 12:18, or even killing, Ju. 8:20.

That fear played a considerable role in the consciousness of the Israelites may be seen in the exclusion of the fearful from the host, Dt. 20:8; Ju. 7:3, the imposing of the death penalty as a deterrent, Dt. 13:11; 17:13; 19:20; 21:21, and esp. texts which reflect consider-able tension between fear of God and fear of men, Ju. 7:9 f.; Jer. 1; Ez. 2. [58] On the other hand, esp. in later Ps. (3:6; 23:4; 27:1, 3; 46:2) one finds freedom from fear as a result of the confident turning of the righteous or the congregation to the God who helps and protects them; this freedom is promised as an eschatological blessing in Is. 54:14.

Man treats with fear and reverent awe esp. persons and places that stand in a special relation to God. Israel is afraid to approach Moses when he comes back from his encounter with God with a radiant face, Ex. 34:30. It fears Joshua because God has made him great in their eyes, Jos. 4:14. Yahweh expects that respect will be shown to those commissioned by him, Nu. 12:8. Israel fears Samuel because he does the works of Yahweh, 1 S. 12:18, and Solomon because divine wisdom was seen in him, 1 K. 3:28. [59] Fear of seeing God, Ex. 3:6, or hearing His voice, Ex. 20:18 ff., may underlie fear of the sites of God's revelation and presence. [60] The Holiness Code can even demand fear of the sanctuary, Lv. 19:30; 26:2.

---

[55] The one exception is Gn. 9:2, where the animal world fears man.
[56] Cf. L. Wächter, "Der Tod im AT," Arbeiten z. Theol., II, 8 (1967), 10-56.
[57] G. Fohrer, Das Buch Hiob, Komm. z. AT, 16² (1963), ad loc.
[58] Plath, 27-31.
[59] In 1 S. 31:4 par. 1 Ch. 10:4; 2 S. 1:14 there is ref. to fear of killing the Lord's anointed but this can hardly be awe at the holiness of the anointed, as against Plath, 108, and it does not have to imply that "sacral kingship" has a share in the numinous, as against Becker, 40.
[60] Cf. also Gn. 28:17; Dt. 5:5; 1 S. 4:7.

3. Fear of God.

a. As men can become a threat and hence an obj. of fear, Yahweh is menacing and hence He is "terror" מוֹרָא to Israel, Is. 8:12 f., and His acts are "terrible acts" מוֹרָאִים for Israel's foes, Dt. 4:34; 26:8; Jer. 32:21. These deeds of Yahweh are נוֹרָא in the true sense for the smitten enemies of Israel but for Israel itself they are Yahweh's saving intervention on Israel's behalf, Ex. 34:10; Dt. 10:21; Ps. 66:3(5), so that LXX can sometimes render this נוֹרָא by θαυμαστός, Ex. 34:10; ψ 64:5. If Yahweh's acts are terrible, so is Yahweh Himself, Ex. 15:11; Ps. 47:2; 68:36; Neh. 1:5; 4:8 etc. and His name is called נוֹרָא, Dt. 28:58; Mal. 1:14; Ps. 99:3; 111:9. His day will also be dreadful and terrible, Jl. 2:11, 31; Mal. 3:23. The term נוֹרָא, which occurs almost exclusively in post-exilic texts, is often combined with גָּדוֹל, 2 S. 7:23; Ps. 145:6 or קָדוֹשׁ, Ps. 99:3; 111:9. From this one may assume that Yahweh is felt to be terrible not through His dreadful works alone but also in His majesty and holiness as He who is above all gods, Ps. 96:4; Dt. 10:17. [61]

b. Since God's acts as well as His power and holiness and majesty not only cause fear but also demand acknowledgment, the term ירא in these contexts [62] denotes not merely elementary fear resulting essentially from threat but also fear relating to the author of the threat, so that it becomes reverence and submissive recognition. This second aspect of the fear of God takes different forms in different theological strata of the OT, and can become independent of the physical aspect. The terms "god-fearing" (verbal adj. with gen. or acc.), "fear of God" יִרְאַת אֱלֹהִים and "to fear God" (verb with acc.) are first found in this special form in the E source of the Pent. and they denote there men whose conduct is orientated to the will of God. There can also be a concrete revelation of the divine will to which man submits in obedience and trust, Gn. 22:12, or fundamental religious demands whose acknowledgment entails specific behaviour in concrete situations, Gn. 20:11. God-fearers are thus reliable men, Ex. 18:21 who in virtue of a basic attitude of this kind act even against their own reason, or indeed an earlier Word of God, Gn. 22:1-13, or the specific will of the ruler, Ex. 1:15-21 (E?). [63]

In Deuteronomic and Deuteronomistic lit., esp. Dt. itself, "to fear God" occurs in a series of formulae which demand piety orientated to the Deuteronomic Law. Fearing God can be a result of hearing and learning God's Word, Dt. 4:10, or keeping the commandments of Yahweh, 8:6, but it can also be equated with the demand to hear Yahweh's voice, 13:5, or to serve Yahweh עָבַד, 6:13; 10:12, 20; 13:5, or to tread His way, 8:6 etc., so that this fear is not just demanded but can also be learned as a statute or commandment, Dt. 14:22 f.; 17:19. [64] The combining of two other words with ירא, namely, אהב "to love" [65] and דבק "to cleave to," Dt. 10:12, 20; 13:5, makes possible a broader understanding of the content of fearing God, esp. since what is said about ירא → 202, 20 ff. applies to אהב and דבק, and the terms are thus more or less interchangeable. Since, however, the norms of the conduct to God and man described by these words can be expressed in the Law, fearing God along with loving God is not just a basic attitude but amounts to the observance of moral and cultic demands. [66] With this development the fear of God loses

---

[61] Cf. Eichr. Theol. AT⁵, II-III, 184-190.

[62] Cf. esp. Ex. 14:31; Is. 25:3; Jer. 5:22, 24; 10:6 f.

[63] The idea that such modes of conduct are not specifically Yahwistic but express the "international humanism" of the chokhmah (Becker, 193) does not really stand up in spite of the "international" setting of Gn. 20:11 and 42:18.

[64] The element of urgent demand in the language of Dt. affects the linguistic use of the root ירא. It is never used as a noun and seldom as a verbal adj., 20:8; 25:18. In all other instances it is a verb.

[65] Cf. Sander, 3-12 but cf. Plath, 39; Becker, 109 f.

[66] As against Becker, 85-124, whose interpretation stands or falls with the tenability of the hypothesis of a covenant formulary.

altogether its original emotional character. There is not even room for fear of the punishment of Yahweh which is suspended over those who do not fear Him, Dt. 6:13-15;
28:58-61.[67]

c. The fear of God occurs in a completely new form in the Wisdom lit. of Israel,
esp. Prv. The predominant use of the noun יִרְאָה with an obj. gen., only יְהוָה in Prv.,
shows already that the concept of the fear of God has left the emotional realm here and
become an object of reflection. If one hearkens to wisdom and inclines to reason one will
understand the fear of Yahweh and attain to knowledge of God, Prv. 2:5. Statements are
made about the fear of Yahweh but it is seldom demanded, Prv. 3:7; 24:21. It is incorporated into the teaching (Ps. 34:11) that tries to offer and establish norms for a
rational and purposeful life which rest on the experience and conviction that the good
brings with it good fortune and affluence while the bad entails disaster, Prv. 13:21 f., and
that a life orientated to wisdom is pleasing to God as the Creator and Upholder of the
cosmic order, Prv. 8:35, indeed, that He Himself grants it to the upright, Prv. 2:5-8. Thus
the fear of Yahweh is the beginning תְּחִלָּה of wisdom, Prv. 9:10, disciplining in wisdom,
Prv. 15:33, the beginning רֵאשִׁית [68] of knowledge, Prv. 1:7, and of wisdom, Ps. 111:10. It
is the presupposition of wisdom or the gift thereof, Prv. 2:1-5. The fear of Yahweh is
equated with knowledge דַּעַת, insight תְּבוּנָה, and wisdom itself, Prv. 1:29; 2:5 f.; 13:14 cf.
14:27; Job 28:28, so that precise differentiation of the terms is barely possible and is
probably not intended. We must rather assume that all the synon. terms relate to the
same basic attitude which is sought in wisdom teaching (→ VII, 487, 1 ff.) and whose
religious aspect is denoted by יִרְאַת יְהוָה. One can grasp the fear of Yahweh, however,
only in concrete manifestations, and here it has a moral orientation. It is the avoidance
of evil, Ps. 34:11, 14; Job 1:1, 8; 2:3; 28:28 יִרְאַת אֲדֹנָי; Prv. 3:7; 16:6, the hatred of evil,
Prv. 8:13, or of sin, Prv. 23:17, so that the one who fears Yahweh can be said to walk
in uprightness יֹשֶׁר, Prv. 14:2, and the way of the יָשָׁר is said to be avoidance of the evil,
Prv. 16:17. The consequences of this moral attitude and hence of the fear of Yahweh
play a comparatively large part in the description of wisdom. An example of this is
Ps. 34:11-14, where the result of moral conduct serves as a spur to it. He who desires
life and loves days that he may see good, let him avoid evil and do what is right. Fear of
Yahweh brings wealth, honour and life, Prv. 22:4. It increases days, 10:27. It is the
spring of life and helps us escape the snares of death, 14:27. It promotes life, security and
confidence, and is a refuge, 14:26; 19:23. Whether these positive and negative results of
a moral attitude are due to a nexus of act and effect guaranteed by Yahweh [69] or to His
retributive justice [70] cannot be deduced from the concept of the fear of Yahweh in the
Wisdom lit. [71]

d. In the Psalter the varied motifs, traditions and genres impose different nuances
of meaning on the root ירא. But one of these stands out in form and content. The Ps.
use the plur. verbal adj. with obj. gen. or suffix: יִרְאֵי יְהוָה etc., for a specific group of

---

[67] The concept of the fear of God plays no part in the priestly tradition. It is commanded
only a few times in the Holiness Code, Lv. 19:14, 32; 25:17, 36, 43, and always in connection
with rules for conduct towards the weak and unprivileged. Cf. on this Plath, 73-76; Becker,
205 f.; C. Feucht, *Untersuchungen z. Heiligkeitsgesetz* (1964), 159-161, with bibl.

[68] רֵאשִׁית is "beginning" in the sense of "first-born," "chief," "principle."

[69] So K. Koch, "Gibt es ein Vergeltungsdogma im AT?" ZThK, 52 (1955), 1-42; Plath,
64-7 etc.

[70] B. Gemser, *Sprüche Salomos, Hndbch. AT,* I, 16² (1963), 7; E. Sellin - G. Fohrer,
Einl. in d. AT (1965), 338 etc.

[71] Qoh. differs from the rest of the Wisdom lit. in relation to the concept of fearing God.
It uses only verbal forms of the root ירא and not the noun customary elsewhere. Fear of God
is not integrated into a theol. wisdom system, and it seems to have a numinous aspect, Qoh.
3:14, cf. J. Hempel, *Gott u. Mensch im AT²* (1936), 25; materially cf. Qoh. 12:13.

persons. [72] Those who fear Yahweh or God in the Ps. are distinguished from their counter-parts in, e.g., the Wisdom lit. by the fact that they are almost exclusively characterised by religious traits; moral features are far less prominent. [73] Those who fear God are those who laud the name of Yahweh, Ps. 22:22 f.; His eye rests on them, Ps. 33:18; Yahweh has pity on them, Ps. 103:13; they hope in His commitment חֶסֶד, Ps. 147:11 etc. Those who fear God are marked by a special relation to Him that is brought out even more strongly by the character of the Ps. as prayers. They belong to the congregation of Yahweh; in the older strata this means that they are members of the cultic community who have proved their cultic worthiness, Ps. 15:4, or who offer sacrifices in the temple, Ps. 66:16. But the ref. might be to the people as the community of Yahweh, Ps. 60:4; 85:9 that assembles for the cultus, Ps. 22:23, 25; 61:5. In the later Ps. the term "those who fear God" usually denotes the righteous in the congregation; the cultic aspect is now less prominent, Ps. 25:14; 33:18; 34:7, 9; 103:11, 13, 17 etc., and commitment to God in contrast to ungod-liness is more strongly emphasised, Ps. 145:19; Mal. 3:16; 20. Ps. 115:11, 13; 118:4 and 135:20 stand apart, for here the term "those who fear Yahweh" refers to various groups of participants in the cultus. [74]

e. As legal piety invades the wisdom of Israel in the post-exilic period the idea of fear of God undergoes a shift in meaning. The man who fears God is now the man who keeps the Law, the man who is faithful to it, Ps. 1:2; [75] 19:7-14; 112:1; 119:33-38, 57-64.

4. The Formula אַל־תִּירָא.

The formula אַל־תִּירָא "Fear not!" occurs 75 times in the OT. It is a common formula of reassurance and assistance in everyday life, spoken by men to one another, Ju. 4:18; 2 S. 9:7 etc., or by God Himself, or a man or מַלְאָךְ commissioned by Him, to an individual or the people in time of trouble, Ex. 14:13; Jer. 42:11 etc. As a formula of this kind אַל־תִּירָא has a place in the oracle of salvation, [76] Is. 41:10, 13 f.; 43:1, 5; 44:2; 51:7; 54:4; Jer. 30:10; 46:27 f.; Lam. 3:57 and in some theophanies to counteract terror at the encounter with the divine, Ex. 20:20; Ju. 6:23; Da. 10:12, 19, but not Gn. 15:1; 21:17; 26:24; 28:13 LXX and 46:3. [77]

III. The Stem פחד in the Old Testament.

1. Linguistic Aspects.

a. The original meaning of the verb פָּחַד — best seen in Job 4:14 — is "to quake," so that the q means "trembling" for fear or joy, or with אֶל "to come trembling to some-one," [78] Hos. 3:5; Mi. 7:17, pi with תָּמִיד "to quake continually," [79] and hi in the causative sense "to cause to quake."

---

[72] Outside the Ps. only Mal. 3:16, 20.

[73] In some sense an exception are Ps. in which legal piety begins to play a role, Ps. 103; 119; Becker, 151 and 153.

[74] Becker, 155-160, esp. 160; Plath, 102 f.

[75] BHK reads יְרְאַת for תּוֹרַת.

[76] J. Begrich, "Das priesterliche Heilsorakel," Ges. Stud. z. AT (1964), 217-231; cf. H. Gressmann, "Die literarische Analyse Deuterojesajas," ZAW, 34 (1914), 254-297, who thinks there were Bab. influences on the form of revelatory utterance.

[77] With Becker, 53. The idea that theophany is the original locus of the formula is in-adequately grounded, as against L. Köhler, "Die Offenbarungsformel 'Fürchte dich nicht!' im AT," Schweizerische Theol. Zschr., 36 (1919), 33-9.

[78] Cf. L. Kopf, "Arab. Etymologien u. Par. zum Bibelwörterb.," VT, 9 (1959), 257 f., who thinks the meaning is "to hurry to someone trembling and seeking refuge."

[79] Jenni, op. cit., 224.

b. The noun פַּחַד, as the only attested noun of the stem formed after the manner of the segholate from the one-syllabled stem, denotes "trembling" and "terror," usually in the sense of fear actually experienced. Only rarely does one find the sense of "respect" so common for יָרֵא, namely, at 2 Ch. 19:7 and perhaps Ps. 36:1. [80]

2. Material Aspects.

a. In the OT the root פחד is found almost exclusively in post-exilic works, probably because the root יָרֵא had at this time acquired so specialised a meaning that other words had to be used to express real fear. The basic sense has given the stem פחד something of the idea of anxious uncertainty and disquiet, Dt. 28:65 ff.; Job 3:25 f., so that the words בֶּטַח "safety," Is. 12:2; Ps. 78:53; Prv. 1:33; 3:24 f., and שָׁלוֹם "intactness," "peace," Job 15:21; 21:9 can be used as the opp. Calamitous situations whose consequences for those concerned cannot be foreseen, or which suddenly engulf men, cause "anxious trembling," "terror," or "panic," cf. the terrors of the night, Ps. 91:4; Cant. 3:8, fear of enemies, Ps. 64:1, or the terror of battle, Job 39:22.

b. פחד can also denote fear and terror at the acts of Yahweh, Is. 19:16 f.; 33:14; Job 23:15, or His Word, esp. prophetic threats, Jer. 36:16, 24; Ps. 119:161. It may ref. also to the terrors of (eschatological) divine judgment, Is. 24:17 f.; Jer. 30:5; 48:43; Lam. 3:47. With מָשַׁל "to rule," Job 25:2, and גָּאוֹן "majesty," Is. 2:10, 19, 21 פחד denotes the "fearfulness" of Yahweh. Terror may be evoked not merely by experiencing the terribleness of Yahweh and His acts but also by Yahweh Himself. פַּחַד יְהוָה and פַּחַד אֱלֹהִים denote the terror caused by Yahweh as this "seizes" נָפַל עַל or "comes upon" הָיָה עַל Israel and its enemies, Ex. 15:16; 1 S. 11:7; 2 Ch. 14:13; 17:10; 20:29, cf. Dt. 2:25; 11:25, or as it may indeed smite an individual, Job 13:11. [81]

c. The divine name פַּחַד יִצְחָק found in patriarchal religion, Gn. 31:42, 53 [82] permits of only two possible meanings for פַּחַד: 1. that it is the obj. of Isaac's reverence in the weaker sense of "respect," [83] or 2. that along the lines of Palmyrene-Aram., Arab. and Ugaritic par. it means "kinsman," [84] which corresponds to theophorous elements in Isr. proper names such as אָב, אָח, עַם etc.

IV. Fear in the Old Testament Apocrypha.

The situation in the apocr. is essentially the same as in the OT. In the narrative sections, where there are many depictions of battles, the fear of war and death and human fear in gen. play a great part, 1 Macc. 2:62; 3:6, 22, 25 etc.; 2 Macc. 12:22; 13:16; 3 Macc. 7:21; Jdt. 1:11; 2:28 etc. We also find fear of the sinister and terrible in depictions of supernatural events, 2 Macc. 3:25, 30; 3 Macc. 6:18; Wis. 11:19; 17:4 etc.; this lies behind the "Fear thou not!" in the angelophany of Tob. 12:16 f. Almost without exception in the apocr. the concept of the fear of God denotes the piety of Dispersion Jews in its various aspects, so that it is a sufficient characterisation of the righteous to say that they are

---

[80] On פַּחַד יִצְחָק → lines 24 ff. The fem. פַּחְדָּה occurs at Jer. 2:19, but this text is probably not in the right order.

[81] Est. uses the same terminology when speaking of the fear of the Jews and of Mordecai, 8:17; 9:2 f.

[82] A. Alt, "Der Gott d. Väter," Kl. Schriften, I³ (1963), 24-26.

[83] Becker, 177-9 with ref. to the proper name צְלָפְחָד.

[84] W. F. Albright, From the Stone Age to Christianity (1957), 248 and n. 71 and O. Eissfeldt, "El. u. Jahwe," Kl. Schriften, III (1966), 392, n. 4, cf. also Alt, op. cit., 26, n. 2.

"god-fearing," Jdt. 8:8; Sus. 2 (→ 202, 20 ff.). In individual books different aspects are stressed acc. to the varying intentions of the authors, e.g., the ethical aspect in Tob. 4:21; 14:2, the religious element in Ps. Sol. (as in the Ps.), cf. 3:12; 13:12 etc., [85] while wisdom and legal piety are essential ingredients of the fear of God in Sir. 1:11-21; 2:15-17 etc. [86] In a few passages the fear of God is equated with Jewish religion as a whole; for the sake of this martyrdom is suffered, 2 Macc. 6:30, and no regard is had to children, 4 Macc. 15:8, while all nations will be converted to it as to the true fear of God, Tob. 14:6.

Two apocr. works, Ep. Jer. and 4 Macc., have as their theme fear as the antithesis of obedience. Borrowing from the vocabulary of the Stoic doctrine of πάθος (→ 195, 33 ff.), 4 Macc. uses examples from history to present the confrontation between fear of death (in the form of martyrdom) and obedience to God. Ep. Jer. 14, 22 etc. tries to ward off the danger of apostasy from God through fascination with other cults, proving on various grounds that idols are no gods and therefore there is no need to fear them.

Wanke

C. Fear in Palestinian and Hellenistic Judaism.

1. The Pseudepigrapha.

a. The hortatory wisdom of Test. XII develops the OT theme of the φόβος κυρίου or θεοῦ (→ 201, 1 ff.) in many formula-like expressions, Test. S. 3:4; L. 13:1; N. 2:9; G. 3:2; B. 10:10 and in some special injunctions. Thus the φόβος τοῦ θεοῦ dwells in the δίκαιος καὶ ταπεινός who eschews doing evil, speaking slander, or offending the Lord φοβούμενος γὰρ μὴ προσκροῦσαι Κυρίῳ, G. 5:3-5. The φόβος τοῦ θεοῦ is seated in the heart, Jos. 10:5, cf. R. 4:1, and leads to love φοβεῖσθε τὸν Κύριον καὶ ἀγαπᾶτε τὸν πλησίον, B. 3:3 → 201, 34 ff. Wisdom that can never be lost is acquired in the fear of God, L. 13:7; the good man τὸν ἔχοντα φόβον Κυρίου ὑπερασπίζει, B. 4:5 β (not in α). The fear of God means renouncing Satan, D. 6:1 and caution in the use of wine; for here φόβος θεοῦ must be coincident with shame (αἰδούμενοι), Jud. 13:2. This motivation of pious and upright action by the fear of the Lord gives evidence of ethical thinking that is new as compared to Hell. and that has its basis in the commandment of God, cf. Jos. 11:1. To be sure, it can said that even τὰ θηρία φοβηθήσονται ὑμᾶς if you do the καλόν, N. 8:4, cf. B. 5:2, but what predominates as compared with the Gk. freedom for self-actualisation is strictness based on the all-embracing power of God. [87] Deuteronomistic statements (→ 201, 28 ff.) are adopted in L. 13:1; R. 4:1. [88]

In Jewish exhortation elsewhere fear of God can result in respect for parents, Ps.-Menand., 4, cf. 16. [89] Fear of God is the beginning of all good things, ibid., 70; he who does not fear Him will be forgotten and one day judged by Him, Test. Iobi 43:9. [90] But

---

[85] Cf. Sander, 56-66. Ps. Sol. 17:40 says the Messiah is strong in the fear of God and 18:6-9 says that under his direction the Messianic generation is one that is filled with the fear of God.

[86] Cf. esp. Haspecker, 45-342; Sander, 25-42; Becker, 276-280.

[87] In the strongly Hellenistically orientated work Jos. and Aseneth (ed. M. Philonenko, *Stud. Post-Bibl.*, 13 [1968]) righteous individuals are called φοβούμενος τὸν θεόν, 27, 2 or τὸν κύριον, 8, 9; 22, 8; φοβέομαι as well as σέβομαι is used for worshipping idols, 2, 5; it also occurs with πρᾶος and ἐλεήμων, 8, 9, and with προφήτης and θεοσεβής, 22, 8. Here as in Ps. Sol. 3:12; 4:23; 12:4 etc., cf. 13:5 (εὐσεβής), φοβούμενος τὸν κύριον etc. is not a tt. (→ 207, 16 ff.) but is used gen. for all the righteous → 207, 1 ff.

[88] On the ethical concern of Test. XII cf. Sander, 42-55, who rightly calls fear a "disposition of the heart towards God," 51, although he underrates the didactic-ascetic character of the exhortation as a whole.

[89] Ed. J. Land, *Anecdota Syriaca*, I (1852), cf. Riessler, 1047, 1049.

[90] Ed. S. P. Brock, *Pseudepigr. Veteris Test. graece*, II (1967).

this basic attitude of fear of God is completely different from harmful fear of death, Test. Abr. 13 f. (p. 118, 8 ff. 24); being afraid perverts the heart, Ps.-Menand. (→ n. 89), 83 f. Here as also in Ep. Ar., 270: μὴ διὰ τὸν φόβον μηδὲ διὰ πολυωρίαν, but διὰ τὴν εὔνοιαν one should serve others, the Hell. criticism of false and unworthy fear exerts an influence (→ 192, 16 ff.), cf. also Wis. 17:12. Yet there can be very uncritical ref. to reverence in sacrifice in Ep. Ar., 95, or holy awe at seeing the priest fully vested, 99, or the θεῖος φόβος which helps to bring all things to their goal, 189.

b. In the apocal. writings hortatory elements are much less prominent. Instead a big part is played by epiphany fear (→ 194, 23 ff.) at visionary revelations of God, His messengers, or other heavenly phenomena, cf. Eth. En. 14:13 f.; 15:1; 21:9; 60:3; Slav. En. 20:1 f.; 21:2 f.; 4 Esr. 10:24, 38, 55; 12:3, 5; S. Bar. 53:12; Apc. Abr. 10:6, 15; 16:2. The fear of God of the righteous [91] does not keep them from being snatched away by death, S. Bar. 14:5 f., but they need not worry about sinners, Eth. En. 95:3, or the assaults of enemies, Apc. Eliae 24 f. (p. 76 f., cf. 115), cf. Slav. En. 43:3; for God heals the suffering, Eth. En. 96:3, and reveals future salvation to them to comfort them, S. Bar. 54:4, cf. Eth. En. 100:5. Whereas sailors fear the power of the sea, sinners are not afraid of the Lord who gives the sea its power, Eth. En. 101:4 ff. For this reason the Last Judgment will plunge them into terror and torment, Eth. En. 48:8; 100:8; cf. 4 Esr. 7:80-87. Gr. En. 13:3 speaks of the τρόμος καὶ φόβος of the fallen angels and 4 Esr. 13:8 of the fear of the hostile army at the One like a Son of Man. Like all other men the righteous will suffer fear in the divine judgment, Eth. En. 1:5; after death, however, the sevenfold pain of sinners does not await them *marcescent in timoribus*, 4 Esr. 7:87, but rather the sevenfold joy of the righteous *gaudebunt non revertentes* (without fear), 7:98.[92] One examines these texts in vain for practical Hell. wisdom or remnants of Stoic philosophy. At the very most there is an echo in the promise of the seer in 4 Esr. 6:33 f.

2. Qumran.

In his prayer the righteous man of the Qumran community knows that he is among those "who fear God" אל יראי בתוך 1 QH 12:3, cf. 1 QSb 1:1; 5:25; Damasc. 10:2 (10:15);[93] 20:19 f. (9:43 f.). The word פחד is used for "terror" at the judgments משפטים of God, 1 QS 10:34; 1 QS 4:2,[94] but it is also combined with other terrors, e.g., בליעל ממשלת in 1 QS 1:17 f., cf. 1 QH 2:36. God Himself is "dreadful" and "terrible" in the holy war ונורא גדול אל 1 QM 10:1, cf. 12:7 (text uncertain), and His works of creation are נוראים, 1 QH 13:15. The children of light are not to be afraid in battle against their enemies, 1 QM 10:3; 15:8; 17:4. In view of the cultic character of the fellowship, wisdom and hortatory aspects of the fear of God are much less prominent in the Dead Sea Scrolls.[95]

---

[91] In acc. with the common adoption of OT motifs we often find humble and obedient fear (of God), cf. S. Bar., 44, 7; 46, 5; *tuum timorem*, 4 Esr. 8:28. In keeping with the usage of the authors of 4 Esr. and S. Bar. elsewhere God is never mentioned as the obj. of fear, cf. B. Violet, "Die Apokalypsen d. Esr. u. d. Bar. in deutscher Gestalt," GCS, 32 (1924), 264, n. on v. 5; 69 f., n. on vv. 3-5.

[92] Lat. versions acc. to L. Gry, *Les dires prophétiques d'Esdras (IV Esdras)*, I (1938), *ad loc*.

[93] J. Maier, *Die Texte vom Toten Meer*, II (1960), *ad loc*. takes אל את ירא to mean "cultically qualified" here.

[94] Acc. to Maier, *op. cit., ad loc*. only the transl. "judgments" makes good sense; K. Schubert, "Die jüd. u. judenchr. Sekten im Lichte d. Handschriftenfunde v. 'En Feščha," *Zschr. f. Kathol. Theol.*, 74 (1952), 45 transl. "statutes."

[95] Cf. Becker, 281 f. with n. 97; on Qumran in gen. cf. Romaniuk Crainte de Dieu, 29-38; S. J. de Vries, "Note concerning the Fear of God in the Qumran Scrolls," *Revue de Qumran*, 5 (1965), 233-7.

3. Rabbinic Writings.

In these works the fear of God denotes the basic attitude of the righteous, bBer., 16b; 17a, 33b, as fear of sin, Ab., 2, 10; 3, 12. In Ab., 1, 3 acc. to a well-known saying of Antigonus of Sokho the מורא שמים rests on those who serve the Lord without expecting any reward, reinterpreted in AbRNat A, 5, 1 (Schechter, p. 26, 2) by the added promise of a double reward. Acc. to bNidda, 16b the fear of God is an attainment of the righteous outside the divine omnicausality. The linking of fearing and loving God in Dt. 6:5, 13 (→ 201, 34 ff.) led to a lively debate whether those who love God stand in a higher relation to Him than those who fear God, Sota, 5, 5; bSota, 31a; jBer., 9 (14b, 45 ff.)), cf. also bSanh., 61b-62a. Hell. influence cannot be rejected out of hand here → 192, 16 ff. [96] Because he loved God Abraham is often set above Job who only feared Him. [97] Nevertheless, fear of God and His judgment must continue in view of man's deficient assurance of salvation, M. Ex., 5, 2 on 17:14 (p. 185, 7 ff.); jChag., 2, 1 (77a, 31 ff.), bBer., 28b. God can be called "the Terrible," היראוי, bBer., 33b, bMeg., 25a. Indeed, the noun יראה in the sense of "object of veneration" can be a term for deity, esp. for false gods, bSanh., 106a; jKid., 1, 7 (61b, 5). [98] Already at 2 Ch. 5:6 the LXX adds to the HT by using οἱ φοβούμενοι for the righteous outside the national fellowship in contrast to ἐπισυνηγμένοι "proselytes." We find the corresponding distinction between יראי שמים and גרים in Rabb. texts when in contrast. to circumcised converts the ref. is to the righteous among non-Jews who stand in a looser relation to the Jewish community but keep part of the Mosaic Law, cf. Dt. r., 2, 24 on 3:25 (Wünsche, 31 f.); M. Ex., 8, 18 on 22:20 (p. 312, 18); Nu. r., 8, 9, on 5:9; jMeg., 3, 2 (74a, 34). Their existence is naturally of special importance in the Diaspora, cf. Jos. Ant., 14, 110, where the Hell. σεβόμενοι (→ 208, 12 ff.) is used, and the passages in Ac. (→ 213, 1 ff.). On σεβόμενοι τὸν θεὸν ὕψιστον → VIII, 615, n. 10; 618, n. 41. Already in the 3rd cent. A.D. the φοβούμενοι τὸν θεόν are no longer clearly differentiated from the proselytes, cf. Gn. r., 28, 5 on 6:7 (Wünsche, 125); cf. → VI, 731, 6 ff.; 734, 5 ff. with examples from inscr.; 740, 32 ff. [99]

4. Philo and Josephus.

a. Although Philo adopts the OT and common Jewish use of fear of God, Migr. Abr., 21; Deus Imm., 69, in good Hell. fashion, adopting the μὴ φοβοῦ of Gn. 28:13 (not HT), he sees in God the weapon of defence against φόβος and every πάθος, Som., I, 173, cf. Conf. Ling., 90; Mut. Nom., 72. [100] For this reason the impelling motive for the righteous is love rather than fear (→ lines 7 ff.), Spec. Leg., I, 300; Deus. Imm., 69. Hence φόβος must be supplemented by θάρσος, Rer. Div. Her., 28, cf. 24. [101] Nevertheless, fear should be present in education, for ἀφροσύνη δ᾽ οὐκ ἄλλῳ ἢ φόβῳ θεραπεύεται, Spec. Leg., II, 239; but φοβούμενοι καὶ τρέμοντες ὑπ᾽ ἀνανδρίας καὶ δειλίας ψυχικῆς are among those who cannot see and hear God, Leg. All., III, 54.

---

[96] Further examples in Str.-B., II, 112 f.

[97] Cf. Sander, 67-138, 125-132, with many examples on the relation of love and fear.

[98] On the question of assurance cf. Str.-B., III, 218-221; on יראה for God v. Levy Wört., s.v., also Becker, 182. The God of Israel does not demand from His people devotion with terror, fear, trembling and quaking but the daily reading of the shema, Lv. r., 27, 6 on 22:27 (Wünsche, 189).

[99] Cf. Str.-B., II, 715-721; K. Thraede, "Beiträge z. Datierung Commodians," Jbch. Ant. Christ., 2 (1959), 96-100; E. Lerle, Proselytenwerbung u. Urchr. (1960), 27-33. Romaniuk Die "Gottesfürchtigen," 66-91; H. Bellen, "Συναγωγὴ τῶν Ἰουδαίων καὶ Θεοσεβῶν, Die Aussage einer bosporanischen Freilassungsinschr. (CIRB, 71) zum Problem d. 'Gottesfürchtigen'" Jbch. Ant. Christ., 8/9 (1965/66), 171-6.

[100] Cf. W. Völker, "Fortschritt u. Vollendung bei Philo v. Alex.," TU, 49 (1938), 127.

[101] Völker, op. cit., 322 [Bertram].

b. In Josephus [102] φόβος occurs 150 times and φοβέομαι 70 times. The word group is often used for fear and terror in war, Bell., 1, 307; 2, 226. 256. 463; 4, 655; 6, 69. 138; Ant., 3, 55; 4, 90; ταραχή, δέος and φόβος occur together in Ant., 6, 24, cf. 6, 5; 9, 94; 11, 175. In this connection we may also ref. to "fear of death" θάνατον φοβηθέντες, Ant., 18, 266, cf. 7, 342 and φόβος in the sense of "danger," Bell., 1, 483 or "deterrent," Bell., 3, 102, cf. 363. "Anxiety" about one's own life is the meaning in Bell., 1, 591; 4, 107 and at the flood in Ant., 1, 97. φόβος occurs alongside οἶκτος in Bell., 6, 263. The senses "respect," "dread," "reverence" are common, e.g., τοῦ κωλύοντος φόβος fear of punishment, Bell., 6, 263, of causing envy, 1, 428, cf. 597 and 609, respect for teachers, Bell., 2, 162. There is an echo of wisdom in the expression: οἱ φόβοι δὲ διδάσκουσιν προμήθειαν, Bell., 1, 374; δοῦλοι should never be witnesses in court οὓς... εἰκός διὰ φόβον μὴ τἀληθῆ μαρτυρῆσαι, Ant., 4, 219. In Jos. φοβέομαι is not usually related to God; only in Ant., 1, 114 do we find φόβος... παρὰ τοῦ θεοῦ. The alternation of ὡς ἄνθρωπον ἐφοβήθημεν and κρείττονά σε θνητῆς φύσεως ὁμολογοῦμεν in Ant., 19, 345, and of καὶ χωρὶς τῆς περιτομῆς τὸ θεῖον σέβειν, Ant., 20, 41; cf. Bell., 1, 111 and πρὸς τὸν θεὸν εὐσέβεια, Ant., 18, 117 shows that Jos. consistently tries to adopt Hell. terminology. Other terms for the fear of God are εὐλαβέομαι in Ant., 6, 259 and δείδω in 2, 23; 3, 321. His approach is particularly clear when he calls passionate Jewish piety δεισιδαιμονία (→ 197, 9 ff.), Ant., 12, 5; Bell., 1, 113; 2, 174 and 277, cf. the judgment on Manasseh after his conversion Ant., 10, 42. [103]

δέος occurs in Jos. 141 times and like φόβος it is mostly used for "fear" of dangers. Bell., 1, 168 and 373; Ant., 6, 151, or punishment, Ant., 18, 81, or it ref. to "anxiety" in gen., Bell., 1, 554 and 615; 2, 157. The meaning "respect" δέος τῆς θρησκείας occurs in Bell., 5, 229.

D. The Word Group in the New Testament.

1. General Usage.

In the NT the word group φοβ- is represented by φοβέομαι 95 times, φόβος 47, ἔμφοβος 5, ἀφόβως 4, φοβερός 3, ἔκφοβος 2 and ἐκφοβέω and φόβητρον once each, a sum total of 158 times. The main use is in the Gospels and Acts; only the noun is rather more common in Paul. As a rule the sense is general and everyday when φοβέομαι is combined with the inf. "to fear to...," Mt. 1:20; [104] 2:22, or with μή "to be afraid that," Ac. 5:26; 23:10; 27:17, 29; 2 C. 11:3; 12:20; Gl. 4:11; Hb. 4:1. We often find fear of specific people, Mk. 6:20; Mt. 25:25; Lk. 19:21; Ac. 9:26, or the whole people, Mk. 11:32; 12:12; Mt. 14:5; 21:26, 46; Lk. 20:19; 22:2; Jn. 7:13; 9:22; 19:38; 20:19; Ac. 5:26; Gl. 2:12; φοβέομαι is in the abs. at Jn. 19:8; Ac. 16:38; 22:29. Beyond the gen. use the context pts. to various special senses which for the most part take up motifs from the OT-Jewish (→ 197, 25 ff.; 205, 15 ff.) and Hell. (→ 189, 14 ff.) traditions.

In the majority of instances what the NT says about fear lies within the framework of traditional ideas. Only a few times does it represent specific concerns of primitive Christianity, and especially so when the relation of faith and fear or love and fear is defined in terms of the Christian life. The significance of fear as a

---

[102] I owe the Jos. ref. to K. H. Rengstorf.
[103] Cf. A. Schlatter, "Wie sprach Josephus von Gott?" BFTh, 14, 1 (1910), 60 f.
[104] As against A. Suhl, "Der Davidssohn im Mt.," ZNW, 59 (1968), 64, who sees here a ref. to awe at the miracle of conception by the Spirit. This is refuted by the saying of the angel in 1:20, which bases μὴ φοβηθῇς παραλαβεῖν on the ref to the πνεῦμα ἅγιον. Hence knowing the Spirit as the One who causes the pregnancy leads not to awe but to acceptance by Mary. Mt. 1:18c can thus be an explanation only for the reader. Fear on Joseph's part is not ref. to until we come to the Prot. Ev. Jc. 14:1:... φοβοῦμαι μήπως ἀγγελικόν ἐστιν τὸ ἐν αὐτῇ.

relational term may be seen in the fact that all hampering anxiety is rejected whereas fear of God cannot be separated from faith as a basic attitude of the man who depends wholly and utterly on God. [105]

2. The Epiphany of God's Kingdom and Fear.

a. The widespread motif of fear at God's epiphany (→ 201, 1 ff.) plays a special role in the NT in accounts of the deeds and destiny of Jesus. The related statements occur chiefly in Mark (8 times), Luke (Lk. 10 times with echoes in Ac. 2:43; 5:5, 11; 19:17) and Matthew (6 times); there is also one each in John's Gospel and Revelation. The concrete occasion for adoption of the motif is to be found in the incomprehensible nature of the mighty work of Jesus which arouses fear both in spectators and also in those more directly concerned. [106] General epiphany and miracle motifs (→ 194, 23 ff.; III, 206, 23 ff.) strengthen this feature. The disciples experience fear at what they cannot understand, [107] but they are also liberated from anxiety for faith, which can entail another reference to fear in a new sense → 213, 17 ff.

Thus after the stilling of the storm Mk. 4:41 says of the disciples: ἐφοβήθησαν φόβον μέγαν, cf. Lk. 8:25: φοβηθέντες δὲ ἐθαύμασαν, while Mt. 8:27 says more briefly: οἱ δὲ ἄνθρωποι ἐθαύμασαν. Similarly the curing of the demoniac in Mk. 5:15 is a reason for fear, which Lk. 8:37 emphasises particularly: φόβῳ μεγάλῳ συνείχοντο. The raising of the νεανίσκος at Nain causes fear among the bystanders, so that they praise God, Lk. 7:16, and the same is true at the healing of the παραλυτικός, where ἔκστασις and φόβος meet and lead to praise of God, Lk. 5:26; here Mk. 2:12 simply has ἐξίστασθαι and Mt. 9:8 ἐφοβήθησαν. Lk. 5:26 finds a more precise reason for the φόβος in the παράδοξον of the event. When the disciples see Jesus walking on the lake, they cry out for fear ἀπὸ τοῦ φόβου — Mk. 6:49 simply has ἀνέκραξαν and Jn. 6:19 ἐφοβήθησαν — because they are startled as at an apparition, Mt. 14:26. The woman with an issue of blood suddenly becomes aware that she is cured: φοβηθεῖσα καὶ τρέμουσα, Mk. 5:33, so that she experiences physical φόβος too and falls down at the feet of Jesus. Lk. 8:47 changes this fear into worry that she is detected: ἰδοῦσα δὲ ἡ γυνὴ ὅτι οὐκ ἔλαθεν τρέμουσα ἦλθεν. The motif of fear plays a special role in the infancy stories in Lk., where fear comes upon the one to whom the ἄγγελος κυρίου appears (Lk. 1:12; 2:9) or who experiences a divine miracle (Lk. 1:65 → 212, 19 ff.).

The theme of epiphany fear is of special significance in the Synoptic Easter stories (→ 210, 14 ff.) and in the account of the transfiguration, in which the disciples are gripped by fear, Mk. 9:6: ἔκφοβοι ἐγένοντο, Lk. 9:34: ἐφοβήθησαν, Mt. 17:6: ἐφοβήθησαν σφόδρα only as a reaction to the voice from the cloud. Luke evidently tries to restrict the fear of the disciples to miraculous phenomena (cf. also Ac. 10:4) or else he explains it psychologically → lines 23 ff.; III, 921, 5 ff. Hence he interprets fear at the transfigured appearance of Jesus as fear at entry into the

---

[105] Cf. also J. Boehmer, *Die neutestamentliche Gottesscheu u. d. ersten drei Bitten des Vaterunsers* (1917).

[106] Also to be noted here is the fact that the ἀρχιερεῖς and γραμματεῖς fear Jesus and the whole people "is beside itself" ἐξεπλήσσετο at His διδαχή, Mk. 11:18. But the disciples, too, are afraid when Jesus predicts His passion, Mk. 9:32 par. Lk. 9:34, and also when He goes up to Jerusalem, Mk. 10:32, for they cannot understand God's plan for Jesus.

[107] R. Otto, *Das Heilige*[14] (1926), 13-23 describes fear as *mysterium tremendum* and a primal experience, cf. G. van der Leeuw / (C. M. Edsman), Art. "Furcht" in RGG[3], II, 1180-1182.

cloud, Lk. 9:34. Mt. in good apocalyptic fashion links fear with the voice from the cloud [108] and by this interpolation strongly emphasises the difference between Jesus and the disciples → 212, 11 ff. [109] He has a general tendency to weaken the element of epiphany fear → 211, 24 ff. and 212, 1 ff. In contrast the fear of the disciples is for Mark a decisive reaction to the deeds and destiny of Jesus understood as the intervention of divine activity → III, 5, 40 ff.; 36, 44 ff. This fear is distinguished, however, from dread at visions (cf. Rev. 11:11) and also from the fear of the wicked at the eschata (Lk. 21:26; Hb. 10:27, 31; Rev. 18:10, 15) by the fact that it does not plunge into despair but leads to δοξάζειν (Mk. 2:12; Mt. 9:8) and προσκυνεῖν (Mt. 28:9, cf. Lk. 24:5; Mt. 17:6). This fear may also be seen in the community's experiences of salvation, Ac. 2:43; 5:5, 11; 19:17. It excludes fear of man (φοβέομαι ἀπό → 195, 40) but causes fear of him who has power to cast into hell, Lk. 12:4 f. par. Mt. 10:28 → 213, 17 ff.

b. According to the Synoptic Easter stories news of the resurrection of Jesus arouses fear and astonishment in the women at the tomb. Interpretation of Mk. 16:8 involves serious problems in this regard. The attested MS text of Mk. ends with the fear of the women at the empty tomb and the message of the angel: ἔφυγον ἀπὸ τοῦ μνημείου, εἶχεν γὰρ αὐτὰς τρόμος καὶ ἔκστασις· καὶ οὐδενὶ οὐδὲν εἶπαν· ἐφοβοῦντο γάρ.

The hypothesis that Mk. planned to end his Gospel with this reference to fear of God [110] is balanced by suggestions that he was hindered from bringing his work to a meaningful conclusion, [111] or that the original ending was lost, [112] or that it had in fact the present ending not found in B ℵ sy^s etc. [113] To-day there is widespread agreement as to the secondary character of Mk. 16:9-20. [114] Linguistically it is not inconceivable that Mk. puts the motif of fear at the end of crucial points in the passion narrative, as also in Mk. 9:32; 10:32. [115] But in this case we should have to reckon with the literary

---

[108] Cf. Loh. Mt., ad loc. At a heavenly voice man falls on his face and is then raised up again by God, Da. 8:17 f., cf. 10:9 f., 15 ff.; Rev. 1:17. An earlier model is provided by Ez., cf. 2:1 f. → 203, 21 ff.; 194, 23 ff.

[109] Cf. on this H. Baltensweiler, "Die Verklärung Jesu," AbhThANT, 33 (1959), 127 f.

[110] Cf. Loh. Mk., ad loc.; O. Linton, "Der vermisste Markusschluss," ThBl, 8 (1929), 229-234; H. Grass, Ostergeschehen u. Osterberichte³ (1964), 16-23. Further bibl. in Pr.-Bauer, s.v. φοβέω; W. G. Kümmel, Einl. in d. NT¹⁵ (1968), 56 f.; Bultmann Trad.⁷, 308 f. and Suppl., 46.

[111] Cf. W. L. Knox, "The Ending of St. Mark's Gospel," HThR, 35 (1942), 13; Zahn Kan., II (1892), 910-938; Zahn Einl., I, 232-240.

[112] M. Hengel, "Maria Magdalena u. d. Frauen als Zeugen," Festschr. O. Michel (1963), 251 conjectures an original protophany to Mary Magdalene; H. E. H. Probyn, "The End of the Gospel of St. Mark," Exp., IX, 4 (1925), 120-5 thinks Ac. 1:6-11 is the lost ending, cf. F. G. Kenyon, "Papyrus Rolls and the Ending of St. Mark," JThSt, 40 (1939), 253-7.

[113] G. Hartmann, "Der Aufbau d. Mk. mit einem Anhang: Untersuchungen z. Echtheit des Markusschlusses," NTAbh, 17, 2-3 (1936), 180 f.; cf. Kümmel, op. cit., 56.

[114] Acc. to Eus. and Jer. vv. 9-20 were not in most Gk. MSS, cf. Oxf. NT, Loh. Mk., ad loc. Dependent on Lk. they belong to the 2nd cent., cf. E. Helzle, Der Schluss d. Mk. (Mk. 16:9-20) u. d. Freer-Logion (Mk. 16:14 W), ihre Tendenzen u. ihr gegenseitiges Verhältnis. Eine wortexeget. Untersuchung, Diss. Tübingen (1959), cf. ThLZ, 85 (1960), 470-4; but cf. also E. Linnemann, "Der (wiedergefundene) Markusschluss," ZThK, 66 (1969), 255-287.

[115] Cf. G. Kittel, "Die Auferstehung Jesu," DTh, 4 (1937), 152. The element of confusion is retained though weakened in Jn. 20:2; Lk. 24:4 f., 22; Mt. 28:8, and related to passing on the news, as against Mk. 16:8. W. C. Allen, "St. Mark 16:8. 'They were afraid' Why?" JThSt, 47 (1946), 46-9; also "'Fear' in St. Mark," ibid., 48 (1947), 201-3 thinks that in virtue of the motif of religious awe Mk. 16:8 was the original ending; cf. K. Tagawa, "Miracles et évangile," Études d'histoire et de philosophie religieuses, 62 (1966), 99-122.

form of aposiopesis, which can hardly be presupposed in Mk.[116] On theological grounds, too, fear and silence can hardly be the last word of the εὐαγγέλιον Ἰησοῦ Χριστοῦ, Mk. 1:1, for, as the present form of the three passion predictions clearly shows,[117] what Mk. expects after the crucifixion of Jesus is not His *parousia* as the Son of Man from heaven[118] but rather, with the primitive Chr. *kerygma* of 1 C. 15:4, His resurrection after three days, Mk. 8:31; 9:31; 10:34. Even if in the tradition fear of God in face of the crucifixion of the Bringer of salvation might have been the primary christological statement,[119] this would still contradict Mk.'s understanding, since he must have spoken of the new reality of the life of Jesus' disciples on the basis of the reality of the resurrection. This post-Easter reality, however, no longer stands under the sign of fear and misunderstanding.[120] In it the pre-Easter hiddenness of the glory of Jesus is pierced by the Easter experience of His epiphany. Mk., however, did not write a second work which might have dealt specifically with the removal of fear and ignorance.

The original ending seems to have been detached later. Perhaps it contained a protophany to Mary Magdalene (→ n. 112), or, more likely, a Galilean appearance to Peter → V, 355, n. 200. A possible reason for removing it prior to the composition of Mt. and Lk. is that, although it was in keeping with the ancient *kerygma* of the Hell. communities (1 C. 15:5), it did not accord with the changed position of Peter in the leadership of the community.[121]

What the women are afraid of in Mk. 16:8 is the empty tomb and the incomprehensible message of the angel. Their fear is in the context of the passion and death of Jesus, which brings only perplexity and horror. The promise of the resurrection has not yet been experienced as the presence of the Risen Lord dispensing salvation. Matthew drastically weakens the strong statement of Mark with his μετὰ φόβου καὶ χαρᾶς μεγάλης (28:8), just as earlier it is only the watchers (τηροῦντες) who are overcome by terror (Mt. 28:4), and not the women, who are mentioned in Mk. 16:5 (ἐξεθαμβήθησαν) and Lk. 24:5 (cf. also Mt. 27:54). Luke eliminates the element of fear altogether (→ 209, 36 ff.) and simply refers later to the astonishment of the disciples (Lk. 24:22, 37 f.) that is turned into χαρά (v. 41).

---

116 Cf. Knox, *op. cit.* (→ n. 111), 20 f. On the other hand short concluding sentences with γάρ are common, cf. Pr.-Bauer, *s.v.* φοβέω, Knox, 14.

117 On this cf. G. Strecker, "Die Leidens- u. Auferstehungsvoraussagen im Mk.," ZThK, 64 (1967), 16-39.

118 So esp. Loh. Mk. on 16:7, who in the saying of the angel to the women at the tomb simply sees a ref. to the close *parousia* of the Lord and not to the appearances of the Risen Lord, cf. W. Marxsen, "Der Evangelist Mk. Stud. z. Redaktionsgesch. d. Ev.," FRL, 67² (1959), 51-9; in criticism of Loh. Mk. cf. esp. W. G. Kümmel, "Verheissung u. Erfüllung," AbhThANT, 6³ (1956), 70-72.

119 Cf. G. Bertram, "Die Himmelfahrt Jesu vom Kreuz aus u. d. Glaube an seine Auferstehung," *Festschr. A. Deissmann* (1927), 187-217; A. Strobel, *Kerygma u. Apokalyptik. Ein religionsgesch. u. theologiegesch. Beitrag z. Christusfrage* (1967), 138-161.

120 Cf. E. Schweizer, "Zur Frage d. Messiasgeheimnisses bei Mk.," ZNW, 56 (1965), 3 f. with n. 17. 7 f.; C. Maurer, "Das Messiasgeheimnis d. Mk.," NTSt., 14 (1967/68), 525 f.; H. R. Balz, "Furcht vor Gott? Überlegungen zu einem vergessenen Motiv bibl. Theol.," EvTh., 29 (1969), 626-644. Acc. to J. Roloff, "Das Marcusevangelium als Geschichtsdarstellung," EvTh, 29 (1969), 73-93 Mk. presented the earthly fellowship between Jesus and the disciples in terms of their lack of understanding (90 f.) and thus closed his account with the final palpable historical datum of the misunderstanding in the epiphany fear of the women (92 f.). Is this kind of abstraction conceivable in a primitive Chr. theologian?

121 In detail cf. E. Schweizer, *Das Ev. n. Mk.*, NT Deutsch, I² (1968), 212-6. A ref. to Peter is put in at Lk. 24:34, cf. U. Wilckens, "Der Ursprung d. Überlieferung d. Erscheinungen d. Auferstandenen," *Festschr. E. Schlink* (1963), 76-80; Grass, *op. cit.*, 38 f.; G. Klein, "Die Berufung d. Petrus," *Rekonstruktion u. Interpretation* (1969), 11-48; also "Die Verleugnung d. Petrus," *ibid.*, 49-98; Bultmann Trad., 314 with n. 1; L. Brun, *Die Auferstehung Jesu Christi in d. urchr. Überlieferung* (1925), 9-11, 52 f.

c. According to the statements of the Synoptists, especially Matthew and Luke, terror at the almighty acts of Jesus and the epiphany of divine power is resolved by the summons not to fear. Whereas in the case of Jairus the call μὴ φοβοῦ, μόνον πίστευε (Mk. 5:36 par. Lk. 8:50) refers to his anxiety about his child, [122] in Mk. 6:50 (par. Mt. 14:27; Jn. 6:20) we have a formula of assurance and comfort (→ 203, 21 ff.) by which Jesus makes Himself known to the disciples: (θαρσεῖτε,) ἐγώ εἰμι· μὴ φοβεῖσθε. In Mark, however, even this word of comfort and revelation cannot dispel the disciples' lack of understanding, Mk. 6:51b-52, whereas in Matthew it leads to fearless faith (→ lines 16 ff.) and to the confession of Jesus as the Son of God, Mt. 14:28-33; → III, 38, 8 ff. [123]

In Matthew the summons not to be afraid is linked to mention of the disciples' fear → 210, 3 f. Thus, diverging from the other accounts, Matthew connects the story of the transfiguration to the summons of Jesus: μὴ φοβεῖσθε, 17:7. Only on this basis dare the disciples rise up and lift up their eyes. Thus the epiphany of Jesus as the Son of God is presented in the apocalyptic style of appearance narratives. The terror of the women at the grave causes them to do obeisance to Jesus. As soon as the One who frightens them makes Himself known to the disciples as the Lord who is devoted to them, fear gives way to proclamation and faith, 28:8, 10.

In the infancy stories in Luke (→ 209, 30 ff.) the angelic appearances are always followed by a summons not to fear, 1:13, 30; 2:10, cf. Ac. 18:9; 27:24 in relation to Paul's visions. The μὴ φοβοῦ of Jesus to Peter in Lk. 5:10 is a reply to the θάμβος which seized them all at the miraculous draught of fishes, 5:9 → III, 6, 26 ff. Perhaps the excision of references to fear from the Easter story in Lk. (→ 211, 28 ff.) is connected with the fact that Lk. drops the account of the appearance of the Risen Lord to Peter which originally contained the motif of epiphany fear.

3. The Fear of God in Formulae.

Luke shows a certain liking for the OT-Jewish formula "to fear God" → 201, 14 ff.; 205, 17 ff. The wisdom-like description of the righteous Jew in Lk. 1:50 is quoted from Ps. 103:13. The parable of the unjust judge describes him as τὸν θεὸν μὴ φοβούμενος καὶ ἄνθρωπον μὴ ἐντρεπόμενος, Lk. 18:2, cf. v. 4. [124] This does not refer to the ungodliness of the judge in general but is alluding to the fact that he fears neither the judgment of men — because he is corrupt? [125] — nor the judgment of God — because he is unjust [126] — and has in view only his own advantage. φοβέομαι relates to the same fear of God's judgment in Lk. 23:40. [127]

---

[122] Naturally there is also ref. to the astonishment of the bystanders when the girl is raised up, cf. Mk. 5:42 par. Lk. 8:55. Mt. (9:25) is consistent here again in eliminating the element of fear → 210, 3 f.

[123] On this cf. H. J. Held, "Mt. als Interpret der Wundergeschichten," G. Bornkamm - G. Barth - H. J. Held, Überlieferung u. Auslegung im Mt., Wissenschaftl. Monographien zum AT u. NT, 1⁵ (1968), 193-5; G. Bornkamm, "Die Sturmstillung im Mt.," ibid., 48-53.

[124] There is a linguistically similar expression in Dion. Hal. Ant. Rom., 10, 10, 7: οὔτε θεῖον φοβηθέντες χόλον οὔτε ἀνθρωπίνην ἐντραπέντες νέμεσιν. Related in meaning is what Jos. says about Jehoiakim in Ant., 10, 83: μήτε πρὸς θεὸν ὅσιος μήτε πρὸς ἀνθρώπους ἐπιεικής.

[125] Cf. Jeremias Gl.⁷, 153.

[126] On this cf. G. Delling, "Das Gleichnis vom gottlosen Richter," ZNW, 53 (1962), 7 with n. 26; W. Grundmann, Das Ev. nach Lk., Theol. Handkomm. zum NT, 3² (1963). ad loc.

[127] We find similar formulae as OT quotations in Rev. 11:18; 15:4; 19:5, and with no direct original in 14:7, in connection with God's eschatological judgment in which the righteous will be delivered, or with the power of God which is to be feared and magnified.

Ac. offers 5 instances of the formula φοβούμενος (-οι) (10:2, 22, 35; 13:16, 26), and 6 of the Hellenistic sounding σεβόμενος (-οι) (→ VII, 172, 18 ff.),[128] with or without θεόν to denote Gentile adherents to the Jewish faith who are open to the primitive Christian mission → 207, 16 ff.

Thus the first conversion of a Gentile under Peter in Ac. 10 is strictly the winning of a marginal member of the Jewish community for the Chr. community.[129] Constant prayer and great liberality are characteristic of the god-fearing centurion Cornelius, Ac. 10:2. He is called εὐσεβής in 10:2 (→ VII, 181, 43 ff.) and δίκαιος in v. 22. It is no surprise, then, if there is an echo of Pauline theology in simplified form in the statement that a man is acceptable to God of whom it may be said: ὁ φοβούμενος αὐτὸν καὶ ἐργαζόμενος δικαιοσύνην, Ac. 10:35. This brings out plainly the Christian starting-point of the Gentile mission as compared to Jewish reserve with ref. to "god-fearers." A clear illustration is to be seen in Luke's account of the missionary practice of Paul, who always preaches at synagogue worship and can thus address the φοβούμενοι better than the Jews themselves, 13:16, 26;[130] cf. 13:43 ff.

4. Faith and Fear.

The tension between fear and fearlessness in the tradition of Jesus (→ 212, 1 ff.) is still maintained in what Paul says about the attitude of believers → VI, 221, 28 ff. If Jesus told His disciples not to be afraid of earthly courts or the threats of existence in the flesh, and yet did not take away their fear of the power of Satan (→ 210, 11 ff.), for Paul, too, fear can be an essential aspect of faith without this implying that the new existence of the believer is fundamentally determined by fear and anxiety. In this regard the menacing seriousness of God's judgment is decisive. How can the Christian community arrogantly exalt itself above hardened Israel if God can inflict the same pitiless penalty of blindness on the new people of God?[131] It is rather to fear: μὴ ὑψηλὰ φρόνει, ἀλλὰ φοβοῦ, R. 11:20. But this fear does not produce the anxiety of helpless men threatened on every hand. This is apparent from the context of 2 C. 5:6 ff., where three times (v. 6, 8, 9) the confidence of Christians in face of an uncertain state after death is asserted, and yet in 5:11 the attitude of hope and assurance can be summed up in the words: εἰδότες οὖν τὸν φόβον τοῦ κυρίου (cf. the analogous ἐλπίς saying in 2 C. 3:12). The believer is not autonomous in relation to God as the unjust judge is (→ 212, 29 ff.) and as are men generally in the sphere of sin, R. 3:18 quoting Ps. 36:1. He is so orientated to God that he gladly accepts suffering in order that he may grow in fear, 2 C. 7:11. This is Paul's situation in relation to the Corinthians: ἐν ἀσθενείᾳ καὶ ἐν φόβῳ καὶ ἐν τρόμῳ πολλῷ ἐγενόμην πρὸς ὑμᾶς (1 C. 2:3, cf. the community itself in 2 C. 7:15). Along with his inner difficulties he mentions φόβοι from without in 2 C. 7:5 because he knows that his preaching is ἐν ἀποδείξει πνεύματος καὶ δυνάμεως (1 C. 2:4) only when the messenger himself is marked by the weakness and folly of the cross and hence by fear.[132] Thus fear as a correlative of faith

---

[128] Ac. 13:43, 50; 16:14; 17:4, 17; 18:7. These "god-fearers" are identical with the "Greeks" of Ac. → VI, 743, 30 ff. After Ac. 13:26 the author consistently has σεβόμενοι for φοβούμενοι.

[129] Cf. Haench. Ag.[14], ad loc. Bibl. in Pr.-Bauer, s.v. σέβω.

[130] On v. 26 cf Haench. Ag.[14], ad loc. with n. 7.

[131] Cf. Lütgert, 165-170. This fear is designed to shatter false security as a caricature of true faith and to confront the believer with the infinite power and freedom of God, to whose gracious address he is totally referred, cf. also on this Bultmann Theol.[6], 321 f.

[132] There is thus a christological reason for the manner of Paul's coming. It cannot be explained simply in terms of human difficulties and fear of conflict, as against O. Glombitza, "Mit Furcht u. Zittern. Zum Verständnis v. Phil. 2:12," Nov. Test., 3 (1959), 101 f.

is not just a spiritual concern. It is so existential a matter that it can be described by the strong expression φόβος καὶ τρόμος which in the NT is found only in the Pauline corpus at 1 C. 2:3; 2 C. 7:15; Phil. 2:12; Eph. 6:5 → 217, 7 ff.; 199, 18 ff.; 206, 18 f. [133] This aspect of fear is particularly evident in Phil. 2:12, where the exhortation commencing with ὥστε (v. 12) catches up the preceding hymn to Christ. The exemplary self-sacrifice of Christ (2:8) makes possible for the believer only the attitude of humble acceptance (μετὰ φόβου καὶ τρόμου) of the will of God, who wants mutual love in the community and not self-assertive zeal, 2:1-4. [134] Trembling and fear bring out the radical and total dependence of the believer on the saving work of God, and this in turn leads to acceptance of the neighbour and is thus the only achievement faith has to offer. [135] God alone, however, is the ἐνεργῶν..., Phil. 2:13; → II, 746, 26 ff.

This spirit of fear no longer has anything to do with the servile anxiety of whose who want to measure up to the *nomos* in all things. It has acquired a new content through the trust of the υἱοὶ θεοῦ in God as their Father: οὐ γὰρ ἐλάβετε πνεῦμα δουλείας πάλιν εἰς φόβον, ἀλλὰ ἐλάβετε πνεῦμα υἱοθεσίας, R. 8:15. For believers who know the presence of Christ in the Spirit, fear has lost the element of anxiety, for anxious fear of suffering (cf. Rev. 2:10: μὴ φοβοῦ, ἃ μέλλεις πάσχειν, cf. 1 Pt. 3:14) or of death (Hb. 2:15: φόβος θανάτου) can have no importance for those who are freed from the bondage of death by Christ (Hb. 2:15), who fearlessly proclaim the Gospel (Phil. 1:14) and who know that God is their Helper in all things (Hb. 13:6 quoting Ps. 118:6, cf. the concrete exposition of the πνεῦμα υἱοθεσίας of R. 8:15 in 8:28 ff.). Nevertheless, for the community of those who have no more to fear from the κόσμος (Jn. 16:33: θαρσεῖτε) God is still to be reverenced and feared as the holy God in both His grace and His wrath. This arises out of gratitude for the salvation promised and granted to believers: ἔχωμεν χάριν, δι' ἧς λατρεύωμεν εὐαρέστως τῷ θεῷ, μετὰ εὐλαβείας καὶ δέους, Hb. 12:28. [136]

5. Fear in Exhortation.

As faith and awe, hope of salvation and fear of judgment, cannot be fundamentally separated in the NT, many primitive Christian injunctions are to be understood in terms of both love and fear. The shifting of emphasis between these basic motifs brings out the tension between spiritual enthusiasm and norm-conscious traditionalism. Between these two extremes stands Paul's exhortation in R. 13:3 f., 7, where φόβος as "fear of punishment" is plainly distinguished from the weaker τιμή "respect," v. 7, cf. 1 Pt. 2:17. This type of gradation is

---

[133] Cf. further Loh. Phil., 102 with n. 1.

[134] As against Glombitza, *op. cit.*, 100-106, who misunderstands an observation in Loh. Phil., 100, cf. Loh.'s transl., 99. Paul cannot be rejecting fear and trembling as the believer's own efforts, for this would contradict the whole structure of Phil. 2:12 and the pt. of the passage. The μή does not go with κατεργάζεσθε but with the elliptical interpolation v. 12b, while the whole sentence is controlled by the imp. κατεργάζεσθε. The meaning is that during Paul's absence the Philippians should remember their own responsibility to his previous proclamation and admonition. An apt interpretation is that of O. Merk, "Handeln aus Glauben. Die Motivierungen d. paul. Ethik," *Marburger Theol. Stud.*, 5 (1968), 183-5.

[135] Cf. K. Barth, *Erklärung d. Phil.* (1928), 60-67. In detail cf. also J. Warren, "'Work out Your Own Salvation,'" *Evangelical Quart.*, 16 (1944), 125-137; E. Kühl, "Über Phil. 2:12, 13," ThStKr, 71 (1898), 557-581; R. Schmidt, "Über Phil. 2:12 u. 13," ThStKr, 80 (1907), 344-363.

[136] This is the only instance of δέος in the NT; M P lat *et al.* supplement the Hell. εὐλάβεια (→ n. 46; II, 753, 20 ff.), which with related constructs occurs in the NT only in Lk. and Hb., with the common Hell. αἰδώς, elsewhere found only in 1 Tm. 2:9.

common in both Rabbinic [137] and also Hellenistic terminology (→ 193, 21 ff.; n. 43) → VIII, 174, n. 24. Its use in R. 13:7 makes it plain that Paul does not have in view a blurred concept of the power of government but the concrete manifestation of this power in specific institutions and rulers. [138] The theological sanctioning of actual power relationships as we have it again in the household tables (→ 217, 1 ff.) is certainly anticipated quite distinctly here: ὁ ἀντιτασσόμενος τῇ ἐξουσίᾳ τῇ τοῦ θεοῦ διαταγῇ ἀνθέστηκεν, R. 13:2. But the motif of fear is decisively relativised as regards the basic fear of authorities: θέλεις δὲ μὴ φοβεῖσθαι τὴν ἐξουσίαν, 13:3. [139] This is addressed to enthusiasts who want to pursue their own path of freedom from the traditional structure of obedience. Paul, however, does not take the Hellenistic route of warning them against anarchy → 193, 35 ff. He counsels obedient subjection to given powers (→ VIII, 43, 25 ff.) in order to rule out the fear of punishment (→ 213, 17 ff.) which is incompatible with the existence of believers: ἐὰν δὲ τὸ κακὸν ποιῇς, φοβοῦ (R. 13:4); οἱ γὰρ ἄρχοντες οὐκ εἰσὶν φόβος τῷ ἀγαθῷ ἔργῳ ἀλλὰ τῷ κακῷ (v. 3). What is at issue, then, is not respect in principle for the institutions or persons who wield power but obedience through perception of the relationships of power and order that God Himself has willed. This perception befits the man for whom "the day is at hand" (13:12; → 213, 23 ff.). He must be on guard against breaking the obedience of fear and understanding and thus encumbering his eschatological existence. [140] Over against both the enthusiastic repudiation of this fear and also the unreflecting acceptance of wrath and punishment Paul sets the work of love which correctly comes to terms with given claims and ordinances as basic demands (13:7 f.) [141] and thus in the last analysis fulfils all claims. [142] Love, then, makes fear unnecessary, [143] cf. also → 82, 17 ff.

---

[137] Cf. Str.-B., III, 304 f.: מוראה and כבוד. In 1 Pt. 2:17 (→ 217, 3 ff.) φοβεῖσθαι relates to God and τιμᾶν to the king. On the problem of fear in R. 13:7 cf. A. Strobel, "Furcht, wem Furcht gebührt. Zum profangriech. Hintergrund v. R. 13:7," ZNW, 55 (1964), 58-62, who adduces Ps.-Aristot. Oec., III, 3 (ed. C. C. Armstrong, The Loeb Class. Library, 287⁴ [1958], 410), which differentiates two kinds of fear of superior authorities, the one cum verecundia et pudore, the other cum inimicitia et odio. The demand for fear of the powers that be is so widespread, however, that Strobel's concrete ref. of R. 13:7 to the Senate's resolution (53 A.D.) concerning the fiscal powers of procurators is most unlikely → 193, 14 ff.

[138] For historical details cf. A. Strobel, "Zum Verständnis v. R. 13," ZNW, 47 (1956), 67-93. His conclusions are accepted by Merk, op. cit. (→ n. 134), 161-4 and cf. also E. Käsemann, "Grundsätzliches zur Interpretation v. R. 13," Exeget. Versuche u. Besinnungen, II² (1965), 218-220. R. Walker's criticism of Strobel in "Studie z. R. 13:1-7," Theol. Ex., NF, 132 (1966), 11-13 etc. is of little positive value here.

[139] It is right to see here a definite statement rather than a question, cf. Walker, op. cit., 34 f. with n. 113 f. Similarly Hb. 11:23, 27 says that in "faith" πίστει the parents of Moses did not fear an order διάταγμα τοῦ βασιλέως, (v. 23) and that Moses himself did not fear the wrath θυμός of the king (v. 27).

[140] The man who does not render the obedience demanded by authorities also rejects obedience to God and thus brings down on himself God's κρίμα, R. 13:2, cf. also Walker, op. cit., 30 f.

[141] It is worth noting that R. 13:8 with its ὀφείλω (→ V, 564, 1 ff.) takes up the vocabulary of v. 7 (ὀφειλή); v. 8 thus gathers together in dialectical antithesis the individual statements of v. 7, cf. Mi. R.¹⁴, ad loc.; Merk, op. cit., 164 f.

[142] The behaviour of Christians under the powers that be is not, then, a model of civil ethics but an example of the concrete actualisation of ἀγάπη in the world, which in spite of all the chaotic elements has not slipped out of the ordaining and overruling hand of God. Paul has Nero in mind. In contrast, 2nd cent. admonitions are more influenced by pragmatism when they demand understanding as well as power in rulers, Just. Apol., 17, 3 f., cf. also Mart. Pol., 10, 2.

[143] Behind this is perhaps the familiar Rabb. motif that love transcends fear → 207, 7 ff.

If primitive Christian enthusiasm may be discerned here in the conquest of fear, it reaches its climax in 1 Jn. 4:17 f.: φόβος οὐκ ἔστιν ἐν τῇ ἀγάπῃ, ἀλλ᾽ ἡ τελεία ἀγάπη ἔξω βάλλει τὸν φόβον, ὅτι ὁ φόβος κόλασιν ἔχει, ὁ δὲ φοβούμενος οὐ τετελείωται ἐν τῇ ἀγάπῃ. He who knows that he is born of God's love no longer knows any fear, for he need not be afraid any more that God will chastise and punish him. Whether or not the κρίσις of v. 17 is to be regarded as an editorial gloss, [144] κόλασις (→ III, 817, 3 ff. with n. 5) means here the fear of being punished (echoed also in R. 8:15 and 13:3 f.) that is indissolubly connected and posited with fear. In contrast, love frees us for παρρησία, [145] i.e., for an attitude of unrestricted freedom and openness in relation to both God and man. [146]

In the later NT writings, which were more strongly under the influence of Jewish exhortation (→ 205, 16 ff.), the motif of fear is a general basis of Christian action. We thus have a development in exhortation which is fully manifested in the writings of the 2nd century (→ 217, 29 ff.) with their heaping up of traditional themes. [147] Thus in the summary in Ac. 9:31: φόβος τοῦ κυρίου and παράκλησις τοῦ ἁγίου πνεύματος offer a general description of the life of the Palestinian churches. [148] In 1 Pt. 1:17 a life in fear is plainly controlled by the seriousness of judgment and effective redemption from the earlier life. Fear, holiness and prayer are the marks of those who are freed from their previous ἐπιθυμίαι. In 1 Pt. 3:2 as well the motif of fear, being connected with the "pure walk" ἁγνὴ ἀναστροφή of wives, leads us into the sphere of the holiness of God with its demand for purity (cf. v. 4: ἐνώπιον τοῦ θεοῦ); in this regard 3:6 makes it plain that fear of God rules out all human intimidation: ἀγαθοποιοῦσαι καὶ μὴ φοβούμεναι μηδεμίαν πτόησιν, cf. Prv. 3:25. φόβος occurs with πραΰτης in 1 Pt. 3:16, which is again a clear indication of the Jewish ideal of the quiet life that is wholly orientated to the will of God (→ 205, 17 ff.; VI, 648, 19 ff.) and that even though aware of moral superiority over others is still anxious about a clear conscience and must shrink from the danger of defilement, cf. Jd. 23: οὓς δὲ ἐλεᾶτε ἐν φόβῳ, μισοῦντες καὶ τὸν ἀπὸ τῆς σαρκὸς ἐσπιλωμένον χιτῶνα (cf. also 2 C. 7:1). [149] 1 Tm. 5:20 refers to the fear of the community at the conviction of sinners, thus strengthening the hortatory character of φόβος, which constantly confronts believers with the seriousness of the divine judgment.

Nor does fear motivate the conduct of the community only in a general and basic sense. It can also play a part in specific situations in life within the structures of authority. In this regard it is the basis both of dependence on God and also of

---

[144] So R. Bultmann, Die drei Johannesbr., Krit.-exeget. Komm. über das NT, 14⁷ (1968), ad loc.; but cf. W. Nauck, "Die Tradition u. d. Charakter d. 1 J.," Wissenschaftl. Untersuchungen z. NT, 3 (1957), 71, 130 f.

[145] For the antithesis of παρρησία and φόβος cf. also Jn. 7:13 → V, 881, 13 ff., 42 ff. and n. 24.

[146] He who is not perfect in love is judged already, cf. Jn. 3:18.

[147] Cf. on this Bultmann Theol.⁶, 561 f.

[148] πορεύομαι (→ VI, 575, 13 ff.), which is a tt. in Lk., is replaced with ἀναστρέφω or ἀναστροφή in the corresponding formulae in 1 Pt. 1:17; 3:2, 16 → VII, 716, 8 ff.

[149] Acc. to Bultmann Theol.⁶, 562, 2 C. 7:1 is interpolated, cf. also G. Bornkamm, "Die Vorgeschichte d. sog. 2 K.," SAH, 1961, 2 (1961), 32; J. Gnilka, "2 K. 6:14 - 7:1 im Lichte der Qumranschriften u. d. Test. XII," Festschr. J. Schmid (1963), 86-99 has drawn attention to the connection with Qumran. W. Schmithals, "Die Gnosis in Korinth. Eine Untersuchung z. d. Korintherbr.," FRL, 66² (1965) thinks the text is Pauline. The connection of ἐν φόβῳ θεοῦ with personal cleansing and sanctification might suggest an exhortation enriched with Jewish themes that is closer to the setting of 1 Pt. than to Paul himself. On the vl. ἐν ἀγάπῃ θεοῦ → 207, 7 ff.; 218, 14 f.

subjection to given authorities, → VIII, 41, 1 ff. The traditional locus of statements to this effect is the schema of the so-called household tables in which the motif of fear occurs seven times in the NT. The traditional exhortation in 1 Pt. 2:17 shows that these demands for respect are linked to the fear of God: πάντας τιμήσατε, τὴν ἀδελφότητα ἀγαπᾶτε, τὸν θεὸν φοβεῖσθε, τὸν βασιλέα τιμᾶτε. Jewish (Prv. 24:21) and Hellenistic materials (→ 193, 21 ff.) are used here, as also by Paul (→ 214, 33 ff.).[150] If in contrast to Prv. 24:21 a distinction is made between respect for the king and fear of God, in typical relationships of subordination, e.g., wives in 1 Pt. 3:2; Eph. 5:33, and slaves in 1 Pt. 2:18; Eph. 6:5; Col. 3:22, fear can denote the obedience demanded by the superior authority of masters or husbands as lords. This fear as a sign of entire dependence on the power of the stronger requires humility from the slave even to the point of suffering unjust treatment (1 Pt. 2:18; → VII, 407, 24 ff.), and yet this is not to be mere dissimulation for the sake of appearance, for strictly it is not shown to the immediate masters, but in the last resort to God Himself in these concrete authorities with their claims: ὑπακούετε τοῖς κατὰ σάρκα κυρίοις μετὰ φόβου καὶ τρόμου ... ὡς τῷ Χριστῷ, Eph. 6:5, cf. Col. 3:22: φοβούμενοι τὸν κύριον. The same applies to wives. Certainly these are to expect love from their husbands rather than anger (Eph. 5:25, 28, 33) and yet they are still to fear in subordination, for they owe this to their exemplary walk (1 Pt. 3:2) or to their husbands ὡς τῷ κυρίῳ (Eph. 5:22, cf. 33). This traditional theme (→ 193, 14 ff.) of subordination is part of the general structure of the household tables, so that it can also be applied to the community in general: ὑποτασσό-μενοι ἀλλήλοις ἐν φόβῳ Χριστοῦ, Eph. 5:21. Yet just because φόβος is due to Christ,[151] the intention of these admonitions does not lie in principial devotion but in the demand for a pure and patient and gentle heart, Col. 3:22; Eph. 6:5; 1 Pt. 3:2, 4.

E. Fear in the Early Church and Gnosticism.

1. The Early Church.

As in biblical usage, the word group is a favourite one in the post-apost. fathers. In distinction from the NT the fear of God is increasingly used in formulae; this is perhaps due to the growing influence of Jewish modes of thought and speech, cf. Barn., 10, 10 f.; 1 Cl., 21, 7; 45, 6; Did., 4, 9; Herm. m., 7, 1 ff.; 10, 1, 6; 12, 3, 1; s., 8, 11, 2 etc. We still find in the NT proclamation (→ 213, 17 ff.) that fear of God vanquishes fear of man: οὐ δεῖ ἡμᾶς φοβεῖσθαι τοὺς ἀνθρώπους μᾶλλον, ἀλλὰ τὸν θεόν, 2 Cl., 4, 4, cf. 5, 1 ff. (based perhaps on Lk. 12:4 f. and par.). Nevertheless, fears of the future judgment of God remains: τὴν μέλλουσαν ὀργὴν φοβηθῶμεν, Ign. Eph., 11, 1, cf. 2 Cl., 18, 2. This fear is already at work in the life of the community, because even the μακροθυμία of God is to be feared, ἵνα μὴ ἡμῖν εἰς κρίμα γένηται, Ign. Eph., 11, 1, and fear of the works of Satan must also determine life: φοβήθητι δὲ τὰ ἔργα τοῦ διαβόλου ὅτι πονηρά ἐστι, Herm. m., 7, 3. Yet Satan himself has no further power over those who fear God: φοβούμενος γὰρ τὸν κύριον κατακυριεύσεις τοῦ διαβόλου, m., 7, 2, cf. 12, 4,

---

150 Cf. on this K. Weidinger, "Die Haustafeln. Ein Stück urchr. Paränese," UNT, 14 (1928), 63 f.; D. Schroeder, Die Haustafeln d. NT. Ihre Herkunft und ihr theol. Sinn, Diss. Hamburg (1959), 6-28, 112-121, 150.
151 This development reaches a climax in Did., 4, 11, cf. Barn., 19, 7: ὑποταγήσῃ κυρίοις ὡς τύπῳ θεοῦ ἐν αἰσχύνῃ καὶ φόβῳ with the concluding warning not to be too hard on slaves lest they lose their fear of God through rising resentment; on Barn., 19, 5 ff. cf. Weidinger, op. cit., 56-8.

6 f.; 12, 5, 2; 12, 6, 1; for we need fear only him who has power: ἐν ᾧ δὲ δύναμις οὐκ ἔστιν, οὐδὲ φόβος, 7, 2. Hence fear is part of faith along with ὑπομονή, μακροθυμία, and ἐγκράτεια, Barn., 2, 2. Indeed, after πίστις it is a decisive ἔργον of those who are saved, Herm. m., 8, 8 f.; with ἐλπίς it is a fruit of the Spirit from baptism, Barn., 11, 11. It helps us to resist evil desires, for ἡ ἐπιθυμία ἡ πονηρὰ ἐὰν ἴδῃ σε καθωπλισμένον τῷ φόβῳ τοῦ θεοῦ ... φεύξεται ἀπὸ σοῦ μακράν (→ 216, 17 ff.), Herm. m., 12, 2, 4, cf. 12, 3, 1. It is no wonder that, esp. in Herm., fear of God is adduced as a motive of Christian action, for it leads to highly-prized abstinence: φοβηθεὶς δὲ ἐγκράτευσαι, m., 1, 2, and through knowledge of one's own works to repentance, s., 8, 11, 2. General fear of God, however, does not itself accomplish this; it can be at the disposal of every-one πᾶσα ἡ κτίσις. A will to do good and keep the commandments must be added to it, m., 7, 4 f. [152] The voluptuousness of pagans who do not want to know fear and sorrow is harmful to the salvation of the δοῦλοι τοῦ θεοῦ, s., 1, 10. Fear, however, leads to observance of the commandments, Barn., 4, 11, cf. 1 Cl., 2, 8. The expression μετὰ φόβου καὶ ἀγάπης occurs in 1 Cl., 51, 2.

The motif of fear has a settled place in household tables, cf. Did., 4, 11 of δοῦλοι, Barn., 19, 5 (and Did., 4, 9), of children, cf. Pol., 4, 2; 1 Cl., 21, 6, of being subject to rulers Barn., 19, 7 (→ 216, 33 ff.). We see here the influence of Jewish (→ 205, 16 ff.) and Hell. (→ 193, 14 ff.) motifs. It is to be noted that Pol., 4, 2 and 1 Cl., 21, 6 f., do not demand that wives should be subject to their husbands (→ 217, 7 ff.) but simply that they should be to them an example of conduct and love. The basic NT freedom from fear is maintained along with Stoic motifs: οἱ ... Χριστιανοὶ καὶ ἄφοβοι καὶ ἀτάραχοι ὑπάρχουσι, Just. Apol., 46, 4.

In later texts, too, the theme of fear is a common one. Thus Cl. Al. takes up the Stoic discussion of the irrationality of fear and claims that in spite of the philosophers it must be called λογικός because it maintains the commandment given by the Logos for the education of man, Strom., II, 7, 32, 1-4, cf. also II, 2, 4, 4; Paed., I, 101, 1. Prv. 1:7 and ψ 110:10 are quoted in Strom., II, 8, 37, 2 → 219, 9 ff. An objection against the Gnostics is that they want to be permeated only by love without uniting fear to faith, Strom., II, 12, 53, 2-5. True fear is not a mere emotion but a reaction to God's commands, IV, 3, 9, 5 - 11, 1, which helps to contain evil, II, 8, 39, 4, cf. VII, 12, 79, 1 f. Three stages of salvation can be distinguished, the πίστις of the Pauline triad being replaced with φόβος, which checks licentiousness, IV, 7, 53, 1 f. Hence φόβος, which comes through the Law, is good, for as obedience to the Law it frees us from the emotions. δέος is awe at the divine and this again is not a matter of emotion but liberates us from bad impulses, II, 8, 39, 1 - 40, 3. At every pt. one may see here the conflict between a post-biblical theology of fear and the Stoic doctrine of the emotions → 195, 33 ff. At the same time, pneumatic enthusiasm must also be resisted with its elevation of freedom fear as an ideal, II, 8, 39, 1. On the connection between fear and penitence cf. Tert. De paenitentia, 2, 1 f.; 5, 3 f.; 6, 14 ff. (CSEL, 76, 4). [153]

2. Gnosticism.

One finds personified Φόβος in the Hermetic Κόρη κόσμου in the words of Σελήνη: ἔλεγε καὶ προπεπαιδοποιηκέναι Φόβον καὶ Σιγὴν καὶ Ὕπνον καὶ τὴν μέλλουσαν αὐτοῖς ἔσεσθαι (π)ανωφελῆ Μνήμην, Herm. Trismeg. Fr., 23, 28 in Stob. Ecl., I, 393, 15 ff. In a conjuration which was orig. Gnostic and influenced by Judaism, but then misapplied to a magical end, a magic pap. contains a cosmogony in which Φόβος καθω-πλισμένος (→ 191, 16 ff.) appears, who in eight instances of divine emanation produces terror (ἐθαμβήθη) of God. In dispute Φόβος can precede the ninefold deity and has the

---

[152] In this regard two kinds of fear of God are distinguished δισσοὶ ... φόβοι according to whether they lead to a godly life or not.
[153] For further ref. cf. P. J. Stöckerl, *Generalregister z. Bibliothek d. Kirchenväter* (1931), 286-8.

same force as the rest, Preis. Zaub., II, 13, 529 and 544, cf. more weakly 13, 192 ff. [154] Hermetic edification can commend "awe" as φόβος τοῦ ἀδήλου, Herm. Trismeg. Fr., 11, 5 in Stob. Ecl., I, 278, 15 and as τῆς ἀποτυχίας τὸ χαλεπὸν φοβηθῆναι, Fr., 23, 46, ibid., I, 401, 1, cf. Fr., 23, 3, I, 386, 1. At the same time it rejects "anxiety": οὐδὲν νοῶ, οὐδὲν δύναμαι· φοβοῦμαι τὴν θάλασσαν..., for this blocks the way to true knowledge, Corp. Herm., 11, 21 → 196, 3 ff.; n. 37.

In the Chr. Gnosticism of Basilides φόβος is the ἔκπληξις of the archon and in Valentinian thinking it is the original fear of cosmic man which Adam himself took over, Cl. Al. Strom., II, 8, 36, 1-4. In both Hipp. Ref., VI, 37, 7 and Cl. Al. Strom., II, 7, 33, 2 the ref. to the LXX: ἀρχὴ σοφίας φόβος κυρίου, Prv. 1:7; ψ 110:10 brings out clearly the connection with the OT-Jewish tradition → 202, 14 ff. Here, however, a sustaining role is played by ancient elements from the mythological (→ 191, 16 ff.) and philosophico-psychological (→ 195, 8 ff.) estimation of φόβος → 218, 24 ff. [155] In the Valentinian system material substance οὐσία arises out of a series of experiences of σοφία, which as the last of the 30 aeons is plunged into the abyss of passion and hence smitten by ἄγνοια, λύπη, φόβος and ἔκπληξις, Iren. Haer., I, 1, 3 (p. 17); cf. I, 1, 7 (p. 34 f.). Finally, however, Jesus cures fallen sophia of πάθη and makes of them δύο οὐσίαι, I, 1, 8 (p. 40 f.). There arise from φόβος, λύπη and ἀπορία, I, 1, 9 (p. 46); cf. I, 1, 7 (p. 35) the corporeal elements ὑλικὴ οὐσία, while φόβος also passes into the ψυχικά, I, 1, 10 (p. 46). Water corresponds in a special way to the movement of tears of φόβος (p. 48). [156] It is no wonder that real Christians διὰ τὸν φόβον τοῦ θεοῦ φυλασσόμενοι... ἁμαρτεῖν are attacked as fools by the Gnostics, I, 1, 12 (p. 56); for they stay at the psychic level and do not have pneumatic perfection (p. 57). There are further hypostatisations of fear as an independent essence in the Apocr. Johannis [157] Cod, II, 18, 18, cf. II, 28, 26 in a depiction of the emanations; in II, 18, 18 Blaomên is called the demon of fear, who, with the other three demons, is nourished on ὕλη, lines 13 ff., and creates the πάθη (→ 195, 34 ff.), line 20, cf. IV, 29, 1; III, 33, 13. The biblical motif of fear of God is echoed in Pist. Soph., 289 (p. 187, 15 ff.), 294 f. (p. 190, 5 f.), cf. Fr. C, p. 334, 1. 13. 21, where the avenging ἄρχοντες experience the μυστήριον of fear at the ψυχή that has left the body after death and goes on to the world of light. In Mandaean statements the righteous man who stands alone against the wickedness and enmity of the world and is plunged into fear, Lidz. Ginza R., 261, 15 ff., need not tremble, for Mandā dHaijē (γνῶσις ζωῆς) liberates him from fear through knowledge of his redemption, 264, 15 ff. Lidz. Ginza R., 183, 24 - 189, 10 is close to the line of thought in →·lines 27 ff.

Balz

---

[154] Text and historical exposition in Dieterich, op. cit. (→ n. 9), 19, lines 92, 102; 20 f., lines 86-93. Developments of Stoic thought undoubtedly lie behind these allegorical emanations, ibid., 85 f. But we also see the influence of syncretistic speculations, esp. those coloured by Judaism → 194, 23 ff. with n. 31.

[155] Cl. Al. Prot., II, 26, 4 hints at a connection with Stoicism when he tries to understand φόβος as a hypostatisation: φιλοσόφων... τινὲς καὶ αὐτοὶ μετὰ τοὺς ποιητικοὺς τῶν ἐν ὑμῖν παθῶν ἀνειδωλοποιοῦσι τύπους τὸν Φόβον καὶ τὸν Ἔρωτα καὶ τὴν Χαρὰν καὶ τὴν Ἐλπίδα.

[156] In detail Iren.'s statements are not very systematic and show how complicated are the underlying systems with their pseudomythology and its philosophical components, cf. also Hipp. Ref., VI, 31-32. Nor does the exposition in Jonas Gnosis, I³ (1964), 366-373 make the train of thought much clearer.

[157] Ed. M. Krause - P. Labib. "Die drei Versionen d. Apokryphon d. Joh.," Abh. des Deutschen Archäolog. Instituts Kairo, Kpt. Reihe, 1 (1962).

**† φρήν, † ἄφρων, † ἀφροσύνη, φρονέω
φρόνημα, † φρόνησις, † φρόνιμος**

Contents: A. Use of the Word Group in the Greek-Hellenistic World: 1. On the History of the Word and Its Oldest Sense; 2. From Homer to the Classical Period; 3. φρόνησις and Cognates in the Philosophical Tradition. B. The Word Group in the Old Testament: 1. The Field of Reason, Insight, Cleverness etc. 2. Negative Expressions; 3. Theological and Ethical Significance of φρόνησις and Cognates. C. The Word Group in Judaism: 1. Dead Sea Scrolls; 2. Hellenistic Judaism: a. Non-Biblical Pseudepigraphical Writings; b. Philo Alexandrinus; c. Flavius Josephus; d. Rabbinic Use of the Word Group. D. The Word Group in the New Testament: 1. φρένες; 2. ἄφρων, ἀφροσύνη: a. The Synoptists; b. The Pauline Corpus; 3. φρονέω, φρόνημα: a. Mark, Matthew, Acts; b. The Pauline Corpus; 4. φρόνησις; 5. φρόνιμος: a. Matthew and Luke; b. Paul. E. The Word Group in the Post-Apostolic Fathers and Apologists.

A. Use of the Word Group in the Greek-Hellenistic World.

1. On the History of the Word and Its Oldest Sense.

φρήν, usually plur. φρένες "diaphragm,"[1] was early regarded as the seat of intellectual and spiritual activity. The diaphragm determines the nature and strength of the breath and hence also the human spirit and its emotions. In Hom. φρένες[2] means "inner part," "mind," "consciousness," "understanding" etc. and like the other terms for inner organs it is the agent of spiritual and intellectual experiences. φρένες and derivates soon lost altogether (or almost so) their physical sense. In Hom.[3] the group is nearly always used for purely intellectual activity; θυμός ref. to emotion or impulse with no rational components, and ἦτορ or καρδία to the disposition. Expressions like κατὰ φρένα καὶ κατὰ θυμόν, Il., 1, 193; 11, 411; Od., 1, 294; 4, 117 etc. are for Hom. typical means of denoting clearly intellectual and emotional involvement.[4]

The meaning "mind" etc. occurs in many compounds such as ἄφρων,[5] "without understanding," or εὔφρων "with a good or cheerful mind," "in a friendly or well-

---

φ ρ ή ν κ τ λ. Bibl. → V, 596, Bibl.; VII, 888, Bibl.; VII, 1097, Bibl.; Liddell-Scott, s.v.; Trench. 188-192; J. Hirschberger, "Die Phronesis in der Philosophie Platons vor dem Staate," *Philol. Suppl.*, 25, 1 (1932); B. Meissner, *Mythisches u. Rationales in d. Psychologie der euripideischen Tragödie*, Diss. Göttingen (1951), 76-98.

[1] The etym. is most uncertain, cf. Boisacq, Hofmann, Frisk, s.v.

[2] φρένες can hardly be related to νεφροί, so Pape, s.v. νεφρός. For a survey of the meaning of the group cf. Pr.-Bauer, s.v.; on the etym. of νεφροί v. Frisk, s.v.

[3] Cf. M. Leumann, "Homerische Wörter," *Schweizerische Beiträge z. Altertumswissenschaft*, 3 (1950), 115-9.

[4] Cf. also J. Latacz, *Zum Wortfeld "Freude" in d. Sprache Homers* (1966), 218 f., who appeals to J. Böhme, *Die Seele u. das Ich im homerischen Epos*, Diss. Göttingen (1929), 38, n. 3.

[5] The α privat. destroys the unity of "to have insight" and "to decide" expressed in φρονέω; hence ἄφρων, ἀφροσύνη belong to the sphere of irrational impulse.

disposed way," cf. the abstract ἀφροσύνη, εὐφροσύνη and the verbs ἀφρονέω "to be irrational," εὐφρονέω "to be well-disposed." We also find the simple φρονέω, [6] which is already common in Hom. esp. in the part. and which usually means "to think" and can also describe the inner attitude. One also finds the sense "to plan" in Hom., but the real development of this is later. In class. times we find the adj. φρόνιμος "understanding," and the two verbal nouns φρόνημα "thought," also "disposition," and φρόνησις "thinking," "reason," "cleverness" etc. φρένες retains for the most part the less precise sense of "inner attitude." In large measure later development is influenced by Hom.

2. From Homer to the Classical Period.

In Hom. Od., 23, 10-14 we find the various possibilities of a sound or sick development of the mind: περίφρων, ἄφρων, ἐπίφρων, χαλιφρονέων, σαοφροσύνη, φρένας αἴσιμος. In Od., 21, 102 ἄφρων means "befooled" (by Zeus); in 5, 761 and 875 it ref. to the behaviour of Ares and Athene. μέγα φρονέω in Il., 8, 533 means "to be high-minded," and in Il., 11, 296 "to be self-conscious." In Il., 6, 79 we find "to fight and counsel" together μάχεσθαί τε φρονέειν τε. Aesch. uses φρήν for "disposition" in Prom., 881, φρένες in 34, φρόνημα in 376. In 879-887 φρενοπληγεῖς μανίαι are described with their physical and mental consequences. In Aesch. Pers., 808, 828 the ref. of φρόνημα is to arrogance and a mind that rejects God. In Pers., 820 φρονέω ref. to presumptuous thinking and in Prom., 1000 to rational thinking. νέα φρονέω in Pers., 782 ref. to "youthful folly." φρήν means "heart," "person," in Soph. Oed. Tyr., 511. ἀφροσύνη is "youthful folly" in Oed. Col., 1230 and in El., 941 ἄφρων means "mad," "out of one's mind." φρόνησις means "purpose" in Oed. Tyr., 664; Phil., 1078, while φρονέω is "to have understanding" in Oed. Tyr., 316. 326. 328 and "to decide" in 617. φρονέω means "to intend" in Eur. Iph. Aul., 332; Phoen., 1128 etc. φρόνησις is used of the divine will in Suppl., 216 and stands in contrast to human arrogance τὸ γαῦρον δ' ἐν φρεσίν. In Hdt., III, 146, 1 οὐκ ἐς τοῦτο ἀφροσύνης ἀπικόμενος means "he was not so foolish," cf. IX, 82, 3. Acc. to VII, 10, 4 the envy of deity does not tolerate μεγά φρονεῖν [7] in anyone. τὠυτὸ φρονέω in I, 60, 1 means "to make common cause," cf. V, 72, 2. ἀφροσύνη in Thuc., I, 122, 4 and τὸ ἄφρον as noun in V, 105, 3 are the opp. of cunning. In VI, 18, 4 φρόνημα is "pride," or, acc. to the standpt., "arrogance." τὸ ἄφρον in Xenoph. Mem., I, 2, 55 means "lack of understanding."

3. φρόνησις and Cognates in the Philosophical Tradition.

a. With Plato one finds a conscious development esp. of φρόνησις in the philosophical tradition. [8] φρήν is used in a physical sense in Tim., 70a etc. It is the inner part of man in Symp., 199a; Theaet., 154d, cf. Eur. Hipp., 612. Acc. to Plat. Phaed., 76c souls had φρόνησις "receptivity" even before being in men. Linguistically Plat. gen. differentiates σοφία (→ VII, 471, 1 ff.) as purely intellectual knowledge from the more practical φρόνησις, but he can use the two with no more precise distinction. φρόνησις can help man in the battle between good and evil, Prot., 352c, and it can heal him, cf. Crat., 411d e. [9] For Socrates, then, φρόνησις denotes the rule of the good over the soul. Under

---

[6] Cf. Leumann, op. cit.; 116-8; v. also Frisk, s.v. φρήν.

[7] W. Aly, Volksmärchen, Sage u. Novelle bei Hdt. u. seinen Zeitgenossen (1921), 167 compares the wisdom saying in the speech of Artabanos with similar sayings in Gk. tragedy, cf. also Is. 2:11-19 and φρόνησις as hubris, Job 5:13 etc.

[8] W. Jaeger, Die Theol. d. frühen gr. Denker (1964), 131 f. transl. φρόνησις in Heracl. Fr., 2 (Diels, I, 151) as "true insight" and interprets φρονέω in Aesch. Ag., 176 as "believing insight," cf. W. Jaeger, Paideia. Die Formung d. griech. Menschen, III² (1955), 289-344.

[9] On good sound thinking as opp. to mania and ecstasy cf. F. Pfister, "Ekstasis," Festschr. F. J. Dölger (1939), 182-7; → VII, 1099, 10 ff. and n. 20; W. Jaeger, Paideia, II³ (1959), 395, n. 145.

the influence of Socrates Plato then answers the question of the unity of virtue by ref. to φρόνησις, the right state of the intellect from which all moral qualities derive. Education is thus admonition in φρόνησις and ἀλήθεια as the knowledge of value and truth. Acc. to Leg., I, 631c, 632c "insight" is the first of divine goods prior to prudence, justice and courage, and all these prior to health, beauty and riches. The resultant dualistic anthropology [10] does not see spirit and body in antithesis; they complement one another in common achievement ἀκμὴ σώματος καὶ φρονήσεως. Like σοφία or φιλοσοφία, φρόνησις is a chief virtue in Symp., 184c d. It holds this position even along with σωφροσύνη, δικαιοσύνη, ἀνδρεία and other virtues, Men., 88a-89a. Acc. to Resp., VI, 505b thinking is orientated to the good and the beautiful, and φρόνησις or ἐπιστήμη is contrasted with the ἡδονή of the crowd which is determined by external things, 506b c. The guardians of the state and the laws should be φρονιμώτατοι, VII, 521b. Experience, understanding and reason belong together as supreme truth, IX, 582a. All culture must link up with the essential rational element in the soul, VII, 530b. The rational soul is good; the bad soul is foolish and unrestrained, Gorg., 507a. What is divine and φρόνιμον should rule men and lead to unity and friendship, Resp., IX, 590d. He who shows curiosity and seeks true insight can direct his mind to immortality and divine things, Tim., 90b c. Νοῦς, φρόνησις is the gift of God which enables the philosopher or statesman to be a lawgiver. [11] Acc. to Resp., IV, 432a φρόνησις is subject to σωφροσύνη (→ VII, 1099, 15 ff.), which as a personal attitude is subordinate to righteousness, in the strict sense a social virtue. Sometimes φρόνησις seems to take the place of σοφία, Leg., VIII, 837c; X, 906b. Plato with slight modifications adopted the cardinal virtues into philosophical ethics and explained them psychologically. Justice (→ II, 179, 14 ff.) [12] is given a superior and unifying position, since it applies to all parts of the soul and all strata of society, cf. Resp., IV, 427c-433e. Plato is perhaps following a Pythagorean lead here. φρόνημα denotes the intellectual or spiritual attitude in Leg., IX, 865d and the disposition in Resp., IX, 573b. In Resp., III, 411c it is self-confidence which can produce unreasoning arrogance if it rests on physical exercise alone, VI, 494d. The adj. ἄφρων occurs with κακός in Resp., V, 452e and with ὑβριστής in Phileb., 45e.

b. Aristotle has φρήν sing. only in quotations, Rhet., III, 15, p. 1416a, 31. The φρένες have a part in φρονεῖν, Part. An., III, 10, p. 672b, 31. φρονέω μικρόν or μικρά means "to think meanly," Pol., V, 11, p. 1313b, 8 f.; 1314a, 16. 29, cf. ἀνθρώπινα, Eth. Nic., X, 7, p. 1177b, 32, [13] θνατά, ἀθάνατα, Rhet., II, 21, p. 1394b, 25. Ability to perceive αἰσθάνομαι is proper to all living creatures, ability to comprehend φρονέω to few, An., III, 3, p. 427a, 19 ff.; b, 7 f. 10, cf. Metaph., 3, 5, p. 1009b, 13. Higher animals are φρόνιμα, Metaph., 1, 1, p. 980a, 28 ff.; Eth. Nic., VI, 7, p. 1141a, 27. Man is the cleverest, Gen. An., II, 6, p. 744a, 30, because he can use his hands, Part. An., IV, 10, p. 687a, 7-21; acc. to p. 686b, 22 all creatures are ἀφρονέστερα in comparison with man. In man, however, ἀφροσύνη is either animal by nature or sick as epilepsy or mania, Eth. Nic., VII, 6, p. 1149a, 5-12. Thus the honest man is rational and the liar foolish, Eth. Eud., III, 7, p. 1234a, 33 f. φρόνησις is a gift of God. It is moral insight and priceless knowledge, Metaph., 1, 2, p. 982b, 22-31, [14] which offers counsel for a good and moral life, Eth. Nic., VI, 5, p. 1140a, 24-31. It is a function of the rational part of the soul, p. 1140b, 26; VI, 12, p. 1143b, 15. As practical acumen it is distinguished in its multiplicity from theoretical and therefore simple wisdom σοφία, VI, 7, p. 1141a, 9-21 (→ VII, 472, 3 ff.). [15] It is

---

[10] F. Cornelius, Idg. Religionsgesch. (1942), 297 f. 260; P. Wilpert, Art. "Autarkie," RAC, I, 1041; Jaeger Paideia, op. cit. (→ n. 9), II, 88. 240.

[11] Jaeger Paideia, III, 303 f. 342; cf. φρόνησις μόνον ἡγεῖται τοῦ ὀρθῶς πράττειν, Plat. Men., 97c.

[12] Wilpert, op. cit. (→ n. 10), 1040.

[13] Aristot. Nic. Eth., cf. F. Dirlmeier's ed.⁵ (1969), 592 on 231, 7.

[14] Dirlmeier, op. cit., 590, on 231, 6.

[15] Ibid., 451 on 128, 1; 452 on 128, 3.

connected with the moral virtues, Eth. Nic., X, 8, p. 1178a, 16-19; Eth. Eud., III, 7, p. 1234a, 29. Acc. to Eth. Eud., I, 1, p. 1214a, 32 φρόνησις, ἀρετή and ἡδονή are called the supreme good from different standpoints. [16]

c. Acc. to Stoic teaching the individual virtues are manifestations of virtue in gen. In Cleanthes the three other cardinal virtues proceed from φρόνησις and in Chrysipp. (→ VII, 889, 14 ff.) from σοφία; the other virtues are subordinate to these, e.g., counsel and understanding to φρόνησις, Diog. L., VII, 126. [17] In Muson. philosophy and virtue are one. Thus φρόνησις with the other cardinal virtues is integral to philosophy, Muson. Fr., 3 (p. 10, 4 - 12, 5); 9 (p. 50, 10 ff.). [18] Epict. Diss., I, 20, 6 borrows from Platonic ideas [19] when he says that φρόνησις knows itself and its opp. [20]

d. In Neo-Platonism, in Plot.'s doctrine of the primal one, φρόνησις is one of the emanations ruled by νοῦς (→ IV, 956, 35 ff.). The It or He is a reality, a thought beyond thought, lying beyond νοῦς, φρόνησις and ζωή, [21] Plot. Enn., VI, 8, 16, 32-34. Cosmological and anthropological statements correspond to the theological statements, IV, 4, 11-13; I, 3, 5. 6; II, 9, 13. 14. Here below there is also a rational life in truth, dignity, and beauty, VI, 6, 18, 22 ff., cf. V, 9, 11, 9 ff. The rational soul is beautiful, the irrational ugly. What grants the soul understanding is νοῦς, V, 9, 2, 22, cf. also V, 8, 2, 1 ff. 38. It is proper to the gods, who are always spirits even when they bave bodies, always to think φρονοῦσι and never to stop doing so ἀφραίνουσιν, V, 8, 3, 24 f. Thought is not proper to the body; if we are really to have a share in it, it must be by itself and identical with itself, VI, 5, 10, 14-16 → VII, 889, n. 8. [22] I, 2, 1, 15 ff. suggests a hierarchy of virtues. In the soul regard for νοῦς (the first emanation) is σοφία and φρόνησις, I, 2, 7, 6 f. φρόνησις is related to the ψυχή because it denotes the intellectual activity of an individualised soul bound to a body. [23]

Acc. to a later tradition traced back to the Cynic Diogenes of Sinope [24] labour and training come before φρόνησις, as the Stoic Hercules typology shows, Diog. L., VI, 71; Sen. Dialogi, II, 2, 1; Epict. Diss., II, 16, 44; III, 26, 31 f. Raised here is a question discussed since Plat. Prot., 323-337, namely, that of the significance of φύσις, ἄσκησις, μάθησις for the attainment of virtue or φρόνησις; Philo (→ 228, 8 ff.), following the OT, proposes a solution in terms of the typical character of each of the three aspects in different persons, Som., I, 167.

e. In the usage of non-literary Hell. documents we sometimes see the influence of popular philosophy, cf., e.g., Ditt. Or., I, 332, 25 (c. 138 B.C.), where practical excellence leading to success is meant as well as ἀρετή and φρόνησις. The adj. φρόνιμος is

---

[16] Aristot. On Virtue, cf. E. A. Schmidt (1965), 56-8.
[17] M. Pohlenz, "Pls. u. d. Stoa," ZNW, 42 (1949), 92 says with ref. to Dio Chrys. Or., 12, 27 ff.: "But the gods have given man the privilege of being able to think about them rationally and to know them."
[18] Understanding and prudence are esp. virtues of the educated → V, 598, 26 ff.
[19] Chr. ethics is for Epict. opposed to the *logos* no less than μανία and ἄνοια. "An ἔθος without λόγος makes no sense to him," A. Bonhöffer, "Epict. u. d. NT," RVV, 10 (1911), 43.
[20] Cf. Plat. Resp., III, 409d e Bonhöffer, *op. cit.*, 168 ref. to the remarkable agreement between Epict. and Paul at 1 C. 2:15. But for Paul the wisdom of this world is empty and his formulation may thus be regarded as original. On φρόνησις conceptually cf. E. Klostermann, "Überkommene Def. im Werke d. Orig.," ZNW, 37 (1938), 61.
[21] ζωή is called ἔμφρων in Plot. Enn., VI, 8, 16, 34; cf. R. Harder, Plotins Schriften übers., IVb (1967), 387.
[22] Harder, *op. cit,* IIa (1962), 66 f., cf. IIb, 418.
[23] The Neo-Platonic doctrine of emanations is also found in Gnosticism, incl. Chr. Gnosticism.
[24] H. Kusch, Art. "Diogenes v. Sinope," RAC, III, 1064.

employed in the same sense. ἀλλότρια φρονήσαντες, Ditt. Or., I, 90, 20 (196 B.C.) occurs here with ref. to apostates. On an execration tablet from Megara φρόνησις is found in a list between σῶμα, πνεῦμα, ψυχή, διάνοια and αἴσθησις, ζοή (sic!), καρδία, Audollent Def. Tab., 41, Col. A, 9-11 (1st/2nd cent. A.D.), cf. 242, 55 f. (3rd cent. A.D.). In a magic pap. we read: τὰς φρένας ἐνοχλήσας διὰ τὸν φόβον "unsettling hearts with fear," Preis. Zaub., II, 12, 65. In the Gnostic context of Corp. Herm., 13, 4 f. we read of οἴστρησις "incitement" par. μανία φρενῶν and ἀπολειφθεὶς φρενῶν. The formula for the preparation of the recipient of revelation in 13, 1 runs: ἀπηνδρείωσα τὸ ἐν ἐμοὶ φρόνημα ἀπὸ τῆς τοῦ κόσμου ἀπάτης. [25] P. Fay., 124, 12 (2nd cent. A.D.) reads: δοκεῖς ἄφρων τις εἶναι, cf. Pap. Grenfell, I, 1, 19 [26] (2nd. cent. B.C.). A legal term obviously current for the competence of a woman testator occurs in a will: νοοῦσα φρονοῦσα, Pap. Wisconsin, I, 13, 2 (2nd cent. B.C.). [27]

B. The Word Group in the Old Testament.

1. The Field of Reason, Insight, Cleverness etc.

There is no single Hbr. original for φρήν and cognates. לֵב (→ III, 606, 3 ff.) seems to correspond only to the orig. psychosomatic range of φρήν. [28] In the LXX we find only plur. φρένες. It is used seven times in Prv. (also φρόνησις 9:16) with negation by ἐνδεής etc. in transl. of חֲסַר־לֵב, and once of כְּסִיל. It means "lack of understanding," "folly," cf. ἄφρων (for חֲסַר־לֵב) at Prv. 17:18. Similarly Prv. 11:29 has φρόνιμος for חֲכַם־לֵב as opp. of ἄφρων (HT אֱוִיל). In Da. 4:34; 36 Θ (no LXX) φρένες is used for the bibl. Aram. מַנְדַּע of Da. 4:31, 33 in the sense of understanding. For מַנְדַּע or מַדַּע we find φρόνησις at Da. 1:4 Θ; 2:21 Θ; 5:12 Θ. OT Hbr. has no term meaning "diaphragm." [29] The root חכם is the original of φρονέω, φρόνησις or φρόνιμος 23 times in the HT, 16 of these being in 3 Βασ. 3-11. [30] בִּין occurs in Is. 44:18 for φρονέω, φρόνιμος and 12 times for the same root in Prv., φρόνησις 15-17 times for בִּינָה, תְּבוּנָה. The root שׂכל [31] is once transl. φρονέω and twice φρόνησις. φρόνησις occurs only once in LXX at Prv. 24:5 for דַּעַת (יָדַע), and once also for רוּחַ at Jos. 5:1. φρόνιμος has a negative accent as a rendering of עָרוּם at Gn. 3:1 with ref. to the subtlety of the serpent, cf. φρόνησις for עָרְמָה at Job 5:13 for "presumptuous cleverness." [32] The prophetic judgment of Is. 44:25 agrees with this. The ref. is to wisdom in government at Ez. 28:4; cf.

---

[25] Reitzenstein Poim., 339 and 341.

[26] Ed. B. P. Grenfell, An Alexandrian Erotic Fr. and other Greek Pap. Chiefly Ptolemaic (1896). Cf. Preisigke Wört., Moult.-Mill., s.v.

[27] Ed. P. J. Sijpesteijn, The Wisconsin Pap. I, Papyrologica Lugduno-Batava, 16 (1967).

[28] For inner organs as the seat of feelings in the OT cf. A. R. Johnson, The Vitality of the Individual in the Thought of Ancient Israel (1949), 5-88; E. D. Freed, "OT Quotations in the Gospel of John," Nov. Test. Suppl., 11 (1965), 24 f.

[29] In Sir. we find tīrtā "diaphragm," "conscience" as an Accad. loan word, cf. A. Adam, "Die Ps. d. Thomas u. das Perlenlied als Zeugnisse vorchr. Gnosis," ZNW, Beih., 24 (1959), 45, 67.

[30] The alternation of φρόνησις and σοφία in 3 Βασ. is sometimes due to different translators, cf. J. A. Montgomery, "The Suppl. at the End of 3 Kingdoms 2 (1 Reg. 2)," ZAW, 50 (1932), 124-9 [Gooding]. On the style of antitheses cf. L. A. Schökel, Estudios de Poética Hebrea (1963), 251-268; T. Boman, Das hbr. Denken im Vergleich mit dem griech.5 (1968), 42-56.

[31] Thus the part. hi is common later for enlightened Jews, cf. Lidz. Ginza R., 225, 20 f.: "They call themselves Jews because they have sinned and clever because they are confounded." But righteous martyrs are in view in Da. 11:33, 35.

[32] 1 C. 3:19, quoting this passage, has πανουργία (→ V, 724, 19 ff.) which with its cognates is also used elsewhere for ערם, cf. the Hexapla transl. of Gn. 3:1.

3 Βασ. 3-11 [33] and Wis. 7:7. ἐν φρονήσεσι... αὐτοῦ καθωδήγησεν αὐτούς ref. to David in Ps. 78:72 'A cf. Σ; in Wis. 6:24 we find the corresponding statement βασιλεὺς φρόνιμος εὐστάθεια δήμου and in Prv. 3:7 the warning μὴ ἴσθι φρόνιμος ('Α Σ Θ σοφός) παρὰ σεαυτῷ, cf. 26:5, 12 LXX. Acc. to Is. 44:28 LXX God has given Cyrus his wisdom as a ruler. In Is. 44:18, 19 we find φρονέω, φρόνησις with negation for the worshippers of idols, cf. Is. 56:10 with ref. to deceivers of the people.

2. Negative Expressions.

Vaunting human reason is folly before God. μωρός (→ IV, 832, 1 ff.) is more prominent in Sir., but the rest of the LXX usually has ἄφρων, ἀφροσύνη. There are many Hbr. originals. נָבָל "fool," [34] with the secondary sense of a "denier of God" who contemptuously disrupts fellowship between God and man, is 11 times transl. by ἄφρων, 5 times in Ps. and sporadically elsewhere. The noun נְבָלָה is transl. 7 times (only historical texts) by ἀφροσύνη, including the interpretation of the name in 1 Βασ. 25:25. The root סכל, found in the HT only twice in Jer. and 20 times in the hagiographa, is transl. by ἄφρων, ἀφροσύνη 9 times in Qoh. Most common is the root כסל. It occurs 3 times in Qoh. and once in Job as the original of ἀφροσύνη, then 40 times in Prv. and 17 in Qoh., at ψ 48:11 and twice in Sir. as the original of ἄφρων (60 times all told); ungodliness can also be meant sometimes in this case too. The same applies to אִוֶּלֶת and אֱוִיל, transl. by ἄφρων and ἀφροσύνη 24 times in Ps. and Prv. פֶּתִי "simple," "inexperienced," is rendered by ἄφρων only 7 times in Prv. At Prv. 1:22a LXX has given a positive turn to the text; v. 22b is adversative: ἄφρονες (לֵצִים scoffers) τῆς ὕβρεως ὄντες ἐπιθυμηταί. HT seems to have in view social abuses, but LXX means "the ungodly," cf. ἀσεβεῖς for כְּסִילִים "fools" in v. 22c. From root זמם comes the noun מְזִמָּה "clever plan," "trick." The word occurs only 19 times in the HT but is rendered by 12 different terms in the LXX, including φρόνιμος at Prv. 14:17. [35] זִמָּה "good purpose" in Job 17:11 elsewhere means "misdeed" and is rendered by ἀφροσύνη at LXX Ju. 20:6 and 10 times by ἀσέβεια, ἀνόσιος, esp. in Ez. Here, too, there is a religious implication.

3. Theological and Ethical Significance of φρόνησις and Cognates.

As true φρόνησις is from God, God's φρόνησις is unsearchable, Is. 40:28, cf. Is. 40:14 'Α Σ Θ (LXX σύνεσις). In His power (ἰσχύς) God has established the earth, in His "wisdom" (σοφία) He has set up the inhabited world, in His "understanding" (φρόνησις) He has spread out heaven, Jer. 10:12. The three terms are to be seen as a unity in view of the Hbr. parallelism. At Prv. 3:19 f. we have σοφία, φρόνησις, αἴσθησις, "wisdom," "understanding" and "knowledge," [36] three virtues which in their theoretically intellectual and practically ethical character cannot be separated conceptually in the OT,

---

[33] On Solomon's wisdom cf. the burial inscr. of Darius on the cliff of Naqš-e-Rostani in Persepolis, which says: "The great (or a great) God is Ahuramazda... who has sent down wisdom and excellence on Darius the king," Inscr. 7, W. Hinz, "Die untere Grabinschr. d. Dareios," ZDMG, 115 (1965), 240.

[34] T. Donald, "The Semantic Field of 'Folly' in Prv., Job, Ps. and Ecclesiastes," VT, 13 (1963), 285-292; W. v. Roth, "nbl," VT, 10 (1960), 394-409; G. Bertram, "Die religiöse Umdeutung altorient. Lebensweisheit in d. gr. Übersetzung d. AT," ZAW, 54 (1936), 153-167; also "Griech. AT u. Entmythologisierung," Deutsches Pfarrerblatt, 66 (1966), 413-8; also "Weisheit u. Lehre in d. LXX," 17. Deutscher Orientalistentag. Vorträge, ZDMG, Suppl., I (1969), 302-310.

[35] On the Hbr. original in its twofold sense cf. B. Gemser, Sprüche Salomos, Hndbch. AT, I, 16² (1963) on 1:4; 12:2; 14:17.

[36] דַּעַת contains the voluntative element; it denotes the understanding which has regard to the will of the one who commissions or reveals, cf. P. Borgen, "Bread from Heaven," Nov. Test. Suppl., 10 (1965), 159 f.

or systematically integrated into a doctrine of virtues, even though the Gk. reader or translator might be inclined to do this under philosophical influence. Rather, the heaping up of terms is an indication of the many-sidedness of aspects. Thus φρόνησις and σοφία and many synon. finally constitute a unity as a depiction of the religiously determined practical wisdom of the OT. The same applies correspondingly to their negative counterparts. φρόνησις is the principle of creation; God gives man a share in the wisdom of the divine Cr●or, cf. esp. Prv. 1-9. When חָכְמָה is transl. by φρόνησις, emphasis on practical reason seems to be in view. Even proverbs which have in the first instance a profane character, e.g., Prv. 10:5 Σ; 12:8 Σ; 11:12; 14:6, 29; 17:27; 18:15; 19:8 etc. acquire in the religiously stressed context their true and definitive significance, for acc. to Prv. 10:23 LXX (HT different) eternal σοφία produces "understanding" φρόνησις in man, cf. 9:6b. Acc. to 8:14 wisdom claims "understanding" as its possession, while the HT sees the two to be identical, cf. 8:1. [37] In both cases LXX subordinates φρόνησις to σοφία.

Sir. 1:4 takes up the wisdom speculations of Prv. 8:22 and posits σοφία and σύνεσις φρονήσεως as eternal values. The macarisms of the numbers sayings in Sir. 25:9-11 have an immanent character, but φρόνησις and σοφία are still subordinate to the fear of God, cf. 19:22, 24. Proverbs like Sir. 20:1, 27; 21:17, 21, 24 f.; 38:4 etc. belong to the sphere of secular practical wisdom. [38] Wis. 7:16, 22, 25 regards σοφία and φρόνησις as hypostases. [39] φρόνησις is under σοφία but retains its metaphysical character. In 8:5 f. it is the architect of creation like wisdom. In 8:7 σωφροσύνη, φρόνησις, ἀνδρεία and δικαιοσύνη are the four chief virtues. In 4 Macc. 1:2 φρόνησις is the supreme virtue; the other three are interpolated in 1:6. [40] Acc. to Wis. 8:8-21 φρόνησις is in v. 21 the presupposition of the ruler recognising as such the divine gift of φρόνησις (v. 18) which is imparted to him in intercourse with wisdom and which as political sagacity determines all his actions. [41]

By way of appendix one might ref. to the usage of Macc. In 1 Macc. 10:20 φρονέω means "to perceive the interests" of someone, cf. Ἐσθ. 8:12b and 2 Macc. 14:8 with γνησίως and 14:26 with ἀλλότρια as the opp. φρόνημα occurs only twice in the LXX at 2 Macc. 7:21; 13:9 with ref. to a noble or barbaric disposition, in each case with the corresponding qualification. The ref. is to conceit or arrogance in 2 Macc. 9:12. ἰσόθεα φρονέω, and 11:4: πεφρενωμένος (no addition). φρήν occurs in the sing. at 3 Macc. 4:16; 5:47 for the "disposition," cf. 4 Macc. 6:17. Acc. to 4 Macc. 7:17 reason lacks understanding in many men οὐδὲ ... φρόνιμον ἔχουσιν τὸν λογισμόν, so that they cannot control their impulses.

C. The Word Group in Judaism.

1. Dead Sea Scrolls.

In the Dead Sea Scrolls we again find the word groups that lie behind φρόνησις in the HT. These are שׂכל, חכמה, חכם, דעת, ידע, בינה, בין, משׂכיל. [42] All things have come

---

[37] On Prv. 8:14 cf. 16:16 and P. de Lagarde, *Anmerkungen z. griech. Übers. d. Prv.* (1863), 28 f., 53. LXX reads קָנִּים "nests" for קנה "to attain"; cf. the image in Plat. Theaet., 197e.

[38] On Sir. 21:15-17 cf. the wisdom saying in Act. Andr. et Matt., 15 (p. 83, 17 f.): φρόνιμος γὰρ ἀκούων λόγους χρηστοὺς εὐφραίνεται τῇ καρδίᾳ.

[39] W. Staerk, "Die sieben Säulen d. Welt u. des Hauses d. Weisheit," ZNW, 35 (1936), 259: λογικὴ δύναμις begotten of God acc. to Just. Dial., 61; Eichr. Theol. AT, II⁴, 50-56.

[40] A. Dupont-Sommer, *Le quatrième livre des Machabées* (1939), 54 f.

[41] Acc. to Wis. 8:21 Solomon already has φρόνησις, cf. 6:15; 8:6; he asks for σοφία as a gift of grace, J. Fichtner, *Weisheit Salomos, Hndbch. AT*, II, 6 (1938), ad loc.

[42] F. Nötscher, "Zur theol. Terminologie d. Qumran-Texte," *Bonner Bibl. Beiträge*, 10 (1956), 52-62; cf. H. Braun, "Spätjüd.-häret. u. frühchr. Radikalismus," *Beiträge z. hist. Theol.*, 24² (1969), esp. I, 15-32: משׂכיל "man of understanding" possibly denotes a rank in the sect, 22, n. 3, cf. 20, n. 3; E. Lohse, "Christologie u. Ethik im Kol.," *Festschr. E. Haenchen* (1964), 167.

into being through God's knowledge דעת, 1 QS 11:11. His eschatologically directed plan for the world is determined by His "insight" שׂכל and "wisdom" חכמה, 4:18, cf. 1 QH 1:7, 14, 19. Acc. to 1 QH 1:21; 14:12 f. the singer has this insight from God Himself, without whose revelation he as a man of dust could not have it. God sends the spirit of truth to "instruct" the upright בין hi in the "knowledge" דעת of God, in the "wisdom" חכמה of the sons of heaven, and to "make them clever" שׂכל hi, 1 QS 4:21 f.; cf. 4:3; 1 QH 1:31, cf. 1:35, where we find ערמה, cf. דעה ומזמת ערמה 1 QS 11:6. [43] חכמה, חכם occur only 18 times in all. בינה and שׂכל best correspond to LXX φρόνησις. [44] We find them in the more legal portions and the hymns. But the dualism between those who walk perfectly and those who are led astray by the spirit of falsehood checks the influence of the OT revelation. Thus he who is outside the community in this time of ungodliness רשׁע is פתי, משׁוגע, אויל, "fool," "madman," "simpleton," Damasc. 15:15 (19:12). In the lists of vices in 1 QS 4:9-11 folly appears among many others. Acc. to 4:24 wisdom and folly do battle in men's hearts, cf. 1 QH 13:4; 1:36 f. In detail the following terms are used for folly: זמם "to plan evil," 1 QH 4:10, 26; 9:20; 1 QpHab 12:6 and 2:17, מחשבות און "wicked plots," 4 Q Florilegium 1:9, משׁגת אונמה "wicked aberration, loc. cit., מזמות בליעל "tricks of Belial," 1 QH 2:16; Damasc. 5:19 (7:19), הולל [45] "folly," 1 QH 4:20. סכלות "foolish laughing" and נבל "foolish talking" are punished acc. to 1 QS 7:9, 14; cf. Damasc. 10:18 (13:2); 1 QS 10:22. פתה means to "lead astray," negatively 1 QH 4:16; 6:19; Damasc. 15:11 (19:10). פתי means "simple" ("led astray"?) [46] in 4 QpHab 12:4 on 2:17, cf. 1 QH 2:9, "foolish," 1 QSa 1:19; Damasc. 13:6 (15:8).

The gifts that embrace theoretical and practical knowledge and combine with other gifts like humility, longsuffering, mercy and goodness, 1 QS 4:3, cf. 2:24, indicate the nomistic impress of the community life and the sharp separation from those without, as do also the vices that might be charged with disruption of fellowship. We see also the eschatological orientation of understanding in 1 QH 11:12, 25 and the hope that evil and folly will be destroyed, 1 QS 4:18, 24 f. But knowledge is primarily and particularly an outworking of possessed salvation. [47]

2. Hellenistic Judaism.

a. Non-Biblical Pseudepigraphical Writings.

In the older writings of Hell. Judaism occurrence of the group is haphazard and rare. ἀγωγή and φρόνησις are found together in Ep. Ar., 124 and σοφοί and φρόνιμοι in 130. What is meant by "direction," "wisdom" and "understanding" here is not stated precisely. Everything is in the superficial style of polite table-talk (deipnosophy). The question whether disposition or virtue can be taught is treated along Platonic lines with a supplementary ref. to the self-knowledge of virtue, 236 (→ n. 20). Acc. to Test. N. 2:8 God has made the heart for understanding [48] as He has made other parts of the body for their physical or spiritual ends, cf. 8:10. In Test. L. 7:2 f. the sin of Shechem is called "folly" as in Dt. 22:21, cf. in Test. S. 2:13 that against Joseph acc. to Gn. 37. ἀφροσύνη occurs

---

[43] Braun, op. cit., I, 22, n. 5; 94 f., n. 8; cf. also 25, n. 5; 26 f.

[44] Nötscher, op. cit., 54 f., 79-92; J. C. Lebram, "Die Theol. d. späten Chokma u. häretisches Judt.," ZAW, 77 (1965), 202-211.

[45] Only in Qoh. in the Hbr. OT, cf. G. Bertram, "Hbr. u. gr. Qoh.," ZAW, 64 (1952), 41.

[46] On the threefold division of men as righteous, wicked and ignorant in Wisdom stories, cf. Lebram, op. cit., 206.

[47] Braun, op. cit., I, 94. 107. 135; G. Bertram, "Das Problem d. gr. Umschrift d. hbr. AT," Die Welt d. Orients, 5 (1970), 153 f.

[48] Cf. the par. לב להבין בינה in the Othioth of R. Akiba (ed. A. Jellinek Bet ha-Midrasch, III³ [1967], 42) in Charles Test. XII, ad loc.

with ὕβρις in Sib., 4, 157 in an eschatological context. ἐνὶ φρεσίν in 4, 170 (→ 221, 7 ff.) [49] imitates Homeric diction, cf. 13, 126, 3, 722 ref. to the folly of idolatry. The saying about the matricidal man who thinks he is cleverer than all other men (5, 366) seems to echo Gn. 3:1. There is an allusion to Gn. 2:9, 17 in the "tree of knowledge" of Gr. En. 32:3. Here φρόνησις (HT דעת) is understood as a basic and critical virtue with a practical aim.

b. Philo Alexandrinus.

Philo's concern is to interpret biblical texts with the aid of the Gk. language and Platonic or Stoic concepts. God possesses the rich fulness of φρόνησις, Mut. Nom., 260, and Himself dispenses on the beholding race the heavenly wisdom which is the true bread from heaven. [50] For allegorical exegesis God's wisdom is the source of virtue in Paradise which then divides into the four chief rivers of the cardinal virtues. Phison (φείδομαι), which nourishes the soul, is φρόνησις, Leg. All., I, 66. The soul is a virgin liberated from passions and vices, including ἀφροσύνη, and bringing forth beings of exceptional beauty, the four cardinal virtues, piety, fear of God and all the rest, Exsecr., 159 f. Here φρόνησις stands in tension with the fear of God → 233, 28 f. As elsewhere in Philo we find both Hell. and biblical influences. [51] From φρόνησις, which shapes man's deeds, come two types, the theoretically clear φρόνιμος, Sacr. AC, 54; Leg. Gaj., 64, and the practically clever thinker φρονῶν, [52] Leg. All., I, 63-7, cf. Det. Pot. Ins., 114. [53] Man as a mixed being, neither animal nor star, encompasses all antitheses, including φρόνησις-ἀφροσύνη, Op. Mund., 73. φρόνησις stands between πανουργία "wantonness" and μωρία "folly," Deus Imm., 164. It is thus a virtuous mean [54] and can be understood as practical wisdom, Ebr., 86 and 140; Sobr., 24; Vit. Mos., I, 236 etc. σύνεσις is equated with it, Op. Mund., 154, cf. Plant., 36 and 40. Acc. to Sobr., 3; Abr., 57 φρόνησις is the eye of the soul; it perishes as the principle of the individual but is eternally imperishable as that of the species, Mut. Nom., 79 f. φρόνησις is the first part of the soul seated in the head and it exerts direction [55] over the whole through ἀνδρεία and σωφροσύνη. Hence δικαιοσύνη finally arises, Leg. All., I, 70-73. φρόνησις is endangered by ἀφροσύνη, which can usurp direction, Leg. All., III, 193; Conf. Ling., 191. Thought, however, consists in words and deeds; there is some polemic against sophistry here, Leg. All., I, 74, cf. 86; Som., II, 180. In contrast with the liberal "disposition" φρόνημα, Vit. Mos., I, 309. 325; Omn. Prob. Lib., 119; Leg. Gaj., 215 etc. of the minority stands the multitude of those who are slaves of their own understanding, Omn. Prob. Lib., 62 f.; Sobr., 23 f., cf. κακὸν ἀθάνατόν ἐστιν ἀφροσύνη, Det. Pot. Ins., 178. The ideal of the friends of φρόνησις is disrupted by the wicked man who lives with ἀφροσύνη, Spec. Leg., II, 48 f.; hence in education ἀφροσύνη is cured only by fear, II, 239. But the final aim of φρόνησις is to establish one's own ἀφροσύνη and that of all creatures. [56] The confession of OT truth is that God alone is wise and hence all man's φρόνησις is ὕβρις.

---

[49] Cf. E. Stauffer, "Probleme d. Priestertradition," ThLZ, 81 (1956), 144 f.

[50] In Abr., 57 etc. Philo links the name Israel with ראה "to behold." On the heavenly bread cf. Wis. 16:20 f. and on Mut. Nom., 259 f. v. Borgen, op. cit., 14 and 32 f.

[51] W. Völker, "Fortschritt u. Vollendung bei Philo v. Alex.," TU, 49, 1 (1938), 30-47, 126-154, 212-226, 325; E. R. Goodenough, By Light, Light. The Mystic Gospel of Hellenistic Judaism (1935), 230-413; also The Politics of Philo Judaeus. Practice and Theory (1938), 64-120.

[52] φρονέω relates to the power of thought in Leg. Gaj., 190; Ebr., 128; Vit. Mos., I, 46; Jos., 166; Spec. Leg., II, 256; IV, 121; Poster. C., 171; Conf. Ling., 93 etc.

[53] On the Stoic distinction cf. the compilation in Stob. Ecl., II, 63, 11 f.

[54] The doctrine of the mean in Philo is taken from Aristot., cf. Eth. Nic., II, 7, p. 1107a, 28 - b, 22; but there is no application to φρόνησις in Aristot.

[55] Cf. the metaphor of steering horses in Plat. Phaedr., 246a-254e.

[56] Cf. the ignorance of Socrates in Plat. Apol., 21d.

The nature of ἀφροσύνη is indicated by many predicates: poison, Vit. Cont., 74, drunkenness, Vit. Mos., II, 162; Som., II, 160. 181. 192, sickness, Leg. All., III, 211; Cher., 10, cf. also Agric., 77; Ebr., 10; Migr. Abr., 169; Virt., 180. God is also the Lord of fools, admonishing or destroying, Mut. Nom., 23, cf. 254. Acc. to Ebr., 110 polytheism leads to atheism among the irrational. With the basic criticism we find ref. to the worthlessness of the attitude of unreason, Fug., 16; Mut. Nom., 153. 170. 175. 195.

c. Flavius Josephus.

φρένες occurs in Ant., 16, 380 as a par. of νοῦς. The soul's power of rational arrangement and orderly understanding has been lost. Bell., 1, 506 ref. to παρακοπὴ φρενῶν καὶ μανία and acc. to Ant., 10, 114 the prophet Jeremiah is disparaged ὡς ἐξεστηκὼς τῶν φρενῶν. ἄφρων is used with θρασύς in Bell., 2, 303 for youthful rashness. In Bell., 1, 630 it means "foolish" in distinction from πανοῦργος "sly." Ant., 2, 307 has ἀφροσύνη as the opp. of κακία and this is the Gk. rendering of Hbr. proper name נָבָל "fool." In 17, 277 the ref. is to the people's "lack of restraint" and in 20, 98 to the simplicity of those who are led astray. In Vit., 323 ἀφροσύνη is equated with ἄνοια. φρονέω is used with ref. to disposition, attitude, or purpose, taking acc. of adj. peaceful, Bell., 3, 30. 458, friendly, 3, 455, liberal, 4, 282, hostile, Vit., 353. Agreement in disposition is expressed by τὸ αὐτὸ φρονέω in Bell., 2, 160 or ὅμοια φρονέω, Ant., 19, 58, cf. Bell., 5, 320. φρονέω τὰ τοῦ... relates to disposition and attitude, esp. political supporters and followers, Ant., 7, 28; 11, 273; 12, 392. 399; 14, 268. We often find μέγα φρονέω "to be high-minded," Ant., 3, 83, to "think highly" of laws (→ IV, 1051, 18 ff.), 17, 41; Ap., 2, 286, also μεῖζον φρονέω "to become high-spirited," Ant., 15, 123, ἔλαττον φρονέω, "to lose heart," Ant., 15, 140, χεῖρον φρονέω "to have a poor spirit, an abject disposition," Bell., 7, 357. Adv. with φρονέω are εὖ in Bell., 3, 440; Ap., 2, 144, ἀνθρωπίνως, Ant., 18, 256, δικαίως, Ap., 1, 45 etc. With the prep. ἐπί, φρονέω means "to plan on," "to be orientated to," Ant., 17, 226; Vit., 56; with περί the obj. of thought is denoted, Ant., 12, 125, e.g., the nature φύσις of God, Ap., 2, 168, or divine providence, Ant., 2, 136. μέγα ἐπ' ἐμαυτῷ φρονέω in Ant., 4, 100; 6, 298 is "to think arrogantly," cf. 7, 301. The noun τὸ φρονεῖν occurs in 2, 156; 8, 21, of God's "understanding," 4, 224. [57]

In Ant., 1, 37 the tree of knowledge is τὸ φυτὸν τῆς φρονήσεως, whereas LXX has τοῦ εἰδέναι for עֵץ הַדַּעַת at Gn. 2:9. The result is that this quality cannot be ascribed to the serpent. φρόνησις is a divine gift. Solomon asks for it: νοῦν ὑγιῆ καὶ φρόνησιν ἀγαθήν, Ant., 8, 23, cf. φρόνησις καὶ σοφία, 8, 34. 42 and ἀρετὴ καὶ φρόνησις, 8, 165. φρόνησις is a right way of thinking orientated to God and it is grouped with σοφία and σύνεσις, 8, 23 f., cf. also 6, 10. φρόνησις and παιδεία are linked in Bell., 7, 399. The unity of φρόνησις and ἀρετή is maintained in Ap., 2, 183; it is the ability to act with insight, i.e., practical wisdom. [58]

φρόνημα is not always sharply differentiated from φρόνησις but it has more of a ref. to action πράγματα καὶ φρονήματα, Bell., 2, 334, cf. Ant., 12, 182; 13, 306. φρόνημα means attitude and disposition, as an inheritance, Ant., 12, 279, cf. Bell., 1, 378, natural tendency and manner. Thus φρόνημα is connected with φύσει δραστήριος in Bell., 1, 204, cf. also Ant., 14, 13. Acc. to Ant., 4, 245 τὰ φρονήματα should be orientated to ἀρετή. σώματά τε καὶ φρονήματα in Ant., 19, 42 means the whole man, body and soul. φρόνημα can often mean "courage" as in Ant., 14, 461; 15, 115; Bell., 5, 342, sometimes with τόλμα, Bell., 3, 22; 4, 90, or θάρσος, Ant., 5, 218, "boldness," Ant., 17, 256,

---

[57] The group is not common in Jos. and is variously used (with qualifying terms) for political, ethical or religious mind or conduct. Often φρόνημα seems to be much the same as φύσις, cf. φρόνημα in Ant., 2, 229. 232 with φύσις in the sense of character or attitude. Bell., 5, 306; Ant., 15, 178.

[58] Jos. presents himself as a champion of Hell. Judaism.

"pride," 15, 44, "arrogance," 15, 81. φρόνιμος, "rational," "clever," "prudent," is rare,
Ant., 4, 36. 259; in diplomacy, 9, 25; 12, 184; the adv. occurs in 19, 112 and the compound
in Bell., 1, 452. In the historian Jos., in keeping with his themes, the word group is esp.
prominent in the field of practical politics.

d. Rabbinic Use of the Word Group.

The area corresponding to Gk. φρόνιμος and cognates in the Rabb. is controlled by
חָכָם "wise," the opp. being שׁוֹטֶה "foolish" = Gk. ἄφρων, Ab., 4, 1. 7. "Knowledge"
דֵּעָה, ידע is finally knowledge of God, 4, 22. Four different kinds of disposition are denoted
by מִדּוֹת בְּדֵעוֹת, 5, 11. מִדָּה, "measure," also "disposition" in the Rabb. and later Hbr.,
corresponds to φρόνημα, which can be a vox media to be filled with good or bad content,
cf. מִדּוֹת בָּאָדָם, 5, 10 f. Acc. to 5, 21 a boy is obligated to keep the commandments at 13;
he thus becomes בַּר־מִצְוָה a "fully responsible" member of the community morally and
legally. This designation first occurs in bBM, 96a but finds gen. acceptance only in the
M. Ages. [59] 5, 21 hands down a group of sayings about the ages of life from Jehuda
b Tema (Tannaite). Here the life of a man of 40 is marked by בִּינָה "understanding,"
while at 60 he attains to עֵצָה, "counsel." With חָכָם comes פִּקֵּחַ [60] "with eyes opened (by
God)" (Ex. 4:11) in the sense of "full of understanding," "prudent," "experienced,"
e.g., bKet., 88a and the parable of the prudent and fools at the king's banquet, bShab.,
153a, cf. esp. Mt. 25:1-13.

D. The Word Group in the New Testament.

1. φρένες. [61]

To give preference to speaking with tongues as an immediate utterance of the
Spirit is childish, 1 C. 14:20. The Corinthians should use their reason, which includes
emotion and will, and achieve perfection therein → VIII, 76, 6 ff. The stage of the
child, that is not yet responsible in its acts, [62] is followed in human development by
that of full understanding, which is the stage of the mature man.

2. ἄφρων, ἀφροσύνη.

a. The Synoptists.

In Lk. 11:40 ἄφρονες [63] "fools" is used by Jesus in a challenge to the Pharisees.
In their rules the Pharisees are concerned about ritual and cultic purity and they
neglect inner, moral purity. The designation, which as such hits at false piety and breaks
off fellowship, must have been all the more offensive and galling to the Pharisees
because of their own claim to be παιδευτὴς ἀφρόνων, R. 2:20. The Lord's saying
is a judgment on the basically false approach of the Pharisees and it uses the common
Rabbinic address "fools" [64] in the sense of "ungodly men"; the Pharisees do not
truly know God as the Creator who makes both what is external and also what is

---

[59] Cf. Schürer, II, 496.
[60] Cf. Str.-B., I, 969. 878.
[61] Cf. Bultmann Theol.[6], 215 on the word group.
[62] Str.-B., III, 462 offers Rabb. examples of the concept "boy."
[63] In Lk. ἄφρων might be the counterpart of the Rabb. בעל תשובה [Rengstorf].
[64] שׁוטה, cf. Str.-B., I, 280; III, 102.

internal. Doubts have been expressed as to whether the vocative ἄφρων, ἄφρονες is an authentic part of the dominical tradition. When God says "Thou fool" to the rich man in Lk. 12:20, He makes it clear to him that he has not reaped anything for himself (ψ 38:7). Lulling himself in false security, the rich man does not reckon with God; this is his folly, his sin. In the sayings about man's outer and inner un-cleanness that follow the dictum of Mk. 7:15, there is a list of vices which includes ἀφροσύνη, 7:21 f. We have here more of an arbitrary and random collection than a systematic grouping, though possibly ἀφροσύνη is put comprehensively at the end as the chief and basic sin. Thus it can be understood as the source of the un-cleanness which arises from within.

b. The Pauline Corpus.

In R. 2:17-20 Paul enumerates the religious and moral claims of Judaism so that he can test the reality by them. [65] Thus the phrase παιδευτὴς ἀφρόνων is not in the first instance Pauline usage. Rather, ἄφρονες along with νήπιοι (→ IV, 919, 31 ff.) contains from the standpoint of the pious Jew a judgment on the pagan world around which is designed to express the accusation of ungodliness → IV, 845, 20 ff.; V, 619, 35 ff. In 1 Cor.15:36 Paul is not pronouncing a definitive judgment with his ἄφρων. It is a rhetorical appeal for true understanding. To cling to the negative view is to adopt the position of the ἄφρων which is close to that of ungodliness, cf. R. 1:22; 1 C. 1:18 ff.; → IV, 845, 12 ff.

In 2 C. 11 and 12 ἄφρων and ἀφροσύνη are used in self-criticism. The apostle's ἀφροσύνη is that in the difficult conflicts with the church or congregation he apparently or provisionally sets himself on the carnal plane of self-boasting rather than on the spiritual plane. This is what Paul has in view when he speaks of his ἀφροσύνη in 2 C. 11: 1. [66] In the situation at Corinth foolish boasting (→ III, 652 13 ff.) before God and men has become necessary for him, 11:16 f. The "clever" Corinthians φρόνιμοι ὄντες have submitted to the reckless claims of fools ἄφρονες, 11:19. [67] But Paul — speaking again in human folly, and hence improperly — will surpass them all, 11:21; 12:11. He does this by pointing to his sufferings. Hence it is no folly, but the truth, 12:6. He thus rejects the term ἄφρων as applicable to him-self, though without developing the same dialectical use of the term as he does in relation to the μωρία (→ IV, 846, 23 ff.; VII, 354, 6 ff.) of the Gospel and of him-self in 1 C. 1:18 ff.

The reference in Eph. 5:17 is to the walk of the community. ἀφροσύνη as foolish or careless conduct is contrasted with σύνεσις as prudent observance of the will of God. Even members of the community can still become ἄφρονες again. ἄφρονες is parallel to ἄσοφοι, which occurs as a hapax legomenon in the NT at 5:15. ἄφρονες, as a warning against an impious or ungodly mind, catches up the ἄσοφοι, just as the exhortation to walk as σοφοί is theologically interpreted by the συνίετε τί τὸ θέλημα τοῦ κυρίου. According to 1 Pt. 2:15 it is God's will that the community

---

[65] Ltzm. R., ad loc.: One gets the impression from v. 19 f. that Paul is quoting the words of a work written for Jewish proselytes, cf. the title of the work by Maimonides, Guide for the Perplexed, cf. A. Weiss (1923/24).

[66] E. Käsemann, "Die Legitimität d. Apostels," ZNW, 41 (1942), 55.

[67] In 2 C. 11:19 Paul describes as "fools" the adversaries to whom the clever Corinthians have subjected themselves.

should silence by good acts the ignorance of men who are without understanding. Faith in God is to bear witness to itself and to overcome ungodliness by good works.

3. φρονέω - φρόνημα.

a. Mark, Matthew, Acts.

Peter's warning, which seeks to restrain Jesus from taking the path of suffering, is very sharply rejected in the Lord's saying, Mk. 8:33 and par.; → IV, 842, n. 17. [68] Peter can grasp only human thoughts that are focused on earthly life and well-being. In Ac. 28:22 the leaders of Jews, in the name of the whole Jewish community in Rome, ask Paul about his position *vis-à-vis* the "sect" of the Christians; they want him to state his own view: ἃ φρονεῖς.

b. The Pauline Corpus.

φρόνημα (R. 8:6; → II, 414, 10 ff.) occurs in the NT only in connection with φρονέω (R. 8:5) and it means the same as the inf. (τὸ) φρονεῖν used as a noun. The τὰ ἐπίγεια φρονοῦντες (Phil. 3:19), cf. ἐν σαρκὶ πεποιθότες (3:3) are entangled in a superstition and their thinking is governed by earthly powers even though they belong to the Christian community. Paul presses toward the mark, his upward calling by God in Christ Jesus, as the prize of victory, Phil. 3:14. This saying about himself gives the τέλειοι (→ VIII, 76, 12 ff.) in the congregation their basic orientation. With the indicative φρονοῦμεν we also find the cohortative φρονῶμεν as a vl. at Phil. 3:15; since the orientation is finally a gift of God's Spirit, the variant is of no material significance. With τὰ ἄνω ζητεῖτε [69] and τὰ ἄνω φρονεῖτε (Col. 3:1 f.) we have the Pauline imperative, obeying which is not left to the will of man, for the basis here is the uniting of the believer in baptism with the Christ event and its eschatological reference. τὸ φρόνημα τοῦ πνεύματος (→ VI, 430, 23 ff.), the gift which determines man, is finally God Himself, R. 8:27. [70]

R. 11:20 warns the community against arrogance in view of the judgment on Judaism: μὴ ὑψηλὰ φρόνει, cf. 11:25: [71] μὴ ἦτε ἐν ἑαυτοῖς φρόνιμοι, → IV, 822, 30 ff. The exhortation in R. 12:16 [72] begins with the admonition to concord, which is granted in faith. A warning against conceit is supplemented by the admonition to identify oneself with the lowly → VIII, 19, 34 ff. The warning against too high a view of oneself is reinforced by the OT formulation from Prv. 3:7, which also lies behind R. 11:25. In R. 12:3 the paronomasia with the fourfold φρονέω directs us to salutary σω-φρονέω (→ VII, 1102, 16 ff.) in place of dangerous ὑπερφρονέω.

---

[68] Hck., Kl. Mk., *ad loc.* Str.-B., I, 748 ref. to a saying of R. Jochanan: "Who is a student of the scribes? He who leaves his business and makes God's business his concern," bShab., 114a.

[69] Lohse, *op. cit.* (→ n. 42), 166-8 ref. to the petition in Col. 1:9-11. The aim is true knowledge and practical action, cf. 1 QS 3:1; 9:17 f. Cf. also Ew. Gefbr., *ad loc.* and Loh. Kol., *ad loc.*

[70] Gennadius of Constantinople in Staab, 382 speaks of σκοπὸς τοῦ πνεύματος. πνεῦμα is the Spirit of God in man (→ VII, 875, 12 ff.). R. 8:27 takes up 8:6; cf. M. Black, "The Interpretation of R. 8:28," *Festschr. O. Cullmann, Nov. Test. Suppl.,* 6 (1962), 166-172.

[71] Cf. Prv. 3:7; Is. 5:21; Gn. r., 44, 2 on 15:1; cf. Str.-B., III, 299.

[72] Marcion does not have R. 12:16a, cf. A. Harnack, "Marcion. Das Ev. vom fremden Gott," TU, 45² (1924), App. III, 109. *

We are not to aspire so high that we miss the set goal; we are to aspire with moderation → 225, 8 ff. At 1 C. 4:6 the φρονέω interpolated into the *koine* MS[73] helps us to understand a difficult text in terms of the familiar warning.[74]

The fundamental demand of Pauline exhortation is a uniform direction, a common mind, and unity of thought and will. In Phil. 2:2 the apostle issues an urgent admonition that we are to seek the same goal with a like mind, establishing the given unity and maintaining a Christian disposition in all things, cf. R. 12:16. According to Phil. 2:5[75] the confession of Christ is itself the standard for the mind of believers whose fellowship is constituted by Christ. In Phil. 4:2 the same admonition occurs in relation to an individual case and with emphasis on fellowship with Christ. In Gl. 5:10[76] Paul expresses confidence that with a like mind the community will reject any other message. In 2 C. 13:11 the exhortation to unity of mind is given a place in the conclusion of the epistle. In R. 15:5 there is a prayerful desire to the same effect with common praise of God as the goal.

In R. 14:6[77] φρονέω means "to observe." The point is that we are not to observe cultic rules and customs but to see to it that decision is made in responsibility to the Lord. φρονεῖν is the practical result of κρίνειν. As the adult sets aside immaturity (→ IV, 919, 8 ff.), so the grown man sets aside childish thoughts and desires, e.g., curiosity regarding falsely extolled gnosis, 1 C. 13:11.[78] He does not do this in his own strength but because he is known by God. In Phil. 1:7; 4:10 φρονέω ὑπέρ or ἐπί is used for care in thought and act. It is almost synonymous with φροντίζω here.

4. φρόνησις.

The noun φρόνησις occurs only twice in the NT, both times in liturgically shaped texts. At Lk. 1:17 φρόνησις comes after the quotation from Mal. 3:23 as a parallel to the first half of the verse and perhaps in reconstruction of the original. To bring back the disobedient to the way of thought and the conduct of the righteous is the eschatological task of the forerunner. In Eph. 1:8[79] the grace of God richly endows us with pure wisdom (→ VII, 523, 2 ff.) and understanding and makes

---

[73] Severian of Gabala in Staab, 239 already offers a similar interpretation.

[74] The admonition to be likeminded, which is constitutive for the Chr. community, leads to the adoption of ὁμόφρων, which occurs in the Gk. Bible only at 1 Pt. 3:8, cf. E. Kühl, *Krit.-exeget. Handbuch über 1 Pt., Jd. u. 2 Pt., Krit.-exeget. Komm. über das NT*, 12⁶ (1897), *ad loc.*; Kn. Pt., *ad loc.* Much later Didymus of Alexandria on 2 C. 13:11 (Staab, 44) uses the noun ὁμοφροσύνη.

[75] The act. is original, the pass. is the koine reading, Dib. Ph., *ad loc.* Acc. to K. Barth, *Erklärung d. Phil.*⁶ (1959), *ad loc.* the point is movement towards unity in spite of strong centrifugal forces. Str.-B., III, 620 quotes Rab Joseph: "Let man always learn from the mind of his Creator קונו מדעת," bSota, 5a. One might supplement Phil. 2:5 along these lines: τοῦτο [φρόνημα] φρονεῖτε ἐν ὑμῖν ὃ [φρόνημα] καὶ [ἦν] ἐν Χριστῷ Ἰησοῦ, cf. R. 15:5 [Moule].

[76] The apostle demands practical determination of thought and uniform orientation in terms of the Gospel, cf. F. Sieffert, *Der Br. an d. Galater, Krit.-exeget. Komm. über d. NT*, 7⁹ (1899), *ad loc.*; Schlier Gl.¹³, *ad loc.*

[77] The second half of R. 14:16 in ℜ is based on the negative ἐσθίων clause, Zn. R., 577, n. 9; Ltzm. R., *ad loc.*

[78] Cf. Jer. 4:22: υἱοὶ ἄφρονες ... σοφοί εἰσι τοῦ κακοποιῆσαι. φρόνιμοι (Is. 44:25) might be better than σοφοί here, since it can also mean "sly," "cunning," on the basis of Gn. 3:1, cf. Lk. 16:8. Copyists obviously changed κακοποιῆσαι to καλῶς ποιῆσαι etc. because of σοφοί.

[79] Ew. Gefbr. on Eph. 1:8: φρόνησις is the "understanding, which, arising from σοφία, makes this profitable for life," cf. Prv. 10:23.

known to us the mystery of the will of God. Here χάρις corresponds to φρόνησις (1:8) or σύνεσις πνευματική (Col. 1:9).

5. φρόνιμος.

a. Matthew and Luke.

In the Synoptic tradition φρόνιμος occurs only in parables or parabolic sayings. Mt. 7:24 compares the doer of the Word to the wise builder (→ V, 137, 17 ff.) who builds his house on a rock. The motif of φρόνιμος is secondary. The point is that the wise servant throws himself into the situation in which he is set, taking directions from his master (Mt. 24:45 and par.). Similarly the Christian who sets Christ wholly before him is wise. In the parable of the ten virgins (Mt. 25:1 ff.) [80] wisdom is preparedness, [81] for everything depends on the actual encounter with the Lord. In the parable of the unjust steward (Lk. 16:8) [82] wisdom has the sense of cunning. Cleverly resolute action is imposed by the hopelessness of the situation and the resultant urgency. In acting as he does, even the worldly man can be a model for the children of light. φρόνιμος in these parables applies to those who have grasped the eschatological position of man. This helps us to see why the term is present in the parable tradition. The metaphor which speaks of the wisdom of serpents (Mt. 10:16) [83] and the simplicity of doves (→ VI, 70, 3 ff.) might well be proverbial. [84] But by association with φρονιμώτατος in Gn. 3:1 it acquires a biblical significance which is underlined by the reading with ὁ ὄφις (→ V, 580, 13 ff.) in the sing.

b. Paul.

Paul finds the word φρόνιμος a help as he tries to express the nature of the believer. In R. 11:25; 12:16 φρόνιμος is par. to φρονέω, R. 11:20; 12:16 → 232, 27 ff. In 1 C. 4:10 φρόνιμοι is employed dialectically. Paul uses μωροί with reference to himself — formally, of course, in view of the plural — while the Corinthians are φρόνιμοι. In 1 C. 10:15 Paul presupposes that the church has the power to judge in the eucharistic question and he addresses it accordingly. Rather different is the admonition in 1 C. 14:20. We are to regard it as irony that in 2 C. 11:19 Paul calls the Corinthians φρόνιμοι when they are taken in so easily → 227, 12 ff.

E. The Word Group in the Post-Apostolic Fathers and the Apologists.

1. Acc. to 1 Cl., 3, 3 the conflicts at Corinth are due to the antithesis of the φρόνιμοι and ἄφρονες. The author calls the adversaries arrogant "fools," 39, 1. 7 f., cf. Job 5:2 f. But better offend them than God, 21, 5. The foolish squabbles cause the Lord's name to be blasphemed among those of other views, 47, 7. φρονέω περί is common in 2 Cl., e.g., 1, 1 f., [85] cf. 12, 5. In both works, as in Paul, there are exhortations to humility, 1 Cl., 13, 1, and concord, 2 Cl., 17, 3. Ign. has φρονέω and acc. in Smyrn., 11, 3: τέλεια, Tr., 4, 1:

---

[80] Jülicher Gl. J., II, 448-459.
[81] Str.-B., I, 969 f.
[82] Jülicher Gl., II, 504: It is Jesus who in Lk. 16:8a commends the unjust steward for his sagacity; cf. also Michaelis, Die Gleichnisse Jesu³ (1956), 227-9.
[83] Str.-B., I, 574 f.; Braun, op. cit. (→ n. 42), II, 30, n. 1: Man's profane acts as a reflection of his attitude to God; II, 102 f., n. 5: 1 QS 9:21-23 expressly demands a hatred that prudently disguises itself as humility.
[84] Cf. Midr. Cant., 2 on 2:14 (Wünsche, 74).
[85] The statements about correct christological thinking still exert an influence in the controversies of the 5th and 6th cent., Kn. Cl., ad loc.

πολλά. An understanding attitude is demanded in Mg., 3, 1: φρόνιμος ἐν θεῷ, and Eph., 17, 2. The aim in Sm., 2, 1; 5, 2 is to ward off docetic thinking; on Ign. Pol., 2, 2 [86] cf. Mt. 10:16; on Tr., 8, 2 cf. 1 Cl., 47, 7. In Ep. Diogn. pagan idolatry is an example of "folly" ἀφροσύνη, 3, 3; 4, 5, cf. φρόνησις, 2, 1. Jewish "thinking" φρονεῖν is initially right, 3, 2. φρονέω with acc. is common in Herm. for right "thinking," m., 3, 4; 9, 12: 10, 3, 1; s., 5, 2, 7; 9, 13, 7. There is "lack of understanding" even among believers, s., 9, 22, 2 f., including Hermas himself, v., 5, 4; m., 4, 2 1; 12, 4, 2; s., 6, 4, 3; 5, 2. "Folly" is enmity against God, m., 5, 2, 2. 4 etc. [87] Behind the irrationality and ungodliness of men stands the angel of wickedness who is also ἄφρων, m., 6, 2, 4. Different as the various peoples of the world are in φρόνησις and νοῦς, through the seal of baptism they receive μίαν φρόνησιν and ἕνα νοῦν. There thus arises a unity of faith and love, s., 9, 17, 2. 4; 9, 18, 4, cf. 9, 29, 2. [88]

2. Aristides Apol., 8, 1; 14, 1 asks what pagans and Jews think about God. Those who pass as wise men are fools. ἀφρονέστεροι than the Gks. are the Egyptians, 12, 1. φρονέω, φρόνησις occur in Just. Dial., 1, 6; 23, 2; 48, 1 etc. esp. in debate with Judaism. Acc. to 3, 3 φρόνησις rests on φιλοσοφία and ὀρθὸς λόγος, 2, 4. 6. Plato's teaching on the soul in Tim., 41 is refuted in Just. Dial., 5, 4 f. with a ref. to the sinfulness and "folly" ἀφροσύνη of souls. On Dial., 12, 3 cf. R. 11:20, 25 → 232, 27 ff. Dial., 112, 2 interprets the serpent of Gn. 3:14; Nu. 21:9; Is. 27:1, which acts ἀφρόνως. φρήν occurs in Just. only in Apol., 39, 4 quoting Eur. Hipp., 612. [89] In his polemic against false gods Athenagoras Suppl., 22, 5 quotes the equation of Athene and φρόνησις, which was common in Hell. theology. [90]

3. In Gnosticism φρόνησις occurs in the development of mythological ideas, Athenag. Suppl., 22, 5 as an emanation of the supreme deity the θεὸς ἄρρητος among the members of the ogdoad. In the system of Basilides we have the series: νοῦς, λόγος, φρόνησις, δύναμις, δικαιοσύνη, cf. Iren. Haer., I, 19, 1 [91] → VII, 896, n. 75. Acc. to Apocryphon Joh. Cod. III, 11, 22 f. [92] there emanate from the divine αὐτογενές the four: χάρις, σύνεσις, αἴσθησις, φρόνησις. In the prayer of anointing in Act. Thom. 27, 5 members are mentioned: νοῦς, ἔννοια, φρόνησις, ἐνθύμησις, λογισμός. The Catholic Epist. Apostolorum, 43-45 [93] contains an interpretation of Mt. 25:1 ff.: The 10 virgins are 10 basic forces. In antithesis to Gnostic views knowledge and understanding are among the foolish virgins. The wise virgins are faith, love, grace, peace and hope.

4. In official church usage φρόνησις is a form of episcopal address [94] in Basil, Athanasius and Isidore, represented by the more common prudentia in the Lat. sphere.

Bertram

---

[86] The serpent is here a symbol of fleshly desire, the dove of what is to be besought spiritually.

[87] In Herm. s., 9, 15, 3 ἀφροσύνη is among the black women. In 15, 2 prudentia is 12th in the Lat. text, σύνεσις 10th in the Gk.

[88] On the innocence of the childlike mind as the climax of piety in s., 9, 29, 2 f. cf. Dib. Herm., ad loc.

[89] Cf. Plat. Theaet., 154d.

[90] W. Kraus, Art. "Athena," RAC, I, 879 f.

[91] P. Hendrix, De alexandrijnsche Haeresiarch Basilides (1926), 38 f.; H. Leisegang, Die Gnosis⁴ (1955), 249.

[92] Ed. M. Krause - P. Labib, "Die drei Versionen d. Apokr. d. Joh.," Abh. d. Deutschen Archäol. Instituts Kairo, Kpt. Reihe, 1 (1962), 64.

[93] Ed. C. Schmidt, "Gespräche Jesu mit seinen Jüngern nach d. Auferstehung. Ein Katholisch-Apost. Sendschreiben d. 2. Jhdt.," TU, 43 (1919), 136-145, cf. 379-383. Whether σύνεσις, ἐπιστήμη or φρόνησις is the original is an open question, cf. Herm. s., 9, 15, 2 (→ n. 87) and the other par. mentioned in Schmidt, 382. Cf. also R. Staats, "Die törichten Jungfrauen v. Mt. 25 in gnostischer u. antignostischer Lit., Christentum u. Gnosis," ZNW Beih., 37 (1969), 98-115.

[94] H. Zilliacus, "Anredeformen," Jbch. Ant. Christ., 7 (1964), 178.

φυλάσσω, φυλακή

† φυλάσσω.

Contents: A. The Verb in Non-Biblical Greek: 1. From Homer to Aristotle; 2. Hellenistic Usage. B. The Old Testament and Judaism: The Greek Old Testament; 2. The Dead Sea Scrolls; 3. Philo and Josephus; 4. Greek Apocrypha and Pseudepigrapha; 5. The Rabbinic Tradition. C. φυλάσσω in the New Testament: 1. The Gospels and Acts; 2. The Epistles. D. Early Christianity.

A. The Verb in Non-Biblical Greek.

1. From Homer to Aristotle.

The verb φυλάσσω, Attic φυλάττω, comes from φύλαξ [1] "watchman" and denotes the activity or office of a watchman whose job is "to protect" those who are asleep from harm during the night. It ref. to deliberate and conscious "watching," "being on the alert," trans. "to guard," Hom. Il., 10, 309 ff., 417 ff. and takes on the sense "to protect," "to watch over," "to care for," Od., 15, 35; we find ῥύομαι with it, Il., 10, 417; Od., 14, 107. Other senses are "to note," "to pay attention to," Il., 2, 251, "to observe," "to follow," 16, 686, or "to keep," 16, 30; 24, 111; 3, 280, finally "to be on guard," "to take care," 23, 343. The mid. means "to take care," "to be on guard against," and is often used like the act., e.g., Soph. Phil., 48. In Hom. Od., 5, 466; 22, 195 the verb means intr. "to be awake," opp. "to be asleep," with ref. to herdsmen. The construction with ἀπό "to guard against" occurs in Xenoph. Cyrop., I, 4, 7. We find μή in Plat. Theaet., 154d or ὅπως μή, Gorg., 480a. φυλάσσω νόμον means "to bear in mind a rule of conduct," Soph. Trach., 616, or "to keep the laws exactly," Plat. [2] Polit., 292a, cf. φυλάττοντες σῴζειν, Resp., VI, 484d, cf. φυλάξαι τοὺς νόμους in Aristot. Pol., III, 15, p. 1286b, 33; φυλάττειν . . . τὴν πολιτείαν, VIII, 1, p. 1337a, 15 f.

2. Hellenistic Usage.

In the everyday Gk. of the pap. there is a rich multiplicity of usage. We find a ref. to guard duty in P. Petr., III, p. 341, 21 f. (3rd cent. B.C.). The pious wish "May God keep you" occurs in P. Masp., I, 67005, 27 (6th cent. A.D.). Often the ref. is to deposited documents, P. Masp., I, 67032, 89 (551 A.D.) or objects, P. Lille, I, 7, 8 (3rd cent. B.C.). There is also a rich legal use in the law of contracts and marriage law. [3]

φ υ λ ά σ σ ω. Hatch-Redpath, Liddell-Scott, Pr.-Bauer, *s.v.*; F. Melzer, *Der chr. Wortschatz d. deutschen Sprache. Eine evangelische Darstellung* (1951), 249; W. Böld, *Die antidämonischen Abwehrmächte in d. Theol. d. Spätjüdt.*, Diss. Bonn (1938), 6-63.

[1] Etym. obscure, cf. perhaps Lat. *bubulcus*, "ox-driver," Walde-Hofmann, *s.v.* and Boisacq, *s.v.* φυλακός, Frisk, *s.v.* φύλαξ. On the formation of the verb cf. Schwyzer, I, 725 [Risch].

[2] W. Jaeger, *Paideia, Die Formung d. griech. Menschen*, III³ (1959), 38.

[3] Preisigke Wört., *s.v.* with many examples; Moult-Mill., *s.v.*

B. The Old Testament and Judaism.

1. The Greek Old Testament.

a. φυλάσσω occurs 471 times in the LXX, 379 times for שָׁמַר [4] and 10 for נָצַר [5]. Both Hbr. verbs embrace essentially the same range of meaning as φυλάσσω. [6]

b. φυλάσσω occurs often, esp. in the mid., in most of the meanings familiar from secular Gk. (→ 236, 10 ff.) but it serves esp. to express the divinely required attitude of man to the divine covenant, Ex. 19:5 etc., and to the cultic statutes, laws, commandments, admonitions and warnings; in this sense it becomes a tt. in the legal traditions from Ex. to Dt. It is also found in the historical books, sometimes with other formulations, e.g., to "keep to" the way of the Lord, Ju. 2:22; 3 Βασ. 2:4; 8:25 (plur.) etc., "to observe or follow" the commandments of the Lord → II, 546, 29 ff. The prophets sometimes have other phrases, e.g., "keeping" knowledge, Mal. 2:7, righteousness, truth, peace, Is. 26:2 f. In the hagiographa there is stress on "keeping," "observing" the ways, testimonies, or commandments of the Lord, Job 23:11; ψ 17:22; 18:12 etc., esp. ψ 118, where φυλάσσω occurs 21 times, cf. also Prv. 2:8; 4:5 etc. We have the negative at ψ 16:4, φυλάσσω with ἀπό [7] at ψ 17:24. In these statements man is the subj.; he is required "to uphold, keep, observe" the divine order after the pattern of Gn. 2:15.

c. The verb also describes God's attitude to man. The ref. is to confident experience of the divine preservation which man remembers and to which he appeals when his own fate seems to be in contradiction with it, Job 10:12; 29, 2. God, who "observes" all the ways of the righteous, Job 13:27; 33:11, "guards" and "protects" him even in suffering and sin, 10:14, and can "shelter" him even from His own wrath in the realm of the dead, 14:13 (HT צָפַן). [8] God "cares" for animals, Job 39:1, and men, Jer. 5:24. Thus Yahweh comes to be portrayed as the "Guardian" and "Shepherd" [9] of Israel in Ἰερ. 38(31):10. We do not find the verb elsewhere in the prophetic message of salvation. In many hymnic statements the Ps. praise God as the Watcher and Guardian of the righteous, who can always turn to Him with a prayer for protection, ψ 11:8; 15:1; 16:8; 24:20; 33:21 etc., cf. also 1 Βασ. 30:23; Prv. 2:8 etc. He who "guards" Israel does not sleep, ψ 120:4. He "keeps" the city, ψ 126:1. He "watches over" aliens, ψ 145:9, the poor, ψ 114:9, the righteous, ψ 96:10, His beloved, ψ 144:20, and praying individuals, ψ 120:7. The Aaronic blessing accords this protection to Israel, Nu. 6:24, cf. Ex. 23:20. We also find sayings

---

[4] שָׁמַר (458 times in HT) is transl. elsewhere in the LXX 13 times by διαφυλάσσω, 10 by προσέχω, 22 by τηρέω and compounds, and 20 by other Gk. verbs.

[5] נָצַר (62 times in HT) is elsewhere in the LXX transl. once by διαφυλάσσω, 12 times by (ἐκ-)ζητέω, 10 by τηρέω and compounds. When we have φυλάσσω and τηρέω together, φυλάσσω corresponds to שָׁמַר and τηρέω to נָצַר, e.g., Prv. 2:11. In Prv. 19:16 שָׁמַר twice is rendered by φυλάσσω and τηρέω and in 21:23 we have φυλάσσω and διατηρέω. שָׁמַר or φυλάσσω has here a personal ref. and נָצַר or διατηρέω a material ref., cf. Prv. 22:5; material obj. are gen. more common with נָצַר.

[6] נָצַר has perhaps a rather sharper sense than שָׁמַר, cf. Job 27:20, where נֹצֵר אָדָם "keeper of men" has in view God's exact, critical observation of men.

[7] Helbing Kasussyntax, 30-32.

[8] There is not even a slight hope of awakening from the sleep of death in Job 14:12. The desire to be hidden in the realm of the dead is unreal, cf. F. Horst, Hiob, Bibl. Komm. AT, 16, 1 (1968), ad loc. Exegesis in the early Church found an intimation of eschatological resurrection in v. 12. G. Hölscher, Das Buch Hiob, Hndbch. AT, I, 17² (1952), ad loc. thinks the v. has undergone revision. But cf. K. Budde, Das Buch Hiob, Hndkomm. AT, II, 1 (1896), ad loc. LXX finds a belief in the resurrection here, esp. in v. 14.

[9] Cf. W. Jost, Ποιμήν. Das Bild vom Hirten in d. bibl. Überlieferung u. seine christologische Bdtg. (1939), 19-21.

with a material obj. God "maintains" His mercy, "keeps" His covenant, 3 Βασ. 3:6; 8:23; 2 Ἐσδρ. 11:5; 19:32; 2 Ch. 6:14 ff.; Dt. 7:9, and "maintains" ἀλήθεια, ψ 145:6. In the Wisdom tradition God's place is taken to some degree by hypostases as powers of blessing which keep man, Prv. 6:22, e.g., wisdom in Wis. 9:11; 10:1, 5, 12, good counsel, Prv. 2:11, the command of the Law, Prv. 6:22, education, Prv. 10:7, righteousness, Prv. 13:6. God is the logical subj. behind pass. formulations, Wis. 19:6; ψ 36:28. As the righteous man is kept for salvation, the ungodly is spared for the day of evil, Prv. 16:9. But the prophetic message contains the promise that God will not chide for ever or be wrathful continually διαφυλάσσω, Jer. 3:5. Thus in the later Gk. transl. of ψ 60:8 E' S' (Field, ad loc.), in a misreading of the difficult HT, we get the confession: "Mercy and truth from Thee (God) keep him (the righteous)." The saying in 1 Βασ. 25:29, which early in Jewish piety was detached from the OT story and viewed as an expression of the hope of eternal life, Σ transl. by φυλάσσω: "May the soul be preserved in a covenant of life with the Lord God," → II, 853, 1 ff.

2. The Dead Sea Scrolls.

שמר in the sense of very loyal keeping of the Law is one of the catchwords of the Qumran community.[10] It is used in the Dead Sea Scrolls of those who keep God's covenant, 1 QS 5:2, 9, who observe His commandments, 1 QpHab 5:5 on 1:12 f.; 1 QH 16:13, 17; Damasc. 3:2 f. (4:2 f.), who "maintain" faithfulness, 1 QS 8:3; 10:25. Damasc. has שמר in relation to the ministry of the sanctuary, 4:1 (5:7), the "observance" of the Sabbath, 6:18 (8:15); 10:16 f. (13:1), the "keeping" of an oath, 16:7 (20:4 f.). In such expressions the community has itself in view. With no casuistry this implies radical rejection of the opp. standpt., 1 QS 10:21; 1 QM 10:1; 1 QH 18:24; Damasc. 2:18, 21 (3:4, 7); 6:14 (8:12). But in the background is God. It is He who "keeps" the righteous, 1 QS 2:3; 1 QM 11:11;[11] 14:4, 8, 10; 18:7;[12] 1 QH fr. 3:7,[13] cf. also 1 QH 15:15,[14] and who thus "keeps" His oath, Damasc. 8:15 (9:23) and "maintains" His covenant and grace, ibid., 19:1 (8:21).

3. Philo and Josephus.

a. Philo in Det. Pot. Ins., 62-8 follows Gn. 4:9 and Nu. 8:26 and thinks "keeping in mind" is the goal which is above "practice" as the means, cf. also Leg. All., I, 53-5 on Gn. 2:15. It is only in the context of the verses mentioned that φυλάττω occurs in Philo. Elsewhere we find προφυλάττομαι in Cher., 34 with ref. to those who give admonition and warning about the uncertainty of the future and the need to observe moderation.

b. The ruling of Dt. 22:5 is repeated in Jos. Ant., 4, 301. The religio-moral admonitions in 8, 120 are a paraphrase of 3 Βασ. 8:58; here Jos. adds τηρεῖν with the acc. to φυλάττεσθαι ἀπό, cf. 8, 395. In Bell., 2, 139 the second point of Essene legislation is the obligation to observe human rights. It is also required in this connection that one should "keep oneself" pure from unholy gain, 2, 141. Of special significance for Jos. is the admonition to "keep" the Law, Ant., 4, 318, to "observe" the statutes, commands,

---

[10] H. Braun, "Spätjüd.-häret. u. frühchr. Radikalismus," *Beiträge z. histor. Theol.*, 24² (1969), I, 99 f.; O. Betz, "Offenbarung u. Schriftforschung in d. Qumransekte," *Wissenschaftl. Untersuchungen z. NT*, 6 (1960), 8 and 32.

[11] With J. Carmignac, *La règle de la guerre des fils de lumière contre les fils de ténèbres* (1958), *ad loc.* and K. G. Kuhn, *Konkordanz z. d. Qumrantexten* (1960), *s.v.* שמר we are to supply [השמ[ו]רתה] here.

[12] On the passages from 1 QM cf. Carmignac, *op. cit.*

[13] Ed. A. M. Habermann, *Megilloth midbar Yehuda* (1959), 135.

[14] Cf. S. Holm-Nielsen, "Hodayot. Psalms from Qumran," *Acta Theol. Danica*, 2 (1960), *ad loc.*

laws and ordinances, to "keep" and "follow" them, 6, 141, and 336 (so also τηρέω, e.g., 8, 120 and 395; 9, 222); 7, 338 and 384; 8, 208; Ap., I, 60 and 317; 2, 156 and 184 etc. The exhortation to "hold fast" to the Law, Ant., 12, 276, and to the customs of the fathers, 16, 36; 19, 285. 288. 290. 304; Ap., 1, 29, and to "protect" them and "keep" peace, Ant., 4, 297, is continually deduced from the history. We are to "maintain" διαφυλάττω piety, 16, 41, to "keep" God's gifts, Ap., 2, 197. Behind all this stands God's "protecting" and "sustaining" power, Ant., 4, 243; 6, 291; 7, 153; 8, 24. 114; 12, 55. We often find a political or military use of φυλάττω in the various senses "to protect or provide for oneself," 6, 207; 7, 32 and 118, "to keep" oaths or treaties, 10, 97; 14, 309; 20, 93 and 349; "to besiege," 12, 318; "to watch over or protect," 11, 47 f.; 12, 333; 13, 202; 20, 155; Ap., 2, 44; Bell., 2, 205; 4, 51, "to preserve," "to spare" Ant., 5, 13; 14, 489; Bell., 2, 321; 5, 565; 6, 208; 7, 334 and 373, "to occupy," 2, 378, "to hold captive," Ant., 13, 17; Bell., 1, 258. In all this Jos. simply follows the gen. use [15] of φυλάττω → 236, 10 ff.

4. Greek Apocrypha and Pseudepigrapha.

The usage of Jewish Hellenism in the apocr. and pseudepigr. presents nothing new. The unfamiliar or ambiguous שׁוּף [16] of Gn. 3:15 is transl. by προφυλάσσω in Sib., 1, 62. "To keep" truth and love is a familiar demand in Sib., 2, 58 and 65. The pious wish that the truth might "keep" you in Test. R. 3:9 is along the lines of the Wisdom tradition in its Hell. form. Elsewhere in Test. XII we read of "preserving" the spiritual heritage of the fathers, Test. R. 4:5; S. 7:3; L. 10:1; Jud. 13:1; 26:1. There is constant warning against various temptations, Test. R. 4:8; 6:1; S. 3:1; 4:5; L. 13:8; Jud. 16:1. Acc. to Jud. 22:3 God "upholds" the kingly power of Judah for ever. In Ep. Ar., 311 the Jewish principle of inviolable keeping of the transmitted Law of God, Dt. 4:2; 13:1, is applied to the Gk. transl. of the Law in the LXX.

5. The Rabbinic Tradition.

The Rabb. are keepers and guardians of the Torah; they establish a tradition extending from Moses to the present, Ab., 1, 1-2. 4; 3-4. In Ab., 4, 5. 11, cf. 2, 8 עשׂה is used with ref. to "observance" of the Law. For the Rabb. observing and following the Law and its commands, of which 613 are listed in M. Ex., 7, 5 on 20:2 (p. 222, 2), is the basis of piety. They thus see it as their task to set a fence about the Law, Ab., 1, 1. Observing all the commandments is possible, [17] so that there may be those who are perfectly righteous, bShab., 55a. Acc. to the Rabb. view the patriarchs, e.g., Abraham, bYoma, 28b, cf. bBB, 17a, and other righteous man of the OT kept the whole Law and thus remained without sin, Qid., 4, 14. In Sheb., 10:3 Dt. 15:9 is quoted with שׁמר "to keep oneself." Bik., 13, 12 speaks of אנשׁי משׁמר, "the men of the service." Shab., 22, 4 has שׁמר "to preserve," but cf. צנע "to preserve," 10:1 etc. and נצל "to save," "to keep," 16, 1 etc. In Aram. שׁמר is replaced by נטר.

C. φυλάσσω in the New Testament.

1. The Gospels and Acts.

Only in the story of the rich young ruler do we find the verb in all three Synoptic Gospels; it is in the mid., Mk. 10:20 and par. What it expresses is a legal piety

---

[15] In Jos. one sees the wide range of the use of φυλάσσω in the 1st cent. A.D. [We owe the material in part to K. H. Rengstorf.]

[16] Cf. Köhler-Baumg., s.v.; LXX has τηρέω, → VIII, 141, 7 ff.

[17] Str.-B., I, 814 and 816, with more material.

which Jesus also acknowledges: "All these have I kept (observed) from my youth."
While Jesus here and elsewhere refers to scrupulous observance of the Law as the
final and supreme content of piety, other NT passages seem to see in the faithful
keeping of given precepts the fulfilling of Christian piety. The ref. in the NT, however, is to God's Word rather than God's Law. Thus we read in Lk. 11:28: "Blessed
are they that hear the word of God (→ IV, 121, 17 ff.), and keep it." This dominical
saying presupposes v. 27 and seems to be an answer to it. [18] God's Word can hardly
be understood as the Torah. From a very early time the sayings of Jesus, the
dominical sayings, were accepted as God's Word by the primitive community. This
may be seen from the claim of Mt. 7:24 ff. and par. ποιέω here (→ VI, 478, 35 ff.)
corresponds to φυλάσσω or τηρέω → VIII, 143, 18 ff. [19] Elsewhere the context
and content of Lk. 11:28 both correspond to the statement in Lk. 8:21, where emphasis is given to those who hear and do God's Word. [20] In Jn. 12:47 [21] "hearing"
and "observing" are christologically orientated: He who does not practise the words
(the logos in v. 48) that he has heard, for him they will become a judgment. To
observe the words of Christ corresponds to the Johannine demand to do the truth,
Jn. 3:21; 1 Jn. 1:6.

In Ac. 7:53 Stephen accuses the Jews of not "fulfilling" the commandments. [22]
In Ac. 21:24 Paul is challenged to show himself to be a loyal "observer" of the
Law. [23] According to 16:4 he publishes the rulings of the so-called Apostolic Council
at Jerusalem in the churches, so that they might be "observed." The reference is to
certain things from which the Gentile congregations are to abstain, Ac. 21:25. Here
as in Lk. 12:15 φυλάσσω is used in the negative sense "to keep oneself from." [24]
According to Lk. 4:10 Jesus is tempted to set Himself under the promise of ψ 90:11:
τοῦ διαφυλάξαι. In Jn. 17:12 it is He Himself who "keeps" those whom the Father
has given Him so long as He dwells among them. The prayer for preservation refers
to the community of the Risen Lord. Jn. 12:25 adopts the Synoptic dictum that
promises the gaining of life to the disciple who sacrifices it.

2. The Epistles.

According to R. 2:26 "observance" of the ordinances of the Law by the Gentiles
effects a reversal of the relation between Jews and Gentiles before God. The Jews
have lost the grace promised to them in the OT since they do not "observe" the
Law, R. 2:25. ἐὰν νόμον πράσσῃς is surely to be taken in the same way [25] as ἐὰν...
τὰ δικαιώματα τοῦ νόμου φυλάσσῃ in the next v.(26): "If (the uncircumcised)

---

[18] Bultmann Trad., 30. Cf. the Gospel of Thomas (ed. A. Guillaumont [1959]), Logion 79
(95, 7 f.): "Blessed are they who have heard the Word of the Father and kept it in truth."
[19] At Dt. 5:15; 1 Ch. 28:7 עשׂה is transl. by φυλάσσω, and at Ex. 12:17; 1 Ch. 22:12;
29:19 שׁמר is transl. by ποιέω. Cf. also Rabb. usage → 239, 26 ff.
[20] Cf. Braun, op. cit., I, Index, s.v. "Tun d. Tora"; II, 29-34.
[21] Bultmann J., ad loc.
[22] H. M. Scharlemann, Stephen: A Singular Saint (1968), 102-104: A full-scale attack on
cultic religion.
[23] Haench. Ag.[15], 542-5.
[24] Bultmann Trad., 360. We find the two sections Lk. 12:13 f. and 16 ff. separately in the
Gospel of Thomas, op. cit. (→ n. 18), cf. Logion 72 (94, 1-6) and 63 (92, 3-9).
[25] πράσσω is used predominantly in an ethically negative sense in the LXX, esp. the
Wisdom tradition. A negative judgment is often connected with this verb in the NT too,
→ VI, 634, 29 ff.; 635, 30 ff.; 636, 1 ff.

comply with the righteous demands of the Law." In Gl. 6:13 Paul has a harsh saying about his Jewish opponents. Though they are zealous for the Law, they do not keep it. [26]

In 1 Tm. 5:21 the demand that the directions of the author should be followed or observed lays emphasis on the binding nature of the admonitions and warnings. Close by we find an admonition to "keep" the Christian faith (→ VIII, 163, 35 ff.), 1 Tm. 6:20, [27] cf. 2 Tm. 1:12, 14. The admonition to "keep oneself from" idols, i.e., to avoid contacts with idolatry or pagan cults (1 Jn. 5:21), [28] is given even stronger emphasis by its opposite, the predication of the true God, 1 Jn. 5:20. Similarly the final sentence 2 Pt. 3:17 contains a general warning against temptation, [29] and 2 Tm. 4:15 warns especially [30] against a certain Alexander. In 2 Th. 3:3 the community is given the promise that the Lord will strengthen and "keep" against evil. Along the same lines is the hope expressed at the end of Jude (v. 24) in what is obviously a liturgically shaped formula: "God, who is able to keep you from falling..." The fact that God preserved Noah and his family when the wicked world was destroyed makes him a preacher of the righteousness of God (2 Pt. 2:5), which here as in the OT (→ 237, 18 ff.) manifests itself in the preservation of the righteous. [31]

Where φυλάσσω is used elsewhere in the NT for "guarding" the palace, Lk. 11:21, or "keeping" the clothes, Ac. 22:20, or in the sense "to hold captive," "to be held captive," Lk. 8:29; Ac. 12:4; 23:35; 28:16, there is no theological ref.; on Lk. 2:8 → 243, 28 ff.

D. Early Christianity.

The word φυλάσσω is adopted esp. in the sense "to keep," cf. Just. Dial., 46, 1 ff. and passim in the debate with Judaism, cf. also 1 Cl., 14, 5; 2 Cl., 8, 4; 9, 3; Dg., 1, 1. Dg., 10, 7 ref. to the true death which is "reserved" for those condemned to eternal fire. Dg., 7, 2 speaks of the "observance" of the cosmic order by the elements and the sun; this is ascribed to the Logos as the Creator of all things. The verb is also common in the sense "to guard oneself," Just Apol., 14, 1 with μή, Dial., 82, 1; Ign. Trall., 2, 3; Eph., 7, 1 with acc.; Herm. m., 5, 1, 7 with ἀπό. The view that the tradition is the true norm for the Church is set forth in Did., 4, 13: "Thou shalt not forsake the commandments of the Lord but keep what thou hast received without adding or subtracting anything," cf. Barn., 19, 11. Here there is stated positively as a principle what is presupposed in Rev. 22:18 f., namely, that the Church is tied to a closed tradition → 240, 2 ff.

† φυλακή.

A. Outside the Bible.

1. φυλακή denotes a. the act of "watching," Hom. Il., 9, 1 and 471; Aesch. Ag., 236, or the "protection" which certain measures offer for the political order, Aristot. Pol., V,

---

[26] Cf. Schlier Gl.[13], ad loc.

[27] B. Weiss, Die paul. Br. u. der Hb.[2] (1902), ad loc. sees the directions in vv. 17-20, Wbg. Past., ad loc. in v. 19 f.

[28] Bl.-Debr. § 149; Johannessohn Präpos., 276 f.; Helbing Kasussyntax, 31 f. There is no question of a Hebraism or Semitism. On the issue cf. Deissmann LO, 96-99.

[29] Bl.-Debr. § 392, 1b.

[30] Cf. Dib. Past. on 4:14.

[31] Cf. O. Kaiser, "Die Begründung d. Sittlichkeit im Buche Jesus Sirach," ZThK, 55 (1958), 51-63; the basis of the distinction between law and wisdom teaching is in Dt. 4:2.

φ υ λ α κ ή . Bibl. → 236, Bibl.

11, p. 1315a, 8; b. the person of the watcher, the "guard," e.g., Plat. Prot., 321d, the "posts" which prevent access to the castle of Zeus, also collectively the "section of the watch," Hom. Il., 10, 408 and 416. φύλαξ is often used instead, Plat. Resp., II, 367a; III, 395b; VI, 504c. The demons are "protectors" of mortal men, Plat. Crat., 398a with a ref. to Hes. Op., 123 and 253. c. φυλακή also denotes the place of watching, the "watch-tower," Hdt., II, 30, 3; Xenoph. Hist. Graec., V, 4, 49, the nadir of a star, Michigan Pap., No. 1, Fr., 3, Col. A, 24 ff. [1] Acc. to Aristot. Cael., II, 13, p. 293b, 3 the Pythagoreans call the centre of the circle of the world the "guard-house" of Zeus, cf. Plat. Prot., 321d → line 2. d. φυλακή is also the place where one is watched, "prison," "hold," Aesch. Pers., 592; P. Oxy., II, 259, 8 (1st cent. A.D.). [2] The word can also ref. to the "keeping" of possessions, Aristot. Eth. Nic., IV, 1, p. 1120a, 9. e. φυλακή can also be used as a measure of time; three or four "night-watches" are distinguished, [3] Hdt., IX, 51, 3. f. φυλακή means "care," "attention," in Plat. Resp., VII, 537d; Ps.-Plat. Alc., II, 149c.

2. Where we have astral notions and read of heavenly guard-houses, posts or watch-men, the ref. is to the planets. Oriental ideas are in the background as we see them in Gnostic and Mandaean traditions, cf. Lidz. Ginza R., 183, 29 ff. [4] The path of the soul [5] past guard-houses blocking access to heaven is described here. The inhabitants are demons. We find similar ideas in Lidz. Ginza R., 209, 23 f. 33 f. etc.; L., 444, 34 ff. When the guard-houses are depicted as prisons or places of punishment we have underlying ideas of hell as in the Turfan texts from a Buddhist source and then again in Judaism and Christianity. [6] The idea of guardian angels (→ I, 82, 5 ff.) who stand beside men as protective powers and help the soul in its ascent out of the prison of the body, as in Procl. In Rem Publ., II, 351, 16, or Iambl. Myst., II, 5, is rather different, though connected with the concept of guard-houses. [7] The incorporating of orig. astral ideas of guard-houses, posts, guardian angels, and angels of punishment or protection [8] into the Hell. redeemer myth, and then into angelology and demonology, has an influence on Judaism and Christianity in very different and often contradictory ways.

B. The Greek Old Testament and Judaism.

1. In the LXX we find the different senses of φυλακή and hence there is no single Hbr. original. שׁמר (→ 237, 3 ff.) is again to the fore. a. φυλάσσω φυλακήν in 4 Βασ. 11:5 means "to keep watch." b. The ref. is to a pers. in 1 Ch. 26:16 and to ἐλεημοσύνη and ἀλήθεια as personifications in Prv. 20:28. Here again φύλαξ is often an alternative

---

[1] Ed. F. E. Robbins, "A New Astrological Treatise: Michigan Pap., No. 1," Class. Philology, 22 (1927), 22 f., cf. 44, ad loc.

[2] It would not be without theological significance if one could distinguish between punitive and protective arrest in antiquity [Moule]. Perhaps there are hints in this direction in Jos.

[3] Cf. Pr.-Bauer, s.v.

[4] Cf. R. Reitzenstein and H. Schaeder, Stud. z. antiken Synkretismus aus Iran u. Griechenland (1926), 27.

[5] In Pist. Soph. we have a description of the path of the soul from chaos to the inheritance on high. Cf. G. Bertram, Art. "Erhöhung," RAC, VI, 22-43.

[6] J. Kroll, "Gott u. Hölle. Der Mythus vom Descensuskampf," Stud. z. Bibliothek Warburg, 20 (1932), 238. 297. 299. 310; F. J. Dölger, Sol Salutis. Gebet u. Gesang im chr. Altertum (1925), 336-364; A. Adam, "Das Sintflutgebet in d. Taufliturgie," Wort u. Dienst, NF, 3 (1952), 9-23; → VIII, 613, 12 ff.

[7] The idea of "watchers" allotted to men is found already in Hes. Op., 121 ff. The men of the Golden Age after they disappeared from the earth became δαίμονες ... ἐσθλοί ... φύλακες θνητῶν ἀνθρώπων. The passage was further developed and interpreted later [Dihle]. Cf. Plat. Crat., 398a.

[8] J. Michl, Art. "Engel, I" in RAC, V, 59; S. Grill, "Synon. Engelnamen im AT," ThZ, 18 (1962), 241-6.

→ VI, 95, n. 8; VII, 610, n. 16. This word is used for a part. of שֹׁמֵר, there being no under-lying noun in acc. with Hbr. word construction. c. "Watch-tower" denotes a place in 2 'Εσδρ. 13:25. d. "Prison" is meant in Gn. 40:3; 3 Βασ. 22:27; 2 Ch. 16:10. e. The word is used for time in Ex. 14:24. f. We have a cultic use along with the verb in Nu. 1:53 etc.: τὰς φυλακὰς φυλάσσω; comprised here are the "care," "maintenance" and "guarding" of the temple and also the minute "observance" of the ritual statutes. In 3 Βασ. 2:3 the ritual formula is taken in a religious and moral sense and thus detached from purely ritual or cultic employment.

2. Astral ideas of heavenly "guard-houses" are present in Bar. 3:34: "The stars shine [9] in their guard-houses." The astral relation makes them watchers themselves. [10] They are often called this in Judaism. These starry spirits are high angels who form a council of "watchers" (Aram. עִיר), [11] Da. 4:14, cf. 1 K. 22:19 ff.; Job 1:6 ff.; Is. 62:6. The φυλακαί or "guard-houses" of the planets are their seat.

3. We are reminded of concepts in the philosophy of antiquity (→ 236, 19 ff.) when Ep. Ar., 125 says that righteous and wise men are the strongest "protection" of the monarchy. Philo in Deus Imm., 17 [12] mentions among the goods which selfish men are not concerned about, along with the safety of one's country etc., the "preservation" φυλακή of the laws, cf. Spec. Leg., I, 154; II, 253; IV, 9. In Spec. Leg., IV, 149 he ref. to the "preservation" of ancient customs and unwritten laws. Deus Imm., 96 speaks of the "preservation" of virtues. Philo ref. to a "prison" δεσμωτήριον of passions, 111, of sins, 113, with special "guards" and overseers. Behind the metaphors is the vividness of myth. In the form of Hell. ideology Philo expresses the Jewish conviction that real life is a glorious death for the "preservation" φυλακή of the laws, Leg. Gaj., 192. In this regard he is adopting ideas taken from the passion piety of Judaism. The statement that bodies are sacrificed as a "protection" φυλακή for the Law, 4 Macc. 13:13, also ref. to martyrdom rather than battle.

C. φυλακή in the New Testament.

1. At Lk. 2:8 it is only in appearance that φυλάσσω φυλακάς puts a cultic phrase (cf. Nu. 8:26 etc. → 237, 5 ff.) to profane use. Based on the special circumstances of shepherd life (→ VI, 499, 14 ff.), the statement that they "kept watch" is to be seen as a presupposition for the discharge of their task.

2. Where φυλακή means a night watch in the NT, the word is to be taken literally in the comparison, but parabolically it carries a reference to the eschaton. [13] One may see this in the parable of the thief and the watching goodman of the house, Mt. 24:43 (→ VIII, 451, 9 ff.), and also in the blessing of those servants who are found watching, Lk. 12:37 f. The parable of the watchful porter in Mk. 13:33-37 uses other terms to express the same eschatological thought. The eschatological element is also suggested, perhaps, in the chronological reference to the "fourth watch" in the walking on the water, Mk. 6:48 and par. [14]

---

[9] Light is personified as a heavenly messenger, cf. F. Nötscher, "Zur theol. Terminologie d. Qumrantexte," Bonner Bibl. Beiträge, 10 (1956), 107.

[10] Bousset-Gressm., 322, n. 2 with other examples.

[11] A. Bentzen, Daniel, Hndbch. AT, I, 19[2] (1952), 43.

[12] E. R. Goodenough, The Politics of Philo Judaeus, Practice and Theory (1938), 16 f.

[13] W. Michaelis, Die Gleichnisse Jesu[3] (1956), 84-6; A. Strobel, "Untersuchungen zum eschatologischen Verzögerungsproblem," Nov. Test. Suppl., 2 (1961), 209, n. 4; 214 and 227-231; Jeremias Gl.[7], 52.

[14] Cf. the exposition in Cramer Cat., I on Mk. 6:48. If the story is an epiphany story similar to the resurrection narrative, the eschatological nature of the chronological ref. is plain, for the revelation of the Risen Lord belongs to the last time.

3. In all the other NT references φυλακή means "prison."

The word has this common meaning in relation to the rebel and murderer Barabbas in Lk. 23:19, 25. Acc. to Mk. 6:17 and par., cf. v. 27 and par., John the Baptist was cast into prison. The apostles in Ac. 5:18-25, Peter in Ac. 12:4-17, and Paul in Ac. 16:23-40 experience a miraculous deliverance when in prison, → III, 175, 4 ff. Several unnamed Christians are also put in "prison" by Paul acc. to Ac. 8:3, cf. 22:4; 26:10, also φυλακίζω in 22:19. Suffering imprisonment is a common fate of the righteous of the OT (Hb. 11:36 ff.) as well as the disciples of Jesus, Rev. 2:10. [15, 16] Peter is ready to accept it, Lk. 22:33, and Jesus predicts it for His followers, Lk. 21:12. It is part of the suffering experienced by Paul acc. to what is almost a formula in 2 C. 6:5; 11:23. In these circumstances it is a duty for Christians to visit those imprisoned "in gaol," Mt. 25:36-44.

In some passages the term "prison" is used figuratively. Thus we read of imprisonment for debt, which in Mt. 18:30 and also in Mt. 5:25 and par. (→ VI, 642, 18 ff.) is referring primarily to an earthly prison, but with a hint of eschatological punishment, especially in the parable of the unforgiving servant, Mt. 18:34, cf. v. 35. In 1 Pt. 3:19 φυλακή means "prison" in the sense of the place where departed spirits are kept, → III, 707, 12 ff.; VI, 577, 11 ff. Satan is bound in his own sphere, which is also his "prison", for a thousand years, Rev. 20:7. Similarly in Rev. 18:2 the shattered city of Babylon becomes the kingdom, the final refuge, and also the place of banishment and the "prison" of unclean spirits and the unclean, hated and sinister birds that are outlawed with them.

Bertram

---

[15] The primary ref. is to the church of Smyrna but the statement has a more general validity, esp. as the devil is called the author of persecution.
[16] Cf. Test. Jos. 1:6; 2:3; 8:4; 1 Cl., 45, 4; Herm. v., 3, 2, 1.

---

† φυλή

A. Profane Greek.

1. As an ancient derivate of the root φῡ- "to be born," "to arise," φυλή [1] first meant a "group bound together by common descent or blood-relationship." This meaning is still found in the neut. τὸ φῦλον, e.g., in the broad sense φῦλον... θεῶν... ἀνθρώπων, the "race of the gods ... that of men," Hom. Il., 5, 441 f., or in the sense of a tribe within a people. Agamemnon arranges the people κατὰ φῦλα, κατὰ φρήτρας "by tribes and clans," Il., 2, 362 f. In φυλή, which is found only after Hom., the element of blood-relationship has almost disappeared. The ref. is simply to a general "sub-division of the people," and it is only with some qualifications that one may cling to the usual transl. "tribe" or "family."

2. Φυλαί are old gentilic groups which occur everywhere in the Ionic and Doric spheres as "sub-divisions" of the total community. [2] In Ionic communities, including Athens, there are traditionally four of these and in the Doric area three except in so far as the number might be increased by including a non-Doric class, e.g., in Argos. On the origin of the division into φυλαί, which seems to have developed only in or after the Doric migration, we have little information. On the one side the older vocabulary of epic does not have the expression φυλή, nor the related φῦλον. On the other hand, the names of the same φυλαί, which represent ancient ethnic designations, [3] occur in almost all the widely scattered areas of immigration. The main significance of the φυλαί, whose relation to the smaller groupings φρατρίαι, γένη, ὠβαί etc. is hard to define, is predominantly in the sphere of sacral law (the same cultic deities), and then in the military and administrative fields. The early disappearance of the element of blood-relationship may be seen from the fact that the orig. inhabitants of the conquered territories were incorporated into the φυλαί. [4] The organising of the city states by Lycurgus in Sparta, Plut. De Lycurgo, 6 (I, 43a) and Solon in Athens, Aristot. Atheniensium Respublica [5], 8, 3 f. did little to alter the structure of the φυλαί. These were not merely electoral districts for the members of the council but also enrollment districts for individual bodies of troops, so that the latter, too, could be called φυλαί, Hdt., VI, 111, 1; Thuc., VI, 98, 4. Cleisthenes carried through greater reforms in Athens. [6] In the interests of consolidating the city

---

φ υ λ ή . [1] On the derivation from φῡ- cf. Hofmann and Frisk, *s.v.* φυλή and φύω, Pokorny, I, 147.

[2] There is no recent monograph on the subject. Cf. H. Bengtson, *Griech. Gesch. v. d. Anfängen bis in d. römische Kaiserzeit, Hndbch. AW*, III, 4 (1950), Index, *s.v.* "Phylen"; G. Busolt - H. Swoboda, *Gr. Staatskunde*, II, *Hndbch. AW*, IV, 1, 1³ (1926), Index "φυλαί, Phylen"; K. Latte, Art. "Phyle," Pauly-W., 20 (1941), 996-1011; cf. also occasional ref. in Dihle.

[3] The names of the Doric φυλαί (the Hylaeans, Dymaeans, Pamphylians and later the Aigialaeans) are given in Hdt., V, 68, 2; on the names of the early Athenian φυλαί supposedly derived from the sons of Ion cf. Hdt., V, 66, 2.

[4] Latte, *op. cit.* (→ n. 2), 996-9.

[5] Ed. F. G. Kenyon (1920).

[6] Bengtson, *op. cit.*, 131-3.

state he replaced the older fourfold division with the newly formed φυλαί, i.e., classes, or district communities, which were organised by residence alone and were then subdivided into smaller districts, δῆμοι. But even so the original gentilic character was retained, for Cleisthenes gave to the new φυλαί the cult of a fictitious hero-ancestor. In the Hell. age the Athenian arrangement became a model for many Gk. cities, e.g., Alexandria, [7] so that the word came to be linked with the idea of a ward or those living in it. Thus φυλή became the accepted transl. for the Roman *tribus,* which gives evidence of a similar development, Dion. Hal. Ant. Rom., 2, 7, 3. If Hdt., III, 26, 1 could still use φυλή for blood-related groups, post-class. Gk. substituted ἔθνος, γένος etc. for it in this sense.

3. In the Egypt. priesthood we find φυλαί as divisions of ministry or classes performing their ministry in turn, [8] Ditt. Or., I, 56, 24 ff. (239/38 B.C.).

B. The Septuagint.

1. Lexical examination presents a uniform picture. Of some 410 instances of φυλή, about 330 can be compared to the Hbr. original. In 170 cases this is מַטֶּה, in about 120 cases שֵׁבֶט, and in 39 cases מִשְׁפָּחָה. Other words occur in seven instances. מַטֶּה and שֵׁבֶט are used interchangeably as tt. [9] for the "tribes" of Israel, [10] and with few exceptions [11] LXX has φυλή, so that this becomes a fixed term for the tribal system of Israel. The common מִשְׁפָּחָה, "family" or "clan," is usually transl. δῆμος, but also πατριά, συγγένεια etc. In most of the 22 instances where φυλή is used for a מִשְׁפָּחָה within Israel, the transl. probably assumed for good or less good reasons that the ref. was to a whole tribe, Lv. 25:49; Nu. 27:11; Am. 3:1, and esp. Zech. 12:12-14 (9 times), where the various families of Judah are called upon to lament. [12] In 17 passages φυλή is used for מִשְׁפָּחָה in the sense of a clan or national group outside Israel, e.g., Abraham's kin in Gn. 24:38, 40 f., [13] the national families in Gn. 10:5, 18, the Edomite tribes in Gn. 36:40. The standpt. here is predominantly, although not exclusively, that of the arrangement of the peoples by blood. The same is true in the great promise to Abraham καὶ ἐνευλογηθήσονται ἐν σοὶ πᾶσαι αἱ φυλαὶ τῆς γῆς, Gn. 12:3; 28:14, cf. ψ 71:17. This use of φυλή (usually plur.) occurs also in the prophets. Am. 3:2; Na. 3:4 vl.; Zech. 14:17 f.; Ez. 20:32. Important for the later period is the use in Da., where φυλή is used as a principle of arrangement in the lists of peoples at Δα. 3:7, 96 and additionally in Θ at 3:4; 5:19; 6:26; 7:14. With γλῶσσα and ἔθνος (Θ λαός), φυλή, based on Aram. אֻמָּה, expresses the arrangement in tribal units. The later transl. of the OT increasingly use φυλή for non-Israelite peoples, Is. 34:1 'ΑΘ; Jer. 51:58 'ΑΘ; ψ 64:8 'ΑΣ; 43:15 Σ. One might thus conclude that the LXX translators understand φυλή less as an independent entity than as the integral part of a larger whole, whether Israel or the nations.

---

[7] For Alexandria and Ptolemais, cf. Mitteis-Wilcken, I, 1, 15-17, 45 f., 49. Further bibl. in Preisigke Fachwörter, 180.

[8] Mitteis-Wilcken, I, 1, 111.

[9] P almost always has מַטֶּה.

[10] שֵׁבֶט, Is. 19:13, ref. without exception to an Egyptian "district."

[11] φυλὴν Λευι, δῆμον τοῦ πατρός σου in Nu. 18:2 is explained by the proximity of the two Hbr. words מַטֶּה לֵוִי שֵׁבֶט אָבִיךָ. On the special use in 1 Βασ. → n. 12.

[12] 1 Βασ. stands apart in the LXX. Here שֵׁבֶט is always σκῆπτρον, 2:28; 9:21; 10:19-21; 15:17. On the other hand, מִשְׁפָּחָה is mechanically rendered by φυλή even though the ref. is plainly to clans within the tribes, 9:21; 10:21; 20:6, 29.

[13] Cf. in analogy φυλή for מוֹלֶדֶת at Gn. 24:4.

2. A special problem, which we cannot discuss in detail here, is posed by the development and history of the twelve tribes of Israel. [14]

a. The tribes achieve historical concreteness only with the entry into Palestine. As the term שֵׁבֶט/מַטֶּה, "staff," "sceptre," indicates, the tribe is a society of men who are bound together not only by common descent but especially by common leadership and law. The tribe is inwardly divided into clans and families and outwardly it may be part of a tribal group. In the course of history some clans might becomes tribes, e.g., that of Manasseh, or weaker tribes might merge into stronger ones, as Simeon did into Judah. The varying lists in Gn. 49 (with Levi and Joseph) and Nu. 1:5-15; 26:5-51 (without Levi and with Joseph divided into Manasseh and Ephraim) display such alterations even though the cultically determined number "twelve" is retained, → II, 321, 26 ff. [15] The names of the tribes are based on personal (Dan, Joseph), geographical (Benjamin, Judah, Ephraim) or historical factors (Issachar, i.e., workmen). If a divine name may perhaps be seen behind some, e.g., Gad and Asher, this might simply imply that all the tribes did not originally worship Yahweh. But already in the wilderness the cultic and legal life of the tribes was shaped by the electing God of the fathers. At the conquest, encounter with the law and cultus of the original population naturally had some influence on the tribal structure.

b. The so-called covenant of Shechem in Jos. 24 was decisive for the mutual relations of the tribes. [16] The Ephraimite Joshua knit the groups into a closed amphictyony under the name of Israel and pledged them to a common confession of Yahweh and to related minimal demands of a cultic, legal and military nature → II, 120, 19 ff. The confession of election by the jealously exclusive covenant God, Yahweh, separated the members of the covenant from the world around. The holy war, [17] associated esp. with the Joseph tribes, united the individual tribes even politically. The annual swearing of the covenant oath subjugated existing Canaanite cults and ancient tribal gods to the common faith in Yahweh. The unified state which developed under Philistine pressure deprived the tribes of their autonomy. David established continuity with the ancient amphictyony by bringing up the ark of the covenant to Jerusalem and thus giving the ancient, private royal city the status of a cultic centre for the tribes. Solomon set up new districts which only in form coincided with the ancient tribal structure. [18] In the age of a standing army (2 S.

---

[14] On what follows cf. A. Alt, "Der Gott d. Väter," Kleine Schriften z. Gesch. d. Volkes Israel, I[3] (1963), 1-78; also "Erwägungen über die Landnahme d. Israeliten in Palästina," ibid., I, 126-175; also "Die Ursprünge d. isr. Rechtes," ibid., I, 278-332; also "Die Staatenbildung der Israeliten in Palästina," ibid., I[3] (1963), 1-65; M. Noth, "Das System d. zwölf Stämme Israels," BWANT, 52 (1930); also Gesch. Israels[5] (1963), 45-217; G. v. Rad, Theol. d. AT, I[5] (1966), 17-97. There are many ref. to other works in Noth and v. Rad. On the many-sided history of a single tribe cf. K. D. Schunck, "Benjamin. Untersuchungen z. Entstehung u. Gesch. eines isr. Stammes," ZAW Beih., 86 (1963).

[15] S. Mowinckel, Zur Frage nach dokumentarischen Quellen in Jos. 13-19 (1946), 22; also "'Rahelstämme' u. 'Lehastämme,'" Festschr. O. Eissfeldt (1958), 129-150, and also J. Hoftijzer "Enige opmerkingen rond het israël. Twaalf-Stammensysteem," Nederlands Theol. Tijdschr., 14 (1959/60), 241-263 even put the system into the post-Davidic period on the basis of the Song of Deborah.

[16] Basic is Noth, op. cit. G. Fohrer, "AT — 'Amphiktyonie' u. 'Bund'?" ThLZ, 91 (1966), 801-816, 893-904 rejects the hypothesis of an amphictyony in view of its weaknesses. Nevertheless, it is difficult to abandon the hypothesis as a whole. R. Smend, "Jahwekrieg u. Stämmebund. Erwägungen z. ältesten Gesch. Israels," FRL, 84[2] (1966) has shown that it is not without validity in a modified form, cf. also M. Weippert, "Die Landnahme d. isr. Stämme in d. neueren wissenschaftlichen Diskussion," FRL, 92 (1967), 105, 139.

[17] Cf. G. v. Rad, "Der Hl. Krieg im alten Israel," AbhThANT, 20[4] (1965); R. de Vaux, Das AT u. seine Lebensordnungen, II[2] (1966), 69-81: Smend, op. cit. (→ n. 16), 10-32, esp. 30.

[18] A. Alt, "Israels Gaue unter Salomo," Kleine Schriften z. Gesch. d. Volkes Israel, II[3] (1964), 76-89; also "Judas Gaue unter Josia," ibid., 276-288.

8:16-18; 20:23) and centralised royal power the system of twelve tribes became increasingly a thing of the past. [19]

c. Already in the pre-exilic period awareness of the faithfulness of the covenant God gave rise to the hope of a new future for the twelve tribes. In the age of the divided kingdom this may be seen in Elijah, who at Carmel made his altar of twelve stones, 1 K. 18:31. The hope is deliberately fostered in P with its emphasis on the common past of all Israel in the desert, Nu. 1-2; 10:12-28; 26:5-51 (order of the camp); Nu. 13:2-16 (the spies); Jos. 4:1-7 (crossing of the Jordan). In the Bab. exile Dt. Is. awaited the day when the Servant of the Lord would re-establish the twelve tribes of Israel (Is. 49:6), while Ezekiel looked forward to a new allotment of the land (Ez. 47:13, 21-23) and named the gates of the new Jerusalem after the twelve tribes, 48:30 ff. The post-exilic period developed this hope. The painstaking genealogies of 1 Ch. 2-9 served it, as did the attempts to maintain the purity of the returning tribes, Ezr. 2; Neh. 7:6-73; 10. From the exile onwards the names of the tribes also began to be used as personal names, Ezr. 10:23, 31, 42. [20] To the expectation that Yahweh sees all the tribes (Zech. 9:1) there corresponds the appeal in prayer to the fact that they are God's possession (Is. 63:17) and the prayer of Sirach for their restoration, Sir. 36:10.

C. Later Judaism.

As a rule the tribes are mentioned only when occasion is given by OT texts, the number "twelve," or the related hope of a regathering of all Israel. [21] Sometimes there is ref. to the genealogical descent of individuals, esp., of course, from Judah or Benjamin. [22]

a. In the pseudepigr. the no. "twelve" plays a role in the ref. to the 72 transl. of the OT, Ep. Ar., 46-50, or in the design of Test. XII. There is prayer for the regathering of all Israel in Sh. E., 10. The apocalyptist expects that the 10 tribes [23] deported to Media acc. to 2 K. 17:6; 18:11 will return, 4 Esr. 13:12 f.; 39-49 and that the Messiah will establish the συναγωγὴ φυλῶν, Ps. Sol. 17:44. In connection with this all nations will appear at the temple, Test. B. 9:2. The tribe of Dan is judged negatively in Test. D. 5:6 on the basis of Ju. 18:30; Gn. 49:17; Satan is its prince.

b. Palestinian Judaism almost always uses שֵׁבֶט, not מַטֶּה. Apart from exeget. passages we find ref. to the tribes in discussions of sacrificial rules, Hor., 1, 5, or of jurisdiction, bSanh., 15b, 16b. There is still a living hope that the 10 tribes will return, though once in bShab., 147b we read that they are being ruined by Phrygian wine and the water of hot springs. Only R. Aqiba, who himself journeyed to Media, voiced a contrary opinion, Sanh., 10, 3; S. Lv. בחוקותי, 8, 1 on 26:38.

c. The Qumran community speaks of the future restoration of a kingdom of twelve tribes, 1 QM 2:2 f.; 3:14 f.; 15:1, 1 QSa 1:15, 29. The no. "twelve" is also reflected in banners arranged acc. to the twelve tribes, 1 QM 3:12 f.

---

[19] M. Noth, "Die Gesetze im Pent.," Gesammelte Stud. z. AT[3] (1966), 42-53, thinks the sacral amphictyonic league lived on independently along with the political organisation, but how far this is true is open to question. Possibly the old traditions simply found a place in the new form of the state.

[20] J. Jeremias, Jerusalem z. Zt. Jesu[3] (1962), 308, 330 with n. 164.

[21] Bousset-Gressm., 237 f.; Volz Esch., 378; Str.-B., II, 606-8; IV, 881 f., 902-6.

[22] Jeremias, op. cit. 309-311.

[23] When S. Bar. 77:17, 19; 78:1 ref to 9$\frac{1}{2}$ or 2$\frac{1}{2}$ tribes the pt. is that Judah, Benjamin and half Levi belong to the Southern Kingdom.

d. Philo, as one would expect from his non-historical thinking and allegorical methods, has little interest in the tribes, Quaest. in Ex., II, 30 on 24, 4b. Levi is mentioned most frequently; this became the priestly tribe in virtue of its zeal on the day of the golden calf, Vit. Mos., II, 160-173; Spec. Leg., I, 79. The tribes as a whole play some part by reason of the perfection of the no. "twelve," Fug., 73 f. and 185.

e. Josephus, who himself came from an eminent priestly φυλή (Vit., 1), keeps to the OT records in his ref. to and depiction of the tribes, cf. the distribution of the land under Joshua in Ant., 5, 80-87 or the deporting of the northern tribes in 9, 280. He knows of vast numbers of the ten tribes remaining by the Euphrates, 11, 133. Jos. also uses φυλή for the Arab tribes, 1, 221.

D. The New Testament.

φυλή occurs 31 times, 21 of the instances being in Rev.

1. On four occasions individuals are said to be descended from a tribe. King Saul belongs to Benjamin (Ac. 13:21), as does also Paul, cf. R. 11:1; Phil. 3:5. The prophetess Anna is of the tribe of Asher (Lk. 2:36), cf. the prophecy of Gn. 30:13: "All daughters call me blessed." Quite early the community came to attach gt. importance to the Davidic descent of Jesus, cf. Mt. 1:1; Lk. 1:27; R. 1:3; Mk. 10:47 f. and par.; 12:35 ff. and par. Similarly Jesus is called the "lion of the tribe of Judah" in Rev. 5:5. For Hb. the fact that Jesus is of the tribe of Judah and not the priestly tribe of Levi is a decisive argument for the dissolution of the Levitical priesthood and of the Law associated with it, [24] Hb. 7:13 f.

2. Most of the references speak of the restoration of the twelve tribes of Israel, → II, 323, 9 ff. The disciples of Jesus, who are now poor and despised, will have seats at the Last Judgment and will play in relation to Israel the role that is ascribed to the elders of this people in relation to the Gentiles, [25] Mt.19:28 and par. This saying reflects the sharp contention between the Christian community and the claim of Israel. The polemical note is completely absent from the similar presentation in Rev. Here the gates of the new Jerusalem will bear the names of the tribes of Israel, Rev. 21:12 → 248, 10 f. In the storms of the end-time the self-surpassing faithfulness of God will preserve not just a few but 12,000 from each of the tribes, 7:4-8 cf. Nu. 1:16. The nature of the apocalyptic imagery, the precedence given to Judah, and perhaps also the omission of the ungodly tribe of Dan [26] (→ 248, 27 f.) suggest that the number 144,000 relates not merely to Israel but to a new community consisting of Israel and the Gentiles [27] → II, 324, 17 ff. This is depicted in vv. 4-8 as the threatened but preserved *ecclesia militans,* while v. 9 f. offers a prospect of the heavenly *ecclesia triumphans.* [28]

Open to debate is the exposition of Jm. 1:1: Ἰάκωβος θεοῦ καὶ κυρίου Ἰησοῦ Χριστοῦ δοῦλος ταῖς δώδεκα φυλαῖς ταῖς ἐν τῇ διασπορᾷ χαίρειν. If here a Jew

---

[24] Cf. esp. Wnd. Hb., *ad loc.*

[25] Examples in Str.-B., IV, 1103 f.

[26] The expectation that the antichrist will come from Dan (Iren. Haer., V, 30, 2, cf. Hipp. De Antichristo, 14) is Chr. exegesis of Rev. 7 or Jer. 8:16.

[27] Though Paul speaks of the salvation of all Israel in R. 11:26, he never uses the image of the twelve tribes.

[28] So Had. Apk., *ad loc.,* but cf. Loh. Apk., *ad loc.,* who thinks the 144,000 are martyrs and the innumerable host is made up of believers and martyrs together.

is writing to Jews, [29] or the Lord's brother to the Jewish *diaspora*, [30] the twelve tribes refer quite literally to the Jewish people. Against this, however, is the fact that the disappearance of the Northern Kingdom leaves the twelve tribes as merely a theme of apocalyptic expectation → 248, 3 ff., 31 ff. Furthermore, at least in the epistle as we now have it, the author is a Christian who is taking issue with mis-understandings of Paul's teaching on justification (2:14, 24) and thus writing to Christians. Another point, illustrated in Rev. 7, [31] is that idealisation of the twelve tribes had established itself in Christian circles too. It thus seems logical to accept a transferred sense [32] which understands the tribes as the new people of God in which OT expectations have come to fulfilment. Since this new people also lives far from its heavenly home and hence in the *diaspora* (→ II, 102, 23 ff.), it is still on the march to the final consummation in spite of all the promises already fulfilled.

3. Passages which, following OT usage (→ 246, 23 ff.) speak of φυλαί among the nations are undoubtedly in the sphere of eschatological expectation. The lament of the families of Judah (Zech. 12:10 ff. → 246, 20 ff.) becomes in Mt. 24:30; Rev. 1:7 the bewailing of the Gentile peoples at the returning Son of Man. The sealed of Rev. 5:9 are redeemed from the Gentile world, which in Rev. too is arranged in φυλαί, γλῶσσαι, λαοί, ἔθνη. The innumerable host of overcomers also comes from this world, 7:9. The bodies of the two witnesses confront it according to 11:9. It is delivered up to the beast from the abyss in 13:7. But it still has the offer of the Gospel, 14:6.

E. The Post-Apostolic Fathers.

NT themes are echoed in the use of φυλή in the post-apost. fathers: for the twelve tribes of Israel, 1 Cl., 43, 2; with the twelve apostles, Barn., 8, 3; this no. ref. to the new people of God, Herm. s., 9, 17, 1; with ref. to the nations of the world in the quotation from Gn. 12:3 at 1 Cl., 10, 1; with ἔθνη and γλῶσσαι, 2 Cl., 17, 4.

Maurer

---

[29] So A. Meyer, "Das Rätsel d. Jacobusbr.," ZNW Beih., 10 (1930), 298 f. with respect to a Jewish original.

[30] Schl. Jk., 1 and 93-5.

[31] τὸ δωδεκάφυλον in Ac. 26:7 is also undoubtedly related to the promises to Israel for the sake of which Paul claims he is on trial.

[32] Dib. Jk.[11], *ad loc.* F. Mussner, *Der Jakobusbr., Herders Theol. Komm. z. NT*, 13, 1 (1964), *ad loc.*

---

† φύσις, † φυσικός, † φυσικῶς

Contents: A. φύσις in Greek Literature: 1. Etymology and Basic Sense; 2. Nature and Constitution: a. Nature; b. Constitution; c. Human and Divine Nature; 3. True Nature and Universal Nature: a. Pre-Socratics; b. Plato; c. Aristotle; d. Hellenism; 4. Nature and Ethics: a. The Antithesis Nature - Law; b. Nature and Education; c. φύσιν ἔχει, κατὰ / παρὰ φύσιν; 5. Nature as a Cosmic and Vital Principle in the Stoics: a. God, World and Nature; b. Man as λόγος and φύσις; c. κατὰ/παρὰ φύσιν in the Stoics; d. Natural Law. B. Jewish Literature: 1. The Septuagint and Pseudepigrapha; 2. Philo: a. God and Universal Nature; b. Nature and Law; 3. Josephus. C. The New Testament: 1. General; 2. Pauline Usage: a. As a Term in General Use; b. Special Meanings; 3. The Rest of the New Testament. D. The Occurrence of φύσις in Other Early Christian Writings: 1. Post-Apostolic Fathers; 2. Apologists; 3. Apocryphal Acts; 4. Gnosticism.

φ ύ σ ι ς κ τ λ.   Bibl.: General: Liddell-Scott, Pr.-Bauer, s.v.; A. Bonhöffer, "Epiktet u. d. NT," RVV, 10 (1911), 146-157 etc.; G. Bornkamm, "Gesetz u. Natur. R. 2:14-16," Stud. zu Antike u. Urchr.² (1963), 93-118; also "Die Offenbarung des Zornes Gottes. R. 1-3," Das Ende d. Gesetzes⁵ (1966), 9-33; B. Gärtner, "The Areopagus Speech and Natural Revelation," Acta Seminarii Neotest. Upsaliensis, 21 (1955), 73-116; R. M. Grant, Miracle and Natural Law in Graeco-Roman and Early Christian Thought (1952); H. Köster, "ΝΟΜΟΣ ΦΥΣΕΩΣ. The Concept of Natural Law in Greek Thought," Festschr. E. R. Goodenough (1968), 521-541; G. Kuhlmann, "Theologia naturalis bei Philon u. bei Pls.," Nt.liche Forschungen I, 7 (1930); H. Leisegang, Art. "Physis," Pauly-W., 20 (1941), 1130-1164; Ltzm. R., 40 f., Exc.; M. Pohlenz, "Pls. u. d. Stoa," ZNW, 42 (1949), 69-104. On A.: J. L. Adams, "The Law of Nature in Greco-Roman Thought," Journ. of Religion, 25 (1945), 97-118; J. W. Beardslee, The Use of ΦΥΣΙΣ in Fifth-Cent. Gk. Lit., Diss. Chicago (1918); G. Bornkamm, "ΟΜΟΛΟΓΙΑ. Zur Gesch. eines politischen Begriffs," Gesch. u. Glaube, I (1968), 140-156; H. Diller, "Der griech. Naturbegriff," Neue Jbch. f. Antike u. deutsche Bildung, 2 (1939), 241-257; W. A. Heidel, "Περὶ φύσεως. A study of the Conception of Nature among the Pre-Socratics," Proceedings of the American Acad. of Arts and Sciences, 45, 4 (1910), 77-133; F. Heinimann, "Nomos u. Physis. Herkunft u. Bedeutung einer Antithese im griech. Denken d. 5. Jhdt.," Schweizerische Beiträge z. Altertumswissenschaft, 1 (1945); D. Holwerda, Commentatio de vocis quae est ΦΥΣΙΣ vi atque usu praesertim in Graecitate Aristotele anteriore, Diss. Groningen (1955); W. Jaeger, Die Theol. d. frühen gr. Denker (1953), 127-146, 196-216, 227 f.; C. Langer, "Euhemeros u. d. Theorie d. φύσει u. θέσει θεοί," Angelos, 2 (1926), 53-59; A. Lovejoy "The Meaning of Φύσις in the Greek Physiologers," The Philosophical Review, 18 (1909), 369-383; D. Mannsperger, Physis bei Platon, Diss. Tübingen (1969); R. Muth, "Zum Physis-Begriff bei Platon," Wiener Stud., 64 (1950), 53-70; H. Patzer, Physis. Grundlegung z. einer Gesch. des Wortes, Marburg (1940); M. Pohlenz, Der hellenische Mensch (1947), Index, s.v. "Natur u. Physis"; also "Nomos u. Physis," Herm., 81 (1953), 418-438; also Die Stoa, I² (1959), Index II, s.v. "Physis"; II³ (1964); K. Reinhardt, Parm u. d. Gesch. d. gr. Philosophie² (1959), 81-125, 223; P. Shorey, "Φύσις, Μελέτη, Ἐπιστήμη," Transactions and Proceedings of the Amer. Philol. Association, 40 (1909), 185-201; O. Thimme, ΦΥΣΙΣ, ΤΡΟΠΟΣ, ΗΘΟΣ. Semasiologische Untersuchung über die Auffassung d. menschlichen Wesens (Charakters) in d. älteren gr. Lit., Diss. Göttingen (1935). On B.: E. R. Goodenough, By Light, Light (1935), Index, s.v. φύσις; H. A. Wolfson, Philo, I (1948), 332-347; II (1947), 165-200. On C.: F. Flückiger, "Die Werke d. Gesetzes bei d. Heiden (nach R. 2:14 ff.)," ThZ, 8 (1952), 17-42; F. Kuhr, "R. 2:14 f. u. d. Verheissung bei Jer. 31:31 ff.," ZNW, 55 (1964), 243-261; M. Lackmann, Vom Geheimnis der Schöpfung. Die Gesch. d. Exegese v. R. 1:18-23; 2:14-16 und Ag. 14:15-17; 17:22-29 vom 2. Jhdt. bis zum Beginn der Orthodoxie (1952), 95-140, 212-235; S. Lyonnet, "Lex

A. φύσις in Greek Literature.

1. Etymology and Basic Sense.

a. The noun φύσις is a verbal abstr. of ἔφῦν, [1] πέφυκα, φύομαι (this is undoubtedly secondary) from the Indo-Eur. root bhū, Sanscr. bhū, e.g., abhūma = ἔφυμεν, Lat. fu-, German bi-n, English be, [2] whose meaning is "to become," "to grow" etc., orig. with ref. to plant growth. φύσις [3] thus means "form," "nature," first with ref. to plants, e.g., Hom. Od., 10, 303, then transf. animals and men. With fresh ref. to the verb there arises the sense "budding," "growth," "development," "parturition." [4] b. In the one instance of φύσις in Hom. it denotes the "external form of nature" of the curative herb moly, Od., 10, 303. [5] The word is first used for man's "external form" [6] in Pind., who in Nem., 6, 5 distinguishes φύσις from νοῦς, cf. Isthm., 4, 49. [7] φύσις has the same sense sometimes in Hippocr., [8] the tragedians, e.g., Aesch. Suppl., 496; Soph. Oed. Tyr., 740 and else-where, cf. Aristoph. Vesp., 1071. [9] c. The meaning "birth" occurs for the first time in pre-Socratic philosophy. Emped. Fr., 8, 1 f. (Diels, I, 312) has φύσις (= γένεσις) as a correlative of τελευτή (= φθορά), [10] cf. Fr., 8, 4 of the "origin" of human members, Fr., 63 (I, 336). The dat. φύσ(ε)ι can thus mean "by birth," so first in Hdt., VII, 134, 2, then the tragic dramatists, cf. φύσει νεώτερος "the younger son," Soph. Oed. Col., 1294 f.; cf. Ai., 1301 f. From this arises the technical use of φύσει to denote "physical descent," either in the sense of the natural claim to legitimacy in contrast to the bastard, Isoc. Or., 3, 42; Isaeus Or., 6, 28, or later for physical descent as opp. to legally established paternity: φύσει μέν... θέσει δέ, Diog. L., IX, 25 [11] and cf. P. Oxy., X, 1266, 33 (98 A.D.); P. Fay., 19, 11 (letter of the emperor Hadrian); Ditt. Syll.³, II, 720, 4 f. (2nd cent. B.C.); Ditt. Or., II, 472, 4; 558, 6 (both 1st cent. A.D.); [12] κατὰ φύσιν occurs

---

naturalis et iustificatio Gentilium," *Verbum Domini*, 41 (1963), 238-242; B. Reicke, "Natür-liche Theol. nach Pls.," *Svensk Exeget. Årsbok*, 22-23 (1957/58), 154-167; R. Walker, "Die Heiden u. das Gericht," *Ev. Theol.*, 20 (1960), 302-314.

[1] Muth, 54 f.

[2] On the etym. cf. Boisacq, Hofmann, *s.v.* φύω, Frisk, *s.v.* φύομαι, Leisegang, 1130, Holwerda, 104-109; G. S. Kirk, *Heraclitus. The Cosmic Fragments* (1954), 228.

[3] On the formation with -σις cf. P. Chantraine, "La formation des noms en grec ancien," *Collection linguist.*, 38 (1933), 283; J. Holt, "Les noms d'action en -σις (-τις)," *Acta Jut-landica*, 13, 1 (1941), 78 f.; W. Porzig, *Die Namen f. Satzinhalte im Griech. u. Idg.* (1942), 333 f.; É. Benveniste, *Noms d'agent et noms d'action en indo-européen* (1948), 78 f.; Pohlenz Mensch, 169 f.; Muth, 54 f.

[4] For the predominance of this sense in orig. usage cf. Thimme, 2; Leisegang, 1130; Patzer, 3 f., 67 (following Holwerda, 104 f.); Diller, 242 f.

[5] Diller, 243, *ad loc.* stresses the connection with plant growth, cf. Leisegang, 1131.

[6] Hom. uses the acc. φυήν for this, preferably as an acc. of relation, e.g. οὐ δέμας οὐδὲ φυήν "neither in form nor growth," Il., 1, 115, cf. Hes. Op., 129 etc. In Pind., however, φυή seems to characterise the inner nature as given by noble descent and developed in ἀρετή, e.g., Pyth., 8, 44, cf. Heinimann, 99.

[7] On φύσις in Pind., cf. Heinimann, 99; Leisegang, 1131.

[8] Cf. φύσις par. μορφή Hippocr. De aere aquis locis, 16 (CMG, I, 1, p. 70, 10).

[9] Cf. ἡ τοῦ σώματος φύσις of man, which one cannot equate with statues and pictures, Isoc. Or., 9, 75.

[10] The attempt to transl. φύσις here by "abiding nature," Lovejoy, 371-3 corresponds to the understanding of the passage in Aristot. Metaph., 4, 4, p. 1014b, 35 - 1015a, 3 but is untenable, cf. Heinimann, 90; Leisegang, 1132; Jaeger, 227 f., n. 5. On the gen. question whether φύσις in the pre-Socratics means "origin" or "substance" cf. J. Burnet, *Early Gk. Philosophy*⁴ (1930), 10-13; F. J. E. Woodbridge, "The Earliest Gk. Philosophy," *The Philosophical Review*, 10 (1901), 164 f.; Heidel, 130-3; Thimme, 44-8; Leisegang, 1138 f.; Pohlenz Nomos u. Physis, 426.

[11] Cf. "by birth" φύσει an Ambracian, by naturalisation δημοποίητος a Sicyonian, Athen., 4, 81 (183d).

[12] The adj. is late in this sense υἱὸς γνήσιος καὶ φυσικός, P. Lips., 28, 18 (381 A.D.); φυσικὸς υἱός "natural son" corresponds to ὁ ἐκ πορνείας γεγονώς opp. γνήσιος υἱός, Thom. Mag. Eclogae Atticarum, ed. F. Ritschl (1832), p. 362, cf. Liddell-Scott, *s.v.* φυσικός.

in the same sense; Hamilcar is Hannibal's father κατὰ φύσιν, Hasdrubal is Hamilcar's son-in-law by marriage, Polyb., 3, 9, 6; 3, 12, 3, cf. 11, 2, 2. d. The adj. φυσικός does not occur in Hom., the tragedians or direct quotations from the pre-Socratics. [13] It is one of the many adj. in -ικος which first become common in the vocabulary of sophistry and science from the 2nd half of the 5th cent. B.C. [14] It is first found in Xenoph. Mem., III, 9, 1 in the sense "natural" as opp. to διδακτός, and first becomes an established part of the vocabulary of philosophy with Aristot. [15]

2. Nature and Constitution.

φύσις is everything which by its origin or by observation of its constitution seems to be a given. To call it "given" φύσις is already to go beyond the sphere of naive description and implies a judgment on its actual constitution or true nature.

a. Nature. The nature and qualities of man are often called φύσις, e.g., "natural tendencies and qualities," such as caring for children, Democr. Fr., 278 (Diels, II, 202 f.), [16] the love of power, Fr., 267 (II, 200), or natural talents οἱ φύσει λογιστικοί, Plat. Resp., VII, 526b. In the tragedians φύσις is often the "inner nature," the "manner" of a man, [17] in which the ἀρετή of the race comes to expression, [18] cf. πρὸς αἵματος φύσιν "of the same blood" (par. φίλων, opp. a stranger), Soph. El., 1125; ironically of the ἐκ πατρὸς ταὐτοῦ φύσις of Chrysothemis, which is so little like the "nature" of her sister, 325, [19] cf. also Soph. Phil., 874; Ai., 1031 f. φύσις is then used for a man's character or nature, without ref. to his birth or descent, in so far as this nature is given and is not dependent on conscious direction or education, e.g., par. ἦθος, Eur. Med., 103 f., [20] cf. Xenoph. Cyrop., I, 2, 2; also of a bad character, Demosth. Or., 20, 140, or a bad "habit," Aristoph. Vesp., 1457 f. [21] It is of special importance when φύσις is used thus for the "true nature" of a man in contrast to his acts. When a man does wrong even though he knows what is right he abandons his φύσις, i.e., his "true nature," Soph. Phil., 902 f., [22] cf. Plat. Crat., 395b; Soph., 265d e.

Dependent on this is the abs. use of φύσις sing. and plur. for a living creature: πᾶσα φύσις "every creature," Xenoph. Cyrop., VI, 2, 29, cf. Plat. Polit., 272c, plur. 306e, beings like Scylla and Cerberus of which the ancient fables tell us, Plat. Resp., IX, 588c. Among plants φύσις means "kind," Theophr. Hist. Plant., VI, 1, 1; Diod. S., 2, 49, 4; Isoc. Areop., 74, and esp. animals: αἱ τῶν ἀλόγων ζῴων φύσεις "the (various) types of irrational animals," Philo Virt., 81, cf. 125, but cf. also various "types" of state constitutions in Isoc. Or., 12, 134, and "features of the soul" in Plat. Leg., VII, 798a, cf. Soph. Oed. Tyr., 674 (each time plur.). Disapprovingly of men "such creatures," supporters of enemies and traitors, Isoc. Or., 4, 113; 20, 11, cf. Aeschin. Tim., 191.

---

[13] Titles likes φυσικά, φυσικὸς λόγος, περὶ φύσεως, commonly mentioned in pre-Socratic quotations, are late, since books still had no titles in the 5th cent. B.C., Leisegang, 1135; on scientific usage → 254, 9 ff.

[14] Cf. P. Chantraine, "Études sur le vocabulaire grec," Études et Comment., 24 (1956), 131 f.

[15] Leisegang, 1135.

[16] Cf. Reinhardt, 85, n. 1.

[17] Only seldom here is φύσις used for the "outer form" and distinguished from the "inner manner" ψυχή, cf. Aesch. Pers. 441 f.

[18] Cf. esp. Leisegang, 1131.

[19] For the play on the senses "descent" and "nature" cf. Lovejoy, 378.

[20] On the use of φύσις in this sense in Eur. cf. Beardslee, 28.

[21] Cf. on this Democr. Fr., 3 (Diels, II, 132); Plat. Resp., VII, 526c; Phaed., 109e; Aristoph. Pl., 273.

[22] On the antithesis "true character" and occasional act cf. Lovejoy, 377.

b. Constitution. To ask what things are in their true constitution is to ask concerning their φύσις. The idea of φύσις in this sense arose in Ionian science. [23] The aim is not to comprehend nature as a whole (→ 256, 19 ff.) but to see the true constitution of individual things, e.g., in the cosmos, the true "nature" of aether or the stars, Parm. Fr., 10, 1 (Diels, I, 241), [24] the "effects" ἔργα and constitution φύσις of the moon, Fr., 10, 4 f. (I, 241). From ethnography comes the question as to the "constitution of the land," φύσις τῆς χώρης, Hdt., II, 5, 2. [25] The issue in φύσις is the distinguishing element in the make-up of foreign countries, cf. also Hdt., II, 19, 1; 35, 2; 68, 1; 71. [26] There is a similar use in Xenoph. Vect., 1, 2; Oec., 16, 2. Above all in medical and scientific speech from the 2nd half of the 5th cent. B.C. φύσις is a term for "original and true constitution" and hence for "proper nature," [27] e.g., of water, Hippocr. De aere aquis locis, 8 (CMG, I, 1, p. 63, 10), of sicknesses, 2 (p. 56, 24), but also of man in gen., 12 (p. 67, 18 f.). [28] In this use of φύσις the aim is to stress what is distinctive in the nature and constitution of individual phenomena, esp. to the degree that this cannot be attributed to divine or social or other human causes. [29] Thus φύσις means "constitution" in Hippocr. De aere aquis locis, 3 (CMG, I, 1, p. 57, 25), 20 (p. 73, 14), [30] or "temperament," Aristot. De divinatione per somnia, 2, p. 463b, 16 f. [31] Usually the question how this nature of individual phenomena relates to natural force in gen. is left in the background. [32] Aristot. adopts this scientific concept of physis and gives it gen. ontological validity: [33] "The φύσις of a thing is what this thing is as the end product of its development" τῆς γενέσεως τελεσθείσης, Pol., I, 2, p. 1252b, 32 ff. This def., then, does not ref. merely to the natural sphere, cf. Part. An., II, 9, p. 655a, 20; 4, p. 651a, 12, [34] but to other things as well, cf. on tragedy Aristot. Poet., 4, p. 1449a, 2-15. [35]

c. Human and Divine Nature. ἀνθρωπίνη φύσις often denotes the ordinary, natural human nature as distinct from non-human phenomena or non-natural phenomena in the human sphere, cf. Hdt., III, 65, 3; 116, 2; VIII, 38. There is also differentiation between the nature of the male and that of the weaker female sex: τὸ ἄρρεν φῦλον... ἰσχυρότερόν ἐστι [τῶν] τῆς θηλείας φύσεως, Xenoph. Resp. Lac., 3, 4, cf. Soph. Trach., 1062;

---

[23] Cf. on this Pohlenz Nomos u. Physis, 426.

[24] Since the tradition is fragmentary one cannot decide how far there may be also a ref. to the origin of things, Leisegang, 1132; Heinimann, 90 f., cf. Lovejoy, 374 f.; Beardslee, 12 f.

[25] Beardslee, 20 thinks that we have the original and basic sense here and elsewhere in Hdt.

[26] Cf. on this Heinimann, 106 f. Possibly Hdt. in this use of φύσις is dependent on Hecataeus, who is to be grouped both chronologically and geographically with Xenophanes and Heracl. We thus have here a further development of the concept of physis in Ionian science, cf. Pohlenz Nomos u. Physis, 425. Thimme, 63 is undoubtedly mistaken when he suggests that we must begin with the idea of "universal nature" if we are to understand the use in Hdt.

[27] On the development of the scientific use of φύσις in medicine cf. Pohlenz Mensch, 175-7.

[28] On φύσις in Hippocrates cf. Beardslee, 31-42, 43-47; Leisegang, 1139-1143.

[29] Leisegang, 1139 f.; on the relation of nature and miracle in medicine, cf. Grant, 11-14.

[30] Cf. also Hippocr. Aphorismi, 3, 2 (Littré, IV, 486); Acut., 43 (Kühlewein, I, 130); Epid., VI, 5, 1 (Littré, V, 314); cf. Beardslee, 32-5.

[31] On the later distinction between φύσις "constitution" and δυνάμεις "individual factors" of which φύσις is made up but which are not themselves substances, cf. H. W. Miller, "'Dynamis' and 'Physis' in On Ancient Medicine," Transactions and Proceedings of the American Philological Assoct., 83 (1952), 184-197.

[32] This relation is wrongly rejected altogether by Beardslee, 39.

[33] There are perhaps reflections of this usage in passages in which a periphrastic use is sometimes suspected, Beardslee, 82-92, cf. Plat. Leg., VII, 845d; Aesch. Ag., 633; Soph. Oed. Tyr., 334 f. For criticism of the supposed periphrastic use v. Holwerda, 15, n. 1.

[34] Cf. τὴν φύσιν "in constitution," Aristot. Part. An., II, 2, p. 648b, 21 f.; 4, p. 650b, 34 f. etc.

[35] On the relation of the individual constitution and nature as a whole → 256, 2 ff.

Oed. Col., 445; Thuc., II, 45, 2.[36] Later usage has what is almost the formula ἀδύνατος γάρ ἐστιν ἡ γυνὴ διὰ ἀσθένιαν τῆς φύσεως, P. Lond., III, 971, 4 (3rd-4th cent. A.D.), cf. P. Oxy., I, 71, Col., 2, 4 (303 A.D.). In particular man's experience of the basic limitation of his existence is expressed with the help of the term. This limitation and vulnerability to surrounding forces are not an accident of present circumstances; they are part of "human nature," cf. ἁ γα φύσις ἀνδρῶν τι ὦν; ἀσκοὶ πεφυσιαμένοι "blown-up bellows," Epicharmus Fr., 10, Diels, I, 200,[37] cf. 2, 9 (I, 196).[38] Such negative statements about human nature are esp. common in Thuc., cf. I, 76, 3;[39] elsewhere cf. Plat. Theaet., 149b-c; Aristot. Pol., III, 10, p. 1286b, 27; Democr. Fr., 297 (Diels, II, 206 f.). The ref. may be specifically to man's mortality: ἡ τῶν ἀνθρώπων φύσις θνητὴ οὖσα, Ael. Var. Hist., 8, 11.[40]

In contrast to man's weak and corruptible nature is everything that transcends this limitation as a sign of participation in the divine nature, cf. the supernatural endowment of the poet Homer which shares in the φύσις θεάζουσα Democr. Fr., 21 (Diels, II, 147).[41] "To enter into the divine nature" εἰς θεῶν φύσιν ἐλθεῖν is equivalent to attaining divinity, says Himerius (4th cent. A.D.) Or., 48, 26 [42] with ref. to Dionysus. Sophistry is the first to distinguish between gods that are so by their true nature and those that become so by human positing, cf. Critias Fr., 25, 19 (Diels, II, 387) and Plat.'s criticism of the atomists who say the gods are τέχνῃ, οὐ φύσει, ἀλλά τισι νόμοις, Leg., X, 889e. The later theory, known as euhemerism and traced back to Euhemerus,[43] that the gods arose through divinisation of worthy rulers, is reported in Diod. S.: The Ethiopians and Libyans believe one part of the gods αἰώνιον ἔχειν καὶ ἄφθαρτον τὴν φύσιν, e.g., the sun and moon, but it is said of the others θνητῆς φύσεως κεκοινωνηκέναι, they came to be revered as gods on account of their good deeds, Diod. S., 3, 9, 1, cf. 6, 1, 2.[44]

---

[36] It is contested whether φύσις was at an earlier time used for the male and esp. the female sex organs, cf. Muth, 69 f., n. 9. The meaning is "nature" in Plat. Leg., XII, 944d, and Symp., 191a. Hippocr. Mul., I, 143 (Littré, VIII, 316) speaks of the womb moving "beyond its natural position" ἐξωτέρω τῆς φύσιος, v. on this Heinimann, 96 f. A ref. to the sex organs is possible in οὕτως ἡ φύσις ἐστὶ φιλόκνισος ἀλλότριος χρὼς καὶ ζητεῖ διόλου τὴν ξενοκυσθαπάτην, Nicand. Fr., 107 (Gow, 164). This is the only basis of the statement in Liddell-Scott, s.v. and Leisegang, 1143 and 1148. But there is rich attestation in the post-Chr. period, cf. Diod. S., 32, 12, 1; 10, 7, esp. female, Artemid. Onirocr., V, 63; Preis. Zaub., I, 4, 318 and 326; P. Osl., I, 1, 83 (both 4th cent. A.D.) etc.; Diod. S., 16, 26, 6; Antonius Liberalis (2nd cent. A.D.?), Μεταμορφώσεων συναγωγή, 41, 5 (ed. E. Martini, Mythographi Graeci, II, 1 [1896], 125).

[37] Epicharmus is dependent here on Parmenides' distinction between the world of truth and that of appearance or constant change, to which man also belongs, Reinhardt, 114 and 119-125.

[38] Cf. par. statements like σκιᾶς ὄναρ ἄνθρωπος, Pind. Pyth., 8, 95 f.; on the whole subj. v. H. Fränkel, "ΕΦΗΜΕΡΟΣ als Kennwort f. die menschliche Natur," Wege u. Formen frühgriech. Denkens² (1960), 23-35.

[39] Cf. Beardslee, 20 f.

[40] Further examples, ibid., 18 f.; Holwerda, 24-26.

[41] Cf. ὡς οὐκ ἐνὸν ἄνευ θείας καὶ δαιμονίας φύσεως οὕτως καλὰ καὶ σοφὰ ἔπη ἐργάσασθαι, Dio Chrys. Or., 53, 1, where the above passage from Democr. is quoted. Further examples in Philo (→ 268, 21 ff.) and Jos. (→ 270, 28 ff.).

[42] Ed. A. Colonna (1951). Pr.-Bauer, s.v. φύσις transl. "to achieve the mode of being of the gods."

[43] Cf. on this K. Goldammer, Art. "Euhemerismus," RGG³, II, 731; H. Dörrie, Art. "Euhemeros," Der kl. Pauly, II (1967), 414 f.; K. Thraede, Art. "Euhemeros," RAC, VI (1966), 877-890; Nilsson, II², 283-9 (bibl.).

[44] In tendency and terminology this Diodor. passage can hardly go back to Euhemerus himself, who was not the radical denier of the gods (Langer, 59) he was supposed to be in antiquity, and whose field was not really that of religious theory and the rationalistic criticism of myth. Rather, he followed the common tendency of the 4th cent. B.C. to use mythology aetiologically and etymologically to give shape to history and to present the political and

3. True Nature and Universal Nature.

The real problems in the Gk. view of φύσις are disclosed by the fact that from an early time the word played a role in the question of being. In accordance with the twofold meaning of φύσις this question developed in two different directions. The first concerned the true nature of things, the second the origin of all being, i.e., universal nature. But the two aspects cannot be separated and they often overlap.

a. The Pre-Socratics. φύσις is first used clearly in the sense of the true nature of things in Heracl. [45] His starting-point is stated in the description of his own enquiry: " ... as I discussed (things), defined each according to its nature κατὰ φύσιν, [46] and explained its being," Heracl. Fr., 1, 8 f. (Diels, I, 150), [47] cf.: "Wisdom is to say and do what is true by perceiving (things) according to their true constitution," Fr., 112 (I, 176). [48] If even in the famous Fr., 123 (I, 178): φύσις ... κρύπτεσθαι φιλεῖ "the true nature loves to hide itself," φύσις does not mean personified universal nature, [49] Heracl. again has in view the true being of things which is not identical with appearances and which remains constant. [50] This is how we are also to understand the title [51] (λόγος) περὶ φύσεως or περὶ φύσεως ἱστορία [52] used for the treatises of Xenophanes, Heracl., Gorg., etc.; [53] περὶ φύσεως means "about the true nature of things" or very gen. "about philosophy." [54] Similarly the title οἱ φυσικοί, used from Aristot., means "the nature philosophers." [55] The question as to the true nature of things seeks to explain phenomena in terms of universal nature and its established laws. [56] Yet it is only c. 400 B.C. that there is a def. of this relation as an explainable result of nature, namely, in Democr., who calls the atoms the true nature of things, Simpl. Comm. on Aristot. Phys., VIII, 9, [57] cf. Aristot. Phys., VIII, 9, p. 265b, 23-29; Democr. Fr., 168 (Diels, II, 178), and among the Pythagoreans, who see the divine nature of all things in numbers, Archytas (early 4th cent. B.C.)

---

cultural acts of powerful rulers, cf. Thraede, op. cit., 879-881. A different verdict must be passed on the Stoic differentiation of the divine world into three, τὸ φυσικόν, natural forces personified as gods, τὸ μυθικόν, the gods of poets, and τὸ νομικόν, the gods of the state religion, Aetius, De placitis reliquiae (ed. H. Diels, Doxographi Graeci [1879]), I, 6, 9, cf. 6, 1-16 and Philo Spec. Leg., I, 32-5. On this view, which goes back to Panaetius, cf. Pohlenz Stoa, I, 197; II, 100; on the related view of Pos. cf. K. Reinhardt, Art. "Poseidonios v. Apameia," Pauly-W., 22 (1954), 808-811.

[45] Cf. esp. Jaeger, 127-146, also Heinimann, 92-4, 106. Parm., though the question is already decisive for him, does not use φύσις in this sense but focuses on the two terms δόξα and ἀλήθεια.

[46] It is an untenable assumption that all κατὰ φύσιν means here is "as one must normally do," Beardslee, 48.

[47] The ref. here is to the true nature of things, Heinimann, 93 f.; Reinhardt, 223, n. 1, not to nature as a person, nor to the being that results organically by growth, Diller, 243.

[48] In interpretation of this Fr. cf. Reinhardt, 223, n. 1.

[49] Leisegang, 1133, but cf. Heinimann, 94; Reinhardt, 88. Heidel's interpretation is not very convincing: "Nature likes to play hide-and-seek."

[50] Cf. the attack on Hesiod in Heracl. Fr., 106 (Diels, I, 174). Similarly Diogenes of Apollonia (middle 5th cent. B.C.) says all things are of like origin and are thus alike in their "true nature," cf. Fr., 2 (Diels, II, 59, 22).

[51] Book titles were not used in the 5th cent. B.C., cf. Beardslee, 54 f. and → n. 13.

[52] So first in Plat. Phaed., 96a.

[53] Cf. esp. Beardslee, 56-59 and also Heidel, 110.

[54] Beardslee, 59 f. Transl. like "On Origin," or "On Primal Substance," Burnet, op. cit., 12 f. do not catch the intention of pre-Socratic thought.

[55] Cf. Aristot. Phys., I, 2, p. 184b, 16 ff.; 4, p. 187a, 12; III, 5, p. 205a, 3 ff. etc. on the pre-Socratics. The term could also be used for later figures; thus Epicurus is ὁ φυσικός in Phylarchus Historicus (3rd cent. B.C.) Fr., 24 (FGrHist, IIa, 167).

[56] Cf. esp. Jaeger, 199 etc.; also Paideia, II³ (1959), 12-16, 25 f.

[57] Ed. H. Diels, Comm. in Aristot. Graeca, 10 (1895), 1318, 31 ff., cf. the transl. Ding an sich in Reinhardt, 85, n. 1.

Fr., 1 (Diels, I, 432, 2-4). [58] Eur., however, expresses already a belief in the normativeness of universal divine nature, esp. in the linking of φύσις and ἀνάγκη, [59] cf. Eur. Tro., 886; Ba., 896. In rationalised and scientific form the Sophists and physicians also speak of the "necessity of nature" → 260, 14 ff.

b. Plato. Plato dealt decisively with the danger of a mechanistic explanation of the world which in his view had been posed in the thought of some pre-Socratics. [60] He has two arguments. The first (1) is that the theory of origins, esp. of the Atomists, lists only nature and contingency as causes: φύσει πάντα εἶναι καὶ τύχη φασί, and rejects such principles as reason, God, or art, Leg., X, 889b-c, cf. 888e-889a. The second (2) is that he who has a materialistic view of φύσις [61] runs the risk of viewing the four primal elements as the beginning of all things καὶ τὴν φύσιν ὀνομάζειν ταῦτα αὐτά, Leg., X, 891c. Against this emphasising of what arises φύσει Plato relativises the distinction between φύσις and τέχνη: "All that is good may have arisen either φύσει or τέχνη . . . ," Resp., II, 381a-b and he contests the validity of calling the material world φύσις, Leg., X, 892b. As νοῦς, τέχνη and νόμος take precedence of what is falsely called φύσις, so, if one wants to describe the primal origin of all things as φύσις, the soul is φύσις in the true sense, 892b-c. [62] As a rule Plato avoids the word φύσις when describing the highest stages of being. It is not a fixed term for him [63] but is used non-technically to denote the true being of a thing and can often have indeed the sense of "idea" or "essential being," [64] e.g., of the body, Phaed., 87e, the soul, Phaedr., 270c. [65] τὸ φύσει δίκαιον is "the idea of righteousness" in contrast to the legal reality [66] established by the legislator, Resp., VI, 501b. [67]

c. Aristotle. Aristot. adopts the two main senses of φύσις, "origin" (→ 252, 13 ff.) and "constitution" (→ 252, 8 ff.) and he seeks to arrive at a uniform def. of the word by clarifying the two components, Metaph., 4, 4, p. 1014b, 16 - 1015a, 19. [68],[69] The elements of φύσις "origin" acc. to Aristot. are: 1. ἡ τῶν φυομένων γένεσις, Metaph., 4, 4, p. 1014b, 16 f., yet "origin" is not nature itself but only the way to the nature of things; [70] 2. that from which anything that grows begins to grow, e.g., the womb, p. 1014b, 17 f.; 3. that from which the first movement comes, that of all the things which are "by

---

[58] Cf. the probably inauthentic Philolaus Fr., very likely from this period, Fr., 1 (Diels, I, 406), 11 (I, 411 f.); here nature is regarded as a divine being, Fr., 6 (I, 408, 13 f.) and Fr., 21 (I, 417, 14), cf. Emped. in Plut. Carn. Es., II, 4 (II, 998c), cf. Diels, I, 362 and on this Leisegang, 1133.

[59] Cf. Heidel, 99 f.

[60] For Plato's debate with the nature philosophers, cf. esp. Leg., X, 886b-899d, v. Leisegang, 1144-1146; Pohlenz Mensch, 68.

[61] Cf. Lovejoy, 379 f. One should not conclude, however, that this was the dominant sense in the nature philosophers.

[62] Plato also says that the soul as the original principle is self-moved and the cause of all movement, Leg., X, 896a, cf. Leisegang, 1146. He thus prepares the way for the decisive element in Aristot.'s def. of φύσις → lines 23 ff.

[63] Beardslee, 96-101. On the difficulties Plato causes hereby cf. Leisegang, 1146 (with Bibl.).

[64] Cf. φύσις par. εἶδος, Plat. Crit., 389b-c; Leisegang, 1147.

[65] Here with a ref. to Hippocr. the nature of the soul is related to that of the universe, cf. Leisegang, 1140; M. Pohlenz, Hippokrates u. d. Begründung d. wissenschaftlichen Medizin (1938), 114, n. 1 on p. 75; 117, n. 1 on p. 89.

[66] Cf. Resp., X, 597c-d, where the one fashioned ἐν τῇ φύσει of God is distinguished from the many individual copies.

[67] Cf. finally some passages in which φύσις seems to be a periphrasis: μισεῖν τὴν τοῦ δικαίου φύσιν "to hate what is just in its essence," Plat. Leg., IX, 862d, cf. also φύσιν ἔχει with inf. "it is the true nature of things," Resp., V, 473a, cf. VI, 489b.

[68] Cf. the simpler version in Phys., II, 1, p. 192b, 8 - 193a, 27.

[69] Cf. esp. Leisegang, 1148-1150; Grant, 6.

[70] ἡ φύσις ἡ λεγομένη ὡς γένεσις ὁδός ἐστιν εἰς φύσιν, Phys., II, 1, p. 193b, 12 f. This passage plainly shows that Aristot. presupposes this kind of use, cf. Jaeger, 227 f., n. 5.

nature" τῶν φύσει ὄντων, inorganic as well as organic, p. 1014b, 18-20. Discussing the components of the sense "constitution" Aristot. begins with the fact that the material "substance," formless and unchangeable in its own quality (→ II, 285, 16 f.), can be called φύσις, e.g., bronze is the φύσις of a statue, p. 1014b, 26 ff. In the same sense the elements, fire, earth etc., are called "nature," p. 1014b, 32 ff. Thus it might seem that φύσις is the same as πρώτη ὕλη. [71] But this equation of φύσις and ὕλη [72] is no more satisfactory than that of φύσις and γένεσις. We are led a step further when φύσις is taken in the sense of οὐσία "essence," namely, the first synthesis of a thing, ἡ πρώτη σύνθεσις. Of the things which are by nature it may be said: οὔπω φαμὲν τὴν φύσιν ἔχειν [73] ἂν μὴ ἔχῃ τὸ εἶδος καὶ τὴν μορφήν, p. 1015a, 4 f., cf. p. 1014b, 35 - 1015a, 5. [74] φύσις in its proper sense of "nature" or "essence" embraces ὕλη, εἶδος and οὐσία. These three denote the "end result of becoming" τὸ τέλος τῆς γενέσεως, p. 1015a, 7-11. Fig., then, every "essentiality" can be called φύσις, p. 1015a, 11-13.

Aristot. thus finishes up yet again with a twofold sense: 1. "the essence" or "form" which is the τέλος τῆς γενέσεως of all things; 2. "the moving primal force" of all things that subsist by nature, even though he does in fact try to view the latter as a force or entelechy inherent in matter itself, [75] cf. Metaph., 4, 4, p. 1015a, 13-19. A further consequence of this view of φύσις is the persistence of the distinction between things which are by nature and things due to other causes, cf. Aristot. Phys., II, 1, p. 192b, 8. For only that which is autonomous is φύσει. [76] Processes due to other causes imitate nature: [77] μιμεῖται γὰρ ἡ τέχνη τὴν φύσιν, Meteor., IV, 3, p. 381b, 3 ff. But even if human morality has natural presuppositions, e.g., the presence of the understanding, it has to operate in a sphere in which the criteria cannot be deduced from nature → 262, 8 ff.

Aristot. could not take from the concept of nature its inner tension. On the one side φύσις is for him the "constitution" of natural things which can be described with exactness → 254, 18 ff. He distinguishes sharply between φυσική and θεολογική ἐπιστήμη, "science" and "theology" or "religious philosophy," Metaph., 10, 7, p. 1064b, 1-14. Only in the latter may the θεῖον be seen, 5, 1, p. 1026a, 18 ff. Scientific questions must be answered φυσικῶς, Phys., II, 7, p. 198a, 23, [78] and abstractly logical questions λογικῶς, III, 5, p. 204b, 4. The order of nature [79] is absolutely valid and allows no operation of supernatural forces within it. Hence anything against nature, but only against it ὡς ἐπὶ τὸ πολύ "as it mostly is," should be called miracle: περὶ γὰρ τὴν ἀεὶ καὶ τὴν ἐξ ἀνάγκης οὐθὲν γίνεται παρὰ φύσιν, Gen. An., IV, 4, p. 770b, 9-12. [80] On the other

---

[71] Cf. ἡ φύσις λέγεται ἡ πρώτη ἑκάστῳ ὑποκειμένη ὕλη, Phys., II, 1, p. 193a, 29 f. and in gen. 193a, 9-30; cf. Leisegang, 1149.

[72] In Metaph., 11, 3, p. 1097a, 9 ff. φύσις and ὕλη are clearly differentiated as two of three οὐσίαι.

[73] Beardslee, 50 pts. out that in older usage ἔχει φύσιν can mean "to be normal." But Aristot. follows Plato, in whom the phrase means "to have one's true being" → n. 67.

[74] Cf. Phys., II, 1, p. 193a, 30 f.; Part. An., I, 1, p. 640b, 4-29, esp. ἡ γὰρ κατὰ τὴν μορφὴν φύσις κυριωτέρα τῆς ὑλικῆς φύσεως, p. 640b, 28 f.

[75] The aim is to overcome the rift between nature philosophy and Plato as this appears in Plat. and Aristot. Plato is right that φύσις comes from εἶδος and τέλος, but the nature philosophers see correctly that φύσις lies in the obj. itself and is not to be viewed as an independent entity, cf. Beardslee, 103 f.; Heidel, 108 f.

[76] Cf. Heidel, 98 f.

[77] All that is τέχνη has its cause in something else, not itself. There are also things which arise τύχῃ or αὐτομάτῳ, cf. Metaph., 11, 3, p. 1070a, 5-8; Phys., II, 6, p. 198a, 5 f.

[78] Cf. the frequently recurring term ὁ φυσικός "scientist," Phys., II, 7, 198a, 22; Metaph., 3, 3, p. 1005a, 31 ff. opp. ὁ φιλόσοφος, and also τὰ φυσικά, cf. Aristot.'s Treatise on Natural Science (Physics), Phys., VIII, 10, p. 267b, 21; Metaph., 7, 1, p. 1042b, 8.

[79] There is no concept of natural law in Aristot., but he tells of the Pythagoreans that they say that they have received numbers from nature as its laws παρὰ τῆς φύσεως εἰληφότες ὥσπερ νόμους ἐκείνης, Aristot. Cael., I,1, p. 268a,13. On the concept of natural law → 265, 23ff.

[80] One cannot base the concept of nature on deformities of nature, Phys., II, 8, p. 199a, 33-b, 9. For a horse to beget a hinny is παρὰ φύσιν, Metaph., 8, 8, p. 1033b, 32 f. On the question of miracle in Aristot. cf. Grant, 6 f.; Beardslee, 105.

hand nature is not just an obj. of scientific concern; it is also an independently operating force which establishes a wise order in its own sphere. [81] There is no disorder in it, Phys., VIII, 1, p. 252a, 11 f.; the organs of sense are excellently καλῶς arranged by it, Part. An., II, 10, p. 656b, 26 f., cf. p. 657a, 8-10 etc. It has furnished individual beings acc. to their ends, II, 16, p. 659a, 11 f., and in so doing has united utility and beauty, II, 14, p. 658a, 32. It has also been constantly at work to invent new things: ἀεὶ γὰρ ἡ φύσις μηχανᾶται, II, 7, p. 652a, 31 f., cf. p. 652b, 19 ff. It is totally in keeping with the basic intention of Aristot.'s view of nature that the common thesis that "nature does nothing without meaning or purpose" [82] should also appear in the form: ὁ δὲ θεὸς καὶ ἡ φύσις οὐδὲν μάτην ποιοῦσιν, Cael., I, 4, p. 271a, 33, cf. πάντα γὰρ φύσει ἔχει τι θεῖον, Eth. Nic., VII, 13, p. 1153b, 32. [83] This does not mean that divine essence is ascribed to visible nature in its totality, nor that personal being is predicated of it. [84] Rather there is expressed here the fact that the ideal form, which acc. to Aristot. is both the origin and the goal of movement, must be seen in indissoluble union with the divine "essence" and also with phenomenal "nature." [85]

d. Hellenism. In contrast to older Gk. lit. φύσις as "universal nature" is in various ways equated with deity in Hellenism. This is so already in Stoicism, where all things are necessarily held together by the best of all essences, including rational things, but ἀρίστη ... φύσις ἡ τὸν κόσμον διοικοῦσα is rational as well as immortal and is thus God, Sext. Emp. Math., IX, 84 f. [86] Although Epic. follows Democr. in his atomistic view of nature and does not ascribe reason to natural events, he can still appeal to nature as a divine being that rules over all things: χάρις τῇ μακαρίᾳ φύσει. Epic. Fr., 469 (Usener, 300). [87] In the school of Epic. this glorification is even stronger in Lucret. De rerum natura, 1, 56, cf. 1, 146 etc. [88] and it is widespread in Hell., esp. in the equation of φύσις with a female deity, cf. ἐπικαλοῦμαι καὶ τὴν τῶν ἁπάντων διογενῆ Φύσιν, δίμορφον... Ἀφροδίτην, Preis. Zaub., I, 4, 3230 ff. (4th cent. A.D.).

φύσις as the highest principle of the visible world is often distinguished from God, cf. God as the πατὴρ τῆς ἀπλάτου φύσεως, which is again differentiated from the κοσμικὴ φύσις, Preis. Zaub., II, 7, 511 f. (3rd cent. A.D.), cf. Herm. Trismeg. Fr., 23, 10-13 in Stob. Ecl., I, 388, 13 - 389, 4, acc. to which God creates Φύσις through His word, and it appears as a beautiful female being which for its part plays a decisive role in the event of creation. [89] We have here the basic elements of the Gnostic distinction between lower nature and the divine world as we have it in Poimandres. To be sure, φύσις is creator here — for she receives the πνεῦμα and brings forth σώματα, Corp.

---

[81] Aristot. constantly speaks of *natura creatrix* as an active divine being, cf. Part. An., II, 8, p. 654a, 24 f.; 9, p. 655a, 17 f.; 16, p. 659b, 35; Eth. Eud., VIII, 2, p. 1247a, 9 f.

[82] Cf. Cael., II, 11, p. 291b, 13; Part. An., II, 13, p. 658a, 8 f. On teleology in the view of nature cf. Pohlenz Mensch, 234; Grant, 29 f.

[83] ἡ γὰρ φύσις δαιμονία, ἀλλ' οὐ θεία Aristot. De divinatione per somnum, 2, p. 463b, 14 f. is certainly inauthentic, cf. nature as δαίμων, Emped. acc. to Porphyry in Stob. Ecl., I, 446, 7 ff. (Diels, I, 362, 7 f.).

[84] Aristot. never calls the world as a whole φύσις but has, e.g., ... περὶ τε τῆς ὅλης φύσεως... καὶ περὶ τοῦ ὄντος, Metaph., 2, 3, p. 1005a, 32, cf. 1, 3, p. 984b, 9; An., III, 5, p. 430a, 10; Cael., I, 2, p. 268b, 11.

[85] One cannot call the personification of nature merely a manner of speaking and dismiss it as inconsistent, Beardslee, 105, cf. in opp. Leisegang, 1150; W. Jaeger, *Aristoteles, Grundlegung einer Gesch. seiner Entwicklung²* (1955), 75-78.

[86] Cf. Jaeger, 237 f., n. 44. But equation of God and nature is rare in earlier Stoicism, → 263, 7 ff.

[87] Cf. on this Leisegang, 1159 f.

[88] Ed. J. Martin (1953). Further examples in Leisegang, 1159 f.

[89] There is a distinctive variation already in Plat. Tim., 50b: περὶ τῆς τὰ πάντα δεχομένης φύσεως. φύσις here denotes the puzzling ἐν ᾧ, the space-matter which receives something from the world of ideas and thus produces the things of the visible world from itself, cf. Muth, 61-70.

Herm., 1, 17 — but as such it comes from darkness, 1, 6, and is no other than the sublunar world from which the *logos* has differentiated itself, so that its elements are ἄλογα, i.e., ὕλη μόνη, 1, 10, cf. 1, 14. Closely related is the ref. to two φύσεις, heaven and earth, sun and moon, light and darkness, night and day, Preis. Zaub., II, 13, 255 f. (346 A.D.). Cf. the identification of the crowd at the cross as κατωτική φύσις in Act. Joh., 100 → 277, 6 f.

The adj. φυσικός is used similarly in Hell. lit., [90] e.g., the true limits of the planetary deities "according to natural law," P. Mich., III, 149, Col. 7, 28 f., cf. φυσικῶς Col., 5, 18 ff. (2nd cent. A.D.), or rays which traverse the cosmos φυσικαὶ ἀκτῖνες, Corp. Herm., 10, 22. In magic, which aims to control natural forces, φυσικά are "magical powers," Geoponica, 2, 18, 8, [91] cf. φυσικά (sc. φάρμακα), Alexander Trallianus Medicus, I, 15 (4th cent. A.D.), [92] also Geoponica (→ n. 91), 2, 42, 3, the adv. 9, 1, 5.

4. Nature and Ethics.

a. The antithesis of nature and law [93] influenced Gk. thought for many centuries. [94] The two were first juxtaposed in Ionian ethnography. [95] This is esp. clear in Hdt., for whom φύσις denotes not only the "constitution of the land" (→ 254, 6 ff.) but also the "cause of the natural distinctiveness of man," II, 45, 2. In distinction is νόμος, "environmental convention," which influences man phenomenologically. [96] This scientific view of man is particularly evident in the work on environment, one of the earliest works of Hippocr., when he describes the peoples that differ ἢ φύσει ἢ νόμῳ, Hippocr. De aere aquis locis, 14 (CMG, I, 1, p. 96, 2), cf. the contrast between "noble by nature" εὔψυχος ... φύσει πέφυκεν, and changed "by laws" ὑπὸ τῶν νόμων, 16 (p. 71, 1 f.). [97] Even when φύσις and νόμος are understood causally and as complementary in their effects, there can be no doubt that the author sees them in basic distinction and antithesis. [98]

We cannot discuss here the relations between the antithesis φύσις / νόμος and Ionian nature philosophy. [99] At any rate the antithesis is first seen in its full sharpness in the Sophists. Though their views are not uniform, older Sophistry, at least in Protagoras, [100]

---

[90] φυσικός means "after its kind" (e.g. a type of plant) in Theophr. Hist. Plant., VIII, 4, 4.

[91] Ed. H. Beckh (1895).

[92] Ed. T. Puschmann, I (1878), 557.

[93] On νόμος in older Gk. usage v. M. Pohlenz, "Nomos," Philol., 97 (1948), 135-142; Heinimann, 59-89; → IV, 1025, 6 ff. On nature and ethics v. A. Dihle, Art. "Ethik," RAC, VI, 649.

[94] For what follows cf. Köster, 524-530.

[95] κατὰ φύσιν "νόμος πάντων βασιλεύς (Pind. Fr., 169, 1)" in Liddell-Scott, s.v. φύσις obviously comes from A. Boeckh, Pindari Opera, II, 2 (1821), 640-642, but κατὰ φύσιν is not part of the quotation, cf. Ael. Arist. Or., 45, 52 (Dindorf, II, 68); Schol., ad loc. (Dindorf, III, 408); Pind. Fr., 169 (ed. O. Schröder [1900], 457 f. with comm.).

[96] A. Dihle, "Hdt. u. die Sophistik," Philol., 106 (1962), 208.

[97] Cf. the "habits" νόμοι and "nature" φύσις of the father as a model in teaching the son, Soph. Ai., 548 f.; cf. Pohlenz Nomos u. Physis, 427 f., as against Heinimann, 38 f.

[98] Cf. Heinimann, 15, 25 f.; Pohlenz Nomos u. Physis, 421-5, who investigates the oldest occurrence of the word in medicine. φύσις as the opp. of νόμος is "only latently present" in Hippocr. Morb. Sacr., Pohlenz, 423.

[99] Parm.'s dualism has the antithesis "appearance" δόξα and "truth" ἀλήθεια, though once Parm. uses νενόμισται "it is accepted as a convention" as the opp. of ἀλήθεια, Fr., 6, 8 (Diels, I, 233), cf. Reinhardt, 81-88; Jaeger, 302, n. 69. φύσει καὶ οὐ νόμῳ, Philolaus Fr., 9 (Diels, I, 410), is inauthentic. καὶ τὸ δίκαιον εἶναι καὶ τὸ αἰσχρὸν οὐ φύσει, ἀλλὰ νόμῳ, Archelaus in Diog. L., II, 16 (II, 45, 6 f.) is certainly not genuine in this antithetical sharpness and is influenced by Hippocr. acc. to Pohlenz Nomos u. Physis, 432 f. On the whole subj. cf. Heinimann, 38-40, 107-114, who takes into account the influence of nature philosophy; as against Heinimann cf. Pohlenz Nomos u. Physis, 425-433.

[100] Heinimann, 114-119 is hardly justified in claiming that the antithesis of *nomos* and *physis* has no place in the thought of Protagoras.

seems to have stressed the utility and blessing of laws, [101] while only some younger Sophists turned against the existing "order" and "its institutions" νόμος in the name of nature. [102] Worth noting here is what Plat. has Hippias say: ἡγοῦμαι ἐγὼ ὑμᾶς συγγενεῖς τε καὶ οἰκείους καὶ πολίτας ἅπαντας εἶναι φύσει, οὐ νόμῳ· τὸ γὰρ ὅμοιον τῷ ὁμοίῳ φύσει συγγενές ἐστιν, ὁ δὲ νόμος τύραννος..., Plat. Prot., 337c-d. [103] The most explicit direct witness is Antiphon Fr., 44 A (Diels, II, 346-355). [104] Here at the beginning of the history of natural law in antiquity we have a plain stand for nature as opp. to law, custom, and convention, ibid., Col., 2, 26-33 (Diels, II, 347 f.). [105] Whereas all the things on the side of law τὰ... τῶν νόμων are called arbitrary ἐπίθετα and arranged, τὰ τῶν φύσει ὄντων have grown up ἀναγκαῖα and φύντα necessarily and naturally, Col., 1, 23 - 2, 1; 2, 10-15 (II, 346 f.), cf. Fr., 44 B, Col., 2, 10-15 (II, 353). It is important that here φύσις and νόμος are two opposing spheres to which man is equally subordinate and subject. [106]

The effects of this view of natural law in the Sophists [107] may be seen plainly in the lit. of the 4th cent. B.C., cf. Isoc. Or., 4, 105, and also in comedy, cf. the description of illicit love as αἱ τῆς φύσεως ἀνάγκαι in Aristoph. Nu., 1075, [108] cf. 1078, and cf. the assertion that all men are created ἐλεύθεροι τῇ φύσει, Philemon Comicus Fr., 95, 2-6 (CAF, II, 508). [109]

b. Already in the pre-Socratics there are statements about the relation of nature and education. Contemplation of teachings "enables one to develop in nature (ἦθος) [110] according to one's disposition (φύσις)," Emped. Fr., 110, 4 f. (Diels, I, 352). [111] It is a platitude that aptitude and education co-operate: [112] "To have a good talent (φύσιν ἔχειν) is best, the next best is to learn something," Epicharmus Fr., 40 (Diels, I, 204), cf.: "Practice does more than ready aptitude (φύσις ἀγαθή)," Fr. 33 (I, 203). Here one finds already the Sophist view that education is of more value than natural talent: [113] Protagoras formulated this in terms of the educational trinity of endowment, practice and instruction: [114] φύσεως καὶ ἀσκήσεως διδασκαλία δεῖται and ἀπὸ νεότητος δὲ ἀρξαμένους δεῖ μανθάνειν, Fr., 3 (II, 264).

Thus Plato is simply repeating what was said before him when he asks whether qualification for a particular office does not demand a specific φύσις as well as τέχνη and ἐπιμέλεια, [115] Resp., II, 374e. [116] In contrast to the Sophists, however, Plato does

---

[101] Cf. K. v. Fritz, Art. "Protagoras," Pauly-W., 23 (1957), 918. On similar Sophist influences in Hdt. v. Dihle, op. cit. (→ n. 96), 209 f., 214-220.

[102] Cf. esp. Pohlenz Mensch, 119 f. and 203 f.

[103] Cf. also the accounts of the Sophist view of nature in Plat. Gorg., 482e-485a and Resp., VI, 501b. There is no reason not to accept these examples of Sophist thought as valid, as against Beardslee, 74 f.

[104] On the train of thought in the Fr. cf. Heinimann, 131-141.

[105] Cf. Leisegang, 1134.

[106] Dihle, op. cit. (→ n. 96), 211.

[107] On the further development of the antithesis in theories as to the origin of culture, in epistemology and linguistic philosophy cf. Heinimann, 147-170, in Gk. and Hell. thought in gen., Grant, 19-28, in Stoicism and Philo → 264, 1 ff.; → 268, 9 ff.

[108] Cf. Heinimann, 131 f.

[109] Cf. Fr. adespotum, 1423 (FAC, IIIa, 520). Cf. also on this thesis the different judgment of Aristot. Pol., I, 4, p. 1254a, 14 f.; 5, p. 1254a, 17 ff.

[110] On the relation ἦθος - φύσις cf. Thimme, 48.

[111] There is a similar thought in Democr. Fr., 33 (Diels, II, 153): "Education recasts man and thus makes his nature," except that φυσιοποιέω is used here, not a combination with ἦθος.

[112] Shorey, 188, 200 f. and passim.

[113] Leisegang, 1133 f.

[114] For an understanding of this trinity v. W. Jaeger, Paideia, I³ (1954), 394-7, cf. also Beardslee, 17 f., n. 4; Jaeger, 199 f.

[115] Cf. ἐπιστήμη, μελέτη, Plat. Resp., II, 374d.

[116] Cf. Shorey, 194-7.

not build on φύσις [117] even though he uses this for "natural disposition," cf. Resp., II, 375e. [118] For the most part φύσις is the aptitude for a specific task and is thus more or less equivalent to ἦθος, cf. II, 375c. [119] As Socrates was interested in ἠθικά but said nothing about nature, Aristot. Metaph., 1, 6, p. 987b, 1 f., cf. Xenoph. Mem., I, 1, 11, so for Plato talk of the κατὰ φύσιν ὀρθὸν βίον is prejudicial to education, Leg., X, 890a. [120] In contrast Plato stresses that νόμος and τέχνη are in truth φύσει, for they are products of the νοῦς ... κατὰ λόγον ὀρθόν, Leg., X, 890d.

Aristot. has the Sophist trinity φύσις, ἔθος, λόγος, Pol., VII, 13, p. 1332a, 39 f. but φύσις is only the presupposition of ethical action, its standard being "understanding" λόγος which man has received from "nature" so as to know right and wrong, I, 1, p. 1253a, 9-13 [121] and which can require acting against "custom and nature" παρὰ τοὺς ἐθισμοὺς καὶ τὴν φύσιν, VII, 12, p. 1332b, 1-10. There is a δίκαιον φυσικόν e.g., love between married couples, Eth. Nic., V, 10, p. 1134b, 18 f., [122] but the virtues are neither φύσει nor παρὰ φύσιν, Eth. Nic., II, 1, p. 1103a, 23 f., cf. p. 1103a, 19; 4, p. 1106a, 9 f.; Eth. M., I, 34, p 1195a, 5-7; one attains them by acting in accordance with the understanding made possible by the logos.

c. φύσιν ἔχει can be used in the weaker sense [123] "it is natural," cf. κῶς φύσιν ἔχει; "how can that be natural?" Hdt., II, 45, 3. [124] Cf. κατὰ φύσιν "according to nature," "normal," cf. Hdt., II, 38, 2; Hippocr. De aere aquis locis, 22 (CMG, I, 1, p. 75, 16), [125] of death which is κατὰ φύσιν in old age, Plat. Leg., XII, 958d. [126] Cf. again παρὰ φύσιν "against nature," "abnormal," ὥσπερ ... ζῷα ἐπίστανταί τινα μάχην ἕκαστα οὐδὲ παρ' ἑνὸς ἄλλου μαθόντα ἢ παρὰ τῆς φύσεως, Xenoph. Cyrop., II, 3, 9, of the fate of the exiled, Eur. Phoen., 395, of a severe illness which causes pain παρὰ φύσιν, P. Mich., III, 149, Col., 6, 30 f. (2nd cent. A.D.).

In particular these phrases are used in ethical judgments, [127] above all with ref. to sexual failings. Already in Plato we find a condemnation of pederasty: "When someone introduced the corresponding law existing before the time of Laius," ἀκολουθῶν τῇ φύσει, Leg., VIII, 836c, cf. II, 636b. This is based on a ref. to animals, among which a male never touches another male for this purpose, διὰ τὸ μὴ φύσει τοῦτο εἶναι, loc. cit. [128] ἡ κατὰ φύσιν ἐπιπλοκή is "normal sexual intercourse," Diod. S., 32, 10, 4. παρὰ φύσιν γάμος

---

[117] Practically and theoretically it is on *physis* that the Sophists base their work as educators, Jaeger, 199.
[118] Acc. to Plato it is esp. negative elements that are proper to all men, both just and unjust, by nature, e.g., avarice, ὃ πᾶσα φύσις διώκειν πέφυκεν ὡς ἀγαθόν, Resp., II, 359c.
[119] On φύσις "character" → 253, 19 ff.; 270, 11 ff.
[120] This is the oldest example of the idea of "natural life" in the Academy, cf. Pohlenz Stoa, I, 112.
[121] Man is not a πολιτικὸν ζῷον by accident or chance, but as the result of his development φύσει, Pol., I, 1, p. 1253a, 2 f. Similarly the *polis* is "by nature" as the result of a historical process of growth, I, 2, p. 1252b, 30-34, cf. ὁ λόγος ἡμῖν καὶ ὁ νοῦς τῆς φύσεως τέλος, VII, 13, p. 1334b, 14 f.
[122] Cf. Leisegang, 1151.
[123] There is a developed use in ἕκαστον δὲ (sc. τῶν νόσων) ἔχει φύσιν τῶν τοιουτέων, καὶ οὐδὲν ἄνευ φύσιος γίγνεται, Hippocr. De aere aquis locis, 22 (CMG, I, 1, p. 74, 17), cf. "where the earth has the natural constitution only for this end," Plat. Leg., XII, 958d-e.
[124] Cf. Beardslee, 51; Holwerda, 76 f.
[125] κατὰ φύσιν "normal" is esp. common in medical lit.; examples in Beardslee, 48 f., cf. Heinimann, 96 f.
[126] Cf. Cic., who hid from the officers to escape death, which came to him only a little before nature οὐ πολὺ πρὸ τῆς φύσεως, Plut. Comparatio Demosthenis et Ciceronis, 5 (I, 888b).
[127] παρὰ φύσιν does not occur in direct quotations from the pre-Socratics. On the basis of available ref. Leisegang, 1134 concludes that here, too, "it related to man and his unnatural desires or acts."
[128] Beardslee, 99 notes this passage in relation to the view that no ancient author forbade the vice.

is used of a marriage in which the woman is in reality a man, 32, 10, 9. [129] ἡ παρὰ φύσιν πρὸς τοὺς ἄρρενας μίξις, Jos. Ap., 2, 273, cf. the complaint against the philosophers that they use Aphrodite παρὰ φύσιν (pederasty), Athen., 13, 84 (605d), whereas it is wholly κατὰ φύσιν that the Spartan Cleonymus takes 200 women as hostages, 13, 84 (605d-e). [130]

5. Nature as a Cosmic and Vital Principle in the Stoics.

a. God, World and Nature.

Stoicism seeks to transcend both theoretically and practically the antitheses that had been getting steadily deeper in Gk. thought from the 5th cent., namely, necessity and contingency, nature and reason, natural life and human arrangement. Nature is not just εἱμαρμένη (ἀνάγκη φύσεως → 257, 1 ff.) but also πρόνοια, Zeno Fr., 176 (v. Arnim, I, 44 f.), and, as Chrysippus adds, Zeus, Fr., 937 (II, 269, 13 f.), cf. 1076 (II, 315, 8 f.). As cosmic divine reason it permeates the economy of the universe, Chrysipp. Fr., 945 (II, 273, 25-28), cf. 912 (II, 264, 7 f.) etc. Similarly the tension in φύσις between universal nature and the individual creature is resolved. The question of the idea of the individual and that of God are a unity, as are the questions of φύσις ἐπὶ μέρους and φύσις τῶν ὅλων, Zeno in Epict. Diss., I, 20, 16 (cf. v. Arnim, I, 46, 10 f.). [131] κοινὴ φύσις is also the κοινὸς λόγος, Chrysipp. Fr., 599 (II, 184, 31 f.). As a universal divine principle φύσις is infinite primal matter, Fr., 599 (II, 185, 1-4), cf. 937 (II, 269, 22 f.) and also φύσις ζωτική, λογική, νοερά, the overseer of a rational world order, Fr., 945 (II, 272, 38 - 273, 1). φύσις and τέχνη are not opposites, cf. the repeated saying of Zeno about nature as an artistic creative fire, Fr., 171 (I, 44, 9 f.). [132] Nature, then, runs its economy in different ways [133] but all it does is artistic and purposeful, cf. καὶ τεχνικῶς ἄπαντα διαπλάττει, Chrysipp. Fr., 1138 (II, 329, 36) and the statement originating in Aristot. (→ 259, 7 ff.): μηδὲν ὑπὸ φύσεως γίνεσθαι μάτην, Chrysipp. Fr., 1140 (II, 330). On the order and beauty fixed by nature for each individual being cf. esp. Epict. e.g., Diss., III, 1, 3 f. [134] Hair and beard styles esp. offer the Stoic diatribe significant examples of a fundamentally illegitimate violation of nature. A man who removes the hairs from his body is complaining against nature that he was born a man, III, 1, 27-30. If hairs are only an "adjunct of nature" τῆς φύσεως ... πάρεργα, they are also σύμβολα θεοῦ by which the nature of each proclaims from afar ἀνήρ εἰμι ... ἰδοὺ τὰ σύμβολα, I, 16, 9-14.

---

[129] Cf. unnatural intercourse with a wife who for physical reasons is not capable of the natural act, Diod. S., 32, 11, 1.

[130] The adj. is used like κατὰ φύσιν: ἀληθὲς καὶ φυσικὸν χρῶμα, Dion. Hal. De Thucydide, 42 (ed. H. Usener - L. Radermacher, Dion. Hal. Opuscula, I [1899], 398).

[131] Hence Epict. can speak of the divine nature of man; he who despises this by his acts is under divine wrath, Diss., II, 8, 14; cf. οὐ μεμνήσῃ ... ὅτι συγγενῶν, ὅτι ἀδελφῶν φύσει, ὅτι τοῦ Διὸς ἀπογόνων; I, 13, 4, cf. Natura nos cognatos edidit, cum ex isdem et in eadem gigneret, Sen. Ep., 15, 95, 52.

[132] Cf. Chrysippus Fr., 1133 (v. Arnim, II, 328, 19 f.), 1134 (II, 328, 26 f.) etc. On the whole subj. cf. Leisegang, 1153 f. A statement based on the Sophist view of the origin of culture, namely, that τέχνη imitates φύσις, is repeated in Cic. Nat. Deor., II, 22, 57 but with a new Stoic sense; creative nature itself as logos makes men capable of τέχνη (Posidonius? Pohlenz Stoa, I, 227; II, 114).

[133] Cf. the fourfold Stoic division of the powers of διοίκησις in which φύσις specifically denotes the growth of plants: τὰ μὲν ἕξει διοικεῖται, τὰ δὲ φύσει, τὰ δ' ἀλόγῳ ψυχῇ, τὰ δὲ καὶ λόγον ἐχούσῃ καὶ διάνοιαν, Chrysipp. Fr., 460 (v. Arnim, II, 150), also Sext. Emp. Math., IX, 81 ff.; Philo Aet. Mund., 75 etc., cf. the proprium hominis given by nature: animus et ratio in animo perfecta, Sen. Ep., 4, 41, 8.

[134] Cf. Epict. Diss., IV, 8, 42; 11, 9; 11, 31 etc. The adj. φυσικός has a similar sense. A horse is unlucky if deprived of the powers proper to it by nature τῶν φυσικῶν δυνάμεων, i.e., running, but not if it cannot call cuckoo, IV, 5, 13, cf. IV, 1, 27.

b. Man as λόγος and φύσις.

The Stoic telos formula [135] is the most pregnant expression of the Stoic view of the relation between man and universal divine nature. In its earliest form τέλος... τὸ ὁμολογουμένως ζῆν, Zeno Fr., 179 (v. Arnim, I, 45, 24 → V, 201, 3 ff.; II, 837, 19 ff.) φύσις is not used, but it occurs in the class. form coined by Cleanthes: [136] τέλος ἐστὶ τὸ ὁμολογουμένως τῇ φύσει ζῆν, Fr., 552 (I, 125, 19). [137] What is meant in both cases is appropriation οἰκείωσις of one's own being, i.e., the logos, so that agreement with nature is abs. agreement or harmony. [138] In the later development of the telos formula [139] special significance attaches to the interpretation of Panaetius: ζῆν κατὰ τὰς δεδομένας ἡμῖν ἐκ φύσεως ἀφορμάς in Cl. Al. Strom., II, 21, 129, 4. [140] What nature demands is thus given already as disposition to every man to provide a basic impulse. [141] Cf. Cleanthes: πάντας γὰρ ἀνθρώπους ἀφορμὰς ἔχειν ἐκ φύσεως πρὸς ἀρετήν, Fr., 566 (v. Arnim, I, 129). In Epict. συμφώνως τῇ φύσει is most common, Diss., I, 2, 6; 4, 14. 18. 29; 6, 21; II, 14, 22. [142] Special stress is placed here on the fact that man has received the logos by nature, Diss., I, 20, 5, i.e., λαβών τις παρὰ τῆς φύσεως μέτρα καὶ κανόνας εἰς ἐπίγνωσιν τῆς ἀληθείας, II, 20, 21, cf. IV, 1, 51. It belongs to man's nature φύσις that he can get what is good for him only by contributing to the profit of all, I, 19, 13. Indeed, Epict. understands ὅτι φύσει ἐσμὲν κοινωνικοί, I, 23, 1. [143] Rational understanding recognises this nature as, e.g., doing good, working together, interceding for others, not biting, trampling, imprisoning, or executing, IV, 1, 122. [144]

c. κατά / παρὰ φύσιν in the Stoics.

From the time of Zeno's statement στοιχεῖα τῆς εὐδαιμονίας (i.e., as the result of ἀρετή) τὴν φύσιν καὶ τὸ κατὰ φύσιν (sc. εἶναι), Fr., 183 (v. Arnim, I, 46), κατὰ φύσιν became in Stoicism a very common summary of the telos formula → lines 1 ff. We thus find the equations τὸ κατὰ φύσιν ζῆν = τὸ καλῶς ζῆν = τὸ εὖ ζῆν = τὸ καλὸν κἀγαθόν = ἡ ἀρετὴ καὶ τὸ μετόχον ἀρετῆς, Chrysipp. Fr., 16 (III, 6, 16-18, cf. 7 ff.), 4 (III, 3). The goal of life as thus formulated is necessarily def. in a purely formal way, since the ref. is to the state of the perfect sage that cannot be grasped empirically. The only thing one learns about its positive content is that it is a righteousness that comes from God and κοινὴ φύσις, Chrysipp. Fr., 68 (III, 17, 4-7), 326 (III,

---

[135] On the form of the telos formula cf. Pohlenz Stoa, I, 116-8; II, 67 f.; on the whole subj. Bornkamm, ΟΜΟΛΟΓΙΑ, 152-6, the earlier history, 139-151; H. Jonas, "Aug. u. das paulinische Freiheitsproblem," FRL, 44² (1965), 27-9; Köster, 527 f.

[136] Cleanthes rejects the etym. play of Zeno, who takes ὁμολογουμένως in the sense of constituent parts, and returns to normal usage, cf. Pohlenz Stoa, I, 113-7.

[137] This form was then adopted by Chrysipp. and interpreted as ζῆν κατ' ἐμπειρίαν τῶν φύσει συμβαινόντων, Fr., 12 (v. Arnim, III, 5, 19 f.).

[138] Not, then, agreement with specific laws of nature confronting man, cf. Bornkamm, ΟΜΟΛΟΓΙΑ, 152-6; on the question how the dialectical relation to ἀρετή is worked out, ibid., 152.

[139] Cf., e.g., the formula of Chrysipp.: ἀκολούθως τῇ φύσει ζῆν, Fr., 6 (v. Arnim, III, 4), cf. Fr., 7-9 (III, 4), and also Epict. Diss., I, 17, 13-18; v. on this Pohlenz Stoa, I, 117 f.

[140] Quoted in Bornkamm Gesetz u. Natur, 105, n. 27; Pohlenz Stoa, I, 200.

[141] Cf. Pohlenz Stoa, I, 200 f. In Panaetius country, climate, circumstances, vocation etc. are also presuppositions, though they, too, derive from nature, Pohlenz Stoa, I, 201.

[142] ὁμολογουμένως τῇ φύσει ζῆν occurs in Epict. only at Diss., III, 1, 25, cf. the older term προαίρεσις often used by Epict., i.e., liberum arbitrium, free moral choice, which must correspond to nature, Diss., I, 4, 18; Pohlenz Stoa, I, 332-4; II, 163 f.

[143] Epict. Diss., II, 20, 13; IV, 11, 1; cf. Aristot.'s saying about the φύσει πολιτικὸν ζῷον → n. 121.

[144] Cf. Epict. Diss., III, 24, 12; IV, 1, 126 etc. An ironic thing about Epic. is that man's nature is so strong that it forced Epic. himself to write what he wrote and hence to accuse himself, Diss., II, 20, 15-20.

80), cf. "everything that it is in our own power to do constantly and steadfastly to attain
to what corresponds primarily to our nature" τῶν προηγουμένων κατὰ φύσιν, Antipater
Fr., 57 (v. Arnim, II, 252 f.). The goal of action κατὰ φύσιν is the perfect development
of one's own essence and, identically with this, perfect insight into nature. [145]

The detailed concrete def. of good acts for the προκόπτων, who is in a depraved
state, is wholly orientated, of course, to nature but with a ref. only to καθῆκοντα. Health,
strength, perfection of the sense organs etc. are κατὰ φύσιν, while sickness, weakness
etc. are παρὰ φύσιν, Chrysipp. Fr., 140 (v. Arnim, III, 34, 14-18), cf. Epict. Diss., II,
5, 24 f. [146] But all these values are only πρῶτα κατὰ φύσιν, Chrysipp. Fr., 140 (III.
34, 20-22), or ἀδιάφορα, Fr., 146 (III, 35). [147] The very rich Stoic conception of rules
for conduct acc. to nature are still put in terms of individual ethics, as in post-Aristot.
philosophy, and simply grant that man must be aware of his character as a social being
→ 264, 2 ff. [148] There is no real move towards social ethics, since κατὰ φύσιν ἔχειν τὴν
διάνοιαν is understood as the loosing of the individual from the bond of relationship,
as constancy εὐσταθεῖν and steadfastness μὴ ταράττεσθαι, Epict. Diss., III, 9, 17-19;
23, 12 etc. Sound common sense tells us what is κατὰ φύσιν and what is παρὰ φύσιν
in the existing order, cf. the criticism of the father who left his sick daughter believing
this was "natural" φυσικῶς, I, 11, 1 ff. [149] Hence the existing order is often in fact the
standard; for Zeno it is παρὰ φύσιν to live with a woman who is legally married to another and thereby to disrupt his house, Fr. 244 (v. Arnim, I, 58, 13-15), and for Epict. κατὰ
φύσιν ἔχοντα αὐτὸν τηρεῖν applies to the state in which one is, Diss., IV, 5, 6.

d. Natural Law.

The older Stoics speak of the λόγος ὀρθός or κοινὸς νόμος [150] but do not use
νόμος φύσεως at all. [151] The closest to the idea of "natural law" is κοινωνίαν... διὰ
τὸ λόγου μετέχειν, ὅς ἐστι φύσει νόμος (with ref. to the world as the city of gods
and men), Chrysipp. Fr., 528 (v. Arnim, II, 169, 26-29). [152] The twofold occurrence in
Epict. is based on an isolated passage in Plato which is deliberately put paradoxically.
Callicles says that the right of the stronger is κατὰ νόμον τὸν τῆς φύσεως, Gorg.,

---

[145] Cf. Pohlenz Stoa, I, 188; Bornkamm, ΟΜΟΛΟΓΙΑ, 155. To be judged similarly are
the def. of κατὰ φύσιν in Diogenes Babylonius Fr., 44 (v. Arnim, III, 219); Archedemus Fr.,
21 (III, 264) etc.
[146] Further examples in Pohlenz Stoa, II, 66.
[147] *Ibid.*, I, 114 and 332; II, 163; Bornkamm, ΟΜΟΛΟΓΙΑ, 153.
[148] Bornkamm, ΟΜΟΛΟΓΙΑ, 155.
[149] The adj. is used in this context of φυσικαὶ σχέσεις like son, father, brother, as distinct
from acquired ones like citizen, neighbour etc.; the two are closely related. τὰ φυσικά also
denotes φυσικὴ θεωρία, the highest of Stoic disciplines next to λογικά and ἠθικά, cf.
Chrysipp. Fr., 44 (v. Arnim, II, 17) etc. Cf. the corresponding book titles, v. Arnim, III, 205,
6 ff. On τὸ φυσικόν for a class of gods → n. 44.
[150] There are many examples, cf. Zeno Fr., 162 (v. Arnim, I, 43, 1 f.); Chrysipp. Fr.,
4 (III, 4, 2 f.), 332 (III, 81, 23 f.), 614 (III, 158, 18-20) and v. Arnim, Index s.v. ὀρθὸς
λόγος.
[151] *Zeno naturalem legem divinam esse censet* occurs first in Cic. Nat. Deor., I, 14, 36.
Lact. Inst., I, 5, 20 and Minucius Felix, Octavius (ed. J. Beaujeu [1964]), 19, 10 cannot be
regarded as independent witnesses, cf. Grant, 21 f. On natural law in Stoicism cf. Köster,
527-530; on the use in Lucretius *v.* K. Reich, "Der historische Ursprung des Naturgesetz-
begriffs," *Festschr. E. Kapp* (1958), 121-134. [I owe useful ref. to Z. Stewart of Harvard
University.]
[152] The example is from Eus. Praep. Ev., 15, 15, 5 quoting Ar. Did; its origin is uncertain.
Most of the other instances of Chrysipp.'s use come either from Cic. (v. Arnim, III, 78, 2-4)
or Philo (III, 79, 38-41; 80, 8-12) → 269, 2 ff. The idea that state laws derive from a gen.
law given by nature φύσει, κατὰ φύσιν comes, of course, from Aristot., cf. Rhet., I, 13,
p. 1373b, 1-18; 15, p. 1375a, 25 - b, 6. Cf. Demosth. Or., 18, 275 for a similar view.

483e. [153] Cf. νόμος οὗτος φυσικὸς τὸν κρείττονα τοῦ χείρονος πλέον ἔχειν, Epict. Diss., III, 17, 6, and νόμος ... τῆς φύσεως καὶ τοῦ θεοῦ, I, 29, 19. [154] These findings show that for Greek speaking Stoics the two spheres of νόμος and φύσις could not be combined without further ado to give the concept of natural law.

As a current term in common use we first find *lex naturae* or *lex naturalis* in Cic. [155] and the equivalent νόμος φύσεως in Philo → 269, 2 ff. [156] Minucius Felix, Octavius (→ n. 151), 19, 10 and Lact. Inst., I, 5, 20 are undoubtedly dependent on the former of these, [157] while the idea of natural law in the Gk. fathers was decisively influenced by the latter. [158]

The whole problem of the Greek concept of nature comes to light in the idea of natural law. To be sure, φύσις is always a final court and never a created thing. On the one side, however, it can be grasped only rationally, so that knowledge of it, including the norms derived from nature, will always be open to discussion. On the other hand it rules out the power of human decision, since the knowledge of nature leads to a close-knit causal nexus from which man cannot escape to the degree that he is himself nature. Freedom is thus possible only in the inwardness or spirituality in which man is either ready for concurrence in virtue of his freedom of soul (as in Middle and Later Stoicism under the obvious influence of Plato and the Academy) or he turns away from the natural world altogether (as in Gnosticism). Only the Jewish and Christian belief in nature as the creation of God was able to solve these problems. And only here did the concept of natural law become significant, since man could relate himself to the Creator and Lawgiver as the ultimate critical court.

B. Jewish Literature.

1. The Septuagint and Pseudepigrapha.

There is no Hbr. equivalent for the word φύσις and hence we find the term only occasionally in LXX works orig. written in Gk. (3 and 4 Macc., Wis.), while the adj. φυσικός does not occur at all. In the pseudepigr. φύσις and φυσικός occur a few times in Test. XII in spite of a possible Hbr. original. Several passages reflect current Gk. usage, "nature" (→ 254, 9 ff.) of water that it can quench, Wis. 19:20, "talent" par. συνήθεια and ἦθος, 4 Macc. 13:27, "species" [159] (or "natures"?) of animals, Wis. 7:20, πᾶσα θνητὴ φύσις "each mortal being," 3 Macc. 3:29, once of God, who has compassion on men "according to (His) nature," 4 Macc. 5:25. In 4 Macc. universal nature which over-

---

[153] On this formulation in Plat. cf. Leisegang, 1144; Grant, 20.

[154] Dion. Hal. Ant. Rom., 3, 11, 3 is dependent on the same ref. in Plat. The only other examples of the idea of a moral natural law in Gk. lit. apart from Jewish and Chr. writings are (Ps.-) Ocellus Lucanus (1st cent. B.C.) De universi natura, 49 (ed. R. Harder, NPhU, 1 [1926]) and Dio Chrys. Or., 80, 5. Cf. Grant, 22; Köster, 523.

[155] Cf., e.g., Nat. Deor., I, 14, 36; Off., III, 6, 27 and 30 f. etc.

[156] Perhaps we are to think of a common source for both even though the development is typically Roman in Cic. and typically Jewish in Philo. A possible common source is the Eclectic Antiochus of Askalon. [I owe this ref. to R. Horsley, Cambridge, Massachusetts.]

[157] On the influence of the idea of natural law in the Latin fathers cf. Pohlenz Stoa, II, 218 and 222.

[158] There are good examples in G. W. H. Lampe, *A Patristic Greek Lex.*, Fasc. 4 (1965), *s.v.* νόμος, II, C, 4.

[159] The meaning "kind" also occurs in 4 Macc. 1:20 with its ref. to two types of impulse, but there is allusion here to the sense of "growth" which is further developed in the terms φυτά and παραφυάδες, cf. 1:28.

rules all life (→ 259, 16 ff.) is contrasted with law and also, in very non-Greek fashion, with reason. In the speech of Antiochus it is the giver of such gifts as good-tasting swine's flesh, 4 Macc. 5:8 f. But the pious and steadfast reason of the mother of the seven martyrs can triumph even over "nature." φύσις ἱερά here is par. to the power of parental love, the ties of birth and their πάθος, 15:13, cf. 16:3 and v. also the advisers in the soul of the mother: nature, birth, love of children, and the agonies of the sons, 15:25.

The sense of "physical nature" occurs in Test. XII, cf. of sleep ἔκστασις φύσεως, Test. R. 3:1, [160] the power of anger which is doubled by sickness παρὰ τὴν τῆς φύσεως, Test. D. 3:5. The adj. is used in the same sense: ἡ φυσικὴ δύναμις as distinct from the help of others and the power of wealth, 3:4, cf. οἱ φυσικοὶ [161] ὀφθαλμοί, 2:4.

Only two passages have any particular importance. Wis. 13:1 says: Μάταιοι μὲν γὰρ πάντες ἄνθρωποι φύσει. [162] Here it is said of the Gentiles that their ignorance of God is "by nature," cf. 13:1 ff. In contrast is Paul's statement in R. 1:19-23, [163] although Paul does not use the word φύσις in this passage (but v. Eph. 2:3 → 274, 25 ff.). [164] Then Test. N. 3:4 f. twice has τάξις φύσεως; the "natural order" is perverted by the "watchers" (Gn. 6:1-6) and also by the Sodomites, and a warning is given not to do such things, "since you have known the Lord in all his works." Here, too, there are obvious connections with R. 1:18-32.

2. Philo.

The word φύσις is extremely common in Philo. As a central concept in his philosophy and his exposition of the Law, φύσις in Philo unites for the first time in Greek literature the elements in OT and Greek thinking which were to be of decisive significance for the thought of the West: God and *natura creatrix*, creation and the natural world, natural law and divine demand. [165]

a. God and Universal Nature.

In Philo nature as the being of all things is personified as the creator and sustainer of the world and it is thus furnished with divine predicates: ἀγένητος and ἀθάνατος, Sacr. AC, 98-100, [166] ἀόρατος and ἀνωτάτω καὶ πρεσβυτάτη καὶ ὡς ἀληθῶς αἰτία, Rer. Div. Her., 115. As "talent" it is the basis of learning to whose summit God alone leads, ἡ ἀρίστη φύσις, Fug., 170-172, [167] cf. Rer. Div. Her., 121. Above all the visible,

---

[160] φύσις par. αἴσθησις as the seat of the spirit of whoredom is to be construed similarly (Test. R. 3:3) unless φύσις means αἰδοῖον here → n. 36.

[161] Here the term occurs only in a few MSS.

[162] φύσει is not found in 545c La Sa Sy; John Damascenus, Sacra Parallela A, 12 (MPG, 96 [1860], 1156d); B, 5 (1277c), but it seems to be original.

[163] Cf. esp. ἐματαιώθησαν ἐν τοῖς διαλογισμοῖς αὐτῶν in R. 1:21, which is closely related to Wis. 13:1.

[164] On the relation between (natural) knowledge of God and guilt in Wis. 13 cf. Bornkamm Offenbarung, 19 f.

[165] On φύσις in Philo cf. esp. Wolfson, I, 332-347; II, 165-200 etc.; Goodenough, 50-53; Köster, 530-540.

[166] In the same context Philo says that everything mortal is distinct from God. Here what is said about nature glides almost imperceptibly into what is said about God, cf. Rer. Div. Her., 114-6, cf. Goodenough, 51 and → n. 169.

[167] On this understanding of nature as γένεσις and ἀρχή cf. Aristot. Pol., I, 2, p. 1252b, 31 ff. etc. and v. Goodenough, 50.

natural world is created and permeated by φύσις: [168] the alternation of day and night, Spec. Leg., II, 100 and 103, light as the connection between the eye and colour, Sacr. AC, 36, the time and measure of fruitfulness, Congr., 4, the fruitful earth, water, mild climate, fruits and plants, Spec. Leg., II, 172 and 205, and esp. the gifts which the course of nature bestows on men, I, 172, cf. II, 173 [169] → 258, 33 ff. Nature fashions man himself by moulding water and earth with divine skill to produce the human form, I, 266, and it gives man the organs of sense, Som., I, 27 etc.: The mother's womb is thus τὸ τῆς φύσεως ἐργαστήριον, Spec. Leg., III, 109. [170]

Of man esp. it may be said that nature has given him the λόγος, Rer. Div. Her., 302; Decal., 132; Cher., 39, [171] thus making him a social and civilised creature able to live in unanimity and fellowship, Decal., 132. He is ἡγεμονικὸν φύσει ζῷον, Op. Mund., 84 [172] and φύσει βασιλεύς, 85. Nature has created all equal and free, Vit. Cont., 70, cf. Decal., 41. Thus we find in Philo a whole set of statements about natural law from the Gk. tradition → 261, 3 ff. [173]

Another development of the term is when it denotes the world of visible things and is thus distinguished from God, whom only reason can contemplate, cf. Abr., 58; Vit. Mos., I, 130. [174] The riches of nature (air, water, [175] harvest) are differentiated from the riches that wisdom confers and from which the virtues develop φύεσθαι by learning, Virt., 6-8. Even more disparaging is the view of φύσις as the unordered οὐσία, without soul or quality, which is the material of the divine work of creation, Op. Mund., 21-23. In dualistic terms ὁρατὴ φύσις [176] is contrasted with ἀσώματος καὶ νοητὴ φύσις, Praem. Poen., 26 [177] or all that has φθαρτὴ φύσις with divine beings θεῖαι φύσεις, Conf. Ling., 154. [178] But man, too, has a share in νοῦς and he thus belongs to the θειότεραι φύσεις, Leg. All., II, 22 f. [179] The soul yearns for the voyage hence which corresponds to its nature ἡ κατὰ φύσιν μετανάστασις, Virt., 76. [180]

---

[168] In all these passages Philo speaks of *physis* as Aristot. does (→ 258, 33 ff.), cf. Goodenough, 51. There is a very different use when Philo follows the Stoic classification (→ n. 133) and φύσις is ἕξις in stones, φύσις in trees, ψυχή in animals and νοῦς καὶ λόγος in men, Aet. Mund., 75; Leg. All., II, 22 f.; Deus Imm., 35-48 (though here God is the origin of this order). A fifth class is obviously Philo's own addition: In good men σπουδαῖοι, φύσις is ἀρετὴ τελειοτάτη, Aet. Mund., 75.

[169] The alternation of φύσις and θεός is esp. noticeable here, cf. Leg. All., I, 28 with Praem. Poen., 9; cf. also Rer. Div. Her., 164.

[170] This expression, a quotation of unknown origin, Aet. Mund., 66, is very common in Philo, cf. Vit. Mos., II, 84; Spec. Leg., III, 33; Leg. Gaj., 56.

[171] For the relating of λόγος to man cf. the Stoic classification → n. 133. Decal, 76 calls man a work of nature that has a soul and hence must not worship anything without a soul.

[172] Cf. Aristot.'s πολιτικὸν ζῷον → n. 121.

[173] Philo also knows the threefold talent, teaching and practice of the Sophists, cf. Sobr., 38; Sacr. AC, 5-7. Cf. the differentiation of Abraham, Isaac and Jacob as types of διδακτική, φυσική (coming from natural talent) and ἀσκητικὴ σοφία, Vit. Mos., I, 76.

[174] All that belongs to the visible world is often called τὰ ἐν τῇ φύσει as in the Stoics, cf. Vit. Mos., I, 130; Omn. Prob. Lib., 108 etc. and sometimes the rational world is included, cf. τὰ ἐν τῇ φύσει κράτιστα, αἰσθητά τε καὶ νοητά, Congr., 52. Often the expression simply means "all that is," Virt., 117; Abr., 35; Decal., 111. There is no real trace of a technical philosophical use, cf. Goodenough, 50.

[175] Earth, water, air and fire are the μέρη τῆς φύσεως, Vit. Mos., I, 143, cf. Omn. Prob. Lib., 43; Som., II, 122.

[176] Related are ὑλικὴ φύσις in Migr. Abr., 192 and αἰσθητὴ φύσις in Praem. Poen., 36.

[177] The distinction of ἀμέριστος and μεριστὴ φύσις in Decal., 103 comes from Plat. Tim., 35a but the terminology is Philo's own.

[178] Cf. ἐναντία φύσει τό τε φθαρτὸν καὶ τὸ ἄφθαρτον, i.e., man and heaven, Op. Mund., 82; λογικαὶ καὶ θεῖαι φύσεις are heavenly powers, Op. Mund., 144; περίγειοι φύσεις are beings under the moon, Spec. Leg., I, 13 f.

[179] The λογικὴ φύσις of man is in conflict with ἄλογος φύσις, Som., I, 106-109.

[180] αἰσθητὸς ἄνθρωπος is φύσει θνητός, ἄνθρωπος κατὰ τὴν εἰκόνα is ἰδέα, νοητός, ἀσώματος . . . , ἄφθαρτος φύσει, Op. Mund., 134.

b. Nature and Law. [181]

Philo speaks in Stoic terms [182] of the τῆς φύσεως ὀρθὸς λόγος as the "constitution" πολιτεία of the cosmos viewed as a city, Jos., 31. But he definitely goes beyond Stoic usage in employing the terms νόμος and οἱ τῆς φύσεως θεσμοί (Jos., 29 f.) [183] for this cosmic polity. [184] Philo has combined here the Stoic legacy and the OT understanding of the Law. The resultant concept of the νόμος φύσεως is at the heart of the attempt to combine the Jewish understanding of God with the Gk. concept of nature, and it is thus a product of Jewish apologetic. [185]

Fundamentally this natural law is always for Philo the Torah by which God has made the world. Op. Mund., 13 [186] and by which He cares for His creation ἐπιμελεῖσθαι γὰρ ἀεὶ τὸ πεποιηκὸς τοῦ γενομένου φύσεως νόμοις καὶ θεσμοῖς ἀναγκαῖον, Op. Mund., 171, cf. Praem. Poen., 42; Spec. Leg., III, 189. In keeping is the equation of the true cosmopolitan with the one who acts acc. to the will of nature, Op. Mund., 3, which again is simply to fulfil the Law as the OT requires. This is shown from the example of Abraham: He "fulfilled" ἐποίησεν all the laws and commandments of God, yet οὐ γράμμασιν ἀναδιδαχθείς, ἀλλ᾽ ἀγράφῳ τῇ φύσει, so that his life corresponded to the Law (νόμιμος), νόμος αὐτὸς ὢν καὶ θεσμὸς ἄγραφος, Abr., 275 f. Many individual laws are presented and established as laws of nature, e.g., Praem. Poen., 108; Spec. Leg., II, 129 f.; III, 112; Decal., 132; Sobr., 25. Very typical is the emphasis on sexual aberrations as a violation of natural law, Abr., 135, cf. Test. N. 3:4 f. → 262, 25 ff. [187]

In accordance with the equation of law and nature νόμιμος, πρέπον, κατὰ φύσιν and ἀκόλουθον τῇ φύσει are used synon., as are ἔκνομος and παρὰ φύσιν, cf. Spec. Leg., III, 47 f.; Abr., 275 f., and also Spec. Leg., III, 39 and 49 f. with Abr., 137. Similarly Philo speaks of the κατὰ φύσιν χρῆσις of the seven natural capacities of man, sexual potency, speech and the five senses, Mut. Nom., 111 f., and following the Stoics, cf. Chrysipp. Fr., 389 (v. Arnim, III, 94) etc., he finds the origin of evil in πάθος, which is def. as ἄλογος καὶ παρὰ φύσιν κίνησις τῆς ψυχῆς, Spec. Leg., IV, 79, cf. Decal., 142 and 150; Ebr., 105. [188]

3. Josephus.

The word φύσις is very common in Jos. and is distributed fairly evenly in his works. It is thus part of his own vocabulary and reflects popular usage in the 1st cent. A.D. It occurs frequently in topographical notes to indicate the "natural setting" of places, cities

---

181 Cf. expressly on this Köster, 532-540.

182 Cf. Chrysippus Fr., 327-332 (v. Arnim, III, 80 f.).

183 Cf. Op. Mund., 143, where the φύσεως ὀρθὸς λόγος is described as θεσμός and νόμος θεῖος. The saying is intentionally old-fashioned, Köster, 532, and perhaps reflects Plat. Phaedr., 248c. Similarly νόμιμα, which is common in this connection, e.g., Migr. Abr., 94, seems to go back to Plato, cf. Phaedr., 265a; Leg., VII, 793a.

184 The stress on God's positing is not at all Stoic, Goodenough, 51 f.

185 On the basic identity of knowledge of God, the world and existence in Jewish apologetic cf. Bornkamm Offenbarung, 16 f. This motif found many echoes in Philo. Conceptually cf. the description of scribal exegesis as ἐπιστήμη καὶ θεωρία τῶν περὶ φύσιν, Vit. Mos., II, 216, the equation of φυσικοὶ ἄνδρες with theologians and scribes, Abr., 99, and also the view of the Therapeutae that the words of Scripture are symbols of "hidden nature" ἀποκεκρυμμένης φύσεως, Vit. Cont., 28 → n. 188.

186 Here νόμος φύσεως is the order of numbers behind creation, cf. Op. Mund., 35, 60 etc.; even God Himself seems to be subject to this, Goodenough, 52 f.

187 Natural law is never simply developed from the so-called Noachic covenant, so Wolfson, II, 183-7, but is of broader and more basic validity.

188 The adj. φυσικός is mostly neutral and means "what is in accord with the natural being of man," Deus. Imm., 80; Spec. Leg., IV, 201 etc. But it can also mean negatively "man's inhumanity," Spec. Leg., II, 93; III, 110. ἡ φυσικὴ πραγματεία is "physics," one of the three branches of philosophy, Mut. Nom., 75. ἡ φυσικὴ ἀπόδοσις is "allegorical exposition," Fug., 108, hence φυσικῶς "allegorically," Leg. All., II, 5; III, 185, cf. Leisegang, 1137; also Art. "Philon," Pauly-W., 20 (1941), 36-9.

etc., or the "natural configuration" of a district, cf. Bell., 1, 22; 2, 191 and 371; 3, 48 f. 161. 290. 419. 516. 521 etc.; Ant., 3, 303; 5, 77. 124; 6, 109. 113; 15, 324; 18, 312; Vit. 187. [189] φύσις also denotes the "specific character" of a thing. Thus part of the φύσις of oil is to heat easily, Bell., 3, 274, cf. the differing φύσις of the Lake of Tiberias and the Asphalt Lake, Bell., 4, 456. 476, the "nature" of war, Bell., 4, 40, cf. Ant., 7, 144, the "nature" of other plagues, Ant., 2, 299. [190] ἰδία (αὐτοῦ) φύσις is the "truly natural state," Ant., 1, 140; 2, 298: Ap., 1, 282. τοῦ δικαίου ἡ φύσις is "right as such," Ant., 17, 118. Closely related to this sense is the use of φύσις for "kind," "type," "genus," e.g., of animals, Ant., 1, 32; 15, 273, or fruits, Ant., 12, 68. φύσις also means "living creature" in Ant., 8, 44.

Used of man φύσις means "character," "true being." φύσεως ἰσχύς is par. to προαίρησις ἀρετῆς in Ant., 1, 8. It is said of Samuel that he was δίκαιος καὶ χρηστὸς τὴν φύσιν καὶ ... φίλος τῷ θεῷ, Ant., 6, 294. [191] In this connection the common dat. φύσει usually means, not "by nature," but rather "in character"; thus it is said of Hyrcanus that he was χρηστός "in character," whereas Aristobulus had "an opposite character" ἐναντίας φύσεως, Ant., 14, 13; the latter saw the cause of Hyrcanus' downfall "in his character" τὴν ἐκείνου φύσιν, 14, 44. In this sense φύσει is used of individuals, cf. φύσει δραστήριος "of resolute character," Bell., 1, 204, [192] and also of groups or whole peoples," cf. ἄνδρες ... φύσει φιλελεύθεροι "men whose love of freedom is a part of their nature," Bell., 4, 246; barbarians are "fundamentally" unfaithful, 1, 255. [193] Jos. often ref. to "man's nature" in the abs., and his view is almost always negative. Thus ἀνθρωπίνη φύσις inclines to self-love and to hatred of those who are superior in ἀρετή, Ant., 5, 215. [194] The Law of Moses was given so that man's φύσις would not lead him through ignorance to what is worse, Ant., 4, 193, cf. 5, 317. It is "human" ἀνθρώπινος τρόπος to be well-mannered so long as there is no chance χρῆσθαι τὴν φύσιν, par. τολμᾶν ὅσα θέλουσιν, Ant., 6, 263, cf. 7, 133. Twice Jos. speaks of higher honours than accrue to man's "mortal nature," ἢ κατὰ τὴν θνητὴν φύσιν, Ant., 15, 372, cf. 19, 345.

The φύσις θεοῦ, par. to God's works or deeds, is distinguished from human nature, Ant., 1, 15. 19. To be able to refrain from justifiable wrath is a sign of "divine nature," Ant., 4, 269. [195] Once emphasis is put on the superiority of the φύσις of angelic beings over human φύσις, Ant., 1, 279. There is ref. to the φύσις of the elements in Ant., 3, 183 f. [196]

In a series of passages φύσις is an independently acting force, e.g., "nature" has made the area around Lake Gennesaret beautiful and fertile, Bell., 3, 518; it does not rejoice in the fellowship of dissimilar things, Ant., 4, 228, cf. 4, 226; 6, 9. ἱερὰ φύσις commands paternal love even in animals, Bell., 1, 465. [197] Jos. speaks of the "law of nature" [198] esp. with ref. to life and death. Natural death is a νόμος φύσεως, Bell., 3, 374; Ant., 4, 322. That all animals want to live is a νόμος φύσεως ἰσχυρός, Bell., 3, 370, cf. 3, 369. The

---

[189] Cf. εὐφυΐα τοῦ χωρίου, Bell., 1, 408.

[190] Cf. also Bell., 4, 472; Ant., 7, 306; 10, 209; 12, 63; 18, 76; often in the phrase τὴν φύσιν "with ref. to his nature," Ant., 3, 134; 4, 95, or φύσει "by nature," 8, 152.

[191] Cf. also Ant., 2, 141; 6, 290. 318; 7, 9. 43. 310 etc.; 8, 49; 9, 1. 178. 260 etc.; Vit., 134.

[192] Cf. Bell., 1, 408, 470; 2, 208; 3, 346 f.; 4, 310 etc.; Ant., 2, 56. 161; 3, 190; 7, 130, 252 etc.

[193] Cf. Bell., 2, 92; 5, 306. 372; Ant., 3, 23; 4, 37; 18, 47; Vit., 87.

[194] Cf. Ant., 6, 59. 136. 341; 10, 241; 19, 296.

[195] φύσις θεοῦ also occurs in Ant., 8, 338; 10, 142; Ap., 1, 224 (opp. φύσις ζῴων ἀλόγων); 2, 168. 180. 250; cf. Ant., 8, 107.

[196] The thesis that Jos.' own account of the law and history of the Jewish people will agree with τῇ τῶν ὅλων φύσει, Ant., 1, 24 is an echo of Philo Op., Mund., 3.

[197] φύσις is par. to γένεσις, "paternity," Ant., 6, 126, εὔνοια, "inclination," Bell., 1, 77. It also denotes the bond between father and son, Ant., 16, 395; cf. 16, 365; Bell., 1, 556. Patricide is an ἀδίκημα καὶ τῆς φύσεως καὶ τοῦ βίου, and he who does not punish it ἀδικεῖ τὴν φύσιν, Ant., 17, 120.

[198] With gen. ref. to the order of nature φύσις is par. to τὸ δίκαιον and ἀλήθεια and the opp. of ἀνομία, Bell., 1, 544.

sons of Herod who made an attempt on his life renounced τῆς φύσεως δικαιώματα, Ant., 17, 108, cf. νόμος φύσεως, 17, 95. He who denies burial transgresses not only the laws of the country but also "the laws of nature," Bell., 4, 382.

κατὰ φύσιν is "everything that corresponds to the order and operation of nature" in contrast to κατ᾽ ἐπίνοιαν ἀνθρώπου, Ant., 1, 54 and τέχνης μιμήματα, 12, 75, Following normal usage Jos. describes menstruation as κατὰ φύσιν, Ant., 1, 322, cf. 3, 261. 275, and also the birth of children, Ant., 2, 292, cf. 3, 88, and marital intercourse, Ap., 2, 199. [199] Similarly bodily deformity is μὴ κατὰ φύσιν, Ant., 7, 303, and sexual lapses are παρὰ φύσιν, Ap., 2, 273 and 275 → 262, 25 ff.

C. The New Testament.

1. General.

The rare occurrence of φύσις in the NT [200] is in itself worth noting. In this regard the NT does not follows the usual pattern of Hellenistic literature, which is marked by frequent use of the word group, whether as an unconscious but common expression of a widespread understanding of existence, or as the conscious result of a corresponding philosophical and theological interpretation of the world and of being. In respect of the comparative paucity of the term the NT belongs linguistically to the side of the OT and of one part of Jewish literature. What we have here, however, is not just a phenomenon accidentally posited with the OT background of the language of the NT. [201] At least in part it is also a deliberate theological decision which rests on the fact that there is no place for "natural theology" in the thinking of the NT. [202]

2. Pauline Usage.

a. As a term in common use φύσις occurs in R. 11:21, 24 in the expressions κατὰ φύσιν and παρὰ φύσιν. In this metaphor of the cultivated olive (Israel) and the wild olive (the Gentiles) φύσις is that which has grown "naturally" and with no artificial intervention. "Against the nature" of that which "by nature" is a wild olive, the branches (→ III, 720, 33 ff.; VI, 989, 16 ff.) have been grafted into a tree of another kind, the good olive. [203] They thus have no advantage over the branches which correspond by nature to this good olive, having grown upon it.

---

[199] The adj. φυσικός is mostly synon. with κατὰ φύσιν and means "given by, or acc. to, nature," cf. Bell., 1, 35; 2, 149; 3, 514; 5, 191; Ant., 5, 71; 12, 190; 13, 310. But elemental disturbances are also φυσικός, e.g., earthquakes, Bell., 1, 377. The desire for freedom is "the most natural" of all feelings, Bell., 4, 175. φυσικός has a special sense only in Ant., 12, 99, where λόγοι φυσικοί are questions of (moral?) philosophy.

[200] The noun occurs 14 times, the adj. 3, the adv. once.

[201] This certainly applies to the Gospels, since their largely Semitic basis leaves no place for the word, and it does not occur at all.

[202] The absence of φύσις from Ac, esp. c. 17, is surprising. It is hardly by chance that the term is not used in R. 1:18-25 → 273, 7 ff.

[203] One should not ask, as Orig. already did (Comm. in R., VIII, 11 on 11:16-24, MPG, 14 [1862], 1195a, in Ltzm. R., ad loc.), whether the grafting of a branch from the cultivated olive on the wild olive would not have been "more natural" for horticultural purposes. For one thing, we do not find this in the raising of olive-trees. but slips from the cultivated olive are used. For another, φύσις ref. simply to "what has grown naturally," not to what corresponds to normal practice. W. M. Ramsay, "The Olive-Tree and the Wild Olive," *Pauline and Other Stud. in Early Christian History* (1906), 219-250, ref. to the practice of grafting the branch from a wild olive on to an old and good tree to revitalise it when it is no longer bearing fruit. But this is not the pt. in Paul's metaphor. Cf. also the bibl. in Mi. R.[13], 275 and Ltzm. R., ad loc.

ἡ ἐκ φύσεως ἀκροβυστία [204] in R. 2:27 refers to the Gentiles who "essentially," "in their true nature," are the foreskin. [205] What is meant is not converted Gentiles but those who really are Gentiles, and have remained such. This is underscored by the ἐκ φύσεως. In context the point is that these real Gentiles rise up in the judgment and by their fulfilment of the Law (on R. 2:14 → 273, 16 ff.) judge the Jew to be a transgressor of the Law in spite of his knowledge of the written Law and his circumcision → III, 586, 18 ff. To be construed in exactly the same way is φύσει Ἰουδαῖοι in Gl. 2:15, although here the reference is more to "the original descent" which determines our being. [206] But this "being a Jew in essence" does not extend to the present, for it has been cancelled by the "coming to faith in Jesus Christ," Gl. 2:16. [207]

b. The notable expression ἐδουλεύσατε τοῖς φύσει [208] μὴ οὖσιν θεοῖς in Gl. 4:8 reminds us of the Hellenistic differentiation of the φύσει and θέσει θεοί → 255, 16 ff. Along these lines Paul with his μὴ οὖσιν would be denying true and proper being to the φύσει θεοί which the Greeks accept and venerate as personified divine forces of the cosmos. But it may be doubted whether Paul really has in view here the specified technical terminology of Hellenism. [209] There is, however, a plain parallel to the στοιχεῖα (→ VII, 684, 9 ff.; 685, 5 ff.; IV, 641, 31 ff.; 1075, 16 ff.; VI, 909, 24 ff.), the personified elements of the world, to which Paul refers in the next v. (Gl. 4:9). [210] As once ignorance of God — Paul uses the typical vocabulary of mission here [211] — was equivalent to bondage to the φύσει μὴ ὄντες θεοί, so now for the Galatians acceptance of the Law would be the same as a return to slavery under the cosmic elements. The ἀσθενῆ καὶ πτωχά contests the claim and power of these elements. In Gl. 4:8 the simple μὴ οὖσιν suffices to deny deity to these supposed gods. The preceding φύσει not only strengthens the negation [212] but makes it clear that these powers do not have any divine quality "essentially," i.e., in their own nature and essence. It is quite possible that Paul is also alluding to the concept of φύσει θεοί.

The only passage in which Paul has φύσις in the nominative and absolute is 1 C. 11:14. Here, of course, "nature" is personified as the teacher of men. Nevertheless, it simply represents the general order of nature and its only task is to remind us of what is seemly and becoming. [213] The idea of a divine creator and sustainer of

---

[204] These words are not in G.

[205] One should not transl.: The Gentiles "who are so by heredity," Pr.-Bauer, s.v., or: "inheritance conditioned by physical descent," Pohlenz Pls. u. Stoa, 77. The term ἀκροβυστία rules this out, since on this interpretation the opp. would not fit the Jews.

[206] Bonhöffer, 148 suggests "what is native in contrast to what is learned later," but this hardly corresponds to what constitutes the essence of the Jew, namely, fulfilment of the Law, cf. Flückiger, 31.

[207] In the context of v. 15 and v. 16 cf. the twofold ἡμεῖς, v. Schlier Gl.[13] on 2:15.

[208] K d m Ir[lat] Ambst omit φύσει to make the unusual expression smoother.

[209] The ref. in Schlier Gl.[13], ad loc. to Luther's Lectures on Galatians (WA, 2, p. 537, 26): non natura sed opinione et errore hominum dii sunt, does not help much, since this verdict applies to the θέσει θεοί, and Paul's term can hardly be regarded as a less apt expression for what is more accurately called θέσει θεοί.

[210] On the connection between worshipping the στοιχεῖα and serving cosmic powers cf. G. Bornkamm, "Die Häresie d. Kol.," Das Ende d. Gesetzes[5] (1966), 140 f.; W. Schmithals, "Die Häretiker in Galatien," Pls. u. d. Gnostiker (1965), 30 ff.; in critical opposition → VII, 684, 9 ff.

[211] Cf. Bultmann Theol.[6], 70 f.

[212] The transl. of φύσει as "really," e.g., in Schl. Gl.[13], ad loc., is hardly adequate.

[213] Cf. the par. πρέπον in 1 C. 11:13 and συνήθεια in 11:16.

the world is completely foreign. The argument is a typical one in popular philosophy and is not specifically Stoic. [214] The fact that nature bears witness to what is fitting in the matter of hair-styles reminds us that in the diatribe the same question was a favourite illustration in discussing what is "natural" → 263, 27 ff. Hence the use of abs. φύσις here can perhaps be regarded as technical, but it is of no theological significance.

In the clearest possible contrast to the way Paul incidentally appeals to φύσις in 1 C. 11:14, φύσις does not occur at all when Paul speaks of the knowledge of God from His works of creation in the visible world, R. 1:18-25. [215] Only in the description of the perversion to which God has delivered man up do we find the term φύσις, and now only in the adverbial παρὰ φύσιν (R. 1:26) and the adjectival φυσικὴ χρῆσις (R. 1:26 f.). The stress on sexual faults corresponds to the so-called Noachic commandments of Rabbinic Judaism [216] but in both tenor and formulation it is in every way Greek in Paul, the idea being that of a violation of the natural order → 262, 25 ff. [217]

The most important and also the most difficult passage in which Paul uses φύσις is R. 2:14: ὅταν γὰρ ἔθνη ... φύσει τὰ τοῦ νόμου ποιῶσιν. [218] Paul is speaking here of the fulfilling of the Law [219] by Gentiles [220] in contrast to the Jew, who is a hearer of the Law but not a doer, R. 2:13. As the ground is indirectly prepared in R. 1:18-32 for the attack on the self-boasting of the Jews, [221] so in R. 2:1 ff. the Jews are expressly included in the "all" mankind that has fallen victim to judgment. The Jew who has the Law has precedence in salvation history only to the degree that judgment overtakes him first; [222] that is to say, he has no real advantage through his possession of the Law. His consciousness of superiority over the Gentiles in

---

214 Pohlenz Pls. u. Stoa, 77, 81; Bonhöffer, 147; A. D. Nock, *Early Gentile Christianity and Its Hellenistic Background* (1964), 95.

215 In par. sayings in Philo φύσις is repeatedly used → 267, 26 ff. Apart from the use of φύσις the sayings about God's natural revelation in R. 1:19 ff. are in full correspondence terminologically with Stoicism and Jewish apologetic, cf. esp. Bornkamm Offenbarung, 12-18; W. D. Davies, *Paul and Rabbinic Judaism*² (1955), 116. For bibl. on the relation between R. 1:18-32 and Hell. Judaism v. S. Schulz, "Die Anklage in R. 1:18-32," ThZ, 14 (1958), 163, n. 2.

216 Cf. *inter al.* Davies, op. cit., 115-7; Gärtner, 76 f.; Str.-B., III, 36-43; Test. N. 3:4 f. (→ 267, 15 ff.) and Philo → 269, 19 f. and → n. 187.

217 There is no technical Stoic use of παρὰ φύσιν, as Bonhöffer rightly emphasises, 149. On the Stoic πρῶτα κατὰ φύσιν → 265, 5 ff.

218 On the many problems of R. 2:14 f., which cannot be discussed in detail here, cf. the basic, rich and convincing study of Bornkamm Gesetz u. Natur, 93-118; cf. also Bonhöffer, 149-157; Pohlenz Pls. u. Stoa, 75-7; Kuhr, 243-261; Ltzm. R., *ad loc.*; for prior exegesis cf. Lackmann, 95-107; K. H. Schelkle, *Paulus, Lehrer der Väter* (1956), 81-5; on the question of the interpretation of συνείδησις in R. 2:15, which is closely related to the understanding of φύσις, → VII, 916, 41 ff.

219 It is a complete mistake to think that τὰ τοῦ νόμου means that the Gentiles do negatively what appertains to the Law by sinning, Walker, 305.

220 The ref. is to the Gentiles in gen. whenever and wherever this doing of the Law by them may be discerned. The introductory ὅταν (not ἐάν) forbids us to conclude that all the Gentiles always act thus, Walker, 304, cf. Pohlenz Pls. u. Stoa, 75; Bornkamm Gesetz u. Natur, 101; Bultmann Theol.⁶, 262. Against the view, common since Augustine, that the ἔθνη are Gentile Christians, cf. Kuhr, 244-252. Luther already in his Lectures on Romans rejected any ref. to Gentile Christians or to sinful Gentiles: *Medios accipio inter impios gentiles et fideles gentiles* (WA, 56, 202, 16).

221 Cf. esp. R. 1:22 and the striking διό in R. 2:1, cf. Bornkamm Gesetz u. Natur. 94-7; Bornkamm Offenbarung, 25, n. 52.

222 Cf. Bornkamm Gesetz u. Natur, 97 f. and on the train of thought in R. 2:11-13 ibid., 99.

virtue of the Law is challenged first of all by the fact that Gentiles, too, practise what the Law demands, R. 2:14, [223] and then by the fact of conscience, v. 15. It is true that Gentiles do not have the Law — the primary reference is to the Law of Moses [224] — and yet they do it φύσει and so they are law to themselves. As R. 2:14 f. in general betrays an unusually strong influence of Greek ideas, [225] φύσει here must be construed as a typically Greek term, although we may not on that account conclude that Paul is advancing specific Stoic teachings. [226] The close relation between φύσις and νόμος [227] points specifically to the context of Hellenistic-Jewish apologetic in which, as in Philo (→ 269, 12 ff.), there could be performance of the Law of Moses "by nature" and the identity of natural law with the revealed Law of the OT could be maintained. Paul does not, of course, appeal to nature as a final court equal to God; [228] his φύσει expresses the fact that what we have here is simply a work of Gentiles corresponding to their nature. In contrast to the awareness of Jews that in the Law they have the blessing of divine salvation — the Jew boasts of the Law *ad maiorem gloriam dei* (R. 2:17) — Paul stresses that the Gentile can point to a similar possession and performance "by nature" [229] even though he does not have the Law of Moses but is law to himself. In the latter expression, which expresses the Greek concept of autonomy, [230] as in the ensuing reference to the law written in the heart of Gentiles, which takes up the Greek idea of the ἄγραφος νόμος, [231] there is no allusion to a divine action. Paul is not trying to show apologetically that the Gentiles have at least a share in the Jewish blessings of salvation. By portraying a wholly secular Gentile possibility of doing what is required by the Law, Paul is simply contesting the soteriological boasting of the Jews on the basis of possession of the Law.

Obviously the terminology of Jewish apologetic is also interpreted critically in Eph. 2:3. The distinctive statement that "we too were τέκνα φύσει ὀργῆς" [232] is to be explained only in terms of these presuppositions. In context the "we" must refer to Jewish Christians, for Eph. 2:1 f. deals with Gentile Christians. [233] Jewish apo-

---

[223] One is not to distinguish between doing the Law (the Jews) in R. 2:13 and serious concern for the works of the Law (the Gentiles) in v. 4; cf. on this → IV, 1070, 17 ff.

[224] νόμον μὴ ἔχοντα means the same as ἀνόμως, v. 12, cf. Bornkamm Gesetz u. Natur, 100 f.

[225] Cf. the decidedly non-Jewish and all the more Gk. expression ἑαυτοῖς εἰσιν νόμος, the Gk. motif of ἄγραφος νόμος and the term συνείδησις, which can be explained only on Gk. presuppositions, Bornkamm Gesetz u. Natur, 101 f.

[226] Bonhöffer, 153 f. and Pohlenz Pls. u. Stoa, 75 f. rightly warn against this.

[227] φύσει goes with τὰ τοῦ νόμου ποιῶσιν and not ἔθνη. Hence one cannot transl.: "The Gentiles in their creatureliness," so Mi. R.[13], *ad loc.*; cf. in opposition Bornkamm Gesetz u. Natur, 103.

[228] For this reason the common exposition that this obedience to the Law is ultimately effected by God (cf. Flückiger, 35 and Lackmann, 218: φύσει, i.e., addressed by God) is mistaken.

[229] Paul thus understands "by nature" Stoically and rationalistically in terms of natural law, not theonomously or in the sense of perceiving "in their *physis* that which is the mystery . . . of their *physis*," Lackmann, 218.

[230] Cf. the Gk. idea of education which can make legislation superfluous, Plat. Resp., IV, 425c; 427a, cf. Jaeger, *op. cit.* (→ n. 56), 314; also Aristot. Eth. Nic., IV, 14, p. 1128a, 31; Pol., III, 8, p. 1284a, 13 f. (→ 261, 19 ff.). On the whole theme *v.* Bornkamm Gesetz u. Natur, 104 f. with further examples 105, n. 24 f. 27; Kuhr, 257 f.

[231] The idea of the law written in the heart can hardly come from Jer. 31:33 since the ref. there is to the eschatological act of divine salvation, cf. Kuhr, 259 f.; on the Gk. origin of the concept, 259; cf. also Bornkamm Gesetz u. Natur, 104-108; E. Norden, *Agnostos Theos* (1913), 11; cf. also → IV, 1022, Bibl. *s.v.* νόμος.

[232] On the position of φύσει cf. Pr.-Bauer, *s.v.*

[233] Dib. Gefbr., *ad loc.*

logetic had claimed that only Gentiles were "by nature" subject to the judgment of God, cf. Wis. 13:1 f. → 267, 11 ff. Jews were freed by the Law from the power of φύσις. [234] The author of Ephesians, however, expressly includes the Jews with the Gentiles in this radical fallenness and he uses the term φύσει to show that the schema of Christian conversion — once sinful, now redeemed by grace — may be applied to Jewish Christians too → V, 435, 22 ff. [235]

3. The Rest of the New Testament.

a. Jm. 3:7 uses φύσις twice in the common Greek sense [236] "every kind of beast" and "human nature" (→ 253, 27 ff.) [237] within a comparison which was widespread in antiquity and which also has parallels in Hellenistic Judaism. [238] ἵνα ... γένησθε θείας κοινωνοὶ φύσεως, said of Christians in 2 Pt. 1:4, presupposes the current Greek distinction between the corruptible, weak and mortal nature of man and the incorruptible divine essence → 254, 24 ff. There is express allusion to this in the accompanying phrase ἀποφυγόντες τῆς ἐν τῷ κόσμῳ ἐν ἐπιθυμίᾳ φθορᾶς. With these and other expressions in 2 Pt. 1:3 f. the epistle makes use of a vocabulary of Hellenistic piety not found in more primitive works; [239] we find something of the same in Christian writings of the 2nd century. [240] The expression "partakers of the divine nature" seems to suggest the non-eschatological understanding of redemption also espoused by Gnosticism. Instead of the primitive expectation of future consummation we now find present participation in the divine nature and its powers, i.e., deification → II, 310, 6 ff. Possibly 2 Pt. took over the term from Gnosticism and tried to work it into his new formulation of future expectation. [241]

b. The adjective φυσικός occurs in 2 Pt. 2:12 and the adverb in the parallel Jd. 10. Both passages are obscure. To explain φυσικῶς ὡς τὰ ἄλογα ζῷα ἐπίστανται in Jd. 10 it is doubtful whether one may simply refer to passages which speak of the natural understanding of men and beasts. [242] Jd. 10, on which 2 Pt. 2:12 is probably dependent, [243] is better interpreted as a polemic against the Gnostic description of pneumatics as φύσει σῳζόμενοι. [244] On this view the Gnostic claim of redemption from nature is countered by the threat of destruction in a merely natural and irration-

---

[234] Cf. Jos. Ant., 4, 193 → 270, 23 ff.

[235] What this pagan nature consists of is shown in Eph. 2:1-3. Hence there is no thought either of natural disposition or of Adamic sonship, as against Pr.-Bauer, s.v.

[236] Bonhöffer, 148.

[237] The first expression occurs in Jewish Wisdom lit., cf. Wis. 7:20 (→ 266, 31), the second in an inscr. of Antiochus I of Commagene, ed. L. Jalabert - R. Mouterde, Inscr. grecques et latines de la Syrie, I (1929), 51, 46 f. (1st cent. B.C.), cf. Deissmann B, 284, n. 3.

[238] Cf. Dib. Jk.[11], ad loc.

[239] Cf. Kn. Pt., ad loc. and esp. Wnd. Kath. Br., Exc. on 2 Pt. 4:3 f.; cf. Bonhöffer, 148. The usage in Jos. is also very closely related → 270, 21 ff.

[240] Examples in Kn. Pt., ad loc.; on φύσις in early Chr. writings → 276, 28 ff.

[241] Cf. how 2 Pt. 3 also gives new pt. to primitive Chr. eschatology as a doctrine and uses it as a weapon against Gnostic heretics.

[242] Cf. Xenoph. Cyrop., II, 3, 9 quoted in Wnd. Kath. Br. and Kn. Pt. on Jd. 10; also φυσικῶς καὶ χωρὶς λόγου in Diog. L., X, 137 in Kn. Pt. on Jd. 10.

[243] For the priority of Jd. cf. Wnd. Kath. Br., Exc. on 2 Pt. 2:1-22; Kn. Pt., 251-3.

[244] Attested in Valentinian Gnosticism acc. to Cl. Al. Exc. Theod., 53, 6 etc. (→ VII, 1000, 17 ff.). Jd. 19 with its ψυχικοί, πνεῦμα μὴ ἔχοντες presupposes the distinction of various classes of mankind (→ ψυχικός) associated with Valentinian Gnosticism. There seems to be ref. to technical Gnostic usage. This is very clear when one compares τῇ ὁδῷ τοῦ Κάϊν in Jd. 11 with τρεῖς φύσεις γεννῶνται, πρώτη μὲν ἡ ἄλογος, ἧς ἦν Κάϊν, Cl. Al. Exc. Theod., 54, 1. On Cain speculation in Judaism cf. Kn. Pt. on Jd. 11.

al knowledge (→ IV, 141, 32 ff.) [245] comparable to that of the beasts. In 2 Pt. 2:12 the word is detached from this context and related merely to the comparison with the beasts, which is set in antithesis to the claim to have γνῶσις. [246]

D. The Occurrence of φύσις in Other Early Christian Writings.

1. Post-Apostolic Fathers.

In the post-apost. fathers φύσις [247] occurs only once in Barn. and twice in Ign. [248] Barn., 10, 7 speaks of the hyena which changes its sex annually; φύσις thus corresponds to γένος or sexus in the par. versions of this fable. [249] In Ign. φύσις is used on both occasions for the "true and proper nature" of Christians. The Ephesians have received their name φύσει δικαίᾳ, Eph., 1, 1 [250] and the Trallians have their unstained conscience οὐ κατὰ χρῆσιν, ἀλλὰ κατὰ φύσιν, Trall., 1, 1. [251]

2. Apologists.

In Just. [252] φύσις is human nature in gen., cf. the wicked desire that is in every man "by nature," Apol., 10, 6; our "own nature" cannot work miracles, Apol., 19, 6, cf. Dial., 10, 2. [253] Closer to philosophical usage is the statement that God is a conception ἔμφυτος τῇ φύσει τῶν ἀνθρώπων, Apol. App., 6, 3, cf. the repeated assertion that the power to distinguish between good and evil is proper to the nature of man, ibid., 7, 6; 14, 2.

The concept of natural law is rare in the older Gk. apologists. Just. Dial., 45, 3 f. equates the Law of Moses with that which is "good, pious and just by nature," cf. 47, 2. A dissolute life can be called παρὰ τὸν τῆς φύσεως νόμον, Just. Apol. App., 2, 4, cf. the idea that natural law directs the mating of animals, Athenag. Suppl., 3, 1, [254] cf. also the sidereal order which God has established and none can violate κατὰ ἀπαραίτητον φύσεως ἀνάγκην, Aristid. Apol., 4, 2. [255] This usage is fully in keeping with that of Jewish apologetic as we have it in Philo → 267, 30 ff. Aristid. Apol., 13, 5 f. should also be quoted in this connection. Here the absurdity of pagan φυσιολογία περὶ τῶν θεῶν is shown; there can be no single φύσις τῶν θεῶν if the gods are in conflict with one another.

3. Apocryphal Acts.

Of the older of these, Act. Jn., Andr. and Thom. use φύσις frequently, [256] while among the later the same is also true of Act. Phil. Sometimes φύσις is the "natural world"

---

[245] On ἄλογος cf. Cl. Al. Exc. Theod., 54, 1 (→ n. 244).

[246] Cf. ἐν οἷς ἀγνοοῦσιν in 2 Pt. 2:12.

[247] φυσικός does not occur at all in the post-apost. fathers and is rare in other Chr. works of the 2nd cent., cf. φυσικὸς λόγος par. θεῖος νόμος in Athenag. Suppl., 3, 1 f.

[248] Ign. Sm., 1, 1 MS A has υἱὸν θεοῦ κατὰ φύσιν (the other MSS κατὰ θέλημα θεοῦ).

[249] Cf. Ael. Nat. An., 1, 25; Tert. De pallio, 3, 2 (CSEL, 76 [1957], 111) and the pertinent ref. in Wnd. Barn., ad loc.

[250] Pr.-Bauer, s.v. cf. Bau. Ign., ad loc., thinks φύσις here means "natural order," from which the Ephesians take their name (ἔφεσις "wish").

[251] On the relation between this and Gnostic usage (→ 277, 18 ff.) cf. H. Schlier, "Religionsgesch. Untersuchungen zu d. Ign.-Br.," ZNW Beih., 8 (1929), 134 f.

[252] Καίσαρος φύσει υἱός, Just. Apol., 1, 1 has the sense of "physical" son found elsewhere in gen. Gk. usage → 252, 18 ff.

[253] Cf. the one occurrence of φύσις in Dg., where our "nature" is too weak to attain life, Dg., 9, 6.

[254] It is worth noting that νόμος τῆς φύσεως, which is very rare in the 2nd cent., is used in De resurrectione (ed. M. Malinine et al [1963]), 44, 20 in opp. to Gnostic knowledge. In the Fr. of the Gnostic work of Epiphanes in Cl. Al. Strom., III, 5, 2 - 9, 3 we do not find φύσις even though there is a strong orientation to natural law.

[255] The wording here is close to the OT, cf. πρόσταγμα ἔθετο, καὶ οὐ παρελεύσεται in ψ 148:6.

[256] φύσις or natura does not occur in Act. Pl., Pt. or Pt. et Pl. φυσικός does not occur at all: naturalis is found only once at Mart. Mt., 14 (p. 233, 24).

as a whole in contrast to God, who is called φύσεως κύριος καὶ κριτής, Act. Thom. 143 (p. 250, 2).[257] "Nature" demands the love of spouses, *ibid.* 62 (p. 179, 3 f.) and "nature, law and conscience" are avengers of adultery, Act. Jn. 35 (p. 168, 34 - 169, 1). Only seldom is nature as such viewed negatively, e.g., as the sphere which has led the soul astray, Act. Andr. 15 (p. 44, 13 f.); cf. ἡ κατωτικὴ ῥίζα, ἀφ' ἧς[258] τῶν γινο-μένων προῆλθεν ἡ φύσις, Act. Jn. 98 (p. 200, 15 f.), cf. ἡ κατωτικὴ φύσις at 100 (p. 201, 1 f.).[259] As a rule φύσις has here the Gnostic sense of "true essence" which remains unchanged and thus irrevocably determines being: οἵα ἡ ὁδός σου τοιαύτη καὶ ἡ ῥίζα καὶ ἡ φύσις, Act. Jn. 84 (p. 193, 23 f.) etc. and cf. Act. Thom. 74 (p. 189, 8 f.). The "true essence" of man which is saved is ἄνωθεν, *ibid.* 61 (p. 178, 11), it is his ἀρχαιό-γονος φύσις, 43 (p. 161, 10). God's healing is granted to those who are of "his own essence," 78 (p. 193, 17 f.). Each must know "his true nature" τὴν ἀληθῆ... φύσιν, Act. Andr. 9 (p. 42, 3). The one to be redeemed is called φύσις σῳζομένη, 6 (p. 40, 24).[260] We also read of the "hidden nature" of the devil which is unmasked by revelation, Act. Andr. 18 (p. 45, 26), esp. in Act. Thom.: the φύσις τοῦ πατρός of the dragon is that of the devil, shown in the fact that he dies of his own poison, Act. Thom. 33 p. 150, 11 f.), cf. 29 (p. 146, 10), 31 (p. 148, 9 f.), 32 (p. 148, 16 f.).[261]

4. Gnosticism.

The same usage may be seen in Egypt. Gnosticism. Acc. to Iren. Haer., I, 1, 14, the Valentinians divide souls into φύσει ἀγαθαί and φύσει πονηραί. Acc. to Cl. Al. Exc. Theod., 54, 1 (→ n. 244), there are three φύσεις deriving from Adam, cf. Iren. Haer., I, 1, 14 and Τρία δὲ γένη ἀνθρώπων, I, 1, 16. Heracleon in Orig. Comm. in Joh., 13, 25 on 4:24 (p. 248, 28 ff.) speaks of the θεία φύσις and of those who belong to it and are thus pneumatics,[262] cf. in contrast the devil whose "nature" is not of the truth, 20, 28 on 8:44 (p. 365, 8 ff.). Among those who belong to the devil there is a distinction between φύσει and θέσει υἱοί, 20, 24 on 8:44 (p. 359, 15 f.), cf. 20, 20 on 8:43 (p. 352, 22 ff.). Basilides says of the spirit of the middle sonship that he is οὐχ ὁμοούσιον οὐδὲ φύσιν εἶχε μετὰ τῆς υἱότητος, Hipp. Ref., VII, 22, 12, but sonship is κατὰ πάντα τῷ οὐκ ὄντι θεῷ ὁμοούσιος, VII, 22, 7. The terms κατά and παρά φύσιν also play a role here; the goal of redemption is the great ignorance into which the cosmos falls back, ἵνα μένη πάντα κατὰ φύσιν καὶ μηδὲν μηδενὸς τῶν παρὰ φύσιν ἐπιθυμήσῃ, VII, 27, 1, cf. 2-5 and VII, 22, 13.[263]

Köster

---

[257] Cf. Act. Jn. 112 (p. 211, 4); Act. Thom. 34 (p. 152, 10).

[258] Acc. to the reading of K. Schäferdiek in Hennecke³, II, 158; Bonnet suggests ἄφες, cf. Apparatus, *ad loc.*

[259] In contrast ἄνω φύσις, Act. Jn. 100 vl. (p. 201, 4) for ἀνθρώπου (emendation for ἄνθρωποι) φύσις, *loc. cit.*

[260] Cf. εὐχαριστοῦμέν σου τῷ χρήσαντι φύσιν φύσεως σῳζομένης, Act. Jn. 85 (p. 193, 8 f.); on the constr. of χρήζω here cf. οὐδὲν οὐδενὸς χρήζει, 1 Cl., 52, 1, cf. Pr.-Bauer, *s.v.* χρήζω.

[261] Cf. also Act. Thom. 48 (p. 164, 13 f.) and the other passages from the Syr. version of Act. Thom. in A. F. J. Klijn, *The Acts of Thomas* (1962), 188 f. Related is the Apocr. Jn. (ed. M. Krause - P. Labib, "Die drei Versionen d. Apokr. d. Joh.," *Abh. d. Deutschen Archäol. Instituts Kairo, Kpt. Reihe,* 1 [1962]), Cod., III, 17, 11 f., acc. to which the names of the powers, given in acc. with truth ἀλήθεια, correspond to their "true nature" φύσις.

[262] Ev. Phil. (ed. W. C. Till. *Patrist. Texte u. Stud.,* 2 [1963]), Saying 30 (106, 26 ff.) has a rather different distinction between those who are begotten "by nature," i.e., children by their father, and those who are begotten by the Spirit, i.e., converted brethren, cf. on this R. McL. Wilson, *The Gospel of Philip* (1962), 94 f.

[263] In the Apocr. Jn. (→ n. 261) there is a similar question as to the time when the soul returns to the "nature" φύσις of its mother, Cod., III, 35, 21, cf. II, 27, 13 f.; IV, 42, 13 f.

φωνή, φωνέω, συμφωνέω, σύμφωνος, συμφωνία, συμφώνησις

φωνή

Contents: A. The Greek World: 1. Cries of Animals; 2. Voice of Man; 3. Speech; 4. Saying; 5. Utterance of Deity. B. The Old Testament: 1. Noise; 2. Sound of Animals; 3. Voice of Man; 4. Voice of Angels; 5. Voice of God. C. Palestinian Judaism: I. Apocalyptic Writings: 1. Noise and Sound; 2. Voice of Man; 3. Voice of Angels; 4. Voice of God; II. Rabbinic Judaism: 1. Noise and Sound; 2. Voice of Man; 3. Thunder; 4. Voice of God at Sinai; 5. Heavenly Voice. D. Hellenistic Judaism: 1. Septuagint; 2. Aristobulus; 3. Josephus; 4. Philo; E. The New Testament: 1. Noise, Sound; 2. Human Voice; 3. μεγάλη φωνή; 4. Cry, Word, Confession, Speech; 5. The Voice of God; 6. The Heavenly Voice. F. Gnosticism. G. Church History.

A. The Greek world.

φωνή [1] is the audible sound produced by living creatures in the throat: φωνή ψόφος τίς ἐστιν ἐμψύχου, Aristot. An., II, 8, p. 420b, 5, cf. 29 ff.; Hist. An., IV, 9. p. 535a. 27 f., ἀὴρ πεπληγμένος, Zeno in Diog. L., VII, 55, ἡ δι' ὤτων ὑπ' ἀέρος ἐγκεφάλου τε καὶ αἵματος μέχρι ψυχῆς πληγὴ διαδιδομένη, "a shock conveyed by air through the ears to the brain and blood and reaching the soul," Plat. Tim., 67b [2] φωνή is usually distinguished from ψόφος, an inarticulate "noise," and φθόγγος, which can refer to the sound of the human voice but is often used in a broader sense.

1. φωνή denotes the cries of animals, Hom. Od., 10, 239; 12, 86, 396, the song of the nightingale, Od., 19, 521, the twittering of the swallow, Anacreontea, 10, 9. [3] Acc. to Aristot. φωνή is the typical means of mutual self-understanding among animals, Hist. An., IV, 9, p. 535a, 26 ff., but its monotony distinguishes it from the human voice; man communicates through articulated φωνή, Probl., 10, 38 f., p. 895a, 4 ff. [4]

2. φωνή is chiefly used for the voice of man and the organ of speech, Aristot. Hist. An., IV, 9, p. 535a, 32 as well as the sound produced by it, Plat. Phileb., 17b. It is said of Prometheus bound ἵν' οὔτε φωνὴν οὔτε του μορφὴν βροτῶν ὄψῃ, Aesch. Prom., 21 f.; a blind man says: φωνῇ ... ὁρῶ, Soph. Oed. Col., 138. The possibility of variation

---

φ ω ν ή . Bibl.: Liddell-Scott, Moult.-Mill., Pape, Passow, Pr.-Bauer, Preisigke Wört., s.v.

[1] φωνή comes with gradation from root φᾱ- Indo-Eur. * bhā, cf. the verb φημί (Doric-Aeolic φᾱμι) "I say" and also Lat. fārī "to speak," fabula, "story," facundus "eloquent," Old High Germ. bannan "to order," ban "command," "prohibition"; cf. too φήμη (Doric-Aeolic φᾱμα) "news," "call," Lat. fama, infamis "infamous," fas "divine right," then "speech," φάτις "rumour," φάσις "speech," cf. Boisacq, Hofmann, but not Frisk, s.v.

[2] Other def. Plut. Plac. Phil., IV, 19 (II, 902b-e); Sext. Emp. Math., VI, 39-41. The etym. φωνή: ... τὰ ἐν τῷ νῷ φωτίζουσα· ἢ τὸ τοῦ νοὸς φῶς Etym. M., 803, 52 f. are edificatory. Cf. also → n. 63.

[3] Ed. K. Preisendanz (1912). Cf. the section on bird sounds in Poll. Onom., V, 89 f.

[4] Poetic texts sometimes call non-living creatures the source of φωνή, e.g., musical instruments, Eur. Tro., 127; Plut. Quaest. Conv., VII, 8 (II, 713c); Poll. Onom., IV, 86 ff.; cf. ὀργάνων φωναί, Plat. Resp., III, 397a, cf. also → n. 9.

is expressed by the corresponding adj., Hom. Il., 18, 219-221; 17, 696; 13, 45; Plat. Tim., 67b; Aristot. Hist. An., V, 14, p. 544b, 12-545a, 22. Equally manifold are the verbs denoting the sound of the voice: ῥήγνυμι, Hdt., II, 2, 3; Aristoph. Nu., 356, ἵημι, Hdt., IV, 23, 2, ἀφίημι, Jos. Ant., 15, 52, ἐπαίρω, Demosth. Or., 19, 336. φωνή is esp. the loud voice, e.g., the call to battle, Hom. Il., 14, 400; 15, 686; (τῇ) φωνῇ means "aloud," Hom. Il., 3, 161; εἶπε τῇ φωνῇ τὰ ἀπόρρητα (what is secret), Lys., 6, 51. μιᾷ φωνῇ is "unanimously," Luc. Nigrinus, 14; μεγάλη τῇ φωνῇ is common for speaking or crying, Achill. Tat., VIII, 1, 1; Polyb., 15, 29, 11. We have transf. use when there is ref. to the φωνή νόμου, Plat. Leg., XI, 938a, φωνή τῶν πολιτειῶν "forms of state," Plat. Ep., 5, 321d e, καιροῦ φωνή, Demosth. Or., 1, 2, or φωνή τῶν πραγμάτων, Plut. De Eumene, 14 (I, 591d).

3. It is noteworthy that Gk. has no special term for speech as a specific form of human life. [5] φωνή is used quite early for the faculty of speech. φαίη δ᾽ ἂν ἡ θανοῦσα... εἰ φωνὴν λάβοι, "if the dead girl could speak she would agree," Soph. El., 548, παρέσχε φωνὴν τοῖς ἀφωνήτοις τινά, Soph. Oed. Col., 1283. To the shrine of Apollo at Epidaurus a παῖς ἄφωνος is brought ὑπὲρ φωνᾶς "to gain the power of speech," Ditt. Syll.[3], III, 1168, 42-48 (4th cent. B.C.). Speaking is articulation of the voice, Plat. Prot., 322a; Aristot. Hist. An., IV, 9, p. 535a, 31. In a lit. pap. that is musical in content φωνὴν ἔχω means "to express oneself articulately" as opp. to ἐνθουσιάω, P. Hibeh, I, 13, 28 f. (3rd cent. B.C.). φωνή can also be the "speech" of a particular people, Diog. L., VIII, 3 or the "dialect" spoken in a certain district φωνὴ Σκυθική, Hdt., IV, 117, φωνή ... μεταξὺ τῆς τε Χαλκιδέων καὶ Δωρίδος ἐκράθη, Thuc., VI, 5, 1, cf. Plat. Ap., 17d; Crat., 398d; P. Giess., I, 40, 27 (3rd cent. A.D.). φωνὴ βάρβαρος is "speech" a Gk. cannot understand, Aesch. Ag., 1051; Plat. Prot., 341c.

4. A single statement, significant saying, or important declaration can be called φωνή: ἡ Σιμωνίδου φωνή, "the statement of Simonides," Plat. Prot., 341b, αἱ σκεπτικαὶ φωναί, Sext. Emp. Pyrrh. Hyp., I, 14. In the forensic sphere φωνή is the "disposition" ἔχομεν δὴ φωνὴν τοῦ Ἀσπιδᾶ, P. Ryl., II, 77, 46 (2nd cent. A.D.), cf. P. Flor., III, 304, 6 (6th cent. A.D.) or the testamentary "disposition" of the father, P. Oxy., I, 131, 16 (6th/7th cent. A.D.). Finally φωνή means "message" πολλάκι[ς] φωνὴν αὐ[τῷ] ἐβάλομεν, ἵνα ἔλθῃ, P. Mich., III, 220, 20 ff. (296 A.D.), cf. VIII, 488, 16 (2nd cent. A.D.).

5. φωνή can also be the utterance of deity, the organ of the divine fiat by which the sun and stars were made, ὁρκίζω σε τὸν φωστῆρα καὶ ἄστρα ἐν οὐρανῷ ποιήσαντα διὰ φωνῆς προστάγματος, Execration Tablet of Hadrumetum, Audollent Def. Tab., 271, 23 f. (3rd cent. A.D.). Like everything divine, the voice of Zeus has numinous force which strikes man like thunder and causes him almost to die of fright. [6] In this light one can understand the argument of Celsus that if Christ were really divine one would have seen Him to be more than man by extraordinary signs like outstanding size, beauty, power and voice ἢ κατὰ μέγεθος ἢ κάλλος ἢ ἀλκὴν ἢ φωνήν, Orig. Cels., VI, 75. God is invisible to man but shows Himself through the voice κἂν ἄποπτος ᾖς ὅμως, φώνημ᾽ ἀκούω, Soph. Ai., 15 f., cf. Eur. Hipp., 86. When Epimenides wanted to build the shrine of the nymphs ῥαγῆναι φωνὴν ἐξ οὐρανοῦ· Ἐπιμενίδη, μὴ Νυμφῶν, ἀλλὰ Διός, Theopompus (4th cent. B.C.) Fr., 69 (FGrHist, IIb, 549). The sanctuary can also be the place where the divine voice goes forth φωνῆς θείας γενομένης ... ἐκ τοῦ μητρῴου (temple of the divine mother), Ael. Arist. Or., 40, 22 (Keil); ἦλθεν φωνὴ ἀπὸ τοῦ ἀδύτου, with the saying following in direct speech, Ps.-Callisth., I, 45, 2 f. cf. ... ἐκ τοῦ ἱεροῦ τοῦ Διὸς φωνὴν ἀκοῦσαι, Plut. Is. et Os., 12 (II, 355e). Acc. to Plut. Ser. Num.

---

[5] Cf. M. Heidegger, Sein u. Zeit[7] (1953), 165.
[6] μικροῦ μὲν ἐξέθανον ὑπὸ τοῦ δέους, εἱστήκειν δὲ ὅμως ἀχανὴς ("with open mouth") καὶ ὑπὸ τῆς μεγαλοφωνίας ἐμβεβροντημένος, Luc. Icaromenipp., 23.

Vind., 32 (II, 567 f.) it sounded forth from a suddenly shining φῶς μέγα. At the birth of Osiris a mysterious voice declared that the Lord of All was manifested: τῇ μὲν πρώτῃ τὸν "Οσιριν γενέσθαι, καὶ φωνὴν αὐτῷ τεχθέντι συνεκπεσεῖν, Plut. Is. et Os., 12 (II, 355e). Artapanus hellenises the story of the call of Moses: At the burning bush a φωνὴ θεία commanded him to take the field against Egypt and to liberate the Jews, Eus. Praep. Ev., 9, 27, 21.

The Delphic Pythia is esp. the mediator of the voice of God. Xenoph. has Socrates ask in his defence: ἡ δὲ Πυθοῖ ἐν τῷ τρίποδι ἱέρεια οὐ καὶ αὐτὴ φωνῇ τὰ παρὰ τοῦ θεοῦ διαγγέλλει; [7] with a ref. to other ways by which the Gks. have sought the direction of the gods, Ap., 12 f. But Socrates also appeals to a voice of God to him as a directive force, Plat. Ap., 31d. This was a serious attack on popular belief in the oracle. Acc. to Socrates God speaks to the individual who apart from external criteria and alien authorities must himself decide whether he will understand and obey the voice of conscience as the voice of God. One finds a similar idea in relation to legislation → IV, 1025, 6 ff. As in the ancient Orient (Hammurapi, the giving of the Law at Sinai), so among the Gks. the legal order can be traced back to the saying of a divine voice. Acc. to Ael. Arist. Or., 45, 11 (Dindorf): οὔκουν φασί γ᾽ ἐκεῖνον οὐδὲν θεῖναι Λακεδαιμονίοις ἄνευ τῆς παρὰ τοῦ θεοῦ φωνῆς and acc. to Oenomaus in Eus. Praep. Ev., 5, 28, 2: ἴδωμεν τὴν θείαν φωνὴν καὶ ἃ ἐδίδαξας τὸν Λυκοῦργον Lycurgus received the laws at Delphi from the voice of God. [8] This thought is weakened when Antiochus I of Commagene (1st cent. B.C.) stated in his introduction to the pronouncements of sacred law made by him: νόμον δὲ τοῦτον φωνὴ μὲν ἐξήγγειλεν ἐμή, νοῦς δὲ θεῶν ἐκύρωσεν, Ditt. Or., I, 383, 121 f. The king is inspired and as such he is God's spokesman. [9]

B. The Old Testament.

In the LXX φωνή is in by far the majority of instances a transl. of Hbr. קוֹל, more rarely of the defective קֹל, Aram. קָל, for which there is, oddly enough, no corresponding Hbr. verb. [10] קוֹל in the OT means everything that can be heard.

1. קוֹל, rarely with art., means "noise," abs. plur. "claps of thunder," Ex. 9:23, 29, 33 f.; 19:16; 20:18; 1 S. 12:17 f.; Job 28:26; 38:25; cf. 1 S. 7:10; Ps. 77:18; Job 38:25; Ex. 9:28. Often קוֹל is more closely def. by a gen., the "roar" of gt. masses of water, Ps. 42:7; 93:3 f.; Ez. 1:24; 43:2, of the primal flood, Hab. 3:10, the "swish" of rain, 1 K. 18:41, the "rolling" of an earthquake, Ez. 37:7, the "sound" of steps, Gn. 3:8; 1 K. 14:6; 2 K. 6:32, esp. of approaching soldiers, 2 S. 5:24; 2 K. 11:13 par. 2 Ch. 23:12, the "trampling" of horses, Jer. 4:29; 47:3; 2 K. 7:6; Ez. 26:10, the "rolling" of wheels, 2 K. 7:6; Ez. 3:13; 26:10; Na. 3:2; Jl. 2:5, the "whistling" of whips, Na. 3:2. קוֹל also denotes the tumult of a large and excited crowd, 1 K. 1:40, 45, a city, 1:41, cf. הֲמוֹן(הַ) קוֹל 1 S. 4:14; Ez. 23:42, the "noise" of a camp, Ez. 1:24, of warriors, 2 K. 7:6, of war, Ex. 32:17; Jer. 50:22, of the battle cry תְּרוּעָה 1 S. 4:6; Ez. 21:27; אֵין קוֹל "no noise" could be heard, 1 K. 18:26, 29;

---

[7] Cf. Ael. Arist. Or., 45, 11 (Dindorf) of the Pythia: ἡ δὲ ἀπεκρίνατο ὡς ἐδόκει τῷ θεῷ.

[8] The Pythia was the organ of the voice of God.

[9] The Memnon colossi in West Thebes, two giant statues of Amenophis III, form a unique phenomenon, since a crack in one of the statues from 27 B.C. caused it to make a sound at sunrise. The many inscr. by visitors describe the puzzling sound as θεία φωνή, Preisigke Sammelb., V, 8213, 2 (130 A.D.), ἱερὰ φωνή, 8349, A 2 (1st/2nd cent. A.D.), φωνή, 8359, 5 (1st/2nd cent. A.D.) etc. [Kelber].

[10] But cf. Accad. qâlū "to speak, cry," Eth. kalha, "to cry," and Arab. qāla "to say." קוֹל is related to Accad. qûlu "call" and Ugaritic ʾql "sound." The same root occurs in Phoenician ql, Arab. qaulun and Eth. qal. The noun קָהֵל (summoned) "assembly" may come from this root, though cf. J. Barr, The Semantics of Bibl. Language (1961), 119-129.

2 K. 4:31. [11] קוֹל can also signify other noises like the "rustling" of the wings of the cherubim on the throne chariot of God, Ez. 1:24 f.; 3:13; 10:5 and of the requickened bones, Ez. 37:7, the "crackling" of fire, Jer. 11:16; Jl. 2:5; Qoh. 7:6, the "rustling" of the leaf, Lv. 26:36, the "grinding" of the millstones, Jer. 25:10; Qoh. 12:4, and finally the soft "rustle" of a slight breath of air, 1 K. 19:12. In a transf. sense קוֹל is the "sound" of the fall of a gt. nation or ruler, Jer. 49:21; Ez. 26:15; 31:16. It is also the "sound" of musical instruments, esp. the "ram's horn" שׁוֹפָר, Am. 2:2; Ez. 33:4 f.; Ex. 19:16; 20:18; 2 S. 6:15; 15:10; 1 K. 1:41; Jer. 4:21; 6:17; 42:14; Ps. 47:5; 98:6; Job 39:24, "trumpets" חֲצֹצְרוֹת, 2 Ch. 5:13, "zithers" כִּנּוֹר, Ez. 26:13, "flutes" עוּגָב, Job 21:12, and the "bells" on the upper garment of the high-priest, Ex. 28:35, cf. Sir. 45:9. קוֹל at the beginning of a sentence or clause is often to be transl. as an interjection "Listen" to draw attention to a noise or voice, [12] Ju. 5:11; Is. 13:4; 40:3, 6; 52:8; 66:6; Jer. 3:21; 4:15; 8:19; 10:22; 31:15; 50:28; 51:54; Mi. 6:9; Zeph. 1:14; Cant. 2:8; 5:2.

2. Often קוֹל denotes the sound made by animals: the "baaing" of sheep, 1 S. 15:14, the "bellowing" of cattle, Jer. 9:9, the "neighing" of horses, Jer. 8:16, the "roaring" of lions, Jer. 2:15; Am. 3:4; Job 4:10; Ez. 19:7, 9, cf. Zech. 11:3, the "cooing" of turtle-doves, Na. 2:8; Cant. 2:14, the "twittering" of birds, Qoh. 12:4; Ps. 104:12; Zph. 2:14 and the "hissing" of snakes, Jer. 46:22.

3. קוֹל means esp. the sound of the human voice קוֹל אָדָם, 2 K. 7:10; Da. 8:16, though not the organ of speech or speech → 279, 12 ff. קוֹל hovers between "sound" and "voice" when there is closer def. by a noun, e.g., "crying" קוֹל בְּכִי Is. 65:19; Ps. 6:8, cf. Job 30:31; Ezr. 3:13, "lamenting" קוֹל צְעָקָה 1 S. 4:14; Jer. 51:54; Ez. 27:28, cf. Zech. 11:3, "fear" קוֹל פְּחָדִים Job 15:21, cf. Jer. 30:5, "groaning" קוֹל אֲנָחָה Ps. 102:6, "jubilation" קוֹל רִנָּה Is. 48:20 and the stereotyped expression "mirth and gladness, the voice of the bridegroom, and the voice of the bride," Jer. 7:34; 16:9; 25:10; 33:11. קוֹל is also the agent of other expressions of mutual relationship and is modified accordingly, e.g., for song, Ex. 32:18; Is. 51:3; Ps. 98:5, cf. Sir. 50:18, greeting, Prv. 27:14; blasphemy, Ps. 44:16 and cursing, Lv. 5:1. The strength of vocal utterance can be expressed by verbal turns of speech. One "utters" נָתַן the voice, Am. 1:2; Prv. 2:3; 8:1, calling aloud, Jer. 4:16; 12:8; 22:20; 48:34; Hab. 3:10, one can "lift it up" נָשָׂא Ju. 9:7, esp. in crying, Gn. 21:16; 27:38; Ju. 21:2; 1 S. 11:4; 24:17; 30:4; 2 S. 3:32; 13:36; Rt. 1:9, 14; Job 2:12, but also joy and rejoicing, Is. 24:14, [13] or one can "raise" it הֵרִים Gn. 39:15, 18; Is. 13:2; 40:9; 58:1; Job 38:34; Ezr. 3:12; Sir. 51:9 and thus "speak haughtily against someone," 2 K. 19:22 par. Is. 37:23. One can speak with a "high" voice (בְּ)קוֹל רָם Dt. 27:14, a "great," i.e., loud voice (בְּ)קוֹל גָּדוֹל Gn. 39:14; 1 S. 28:12; 2 S. 15:23; 19:5; 1 K. 8:55; 18:27 f.; 2 K. 18:28 par. Is. 36:13; Ez. 8:18; 11:13; Prv. 27:14; Ezr. 3:12; 10:12; Neh. 9:4; 2 Ch. 32:18, or with a "lovely voice" יְפֵה קוֹל, Ez. 33:32, or can make the voice friendly חָנַן, Prv. 26:25, or send it forth, הֶעֱבִיר, publish something in the camp, city, or land, Ex. 36:6; Ezr. 1:1; 10:7; 2 Ch. 30:5; 36:22. The voice is individual. It enables us to recognise the speaker, cf. the voice of Jacob in Gn. 27:22, cf. Ju. 18:3; 1 S. 24:17; 26:17.

קוֹל also occurs with ref. to dealings between man and God. In the abs. it denotes "petition," Dt. 26:7; 33:7; Ju. 13:9; 1 S. 1:13; 2 S. 22:7; 1 K. 17:22; Is. 58:4; Ps. 5:3; 119:149; 130:2; Jon. 2:3, or shows itself in context to be complaint in prayer, Dt. 1:45; Ps. 55:17, or vow, Nu. 21:2 f. A gen. attribute indicates often that the prayer is esp. loud or fervent, Ps. 5:3; 28:2, 6; 31:22; 86:6; 116:1; 140:7. The utterance may be defined as thanksgiving,

---

[11] We find groups of noises in Ez. 32:17 f.; 1 K. 1:40-45; 2 K. 7:6; Ez. 1:24; 3:13; 26:10; Na. 3:2; Jl. 2:5.

[12] קוֹל is not taken as an interjection, of course, in LXX and Targum, cf. Is. 40:3, 6; 52:8.

[13] Nu. 14:1; Is. 3:7; 42:2, 11; Job 21:12 have the expression without קוֹל.

Jon. 2:10, rejoicing, Ps. 42:4; 47:1; 118:15, or praise, Ps. 66:8. קוֹל קָרָא in Ps. 3:4; 27:7, cf. 142:1; Ez. 8:18 means "to pray aloud," cf. also the recitation of benediction in 1 K. 8:55 and cursing in Dt. 27:14. קוֹל is the vocal utterance of the whole people in response to God, Dt. 26:7, or in weeping before Him, Ju. 2:4, or lamentation, Nu. 14:1, or crying for help, Nu. 20:16, or united promise of obedience, Ex. 24:3, or common praise, 2 Ch. 5:13, or rebellion against Him, Dt. 1:34; Jer. 12:8.

4. קוֹל is related to angels with relative infrequency, although the heavenly world was not thought to be without voice or language. Acc. to Ps. 19:2 f. the heavens declare the glory of God and the firmament displays His handiwork. Days and nights cry out God's praise to one another, and in this way maintain an unbroken tradition from the beginning of creation. [14] It is true that no one can hear their voice, v. 4. On the other hand, the cries of the seraphim as they magnify God can be understood, and they are so loud that they cause the lintels of the temple to shake, Is. 6:3 f. Similarly the sound of the words that the interpreting angel speaks to Daniel is as the sound of a tumultuous mob, Da. 10:6, cf. v. 9. In many cases the heavenly speaker remains anonymous; the prophet hears only a directive voice, Is. 40:3, 6, cf. Ez. 1:28. In Da. 4:28 a voice comes from heaven and declares the judgment on Nebuchadnezzar.

5. God's self-revelation can take audible form. God is neither seen nor apprehended, but He is heard. [15] In distinction from the naive mythological speech of God, when He addressed Himself like a man to the patriarchs, Moses and Joshua, [16] the word קוֹל points to the superhuman and numinous power of the divine revelation, with less emphasis on the wording than in the older tradition.

In about 50 of some 560 instances God is the author of קוֹל. The angels hear the "sound" of His Word of command, Ps. 103:20. God is also a voice to Moses speaking to him from the cover of the cherubim throne, Nu. 7:89. The sound of thunder is God's voice in Am. 1:2; Is. 29:6; 30:30 f., cf. Jer. 25:30; Jl. 2:11; 3:16; 2 S. 22:14 par. Ps. 18:13; "he thunders with his lofty voice," Job 37:4; cf. 1 S. 7:10. The rustling of the wings of the cherubim is like "the voice of the Almighty when he speaks," Ez. 10:5, cf. 1:24. Ancient Israel shares this idea with the Assyrians [17] and Canaanites. [18] Yahweh's voice in the

---

[14] G. v. Rad, Theol. d. AT, I[5] (1966), 373. These vv., which remind us of the Gk. idea of the music of the spheres, find a par. in the Ugaritic texts. Gordon Manual 'nt, III, 21 f. = Baal, V, III, 39 f. (G. R. Driver, Canaanite Myths and Legends [1956], 87) = V, AB, C, 21 f. (J. Aistleitner, Die mythol. u. kultischen Texte v. Ras Schamra[2] [1964], 27) tells of the "sighing and murmuring of heaven to earth, of the oceans to the stars." The term tant, however, is used rather than ql, cf. C. H. Gordon, Before the Bible (1962), 192.

[15] K. Barth, K.D., I, 1[6] (1952), 93 (C.D., I, 1 [1936], 101 ff.).

[16] J. Lindblom, "D. Vorstellung vom Sprechen Jahwes z. d. Menschen im AT," ZAW, 75 (1963), 263-288.

[17] We find the equation of thunder and the voice of God on the Kurba'il statue of Shalmaneser III discovered at Nimrud in 1961 (cf. J. V. Kinnier Wilson, "The Kurba'il Statue of Shalmaneser III," Iraq, 24 [1962], 93-6). Here the storm-god Hadad is lauded as the bold one whose voice (pî, literally "mouth") is of incomparable power, line 2, who causes the rain to fall, the lightning to flash and the plants to grow, line 5, at whose voice (pi-šu) the hills shake and the seas rise up, line 6.

[18] The storm-god Baal "lifts up his voice in the clouds" w⟨y⟩tn qlh b'rpt, Gordon Manual, 51, V, 70 = Baal, II, V, 8 (Driver, 97) = II, AB, IV-V (Aistleitner, 41), cf. Ps. 18:13. Since in so doing he gives abundant rain, he lifts up his "voice for good," Gordon Man., 1 Aqht, I, 46 = Aqhat, I, I, 46 (Driver, 61) = I, D, 46 (Aistleitner, 77). When the prophets of Baal at Carmel seek "a voice and answer" from their god in 1 K. 18:26, they are obviously hoping for a storm to break the drought. Cf. also in the Babyl. creation epic Enuma eliš, Tabl. 7, 47 (Ancient Near Eastern Texts Relating to the OT, ed. J. B. Pritchard[2] [1955], 72), where we have the wish: "May his (sc. the god Addu) beneficent roaring be heavy upon the earth!"

thunder causes the earth to tremble [19] when He rides on the wind and clouds, Ps. 18:7-15 par. 2 S. 22:8-16; Ps. 68:34; Hab. 3:15 f. [20] and proclaims His power through the sound of thunder, Is. 29:6; Job 37:2-5; 40:9. [21]

The (thunder) voice of Yahweh is expressly depicted in Ps. 29 with its description of a storm from the west. The double sense of קוֹל comes to full expression here. The "thunder" is not just a natural force [22] but the rumbling majestic voice of God, the Creator of the world, the Judge and the Holy Warrior, to which the chorus of heavenly beings responds in wonder and praise, v. 9b and which strikes with terror the enemies of Israel and the power of chaos. At creation the waters of the primal flood are chased from the earth by the rebuke of God's voice of thunder, Ps. 104:7. In the days of the monarchy Israel's deliverance at the Red Sea is viewed as a victory of this voice of Yahweh over the flood of chaos, Ps. 77:16-20. Israel's foes, the agents of chaos, are frightened by the voice of Yahweh in the holy war, 1 S. 7:10; Jl. 2:11; Ps. 46:6. This voice declares judgment on the nations and executes it, Jl. 3:16; Is. 30:30 f.; Jer. 25:30 f.

When the classical prophets speak of receiving the Word of God, rather remarkably they do not mention the voice of Yahweh. The reason for this is not to be sought merely in the non-Israelite origin of the idea but more esp. in the fact that while the voice of thunder (→ 282, 25 ff.) presents God as *numen tremendum* it does not reveal His direction or clear Word, and the prophet takes himself to be the messenger of this Word. [23] Only Is. (6:8) and Ez. (1:28 f., cf. 10:5) speak of God's voice in their visions of calling and in connection with the act of sending. קוֹל, then, is the appeal or reference to God's mighty presence; it is not yet word, revelation, direction, or oracle.

This also applies to the older Sinai tradition in Ex. 19:16-20; 20:18-21 (E). Here the claps of thunder קֹלֹת, the lightnings and the sound קוֹל of the ram's horn are signs of God's coming in the concealment of thick cloud. God answers Moses בְקוֹל in Ex. 19:19, and here the ref. is not just to the noise of thunder but also to the intelligible "voice" of God, [24] cf. Sir. 45:5. The people is unable to hear God's speaking in the storm, Ex. 20:18 f. The sound of the ram's horn has the significance of an epiphany in 2 S. 6:15; Ps. 47:5; 81:3; 98:6, and it has been suggested that this was brought into the Sinai tradition of a storm theophany under the influence of the cultus. [25]

---

[19] Cf. the idea of the sacred voice which in its echo causes the earth to quake and shakes the heights to east and west, Gordon Man., 51, VII, 29-34 = Baal, II, VII, 29-34 (Driver, 101) = II, AB, VII, 29-34 (Aistleitner, 45).

[20] For the relation of storm and earthquake in Ps. 18:7 ff.; 29:3 ff.; Ex. 19:16 ff. and in Canaanite texts cf. M. Blankenhorn, "Neue Erdbeben in Jerusalem," ZDPV, 51 (1928), 124 f.

[21] In the Tammuz liturgies (ed. M. Witzel, "Tammuzlit. u. Verwandtes," *Analecta Orientalia*, 10 [1935]), p. 9, 64 f.; 121 ff.; 157, 7 f. the complaint of the god that has been attacked by the underworld finds expression as a roaring storm going forth from the sanctuary and spreading over the earth.

[22] The OT can use רַעַם "roaring," "noise" for thunder. Some thunder is thought to be caused by God but is not experienced as His voice. Thus Yahweh brings the disaster of thunder and hail on the Egyptians, Ex. 9:23 f., or He uses a man of God to send untimely thunder and rain, 1 S. 12:17 f.

[23] A theology of the Word developed later, G. Fohrer, *Elia* (1957), 46. On the many formulae which the prophet uses to describe reception of God's Word cf. Lindblom, *op. cit.*, 282 f. and C. Westermann, *Grundformen prophetischer Rede*² (1964).

[24] In the comm. there is vacillation between "thunder," so O. Eissfeldt, *Hexateuchsynopse* (1922), *ad loc.* and "audible voice," so M. Noth, *Das zweite Buch Mose, AT Deutsch,* 5⁴ (1968), *ad loc.*, so also H. Schmid, "Mose, Überlieferung u. Gesch.," ZAW Beih., 110 (1968), 57. Undoubtedly the voice is meant but there is some ambivalence as between thunder and voice.

[25] Cf. W. Beyerlin, *Herkunft u. Gesch. d. ältesten Sinaitradition* (1961), 155.

Dt. strengthens the visual phenomena of the Sinai theophany, 4:11 f.; 5:22 f. but the decisive pts. are still the voice of God and the event of receiving the Word of which the whole people, including the present generation, is a witness, cf. Dt. 5:4; 9:15 with Ex. 3:2; 33:11. It perceives no form but only the "sound of words," 4:12. God causes His voice to be heard in order to instruct Israel, 4:36; He pronounces the decalogue from out of the fire, 4:12 f., 33; 5:22-24. Acc. to Dt. 5:25 f. קוֹל is the "voice" with which God makes known His will to assembled Israel and there is no further mention of the thunderings of Ex. 19; 20. This is an unheard of wonder, for never has a corporeal being heard the voice of God from the midst of the fire and lived, 5:26.

In 1 K. 19 the phenomena of theophany and the speaking of Yahweh are separated. It is true that God's coming to Horeb is intimated by cosmic signs, the wind, the earthquake and the fire. But He is not in these, v. 11 f. Elijah perceives the presence of God by the "sound of a still small blowing" קוֹל דְּמָמָה דַקָּה, [26] v. 12b; God speaks to Him through a voice, v. 13. When God declares His will to the prophet, this is done through a whispered word, Ez. 3:10; Job 26:14; Is. 50:4 f. The Ps. attest to the continued life of the Sinai tradition in the cultus, esp. in Ps. 50 and 81. The storm theophany is depicted in 50:3, cf. 81:7, but the dominant pt. is the Word of God that all can understand: the call to judgment in 50:4-6, God's accusation in 50:7-23, and the recitation of His saving acts by an unknown voice in 81:4-16.

This path from a numinous How of revelation to a clearly intelligible What is completed in the pre-exilic period, especially in Jeremiah, Deuteronomy and the Deuteronomic histories. The phrase "hearkening to the voice of God" becomes a stereotyped one in exhortation and preaching. [27] Since the basic revelation of God's will is well back in time, it has to be actualised in preaching and proclaimed as the summons of God issued here and now. Thus in Ps. 95:7 the voice of God is the Word which was commanded by Moses but which is preached and which calls for decision to-day. Keeping the traditional Law of the covenant is described as "hearkening to the voice of God," a formula which may be traced back to the cultic reading of the Law, Dt. 4:30; 8:20; 13:5, 19; 15:5; 26:14; Ju. 2:2; 6:10; 1 S. 12:14; 15:1 ff.; 2 K. 18:12. This "hearing the voice of God" is the quintessence of Yahweh worship (Jos. 24:24) and true obedience (Jer. 3:13, 25; 7:23, 28; 18:10; 22:21; 26:13; 40:3; 42:6, 13, 21). It decides Israel's weal or woe, Dt. 8:20; 28:45; 30:20; Jos. 5:6. It is more or less equivalent to keeping God's commandments, Dt. 13:5; 26:17; 27:10; 28:1, 15, 45; 30:8, 10, or keeping His covenant, 2 K. 18:12.

In another area of Israel's religion the voice of Yahweh finds actualisation in the preaching Word of personified wisdom. In open places, Prv. 1:20, on high places by the

---

[26] The still small breathing must be atmospheric, cf. Ps. 107:29, where דְּמָמָה is the opp. of "storm" סְעָרָה. LXX transl. 1 K. 19:12b by φωνὴ αὔρας λεπτῆς, cf. Job 4:16 and v. Rad, op. cit., II⁴ (1965), 28 f. How this is connected with the other Sinai traditions is not altogether clear. Is there intentional antithesis between 1 K. 19 and Ex. 19, so Fohrer, op. cit., 58 f. but not R. de Vaux, Élie le prophète (1956), 67? Perhaps 1 K. 19 is stressing the difference between the revelation of Yahweh and that of the thunder god Baal. Yahweh also sends fire, 1 K. 18:38, cf. 2 K. 1:9-12, along with cloud, storm and rain, 1 K. 18:45. But He is not tied to them and can show His power also by closing heaven, so that neither dew nor rain will fall, 1 K. 17:1 and by silencing the storm god Baal, 1 K. 18:26, 29. In particular the ambivalence of Ex. 19 is resolved. "God passes by in the storm, the earthquake and the fire, but He tarries only when He causes Elijah to hear Him from the stillness," H. Gese, "Bemerkungen zur Sinaitradition," ZAW, 79 (1967), 145 f.

[27] Cf. already Ex. 19:5 unless it is a later addition there. Beyerlin, op. cit., 78-90 regards שָׁמַע בְּקוֹל יהוה as at any rate pre-Deuteronomistic. It is one of the most important features in the exhortations of Dt. and the Deuteronomic histories.

way and in the middle of the paths it causes its voice to sound forth, Prv. 8:1. In the forms of prophetic proclamation we sometimes find the same cry of wisdom as it demands a hearing, Is. 28:23; 32:9, cf. Ps. 49:1 f. We also recall at this pt. the Servant of the Lord in Dt. Is., who when he brings truth to the peoples "does not cause his voice to be heard in the streets," Is. 42:1 f.

C. Palestinian Judaism.

I. Apocalyptic Writings.

The use of קוֹל or equivalents in the apocal. writings is often shaped by the OT, esp. in the case of Qumran. But there is a shift from the sense of "noise" to that of "voice" which is important in relation to the concept of God's voice.

1. Noise and Sound. קוֹל denotes "noise," e.g., the "roaring" of many waters, 1 QH 2:16. This ref. to the fuming of enemies and it sets them in the sphere of chaos, [28] cf. Ps. 93:4, to whose eschatological manifestations the "noise" of clouds also belongs, 1 QH 3:13, cf. 3:16. קוֹל is mentioned esp. in connection with the war of the end-time with its "sound of a gt. multitude and noise of divine beings and men," 1 QM 1:1, the sounding of ram's horns with which the hosts produce a terrible din of battle, 1 QM 8:10 f.; 9:1, and finally the distinctive signal of the trumpets blown by the priests (→ VII, 82, 2 ff.), 8:5, 7, 9, 12, 14; 16:5, 7; 17:10. [29] In the vision of the eagle in 4 Esr. two of the beasts have a voice, the eagle (i.e., Rome) and the lion (i.e., the Messiah), which announces judgment to the former with a man's voice, 11:37-45, cf. 12:32.

2. Voice of Man. קוֹל is more important as a vocal utterance of man whether as jubilation in praise of God's gt. deeds, 1 QH 11:25 f.; Test. Jos. 8:5, triumph at the final victory, 1 QM 12:15, cf. 11:25 f., sighing at present affliction, 1 QH 9:4, foolish laughter, 1 QS 7:14, or the voicing of prayer, Test. Jos. 9:4. Man's faculty of speech is designed esp. for the service of God's praise, 1 QH 1:28-30. Early reflection on the faculty has a Hell. tinge. Speech is a miracle of creation in 1 QH 1:27-29. The time before creation is characterised as a period in which the *sonus vocis hominum nondum erat,* 4 Esr. 6:39. The last time will bring miraculous phenomena of speech. Children one year of age will speak with their voices, 4 Esr. 6:2 [30] and the stones will lift up their voices, 5:5. Gn. 4:10 is interpreted in terms of a belief just entering Palestine at the time, the belief in the continued existence of the soul. The soul of Abel lifts up its voice in the realm of the dead so that it is heard in heaven, Eth. En. 22:5 f. [31]

3. Voice of Angels. The angels praise God with one voice. Eth. En. 47:2; 61:7, 9, 11, cf. Apc. Abr. 18:2; Slav. En. 19:6. Heavenly voices laud the faithfulness of man, e.g., of Abraham, Jub. 17:15, and Michael, the Revealer of Jub., speaks with the voice of God baqāla 'ĕgziabḫēr, Jub. 2:1. Michael mediates to Abraham the divine command that he must leave his homeland, Jub. 12:22, cf. Gn. 12:1-3; an angel tells Ezra "to hearken to his voice," 4 Esr. 8:19. The demons also hearken to the "voice" of Mastema, Jub. 10:8. The voices of the heavenly hosts that go forth for the eschatological war are raised in a battle-cry, 1 QH 3:35, cf. 1 QM 1:11. Acc. to 4 Esr. 13:3 f. the voice of the One like the Son of Man causes all foes to melt away like wax, cf. 13:10 (based on Is. 11:4) and 13:33 → VIII, 427, 15 ff.

---

[28] But cf. the hymn to the Creator in 11 QPsa Col. 26, 10 (DJD, IV [1965], 47), where הֲמוֹן מַיִם רַבִּים is thought of in terms of theophany.

[29] The horses must be trained so that they can stand any kind of noise, whether trumpet blasts or the noise of battle, 1 QM 6:13.

[30] Cf. on this Eth. En. 106:3: Reborn Noah prays to God.

[31] We also find the belief that the blood of the righteous cries for retribution, Jub. 4:3; 2 Macc. 8:3 f.; Eth. En. 47:1.

4. Voice of God. The apocal. view of God's voice is influenced on the one side by expectation of a new eschatological revelation and on the other by heightened awareness of the divine transcendence. The miracle of God's voice is recounted both of the remote past and also of the near future. The OT tradition is interpreted accordingly. Thunder (→ 282, 25 ff.) is separated from the revelation of the Word. [32] It is sent by God, Sib., 3, 1. 302. 433, and like lightning it is a blessing or a curse acc. to God's behest, Eth. En. 59:1-3. But the "voices of thunder" which are laid up in heaven (Eth. En. 69:23) are under the control of specific angels (Jub. 2:2) and are treated like other natural phenomena. [33] Special emphasis is laid on the revelation by Word in exegesis of the events at Sinai. It is said of the congregation there: μεγαλεῖον δόξης εἶδον οἱ ὀφθαλμοὶ αὐτῶν καὶ δόξαν φωνῆς αὐτοῦ ἤκουσεν τὸ οὖς αὐτῶν, Sir. 17:13. Moses esp. has seen God's glory and heard His voice, 45:3-5, cf. Ps.-Philo, 11, 6. 14.

Similarly in a hymnal passage in the War Scroll the representatives of the true Israel are called "hearers of the divine voice" and "those who saw the (holy) angels," 1 QM 10:10 f. 1 QH Fr. 12:5 [34] speaks of the "glorious voice." We are reminded of Deuteronomistic usage in the employment of קול in Damasc. The Israelites led by Moses hearkened "to the voice of their Creator, to the commandments of their teacher," 3:7 f. (4:7), Moses being the teacher and interpreter of God's voice. To-day God's voice comes through the teacher of the sect and obedience to the Torah is seen as "hearkening to the voice of the teacher of righteousness," 20:32 (9:53), cf. 20:28 (9:50). [35] The transcendence of God is seen esp. when in Haggadic accounts mysterious OT figures are addressed by a voice from heaven behind which stands God as the author, cf. Enoch in Eth. En. 13:8, Noah in 65:4 and Baruch in S. Bar. 13:1; 22:1. When the high-priest of the end-time is instituted the heavens open and from the sanctuary of glory holiness will come down on him μετὰ φωνῆς πατρικῆς ὡς ἀπὸ ᾿Αβραὰμ πρὸς ᾿Ισαάκ, Test. L. 18:6, i.e., God speaks to him as a father to his son, cf. Gn. 22:2, 7 f. The proclamation of the last judgment has universal validity, cf. 4 Esr. 5:7: et dabit vocem noctu, quem [36] non noverunt multi, omnes autem audient vocem eius. In 4 Esr. 6:13-29 a mighty voice whose sound is as that of many waters (6:17) is known by its content to be the voice of the world-judge, 6:18-29.

II. Rabbinic Judaism.

In Rabb. Judaism, too, קול has the same range of meaning as in the OT. It never means "speech" לָשׁוֹן or "word" דִּבּוּר but it denotes everything else that may be heard, "noise," "sound," "voice."

1. Noise and Sound. קול is "noise," e.g., of a door opening, Tamid, 3, 7 f., of the shovel, 3, 8, or excavation, BQ, 5, 6, the disruptive noise of a hammer, millstones, playing children, or men going in and out, BB, 2, 3, lamentation, Ber., 9, 3. Three noises are not

---

[32] Apc. Abr., in a hymnal prayer, says that God's voice is like thunder, but in 18:13 Abraham hears His voice as that of a man. There is no ref. to thunder in the (brief) allusions to Sinai in Jub. 1:1-3; 1 Q 34bis Col. 2:6 f. (DJD, I, 154); 4 Esr. 1:18 f. It is one of the elements in the depiction of the external accompaniments in Ps.-Philo, Antiquitates Biblicae, 11, 5 (ed. G. Kisch, Publications in Mediaeval Studies, 10 [1949]).

[33] It is worthy of note that in Jub. 2:2 "voices" are mentioned with thunder and lightning, i.e., קול carries the sense of both thunder and voice.

[34] Ed. A. Habermann, Megilloth midbar Yehuda (1959), 140.

[35] Perhaps at 1 QH 14:17 one should supplement as follows: "for they (have) not (hearkened to) thy (voice)," so J. Licht, Megillath ha-Hodayoth (1957), 94. The "beloved of the Lord" promised in Test. B. 11:2 is characterised in some MSS as ἀκούων τὴν φωνὴν αὐτοῦ (sc. κυρίου). In Bar. 1:18, 21; 2, 5 ff.; 3, 4 the Deuteronomistic expression "hearkening to the voice of Yahweh" is the epitome of proper obedience to the Torah, cf. A. Kahana, הספרים החיצונים, II[3] (1960), 355-361.

[36] MS quam, emended by G. H. Box, "IV Ezra," R. H. Charles, The Apocr. and Pseudepigr. of the OT, II (1913), ad loc.

heard even though they move from one end of the earth to the other: that of the wheels of the sun-chariot, that of the city of Rome, and that of the soul parting from the body at death, bYoma, 20b. קוֹל is also the "sound" of the ram's horn, RH, 3, 7 and other musical instruments, Tamid, 3, 8.

2. Voice of Man. קוֹל is esp. the "voice" [37] by which man communicates, bBer., 24b. קוֹל is a principle of individuation. Along with appearance and thought it is an essential mark of the individual, bSanh., 38a. The voice can rejoice the heart, bBer., 57b; God wants to hear the beloved voice of Israel, M. Ex., 7, 3 on 19:17 (p. 215, 1). Dear is the voice of Israel in prayer, ibid., 2, 2 on 14:13 (p. 94, 12) acc. to Cant. 2:14. In contrast to the OT a loud voice is regarded as unseemly in prayer and worship since it may spring from man's need to assert himself. [38] But because of heretics it is ordered that the "Hear, O Israel" be recited out loud, bPes., 56a. He who does good makes no noise, Gn. r., 16, 3 on 2:13. קוֹל can also mean "report" (jJeb., 1, 1 [13c, 46]; jKet., 6, 1 [30c, 55]), or "rumour" (bGit., 89a b). In a transf. sense we find the voice of the scroll in RH 3:7 and Gehinnom in bAZ, 17a. Sarah's voice is declared to be that of the Holy Ghost in Gn. r., 45, 2 on 16:2. Acc. to Pesikt. r., 35 (161a) Elijah will appear three days before the coming of the Messiah, setting himself on the mountains of Israel (cf. Is. 52:7) and causing his voice to be heard from one end of the world to the other. He proclaims to all men the revelation of the glory and kingship of God.

3. Thunder. קוֹל in the abs. means "thunder," esp. in the plur., bBB, 16a; M. Ex., 7, 1 on 19:2 (p. 205, 20). The understanding of the "voices of thunder" קוֹלוֹת is important. They come from God (bBB, 162) and may have significance as a means of universal declaration. For three whole hours the death of a rabbi is proclaimed by thunder and lightning, jPea, 1, 1 (15d, 40 f.). Claps of thunder are the sixth of the seven signs that intimate the coming of the Messiah, bSanh., 97a; bMeg., 17b.

4. Voice of God at Sinai. Rabb. exegesis examined closely the events at Sinai and the קּלֹת of Ex. 19 f. While M. Ex. sees in Ex. 19:16 a ref. to various "claps of thunder" קוֹלֵי קוֹלוֹת, 7, 3, ad loc. (p. 214, 7 f.), cf. Tanch. לך לך, 6 on Gn. 14:1 (Buber, 63), and while bYoma, 4b thinks the ref. is to the voice of God that Moses alone can hear, Ex. r., 28, 6 on 20:1 thinks that at Sinai God spoke to Israel directly and not through a Bath Qol → 288, 8 ff.; the people saw His glory and heard His voice, Ex. r., 29, 4 on 20:2. In the light of the more drab present with its poverty of revelations, the events at Sinai seem to be full of wonders, Ex. r., 5, 9 on 4:27. Speculation is aroused esp. by the plur. "voices" in Ex. 19:16 and by the fact that they could be seen, 20:18. There is a twofold development. Stress is laid on the numinous power and also on the universal range [39] and adaptability of the voice of God. The power of the divine voice caused the souls of the hearers to melt, Ex. r., 5, 9 on 4:27 (Wünsche, 56); 29, 4 on 20:2. Its visibility was explained by R. Akiba to mean that the flaming Word struck the tablets and wrote on them the commandments, M. Ex., 7, 9 on 20:15 (p. 235, 8-10). It is also maintained that God's voice went around the whole world, that the Israelites received it successively from the four quarters of

---

[37] For the cries of animals the word is used, e.g., of the raven in Qoh. r., 10 on 10:20 and sheep in Qinnim, 3, 6.

[38] He who recites the tephillah audibly is regarded as weak in faith, and he who does so with a loud voice is viewed as a lying prophet, bBer., 24b. The Amen of the responsio should not be louder than the blessing nor the transl. louder than the reading. For acc. to Ex. 19:19 God accommodated His voice to that of Moses (בְּקוֹל is construed thus), bBer., 45a, cf. M. Ex., 7, 4 on 19:19 (p. 216, 16).

[39] The thunder fills the world. The Torah was intentionally given in the wilderness rather than the land of Israel, i.e., in a neutral place accessible to all peoples, in order that any nations might receive it without prejudice, M. Ex., 7, 1 on 19:2 (p. 205, 16-18) and 7, 5 on 20:2 (p. 222, 2-6) etc.

heaven, from heaven and earth, that they welcomed it and received it gladly, Ex. r., 5, 9 on 4:27. R. Jochanan b Nappacha (c. 250 A.D.) explains on the basis of the plur. קֹלֹת that God's voice split up into 70 voices acc. to the 70 languages of the earth, so that each people could hear it in its own tongue, loc. cit.,[40] cf. bShab., 88b (school of R. Yishmael c. 130 A.D.).

5. Heavenly Voice. After the destruction of the second temple there developed among the Rabb. the idea that with the last prophets Hag., Zech. and Mal. the Holy Spirit left Israel (→ VI, 385, 26 ff.) and in His place [41] God caused the voice from heaven to come forth, T. Sota, 13, 2 f. (Zuckermandel, 318 f.); bSota, 48b; bSanh., 11a; [42] bYoma, 9b. The term בַּת קוֹל, Aram. בְּרַת קָלָא, ref. to the echo, audible on earth, [43] of a voice that usually comes from heaven and declares God's judgment. Ancient oriental, [44] OT [45] and esp. apocal.-visionary (→ 286, 20 ff.) traditions are adopted here and developed and formalised under the impress of the divine transcendence. [46, 47] The belief in oracles, popular in the Hell. world, also had some influence. The Rabb. Bath Qol is not to be regarded as in any sense a continuation of the revelation of God in the Torah and the prophets. This was now regarded as closed. Nor is the voice a substitute for prophecy or the Holy Spirit. [48] In apocalyptic, the NT and Jos. there is, however, little trace of critical distance; [49] here we find the undiluted קוֹל or φωνή. The same applies to the Tannaite period, esp. the school of Hillel. [50] Thus the long debate between the schools of Shammai and Hillel was

---

[40] Cf. Tanch. שמות on Ex. 4:27 (Buber, 13 f.), where God's voice first divided into 7 voices on the basis of Ps. 29 with its sevenfold קוֹל. Acc. to S. Dt., 343 on 33:2 God revealed Himself in 4 languages when He gave the Torah, cf. M. Ex., 7, 5 on 20:2 (p. 221, 9 ff.).

[41] The relation between the Bath Qol and the H. Spirit may be seen from a comparison of Cant. r., 8 on 8:10 with Lv. r., 6, 1 on 5:1, also bGit., 57b with Eka r., 1, 423 on 1:16 (Wünsche, 86). The fact that acc. to bBer., 3a, cf. Tg. on Cant. 2:12 the Bath Qol coos like a dove seems to support the relationship, cf. the H. Spirit as a dove in Mk. 1:10 (→ VI, 68, 11 ff.) and Gn. 1:2. On this whole matter v. Bacher Term., II, 206.

[42] מַשְׁמִיעִין (the plur. denotes God as author), T. Sota, 13, 2 (Zuckermandel, 318) is older than מַשְׁמִשִׁין, bSanh., 11a. The thesis that the Spirit withdrew is also aimed at the claim of the Qumran sect, the Zealots and Christians to have the Spirit. The H. Spirit, who is for the Rabb. the Spirit of prophecy, will be given again only in the end-time.

[43] Cf. at any rate Ex. r., 29, 9 on 20:2 (Wünsche, 214), which ref. to the echo of the human voice. Whether בַּת (for בֶּן) is meant to denote the weakness of the echo is doubtful. Acc. to M. Maimonides, Moreh Nebuchim, 2, 42 (ed. J. Goldmann [1960]) Hagar and Manoah and his wife simply heard a Bath Qol, since they were not prophets.

[44] In the form of the saga of the Bab. flood hero found in Berossus his rapture to the gods was made known to those left behind by a heavenly voice φωνὴ ἐκ τοῦ ἀέρος, Fr., 4 (FGrHist, IIIc, 380).

[45] Cf. Nu. 7:89; Is. 40:3, 6; 1 K. 19:12 f. and esp. Da. 4:28: "A voice fell from heaven."

[46] בַּת קוֹל is at least meant to correct the impression that God's voice is heard speaking directly.

[47] Usually the voice from heaven is introduced by the stereotyped phrase: "A Bath Qol went forth (from heaven) and spoke יָצְאָה בַּת קוֹל (מִן־הַשָּׁמַיִם) וְאָמְרָה. Aram. נְפַקַת בְּרַת קָלָא cf. ἦλθεν οὖν φωνὴ ἐκ τοῦ οὐρανοῦ, Jn. 12:28 and רוּחַ הַקֹּדֶשׁ אָמְרֶת → n. 41. The content of the message is short and usually stereotyped.

[48] Cant. r., 8 on 8:10 (Wünsche, 187) sees in the Bath Qol a small remnant (cf. Is. 1:9) of prophecy.

[49] Dalman WJ, I, 168 thinks that originally the Bath Qol was not regarded as lower grade revelation.

[50] Acc. to T. Nazir, 1, 1 (Zuckermandel, 283), the school of Shammai in halachic questions allowed no witness on the basis of a Bath Qol אֵין מְעִידִים עַל בַּת קוֹל while the school of Hillel did. Cf. A. Guttmann, "The Significance of Miracles for Talmudic Judaism," HUCA, 20 (1947), 363-406.

settled by a Bath Qol in favour of the latter, jBer., 1, 7 (3b, 75 f.); bErub., 13b. On the other hand R. Jehoshua b Chananya (2nd cent. A.D.) rejected an intervention of the heavenly voice in favour of the halachic judgment of R. Eliezer b Hyrcanos in the light of the Torah given at Sinai and the majority decision demanded by it (Ex. 23:2), bBM, 59b, Bar.; bSanh., 104b. [51] In distinction from the gift of the Spirit the Bath Qol sets up no lasting relation between God and men. Nor does it apply to certain elect but can come to Gentiles and the ungodly too. It occurs chiefly in the sphere of popular and legendary haggada and biblical exegesis embroidered for edification. Usually the Bath Qol comes from heaven, bChag., 14b; bBB, 74b; bSanh. 11a etc. More rarely other places of God's presence are the points of origin, e.g., Sinai/Horeb, Ab., 6, 2; bBer., 17b, the holiest of all in the temple, T. Sota, 13, 5 (Zuckermandel, 319); bSota, 33a; jChag., 2, 1 (77b, 60 f.), cf. Ez. 43:6 f.; Jos. Ant., 13, 282. In many instances it is clear that God Himself is the speaker. [52] Sometimes there are accompanying phenomena as in an OT theophany, e.g., thunder, jPea, 1, 1 (15d, 40 f.) or earthquake, bMeg., 3a; jChag., 2, 1 (77a, 69 f.). Yet there is a differentiating trend when it is said that evil is declared by the Bath Qol but nothing bad can come from God's mouth, Tg. on Lam. 3:38. It is the task of the Bath Qol to make known an important judgment which either is not compelling to the mind of man or is contrary to the common view. It is often addressed to the world and calls from the mountain-tops in all directions, Lv. r., 27, 2 on 22:27 and sometimes by day and night, Ab., 6, 2; bBer., 3a; 17b. The form of the message frequently recalls prophetic sayings, e.g., a call to repentance, Eka r. Intr., 25, 10 (Wünsche, 32), a cry of disaster, Ab., 6, 2, rejection of penitence, bChag., 15a, or a pious wish, Tanch. אב, 2 on Dt. 26:16 (Buber, 45). It accuses the world, Ab., 6, 2; bBer., 17b and is Israel's advocate among the peoples, Cant. r., 8 on 8:10 (Wünsche, 187). It pronounces oracles on the dawn of the Messianic time, bSanh., 94a. Usually the content of its message relates to individuals. God's punishment is announced to the arrogant ruler — Nebuchadnezzar is a cover for Titus — in bGit., 56b and to the Messianic pretender, Bar Cosibah, jTaan., 4, 8 (68d, 73). It rejects the wilful transgressor of the Law, Elisha bAbuya, bChag., 15a, and comforts the harassed rabbi, Qoh. r., 9 on 9:7 (Wünsche, 121 f.). Above all it proclaims God's acceptance to the misunderstood righteous and thereby corrects the superficial judgment of the world. It honours the scholar Hillel, T. Sota, 13, 3 f. (Zuckermandel, 318 f.); bSota, 48b; bSanh., 11a and reveals the cosmic merit of the modest ascetic Chanina, bBer., 17b; bTaan., 24b. It anticipates the verdict of the last judgment by promising a share in the life of the world to come. It does this esp. at the hour of martyrdom, bBer., 61b; bGit., 57b; Eka r., 1, 423 on 1:16 (Wünsche, 86); bAZ, 10b; 18a. Exegetes also see the Bath Qol playing a role in the story of ancient Israel. Qoh. r., 9 on 9:7 (Wünsche, 121); bSota, 10b; bYoma, 22b; bMak., 23b; bShab., 149b; S. Dt., 357 on 34:5; bShab., 56b; bYoma, 22b (Rab); T. Sota, 13, 5 (Zuckermandel, 319); jSota, 9, 15 (24b, 27 f.), cf. Jos. Ant., 13, 282 f.; bBB, 3b. The Bath Qol was always operative when a man not a prophet received knowledge that made him God's instrument, bMak., 23b. The desire to make a mere idea more concrete brought the Bath Qol close to the oracle and divination. Even an unexpected human word could be regarded as a divine hint and hence as a Bath Qol, e.g., the chance repeated Yes or No of a man in the city or a woman in the field, bMeg., 32a, or the voice of a child [53] reciting a v. of Scripture, jShab., 6, 1

---

[51] Growing scepticism about signs and wonders, bHullin, 43a; bYeb., 121b; bBer., 60a may also be based on opposition to Christianity, cf. B. Gerhardsson, "Memory and Manuscript," Acta Seminarii Neotest. Upsaliensis, 22 (1961), 213.

[52] So, e.g., when the Bath Qol is brought in as subj. and in the OT God Himself is the speaker, Tg. on Cant. 2:14; on Lam. 3:38, or when acc. to bGit., 56b it proclaims what God Himself says in the par. passages, Gn. r., 10:7 on 2:1 (Wünsche, 43); Lv. r., 22, 3 on 17:3; Nu. r., 18, 22 on 16:35 (Wünsche, 457). Use of the 1st pers. also indicates that God is the speaker, e.g., "my children," bBer., 3a or "my secret," bSanh., 94a.

[53] Cf. on this the judgment of R. Jochanan b Nappacha (3rd cent.): "From the day the sanctuary was destroyed, the gift of prophecy was taken from the prophets and given to fools and children," bSanh., 11a.

(8c, 56), cf. bChul., 95b. Only rarely does the Bath Qol interject itself into the work of the Rabb. It may censure lack of interest in hidden things, jSota, 7, 5 (22a, 9 f.), or forbid the publication of a Tg. for the Ketubim, bMeg., 3a, or show that it is right to add an additional month, PREl, 8 (p. 58 f.), or show the right path in an insoluble legal case, Jeb., 16, 6. Here, too, its judgment is situational. The direction never becomes a generally valid halacha, cf. bSanh., 104b.

The Bath Qol often gives such direction through a text, bSota, 21a; bSanh., 104b; bGit., 57b; certain texts are said to be utterances of a Bath Qol, e.g., Is. 35:3 f. acc. to Lv. r., 19, 5 on 15:25; Zech. 11:17 acc. to Eka r., 2, 64 on 2:1 (Wünsche, 101); Jer. 3:14 acc. to Rt. r., 6, 4 on 3:13. The Bath Qol also actualises God's Word, applying it to a specific case in the present, bGit., 56b; jShab., 6, 8 (8c, 55. 69 f. 72). It also explains a striking circumstance in the text, bSanh., 94a, or a difficult saying of the OT, bMeg., 29a; bShab., 56b, also passages where objection might be made to God's righteousness, bSanh., 94a, cf. Eka r., Intr. 24, 19 (Wünsche, 29). [54]

D. Hellenistic Judaism.

1. Septuagint. Apart from a few specifically Semitic expressions, [55] the LXX follows the OT use of קוֹל. It almost always transl. the term קוֹל by φωνή, although in Gk. (→ 278, 13 ff.) this is more sharply limited to the oral intimations of living creatures. We have a Gk. concept when φωνή is used for דְּבָרִים at Gn. 11:1 and לָשׁוֹן at Dt. 28:49 in the sense of "language," cf. also 2 Macc. 7:8, 21 and ἡ 'Εβραΐς φωνή at 4 Macc. 12:7. The plur. קוֹלוֹת "claps of thunder" is transl. φωναί at Ex. 9:23; 19:16, but φωνή at 20:18, where the ref. is to God's "voice." [56] The revelation of God takes place exclusively by the Word. OT passages which speak or seem to speak of the vision of God are often rendered by the LXX in such a way that the vision drops out, cf. Ex. 24:9-11; Job 19:25-27; 35:13 f.; ψ 16(17):15; 41(42):3, though cf. Is. 6:1, 5. [57] Hence φωνή κυρίου is used at Gn. 15:4 for דְּבַר יהוה; פִּי יהוה (עַל) can sometimes be transl. by διὰ φωνῆς κυρίου, Nu. 3:16, 39, 51; 4:37, 41, 45; 9:20; 10:13.

2. Aristobulus. Aristob. (170-150 B.C.) guards against an anthropomorphic view of the divine voice, Eus. Praep. Ev., 13, 12, 3 f. He thinks the voice of God is to be understood in terms of operation rather than the spoken word, for the creation of the world is described as "divine words" by Moses, 13, 12, 3. Pythagoras, Socrates and Plato follow Moses' teaching when they mention God's voice in contemplation of the cosmic structure continually made and sustained by God, 13, 12, 4.

3. Josephus. Jos. also uses φωνή for "speech" → 279, 12 ff.: ἡ 'Ελληνικὴ φωνή, Ap., 1, 1, cf. 1, 50. 73. He says of Balaam's ass: φωνὴν ἀνθρωπίνην ἀφεῖσα κατεμέμφετο τὸν Βάλαμον, Ant., 4, 109. While avoiding φωνὴ θεοῦ, he uses the idea of God's voice to express more clearly the distance between God and man. It is a θεία φωνή rather than God Himself that gives Abraham the bad news of the future imprisonment of Israel in Egypt, Ant., 1, 185, cf. Gn. 15:13. Jos. explains the summons of God out of the burning bush as an act of fire that found a voice and used words, Ant., 2, 267. The claps

---

[54] Further instances in Bacher Term., II, 206 f.

[55] On the transl. of the interjectional קוֹל → n. 12. Formally, too, הֶעֱבִיר קוֹל is not given a true equivalent, but the transl. is materially correct.

[56] Worth noting is the embellishment of Ex. 19:13b HT: "When the ram's horn sounds, they are to go up on the mountain," LXX: ὅταν αἱ φωναὶ καὶ αἱ σάλπιγγες καὶ ἡ νεφέλη ἀπέλθῃ ἀπὸ τοῦ ὄρους, ἐκεῖνοι ἀναβήσονται ἐπὶ τὸ ὄρος.

[57] For the revelation of the Word cf. Jer. 25:30 HT, where God will lift up His voice with a roar, 'Ιερ. 32:30: κύριος ἀφ' ὑψηλοῦ χρηματιεῖ (HT יִשְׁאָג), ἀπὸ τοῦ ἁγίου αὐτοῦ δώσει φωνὴν αὐτοῦ.

of thunder at the Sinai theophany are called κεραυνοί [58] and have nothing to do with God's speaking, 3, 80-88. At Sinai Moses alone first perceived an ἄφθαρτος φωνή, 3, 88, and then Israel heard φωνῆς ὑψόθεν παραγενομένης εἰς ἅπαντας that proclaimed the decalogue, 3, 90. This direct revelation was designed to protect the nobility of God's words from being injured or distorted by human rendition, 3, 89. [59] The mysterious still small voice of 1 K. 19:12 is said to be a φωνὴ θεία that broke the silence, 8, 352. Already before the earthquake Elijah was addressed at Horeb by a φωνή τις ἐξ ἀδήλου, 8, 350, cf. 1 K. 19:9. We also read of the voice of God in the post-bibl. period; Jos. was perhaps influenced by the idea of the Bath Qol → 288, 8 ff. Acc. to him the voice issued forth from the temple. [60] Hyrcanus I at the offering of incense heard a voice announcing the victory won for him by his sons; the Word of the Godhead came to him therewith, 13, 282. Before the outbreak of the Jewish War the priests in the temple heard movement and knocking and then a voice as it were calling from a mouth φωνῆς ἀθρόας: "Let us depart hence," Bell., 6, 299. [61] Of the same foreboding significance was the voice that Jesus son of Ananos heard and made known 4 yrs. before the war began: φωνὴ ἀπὸ ἀνατολῆς, φωνὴ ἀπὸ δύσεως, φωνὴ ἀπὸ τῶν τεσσάρων ἀνέμων, φωνὴ ἐπὶ Ἱεροσόλυμα καὶ τὸν ναόν, φωνὴ ἐπὶ νυμφίους καὶ νύμφας, φωνὴ ἐπὶ τὸν λαὸν πάντα, Bell., 6, 301, cf. Ἱερ. 7:23, 34.

4. Philo. Philo's use of φωνή for the audible utterance of living creatures betrays Gk. influence → 278, 14 ff. Philo reflects scientifically on the human voice, which cannot evade the critical faculty, Som., I, 28. [62] He thus pays more regard to the process of speaking than to its effect in various situations. The empirical and scientific approach goes hand in hand with a theological and speculative. The voice is to serve the exalting of the Creator of all things, for the ὄργανα τῆς φωνῆς are not a human possession, since a slight ailment can cripple the tongue, Cher., 116. The human voice is an instrument of reason, the νοῦς. Among the creatures man alone has an articulate voice φωνὴ ἔναρθρος which can be the κήρυξ and ἑρμηνεύς of the νοῦς; λόγος, rational speech, is thus an expression of the φωνὴ ἔναρθρος directed by the νοῦς, Som., I, 29, cf. Vit. Mos., II, 16. The voice reveals all thoughts like a light; hence Philo calls it φωνὴ τηλαυγεστάτη, "the voice that shines afar," Det. Pot. Ins., 128. [63] For Philo the process of prophetic inspiration is analogous to the production of νοῦς-informed speech. The divine spirit uses man's vocal apparatus as a medium and causes it to resound and sound forth, Spec. Leg., IV, 49.

For Philo φωνή can also mean "language." The serpent in Paradise spoke with "human speech" ἀνθρώπου προϊέμενος φωνήν, Agric., 96. Mankind had one language before the confusion of tongues, Conf. Ling., 1 (Gn. 11:1).

The bibl. account of the Sinai incident gives Philo the opportunity to draw attention to the uniqueness of the divine voice. He must have been familiar with many of the traditions that are found in Rabb. speculations on the voice of God (→ 287, 26 ff.) but exegetically he takes a different path. Like the Rabb. he stresses the miracle of the divine voice, Decal., 33, and also of the accompanying thunder and lightning, 44. He clearly distinguishes between the two. The voice of God is again a vehicle of revelation through which God proclaims the ten commandments to assembled Israel, 32. But the process of

---

[58] Or ψόφος Ant., 3, 81. It is up to the reader whether he believes the theophany or not.

[59] The mediatorial role of Moses is basically maintained. Israel is to know the divine author in the Law even though it is proclaimed by a human tongue, Ant., 3, 85. God Himself was heard in all Moses' utterances, 4, 329.

[60] Cf. Sir. 45:5; Rev. 16:1, 17; 19:5; 21:3.

[61] What is meant is the departure of the divine glory with the cherubim; this is an intimation of approaching judgment, cf. Ez. 10:18-22; 11:22 f.

[62] Cf. also Vit. Mos., II, 239; Spec. Leg., I, 147; IV, 49; Migr. Abr., 47; Sacr. AC, 23; Deus Imm., 25; Poster. C., 106; Op. Mund., 121.

[63] Stoic influence may be detected here, for φωνή is understood as φῶς τοῦ νοῦ in the Stoa, H. Steinthal, Gesch. d. Sprachwissenschaft bei d. Griechen u. Röm., I² (1890), 285.

revelation is not understood as an audible proclamation of Word. It is a visually depicted event directed to the soul. Speaking and hearing are expressly ruled out, Migr. Abr., 47 ff.; Decal., 33 ff. This is based on the nature of God's voice, which Philo describes as a unique phenomenon. Unlike a human voice, it is not produced by an organ of speech, Decal., 32 f. Hence it needs no ear to receive it, 35. As a spiritual construct it affects the soul of man. God's voice at Sinai was specifically created by God as ἦχος ἀόρατον and ψυχὴ λογική. As a soul endowed with reason it was capable of speech and caused an articulate voice φωνὴ ἔναρθρος to sound forth like a breath of air, 33. Unlike the human voice God's voice increased rather than decreased with distance, since it struck the ear of the spirit filled with God, 35. Philo makes much of the visibility of God's voice, Ex. 20:18, 22; Dt. 4:12, but here, too, he has a plain tendency towards psychological and ethical interpretation. Fundamentally God's voice is visible and it changes into a fiery flame at Sinai, Decal., 33, since God speaks deeds rather than words, 47. Acc. to Migr. Abr., 47 Israel saw God's voice as a light. [64] For God's words are a radiant shining of virtue and a source of reason. From Dt. 4:12 it is deduced that God's voice is not grasped in concepts nor heard with the ear but seen with the eye, Migr. Abr., 48 and 52. [65] That it came forth from the fire acc. to Dt. 4:36 is expounded as follows. God's words are purified as gold in the fire and when received they work like a fire that both illumines and also burns. To the obedient they become as light but the ungodly are consumed by the fire of lusts, Decal., 48 f. The optical depiction simply serves to stress the objectivity of God's voice, which otherwise would be spiritualised and related to individuals. The universality of the giving of the Law at Sinai is restricted to the sound of the trumpet which startles even those not present and calls their attention to the greatness of the event, Spec. Leg., II, 189. Revelation, however, applies only to Israel, which acts like the initiate who "sees being without voice and by the soul alone" ἄνευ φωνῆς μόνη ψυχῇ τὸ ὂν θεωρεῖν, Gig., 52, cf. the ideal of the seeing sage in Migr. Abr., 38 and the βίος θεωρητικός, 47. [66]

E. The New Testament.

1. Noise, Sound. In the NT — mostly in passages influenced by the OT — φωνή means first "noise," "sound."

It may be the "rush" of wings and the "rolling" of wheels, Rev. 9:9, or the "grinding" of millstones, Rev. 18:22, cf. also the "sound" of many waters, 1:15; 14:2; 19:6, the "reverberation" of thunder, 6:1; 14:2; 19:6, or the tumult of a countless multitude, 19:1, 6, which suggests the numinous force of the voices of heavenly beings. Again φωνή is the "rushing" of the wind, Jn. 3:8, perhaps also Ac. 2:6. It can also denote the "melody" of musical instruments, e.g., flutes and zithers in 1 C. 14:7, or the "signal" of trumpets, 1 C. 14:8, where it is distinguished from φθόγγος, the single "note." [67] φωνή is the "sound" of trumpets in Rev. 1:10; 4:1; 8:13b, of singing players on the zither in 14:2, of players on the zither, singers, flautists and trumpeters in 18:22. It can then ref. to the "sound" of spoken words, Lk. 1:44; Hb. 12:19, and the cry of grief in Mt. 2:18. In Rev. 10:3 it denotes a loud "calling" that can be compared to the roaring of a lion.

---

[64] Acc. to Ex. 20:18 with sing. φωνή as in LXX.

[65] Cf. Vit. Mos., II, 213: God spoke the command of Sabbath sanctifying ἄνευ προφήτου ... διὰ φωνῆς — τὸ παραδοξότατον — ὁρατῆς.

[66] On the basis of Ex. 6:12 Philo presents Moses as a man "without speech," Det. Pot. Ins., 38. He could grasp thoughts without words, an ability of the gods acc. to Pos., cf. Cic. Divin., I, 57, 129 and Leisegang, Philo v. Alex., Die Werke in deutscher Übers., ed. L. Cohn, et al., III² (1962), ad loc.

[67] φωνή is what the instrument "has to say," the orderly sequence of notes, "melody." In R. 10:18, quoting Ps. 19:5, φθόγγος is for Paul the "sound" of the universal proclamation of the Word of God.

2. Human Voice.

Human voices can be distinguished. The maid Rhoda can tell Peter by his voice, Ac. 12:14; the sheep know the voice of the shepherd who calls φωνεῖ them by name (→ V, 281, 17 ff.), Jn. 10:3 f. The friend of the bridegroom rejoices when he hears the bridegroom's voice, Jn. 3:29. [68] The desolation of Babylon (= Rome) in Rev. 18:23 is indicated by the OT image that the voice of the bridegroom and the voice of the bride are no longer heard there. Paul wants to have ἀλλάξαι τὴν φωνήν in his dealings with the Galatians, i.e., he wants to speak to them in another tone of voice, Gl. 4:20.

φωνή means "voice" in OT quotations. Mt. has the voice of Rachel lament at the slaughter of the innocents at Bethlehem, 2:18. [69] John the Baptist is the eschatological figure crying in the wilderness φωνὴ βοῶντος, Mk. 1:3 and par. [70] His ministry is regarded as so important in the Fourth Gospel that the Baptist himself is called the "voice of one that crieth in the wilderness" (→ II, 659, 28 ff.), an indication of his eschatological mission, Jn. 1:23, cf. Just. Dial., 88, 7. Mt. 12:18-21 quotes Is. 42:1-4, relating the οὐδὲ ἀκούσει τις ἐν ταῖς πλατείαις τὴν φωνὴν αὐτοῦ to the command to keep silence taken from Mk. 3:12, and thus providing a biblical basis for this command.

Expressions denoting raising the voice, loud speaking and crying remind us of the LXX though they are found in other Gk. too → 279, 4. Lk., whose style is esp. strongly orientated to the LXX, likes the expression (ἐπ)αίρω (τὴν) φωνήν Hbr. קוֹל נָשָׂא, followed by a verb of speech, cf. the lepers who cry out for mercy in Lk. 17:13 or the prayer of the first community in Ac. 4:24. The ref. may also be to emotional crying out under the influence of the spirit of blindness or of the Holy Spirit, cf. the deifying of the apostles in Lystra, Ac. 14:11, or the demand of the incensed Jews in Ac. 22:22, which reminds us of the "Crucify him," or the speech of Peter at Pentecost under the inspiration of the Spirit, Ac. 2:14, or the macarism of the woman with ref. to Jesus, which is to be regarded as inspired, Lk. 11:27. Also Semitic are ἐλάλησαν ... τὰς ἑαυτῶν φωνάς in Rev. 10:3 and λαλέω μεγάλα "to speak haughtily" in 13:5, cf. Da. 7:8, 11. To the instrumental בְּקוֹל קָרָא correspond λέγω, κράζω, κηρύσσω (ἐν) φωνῇ μεγάλῃ, again common in Lk. and used of the speech of men who are either agitated or moved by the Spirit, Lk. 23:23; Ac. 7:57, 60; 26:24. μεγάλη φωνῇ is connected esp. with the praise of God, Lk. 17:15; 19:37; Rev. 7:10. [71]

3. μεγάλη φωνή.
A very important use of μεγάλη φωνή is in relation to the speech of angels, spirits, or bearers of the Spirit.

Connected with this is the fact that acc. to Rev. 6:10 the souls of the martyrs cry out with a loud voice for retribution. [72] The angels praise God μεγάλη φωνῇ in Rev. 5:12,

---

[68] Behind Jn. 3:29 f. there is perhaps a play on the Aram. words קָלְא "voice," כַּלְּתָא "bride," קְלַל "to take from," and כְּלַל "to be full," M. Black, An Aram. Approach to the Gospels and Acts[3] (1967), 147.

[69] This is further developed in Just. Dial., 78, 8.

[70] Eschatological interpretation of Is. 40:3 is common to Qumran and the Gospels. But the Evangelists stress the introductory קוֹל קוֹרֵא, which is left out in 1 QS 8:14 vg. 9:16, and following LXX against HT they link the topographical "in the wilderness" with the one who cries: The Baptist is in the wilderness and from there issues his call to the world, whereas preparation of God's way, which for Qumran means going into the desert, is spatially indefinite in the Gospels and can be done anywhere, cf. O. Betz, "Offenbarung u. Schriftforschung in d. Qumransekte," Wissenschaftl. Untersuchungen z. NT, 6 (1960), 155-8.

[71] Because praise is rendered in pneumatic joy, it is uttered μεγάλη φωνῇ, cf. R. Deichgräber, "Gotteshymnus u. Christushymnus in d. frühen Christenheit," Stud. z. Umwelt d. NT, 5 (1967), 213.

[72] This passage reminds us of the soul of Abel lamenting in the realm of the dead, Eth. En. 22:5-7. The blood of Christ is said to speak more loudly than that of Abel in Hb. 12:24, though this is in intercession rather than accusation.

or proclaim in this way an eschatological judgment of God, so that it may be heard by all the dwellers on earth, 14:7, 9; 18:2, cf. 8:13; 14:18. [73] The strength of the voices of these superhuman beings is also expressed by comparisons in which transfer is made from God's speaking in the OT to that of His messengers. Thus calling out μεγάλη φωνῇ is like the "roaring" of a lion, 10:3 cf. Am. 1:2; Hos. 11:10, or the "sound" of a trumpet, 1:10, or the "noise" of many waters, 1:15; 14:2; 19:6 cf. Ez. 1:24; 43:2. One of the beasts on the throne chariot speaks ὡς φωνῇ βροντῆς 6:1. [74] We can thus see why the voice from heaven in Jn. 12:29 f. might be regarded as angelic speech by some hearers and as a clap of thunder by others → I, 640, 24 ff. The voice of the exalted Son of Man is as the "noise" of many waters in Rev. 1:15. [75] Among the phenomena accompanying the return of Christ are the "peal" of the trumpet of God and also the "voice" of the archangel, 1 Th. 4:16 → III, 657, 37 ff.

In this light it is probable that Mark regarded as an epiphany the loud cry with which Jesus died on the cross. For the ἀφεὶς φωνὴν μεγάλην in Mk. 15:37 ends the darkness and is brought into material connection with the centurion's confession that He is the Son of God, 15:37, 39. [76] It is also quite possible that Jl. 3:15 LXX stands behind this account. [77] Later the wordless cry was handed down as a final saying of Jesus on the cross. In Mt. 27:50 it is connected by πάλιν with v. 46, in which Jesus cries out Ps. 22:1 φωνῇ μεγάλη. In Lk. 23:46 Jesus dies after a prayer spoken φωνῇ μεγάλη (Ps. 31:5, cf. Ac. 7:59).

Acc. to Ac. 12:21 f. Agrippa's speech about the men of Tyre and Sidon is celebrated with the cry: θεοῦ φωνὴ καὶ οὐκ ἀνθρώπου. The king is punished by God because he lets himself be honoured as a spokesman of deity or even perhaps as its incarnation, [78] 12:23. Unclean spirits or demons, as supernatural beings, also have the power of a loud voice. κράζω, φωνέω or βοάω φωνῇ μεγάλη is esp. mentioned as an accompanying phenomenon when they are driven out of the possessed, Mk. 1:26; Ac. 8:7, and they are also means by which the demon resists the exorcist, Lk. 4:33; Mk. 5:7, cf. Lk. 8:28 → III, 900, 37 ff.

---

[73] In Rev. 8:13 an eagle is the messenger of judgment and it sounds forth a cry of woe φωνῇ μεγάλη; in 14:18 a command is issued to one of the angels of destruction in the same way, cf. 7:2; 14:15. The instrumental ἐν, Hbr. בְּ, is Semitic in 14:7, 9, 15; 18:2.

[74] The noise of the movement of the throne chariot is transf. here to the speech of one of the beasts, cf. Ez. 1:24.

[75] Like that of a lion acc. to 4 Esr. 11:37. A later Midr. says that the enthroned Messiah will proclaim בְּקוֹלוֹ that salvation has drawn nigh קָרְבָה יְשׁוּעָה, A. Jellinek, Bet ha-Midrasch, III (1855), 73.

[76] Orig. interpreted the confession as follows: Et vide, si dicere possumus secundum unum quidem modum, quia miratus est in his, quae dicta fuerant ab eo ad deum cum clamore et magnitudine sensuum, secundum quod capiebat intelligere suspicans admiratus est et dixit: 'Vere hic homo Filius erat Dei,' Orig. Comm. in Mt., 140 on 24:57 (GCS, 38, 290). Origin. the φωνὴν μεγάλην of Mk. 15:37 related to the recitation of Ps. 22:1 in v. 34 and the impression of an inarticulate death-cry arose only through insertion of the misunderstanding about Elijah acc. to H. Gese, "Ps. 22 u. d. NT," ZThK, 65 (1968), 16; T. Boman, Die Jesusüberlieferung im Lichte d. neueren Volkskunde (1967), 226-8, G. Bertram, "Die Leidensgesch. Jesu u. der Christuskult," FRL, 32 (1922), 78 and 90-92.

[77] After announcement of the darkness of the sun and moon it is said that the Lord will cry from Zion and raise up His voice from Jerusalem, so that heaven and earth will be shaken, Jl. 3:15 f. LXX.

[78] S. Lösch, Deitas Jesu u. antike Apotheose (1933), 14 f. thinks in terms of the divine veneration common in the ruler cults of antiquity and esp. the equation of Agrippa with the sun-god, for in the par. Jos. Ant., 19, 344 f. there is ref. to the radiance emitted by the king, cf. also Dio C., 59, 7, 1; 29, 5-7 of Caligula.

The wonder-working power of God in man can also be proclaimed with a loud voice.

Paul in Lystra issues μεγάλη φωνῇ the command that the lame man stand on his feet, Ac. 14:10. Along with the healing the powerful voice may also express the judgment of pagans that they are witnesses of an epiphany, v. 11. When Jesus with a loud voice summons Lazarus to come forth from the tomb in Jn. 11:43, He anticipates the voice of the Son of Man that will pierce graves and summon the dead to life and judgment, Jn. 5:28 f. [79]

Paul's vision of calling on the Damascus road is portrayed as an audition too by Lk. A voice is heard, Ac. 9:4, 7; 22:7, 9; 26:14. It is thought to come from heaven, and shows itself to Paul to be the voice of Christ, 9:5. Acc. to Ac. 9:7 Paul's companions hear the "voice" ἀκούοντες τῆς φωνῆς but see no man, [80] though cf. 22:9. The common pt. in the accounts here is that the reality of the theophany was apparent to the companions but they did not understand the revelation as such; only the chosen one does this, Ac. 22:14.

4. Cry, Word, Confession, Speech. In content φωνή is also the specific cry, the significant and authoritative word, the solemn confession, and speech.

The Ephesians' confession of the local goddess Artemis rang out as a "unanimous cry" and "acclamation" φωνὴ ἐγένετο μία ἐκ πάντων, Ac. 19:34. The φωνὴ ἐκ τοῦ στόματος αὐτοῦ mentioned in Ac. 22:14 is not the voice of Jesus as in 9:4, 7 but the Word of calling given by Him. Similarly the φωνὴ ἐνεχθεῖσα αὐτῷ of 2 Pt. 1:17 is the "declarative word" issued at the transfiguration of Jesus, although "voice" is a possible transl. Acc. to Ac. 13:27 the φωναὶ τῶν προφητῶν are sounded forth as Scripture readings at Jewish Sabbath worship; the witness of Moses and the prophets is actualised as the summons of God's Word. In Ac. 24:21 the μία αὕτη φωνή that Paul called out before the Sanhedrin is defined in content as a solemn "confession" of the resurrection. This usage is related to the Gk. employment of φωνή in the sense of the "maxims" of a philosopher, → 279, 25 ff. In 2 Pt. 2:16, where the speaking of Balaam's ass is depicted as follows: ὑποζύγιον ἄφωνον ἐν ἀνθρώπου φωνῇ φθεγξάμενον, φωνή means "speech" and ἄφωνος "dumb." [81] The two terms are used similarly in 1 C. 14:7 f., 10 f. where Paul compares uninterpreted speaking in tongues to the unintelligibility of foreign languages τοσαῦτα εἰ τύχοι γένη φωνῶν εἰσιν ἐν κόσμῳ, καὶ οὐδὲν ἄφωνον, "there are many languages in the world and none is without speech," v. 10. [82] But one must know the δύναμις τῆς φωνῆς i.e., the meaning of a given language, if one is not to be as a βάρβαρος to the speaker, v. 11.

5. The Voice of God. In the NT, too, there are references to the voice of God of the Sinai tradition. For on the one side the eschatological speaking of God through Christ must be related to apocalyptic expectation of a direct encounter with God in the end-time and on the other it must be asserted in opposition to the Rabbinic dogma of a definitive revelation at Sinai that can never be repeated. [83]

---

[79] Faith in the miraculous power of Jesus' voice may be seen esp. in Act. Phil., where Jesus speaks from heaven and startles the crowd because His voice is stronger than that of thunder. Philip cures the blinded high-priest Ananias with the words "in the name of the power of the voice of my Lord Jesus," Act. Phil. 22.

[80] The terminology in Ac. 9:7 reminds us of the Sinai tradition, Dt. 4:12.

[81] Cf. Jos. Ant., 4, 110.

[82] In 1 C. 14 the term γλῶσσα "speech" is replaced with φωνή because it is used for "tongue" in relation to glossolalia. οὐδὲν ἄφωνον does not ref. to living creatures in gen. but to human language-groups or nations.

[83] Paul opposes to this the universal validity of the kerygma; this is illustrated by the speaking of the heavenly beings in ψ 18, which Paul relates to the proclamation of the Gospel: εἰς πᾶσαν τὴν γῆν ἐξῆλθεν ὁ φθόγγος αὐτῶν, R. 10:18.

In Revelation the voices of thunder are said to speak. This is along the lines of Rabbinic speculation on the tradition of Ps. 29:3-9 and the related voice of God at Sinai → 287, 39 ff. In Rev. 10:3 seven voices of thunder reply in their own speech to the cry of a gigantic angel. But this speech is not written down (v. 4), probably because it cannot be understood. The opposite is true of what the exalted Son of Man proclaims with a loud voice like the sound of a trumpet, 1:10-12. This Word is revelation for the community which through the death of Jesus has become the kingdom and the priestly people of God and has thus inherited the Sinaitic promise, 1:6, cf. Ex. 19:6. 1:12 reminds us of Ex. 20:18 with its seeing of a heavenly voice; the voice is again that of the Son of Man, v. 15. In the end-time, then, God's speaking is replaced by the direction of the Son of Man. In plerophorous expressions the signs of the theophany at Sinai are transferred to the world-shaking catastrophe of the last judgment; alongside one another we find βρονταὶ καὶ φωναὶ καὶ ἀστραπαὶ καὶ σεισμός, Rev. 8:5; cf. 4:5; 11:19; 16:18, cf. also Jub. 2:2.

The Lucan account of the first Pentecost (→ VI, 44, 2 ff.) of Christians in Ac. 2 reminds us of the universal interpretation of the Sinai tradition, [84] The sound from heaven and the mighty wind in v. 2 are elements in theophany like the fire, cf. Is. 66:15 ff. and they herald the revelation of the Word. The fiery tongues in v. 3 recall the fact that God spoke from out of the fire at Sinai, Dt. 4:12, and of Philo's exegesis. [85] The miracle of tongues in the disciples' preaching is similar to the Rabb. miracle of God's voice at Sinai (→ 288, 2 ff.), [86] though this is attested only later. The φωνή of v. 6 is to be related to the miracle. [87] God's speech is replaced with the inspired witness of the disciples and to that degree "demythologised." Instead of the Law we have the Gospel of the great acts of God in Christ.

The claim of the Jews that they alone possess and fully understand God's will is plainly rejected in the Fourth Gospel. In apparent contradiction of Dt. 4:12 the Johannine Jesus declares to the Jews: οὔτε φωνὴν αὐτοῦ πώποτε ἀκηκόατε οὔτε εἶδος αὐτοῦ ἑωράκατε, Jn. 5:37. [88] John understands Scripture as prophetic revelation and advance proclamation of the message of Christ (cf. R. 1:2). For him the voice of God is uttered in the present with the witness of the Spirit and special stress is laid on listening to the voice of Jesus, 5:25, 28; 10:3, 16, 27; 18:37. For with the coming of the Logos the event of revelation reaches its climax and this will decide the future too. One may see this from a comparison of 5:28 and v. 25: ἀμὴν ἀμὴν λέγω ὑμῖν ὅτι ἔρχεται ὥρα καὶ νῦν ἐστιν ὅτε οἱ νεκροὶ ἀκούσουσιν τῆς φωνῆς τοῦ υἱοῦ τοῦ θεοῦ καὶ οἱ ἀκούσαντες ζήσουσιν. He who receives the voice that now calls with faith moves out of the sphere of the dead into the realm of life, of eschatological existence, 5:24, cf. 6:63, 68; 10:3, 28; 12:47. This entails a protest against the Jewish belief in life-giving obedience to the Torah. A deepened interpretation of ἀκούω τῆς φωνῆς also governs the address on the Good Shepherd

---

[84] Worth noting is the fact that Jub. 6 puts the making of the OT covenant in the feast of weeks and Qumran expects an eschatological outpouring of the Spirit by God, 1 QS 4:20-22 (based on Ez. 36). On Pentecost cf. G. Kretschmar, "Himmelfahrt u. Pfingsten," ZKG, 66 (1954/55), 209-253; A. Jaubert, La notion d'alliance dans le Judaisme aux abords de l'ère chrétienne (1963).

[85] Philo Decal., 33 → 292, 12 f.

[86] Cf. Ex. r., 5, 9 on 4:27; bShab., 88b. The magnifying of God's great acts in Ac. 2:11 is part of the liturgy of the covenant feast.

[87] Thes. Steph., s.v. and after him Δ.Δημητράκος, Μέγα λεξικὸν τῆς Ἑλληνικῆς γλώσσης, IX (1951), s.v. understand φωνή in Ac. 2:6 as "report."

[88] Acc. to A. Guilding, The Fourth Gospel and Jewish Worship (1960), 77, 83 the first cc. of Dt. are the liturgical background of Jn. 5, Dt. 4:12 and Jn. 5:37 being linked.

in Jn. 10. To hear the voice of the Shepherd (v. 2f., 16, 27) is εἰδέναι τὴν φωνὴν αὐτοῦ and to follow it, v. 4. In contrast the sheep escape from the unknown voice of a stranger by flight, v. 5. National limits are set aside. Even outside the flock there are sheep who will hear the voice of the Shepherd and who will thus come to join the flock, v. 16. Only he who is of the elect can hear the voice of Jesus and in faith and obedience receive it as the eschatological Word of grace and truth. The reference is also to the elect in the declaratory statement with which Jesus ends the dialogue with Pilate: πᾶς ὁ ὢν ἐκ τῆς ἀληθείας ἀκούει μου τῆς φωνῆς, 18:37. One must stand in the realm of truth and not see oneself in the light of the world's reality if one is to be able to hear God speaking in the voice of Jesus, 8:47, cf. 3:3, 21.

Jn. 3:8 also has in view the voice of the Revealer. Here the metaphor of the wind [89] is used for the inconceivable miracle of regeneration by the Spirit: τὸ πνεῦμα ὅπου θέλει πνεῖ, καὶ τὴν φωνὴν αὐτοῦ ἀκούεις, ἀλλ' οὐκ οἶδας πόθεν ἔρχεται καὶ ποῦ ὑπάγει. The Logos belongs to the world of the Spirit and the Jews do not know whence He comes or whither He goes (8:14); they do not hear His φωνή.

The terms "speaking" and "hearing" are also important in Hb. [90] The Sinai incident should make clear to Christians the meaning of the new covenant and of the eschatological encounter with God. [91] In the depiction of the theophany in Hb. 12:18-21 we find not only two pairs of visible phenomena, fire and thick cloud, darkness and stormy wind (v. 18), but also a third ἦχος σάλπιγγος (cf. Ex. 19:19) καὶ φωνὴ ῥημάτων (cf. Dt. 4:12), Hb. 12:19. The revelation of the Word as the final member is the formal climax, but the emphasis is on the numinous power of the theophany [92] which will be manifested with incomparably greater strength at the imminent coming of God to final judgment. If God's voice then caused the earth to quake, heaven will now be shaken as well, cf. Hag. 2:6, and everything created will be changed, Hb. 12:25-29. [93] The revelatory character of God's voice at Sinai is less prominent and there is more emphasis on the hortatory use of theophany. At Sinai the Word was spoken by angels, Hb. 2:2, cf. Gl. 3:19. God spoke to the fathers through the prophets, Hb. 1:1, and it was God's works that Israel saw in the wilderness, 3:9. The admonition to stand fast in the final evil times is supported in Hb. 3:7 f., 15; 4:7 by a ref. to ψ 94:7 f.: σήμερον ἐὰν τῆς φωνῆς αὐτοῦ ἀκούσητε, μὴ σκληρύνητε τὰς καρδίας ὑμῶν... Now that God has spoken eschatologically through the Son (Hb. 1:2) the gt. "to-day" (→ VII, 274, 27 ff.) has dawned

---

[89] Jn. 3:8 reminds us formally of OT and later Jewish statements in which God's incomprehensible rule is compared to the movement of the wind, Qoh. 11:5; Prv. 30:4; Sir. 16:21; 4 Esr. 4:5-11.

[90] E. Grässer, "Der Glaube im Hb.," Marburger Theol. Stud., 2 (1965), 24, n. 64.

[91] In contrast to the tangible or earthly Sinai in Hb. 12:8 we have the (invisible) Zion and the heavenly city of God (v. 22), in contrast to the earthquake of the theophany the eschatological shaking of heaven and earth (v. 26), in contrast to the cultic community of Israel the festal assembly of the elect and of angels (v. 22), and in contrast to the God who gives direction on earth the God who speaks from heaven (v. 25).

[92] The hearers refused to listen to the voice any more, cf. Ex. 20:18 f.; even Moses was full of fear and trembling, v. 21, cf. Dt. 9:19.

[93] The Sinai tradition is eschatologically transcended esp. under the influence of Is. 65:17; 66:22; Da. 7. Expectations may be seen that are also found in apoc. writings, cf. Eth. En. 1:4-9, for the earthquake at Sinai 4 Esr. 1:18, for the cosmic catastrophe 1 QH 3:13-15, 19-36, cf. O. Betz, "The Eschatological Interpretation of the Sinai-Tradition in Qumran and in the NT," Revue de Qumran, 6 (1967), 89-108.

which will end with the Sabbath rest of the eschaton (→ VII, 19, 22 ff.; 34, 12 ff.). Until this is reached God's voice sounds forth in the preaching of the community to warn and to comfort.

6. The Heavenly Voice. In Rev. we often read that a voice rang out from heaven (10:8; 11:12; 14:13, cf. 4:1) or in heaven. The heavenly sanctuary (16:1, cf. Is. 66:6) and the neighbouring throne of God are esp. mentioned as the points of origin (19:5; 21:3; the two together in 16:17, the altar in 9:13). Things are not yet as abstract and stereotyped as with the Rabb. Bath Qol. Often the voice is briefly characterised, 1:10; 4:1; 11:15; 14:2; 16:1. The speaker may also be inferred from the context, e.g., the Son of Man in 1:10-13; 4:1, the four beasts by God's throne in 11:15; God in 16:17, cf. 10:8. Finally the human hearer is inspired by the Spirit, 1:10. In content the voice seldom gives revelation or elucidation. Much more often we have a command to the hearer respecting revelation, 1:11, cf. 14:13; 10:4, 8 f., or a charge to heavenly beings that is part of the course of the heavenly drama, 9:13 f.; 16:1, or finally an assertion which confirms the conclusion of an eschatological act, 11:15; 12:10; 16:17, cf. 21:3. In 4:1 the bearer of the voice introduces to heavenly mysteries; in 18:4-20 he issues threats; in 19:5 he calls for praise of God.

The enhanced sense of God's transcendence is often expressed in Ac. by a ref. to the voice from heaven. In Ac. 7:31 the self-revelation of God at the burning bush is introduced by the expression ἐγένετο φωνὴ κυρίου. [94] Along with a vision a voice comes to Peter making known to him an unheard of and indeed objectionable halachic decision [95] and brushing aside his protest with a categorical declaration of God's acts, Ac. 10:13-15; this is repeated three times, v. 16. In 11:9 the voice is called a φωνὴ ἐκ τοῦ οὐρανοῦ, but it is distinguished from the Bath Qol by the fact that dialogue is possible and closer personal identification may be made; Peter sees that the speaker is the Lord, 10:14; 11:8.

Closer to the Rabbinic Bath Qol (→ 288, 8 f.) is the voice from heaven which is mentioned in the Synoptic accounts of the baptism and transfiguration of Jesus and which binds these stories closely together. The point of the heavenly voice is divine confirmation of the preceding witness to the Messiahship of Jesus by human lips (Mk. 1:7 and par.; 8:29-33 and par.). The introductory formula denotes the place of origin: φωνὴ ... ἐκ τῶν οὐρανῶν (Mk. 1:11 and par. → V, 530, 20 ff.; VIII, 367, 23 ff.), with the Rabbinic addition λέγουσα (Mt. 3:17), and in the account of the transfiguration: φωνὴ ἐκ τῆς νεφέλης (Mk. 9:7), with the addition λέγουσα (Mt. 17:5 and par.). Unusual are the direct address σὺ εἶ (Mk. 1:11 and par.) [96] and the Messianic declaration, [97] which shows that God Himself is conceived to be the heavenly speaker. [98] In distinction from the Bath Qol, which is usually addressed to all, Jesus is the specific recipient, especially in Mk.'s account. [99] The limitation of the circle of hearers is counterbalanced by the directness and the unrestricted authority of the heavenly voice. In the glory of the transfiguration the admonition of the voice from heaven: ἀκούετε αὐτοῦ (Mk. 9:7), transfers the

---

[94] Cf. Jos. Ant., 2, 267.

[95] Gerhardsson, op. cit. (→ n. 51), 231.

[96] But cf. Mt. 3:17; Mk. 9:7 and par.

[97] All accounts have ὁ υἱός μου ὁ ἀγαπητός, only Lk. 9:35 ὁ υἱός μου ὁ ἐκλελεγμένος, cf. Jn. 1:34 Cod ℵ* sy⁵ᶜ etc. Cf. bBer., 17b.

[98] It is formed of OT material seen as prophecy of the Messiah. Important par. are Test. Jud. 24 and the institution of the eschatological high-priest in L. 18:6, where God speaks μετὰ φωνῆς πατρικῆς ὡς ἀπὸ ᾿Αβραὰμ πρὸς ᾿Ισαάκ, cf. Gn. 22:2, 7 f.

[99] Lk. 3:21 f. has an audience, the declaration in Mt. 3:17 is a proclamation in the 3rd person, in Mk. 9:7 f. and par. the voice from heaven is heard by the disciples but not understood in its true sense, cf. H. Baltensweiler, Die Verklärung Jesu (1959), 115; S. G. F. Brandon, Jesus and the Zealots (1967), 277.

authority of Moses to Jesus (Dt. 18:15). According to 2 Pt. 1:16-18 the author of the letter was an eye-witness of the glorification of Jesus and a hearer of the voice from heaven addressed to Him. It is now assumed that the disciples present have a full understanding of the divine voice and this is a pledge of the truth of the apostolic message about Christ: ταύτην τὴν φωνὴν ἡμεῖς ἠκούσαμεν ἐξ οὐρανοῦ ἐνεχθεῖσαν, v. 18. [100] The transfiguration took place on the holy mount (v. 18); there is perhaps an allusion to Zion here. [101]

> The Synoptic tradition of the baptism of Jesus is given a unique interpretation in John's Gospel. The task of the heavenly voice is taken over by a human messenger and changed into proclamation, 1:33 f. The recipient is no longer Jesus Himself, esp. as He is omniscient in this Gospel. The transfiguration undergoes a similar change in 12:20 ff. The voice from heaven conveys God's answer to the prayer of Jesus for glorification. It no longer declares the long-known Messiahship but the fact of glorification, which is understood as glorification of the name of God: ἦλθεν οὖν φωνὴ ἐκ τοῦ οὐρανοῦ· καὶ ἐδόξασα (sc. τὸ ὄνομά μου) καὶ πάλιν δοξάσω, v. 28. It is expressly said that the voice was given for the sake of the crowd and not for Jesus' sake, v. 30. But, as in the Synoptic account, it is not understood. According to the judgment of the hearers it simply thundered or an angel spoke, v. 29. Here the Evangelist shows that God's direct speaking from heaven founders on the incapacity of the human hearers. Thus the idea of a voice from heaven is rejected and with it Jewish speculation about the reception of the voice of God at Sinai.

F. Gnosticism.

In Gnostic works the otherworldly power of redemption manifests itself as a "voice" or "call" (Syr. and Mand. qālā, Cpt. t-smē, p-hrai, p-hrou). Mandaean and Manichaean Gnosticism can be described as religions of calling or hearing. [102] Since the true God of Gnosticism is remote and unknown, His voice cannot be heard directly. Hence man's redemption takes place through a heavenly envoy or the call from above. Unmistakable here is the influence of Jewish ideas, namely, that of the *angelus interpres* of apocalyptic, of wisdom's preaching on earth and of the Rabb. Bath Qol → 286, 20 ff.; 288, 8 ff. Yet the Gnostic understanding of the call goes beyond these.

1. In man qālā is the loud "voice" of the one who begs for redemption, O. Sol. 42:19 f., cf. Pist. Soph., 39 (GCS, 45, p. 39, 17); 40 (p. 41, 16); Ps. of Heraclides, [103] 188, 7 (φωνή untransl.), of the oppressed weak, of mighty warriors, or of cursing and bewitching women. Mandaean Mag. Texts, 1a, 4-8; 2. [104] In Gk. fashion t-smē as the equivalent of φωνή in Sophia of Jesus Christ, 81, 13 [105] means the teaching of philosophers. Acc. to Corp. Herm., 12, 13 the animal also has φωνή but only man has λόγος as the meaning of speech.

2. Much more often qālā or t-smē is the supraterrestrial, non-worldly voice, the call that brings redemption. Biblical traditions are speculatively exegeted. A φωνή ἀπὸ τοῦ φωτός orders Elohim to enter the heavenly world, Hipp. Ref., V, 26, 16 (Justin's system), cf. Corp. Herm., 1, 4-5. A voice comforts despairing Sophia by a brief word of revelation,

---

[100] φέρομαι (→ 57, 29 ff.) is used for the proclamation of divine speech or an inspired message, cf. 2 Pt. 1:21; 2:11. On 1:17 f. cf. Plut. De Caesare, 1 (I, 707e).
[101] Cf. Ps. 2:6; Jn. 12:28.
[102] Jonas Gnosis, I, 120.
[103] Ed. C. R. C. Allberry, *A Manichaean Psalm-Book*, II (1938), 187-202.
[104] Ed. M. Lidzbarski, *Ephemeris f. semitische Epigraphik*, I (1902), 90 and 96.
[105] Ed. W. C. Till, "D. gnost. Schriften d. kpt. Pap. Berolinensis 8502," TU, 60 (1955).

Apocryphon of John, *op. cit.* (→ n. 105), 47, 14-16 = Cod. II, 14, 13-15;[106] it orders Noah to build the ark, Lidz. Ginza R., 409, 2. In O. Sol. 24:1-6 the heavenly voice of the Synoptic baptism story is interpreted as the voice of the dove which goes out into the whole world and even penetrates to the underworld. Acc. to Ev. Pt. 9:35 a gt. voice from heaven rang forth just before the resurrection of Christ, and then a second voice from heaven asked: "Hast thou preached to them that sleep (i.e., the dead)?" 10:41. The voice of the Redeemer Christ, standing on a high mountain, carries even to the ends of the earth, O. Sol. 33:3; His voice has called forth life, Ev. Veritatis,[107] 31, 15 f. Gnosticism can also emphasise that while the figure of the Redeemer is not seen in Hades His voice is heard there, Cl. Al. Strom., VI, 6, 45, 1 f., cf. Adumbrationes in ep. canonicas on 1 Pt. 3:19 (GCS, 17, 205) and the corresponding statement about the voice of the heavenly man in the Naassene Sermon, Hipp. Ref., V, 8, 14. In the sacrament of anointing Christ has revealed Himself to the sealed alone through His voice, Act. Thom. 27, and Jn. simply heard the divine voice of the Crucified but did not see His figure.[108] The children of the Bridegroom are allowed to enter the bridal chamber whereas others merely hear the voice of the bride, Ev. Phil.[109] 130:20.

Among the Mandaeans the transcendence of the call that brings salvation is described spatially. It comes from the upper kingdom, Lidz. Ginza L, 547, 14-19, from on high, *loc. cit.*; Lidz. Jn., 217, 16, from concealment, 186, 3, from without, 225, 5, from the place of light, Lidz. Ginza R, 367, 11. The otherworldly and salvific effect of this call or voice is expressed by adj. The voice is bright, *ibid.*, 464, 7, sublime, R, 16, 7, pure, 322, 36, wonderful, 130, 24 f.; 302, 29, soft, 112, 28, lovely 367, 10; 395, 29-32, loud, Lidz. Jn., 186, 3. Sometimes the call is issued by specific saviours, Mandā de Hayyē, who stands at the ends of the earth and calls for the elect, Lidz. Ginza R, 397, 16-20, the emissary of light, 58, 5-9, and other heavenly messengers, 92, 20-36; 112, 26-29, helpers and companions of the soul, 308, 21 f.; L, 464, 7-25, the shepherd, Lidz. Jn., 43 f. and the pure fisherman, 160 f. Among the Manichees the "first sacred call," the "great call," is Christ, Psalm-Book (→ n. 103), 138, 7. The heavenly messenger can be named "Call," 199, 9. Esp. important is the "call of life," qālā dě hayyē, Lidz. Jn., 170, 16; 171, 14-16; Lidz. Ginza R, 5, 12 f.; 18, 14; 68, 24 etc.; Lidz. Liturg., 151, 9 f., which owes its name to the fact that it comes from the place of light and grants life, cf. Lidz. Ginza R, 275, 13-20. "Call" is par. to "address," L, 464, 7-9. Mandaean teaching is traced back to the extra-terrestrial call which contains the sum of redemptive revelation, R, 322, 20 ff.; 381, 21 ff. and the basic rules of authentic existence, Lidz. Jn., 225 f.; Ginza R, 58, 9-12; 387, 1 - 388, 2. The first duty of man is to hear this call in faith, Lidz. Ginza R., 253, 23 f.; 225, 36 and to secure its acceptance, i.e., to spread Mandaean teaching, 68, 24; 92, 10; 141, 22.[110] Sin is turning away from the call. 130, 36 f. The awakening call from without is necessary because man is in the sleep (→ VIII, 556, 9 ff.) of forgetfulness. In Gnosticism the idea of souls sleeping in the underworld is transferred to earth and the world of men. A Peratic Fr. begins: "I am the call of awakening from sleep in the aeon of the night," Hipp. Ref., V, 14, 1. The letter sent to the king's son of the Pearl Song[111] is "speech," and at its "voice" the sleeper wakes up, 51 f.; 64. and the radiant garment causes the sound qālā of its melodies to be heard, 88-90. The Mandaean "call" wakens Adam from the sleep of

---

[106] Ed. M. Krause - P. Labib, "Die drei Versionen d. Apokryphon d. Joh. im kpt. Museum zu Alt-Kairo," *Abh. d. Deutschen Archäol. Instituts Kairo, Kpt. Reihe,* 1 (1962).

[107] Ed. M. Malinine, H. C. Puech, G. Quispel (1956).

[108] σχῆμα μὴ ἔχοντα ἀλλά τινα φωνὴν μόνον, φωνὴν δὲ οὐ ταύτην τὴν ἡμῖν συνήθη, ἀλλά τινα ἡδεῖαν καὶ χρηστὴν καὶ ἀληθῶς θεοῦ, λέγουσαν πρός με..., Act. Jn. 98, cf. 99: οὔτε ἐγώ εἰμι ὁ ἐπὶ τοῦ σταυροῦ, ὃν νῦν οὐχ ὁρᾷς ἀλλὰ μόνον φωνῆς ἀκούεις.

[109] Ed. W. C. Till, *Patristische Texte u. Studien,* 2 (1963).

[110] "Caller of calls" is a title for Manichaean missionaries and cf. the similar usage in Islamic missions, Jonas Gnosis, I, 120, n. 1.

[111] Cf. A. Adam, "Die Ps. d. Thomas u. d. Perlenlied als Zeugnisse vorchr. Gnosis," ZNW Beih., 24 (1959), 49-54.

forgetfulness, Lidz. Jn., 245f., and startles sleeping, i.e., errant souls, Lidz. Ginza R, 308. 21-26. It keeps believers from stumbling, L, 561, 7; 564, 6, and strengthens, R, 322, 37 and enlightens them, 370, 16. It ensures the return of the soul to its heavenly home, 275, 13-23. The Gnostic call thus discharges a similar task to that of the OT Torah, though for the anti-Jewish Mandaeans this is a book of wickedness and deception, Lidz., Jn., 198 f. The task is also the same as that of the enlightening and keeping Holy Spirit, who is, however, decried as the opposite: The malevolent ones of Rūhā, the demons, want to hamper and set aside the call of life, Lidz. Ginza R, 383, 9, cf. 120, 32.

3. The idea of the call also dominates Gnostic dualism. The opp. of the voice of heavenly messengers and the saving call is to be found in the voices of wicked forces and the "rebellious call," Lidz. Liturg., 272 10, or the "vain call," Lidz. Ginza R, 25, 6; 362, 28. On the appearing of Jesus Rūhā lets a call sound forth over Him as a witness, 50, 37. Mohammed issues a "call that is no call," 30, 15 f. Conversely the call can take form; the planets and signs of the zodiac are "calls" in the form of concrete beings, 90, 26-34.

G. Church History.

Ign. uses the metaphor of a choir in unison to strengthen the unity of members of the community, who σύμφωνοι ὄντες ἐν ὁμονοίᾳ... ἐν φωνῇ μιᾷ are to praise the Father through Christ, Eph., 4, 2. He probably has in mind the Trishagion of the liturgy sung in unison, cf. 1 Cl., 34, 5-7 and Pass. Perp. et Fel., 12, 1.[112] Ign. can call himself the medium of God's voice when the inspired bishop μεγάλη φωνῇ, θεοῦ φωνῇ seeks to bind members of the community to the bishop, presbyters and deacons, Phld., 7, 1.[113] To Polycarp when he enters the stadium there calls out a φωνὴ ἐξ οὐρανοῦ that only the Christians present can hear: "Ἴσχυε, Πολύκαρπε, καὶ ἀνδρίζου, Mart. Pol., 9, 1.[114] Barn., 9, 2 has an agraphon that makes the attainment of eternal life dependent on exact hearing of the "voice of the Son" ἀκοῇ ἀκουσάτω τῆς φωνῆς τοῦ παιδός μου. We have here a hortatory use of the voice from heaven at the transfiguration of Jesus, cf. also Dt. 18:15-18.

In the Apologists there is a combination of Gk. and OT use. φωνή is "spoken word" in contrast to deed in Just. Dial., 131, 2 and "speech" in Apol., 31, 1. 3. 4; Tat. Or. Graec., 1, 3; 37, 1. The φωνὴ τοῦ θεοῦ is proclaimed by the prophets and made known afresh by the apostles of Christ, Just. Dial., 119, 6. φωνή is also the "call" with which Christ once called Abraham out of the wicked world (Gn. 12:1) and with which He similarly calls Christians, 119, 5. OT quotations are called αἱ φωναί (αὐτοῦ, sc. God) in Just. Dial., 21, 1; 33, 1, cf. οἱ λόγοι in the same sense in 64, 7 and αἱ φωναὶ τῶν προφητῶν in Athenag. Suppl., 9. It is important that Papias calls the oral tradition of Jesus the "living voice." He values τὰ παρὰ ζώσης φωνῆς καὶ μενούσης more highly than τὰ ἐκ τῶν βιβλίων; by the former he means τοὺς τῶν πρεσβυτέρων... λόγους, which are for him authentic and reliable tradition, Eus. Hist. Eccl., III, 39, 4.

φωνέω.

1. The Greek World.

φωνέω denotes the production of a sound or noise by musical instruments, animals, or men. A musical instrument φωνεῖ, Eur. Or., 146; the φωνεῖν of thunder means that it

---

[112] Cf. Eth. En. 39:12 f. and D. Flusser, "Sanctus u. Gloria," *Festschr. O. Michel* (1963), 133.
[113] Cf. Ant. Christ, V, 220.
[114] The voice from heaven also occurs in other stories of martyrs, promising them heavenly glory, cf. H. Günther, *Die chr. Legende d. Abendlandes* (1910), 134.

has something significant to say or serves as an oracle, Xenoph. Ap., 12. As a rule, however, the verb is used only of living creatures with a lung and throat. Thus animals make a sound, Aesopus Fab., 249; [1] Aristot. Hist. An., VI, 28, p. 578a, 32. The ref. may also be to the song of birds, VIII, 3, p. 593a, 14, though ψοφέω rather than φωνέω is used for the noise of cartilaginous creatures, IV, 9, p. 535b, 25 f. Man, however, is the chief subj. of φωνέω. The first sense here is "to lift up the voice," "to address": ὄπα φωνέω "to cause the voice to sound forth," Hom. Il., 2, 182; 10, 512; Od., 24, 535. Usually a second verb of speaking follows, e.g., προσηύδα, Hom. Il., 1, 201; 2, 7; 4, 284, φωνήσας προσέφη, Il., 14, 41, in reverse order ἔπος φάτο φώνησέν τε, Od., 4, 370. When it introduces what is said directly φωνέω can also mean "to speak," Aesch. Sept. c. Theb., 434, cf. Ag., 205 and 1334; Choeph., 314; Prom., 1063, μέγα φωνέω "to boast," Eum., 936, ἀνήρ... φωνέων μέγιστον "a man who has the loudest voice," Hdt., IV, 141, cf. VII, 117, 1. In the abs. φωνέω means "to cry out loud," e.g., for joy, Soph. Trach., 202, "to sing," Theocr. Idyll., 16, 44, "to begin to speak," cf. the rules of the religious society of the Iobacchi: μηδεὶς δ' ἔπος φωνείτω μὴ ἐπιτρέψαντος τοῦ ἱερέως ἢ τοῦ ἀνθιερέως, Ditt. Syll.[3], III, 1109,. 108 f. (178 A.D.), cf. 1 QS 6:12 f. Then φωνέω means "to summon" an assembly for a proposal or report: οἱ βουλευταὶ ἐφώνησαν, P. Oxy., XVII, 2110, 6 (370 A.D.), cf. BGU, III, 925, 8 (3rd cent. A.D.). τὰ φωνηθέντα are "spoken words," Plat. Soph., 262c; Tim., 72a. With dat. of person φωνέω is "to call to," "to reply to," Soph. Oed. Tyr., 1121, or "to invoke" the deity in prayer, Oed. Col., 1485. When used with acc. of person it means "to call," "to call by name," Soph. Ai., 73, pass. "to be called," Nicander (3rd cent. B.C.) Fr., 2 (FGrHist, IIIa, 87). If an inf. follows the acc. of person φωνέω means "to order," Soph. Ai., 1047. With acc. of obj. φωνέω means "to speak of something," "to tell something," Soph. Oed. Col., 1402 f.; Aesch. Choeph., 283, also "to cite," Ps.-Plat. Ax., 366c.

2. Hellenistic Judaism.

a. φωνέω is rare in the LXX; [2] in a mere 10 instances do we find it for a Hbr. or Aram. term. It denotes the "pealing" of trumpets in Am. 3:6; 1 Macc. 9:12, the "crying" of animals, Is. 38:14; Jer. 17:11; Zeph. 2:14. In particular it means "to speak." Thus idols cannot "make a sound in the throat," ψ 113:15, cf. 134:17; 3 Macc. 2:22. Again, φωνέω ἐκ τῆς κοιλίας is used in Is. 8:19 for the strange "muttering" (HT הגה hi) of the spirits of the dead and of soothsaying. Spirits of the dead אֹבוֹת are themselves interpreted as οἱ ἀπὸ (ἐκ) τῆς γῆς φωνοῦντες in Is. 8:19; 19:3. This phrase is used for sing. אוֹב in Is. 29:4. Da. 5:7 has ἐφώνησε φωνῇ μεγάλῃ for קְרָא בְחַיִל. In 4 Macc. 15:21 φωνέω denotes the loud crying of the voices of the seven martyred brothers. In 1 Ἐσδρ. 9:10 it is the assent of an assembled company. In 1 Ἐσδρ. 4:41 the ref. is to the hymnal, in 9:47 Cod. B to the liturgical "speaking" of the people, and in 1 Ch. 15:16 to the "singing" or "playing" of the Levites. At Sir. 45:17 it denotes the "instruction out loud" of the people in the Law, though we should read the φωτίσαι of Cod. A for φωνῆσαι in BS. Finally φώνησον αὐτὸν πρός με means "call him to me," "make him come to me," Tob. 5:9 Cod. BA.

b. In Philo φωνέω means "to lift up the voice," "to speak openly," and it serves the λόγος προφορικός which expresses and translates thoughts. The νοῦς needs the tongue and other φωνητήρια ὄργανα in order that thoughts may be born and brought to light, Det. Pot. Ins., 127. In a transf. sense φωνέω is used by Philo for the claiming, impressing and capturing of the human senses by the objects of the visible world, Leg. All., III, 44.

φωνέω. [1] Ed. A. Hausrath, Corpus Fabularum Aesop., I, 2² (1959).
[2] καλέω is mostly used for קרא and βοάω for קרא, צעק, זעק.

3. The New Testament.

a. φωνέω, which does not occur in the Epistles, denotes the "loud speaking," "calling," or "crying" of men, angels, or demons. It can be strengthened by φωνῇ μεγάλῃ, Mk. 1:26; Lk. 23:46; Ac. 16:28; Rev. 14:18; in these passages it means the same as κράζω → III, 900, 29 ff. In Luke φωνῆσαι "to raise the voice" emphasises the urgency of what is said, Lk. 8:54; 16:24; Ac. 10:18; 16:28. In Lk. 23:46 it denotes loud crying in prayer. Lk. 8:54 has in view the Messiah's Word of eschatological power which raises the dead. Lk. and Jn. also employ φωνέω with the acc. of person in the sense of καλέω (→ III, 488, 14 ff.) and προσκαλοῦμαι (→ III, 500, 20 ff.) "to summon," "to send for," "to cause to come," Lk. 16:2; 19:15; Ac. 9:41; 10:7; Jn. 2:9; 4:16; 9:18, 24. When some Jews at the foot of the cross think that Jesus is calling for Elijah they have in view the summoning of the Deliverer and the Bearer of eschatological salvation, Mk. 15:35 and par. → I, 627, 11 ff. At Mk. 10:49 the blind man is called by others, but the call is understood to be that of Jesus, who is the turning-point for those who seek deliverance. φωνέω here, like καλέω, is qualified eschatologically as the mighty summons to the place of salvation. The same is true when Philip summons Nathanael to Jesus in Jn. 1:48, cf. v. 45, or when Martha secretly "calls" her sister and says to her: ὁ διδάσκαλος πάρεστιν καὶ φωνεῖ σε, Jn. 11:28. Those whom the Good Shepherd calls by name (Jn. 10:3) know by this mark that they are bound to Him and that they are called into the sphere of salvation. We have an analogy to Lk. 8:54 (→ lines 7 ff.) when Jesus calls Lazarus forth from the tomb; the meaning is the same as ἐγείρω ἐκ νεκρῶν, "to awaken from the place of the dead, from Hades," Jn. 12:17. φωνέω τοὺς φίλους in Lk. 14:12 means "to invite friends"; normally καλέω is used for this (→ III, 488, 14 ff.), cf. 14:8, 10, 12 f. Finally φωνέω in a similar construction means "to name or address as": φωνεῖτέ με· ὁ διδάσκαλος, Jn. 13:13 → III, 1093, 34 ff.

b. φωνέω is the "crowing" of the cock in Mk. 14:30, [3] 68, 72; [4] Mt. 26:34, [5] 74 f.; Lk. 22:24, 60 f.; Jn. 13:38; 18:27. Since in Palestine the cock usually crows just before dawn, i.e., from soon after midnight to about 2.30 a.m., [6] the third watch from midnight to 3 a.m. is called ἀλεκτοροφωνία "the time of the crowing of the cock" (קְרִיאַת הַגֶּבֶר). [7]

4. The Post-Apostolic Fathers.

Rather oddly φωνέω does not occur at all in early Christian works outside the NT, whether in the so-called post-apost. fathers or in the Apologists.

---

[3] The Fayyum Fr. (ed. E. Klostermann, Apocrypha, II, KlT, 8³ [1929], 23) has κοκκύζω here for the crowing of the cock, cf. Poll. Onom., V, 89.

[4] At Mk. 14:68 ℵ BL W sy⁵ etc. do not have the crowing of the cock. D Θ lat etc. assimilate to the δίς or ἐκ δευτέρου φωνεῖν of v. 30, 72.

[5] L λ Or have πρὶν (πρὸ) ἀλεκτοροφωνίας (cf. Mk. 13:35) for πρὶν ἀλέκτορα φωνῆσαι.

[6] Cf. Dalman Arbeit, I, 2, 636-8; H. Kosmala, "The Time of Cock-Crow," Annual of the Swedish Theol. Institute, II (1963), 118 f.; Str.-B., I, 993. Acc. to BQ, 7, 7; TBQ, 8, 10 (Zuckermandel, 361) no hens were to be kept in Jerusalem lest they might endanger the purity of the sacrificial beasts, cf. C. Albeck, ששה סדרי משנה, IV (1958) on BQ, 7, 7; but the Sadducees and the people can hardly have kept this rule, Dalman Orte, 299.

[7] At Lk. 1:42 BWAD ℜ etc. have ἀναφωνέω for ἀναβοάω. Normative here is LXX usage which has ἀναφωνέω for striking up praise and playing on harps and lutes, 1 Ch. 15:28; 16:4 f., 42; 2 Ch. 5:13. Luke also wants to bring out the fact that the speaker is filled with the Spirit, v. 41. The liturgical ἐπιφωνέω of the LXX at 1 Ἐσδρ. 9:47; 2 Macc. 1:23; 3 Macc. 7:13 "to shout aloud to," occurs in Ac. 12:22 in the scene when Herod Agrippa is deified; what is meant is "to acclaim."

† συμφωνέω,   † σύμφωνος,   † συμφωνία,   † συμφώνησις.

A. The Greek World.

1. συμφωνέω.

a. συμφωνέω means "to agree, to be in harmony or concord with." Lit. it may denote the "harmonious sound" of many musical instruments, e.g., zithers, Callixenus (3rd cent. B.C.) Fr., 2 (FGrHist, IIIc, 175, 12). Plat. Resp., X, 617b says of the music of the spheres: ἐκ πασῶν (sc. sirens) μίαν ἁρμονίαν συμφωνεῖν. The consonants are called συμφωνούμενα because they are in harmony with the vowels Dion. Hal. De Demosthene, 43. [1] Similarly συμφωνέω denotes the "fitting together" of stones in a building: θριγκούς ... συμφωνοῦντας πρὸς ἀλλήλους δοκίμως, Ditt. Syll.[3], III, 972, 80-85 (175-172 B.C.); συμφωνοῦσιν αἱ ἁρμογαί, Herm. v., 3, 5, 1; συμφωνοῦντες ταῖς ἁρμογαῖς αὐτῶν μετὰ τῶν ἑτέρων λίθων, 3, 5, 2, cf. 2, 6; μὴ συμφωνοῦντες (sc. λίθοι) τοῖς ἑτέροις λίθοις, s., 9, 6, 4.

b. More common is the transf. sense "to be in agreement or harmony with." The original and copy of two texts agree, P. Oxy., VIII, 1115, 18 f. (284 A.D.); "to agree with statements made earlier" τοῖς προειρημένοις συμφωνέω, Plat. Resp., III, 398c, cf. Leg., IX, 860e. Negated συμφωνέω denotes discrepancy: τὰ ἔργα οὐ συμφωνεῖ ἡμῖν τοῖς λόγοις, Plat. La., 193e; οὐ ... συμφωνοῦσι πραγματεῖαι καὶ φροντίδες καὶ ὀργαὶ καὶ χάριτες μακαριότητι, Epic. Ep., 1, 77 (Usener, 28); ἔσχε (sc. Agesilaus) γὰρ διττὰς ἐπιθυμίας ... οὐ συμφωνούσας ... ἀλλήλαις, Isoc. Or., 5, 87. In the sphere of human thought and judgment the act. and mid. means "to champion the same view," the opp. being διαφωνέω, Plat. Phaed., 101d or ἀμφισβητέω, Diod. S., 5, 69, 1; ἐν μὲν ἄρα τοῖς συμφωνοῦμεν, ἐν δὲ τοῖς οὔ, Plat. Phaedr., 263b; as regards the divine origin of the legal order μιᾷ δὲ φωνῇ καὶ ἐξ ἑνὸς στόματος πάντας συμφωνεῖν ὡς πάντα καλῶς κεῖται θέντων θεῶν, Plat. Leg., I, 634e; ταῦτα ... σχεδὸν συμφωνοῦσι πάντες "almost all agree," Theophr. De causis plantarum, VI, 9, 2, mid., I, 1, 1; ἔδοξε τῇ ... συμφωνεῖν κρίσει, Ditt. Syll.[3], II, 827, Col. 5, 9 (116-117 A.D.); ξυμφωνέω περί τινος, Democr. Fr., 107 (Diels, II, 164); Dion. Hal. Ant. Rom., 2, 47, 2. The pass. συμφωνεῖται means "it may be regarded as settled," Diod. S., 1, 26, 8, cf. 20, 5.

c. συμφωνέω "to reach agreement," "to come to terms" is used when political treaties are concluded and esp. economic contracts: συμφωνήσας Ἡρακλείδης μετὰ Θοτέως, Pap. Cairo Zeno, III, 59330, 2 f. [2] (3rd cent. B.C.); συμφωνέω περί τινος, Polyb., 2, 15, 5; ἐννόμιον συνεφωνήθη μὴ δεῖν πράσσειν ἐγχωρίους, "by agreement no lease had to be paid by natives," Ditt. Or., II, 629, 173 f. (2nd cent. A.D.). Like τὸ συμφώνημα, τὸ συμφωνηθέν means "agreement," Diod. S., 30, 19, plur. τὰ συμφωνηθέντα ἐμοὶ καὶ Ἀντιφάνει, P. Oxy., II, 260, 7 (59 A.D.); ἀπέχω τὴν συμπεφωνημένην αὐτοῦ τειμήν, BGU, VII, 1643, 20 (2nd cent. A.D.); μισθοῦ τοῦ συμπεφωνημένου, ibid., IV, 1125, 5 (13 B.C.). Finally συμφωνέω means "to unite" for a bad purpose, "to conspire": οὐθὲν γὰρ φοβερὸν μήποτε συμφωνήσωσιν οἱ πλούσιοι τοῖς πένησιν ἐπὶ τούτους (sc. τοὺς μέσους, i.e., to suppress the middle class), Aristot. Pol., IV, 12, p. 1296b, 40 f.

2. σύμφωνος.

a. σύμφωνος means "harmonious" in sound, "agreeing," "consonant": φθόγγοι ... σύμφωνοι δι' ὁμοιότητα, opp. ἀνάρμοστος, Plat. Tim., 80a, cf. Leg., VII, 812d-e.

συμφωνέω κτλ.   [1] Ed. H. Usener and L. Radermacher, Dion. Hal. Opuscula, I (1899), 226.
[2] Ed. C. C. Edgar, *Catalogue général des antiquités Égypt. du Musée du Caire*, 85 (1928).

Of a cry σύμφωνος means "echoing," Soph. Oed. Tyr., 421. In the doctrine of harmony σύμφωνος is distinguished from ἀντίφωνος, Aristot. Probl., 19, 16, p. 918b, 30, and also ὁμόφωνος, 19, 39, p. 921a, 7.

σύμφωνος is mostly used in a transf. sense. In the sphere of acoustics we read of "harmonious numbers" ἐπισκοπεῖν τίνες σύμφωνοι ἀριθμοὶ καὶ τίνες οὔ, Plat. Resp., VII, 531c, cf. also σύμφωνοι εἰκόνες, Ps.-Aristot. Mund., 5, p. 396b, 14 f. and σύμφωνοι φοραί ("movements," "impulses"), Aristot. An., I, 3, p. 406b, 31. In gen. σύμφωνος denotes the pertinent and proper relation between two statements or things: σύμφωνα οἷς τὸ πρῶτον ἔλεγες, Plat. Gorg., 457e; σύμφωνος τῷ ὀνόματι, Crat., 395e. Theory agrees with observed facts, Theophr. Ign., 8, 61; σύμφωνον τοῖς φαινομένοις, Epic. Ep., 2, 112 (Usener, 52), cf. 2, 86 (36). Two records agree with one another: ἐξέλαβα τὰ προκίμενα σύμφωνα τοῖς ἐν καταχωρισμῷ, "I found the present document to be a faithful transcript of the original in the archives," BGU, II, 562, 22 (2nd cent. A.D.). σύμφωνος is esp. important in ethics; the opp. here is ἀσύμφωνος, Plat. Resp., III, 402d. In life words and deed should be in harmony ὁ βίος σύμφωνος τοῖς λόγοις πρὸς τὰ ἔργα, Plat. La., 188d. The inner harmony of the wise arises above all from the fact that feelings of desire and pain agree with the commands of the *logos* τὸν τὰς ἡδονὰς καὶ λύπας κεκτημένον συμφώνους τοῖς ὀρθοῖς λόγοις καὶ ἑπομένας, Leg., III, 696c. Polyb., 31, 25, 8 says of Scipio: ὁμολογούμενον καὶ σύμφωνον ἑαυτὸν κατασκευάσας κατὰ τὸν βίον. σύμφωνον is used impersonally to express agreement between two parties σύμφωνόν ἐστί τινι πρός τινα, Polyb., 6, 36, 5; σύμφωνός εἰμί τινι, 30, 8, 7. ἐκ συμφώνου [3] means "in mutual agreement," "by consent," Pap. Primi, 1, 22 [4] (108 A.D.); P. Greci e Latini, 13, 1341, 18 (5th cent. A.D.); καθὼς ἐκ συμφώνου ὑπηγόρευσαν "in accordance with what the contracting partners by consent dictated to the notary," P. Lond., II, 334, 18 f. (166 A.D.); P. Hamb., I, 15, 8 (209 A.D.); P. Strassb., I, 14, 13 f. (211 A.D.); BGU, II, 446, 13 (2nd cent. A.D.).

b. τὸ σύμφωνον means "agreement," "arrangement" [τὸ σύ]μφωνον κύριον, "the agreement should be valid," Preisigke Sammelb., I, 5810, 19 (322 A.D.); τῶν... ἀνενεγκόντων ὡς μὴ πληρωθέντων τοῦ συμφώνου τοῦ πρὸς αὐτούς, "they reported that they had not been paid acc. to the arrangement," P. Oxy., VIII, 1103, 6 (360 A.D.). τὰ σύμφωνα are the "arrangements" reached, *ibid.*, VI, 914, 9 (5th cent. A.D.); καὶ οὐ συνέθετο σύνφωνα ἐργάσασθαι, [5] ἀλλὰ πρὸς ἡμέραν "he did not make any contract (fixed terms for a longer period), but per day," P. Gen., I, 76, 17 ff. (3rd-4th cent. A.D.).

c. The adv. συμφώνως occurs in Ps.-Plat. Epin., 974c, cf. Diod. S., 1, 98, 9; 15, 18, 2, συμφώνως ἔχω τινί, Ptolemaus Geographia [6], I, 17, 2.

d. When σύμφωνος is used pass. it means "arranged"... ἕως συνθήκας ποιησάμενοι συμφώνους ὅρους ἔθεντο τῆς χώρας, Diod. S., 5, 6, 4. Its meaning is thus the same as that of ὁμόλογος, cf. σύμφωνον καὶ ὁμόλογον ταῖς πόλεσιν ὑπὲρ τῆς πανηγύρεως, Ditt. Or., II, 444, 1 (2nd/1st cent. B.C.).

3. συμφωνία.

a. συμφωνία occurs first in Plat. and its primary ref is to the "harmony" of sounds in music τὴν ἐν τῇ ᾠδῇ ἁρμονίαν ἣ δὴ συμφωνία καλεῖται, Plat. Crat., 405c d, cf. Tim., 67c; Symp., 187b, opp. ἑτεροφωνία, Leg., VII, 812d and then the "agreement" of

---

[3] Cf. Deissmann NB, 82 f., cf. LO, 176.
[4] Ed. E. Kiessling, *Sammelbuch griech. Urkunden aus Ägypten, Beih. 2* (1961).
[5] The reading of U. Wilcken, "Zu den Genfer Pap.," APF, 3 (1906), 402 for ἐργάσαιτο, cf. F. Preisigke, *Berichtigungsliste d. griech. Papyrusurkunden aus Ägypten,* I (1922), 167.
[6] Ed. C. Müller, I, 1 (1883).

two sounds, "accord," Resp., VII, 531a c. Aristot. An. Post., II, 2, p. 90a, 18 f. defines συμφωνία as λόγος ἀριθμῶν ἐν ὀξεῖ ἢ βαρεῖ, also as κρᾶσις ... λόγον ἐχόντων ἐναντίων πρὸς ἄλληλα, Probl., 19, 38, p. 921a, 2 f. He distinguishes συμφωνία as the harmony of different voices from mere "unison" ὁμοφωνία, Pol., II, 5, p. 1263b, 35. The Pythagorean doctrine of the music of the spheres he describes as οἱ τῶν συμφωνιῶν λόγοι, Cael., II, 9. p. 290b, 22; thus συμφωνία is for him the harmony of many sounds. [7]

b. Later συμφωνία in the "concert" of many instruments, Paradoxographus Florentinus, [8] 43 and concretely an "orchestra," P. Flor., I, 74, 5 (181 A.D.); P. Oxy., X, 1275, 9 (3rd cent. A.D.). A single instrument can also be meant, perhaps when Polyb., 30, 26, 8 recounts of Antiochus Epiphanes: καὶ τῆς συμφωνίας προκαλουμένης (sc. ὁ βασιλεύς) ἀναπηδήσας ὠρχεῖτο, and certainly in 26, 1, 4: ἐπικωμάζων μετὰ κερατίου καὶ συμφωνίας. Suet. Caes., IV, 37 tells similarly of Caligula: discumbens de die inter choros et symphonias, cf. Pos. Fr., 14 (FGrHist, IIa, 229): χορῷ μεγάλῳ καὶ παντοίοις ὀργάνοις καὶ συμφωνίαις. Acc. to Plin. Hist. Nat., 8, 64, 157 symphonia must be a wind instrument, acc. to Isidor. Etymologiae, [9] 3, 22, 14 a percussion instrument. [10]

c. Trans. συμφωνία is the "harmony" of true thought and life. Epicurus uses it for the "agreement" of theory with observed facts: ἔχειν τοῖς φαινομένοις συμφωνίαν, Ep., 2, 86 (Usener, 36). An Epicurean mentions τὴν πρὸς τὰ πάθη συμφωνίαν, Polystratus, Περὶ ἀλόγου καταφρονήσεως, [11] Col. 7b, 4 f. Acc. to Stob. Ecl., II, 74, 4 f. the Stoics give the following def.: συμφωνίαν δὲ εἶναι ὁμοδογματίαν περὶ τῶν κατὰ τὸν βίον, Gal. Comm. on Hippocr. De natura hominis, II, 6, 134 (CMG, V, 9, 1, p. 69) speaks of a συμφωνία τῶν ἱστορησάντων and calls the opp. διαφωνία, Comm. on Hippocr. Acut., I, 14, 440 (V, 9, 1, p. 127 f.). Wisdom, acc. to Plat., consists in harmony of thought: πῶς ... ἄνευ συμφωνίας γένοιτ᾽ ἂν φρονήσεως καὶ τὸ σμικρότατον εἶδος; οὐκ ἔστιν, ἀλλ᾽ ἡ καλλίστη καὶ μεγίστη τῶν συμφωνιῶν μεγίστη δικαιότατ᾽ ἂν λέγοιτο σοφία, Leg., III, 689d, cf. συμφωνία τῷ καλῷ λόγῳ, Resp., III, 401d and συμφωνία (sc. τῆς ψυχῆς) ἑαυτῇ, Tim., 47d. Like the strings of an instrument the wise man tunes the rational and sensory powers of the soul acc. to the measure of understanding and brings feelings and desires into harmony with the commands of the logos. There thus arises the inner balance or harmonious agreement of man with himself, Plat. Leg., III, 689d, cf. 696c; Resp., VIII, 554e. The beauty of soul formed by understanding should find harmonious correspondence in a beautiful bodily figure to give rise to the ideal man, Resp., III, 402d; IX, 591d; Gorg., 479b. συμφωνία τῷ καλῷ λόγῳ as the goal of human culture is illustrated by music. Education in music should come first, for rhythm and harmony can best find the way to the soul and give training in judgment, Resp., III, 401d e. Gk. philosophy discovers συμφωνία as the harmonious order which constitutes the essence of the cosmos and ensures its consistence. The world's harmony rests on the co-presence and co-operation of opposing ἐναντία entities, Ps.-Aristot. Mund., 5, p. 396a, 33 - 397b, 8, cf. Plat. Symp., 187a. In this regard Heracl. [12] is accepted as the father of the idea that opposing forces make the world a united entity.

d. In economic dealings συμφωνία, like τὸ σύμφωνον and τὸ συμφώνημα, is an "agreement" or "contract": ἀπὸ τῆς συμφωνίας ἧς ἐποίησας πρὸς τοὺς ἐργάτας, P. Lond., III, 1173, 7 (125 A.D.), cf. Ostraka, 364 (1st cent. A.D.).

---

[7] συμφωνία is also the agreement of foods, cf. on a cook Damoxenus (4th/3rd cent. A.D.) Fr., 2, 54 (FAC, IIIa, 214): μείξας πάντα κατὰ συμφωνίαν.
[8] Ed. H. Öhler, Diss. Tübingen (1913); on the usage p. 146.
[9] Ed. W. Lindsay (1911).
[10] On the use of symphonia for a musical instrument cf. the examples in P. Barry, "Da. 3, 5 sumphonyah," JBL, 27 (1908), 103-8.
[11] Ed. C. Wilke (1905).
[12] Cf. Fr., 10 (Diels, I, 153).

B. The Old Testament and Judaism.

1. In the LXX συμφωνέω denotes common action and planning: the gathering (HT חָבַר) of the conspiring kings in the valley of Siddim, Gn. 14:3, the encampment of the Syr. army in Ephraim, transl. συνεφώνησεν Αραμ πρὸς τὸν Εφραιμ in Is. 7:2 because of the joint action of Syria and North Israel. In 4 Βασ. 12:9 συμφωνέω ref. to common acceptance of the royal command, while in 4 Macc. 14:6 common readiness for martyrdom is συνεφώνησαν πρὸς τὸν θάνατον. The adj. σύμφωνος denotes the agreement of conduct with a given norm. At Qoh. 7:14 it is used for לְעֻמַּת "corresponding": God has ordained good and bad for man in equal measure: τοῦτο σύμφωνον τούτῳ ἐποίησεν. The priest Eleazar is lauded: ὦ σύμφωνε νόμου καὶ φιλόσοφε θείου βίου, 4 Macc. 7:7, and so are the seven brothers: ὦ πανάγιε συμφώνων ἀδελφῶν ἑβδομάς, 4 Macc. 14:7. The resolve to suffer martyrdom is here compared to the harmonious obedience of members of the body to the commands of the soul: καθάπερ αἱ χεῖρες καὶ οἱ πόδες συμφώνως τοῖς τῆς ψυχῆς ἀφηγήμασιν κινοῦνται, οὕτως οἱ ἱεροὶ μείρακες ("young men") ἐκεῖνοι ὡς ὑπὸ ψυχῆς ἀθανάτου τῆς εὐσεβείας πρὸς τὸν ὑπὲρ αὐτῆς συνεφώνησαν θάνατον, 4 Macc. 14:6. συμφωνία in the sense of "agreement" or "harmony" occurs only in 4 Macc. 14:3 with ref. to the concord of the seven brothers. At Δα. 3:5, 15 cf. Da. 3:5, 7, 10, 15 Θ the word is used for a musical instrument which was adopted as a loan word by the Aram. or Hbr., Aram. סוּמְפֹּנְיָה in Da. 3:5, 15; סִימְפֹּנְיָה Ketib, סוּמְפֹּנְיָה Qerē' Da. 3:10. What is meant is a kind of double flute [13] or bagpipe. [14]

2. Acc. to Rabb. texts the סִימְפֹּנְיָה is made of metal or is covered with metal and has a case, Kelim, 11, 6 (par. flute), cf. 16, 8 and T BM, 1, 7 (Zuckermandel, 579).

3. For Philo συμφωνία is the "harmony" of musical instruments, Sacr. AC, 74, of fourths, fifths and eighths, Som., I, 28. The best harmony, which does not consist in the raising and sounding of a melodious voice ἐμμελοῦς φωνῆς but in the concord ὁμολογία of the acts of human life, is produced by a well-tempered soul τὴν πασῶν ἀρίστην συμφωνίαν ἀπεργάσεται, Deus Imm., 25.

4. Jos. uses συμφωνέω for the "agreement" of accounts given by various historians, Ant., 1, 107; [15] Ap., 1, 17, and for the common striving of authentic Gk. philosophers and Jews to achieve a true and fitting concept of God, Ap., 2, 255. He extols the glorious συμφωνία in thought and life of the Jewish people, which is grounded in the uniformity of their way of life and a common view of God in agreement with the Law εἷς δὲ λόγος ὁ τῷ νόμῳ συμφωνῶν περὶ θεοῦ, Ap., 2, 179-181.

5. In the vocabulary of the OT and later Judaism we do not find the terms deriving from the Gk. doctrine of harmony (→ 305, 41 ff.) nor is there any trace of a theoretical consideration of music. Note is taken, however, of the harmonious order of the world as God created it. Already in pre-Chr. apoc. circles this arose through concern about the calendar and expectation of a new creation of the world at the end of time, Eth. En. 2-5, 72-82. But while Gk. philosophy attained its picture of a harmonious cosmos by empirical study and a rational understanding of individual phenomena (→ 306, 36 ff.), the Jew studied the Law of God that was set before him and used it as an aid and standard in

---

[13] So G. F. Moore, "Συμφωνία not a Bagpipe," JBL, 24 (1905), 166-175; C. Albeck in ששה סדרי משנה, VI (1958) on Kelim, 11, 6 suggests a kind of "flute." Str.-B., IV, 396, 400: "double flute," "bagpipe"; Jastrow, s.v.: "a wind instrument," "double flute," "bagpipe."
[14] So A. Bentzen, Daniel, Hndbch. AT, I, 19² (1952), ad loc.; P. Barry, "On Lk. 15:25, συμφωνία: bagpipe," JBL, 23 (1904), 180-190; Barry, op. cit., 99-121.
[15] συμφωνοῦσιν τοῖς ὑπ' ἐμοῦ λεγομένοις, Ant., 1, 107 means the same as μαρτυροῦσι δέ μου τῷ λόγῳ, loc. cit.

contemplation of the world. Hence the will of God revealed in the Law was also a norm of true life and conduct, and when later, under Gk. influence, use was made of the present word group, the ideal man was called a σύμφωνος νόμου, 4 Macc. 7:7, cf. Jos. Ap., 2, 181. For the rest the divine order set up in the world could be seen not so much in the life of the individual but rather in the society shaped by the Law. An example is the Qumran community, in which terms like סֶרֶךְ and תְּכוּן ("rule," "order") play an important role, e.g., 1 QS 2:21; 5:1; 6:8 f.; 8:4.

C. The New Testament.

1. In the NT συμφωνέω means "to correspond with," "to be at one," "to agree," whether with reference to things, words, or persons. Luke adds to the parable of the patch on the old garment the further point that a piece taken from a new garment does not fit in with the old τῷ παλαιῷ οὐ συμφωνήσει, 5:36. συμφωνέω is used similarly in Ac. 15:15. According to the view of James at the Apostolic Council the words of the prophets agree with the wonderful events on the mission field: τούτῳ συμφωνοῦσιν οἱ λόγοι τῶν προφητῶν. This harmony between the word of Scripture and eschatological events is grounded in God's plan of salvation, cf. ὁ θεὸς ἐπεσκέψατο, 15:14. [16] In Mt. 18:19 συμφωνέω is used with reference to the content of common prayer: ἐὰν δύο συμφωνήσωσιν... περὶ παντὸς πράγματος οὗ ἐὰν αἰτήσωνται. God's assent follows man's agreement and is imparted as Christ is where two or three are gathered in His name, v. 20. Agreement in a wicked plan is disclosed by Peter in his question to Sapphira: τί ὅτι συνεφωνήθη ὑμῖν πειράσαι; "Why have you agreed?" Ac. 5:9 → VI, 408, 18 ff. [17] In the parable of the husbandmen συμφωνέω denotes a successful economic arrangement (→ 304, 31 ff.) though this is only an oral agreement as to the wage for a single day, Mt. 20:2, 13. [18]

2. The phrase ἐκ συμφώνου, which is mainly used in economic contracts and almost as a tt. (→ 305, 22 f.), expresses in 1 C. 7:15 the consent of two partners in a matter of practical piety. Paul advises married couples: μὴ ἀποστερεῖτε ἀλλήλους, εἰ μήτι ἂν ἐκ συμφώνου πρὸς καιρὸν ἵνα σχολάσητε τῇ προσευχῇ. This agreement corresponds to the order of v. 4 in terms of which neither partner has autonomous control of his own body.

3. The brother of the Prodigal Son can tell that there is festivity in his father's house from the fact that he hears συμφωνία καὶ χοροί "flute-playing and dancing," Lk. 15:25. The meaning of συμφωνία is contested. [19] Possibly the double flute is in view, → 307, 17 ff.

---

[16] In the middle of a series of five rhetorical questions we find in 2 C. 6:15: τίς δὲ συμφώνησις Χριστοῦ πρὸς Βελιάρ; The rare συμφώνησις is used here in the same sense as μετοχή and κοινωνία. The questions are couched in the vocabulary of Qumran, esp. 1 QS 3:13 - 4:26.

[17] This pass. constr. differs from that normally found in the pap. where a prep. or ὥστε and inf. links the thing agreed upon, and it is more like the Lat. convenit inter vos with inf.; this is even clearer in the συνεφώνησεν ὑμῖν of Cod. D.

[18] The constr. is not quite the same in the two cases. The contracting partner is linked to συμφωνέω either by a prep. μετὰ τῶν ἐργατῶν, v. 2 or by a simple dat.: οὐχὶ... συνεφώνησάς μοι; v. 13. The agreed wage is put similarly: ἐκ δηναρίου, v. 2, a simple gen. pretii δηναρίου, v. 13.

[19] Hier. Ep., 21, 29 suggests "common song" consonantia. Wellh. Lk. favours "bagpipe." A. Merx, Die vier kanon. Ev. nach ihrem ältesten bekannten Texte, I (1897), transl. "symphony" and explains that this is a "shepherd's pipe," II, 2 (1905), ad loc.; M. J. Lagrange, Ev. selon S. Luc, Études Bibl.8 (1948), ad loc. transl. "des instruments"; Kl. Lk., ad loc. "Musik." In discussion cf. Barry, op. cit., 103-8 and Moore, op. cit. (→ n. 13), 166-175.

D. Church History.

1. Ignatius of Antioch uses the group συμφωνέω, συμφωνία, σύμφωνος to portray the unity of the Church. In so doing he obviously recalls the original ref. of the terms to playing on strings and choral singing → 305, 1 f.; 306, 3 ff. To the Ephesians he writes that Jesus Christ should be sung among them ἐν τῇ ὁμονοίᾳ ὑμῶν καὶ συμφώνῳ ἀγάπῃ, 4, 1, and he admonishes them to be a choir ἵνα σύμφωνοι ὄντες ἐν ὁμονοίᾳ, χρῶμα θεοῦ λαβόντες ἐν ἑνότητι, ᾄδετε ἐν φωνῇ μιᾷ διὰ ᾽Ιησοῦ Χριστοῦ, 4, 2. The unity of the Church is already achieved by Christ but is to be kept by the members of the community with a common mind; this is the pt. of the metaphor of the choir. The harmonious unity of the Church does not rest on monotonous uniformity but on the validity of hierarchically ordained relations; the members to the bishop, the bishop to Christ, Christ to God, ἵνα πάντα ἐν ἑνότητι σύμφωνα ᾖ, 5, 1. On συμφωνέω in Herm. → 304, 11 ff.

2. συμφωνέω and σύμφωνος are used in the cosmogonic speculations of Gnosticism to express the harmonious agreement of the heavenly aeons as opp. to the chaos of the material world. The words often occur untransl. in the Berlin Cpt. Cod., 8502, a collection of Gnostic tractates. [20] The aeons, powers and kingdoms created by the immortal man, i.e., God (→ VIII, 475, 14 ff.), agree with one another συμφωνεῖν, Sophia of Jesus Christ (→ n. 20), 109, 14, and the Son of Man agreed with Sophia, His opposite number, when He revealed Himself, 102, 15-18. Lack of harmony, or autonomous action within a syzygy, brings doom. Acc. to the Apocr. Jn. (→ n. 20) Sophia, the last of the heavenly aeons, must regret having given rise to a being from itself even though its partner, the male virgin Spirit (37:5), did not agree with her, 45:2-4, cf. 46:12-14. This error led to the origin of the material world. In Apocr. Jn. the partner σύζυγος of Sophia is called σύμφωνος (37:7, 9).

Betz

---

[20] Ed. W. C. Till, "Die gnost. Schr. d. kpt. Pap. Berolinensis, 8502," TU, 60 (1955).

---

† φῶς, † φωτίζω, † φωτισμός,
† φωτεινός, † φωσφόρος, † φωστήρ,
† ἐπιφαύσκω, † ἐπιφώσκω

Contents: A. The Word Group in Greek: 1. Usage; 2. Meaning; 3. Light and Illumination in Philosophy; 4. Light in the Cultus. B. The Word Group in the Old Testament: 1. Ancient Oriental Background; 2. Usage; 3. General; 4. God; 5. The World; 6. Eschatology; 7. Anthropology. C. Judaism (Apart from Philo): 1. General; 2. Special Features; 3. Dead Sea Scrolls; 4. Rabbinic Literature. D. Hellenism, Gnosticism: 1. General; 2. Philo; 3. Gnosticism: General Features; 4. Corpus Hermeticum; 5. The Mandaeans; 6. Manicheeism; 7. Odes of Solomon; 8. Christian Gnosticism. E. The New Testament: I. Occurrence; II. Synoptic Gospels and Acts: 1. Literal; 2. Figurative; 3. Transferred; III. The Pauline Corpus: 1. Paul; 2. Ephesians and Colossians; 3. The Pastorals; IV. John's Gospel and Epistles: 1. The Gospel; 2. 1 John; V. The Rest of the New Testament: 1. Hebrews; 2. James; 3. 1 Peter. F. The Early Church: 1. Post-Apostolic Fathers; 2. Baptism as φωτισμός.

φ ῶ ς κ τ λ . Note: R. Bultmann placed his rich collections of material at our disposal. Bibl.: → VII, 423, Bibl.; General: G. Mensching, "Die Lichtsymbolik in d. Religionsgesch.," *Studium Generale*, 10 (1957), 422-432. On A. and D.: → 7, Bibl.; C. Baeumker, "Witelo," *Beiträge z. Gesch. d. Philosophie d. MA*, 3, 2 (1908), 357-514; G. P. Wetter, "Phos," *Skrifter ·utgifna af Kungliga Humanistika Vetenskaps-Samfundet i Uppsala*, 17, 1 (1915); F. J. Dölger, "Die Sonne d. Gerechtigkeit u. d. Schwarze," *Liturgiegesch. Forschungen*, 2 (1918), 37-48; A. Schneider, "Die mystisch-ekstatische Gottesschau im griech. u. chr. Altertum," *Philosophisches Jbch.*, 31 (1918), 24-42; also "Der Gedanke d. Erkenntnis des Gleichen durch Gleiches in antiker u. patristischer Zeit," *Festschr. C. Baeumker* (1923), 65-76; F. J. Dölger, "Sol Salutis. Gebet u. Gesang im chr. Altertum," *Liturgiegesch. Forschungen*, 4/5² (1925); J. Stenzel, "Der Begriff d. Erleuchtung bei Plat.," *Die Antike*, 2 (1926), 235-257; Reitzenstein Hell. Myst., 220-334; J. Pascher, Η ΒΑΣΙΛΙΚΗ ΟΔΟΣ. Der Königsweg zu Wiedergeburt u. Vergottung bei Philo v. Alex.," *Stud. z. Gesch. u. Kultur d. Altertums*, 17, 3/4 (1931), Index, *s.v.* "Lichtgott," "Lichtkleid," "Lichttheologie"; Ant. Christ., V, 1-43; E. Bevan, *Symbolism and Belief* (1938), 129-250; W. Völker, "Fortschritt u. Vollendung bei Philo v. Alex.," TU, 49, 1 (1938), 178-192, 304-307; H. Westhoff, *Die Lichtvorstellung in d. Philosophie d. Vorsokratiker*. Diss. Erlangen (1947); R. Bultmann, "Zur Gesch. d. Lichtsymbolik im Altertum," *Exegetica* (1967), 323-355; W. Beierwaltes, *Lux intelligibilis. Untersuchung z. Lichtmetaphysik d. Griechen*, Diss. Munich (1957); D. Torrant, "Greek Metaphors of Light," *The Class. Quarterly*, 54 (1960), 181-7; W. Burkert, "Iranisches bei Anaximandros," *Rhein. Museum*, 106 (1963), 97-134; M. Treu, "Licht u. Leuchtendes in d. archaischen griech. Poesie," *Studium Generale*, 18 (1965), 83-97; C. J. Classen, "Licht u. Dunkel in d. früh.-gr. Philosophie," *ibid.*, 18 (1965), 97-116. On B.: C. Clemen, *Fontes historiae religionis Persicae* (1920); also *Die gr. u. lat. Nachrichten über die persische Religion* (1920); F. Cumont, *Die Mysterien d. Mithra³* (1923), Index, *s.v.* "Sonne"; E. Benveniste, *The Persian Religion acc. to the Chief Gk. Texts* (1929), 69-117; O. G. v. Wesendonck, "Bemerkungen z. iranischen Lichtlehre," ARW 31, (1934), 177-187; J. Bidez - F. Cumont, *Les mages hellénisés*, II (1938), 72-9; H. G. May, "The Creation of Light in Gn. 1:3-5," JBL, 58 (1939), 203-211; T. Hopfner, *Plut. über Isis u. Osiris*, II (1941), 201-211; G. Widengren, "Stand u. Aufgabe d. iranischen Religionsgesch.," *Numen*, 1 (1954), 16-83, 2 (1955), 46-134; W. v. Soden, "Licht u. Finsternis in d. sumerischen u. bab.-assyr. Religion," *Studium Gen.*, 13 (1960), 647-653; J. Hempel, "Die Lichtsymbolik im AT," *ibid.*, 352-368; W. Hinz, *Zarathustra* (1961), 166-203; E. Hornung, "Licht u. Finsternis in d. Vorstellungswelt Altägyptens," *Studium Gen.*, 18 (1965), 73-83; C. Colpe, "Lichtsymbolik im alten Iran u. antiken Judt.," *ibid.*, 116-133. On C.: S. Aalen,

A. The Word Group in Greek.

1. Usage.

a. The noun φῶς [1] "light" is found from Hom. [2] But the derivates that call for notice here are mostly rare and late. b. φωτίζω intr. means "to shine" of flame, Theophr. Ign., 4, 30, trans. "to illumine," "to bring to light," of the sun δοκεῖν... φωτίζειν τὸν κόσμον, Diod. S., 3, 48, 4, transf. "to make known," e.g., ὡς ἂν πεφωτισμένων τῶν πραγμάτων ὑπὸ τῆς ἀληθείας, Luc. De calumnia, 32, ἡ μὲν οὖν ἀνθρωπίνη βοήθεια παντάπασιν ἦν ἀσθενής, ἡ τύχη δὲ ἐφώτισε τὴν ἀλήθειαν ἧς χωρὶς ἔργον οὐδὲν τέλειον, Charito, III, 8, [3] cf. Polyb., 30, 8, 1; Epict. Diss., I, 4, 31; ἐπεὶ δὲ ἡ τοῦ δαιμονίου πρόνοια... τὰ κεκρυμμένα βουλεύματα... εἰς φῶς ἄγει, Dion. Hal. Ant. Rom., 10, 10, 2. Jewish influence may be seen in Audollent Def. Tab., 242, 13 (3rd cent. A.D.): ὁρκίζω σε τὸν θεὸν τὸν φωτίζοντα καὶ σκοτίζοντα τὸν κόσμον. The mysteries use the word, e.g., Vet. Val., IX, 15 (p. 359, 22): πεφωτισμένη τὴν μυσταγωγίαν ἐκτήσω, cf. VII, 2 (p. 271, 14 ff.). c. φωτισμός "shining," "gleaming," is rare. There are instances from

---

"Die Begriffe 'Licht' u. 'Finsternis' im AT, Spätjudt. u. im Rabbinismus," *Skrifter utgitt av det Norske Videnskaps-Akad. i Oslo, Historisk-filosofisk Klasse,* 1951, 1 (1951); K. Schubert, *Die Religion d. nachbibl. Judt.* (1955), 87-94; Index, *s.v.* "Licht"; G. Scholem, *Die jüd. Mystik in ihrer Hauptströmungen* (1957), 43-86. On D.: J. Kroll, "Die Lehren d. Herm. Trismeg.," *Beitr. z. Gesch. d. Philosophie d. MA,* 12, 2-4 (1914); W. Bousset, Review of J. Kroll, *op. cit.* in GGA, 176 (1914), 697-755; C. H. Dodd, *The Bible and the Gks.* (1935), Index, *s.v.* φῶς; T. Säve-Söderbergh, *Stud. in the Coptic Manichaean Psalm-Book* (1949), 155-163; A. J. Festugière, *La révélation d'Herm. Trismég.,* I² (1950); II (1949); III (1953); IV² (1954); A. Adam, "Texte z. Manichäismus," KlT, 175² (1969); J. Daniélou, *Philon d'Alex.* (1958), 149-153; A. Adam, "Die Psalmen d. Thomas u. d. Perlenlied als Zeugnisse vorchr. Gnosis," ZNW Beih., 24 (1959), 34 f., 42-44, 56, 68-72; E. S. Drower, *The Secret Adam* (1960), 56-64; K. Rudolph, "Die Mandäer, I. Prolegomena: Das Mandäerproblem," FRL, 56 (1960), Index, *s.v.* "Lichtsymbolik" etc.; II. "Der Kult," FRL, 57 (1961), Index, *s.v.* "Lichtgewand," "Lichtwelt" etc.; S. Schulz, "Die Bdtg. neuerer Gnosisfunde f. d. nt.liche Wissenschaft," ThR, NF, 26 (1960), 209-266; A. Wlosok, *Laktanz u. d. philosoph. Gnosis,* AAHdbg., 1960, 2 (1960); F. N. Klein, *Die Lichtterminologie bei Philon v. Alex. u. in d. hermetischen Schr.* (1962). On E. II: S. Aalen, "Der Begriff d. Lichtes in d. synpt. Ev.," *Svensk Exeget. Årsbok,* 22/23 (1957/58), 17-30. On E. IV, 1: G. P. Wetter, "Ich bin das Licht d. Welt," *Beitr. z. Religionswissenschaft,* I, 2 (1913/14), 166-201; H. Preisker, "Jüd. Apokalyptik u. hell. Synkretismus im Joh.-Ev., dargelegt am Begriff 'Licht,'" ThLZ, 77 (1952), 673-8; E. Haenchen, "Aus d. Lit. z. Joh.-Ev.," ThR, NF, 23 (1955), 295-335; H. Becker, "Die Reden d. Joh.-Ev. u. der Stil d. gnostischen Offenbarungsrede," FRL, 68 (1956); R. E. Brown, "The Qumran-Scrolls and the Johannine Gospel and Epistles," *The Scrolls and the NT,* ed. K. Stendahl (1957), 183-207; F. M. Cross, *The Ancient Library of Qumran* (1958), 153-162; S. Schulz, "Die Komposition d. Joh.-Prologs u. d. Zusammensetzung d. 4. Ev.," *Stud. Evangelica,* I, TU, 73 (1959), 351-362; also "Komposition u. Herkunft d. joh. Reden," BWANT, 81 (1960), 99-102; K. G. Kuhn, "Joh.-Ev. u. Qumrantexte," *Festschr. O. Cullmann* (1962), 111-122; H. Braun, *Qumran u. d. NT,* 1 (1966), 96-138. On E. IV, 2: O. Schaefer, "'Gott ist Licht,' 1 Jn. 1:5. Inhalt u. Tragweite d. Worts," ThStKr, 105 (1933), 467-476; C. H. Dodd, "The First Ep. of John and the Fourth Gospel," *The Bulletin of the John Rylands Libr.,* 21 (1937), 129-156; J. Dupont, "Jésus-Christ. Lumière du monde," *Essais sur la christologie de S. Jean* (1951), 61-105; E. Haenchen, "Neuere Lit. z. d. Joh.-Br.," *Die Bibel u. wir. Gesammelte Aufsätze,* II (1968), 235-311.

[1] φῶς is contracted from φάος (→ n. 2), which comes from *φάϝος. It belongs to aor. φά(ϝ)ε the dawn "appeared," Hom. Od., 14, 502 and the reduplicated pres. πιφαύσκω, Hom. Od., 11, 442 and later poets, "to bring to light," mid. "to show." It is also associated with φαίνω (→ 1, n. 1) "to show," φαίνομαι "to appear," aor. ἐφάνην, perf. πέφηνα (→ *loc. cit.*), but the relation of φαϝ- to φαν-, which reminds us of χάος and χαίνω, perf. κέχηνα "to open, gape," is not clear. For other cognates *v.* Boisacq, Hofmann, Frisk, *s.v.* φάος. In Attic φωτός, φωτί etc. for φάεος, φάει etc. were also constructed afresh from φῶς [Risch].

[2] Hom. never has φῶς but either φάος, e.g., Od., 23, 371, which also occurs later, e.g., Aristoph. Eq., 973, or φόως, Od., 5, 2, *v.* Liddell-Scott, *s.v.* φάος.

[3] Ed. W. E. Blake (1938). Other examples in Festugière, IV, 100, n. 1.

c. 300 B.C., e.g., Plut. Fac. Lun., 16 (II, 929d); 18 (II, 931a). [4] d. The same is true of φωστήρ "body of light," "gleam." This is used esp. in relation to stars: οἱ δύο φωστῆρες (sc. sun and moon), Simpl. in Epict., 27 (Dübner, 72, 6 f.), ὁρκίζω σε τὸν φωστῆρα καὶ ἄστρα ἐν οὐρανῷ ποιήσαντα Audollent Def. Tab., 271, 23 f. (3rd cent. A.D.). [5] In a transf. sense a king is called φωστήρ, Themist. Or., 16, 204c. Vett. Val., II, 36 (p. 110, 22) ref. to the eyes as φωστῆρες. The sense of "gleam" occurs from Anth. Graec., 11, 359, 7. e. φωσφόρος as adj. means "bringing morning light" of Ἕως, Eur. Ion, 1157, Dionysos, Aristoph. Ra., 342. As noun it means "morning-star," Tim. Locr., 96e; 97a; Ps.-Aristot. Mund., 2, p. 392a, 27; Cic. Nat. Deor., II, 20, 53. [6] f. φωτεινός (→ VII, 424, n. 7) "light" is the opp. of σκοτεινός and is used both lit. and transf., of the sun, Xenoph. Mem., IV, 3, 4, in antithesis to σκοτεινός III, 10, 1; Plut. Col., 7 (II, 1110b). [7] Transf. φωτεινός means "clear," of the λόγος, Plut. Lib. Educ., 13 (II, 9b). g. ἐπιφαύσκω and ἐπιφώσκω [8] "to shine forth," are rare and late. Obviously they replace the older διαφαύσκω (-φώσκω) and ὑποφαύσκω "the days dawns," e.g., ἅμ' ἡμέρη . . . διαφωσκούσῃ, Hdt., III, 86, 1, ὑποφωσκούσης (vl. ὑποφαυσκούσης) ἕω, Aristot. Probl., 25, 5, p. 938a, 32, ὑποφαύσκοντος, 8, 17, p. 888b, 27, ἄρτι διαφαύσκοντος, Polyb., 31, 14, 13, v. also Orph. Hymn. (Quandt), 50, 9; Act. Thom. 34 (p. 151, 11).

2. Meaning.

As regards the noun φῶς we find lit. transf. and fig. meanings from the earliest period. Related words like αὐγάζω (→ I, 507, 31 ff.), λάμπω (→ IV, 16, 1 ff.), σέλας, φέγγος etc., should also be considered with ref. to the phenomenon of light → n. 135. Lit. φῶς means a. "daylight" ἤδη μὲν φάος ἦεν ἐπὶ χθόνα, Hom. Od., 23, 371, τὸ ἡμερινὸν φῶς Plat. Resp., VI, 508c. ἐν φάει means "openly," Hom. Od., 21, 429, ἅμα φάει "with the dawn," Plut. De Aristide, 15 (I, 327d). The opp. is νύξ, Aesch. Prom., 24, ζόφος, Hom. Od., 3, 335. It then means b. "sunlight" κατέδυ λαμπρὸν φάος ἠελίοιο, Hom. Il., 1, 605 or the "light" of other heavenly bodies σελάνας ἐρατὸν φάος, Pind. Olymp., 10, 75, cf. Plat. Resp., VII, 516a-b. Then c. it means "brightness" on earth; return from Hades is return to the light, Soph. Phil., 624 f.; El., 419. It can ref. d. to the "shining" of lights, Hom. Od., 19, 33 f.; Aesch. Choeph., 863. Then it denotes e. the "lights" themselves, "lamps," φῶτα, BGU, III, 909, 16 (359 A.D.), φῶς ποιέω "to kindle fire," Xenoph. Hist. Graec., VI, 2, 29. [9]

Light is not just a medium of sight, Plat. Resp., VI, 508a; Epict. Diss., I, 6, 6. 8 but also its object, cf. the attributes given to it: φάος ἱερόν, Hes. Op., 339, ἡμέρας . . . ἁγνὸν φάος, Eur. Fr., 443 (TGF, 495), cf. Soph. El., 86, οὐράνιον, Soph. Ant., 944, γλυκερόν, Hom. Od., 16, 23, ἡδὺ γὰρ τὸ φῶς βλέπειν, Eur. Iph. Aul., 1218 f., φέγγος ἱλαρόν, Aristoph. Ra., 456, καθαρόν, Pind. Pyth., 9, 90, λαμπρόν, 8, 97. [10] This com-

---

[4] Other examples in Pass., Liddell-Scott, Pr.-Bauer, s.v.

[5] On the examples from the LXX → 318, 19 ff.; for Judaism cf. also Sib., 3, 88; Test. L. 14:3; Jud. 25:2; Gr. En. 104:2 (ed. C. Bonner, "The Last Chapters of Enoch in Greek," Stud. and Documents, 8 [1937]), in the NT Phil. 2:15. φωστήρ means "radiance" in 1 Ἐσδρ. 8:76; Rev. 21:11.

[6] Cf. Wnd. Kath. Br. on 2 Pt. 1:19. Dölger thinks in Ant. Christ., V, 1-43 that φωσφόρος means sun, rather than morning-star which fits the context better. But his examples of this usage are precarious.

[7] On the formation of the word → VII, 424, n. 7.

[8] Only later lexicographers have the simple φαύσκω, φώσκω, e.g., Etym. M., 673, 51, though Hom. and later poets have a trans. πιφαύσκω → n. 1. The ω of -φωσκω may be interpreted as a borrowing from φῶς [Risch].

[9] Ant. Christ., V, 27, n. 72.

[10] The attributes are collected in Beierwaltes, 99 f. "In part we find words that indicate the numinous character of light, in parts laudatory terms deriving from thanks for the gift of light . . . in part terms that offer a gen. characterisation of its nature," Beierwaltes, 99 and v. Dölger Sol, 358, n. 1; Ant. Christ., V, 1-43.

pletely distinguishes the Gks from Orientals. [11] The basic connection between light and vision may be seen in phrases like φάος ὀμμάτων "light of the eyes," Pind. Nem., 10, 40 f., φάεα "the eyes," Hom. Od., 16, 15, ὄσσε φαεινώ "the bright eyes" of Zeus, Il., 16, 645, cf. of the inner eye τὴν τῆς ψυχῆς αὐγήν, Plat. Resp., VII, 540a. On light and seeing → 315, 4 ff. [12] Light is the possibility of grasping and hence of mastering the world. Seeing light is life ὄφρα δέ μοι ζώει καὶ ὁρᾷ φάος ἠελίοιο, Hom. Il., 18, 61, 442, [13] separation from it death, → VII, 19 ff.; 424, Hom. Il., 18, 10 f.; Aristoph. Ach., 1185. The fig. and transf. sense of the term results from this relation to light as the possibility of life not merely as existence but as full life: ὅτι γὰρ ἀσμένοις τοῖς ἀνθρώποις καὶ ἱμείρουσιν ἐκ τοῦ σκότους τὸ φῶς ἐγίγνετο, ταύτῃ ὠνόμασαν "ἱμέραν" (i.e., ἡμέραν), Plat. Crat., 418c-d. There is an indication here that light's existence is not self-evident. For φῶς and direction cf. Plat. Resp., VII, 518a (on the process of seeing): ἐκ φωτὸς εἰς σκότος — ἐκ σκότους εἰς φῶς. φῶς is used to denote well-being in gen. It can be an obj. of praise, e.g., the shining light of freedom, Aesch. Choeph., 809 f. This expresses the fact that man is not already in health. Light is the world of the gods, cf. Hom. Od., 6, 43 ff.; Ps.-Aristot. Mund., 6, p. 400a, 6 ff. [14] It is deliverance φάος δ' ἐτάροισιν ἔθηκεν, Hom. Il., 6, 6 and hope, Soph. Ant., 599 f. The deliverer appears as light καὶ τῷ μὲν φάος ἦλθεν, Hom. Il., 17, 615, cf. 16, 39; Soph. El., 1224. 1354 f., and so, too, the happy man ἦλθες, Τηλέμαχε, γλυκερὸν φάος, Hom. Od., 16, 23. φάος is synon. with joy, Aesch. Pers., 300; φῶς ... μακάριον (sc. the wedding) τῇ παρθένῳ, Eur. Iph. Aul., 439. A woman is φῶς τῆς οἰκίας, Ditt. Syll.³, III, 1238, 2 (c. 160 A.D.). The sense is also positive when light seems neutrally to denote what is "public or known," Pind. Nem., 4, 37 f., ἐς φῶς ... εἶμι, Soph. Phil., 1353; ἐς φῶς λέγω, 581, cf. Athen., 11, 114 (506c); Plat. Leg., IV, 724a; VI, 788c, transf. also Plat. Phaedr., 261e. The sense of good is also present when one observes the opp. σκότος (→ VII, 424, 1 ff.) as the unknown that needs illumination: κλεπτῶν γὰρ ἡ νύξ, τῆς δ' ἀληθείας τὸ φῶς, Eur. Iph. Taur., 1026. The idea of the open is close to that of "fame," Pind. Pyth., 4, 271.

Light accompanies the manifestation of the divine, Eur. Ba., 1082 f. At the translation of Emped. there shines φῶς οὐράνιον καὶ λαμπάδων φέγγος, Diog. L., VIII, 68. [15] The orig. meaning persists when intellectual illumination by the light of knowledge is described, Plut. Aud., 17 (II, 47c); Quomodo quis suos in virtute sentiat profectus, 5 (II, 77d); Plat. → 314, 33 ff. Knowledge leads to self-understanding in the world; it is assumed that this must first be discovered, and hence the metaphors of the way (→ 322, 32 ff.) and the use of verbs like "to shine" in describing the process of knowledge. The direction of the way is indicated by prep., that of διάνοια being ἐκ τῶν σκοτεινῶν καὶ ταρακτικῶν πρὸς τὰ φωτεινὰ καὶ λαμπρά, Plut. Consolatia ad uxorem, 8 (II, 610e).

3. Light and Illumination in Philosophy.

a. The pre-Socratics occasionally speak of light but it is not seen as an element or developed into a concept. This is connected with the total approach. The concern is being, which is sought first as primal matter. [16] φῶς is simply explained as a physical phenomenon

---

[11] In the OT one finds a predicate only in some late passages, Qoh. 11:7: "And sweet is light and precious to the eyes to behold the sun."

[12] Bultmann, 337 f.

[13] Cf. Aesch. Pers., 299; Choeph., 61 ff.; Soph. Oed. Tyr., 375: μηκέτ' ὄντα ... ἐν φάει, Phil., 415.

[14] Beierwaltes, 13.

[15] Beierwaltes, 14-17, though he is wrong simply to equate light and radiance.

[16] Hardly tenable is the thesis of Westhoff, 5 f. 56 that the cult of the sun is the original locus of the Gk. metaphysics of light and the pre-Socratic idea of light is a direct continuation of this cult. He relies on Plat. Crat., 397c-d. But this will not bear the weight put on it. There was no cult of the sun in ancient Greece, Nilsson, II, 839; Bultmann, 332; Beierwaltes, 4. The prayers to the sun in Festugière, IV, 245, n. 3 do not alter this. Westhoff, 6. 15f. 55-7 wrongly equates light and fire. These are to be basically distinguished in spite of Emped. Fr., 84, where the identification serves to explain sight, i.e., by the streaming of fire from the eyes.

in terms of the element of fire → VI, 930, 13 ff. It moves and is an emanating substance, Emped. in Aristot. An., II, 7, p. 418b, 20 ff.; Aristot. himself takes issue with this, *loc. cit.* φῶς is thus an obj. and not a principle of explanation. [17] The theoretical difficulty is that experience of light and dark is different from that of hot and cold. It is not direct in the same way. Light is first a medium and not an obj. of perception. It is not adapted to different forms of perception. We find a transf. sense in Heracl. Fr., 26 (Diels, I, 156): ἄνθρωπος ἐν εὐφρόνηι φάος ἅπτεται ἑαυτῶι ἀποσβεσθεὶς ὄψεις, "man kindles a light in the darkness when his sight is extinguished." [18] The decisive step is taken by Parmenides. In the famous Fr., 1 (Diels, I, 228) he describes the way from the house of night to the light, the way of truth as the way to being which is *eo ipso* being light. [19] The mythical starting-pt. may still be seen when illumination leads back to God. In reality it is the experience of pure thought in which being is known. Light is the necessary presupposition of all understanding. "But after all things were named light (φάος) and night (νύξ), and what is proper to their powers was imparted to them as names, so everything is full both of light and also of invisible (ἄφαντος) night, which are equally important, for nothing is possible which does not stand under one of the two," Parm. Fr., 9, 1 ff. (I, 240 f.). This is not meant morally. Darkness is not guilt but the mere antithesis of light, Fr., 8, 54 (I, 239). The structure of the cosmos corresponds to that of the organ of knowledge. [20] The principle obtains that like is known by like, Parm. acc. to Theophr. De sensu, 1, 3, cf. Plat., Resp., VI, 508b.

b. Basically early dualism does not carry the concept much further. Acc. to the Orphics we first have chaos and night and dark Erebus and broad Tartarus, Aristoph. Av., 693 ff.; Hipp. Ref., IV, 43, 12; 44; 1; Orph. Fr. (Kern), 65, cf. Aristot.'s polemic against this, Metaph., 11, 6, p. 1071b, 20 ff. [21] Sex is brought to light through the coupling of Eros and Chaos. In spite of the figures of the god Phanes and his daughter Nyx the antithesis is not developed terminologically.

c. Among the Pythagoreans light and darkness are among the ten antithetical principles, Alcmaion acc. to Aristot. Metaph., 1, 5, p. 986a, 22 ff.; φῶς is ἐπιφάνεια "visible surface," this is χρῶμα, and this again is πέρας, [22] cf. Aristot. De sensu et sensibilibus, 3, p. 439a, 30 f. Alexander Polyhist. says about the Pythagoreans: ἰσόμοιρά τ' εἶναι ἐν τῷ κόσμῳ φῶς καὶ σκότος, καὶ θερμὸν καὶ ψυχρόν, καὶ ξηρὸν καὶ ὑγρόν, Fr., 93, 26 (FGrHist, III, n. 116). [23]

d. Plato develops a definite metaphysics of light. [24] Light is not just a figure for true being but true being is light; hence it can shine and man attains illumination by ascent to being. Resp., VII, 517b; 521c, speaks of an ascent to light. [25] Knowledge presupposes that

---

[17] Cf. Aetius De placitis reliquiae, VI, 15 (ed. H. Diels, Doxographi Graeci [1879], 405 f.): εἰ ὁρατὸν τὸ σκότος.

[18] What is meant is the light of wisdom, Beierwaltes, 94, n. 3, or the torch of the *logos*, F. J. Brecht, *Heraklit* (1936), 54.

[19] Cf. W. Kranz. "Über Aufbau u. Bdtg. d. Parmenideischen Gedichtes," SAB, 1916, 47 (1916), 1158-1176; W. Jaeger, *Paideia*, I³ (1954), 240; also *Die Theol. d. frühen griech. Denker* (1953), 122; B. Snell, *Die Entdeckung d. Geistes³* (1955), 197-200; H. Fränkel, "Parmenidesstud.," NGG, 1930 (1930), 153-192; also *Dichtung u. Philosophie d. frühen Griechentums³* (1969) 398-422; Beierwaltes, 34-36; K. Deichgräber, "Parmenides' Auffahrt z. Göttin d. Rechts," AA Mainz (1958), 629-724; A. Schwabe, "Hes. u. Parm.," *Rhein. Mus.*, 106 (1963), 134-142; W. Burkert, "Das Prooem d. Parm. und d. Katabasis des Pythagoras," *Phronesis,* 14 (1969), 1-30.

[20] Beierwaltes, 34-36.

[21] Dölger Sonne, 42-44.

[22] Cf. Jaeger Theol., *op. cit.,* 79 and 126; Beierwaltes, 30-33.

[23] Cf. on this F. Jacoby, FGrHist, IIIa, 293 f.

[24] Cf. esp. the conclusion of Resp. VI and beginning of Resp. VII, also Ep., 7 (the question of authenticity need not be discussed here).

[25] P. Friedländer, *Platon,* I³ (1964), 69.

ideas are light, and knowledge illumines being. The ἀγαθόν is τοῦ ὄντος τὸ φανότατον, Resp., VII, 518c, cf. the beautiful, Phaedr., 250d. On the identity of the good and the beautiful, cf. Resp., VI, 508a-509d with Symp., 210e-212a. [26] Light and truth correspond: ὅν (sc. the sun) τἀγαθὸν ἐγέννησεν ἀνάλογον ἑαυτῷ, Resp., VI, 508b. Resp., VII, 540a speaks of the vision of the good and its character as light: ... ἀνακλίναντας τὴν τῆς ψυχῆς αὐγὴν ("eye") εἰς αὐτὸ ἀποβλέψαι τὸ πᾶσι φῶς παρέχον, καὶ ἰδόντας τὸ ἀγαθὸν αὐτό, παραδείγματι χρωμένους ἐκείνῳ ... [27] Suddenness is an element in illumination, Ep., 7, 341c. [28] Illumination it not a subj. experience; it opens up the mutual understanding of those who know. The sense is wholly rational rather than mystical, ontological rather than moral. [29] In enquiry man understands himself in the light of the disclosure of the obj. Neither the contours of things nor those of the subj. nor the limits between subj. and obj. are effaced — in spite of the extreme possibility of blinding, Resp., VII, 516a. [30] This is true even when Plato uses the language of the mysteries, Symp., 210a; τελέους ἀεὶ τελετὰς τελούμενος, Phaedr., 249c. [31] Plato knows no dark primal ground or non-ground, [32] cf. the depiction of ascent: γνῶναι ἂν ὅτι ἐκεῖνός ἐστιν ὁ ἀληθῶς οὐρανὸς καὶ τὸ ἀληθινὸν φῶς καὶ ἡ ὡς ἀληθῶς γῆ, Phaed., 109e.

e. Aristot. defines the nature of light as follows: φῶς δέ ἐστιν ἡ τούτου ἐνέργεια τοῦ διαφανοῦς ᾗ διαφανές, δυνάμαι δέ, ἐν ᾧ τοῦτ' ἐστί, καὶ τὸ σκότος, An., II, 7, p. 418b, 9 ff.; δοκεῖ ... τὸ φῶς ἐναντίον εἶναι τῷ σκότει, 418b, 18. Cf. also ἡ γὰρ αὐτὴ φύσις ὁτὲ μὲν σκότος ὁτὲ δὲ φῶς ἐστιν, 418b, 31 f., ἔστι δὲ τὸ σκότος στέρησις τῆς τοιαύτης ἕξεως ἐκ διαφανοῦς, ὥστε δῆλον ὅτι καὶ ἡ τούτου παρουσία τὸ φῶς ἐστιν, 418b, 18-20, and also 419a, 11; III, 3, p. 429a, 3. In III, 5, p. 430a, 14 f. the activity of the νοῦς is compared to a light; Plato proceeds from the fact that things are light, in Aristot. the νοῦς illumines a thing. [33]

4. Light in the Cultus.

Light effects play a role in the cult of the dead. Light drive out demons. [34] Esp. instructive are the mysteries, e.g., the Eleusinian, Hipp. Ref., V, 8, 40, cf. Firm. Mat. Err. Prof. Rel., 22, 1. [35] One may detect a certain development. A constant feature is the hailing of newly streaming light ἄι]δε, [36] νύμφε, χαῖρε, νύμφε, χαῖρε νέον φῶς, Firm.

---

[26] Beierwaltes, 80-82; C. Krüger, Einsicht u. Leidenschaft (1939), 157-165.

[27] Beierwaltes, 52: "Intelligible light is logically and ontologically prior to sensory light." Stenzel, 243: "Rather than that a too bright light causes this world to vanish in darkness, all vision of the eternal and immutable is constantly used to penetrate it. This world is transparent in its present divinity precisely through the indication of a hidden intellectual and sensory core and the light of vision directed on it streams back to itself from its innermost ground."

[28] Stenzel, 252. On the understanding of truth as hiddenness (with M. Heidegger, Platons Lehre von d. Wahrheit [1947] as against Friedländer, op. cit., I, 233-248): Beierwaltes, 74-9; E. Heitsch, "Wahrheit als Erinnerung," Herm., 91 (1963), 36-52. For metaphorical use in Plato cf. Phaedr., 261e; Ep., 7, 341d; Leg., VII, 788c.

[29] Stenzel, 257: "Illumination as to good and evil means for Plato knowledge of the world through very scientific knowledge; it is not the stimulation of the responsible conscience, nor redemption by divine grace, nor guidance by a charismatically endowed leader."

[30] One can see this from the continuation of the passage quoted, where being in light is contrasted with being in darkness and the stages of knowledge up to vision of the ἀγαθόν are depicted, Resp., VII, 516c-518d.

[31] Beierwaltes, 25; Bultmann, 342.

[32] Beierwaltes, 77.

[33] Ibid., 95.

[34] Cumont, 47 and 54.

[35] Rohde, I, 285; Wetter Phos, 98-101.

[36] The reading ἰδέ (for ἄιδε) is championed by M. J. Vermaseren, Mithras. Gesch. eines Kults (1965), 117; on νύμφε for νύμφιε cf. Bidez-Cumont, 154.

Mat. Err. Prof. Rel., 19, 1. [37] In the class. period light means epiphany or the vision of light rather than personal illumination. An epiphany of Dionysos is described in Soph. Ant., 1146 ff.; Oed. Col., 1047 ff.; Eur. Ba., 594 ff.; Aristoph. Ra., 343 ff. → 348, n. 315; IV, 17, 33 ff. The element of epiphany persists in the later period. But here the way through the mystery becomes mystical ascent, Apul. Met., XI, 23, with interchange of light and darkness: σκότους τε καὶ φωτὸς ἐναλλὰξ αὐτῷ (i.e., the initiate) φαινο-μένων, Dio Chrys. Or., 12, 33. Interest focuses, not on the antithesis of light and dark-ness, but on the goal, cf. Apul. Met., XI, 23. This may be seen already in the effect of mystery motifs on the light symbolism of the class. age → 315, 13 ff., cf. also Plut. Is. et Os., 77 (II, 382c-d); ἐλλάμπω is almost a tt. in Iambl. Myst., e.g., II, 6 (p. 81).

B. The Word Group in the Old Testament.

1. The Ancient Oriental Background.

One sees everywhere here the original understanding of light as the natural brightness of day. Oriental usage does not break loose from the connection of light and bodies of light. It is rooted in nature. Sun, light, life and salvation go together. [38] The main ref. is to the sun. An example of this connection is the hymn of Echnaton. [39] Only on this basis are the predicates of light transferred to other bearers. [40] In spite of very different cosmology the same holds good in Babylonia. Here, too, light is linked to its bearer. Light predication is found esp. in hymns. Šamaš is the "lighter of darkness, the illuminator of obscurity, who breaks through the darkness, illumines the broad earth, makes the day bright." [41] Prayer is made to him (by Nabonidus): "Grant me a life for the furthest days, that I may dwell for ever in thy light." [42] The extreme limit of reflection attainable in oriental thought is the paradox that in light one can be wrapped in darkness. The so-called Sumerian Job

---

[37] On the issuing of the call v. Ant. Christ., V, 1-43 passim. For lychnomanticism cf. Preis. Zaub., I, 4, 978 f. (4th cent. A.D.): ὁρκίζω σε, ἱερὸν φῶς, ἱερὰ αὐγή, πλάτος, βάθος, μῆκος, ὕψος, αὐγή (cf. Eph. 3:18), v. also 959 ff.; Nilsson, II, 508.

[38] Physical and true life are not distinguished where the idea of an after life is dominant, as in Egypt. True life is happy, full life in this world. On cosmology and the world to come cf. Hornung, 73-81; also Nacht u. Finsternis im Weltbild d. alten Ägypter, Diss. Tübingen (1956).

[39] Cf. AOT, 15. Further songs in A. Erman, Die Lit. d. Ägypter, (1923), 187-192. How little light is abstracted from the sun is shown by this hymn, Ancient Near Eastern Texts relating to the OT, ed. J. B. Pritchard² (1955), 367 f. (→ VII, 426, n. 31). The monuments are also instructive, cf. J. B. Pritchard, The Ancient Near East in Pictures (1954), No. 408 f., 411, on the hands of the sun-god that send forth the divine light-power-fluid cf. F. Preisigke, "Vom göttlichen Fluidum nach ägypt. Anschauung," Pap.-Institut Heidelberg, I (1920), 6-10, cf. E. R. Goodenough, Jewish Symbols in the Greco-Roman Period, V (1956), 146 f.; V, Ill., 183 (sun, emission of water, sign of life ankh, on this cf. p. 186). Cf. also A. Massart, "L'emploi, en Égyptien, de deux termes opposés pour exprimer la totalité," Festschr. A. Robert (1957), 38-46.

[40] Hymn to the Nile (Erman, op. cit., 195): "Thou light that comest from the darkness, thou feed for the cattle." Acc. to Hornung, 81 darkness is not personified apart from the god Kuk. But light is constantly personified in the sun, stars, "the king, the cultic flame, as an eye or a serpent."

[41] A. Falkenstein and W. v. Soden, Sumerische u. akkad. Hymnen u. Gebete (1953), 247, cf. AOT, 247.

[42] Falkenstein-Soden, 288. There is already something similar among the Sumerians: "... The gt. [lady of] heaven, Inanna, will I greet, holy light, that fills the heaven, will I greet, Inanna, that shines afar as the sun ... the heroine of heaven that pours forth full light ...," Falkenstein-Soden, 90. "Thy prince is a lofty light, a gt. storm," 132. "The pure and blinding sunlight is he," says the temple-building hymn of Gudea of Lagaš, 156. Šamaš is "the true protector of right since his streaming light pierces all things," Soden, 649. Light becomes a special god, Kusku, chamberlain of Enlil, ibid., 651 f.

says: "My God, thy day beams in splendour over the land. For me the day is dark," Inscr. of Nippur, line 68 (c. 1700 B.C.). [43]

In Iran light and darkness play no part in the older Avesta, the Gathas. They do not figure in the passage on the two spirits which are so important in historical evaluation of the Dead Sea Scrolls → 325, 15 ff. [44] There is a bright sphere of salvation and a dark one of ruin, [45] but no terminological development of the antithesis. [46] The one passage which in some sense approaches this is Yasna, 44, 5: [47] "I ask thee this, vindicate me openly, Lord. What master created the lights and darkness? What master created sleep and waking? Who is it by whom morning, mid-day and evening exist, to summon the one aware of responsibility to his duty?" [48] In Zarathustra, as in the rest of the ancient Orient, light is not detached from the natural sub-stratum. Hence it is doubtful whether one can trace back the Jewish, Chr. or Gnostic dualism of light and darkness to Persian religion, esp. as a development may be traced within Judaism itself → 323, 16 ff. In any case, there is no source material for the period in question. [49]

Nevertheless, there are arguments for an early dating of light-darkness terminology in Iran. It plays an important role in the later Avesta and completely dominates the Mandaean writings. [50] This suggests an earlier origin. [51] Gk. accounts of Persian dualism

---

[43] Cf. S. N. Kramer, "Man and his God," Festschr. H. H. Rowley, VT Suppl., 3 (1955), 170-182.

[44] Yasna, 30, 2-5: "... Receive supreme values with the ears, consider with bright mind the two confessions of decision ... The two spirits at the beginning, the twins, revealing themselves by a dream, are the better and the bad in thinking, speaking and acting. The prudent choose well between the two, not fools. But when the two spirits clashed, they established life and death ... an evil fate awaits the servants of falsehood at the end, but the best mind is reserved for those who believe aright. From these two spirits the lying spirit selected himself to do his worst, but the holy spirit who has the firmest heaven as his garment (elected) divine right" cf. Hinz, 169 f. Cf. K. G. Kuhn, "Die Sektenschr. u. d. iranische Religion," ZThK, 49 (1952), 296-316; H. Lommel, Die Religion Zarathustras (1930), 22 f.; H. S. Nyberg, "Die Religionen d. Alten Iran," Mitteilungen d. Vorderasiatisch-Ägypt. Gesellschaft, 43 (1938), 102-9; Hinz, 107-9.

[45] Festugière, III, 24, cf. 87, n. 2 thinks Iranian dualism is within the world whereas Greek dualism is between this world and a spiritual world, but the findings (cf. Yasna, 28, 2 f.; Hinz, 168) do not support this.

[46] Yasna, 43, 16 (Hinz, 184): "In the sunlit world there may be devotion (armaiti)"; Yasna, 31, 7 (172): "He who thought first of flooding the blessed fields with lights," cf. the comm., Hinz, 205 and 212; Nyberg, op. cit., 127. Yasna, 50, 10 (200): "The lights of the sun, the dawn light that gives flame to the day." Yasna, 31, 20 (174): "He who ranges himself with true belief names joyous fortune in the future (H. Humbach Die Gathas d. Zarathustra, I [1959] 94: "ray of fortune") his own. Long pining in darkness, poor food, lamentation — to such a plight, servants of falsehood, will your own nature bring you on account of your deeds."

[47] Hinz, 185.

[48] The similarity to Is. 45:7 is so gt. that one may suspect Persian influence on Dt. Is., cf. R. Mayer, "Die biblische Vorstellung vom Weltenbrand," Bonner Orient. Stud., NS, 4 (1956), 128. Yet the detachment from a basis in nature, is surely the decisive pt. here. Cf. for Zarathustra Lommel, op. cit., 199 f. Acc. to O. G. v. Wesendonck, Das Weltbild d. Iranier (1933), 212 light religion occurs expressly only in the later Avesta.

[49] How examples can be found may be seen from Nyberg, op. cit., 130: "Hertel's (J. Hertel, "Die Sonne u. Mithra im Avesta," Indoiran. Quellen u. Forschungen 9 [1927], 17 and 78, also "Beiträge z. Erklärung d. Awestas u. d. Vedas," ASG, 40, 2 [1929], 20) transl. of asa as 'light of salvation' cannot be justified etym. as he thinks, and it is also one-sided, but materially it is not incorrect and it corresponds to an important aspect of the meaning of asa."

[50] On the later Avesta → n. 48; Wesendonck, passim. The Parthian-Gnostic texts may be found in C. Colpe, "Die religionsgeschichtliche Schule," FRL, 78 (1961), 72-88 (bibl.); G. Widengren, "Iranisch-semitische Kulturbegegnung in parthischer Zeit," Arbeitsgemeinschaft f. Forschung des Landes Nordrhein-Westfalen, 70 (1960). On Manicheeism → 339, 4 ff.

[51] Manichaean vocabulary cannot be traced back to the Chr. tradition. On the other hand we must beware of conclusions from Manichaean works: "It should be added that the

pose a special problem. [52] Acc. to Plut. Is. et Os., 46 f. (II, 369e-f) Zarathustra has two gods: ... τὸν μὲν ἐοικέναι φωτὶ μάλιστα τῶν αἰσθητῶν, τὸν δ' ἔμπαλιν σκότῳ καὶ ἀγνοίᾳ... ὁ μὲν Ὡρομάζης ἐκ τοῦ καθαρωτάτου φάους ὁ δ' Ἀρειμάνιος ἐκ τοῦ ζόφου γεγονὼς πολεμοῦσιν ἀλλήλοις. The one god is like light, the other like darkness and ignorance; between is Mithra as μεσίτης (→ IV, 604, 44 ff.). [53] Hipp. Ref., I, 2, 12 offers another example: Διόδωρος δὲ ὁ Ἐρετριεὺς καὶ Ἀριστόξενος [54] ὁ μουσικός φασι πρὸς Ζαράταν τὸν Χαλδαῖον ἐληλυθέναι Πυθαγόραν. τὸν δὲ ἐκθέσθαι αὐτῷ δύο εἶναι ἀπ' ἀρχῆς τοῖς οὖσιν αἴτια, πατέρα καὶ μητέρα. καὶ πατέρα μὲν φῶς, μητέρα δὲ σκότος. Zaratas is supposed to have taught δύο δαίμονας εἶναι, τὸν μὲν οὐράνιον, τὸν δὲ χθόνιον, I, 2, 13. [55]

2. Usage.

Dominant is the word group אוֹר, which is used in a lit. sense for light and its shining and also in a transf. sense.

The verb אוֹר q "to shine" denotes the break of day, 2 S. 2:32, the brightening of the eyes, 1 S. 14:27, 29, cf. hi Ps. 13:3. אוֹרִי has a transf. sense at Is. 60:1. Similarly the hi means "to cause to shine," "to light up." The night will shine, give out light, as the day, Ps. 139:12. Prayer is made to God that He will cause His face to shine, Ps. 31:16. His commandment gives light to the eyes, Ps. 19:8.

The noun אוֹר denotes daylight in Ju. 16:2 and the light of the stars in Is. 30:26, cf. also מָאוֹר "star" in Gn. 1:14, 16 (LXX φωστήρ → 312, 1 ff.) and also in Wis. 13:2;

Manichaean view of light and darkness is not a necessary deduction from Zoroastrian or Zervanian presuppositions," Colpe, op. cit., 126. Ref. should also be made to the developed light and light/darkness terminology of Indian texts. Light is being, salvation. "We have now drunk soma, we have become immortal. We have attained to light, we have found the gods," Rigveda, VIII, 48, 3, cf. K. F. Geldner, "Vedismus u. Brahmanismus," Religionsgesch. Lesebuch, ed. A. Bertholet, 9² (1928), 57. "From non-being lead me to being, from darkness lead me to light, from death lead me to immortality," S'athapatha-Brāhmana, 14, 4, 1, 30, Geldner, 75, cf. Index, s.v. "Licht" etc.; cf. I. Gonda, Die Religionen Indiens, I (1960), 91-5.

[52] Clemen Fontes, passim; Clemen Nachrichten, passim; Benveniste, passim; Bidez-Cumont, I and II, passim. The supposed Basilides Fr. in Hegemonius Acta Archelai (ed. C. H. Beeson, GCS, 16 [1906], 67, 7-11) is worthless. Basilides presents the doctrine of two principles, light and darkness, as that of barbarians, i.e., Persians. The anti-Manich. production has no value as a source either for Basilides (H. Leisegang, Die Gnosis⁴ [1955], 204, though cf. C. H. Dodd, The Interpretation of the Fourth Gospel² [1953], 103 f.) or for Persian religion, whose Manichaean modification is presupposed. Cf. the account of Mani in Hegemonius, 7, 1 - 13, 3.

[53] Keen note is taken of this ref. because Theopompus is quoted in the vicinity. If the account comes from him we have another example from the 4th cent. B.C. But analysis shows that it does not. The express naming of Theopomp. shows that he is not the source of what precedes, cf. F. Jacoby, FGrHist, IId, 365 on Theopomp. Fr., 65. Bidez-Cumont, II, 72-9 show that Plut.'s account is not a unity, though cf. Benveniste, 112 f., who takes it to be an authentic account of Zervanism. This assertion is overthrown already by the false etym. of Mithra, cf. also Hopfner, II, 155-169. One might also ask how far Gk. terminology has penetrated the presentation to express the generally known dualism of the Persians, cf. also Plut. Quaest. Rom., 25 (II, 270c) and esp. Diog. L. prooem, 8 (Bidez-Cumont, II, 9), who appeals to Aristot. De philosophia Fr., 6 (ed. R. Walzer [1934]) and Eudoxus of Cnidus and speaks of two principles but does not mention light/darkness terminologically. On the question of Gk. accounts of oriental matters v. also J. Kerschensteiner, Plat. u. d. Orient (1945), 66 f.

[54] A pupil of Aristot.; Bidez-Cumont, I, 33.

[55] Clemen Nachrichten, 187 f. thinks the naming of the father as light and the mother as darkness is a transferring of Pythagorean teaching to Zarathustra. Materially cf. Plut. De animae procreatione in Timaeo, 2 (II, 1012e); Hipp. Ref., VI, 23, 4; also Cl. Al. Strom., I, 15, 69, 6 - 70, 1 (Bidez-Cumont, II, 36) appealing to Alexander Polyhist. Fr., 94 (FGrHist, III, A 118).

Sir. 43:7. Light characterises natural life, Ps. 38:10; 56:13, and also spiritual life, Ps. 37:6; 97:11; 112:4; 119:105. God enfolds Himself in light, Ps. 104:2 → 320, 4. He is the light of the righteous, Mi. 7:8 f. [56] and the possibility of life: In His light we see light, Ps. 36:9. Illumination is by the Word and hence by the Torah, Ps. 19:8.

The most important further terms are נֵר "light," Ps. 119:105, נגה "to shine," Is. 9:1, נֹגַהּ "radiance," Is. 60:19, נהר "to shine," Is. 60:5 and יפע "to shine forth," Dt. 33:2. Of the 200 [57] instances of root אור in the HT, 137 are transl. by φῶς (110 times) and cognates. Elsewhere various Gk. words are used which almost all belong to the same field and may just indicate the time of day. In contrast φῶς, esp. in the Wisdom lit. and Is., denotes the divinely given sphere of human life acc. to creation (Job). [58]

Light is not itself an obj. of sight as among the Gks. Nor, rather oddly, does it have any attributes. [59] Only with reservations can one speak of a theological development of light terminology. [60] The transf. use presupposes for its part a definite understanding of man's existence in the world, namely, as movement in a space which may be a sphere of light or darkness. There is always in view the twofold possibility of salvation or perdition, and thought is naturally orientated, not to ever imminent disaster, but to the salvation that has always to be sought and protected. For the rest, this structure of under-standing is largely the same as that found in early Gk. thought.

3. General.

Light is first physical, experienced brightness, the sphere of natural life (→ 313, 5 ff.) with its rhythm of day and night. [61] But it is not considered as a phenomenon nor experienced as a state in which seeing, movement, and care for life are possible. [62] Life is existence here and now. [63] The world is not contrasted with a world of light beyond, nor is earthly light derived from such transcendent light. God is surrounded by brightness, but is is worth noting that there is little contact between references to God's כָּבוֹד (→ II, 245, 33 ff.) and light. Even where they are combined, the terms are not synon., e.g., in Ps. 104:1, where we find הוֹד וְהָדָר for כָּבוֹד. The distinction, and relation, are plain to see in Is. 60:1-3. The "glory" is around and in Yahweh; it constitutes His being. But this cannot be said of light. Yahweh is not light. What is said of this is that "the Lord is my light" (Ps. 27:1). He is the One who causes His light to shine, Job 37:3. Light denotes a relation, not being. Light is a term for life in the absolute sense, not as mere existence, but as possibility. It thus denotes salvation, cf. light and life in Ps. 36:9; 56:13. To see light (→ 313, 6 ff.) is to live.

---

[56] B. Reicke, "Mik. 7 såsom 'messiansk' Text, med särskild hänsyn till Mt. 10:35 f. och Lk. 12:53," Svensk Exeget. Årsbok, 12 (1947), 263-286.

[57] Acc. to Mandelkern.

[58] Lines 8-10 are by Bertram.

[59] The only instance of characterisation by an adj. in a predicative position is late and shows Hell. influence, namely, Qoh. 11:7 (→ n. 11), cf. Eur. Iph. Aul., 1218.

[60] As against Aalen Licht u. Finsternis, 3. The concept of light has no significance in relation to the Law (apart from the individualistic view of it in Wisdom) or history. Thus in the Hexateuch it occurs only in a profane sense except in the Sinai theophanies. In the LXX perhaps Hos. 10:12 is of interest (→ I, 700, n. 50); נִיר וְעֵת is read as נֵר דַּעַת and transl. φωτίσατε ἑαυτοῖς φῶς γνώσεως. Do we have here the trace of a model for the Philonic idea of illumination in Alexandrian Judaism? Cf. Wlosok, 83, n. 60.

[61] Hempel, 352 stresses that the alternation of light and darkness in the OT is a daily rather than an annual experience.

[62] On "to see light" and "light of the eyes" → 313, 1 ff.

[63] In contrast to Judaism → 323. 6 ff.

Job 3:16; 33:28, 30. [64] Part of salvation is to be in the light. In the OT, too, light means self-understanding and freedom from care: "Light streams on the righteous and joy on the upright in heart," Ps. 97:11.

The existential character of references to light may be seen from the way it is spoken of. It is extolled in Ps. 104:2. Theophany is the object in Job 37:15 and creation in Is. 45:7. God's manifestation must be set forth with praise. [65] The petitioner speaks of light in Ps. 43:3 and the teacher of wisdom in Prv. 4:18. Formally light is the sphere in which man moves and it is also movement, esp. when verbs are used: "Light shines forth," Is. 9:1; "that I may walk before God in the light of life," Ps. 56:13.

4. God.

God is the sovereign Lord of light and darkness, Am. 5:8. Light is His sphere or garment, Ps. 104:2. [66] He has created the world-order with the firm rhythm of day and night. But He breaks this when He wills, sending darkness on Egypt or causing the sun to stand still, Jos. 10:12 f. Light is Yahweh in action, Ps. 44:3. Also to be mentioned in this connection is the shining of His countenance, Ps. 4:6, cf. Nu. 6:25 f.; Ps. 80 *passim;* Ps. 31:16; 67:1; 119:135. So, too, is His manifestation in the cloud that sends forth light, Job 37:15 and in the appearance of the fiery pillar, Ps. 78:14. So, too, is theophany, Ex. 24:15 ff.; Ps. 29; 97:1 ff.; Ez. 1:1 ff. [67] Yahweh irradiates light, Hab. 3:4. He is resplendent, Is. 42:16 ff. Hence no darkness can hide from Him, Ps. 139:11 f. He brings what is hidden to light, Job 12:22, cf. 28:11; 34:22. Natural relations pursue their course in His sphere.

5. The World.

The beginnings of reflection on light/darkness and God come to their clearest development when the world is described as creation. Though various philosophical motifs intermingle, the one intention is to bring out God's absolute sovereignty. Even when darkness is the original state, and the mythical chaos motif is thus the basis, the point is not that the world was once autonomous but that it is now an integrated entity. On Gn. 1:1 → 321, 5 ff.; Job 38:8 f., 19 → 321, n. 72. [68]

---

[64] Aalen Licht u. Finsternis, 65 tries to distinguish between "to see the light" as to live and "to see light" as to experience salvation. But when light is spoken of in relation to life this is not understood neutrally. One may see this in the expression "light of the eyes" (→ 322, 25), Ps. 13:3; 38:10. Like life in gen. the light of the eyes is a wonderful gift of God, Prv. 29:13, cf. 15:30. אוֹר has a transf. sense at Ps. 19:8: "The Law of Yahweh is pure; it gives light to the eyes." The opp. (→ VII, 428, 20 ff.) may be seen in Lam. 5:17.

[65] This is the point in the transition from hymnal to didactic form in Gn. 1.

[66] The list is origin. Egyptian but the mention of light is new.

[67] A. Weiser, "Die Darstellung d. Theophanie in d. Ps. u. im Festkult," *Festschr. A. Bertholet* (1950), 513-531.

[68] Job 26:10 is difficult: "God drew a circle about the waters until the completion of light and darkness." There are three possible meanings: a. Inside is light and outside darkness, so G. Hölscher, *Das Buch Hiob, Hndbch. AT,* I 17² (1952), *ad loc.;* b. By day light is inside and darkness outside, *vice versa* by night, K. Budde. *Das Buch Hiob, Handkomm. AT,* II, 1² (1913), *ad loc.:* "Until the cessation of light with darkness"; c., and more probably, light and darkness are separate within the horizon; outside is nothing, cf. v. 7. In the background is the idea of the turning of the sun, Ps. 19:6; Qoh. 1:5, the Egypt. circuit of the sun. In v. 11 there is ref. to the pillars of heaven between which the sun comes forth [Galling].

The highest level of reflection occurs in two passages with very different concepts. The first is Is. 45:7: God created light and darkness, salvation and destruction. [69] Here the cosmology is a basis and foil for the statement about God working to save and to destroy. For the first time, then, we have a clear consideration of the relation between cosmology and soteriology. [70] The second passage, which works with a different set of ideas, is Gn. 1. This is aimed against Bab. cosmogony (→ n. 72), whose concepts may be detected but are defused. The motif here is that of the creation of the world by the Word [71] and differentiation between light and light-bearers. Light is created before the stars. This gives us a view for which there is no parallel in the ancient East. [72] The tension between material and rational construction may be seen in the presentation, esp. as the material itself is not one and the same. At the outset light is separated from darkness and each is assigned to its own place. Then light is carried by the sun and moon and this establishes the rhythm of day and night. Space is dominant in the one case, time in the other. [73] But the haziness

---

[69] In analysis cf. K. Elliger, "Dtjs in seinem Verhältnis zu Tritjs," BWANT, 63 (1933), 244 f., acc. to whom vv. 1-7 are a Cyrus song; cf. R. Rendtorff, "Die theol. Stellung d. Schöpfungsglaubens bei Dtjs," ZThK, 51 (1954), 3-13. The passage is polemical but can hardly be directed against Iranian dualism. The statement is strikingly reminiscent of Yasna, 44, 5, cf. Hinz, 185; → 317, 7 ff. Spiritualisation is advanced by the sing. "light and darkness." If the pt. is ethical in Zarathustra, it is soteriological in Dt. Is. God is sovereign over salvation and destruction. In the juxtaposition of יצר and ברא do we simply have poetic alternation? This is supported by the combination of ברא and חֹשֶׁךְ, cf. later ברא and עֹשֶׂה and the summarising in (כָּל־אֵלֶּה) עֹשֶׂה. The polemic is against Bab. polytheism (and the mythicising of chaos?).

[70] On the use of creation terminology → III, 1006, 22 ff.; on the analogy of the world and the history of Israel, v. Rendtorff, op. cit., passim, and cf. the intensity of the light-sayings about the servant of Yahweh in Is. 42:6; 49:6.

[71] On the historical background cf. G. v. Rad, Theol. d. AT, I⁵ (1966), 156 f. As in Is. 45:7 we find the catchword ברא. v. Rad observes that no prior matter is mentioned in connection with the work of creating.

[72] Light is thus a condition of creation, cf. G. v. Rad, Das erste Buch Mose, AT Deutsch, 2/4⁸ (1967), 39 on 1:3-5: "Without light no creation; only light brings out the contours of things hovering in darkness." On the distinction between light and the stars, loc. cit.: "The remarkable separation of light and the stars was a not impossible idea for the oriental, since he did not relate light and darkness so exclusively to the heavenly bodies, Job 38:19 f." There is an actual relation to Job 38:19 f. (light and darkness have their places), cf. Hölscher, op. cit., ad loc. But here their relation to the stars is not considered as in Gn. 1. On the separation of light and darkness, note that acc. to Berosus Fr., 1 (FGrHist, IIIc, 371) Bel pierces the darkness. But this ref. is not reliable. J. Bidez, "Les écoles chaldéennes sous Alexandre et les Séleucides," Annuaire de l'Institut de Philologie et d'Histoire Orient., 3 (1935), 48-52 suspects Iranian influence. F. Dornseiff, "Antikes z. AT," Kleine Schriften, I (1956), 211 f. sees a trace of the idea in Hes. Theog., 371 f.: Helios, Selene, and Eos are children of Theia (θέα "view," "light"). But Theia is only one of many figures and "she bore these bound to Hyperion in love," 374. The ref. (F. Dornseiff, "Altorientalisches in Hes. Theog.," ibid., 48, n. 25) to Sanchunyaton acc. to Philo of Byblos in Eus. Praep. Ev., I, 10, 1 ff. is also off the mark. Here we have in the beginning dark air and chaos. Then Mot arises like an egg and shines forth, similarly the sun, moon etc. When the dark air becomes bright καὶ τοῦ ἀέρος διαυγάσαντος the clouds come into being, cf. O. Eissfeldt, "Sanchunjaton v. Berut u. Ilumilku v. Ugarit," Beiträge z. Religionsgesch. d. Altertums, 5 (1952), 9, 59-67. May, 206-9 ref. to the Ugaritic Baal whose battle with the waters takes place in darkness and after the battle the day of creation, of light, comes. Egypt. analogies are also no help in spite of S. Herrmann, "Die Naturlehre d. Schöpfungsberichtes," ThLZ, 86 (1961), 413-424, cf. the materials adduced by him and S. Morenz, Ägypt. Religion (1960), 184 f. On the danger of star-worship averted by the separation of light and darkness cf. Job 31:26 ff. One also finds the same idea as in Gn. 1 (light's independence of the heavenly bodies) (May, 211) in Is. 24:23; 60:19 f.; Zech. 14:7 → 322, 9 f.

[73] G. v. Rad, op. cit. (→ n. 71), 157, notes that day and night are differently structured. The one is the remnant of the darkness of chaos, whereas the other is light from the light of creation. This may be true. But tension is not removed by the motif of rhythmic balance,

of the concept shows that the mythical originals have been robbed of their force. Above all the separation of light from the heavenly bodies also controls the relation to darkness → VII, 429, 18 ff.

6. Eschatology.

The sharp thesis of Amos that the Day of Yahweh is darkness and not light (Am. 5:18, 20 → VII, 430, 3 ff.) presupposes expectation that the Day will be light and salvation. This idea persists even through the threat. If the beginning of the end-time is dark, there is still hope of a wonderful age of light for Israel. The sun and moon will shine miraculously (Is. 30:26) [74] and the alternation of day and night will cease (Zech. 14:6 f.). [75] Most strongly spiritual is Is. 60:19 f.: "The sun shall no more serve as thy light by day, neither for brightness shall the moon give light to thee. For Yahweh shall be unto thee an everlasting light, and thy God thy glory ... and the days of thy mourning shall be ended," cf. 60:1-5.

7. Anthropology.

Elements of wisdom style are to be noted in the prophets as well as Prv., Ps., Job, Wis. and Sir. [76] Here, too, the primary emphasis is a positive one on light and the process of illumination. Formally light is described as present on the one side and as coming on the other → lines 5 ff. The distinctive thing is the use of the terms within the understanding of life in this literature, especially its ideal of culture. [77] The wise man is the enlightened man, i.e., righteous, good, and happy. Wisdom is compared to light; radiance φέγγος shines forth from it (Wis. 7:10), cf. the simile in Qoh. 2:13: Wisdom excels folly as light does darkness. One is illumined by it, Qoh. 8:1. The same point is made by similar combinations like light and truth, Ps. 43:3, light and righteousness, Wis. 5:6; Sir. 32:16, or by predicating the Law as light: "The commandment of the Lord is pure, enlightening the eyes," Ps. 19:8, cf. Prv. 6:23. Light is regarded as already present: "Walk in the light of life," Ps. 56:13, and yet also as coming: "Unto the upright there ariseth light in the darkness," Ps. 112:4. Notwithstanding the many nuances, there is a single substratum. Wisdom is the fear of the Lord (→ 197, 26 ff.) and it is thus knowledge of God's will. Having this is no simple thing. One has to acquire it by learning and one has to tread its path, the path to fortune. Representative is Ps. 119, the song of the Torah as enlightening power: "Thy word is a lamp unto my feet, and a light unto my path," v. 105, cf. v. 130. The idea of the path can be presented differently, i.e., as going in the light (Prv. 4:18; Qoh. 2:13 f.) or as going in the darkness with a light (Job 29:3).

Two main stylistic forms may be distinguished, although naturally they overlap. The first is the style of prayer, [78] in which Yahweh is asked for light, Ps. 4:6; 43:3.

K. Galling, "Der Charakter d. Chaosschilderung in Gn. 1:2," ZThK, 47 (1950), 145-157. Hempel, 356 calls the attitude of God to darkness "ambivalent": Darkness is not made but restrained and hence recognised; it becomes a constituent part of day.

[74] The naive gloss "as the light of seven days" is not in the LXX. The passage may be late; our present concern is only with the development of the concept.

[75] On the uncertain text v. E. Sellin, Das Zwölfprophetenbuch, Komm. AT, 12[2, 3] (1929), and F. Horst, Die Zwölf kl. Propheten, Hndbch. AT, I, 14[3] (1964), ad loc.

[76] J. Fichtner, "Js. unter d. Weisen," ThLZ, 74 (1949), 75-80; J. Lindblom, "Wisdom in the OT Prophets," Festschr. H. H. Rowley, VT Suppl., 3 (1955), 192-204.

[77] On wisdom as a way of mastering life cf. v. Rad, op. cit. (→ n. 71), 430-454.

[78] Naturally prayer style occurs esp. in the Ps. On these cf. A. M. Gierlich, "Der Lichtgedanke in den Ps.," Freiburger Theol. Stud., 56 (1940).

The second is true wisdom style which is governed by the theme of individual morality and the wise handling of life and its situations. In both cases there is conviction that conduct and condition are related. [79] The interpretation of history in Wis. 17 f. (→ 324, 27 ff.) stands apart; materially it belongs already to the phase of Judaism.

C. Judaism (Apart from Philo).

1. General.

The terms are used in the same fields as in the OT, namely, cosmology (→ 320, 23 ff.), eschatology (→ 322, 4 ff.) and ethics (→ 322, 14 ff.). The formal sense also remains the same. Light is the brightness of the world, salvation, and transf. wisdom, or the possibility of man's enlightenment by this. God causes His light to shine (Eth. En. 38:4), τοῖς ἐκλεκτοῖς ἔσται φῶς καὶ χάρις (Eth. text "joy") καὶ εἰρήνη ... δοθήσεται τοῖς ἐκλεκτοῖς σοφία (Gr. En. 5:7 f.); God gives light to the understanding (S. Bar. 38:1). The connection with wisdom and the Law is maintained, as is also that with the world, its order, and self-understanding in relation to it. Nevertheless, there are profound changes. The world-view has altered and the spatial aspect is predominant. [80] The world is viewed statically and the idea of regularity is abstract → VII, 431, n. 58 f. [81] Salvation is in this world and it is seen primarily as the salvation or loss of the individual. To be sure, the idea of the people of God does not evaporate. But it acquires a new sense. It denotes the totality of elect individuals who have a share in the salvation of the world to come. The duality is sharper. In antithesis to the light of the Law is the darkness of Adam, S. Bar. 17 f. [82]

The change may be detected in the new depiction of creation. [83] The separation of the creation of light from that of the stars is put earlier in Jub. 2:2 ff. and the separation of light and darkness then follows in v. 8, both being presented spatially in 2:16. Movement is replaced in Jub. with the enumeration of static cosmic factors. [84] There is a modification in Slav. En. 25 ff. Primal light comes first, and then the sun is made, 29:1. The stars thus take on enhanced importance. The order of the world is bound to their

---

[79] It is not appropriate to speak of a dogma of retribution functioning quasi-mechanically. In the very act of prayer the connection is shown to be ambivalent when the afflicted man pts. to his uprightness. (On the understanding of uprightness cf. v. Rad, op. cit. [→ n. 71], 382-430.) The connection stands, not as theoretical causality, but as a situation of address. The "dogma" is theoretically developed only when it is already under attack, i.e., in Job. On the other hand one may affirm that the ref. to God as the author of good or evil fortune becomes less prominent. This is connected with the total world-view of wisdom, which handles the phenomenon empirically, and thus from outside, v. Rad, 398. The dominant understanding is that of misfortune, not as God's punishment, but as the result of unrighteous deeds. He who curses his parents, his light will go out in darkness, Prv. 20:20, cf. the challenge to this view in Job 21:17 f.

[80] Aalen Licht u. Finsternis, 96.

[81] Ibid., 159-161. Aalen's view of a cosmic balance determining the Jewish view of the world goes beyond the textual evidence, cf. N. A. Dahl, "Begrepene 'lys' og 'morke' i jodedommen," Norsk teologisk Tidsskrift, 53 (1952), 77; J. Jervell, "Imago Dei," FRL, 76 (1960), 32, n. 51.

[82] Cf. on the Dead Sea Scrolls and the Test. XII → 325, 14 ff.

[83] J. B. Schaller, Gn. 1:2 im antiken Judt., Diss. Göttingen (1961).

[84] Aalen Licht u. Finsternis, 101 and 164. In Sir. 43:1 ff., unlike Ps. 19, the parallelism of day and night is broken. The heavenly lights are taken out of the time schema and made spatial obj., ibid., 161, cf. Eth. En. 69:16-25; Sib., 1, 1 ff.

courses and not so much to the alternation of day and night. [85] The annual rhythm is more important than the daily rhythm. [86] The inner consequence may be seen when light alone is exempted from creation. It is not created but had prior existence as primal light in the containers, cf. the "council-chambers of light" in S. Bar. 59:11, primal light, 4 Esr. 6:38-40; [87] Ps.-Philo Antiquit. biblicae, [88] 28, 8 f.; Hb. En. 48 A 1; [89] Slav. En. B 29:1 (Bonwetsch, 80), where the sun is formed of the gt. light; also Ps.-Clem. Recg., [90] II, 61, 1; 49, 1 - 51, 1, cf. 61, 5: *lumen immensum . . . , cui tenebrae nullae succedunt.* [91] At the same time there is a tendency not to assume any תֹּהוּ before creation. [92] Light and darkness are spatially neutralised as cosmic matters, Jub. 2:16; 4:6. On the places of lights cf. Eth. En. 17:3; 41:3 ff.; 60; 71:4; 72 ff.; 4 Esr. 6:40. Light is put first.

The spatial orientation in cosmology is accompanied by an intensifying of the time element in eschatology, which now adopts the style of apocal., Eth. En. 58:6; 38:7; 92:4 f.; 108:11 ff. [93] In contrast to the world is a world to come. Already in the OT the last time could be portrayed as one of brightness. Now we have the brightness of a world beyond and this world is dark, → I, 204, 25 ff. Darkness is destroyed. Eth. En. 58:6; 92:4 f. Eternal brightness reigns, 38:2. The alternation of light and darkness ceases, 4 Esr. 7:39 ff. The first time and the last time correspond. The enlightenment of the blessed is part of the expectation of salvation, S. Bar. 51:3, 10. On the contrast between this world and the world to come cf. S. Bar. 48:50.

The same unmistakable style dominates anthropology and ethics too. The Torah is still light, [94] S. Bar. 17 f. It is the power confronting darkness, Wis. 18:4; Test. XII (→ 326, 17 ff.). It is symbolised by the menorah. [95] The connection between wisdom and Law also remains. [96] There is simply added an anchoring in the cosmic order. Light and darkness become moral qualities. [97] The idea of separation is given added emphasis, S. Bar. 18:1 f.; Test. XII.

2. Special Features.

In Hell. form we find the idea of wisdom as the primal light in Wis. 7:29 f. [98] In the same book the light-darkness vocabulary occurs in a historical picture with an eschatological

---

[85] Cf. the dominant position of the sun in the admittedly unreliable Slav. En. A 27:3 f. (Bonwetsch, 25). Astronomy is important in understanding the world, cf. Eth. En. 72:82.

[86] Cf. the importance of the calendar problem in Jub. and the Qumran Writings. It is typical that on the other hand the stars are personified, Eth. En. 43:1 etc. The spatial view and the link to the stars raises the question where these are when not in the firmament, Eth. En. 72:5. Acc. to Vit. Ad., 19 the heavenly lights have souls; Eve prays to them. Cf. Apc. Mos. 34-36: Sun and moon intercede for Adam. But they lose their light in face of the light of all things, the Father of lights [Bertram].

[87] On the text cf. Aalen Licht u. Finsternis, 167, n. 3.

[88] Ed. G. Kisch, *Publications in Mediaeval Studies,* 10 (1949).

[89] Cf. Odeberg, III, 63.

[90] Ed. J. Behm, GCS, 51 (1965).

[91] H. J. Schoeps, *Theol. u. Gesch. d. Judenchristentums* (1949), 312.

[92] Aalen Licht u. Finsternis, 163. The sea is the power of chaos in Eth. En. 60:7 f.; 69:18; Slav. En. 28:4. But these are only echoes. Acc. to Eth. En. 69:16 ff. the sea is created and the depths are established.

[93] On the rise of apocalyptic cf. O. Plöger, "Theokratie u. Eschatologie," *Wissenschaftliche Monographien z. AT u. NT,* 2³ (1968).

[94] G. Vermes, "The Torah is a Light," VT, 8 (1958), 436-8.

[95] On the menorah cf. Phil. Rer. Div. Her., 221-5; Vit. Mos., II, 102 f. and Jos. Bell., 5, 217; Ant., 3, 144-6 and 182; cf. the Rabb. examples in Str.-B., III, 716-8. The light was put out with the destruction of the temple acc. to 4 Esr. 10:21 f. But the continued existence of the Torah is recorded in fig. representations, for material cf. Goodenough, op. cit. (→ n. 39), esp. III, Ill. 59 f., 440, 639 (cf. IV, 136), and III, 292 (IV, 119); interpretations of the menorah in Philo and Jos., IV, 82-8, the Rabb. IV, 88-92, cf. III and IV, Index, s.v. "Menorah."

[96] Cf. the whole of Sir.

[97] Cf. Aalen Licht u. Finsternis, 178-183.

[98] U. Wilckens, "Weisheit u. Torheit," *Beiträge z. histor. Theol.,* 26 (1959), 188-190.

thrust, 17 f. [99] The bibl. creation story is expounded with the help of Gk. philosophy. God gave us the seventh day: ἤ δὴ καὶ πρώτη φυσικῶς ἄν λέγοιτο φωτὸς γένεσις, ἐν ᾧ τὰ πάντα συνθεωρεῖται. μεταφέροιτο δ᾽ ἄν τὸ αὐτὸ καὶ ἐπὶ τῆς σοφίας· τὸ γὰρ πᾶν φῶς ἐστιν ἐξ αὐτῆς, Aristobul. in Eus. Praep. Ev., 13, 12, 9 f. To be noted is the fashioning of a conversion idiom that borrows from the cosmological field of expression, Test. XII → 326, 17 ff. The best examples are in Jos. and Aseneth, [100] 8, 10 f.: Κύριε... ὁ ζωοποιήσας τὰ πάντα καὶ καλέσας ἀπὸ τοῦ σκότους εἰς τὸ φῶς καὶ ἀπὸ τῆς πλάνης εἰς τὴν ἀλήθειαν καὶ ἀπὸ θανάτου εἰς τὴν ζωήν, σὺ αὐτὸς Κύριε ζωοποίησον καὶ εὐλόγησον τὴν παρθένον ταύτην. καὶ ἀνακαίνισον τῷ πνεύματί σου, cf. also 15, 13. Also worth noting is the idea of the inner light: ὅτι πᾶσαν ἀποκρυβὴν αὐτὸς (sc. Joseph) ὁρᾷ καὶ οὐδὲν κρυπτὸν λέληθεν αὐτῷ διὰ τὸ φῶς τὸ μέγα τὸ ὂν ἐν αὐτῷ, 6, 3. Gnosticising may already be seen here, cf. Philo Spec. Leg., IV, 192. Note should also be taken of the ethical use in lists of virtues and vices. [101]

3. Dead Sea Scrolls.

a. The marks that characterise Judaism in gen. may be seen here too, but there is also an explicit dualistic use. [102] The traditional way of speaking, which is orientated to the positive concept of light and to movement, shining forth, is naturally not eliminated → VII, 432, n. 64. [103] A special feature connected with dualism is detachment from the natural phenomena. Where these are described, "light" and "darkness" are less prominent, 1 QH 1:10 f.; 1 QM 10:11 f. In the foreground is the dualism of eschatological decision which controls all the writings, although, of course, it introduces a light-darkness vocabulary only into a relatively small selection, 1 QS 3:13 ff.; 1 QM 1:1 ff.; 13:5; 9 ff. [104] Can this be traced back to Iranian influence? We have already hinted at the problem above → 317, 3 ff. There is no direct Iranian material from the earlier period. On the other hand, the dualism

---

99 The eschatological thrust affects the style of presentation, cf. G. Kuhn, "Beiträge z. Erklärung d. Buches d. Weisheit," ZNW, 28 (1929), 335 f.; Aalen Licht u. Finsternis, 173, n. 2 emphasises that the Egypt. darkness comes from the underworld and is not just a plague; it has an ethical dimension. Similarly on the other side the light is that of the Law.

100 Ed. M. Philonenko, Studia Post-Biblica, 13 (1968).

101 A. Vögtle, "Die Tugend- u. Lasterkataloge im NT, exeget., religions- u. formgeschichtlich untersucht," NT Abh., 16 4/5 (1936); S. Wibbing, "Die Tugend- u. Lasterkatal. im NT," ZNW Beih., 25 (1959), 33-42, 61-64. Wibbing, 12 investigates the religio-historical presuppositions of the dualistic arrangement of Paul's lists and for this purpose uses the twofold list in 1 QS 4:3 ff. It is obvious that there is a historical connection with later Jewish dualism and this comes out esp. in the use of light and darkness. But the form in the Qumran work is a problem of its own. Elsewhere the tradition of a list belongs exclusively to Hell. Judaism, which took it from the popular philosophical ethics of Hellenism. It is correct to pt. out that there is a material relation to the two-way schema. But this is not the pt. of origin of contrasting lists of virtues and vices.

102 Cf. also Eth. En. 41, where the separation between light and darkness corresponds to that between the spirits of men, and also 108:11 ff. Very dualistic is Slav. En. 25 f. The light is the aeon in which all creation is contained. It is commanded upward, a dark aeon downward, Dodd Bible, 111-3; E. Haenchen, "Aufbau u. Theol. d. 'Poimandres'," Gott u. Mensch (1965), 341, n. 5 thinks we have the incursion of a non-Jewish aeon doctrine. But there are possible presuppositions in Judaism itself. On the continuation of Qumran dualism in the Ps.-Clem., v. O. Cullmann, "Die neuentdeckten Qumrantexte u. das Judenchristentum d. Ps.-Clem.," Festschr. R. Bultmann, ZNW Beih., 21² (1957), 38.

103 O. Betz, "Offenbarung u. Schriftforschung in d. Qumransekte," Wissenschaftliche Untersuchungen z. NT, 6 (1960), 111-4.

104 Elsewhere light dominates, cf. also 1 Q Livre des Mystères, 1:1, 5 f. (DJD, I, 103). In relation to the form אורתום or אורתים in 1 QH 4:23 the question arises whether this denotes the primal light. But R. Meyer, reviewing H. Bardtke, Hbr. Konsonantentexte in ThLZ, 80 (1955), 420, thinks we have here a dialect form of 'ôrātām "their illumination," cf. also G. Jeremias, "Der Lehrer d. Gerechtigkeit," Stud. z. Umwelt d. NT, 2 (1963), 204, n. 6.

of the dualistic passages in the Dead Sea Scrolls does manifest Iranian features. [105] Is it by chance that dualistic language occurs in the section about the two spirits (→ VI, 388, 6 ff.)? [106] Provisionally we might simply assert the syncretistic process as such. [107] It should be noted that the dualism of decision is more than matched by an enhanced monotheism in the cosmology. [108]

Light and darkness are determinative spheres but also paths one can take. Decision between the two ways (→ V, 53, 49 ff.) is anticipated by the two spirits. The summons to the individual is sharpened rather than eliminated thereby. [109] The "children of light" (→ n. 303) in 1 QS 1:9; 2:16; 3:13, 24 f.; 1 QM *passim* give conscious expression to their being by looking back to the past and also by repeating the confession of sins, by hymnic thanksgiving for salvation, [110] and by the doing of works of light, which is possible only through placing in the light. Esp. should one mention here separation from the children of darkness and hatred for them, 1 QS 1:3 f. etc. Eschatology is part of the dualism. The present war is an anticipation of the final war, cf. the War Scroll 1 QM. The two possibilities of human being are definitive: eternal life in eternal light or eternal perdition. 1 QS 4:7 f., 17 f.

b. Related but with a stronger Hell. tinge, [111] are the Test. XII. Here the wisdom tradition is evident. Light again dominates, cf. the light of the Law in Test. L. 14:4, of knowledge in 4:3; 18:3, or righteousness in Zeb. 9:8. But there is a tendency to mention the other side too, L. 14:4; 18:3; Jos. 20:2. The most important elements are the idea of order in N. 2:7; A. 5:2 and the resultant demand for decision, cf. ἐκλέξασθε ἑαυτοῖς ἢ τὸ φῶς ἢ τὸ σκότος, ἢ τὸν νόμον ἢ τὰ ἔργα τοῦ Βελίαρ, L. 19:1. Here again it is true that being precedes works; one can do the works of light only when one is in the sphere of light, or enlightened, N. 2:10, cf. the context. The idea of individual conversion (→ 325, 4 ff.; 332, 15 ff.) is developed; μετάνοια drives out darkness, G. 5:7.

4. Rabbinic Literature. [112]

Jewish development continues. [113] We do not find here the intensity of the Dead Sea

[105] Kuhn, *op. cit.* (→ n. 44), 296-316; E. Kamlah, "Die Form d. katalog. Paränese im NT," *Wissenschaftliche Untersuchungen z. NT*, 7 (1964), 163-171.

[106] An answer is made more difficult by the fact that the most important section in 1 QS 3:13 - 4:26 is not a unity. There is a break at 4:14. Before this the main idea is that of double predestination whereby we belong to the one spirit or the other. After it the ethical aspect is to the fore, so that man has a part more or less in both spheres. The terms light and darkness are not used after the break, cf. J. Becker, "Das Heil Gottes," *Stud. z. Umwelt d. NT*, 3 (1964), 83-9.

[107] On different strata of dualism at Qumran cf. H. W. Huppenbauer, "Der Mensch zwischen zwei Welten," AbhThANT, 34 (1959); on the influence of Iranian light mysticism on Judaism, Colpe, 133: (provisionally) "I make a plea that we speak of convergence rather than influence," cf. also Hinz, 161-5.

[108] The תהומות are also made, 1 QH 1:13 f., cf. also 1 QM 10:13.

[109] This may be seen from the structure of the concept of election. The doctrine of predestination is imparted to a member of the elect group as a basis of membership. His situation with its rigorous demands is disclosed to him thereby → VII, 433, n. 70-72.

[110] On the relation between style and content in the Qumran Ps. cf. S. Schulz, "Zur Rechtfertigung aus Gnaden in Qumran u bei Pls.," ZThK, 56 (1959), 166-177; Jeremias, *op. cit.* (→ n. 104), 168-267.

[111] Cf. the psychological terms διάνοια, Test. R. 3:12 etc. and νοῦς, R. 3:8 etc.

[112] Jastrow, Levy Chald. Wört., *s.v.*; Aalen Licht u. Finsternis, 258-324; Str.-B., I, 161 f., 236-8; II, 427 f.; II and IV, Index, *s.v.* "Licht."

[113] It is sometimes asked whence light was made, Gn. r., 3, 4 on 1:3; v. Bacher Pal. Am., I, 120, 545, n. 4; H. F. Weiss, "Untersuchungen z. Kosmologie d. hell. u. paläst. Judt.," TU, 97 (1966), 107-110; V. Aptowitzer, "Zur Kosmologie d. Agada. Licht als Urstoff," MGWJ, 72 (1928), 363-370, as against Weiss, 107-110.

Scrolls. [114] The new thing lies not so much in the formal use [115] as in the further development of the understanding of things that can be described in terms of light, esp. the Law.
Light is used for the time of salvation and for the Messiah: "In that hour (i.e., when the
Messiah manifests Himself) God will cause the light of the king, the Messiah and Israel
to shine, and all the peoples of the world are in darkness and obscurity. Then they will
all come to the light of the Messiah and Israel," Pesikt. r., 36 (162b). [116] The light of the
Messiah can be identified as the primal light that God withdrew and reserved for the
righteous, *loc. cit.* (161a). [117] "Light of the world" אוֹרוֹ שֶׁל עוֹלָם or נֵרוֹ is used for God
in Nu. r., 15, 5 on 8:2, Israel in Cant. r., 1 on 1:3 (Wünsche, 22), individual men in
Rabb. AbRNat A 25 (Schechter, p. 79), the Law in bBB, 4a, the temple in bBB, 4a. [118]
The works of the righteous are light, cf. the exposition of Gn. 1:3: "From the beginning
of the creation God has looked upon the works of the righteous and the works of the
unrighteous . . . , 'the earth was waste and empty,' this ref. to the works of the unrighteous.
'And God said, Let there be light,' this ref. to the works of the righteous," Gn. r., 2, 5 on
1:3. [119] Light surrounds the birth of the man of God, the son (Moses), bSota, 12a; 13a. [120]
Finally the human soul is light: "What thou thinkest in thine heart, the soul imparts all
words to him (sc. God), the soul of man is a lamp of God," Pesikt. r., 8 (29a). [121]

D. Hellenism, Gnosticism.

1. General.

It is hard to fix the transition from the classical age to Hellenistic thought. Great
diversity exists, since the classical tradition and classical usage continue on the one
side, but doctrines of salvation in religious style, yet with an intermingling of philosophical elements (cf. the colourful picture in the Hermetica), increasingly come to
expression. Thus references to light are still figurative on the one side. Light
signifies what is grasped philosophically and speculatively → 313, 38 ff. On the
other side, however, light in the doctrine of salvation is the reality of saving power
which can again be depicted as the sphere of salvation. No rules can be set up
whereby to delimit the religious type from the philosophical type. Only as the final
product of the whole development does there clearly emerge the typical light
metaphysics of later antiquity. [122]

---

[114] Partial exceptions are texts under Gnostic influence like Gn. r.; Hb. En. On Jewish
Gnosticism cf. M. Friedländer, *Der vorchr. jüd. Gnosticismus* (1898); Scholem, 43-86; Schubert,
87-94. We do not find dualistic antithesis to darkness.

[115] Naturally light is here too equivalent to salvation, cf. Tg. Pro. on Is. 60:1, *v.* Str.-B.,
II, 427 f., or the Torah, e.g., bBB, 4a, Str.-B., I, 237.

[116] Str.-B., I, 151, cf. 161 f.; II, 348.

[117] *Ibid.*, II, 348. Light is used of the pre-existent soul of the Messiah in Gn. r., 85, 1 on
38:1, cf. Str.-B., II, 346, and in exposition of Scripture, though not terminologically, we also
find it for the Messiah, Gn. r., 1, 6 on 1:1, Str.-B., I, 67.

[118] Str.-B., I, 236-8. On a mosaic in the Beth-Alpha synagogue (6th cent. A.D.) God is
hidden in a cloud that radiates light, Goodenough, *op. cit.* (→ n. 39), III, Ill. 638 (cf. I, 246-8
in interpretation). On the Torah cf. also Str.-B., II, 357 and on menorah-symbolism → n. 95.

[119] Str.-B., I, 239, cf. Mt. 5:16.

[120] R. Mach, *Der Zaddik in Talmud u. Midr.* (1957), 69 f.

[121] Str.-B., I, 432.

[122] Wetter Phos, 103-6 attributes the development to oriental influence. The examples
are mostly late, but go back to an earlier time, esp. cultically. Oriental influence can hardly
be disputed in the case of Gnosticism. Inner development in Hellenism must also be taken into
account. To present external influence and internal development as alternatives is too simple
and causal.

The development may be traced in various fields (→ lines 29 ff.) and at various literary stages. The difference should be kept in mind as texts are evaluated. An example from a magic pap. should not be regarded as typical of Hellenism in gen., and in no sphere is the development a consistent process. The class. tradition may be seen in Plut., who in essentials offers a Platonic popularisation. We find the soul compared to a light in Plut. Def. Orac., 18 (II, 419 f.), or truth in 42 (II, 433d), or knowledge in Lat. Viv., 4 (II, 1129a-b); 6 (II, 1130b) goes a step further. There are many antitheses, including φωτίζομαι and πικραίνομαι in Col., 7 (II, 1120e). Plat. is a model when illumination is linked to the vocabulary of the mysteries (→ 315, 23 f.): ὥσπερ γὰρ οἱ τελούμενοι κατ' ἀρχὰς μὲν ἐν θορύβῳ καὶ βοῇ συνίασι πρὸς ἀλλήλους ὠθούμενοι, δρωμένων δὲ καὶ δεικνυμένων τῶν ἱερῶν προσέχουσιν ἤδη μετὰ φόβου καὶ σιωπῆς, οὕτω καὶ φιλοσοφίας ἐν ἀρχῇ καὶ περὶ θύρας πολὺν θόρυβον ὄψει... ὁ δ' ἐντὸς γενόμενος καὶ μέγα φῶς ἰδών..., Plut. Quomodo quis suos in virtute sentiat profectus, 10 (II, 81d-e), cf. De anima, 2. [123] The brightness of the world beyond is described in literary myths, Ser. Num. Vind., 22-24 (II, 563b-564d); [124] Gen. Socr., 21 (II, 589 f.); [125] Fac. Lun., 26 (II, 940f-942d). [126] Is. et Os. is of special importance, above all 51 ff. (II, 371 ff.). Osiris is Nous and Logos, the first Noeton in the shape of light. [127] True philosophical development leads, however, by way of men like Philo to Neo-Platonism. [128] Early Chr. lit. is closer to the edificatory writings of Hellenism, esp. the Hermetica (→ 334, 8 ff.). The lowest stage is magical lit. with its echoes of light metaphysics and its vocabulary. There is stronger Jewish influence, cf., e.g., Audollent Def. Tab., 242, 13 (3rd cent. A.D.) → 311, 11 f. Gnosis is an entity *sui generis*. On the margin we find many nuances in more philosophical or more edificatory style and also many syncretistic transitional phenomena, but at its heart one may discern a self-enclosed totality which affects even the marginal phenomena. Oriental influence is palpable in Gnosticism. [129]

In Hellenism light naturally means salvation. But this is now understood differently and located differently, and the idea of light changes accordingly. Light is now viewed as a sphere and yet also as a substance. We find the first motif in cosmology, the antithesis of this world and the upper world of light; we find the second in the idea of the light-soul. A synthesis is achieved in the concept of the

---

[123] Ed. G. N. Bernardakis, Plut. Moralia, VII (1896), 23, 7 ff. Cf. Beierwaltes, 25 on the passage. For a short survey of the history of Platonism cf. H. Dörrie, Art. "Platonismus," RGG³, V, 411-5 with bibl.

[124] Plut. borrows here from the myth in Plat. Resp., X, 614b-615d, but with Pythagorean and Heraclitian elements and personal invention too, cf. K. Ziegler, Art. "Plut.," Pauly-W., 21 (1951), 849 f.; G. Méautis, *Plutarque. Des délais de la justice divine* (1935), 57-74.

[125] This is based on Plat. Phaedr., Ziegler, *op. cit.*, 891.

[126] Ziegler, 855 f.; W. Hamilton, "The Myth in Plut.'s De facie," *The Class. Quarterly*, 28 (1934), 24-30.

[127] On the interchange between mystical Plato interpretation and the philosophical exposition of real experience in the mysteries cf. Wlosok, 56-9. Cf. also Apul. De Deo Socratis, 3 and Max. Tyr., 11, 9a-10e, Wlosok, 226, 255 f. In the last passage we have an esp. fine example of the mystical style of Plato exposition, Phaedr., 247c.

[128] We shall not deal with Neo-Platonism here except in so far as some passages may illustrate Hellenism in gen. For material cf. Wetter Phos, 46-97 and Baeumker, 357-371. On Proc. and Iambl. cf. Nilsson, II, 652 f.

[129] This is true in spite of all the disagreement regarding the origin of individual motifs and the strength of component elements. For motifs cf. Reitzenstein Hell. Myst., Index, *s.v.* "Gnosis," "Gnostizismus," etc.; Reitzenstein Poim., 58-160; W. Bousset, "Hauptprobleme d. Gnosis," FRL, 10 (1907), *passim;* F. Cumont, *Die orient. Religionen im röm. Heidentum⁴* (1959), Index, *s.v.* "Gnosis"; Nilsson, II, 582-622 and *passim;* H. Junker, "Über iranische Quellen d. hell. Aionvorstellung," *Vorträge d. Bibliothek Warburg*, 1921/22 (1923), 145 f. Hermeneutically Jonas Gnosis, I, 1-80 is basic.

ascent of the soul. [130] Illumination is ascent and also change, Corp. Herm., 1. It is the condition of knowledge. [131] As the upper and lower (sublunary) spheres are sharply divided, so the dominant antithesis is not between light and darkness but rather between the divine light and the earthly or human light, Philo Rer. Div. Her., 264. [132] Except in a distinct part of Gnosticism, darkness is not an active opponent but the sphere and situation one leaves behind, ἄγνοια → I, 118, 42 ff. [133] Thought is orientated not to the presence of the antithesis but to the movement and event of epiphany, to shining, illumination. If light is true and transcendent being, earthly light is σκοτεινὸν φῶς in relation to it → VII, 433, 18 ff. [134] We are thus in process of transition to Gnosticism.

Light metaphysics may be found in Plato → 314, 33 ff. But whereas light is in Plato the constitution of the world of ideas, in Hellenism it becomes the formless sphere of light. A new thought is that divine power is light and illumination is deification. As the relation between the sphere of light and the world changes, so does the understanding of the process of knowledge. One now attains to the light, not by rational knowledge, but by translation into a transcendent substance. The philosophy of illumination and the religion of light draw close to one another.

2. Philo.

Philo belongs to the illumination type rather than the antithesis type. This is shown already by his use of the σκότος group → VII, 434, 6 ff. [135] If the Platonic tradition

---

130 W. Bousset, "Die Himmelsreise d. Seele," ARW, 4 (1901), 136-169, 229-273. Later antiquity sees the incursion of astral devotion from the East. We now have a cult of the sun and stars that was alien to the class. age. Though dualism is heightened, this is not yet Gnosticism, cf. Cumont, op. cit., 112-123; also Astrology and Religion among the Greeks and Romans (1912), 73-102; F. Boll, Sternglaube u. Sterndeutung (1931), 15-29; Bultmann, 345-352; also Das Urchr. im Rahmen d. antiken Religionen (1949), 163-180.

131 The ancient principle that "like is known by like" now takes on a new sense. To be able to see light, not only must it shine but the one who sees must be of like substance with it, Philo Deus Imm., 78; Plut. Is. et Os., 77 (II, 382d-e); Ascl., 18 and 32; cf. the complaint of souls ἄθλιαι γὰρ κατεκρίθημεν καὶ τὸ βλέπειν ἡμῖν οὐκ ἄντικρυς ἐχαρίσθη, ὅτι χωρὶς τοῦ φωτὸς ἡμῖν τὸ ὁρᾶν οὐκ ἐδόθη, Herm. Trismeg. Fr., 23, 36 in Stob. Ecl., I, 396, 12 f. On illumination cf. Festugière, IV, 241-257.

132 Cf. the construct ἀφώτιστος. The orig. negative word now becomes positively bad, Wetter Phos, 63; cf. the analogous ἄγνωστος, ἀχάριστος (→ χάρις).

133 Corp. Herm., 1, 28; 7, 2, cf. ὥσπερ γὰρ ἡλίου καταλάμψαντος οὐ πέφυκε τὴν αὐγὴν ὑπομένειν τὸ σκότος, ἐξαίφνης δὲ ἀφανὲς ἄρδην καθίσταται..., Iambl. Myst., III, 13 (p. 130, 9 f.), cf. Philo Deus Imm., 123.

134 On the connection between light and life, Corp. Herm., 1, 32 (→ 334, 14 ff.; II, 842, 13 f.), on light and the world or men, W. Bousset, "Kyrios Christos," FRL, 21² (1921), 173; Wetter Licht der Welt, 166-201. Alexander of Abonuteichos, has his god Glycon present himself: εἰμὶ Γλύκων, τρίτον αἷμα Διός, φάος ἀνθρώποισιν, Luc. Alex., 18, v. O. Weinreich, "Alexandros der Lügenprophet u. seine Stellung in d. Religiosität d. 2. Jhdt. n. Chr.," NJbchKlAlt, 47 (1921), 145: "I do not doubt that if the god had spoken in prose rather than an oracular hexameter he would have said ἐγὼ εἰμι etc." Cf. Luc. Alex., 43 and Macrob. Sat., 1, 23, 21: "Ἥλιε παντοκράτορ, κόσμου πνεῦμα, κόσμου δύναμις, κόσμου φῶς. On Isis → n. 341; for Gnosticism cf. Corp. Herm., 1, 6 (→ n. 187); 13, 19; "I was named the Enlightener, the Son of God," O. Sol. 36:3, cf. also Cl. Al. Exc. Theod., 34, 1 - 35, 1; on Mandaica → 336, 5 ff. We find combination with the idea of the primal man in Zosimus Fr., 49, 10 (Berthelot, 232): καὶ ταῦτα μόνοι Ἑβραῖοι καὶ αἱ ἱεραὶ Ἑρμοῦ βίβλοι περὶ τοῦ φωτεινοῦ ἀνθρώπου καὶ τοῦ ὁδηγοῦ αὐτοῦ υἱοῦ θεοῦ, καὶ τοῦ γηίνου Ἀδάμ, καὶ τοῦ ὁδηγοῦ αὐτοῦ ἀντιμίμου τοῦ δυσφημία λέγοντος ἑαυτὸν εἶναι υἱὸν θεοῦ πλάνη. Cf. τὸ δὲ προσηγορικὸν αὐτοῦ (sc. the primal man) ὄνομα φῶς καλεῖται... ὅτε ἦν φῶς ἐν τῷ Παραδείσῳ..., 49, 6 f. (p. 231).

135 φῶς and derivates occur some 250 times. We also find synon. like αὐγή, φέγγος etc. with compounds. The verb φωτίζω plays no part except at Fug., 139; instead we have

is plain (→ 314, 33 ff.), [136] so is the continuation and development of this tradition in the Hell.-protognostic style [137] (→ 327, 19 ff.): σοφία δὲ οὐ μόνον φωτὸς τρόπον ὄργανον τοῦ ὁρᾶν ἐστιν, ἀλλὰ καὶ αὐτὴν ὁρᾷ, Migr. Abr., 40, cf. Det. Pot. Ins., 117; wisdom is the light of the soul, Spec. Leg., I, 288; Congr., 47; Quaest. in Ex., II, 7, cf. Spec. Leg., III, 6. The development may be seen when one studies Philo's concept of God and the relation between wisdom and *logos*. Aaron is interpreted as *logos* and Mt. Hor (LXX Ωρ) in Nu. 20:25 is naturally light: τὸ γὰρ τέλος τοῦ λόγου ἀλήθειά ἐστιν ἡ φωτὸς τηλαυγεστέρα, εἰς ἣν σπουδάζει ὁ λόγος ἐλθεῖν, Leg. All., III, 45. φῶς and σκότος are important in cosmology, cf. esp. Op. Mund., *passim* and ἐκ δὲ σκότους φῶς ἐργασάμενος, Spec. Leg., IV, 187. On the use with ἐκ → 313, 35 f. There is Stoic influence in Abr., 205: καὶ τὸ φῶς ἐν οὐρανῷ μὲν ἄκρατον καὶ ἀμιγὲς σκότους ἐστίν, ἐν δὲ τοῖς ὑπὸ σελήνην ἀέρι ζοφερῷ κεκραμένον φαίνεται, cf. 156 ff. [138] The Jewish element is the view of the world as creation. [139] The chief contrast is between heavenly and earthly light rather than light and darkness. Philo, too, has a specific light metaphysics. That the divine world is light is the presupposition of earthly light and of sight as also of the supernatural possibility of the vision of light in the mystical ascent, Op. Mund., 71. The idea of light is formed prior to visible light ἀόρατον καὶ νοητόν, Op. Mund., 31. [140] We find a sharp distinction between the first and the second light in Som., I, 115-117. [141] God is the source of the purest radiance, Mut. Nom., 6. This sounds emanationist, [142] esp. as Philo can say in Platonic fashion that God is light, Som., I, 75; He is the sun of the sun. [143] But the emanationist concept is qualified by the assertion that God is not the archetype of all other light but is before every other archetype, Som., I, 75, and also by the doctrine of the δυνάμεις; the divine forces shine forth, not God Himself. [144] The *logos* is also a middle being, for it, too, is light. Intelligible light is the εἰκών of the divine *logos*, Op. Mund., 31. "Image" denotes a connection in terms of substance. The *logos* is φῶς ψυχικόν, Leg. All., III, 171 and it is the prototype of the sun, Som., I, 85, cf. I, 75, where God is the prototype, and I, 87, where the sun is the symbol of God. In Philo there are two concurrent schemata: a. being — ideas = divine light, and b. being — divine light — ideas — world. The second type occurs in Op. Mund., 69 ff.; Mut. Nom., 178 ff.; Rer. Div. Her., 263 ff.; Gig., 52 ff. [145] When light is called divine,

---

compounds of synon. and also λάμπω (→ IV, 16, 1 ff.) and compounds, ἀνατέλλω, ἀναφαίνομαι etc., Klein, 50-61. Philo's typical way of speaking of light and darkness is: ἐπεὶ καὶ φωτὸς ἐπιλάμψαντος ἀφανίζεται τὸ σκότος, Deus Imm., 123. Acc. to Kuhn, 23, 32 f. darkness is simply absence of light.

[136] We cannot discuss here other influences and their mutual relationship. Spec. Leg., I, 288 is Platonic: διανοίας δὲ φῶς ἐστι σοφία... The antithesis is ἀφροσύνη as σκότος. We have transf. use in the style of the Gk. tradition at Leg. All., III, 167: φῶς δὲ ψυχῆς ἐστι παιδεία, cf. on ἄγνοια, Ebr., 154-161.

[137] On this *v.* esp. Jonas Gnosis, II, 1, 70-121 and Wlosok, 50-114.

[138] On the concept of air cf. H. Leisegang, *Der Heilige Geist* (1919), 24-36.

[139] This is esp. plain in the exposition of the bibl. creation story in Op. Mund., with Plat. Tim., 28a as a basis of the synthesis. But this is still new. On the exposition of Plat. Tim., 28a in antiquity cf. Wlosok, 252-6.

[140] Klein, 39.

[141] Völker, 178.

[142] F. W. Eltester, "Eikon im NT," ZNW Beih., 23 (1958), 32-4. 105 f.

[143] ὁ δὲ θεὸς καὶ νόμων ἐστὶ παράδειγμα ἀρχέτυπον καὶ ἡλίου ἥλιος, νοητὸς αἰσθητοῦ, παρέχων ἐκ τῶν ἀοράτων πηγῶν ὁρατὰ φέγγη τῷ βλεπομένῳ, Spec. Leg., I, 279. The *logos* is passed over here, Wlosok, 91; Klein, 31-3, 37.

[144] Pascher, 191-228; Völker, 283 f.; H. A. Wolfson, *Philo*, II² (1963), Index, *s.v.* δύναμις, Daniélou, 149-153. Klein, 17 emphasises that the identification of God and light is only loose and metaphorical.

[145] Pascher, 167. On the material relation of the two series with and without the *logos* cf. Wlosok, 90: "The *logos* as the prototype of light or the sun is the divine light itself." Acc. to Eltester, *op. cit.*, 33, Philo, when he calls the things of the intelligible world εἰκόνες, differs from Plato, who speaks of εἰκόνες only within the sensory world. An epiphany of the image of God is described in Vit. Mos., I, 66, cf. Klein, 66-8.

this is good Greek (→ 313, 15 f.), but the meaning is different, Migr. Abr., 39; Rer. Div. Her., 264 (→ 329, 2 ff.), cf. Som., I, 72; Deus Imm., 78. In these terms cosmological dualism is impossible. [146]

Development of the transcendence of God brings with it transposition of Plato's understanding of the world and the rise of a new cosmology. The world, including the world of ideas, is bracketed by the concept of God. [147] We do not have mere formal extension but qualitative change. Both the world of ideas and the empirical world are put in another place. Being in the world is understood differently. The highest possibility of transcendence in Plato was the idea of the good, Resp., VI, 509b. [148] The negative attributes of light are an indication of enhanced transcendence in Philo, ἀσώματον in Conf. Ling., 61, ἀγένητον, Ebr., 208, [149] ἀόρατον, Op. Mund., 31. [150]

Cosmology and anthropology correspond. The being of the *logos* as light implies the possibility of revelation while protecting transcendence. The *logos* is the enlightening power in conversion, Conf. Ling., 63. Garment allegorising can lead to the anthropological significance of the *logos*, Fug., 108 ff.; [151] Som., I, 216 ff. [152] In anthropology and epistemology, too, Philo goes beyond Plato. There is in the first instance formal agreement when knowledge is understood as illumination: ἡ θεία σύνταξις αὕτη τὴν ὁρατικὴν ψυχὴν φωτίζει τε ὁμοῦ καὶ γλυκαίνει, φέγγος μὲν τὸ ἀληθείας ἀπαστράπτουσα, πειθοῖ δέ, ἀρετῇ γλυκείᾳ, τοὺς διψῶντας καὶ πεινῶντας καλοκἀγαθίας ἐφη-δύνουσα, Fug., 139, cf. 137 f. and Leg. All., I, 46; III, 171; Virt., 164. We find the principle that like is known only by like, light only by what is essentially light-like, Spec. Leg., I, 42. This is an ancient Gk. principle (→ 312, 33 ff.). There is an ontological connec-tion between knowledge and its object. But now in Philo this is given a distinctive twist: "God is His own light and He is seen by this alone ... only those attain to truth who reach the idea of God through God, the idea of light through light," Praem. Poen., 45 f., [153] cf. Cher., 97; Deus Imm., 58 f. and the closeness of φῶς, λόγος, σοφία and πνεῦμα to one another, e.g.: Wisdom is θεοῦ τὸ ἀρχέτυπον φέγγος, Migr. Abr., 40. [154] Another formal agreement with Plato is that the eye is blinded by the over-fulness of the divine light, Op. Mund., 69-71; Quaest. in Ex. Fr., 1, [155] cf. Migr. Abr., 38-42. [156] But again Philo goes further, for, when he sees, man transcends himself. The condition of sight is the impelling of the human νοῦς by the divine πνεῦμα. When the divine light shines forth, the human light goes out, Op. Mund., 69-71; Som., I, 118: ἐξοικίζεται μὲν γὰρ ἐν ἡμῖν ὁ νοῦς κατὰ τὴν τοῦ θείου πνεύματος ἄφιξιν, κατὰ δὲ τὴν μετανάστασιν αὐτοῦ πάλιν εἰσοικίζεται· θέμις γὰρ οὐκ ἔστι θνητὸν ἀθανάτῳ

---

146 The antitheses in Rer. Div. Her., 207 ff.; Gig., 41 do not prove the contrary, cf. the context.

147 Cf. Jonas Gnosis, I, *passim* and II, 1, 87 f. Eltester, *op. cit.*, 33: "The Platonic idea, which in Tim. is a prototype outside itself for the demiurge, now becomes the concept of God's creation." Cf. Op. Mund., 24.

148 Cf. Phaedr., 247b c, Beierwaltes, 46.

149 For the ideas cf. Plat. Tim., 52a, also 28a, 29a.

150 On the relation to Plato cf. Wolfson, *op. cit.*, I, 200-217, who differentiates an un-created world of ideas (Plato) from a created world of ideas. This is a simplification acc. to Daniélou, 169. The world of ideas rather shares the ambiguity of the *logos* itself.

151 Pascher, 61-4.

152 *Ibid.*, 174-184.

153 Cf. on this Jonas Gnosis, II, 1, 86-88. When Völker, 163, n. 7 says the ref. to illumina-tion as a condition of knowledge is fig., he misses the real pt.

154 Cf. Corp. Herm., 2, 12 vl. (Nock-Fest., I, 37, 6, cf. I, 40, n. 16); Pascher, 135 f. In this connection cf. also the fact that seeing takes precedence of hearing, Migr. Abr., 38 ff. and 47 ff.; Jonas Gnosis, II, 1, 95-7, though *v.* also Klein, 48 f.

155 Ed. R. Marcus, *Philo Suppl.*, II (1961), 258.

156 Völker, 178; Pascher, 13-23, 162. We find a basis in Plat. Resp., VII, 516a; Soph., 254a, but while there is the possibility of domestication in Plat., cf. Resp., VII, 516a, man's possibilies are transcended in Philo.

συνοικῆσαι. διὰ τοῦτο ἡ δύσις τοῦ λογισμοῦ καὶ τὸ περὶ αὐτὸν σκότος ἔκστασιν καὶ θεοφόρητον μανίαν ἐγέννησε, Rer. Div. Her., 265, cf. 263 f. [157] The royal way leads via the world of ideas to the vision of God. Direct knowledge of God excels indirect knowledge from His works. Leg. All., III, 101. The bracketing of the world in cosmology finds a par. in anthropology. Walking in the light is described in Abr., 70, [158] the way to the God of light in Mut. Nom., 4 ff. [159] Platonic knowledge is enveloped in mysticism. [160] Philo goes almost to the point of asserting deification, Quaest. in Ex. (→ n. 155), Fr. 1. [161] But he does not transgress the limit, for ascent and knowledge presuppose revelation, which has to come first, Plant., 23-27. [162] The ontic presupposition of enlightenment of the soul is the being of God as the spiritual sun, Virt., 164, cf. Leg. All., I, 46; Conf. Ling., 60 f. There is also the corrective that the concept of light is linked to the Law, Spec. Leg., I, 279 cf. Plat. Resp., VI, 509a; Fug., 137-139 (→ 324, 20 ff.) [163] Knowledge includes knowledge of God's claim. This finds expression in Gk. fashion as the light of virtue, Leg. All., I, 18 and 46; Plant., 40. [164] Knowledge leads to the uncovering of the sinner, Deus Imm., 135. Finally one should ref. to the vocabulary of conversion → 325, 4 ff. Conversion is a transition from darkness to light: ... ὥσπερ ἐκ βάθεος ὕπνου διοίξας τὸ τῆς ψυχῆς ὄμμα καὶ καθαρὰν αὐγὴν ἀντὶ σκότους βαθέος βλέπειν ἀρξάμενος ἠκολούθησε τῷ φέγγει καὶ κατεῖδεν, ὃ μὴ πρότερον ἐθεάσατο, τοῦ κόσμου τινὰ ἡνίοχον καὶ κυβερνήτην ἐφεστῶτα καὶ σωτηρίως εὐθύνοντα τὸ οἰκεῖον ἔργον..., Abr., 70. [165]

---

[157] Klein, 21 f. It is not enough to say that the nous is purified on the one side and negated on the other, Völker, 303 f. There are in fact contradictions, but these need explanation. They arise because it is hard to express the present thinking in Platonic terms and their presuppositions, which underlie Gk. theory, cf. Jonas Gnosis, II, 1, 79 f. On the one side the condition of this knowledge is desecularisation. But on the other it must be shown that it is man who has thus attained his goal. We thus have the contradiction that the nous is the eye of the soul (cf. Plat. Resp., VII, 533d; Soph., 254a, also Symp., 219a, on the spread of this expression cf. Kroll, 18-21; Dib. Gefbr. on Eph. 1:18) and therefore the organ of knowledge, but that the human possibility, and hence the nous, has to be transcended. On the one side it is maintained along Gk. lines that God can be grasped only by the nous, Philo Spec. Leg., I, 20, cf. Plat. Phaedr., 247c, while on the other He cannot be grasped by the nous either, Philo Deus Imm., 62, cf. Quaest. in Ex., II, 45 on 24:16; for the one side cf. also Mut. Nom., 6 and for the other 7. Thus the unity of knowledge of God and self can no longer be viewed in Platonic or Stoic fashion. Only Christianity and Gnosticism, however, develop the concepts in which to present this unity as a transcendent possibility. There is an attempt at mediation in Som., II, 231 ff. The nous stands here between God and man. But the paradox of Poster. C., 15 does the matter greater justice: καταλαβεῖν (the soul that seeks and loves God is the subj.) ὅτι ἀκατάληπτος ὁ κατὰ τὸ εἶναι θεὸς παντὶ καὶ αὐτὸ τοῦτο ἰδεῖν ὅτι ἐστὶν ἀόρατος, cf. Som., I, 66. Cf. also Abr., 119; Som., I, 118 f. and Jonas Gnosis, II, 1, 105, n. 1.

[158] Pascher, 140 compares with this Yašt 22 (cf. J. Darmesteter, "The Zend-Avesta, II" SBE, 23, 314-323; cf. also G. Widengren, Iranische Geisteswelt [1961], 171-5).

[159] Pascher, 13-36.

[160] If Philo depicts the supreme possibility in the vocabulary of the mysteries this does not means that he adopts a mystery; he is just following the Platonic tradition. There is a Platonising mystery theology, Wlosok, 58. To be noted is the connection between mystery speech and the self-understanding of a society, Som., II, 252; Cher., 27, 42 and 48; Migr. Abr., 35; Wlosok, 97-100.

[161] Statements about one's personal future (immortality) are less prominent than illumination mysticism, though cf. Vit. Mos., II, 288.

[162] Leisegang, op. cit. (→ n. 138), 221-9.

[163] E. R. Goodenough, By Light, Light (1935), 72-94; Wlosok, 97-107. The connection between light and the Law is not so explicit but may be seen in the use of the logos concept.

[164] But the Gk. doctrine of virtue loses its substance. The way to God does not lead by way of self-fulfilment but by way of self-surrender in knowledge of one's own nothingness, Rer. Div. Her., 30; Mut. Nom., 54, cf. Jonas Gnosis, II, 1, 38-43.

[165] Cf. the continuation and Klein, 22-4; Wlosok, 81-4. Cf. the summons to awake in Som., I, 165; Wlosok, 137-9, 149, 159-164; Virt., 179, cf. Corp. Herm., 1, 23; 7, 1-3 (→ 335, 20 ff.).

3. Gnosticism. General Features.

Basic to an understanding of Gnostic light metaphysics is a distinction between the two main types, the Syr.-Egypt. and the Iranian. [166] In the first the movement is from above to below, from primal light to darkness by means of emanation, i.e., weakening or a fall, or the combination of both. In the second type the movement begins with the revolt of primal darkness against the world of light. Here darkness does not come into being; it is pre-existent. The Syr.-Egypt. type is the normal one; its schema of the world and redemption is genuinely Gnostic. In the Iranian type a dualistic schema and the motif of conflict are given factors that then undergo a Gnostic-soteriological change. [167] This type is represented by the Mandaean writings and, of course, Manicheeism. There also seems to have been Iranian influence on the Peratae (Hipp. Ref., V, 12-18) and the Sethians (V, 19-22). [168]

Only in the second type can light and darkness confront one another dualistically in the strict sense. In the first, darkness, understood existentially, is the whence of the process of redemption. The focus here is primarily on light as the goal of the way of gnosis → I, 694, n. 21. Thus the almost exclusive ref. in liturgy, prayers and hymns is to light. The quantitative and intensive distribution of its negative counterpart, the ref. to darkness, corresponds to the degree of theoretical reflection on the whence of redemption. [169] This retrospective glance of the illumined to his lostness finds existential expression in the complaint of the wandering soul. [170] The more strongly this is developed, the stronger is the dualistic tension in this type, though not to the pt. of the Iranian antithesis. The most important documentation of the lament out of darkness is in Pist. Soph. → 342, 39 ff.; VII, 437, 16 ff.

What is prepared in non-Gnostic Hellenism is completed in Gnosticism. Light is the formless space of the world and the substance irradiating from it. [171] It is the self of those to be redeemed or already redeemed. He who is of the light, or is himself light, is at the goal, in the light, Corp. Herm., 1, 17. In Gnostic dialectic illumination is the awakening of the spark of light imprisoned in darkness (matter) and it is also fulfilment with the substance of light, transformation in light, deification. [172] Redemption, again dialectically, is the ascent of the redeemed to the light, Corp. Herm., 1, 32, the return home, 7, 2: ζητήσατε χειραγωγὸν τὸν ὁδηγήσοντα ὑμᾶς ἐπὶ τὰς τῆς γνώσεως θύρας, ὅπου ἐστὶ τὸ λαμπρὸν φῶς, τὸ καθαρὸν σκότους. [173] The inner relation of the heavenly origin, self-alienation, awakening by the call (→ 299, 22 ff.) or the heavenly letter, and return to oneself, can be depicted by the motif of the heavenly garment as one's true self,

---

[166] Jonas Gnosis, I, 256 f., 283 f., 328-331.

[167] *Ibid.*, 283, 328-331.

[168] *Ibid.*, 341 f.

[169] Along the lines of the Valentinian schema. Cl. Al. Exc. Theod., 78, 2: ἡ γνῶσις, τίνες ἦμεν, τί γεγόναμεν· ποῦ ἦμεν [ἢ] ποῦ ἐνεβλήθημεν· ποῦ σπεύδομεν, πόθεν λυτρούμεθα· τί γέννησις, τί ἀναγέννησις, cf. Jonas Gnosis, I, 261.

[170] Here, too, dialectic rules. The complaint presupposes insight into the heavenly origin and present lostness, and hence knowledge. In reality it is retrospective, although at the border. The redeemed have no time between redemption and the present, for the whole schema of redemption is timeless.

[171] Otherworldliness is stronger compared to non-Gnostic dualism. The world of ideas or spirit is put in the present cosmos and confused with it, Jonas Gnosis, I, 161-170.

[172] The pre-existence of the soul and transformation are intrinsically contradictory. One sees here the tension between the mode of expression and the real point. The point is redemption, newness. The metaphysical basis fits this only in intention and not in conception. It is the same contradiction as that between timelessness and the relics of a time schema in retrospect and prospect. The principle that like is known by like occurs in Corp. Herm., 11, 20 → 331, 20 f.; n. 131 [Bertram].

[173] Gnostic reflection may be seen in the fact that the ascent is broken. It leads through the cosmic wall separating the world and the sphere of light, through the gates and past the guards → 242, 14 ff., Jonas Gnosis, I, 146-156, 205-210 and *passim*.

as is finely done in the Song of the Pearl, Act. Thom. 108-113.[174] Light and life are not just related; they are identical. As light, life is beyond and otherworldly → II, 841, 12 ff.[175]

Light is the Gnostic alien, formless God who is identical with the sphere of light, Corp. Herm., 1; 13, 18, the self of those to be redeemed, the light of illumination γνῶσις ἁγία, φωτισθεὶς ἀπὸ σοῦ, διὰ σοῦ τὸ νοητὸν φῶς ὑμνῶν χαίρω ἐν χαρᾷ νοῦ, 13, 18, namely, knowledge of the inheritance of light. Hence the Gnostic has retrospective knowledge of the origin, 1, 21 and prospective knowledge of the goal, 1, 32.

4. Corpus Hermeticum.

Here, although the motifs are much the same as in Philo (→ 329, 18 ff.), the Gnostic transformation may be seen much better. Light terminology is restricted to the dualistic tractate[176] Corp. Herm., 1, 4. 6. 7. 13.[177] In 1 darkness is typically bracketed by light, 1, 1-4.[178] Darkness comes from it alone.[179] Light is both a sphere — hence cosmogony — and also a substance, as seen in anthropology.[180] Compared to true light earthly light is only σκοτεινὸν φῶς, 1, 28.[181] What unites cosmology and anthropology in Poim. too is the Logos, which as God's Son is φωτεινός, 1, 5 f.,[182] corresponding to Anthropos,

---

[174] Cf. Adam Thomas-Ps. 49-54. On the garment motif cf. Reitzenstein Hell. Myst., Index, s.v. "Gewand"; Klein, 61-66.

[175] Bultmann J., 25 f. E.g., Corp. Herm., 1, 9. 12. 17. 21; 13, 9. 12. 18 f. There are infinite variations in the Mandaeans, cf. the formula: "In the name of the gt. life hallowed by the majestic light," Lidz. Joh., 4, 13 f.; 12, 1; 17, 11 f. and passim; Ginza R., 271, 18; Lidz. Liturg., 177, 5; 190, 1 etc., cf. Ginza R., 54, 25 etc.

[176] The tractates are divided into dualistic (→ line 10) and monistic (2. 5. 8. 14; Ascl.), cf. Bousset, 749. Tractates 9. 10. 12. 16 are mixed.

[177] Klein, 18 f. σκότος is not found in hymns (e.g., Corp. Herm., 13, 17-20) or prayers (1, 31 f.). One may see here the difference of structure between the two ways of Gnostic self-actualisation, the liturgical orientated to the way to light and the ethical that is in conflict with darkness; this then finds theoretical expression. To determine the concept of light we need not discuss how far Corp. Herm., 1 is dependent on Gn. 1. There are echoes, cf. 1, 5. 7. 11 f. 17 f. 19. But they are only external. Literary dependence cannot be proved, as against Dodd Bible, 147, cf. Eltester, op. cit., 81 f. The cosmogony is basically different from that of the Bible. Light is at the beginning, not chaos. Dodd Bible, 107 thinks the sequence of Gn. 1 has been intentionally reversed. What we really have is a cosmogony that has nothing to do with Gn. 1. Creation is emanation from primal light. A duality arises thereby, since darkness is posited out of light. For a material evaluation of echoes and differences cf. Haenchen, op. cit., (→ n. 102), 340-344.

[178] Festugière, IV, 41 f. Haenchen, op. cit., 341 rightly argues against Dodd Bible, 108 that light not only symbolises the divine but is the divine, cf. Corp. Herm., 1, 6. 12. 21.

[179] The origin of the themes in the cosmogony of Poim. has not been cleared up. Scott, II, 6 and 123-6, cf. Haenchen, op. cit., 342 f., thinks the elements are Stoic (four), but Klein, 87-89 says Iranian (five). The no. five can only be postulated, however, and not proved. If the basis is Iranian, one must still say that the attack of darkness on light which one would have expected has been completely changed. Darkness does not come from below but from above σκότος κατωφερές, Corp. Herm., 1, 4, cf. Haenchen, op. cit., 341. Nor does it have the same primal existence as light, Klein, 93. It is not abs. pre-existent; it is so only in relation to the human body, Corp. Herm., 1, 20. Conflict first arises between the two, not in cosmogony, but in ethics, in the expulsion of the τιμωρίαι by the δυνάμεις, 13, 11 f. 17 ff., cf. σκοτο-μαχέω in 1, 23 as an ethical conflict.

[180] Corp. Herm., 13 can present its soteriology without the mythical and cosmological props of 1, cf. Klein, 107-116.

[181] Basically this expression goes beyond Philo Som., I, 79, which is only a relational def. and not a direct designation of αἰσθητὸν φῶς. Here and in the view of σῶμα is the starting-pt. of an ascetic ethics aimed at desecularisation.

[182] The text of Corp. Herm., 1, 6 is uncertain; one should read with Nock, I, 8, 18 f.: τὸ ἐν σοὶ βλέπον καὶ ἀκοῦον.

1, 17. [183] Between God and man in need of redemption is light, esp. in the typical combination "light and life" → n. 175. [184] In Poim. the light-nous is bisexual, 1, 9. [185] Life is the female principle in man and light is the male principle: ὁ δὲ ῎Ανθρωπος ἐκ ζωῆς καὶ φωτὸς ἐγένετο εἰς ψυχὴν καὶ νοῦν, ἐκ μὲν ζωῆς ψυχήν, ἐκ δὲ φωτὸς νοῦν, 1, 17. But this is secondary speculation. Originally light and life are a primal unity, cf., 1, 32. The relation of light as sphere and substance, of teaching on the world and on redemption, also finds expression in the doctrine of the δυνάμεις. These constitute the kingdom of light and in their totality they also constitute man, 13. 8 f., cf. 1, 9; 13, 18-20. [186]

In the process of revelation light cosmology is the first answer to the yearning for knowledge, 1, 3, which includes self-knowledge, as the presentation in Poim. shows. In knowledge man finds his origin in light and the way to return thereto. [187] Illumination is the presupposition of knowledge and this is the influx of power, 1, 32; 13, 21, [188] deification: τὸ πᾶν τὸ ἐν ἡμῖν, σῷζε ζωή, φώτιζε φῶς, 13, 19. [189] This is anticipated in ecstasy. [190] The inner tension of Gnostic anthropology (→ n. 190) vanishes in the idea of regeneration. [191] The organs must be changed to be able to know, cf. Preis. Zaub., I, 4, 529 ff. (4th cent. A.D.); Corp. Herm., 13, 3. The presupposition of this is man's original being as light. This is how the process of finding oneself out of radical self-alienation is depicted. The practical outworking of this self-understanding is in asceticism. In this the self confronts itself as a heavenly being.

The total picture includes the missionary concept with the vocabulary of conversion, 1, 27-32; 7. [192] This starts with the Gnostic idea that the saved are few [193] and that they must be awakened by the call — 299, 22 ff. [194] Only the illuminated can be awakened.

---

[183] Cf. Just. Dial., 121, 2 and the function of the πνεῦμα in the Sethians, Hipp. Ref., V, 19, 2, also φωτεινὸν πνεῦμα in V, 19, 17. On the relation of Logos, Second Nous (Demiurge) and Anthropos, v. Haenchen, op. cit., 351 f., 356 f.

[184] Dodd Bible, 133-6; Dodd, op. cit. (→ n. 52), 345-354; E. Peterson, Εἷς Θεός, FRL, 24 (1926), 38 f.

[185] Cf. Nock-Fest., I, 20, n. 24.

[186] Cf. Philo → 330, 21 ff. with n. 144; on the series in Herm. s., 9, 15, 3 cf. Festugière, III, 153-174, on the hymn Corp. Herm., 13, 18-20, ibid., 246-251. One finds the non-Gk. element: The δυνάμεις establish themselves in man as an alien force. Virtue is a divine power that man cannot achieve on his own. Ethical existence is a transmundane possibility. Moral and mystical concepts merge into one another in Corp. Herm., 13, 8 f. The life-style of Gnosticism is reflected here. This is not a moralising of mysticism; it is a new morality presupposing transformation.

[187] The self-presentation with which the revelation begins τὸ φῶς ἐκεῖνο... ἐγώ, Corp. Herm., 1, 6 cannot be compared with the Johannine ἐγώ εἰμι. It is just a matter of the style adopted to identify the light already manifested. Rather different is the ἐγώ εἰμι ὁ Ποιμάνδρης, 1, 2.

[188] Cf. also ἧκέ μοι, τὸ πνεῦμα τὸ ἀεροπετές... καὶ ἔμβηθι αὐτοῦ (sc. of the child that serves as a medium) εἰς τὴν ψυχήν, ἵνα τυπώσηται τὴν ἀθάνατον μορφὴν ἐν φωτὶ κραταιῷ καὶ ἀφθάρτῳ, Preis. Zaub., II, 7, 559-564 (3rd cent. A.D.).

[189] The continuation πνεῦμα θεέ is corrupt. Should one read πνευμάτιζε θεέ with B. Keil, cf. Nock-Fest., II, 208 on line 17? Cf. Klein, 114 f.

[190] Jonas Gnosis, I, 200-203. In Corp. Herm., too, there is tension between return to the true origin in light and transformation (→ n. 172), cf. 1, 6. 17 with 1, 26 and εἰς ζωὴν καὶ φῶς χωρῶ, 1, 32. This reflects the Gnostic contradiction that I am not who I should be and can come to myself only by surrendering myself as illustrated by destruction of the σῶμα and effected by asceticism.

[191] This is the theme of Corp. Herm., 13 and cf. Mithr. Liturg., 165 f.

[192] Cf. Philo (→ 332, 14 ff.), Test. XII (→ 326, 24 f.) and Jos. and Aseneth (→ 325, 4 ff.).

[193] Corp. Herm., 9, 4; Ascl., 9. 22; Herm. Trismeg. Fr., 11, 4 in Stob. Ecl., I, 277, 21 f.

[194] ... ἦργμαι κηρύσσειν τοῖς ἀνθρώποις τὸ τῆς εὐσεβείας καὶ γνώσεως κάλλος, ῏Ω λαοί, ἄνδρες γηγενεῖς οἱ μέθῃ καὶ ὕπνῳ ἑαυτοὺς ἐκδεδωκότες καὶ τῇ ἀγνωσίᾳ τοῦ θεοῦ, νήψατε παύσασθε δὲ κραιπαλῶντες θελγόμενοι ὕπνῳ ἀλόγῳ, Corp. Herm., 1, 27, cf. 7, 2. On the Gnostic call to awake cf. Jonas Gnosis, I, 120-122; Becker, 21 f.; → 338, 5 ff.; n. 312.

Mission is their duty; ecstasy is prophetic consecration: ... ἐνδυνάμωσόν με, καὶ τῆς χάριτος ταύτης φωτίσω τοὺς ἐν ἀγνοίᾳ τοῦ γένους, μοῦ ἀδελφούς, υἱοὺς δὲ σοῦ. διὸ πιστεύω καὶ μαρτυρῶ· εἰς ζωὴν καὶ φῶς χωρῶ, 1, 32. Decision is not ruled out by the pre-existence of souls: it is in fact presented in these terms. [195]

5. The Mandaeans.

The data are abundant, but not uniform, since the Syr.-Egypt. and Iranian types are combined in the Mandaean writings (→ 333, 1 ff.), the former having historical and hermeneutical precedence. [196] Note has also to be taken of the forms and genres: cosmogonic depiction, mission of the Revealer, hymns of complaint and jubilation, calls to awake, prayers etc. The soteriology can be detached from its mythical garb and take a pure form (→ 337, 7 ff.) as in the liturgies and hymns of Ginza L., where the structure of the process of redemption is very plain. The pre-existent soul of light has been cast into Tibil, 454, 17 f. etc. [197] and it laments, is summoned, [198] is awakened, and rises up, e.g., 459, 20 - 460, 34 → n. 218. [199]

· Light is transcendent. With light nhur we find the largely synon. "radiance" ziw and "glory" 'qar, e.g., Lidz. Ginza R., 6, 8 ff., cf. 11, 4 ff. "Life rests in its own radiance and light," Lidz. Liturg., 95, 8. The "king of light" is "pure radiance and the gt. light that does not go out," Ginza R., 5, 18 f. Light and radiance are synon. when ref. is made to the garment of light; the sent one is clothed in light or radiance, Ginza R., 143, 9 f. 32; 145, 27 ff. Recipients of revelation are told: "Clothe yourselves with radiance and clothe yourselves with light and set forth on the way of life," R., 255, 30 ff. [200] Liturg., 8, 10 ff. is a good example of the style: "In the name of life. The light shone, the light shone, the light of the great first life shone. Wisdom and illumination shone, understanding and praise of the first Mānā that came from his place." Except in the Iranian parts light is before darkness. It is without form or limit. [201] Light and Godhead are identical. The latter, too, is without personality. It is formless being, life. It can be described only by infinite light and life predications, cf. the formula: "In the name of the gt. life hallowed be the majestic light" → n. 175. "He is the light in whom is no darkness, the living one in whom is no death, the good one in whom is no wickedness...," Ginza R., 6, 26 ff. [202] The otherworld-

---

[195] Note that the Gnostic I, like the Gnostic God, is without form, a negation of individuality rather than an individual.

[196] Esp. in the twofold cosmogony Lidz. Ginza R., Book 3, cf. the analysis in Jonas Gnosis, I, 262-283 and Ginza R., 277-280. The Iranian portions are not the original, Jonas Gnosis, loc. cit.; Rudolph, I, 145. We can concentrate on the first type since the second will be dealt with under Manicheeism → 339, 3 ff. On the role of the Mandaeans in the rise of Manicheeiem cf. Rudolph, I, 176-195; → 339, 4 ff.

[197] Jonas Gnosis, I, 106-109.

[198] On the sequence of call and lament → 338, 15 ff.

[199] On the mass for the dead Masiqtā, i.e., the ascent of the soul, cf. Rudolph, II, 259-278.

[200] There are naturally variations. When the sent one is clothed with light, his radiance shines forth, Lidz. Liturg., 233, 7 - 234, 6, cf. Ginza R., 143, 10 with 143, 32. But it is artificial to see in light the masculine aspect and in radiance the feminine aspect (→ 335, 2 ff.), so Alf Trisar Suialia, II, 3b (transl. E. S. Drower, "The Thousand and Twelve Questions," Deutsche Akad. d. Wissenschaften zu Berlin, Institut f. Orientforschung, 32 [1960], 211), and Drower, 6. Radiance is personified in Ziwa or Jawar-Ziwa, ibid., 15 f.

[201] Lidz. Ginza R., 75, 16 ff.: "For life there is no limit, and it was not known when it arose." Cf. Lidz. Liturg., 91, 2: Nothing was when light was not. The pt. is naturally not that of primal nothingness but rather the primal nature of light. If darkness is also original and autogeneous in Lidz. Joh., 216, 14 f.; Ginza R., 277, this is due to Iranian influence, Jonas Gnosis, I, 268.

[202] Jonas Gnosis, I, 243-251; Rudolph, I, 122.

liness of this world and this God may be seen in such predications. [203] The characteristic attribute of life, and hence of the emissary of life, is "alien," e.g., in the fixed formula. "In the name of the gt. alien life from the worlds of light, the lofty one above all works (sc. the world)," R., 31, 2 f.; 65, 21 f.; 149, 1 f.; 251, 6 f.; 239, 25 f.; cf. 251, 1 f.; 15, 28 f.; Liturg., 3, 4 f. [204] Light has nothing whatever to do with earthly brightness; the two are even hostile to one another. [205]

Among the Mandaeans mythical cosmogony also has soteriological significance though this is often obscured by wild fantasy. [206] Primal light develops and original being enters into a movement that cannot be halted. [207] Another not wholly compatible idea is that of the fusion by which the world comes into being: "Then they brought living water and poured it into muddy water; they brought shining light and threw it into black darkness," Lidz. Joh., 56, 15-17. Since the world has light only through the particles of light dispersed in it — a state of abs. perversion — it has its own interest in light → VII, 436, 1 ff. [208] The world collapses when the particles of light are withdrawn, Ginza L., 517, 8 ff.

Mythically depicted, light is the living power of the world in the creation of Adam, Ginza R., 108, 16 ff. The body created by the planets (→ n. 205) lives only when the heavenly substance of life is given to it. Light cannot be lost. But this is no consolation so long as the soul is imprisoned. The soul knows it cannot be lost only through the call; then this truth gives assurance to the Gnostic. In warning it is also said that a man can be torn from it, R., 324, 15.

The myth depicts the destiny of the individual soul. Man even in his dark house lives by the light, which is in him and thus constitutes his true being, Ginza L., 514, 13 ff.; Liturg., 102, 12. Redemption comes to him through the envoy from the kingdom of light. [209] This envoy is clothed with light and radiance and comes down into the world, R., 142 ff., as "the strange man who penetrated the worlds, came, clove the firmament, and revealed himself," R., 197, 15 ff. The cosmic wall symbolises the otherworldliness of revelation → n. 205. The sent one is the image of the Father, R., 152, 28 ff. The clothing represents his being and is thus a symbol of the supernatural revelatory character of redemption. [210] Related is the symbol of the sweet savour, R., 327, 31 ff. The revealer conceals himself on descending, Liturg., 184, 1 f. etc. [211]

Revelation is the self-revelation of the sent one. He issues the cry: "I am the envoy of light, whom the Great One has sent into this world ... He who accepts His message, his eyes fill with light," Ginza R., 58, 17 ff., cf. 59, 1 f. "I am the life that was from hence,

---

[203] The king of light — special problems relating to the parts about him may be ignored here — is also without form. Drower, 56 says about him and his pendant, the king of darkness: "But these are epithets, descriptive of characteristics rather than names of beings." The personified emanations of light, the uthras, and the envoys are also without form. The name of the chief envoy, Manda d'Haijē, is enough to show this.

[204] Jonas Gnosis, I, 96 f.

[205] The exponents of cosmic and sidereal brightness, the planets, belong to darkness, i.e., the world. The symbol showing that light is alien to the world is the cosmic wall which must be pierced by the revealer → lines 25 f.; Lidz. Ginza R., 197, 15 etc.

[206] We need not present the mythical side, since the meaning of "light" is esp. clear in the non-mythical parts, e.g., Ginza L.

[207] Jonas Gnosis, I, 263. Cf. Ginza R., 66, 14 ff. The uthras are the personified representation of movement, Drower, 56-65. These "left the fellowship of light and loved the fellowship of darkness," Ginza R., 69, 10 f. For details cf. esp. Ginza R., Book 3 and Jonas Gnosis, I, 262-283. The change from the passivity of darkness to activity is depicted in Ptahil-Uthra, Jonas Gnosis, I, 272. The movement is a fall; note the expression "to be thrown." The soul laments: "Why did they strip me of my radiance, bring me hither and put me in the garment of the body?" Ginza L., 461, 6 f. etc.

[208] Lidz. Joh., 216, 14 ff. (Iranian).

[209] On the sending cf. esp. Lidz. Ginza R., Book 5.

[210] On the image and garment motifs cf. esp. the Pearl Song, 2. 8. 14. 61. 70-85. 95-97 (Adam Thomas-Ps., 49-54).

[211] This motif is also common, Asc. Is. 9:13 ff.; 10:14 ff., cf. H. Schlier, "Religionsgesch. Untersuchungen z. d. Ignatiusbriefen," ZNW Beih., 8 (1929), 7-17.

I am the Kušta (→ I, 240, 16 f.) ... I am the radiance, I am the light," R., 207, 34 ff. [212] Revelation is illumination: "The heart in which I found a place lit up and shone beyond measure ... He who lets himself be enlightened by illumination, will be set at the place of light," R., 327, 33 ff. [213] Illumination thus makes known the ascent: [214] "Hail to the True Ones! They rise up and see the place of light," R., 376, 11 ff. The content of revelation can be put in the form of the call to awake → 335, 20 ff.: "Stand up, you that lie ... stand up, honour and extol the gt. life, praise the image, the image of life, that beams and shines in glorious light," Liturg., 178, 3-5 → n. 194. To the soul is disclosed its origin from light: "Thou art a part of the light-earth," Ginza L., 458, 22. "Thou, elect, didst not come from here ... Thy place is the place of life, thy dwelling is the dwelling of light," Liturg., 158, 6 f. The course of redemption is determined by the fact that the revealer and the summoned are identical in substance. [215] The redeemer thus gathers himself. [216] The identity is expressed in the use of the image idea. The image is the revealer (→ 337, 31 ff.) [217] and also the awakened one: "I go towards my image and my image goes towards me," Ginza L., 559, 29 ff. "Image" denotes unity of substance.

The summons to awake first kindles in the awakened a knowledge of lostness and the complaint of the lost soul: "When Adam heard this, he bewailed himself and wept," Ginza L., 431, 4. This mythical process of awakening is the material presupposition when the complaint comes first and the heavenly revelation and redemption is the answer. The lamentations are songs of the Gnostic. He who laments is already awake, cf. esp. Ginza L., Book 2. [218] Lamentation is followed by jubilation in self-knowledge: "I have gone forth from the place of light," R., 377, 31. The one illumined calls to the cosmos: "I and the root of my Father rise up; the house is left to you," L., 457, 23 f. Light is finally victorious. The practical side of this teaching is the worship of light. [219] Along with water symbolism, light symbolism serves to interpret baptism. [220]

Related [221] to the Mandaean writings are the Thomas Ps. from the Coptic Manichaean Psalm-Book, [222] which stand out against their purely Manichaean background. [223] Although these belong to the Iranian type, in many respects they reflect a proto-Manichaean or

---

[212] Analysis in E. Schweizer, "Ego Eimi," FRL, 56² (1965), 70-72.

[213] Cf. Lidz. Ginza R., 145, 27 ff.; 381, 35 ff.; Ginza L., 441, 12 ff. In practice illumination leads to worship and to Mandaean morality.

[214] Cf. Lidz. Ginza L., 513, 23 ff. The Kušta is addressed in the psalm, Ginza R., 271, 26 f.: "Thou art the way of perfection, the path that leads to the place of light." The symbol of the way is common to Gnosticism; gnosis is def. as γνῶσις ὁδοῦ → I, 694, n. 21; V, 47, 3 ff., cf. Lidz. Ginza R., 20, 3; 23, 2; 68, 10; 148, 10; 264, 7 etc.

[215] The primal man as the head of the race of souls, Lidz. Ginza R., 242, 34 ff., Rudolph, I, 152 f. For the identity of the primal man and the soul cf. L., 486, 14 ff. etc. Since there is no individuation Mānā is both the collective and the individual soul, R., 333, 23 ff. The fact that light and soul have no form finds expression in the idea of fellowship laufā: sin breaks this, being lost is being cut off, Rudolph, II, 149-153; Bultmann J., 409, n. 6.

[216] Rudolph, I, 159.

[217] The "helper" speaks: "Thou art mine image. I will lift thee up and keep thee in my garment," Lidz. Ginza L., 461, 31 f.

[218] Lidz. Ginza L., 454, 14 - 455, 26: "I am a Mānā of the gt. life. Who has caused me to dwell in Tibil? ... When the Mānā said this, his cry rose up to the place of light. Manda d'Haijē heard his cry and sent his messenger to me ..." This calls: "Shine and light up, Mānā. I have come to thee and will not leave thee. When thou art called, rise up to the place of light."

[219] Rudolph, II, 217. White sacral attire is part of the cult, 50.

[220] Ibid., II, 103: "The world of light is there in baptism and its actions," cf. 62 f.

[221] Säve-Söderbergh, 155-163.

[222] Cf. C. R. C. Allberry, "A Manichaean Psalm-Book, II," Manich. Manuscripts in the Chester Beatty Collection, II (1938), 203-228; Adam Thomas-Ps., 2-28.

[223] Chronologically cf. Adam Thomas-Ps., 32, though his conjecture that Wis. 18:14-16 is dependent on Thom.-Ps. (→ n. 222), 1 (p. 203, 1 - 205, 9) is not convincing. Wis. may be left out of account in the question of dating.

Mandaean stage. [224] They share with Manicheeism the revolt of darkness, the dramatic victory of light, and the structure of redemption as a drama. [225]

6. Manicheeism (→ VII, 437, 1 ff.).

As distinct from Syr.-Egypt. Gnosticism, including the Mandaeans, Manicheeism presents the metaphysical in the form of a nature-system. [226] The Syr.-Egypt. type def. the antithesis as that of true and transcendent light and false this-worldly light → 333, 2 ff. [227] In the Manichaean system the world itself is divided. The visible light of the sun and moon is true light. The heavenly bodies have a firm place in the process of redemption, namely, in separating the two elements of light and darkness. [228] Duality does not arise through fall and guilt, i.e., through a movement from above downwards; rather two primal spheres confront one another. [229] Conflict rather than movement is the basic motif, Kephalaia (→ n. 228), Intr. p. 4, 1 ff. The antithesis is absolute. [230] As there are no gradations but only conflict in cosmology, so there are no shadings of good and bad but only an either-or in psychology and ethics. [231] Darkness is not for a single moment passive. Through its assault on primal man and triumph over him there is a mingling of the elements, Psalm-Book (→ n. 222), 223 (p. 10, 6 ff.). [232] Hence the process of separation is both necessary and possible. It is a cosmic process in which the sun and moon and the zodiac provide transport for light → VII, 437, n. 122. The outcome of the battle is sure. Light is superior to darkness, since the latter aspires beyond itself and is inwardly divided, while light is at one with itself and desires only itself → VII, 437, n. 123 f. [233] "When they (sc. the five houses of darkness, the pendant of the five magnitudes of light) waged war among themselves, they dared to lay their hands on the land of light; they thought they could conquer it, but did not realise that what they had in mind they would bring down on themselves," Psalm-Book (→ n. 222) 223 (p. 9, 21 ff.). [234]

---

[224] Adam Thomas-Ps., 30 notes in relation to the mythological Ps. 1: "We undoubtedly have dualism, but in an undeveloped form; the system might equally well lead to monism as dualism." On the historical relation between the Mandaeans and Manicheeism cf. Rudolph, I, 176-195.

[225] The Father is joyous light, Thomas-Ps. (→ n. 122) 1 (p. 203, 3-6). He summons the aeons of light and the drama begins. The goal: "Then shall the light come to light and darkness shall be destroyed from its place," Thomas-Ps. 9 (p. 215, 24 ff.).

[226] Jonas Gnosis, I, 316 f.

[227] Historically considered the Syr.-Egypt. type is the Gnostic transformation of Iranian dualism (→ VII, 437, n. 119). It is not basically Gnostic but a later adaptation, Jonas Gnosis, I, 329.

[228] Kephalaia, 1 (ed. H. J. Polotsky-A. Böhlig, *Manichäische Hdschr. d. Staatlichen Museen Berlin,* I [1940]), 65 (p. 158, 31 f.): The sun is the "gate of life and the vehicle of peace to this gt. aeon of [light]," Psalm-Book (→ n. 222) 223 (p. 10, 30-32), cf. Adam Texte, 41: "The sun and the moon will be set up and placed on high so that the soul may be purified. Daily that which is purified will be raised up on high."

[229] Book of Giants, from extracts in Severus of Antioch, Hom., 123 (Syr.), cf. Adam Texte, 11. The movement of darkness is one of revolt → VII, 437, 5 ff. with n. 121.

[230] Cf. the confrontations in Kephalaia (→ n. 228), 4 f. (p. 25, 7 - 30, 11): Psalm-Book (→ n. 222) 223 (p. 9, 12 ff. cf. Adam Texte, 39-42).

[231] That cosmology and anthropology correspond is naturally true of Manicheeism too, cf. the cosmos and the body, Kephalaia (→ n. 228), 70 (p. 169, 24 ff.). In Manicheeism, too, man simply subsists as the non-worldly and formless self, which is not defined abstractly as being but in respect of its need of redemption and capacity for it. On the self v. Colpe, op. cit. (→ n. 50), 91-6. Man is not a being that has virtues and vices; he is in his virtues and vices as their sum. This is finely presented in the motif of the *alter ego,* cf. Reitzenstein Hell. Myst., 265-275; cf. the δυνάμεις, Corp. Herm., 13, 8 f. 18 ff. (→ n. 186); Col. 3:5 ff.

[232] Adam Texte, 40.

[233] Kephalaia (→ n. 228), 52 (p. 128, 3 ff.); Jonas Gnosis, I, 290.

[234] Adam Texte, 39 f.

The soteriological drama is portrayed mythically — with a monstrous apparatus of hypostases, envoys, virgins of light etc. [235] — as the sending and fall of the first emissary and then his liberation. It is also portrayed existentially as call and answer and also as illumination with complaint and jubilation: "May the gt. radiance come and light up the way before me," Manich. Homilies, p. 6, 19 f. [236] The Manichaean redeemer, too, is consubstantial with those who are called, and thus gathers himself. [237] The drama is eschatologically orientated, i.e., to the final state of the separation of the hostile elements, the triumph of light, and the end of darkness, which is nothing.

The point of the dualism is decision on the basis of the insight that decision is already made, since the self derives from light. Missionary feeling is dominant, for the disclosure of the world process by preaching is itself an act of separation or redemption → VII, 437, 13 ff. with n. 125. The elect individual actualises it in ethical action emotionally charged by the dimension of what is to be attained.

7. Odes of Solomon (→ VII, 435, 12 ff.). [238]

Light is the place of the redeemed. "And I was lifted up to the light and passed before His (sc. the Lord's) face," 21:6. "I rose up to the light of truth as on a chariot," 38:1. On the way or walk into light cf. 11:18 f.; 7:13 f., on the ascent of the soul, 35:7. Light is also the essence of the redeemed. This is depicted again as the garment: "And I I came out of darkness and put on light," 21:3. [239] Light is transcendent, God's light, which drives out darkness. "For He is my sun, and His rays have caused me to arise, and His light has dispelled all darkness from my face," 15:2. Where Judaism governs the thought of the Odes, the world is not abandoned, for it is creation. The Jewish tradition and Gnosticising may also be seen in the concept of light, the combining of light and life, 10:1 f.; 38:1 ff.; 41:11 f. Light is knowledge, 6:17 f.; 7:13 f., truth, 12:1 ff.; 25:7, 10; 38:1, joy, 15:1 ff. 32:1; 41:1 ff., love, 41:6. All these concepts are shaped by the fact that light is revelation, and revelation proclaimed in the Word, 6:7; 10:1; 32:1 f. [240] The Word can be explicitly called light: "For as its (light's) effect, so its expectation; for it is light and brightness for thought," 12:7, cf. 12:3 and also 41:14: "And light beamed forth from the Word that was previously in it." In relation to this myth recedes into the background. [241]

The relation between redeemer and redeemed is Gnostic; the same statements can be made about both. Both are the shining one, the Son of God, 36:3. "And our face shall shine in his light," 41:6, i.e., the redeemed transformed into light. [242]

---

[235] Cf. the interpretation of all the fathers of light in Kephalaia (→ n. 228), 11 (p. 43, 23 - 44, 18). There is a survey in Psalm-Book (→ n. 222) 223 (p. 9-11, Adam Texte, 39-42) and cf. the account of Theodore bar Konai, Liber scholiorum, 11 (Adam Texte, 15-23). Cf. the dialogue between the envoy and primal man, Psalm-Book, p. 197, 9 - 202, 9.

[236] Ed. H. J. Polotsky, *Manich. Manuscripts in the Chester Beatty Collection*, I (1934).

[237] Colpe, *op. cit.* (→ n. 50), 93. Man. Homilies (→ n. 236), p. 7, 11 ff.: "He gave us knowledge of the beginning; he taught us the [mysterie]s (??) of the middle and the separation of the end."

[238] R. M. Grant, "Notes on Gnosis," *Vigiliae Christianae*, 11 (1957), 149-151, on the basis of a comparison of the Odes with the Ev. Veritatis (ed. M. Malinine, H. C. Puech, G. Quispel [1956]), thinks they are Valentinian; cf. O. Sol. 23:1-4 with Ev. Veritatis, 16, 31-35; O. Sol. 38:6-12 with Ev. Ver., 17, 14-16, 19-21; 18, 20 f. 24; 41, 17 ff. 26; 42, 33-35.

[239] The familiar conversion style (→ 335, 20 ff.) is echoed, cf. 11:11; 25:7 f. and the missionary preaching of O. Sol. 33 with the end of Poimandres, Corp. Herm., 1, 27-32.

[240] Bultmann J., 24, n. 4.

[241] It is in the background as a representation, cf. the odes about the Word and the manifestation of goodness, O. Sol. 12, 33.

[242] Cf. the statements of the Gnostic I about itself, which are mostly redeemer predications, e.g., O. Sol. 17, also 9:2; 10; 31:8-13; 42. On the identity of redeemer and redeemed cf. Colpe, *op. cit.* (→ n. 50), 180 f. In 8:22; 42:18 we find the redeemed redeemer, Adam Thomas-Ps., 34 f. though cf. H. M. Schenke, *Der Gott "Mensch" in d. Gnosis* (1962), 30, n. 120.

8. Christian Gnosticism. [243]

Chr. Gnosticism contributes nothing new to the understanding of light but simply offers variations on traditional ideas of light, its emanations, phenomena, and exponents, and also the counterforces, the archons, the fall (mostly of sophia), and then the ascent and the way past the archons. Use of the terminology is not uniform. Thus it is not at all prominent in the Gospel of Thomas. [244] In this case the reason is the link with Synoptic materials. When there is ref. to light the Gnostic character is patent. Synoptic light-sayings (Mt. 5:14, 16; 6:22 f.) are Gnosticised: "There is light in a man of light and it shines on the whole world. When it does not shine there is darkness," Gospel of Thomas (→ n. 244) Logion 24 (86, 7 ff.). The pt. is the same in Logion 77 (94, 22 ff.): "Jesus said: I am the light that is over all. I am the all," and also 50 (89, 33 ff.): "We have come from the light, the place where light has come into being of itself." [245] Jesus is consubstantial with the Father, cf. Ev. Veritatis (→ n. 238) 31:13 f.: "Through his (Jesus') voice light spoke and its voice, which had begotten life." Too much importance should not be attached to the statistics. What counts is the character of the terms and their use. [246]

Common to the disparate Gnostic forms and schemes [247] is the basic pt. that in most documents movement is from above downwards by emanation from primal light, Apocr. of Jn. (→ n. 247) 32:19 - 33:7 [248] and the fall of sophia. [249] Though the antithesis of light and darkness can be very strong (→ VII, 437, 16 ff.), [250] the priority of light as primal

---

[243] Sources include not only Ev. Veritatis and the other works adduced but also the Work without Title on the origin of the world, ed. A. Böhlig - P. Labib, *Deutsche Akad. d. Wissenschaften zu Berlin, Institut f. Orientforschung*, 58 (1962); Hypostasis of Archons, ed. R. A. Bullard, *Patrist. Texte u. Stud.*, 10 (1970), cf. J. Leipoldt - H. M. Schenke, "Kpt.-gnost. Schriften aus den Pap.-Cod. v. Nag-Hamadi," *Theol. Forschung*, 20 (1960), 71-78; the Apocalypses of Paul, James I and II and Adam, ed. A. Böhlig - P. Labib, "Kpt.-gnost. Apokal. aus Cod. V v. Nag Hammadi," *Wissenschaftliche Zschr. d. Martin-Luther-Univ. Halle-Wittenberg, Special Vol.* (1963); De resurrectione, ed. M. Malinine *et al.* (1963); Ep. Iacobi Apocr., ed. M. Malinine *et al.* (1968). In gen. cf. H. C. Puech in Hennecke[3], I, 158-271; W. C. v. Unnik, *Ev. aus d. Nilsand* (1960); J. M. Robinson, "The Coptic Gnostic Library Today," NTSt, 14 (1967/68), 356-401.

[244] Ed. A. Guillaumont *et al.* (1959). Bibl. in E. Haenchen, "Lit. z. Thomas-Ev.," ThR, NF, 27 (1961), 147-178, 306-338.

[245] Cf. the Gospel of Philip, ed. W. C. Till, *Patrist. Texte u. Stud.*, 2 (1963), Logion 10 (101, 14 ff.); Ev. Veritatis (→ n. 238), 35, 1 ff.; R. McL. Wilson, *Stud. in the Gospel of Thomas* (1960), 106 f.; also The Gospel of Philip (1962), 72 f.; B. Gärtner, *The Theology of the Gospel of Thomas* (1961), 206-9; E. Haenchen, *Die Botschaft d. Thomas-Ev.* (1961), 39 f.

[246] Thus the no. of instances in the Gospel of Philip (→ n. 245) is small. But we find Gnostic motifs there: predication as perfect, Logion 77 (118, 5); 106 (124, 27); 125 (133, 16. 18. 26), the garment motif, 106 (124, 25 ff.). The Gnostic idea of predestination is also present: "When one who is blind and one who sees are in the dark, there is no difference between them. When light comes, the one who sees will see the light and the one who is blind will remain in the dark," Logion 56 (112, 5-9). Cf. also: "Thou who hast united the perfect, light, with the Holy Ghost (sc. Achamot, cf. Iren. Haer., I, 1, 7 f.), unite the angels with us too, the images (εἰκών)," 26 (106, 11-14).

[247] Thus we find wild and artificial speculations, cf. Pist. Soph., the two books of Jeû (cf. C. Schmidt and W. Till, GCS, 45[3] [1959]), the Ancient Anon. Gnostic work (Schmidt-Till, *op. cit.*), the Gospel acc. to Mary (ed. W. Till, TU, 60 [1955]), the Apocr. of Jn. (Till, *op. cit.*) and the Sophia of Jesus Christ (Till, *op. cit.*). We also have songs, e.g., O. Sol., in which the Gnostic self-understanding finds clear expression, and meditations like the Ev. Veritatis (→ n. 238), nor should one forget the Gnostic Gospels, to which this incorrectly named work does not really belong.

[248] Cf. the Nag-Hamadi versions in M. Krause - P. Labib, "Die drei Versionen d. Apokr. d. Joh.," *Abh. d. Deutschen Archäol. Instituts Kairo. Kpt. Reihe*, 1 (1962).

[249] This is true even when darkness is shown to be in revolt, cf. Pist. Soph. 15 f. (GCS, 45 p. 15, 3 - 16, 2).

[250] The Sethians and Peratae represent the Iranian type (→ 333, 8 ff.). On the form of Sophia in the Copt.-Gnostic texts → VII, 511, 23 ff.

being is preserved. 251 Its formlessness may be seen from the negative descriptions of God or light in Apocr. of Jn., 22:19 - 25:8; 26:2, 12, cf. Sophia of Jesus Christ (→ n. 247), 84:1 - 86:1. The language is always strict and not fig.: Light *is* God and His world, revelation, the Gnostic self. The true God is in pure light, in which no light of the eyes may be seen, Apocr. of Jn. (→ n. 247) 22:23 - 23:2. He is immeasurable light, 24:6 f. "He who attains (only) to himself, in the perfection of light, comprehends (νοεῖν) pure (ἀκέραιον) light," 25, 9-12. 252 The attributes of light pt. to its nature: It is indescribable, Pist. Soph., 143 (GCS, 45, p. 245, 35), infinite, Book II of Jeû (→ n. 247), 45 (p. 309, 2), incorruptible, Ancient Anon. Gnostic work (→ n. 247), 9 (p. 345, 25), immeasurable, Apocr. of Jn. (→ n. 247) 24; 6 f., perfect, Gospel of Philip (→ n. 245), Logion 77 (118, 5); 106 (124, 27 f.). 253 Salvation is experienced as illumination. Here we again find the older vocabulary of conversion (→ 335, 20 ff.). Conversion is transition from darkness to light, Act. Thom. 28 (p. 145, 13 f.); 157 (p. 267, 1). Among the Valentinians light is received through the sacrament of the bridal chamber, Gospel of Philip, Logion 127 (134, 4-18). How the strict sense may be retained even with spiritual exegesis of the NT may be seen from the school of Basilides: ἐπέλαμψεν ⟨οὖν⟩ ὁ υἱὸς τοῦ μεγάλου ἄρχοντος τῷ υἱῷ τοῦ ἄρχοντος τῆς ἑβδομάδος τὸ φῶς, ὃ εἶχεν ἅψας αὐτὸς ἄνωθεν ἀπὸ τῆς υἱότητος, καὶ ἐφωτίσθη ὁ υἱὸς τοῦ ἄρχοντος τῆς ἑβδομάδος, καὶ εὐηγγελίσατο τὸ εὐαγγέλιον τῷ ἄρχοντι τῆς ἑβδομάδος, Hipp. Ref., VII, 26, 5. Light comes further even to Jesus: καὶ ἐφωτίσθη συνεξαφθεὶς τῷ φωτὶ τῷ λάμψαντι εἰς αὐτόν. τοῦτό ἐστι, φησί, τὸ εἰρημένον πνεῦμα ἅγιον ἐπελεύσεται ἐπὶ σέ, VII, 26, 8 f. If the direct attributes of light are mostly negative (→ 336, 25 ff.), the positive side, which is negative to the world in the Gnostic sense, may be seen along with existential concepts like knowledge (Ev. Veritatis 30:4 ff.) and truth. Jesus Christ "enlightened those who are in darkness by reason of oblivion. He enlightened them. He gave them a way. But this way is truth," 18:16 ff., cf. 36:11. 254 The terms (eternal) life, seed, pleroma, spirit etc. are piled up in 43:9 ff.: "It is they that are revealed in truth, that are in true and eternal life. And they speak about the light that is perfect, that is full of the seed of the Father, that is in his heart and in the pleroma. His spirit rejoices in him, and he praises the one in whom he is; for he is good. And his children are perfect and are worthy of his name; for they are children such as he the Father loves." 255 Here, too, knowledge is knowledge of self as a being of light. "When the light shines, this man (i.e., he who has dreamed) knows with ref. to the fear he has experienced that it is nothing," 28:28 ff. On the other side is ontologically judged negative matter which is an active factor as darkness → VII, 438, 7 ff. 256

In the confused speculations about the cosmos and forces, and the fantastic personifications of Gnostic powers and pseudo-powers which often arise simply by making speculation autonomous, one may always discern the Gnostic schema of existence. Original being, affected by the reflection of incorruptibility below in water, Nature of Archons, 135, 11 ff., is set in a downward motion. There follows the lament of fallen sophia or the soul: "O light of lights, in whom I have believed from the beginning, attend now. O light, to my μετάνοια," Pist. Soph., 32 (GCS, 45, p. 28, 24-31). When deliverance begins we read:

---

251 Work without Title (→ n. 243) 145, 24 ff. has a thematic treatment of these questions with an attack on the idea that chaos came first. Chaos arises out of the shadow — it is thus non-being — on the outer side of primal light. It thus owes its existence to this.

252 There are many examples in Pist. Soph. and other Copt.-Gnostic works, cf. the Index in Schmidt-Till, GCS, 45, *s.v.* "Licht," Till, TU, 60, *s.v.* ογο(ε)ιν.

253 Further examples in Schmidt-Till, GCS, 45, Index, *s.v.* "Licht," "Lichtjungfrau," "Lichtreich," "Lichtschatz" etc.

254 P. 33-36, which are not in the edition cited → n. 238, may be found as a Suppl. ed. M. Malinine *et al.* (1961).

255 Cf. also the Index in Schmidt-Till, *op. cit.* (→ n. 247), Till, *op. cit.* (→ n. 247), Malinine *et al., op. cit.* (→ n. 238), *s.v.* ογλειν "life," ωνϩ "seed," σπέρμα, πλήρωμα, "Geist," πνεῦμα.

256 Cf. Pist. Soph. Index, *s.v.* "Finsternis."

"I cry to thee, O light of lights, in my affliction, and thou dost hear me," 52 (p. 63, 31 f.). "I am delivered from chaos and redeemed from the bonds of darkness. I have come to thee, O light," 68 (p. 96, 1 f.), cf. also Apocr. of Jn. (→ n. 247) 46:13-15. Hearing the complaint, God has pity on the imprisoned particle of light, Apocr. of Jn. 52:17 ff. and sends revelation from above, redemption. "Then his disciples spoke to him: 'Rabbi, reveal to us the mystery of the light of thy Father, since we heard thee say: There is also a baptism of fire and there is also a baptism of the Holy Spirit of light, and there is a spiritual anointing which leads souls to the treasure of light . . . ' Jesus said to them: 'There is no mystery more excellent than this mystery about which you ask, for it will lead your souls to the light of lights, to the place of truth and goodness, to the place of the holy one of all holy ones, to the place in which is neither female nor male, nor are there figures (μορφαί) in that place but a constant and indescribable light,'" Pist. Soph., 143 (GCS, 45, p. 245, 20-35).

E. The New Testament.

I. Occurrence.

The noun φῶς is the most common, the verb φωτίζω occurs 11 times, twice in quotations at Rev. 21:23; 22:5, φωτισμός is found at 2 C. 4:4, 6, φωτεινός at Mt. 6:22 and par. and 17:5, φωστήρ at Phil. 2:15; Rev. 21:11, φωσφόρος at 2 Pt. 1:19, ἐπιφαύσκω at Eph. 5:14, ἐπιφώσκω at Mt. 28:1; Lk. 23:54. Only the noun φῶς has theological rank and this only in Jn. and 1 Jn. The use of the verb φωτίζω remains within modest limits. An average Hell.-Jewish use is presupposed; this is transferred to Christians. No theory of illumination is developed.

II. Synoptic Gospels and Acts.

1. Literal. We sometimes have a lit. use, as in the common motif of the appearance of light at an epiphany, Mt. 17:5. This is the basis of the comparison λευκὸς ὡς τὸ φῶς at Mt. 17:2. Materially cf. also Ac. 12:7. [257] Light from heaven [258] shines when Christ appears on the Damascus road, Ac. 9:3; 22:6, 9, 11; 26:13. φῶς can also be used for a carrier or body of light, fire in Mk. 14:54; Lk. 22:56 → 312, 31 f., lamp in the comparison in Lk. 8:16, torch in Ac. 16:29. [259] There is obvious borrowing from Jewish usage when God is called the "Father of lights," i.e., the stars, in Jm. 1:17 → V, 1013, 17 ff. [260] The use is again literal in Mt. 6:23 and par. [261] An empirical principle is obviously the basis and this is applied to the inner light. [262] Light is not the element here, but the source of light. There is no dualistic an-

---

[257] Beierwaltes, 14-16. How strong the tradition of this motif is may be seen from the fact that it could come into Gnosticism even though the Gnostic view is opposed to it, for visible light is no true light for the Gnostics, apart from the Mandaeans. Yet light still appears at an epiphany, cf. Pist. Soph., 2 (GCS, 45, p. 3, 16 ff.).

[258] Xenoph. Cyrop., IV, 2, 15; Dio Chrys. Or., 12, 29, cf. also the heavenly light at the rapture of Empedocles, Diog. L., VIII, 68.

[259] Cf. the lamps of Ac. 20:8.

[260] Apc. Mos. 36, 38 (→ n. 388).

[261] E. Sjöberg, "Das Licht in dir," Studia Theol., 5 (1951), 89-105; H. J. Cadbury, "The Single Eye," HThR, 47 (1954), 69-74; C. Edlund, Das Auge der Einfalt (1952); Jeremias Gl.⁷, 162 f.; Aalen Licht in Synpt., 21-3. At Lk. 11:33 the reading φῶς for φέγγος is now supported by p⁷⁵.

[262] Cf. also Beierwaltes, 42, n. 3; Sjöberg, op. cit., 94, though he takes the "light in thee" to be a share in the world's light, 103 f. This does not have any bearing on the interpretation, however, and the par. in Joseph and Aseneth (→ n. 100), 6, 3 can relate only to the inner light and the ability of the Gnostic to see what is within; nothing is hid from Joseph διὰ τὸ φῶς τὸ μέγα (!) τὸ ἐν αὐτῷ, cf. Philo Spec. Leg., IV, 192 and also Prv. 20:27.

thropology. As the interpretation shows, Mt. is obviously taking v. 22 and v. 23a to be already an allegory of the inner light. [263]

2. Figurative. φῶς is used fig. in the paradoxically intended rendering of Is. 8:23 f. in Mt. 4:16. [264] ἀνατέλλω is the key word. [265] The question whether light symbolises the person or the teaching of the Messiah [266] misses the relation between the two in Mt. and the position of the quotation in context. The light symbolism should not be restricted to the person; the teaching is included. [267] There is a model for the description of persons as light (Mt. 5:14, 16) in the OT (Is. 42:6; 49:6) and there are also parallels in Judaism [268] and the Greek world → 313, 17 f. Other NT instances are at Lk. 2:32; [269] Ac. 13:47; R. 2:19 → 345, 22 ff. The term "light of the world" in Jn. 8:12; 12:35 is also Jewish → 327, 8 f.; VII, 392, 10 ff. [270] Mt. fixes the sense of Mt. 5:14 ff. by the comparison that follows and also v. 16. Since he himself seems to have formulated both v. 14a and v. 16 (cf. Mk. 4:21; Lk. 8:16 → IV, 326, 1 ff.; 11:33), the shift from light = the disciples in v. 14a to light = their works in v. 16 is only apparent. The person is not an entity existing apart from the works. [271]

3. In a transferred sense "light" signifies openness, Mt. 10:27 and par. [272] Is an originally secular warning adopted (→ III, 705, 4 ff.; 709, 22 ff.; V, 553, n. 93)? [273]

---

[263] But not Lk., cf. Jeremias Gl.⁷, 162 f.

[264] The text cannot come from LXX. HT has the verbs in the perf. רָאוּ or נָגַהּ, LXX in the impf. aor. or fut. ἴδετε or λάμψει, Mt. aor. εἶδεν or ἀνέτειλεν. K. Stendahl, "The school of St. Matthew," *Acta Seminarii Neotest. Upsaliensis,* 20 (1954), 104-6 rightly argues that the choice of the aor. is deliberate and pts. to the fulfilment of the promise. Worth noting is the working out of the paradox: Revelation takes place in the despised land, v. E. Lohmeyer, *Galiläa u. Jerusalem* (1936), 36 f. G. Strecker, "Der Weg der Gerechtigkeit," FRL, 82² (1966), 63-6 ascribes the novel version to a collection of quotations used by Mt.

[265] φῶς μέγα is also used in different senses: Aesch. Pers., 300 f. transf. ἐμοῖς μὲν εἶπας δώμασιν φάος μέγα καὶ λευκὸν ἦμαρ νυκτὸς ἐκ μελαγχίμου (= μέλανος), on "speaking light" cf. Ac. 26:23 → 345, 4 f. There is another use in Luc. Nigrinus, 4; ἔχαιρον δ' αὖ ὥσπερ ἐκ ζοφεροῦ τινος ἀέρος τοῦ βίου τοῦ πρόσθεν ἐς αἰθρίαν τε καὶ μέγα φῶς ἀναβλέπων, cf. Joseph and Aseneth, 6, 3.

[266] Cf. Kl. Mt., ad loc.

[267] This is true in spite of Jewish Messianic light symbolism → 324, 11 ff.; 327, 3 ff.; Str.-B., I. 161 f.

[268] E.g., Test. L. 14:3α: You are the φωστῆρες of Israel; Str.-B., I, 237; Aalen Licht in Synpt., 25-27.

[269] Cf. Test. L. 18:3. φῶς is probably in apposition to σωτήριον, so Kl. Lk., ad loc., and is thus par. to δόξα.

[270] The world is naturally the world of men, not the cosmos, cf. the Rabb. נרו של עולם or אורו, Str.-B., I, 237. The saying is given a Gnostic twist in Gospel of Thomas (→ n. 244), Logion 24 (86, 7 ff.), cf. 50 (89, 33 ff.); → 341, 7 ff. Mt. adopts the Jewish sense of election and applies it to the disciples.

[271] In the comparison light cannot be detached from its source; linguistically the two go together in Hbr. and Aram. as well as Gk. Aalen Licht in Synpt., 17-19 observes that the pt. of the metaphor is not that a room becomes bright; what matters is that there is a point of light and this shines forth. He thus says: "It is not that the disciples are to cause their light to shine by doing good works but that when they cause their light to shine they do good works," 31. The walk is already described as a light in Prv. 4:18. The objection that teaching rather than walk should be the light (Wellh. Mt., ad loc.) is without foundation: "This misses the point that the ref. is not to the lampstand or lamp but to the light φῶς, that v. 14 f. also denies any distinction between teaching and walk, and finally that there is a very similar OT saying ... (Prv. 4:18)." Loh. Mt. on 5:16.

[272] There are class. and Jewish par. → 313, 22 ff.; 327, 8 ff.

[273] Bultmann Trad., 99 f.

At any rate in both the sayings source [274] and Mk. the saying is a promise reflecting two different epochs in the history of salvation as christologically understood. Mt. deviates: What Jesus has taught will be proclaimed by the disciples. Luke has it that what has been heard in secret will be said in public → VII, 441, 7 ff. [275] How refined the sense can be when light denotes openness may be seen from the expression "to proclaim light" in Ac. 26:23. [276] The familiar missionary style of Judaism and Gnosticism is adopted here, Ac. 26:18. [277] Conversion (→ VII, 728, 1 ff.) is a movement from darkness to light, Eph. 5:8; 1 Pt. 2:9 → VII, 441, 26 ff. [278]

A singular expression in the Synoptists is "children of light," Lk. 16:8. The only instances elsewhere are at Jn. 12:36; 1 Th. 5:5; Eph. 5:8, cf. also Ign. Phld., 2, 1. [279] The meaning is not uniform in the NT. One can hardly speak of a technical use. In distinction from the Dead Sea Scrolls (→ 326, 8 ff.), the context furnishes the sense. Lk. contrasts the "children of light" with the "children of this aeon" rather than the children of darkness. How this is to be understood may be seen from Lk. 20:34. [280]

III. The Pauline Corpus.

1. Paul. Paul's usage [281] lies essentially within the bounds of the common Jewish use. The meaning is hardly technical in given verses. It is fixed by the — generally eschatological — context. This is also true of the verb φωτίζω. The last day (→ II, 952, 7 ff.) is the day which will bring to light what is concealed... ἕως ἂν ἔλθῃ ὁ κύριος, ὃς καὶ φωτίσει τὰ κρυπτὰ τοῦ σκότους, 1 C. 4:5. What Paul means may be seen from the parallel continuation καὶ φανερώσει τὰς βουλὰς τῶν καρδιῶν and 2 C. 5:10. [282] The Jewish view of Israel as the light of the peoples (→ 327, 8 f.) and of the light of the Torah/knowledge (→ 324, 22 f.; 327, 3 f.) governs the exposition in R. 2:19, which adopts the Jewish view in polemic against the claim of Judaism → 231, 12 ff. [283] The Jewish picture of the world underlies 2 C. 11:14. Satan, the Lord of darkness, and the angels of light, are in conflict, and the former uses the device of appearing as an angel of light. [284] With apocalyptic Phil. 2:15 depicts eschatological existence as the illuminating of the elect. [285] The new thing is

---

[274] Vv. 26 and 27 are already related in Q, cf. Lk. 12:2 f.

[275] The connection with the view of history is plain in both cases; for Mt., cf. Strecker, op. cit. (→ n. 264), 190.

[276] Aesch. Pers., 300 f. → n. 265.

[277] There are models in Is. 35:5; 42:7, 16, cf. 61:1 (Lk. 4:18). H. Windisch, "Pls. u. Christus," UNT, 24 (1934), 137 notes the adoption of motifs from the call of Jeremiah, Jer. 1:7, and the Servant of the Lord, Is. 42:7, 16.

[278] The expression is class. and Jewish → 316, 1 ff.; 325, 4 ff. Cf., e.g., καὶ ἤγαγε (sc. Κύριος) αὐτοὺς ἐκ σκότους εἰς φῶς in Test. Jos. 19:3 for conversion phraseology.

[279] Qumran (→ 325, 22 ff.) offers the bestknown formal par., but cf. also Gnostic examples → n. 303.

[280] We have here the familiar dualism of this world and the next. The expression is analogous to the Rabb. "son of the world to come," v. Str.-B., II, 219; H. Braun, Spätjüd.-här. u. frühchr. Radikalismus, II, Beiträge z. hist. Theol., 24² (1968), 39, n. 1.

[281] We are ref. here to R., 1 and 2 C., Gl., Phil., 1 Th. and Phlm.

[282] Cf. Wnd. 2 K., ad loc. The parallelism in 1 C. 4:5 raises the pt. whether we have here a quotation from some apocr. work, Joh. W. 1 K. and Ltzm. K., ad loc.

[283] The Jewish colouring is so strong that Ltzm. R., ad loc. thinks a Jewish missionary work was the basis. Materially cf. Eth. En. 105; Wis. 18:4; Jos. Ap., 2, 291 ff.

[284] Cf. Wnd. 2 K., ad loc.; for the dualism cf. 1 QS 3:20 f.; 1 QM 13:10 ff. We also find Satan's deceitful transformation in Vit. Ad. 9; Apc. Mos. 17.

[285] Δα. 12:3; Wis. 3:7; Eth. En. 108:11 ff.; 4 Esr. 7:97, 125; S. Bar. 51:1 ff., cf. Bousset-Gressm., 277.

that for Paul it is already present. This existence is now worked out in the relation of the community to the world. Paul thus transfers the concept of Israel in its eschatological form to the community. [286]

Paul also adopts the expression "children of light" (→ 345, 9 ff.; n. 279) and uses it in the same sense, 1 Th. 5:5; → II, 953, 20 ff.; IV, 1129, 41 ff. [287] Related is R. 13:12, but the movement here is the reverse. In 1 Th. the way leads from traditional eschatology to actualisation in exhortation. Now, however, broad exhortation is given an eschatological foundation. [288] The starting-point is the imminence of the day. Then light and darkness appear as two spheres or qualifying forces. [289] The change from ἔργα on the negative side to ὅπλα (→ V, 294, 14 ff.) on the positive side is surely intentional and underscores the ethical appeal. [290]

The most important passage is 2 C. 4:4-6 with its εἰκών christology and its dualism of decision, [291] which is transcended by the concept of the Creator. Judaism had already developed a relation between the language of creation and that of conversion, → 325, 4 ff.; VII, 26 ff. [292] Paul works this out even further with the idea of the new (→ III, 449, 12 ff.) creation, [293] which again expresses the presence of the event of eschatological salvation. [294] The point of φῶς may be gathered from the link with γνῶσις and the verb λάμπω → IV, 25, 11 ff. This does not refer to light as an element but to the movement released, the process and effect of shining, [295] knowledge. [296] There may be doubt as to the authenticity of the dualistic exhortation in 2 C. 6:14 ff. [297] This deals formally with the impossibility of κοινωνία ἀνομοίων. Materially it marks off the elect from unbelievers by an ethical appeal.

---

[286] Loh. Phil., ad loc. does not think φωστήρ ref. to the stars and their light. He construes φαίνομαι as "to appear" (→ 1, 25 ff.) rather than "to shine": "Among whom you appear as lights in the world." But φωστήρ for "star" is well attested → 312, 1 ff. The addition ἐν κόσμῳ controls the sense here.

[287] The theme is eschatology as such, 1 Th. 5:1. It is given a hortatory application. In 5:2 ἡμέρα is the day of eschatological judgment. But then the ref. is to the day as brightness with the possibility of conducting one's life, opp. νύξ, v. Dib. Th., ad loc. Pl. adopts the traditional style of eschatological exhortation, cf. Lk. 21:34-36. Typical of Paul is the detachment of hope from specific views of the end-process by the εἴτε - εἴτε clause, 1 Th. 5:10.

[288] Cf. Phil. 4:5; Hb. 10:25 ff.; 1 Pt. 1:5 ff.; Did., 16; Barn., 21, 3; Ign. Eph., 11:1; Herm. v., 2, 3, 4. On the metaphor of arming cf. Dib. Gefbr. on Eph. 6:10 → V, 296, 34 ff.

[289] The gen. with ἔργα and ὅπλα are to be taken in the same sense as ἔργα τῆς σαρκός and καρπὸς πνεύματος. Gl. 5:19, 22. 1 QM 15:9: ". . . and in darkness are all their works." They are thus qualified thereby.

[290] Cf. again Gl. 5:19 ff. ἔργα is not part of the metaphor, unlike 1 QM 15:9 → n. 289.

[291] The expression ὁ θεὸς τοῦ αἰῶνος τούτου is dualistic. cf. 1 C. 2:8; Eph. 2:2; Jn. 12:31.

[292] Gn. 1:3 is refashioned acc. to Is. 9:1 or 2 Βασ. 22:29. Materially cf. → 325, 4 ff.; R. 2:19; 1 Th. 5:4 f.; Eph. 5:8; 1 Pt. 2:9.

[293] Cf. 2 C. 5:17. The catchword καινός occurs in a conversion context in Joseph and Aseneth (→ n. 100) 8. 11 in the compound ἀνακαινίζω, cf. Barn., 6, 11.

[294] The theme in context is the legitimacy of the apostle's office. Illumination is related to proclamation, and this is validated by the fact that the preacher proclaims not himself but the Lord.

[295] Ltzm. K., ad loc. twice takes λάμπω to mean "to shine." But in the second case it means "to cause to become bright." cf. Philo Praem. Poen., 25: . . . πλὴν οἷς ἂν ὁ θεὸς αὐγὴν ἐπιλάμψῃ τῆς ἀληθείας, and Eltester, op. cit. (→ n. 142). 132, n. 8. φωτισμός has in v. 4 an act. intr. sense: the shining of the Gospel, and in v. 6 a pass. sense: knowledge is lit up, i.e., it arises as light, v. Eltester, 132, n. 9, but cf. Wnd. 2 K., ad loc., who twice takes φωτισμός to mean "radiance."

[296] For this thought in the OT → 322, 18 ff.; in Test. XII → 326, 18 f., in Corp. Herm. → 335, 9 ff., in O. Sol. → 340, 22 ff.

[297] The style reminds us of Test. XII, cf. L. 19:1 → 326, 20 f.; J. Gnilka, "2 K. 6:14 - 7:1 im Lichte d. Qumranschr. u. d. Test. XII," Festschr. J. Schmid (1963), 97 f.

2. Colossians and Ephesians. Current usage is presupposed here. Eph. has strong colours that remind us of 2 C. 6:14 (→ 346, 20 ff.) and hence also of Qumran and Test. XII → 326, 6 ff. [298] In Col. 1:12 φῶς is the transcendent sphere of light which is more narrowly defined as the βασιλεία of Christ. As a sphere it is obviously a realm of power here again [299] → VII, 442, 19 ff. In interpretation note should be taken of conversion style. [300] Realised eschatology of place — translation into light as deliverance already effected — should not lead to a spiritual exposition of light or kingdom → I, 107, 22 ff. [301] The presence of salvation removes neither the realistically viewed transcendence of the domain of light nor the fact that even the redeemed are still engaged in an upward movement, Col. 3:1 ff., 5 ff.

The style of eschatological light-exhortation (→ 346, 6 ff.) is adopted in Eph. 5:8-10 and integrated into the schema of the antithesis between once (σκότος) and now (φῶς). [302] In itself the statement "You are light" would suggests a Gnostic interpretation, so that "children of light" would also have to be taken Gnostically: "You are of heavenly origin." [303] But φῶς is not a substance here → n. 302. It is a sphere, and even this only in the weaker form of a metaphor. [304] The idea is not the pre-existence of the light-ego but new creation along the lines of Eph. 2:9 f. [305] The closer definition ἐν κυρίῳ should be noted [306] and also the Pauline rather than Gnostic basis of the expressions τέκνα (1 Th. 5:5) and καρπός (Gl. 5:22, cf. R. 13:12) τοῦ φωτός. Being light is worked out in conduct. Hence the Pauline relation between indicative and imperative is sustained. Separation from darkness is actualised in a new way of life. [307] The act of illumination, which by means of the metaphor of the eye of the inner organ of perception (→ IV, 966, n. 14) is described as the illumination of the eyes of the heart (Eph. 1:18), [308] constitutes the transition from the once to the now and the presupposition of the new existence. What is meant by this illumination is the capacity for active gnosis as this is meditatively achieved in Eph. Characteristic is the adoption of the μυστήριον schema (→ IV,

---

298 K. G. Kuhn, "Der Eph. im Lichte d. Qumrantexte," NTSt, 7 (1960/61), 334-346.

299 On the cosmological sense cf. Eph. 6:10 ff., v. Dib. Gefbr., ad loc. Acc. to 1 Tm. 6:16 God dwells in a φῶς ἀπρόσιτον, cf. ἀπρόσιτον φῶς, Cl. Al. Exc. Theod., 12, 3, lumen inaccessibile, Act. Verc., 20 (p. 66, 26). For the counterpart in the traditional view of the world cf. Ps. Sol. 14:9: ἡ κληρονομία αὐτῶν ἅδης καὶ σκότος καὶ ἀπώλεια, cf. 14:5.

300 Cf. 1 Pt. 2:9, though in a transf. sense. On the style cf. E. Käsemann, "Eine urchr. Taufliturgie," Exeget. Versuche u. Besinnungen, I⁵ (1968), 44-46.

301 Cf. rather the total eschatology of Col. We are already risen with Christ, 2:12, but this means that we can seek what is above. We have life, but it is hidden with Christ in God, 3:1 ff.

302 Kuhn, op. cit. (→ n. 298), 339 f. stresses that the dualism is that of decision not substance.

303 ὅτι ἄυλος ὑπάρχεις, ὅτι ἅγιος, ὅτι φῶς, ὅτι συγγενὴς τοῦ ἀγεννήτου, Act. Andr. 6. The term "sons or children of light" is found in Gnosticism, e.g., 1 Apc. Jm. (→ n. 243), 25, 17 f.; Nature of Archons, 145, 14, cf. Thomas Ps. (→ n. 222), 1 (p. 204, 9); 2 (p. 205, 24) etc. [Kelber].

304 Dib. Gefbr., ad loc. Note the influence of Paul's parenetic tradition in which φῶς is used metaphorically.

305 For further development in Cl. Al. and Lact. cf. Wlosok, 222, n. 104.

306 In Eph. the ἐν formula also pts. to Christ extra nos, F. Neugebauer, In Christus (1961), 175-181, who does not see any clear differences between Paul and Col./Eph.; M. Bouttier, En Christ (1962), 139-142.

307 In the Pauline tradition the demanded good is indicated in terms from popular ethics. The list provides a more exact material explanation.

308 The metaphor of the illumination of the eye is ancient (→ 313, 1 ff.). For "eye of the heart" cf. Dib. Gefbr., ad loc.; 1 Cl., 36, 2; 59, 3; Corp. Herm., 4, 11; 7, 7.

820, 10 ff.), which occurs already in Col., at Eph. 3:9. [309] Disclosure is denoted by the verb φωτίζω "to bring to light," 1 C. 4:5; 2 Tm. 1:10. [310] The content of knowledge is the economy of salvation.

A special problem is posed by Eph. 5:14 (→ III, 990, 8 ff.; VIII, 500, 12 ff.) [311] with the rare ἐπιφαύσκω (→ 312, 13 ff.), especially as we have here a quotation, three lines with homoioteleuton. [312] The form of the call to awake and the material parallels suggest a Gnostic milieu. [313] The parallels from the Dead Sea Scrolls [314] do not suffice for interpretation. In the present context an ethical thrust is given to the concept. But beneath this a physical substratum may be discerned. [315]

---

[309] The schema of once hidden and now revealed is broadly worked out in R. 16:25-27, cf. E. Kamlah, *Traditionsgeschichtliche Untersuchungen z. Schlussdoxologie d. Römerbriefs,* Diss. Tübingen (1955).

[310] Schlier Eph.³ on 3:9.

[311] Cf. Dib. Gefbr., *ad loc.;* Schlier Eph.³, *ad loc.;* Peterson, *op. cit.* (→ n. 184), 132 f.; B. Noack, "Das Zitat in Eph. 5:14," *Studia Theol.,* 5 (1951), 52-64; Kuhn, *op. cit.* (→ n. 298), 341-5. It is not clear to what the διό in the introduction of the quotation refers, i.e.,, what is to be established. A ref. to v. 8a (Dib. Gefbr., *ad loc.*) is not easy, *v.* Kuhn, 342.

[312] Reitzenstein Ir. Erl., 135-7, cf. 6 and Hell. Myst., 64, thinks it is a Gnostic summons; he compares the Manichean Turfan Fr. M., 7, 89-95 (ed. F. C. Andreas - W. Henning, "Mitteliranische Manichaica aus Chinesisch-Turkestan," SAB, 1934 [1934], 872): "Heavy is the drunkenness in which thou dost slumber, wake up and look on me. Hail to thee from the world of peace from which I am sent on thy behalf," cf. Reitzenstein Hell. Myst., 58 and Colpe, *op. cit.* (→ n. 50), 41 f., 69. He also compares an alchemistic work lines 125-8 (ed. R. Reitzenstein, "Zur Gesch. d. Alchemie u. d. Mystizismus," NGG, 1919, 1 [1919], 17: τότε φωτίζεται τὸ σῶμα καὶ χαίρεται ἡ ψυχὴ καὶ τὸ πνεῦμα ὅτι ἀπέδρα τὸ σκότος ἀπὸ τοῦ σώματος καὶ καλεῖ ἡ ψυχὴ τὸ σῶμα τὸ πεφωτισμένον· ἔγειραι ἐξ Ἅιδου καὶ ἀνάστηθι ἐκ τοῦ τάφου καὶ ἐξεγέρθητι ἐκ τοῦ σκότους, cf. Reitzenstein Hell. Myst., 314. There is a third par. in the Song of the Pearl, Act. Thom. 110 f. (Adam Thomas-Ps. 51 f.): "Rise up and stand from thy sleep ἀνάστηθι καὶ ἀνάνηψον ἐξ ὕπνου and receive the word of our letter ... And as he had wakened me with his call, so he led me also with his light." Adam Thomas-Ps. 59 suggests dependence of the original of Eph. 5:14 on the Song of the Pearl.

[313] The call to awake does not belong to apocalyptic, as Nock, *op. cit.,* 62 avers. The passage adduced from Syr. Didasc., 21 (cf. H. Achelis - J. Flemming, TU, 25, 2 [1904], p.110, 5-7, cf. Didasc., V, 16, 4): "You have already become believers and been baptised into him and a great light has arisen over you," is not compelling. On the summons cf. also Corp. Herm., 1, 28: τί ἑαυτούς ὧ ἄνδρες γηγενεῖς, εἰς θάνατον ἐκδεδώκατε ...; O. Sol. 8:3: "Stand up and stand fast, you who have been recumbent." In content cf. also O. Sol. 11:13 f.; 15:1 ff.; 41:13 f. Cf. Jonas Gnosis, I, 126-133; Becker, 21 f.; G. Schille, *Frühchr. Hymnen* (1962), 94-101.

[314] 1 QH 4:5 f.: "I praise thee, Lord, that thou hast lightened my countenance for thy covenant..., and as surely as the dawn hast thou appeared as my li[ght] לאורתי‎ (→ n. 104). cf. 1 QH 4:23, *v.* Kuhn, op. cit., 341-5.

[315] Perhaps there is another hint as to the origin in Cl. Al. (cf. Dölger Sol, 364-370), Wlosok, 159-164; for Cl. Al. quotes Eph. 5:14 with a κύριος added to χριστός, and then three more lines ὁ τῆς ἀναστάσεως ἥλιος, ὁ πρὸ ἑωσφόρου γεννώμενος, ὁ ζωὴν χαρισάμενος ἀκτῖσιν ἰδίαις. Cl. Al. Prot., IX, 84, 2. Just before there is a summons in two three-line sections, VIII, 80, 1 ff. that make use of Prv. 6:9, 11a. The ideas and language suggest Alexandrian Judaism. This is even clearer if we assume that the original was κύριος rather than χριστός. Wlosok, 161 suggests the influence of Dionysiac-Orphic speech (ἐπιφαύσκω), cf. also the mystery call in Aristoph. Ra., 340 ff.: ἔγειρε φλογέας λαμπάδας ἐν χερσὶ γὰρ ἥκει τινάσσων, Ἴακχ' ὧ Ἴακχε, νυκτέρου τελετῆς φωσφόρος ἀστήρ. φλογὶ φέγγεται δὲ λειμών, though this is not a direct model, as against J. Leipoldt. "Die altchr. Taufe religionsgeschichtlich betrachtet," *Wissenschaftliche Zschr. d. Karl-Marx-Univ. Leipzig. Gesellschafts- u. sprachwissenschaftliche Reihe,* 3 (1953/54), 72, cf. G. Wagner, "Das religionsgesch. Problem von R. 6:1-11," AbhThANT, 39 (1962), 82 f.; G. Delling, *Der Gottesdienst im NT* (1952), 51.

3. The mystery schema also underlies 2 Tm. 1:10. Christ has brought life to light, i.e., not only shown it, but effectively manifested it. [316]

IV. John's Gospel and Epistles.

The story of recent Johannine research [317] is also that of differing historical backgrounds. The following are championed: the OT, Jewish Alexandrian religious philosophy (Philo), Stoic (Logos) and Platonic (dualism) components variously estimated, Gnosticism (Hermetica, O. Sol., Mandaica). The problem has been posed afresh with the Qumran texts. To understand the concepts of light and darkness an OT milieu seems no more adequate than it does for that of the Logos, although it still finds advocates. [318] In no sense are the relations to be understood in purely literary terms, in the sense of direct dependence on specific writings. This applies no less in respect of the Dead Sea Scrolls than it did earlier in respect of the Hermetica and Mandaica.

As regards motifs and thought-structures the concept of dualism is too simple to play an effective expository role. We find very different dualisms, e.g., the Platonic and the Iranian (→ 333, 8 ff.), which is modified in Qumran. Common to the Dead Sea Scrolls and John's Gospel is a non-mythical dualism of decision → 325, 20 ff. In Jn., however, the figure of the Revealer is at the centre; this is not so in the Scrolls, for here the Messiahs and the Teacher of Righteousness are not revealers. The doctrine of two spirits in 1 QS (→ VI, 390, 6 ff.) finds no equivalent in Jn.'s Gospel. We cannot do justice to the Johannine material without a concept of gnosis that is orientated to the phenomenon. [319]

1. The Gospel. The NT use of light and darkness culminates in the Johannine writings. Here, too, we find the literal sense. φῶς is the natural light of the lamp, Jn. 5:35. It is brightness, 3:20 f. → VI, 557, 14 ff., [320] which is avoided by the wicked as those who shun the light. One cannot always distinguish clearly between the figurative and the literal sense. There is vacillation between the two, between the light of day and the true light, in 12:35 f. → VII, 444, 5 ff. [321] φῶς [322] is the brightness of day, and this is a figure for the presence of revelation, which is later shown to be identical with the Revealer. Revelation is again the illumination that makes

---

[316] Cf. Dib. Past.4, ad loc. The fixed linguistic conjoining of light and life affects the formulation, Corp. Herm., 13, 19 (→ 335, 14 f. with n. 189), cf. 13, 9. 13; Philo Fug., 139 (→ 331, 16 ff.), cf. the usage (→ 328, 27 ff.).   ...

[317] W. F. Howard, The Fourth Gospel in Recent Criticism and Interpretation4 (1955); P. H. Menoud, L'Évangile de Jean d'après les recherches récentes2 (1947); also "Les études johanniques de Bultmann à Barrett," L'Év. de Jean, Recherches bibl., 3 (1958), 11-40; Dodd, op. cit. (→ n. 52), passim.

[318] Cf. J. Dupont, Essais sur la christologie de S. Jean (1950), 95-105.

[319] Jonas Gnosis passim, Bultmann J., 9-12 and passim. Breaking up the individual Gnostic writings into groups (Dodd, op. cit., 10-130) does not provide a satisfactory picture.

[320] On the various meanings in Jn.'s Gospel cf. Bultmann J., 23. We again have literal usage at Jn. 5:35, where λύχνος is primarily a figure that is then developed with φῶς as a metaphor, 199, n. 5. The lamp is a symbol of the transitory, Lidz. Ginza R., 256, 8 f.: "These other souls (who) die come to an end and go out like a lamp." On Jn. 11:9 f. "light of this world" — inner light, cf. Philo Spec. Leg., IV, 192, in analysis v. Bultmann J., ad loc., who thinks the ὅτι clauses are the Evangelist's glosses on his source. We have fig. use at Jn. 3:20 f. Cf. also the specific Johannine use → 353, 1 ff.

[321] Bultmann J., 271. Acc. to ibid., 237. 271, n. 2. 304, n. 1 this is the conclusion of an address on light taken from the source of revelation addresses whose fr. are scattered across cc. 8-12. Becker, 114-6 takes the same view, though his reconstruction differs in detail; he attaches 8:30 ff. to 12:36. On the style (imp., characterising of believers in part.) cf. Becker, 65 f.

[322] σκοτία without art. forces us to take the passage fig. and the imp., as noted in Bultmann J., ad loc., also denotes a metaphorical sense.

movement possible. Its presence is limited to a specific time, which in historical context is that of the presence of Jesus, cf. 9:5. But this is only a primary statement. Light now shines forth in the community, in preaching. Yet the present shining of light is also not without limits, i.e., it is not at our disposal. The offer of revelation cannot be put off. What comes to expression here is the idea of decision, of its once-for-allness, of the contingency of revelation. In the call to take the one chance lies the true significance of light. This may be seen in the summons to believe in the light (12:36) and in the combination of the subject and object of faith in the expression υἱοὶ φωτός → 325, 23 ff.; n. 303. [323] The identification of light with revelation and of revelation with the Revealer [324] means the exclusion of all metaphysical and cosmological speculation. Herein lies the basic distinction between Jn.'s Gospel and Gnosticism → 333, 24 ff. No factual statement is made about the world of light. Jn. does not call God light, [325] but God's manifestation in Jesus. [326] Light is a pure concept of existence. Its knowledge, with no metaphysical traces at all, can be fully indicated by defining it as faith and perception. [327] Concentration on the person of the Revealer comes to its clearest expression in the self-predication ἐγώ εἰμι (→ II, 352, 14 ff.) τὸ φῶς τοῦ κόσμου, 8:12. [328] Irrespective of the debate whether ἐγώ is subject or predicate (→ n. 328), these statements are meant literally and not metaphorically. Jesus is not just light in a figurative way, nor is He just a light, or an illuminator. He is the true light. [329] The definite article denotes the exclusiveness of revelation. [330] The article does not occur, of course, in the two repetitions of the statement, 9:5; 12:46. [331] This is simply in accordance with the

---

[323] On the nuances of meaning in the NT cf. 1 Th. 5:5; Eph. 5:8; Lk. 16:8. For the Johannine sense cf. Jn. 1:12 f. In the context of Jn. this thoroughly Jewish expression is controlled by the idea of the new birth, Jn. 3:1 ff.

[324] "Revelation never becomes what is revealed; the light that the believer has is always the light that is Jesus," Bultmann J. on 8:12, as opp. to H. H. Malmede, *Die Lichtsymbolik im NT*, Diss. Bonn (1959), 331.

[325] Only 1 Jn. does this, and again non-speculatively.

[326] The relation of God and revelation is not described as an emanation of revelation from light but as sending.

[327] In this regard Jn. clearly differs from the Qumran texts, cf. what is said about Satan or Belial (→ VII, 152, 3 ff.), about the two spirits (→ VI, 389, 35 ff.) and the Qumran passages in which light is the sphere of the blessed. Jn. never speaks of passing over into light but of entering into life, Jn. 5:24. The relation of φῶς and δόξα confirms this, cf. Dodd, *op. cit.*, 201-212. δόξα, too, is a manifestation term, not a describable substance or sphere, Bultmann J., 44. n. 1.

[328] Schweizer, *op. cit.* (→ n. 212), 164 etc.; Bultmann J., 167 f., n. 2 and *passim*. Bultmann regards Jn. 8:12 as a kind of recognition formula (ἐγώ εἰμι as an answer to the question: Who is the expected one?). Here ἐγώ is the predicate. But Bultmann admits that ἐγώ might have been the subj. in the source used. Apart from the question whether a source is actually used, ἐγώ is surely to be taken as subj. in the context. The fact that it is stressed in the saying is no argument to the contrary. The transl. is not: "The true light am I," but: "I am the true light." The statement is thetic rather than polemical. It is a presentation of the speaking I (cf. Bultmann J., 261), as in the Mandaean par. adduced in Bultmann J., 167 f., n. 2 and Schweizer, 64-80. τὸ φῶς ἐκεῖνο ἐγώ, Corp. Herm., 1, 6 is no true par., for here the light that has appeared is later interpreted as the appearance of Poimandres.

[329] Bultmann J., 261: "He gives light and He also is light; He gives it as He is it, and He is it as He gives it." Ref. to the ancient oriental theme of the shining of the king (C. Spicq. "Agapè dans le NT, III," *Études Bibl.* [1959], 42, n. 3) is irrelevant, notwithstanding the βασιλεύς of Jn. 18:37.

[330] Other claims to be revelation are in fact negated, but this is no reason why ἐγώ should be regarded as the predicate.

[331] Bultmann J., 236 f. adopts the sequence 9:1-41; 8:12; 12:44-50. He does not include 12:46 in the source but thinks it is a mere variation on 8:12. On 9:5 cf. Becker, 115.

context. 9:5, based on the figure in 9:4, is formulated in such a way that the temporal nature of revelation (→ 352, 8 ff.) is also indicated; the stress is wholly on light. 12:46 is formulated in relation to the aim of revelation (ἵνα...).[332] The genitive τοῦ κόσμου means "for the world."[333] The expression "light of the world" is only outwardly similar to the same Rabbinic phrase → 327, 8 ff.[334] The Johannine statement can be called dualistic to the degree that light confronts the unenlightened world orientated to illumination. In this regard it is close to the light-sayings of Qumran (→ 325, 20 ff.),[335] but with the difference already indicated, namely, that there is no teaching about a sphere of light independent of the Revealer. The concept of faith is thus accentuated.[336]

The description of the deity or the Revealer as the light of the world cannot be derived from the OT or the Greek tradition.[337] Instances lead us into the world of Hellenistic syncretism (→ 329, 11 f.) and Gnosticism (→ 334, 3 f.; n. 134). The meaning of this being as light is indicated by the term ζωή (→ II, 872, 7 ff.),[338] which signifies life-giving power rather than mere life (being alive) as such.[339] The linking of the two concepts governs the Prologue (1:1-18).[340] Two equations stand alongside one another: a. The life was the light of men;[341] b. the Logos was the (true) light. The starting-point is the concept of life. Obviously the meaning of light, which is felt to be a problem, is being fixed.[342] The genitive τῶν ἀνθρώπων (1:4) corresponds to the genitive τοῦ κόσμου (8:12): The world is the world of men.[343] In the chain-like style of the Prologue[344] the second catchword of v. 4b is taken up in such a way that the previous predicate becomes the subject: καὶ τὸ φῶς ἐν τῇ

---

[332] Bultmann J., 262, n. 6 finds the absence of the art. difficult in terms of his source analysis. But it is explained by the context.

[333] Cf. 1:4: τῶν ἀνθρώπων (→ line 19 f.). Rather different is the gen. in 8:12: τῆς ζωῆς, which is to be taken epexegetically: "Light that is life." Quite different is 11:9.

[334] The Rabb. expression is fig.

[335] Braun, 122-124.

[336] It is no accident that Qumran has no concept of the world corresponding to that of Jn. אוֹר עוֹלָמִים in 1 QS 4:8; 1 QM 17:6; 1 QH 12:15 means "eternal light," cf. "to the light of perfect illumination for ever," 1 QH 18:29. In turn there is nothing like this in Jn.

[337] Braun, 123 and 127 f. as against F. Nötscher, "Zur theol. Terminologie d. Qumrantexte," Bonner Bibl. Beiträge, 10 (1956), 92-103 etc.

[338] We find light and life combined in various places. For the Gk. world → 313, 6 ff.; the OT Job 33:30; Ps. 36:9; Judaism Ps. Sol. 3:12; Eth. En. 58:3; the Hermetica → 335, 1 ff., the Mandaica → 336, 15 ff.; the O. Sol. → 340, 22 ff.; v. Dodd, op. cit. (→ n. 52), 345-354. In the Dead Sea Scrolls we find "light of life" in 1 QS 3:7, but "life" is not a central salvation concept, Braun, 112, cf. 96-98, and therefore the antithesis of life and death does not play any part.

[339] Bultmann J., 21 with n. 3.

[340] For recent analysis cf. E. Käsemann, "Aufbau u. Anliegen d. joh. Prologs," Exeget. Versuche u. Besinnungen, II³ (1968), 155-180; R. Schnackenburg, "Logos-Hymnus u. joh. Prolog," BZ, NF, 1 (1957), 69-109; Schulz Joh. Reden, 7-56; Schulz Joh.-Prolog; J. A. T. Robinson, "The Relation of the Prologue to the Gospel of John," NTSt, 9 (1962/63), 120-129; E. Haenchen, "Probleme d. joh. 'Prologs'" Gott u. Mensch (1965), 114-143.

[341] Isis is φῶς πᾶσι βροτοῖσι, Anubis-Hymn of Kios, line 7 (1st/2nd cent. A.D.), ed. W. Peek, Der Isishymnus v. Andros u. verwandte Texte (1930), 139. Sarapis is called κοινὸν πᾶσιν ἀνθρώποις φῶς, Ael. Arist. Or., 45, 39 (Keil).

[342] Bultmann Theol.⁶, 372 f.: "The concepts light, truth, life and freedom mutually explain one another, as do also the opposite concepts darkness, falsehood, death and bondage."

[343] Previously the Logos is the mediator of creation, now the light of men. Note how κόσμος and ἄνθρωπος are interchanged in vv. 9-11 and τὰ ἴδια and οἱ ἴδιοι, cf. 3:19; Bultmann J. on 1:10.

[344] Bultmann J., 2 f.

σκοτία (→ VII, 443, 5 ff.) φαίνει καὶ ἡ σκοτία αὐτὸ οὐ κατέλαβεν (1:5). [345] The activity of light, which is posited by its being as such and exhausted therein, is indicated by the verb φαίνω (v. 5 → 1, 4 ff.), and its positive effect by φωτίζω (v. 9). Here the Prologue expands the promise of 8:12.

The tenses cause difficulty, ἦν [346] twice in v. 4, then the pres. φαίνει and the aor. κατέλαβεν in v. 5, ἦν again in the interpolated vv. 6-8, and then φωτίζει in v. 9. Explanation is hampered by the uncertainty of analysis. V. 9 seems to belong to the source, while v. 5 might come from the Evangelist as a transition to vv. 6-8. He is making here the transition from pre-existence to the historical epiphany. In this light one can understand the tenses. The aor. refers to the historical destiny of Jesus, while the pres. affirms that revelation nevertheless endures. V. 9 is more difficult in the present version of the Prologue, [347] but critical analysis helps to elucidate it. The subj. is the same as in v. 5 or 4. [348] Thus the pres. φωτίζει poses the same question as in v. 5, here undoubtedly for the source: Does this, coming after v. 4, deal already with the historical revelation? [349]

ἀληθινός (→ I, 250, 29 ff.), the attribute of light in v. 9, is to be taken exclusively. Only this light is really light. [350] The idea is elucidated by Gnostic analogies. Nevertheless, there is absolutely no idea of substance in Jn. nor is there any speculative cosmology → 328, 27 ff. [351] The prose interlude in vv. 6-8 refutes the hypothetical or actual assertion that another, namely, the Baptist, is the light, the Revealer. [352] φωτίζω (1:9) means "to fill with light"; the enlightened are the children of light → 350, 7 f. Only illumination makes awareness of darkness possible.

---

[345] καταλαμβανω (→ IV, 9, 33 ff.) can mean "to grasp," "fall upon." It is also used of darkness or night in relation to light or day in Jn. 12:35, cf. τῆς δὲ νυκτὸς ἤδη καταλαμβανούσης, Diod. S., 20, 86, 3. Many expositors (→ IV, 10, 22 ff., cf. Schl. J., ad loc.) thus find in Jn. 1:5 a mythical conflict motif: Darkness could not "vanquish" light. But the meaning "vanquish" is not attested, and "surprise" is not appropriate. In spite of 12:35 we should construe "comprehend" in the light of the analogous οὐκ ἔγνω in 1:10 and οὐ παρέλαβον in 1:11. Recourse to an Aram. original leads to the same result as against W. Nagel, "'Die Finsternis hat's nicht begriffen' (Jn. 1:5)," ZNW, 50 (1959), 132-7. M. Black, An Aram. Approach to the Gospels and Acts³ (1967), 10 f. thinks there is a play on words in Aram. לָא קַבְּלֵיהּ קַבְלָא. Materially cf. O. Sol. 42:3 f.: "... because I should hide myself from those who do not comprehend me, but I will be among those who love me."

[346] The vl. ἐστίν א D it syᶜ is secondary.

[347] In the preceding statement the Baptist is the subj., in v. 9 again the Logos, though this is not formally indicated. The difficulty remains even if φῶς is taken to be the subj.: "The true light that lightens every man was such as comes into the world," Bau. J., ad loc. This is improbable. The argument that only light comes into the world is refuted by the fact that world is a current Jewish circumlocution for men.

[348] Christ the light: κατὰ οὖν τοῦ μόνου ἀμώμου καὶ δικαίου φωτός, τοῖς ἀνθρώποις πεμφθέντος παρὰ τοῦ θεοῦ, Just Dial., 17, 3. Cf. also Act. Phil. 18, 112, also 20 and 124 and Ant. Christ., V, 8-43. Orig. Comm. in Joh., 1, 25 on 1:1 (p. 30, 33 ff.) spiritualises: The σωτήρ is the light of the spiritual world and the true sun: Dölger Sol, 157-170.

[349] So Käsemann, op. cit. (→ n. 340), 166 ff., who thinks the source ends at v. 12. Thus v. 5 in the source ref. to the historical revelation and the tenses cause no difficulty.

[350] ἀληθινός is said of God in Jn. 17:3; it is an attribute of light in Plot. Enn., VI, 9, 4. 20; Sen. Ep., 15, 93, 5 (vera lux). On Plat. → 314, 33 ff.

[351] On the relation to the Mandaean understanding of light as substance cf. K. Schaedel, Das Joh.-Ev. u. die Kinder des Lichts, Diss. Vienna (1953), 52-64; Schulz Joh. Reden, 101.

[352] J. A. T. Robinson, "Elijah, John and Jesus," Twelve NT Studies (1962), 28-52, does not agree that there is any real polemic, since John after his death had no disciples who were not also Christians. But cf. R. Schnackenburg, "Das vierte Ev. u. d. Johannesjünger," Historisches Jbch. der Görres-Gesellschaft, 77 (1957), 21-38.

The non-mythological meaning comes out in 3:19. The manifestation of light is judgment (→ III, 938, 35 ff.), [353] which works itself out as cleavage between faith and unbelief. Man's decision is not free in the sense of a *liberum arbitrium*. Wicked works precede it. [354] The argument that they hated (→ IV, 691, 24 ff.) the light because their works were evil [355] is not meant psychologically; it points to a prior decision. This is shown by the further argument in the experiential statement v. 20. There is a play here on the meaning of φῶς. The common idea that evil is afraid of the light is adopted, [356] and we have a variation along the lines of decision dualism. [357] Revelation brings to light what man really is. This is the crisis. [358] Works are qualified by their place. [359] Conversely light and darkness are understood non-speculatively as the place of works. Thus the rise of darkness is not explained cosmologically; it is explained in terms of salvation history.

2. 1 John. While generally Johannine, 1 John differs somewhat from the Gospel. [360] Only the noun occurs, and this only in two passages, 1:5, 7 and 2:8-10, with the opposite σκοτία at 2:11.

Assessment of the passages is dependent on literary analysis. Even if analysis can show [361] that 1:5-10 apart from 5a, 7c, 9d, and also 2:9-11, belong to a source stratum, the revelation addresses, while 2:7 f. give evidence of the style of a homiletical reworking of this source by the author of the epistle, [362] the source [363] is still to be regarded as a Chr. document. [364] This destroys one important criterion of source differentiation. [365]

---

[353] With 5:24 f. this is one of the programmatic formulations of Johannine eschatology, Bultmann J., 113 with n. 1.

[354] The concept of predestination is part of revelation dualism. Here, too, there is formal agreement with the Qumran texts → n. 109.

[355] "To love more than . . ." in Jn. 3:19 is again meant exclusively, as the context and the catching up of "hate" again in the next v. show, cf. Lidz. Ginza R., 285, 31 f.: "who ignore the call of life and love the call of darkness." The par. with 1 QS 4:24 f. "hatred of wickedness" is only apparent and formal.

[356] Prv. 7:9; Job 24:16; 38:15; Sir. 23:18 f.; κλεπτῶν γὰρ ἡ νύξ, τῆς δ' ἀληθείας τὸ φῶς, Eur. Iph. Taur., 1026, cf. Philo Spec. Leg., I, 319-323. "The wicked are blind and do not see. I call them to the light, but they bury themselves in darkness. 'O ye wicked,' I cry to them, who sink into darkness, rise up and do not fall into the abyss,'" Lidz. Joh., 203, 19-23.

[357] Philo Spec. Leg., I, 54: σκότος αἱρούμενοι πρὸ αὐγοειδεστάτου φωτός, is only formally akin, since the characteristic dualism is not present.

[358] Cf. the interchanging of ἐλέγχω and φανερόω, cf. Eph. 5:11, 13.

[359] "They are the congregation of iniquity, and in darkness are all their works, their desire is for it," 1 QM 15:9. οὐδὲ ἐν σκότει ὄντες δύνασθε ποιεῖν ἔργα φωτός, Test. N. 2:10, cf. Test. L. 19:1 (→ 326, 21 f.). "In the decision of faith or unbelief is manifested what man really is and always was already. But it is manifested in such a way that now for the first time he decides," Bultmann J., 115.

[360] Dodd Epistles of Jn., 155 f.: Haenchen Joh. Br., 226 f., 282; R. Bultmann, *Die drei Johannesbr., Kritisch-exeget. Komm. über d. NT,* 14⁸ (1969), 9; but cf. Schnckbg. J.², 34-38.

[361] R. Bultmann, "Analyse d. 1 Jn.," *Exegetica* (1967), 106 f., cf. also Wnd. Kath. Br., ad loc.

[362] R.Bultmann, "Die kirchliche Redaktion d. 1 Jn.," *Exegetica* (1967), 381-393 modifies the earlier analysis, putting καὶ τὸ αἷμα κτλ. 1:7c in the third stratum of later church glosses. The pas., he thinks, disrupts the rhythm and thought and thus does not belong to the source, nor is it from the author, since it would also disturb the context fashioned by him.

[363] As against Bultmann, op. cit. (→ n. 361), 121, who thinks it is pre-Chr. Gnostic.

[364] H. Braun, "Literaranalyse u. theol. Schichtung im 1 Jn.," *Gesammelte Stud. z. NT u. seiner Umwelt*² (1967), 214.

[365] E. Käsemann, "Ketzer u. Zeuge," *Exeget. Versuche u. Besinnungen,* I⁵ (1967), 182, n. 47; Haenchen Joh.-Br., 254.

But even if we cling to the distinction, 1:9 does not fit the source. [366] It is thus as well to interpret the passage without regard to source hypotheses. [367]

The main thesis is that God is light, 1:5. The light predication of the Evangelist is thus transferred to God. This is more than a formal change, since the meaning of light is altered thereby; there is no article. The point is not the exclusiveness of God as the true light (in spite of 2:8; → 355, 7 f.). It is the definition of His nature along the lines of the tradition: φῶς is used in a transferred rather than a literal sense in 1:5 → VII, 444, 10 ff. The absence of metaphysical speculation about light is truly Johannine. [368] The statement is buttressed by negation of the opposite. [369] One change as compared with the Gospel is that light is not brought into relation to the concept of the world. [370] The aim of the saying is hortatory. [371] With Gnosticism in view, there is drawn from the statement that God is light [372] the conclusion that fellowship with God may be seen in a walk in the light, [373] in truth [374] (→ I, 240,

---

[366] Braun, op. cit. (→ n. 364), 214 argues from the plur. τὰς ἁμαρτίας and the concept of forgiveness. The antithetical structure of 1:8-10 no longer provides a criterion for differentiation.

[367] We must insist on this in spite of the analysis of W. Nauck. "Die Tradition u. der Charakter d. 1. Jn.," Wissenschaftliche Untersuchungen z. NT, 3 (1957), cf. Haenchen Joh.-Br., 242-255. Nauck builds on the alternation, noted already by Bultmann, op. cit. (→ n. 361), 111 etc., of the conditional style (ἐάν...) and the participial style in the two passages at issue. But in spite of the sequences there is no poetry or poetic source, only prose, Haenchen Joh.-Br., 245, which is composed by the author ad hoc. The par. noted by Nauck, 23-8, merely throw light on the stylistic tradition, cf. the antitheses: "Every man who is found sinless will mount up to the place of light. He who is not found sinless...," Lidz. Joh., 84, 2 ff. On the conditional style cf. Lidz. Ginza R., 20, 19 ff.: "If you, my elect, hear what I say to you... I will grant you brightness from me in fulness and light from me without end. 'If you do not hearken to what I say to you...'" On the participial style cf. Ginza R., 237, 3 ff.: "Whoever reveals this form to men that are unworthy... will not see the light. But whoever..."

[368] This is shown by comparison with passages like Philo Som., I, 75 → 330, 19 ff.

[369] Taken alone, this can be construed gnostically. It is obviously formulated against Gnosticism to rob opponents of their claim to be men of light. On the style cf. Lucretius De rerum natura (ed. J. Martin [1953]), I, 4 f. 22 f. "He is the light in whom is no darkness, the living one in whom is no death...," Lidz. Ginza R., 6, 26 ff., cf. Test. L. 19:1 (→ 326, 21 f.); Test. N. 2:7; Eth. En. 58:3 ff.; ὅνπερ τρόπον καὶ τὸ φῶς ἐν οὐρανῷ μὲν ἄκρατον καὶ ἀμιγὲς σκότους ἐστίν, Philo Abr., 205. Cf. also 1 QS 11:11; 1 QH 1:8; 10:9, though in Qumran the dualism did not produce antitheses comparable to those in Jn., Haenchen Joh.-Br., 260.

[370] As in the Prologue of Jn. and the expression φῶς τοῦ κόσμου → 350, 17. In Jn. the κόσμος is creation, the place into which light shines; even though fallen it is sustained by God → III, 894. 9 ff. God loved it and therefore sent His Son to it. In 1 Jn. the κόσμος is the present world from which believers must keep apart → III. 895. 29 ff.

[371] Braun, op. cit. (→ n. 364), 214: Nauck, op. cit. (→ n. 367), 59-62: The ethical motifs determine the metaphysical and not vice versa. This does not mean that the concept of God is ethicised, as F. Mussner, "ZΩH. Die Anschauung vom 'Leben' im Vierten Ev.," Münchener Theol. Stud., I, 5 (1952), 169 f., ad loc. opines: God is light "to the degree that he is the embodiment of the moral good." On the contrary, the ethical is derived from an existing datum. The exposition of Schnckbg. 1 Jn., ad loc. is speculative and restrictive: Light signifies "the fulness of the divine nature and moral holiness." The saying is not a def. but rather the refusal of a def. Cf. the formulation in 1:7.

[372] One may amplify: We "are" not light in the sense of Gnostic self-awareness.

[373] On the interchangeability of being and doing cf. 1 QS 3:13 f. With a hortatory goal it is now said that God is "in the light," 1 Jn. 1:7, cf. 1 Tm. 6:16. Here, then, light is the world beyond. The conjunction of v. 6 and v. 7 proves the non-speculative tendency. In Jn. 8:12 περιπατέω ἐν τῷ φωτί means life in gen., in 1 Jn. 1:7 a specific form of light.

[374] πᾶσα ἀλήθεια ὑπὸ τοῦ φωτός ἐστιν, Test. A. 5:3. The schema of the two ways, which is developed in 1 QS 3:13 ff., is the background in 1 Jn.

26 ff.), i.e., in love. This takes concrete shape in fellowship μετ' ἀλλήλων, 1:7. [375]
The walk is paradoxical in structure. Part of walking in the light, in sinlessness,
is continually confessing one's sins → I, 307, 16 ff. [376] The alternative between the
two possibilities of walking is absolute; there are no gradations of light and darkness. [377] 2:7 develops the thought and establishes the requirement by a reference to
the old and new commandment → II, 555, 1 ff. [378] If φῶς previously serves to
characterise human conduct, it now defines the relation to God. [379] Walking is
possible because the "true [380] light" (2:8 → I, 250, 33 ff.) now shines. Darkness is
being dispelled. [381] Brotherly love (2:9 → IV, 692, 1 ff.; 693, 10 ff.), keeping the
commandments, is the ontic and not just the noetic ground of fellowship with God.
This is attained by walking in the light. [382]

V. The Rest of the New Testament.

1. Hebrews. Hb. uses the verb φωτίζω twice of Christians, the reference being
to the beginning of the Christian life, 6:4; 10:32; → I, 382, 21 ff.; IV, 1005, 35 ff.
Baptism is in view. But the use of the verb is not developed and there is no fixed
baptismal terminology → 357, 19 ff. [383] Illumination takes place at baptism, but the
verb does not denote this technically; [384] it simply refers to the process of illumination as such. [385]

2. James. At 1:17 f. the statement that all good gifts are from above. [386] is based
on the reference to God as the "Father of lights." [387] There are hardly any other

---

[375] This is the true reading, Bultmann, op. cit. (→ n. 362), 392, n. 12; Käsemann, op. cit.
(→ n. 365), 183, n. 47.
[376] The stress is on confession of sin rather than awareness of it. This is in antithesis to
Gnostic enthusiasm. 1 Jn. is distinguished from the confessions of the righteous in Qumran
by the link with christology, which changes the structure, Haenchen Joh.-Br., 260.
[377] There is agreement here with Qumran, cf. 1 QS 4:17 f.
[378] The wording again comes from Jn. 13:34, but the eschatological meaning of newness
is now changed into an idea of church tradition: The commandment is new because it was
brought by Jesus — its presence in the OT is disregarded — and it is old for existing believers
since it already has a church tradition.
[379] Bultmann, op. cit. (→ n. 361), 111.
[380] φῶς ἀληθινόν echoes Jn. but in a polemical sense rather than the strict sense of Jn.
(→ 352, 15 ff.). The antithesis is not between light and darkness; it is between true light and
false light. The meaning of ἀληθινός is determined by the preceding antithesis of → ψεῦδος -
ἀλήθεια.
[381] Light has its time, as in Jn., but in Jn. it is measured eschatologically with stress on
the danger of "too late," while in 1 Jn. the measure is the history of the church.
[382] Braun, op. cit. (→ n. 364), 223, who appeals, of course, to the reading μετ' αὐτοῦ,
but whose exegesis is right irrespective of this.
[383] As against E. Käsemann, "Das wandernde Gottesvolk," FRL, 55² (1957), 119, n. 4.
[384] Cf. Wnd. Hb. on 6:4: "Illumination here is not the wonderful new knowledge which
comes by listening to preaching, nor is it the act of baptism itself." But one may question his
further statement that "the heavenly gift is not the totality of salvation proffered in Christ
(Riggenbach) but something concrete, probably the Holy Spirit as in Ac. 2:38; 10:45; 11:17;
1 Pt. 1:12 (ἀπ' οὐρανοῦ); for there is synon. parallelism of members in γευσαμένους
τε ... καὶ μετόχους γενηθέντας."
[385] Philo Fug., 139; Klein, 53 f. Cf. also Ign. R., inscr.; Reitzenstein Hell. Myst., 292.
[386] H. Greeven, "Jede Gabe ist gut. Jk. 1:17," ThZ, 14 (1958), 1-13.
[387] On the negation of darkness → 329, 8 ff.; Ps.-Aristot. Mund., 6, p. 400a, 9.

examples of this expression; it has an apocalyptic ring. [388] Whether besouled stars
are in view (→ V, 1013, 23 f.) one can hardly say. [389] In itself cosmological, the
statement is linked with a soteriological saying. This gives it a Jewish-Gnostic
ring. [390]

3. 1Peter. 1 Pt. 2:9 (→ III, 41, 14 ff.) is an example of the conversion style
adopted from Judaism → 325, 4 ff. [391] The apocalyptic motif of the brightness of
the end-time, in which God or His representative is light, finds a par. in Rev. 18:1,
cf. 21:23; 22:5. [392]

F. The Early Church.

1. Post-Apostolic Fathers. [393]

Light terminology plays no gt. part here. These works are interesting rather as links
in the chain of tradition. The blossoming of light symbolism begins with Cl. Al. Light
occurs a few times in quotations from the OT but with no further development, 1 Cl., 16,
12; Barn., 3, 4; 14, 7 f. How OT usage is continued and becomes stock phraseology may
be seen in 1 Cl., 36, 2: [394] (ψ 49:16-23 is first quoted) ... διὰ τούτου (sc. Jesus Christ)
ἠνεῴχθησαν ἡμῶν οἱ ὀφθαλμοὶ τῆς καρδίας, διὰ τούτου ἡ ἀσύνετος καὶ ἐσκοτω-
μένη διάνοια ἡμῶν ἀναθάλλει εἰς τὸ φῶς, διὰ τούτου ἠθέλησεν ὁ δεσπότης τῆς
ἀθανάτου γνώσεως ἡμᾶς γεύσασθαι (Hb. 1:3 f. is then quoted). φῶς here is transf.
and denotes illumination as a state. The linking of φῶς, γνῶσις, life (ἀθάνατος as an

---

[388] The expression occurs only in Apc. Mos. 36 Cod. D (ed. A. Ceriani, Monumenta
sacra et profana, V, 1 [1868], 23) and Arm. transl., cf. c. 38 of the Arm. transl. in E.
Preuschen, "Die apokr. gnost. Adamschr. aus dem Arm. übersetzt u. untersucht," Festschr.
B. Stade (1900), 182, who twice transl. "Father of light," cf. Kautzsch Apkr. u. Pseudepigr.,
II, 526; also Test. Abr. B 7 (p. 111, 11). φῶτα are stars ψ 135:7; Ἰερ. 4:23. On the use
of the word father cf. Job 38:28, also τοῦ κόσμου πατήρ, Philo Spec. Leg., 1, 96. שׂר אורים
in 1 QS 3:20 is no par.

[389] We find related motifs in Philo: Father and stars, Op. Mund., 56 f.; Som., I, 73, the
immutability of God, Poster. C., 19, 3, the antithesis between this and the mutability of
creation as a reason for faith, Leg. All., II, 89. On the motif of immutability cf. 1 QS 3:15 ff.;
Dib. Jk.11. 133, n. 3.

[390] On βουληθεὶς ἀπεκύησεν ἡμᾶς ... Jm. 1:18, v. H. Schammberger, Die Einheitlichkeit d. Jk. im antignost. Kampf (1936), 58 f., though he wrongly affirms that ἀποκυέω can
be said only of the feminine principle, cf. against this πατὴρ ὁ Νοῦς ... ἀπεκύησεν
Ἄνθρωπον, Corp. Herm., 1, 12, with no immediate ref. to the gynandrous character of
the Hermetic God, and also Corp. Herm., 1, 9. Light and generation are linked in Corp. Herm.,
1, 9. 12; 9, 3. For one-sided soteriological exegesis cf. Schrenk (→ V, 1013, 17 ff.), for one-
sided cosmological exegesis C. M. Edsman, "Schöpferwille u. Geburt Jk. 1:18," ZNW, 38
(1939), 11-44. For a hardly adequate attempt to derive from the OT cf. L. Elliott-Binns,
"James 1:18: Creation or Redemption?" NTSt, 3 (1956/57), 148-161. A. Meyer, "Das Rätsel
d. Jk.," ZNW Beih., 10 (1930), 279-281 tries to interpret the passage in terms of the tradition
of Joseph's dream. Here Jacob appears as the father of the stars. In Meyer's structuring of the
epistle the whole section is controlled by the symbolism of Reuben, the first-born ἀπαρχή.

[391] Cf. Ac. 26:18; J. H. Elliott, "The Elect and the Holy," Nov. Test. Suppl., 12 (1966),
43 f.

[392] Cf. Is. 60:11 ff., 19 f.; Ez. 43:2.

[393] Bibl.: F. X. Funk - K. Bihlmeyer, Die Apost. Väter² (1956), LII-LIV; J. A. Fischer,
Die Apost. Väter, Die Schriften d. Urchr., I⁵ (1966), 6-23, 119-141.

[394] Kn. Cl., ad loc.: v. 1 f. gives evidence of liturgical development and differs in style
and content from the average morality of 1 Cl. In analysis cf. also A. v. Harnack, Einführung
in d. alte Kirchengeschichte (1929), 113 f.; v. 2b goes better with v. 1 than 2a; has 2a been
interpolated by the author? An argument to the contrary is that the whole is an elucidation of
σωτήριον.

attribute of γνῶσις) is now stereotyped, cf. 1 Cl., 59, 2 [395] with the favourite conversion style: The beloved παῖς Jesus Christ [our Lord], [396] δι' οὗ ἐκάλεσεν (sc. God) ἡμᾶς ἀπὸ σκότους εἰς φῶς, ἀπὸ ἀγνωσίας εἰς ἐπίγνωσιν δόξης ὀνόματος αὐτοῦ → 325, 4 ff. [397] How the vocabulary develops may be seen from 2 Cl., 1, 4: τὸ φῶς γὰρ ἡμῖν ἐχαρίσατο, [398] cf. also Dg., 9, 6, where in a long list Jesus is also called light. Acc. to Ign. R. inscr. the addressed community is beloved and enlightened; in R. 6, 2: ἀφετέ με καθαρὸν φῶς λαβεῖν, φῶς means the heavenly place of light, as the continuation ἐκεῖ παραγενόμενος ἄνθρωπος ἔσομαι shows. The motif of the heavenly journey is hinted at, [399] but in altered form along the lines of Ign.' concept of martyrdom; [400] Phld., 2, 1: τέκνα οὖν φωτὸς ἀληθείας, φεύγετε τὸν μερισμὸν καὶ τὰς κακοδιδασκαλίας. Of greater interest is Eph., 19, 2 f., though here the meaning of the verse does not depend on the concept of light as such but on the mythical framework, the cosmic depiction of the birth of the Redeemer. [401]

Did., 1-6 and Barn., 18-21 adopt Jewish teaching on the two ways. [402] Light is thrown on the meaning if we compare Did., 1, 1: ὁδοὶ δύο εἰσί, μία τῆς ζωῆς καὶ μία τοῦ θανάτου [403] with Barn., 18, 1: ὁδοὶ δύο εἰσὶν διδαχῆς καὶ ἐξουσίας, ἥ τε τοῦ φωτὸς καὶ ἡ τοῦ σκότους. [404] διαφορὰ δὲ πολλὴ τῶν δύο ὁδῶν. ἐφ' ἧς μὲν γάρ εἰσιν τεταγμένοι φωταγωγοὶ ἄγγελοι τοῦ θεοῦ, ἐφ' ἧς δὲ ἄγγελοι τοῦ σατανᾶ.

2. Baptism as φωτισμός. [405]

The technical use of φωτισμός for baptism, which does not occur in the NT (→ 355, 13 ff.), [406] is developed by Justin: καλεῖται δὲ τοῦτο τὸ λουτρὸν φωτισμός, ὡς φωτιζο-

---

395 Beginning of the gt. concluding prayer 1 Cl., 59, 2 - 61, 3, stylistically opened with the predication of God as Creator, the ref. to election and calling being then added. The style is more typical of liturgy than of the author.

396 Cf. Funk-Bihlmeyer and Fischer, op. cit. for text and apparatus.

397 V. 3 echoes Eph. 1:17 f.

398 Within the schema of once and now the once is depicted as idolatry, death and darkness, 2 Cl., 1, 6; transition to light is denoted by ἀναβλέπω. Traditional, too, is the ref. to creation terminology, the call out of non-being into being, 1, 8.

399 Cf. O. Sol. 21:5: "I was raised up into light"; 38:1: "I soared up to the light of truth as on a chariot."

400 Cf. Schlier, op. cit. (→ n. 211), 136-140, 172 f.

401 Christ is the new star with an ineffable light by which ἄγνοια is destroyed, Ign. Eph., 19, 2 f., cf. also καινὸς ἄνθρωπος, 20, 1; Schlier, op. cit., 28-32.

402 On the origin and spread of the two-way schema and its connection with light and darkness → V, 42, 1 ff.; Slav. En. A 30:15 (Bonwetsch, 29): "And I showed him two ways, light and darkness." On the Qumran texts, esp. 1 QS 3:19 ff. → 325, 20 ff. As there each way has its personal representative (spirit), so in Barn., 18, 1 φωταγωγοὶ ἄγγελοι τοῦ θεοῦ are set over the way of light and angels of Satan over the way of darkness, of the black one, 20, 1. Dualism is restricted by the fact that the representatives are plural. In contrast Did., 1, 1 Lat. (v. apparatus, ad loc.) has the sing.: in his constituti sunt angeli duo, unus aequitatis, alter iniquitatis. L. W. Barnard, "The Epistle of Barnabas and the Dead Sea Scrolls," The Scottish Journ. of Theology, 13 (1960), 45-49.

403 The Lat. text adds lucis et tenebrarum, J. P. Audet, "La Didachè," Études Bibl. (1958), 154 thinks the Lat. text is not a transl. of Gk. Did. but of the common original of Did. and Barn., cf. Barn., 19, 2, which has θανάτου, cf. Did., 5, 1.

404 Also Barn., 19, 1 and 19, 12, cf. Did., 4, 14. On the opp. side 20, 1 does not have σκότος but the personification of blackness.

405 F. Cumont, Lux perpetua (1949), 422-8; Beierwaltes, 104-7; Malmede, op. cit. (→ n. 324), 318-325, 576-600; Wlosok, 249 f.; Nauck, op. cit. (→ n. 367), 61 f.; J. Ysebaert, Greek Baptismal Terminology (1962), 158-178.

406 A model might be found in Hb. 6:4; 10:32 → 355, 13 ff. The Syr. transl. deviate in this sense. On the connection of light and baptism cf. also Col. 1:12 ff.; Eph. 5:14.

μένων τὴν διάνοιαν τῶν ταῦτα μανθανόντων, Apol., 61, 12, cf. 65, 1; Dial., 122, 5. [407]
Another explanation is offered in Cl. Al. Paed., I, 6, 26, 2, where baptism is φώτισμα:
φώτισμα δὲ δι' οὗ τὸ ἅγιον ἐκεῖνο φῶς τὸ σωτήριον ἐποπτεύεται τουτέστιν δι'
οὗ τὸ θεῖον ὀξυωποῦμεν. [408] The working out of the light motif can change; light can
take the form of phenomena of light. [409] One sees this sometimes in the NT account, [410]
and cf. the apocr. Gospels, [411] e.g., Ev. Eb. acc. to Epiph. Haer., 30, 13, 7. [412]

Conzelmann

---

[407] Wetter Phos, 1. Reitzenstein Hell. Myst., 265 thinks that Justin's explanation is a
rationalistic reinterpretation and that the use originally developed from the light garment
in which the initiate was clothed. But Wlosok, 249 objects that the expression cannot have
been derived from the mysteries since it is not attested there: "the appended explanation
reproduces crisply the understanding of light in philosophical Gnosticism which we find in
Hell. Judaism and which was familiar to Justin acc. to the testimony of Dial., 121, 2."

[408] Cf. Wetter Phos, 16 f.; Wlosok, 249 f.; Beierwaltes, 105.

[409] Act. Pl. (Gk.) 2:28-36 (p. 34); Act. Thom. 25 (p. 140, 18; the tradition vacillates
between ἐβάπτισεν and ἐφώτισεν), cf. 119 (p. 229, 15 f.); Act. Pl. et Thecl. 34. Cf. C. M.
Edsman, "Le baptême du feu," *Acta Seminarii Neotest. Upsaliensis*, 9 (1940), 158-174, 182-
190, πῦρ being dominant. On Jesus as guiding light cf. E. Peterson, "Einige Bemerkungen
z. Hamburger Papyrusfr. d. Act. Pl.," *Frühkirche, Judt. u. Gnosis* (1959), 192-8.

[410] Mt. 3:15a (g¹). C. Peters, "Nachhall ausserkanon. Ev.-Überlieferung," *Acta Orientalia*,
16 (1938), 258-294; on the relation to Tat. cf. also his "Das Diatessaron Tat.," *Orientalia
Christ. Analecta*, 123 (1939), 151 f. Cf. Just. Dial., 88, 3: κατελθόντος τοῦ 'Ιησοῦ ἐπὶ τὸ
ὕδωρ καὶ πῦρ ἀνήφθη ἐν τῷ 'Ιορδάνῃ.

[411] H. Waitz, "Neue Untersuchungen über die sog. judenchr. Ev.," ZNW, 36 (1937),
60-81; P. Vielhauer in Hennecke³, I, 75-90.

[412] καὶ εὐθὺς περιέλαμψε τὸν τόπον φῶς μέγα, Ev. Eb. Fr. 3 (Klostermann, 14),
cf. Fr. 4, Hennecke³ (I, 103).

χαίρω, χαρά, συγχαίρω, χάρις, χαρίζομαι,
χαριτόω, ἀχάριστος, χάρισμα, εὐχαριστέω,
εὐχαριστία, εὐχάριστος

χαίρω, χαρά, συγχαίρω.

Contents: A. The Word Group in Profane Greek: 1. Usage; 2. Philosophy; 3. Religious Connection. B. The Old Testament. C. Judaism: 1. Qumran; 2. Rabbinic Writings; 3. Philo. D. The New Testament: 1. Usage; 2. The Synoptics and 1 Peter; 3. The Pauline Corpus; 4. The Johannine Writings. E. The Post-Apostolic Fathers. F. Gnosticism.

A. The Word Group in Profane Greek.

1. Usage.

a. As a phenomenon, a direct feeling or better self-perception, as self-being in self-transport, [1] joy is uniform, and so are its manifestations even to tears of joy, Aesch. Ag., 270 and 541. It is everywhere a culmination of existence: "Joy, beauteous spark divine." It strains beyond itself. [2] As direct feeling it creates no problems. These arise only when man in ethical self-reflection sees himself as mastered by desire (→ II, 911, 12 ff.) and plunged into bondage.

χ α ί ρ ω κ τ λ. Bibl.: On A.: O. Loew, Χάρις, Diss. Marburg (1908); E. Norden, *Die Geburt des Kindes* (1924), 57 f.; H. G. Gadamer, *Platos dialektische Ethik, Phänomenologische Interpretationen zum "Philebos"* (1931), 131-159; M. Pohlenz, *Die Stoa*, I[2] (1959), Index, s.v. χαρά; J. Latacz, *Zum Wortfeld "Freude" in d. Sprache Hom.* (1966). On B.: S. Mowinckel, *Psalmenstud.*, II (1921), 18 f., 130-145; K. Grzegorzewski, *Elemente vorderorient. Hofstils auf kanaanäischem Boden*, Diss. Königsberg (1937), 34-44; L. Köhler, *Theol. d. AT*[4] (1966), 137 f. On C.: H. v. Arnim, "Quellenstud. zu Philo v. Alex.," PhU, 11 (1888), 127-130; H. Windisch, *Die Frömmigkeit Philos* (1909), 52-60; H. Lewy, "Sobria Ebrietas," ZNW Beih. 9 (1929), 34-40; W. Völker, *Fortschritt u. Vollendung bei Philo v. Alex.*, TU, 49, 1 (1938), 260-350. On D.: A. Fridrichsen, "Le problème du miracle dans le christianisme primitif," *Études d'histoire et de philosophie religieuses*, 12 (1925), 94-6; E. Gulin, "Die Freude im NT, I. II.," *Annales Acad. Scientiarum Fennicae Ser. B*, 26, 2 (1932); 37, 3 (1936); S. Lyonnet, "χαῖρε κεχαριτωμένη, *Biblica*, 20 (1939), 131-141; J. Schniewind, "Die Freude im NT," *Nachgelassene Reden u. Aufsätze* (1952), 72-80; J. D. Plenter, *De blijdschap in Paulus' brieven*, Diss. Groningen (1953); W. Nauck, "Freude im Leiden," ZNW, 46 (1955), 68-80; A. B. du Toit, *Aspekte d. Freude im chr. Abendmahl*, Diss. Basel, (1965).

[1] It needs no object. It can have this, but even then it means the harmony of self-rejoicing. On the occasion cf. Gadamer, 154 f. It is a. anticipatory joy with a view to something fut., b. joy over something pres., c. pure joy only as joy at something present. It can create fellowship, esp. as festal joy, cf. the feast of peace in Aristoph. Pax, 291.

[2] Gadamer, 131: "Joy is not just a state or feeling but a way of making the world manifest. Joy is determined by the discovery of being in its joyousness."

b. χαίρω³ means "to rejoice," "to be merry."⁴ For Hom. the seat of the emotion is the θυμός in Il., 7, 191 f. and then other anthropological locations.⁵ The aor. occurs from Hom., e.g., Il., 7, 54, normally ἐχάρην, fut. χαρήσομαι. From the pres. the fut. χαιρήσω is formed from Hom., e.g., Il., 20, 363, and occ. aor. ἐχαίρησα.⁶ The mid. χαίρομαι is used as a barbarism in Aristoph. Pax, 291. Constr. is with dat. of pers., Hom. Od., 3, 52, εἰκότως σοι χαίρουσιν οἱ Λακεδαιμόνιοι ἅτε πολλὰ εἰδότι, Plat. Hi., I, 285e, or dat. of obj., e.g., νίκῃ, Hom. Il., 7, 312, also ἐπί with dat., Xenoph. Cyrop., VIII, 4, 12; Eur. Ba., 1039 f., or πρός with dat. of obj., Eupolis Fr., 327 (CAF, I, 345). It is seldom combined with ἐν, Aesch. Eum., 996 or acc. and part., χαίρω δέ σ᾽ εὐτυχοῦντα, Eur. Rhes., 390. We find χαρὰν χαίρω with acc. of inner obj.: χαίροντες ἀνδραπόδων τινὰ χαράν, Plut. Suav. Viv. Epic., 8 (II, 1901e), with part. χαίρω... ἀκούσας Hom. Il., 19, 185, with ὅτι, Hom. Od., 14, 51 f. In the neg. we esp. find χαίρω in the fut. οὐ... χαιρήσεις "thou wilt regret that," Aristoph. Pl., 64. Like all terms for emotions the word is often associated with related expressions, esp. εὐφραίνω (→ II, 773, 12 ff.), cf. ἥδομαι καὶ χαίρομαι (→ 361, 6 ff.) κεὐφραίνομαι, Aristoph. Pax, 291, cf. also the noun χαρά, e.g., ἡδονὴ καὶ τέρψις καὶ χαρά, Plat. Phileb., 19c. χαῖρε is already a greeting in Hom., esp. on meeting, Od., 1, 123, with the reply χαίρω, Aesch. Ag., 538 f., but also on parting, Od., 5, 205, cf. also ἐάω χαίρειν τι "to give up something," Plat. Prot., 347e, at death, Soph. Ai., 863; Plat. Phaed., 116d, on funerary inscr., e.g., IG¹, 7, 203 etc.⁷ Hesych. notes s.v. χαίρειν: ἐρρῶσθαι. τὸ χαίρειν ταῖς ἐπιστολαῖς (→ n. 9) προσετίθεσαν. ἔστι δὲ καὶ ἀπαλλασσομένων προσαγόρευσις. In Luc. Pro lapsu inter salutandum, 1 ff. the morning greeting χαῖρε is sharply if ironically distinguished from the evening greeting ὑγίαινε; similarly Suet. Caes., VII Galba, 4 differentiates salvere and valere. On the evening blessing of light χαῖρε, νέον φῶς → 362, 12 f. χαῖρε is above all a greeting to the gods. It is a stereotyped expression in hymns, as a conclusion, Hom. Hymn. Merc., 579 etc., at the beginning, e.g., in the hymn to Helios, Preis. Zaub., I, 4, 640 f. (4th cent. A.D.).⁸ χαίρειν is an epistolary formula in the model: sender to recipient χαίρειν, → 394, 1.⁹

c. The noun χαρά¹⁰ is nomen actionis: "rejoicing," "merriness," Soph. Ant., 392.¹¹ The mood can be emphasised by the expression "to fill with joy," the verbs for this being πληρόω, Jos. Bell., 3, 28; Ac. 13:52; 2 Tm. 1:4; Dg., 10, 3, ἀναπίμπλαμαι, Philo Det. Pot. Ins., 123, ἐμπίμπλημι, Eur. Phoen., 170; Jos. Ant., 3, 99, cf. Mart. Pol., 12, 1;

---

³ Etym.: Indo-Eur. root *g'her- "to desire," "to like," Germ. "gern," "(be)gehren [Risch]. Cf. also Hofmann, s.v.; Schwyzer, I, 714; Frisk, s.v.

⁴ Opp. λυπέομαι (→ IV, 313, 1 ff.) Soph. Ai., 555; Demosth. Or., 18, 292; μισέω (→ IV, 683, 20 ff.) Plat. Leg., II, 656b. Latacz, 125 f.

⁵ Cf. χαίρων ἐνὶ θυμῷ, Od., 8, 395. χαρείη δὲ φρένα μήτηρ, Il., 6, 481. ὁ δὲ φρεσὶν ᾗσι χάρη, Il., 13, 609. κῆρ, Od., 20, 89. Cf. Liddell-Scott, s.v. χαίρω.

⁶ [Risch]. Cf. Liddell-Scott, s.v.; Schwyzer, III, Index, s.v. ἐχάρην, ἐχαίρησα, χαιρήσω.

⁷ W. Peek, "Griech. Grabgedichte," Schriften u. Quellen d. Alten Welt, 7 (1960), mark of the beginning of the poem, s.v. χαῖρε.

⁸ In spite of Plat. Ep., 3. 315c.

⁹ The inf. is not imper. but elliptic: ὁ δεῖνα τῷ δεῖνι χαίρειν, sc. λέγει vel εὔχεται, cf. G. A. Gerhard, "Untersuchungen z. Gesch. d. griech. Briefes, I," Philol., 64 (1905), 27-65, esp. 27-38; Bl.-Debr. § 389; 480, 5. On the greeting in gen. cf. F. Ziemann, De epistularum Graec. formulis solemnibus quaestiones selectae. Diss. phil. Hal., 18, 4 (1910); Wendland Hell. Kult., 411-417; O. Roller, "Das Formular d. paul. Br.," BWANT, 58 (1933), 61 f., 447-459; A. Strobel, "Der Gruss an Maria (Lk. 1:28)," ZNW, 53 (1962), 92, n. 30 (Bibl.). Examples also in Moult.-Mill., s.v. The formula occurs in the NT at Ac. 15:23; 23:26; Jm. 1:1; elsewhere we always have a two-membered form of greeting with χάρις → 393, 23 ff.

¹⁰ Suid., s.v. χαρά (Adler, IV, 786): ἡδονή, εὐφροσύνη, τέρψις. Hesych., s.v. χαρά: ἡδονή, ἀγαλλίασις, εὐφροσύνη. It will be seen that the moods and expressions overlap.

¹¹ In the NT χαρά is also metonymically the reason for joy: "Lo, I proclaim to you great joy," Lk. 2:10.

Demosth. Or., 18, 217: ζήλου καὶ χαρᾶς καὶ ἐπαίνων ἡ πόλις ἦν μεστή. Prepos. expressions offer fine flourishes μετὰ πολλῆς χαρᾶς, BGU, IV, 1141, 3 (13 B.C.).[12]

2. Philosophy.

a. In philosophy joy is an obj. of reflection. In Plato χαρά and ἡδονή are barely distinguished → II, 911, 17 ff.; 920, n. 65. The noun is less common than the verb.[13] Plato offers an etym. of the two terms: ἥ τε γὰρ "ἡδονή," ἡ πρὸς τὴν ὄνησιν ἔοικε τείνουσα πρᾶξις τοῦτο ἔχειν τὸ ὄνομα... There follow λύπη etc.; "χαρά" δὲ τῇ διαχύσει καὶ εὐπορίᾳ τῆς ῥοῆς τῆς ψυχῆς ἔοικε κεκλημένη, Crat., 419b c. Then come τέρψις, εὐφροσύνη.[14] The theme of pleasure (or the reverse) and the good is dealt with in Phileb., cf. the thesis of Philebus: Φίληβος μὲν τοίνυν ἀγαθὸν εἶναί φησι τὸ χαίρειν πᾶσι ζῴοις καὶ τὴν ἡδονὴν καὶ τέρψιν, 11b.[15] Typical is Resp., V, 462b: οὐκοῦν ἡ μὲν ἡδονῆς τε καὶ λύπης κοινωνία συνδεῖ, ὅταν ὅτι μάλιστα πάντες οἱ πολῖται τῶν αὐτῶν γιγνομένων τε καὶ ἀπολλυμένων παραπλησίως χαίρωσι καὶ λυπῶνται; against this works differentiation ἰδίωσις, ὅταν οἱ μὲν περιαλγεῖς, οἱ δὲ περιχαρεῖς γίγνωνται ἐπὶ τοῖς αὐτοῖς παθήμασι τῆς πόλεώς τε καὶ τῶν ἐν τῇ πόλει, loc. cit.

b. In Aristot. χαρά is almost completely replaced by ἡδονή. There is a trace of distinction in Eth. Nic., II, 4, p. 1105b, 19 ff. in the def. of virtue: In the soul are πάθη, δυνάμεις, ἕξεις. χαρά is one of the πάθη which ἡδονή or λύπη follows.[16]

c. In the Stoics χαρά is a special instance of ἡδονή, which is one of the four basic affections, λύπη, φόβος, ἡδονή, ἐπιθυμία. Since the Stoics, unlike Platonists and Peripatetics, think all emotions are defective judgments of the λόγος, χαρά is viewed negatively.[17] To mitigate this view, which is so contrary to common opinion, the Stoics develop the doctrine of the εὐπάθειαι or "good moods" of the soul as distinct from affections πάθη.[18] χαρά is an εὐπάθεια:[19] εἶναι δὲ καὶ εὐπαθείας φασὶ τρεῖς,

---

[12] Moult.-Mill., s.v. χαρά. Cf. μετὰ παρρησίας πάσης, Ac. 4:29; ἐν πάσῃ ἀσφαλείᾳ, Ac. 5:23, cf. Ditt. Syll.³, II, 547, 30 (3rd cent. B.C.). Cf. also μετὰ πάσης προθυμίας, ibid., I, 532, 6 f. (218/217 B.C.). Such expressions are customary in inscr. of honour and from there they come into rhetorical historical writing, E. Skard, "Epigraphische Formeln bei Dion. Hal.," Symb. Osl., 11 (1932), 55-60, esp. 57.

[13] The main term under which the problem of pleasure and fortune or virtue is handled in Aristot. is ἡδονή.

[14] In explanation cf. Crat., 415c d: ἀρετή means πρῶτον μὲν εὐπορίαν, ἔπειτα δὲ λελυμένην τὴν ῥοὴν τῆς ἀγαθῆς ψυχῆς εἶναι ἀεί. There is another etym. in Plat. Leg., II, 654a; Aristot. Eth. Nic., VII, 12, p. 1152b, 6 f.

[15] Cf. ἡδονή, τέρψις, χαρά, Phileb., 19c. Opp. are ἀλγέω, 35e; 36a, cf. ἀνιάομαι, Gorg., 497a, λυπέομαι, 494b, λύπη, Phileb., 36a. The epistemological problem of true and false pleasure or the reverse, with the underlying problem of true and false concepts, is discussed in Phileb., 36e-38a.

[16] But cf. 4 Macc. 1:22: χαρά follows ἡδονή, resulting from satisfied desire.

[17] Cf. v. Arnim, 128 f.

[18] [Dihle].

[19] There are already approaches to differentiation in the Pre-Socratics, cf. Suid., s.v.: χαρά· ἡδονή, εὐφροσύνη, τέρψις. τινές φασι κατὰ τὸ ὑποκείμενον ταὐτὸν σημαινόμενον εἶναι. Πρόδικος δὲ ἐπειρᾶτο ἑκάστῳ τῶν ὀνομάτων τούτων ἴδιόν τι σημαινόμενον ὑποτάσσειν, ὥσπερ καὶ οἱ ἀπὸ τῆς Στοᾶς, χαρὰν μὲν λέγοντες εὔλογον ἔπαρσιν, ἡδονὴν δὲ ἔπαρσιν ἄλογον, τέρψιν δὲ τὴν διὰ θεωρίας ἡδονήν, εὐφροσύνην δὲ τὴν διὰ λόγων ἡδονήν. νομοθετούντων δέ ἐστι τοῦτο. τὸ μὲν γὰρ εἰπεῖν ἡδονὴν χαρὰν οὐχ ἁμάρτημα, ὥσπερ οὐδὲ τὸ τὴν μονάδα ἀδιαίρετον· οὐδὲ γὰρ τὸ τὴν χαρὰν χαρὰν εἰπεῖν ἢ τὴν μονάδα μονάδα. In transition to Stoicism there is discussion of the true obj. of joy, Gnomologium Vaticanum (ed. L. Sternbach, Texte u. Komm., 2 [1963]), No. 497: Ὁ αὐτὸς (sc. Socrates) εἶπεν· εἰ [ἐν] τῷ πλουτεῖν τὸ χαίρειν συνῆν, πολλοῦ ἂν ἦν ἄξιον· νῦν δὲ ταῦτα χωρίζεται· ὁ γοῦν Μενέλαος παρὰ τῷ ποιητῇ (cf. Hom. Od., 4, 93) φησιν· ὡς οὗτοι χαίρων τοῖσδε κτεάτεσσιν ἀνάσσω, cf. Stob. Ecl., V, 766, 16 ff.; Plut. Aud. Poet., 6 (II, 25a).

χαράν, εὐλάβειαν, βούλησιν. καὶ τὴν μὲν χαρὰν ἐναντίαν φασὶν εἶναι τῇ ἡδονῇ, οὖσαν εὔλογον ἔπαρσιν (cf. Philo Spec. Leg., II)· τὴν δ' εὐλάβειαν τῷ φόβῳ, οὖσαν εὔλογον ἔκκλισιν, Diog. L., VII, 116. [20] Joy is among the prima bona, Sen. Ep., 7, 66, 5; it is reserved for the wise: gaudium nisi sapienti non contingere; est enim animi elatio suis bonis verisque fidentis, 6, 59, 2. χαίρειν is a κατόρθωμα, Stob. Ecl., II, 96, 20 f. Plut. says of the Stoics: αἰδεῖσθαι τὸ αἰσχύνεσθαι καλοῦσι καὶ τὸ ἥδεσθαι χαίρειν καὶ τοὺς φόβους εὐλαβείας, De virtute morali, 9 (II, 449a). [21] In the Cyrenaics χαρά is defined as a τέλος: τέλος δ' ὑπελάμβανε χαρὰν καὶ λύπην. τὴν μὲν ἐπὶ φρονήσει, τὴν δ' ἐπὶ ἀφροσύνῃ· ἀγαθὰ δὲ φρόνησιν καὶ δικαιοσύνην, κακὰ δὲ τὰς ἐναντίας ἕξεις, μέσα δὲ ἡδονὴν καὶ πόνον, Theodorus in Diog. L., II, 98.

3. Religious Connection.

Religiously χαρά denotes festal joy in Hell. It is a basic mood in mystery piety → n. 111, and there is thus transmitted as a mystery summons χαῖρε νύμφε, χαῖρε νέον φῶς, Firm. Mat. Err. Prof. Rel., 19, 1, while in the Osiris mysteries we have the cry εὑρήκαμεν, συγχαίρομεν, Athenag. Suppl., 22, 6; Firm. Mat. Err. Prof. Rel., 2, 9, cf. Apul. Met., XI, 24, 5. The Attis cult has its hilaria on March 25, Macrob. Sat., I, 21, 10. [22] The eschatological intention in joy as such appears now as an eschatological concept, e.g., expectation of the world-saviour → VII, 1012, 3 ff. [23] We are thus in the emotional milieu of the story of Jesus' birth in Lk. 1 f. → 367, 4 ff.

B. The Old Testament.

In the OT [24] the experience and expression of joy are close to one another. One can see this in the juxtaposition of related expressions and their transl. into Gk. The usual

---

[20] Cf. Ps.-Andronicus Rhodius, De passionibus, I, 6, ed. X. Kreuttner, Diss. Heidelberg (1885), 20, cf. v. Arnim, III, 105, 28.

[21] Cf. on the whole subj. A. Bonhöffer, Epictet. u. d. Stoa (1890), 293 f.

[22] H. Hepding, "Attis," RVV, 1 (1903), 167 f.; F. Cumont, D. orient. Religionen im röm. Heidentum (1930), 53-5.

[23] The roots are old. Hom. Hymn. Ap., 90: Δῆλος μὲν μάλα χαῖρε γόνῳ ἑκάτοιο ἄνακτος, cf. 125 f. Theogn., I, 9 f. of the birth of Apollo: ἐγέλασσε δὲ Γαῖα πελώρη γήθησεν δὲ βαθὺς πόντος ἁλὸς πολιῆς, Ditt. Syll.³, II, 797, 5-9 (37 A.D.): ἐπεὶ ἡ κατ' εὐχὴν πᾶσιν ἀνθρώποις ἐλπισθεῖσα Γαΐου Καίσαρος Γερμανικοῦ Σεβαστοῦ ἡγεμονία κατήγγελται, οὐδὲν δὲ μέτρον χαρᾶς εὕρηκ[ε]ν ὁ κόσμος, πᾶσα δὲ πόλις, καὶ πᾶν ἔθνος ἐπὶ τὴν τοῦ θεοῦ ὄψιν ἔσ[π]ευκεν, ὡς ἂν τοῦ ἡδίστου ἀνθρώποις αἰῶνο[ς] νῦν ἐνεστῶτος... Best known is Verg. Ecl., 4, 50 ff. The expectation goes back to the ancient Orient, v. H. Windisch, Die Orakel d. Hystaspes (1929), 65, n. 2; Norden, 57. From Egypt cf. the Hymn to Osiris: "The two lands rejoiced that he (sc. Osiris) has appeared on the throne of his father," cf. H. Kees, Religionsgesch. Lesebuch, ed. A. Bertholet, 10² (1928), 28, from Assyria the inscr. of Assurbanipal, Col. II, lines 13-15, ed. M. Streck, "Assurbanipal," Vorderasiat. Bibliothek, 7, 2 (1916), 261, who says of himself: "Through the naming of my weighty name the four corners of the earth rejoiced and were glad. The kings of the upper and lower sea... sent messages of joy by reason of the exercise of royal power by me," cf. also W. Staerk, "Die Erlösungserwartung in d. östlichen Religionen." Soter, II (1938), 242, cf. 370. Cf. also Sib., 3, 785: εὐφράνθητι, κόρη, καὶ ἀγάλλεο, 8, 474 f.: τικτόμενον δὲ βρέφος ποτὶ δ' ἔπτατο γηθοσύνη χθών, οὐράνιος δ' ἐγέλασσε θρόνος καὶ ἀγάλλετο κόσμος.

[24] In ancient Egypt joy at the beauty of the god is a motif, cf. the prayer to the sun in the Book of the Dead of Night: "The divine world rejoices at thy rising and the earth is glad at the sight of thy rays. Mankind daily rejoices to see thy beauty," cf. G. Roeder, Urkunden z. Religion d. alten Ägypten (1915), 3. Then a reason for joy is the beauty of the king as a reflection of divine beauty, Grzegorzewski, 38. To see this beauty means life: "Their arms worship thy Ka, for thou dost quicken hearts by thy beauty," Little Hymn to Aton. Roeder, 67.

Hebr. equivalent is שָׂמַח, שִׂמְחָה, cf. חדה and terms for the expression of joy שׂושׂ, גִּיל, רנן, עלץ etc. [25] In the Ps. שׂמח is transl. by εὐφραίνομαι → II, 773, 12 ff. [26] It is often combined with ἀγαλλιάομαι (→ I, 19, 1 ff.), ψ 9:3; 30:8; 89:14. [27]

Joy is not just inward. It has a cause and finds expression. It thus aims at sharing, especially as festal joy → lines 14 ff. It is a disposition of the whole man. This is the point when the heart is called its organ (→ III, 605, 19 ff.), Hab. 1:15 LXX, cf. ψ 83:3. [28] Occasions and objects are manifold, e.g., God and His saving acts, Ps. 5:11; 9:2; 16:9; 32:11; 33:1; 40:16; 63:11; 64:10; Neh. 8:10; Is. 35:10; 51:11; 65:18. The specific reason is to be found in concrete demonstrations of salvation. God helps, cf. Ex. 18:9-11; 1 S. 2:1 f.; Ps. 33:21; 149:2. God's Law is the object in Ps. 119:14 and God's Word in Jer. 15:16. Conversely joy is the reward for faithfulness to the Law in Is. 65:13 f.; Prv. 10:28. [29] Naturally the OT mentions secular joy, e.g., at weddings, Jer. 25:10, and cf. the reference to wine that makes glad the heart of man in Ps. 104:15. Most common, however, is the use in a cultic relation, joy as festal joy and its expression. [30] This is the reference in Ps. 33; 95; 98:4. Joy in harvest is ritually celebrated, Is. 9:2; Ps. 126:5 f.; cf. ritual weeping at sowing, Ps. 126:5 f. God Himself rejoices, Is. 65:19; 62:5; Zeph. 3:17. Joy is called for as the rendering of thanks to Him, Dt. 16:13-15, cf. 12:6 f.; 2 Ch. 30:21 ff., cf. Jub. 49:22. In feasts one may see what it is to be glad before God (Dt. 12:7; Ps. 16:11) and what it means that God Himself is the object of joy (Ps. 84:2; 89:16; 149:2). God is not just power in a neutral sense; in the first instance He is salvation in a positive sense. [31] Orientation to Him finds utterance as hymnal jubilation, Jl. 2:21, 23; ψ 95, cf. Ps. 89:12; 98:8. In Wisdom literature joy in the Law is extolled and it is exercised thereby, Ps. 119:14, cf. 1:2. In comparison to the original forms of utterance we have here a secondary stage of reflection. [32]

It corresponds to the inner intention of joy itself that OT usage culminates in eschatology (Ps. 14:7 = 53:6; Ps. 126:2, 5 f.; Is. 9:2; 12:6; 25:9; 51:3; 61:10; 65:17-19; 66:14; Zech. 2:14; 8:19; → n. 34). The roots are to be found in the connection between joy and kingship. [33] High-points are passages in the prophets in which we have the call: χαῖρε (Zeph. 3:14-17; Jl. 2:21-27; Zech. 9:9 f.). [34]

---

25 For material cf. P. Humbert, "Laetari et exultare dans le vocabulaire de l'AT," Rev HPhR, 22 (1942), 185-214.

26 In Dt. Is. we usually find εὐφραίνομαι for רנן, while ἀγαλλιάομαι is used for גיל at Is. 49:13 etc. and for התהלל at 41:16.

27 Cf. also the synon. in Is. 66:10: εὐφράνθητι, Ιερουσαλημ, καὶ πανηγυρίσατε ἐν αὐτῇ, ...χάρητε χαρᾷ...

28 ἡ καρδία (HT לֵב) μου καὶ ἡ σάρξ (HT בְּשָׂר) μου ἠγαλλιάσαντο ἐπὶ θεὸν ζῶντα.

29 Cf. οὐκ ἔστιν χαίρειν τοῖς ἀσεβέσιν, Is. 48:22; 57:21.

30 Mowinckel, 18 f., cf. 130-145. Humbert, op. cit. assumes that the technical cultic sense of שׂמח and גיל has a pagan origin, Ju. 16:23: the princes of the Philistines gather לְזְבֹּחַ זֶבַח־גָּדוֹל לְדָגוֹן אֱלֹהֵיהֶם וּלְשִׂמְחָה, cf. also Hos. 9:1; 2 S. 6:12; 2 K. 11:14, 20; Is. 9:2; 22:13; 30:27 ff.

31 Salvation is a display of grace in Ps. 4:7; 92:5, e.g., forgiveness, Ps. 32; 51.

32 Köhler, 198.

33 Esp. gt. is joy at birth or accession. The time of rule is esp. characterised as a time of salvation, cf. Grzegorzewski, 34-44; G. v. Rad., Theol. d. AT, I⁶ (1969), 334.

34 Basic is Zeph. 3:14-17; v. 14 f. seems to be an accession song, cf. also vv. 16-18a, K. Elliger, Das Buch d. zwölf kleinen Propheten, II, AT Deutsch, 25⁵ (1964), ad loc.

C. Judaism.

1. Qumran.

The OT synon. occur here too; we find שׂמח with שׂושׂ and גיל, 1 QM 13:12 f. OT motifs also recur, joy in God, 1 QM 4:14, in His mighty hand, 13:12 f., God Himself rejoicing: "May the soul of thy servant be glad in thy truth (אמת)," 1 QH 11:30. The eschatological character of joy is dominant, being expressed in conscious reliance on the Bible: "Rejoice (שׂמח) greatly, Zion, appear with jubilation (רנה), Jerusalem, and all the cities of Judah, be glad (גיל)," 1 QM 12:13, cf. Ps. 97:8; Zech. 9:9. Joy is a sign of the age of God, cf. esp. 1 QM 1:9: "Peace and blessing, glory and joy (שׂמחה) and length of days for all the sons of light," 35 cf. 14:4. "Everlasting joy" is a fixed catchword, 1 QS 4:7; 1 QH 13:6; 18:15; 1 QH fr. 36 7:5. The elect know already that they are under God's protection and can rejoice in spite of present suffering: "And thy correction became joy שׂמחה and delight שׂושׂון to me and my plagues became healing ... and the scorn of my enemies became a crown of honour and my stumbling everlasting strength," 1 QH 9:24 f., cf. 1 QM 13:12 f. 37

2. Rabbinic Writings. 38

Here, too, joy is also festal joy → 363, 14 ff. 39 Its giver is God: "So the God of Israel prepared joy for Israel when He redeemed them (from Egypt). God said Whosoever loves my children, let him come and rejoice with my children," Ex. r., 18, 10 on 12:29 (Wünsche, 143). "Blessed be He who has given His people Israel feast-days for rejoicing and remembrance," bBer., 49a. It is thus a duty to rejoice: "It is a duty to gladden thy children and members of thy family at the feast (Dt. 16:14). How does one gladden them? With wine," bPes., 109a. One should serve God with joy; Midr. Ps., 100, 3 on 100:2 40 compares: "Serve God with joy" (Ps. 100:2) and: "Serve the Lord with fear" (Ps. 2:10). God will rejoice at the works of the righteous and Israel at the acts of God, Pesikt., 27 (171a). 41 Joy is joy before God 42 שׂמחה בשׂמים, M. Ex. משׂפטים, 20 on 23:15 (p. 333, 12). "It is joy before God when those who anger Him vanish from the world," S. Nu., 117 on 18:8 (Kuhn, 371). Here as in Lk. 15:7 joy before God is in the first instance joy in heaven. But "joy for Israel is as joy before God," M. Ex. בשׂלח, 2 on 17:15 (p. 186, 12). The meal is part of the festival: 43 "There is no joy 44 without eating and drinking,"

---

35 Cf. also ὅτι ἀγαθὰ καὶ ἡ χαρὰ καὶ ἡ τ[ιμὴ] ἡτοίμασται καὶ ἐγγέγραπται ταῖς ψ[υχαῖς] τῶν ἀποθανόντων εὐσεβῶν Gr. En. 103:3 (ed. C. Bonner, The Last Chapters of Enoch in Greek, Studies and Documents, 8 [1937]). On the eschatological strand in Hell. Judaism → 365, 19 ff.

36 Sukenik, 55.

37 4 Esr. 7:88 ff. mentions 7 joys of the righteous corresponding to the 7 torments of the damned (7:81 ff.).

38 Cf. Levy Wört., s.v. שׂמח; שׂמחה/שׂמחי, חדי, חדא/חדי, חדו, חדוא, חדותא, חדותא, cf. Jastrow, s.v.

39 The Passover esp. is viewed as a feast of joy, cf. Ex. r., 18, 11 on 12:41 and the material in B. Reicke, "Diakonie, Festfreude u. Zelos," Uppsala Univ. Arsskrift, 1951, 5 (1951), 182-5. On the link between expectation of salvation and feasting in Israel cf. Moore, II, 40-51, the Passover, A. Strobel, "Die Passa-Erwartung als urchr. Problem in Lk. 17:20 f.," ZNW, 49 (1958), 164-171; on Tabernacles in gen. J. Jeremias, "Golgotha," Angelos Beih., 1 (1926), 81-4; H. Riesenfeld, "Jésus transfiguré," Acta Seminarii Neotest. Upsaliensis, 16 (1947), 24-28, 43-53, 278 f.; Str.-B., II, 774-812, on its joyous character, 804-807.

40 Str.-B., IV, 844.

41 Ibid., 851.

42 The following examples are from Str.-B., II, 209.

43 Ibid., 143 f.

44 Cf. ibid., 143; L. Goldschmidt, Der bab. Talmud, III (1933) transl. שׂמחה by "festivity."

bMQ, 9a. This is even worked out linguistically, for שמחה takes on the sense of "feast,"
esp. the wedding: [45] "Like a king who made a שמחה for his son and slew his enemies.
The king said: Whosoever has made me glad, let him come to the שמחה of my son ... ,"
Ex. r., 18, 10 on 12:29 (Wünsche, 143).

Significant for Johannine usage is the idea of "perfect joy" שמחה שלימה: [46] "Joy in
this world is not perfect; but in the future our joy will be perfect," Pesikt., 29 (189a b).
"But when they (sc. the prophets) say to you: Lo, thy king comes to thee, righteous and
full of salvation (Zech. 9:9), [47] they will then say: This is a perfect joy" הא חדותא שלימה
Midr. Cant., 1 on 1:4 (Wünsche, 29).

3. Philo.

In Philo the word group [48] is of gt. significance. [49] There is a gen. def. in Leg. All.,
III, 86 f. The specifically religious character of joy [50] may be seen from its close connection with religious "intoxication," Rer. Div. Her., 315. [51] Relations to other concepts
bring out its structure: ἀρετή, εἰρήνη and εὐπάθεια in Leg. All., I, 45, εὐπάθεια
in Abr., 201, εὐφροσύνη in Leg. All., III, 81 and 87. Joy is the fruit of virtue, Leg. All.,
III, 247; Abr., 204; Praem. Poen., 27 and 31, cf. Det. Pot. Ins., 120 f. or δικαιοσύνη,
123. χαρά and ἐλπίς come under the master concept of εὐπάθειαι in Det. Pot. Ins., 120,
cf. Leg. All., III, 86 → 366, 4 ff. χαρά can also be called the supreme εὐπάθεια, Praem.
Poen., 32. [52] The terms relate to the present and future possession of the good: τὸ μὲν
οὖν ἔχειν ἀποτελεῖ χαράν, κτημάτων τὸ κάλλιστον, τὸ δὲ σχήσειν προσδοκᾶν
τὴν τροφὴν φιλαρέτων ψυχῶν ἐλπίδα, Det. Pot. Ins., 120. The corresponding negative
concepts are λύπη (→ IV, 319, 19 ff.) and φόβος (→ 207, 29 ff.). In this def. of
relations Philo differs from Stoicism → 361, 20 ff. Isaac is the OT symbol of joy. [53]
Joy is at work already when it is proclaimed, Leg. All., III, 87, cf. ἐλπὶς χαρὰ πρὸ
χαρᾶς, Mut. Nom., 163. It is the situation of the blessed wise, Det. Pot. Ins., 135; Plant.
38. [54] Joy is def. as τέλος in Rer. Div. Her., 315. The religio-psychological description of
joy is made theological by the tracing back of joy to God. This is not just a formal
assertion from tradition. It is shown by the phenomenon itself. Its objects are, e.g., health,
freedom, honour, Leg. All., III, 86, the good and beautiful, Praem. Poen., 32, cf. Mut.
Nom., 163; Spec. Leg., II, 48. God, Praem. Poen., 32; Ebr., 62; worship. Rer. Div. Her.,
7. How these obj. relate to the fact that joy needs no point of reference may be seen from
the basic exposition in Det. Pot. Ins., 135-7. The grounds and references of joy are fundamentally non-objective. The sage knows this. He accepts the truth: ἐπεὶ οὖν ἐν τοῖς

---

45 Str.-B., I, 972 f.; Dalman WJ, I, 96 → 367, n. 69.
46 Str.-B., II, 429 and 566.
47 On Zech. 9:9 in Rabb. lit. cf. Str.-B., I, 842-4.
48 Apart from χαίρω, χαρά note esp. γέγηθα. Laughter expresses spiritual joy, Abr.,
201; the link comes out in the name Isaac.
49 Windisch, 56: "This mood of soul denotes religious experience in its purest and most
perfect form; it is esp. characteristic of Philo's view of God and the world, of his piety."
50 Ibid., 59: "Thus joy is a specifically religious mood for Philo."
51 Lewy, 34-37. Naturally the two states are not identical. χαρά denotes both a momentary
outbreak and also a lasting disposition. Intoxication, on the other hand, is by nature momentary. It also has more strongly in view the stimulus, the πνεῦμα, Lewy, 36. n. 3. χαρά
embraces every degree of intensity. Only at the highest level does it coincide with "sober
intoxication," Lewy, 37.
52 Cf. v. Arnim, 127.
53 The name Hannah, usually explained in terms of χάρις (→ 389, 20 f.), is also related
to joy in Ebr., 145 f.; γέγηθεν.
54 E. Bréhier, Les idées philosophiques et religieuses de Philon d'Alex.³ (1950), 234 f.,
254 f.; Windisch, 56 f.

τῆς ψυχῆς μόνοις ἀγαθοῖς ἡ ἀνόθευτος χαρὰ καὶ ἀκιβδήλευτος εὑρίσκεται, ἐν ἑαυτῷ δὴ πᾶς σοφὸς χαίρει, οὐκ ἐν τοῖς περὶ αὐτόν, 137. When it is shown that joy is God's gift, Leg. All., III, 219; Abr., 203 ff.; Spec. Leg., II, 53-55; Quaest. in Gn., IV, 19, even the anthropological analysis changes. This leads Philo into opposition to Stoicism even though he accepts its def. of joy as εὐπάθεια → 365, 17 ff. The Stoic sage tries to attain joy as harmony of soul [55] through his own activity. Philo advocates instead the radical ref. of even the sage away from himself. Joy is native to God alone τὸ χαίρειν μόνῳ θεῷ οἰκειότατόν ἐστιν, Abr., 202. It is found only in God, Cher., 86. [56] To know this is wisdom. Thus the understanding of wisdom is quite different from that of the Stoics → VII, 500, 7 ff. [57] This may be seen in the concept of virtue. He who has virtue has lasting joy, Mut. Nom., 167; joy is not granted to the wicked, 168-171. Virtue and wisdom are firmly linked. Wisdom fashions joy, Mut. Nom., 264. What applies to God alone, i.e., that joy is native to Him, can be transferred to the wise: σοφοῦ τὸ χαίρειν ἴδιον, Det. Pot. Ins., 138. [58] Thus the possibility of the wise transcends human possibilities. [59] How both the Gk. and the OT tradition are carried further here may be seen at the pt. of contact: What is proper to God reaches man only in mystical union with Him, Cher., 86 f.; Som., II, 249 → line 8. The ancient possibility of an ascent of the soul to God is qualitatively transcended by the thought of perfection. [60] The moment of mediation between God and man comes in the form of the Logos as the giver of joy, Som., I, 71; II, 249. Only on these presuppositions can there be the countermovement of man giving joy to God, namely, through virtues, Som., II, 178 f. God rejoices in these, not in sacrifices, for He has no needs, Spec. Leg., I, 271, cf. II, 35.

D. The New Testament.

1. Usage.

Whereas ἀγαλλιάομαι (→ I, 19, 1 ff.) is used in the biblical tradition in a religious sense, χαίρω is intrinsically a secular term. Yet it is coloured by the specific context and can be used synon. with ἀγαλλιάομαι, Rev. 19:7.

As in profane Gk. and the OT χαίρω is associated with related verbs: ἀγαλλιάομαι, Mt. 5:12; 1 Pt. 4:13; Rev. 19:7, εὐφραίνομαι, Lk. 15:32; Rev. 11:10. The part. qualifies acts in Lk.: "full of joy," Lk. 19:6 etc.; we find the acc. of inner obj. at Mt. 2:10: χαρὰν χαίρω, [61] cf. φόβον φοβέομαι, Mk. 4:41 → 209, 16 f., with dat. [62] χαρᾷ χαίρω, Jn. 3:29, cf. Is. 66:10. The obj. or reason may be indicated by the prep. ἐπί with dat., Mt. 18:13; Lk. 1:14; 13:17; Ac. 15:31; R. 16:19; 1 C. 13:6; 2 C. 7:13; Rev. 11:10, διά with acc., Jn. 3:29; 1 Th. 3:9. and ἐν, Phil. 1:18a, by ὅτι, Lk. 10:20 (twice); Jn. 11:15; 14:28;

---

[55] Sen. Ep., 6, 59, 14; Lewy, 36, n. 2.

[56] The same may be said of the Logos, Det. Pot. Ins., 129 and 131. One has to wonder that man can achieve festal joy in this sea of troubles, Spec. Leg., II, 53, cf. 52; Windisch, 56.

[57] The structural alteration affects cosmology too. Laughter must come into the world; it must be created, Det. Pot. Ins., 124. In mitigation God mixes joy into the troubles of what has come into being, Abr., 207. Genuinely Jewish motifs are used here, Mut. Nom., 169 quoting Is. 48:22; Som., II, 175 f. with Dt. 30:9 f., cf. Quaest. in Gn., IV, 138; Praem. Poen., 32 with Ps. 9:2; 32:11; 104:34; 149:2. But it is still a true innovation.

[58] Sarah laughs and is afraid she has infringed God's prerogative. But she still shares the promised joy, Abr., 204 ff. God gives what is His, Mut. Nom., 131; Windisch, 56 f.

[59] Basic here is Jonas Gnosis, II, 1, p. 38-43.

[60] One may see this from the description of the gifts the righteous receive: πίστις, χαρά, ὅρασις θεοῦ, Praem. Poen., 24-51. Lewy, 35 f.; Jonas Gnosis, II, 1, p. 70-121.

[61] Cf. Jon. 4:6, v. Bl.-Debr. § 153, 1. Cf. with attraction 1 Th. 3:9: ἐπὶ πάσῃ τῇ χαρᾷ ᾗ χαίρομεν.

[62] Bl.-Debr. § 198, 6.

2 C. 7:9, 16; Phil. 4:10; 2 Jn. 4, cf. 2 C. 13:9, or by part., Mt. 2:10; Lk. 23:8; Jn. 20:20; Ac. 11:23; Phil. 2:28; Mk. 14:11, cf. Ac. 13:48; Col. 2:5; 3 Jn. 3. [63]

The Greek formula of greeting with χαίρειν (→ 360, 27 f.) occurs in the NT only three times, Ac. 15:23; 23:26; Jm. 1:1. Use of the Greek greeting (→ 360, 16 ff.) χαῖρε (Mk. 15:18; Mt. 26:49; 27:29; Jn. 19:3) [64] raises a problem only at one point, namely, when the angel greets Mary χαῖρε κεχαριτωμένη, Lk. 1:28. Many exegetes think χαῖρε here does not mean: "Greetings," [65] but "Rejoice." [66] The deeper meaning of the statement, however, does not lie in the sense of χαίρω alone but in its association with κεχαριτωμένη → 393, 11 ff. [67] The aspect of greeting also occurs in the imperative plural, Phil. 3:1a; 4:4. [68] The specific sense of both verb and noun [69] is not to be sought in the literal meaning as such but in the material contexts in which "joy" occurs. [70]

2. The Synoptics and 1 Peter. [71]

The group is more common only in Lk. [72] There is joy at finding what is lost, Lk. 15:5-7, 9 f., 32 → VI, 492, 1 ff., or at the knowledge that one's name is written in heaven, Lk. 10:20 (→ I, 770, 1 ff.), cf. 10:17. [73] In the infancy stories in Lk. (1:14; 2:10) the dominant mood is that of joy in the sense of Hellenistic σωτήρ piety → 352, 17 ff. → VII, 1015, 20 ff. [74] But this mood persists throughout the Gospel as joy at the acts of Jesus, 13:17; 19:6. It is the mood of the people in 18:43; 19:37. Luke adds a final accent when the disciples return to Jerusalem μετὰ χαρᾶς

---

[63] Pr.-Bauer, s.v. χαίρω.

[64] Cf. 2 Jn. 10 f.: A greeting, i.e., fellowship, is not to be extended to false teachers, cf. Mt. 10:12 f. Cf. the Jewish principle that one is not to talk with false teachers. Just. Dial., 38, 1.

[65] Esp. if they think there is a basic Hbr. text.

[66] Lyonnet, 132-5, who ref. to the 4 OT texts with imp. χαῖρε, Zeph. 3:14; Jl. 2:21; Zech. 9:9; Lam. 4:21, though cf. Tob. 13:15 Cod. AB (→ 363, 29 f.), thinks χαῖρε does not correspond to the simple Hbr. "Peace" but to the intimation of Messianic joy. εἰρήνη would correspond to the Hbr. greeting. Along the same lines cf. R. Laurentin, Struktur u. Theol. d. lk. Kindheitsgeschichte (1967), 75-8. Lyonnet, 134 finds alliteration and thinks מוּחָנָה רָנִּי is the Hbr. original, cf. also H. Sahlin, "Der Messias u. d. Gottesvolk," ̔Acta Seminarii Neotest. Upsaliensis, 12 (1945), 380-2: רָנִּי חֲנִינָה.

[67] Strobel, op. cit. (→ n. 9), 86-110; 87, n. 5 Bibl. His argument that a summons to joy would demand the imp. of the aor. is not convincing in view of the OT flavour of the passage.

[68] On the imp. χαίρετε cf. Gulin, I, 171-6. Phil. 3:1a is perhaps introducing the final salutation, v. G. Friedrich, Der Br. an die Phil., NT Deutsch, 8¹² (1970), ad loc. 4:4 comes in the final salutation, esp. if 4:10 ff. is assigned to another letter, ibid. on 4:10.

[69] One finds metonymic as well at lit. use: the obj. or state of joy, e.g., Mt. 25:21, 23. Others on the basis of Rabb. usage (→ 364, 17 ff.) take χαρά here to mean "joyous festival," "feast," cf. Dalman WJ, I, 96, who compares inter al. 2 Ch. 30:23; Neh. 12:27.

[70] As God's joy, Lk. 15:7, that of Jesus, Jn. 15:11; 17:13, in connection with the Holy Spirit, Gl. 5:22 etc.

[71] Gulin, I, 101, n. 1: In Mk. we do not find joy in a soteriological context at all, in Mt. only at 18:13 and perhaps also 2:10. But Gulin's presentation of the data is not quite correct. Joyful reception of the Word in Mk. 4:16 is mission style, cf. 1 Th. 1:6. The wedding (Mk. 2:18 ff.) is a time of joy and serves as a metaphor as such. On joy at sufferings in Mt. 5:12 → 368, 14 ff.

[72] Gulin, I, 95-108; A. Harnack, Beiträge z. Einleitung in d. NT, III; Die Ag. (1908). 207-210.

[73] In contrast thaumaturgical power is disparaged.

[74] For Judaism cf. Sib., 3, 785 f. (cf. Zech. 2:14); 3, 619; 6, 20; 8, 474 f. On "great joy" as a sign of the time of salvation cf. M. Dibelius, "Jungfrauensohn u. Krippenkind," Botschaft u. Gesch., I (1953), 61 f.

μεγάλης after the ascension, 24:52. This also denotes the beginning of the age of the Church. The joy persists even when the Church is exposed to suffering → lines 6 ff. [75] Against the background of momentary terror (→ 369, 22 ff.) [76] joy is the state initiated by epiphany: ἐχάρησαν χαρὰν μεγάλην σφόδρα, Mt. 2:10. In keeping is the fact that the acts of Jesus are depicted in epiphany style. [77]

The apparently paradoxical thought of joy in suffering was developed in Judaism. [78] It takes different, though related, forms. Jm. 1:2 is in the tradition of Jewish Wisdom: πειρασμοί are a reason for joy → VI, 29, 26 ff. They are educational instruments of God and provide occasion for proving. [79] That there is a solid tradition is shown by the related 1 Pt. 1:6 f. [80] Here the general concept of suffering is given concrete shape as suffering for the faith and the testing is that of faith. [81] Suffering is given a christological basis in 1 Pt. 4:12-14. It is participation in the sufferings of Christ. [82] 1 Pt. 2:20-24 and 3:17 (cf. 4:1) develops this thought in terms of the exemplary nature of Christ's suffering. [83] The motif of "joy in suffering" is even more strongly developed as "joy at suffering" in Ac. 5:41. Unjust suffering is χάρις παρὰ θεῷ, 1 Pt. 2:20 cf. the christological continuation. The linking of joy and persecution is an established element in the NT understanding of faith, Mt. 5:11 f. and par. [84] Another component part of faith is present in 1 Pt. 4:12-14. This is the eschatological element, the hope of future δόξα. [85] The same tradition — suffering μετὰ χαρᾶς for faith's sake and with a view to imminent deliverance — is also present in another form in Hb. 10:32-39, with emphasis on the fellowship of the Church. [86]

---

[75] Gulin, I, 121 thinks that "in Ac, we seek in vain for the soteriological joy of the Third Gospel." He overlooks the specific purposes of the two books and the transferring of the salvation event into Church style. Cf. also ἀγαλλιάομαι → I, 20, 19 ff.

[76] We also find the combination of joy and terror in Orph. Hymn (Quandt), 73, 6 ff.

[77] Gulin, I, 100 f. In Aristoph. Pl., 637 f. the chorus says of the accomplished miracle: λέγεις μοι χαράν, λέγεις μοι βοάν, and Carion answers: Πάρεστι χαίρειν, ἤν τε βούλησθ' ἤν τε μή.

[78] 2 Macc. 6:30 and 4 Macc. 10:20 etc.; S. Bar. 48:48-50; 52:5-7; 54:16-18. H. W. Surkau, "Martyrien in jüd. u. frühchr. Zeit," FRL, 54 (1938); E. G. Selwyn, The First Ep. of St. Peter² (1947), 126-9, 301, 439-459; Nauck, 73-9.

[79] On the idea of proving in trial cf. Wis. 3:4-6; Test. Jos. 2:7. On 1 QH 9:24 f. → 364, 11 ff.

[80] ἀγαλλιᾶσθε is not to be taken as an imp. after the manner of v. 8 but as an ind., and strictly so, not as a future pres. ἐν ᾧ is most simply understood in a gen. way, e.g., as "on that account," Nauck, 71. The similarity between Jm. 1:2 and 1 Pt. 1:6 is not due to the literary dependence of either work on the other but to the influence of related traditions, cf. E. Lohse, "Paränese u. Kerygma im 1 Pt.," ZNW, 45 (1954), 68-89.

[81] There is a model for this variation too in Judaism, cf. 1 QS 10:17; 1 QH 9:24 f. (→ 364, 11 ff.); Jdt. 8:25.

[82] On fellowship of suffering with Christ cf. Phil. 3:10; R. 8:17; Col. 1:24 and E. Lohse, Die Br. an d. Kolosser u. an Philemon, Krit.-exeget. Komm. über d. NT, 9, 2¹⁴ (1968), ad loc.; on the relation between Christ's suffering and martyrdom cf. Lohse's "Märtyrer u. Gottesknecht," FRL, 64² (1963), 193-203; also op. cit. (→ n. 80), 82-85 and 88 f.

[83] Selwyn, op. cit., ad loc.; Bultmann Theol.⁶, 532.

[84] On the uniform style of the passage cf. Nauck, 69-73; J. Dupont, Les Béatitudes¹ (1954), 96-101, 128-141; also Les Béatitudes, I² (1958), 223-243, 244-250. The distinction of tenses is important: Mt. has the imp. pres., Lk. the aor., cf. Bl.-Debr. § 335. The aor. corresponds to the pointed addition ἐν ἐκείνῃ τῇ ἡμέρᾳ, on which there is a comment in Ac. 5:41.

[85] Materially cf. R. 8:17 ff.; S. Bar. 48:50; 52:6 f.

[86] In terms of the theme of God's pilgrim people. On the conclusion of Hb. cf. E. Käsemann, "Das wandernde Gottesvolk," FRL, 55² (1957), 8-39. In Hb. 12:11 suffering is explained in terms of παιδεία (→ V, 621, 23 ff.): This is experienced as λύπη; the positive result is disclosed later. A commonplace of antiquity is adopted here, Wnd. Hb., ad loc.

3. The Pauline Corpus.

a. Here χαρά [87] is never a profane mood. In Paul it is bound up with his work as an apostle. It is χαρὰ τῆς πίστεως, Phil. 1:25, [88] a fruit of the Spirit, Gl. 5:22. There is thus reference to the eschatological and paradoxical element in it. [89] "The kingdom of God is righteousness and peace and joy," R. 14:17 → II, 416, 10 ff. [90] The eschatological significance may also be seen in the connection with ἐλπίς, R. 12:12; 15:13 → II, 417, 11 ff. [91] The material relation between the two is brought out in R. 5:1 ff. with the help of the opposite concept of θλῖψις. [92] Joy is the actualisation of freedom, which takes concrete form in fellowship, R. 12:15. [93] The dialectic is worked out most sharply in 1 C. 7:30. Those who rejoice should be ὡς μὴ χαίροντες. [94] Joy is an essential factor in the relation between apostle and community. Paul asks the Roman church to pray that he might come with joy, R. 15:32. Joy is reciprocal, Phil. 2:28 f.; 2 C. 2:3 in contrast to λύπη. It is a matter of more than mood. In 1 Th. 3:9, with a play on εὐχαριστέω, joy is in God, and in Phil. 3:1; 4:4, 10, with the formula ἐν κυρίῳ, which has ecclesiological significance, it is in the Lord. Joy in the relation between apostle and community is eschatological. In the *parousia* the community will be manifested as the apostle's work, 1 Th. 2:19, cf. Phil. 4:1. The same thought stands behind the prologue to Phil. In Phil. 2:17 f. we find συγχαίρω alongside the simple χαίρω; this reflects the mutuality → lines 21 ff.

Phil. deserves special attention. [95] Already at the outset the "mood" is characterised by μετὰ χαρᾶς, 1:4. [96] It is given a Church basis in 1:18, growing out of the fact that Christ is proclaimed. The play between the present χαίρω and the future χαρήσομαι directs our gaze to the future judgment and the account that will have to be given, 2:16; 4:1. The point is that this joy is not just preliminary joy. It is a reference to the future experienced as joy in the present. [97] As χαρὰ πίστεως (1:25,

---

[87] Opp. λύπη, λυπέομαι, 2 C. 6:10; 7:4 ff., κλαίω, R. 12:15.

[88] Loh. Phil., *ad loc.*

[89] Cf. the context of Gl. 5:22. χαρά is in the list of virtues, with which the list of works of the flesh is contrasted. Even if the list is not arranged systematically, the proximity to εἰρήνη should be noted, cf. R. 14:17 (→ lines 4 ff.); 15:13. Cf. Is. 55:12; Philo (→ 365, 11 ff.); also Jub. 23:29; Eth. En. 5:7, 9; *v.* Bultmann J., 386, n. 5.

[90] This does not mean that God's kingdom is a spiritual entity but that the eschaton determines the present. On the eschatological meaning cf. 1 C. 6:9 and 1 C. 4:20. The addition ἐν πνεύματι ἁγίῳ characterises righteousness, peace and joy as blessings of eschatological salvation; there is no reason to relate it to joy alone.

[91] τῇ ἐλπίδι in R. 12:12 does not mean "at hope" but "in hope," cf. the par. τῇ θλίψει ὑπομένοντες, Bl.-Debr. § 196. In R. 15:13 ἐλπίς is the result of χαρά, though one may doubt whether the text should be pressed too literally.

[92] The combination of ἐλπίς and χαρά has a very different, namely, a psychological sense in Philo → 365, 23 ff.

[93] In itself the summons has the style of Jewish Wisdom, cf. Sir. 7:34 and also the Hell. version in Epict. Diss., II, 5, 23. It can be the expression of opportunism: Trim your sails according to the wind. But in the context of the understanding of the Church it is a call to positive participation in the life of the community. For Jewish materials cf. Str.-B., III, 298.

[94] On the comprehensive presentation of the eschatological relation to the world *v.* Bultmann Theol.[6], 352 f.

[95] The question of the literary unity of the epistle can be left on one side, since the word group occurs throughout.

[96] Cf. Col. 1:11. In analysis cf. Dib. Gefbr., *ad loc.* ἐπί goes with "to ask."

[97] Bultmann Theol.[6], 340. This intention is expressed indirectly in the εἴτε - εἴτε clause, Phil. 1:20 (cf. 2 C. 5:9): Salvation does not depend on Paul's human destiny. Loh. Phil. on

cf. Ac. 8:39; 13:48; Mt. 13:44) it includes within itself readiness for martyrdom; physical destruction cannot nullify it.

The paradox in joy is no other than that of the eschatological mastering of the world. χαρά is maintained in the face of θλῖψις, 2 C. 7:4-16, cf. Phlm. 7; 1 Th. 1:6; 2 C. 8:2; 6:10. [98] Paul points to the example (→ IV, 670, 1 ff.) of himself and the Lord (1 Th. 1:6 → IV, 667, 13 ff.). The word reflects the dialectic of apostolic authority (2 C. 1:24 → III, 1097, 37 ff.) and the determination of apostolic existence as worldly impotence, 2 C. 13:9.

b. There is nothing materially new in the later Pauline writings. χαίρω occurs in Col. 1:24; 2:5, χαρά in Col. 1:11; 2 Tm. 1:4. The most important aspect here is the motif of joy in suffering → 368, 6 ff.; → n. 82.

4. The Johannine Writings.

Jn. 4:36 adopts the image of harvest joy → 363, 12 ff. The point in Jn. is the simultaneity of sowers and reapers. Similar to this is adoption of the widespread theme (→ 363, 12 f.; I, 654, 25 ff.; IV, 1101, 2 ff.) of the joy of marriage, Jn. 3:29. [99] What Jn. has in view is that the ancient time has run its course and the time of joy is present with Jesus. [100] The statement that joy (sc. that of the Baptist) *is* fulfilled gives us the specific Johannine sense. Fulfilled (→ VI, 297, 28 ff.) does not mean that joy has reached a climax but that its object has appeared. [101] Throughout John's Gospel fulfilment and joy are related to the person of Jesus. In Jn. 8:56 χαίρω is distinguished from ἀγαλλιάομαι, the one being the anticipation and the other the state of fulfilment. The form of expression in 3:29 makes it likely that there is already here a reference to perfect joy (→ 365, 5 ff.), [102] which is the climax of Johannine usage, Jn. 15:11; 16:24; 17:13; 1 Jn 1:4; 2 Jn. 12. [103] In the Parting Discourses Jn. 14:28 prepares the ground for discussion of this joy. The disciples should rejoice at Jesus' death, for it means exaltation, and through it Jesus can prepare for His own dwelling with the Father. The link between the disciples and Jesus is not defined psychologically; it does not refer to His earthly person. To be sure, their λύπη is not censured. But it, too, is lifted up to the theological plane. It arises out of the change in the form of revelation. λύπη (→ IV, 321, 32 ff.) and χαρά clash (Jn. 16:20-22) and the theological function of λύπη is to show that death is not annulled but made into an act of salvation by the resurrection. The eschatological nature of this joy can be seen from its association with εἰρήνη, Jn. 14:27. [104] It is *gaudium alienum*, Jesus' joy in them, 15:11. The attribute "perfect" expresses this,

---

1:18 etc. thinks that throughout the letter joy has the special sense of joy in martyrdom. But we should start quite simply with the formal sense of "joy"; the context will then determine the specific sense.

[98] Cf. Bultmann Theol.[6], 351; on the style of 2 C. 6:10 cf. Wnd. 2 K., *ad loc.* R. 8:31 ff. exhibits the same material connection, though the term χαρά is not used.

[99] Gulin, II, 34. On the expression χαρᾷ χαίρω → 366, 30 f.; Radermacher, 128 f. Cf. the mystery call → 362, 12 ff.

[100] Though cf. Mk. 2:18-20: Now is the time of joy; then a time of sorrow follows as an intervening stage. This motif is taken up in the Parting Discourses in Jn. But it is also changed, for here the intervening time is only for a moment.

[101] Gulin, II, 34.

[102] Bultmann J., 127.

[103] *Ibid.*, 387, n. 1 and 2; Schl. J., 108 f. On Rabb. models for the expression → 365, 5 ff.

[104] Bultmann J., 386, n. 5.

cf. 16:24. The fact that this joy is attained by keeping the commandments does not mean that ethical action is the way of salvation; it is to be understood in the framework of all that is said about the commandment of love. Love is not a means to win through to eschatological existence. It is rather the leading of this life. The nature of joy is brought into relief by the cosmos. For the cosmos the λύπη of the disciples is joy (16:20) because it thinks it has triumphed by destroying Jesus. Its victory, however, is only for the moment. [105] By promise the community already has behind it the movement through λύπη to χαρά. But this is not so empirically, for the hatred of the world (→ IV, 691, 31 ff.) remains and it governs the situation of the Church in the world, 15:18 f.; 17:14. This very fact, however, shows that joy cannot be lost. The presupposition of its perfection is the very fact that it has no perceptible basis. [106] In practice joy is the possibility of prayer, which carries with it fulfilment, 16:24. [107]

E. The Post-Apostolic Fathers.

All we need do is give a few examples. "God has adorned Himself with good works and rejoiced (sc. by creating the world)." The righteous have done the same, and we ought to act according to these examples, 1 Cl., 33, 7 f.; [108] μία προσευχή, μία δέησις, εἷς νοῦς, μία ἐλπὶς ἐν ἀγάπῃ, ἐν τῇ χαρᾷ τῇ ἀμώμῳ (cf. Ign. Eph. Inscr.), ὅ ἐστιν Ἰησοῦς Χριστός, οὗ ἄμεινον οὐθέν ἐστιν, Ign. Mg., 7, 1. [109] Joy is a reward for excess good works, Herm. s., 5, 3, 3. [110]

F. Gnosticism.

There is joy at the vision of God. [111] In Gnosticism, as in the mysteries (→ 362, 11 ff.), enlightenment and vision determine joy. The new thing is the change in ontology and anthropology. Joy is no longer a state but a constituent part of man, one of the δυνάμεις that make up his nature. [112] Some instances from Chr. Mandaean and Manichaean Gnosticism may be quoted. "As the course of wrath against iniquity, so (is) the course of joy with the beloved, and it gathers their fruits unhampered. My joy is the Lord and my course is to him," O. Sol. 7:1 f., cf. 7:17; 8:1; 23:1; 31:3 par. "life," 31:6 f. "In the saints joy (comes) from their hearts and light from him that dwells in them,"

---

105 For the metaphor of joy at the birth of a child (16:21) → n. 23.

106 Bultmann J., 449: "Eschatological joy has no specific ground. It does not rejoice in anything in particular — from the standpoint of the κόσμος." Cf. Philo → 365, 28 ff.

107 Bultmann J., 450 f.: "God grants fulfilment in that He thereby confesses Jesus, His own work of revelation."

108 Cf. also χαρά par. ἀγαλλίασις, 1 Cl., 63, 2.

109 Cf. also joy in the Prescr. of Ign. Phld.

110 Cf. Herm. v., 1, 3, 4; 3, 3, 2; 12, 3; s., 1, 10.

111 The vision of the initiate is full of ἡδονή and χαρά, Mithr. Liturg., 10, 21 f., cf. also the final prayer of the Λόγος τέλειος, Preis. Zaub., I, 3, 599 f., v. Reitzenstein Hell. Myst., 285 f.; Bultmann J., 387, n. 1. We find much the same in the description of the Isis mystery in Apul. Met., XI, 24, 6.

112 χαῖρε λοιπόν, ὦ τέκνον ... ἦλθεν ἡμῖν γνῶσις χαρᾶς. παραγενομένης ταύτης, ὦ τέκνον, ἡ λύπη φεύξεται εἰς τοὺς χωροῦντας αὐτήν, Corp. Herm., 13, 8. In contrast λύπη is the second of the τιμωρίαι. Filled with joy the initiate can praise God χαίρω ἐν χαρᾷ νοῦ, 13, 18; God rejoices in hymns, Herm. Trismeg. Fr., 23, 69 in Stob. Ecl., I, 407, 11 ff. We find the revelation style of Gnosticism in Fr., 23, 29 f. 51 in Stob. Ecl., I, 393, 26 ff.; 402, 14 ff. God rejoices that His works move. With the doctrine of the δυνάμεις the structure of ethics is changed basically. Virtues are no longer qualities of the subj. They rather constitute this in such a way that it only exists in them and is rather than has salvation. The opp. is also true. Cf. A. J. Festugière, La révélation d'Hermès Trismégiste, III (1953), 153-174.

32:1. In Act. Thom. erotic symbolism and light symbolism are gnosticised, compactly in the marriage song 6 f. (p. 109, 1 - 110, 20), cf. also 14 (p. 120); 27 (142, 15 f.). The so-called Ev. Veritatis begins: "The Gospel of Truth is joy for those who have received grace from the Father of truth," Ev. Verit. [113] 16:31. From Coptic Gnostic works one may quote: "And it (sc. the all) rejoiced and exulted and bore myriads and myriads of aeons in its joy; they were called 'the births of joy,'" Ancient Anon. Gnostic Work, 2 [114] (p. 337, 23 ff.). "And he gave them praise, joy, jubilation, merriness, peace (εἰρήνη), hope (ἐλπίς), faith (πίστις), love (ἀγάπη) and unalterable truth (ἀλήθεια)," 15 (p. 357, 1 ff.).

The Mandaean works seldom speak of joy. Where it occurs it is a self-evident mark of salvation: The blessed in the world of light rejoice and leap and spring, Lidz. Liturg., 38. There is also ref. to the "great day of joy," 134. Joy is par. to life in 196, cf. O. Sol. 31:6 f. For the Manichees redemption is ascent into the ἀήρ of joy. [115]

χάρις, χαρίζομαι, χαριτόω, ἀχάριστος.

Contents: A. Profane Greek: 1. Usage; 2. Special Developments in Hellenism. B. Old Testament: 1. חָנַן and Derivates; 2. חֶסֶד. C. Judaism: 1. Qumran and Testaments of the Twelve Patriarchs; 2. Rabbinic Writings; 3. Septuagint; 4. Philo. D. New Testament: 1. Luke; 2. Paul; 3. Deutero-Pauline and Other Epistles apart from the Johannine; 4. John. E. Post-Apostolic Fathers. F. Gnosticism.

---

[113] Ed. M. Malinine et al. (1956).

[114] Transl. C. Schmidt - W. Till, Kpt.-gnost. Schriften, GCS, 45³ (1959). Further material in W. C. Till, Die gnost. Schr. d. kpt. Pap. Berolinensis 8502, TU, 60 (1955), Index, s.v. ⲣⲁϣⲉ. Cf. also the Indexes of the works mentioned → 341, n. 243-5, s.v. ⲣⲁϣⲉ or ⲣⲉϣⲉ.

[115] A Manichaean Psalm-Book, 245, ed. C. R. C. Allberry, Manichaean Manuscripts in the Chester-Beatty-Collection, II (1938), 52, 18. Cf. also Manichäische Homilien, ed. H. J. Polotsky, Manich. Hdschr. d. Sammlung Chester-Beatty, I (1934), Index, s.v. ⲣⲉϣⲉ; Kephalaia, e.g., 83 (p. 200, 27 f.); 84 (p. 205, 20; 206, 9), ed. H. J. Polotsky - A. Böhlig, Manichäische Hdschr. d. staatlichen Museen Berlin, 1 (1940).

χάρις κτλ. Bibl.: General: G. P. Wetter, "Charis," UNT, 5 (1913). On A.: O. Loew, χάρις, Diss. Marburg (1908); J. Stenzel, Review of F. Taeger, Thukydides in GGA, 188 (1926), 203 f. On B.: N. Glueck, "Das Wort hesed im at.lichen Sprachgebrauch als menschliche u. göttliche gemeinschaftsgemässe Verhaltungsweise," ZAW Beih., 47² (1962); W. F. Lofthouse, "Ḥen and Ḥesed in the OT," ZAW, 51 (1933), 29-35; L. Gulkowitsch, Die Entwicklung des Begriffes ḥāsîd im AT (1934); C. H. Dodd, The Bible and the Gks.² (1954), 59-65; J. A. Montgomery, "Hbr. hesed and Greek charis," HThR, 32 (1939), 97-102; N. H. Snaith, The Distinctive Ideas of the OT (1944), 94-130; H. J. Stoebe, Gottes hingebende Güte u. Treue חֶסֶד וֶאֱמֶת I: Bdtg. u. Gesch. d. Begriffes חֶסֶד, Diss. Münster (1950); also "Zu Js. 40:6," Wort u. Dienst, NF, 2 (1950), 122-8; also "D. Bdtg. d. Wortes ḥäsäd im AT," VT, 2 (1952), 244-254; W. L. Reed, "Some Implications of ḥen for OT Religion," JBL, 73 (1954), 36-41; A. R. Johnson, "Hesed and ḥāsîd," Festschr. S. Mowinckel (1955), 100-112; D. R. Ap-Thomas, "Some Aspects of the Root hnn in the OT," Journal of Semitic Stud., 2 (1957), 128-148; G. Farr, "The Concept of Grace in the Book of Hosea," ZAW, 70 (1958), 98-107; E. E. Flack, "The Concept of Grace in Biblical Thought," Festschr. H. C. Alleman (1960), 137-154; A. Jepsen, "Gnade u. Barmherzigkeit im AT," Kerygma u. Dogma, 7 (1961), 261-271; K. Koch, " ... denn seine Güte währet ewiglich," Ev. Theol., 21 (1961), 531-544; K. W. Neubauer, Der Stamm ch n n im Sprachgebrauch d. AT, Diss. Berlin Kirchliche Hochschule (1964); A. E. Goodman, "חסד and תורה in the Linguistic Tradition of the Psalter," Festschr. D. W. Thomas (1968), 105-115. On D.: Trench, 99-104; J. Moffatt, Grace in the NT (1931); W. Manson, "Grace in the NT," in The Doctrine of Grace, ed. W. T. Whitley (1932), 33-60; A. Lang, "Die Gnade in d. joh. Schriften," Christentum u. Wissenschaft, 8 (1932), 408-414; J. Wobbe, "Der Charis-Gedanke bei Pls.," NTAbh., 13, 3 (1932);

A. Profane Greek.

1. Usage.

a. The basis of the usage is the relation to χαίρω.[1] χάρις is what delights[2] ναυσιφορήτοις δ' ἀνδράσι πρῶτα χάρις ἐς πλόον ἀρχομένοις πομπαῖον ἐλθεῖν οὖρον (favourable wind), Pind. Pyth., 1, 33 f.; ὄλωλα, τέκνον, οὐδέ μοι χάρις βίου, "life has no more charm for me," Eur. Hipp., 1408. It may be a state causing joy or an act accompanying it → 360, 29 ff. On χαίρω and χάρις[3] cf. Eur. Ion, 646 f.; ἔα δ' ἔμ' αὐτοῦ ζῆν· ἴση γὰρ ἡ χάρις, μεγάλοισι χαίρειν σμικρά θ' ἡδέως ἔχειν, Hippocr. De aere aquis locis, 22 (CMG, I, 1, p. 75, 8 ff.): τιμώμενοι χαίρουσιν οἱ θεοὶ καὶ θαυμαζόμενοι ὑπ' ἀνθρώπων καὶ ἀντὶ τουτέων χάριτας ἀποδιδοῦσιν. Here one may see the typical motif of response. In χάρις the specifically Gk. relation to the world comes into view. It is joyous being, "charm,"[4] understood not in terms of the beautiful but of the element of the delightful in the beautiful, Aesch. Ag., 417, cf. 421 f.; Plat. Leg., II, 667b-d; it is the happy state, the "favour" of fortune, Aesch. Ag., 484, the charming element in pers., Eur. Ba., 236 → line 18; cf. also Plut. Amat., 5 (II, 751d): χάρις ... ἡ τοῦ θήλεος ὕπειξις τῷ ἄρρενι κέκληται πρὸς τῶν παλαιῶν. In Hell. χάρις is the magic of love (→ 376, 8 f.), Luc. Alex., 5, cf. Preisigke Sammelb., I, 4324, 7 f. The use is similar in the plur.: οἰνῶπας ὅσσοις χάριτας Ἀφροδίτης ἔχων, Eur. Ba., 236, of words, Hom. Od., 8, 175; Demosth. Or., 4, 38. Here, too, the element of the pleasing is the starting-pt., e.g., Plat. Gorg., 462c, where χάρις is used with ἡδονή. χάρις as an effect is favour shown and received, the showing and receiving being seen together χάρις χάριν γάρ ἐστιν ἡ τίκτουσ' ἀεί, Soph. Ai., 522, cf. Oed. Col., 779; Eur. Herc. Fur., 134; Aristot. Rhet., II, 7, p. 1385a, 16. The same holds true of the gods, Hippocr. De aere aquis locis, 22 (CMG, I, 1, p. 75, 8 ff. → lines 9 f.), cf. Ditt. Syll.[3], II, 708, 25, 30 f. (c. 100 B.C.). χάρις can be a mood or emotion, e.g., "sympathy," (→ 374, 22 ff.)[5] plus its expression in gestures and deeds, "kindness," Hom. Od., 5, 307, cf. χαρίζομαι (→ 375, 4 ff.), Plat. Tim., 20b, with obj. gen. "out of kindness to" ... τῶν Μεσσηνίων χάριτι πεισθείς, Thuc., III, 95, 1. As kindness χάρις is an act that causes pleasure μίαν δὲ νῷν δὸς χάριν, ἄναξ, ἱκνούμεθα, Eur. Herc. Fur., 321, cf. 327. There is a political ref. in Pericles' speech in Thuc., II, 40, 4:[6] The χάρις of Athens to other states by its concession becomes an ὀφείλημα. Even when the ref. is to the χάρις of the gods, this is seen in terms of its obj. gladdening effect, Aesch. Ag., 182; 581. Related verbs are

---

R. Winkler, "Die Gnade im NT," ZSTh, 10 (1933), 642-680; R. Homann, "Der Begriff d. Gnade in d. synpt. Ev.," ZSTh, 11 (1934), 328-348; Bultmann Theol.[6] 281-305 and Index, s.v. "Gnade" and χάρις; C. R. Smith, The Bible Doctrine of Grace (1956); W. Grundmann, "Die Übermacht d. Gnade," Nov. Test., 2 (1958), 50-72. On E.: A. Harnack, "'Sanftmut, Huld u. Demut' in d. alten Kirche," Festschr. J. Kaftan (1920), 113-129; N. Bonwetsch, "Zur Geschichte d. Begriffs Gnade in d. alten Kirche," Festschr. A. Harnack (1921), 93-101; W. Roslan, "Die Grundbegriffe d. Gnade nach d. Lehre d. Apost. Väter," Theol. Quart., 119 (1938), 200-225, 275-317, 470-503; T. F. Torrance, The Doctrine of Grace in the Apostolic Fathers (1948).

[1] On the etym. → 360, n. 3, though forms with -ι- or -ιτ- (gen. χάριτος, acc. χάριν and χάριτα) are singular [Risch]. The mixture of the dental and vocal stem in χάριν and ἔριν is ancient, Schwyzer, I, 464; Bl.-Debr. § 47, 3. The NT mostly has χάριν, but χάριτα at Ac. 24:27 Cod. B et al.; Jd. 4.

[2] χάρις thus has trans. significance. "Merriness" is χαρά, Loew., 32.

[3] Cf. Hesych., s.v. χάρις, δωρεάς.

[4] The word is associated with similar terms, e.g., κάλλος, Hom. Od., 6, 237; Sir. 40:22, κόσμος, Plut. De Demosthene, 7 (I, 849b). Opp. is λύπη, Soph. El., 821; Tob. 7:17. Charm is, of course, fleeting: ἐρωτηθεὶς τί τάχιστα γηράσκει εἶπε (sc. Aristot.) "χάρις," Gnomologium Vaticanum, ed. L. Sternbach, Texte u. Komm., 2 (1963), No. 138.

[5] It occurs with εὔνοια in Plat. Leg., XI, 931a, πραότης, Plut. Col., 2 (II, 1108b), ἐπιείκεια, Isoc. Or., 4, 63, ἔπαινος, Plut. Adulat., 11 (II, 55b). The opp. is ἔχθρα, Demosth. Or., 19, 85, ὀργή, 19, 91, φόβος, Thuc., I, 9, 3.

[6] Stenzel, 204.

δίδωμι, Aesch. Prom., 821 f.; Eur. Herc. Fur., 321; Menand. Epit., 55, ἀποδίδωμι, Ditt. Syll.³, III, 1268, Col. 1, 14 (3rd cent. B.C.), φέρω, Hom. Il., 5, 211, from the standpt. of the recipient ἐξαιτέομαι, Soph. Oed. Col., 586, λαμβάνω, Soph. Oed. Tyr., 1004, εὑρίσκω in the LXX → 389, 3. The element of reciprocity leads to the senses of demonstration due with ὀφείλω, Aesch. Prom., 985 and demonstration achieved, "thanks," Soph. Ant., 331, cf. the expression τοῖς θεοῖς χάρις, Xenoph. An., III, 3, 14. This is not a primary sense but derives from the idea of gratia reddita: φιλότητος ἀμειβόμεναι χάριν, Soph. El., 134; τὴν ἀμοιβὴν τῆς πρὸς τοὺς εὐεργέτας χάριτος, Diod. S., 1, 90, 2. There is play on the two senses of gift and thanks in Soph. Oed. Col., 779; Al., 522, while the idea of reciprocity occurs in Aristot. Eth. Nic., V, 8, p. 1133a, 3-5. Voluntariness can also be stressed, Aristot. Rhet., II, 7, p. 1385a, 17 ff. → lines 29 ff. This sense is also expressed in the associated verbs: χάριν ἔχω "to stand in favour," Eur. Or., 244 and "to thank," Xenoph. An., II, 5, 14; in the epistolary expression χάριν ἔχω θεοῖς πᾶσιν, P. Oxy., I, 113, 13 (2nd cent. A.D.), [7] often οἶδα e.g., Hdt., III, 21, 3, [8] γιγνώσκω, Philostr. Vit. Ap., II, 17 (p. 60, 5), ἀποδίδωμι, Plat. Resp., I, 338b, popularly of the piety due: The one who dies young cannot show his parents the thanks due, he died οὐδὲ γονεῦσιν ἑοῖς ἀποδοὺς χάριν, Gr., VI, I, 1822, 7 (2nd cent. B.C.). [9] Prepos. phrases are ἐς χάριν, Soph. Oed. Tyr., 1353, πρὸς χάριν, with πράσσω, Soph. Oed. Col., 1774 ff., with λέγω, Eur. Hec., 257. χάριν with gen. means "for the sake of," [10] "to oblige someone," μηδὲ ψεύδεσθαι γλώσσης χάριν, Hes. Op., 709, "for the tongue's sake," "out of consideration for it"; "out of regard for," "on account of."

The word is widely used in the class. age. χάρις is the "favour" of the gods in Aesch. Ag., 182, 581. [11] It is very common in Eur., e.g., Ba., 534-6, [12] in prose, Plat. Leg., VII, 796c; VIII, 844d. Though there is ref. to the favour of the gods χάρις is not a key religious term → n. 11. Nor is it a philosophical term, cf. Plat.; thus it means "goodpleasure" in Gorg., 462c; Soph., 222e, "favour," "good-will," Symp., 183b, "joy," "pleasure," Phaedr., 254a, "what pleases" (the gods), Leg., VII, 976c "favour," Leg., VIII, 844d, "thanks" χάριν ἔχω, Phileb., 54d; cf. the verb χαρίζομαι → 375, 4 ff. Aristot. then defines the term, Rhet., II, 7, p. 1385a, 17 ff.: ἔστω δὴ χάρις, καθ' ἣν ὁ ἔχων λέγεται χάριν ὑπουργεῖν δεομένῳ μὴ ἀντί τινός, μηδ' ἵνα τι αὐτῷ τῷ ὑπουργοῦντι, ἀλλ' ἵνα ἐκείνῳ τι, cf. Eth. Nic., V, 8, p. 1132b, 21 ff. [13] The Stoic Cleanthes is said to have written a work περὶ χάριτος, Diog. L., VII, 175. [14] Stoicism stresses the disposition: itaque negamus quemquam scire gratiam referre nisi sapientem: non magis quam beneficium dare quisquam scit nisi sapiens, Sen. Ep., 10, 81, 10. But the basic aesthetic sense persists even in ethics: χάρις adds to ἀρετή only what καλός does to ἀγαθός. [15]

---

[7] Cf. Preisigke Wört., s.v. χάρις. Cf. Hb. 12:28.

[8] "To be thankful" is not quite the sense, since χάρις received rather than rendered is in the mind of the Gk., thus: scio gratum mihi factum esse, Loew, 9. The reason can be put in the gen., Xenoph. Cyrop., I, 6, 11 or the dat., Plut. Alex., 62 (I, 699 f.) or the part. σωθέντες, Xenoph. An., II, 5, 14.

[9] Cf. W. Peek, Griech. Grabgedichte (1960), 160, 7. Cf. Gr., VI, I, 1680, 10 (3rd/2nd cent. B.C.; Peek, 163, 10). The deceased cheats his parents out of the reward for their proofs of affection; he lies in the grave τὰς γονέων ψευσάμενος χάριτας, Gr., VI, I, 1584, 4 (2nd/1st cent. B.C.; Peek, 211, 4).

[10] Schwyzer, II, 551 f.: χάριν is origin. appos. "as kindness," cf. gratia; κακῆς γυναικὸς χάριν ἄχαριν ἀπώλετο, Eur. Iph. Taur., 566.

[11] The motif of the favour of the gods must be seen alongside the idea of divine righteousness, cf. H. Patzer, Die Anfänge d. griech. Tragödie (1962), 169.

[12] Cf. Moffatt, 27 on this.

[13] A. Dihle, "Die Goldene Regel," Studienhefte z. Altertumswissenschaft, 7 (1962), 66, n. 3.

[14] There are fr. of this in Sen. Ben., VI, 12, 2; 10, 2; V, 14, 1. Chrysipp. writes περὶ χαρίτων, cf. v. Arnim, III, 205, 27 ff. and the list of fr. from this. On charis in Stoicism cf. M. Pohlenz, Die Stoa, I³ (1964), 141; on the broader tradition to Sen. Ben., cf. Pohlenz, I, 317 f.

[15] Stenzel, 203.

In the hermeneutics of historiography χάρις and ἀπέχθεια are motifs which can cause the historian to garble the facts, Luc. Quomodo historia sit conscribenda, 38. [16] They correspond to *studium* and *ira* in the famous assertion in Tac. Ann., I, 1, 3.

b. The verb χαρίζομαι is def. in terms of the noun: "to show pleasure," "to show oneself to be pleasant" in word or deed, Hom. Od., 14, 387; Ditt. Syll.[3], I, 354, 5 (3rd cent. B.C.); Diod. S., 14, 11, 1; Jos. Ant., 17, 222. It takes the dat. [17] of pers., e.g., τοῖς θεοῖς, Xenoph. Mem., IV, 3, 16, cf. Cyrop., III, 2, 29, the acc. of obj., e.g., δῶρα Hom. Od., 24, 283. In the pass. it means "to be agreeable," esp. in the perf.: κεχάριστο δὲ θυμῷ, Hom. Od., 6, 23, so esp. the perf. part. of a pers.: ἐμῷ κεχαρισμένε θυμῷ, Hom. Il., 5, 243, things: κεχαρισμένα δ᾿ αἰεὶ δῶρα θεοῖσι δίδωσι, 20, 298 f., cf. Plat. Euthyphr. 14b. [18]

c. χαριτόω is not found prior to LXX Sir. 18:17.

d. ἀχάριστος means "without charm," of words, Xenoph., An., II, 1, 13; it also means "ungrateful," Hdt., I, 90, 4. [19]

2. Special Developments in Hellenism.

a. The development in later antiquity, [20] which is important for the NT, is along two lines. [21] χάρις is a fixed term for demonstrations of a ruler's favour, often used in inscr.: τῆι τοῦ θεοῦ Κλαυδίου χάριτι, edict of Tiberius Alexander, Ditt. Or., II, 669, 28 f. (68 A.D.), cf. in relation to emperor worship Ditt. Syll.[3], II, 798, 8 ff. (age of Caligula): οὗτοι δ᾿ ἐ(κ) τῆς Γαΐου Καίσαρος χάριτος εἰς συναρχίαν τηλικούτων θεῶν γεγόνασι βασιλεῖς, θεῶν δὲ χάριτες τούτῳ διαφέρουσιν ἀνθρωπίνων διαδοχῶν ᾧ ἡ νυκτὸς ἥλιος καὶ τὸ ἄφθαρτον θνητῆς φύσεως, cf. also *ibid.*, II, 814, 17 ff. (speech of Nero). Mostly we have the pir. in the concrete sense of "gift," with δωρεαί, *ibid.*, II, 814, 18 f. In the sing. χάρις can also mean "gracious disposition," with φιλανθρωπία → 108, 3 ff. Ditt. Or., I, 139, 20 f. (2nd cent. B.C.), but demonstration can also be stressed, cf. ἔργα χάριτος, *ibid.*, I, 383, 9 (1st cent. B.C.). χάρις as "gracious gift" is distinguished from εὔνοια in Ditt. Syll.[3], II, 814, 20 ff. The ethical sense naturally persists in later antiquity. In Plut. we find the word with πραότης, Col., 2 (II, 1108b), εὔνοια, Adulat., 34 (II, 72 f.); De Romulo, 15 (I, 26b); De amicorum multitudine, 2 (II, 93 f.), φιλία, De Lycurgo, 4 (I, 41c). It is also used of other dignitaries, as in the inscr. in honour of the prefect of Egypt, Ditt. Or., II, 666, 7 f. (age of Nero): διὰ δὲ τὰς τούτου χάριτας καὶ εὐεργεσίας, line 21: τὰς ἰσοθέους αὐτοῦ χάριτας. A special use is for the showing of grace in court. In P. Flor., I, 61, 61 f. (c. 87 A.D.) is as follows: χαρίζομαι δέ σε τοῖς ὄχλοις (sc. for decision). [22] In pagan martyrology [23] we read: καὶ τοῦτο ἡμῖν χάρ[ισ]αι, Κύριε Καῖσαρ, P. Oxy., I, 33, Col. 2, 15 f. (2nd cent. A.D.). Naturally the inscr. do not speak of the "grace" of God but we find this in philosophy, Epict. Diss., I, 16, 15. The philosophical schools debate

---

[16] G. Avenarius, *Lukians Schr. z. Geschichtsschreibung* (1956), 49-54.
[17] On the dat. with verbs of friendly or hostile attitudes and their expression cf. Schwyzer, II, 144 f.
[18] Pass in the NT: 1 C. 2:12; Phlm. 22; Ac. 3:14; *v.* Bl.-Debr. § 311, 2.
[19] The verb ἀχαριστέω occurs in Ditt. Syll.[3], I, 495, 159 (c. 230 B.C.), in a magical context τοὺς δὲ ἀπαλλαγέντας καὶ ἀχαριστήσαντα[ς], BGU, IV, 1026, 22, 16 (4th cent. A.D.).
[20] Wetter, *passim;* Moffatt, 52-67.
[21] The technical use of χάρις for "deed of gift," e.g., εἰς ἕτερόν τι δαπανῆσ[εσ]θαι τὴν χάριν "to use the deed of gift for another purpose," P. Oxy., IV, 705, 63 (c. 200 A.D.) may be disregarded here.
[22] Cf. Mk.15:15; *v.* Deissmann LO, 229.
[23] Cf. H. Musurillo, Acta Alexandrinorum (1961), 54.

God's *ira* and *gratia* (→ V, 389, 14 ff.), cf. Lact. De ira dei, 2, 7 f.; 4, 1-5, 7. The Epicureans contest both, *neque ira neque gratia teneri,* Cic. Nat. Deor., I, 17, 45. The Stoics, however, ascribe *gratia* to God but not *ira,* Lact. De ira dei, 2, 8. In relation to the recipient of grace χάρις means "thanks" to the benefactor; the principle of appropriateness applies χάριτας ἀξίας ἀποδιδόναι τοῖς εἰς [αὐ]τοὺς εὐεργετοῦσι, Ditt. Syll.³, II, 613, 36 f. (c. 185 B.C.).

b. The second development is that χάρις becomes power in a substantial sense. 24 Naturally a "power" dwells in χάρις from the outset 25 and this is a supernatural power, that of love, Eur. Hipp., 527, or the oath, Eur. Med., 439. In Hell., however, there is a radical change in the concept of power. 26 It is now a potency that streams down from the world above, a religious quality, Corp. Herm., 1, 32; 13, 12; Ascl., 41. 27 It appears in the θεῖος ἀνήρ 28 and expresses itself in magic. 29

Conzelmann

B. Old Testament.

The LXX (→ 389, 1 ff.) uses χάρις esp. for Hbr. חֵן.

1. חנן and Derivates.

a. The noun חֵן as an inf. substantive of the form qill derives from the verb חנן. 30 If an attempt has been made 31 to derive חנן as a denomin. verb from an original חֵן, this hardly does justice to the broad and early spread of the verbal stem, with no corresponding spread of the noun חֵן. The verbal stem is attested as ḫanānu in Middle and New Babylonian 32 and as enēnu(m) (enānum) in Ancient Accadian, Ancient and Later Babylonian, and Ancient Assyrian, in the sense "to grant favour." 33 In the El-Amarna texts 34 Rib-Addi of Byblos writes to Pharaoh: "If the king, my lord, has mercy on me (yi-iḫ-na-nu-ni) and brings me back to the city, I will protect it as formerly," Tabl., 137, 81 ff. and in a piece written

---

24 Wetter, 40-46 gives an account of the development.

25 Moffatt, 21-9, who thinks that from the very first χάρις has a chthonic aspect, 29. This would explain why χάρις, "favour" from a supernatural source, could acquire the specific religious sense midway between force and magic. He ref. to Aesch. Sept. c. Theb., 702 f.; Soph. Oed. Col., 1751 f.; Eur. Heracl., 1036 f. But the qualitative change in thinking is missed here.

26 This is a comprehensive change and may be seen in other terms, e.g., πνεῦμα (→ VI, 351, 8 ff. etc.), δόξα (→ II, 252, 1 ff.) and all manifestation words. The analogous change in concepts of form, μορφή (→ IV, 742, 1 ff.), σχῆμα (→ VII, 954, 1 ff.), εἰκών (→ II, 388, 27 ff.) etc., should also be noted. There is a veritable revolution not merely in thought and world-view but also in the presuppositions of the world-view. Gk. ontological categories are set aside, as may be seen most clearly in Gnosticism. On Philo cf. Wetter, 46. Cf. the relation of grace or goodness in O. Sol. 33 to γνῶσις in Corp. Herm., 1, 26; 13, 8, νοῦς, *ibid.,* 4, 2 f., Wetter, 111.

27 Moffatt, 52-5.

28 L. Bieler, ΘΕΙΟΣ ANHP, 1 (1935), 52-6. χάρις finds expression in the beauty of the θεῖος ἀνήρ, Porphyr. Vit. Pyth., 18, cf. already Hom. Od., 6, 235 f. It may also be seen in speech, Luc. Demon., 6, cf. Philostr. Vit. Ap., V, 37 (p. 198, 26 f.). We find related motifs in Chr. lit., Prot. Ev. Jc. 7:3; Act. Pl. et Thecl. 3, cf. Bieler, 50-52.

29 δός μοι πᾶσαν χάριν, πᾶσαν πρᾶξιν (→ VI, 643, 1 f.), Preis. Zaub., I, 4, 3165; δὸς δόξαν (→ II, 252, 1 ff.) καὶ χάριν, 4, 1650. Cf. also 4, 198. 1616 f., 2437 ff. and the examples in Wetter, 131-140.

30 H. Bauer - P. Leander, *Histor. Grammatik d. hbr. Sprache d. AT* (1922) § 61d.

31 W. J. Gerber, *Die hbr. Verba denominativa, insbes. im theol. Sprachgebrauch d. AT* (1896), 207.

32 B. Meissner - W. v. Soden, *Akkad. Handwörterbuch,* I (1965), *s.v.* ḫanānu.

33 *Ibid., s.v.* enēnum, I.

34 Ed. J. A. Knudtzon, *Vorderasiat. Bibliothek,* 2, 1 (1915).

by Labaya protesting his innocence to Pharaoh we read similarly: "May the king be gracious (yi-en-ni-nu-nu-mi) to us," Tabl., 253, 24 f. The verb is also found in Ugaritic, Aram., Syr. and Arab. [35]

b. In the basic stem [36] the verb חנן occurs 56 times [37] and denotes the kind turning of one person to another as expressed in an act of assistance. The root meaning "to stoop," "to be inclined" has been conjectured. [38] But חנן does not just denote the kind disposition and then the outer act as something detached from the inner mood. It rather means the attitude of a person in its direction to another in a specific gracious action. [39] This may be seen plainly, e.g., when the gift which manifests the movement is put in a constr. with double acc. and no further prepos. with acc. Thus in Gn. 33:5 (E) Yahweh has been gracious to Jacob in giving him children. Acc. to Ps. 119:29 Yahweh is gracious with the Law. [40]

Usually, of course, חנן is simply construed with acc. of the person to whom it applies. This shows the thrust of the verb; it expresses gracious address to another. Only on the margin do we find an impersonal obj., as in Ps. 102:14, where the servants of Yahweh "love" רצה the stones of Zion and there is sorrow חנן po'el at the dust of Jerusalem. [41] It has been heavily underlined that in the development of חנן the obj., the recipient of the act, is decisively included as well as the subj.; חנן replies to a need, a question. Thus it can be replaced by ענה "to answer." [42] What is in view is the process whereby one who has something turns in grace to another who has nothing, nor is this just an impersonal transfer of things, but a heart-felt movement of the one who acts to the one acted upon.

Initially חנן is not a theological term. In the Wisdom field esp. the one in view is man having mercy on the poor אֶבְיוֹן, Prv. 14:31, and lowly דָּל, 28:8, by giving נוֹתֵן, Ps. 37:21 or lending מַלְוֶה, Ps. 37:26; 112:5, cf. Prv. 19:17. One also finds חנן in war when the armed man encounters the defenceless. [43] This "sparing" of the weak takes permanent form when a covenant is made with those who are overthrown, Dt. 7:2. חנן is also demanded by Job when, smitten by God, he is pressured by his friends, Job 19:21. More weakly חנן can also be used to denote friendly speech, Prv. 26:25.

c. The verb undergoes its true development, of course, when it is related to statements about God. In 41 of the 56 occurrences of the basic stem in the OT canon Yahweh is the subject of the saying. 26 of these instances are in Ps. where חָנֵּנִי is found no less than 19 times in prayers of complaint. [44] Yahweh, who is often

---

[35] Neubauer, 5-9 with n. 23-45.

[36] On the hitp → 379, 5 ff. We find the ho at Is. 26:10 and Prv. 21:10, the pi at Prv. 26:25, the po'el at Ps. 102:14 and Prv. 14:21. The apparent ni in Jer. 22:23 is a mistake in the text.

[37] In LXX חנן q is 43 times transl. by ἐλεέω or ἐλεάω, 10 by οἰκτ(ε)ίρω and once each by δέομαι, Mal. 1:9 and προσκαλέομαι, Job 19:17; one also finds ἀνθέξεται in the very free rendering of Job 33:24.

[38] Ges.-Buhl, s.v.; Ap-Thomas, 128-130.

[39] The more developed thesis of Neubauer, 55 that in its main early sense ch n n expresses an obligation of the lord in the form of social dealings with his servant introduces an element alien to the verb חנן by its stress on obligation.

[40] We may thus ask whether אוֹתָם (masc.) should not be left at Ju. 21:22 and the statement thus taken to mean that the inhabitants of Shiloh, robbed of their daughters, should be gracious to the men of Benjamin by letting them have them.

[41] Here it might seem at a first glance that חנן simply ref. to an inner feeling. The helpful act is then expected from Yahweh acc. to v. 16. But then in v. 17 we see that the men grieved by the need of Jerusalem help to turn the fate of Zion by more than an emotion, i.e., by their intercession, cf. also Job 33:24.

[42] Stoebe ḥäsäd, 245 and n. 4.

[43] Cf. the negative statements in Dt. 28:50; Lam. 4:16.

[44] Ps. 9:13 is to be read thus. Cf. the double חָנֵּנוּ of Ps. 123:3.

expressly named in the prayers, [45] is called upon to hear the prayer 4:1, to heal 6:2; 41:4, to look upon the plight of the petitioner in the face of his foes 9:13, to redeem him 26:11, to set him up 41:10, to pardon his sins 51:1, to grant strength to his servant 86:16. The reason adduced for the request may be the weakness of the petitioner 6:2, his loneliness 25:16, his affliction 31:9; 123:3, his crying 86:3 and also his keeping of the commandments 26:11. In the first group of reasons we see the assurance of OT faith that Yahweh always loves especially to turn to the weak and lost. The specifically OT form of this cry for help, for which there are rich parallels in the prayers of all nations, is to be seen when the petitioner appeals to the grace of the covenant [46] or to Yahweh's own Word. [47] It is against this background that the blessing of the priest when he prays for the gracious intervention of Yahweh acquires its true significance. If in Joseph's saying to Benjamin "God be gracious unto thee, my son" (Gn. 43:29), we seem to have a more general and common blessing, the blessing of Aaron (Nu. 6:25), [48] in which the name of Yahweh is put upon the people (v. 27), refers to the gracious will of Yahweh, who has pledged Himself to His people in His special covenant. But this graciousness is always God's free gift, as is said with almost offensive severity in the word to Moses, the mediator of the covenant: "I am gracious to whom I am gracious, and have mercy on whom I have mercy," Ex. 33:19. [49] Here as often (Is. 30:18; 27:11, cf. also Ps. 102:13) we find חנן alongside the related רחם. That Yahweh's mercy may also be associated with judgment is to be seen at Am. 5:15, where as the last conceivable possibility of mercy we find the graciousness of Yahweh to the "remnant of Joseph." It is striking, however, that apart from this passage there is no mention at all of חנן in the great writing prophets and their declarations of overthrow and salvation. [50]

The significance of what is said about Yahweh's graciousness for OT faith may also be seen from the important predication חַנּוּן וְרַחוּם, [51] which is so at home in liturgical use. In this rhyming construction, which again combines חנן and רחם, we have one of the comparatively rare adjectival predications of Yahweh. In keeping with the meanings of חנן and רחם, it is to be understood as a statement about Yahweh's acts rather than His being. In comparison with the 11 instances of the double formula [52] there are only two with חַנּוּן alone. [53] Apart from Ps. 112:4 [54] the

---

[45] The proper name יהוה occurs in Ps. 6:2; 9:13; 30:10; 31:9; 41:4, 10; 123:3, אֱלֹהִים in 51:1; 56:1; 57:1, אֲדֹנָי in 86:3.

[46] כְּחַסְדֶּךָ in Ps. 51:1 → 384, 20.

[47] כְּאִמְרָתֶךָ in Ps. 119:58. 2 K. 13:23 ref. openly to Yahweh's mercy for the sake of His covenant with the fathers.

[48] It is echoed in Ps. 67:1.

[49] Hence it is as well not to relate חנן in its theological significance quite so closely with the covenant as Neubauer does, 145: "The stem ch n n in both its theological and also its secular use expresses the social attitude of the lord to his faithful servant." Cf. also → n. 39.

[50] It is in the q at Is. 27:11; 30:18 f.; 33:2, the ho in a secondary sense at 26:10. Jer. 22:23 is a textual error. The hitp occurs in Hos. 12:5 → 379, 12. We find it in a late offshoot of prophecy at Mal. 1:9.

[51] The order of the words can also be reversed.

[52] Ex. 34:6; Jl. 2:13; Jon. 4:2; Ps. 86:15; 103:8; 111:4; 112:4; 145:8; Neh. 9:17, 31; 2 Ch. 30:9.

[53] Ex. 22:26; Ps. 116:5. In the latter v. one may easily see in the ensuing מְרַחֵם an echo of the corresponding רחום.

[54] The use of the formula for the righteous here may perhaps be explained in terms of the borrowing of Ps. 112 from Ps. 111, cf. 112:3b with 111:3b, also 112:8a with 111:8a. Cf. W. Zimmerli, "Zwillingspsalmen," Festschr. J. Ziegler (1972).

reference is always to God. The formula finds its true locus in liturgical description and praise of Yahweh. We thus find it in the very solemn proclamation of Yahweh's name in the events at the making of the covenant at Sinai, Ex. 34:6. The passage might be regarded as the aetiology of a liturgical event in the sanctuary.

d. Along with the basic stem of חנן we esp. find the hitp with 17 examples. [55] This better describes the action of him who utters the חִנְנִי. Here again it is to be noted that the verb is by no means restricted to the religious sphere. It tells how Joseph besought his brethren in his need, Gn. 42:21, or how the threatened captain besought Elisha, 2 K. 1:13, or how the sick Job besought his servants, Job 19:16, or how Esther made her request to the king, Est. 4:8; 8:3. There is also a group of passages which speak of beseeching Yahweh. Moses asks Him that he might see the land, Dt. 3:23. In connection with the dedication of Solomon's temple there are many such references, 1 K. 8:33, 47, 59; 9:3; 2 Ch. 6:24, 37. We also read of Jacob's supplication in Hos. 12:4 and that of the psalmist in Ps. 30:8; 142:2. Prayer can be denoted by this verb.

e. Two nouns with t-prefix are then to be construed in terms of the hitp of חנן. [56] The replacement of תְּחִנַּת עַבְדְּךָ in 1 K. 8:30 by תַּחֲנוּנֵי עַבְדְּךָ in the par. 2 Ch. 6:21 shows that תַּחֲנוּנִים was more common later. But it also shows that at a later time the two words were taken to have the same sense. The words also show how freely the reference might be to beseeching men on the one side or God on the other. The story of Baruch can describe both Jer.'s request to Zedekiah and also the prayer of the people to God as תְּחִנָּה, cf. Jer. 37:20; 38:26 with 36:7. תַּחֲנוּנִים can also be used for the supplication of the poor to the hard-hearted rich, Prv. 18:23, while elsewhere, esp. in the Ps., it denotes prayer to Yahweh, Ps. 28:2, 6; 31:22 etc.

It should be recognised, of course, that תְּחִנָּה can also be used for the "mercy" of the conqueror on the conquered (Jos. 11:20) and for that of Yahweh on His people (Ezr. 9:8). It thus provides the hitherto missing substantive for the basic stem of חנן. Once at Jer. 16:13 we find in the same sense a word for grace or mercy not attested anywhere else, namely, חֲנִינָה. In an important noun formulation נתן חֲנִינָה represents here the simpler חנן.

f. One would primarily expect to find a noun equivalent to the verbal חנן in the inf. חֵן as noun → 376, 16 f. In analogy to the נתן חֲנִינָה of Jer. 16:13 the expression נתן חֵן seems a natural one. As a fuller development of חנן it would appear to express in noun form the gracious action stated in terms of a subj. with reference to the recipient. Now נתן חֵן does in fact occur several times, Gn. 39:21; Ex. 3:21; 11:3; 12:36; Ps. 84:11; Prv. 3:34; 13:15. Closer examination, however, leads to the surprising conclusion that the phrase does not have the same ref. as the נתן חֲנִינָה of Jer. 16:13 and is connected with a different development of חֵן as compared with חֲנִינָה. If חֲנִינָה remains under the influence of the verb חנן and indicates the gracious act from the standpt. of the giver, thus carrying a ref. to the giver, חֵן manifests a wholly astonishing detachment from the giver and his gracious act and relates the value established thereby to the recipient. [57] חֵן is the "gracefulness" of the one gifted with חֵן. Often with a strong aesthetic emphasis, it denotes his "beauty" or "charm." Thus Yahweh will give the departing Israelites "attractiveness" in the eyes

---

[55] LXX has (κατα-) δέομαι for the hitp, in 'Εσθ. παραιτέομαι at 4:8 and ἀξιόω at 8:3.

[56] Cf. Bauer-Leander, op. cit. (→ n. 30) § 61nη; χη.

[57] This shift in the structure of חֵן compared with the verb formulation is often overlooked in discussions of חֵן. cf. Snaith, 94-130; Reed, 36-41.

of the Egyptians so that these will give them costly equipment for the exodus, Ex. 3:21; 11:3; 12:36. Ps. 84:11 says that Yahweh will give His people grace and glory. As כָּבוֹד denotes the *gravitas* of man, his distinctive dignity and worth, חֵן is the "pleasantness" which others perceive in him. If in Prv. 3:34 one sees more of the older relation between rich giver and poor recipient such as is typical of the verb חנן, and if here Yahweh gives חֵן specifically to the poor, it is evident that what is in view in Prv. 13:15 is a good that distinguishes man and inheres in him when we are told that a good understanding brings "favour." This aspect is very plain in Gn. 39:21, the one v. that has חֵן with suffix. We read here that Yahweh was with Joseph "and gave him favour וַיִּתֵּן חִנּוֹ in the sight of the keeper of the prison." The suffix of חֵן does not relate to the dispenser of favour, as one would expect in the light of the verb חנן, but to the recipient, or should we say to the possessor of חֵן, חֵן radiates from the bearer to a third person. In the חֵן given by Yahweh there is no longer reflected the relation between giver and recipient but that between the bearer of חֵן and a third person in whose eyes the חֵן of him who bears it has its effect.

g. This relation is then very plain in the phrase that occurs in no less than 43 of the 70 חֵן passages in the Hbr. canon: "to find grace in the eyes" of another . . . מָצָא חֵן בְּעֵינֵי. The ref. here is no longer to an activity of the dispenser of חֵן such as we have in the basic form of the verb חנן. חֵן is a qualification which the bearer of it achieves, or, as the formula puts it, can "find," "in the eyes of," i.e., as considered by, another person, Since מצא does not say precisely how חֵן comes to a man, there is a veil of mystery over this process.

The formula can also be used with reference to man and God. "Noah found grace in the eyes of the Lord," Gn. 6:8 (J). Undoubtedly there is implied here the mystery of the free divine decision whereby Noah came to have this attractiveness for God. The same is true when Yahweh says to Moses in Ex. 33:12: "I know thee by name (→ I, 698, 29 ff. with n. 37), and thou hast also found grace in my sight." [58] Other passages show that the phrase can sound much more like a formula. When Moses in striking oxymoron can say in Nu. 11:15: "Kill me (i.e., let me die) if I have found favour in thy sight," the meaning might well be: "Do me the favour," or: "Please, please, kill me."

The phrase, however, is far more common in secular speech. Jacob sends Esau gifts and gives as a reason: "That I may find grace in thy sight," Gn. 32:5, cf. 33:8. The ref. is to his intention to reconcile his angry brother, which reminds us of the meaning of חנן mentioned earlier → 378, 6 ff. The same formula is used for the favour which Joseph found in the house of Potiphar, Gn. 39:4 or for the favour that a wife wins or does not win with her husband, Dt. 24:1. [59] We also find examples in which the phrase, esp. in the conditional form: "If I have found grace in thine eyes," is reduced to mere politeness. [60]

h. How little of the full weight of the grace of God remains in the term חֵן may be judged from the fact that in the Ps. with their full use of the verb חנן the word does not occur at all in the context of petition. In all it occurs only twice in Ps., once in the saying already quoted from Ps. 84:11, namely, that God will give grace and glory, and once when there is ref. to "charm" on the lips of the royal bridegroom in Ps. 45:2. In contrast to the virtual absence of חֵן from the Ps. is the fair total of 13 instances in Prv., where we read of the favour one achieves with God and man, 3:4, of the chain of grace לִוְיַת חֵן

---

[58] The formulation is repeated no less than four times in Ex. 33:13, 16 f., cf. also 34:9, and it forms the basis for the bold requests of Moses.

[59] Cf. esp. also Est. 2:15, 17; 5:2 with its later formula נשׂא חֵן.

[60] In this polite usage one also finds the humble self-designation "thy servant," Gn. 19:19 → V, 658, 15 ff.

1:9, 3:9, of the adornment for the neck חֵן לְגַרְגְּרֹתֶיךָ 3:22, and of the graceful roe, 5:19, חֵן being given a purely aesthetic emphasis here. In 31:30 it is par. to יֳפִי. In Qoh., however, the term denotes the "favour" that comes to a man, 9:11; 10:12.

The word חֵן, which is hardly ever used with an article or in the plural, has thus undergone a distinctive change of sense. In the demonstration of grace expressed by the verbal stem (→ 377, 4 ff.) the implied element of conferring a good has broken free and changed into a qualification of the recipient, with, in part, a strong aesthetic accent. In the חֵן חֵן of Zech. 4:7 with which the community hails the laying of the foundation stone for the new temple, [61] one may infer an independent: "Good, good," or: "Beautiful, beautiful!" [62] A closer approximation to the basic sense of חנן seems to be present only in Zech. 12:10. This refers to the outpouring of a רוּחַ חֵן וְתַחֲנוּנִים in which the house of David and the inhabitants of Jerusalem are moved to bewail the mysterious stranger whom they have pierced. Seeing that the link with תַחֲנוּנִים involves a play on words, it seems that חֵן is again understood here in the light of its verbal origin. In place of the hardness of the men of Jerusalem comes the capacity for mercy [63] and supplication. In this v., then, we are to relate חֵן to חֲנִינָה and the secondary meaning of תְּחִנָּה.

The surprising development of the meaning of חֵן, which separates it sharply from חנן in its normal use, leaves a perceptible gap in the range of the stem חנן. Among its derivates, there is no noun clearly corresponding to it. The occasional use of תְּחִנָּה and חֵן (which normally has a very different stress) gives evidence of a very scattered attempt to fill the gap with a derivate of חנן. If this is not successful, it is because another noun which could effectively fill the gap enters the field. This is חֶסֶד, which the LXX usually renders by ἔλεος. This transl., which offers a Gk. term related to ἐλεέω, the LXX equivalent of חנן, shows clearly the relation between the two words. חֲנִינָה, however, can also be transl. by ἔλεος.

2. חֶסֶד (→ II, 479, 1 ff.).

a. The present treatment of חֶסֶד is also suggested by the consideration that in the later speech of the OT there is a remarkable merging of חֵן and חֶסֶד [64] in which חֶסֶד loses its earlier distinctiveness in favour of the meaning of חֵן, and furthermore that the later translators with increasing firmness connect חֶסֶד and χάρις. [65]

The thesis mentioned in → II, 479, 3 ff., [66] namely, that חֶסֶד is a mode of conduct corresponding to a relation of right and duty, has been hotly debated in recent times. [67] On the one hand חֶסֶד is taken to be a term for kindliness or friendliness. [68] Since we also read of a demonstration of (עָשָׂה חֶסֶד) חֶסֶד, one may see the secondary influence of the

---

[61] K. Galling, "Die Exilswende in der Sicht d. Propheten Sach.," VT, 2 (1952), 27.
[62] E. Sellin, Das Zwölfprophetenb., Komm. AT, 12², ³ (1930) transl. "Bravo, bravo."
[63] T. H. Robinson - F. Horst, Die Zwölf Kleinen Propheten, Hndbch. AT, I, 143 (1964) transl. "sympathy," K. Elliger, Das Buch d. Zwölf Kl. Proph., II, AT Deutsch, 25⁵ (1964), ad loc. and Sellin, op. cit. (→ n. 62) have "compassion."
[64] This is esp. clear in Est. 2:17. Acc. to Neubauer, 29 f. חֵן and חֶסֶד can hardly be distinguished even in origin; → n. 39, 49.
[65] Dodd, 61; Montgomery, 100.
[66] Glueck, 3-21 and passim.
[67] Stoebe häsäd, 247 f.; Jepsen, 264-7.
[68] Stoebe häsäd, 247 f.

related רַחֲמִים (→ V, 160, 7 ff.), which from the very first means the individual good act. On the other hand [69] the logical sundering of good will and good work is rejected and it is claimed that the content of חֶסֶד is complex, so that uniform rendering is almost impossible. Here too, however, the linking of חֶסֶד with the covenant relation is decisively rejected, and it is pointed out that there are few examples of any linking of חֶסֶד and בְּרִית in the OT. [70]

This rebuttal is undoubtedly right when directed against too rigidly legal a view of חֶסֶד and too narrow a connection of this with a fixed covenant. חֶסֶד always contains an element of spontaneous freedom in the demonstration of goodness or in kindly conduct, and it cannot be reduced to what is owed or to a duty. On the other hand, the polemic constantly ignores something that is plain in the texts, namely, that the nature of חֶסֶד is conduct in relation, and in demonstration of this relation. It is grace shown, or ready to show itself, in relation. Even though orientation to the giver of חֶסֶד may be seen again and again in the suffix, חֶסֶד is not thought of merely in individual terms. It presupposes an ongoing fellowship, and is distinguished hereby from חֵן, in which we have movement from the one to the other (→ 377, 14 f.) but not the maintaining of a relation of fellowship. Thus we find חֶסֶד between host and guest in Gn. 19:19, relatives in Gn. 47:29, those in covenant in 1 S. 20:8, ruler and subject in 2 S. 16:17, the one bound to another by an act of assistance and that other in Ju. 1:24; Jos. 2:12, 14. [71] This kindness in a specific relation may also be seen in 1 K. 20:31, a text where one might most easily discern unobligated mercy. If here the advisers of Benhadad, whose life is threatened in conquered Aphek, tell the king that he should put sackcloth on his loins and a rope on his head and go out to the king of Israel because the kings of the house of Israel are known to be מַלְכֵי חֶסֶד, they are advising the king to adopt the position of a suppliant even in outward dress, trusting that the king of Israel will accept this specific relation between men, and grant the grace of the protector.

The freedom with which, esp. in the earlier narrative texts, חֶסֶד occurs in the most varied human relationships with no special theological emphasis, suggests that in the first instance the native habitat of חֶסֶד is the sphere of intra-human relations. So far it has not been possible to get a more precise etym. explanation of the word, which seems to come from a sociologically closely intertwined group of peoples. We find it again in post-biblical Hbr., Jewish Aram. and Syr., [72] but nothing corresponding to it has been found in the older Semitic languages. Connection with the Arab. ḥśd "to act together to help someone," [73] is doubtful. [74] In Hbr. there is no verb corresponding to the noun. [75]

חֶסֶד as used in the sphere of human relations is then brought into the vicinity of covenant statements. But the question whether חֶסֶד is the presupposition of a covenant [76] or a covenant the presupposition of חֶסֶד [77] is a false one, as comparison of Gn. 21:23 and 1 S. 20:8 shows. In the former v. Abimelech asks Abraham to show him חֶסֶד as he has

---

[69] Jepsen, 266.

[70] Ibid., 265.

[71] Johnson, 107 f., fumbles for the right term for חֶסֶד, which has to be between grace, mercy and duty, and suggest the words "loyalty" and "devotion," which stress one aspect of חֶסֶד.

[72] Ges.-Buhl, s.v. חסד I.

[73] So Glueck, 67 f., following F. Schulthess, Homonyme Wurzeln im Syr. (1900), 32, but cf. Snaith, 95-8, who pts. to Arab. ḥsd "to envy," from which חֶסֶד "outrage" in Lv. 20:17 is supposedly derived also.

[74] Cf. the doubts of T. Nöldeke, Neue Beiträge z. semit. Sprachwissenschaft (1910), 93.

[75] The hitp of Ps. 18:25 = 2 S. 22:26 is denominated.

[76] What Stoebe ḥāsäd, 247 f. says might be understood along these lines.

[77] Cf. Snaith, 9: "אַהֲבָה is the cause of the covenant; חֶסֶד is the means of its continuance."

already done and hence to make a covenant with him. In the latter David appeals to the covenant Jonathan has made with him and asks Jonathan to show him חֶסֶד for the sake of this covenant. Both passages show that on the basis of a demonstration of חֶסֶד or a בְּרִית the counterdemonstration of חֶסֶד can be asked for. In such cases one may rightly detect an element of duty in חֶסֶד.

It is significant that already in secular usage חֶסֶד can easily be linked with אֱמֶת (→ I, 232, 26 ff.; VI, 185, 34 ff.). The element of constancy and of loyalty native to חֶסֶד is expressly brought out in a duplicate term. [78]

b. In the OT the word חֶסֶד achieves its distinctive sense, however, in its relation to Yahweh. It is particularly adapted to denote what takes place in the covenant between Yahweh and Israel. Note should be taken of the fact that it finds a place in the great hymnal predications of Yahweh in which OT faith tries to describe the nature of Yahweh. In the second predication of the Decalogue appended to the second commandment (Ex. 20:5b-6) the inner tension that comes to resolution in the story of the covenant people of the OT before God may be seen in the combination of two statements about Yahweh: Yahweh, who turns to His people in the covenant, is also the One who is jealous for His rights (אֵל קַנָּא). [79] The חֶסֶד statement is one of those that express Yahweh's covenant grace to His people. Thus Yahweh is predicated as the God "who shows covenant grace (עֹשֶׂה חֶסֶד) to thousands of generations [80] of those that love me and keep my commandments." The use of עֹשֶׂה חֶסֶד makes it plain that this is not an ontic description but a reference to grace converted into act. In the "to thousands" it is maintained that חֶסֶד, which is given its historical explication in the first preamble to the Decalogue (Ex. 20:2) with its reference to the credo-event of the deliverance out of Egypt, is incomparably stronger than the burning wrath of the jealous God. Hence חֶסֶד occurs elsewhere in Yahweh predications whether they contain a reference to the One who visits sin or are limited on the other hand to salvation formulations. Instead of the simple עֹשֶׂה חֶסֶד (Ex. 20:6; Dt. 5:10; Jer. 9:23; 32:18) we also find the stronger רַב חֶסֶד וֶאֱמֶת (Ex. 34:9; Ps. 86:15) [81] or נֹצֵר חֶסֶד (Ex. 34:7) or חָפֵץ חֶסֶד (Mi. 7:18). חֶסֶד can be expressly supplemented by a reference to the covenant. [82]

The other elements in the predication explain, however, what is meant by the חֶסֶד action of Yahweh. The חַנּוּן (→ 378, 26 ff.) in אֵל רַחוּם וְחַנּוּן shows the inner proximity of חַנּוּן to the עֹשֶׂה חֶסֶד. In אֶרֶךְ אַפַּיִם, which is often the first member before רַב חֶסֶד (וֶאֱמֶת) (Ex. 34:6; Nu. 14:18; Jl. 2:13; Jon. 4:2; Ps. 86:15; 103:8; Neh. 9:17), there is expressed, as in נֹשֵׂא עָוֹן וָפֶשַׁע וְחַטָּאָה (Ex. 34:7), the grace that forgives sins, cf. also טוֹב וְסַלָּח in Ps. 86:5 and אֱלוֹהַּ סְלִיחוֹת in Neh. 9:17. The הָאֵל הַנֶּאֱמָן of Dt. 7:9 brings out even more fully the

---

[78] D. Michel, "'Ämät. Untersuchung über 'Wahrheit' im Hbr.," *Archiv. f. Begriffsgeschichte,* 12 (1968), 56: "In the use of häsäd and 'ämät the latter ref. to the fulfilment of a promise, oath, blessing, or sign. Hence the two terms are not paratactic in this expression but 'ämät is to be construed as in qualifying apposition to häsäd. There is thus a material reason for the fixed order of the two. An adj. would perhaps best bring out the sense: "promised, sworn, covenanted etc. häsäd."

[79] W. Zimmerli, *Das Gesetz u. d. Propheten. Zum Verständnis d. AT, Kleine Vandenhoeck-Reihe,* 166/168² (1969), 88-91.

[80] Dt. 7:9 expressly elucidates the לַאֲלָפִים of Ex. 20:6 by לְאֶלֶף דּוֹר.

[81] Without אֱמֶת Nu. 14:18; Jl. 2:13; Jon. 4:2; Ps. 86:5; 103:8. גְּדָל־חֶסֶד is the term in Ps. 145:8.

[82] שֹׁמֵר הַבְּרִית וְהַחֶסֶד, Dt. 7:9; 1 K. 8:23; Da. 9:4; Neh. 1:5; 9:32, cf. Dt. 7:12.

element of faithfulness elsewhere implied in אֱמֶת. Awareness of the turning-pt. of disaster comes to expression in the post-exilic age in the נִחָם עַל־הָרָעָה of later formulations such as Jl. 2:13 and Jon. 4:2.

The full life of the believer and suppliant in face of the divine חֶסֶד is then developed especially in the Psalms. If חֵן is very rare in the Ps., the occurrence of חֶסֶד is so much the richer. No less than 127 of the 237 instances of חֶסֶד in the Hbr. canon occur in the Ps. alone. [83] Of these 127 examples only three refer to חֶסֶד between men, 109:12, 16; 141:5. In express invocation of the divine חֶסֶד which as God's total attitude is presented here as the broad background for individual proofs of חֶסֶד, [84] the psalmist prays to God and asks Yahweh to hear (119:149), to save (109:26), to redeem (44:26), to give life (119:88, 159), to forgive (25:7). Thanksgivings can extol Yahweh because in His great חֶסֶד He has let the psalmist visit the sanctuary (5:7) or has repented of the evil (106:45). Verbal statements can recount how God in His חֶסֶד has had regard to the plight of the suppliant (31:7), has supported him (94:18), has not let him fall (21:7), has saved him from the enemies (59:10), has destroyed his enemies (134:12), has exercised righteous judgment (62:12), has saved the suppliant from death (86:13). With חֶסֶד וֶאֱמֶת (25:10; 40:10; 57:3; 61:7; 85:10; 86:15; 89:14; cf. 26:3; 57:10; 69:13; 115:1; 117:2; 138:2; 77:9 vl.) we find טוֹב וָחֶסֶד (23:6) and חֶסֶד וּמִשְׁפָּט (101:1). Parallels to חֶסֶד are "salvation" יְשׁוּעָה (13:5; 18:50; 119:41), "mercy" רַחֲמִים (25:6; 40:11; 51:1; 103:4 cf. Lam. 3:22), "righteousness" (i.e., salvation) צְדָקָה (Ps. 36:10; 103:17, cf. 40:10), "righteousness and right" (33:5), "redemption" (130:7), "faithfulness" (36:5; 88:11; 89:1 f., 33; 92:2; 100:5, cf. 40:10; 89:49). How little חֶסֶד is a mere, self-evident obligation of the covenant Lord may be seen from its connection with references to miracles (107:8, 15, 21, 31) or the request for the miracle of חֶסֶד (17:7; 31:21) or the fact that joy (31:7; 90:14; 101:1) and praise (138:2) arise at חֶסֶד and it can be spoken of as a crown (103:4). In spatial categories we read of the extent of חֶסֶד: the earth is full of it (33:5; 119:64) and it reaches even to heaven (36:5; 57:10; 103:11; 108:4). Yahweh's חֶסֶד endures for ever (89:2; 103:17, 138:8). From the depths of despair the author of Lamentations dares to believe that even now חֶסֶד cannot have come to an end, Lam. 3:22.

Only apparently is a limit set: "Shall thy covenant grace חֶסֶד be recounted in death, thy faithfulness in the realm of the dead?" Ps. 88:11. If it would seem from this that man with all his strength must grasp after life as the supreme good that encounter with חֶסֶד makes possible for him, even then, in a most illogical way that is most instructive for the meaning of חֶסֶד, we find the opposing statement that "thy covenant grace חַסְדְּךָ is better than life," Ps. 63:3. This shows how fully Israel's faith is in the last analysis set on the turning of Yahweh expressed in חֶסֶד. Alongside this a life isolated from חֶסֶד is empty and not worth wanting.

The חֶסֶד of Yahweh can then be spoken of almost as a person. Yahweh sends it (57:3). It is ordered (42:8). It comes (59:10, 17 vl.; 89:14). It meets man (85:10). It follows him (23:6). In relation to it man must remember (106:7), consider (48:9) and understand (107:43). He must also — and here again we see the freedom with which Yahweh shows

---

[83] There are also two instances in Lam. at 3:22 and 3:32.

[84] Ps. 6:4; 44:26, עַל־חַסְדְּךָ; 115:1, כְּחַסְדְּךָ; 25:7; 51:1; 109:26; 119:88, 124, 149, 159, בְּחַסְדֶּךָ 31:16, בְּרֹב־חַסְדֶּךָ 69:13, כְּטוּב חַסְדֶּךָ 109:21 vl.; 69:16 vl. Cf. also לְמַעַן טוּבְךָ in 25:7.

His חֶסֶד as no mere duty — wait for it (33:18, 22; 147:11). [85] If חֶסֶד is connected with the covenant with Israel in 106:45, it is also brought into special relation to the covenant with David in 89:28. [86]

The extolling of Yahweh for the riches of His חֶסֶד takes on fixed liturgical form. We might mention here the antiphonal refrain: "For his חֶסֶד endureth for ever," [87] which has its place in the singing of hymns of salvation history (Ps. 136) by the congregation but can also be a response to the narrative in individual thanksgivings (107). The individual lets his own reason for thanksgiving be caught up in the praise of the community. According to the Chronicler the same refrain sounds forth on great liturgical occasions (1 Ch. 16:34; 2 Ch. 5:13; 7:3, 6; Ezr. 3:11) and even in the holy war, which leads to victory with this chant (2 Ch. 20:21). Then the day of the future turning-point of destiny can be depicted as the day when this song will be sung (Jer. 33:11, cf. also Sir. 51:12a-o). [88]

If the Ps. are controlled by the ref. to divine חֶסֶד elsewhere one finds discussion of the relation between divine and human חֶסֶד. The ripest formulations in this regard are in the story of Gn. 24 and the little book of Ruth. Here, although the connection is not made explicitly, one may see how, in the sphere of Yahweh's proofs of grace, [89] in which He can lead men mysteriously through apparent chances, [90] men too are in a position to show חֶסֶד to one another, Gn. 24:49; Rt. 1:8; 3:10.

c. The prophets have still to be mentioned. One may regard it as simply a confirmation of the view of חֶסֶד presented here that חֶסֶד statements — apart from liturgical predications of Yahweh — are to be found most impressively in the three prophets who also speak of the covenant, namely, Hos., Jer. and Dt. Is. [91] It should also be said, however, that a new turn is now given to what is said about חֶסֶד. If the original statements speak about חֶסֶד between men, and then the OT refers specifically to the חֶסֶד of Yahweh, the basis here being confession of the covenant relation of Yahweh to Israel, we now find a new reference, i.e., to man's חֶסֶד towards God. [92] Thus Hos., when he accuses Israel in terms of the Decalogue (4:2), opens with the profound summary (4:1) that "there is no faithfulness אֱמֶת, love חֶסֶד, nor knowledge of God in the land." Even more plainly in 6:4, when the people returns to Yahweh with a moving song of penitence, the reply is given: "Your love חַסְדְּכֶם is as a morning cloud, and as the early dew it goeth away." In both passages the prophet obviously has in mind the covenant conduct of Israel before God, which ought to be powerfully at work in free, spontaneous love. Then Jer., who follows in the steps of Hos., can use אַחֲבָה par. to חֶסֶד in depiction of the early and happy days of Israel's espousals, 2:2. This is the period consciously expressed in the command of Dt. 6:5; 11:1 to love Yahweh, though חֶסֶד is not used for this love of man for Yahweh in Dt. When

---

[85] W. Zimmerli, *Der Mensch u. seine Hoffnung im AT, Kl. Vandenhoeck-Reihe,* 272 (1968), 33-48 etc.

[86] With the sing. ref. (Ps. 89:1, 49, cf. Is. 55:3) we also find plur. ref. to demonstrations of (covenant) grace, e.g., Ps. 17:7; 25:6; 106:7, 45; 107:43; 119:41, cf. also Lam. 3:22.

[87] Koch, 531-544.

[88] Ed. I. Lévi, *The Hebrew Text of the Book of Ecclesiasticus, Semitic Study Series,* 3³ (1969), 73 f.

[89] Gn. 24:12, 14, 27; Rt. 2:20. As against Glueck, 6 f. חַסְדּוֹ should be related to Yahweh here, cf. W. Rudolph, *Das Buch Ruth, Das Hohe Lied, Die Klagelieder, Komm. AT,* 17, 1-3 (1962), *ad loc.*

[90] Cf. קרה in Gn. 24:12; Rt. 2:3.

[91] Echoed also in Tt. Is. at 57:1; 63:7.

[92] Incorrectly contested by Jepsen, 269.

Hos. in 2:19 f. speaks of חֶסֶד as well as righteousness and judgment and mercy and faithfulness and the knowledge of God as the dowry which God Himself paid, he is seeking to express the fact that full חֶסֶד is possible in God's people only as the gracious gift of God Himself, cf. also Hos. 6:6; 10:12; 12:7; Jer. 9:23; 16:5; 31:3. The salvation character of חֶסֶד is esp. clear in Dt. Is. where the covenant with Noah (54:8 f., 10) and the Davidic covenant (55:3) are brought in to elucidate what is meant by the covenant grace of Yahweh towards Israel. [93] It is worth noting that the assurance of covenant grace is not based on the covenant of the Mosaic age with its mediation of the Law and its consequent reminder of אֵל קַנָּא. The Noachic and Davidic covenants mentioned here are pure covenants of grace. חֶסֶד is gracious condescension.

The חֶסֶד of Is. 40:6 poses a problem. LXX is perhaps on the right track with its transl. πᾶσα δόξα ἀνθρώπου. It does not find human action in חֶסֶד here, but has in mind the collapse of human glory. [94] If this is correct, then חֶסֶד here is close in meaning to חֵן, which is linked with כָּבוֹד (LXX δόξα) in Ps. 84:11. This surprising approximation of חֶסֶד to the sense of חֵן is certainly to be found in later passages. In Est. 2:9, 17 חֶסֶד has been completely swallowed up by חֵן and denotes the favour that Esther found before the keeper of the harem and the Persian king. [95] In consequence the word loses its function as a substitute in the sphere of the verb חנן.

d. Over the broad range of other OT statements, however, חֶסֶד can still play this role as a substitute. To be sure, as a term orientated originally to relations between men, it cannot be an absolute synonym for the noun of the verb חנן, which is missing apart from a few instances of תְּחִנָּה or חֵן in a secondary sense. This verb expresses approach to one who is weaker and poorer and more afflicted, with an emphasis on the direction of the movement from stronger to weaker. In contrast חֶסֶד has in view right conduct in free kindness within a given relation. Nevertheless, since this carries with it the idea of a movement to the other in a relation of kindness, חֶסֶד can play its role as a substitute for the noun of חנן, which is missing in this sense.

In conclusion it must be stated that the content of חֶסֶד is decisively controlled by the nature of the social relationship to which it refers. When in its theological use חֶסֶד is orientated to the covenant (→ II, 109, 16 ff.) its understanding depends on that of the presupposed covenant. Neh. 13:14 can show how, when legal fulfilment of the commandment begins to determine the covenant, what is said about man's demonstration of חֶסֶד is also controlled by the commandment and its fulfilment.

e. By way of appendix something must be said about the adj. derived from חֶסֶד, namely, חָסִיד. [96] Like חֶסֶד, it occurs esp. in the Ps. (25 instances compared to only 7 in other books). [97] חָסִיד shares in the movement of the noun. When in Jer. 3:12 Yahweh in His appeal to apostate Israel says: "I will not give you black looks, for I am חָסִיד ..., I do

---

[93] In both passages חֶסֶד is par. to בְּרִית.

[94] Stoebe Wort u. Dienst, 124 explains this in terms of man's faithfulness or unfaithfulness, but this is not convincing. Snaith, 105, dropping the theological accent, thinks of man's steadfastness (or the reverse) in terms of the lack of endurance native to man.

[95] Cf. also Da. 1:9. Is Gn. 39:21 already to be construed along these lines?

[96] Gulkowitsch, passim. For חָסִיד the LXX mostly has ὅσιος, once each εὐλαβούμενος and εὐσεβής. With ref. to God ἐλεήμων is used in Jer. 3:12, and cf. once ὅσιος, Ps. 145:17, Dodd, 60; Snaith, 123-7.

[97] Basically 1 S. 2:9; 2 S. 22:26; 2 Ch. 6:41 may be grouped with the Ps.

not bear anger for ever," this is simply expressing the generous covenant grace of Yahweh after the manner of Yahweh predications and many statements in the Ps. Yahweh is the act. giver of חֶסֶד. In relation to men the ref. might be either to the recipients of the divine חֶסֶד (pass.) or to those who themselves show חֶסֶד (act.). Both are possible grammatically. Significant either way is Ps. 50:5, where Yahweh calls for a gathering of His חֲסִידִים who have made a covenant in sacrifice. It seems that the term חָסִיד has a special place at the conclusion of a covenant.

Zimmerli

C. Judaism.

1. Qumran and Testaments of the Twelve Patriarchs.

a. In the Qumran writings [98] חסד is dominant → 381, 28 ff. From the stem חנן (→ 376, 16 ff.) we find only once the noun חנינה 1 QH 11:29 and 15 times the verb חנן, e.g.: "And me, thy servant, hast thou favoured with the spirit of knowledge," 1 QH 14:25. To be noted is the link with "righteousness": Lo, thou hast begun to show favour חסד to thy servant, thou art gracious חנן to me in the spirit of thy mercy רחמים... and for thy righteousness' sake. Thine, yes thine is the righteousness; for thou hast done all," 1 QH 16:8 f. We also find this link in the case of חסד, most clearly in 1 QS 11:12-14: "When I waver, God's acts of grace חסדים are my help for ever. When I stumble through the fault of my flesh, my justification through God's righteousness abides for ever, when He looses mine affliction ... and in His mercy lets me draw nigh. By His grace חסדים my justification comes, in His true righteousness He directs me. In the plenitude of His goodness טוב He expiates all my sins and by His righteousness He purifies me ... " In sense חסד is hard to distinguish from רחמים and חנן. Grace and mercy complete righteousness, 1 QH 7:18 f.; 11:4-9, 30 f. → n. 182. [99] חסד is on the one side the norm of conduct towards fellow-members of the covenant (→ 382, 27 ff.); hence the expression אהבת חסד in 1 QS 2:24; 5:4, 25; 8:2; 10:26, and in the same sense רוב חסדים, 4:5. [100] On the other side חסד is the basic term for God's dealings → 383, 9 ff. In ever new phrases the "God of graces" (1 QM 14:8), "the fulness of His grace" (1 QS 4:4, cf. 5) and "His eternal graces" (1 QS 10:4) are extolled. The righteous man relies on His grace, 1 QS 10:16. [101] He clings to it, 1 QH 7:18, cf. Ps. 33:18; 147:11 and cf. also 1 QH 9:14. It proves itself in trouble. [102] But the concept of grace never breaks out of the framework of the Law; on the contrary, it constitutes a sharpening of the Torah. The insight into dependence on God's grace is negated by the principle of legal attainment. [103]

b. The findings in the Test. XII are of little significance. Joseph εὗρεν χάριν (→ 374, 3 f.; 389, 2 f.) ἐνώπιον θεοῦ καὶ ἀνθρώπων, Test. R. 4:8, cf. S. 5:2. Test. S. 4:5: Walk in ἁπλότης that God may give you χάρις, δόξα and εὐλογία. Test. L. 18:9: φωτισ-

---

[98] F. Nötscher, "Zur theol. Terminologie d. Qumran-Texte," *Bonner Bibl. Beiträge*, 10 (1956), 161 f., cf. 183 f.; H. Braun, "Spätjüd.-häret. u. frühchr. Radikalismus, I," *Beiträge z. hist. Theologie*, 24 1² (1969), Index, *s.v.* חסד; W. Zimmerli, "חסד im Qumranschrifttum," *Festschr. A. Dupont-Sommer* (1971).

[99] Nötscher, *op. cit.*, 183 f.

[100] Braun, *op. cit.*, 37, n. 10.

[101] And also His truth, 1 QH 10:17.

[102] Braun, 45, n. 1.

[103] *Ibid.*, 46 f.

θήσονται (sc. the peoples) διὰ χάριτος θεοῦ. Test. Jud. 2:1: καὶ ἔδωκέ μοι Κύριος χάριν ἐν πᾶσι τοῖς ἔργοις μου, cf. B. 4:6: καὶ τὸν ἔχοντα χάριν ἀγαθοῦ πνεύματος ἀγαπᾷ κατὰ τὴν ψυχὴν αὐτοῦ.

2. Rabbinic Writings.

There is no development of sense in the Rabb. → 376, 14 ff. [104] The noun חסד means "favour," "attractiveness," [105] the verb חנן "to be favourable to, to have mercy on someone" ואיחון למן דאיחון, Tg. O. on Ex. 33:19. Typical is the morning prayer, bBer., 60b: "Today and every day make me חן and חסד and רחמים in thine eyes and the eyes of all who see me. Show me thy good graces. Blessed be thou, Yahweh, who shows good graces to His people Israel." God draws over men the thread of favour חוט של חסד, bTamid, 28a with a ref. to Prv. 28:23, which has חן. [106]

The central problem is the relation between grace and works. The principle applies: "One receives a reward only for an act," M. Ex., 1, 5, on 12:6 (p. 14, 12 f.). [107] "Grace is what thou hast done to us because there were no good works in our hands," M. Ex., 3, 9 on 15:13 (p. 145, 15). That is, grace arises only where there are no works; it is supplementary. [108] This is true even though the need of man can be set very high. "Do grace to my lord Abraham (Gn. 24:12) ... R. Chaggai has said in the name of R. Yizchaq: All need grace; even Abraham, for whose sake grace rules in the world, needed grace," Gn. r., 60, 2 on 24:12. [109] The freedom of the divine giving is also emphasised. [110] Basically, however, the concept of grace remains caught in the schema of the Law. [111] In the understanding of grace no line can be drawn from the Synagogue to the NT. [112] Judaism cannot accept the alternative of works or grace. [113]

---

[104] Cf. Levy Wört., Jastrow, s.v. חַנַן, חִנָּא, חַנְנָא.

[105] bSota, 47a: "There are three kinds of attractiveness: the attractiveness of a place for its inhabitants, the attractiveness of a wife for her husband, and the attractiveness of wares for the buyer."

[106] Str.-B., I, 788.

[107] Ibid., III, 201.

[108] Cf. the examples in H. J. Schoeps, Paulus (1959), 217.

[109] A. Meyer, "Das Rätsel d. Jk.," ZNW Beih., 10 (1930), 100 f.

[110] Tanch. ואתחנן, 3 (Sundel, 101a): "Why did Moses pray only with the word 'beseech' תחנונים, as it is said: Then I besought ואתחנן (Dt. 3:23) ... (ref. to Ex. 33:19)? God said to him: I am under obligation to no man, no matter what a man do in fulfilment of the Law, I repay him freely חנם." Cf. Dt. r., 2, 1 on 3:23 (Wünsche, 18 f.). On Ex. 33:19 in Rabb. lit. v. Str.-B., IV, 489.

[111] Grace does not overthrow thinking in terms of works and merit. On the relation between the order of rewards and that of grace cf. Str.-B., IV, 490: "The ancient Synagogue did not uphold the idea of a reward of grace. This was because its doctrine of rewards became completely independent of its doctrine of justification." Cf. also Moore, II, 93-95.

[112] As against Schoeps, op. cit., 217: "Fundamentally Paul was merely putting in his own words an ancient Jewish opinion," cf. ibid., n. 1: "Basically one has only to open the Jewish Prayer-Book." The examples adduced by him prove the opposite, e.g., Pesikt. r., 21 (98b): "Even when we consider our pious works, we are ashamed at their paltriness compared to God's good deeds for us." In the upshot Schoeps is logically forced to repudiate Paul's doctrine of grace.

[113] By way of supplement Moffatt, 33-6 observes that in the Jewish use of the word associations developed which did not immediately commend it to Paul, esp. that of the capriciousness of the giver and that of merit in the recipient.

3. Septuagint. [114]

a. χάρις is not the transl. of חֶסֶד [115] but חֵן → 376, 16 f. [116] The mode of expression is shaped by the Hbr.: χάριν εὑρίσκω, Gn. 6:8 etc., δίδωμι, Ex. 3:21; ψ 83:12 etc. In comparing sense distribution one should recall that Hbr. and Aram have no term for thanks or gratitude. [117] In distinction from profane Gk. and the Hbr. חֵן the concept is not developed. [118] One may see this from Prv., in which HT and LXX deviate widely: "attractiveness," Prv. 1:9; 3:22, "charming speech," 10:32, "favour shown," 3:34; doing good is the way to achieve "favour" with God and hence happiness, 11:27, cf. 12:2; prayer for "grace," 30:7, "favour," 22:1, "thanks," 28:23. Wis. follows the normal pattern too, 3:9, 14; 4:15; 8:21; 14:26; 18:2. Sir. shows a certain liking for the term; it occurs here 31 times, without the prep. χάριν. [119] χάρις is never a theological word in the LXX.

b. The word χαρίζομαι, found only in Sir. and Macc., simply means "to give," Sir. 12:3; 2 Macc. 3:31, 33 etc. [120]

4. Philo. [121]

The complex character of Philo's thought is reflected in the word χάρις. [122] Both dependence on the OT and also further development may be seen, e.g., in discussion of the phrase χάριν εὑρίσκω, Leg. All., III, 78 → 390, 8 ff. At Gn. 6:8: Νῶε εὗρε χάριν, the alternative is posed: ἆρ' οὖν τοιοῦτόν ἐστι τὸ δηλούμενον, ὅτι χάριτος ἔτυχεν, ἢ ὅτι χάριτος ἄξιος ἐνομίσθη; Deus Imm., 104 (→ 390, 12 f.), cf. Quaest. in Gn., I, 96. [123] The symbolical figure in the OT is Hannah, Deus Imm., 5; Ebr., 145; Som., I, 254 (→ 365, n. 53), and cf. Enoch, whose name, Poster. C., 35, 41; Conf. Ling., 123, is transl. "thy grace." God's χάριτες are all His good gifts, Deus Imm., 108, and χάρις is the power behind them, Congr., 96. [124] χάρις is not a specific, definable gift. Its content derives from the total understanding of God's rule as Creator, Preserver, World-Governor

---

[114] On the doctrine of grace in Hell. Judaism cf. A. D. Nock, *Paul* (1938), 76 f.

[115] This group is transl. by ἔλεος (→ II, 479, 1 ff.). An exception is Est. 2:17, where חֵן וָחֶסֶד is simply transl. χάρις.

[116] 62 of the total of 70 instances of חֵן in the Hbr. canon are transl. by χάρις, cf. also εὐχάριστος in Prv. 11:16 and ἐπιχαρής in Na. 3:4, also ἔλεος in Gn. 19:19; Nu. 11:15 and ἐλεήσει in Job 41:4 [Zimmerli].

[117] P. Joüon, "Reconnaissance et action de grâces dans le NT," *Recherches de Science Relig.*, 29 (1939), 112-4.

[118] Manson, 36-38. To be sure, the word now ref. to God's acts, but χάρις is not their basic characteristic.

[119] The Hbr. equivalents, available in 13 instances, show very broad distribution. חֵן holds the field numerically, 4:21; 7:19, 33; 32:10 (HT 35:10); 41:27 (HT 42:1c); 45:1 (HT 44:23 f.), but cf. also טוב 3:31 (?), טובה 8:19; 12:1; 20:13, רחמים 3:18; יפי 40:22 and חסד 40:17 [Zimmerli].

[120] Schlier Gl.[13], 149, n. 3: In the LXX χαρίζομαι simply means "to give"; the sense "to show oneself gracious" is found for the first time in Ep. Ar., 38 and 228.

[121] H. Windisch, *Die Frömmigkeit Philos* (1909), 15-23, 104-113; Wetter, 44-6 and Index, *s.v.* "Philo"; Moffatt, 45-51; H. A. Wolfson, *Philo*, I (1948), 445-455; J. Daniélou, *Philon d'Alex.* (1958), 175-181; Torrance, 6-10.

[122] This is why opposing judgments of scholars on his understanding of grace arise. The ambivalence of his statements is favoured by the convergence of חֵן and χάρις in the sense of "charm," "favour."

[123] Cf. the Gk. text. in P. Wendland, *Neu entdeckte Fr. Philos* (1891), 49 f.

[124] E. Bréhier, *Les idées philosoph. de Philon d'Alex.*[3] (1950), 148 f.

and Redeemer. [125] Ability to receive the gift varies, Ebr., 32. [126] But the systematic stress is on the fact that God is always act.: τὸ δὴ "θεὸς αἰώνιος" ἴσον ἐστὶ τῷ ὁ χαριζόμενος οὗ ποτὲ μὲν ποτὲ δὲ οὔ, ἀεὶ δὲ καὶ συνεχῶς, ὁ ἀδιαστάτως εὐεργετῶν, ὁ τὴν τῶν δωρεῶν ἐπάλληλον φορὰν ἀπαύστως συνείρων, ὁ τὰς χάριτας ἐχομένας ἀλλήλων ἀνακυκλῶν δυνάμεσιν ἑνωτικαῖς καθαρμοσάμενος, ὁ μηδένα καιρὸν τοῦ ποιεῖν εὖ παραλείπων, ὁ κύριος ὤν, ὡς καὶ βλάπτειν δύνασθαι, Plant., 89, cf. the ongoing operation of His χάριτες, Spec. Leg., I, 285; Conf. Ling;, 182. [127] χάρις is the endowment of man by creation; [128] the pious regard this as χάρις → n. 128. The meaning of χάριν εὑρίσκω (→ 387, 21 f.; 389, 2 f.) is explained as follows: τὸ δὲ χάριν εὑρεῖν οὐκ ἔστιν μόνον... ἴσον τῷ εὐαρεστῆσαι, ἀλλὰ καὶ τοιοῦτον· ζητῶν ὁ δίκαιος τὴν τῶν ὄντων φύσιν ἐν τοῦτο εὑρίσκει ἄριστον εὕρημα, χάριν ὄντα τοῦ θεοῦ τὰ σύμπαντα, γενέσεως δὲ οὐδὲν χάρισμα, Leg. All., III, 78, cf. Deus Imm., 104-108. The new thing in Philo is his development of the notion of the δυνάμεις [129] to the point of hypostatisation.

The view of grace reaches a climax in the doctrine of redemption. This is marked by Philonic ambivalence. Man can purify himself and yet he is incapable of this. [130] The impossible is possible for God, Spec. Leg., I, 282. There is no merit, Sacr. AC, 54-57. God's gifts are also perfect, Sacr. AC, 57; Migr. Abr., 31. Yet Philo can say that χάρις is only for the righteous, Leg. All., III, 14. One must be worthy of it, otherwise it vanishes. [131] In view of this some see in Philo a "Catholic" vacillation between grace and man's own work, [132] while others speak of Hell.-Jewish synergism to the degree that grace is in fact a help in the attainment of virtue. It cannot be maintained, however, that outstanding individuals do not need grace. [133] Rather God grants individuals perfection in order that they may have virtue without their own effort. [134] The normal situation, of course, is that man should exert himself. But even here one can at most speak of a synergism only outwardly. Nor would such an objectifying consideration of man's activity really do justice to what Philo has in mind. For the struggle for virtue in Philo carries with it as

---

[125] Philo distinguishes in God the gracious aspect θεός and the ruling, judicial aspect κύριος: τὰς δὲ τοῦ ὄντος πρώτας δυνάμεις, τήν τε χαριστικήν, καθ' ἣν ἐκοσμοπλάστει, ἣ προσαγορεύεται θεός, καὶ τὴν κολαστικήν, καθ' ἣν ἄρχει καὶ ἐπιστατεῖ τοῦ γενομένου, ἣ προσονομάζεται κύριος, Rer. Div. Her., 166, cf. Som., I, 162 f.; Spec. Leg., I, 307. Wetter, 13: "Χαριστικός is not, then, an essential but an act. attribute, an expression for God's creative (as θυμός and κολάζειν are for His judicial) activity, not for a divine disposition." Note the exposition of Gn. 17:4 in Mut. Nom., 57-59 and cf. Epict. Diss., I, 16, 15-21.

[126] Bréhier, op. cit., 278.

[127] Cf. Jos. Ap., 2, 190: God is ἔργοις μὲν καὶ χάρισιν ἐναργής.

[128] Two races confront one another, that of Cain that maintains, δωρεὰν εἶναι τῆς ἑαυτῶν ψυχῆς πάνθ' ὅσα ἐν τῷ νοεῖν ἢ αἰσθάνεσθαι ἢ λέγειν, and that of Seth: οἱ δ' ὅσα ἐν γενέσει καλὰ μὴ σφετεριζόμενοι, χάρισι δὲ ταῖς θείαις ἐπιγράφοντες, Poster. C., 42, cf. Conf. Ling., 123 and 127.

[129] The virgin daughters of God, Migr. Abr., 31. χάριτες, ἀρεταί, λόγοι and δυνάμεις are related, Wetter, 46. The idea of power is basic.

[130] On the sighing of those who repent and seek God's help cf. Leg. All., III, 211-213 and cf. 215 building on Ex. 20:24: ὁρᾷς ὅση τοῦ αἰτίου (author, sc. of all things) ἡ χάρις φθάνοντος τὴν ἡμετέραν μέλλησιν καὶ προαπαντῶντος εἰς εὐεργεσίαν παντελῆ τῆς ψυχῆς, cf. also Som., II, 25.

[131] Cf. the consequences of the fall, Op. Mund., 168: νυνὶ δὲ αἱ ἀέναοι πηγαὶ τῶν τοῦ θεοῦ χαρίτων ἐπεσχέθησαν, ὅτε ἤρξατο κακία τὰς ἀρετὰς παρευημερεῖν, ἵνα μὴ ὡς ἀναξίοις χορηγῶσιν.

[132] Wetter, 45.

[133] Cf. Wolfson, op. cit. (→ n. 121), I, 447-452, who ref. to Noah in Leg. All., III, 77 and Moses in III, 135.

[134] This distinguishes Moses from Aaron: Moses does not get the thigh ὅτι ὁ μὲν τέλειος ὢν βραχὺ καὶ ταπεινὸν οὐδὲν φρονεῖ..., Leg. All., III, 134 (expounding Lev. 7:34); ἄπονος δ' ἐστὶν ᾧ ὁ θεὸς χαρίζεται κατὰ πολλὴν περιουσίαν τὰ ἀγαθὰ τέλεια, 135. Cf. III, 77 f. for Noah.

a constitutive factor the confession that it is God's achievement and not our own.[135] Man begins when he recognises and admits his nothingness and the way of virtue is the actualisation of this confession. Thus the understanding of virtue has changed completely in comparison with the Gk. view (→ 375, 17 ff.), not just by way of development, e.g., by combination with Jewish concepts, but by leaping to a new level of reflection.[136] I experience myself by confessing God. In the light of this starting-pt. we do not find a systematic unity of all statements about man and his abilities. We have rather a central pt. which gives the varied statements their reference and produces a new, consistent, and subjective style of thought in which the alternative of χάρις and self-activity is resolved. The emphasis on distance, or sin,[137] thus becomes distinctively radical.[138] The greatness of grace stands out in relief against this background.[139] He who is pious in the sense of confession and self-renunciation is impelled by divine forces, Congr., 38, and protected against evil, Leg. All., II, 32. Hence he never leaves the sphere of χάρις.

D. New Testament.

The noun χάρις does not occur in Mk., Mt., 1 and 3 Jn. In Jn. we find it only at 1:14-17, and in 1 Th. and Phlm. only in salutations.[140] The verb χαρίζομαι occurs only in Lk. and Pl. (incl. Col. and Eph.),[141] χαριτόω in Lk. 1:28; Eph. 1:6. The prep. χάριν[142] (→ n. 10) is common in the koine but rare in the NT; in contrast to koine use and unlike ἕνεκα it comes after in Lk. 7:47;[143] Gl. 3:19; Eph. 3:1, 14; 1 Tm. 5:14; Tt. 1:5, 11; we find it before at 1 Jn. 3:12.

To refer to OT חֵן (→ 376, 14 ff.) does not help much in determining the sense in the NT. The OT background is clear in Lk. (→ 392, 10 ff.) but where this is true χάρις is not a theological term. Nor does חֶסֶד [144] (→ 381, 28 ff.) help much, since it points us to ἔλεος (→ II, 479, 1 ff.). In distinction from Jewish antecedents,

---

135 ... ὅτι δεῖ τὸν ὑπὲρ ἀρετῆς πόνον μὴ ἑαυτῇ προσάγειν τὴν ψυχήν, ἀλλ' ἀφελεῖν ἀφ' ἑαυτῆς καὶ θεῷ ἀνενεγκεῖν, ὁμολογοῦσαν ὅτι οὐχ ἡ ἰσχὺς αὐτῆς οὐδὲ ἡ δύναμις περιεποίησε τὸ καλόν, ἀλλὰ ὁ καὶ τὸν ἔρωτα χαρισάμενος, Leg. All., III, 136, cf. Agric., 168 f.

136 Jonas Gnosis, II, 1 speaks of a gnosticising "undermining of the Gk. concept of virtue," 41. "Non-orientation to the I is constitutive," 39. "The execution or non-execution of that reflection on nothingness on the part of the self in performing the acts that formerly represented the goods of the soul or values of the personality is what decides whether virtue or its opposite is effected in them," 39. "Whereas for the Gk. world from Plato to Plotinus the way to God is via man's moral self-perfecting, in Philo it is via self-renunciation in recognition of one's own nothingness," 41 f. Cf. the contrasting of the two human possibilities in Sacr. AC, 2.

137 Daniélou, op. cit., 176.

138 "λάβε μοι" (Gn. 15:9) ... πρῶτον μέν, ἴδιον, φησίν, οὐδὲν ἔχεις ἀγαθόν, ἀλλ' ὅ τι ἂν νομίσῃς ἔχειν, ἕτερος παρέσχηκεν, ἐξ οὗ συνάγεται ὅτι θεοῦ τοῦ διδόντος κτήματα πάντα, ἀλλ' οὐ τῆς μεταίτου καὶ τὰς χεῖρας εἰς τὸ λαβεῖν προτεινούσης γενέσεως. δεύτερον δέ, κἂν λάβῃς, λάβε μὴ σεαυτῷ, δάνειον δὲ ἢ παρακαταθήκην νομίσας τὸ δοθὲν τῷ δοθέντι καὶ συμβαλόντι ἀπόδος, πρεσβυτέραν χάριν χάριτι νεωτέρᾳ, προκατάρχουσαν ἀντεκτινούσῃ δικαίως καὶ προσηκόντως ἀμειψάμενος, Rer. Div. Her., 102-4.

139 τί οὖν ἂν ἐπιλίποι καλὸν τοῦ τελεσφόρου παρόντος θεοῦ μετὰ χαρίτων τῶν παρθένων αὐτοῦ θυγατέρων, ἃς ἀδιαφθόρους καὶ ἀμιάντους ὁ γεννήσας πατὴρ κουροτροφεῖ; τότε μελέται μὲν καὶ πόνοι καὶ ἀσκήσεις ἡσυχάζουσιν, ἀναδίδοται δὲ ἄνευ τέχνης φύσεως προμηθείᾳ πάντα ἀθρόα πᾶσιν ὠφέλιμα. καλεῖται δ' ἡ φορὰ τῶν αὐτοματιζομένων ἀγαθῶν ἄφεσις, ἐπειδήπερ ὁ νοῦς ἀφεῖται τῶν κατὰ τὰς ἰδίας ἐπιβολὰς ἐνεργειῶν... Migr. Abr., 31 f.

140 Hence Wetter, 2: "This word, which plays so small a role in the NT."

141 On the pass. → n. 18.

142 Bl.-Debr. § 216, 1.

143 The οὗ χάριν is meant causally here acc. to Bl.-Debr. § 456, 4.

144 Dodd, 61 f. In NT times χάρις is more akin to חֶסֶד than חֵן.

χάρις shows affinity to the ordinary use of πνεῦμα. χάρις, like πνεῦμα, is given both for the moment and also lastingly → VI, 406, 10 ff. [145]

1. Luke.

In the Synoptists use of the word group is limited to Lk. Whether he took it from his special tradition is an open question.

a. The profane sense of "favour," "pleasure," with the hint of something dubious, occurs in Ac. 24:27; 25:3, 9. [146] Also profane is the use in Ac. 2:47; 4:33: The Chr. community enjoys "favour" among the people. [147] Cf. also χάριν ἔχω "to be grateful" in Lk. 17:9.

b. The religious use is in the first instance dependent on the OT → 376, 14 ff., cf. "to find grace" in Lk. 1:30; [148] Ac. 7:46, "to give," Ac. 7:10, cf. Gn. 39:21. God's "grace" rests on the child, Lk. 2:40. [149] Traces of the θεῖος-ἀνήρ motif (cf. Ac. 7:20 ff.) run through the OT wording: προέκοπτεν ἐν τῇ σοφίᾳ καὶ ἡλικίᾳ καὶ χάριτι παρὰ θεῷ [150] καὶ ἀνθρώποις, Lk. 2:52. [151] The meaning is also religious in Lk. 6:32, 33, 34: ποία ὑμῖν χάρις ἐστίν; cf. τίνα μισθὸν ἔχετε; Mt. 5:46. Lk. wants to bring out the element of divine "good-pleasure." [152]

c. Where Lk. himself is responsible, certain intentions are recognisable. χάρις characterises the message of salvation, or the message as a message of salvation. "Words of grace" [153] is in Lk. 4:22, [154] cf. Ac. 20:24, [155] 32; Col. 4:6, a term for the Gospel, whose content may be gleaned from the context. Mighty works confirm the Gospel, Ac. 14:3. [156] χάρις can also depict the Spirit-filled man. Stephen is πλήρης χάριτος καὶ δυνάμεως, Ac. 6:8. [157] The overruling of grace may be seen in the spread of the Church, Ac. 11:23, with a play on χαίρω. Beyond the idea of the Church the word may be used generally for the state of grace, cf. προσμένω τῇ χάριτι τοῦ θεοῦ, Ac. 13:43. [158] There is commendation to the grace of God (Ac. 14:26) or the Lord (15:40). [159] Ac. 15:11 sounds Pauline: διὰ τῆς χάριτος κυρίου Ἰησοῦ πιστεύομεν σωθῆναι, [160] though the specific Pauline sense is blunted into a

---

145 Wetter, 126.

146 On the acc. χάριτα in Ac. 24:27; Jd. 4 → n. 1.

147 Wetter, 146 f. and Haench. Ag.6 on 4:33 propose "grace." The analogy to δύναμις supports this but cf. Ac. 2:47 → line 7 f.

148 Lk. 1:30 explains κεχαριτωμένη in 1:28 → 393, 11 f.

149 D has ἐν αὐτῷ for ἐπ' αὐτό. We find ἔλεος with ἐπί c. acc. in Ps. Sol. 4:25; 11:9; 13:12.

150 Cf. Hbr. בְּעֵינִי, e.g., Ex. 33:12 (LXX παρ' ἐμοί).

151 On the motif cf. 1 S. 2:26. σοφία and χάρις also occur together in Ac. 7:10, cf. σοφία καὶ πνεῦμα, 6:10, πίστις καὶ πνεῦμα, 6:5, χάρις καὶ δύναμις, 6:8.

152 But cf. Pr.-Bauer, s.v. χάρις: "What kind of favour will be yours then?" cf. 1 C. 9:16 vl.; 1 Pt. 2:19; Did. 1, 3; Ign. Pol., 2, 1; 2 Cl., 13, 4. These passages show that this use of χάρις is not specifically Lucan. H. Köster, "Synpt. Überlieferung bei d. Apost. Vät.," TU, 65 (1957), 44, 224 f. is inclined to think that the Lucan passages are Lk.'s own redaction. This carries with it the serious conclusion that the prototypes of Did. and Ign. knew Lk. → 399, 21 ff.

153 χάρις is intentionally ambivalent ("charm" or "grace"). Attractive words are in view in ψ 44:3: ἐξεχύθη χάρις ἐν χείλεσίν σου.

154 Wetter, 147-9 would take χάρις dynamically here too, i.e., "mighty words," cf. Just. Dial., 9, 1: οὐ κενοῖς ἐπιστεύσαμεν μύθοις οὐδὲ ἀναποδείκτοις λόγοις, ἀλλὰ μεστοῖς πνεύματος θείου καὶ δυνάμει βρύουσι καὶ τεθηλόσι χάριτι.

155 Haench. Ag.6 on 20:24 suggests a Pauline term but the expression is Lucan.

156 χάρις and δύναμις should be more clearly distinguished than in Wetter. They are distinct in relation to the message, close in relation to the pneumatic.

157 The durative πλήρης alternates with the momentary πλησθείς without clear distinction, cf. πλήρης in Mart. Pol., 7, 3 and πεπληρωμένος in Ign. R. Inscr.

158 Cf. προσμένω τῷ κυρίῳ, Ac. 11:23.

159 Cf. παρατίθεμαι ὑμᾶς τῷ κυρίῳ καὶ τῷ λόγῳ τῆς χάριτος αὐτοῦ, Ac. 20:32.

160 On πιστεύομεν σωθῆναι cf. Bl.-Debr. § 397, 2. "By grace" goes with σωθῆναι, not πιστεύομεν.

current term in edification. [161] Ac. 18:27 is not very clear: συνεβάλετο (sc. Apollos) πολὺ τοῖς πεπιστευκόσιν διὰ τῆς χάριτος. [162]

d. The verb χαρίζομαι occurs twice in a legal context for showing favour in a trial, though in directly opposite ways. Thus Barabbas is "given" to the people, i.e., set free, in Ac. 3:14, [163] but Paul is to be given up to the Jews, a fatal favour on the part of the Jewish procurator, Ac. 25:11, 16. [164] God grants Paul the lives of those who travel with him, Ac. 27:24. We find typically Lucan style in the brief summary of Jesus and His work in Lk. 7:21. [165] This is elucidated by Lk. 4:22, or Lk. 7:21 is a paradigm for the programme there. Miracle again serves to accredit. [166] Lk. 7:42 f. is again typically Lucan.

e. χαριτόω "to show grace." "to bless," is used in the NT only in connection with divine χάρις: [167] χαῖρε κεχαριτωμένη, Lk. 1:28 → 366, 25 ff.; 392, n. 148. [168]

f. ἀχάριστος "ungrateful" in Lk. 6:35 is perhaps editorial. The use of the word is dependent on χάρις in v. 32, 33, 34 → 392, 13 f. [169]

2. Paul.

In Paul χάρις is a central concept that most clearly expresses his understanding of the salvation event. [170] It is worth nothing that the singular predominates in usage. [171] Naturally the term does not have in every passage the specific sense of Paul's doctrine of grace. It can means "thanks" in the expression χάρις τῷ θεῷ, R. 6:17; 7:25; 1 C. 15:57; 2 C. 8:16; 9:15. [172] Then as a term for the collection it means "thank-offering," 1 C. 16:3; 2 C. 8:1 ff. 1 C. 10:30 is obscure: "to enjoy with thanks." [173]

a. The word occupies a special place in the salutation [174] χάρις ὑμῖν καὶ εἰρήνη (R. 1:7 etc.) and similarly in the final greeting (1 Th. 5:28 etc.).

---

[161] The speaker is Peter. He speaks like Paul in 13:38 f. The Pauline antithesis of grace and works is missing.

[162] διὰ τῆς χάριτος can go with συνεβάλετο, "he was a great help to believers by grace," or less plausibly with τοῖς πεπιστευκόσιν: "to those who had come to believe through grace."

[163] Jewish opposition and guilt are emphasised by the contrast: τὸν ἅγιον καὶ δίκαιον ἠρνήσασθε — ἄνδρα φονέα. Cf. Diod. S., 13, 59, 3: ἐχαρίσατο δ' αὐτῷ τοὺς συγγενεῖς and also Jos. Vit., 355.

[164] Cf. the noun χάρις, Ac. 24:27; 25:3, 9. Materially cf. Jos. Vit., 53; P. Flor., I, 61, 61 (c. 87 A.D.); → n. 194.

[165] Cf. Ac. 10:38: Jesus as εὐεργετῶν καὶ ἰώμενος. This is θεῖος-ἀνήρ style, v. H. Conzelmann, Die Apostelgesch., Hndbch. NT, 7 (1963), ad loc.

[166] But the scandal is not forgotten, v. 23, v. H. Conzelmann, "Die Mitte d. Zeit," Beiträge z. histor. Theol., 17⁵ (1964), 178 f.

[167] Pr.-Bauer, s.v.

[168] M. Cambe, "La ΧΑΡΙΣ chez S. Luc.," Rev. Bibl., 70 (1963), 193-207.

[169] J. Dupont, Les béatitudes² (1958), 151, n. 1, Wetter, 119: ἀχάριστος, like ἀγνωσία θεοῦ, is a "positive" term, cf. Just. Dial., 96, 3: τὸν ἥλιον αὐτοῦ ἀνατέλλοντα ἐπὶ ἀχαρίστους καὶ δικαίους.

[170] Bultmann, Theol.⁶, 281-5, 287-291; Moffatt, 131-296.

[171] Wetter, 27: "It is as though Paul wanted to avoid the plur. of χάρις." When he speaks of a multiplicity of gifts he uses χαρίσματα (→ 404, 20 ff.), R. 11:29.

[172] Ibid., 206 f.; Bl.-Debr. § 128, 6.

[173] Acc. to Ltzm. K., ad loc. we have here the exclamation of one of the strong, but cf. Bultmann Theol.⁶, 220.

[174] On the Gk. epistolary formula cf. O. Roller, "Das Formular d. paul. Briefe," BWANT, 58 (1933), 46-91; Wendland Hell. Kult., 411-417. On Paul's formula cf. E. Lohmeyer, "Briefliche Grussüberschriften," ZNW, 26 (1927), 158-173; G. Friedrich, "Lohmeyers These über d. paul. Briefpräskript kritisch beleuchtet," ThLZ, 81 (1956), 343-6.

χάρις echoes here the key-term χαίρειν in the greeting in Gk. letters → 360, 27 f. But it is integrated into the two-membered oriental formula of greeting as in Da. 4:1 Θ. Paul adopts the greeting of peace and supplements it by a greeting of grace. [175] Paul's salutation has been called a pre-Pauline liturgical formula. [176] The usage, lack of article and also the theology are not Pauline. The omission of the art. is indeed found in the liturgical style of early Christianity. [177] A difference from related oriental material is that in Paul the whole prescript is a constituent part of the letter, whereas in the Orient the naming of the sender מ‍—ל is originally a dictation formula. [178]

b. Specifically Pauline is the use of the word to expound the structure of the salvation event. The linguistic starting-point is the sense of "making glad by gifts," of showing free unmerited grace. The element of freedom in giving is constitutive, δωρεάν, R. 3:24 f.; cf. 4:1 ff.; 5:15, 17. Unlike Philo (→ 389, 14 ff.), Paul orientates himself, not to the question of the nature of God, but to the historical manifestation of salvation in Christ. He does not speak of the gracious God; he speaks of the grace that is actualised in the cross of Christ (Gl. 2:21, cf. vv. 15-20) and that is an actual event in proclamation. [179] If God's favour is identical with the crucifixion, then its absoluteness is established. We are saved by grace alone. [180] Grace is shown to the sinner, R. 3:23 f.; 5:10, cf. Gl. 2:17-21; R. 11:32. It is the totality of salvation, 2 C. 6:1. Every Christian has it, 1 C. 1:4. To the embodiment of grace in Christ corresponds that of the *sola gratia* (R. 4:4) [181] in the *sola fide* (R. 3:24 ff.; 4:16), and hence in the self-understanding of the believer and the special self-understanding of Paul as an office-bearer. The *sola fide* excludes the Law as a way of salvation (R. 3:21 ff.; 4:16), since the Law is in opposition to χάρις (R. 6:14 f.; Gl. 2:21; 5:4). In R. 4:14-16 χάρις and πίστις together are set in antithesis to the νόμος. The understanding of *sola gratia* might remain formal without establishment by the *sola fide*, i.e., it might remain in the sphere of the Law, the attainment of salvation by works. [182]

---

[175] Does Paul borrow from the use of ἔλεος for the customary εἰρήνη? Cf. the combination of the two terms in S. Bar. 78:2: "Thus saith Baruch, the son of Neriyas, to the brethren who are imprisoned: Mercy and peace be with you."

[176] Lohmeyer, *op. cit.* (→ n. 174), 161 f.

[177] Friedrich, *op. cit.* (→ n. 174), 344-6.

[178] *Aramaic Documents of the Fifth Cent. B.C.*, ed. G. R. Driver[2] (1957), No. 2, 3, 13; cf. also Pap. Murabbaʿât, 17A (8th cent. B.C.; DJD, II, 96).

[179] Grace is not a hitherto unknown gracious disposition but the present demonstration of grace on the part of the judge in justifying the guilty, Bultmann Theol.[6], 284. Worth noting is the lack of any tension or confrontation between grace and wrath. The opp. of ὀργή is not χάρις but δικαιοσύνη, R. 1:17 f., cf. the train of thought in R. 4:15 f., the only place where ὀργή and χάρις occur together. The philosophical question of God's affections (→ 375, 37 ff.; V, 386, 18) does not help us to understand the Pauline concept.

[180] Grace does not support man's striving for the good. It makes the effort to stand on one's own futile, Bultmann Theol.[6], 284. An aspect of grace is its newness. It is not tied to any human presupposition, but negates all human preparation. It is the instantaneous new creation of the recipient of the message of grace. It makes him a justified sinner. Hence the use is to be understood in a wholly non-mystical sense.

[181] Cf. Gn. 18:3. The idea is not, of course, developed from χάρις but from πίστις and δικαιοσύνη.

[182] Cf. the concept of grace in the Qumran writings → 387, 9 ff. The interrelation of *sola gratia* and *sola fide* may be seen esp. from 2 C. 2 C. 8 illustrates Paul's development of the term, cf. Wnd. 2 K. on 8:1: "χ. is (1) the divine loving-kindness and its objective demonstration for all men, v. 9; (2) the special proof of grace imparted to individual Christians, 8:1, personal possession of the power of grace, 8:1; 9:8, 14, cf. 1 C. 1:4; 15:10; and finally (3) the Chr. work of grace or love originated by divine grace," the outworking of grace, 8:4, 6, 7, 10, cf. 1 C. 16:3.

Grace is not just the basis of justification (R. 3:24 f.; 5:20 f.). It is also manifested therein. For justification is not the subjective appropriation of the salvation object- ively effected in Christ. The event of salvation is in itself orientated to the sinner and carries justification with it; hence it is received in faith. The scope of justifica- tion as the transmission of life in face of death may be seen in R. 5. [183] We find here the connection between grace as event and grace as possession or "state," R. 5:2. [184] That this "state" (→ VI, 218, 20 ff.) is not habitual is implicit in the term of "grace" itself, for grace remains a gift and it is allotted in the Word. [185] A man is called into it (Gl. 1:6, 15). [186] Hence he has neither claim nor desert. It comes to view in the destruction of self-glorying and paradoxical self-glorying in the Lord (1 C. 1:29, 31), in the cross (Gl. 6:14), in weakness (2 C. 12:9). Grace "is sufficient." Two thoughts intertwine in 2 C. 12:9: a. You will get no more, Paul's request being denied, and b. You need no more, cf. the positive explanation: ἡ ... δύναμις ἐν ἀσθενείᾳ τελεῖται. According to the theology of the cross in this sense χάρις determines the form of proclamation and also therewith of both proclaimer and believer. Boasting is also ruled out by the fact that although one can be sure of grace — the element of assurance of salvation is also contained in the concept itself — one does not have it for certain (→ VI, 168, n. 9). It is possible to fall from grace, Gl. 5:4. [187]

c. The power of grace (→ 376, 7 ff.) is displayed in its work, the overcoming of sin, R. 5:20 f. [188] The understanding of its superiority is not quantitative, but qualitative and structural. It is not just superior to sin and its result, death. It is also structurally different. It does not come in the form of destiny, like death. It is free election, R. 11:5 f. Hence, quantitatively considered, it is the exception. [189] The understanding of grace as a power is historical. It actualises itself in the Church (Phil. 1:7), e.g., in the collection that Paul makes for the original community, 2 C. 8.

---

183 Wetter, 40 thinks sin, death and grace are hypostases in R. 5. But what we have here is simply the common personifying mode of expression. The transition to the sense of "gift" is plain. The movement of thought may be seen at the beginning of the c. R. 5:1 ff. expounds the confessional statement in 4:25. From this it is deduced that we stand in peace, i.e., in eschatological salvation, through Christ, through whom we have access into this state of grace. χάρις is gift, operation and result of the operation at one and the same time. The unity of these elements is provided by the identification of grace with Christ's work.

184 The text is uncertain: Is τῇ πίστει original? The idea of standing in grace also deter- mines the expression "under grace" in R. 6:14, cf. the opp. "under the Law," and also "in grace," 2 C. 1:12, where the sense is again non-habitual. Wetter, 76 takes this ἐν locally, cf. "in Christ." But in neither case is the ἐν local; it can very well be instrumental, Gl. 1:6; Col. 3:16; 4:6; 2 Th. 2:16. On ἐν χάριτι cf. also Ign. Eph., 20, 2; Mg. Inscr.; Sm., 9, 2; 13, 2, and cf. ἐν γνώσει in Corp. Herm., 9, 4 and ἐν ἀγνοίᾳ, 1, 32.

185 The event character comes to expression in the combination of χάρις and δίδωμι, esp. when Paul speaks of his office (→ 396, 11 ff.) but also with ref. to the grace given to the community, 2 C. 8:1, cf. 1 C. 1:4.

186 Materially cf. 1 C. 15:10. The one who calls is God, Ltzm. Gl. on 1:6, or possibly Christ, cf. R. 1:6; but cf. Schlier Gl.13 on 1:6. In Gl. 1:6 the ἐν is to be taken instrumentally, cf. 1:15. "Called to grace" is also possible, cf. 1 C. 7:15. O. Glombitza, "Gnade — das ent- scheidende Wort. Erwägungen z. 1 K. 15:1-11," Nov. Test., 2 (1958), 281-290.

187 "To fall from" is not meant locally; it is a fig. of speech. Cf. ἐκπεσεῖν καὶ στέρεσθαι τῆς πρὸς τὸν δῆμον εὐνοίας, Plut. Tib. Gracch., 21 (I, 834e). Materially cf. 1 C. 10:12.

188 Cf. ὑπερεπερίσσευσεν (→ VI, 60, 16 ff.) and also περισσεύω, 2 C. 4:15, and on this B. Noack, "A Note on 2 C. 4:15," Studia Theologica, 17 (1963), 129-132. Materially cf. Grundmann, 50-72.

189 Grace is not merely the exception in the sense that the elect are a small group. The small number shows that election is a miracle, not the normal case on which we can count.

It makes generosity possible, 2 C. 8:1, cf. 9:8. Its goal is "every good work," 2 C. 9:8. It becomes a demand (2 C. 6:1; Gl. 5:4 ff.) and it does so in such a way as to make compliance possible. Hence compliance cannot set itself up independently as a work; even as achievement it holds the believer fast in the fellowship of grace. The radical consequences of this understanding of grace — Christ the end of the Law — are defended by Paul in Gl. and R. In R. 6:1 he deals with the actual or possibly assumed charge that absolutising the concept will lead to libertinism. Paul refutes this only in a formal and sweeping way; he does not argue in detail. This is appropriate, for the opposing logic is only pseudo-logic. It fails to see that grace is impartation, and that as such it is the destruction of sin. [190]

d. Paul's special grace is his apostolic office [191] χάρις καὶ ἀποστολή, R. 1:5. He has received it (R. 1:5); it was given to him (R. 12:3; 15:15, cf. 1 C. 3:10). [192] The fact of the discharge of his office is grace (2 C. 1:12). His visit to a church is a grace (2 C. 1:15).

e. The verb χαρίζομαι does not have the precise sense of the noun. It is always to be construed in terms of the basic sense "to give." The Pauline element lies in the context rather than the usage, cf. Gl. 3:18. [193] The word stands in a soteriological context in R. 8:32, namely, an exposition of the kerygma. In 1 C. 2:12 the part. denotes the subject-matter of theology and the sense is thus close to that of the noun. Suffering is a gift (Phil. 1:28 f., cf. 2:17; 1 Pt. 4:12 f. → 399, 3 ff.). Phil. 2:9 seems to be pre-Pauline → VIII, 18, 10 ff.; 608, 20 ff. The institution of Jesus into the dignity of the κύριος is a reward given for His obedience. On the basis of the primary sense we find a special form of giving, namely, pardoning, in 2 C. 12:13 → 397, 17 ff.; I, 155, 23 ff. [194]

3. Deutero-Pauline and Other Epistles apart from the Johannine. [195]

a. In Col. 1:6 χάρις means the Gospel, saving doctrine; to hear and perceive God's χάρις is to become a Christian. Since the meaning has already become rather more general we should not try to construe too precisely the singular expression

---

[190] Cf. the emphasis: We are — in freedom — under grace, R. 6:14 f.

[191] A. Satake, "Apostolat u. Gnade bei Pls.," NTSt, 15 (1968/69), 96-105.

[192] For the sense cf. 1 C. 15:10; Gl. 2:9.

[193] Schlier Gl.[13], ad loc. overstresses the emotional aspect: "God has shown Himself gracious to Abraham by promise," cf. n. 3: Perhaps there is an allusion to the vocabulary of inheritance: The testator retains the right ἢ προσδιατάσσων ἢ ἑτέροις χαριζόμενος ἢ καὶ ἄλλο τι βουλόμενος, Mitteis-Wilcken, II, 2, No. 305, 26 (deposition, 156 A.D.). Pr.-Bauer, s.v. χαρίζομαι suggests two possibilities: a. "to give by grace," if τὴν κληρονομίαν is to be supplied from the context; b. "to show oneself gracious to someone." Examples in Pr.-Bauer.

[194] For examples of the sense "to pardon" v. Pr.-Bauer, s.v. Hence one should not assume too limited an origin for the sense, as Loh. Kol.[13], 115, n. 2 does: "This nuance, which is distinctively Pauline in the NT, seems to derive from the law of debt." He ref. to Lk. 7:42; cf. also Philo Spec. Leg., II, 39: τὰ δάνεια χαρίζεσθαι and P. Flor., I, 61, 61 (c. 87 A.D.).

[195] Cf. the summary in Bultmann Theol.[6], 559: "Very generally there is not infrequent reference to divine χάρις, 2 Th. 1:12; 2:16; 1 Tm. 1:14; Ac. 11:23; 14:26; 15:40; 1 Cl., 30, 2 f.; 50, 3; 2 Cl., 13, 4; Ign. Sm., 12, 1; Pol., 2, 1; Herm. m., 10, 3, 1. χάρις can hardly be distinguished here . . . from ἔλεος. They are combined not just in salutations (1 Tm. 1:2; 2 Tm. 1:2; Tt. 1:4 vl.; 2 Jn. 3; Ign. Sm., 12, 2) but elsewhere too (Hb. 4:16); ἔλεος can replace χάρις (Eph. 2:4; Tt. 3:5). χάρις can also be seen in the granting of repentance (1 Cl., 7, 4, which obviously is not thinking only of baptismal repentance like Ac. 5:31; 11:18)."

ἐν τῇ χάριτι ᾄδοντες in Col. 3:16 → I, 164, 38 ff. [196] In Col. 4:6 the word might mean "grace" or "charm." The context seems to favour the latter sense. [197]

Eph. 4:29 takes the word in the sense of grace. In the preface, which is in hymnal style, there is a play on words: εἰς ἔπαινον δόξης τῆς χάριτος αὐτοῦ, ἧς [198] ἐχαρίτωσεν ἡμᾶς ἐν τῷ ἠγαπημένῳ ... κατὰ τὸ πλοῦτος τῆς χάριτος αὐτοῦ, 1:6 f. χάρις is the divine "favour" shown in Christ. Its content is described in terms of baptismal teaching: ἀπολύτρωσις, ἄφεσις τῶν παραπτωμάτων, 1:7, cf. Col. 1:14, 20. Important from the standpoint of historical theology is 2:5-8. The style of v. 7 reminds us of the preface. But the section contains two distinctively Pauline passages [199] safeguarding the "orthodox" understanding of grace. [200] Pauline elements with a similar shift of sense may be seen in Eph. 3:2, 7 f. [201] Paul's concept of office is developed along the lines of the specific Ephesian concept of the Church and tradition. The combination with δίδωμι in 4:7, 29 is stereotyped → 373, 32 ff. [202]

2. Th. contributes nothing materially new. 2:16 has a Pauline ring. 1:12 is obscure. Are we to translate "according to the grace of our God and of the Lord Jesus Christ," or "according to the grace of our God and Lord Jesus Christ"? [203]

The verb χαρίζομαι means "to pardon" in Col. 3:13. Forgiveness is mutually required in the community. The demand is based on the model of the giving of Christ. Eph. puts this in its own way: God's gift in Christ, 4:32. The verb denotes the gracious remission of faults, Col. 2:13 → VII, 785, 18 ff.; 792, 25 ff. [204]

χαριτόω occurs in Eph. 1:6 for "to bless." The sense is established by the link with χάρις → 393, 11 ff.

b. In the Pastorals [205] χάρις has the profane sense of "thanks" at 1 Tm. 1:12. [206] It is typically combined with ἔλεος in salutations → n. 195. In 2 Tm. 2:1 χάρις is

---

[196] Wetter, 77 f. takes ἐν locally. But the strongly realistic concept of grace is not dominant in Col. as Wetter thinks. The usage is simply that of popular Paulinism. Dib. Gefbr.², ad loc. transl. "with thanks" acc. to the context (εὐχάριστοι — χάριτι — εὐχαριστοῦντες). The def. art. (p⁴⁶ B D* G) is, however, against this, and hence Dib. Gefbr.³, ad loc. transl. "Sing, since you are in grace." This does in fact correspond to the average use of χάρις for the Chr. state.

[197] The continuation ἅλατι ἠρτυμένος supports this.

[198] A matter for debate is how ἧς ἐχαρίτωσεν is to be explained: ᾗ or ἥν? Bl.-Debr. § 294, 2 cautiously favours ᾗ, and Wobbe, 49 supports this as follows: "The favour of God is not, however, the content but the basis of the blessing. Hence ἧς arose from the dat. ᾗ."

[199] Note the alternation of pers.

[200] To understand the section we need to take Col. 2:9 ff. into account. The Pauline element wards off a possible Gnostic interpretation of Col. by transferring the resurrection from the future to the past, Col. 2:12, cf. the polemic in 2 Tm. 2:18. Eph. adopts the aor. συνήγειρεν of Col. in Eph. 2:6, but establishes a non-Gnostic sense. Yet post-Pauline features have been seen even in the Pauline elements. Eph. has σεσῳσμένοι, not δικαιωθέντες. δικαιόω does not occur at all in Col. or Eph. and δικαιοσύνη is ethicised, cf. Bultmann Theol.⁶, 529.

[201] Cf. Dib. Gefbr.³ on 3:2, 8. The Paulinising tendency may be seen from comparison with Col. 1:25, where χάρις is not used.

[202] Wetter, 122 pertinently notes that in 4:29 grace is a weaker "pneumatic concept." The same applies to 4:7 as well, and cf. also Jm. 4:6; 1 Pt. 5:5.

[203] If the art. is correctly used only the second transl. is possible. In support of the first one may pt. out that the expressions "God and the κύριος" and "κύριος Ἰησοῦς Χριστός" are fixed, so that the author might not have noticed that the art. should be added, C. Masson, Les deux Ép. de S. Paul aux Thess., Comment. du NT, 11a (1957), ad loc.; B. Rigaux, Les Ép. aux Thess., Études Bibl. (1956), 643.

[204] This is a paraphrase of R. 6:1-11 except that our resurrection with Christ is put in the past, being equated with the forgiveness of sins (in baptism), cf. Col. 1:14.

[205] Moffatt, 303-313; Manson, 52-5; Bultmann Theol.⁶, 535 f.

[206] Moffatt, 304 pts. out that the expression χάριν ἔχω is not Pauline.

the grace of office. Pauline development may be seen in 2 Tm. 1:9. The antithesis of χάρις and ἔργα is adopted but modified by a formula of confession in epiphany style. [207] χάρις is again used for the self-awareness of the apostle according to the successor's view. [208] The same epiphany style controls Tt. 2:11: Revelation is the epiphany of grace. [209] The related Tt. 3:4-7 shows that χάρις can be replaced with χρηστότης, φιλανθρωπία → 111, 11 ff.; ἔλεος is also used in v. 5. Here again the antithesis to works is adopted and the connection between grace and justification is stressed. In the context, however, χάρις is specifically related to the grace of baptism. [210] In 1 Tm. 1:14 the triad of faith, love and hope is changed into χάρις, πίστις and ἀγάπη. [211]

c. Hb. [212] too uses χάρις with ἔλεος, 4:16, cf. 1 Tm. 1:2 etc. → n. 195. Grace is embodied in Christ, the High-priest; one receives it at the throne of God, cf. 7:25. [213] The characteristic themes and motifs may be seen in context. The main soteriological concept is διαθήκη rather than χάρις, → II, 131, 5 ff. The christological theme occurs in the difficult 2:9 → V, 934, 11 ff. [214] Hb. does not speak of the grace of Jesus Christ but rather of His suffering through God's favour. [215] The relationship between the death (or blood) of Christ, the covenant and grace is developed in Hb. 10:29. [216] The antithesis of grace and meats is part of the contrast between the old covenant and the new, 13:9. The new covenant is a crisis for the

---

[207] Cf. on this Dib. Past.[4], ad loc.; E. Pax, "ΕΠΙΦΑΝΕΙΑ," Münchener Theol. Stud., I, 10 (1955), 239-241. Though the wording might suggest that grace is a hypostasis, cf. esp. O. Sol. 33, the context shows that it is the gift of salvation, like ἀγάπη in 1 C. 13; cf. C. Spicq, "Agapè dans le NT, III," Études Bibl. (1959), 20.

[208] On succession in the Past. cf. Moffatt, 312.

[209] Tt. 2:11 reminds us of the epiphany of the Logos in Jn. 1:1 ff., but one is not to see any hypostatising either here or in 2 Tm. 1:9 (→ n. 207). In context the ref. to revelation has a paraenetic thrust.

[210] Moffatt, 308, though he speaks of personification in the light of v. 4 (306). On the characterising of grace as σωτήριος in Tt. 2:11 cf. Spicq, op. cit., 21, n. 1.

[211] Wetter, 114 f.

[212] Moffatt, 345-357. χάρις means "thanks" in Hb. 12:28, cf. 1 Tm. 1:12.

[213] On προσέρχομαι in this connection cf. E. Käsemann, "Das wandernde Gottesvolk," FRL, 55[4] (1961), 31. On the throne of grace cf. τὸν ἐλέου βωμόν, orientated not to God's salvation in Christ but to the sins of men.

[214] Wnd. Hb., ad loc. transl.: "so that by God's grace he might taste of death for every man." He asks whether there is perhaps a lacuna in the text: "in any case the ὅπως clause is not in the right place." The context is against the vl. χωρὶς θεοῦ, cf. v. 10; χωρίς is defended by J. C. O'Neill, "Hebrews 2:9," JThSt, NS, 17 (1966), 79-82. H. Strathmann, Der Br. an d. Hb., NT Deutsch, 9[9] (1968), ad loc.: The section is governed by v. 10: "It was proper for God." Thus the main statement in v. 9 relates to suffering, v. 10 being the basis. Yet there seems to be a ref. to exaltation here. Hence the final clause does not fit in. Death is before exaltation. The solution is that glory and honour relate, not to exaltation, but to high-priestly worth, cf. 5:4 f.; Ex. 28:2. The final clause is to be taken strictly; it explains the "in virtue of the suffering of death." v. 10 can be linked to "through God's grace."

[215] On the significance of Christ's death in Hb. v. Käsemann, op. cit. (→ n. 213), 98-105. As against Strathmann, op. cit. on 2:9, he retains the thought of exaltation. This makes it plain that the death of Jesus has a different character from that of other men. The grace that exalts and crowns Christ shows that Jesus suffered death, and had to suffer it, ὑπὲρ παντός. For it appointed Him Leader and could perfect Him as such only through suffering, Käsemann, 103. Only through suffering could the power of matter be broken.

[216] A. W. Argyle, "Grace and the Covenant," Exp. T., 60 (1948/49), 26 f. compares 1 K. 8:23; Neh. 1:5; 9:32; Da. 9:4 for the linking of grace and covenant חֶסֶד and בְּרִית, cf. also Damasc. 19:1 (8:21). The expression πνεῦμα τῆς χάριτος reminds us of Zech. 12:10 LXX· πνεῦμα χάριτος καὶ οἰκτιρμοῦ.

cultus as it is a crisis for the Law in Paul. [217] From this results the exhortation to God's wandering people, the warning against the danger of lagging behind, 12:15.

d. 1 Pt. also speaks quite naturally of χάρις (1:10), [218] but the term has little influence on the development of theological thinking here. [219] The stress is on the hortatory fruit, the understanding of suffering as grace, 2:19 f. → 368, 6 ff.; 396, 20 f.; IV, 322, 10 ff. The meaning is elucidated by the appended catchword κλέος. [220] A Hellenising trend may be discerned when χάρις is combined with γνῶσις in 2 Pt. 3:18. [221] Jm. 4:6 is obscure: μείζονα δὲ δίδωσιν χάριν. [222]

4. John.

The Johannine writings very seldom use the word group. [223] Apart from greetings formulae like 2 Jn. 3, where we find χάρις with ἔλεος and εἰρήνη, and Rev. 1:4; 22:21, the only instances are Jn. 1:14, 16 f. Here the word denotes the result of the revelation of the Logos. Paul's antithesis of grace and Law is adopted, [224] but it is not developed. The statement is unique in John's Gospel. The sense is determined by the combination with ἀλήθεια (→ I, 245, 1 ff.) [225] and πλήρωμα (→ VI, 302, 33 ff.). [226]

E. Post-Apostolic Fathers. [227]

The NT salutation is adopted from 1 C. and 1 Pt. in 1 Cl. Inscr., cf. the final greeting in 65, 2 and also the formulae in Barn., 21, 9; Pol., 14, 2; Ign. Sm., 13, 2. χάρις occurs with ἔλεος, εἰρήνη and ὑπομονή in Ign. Sm., 12, 2. Elsewhere we find the normal use (→ n. 195) of χάρις for "thanks," "favour," "reward." One may see it in the history of the transmission of the logion Mt. 5:46 and par. (→ n. 152). The saying appears in

---

[217] Is the attack directed against Jewish rules on meats (Wnd. Hb., ad loc.) or against Judaistic Gnosticism (Mi. Hb.[12], ad loc.)?

[218] On χάρις εἰς cf. 1 C. 15:10. The average view also lies behind οἰκονόμοι... χάριτος in 1 Pt. 4:10: Grace is the power of common life in the community, cf. 5:10.

[219] χάρις is practically synon. with σωτηρία, Wetter, 84; Bultmann Theol.[6], 532. Bultmann pts. out that there is no further ref. to justification; apart from 1:10 cf. 1:13; 5:12.

[220] One may perhaps detect an idea of reward here, E. G. Selwyn, The First Ep. of St. Peter[3] (1949), 176, cf. Wetter, 209, but this is not in view. The pt. is the understanding of suffering by sufferers, not by distant observers.

[221] Cf. Jd. 4.

[222] The meaning is uncertain. Wnd. Kath. Br., ad loc. assumes that the text is corrupt. Dib. Jk.[11], ad loc. thinks the statement is transitional, preparing the ground for the next quotation: "If you are faithful he will give you the greater grace."

[223] χαρίζομαι and χαριτόω do not occur. We find εὐχαριστία at Rev. 4:9; 7:12, εὐχαριστέω at Jn. 6:11, 23; 11:41; Rev. 11:17 → 411, 3 ff.

[224] E. Haenchen, "Probleme d. joh. 'Prologs'," Gott u. Mensch (1965), 132 f. ascribes v. 17 to a source closer to Paul than the author of the Fourth Gospel. But the v. is not really Pauline. Bultmann J., 53, n. 4 rightly states that the meaning of χάρις in Jn. 1:17 is nearer the Pauline πνεῦμα.

[225] L. J. Kuyper, "Grace and Truth," The Reformed Review, 16 (1962), 1-16 finds the origin of this in the OT combination of חֶסֶד and אֱמֶת.

[226] πλήρης in v. 14 is difficult. Bultmann J., 49, n. 2 does not think it goes with δόξα but possibly with ὁ λόγος (certainly so if v. 14 originally belongs together with v. 16, Bultmann J., 49, n. 1) or as indeclinable with αὐτοῦ. On the Logos cf. Philo Som., I, 75; II, 245; Rer. Div. Her., 188. God's διαθήκη is πλήρης χαρίτων, Som., II, 223, cf. 183. In the prophetic consecration of the Marcosites revelation is represented as reception of χάρις: λάμβανε πρῶτον ἀπ' ἐμοῦ, καὶ δι' ἐμοῦ τὴν χάριν... ἰδοὺ ἡ χάρις κατῆλθεν ἐπὶ σε, Iren. Haer. I, 7, 2 (I, 118), cf. Corp. Herm., 1, 32; Ascl., 41; Did., 10, 6 → 400, 5 ff. The phrase χάριν ἀντὶ χάριτος expresses the inexhaustibility of grace, cf. Philo Post. C., 145, and cf. χάρις ἐπὶ χάριτι in Sir. 26:15.

[227] Bonwetsch, 93-6; Torrance, 36-132.

Did., 1, 3 in the version: ποία γὰρ χάρις, ἐὰν ἀγαπᾶτε τοὺς ἀγαπῶντας ὑμᾶς; [228] and then in 2 Cl., 13, 4a in the form: οὐ χάρις ὑμῖν, εἰ ἀγαπᾶτε τοὺς ἀγαπῶντας ὑμᾶς, ἀλλὰ χάρις ὑμῖν, εἰ ἀγαπᾶτε τοὺς ἐχθροὺς καὶ τοὺς μισοῦντας ὑμᾶς, [229] cf. Ign. Pol., 2, 1: καλοὺς μαθητὰς ἐὰν φιλῇς, χάρις σοι οὐκ ἔστιν. [230]

In the Did. [231] 10, 6 [232] is of interest: ἐλθέτω χάρις καὶ παρελθέτω ὁ κόσμος οὗτος. If χάρις is to be read, [233] it denotes sacramental grace and hence the sum of Messianic salvation, or, less probably, the Lord Himself, in which case χάρις would be a synon. of λόγος. [234] In 1 Cl. [235] "grace" is the saving result of conversion. [236] The prophets are οἱ λειτουργοὶ τῆς χάριτος τοῦ θεοῦ, 8, 1. [237] The Chr. state is the "yoke (→ II, 896, 7 ff.) of his grace," 16, 17. There is no antithesis to works. On the contrary, instruction is given on how to achieve grace by right conduct, 30, 2 f. In this connection one may ref. to the summons to unity on the basis of the one God, the one Christ, the one Spirit of grace, the one calling to Christ, 46, 6. [238] The data in relation to Ign. are richer only in appearance. [239] In reality the weaker gen. use prevails here too. Grace is a power at work in the community, Sm., 9, 2; 13, 2; R. Inscr.; Mg., 8, 2 and esp. in the ordained bishop, Mg., 2, 1; Pol., 1, 2. [240] It is the totality of salvation, Eph., 11, 1; Mg., 8, 1; Sm., 6, 2, the gracious will of God or of Christ, R., 1, 2; Phld., 8, 1; 11, 1; Sm., 11, 1. Here again, as in the case of πίστις, there is no antithesis to works. [241] Grace is the motif in the call to unity, Eph., 20, 2 [242] and the warning against heterodoxy, Sm., 6, 2. Sometimes a personal note may be detected. Ign. trusts in God's grace with ref. to the community, Phld., 8, 1, cf. Pol., 7, 3 and esp. R., 1, 2: It is grace when he achieves his destiny, martyrdom, 6, 2. [243] Pol., 1, 3 reproduces the antithesis to works but with no theological point, cf. Eph., 2, 8 f.; Tt. 3:5; 1 Cl., 32, 3. Barn., [244] 2 Cl. [245] and Herm. [246] add no new features to the general picture.

---

[228] On the relation to the tradition cf. Köster, op. cit. (→ n. 152), 224 f. From this ref. alone there can be no certainty whether the collection used Lk. as well as Mt., or along with Mt. only free tradition. J. P. Audet, La Didachè (1958), 183-6 contests the influence of Mt. and Lk.; he also regards Did., 1, 3b-5 as an interpolation.

[229] Köster, op. cit., 75-7 thinks 2 Cl. knows Lk. and adduces the passage from memory.

[230] Ibid., 44 f. Without χάρις in Just. Apol., I, 15, 9: εἰ ἀγαπᾶτε τοὺς ἀγαπῶντας ὑμᾶς, τί καινὸν ποιεῖτε; cf. E. Massaux, "Le texte du Sermon sur la montagne de Matthieu utilisé par S. Justin," Ephemerides theol. Lovanienses, 28 (1952), 428-431; J. C. O'Neill, The Theology of Acts (1961), 32.

[231] Torrance, 36-43.

[232] The Coptic version presupposes κύριος, not χάρις. M. Dibelius, "Die Mahl-Gebete d. Did.," Botschaft u. Gesch., II (1956), 125 prefers this, but not H. Lietzmann, Messe u. Herrenmahl³ (1955), 237.

[233] Cf. the confrontation with κόσμος.

[234] Cf. Lietzmann, op. cit. (→ n. 232), 237, n. 2; F. J. Dölger, Sol Salutis (1952), 204-9.

[235] Torrance, 44-55.

[236] 1 Cl., 7, 4 is elucidated by 12, 7; 49, 6. χάρις occurs with ἔλεος, 50, 2 f.

[237] Cf. 1 Cl., 23, 1: The all-merciful and benevolent Father lavishes His "graces." On the plur. cf. Philo → 389, 22 f.

[238] For this extension of a triadic formula cf. Eph. 4:4-6.

[239] Torrance, 56-89.

[240] Wetter, 70 thinks χάρις is a hypostasis in Mg., 2, 1, cf. Eus. Hist. Eccl., II, 1, 10; V, 1, 6. The context is against this. Cf. χάρισμα in Ign. Sm. Inscr.; Ign. Pol., 2, 2; Bultmann Theol.⁶, 547.

[241] Bultmann Theol.⁶, 547.

[242] But it is only a secondary motif, the chief one being unity of belief.

[243] Ign. Sm., 11, 1 is obscure: "I am not worthy to be from there (sc. Antioch) ... κατὰ θέλημα (God's) δὲ κατηξιώθην, οὐκ ἐκ συνειδότος, ἀλλ' ἐκ χάριτος θεοῦ, ἣν εὔχομαι τελείαν μοι δοθῆναι. Bau. Ign., ad loc.: "Either the sole-operative grace of God rules out all human 'co-knowledge' or Ign. feels that in spite of his 'conscience' he is accepted as worthy by divine grace."

[244] Torrance, 100-110. Apart from Barn., 5, 6; 9, 8; 14, 9 cf. ἔμφυτον τῆς δωρεᾶς πνευματικῆς χάριν εἰλήφατε, 1, 2, Wetter, 125, and the final greeting in 21, 9. At 14, 9 χάρις is an addition to the quotation from Is. 61:1 f.

[245] Torrance, 126-132. χάρις occurs only in the dominical sayings at 2 Cl., 13, 4, → line 2 f.

[246] Torrance, 111-125.

Things are similar with the verbs χαρίζομαι [247] and χαριτόω. The former denotes God's giving, e.g., in the sacrament, Did., 10, 3, [248] cf. also Ign. Eph., 1, 3; 2 Cl., 1, 4; Herm. s., 9, 28, 6. χαριτόω is used in the same way in Herm. s., 9, 24, 3. [249]

F. Gnosticism.

χάρις is not a basic term. The features of later antiquity are plain. χάρις is power → 376, 7 ff. [250] Gnostic intensification may be seen in the view of the inflowing of this power, of illumination, cf. the closing prayer of Poim., Corp. Herm., 1, 32. [251] χάρις is also hypostatised, [252] very finely in O. Sol., in which taibutha "grace" [253] appears as a person, 33. [254] The same figure, which is simply a variation on Sophia (→ VII, 507, 20 ff.), may be seen in the background of the epicleses of Act. Thom. 27 and 50, where it is called εὐσπλαγχνία. [255] The occasional use of the word in Act. Thom. is non-specific. [256] The same is true in Act. Joh., cf. the hymn of Jesus: δόξα σοι χάρις, 94. We find the term in lists of soteriological concepts, 98 and 106.

The following survey will perhaps shed light on the relation between χάρις as gift and hypostasis. It is a gift in the eucharist of the Marcosites. Participants drink the blood of χάρις: ἡ πρὸ τῶν ὅλων ἡ ἀνεννόητος καὶ ἄρρητος Χάρις πληρῶσαι σου τὸν ἔσω ἄνθρωπον, καὶ πληθύναι ἐν σοὶ τὴν γνῶσιν αὐτῆς... λάμβανε πρῶτον ἀπ' ἐμοῦ, καὶ δι' ἐμοῦ τὴν χάριν, Iren. Haer., I, 7, 2, (I, 117 f.). It is also a gift in the Coptic-Gnostic writings. In the Gospel of Mary 9:16 [257] the disciples ask how they are to preach the Gospel to the Gentiles. Mary answers: "Do not weep... for his χάρις will be with you all." If one may detect in the Marcosites a connection between soteriology — grace as gift — and hypostatising, this is worked out clearly in the Valentinians: "The perfect will become pregnant and give birth through a kiss. This is why we kiss one another. We become pregnant through the grace that we have among us," Gospel of Philip,

---

[247] In the Apologists cf. τὰ μυστήρια χαρίζεσθαι ὑμῖν τοῦ θεοῦ in Just. Dial., 131, 4, cf. also 119, 5; it is said of idols πῶς ἄλλοις σωτηρίαν χαρίσονται; Aristid. Apol., 3, 2 [Bertram].

[248] ἔδωκας is used with ref. to the par. gifts of creation "food" and "drink."

[249] Cf. Jm. 1:5 and Wnd. Kath. Br., ad loc.

[250] Eus. Hist. Eccl., II, 1, 10: Philip comes to Samaria, θείας τε ἔμπλεως δυνάμεως κηρύττει πρῶτος τοῖς αὐτόθι τὸν λόγον, τοσαύτη δ' αὐτῷ θεία συνήργει χάρις, ὡς καὶ Σίμωνα τὸν μάγον μετὰ πλείστων ὅσων τοῖς αὐτοῦ λόγοις ἑλχθῆναι.

[251] ἐπίνευσόν μοι καὶ ἐνδυνάμωσόν με, καὶ τῆς χάριτος ταύτης φωτίσω τοὺς ἐν ἀγνοίᾳ τοῦ γένους, μοῦ ἀδελφούς, υἱοὺς δὲ σοῦ, Corp. Herm., 1, 32. On illumination → 335, 9 ff. Cf. the closing prayer in Ascl., 41: gratias tibi summe, exsuperantissime; tua enim gratia tantum sumus cognitionis tuae lumen consecuti, and on this Reitzenstein Hell. Myst., 286 f.

[252] G. Bornkamm, "Mythos u. Legende in d. apokr. Thomas-Akten," FRL, 49 (1933), 94: "It is of the nature of these hypostatic figures that now they are the deity itself and now the divine operation, now a definite figure and now a χάρισμα."

[253] The equation of taibutha and χάρις is directly attested by the Coptic text of Ode 25:4 and the newly discovered Gk. text of 11:1, ed. M. Testuz, Pap. Bodmer X-XII (1959), 60, cf. also A. Adam, "Die urspr. Sprache d. Salomo-O.," ZNW, 52 (1961), 146 f.

[254] Like wisdom it is a virgin. Note that the usual sense of "gift" also occurs in O. Sol. 34:6; 24:3; "Without payment I received thy grace," 5:3 Syr. version.

[255] Bornkamm, op. cit., 89-94: "Celebration of the eucharist is wholly along the lines of the ἱερὸς γάμος, so we may equate at once Χάρις and the Ἀχαμώθ of the νυμφῶν sacrament (sc. of the Valentinians)." Bornkamm, 93 f. quotes O. Sol. 33 and also the Ophite magic saying of the soul passing through the kingdom of the aeons; every petition contains ἡ χάρις συνέστω (μοι), (ναὶ) πάτηρ, συνέστω, Orig Cels., VI, 31. But there is no hypostatising here.

[256] Grace goes with Thomas: "Come to the truly good that you may receive grace through it and set its sign in your souls," 28 (p. 145, 14 ff.).

[257] Ed. W. C. Till, "Die gnost. Schr. d. kpt. Pap. Berolinensis, 8502," TU, 60 (1955).

Saying 31 (107, 2 ff.). [258] Cf. Gospel of Truth [259] 35:36 ff.: "Similarly the πλήρωμα, which is without lack, fills the lack. He (the Father) has given it (the πλήρωμα) of Himself to fill up what he (the needy one) lacks in order that he may receive grace. For at the time he suffered want he did not have grace," and also the accounts in the fathers: The Αὐτοπάτωρ, who in the beginning enclosed the all in Himself ... ὃν καλοῦσί τινες Αἰῶνα ἀγήρατον, ἀεὶ νεάζοντα, ἀρρενόθηλυν, ὃς πάντοτε περιέχει τὰ πάντα καὶ οὐκ ἐνπεριέχεται, τότε ἡ ἐν αὐτῷ Ἔννοια ἠθέλησεν — ἐκείνη, ἥν τινες Ἔννοιαν ἔφασαν, ἕτεροι Χάριν· οἰκείως, διὰ τὸ ἐπικεχορηγηκέναι αὐτὴν θησαυρίσματα τοῦ Μεγέθους τοῖς ἐκ τοῦ Μεγέθους, οἱ δὲ ἀληθεύσαντες Σιγὴν προσηγόρευσαν, Epiph. Haer., 31, 5, 3 f.; τοῦτον (the Aeon) δὲ καὶ προαρχὴν καὶ προπάτορα καὶ Βυθὸν καλοῦσιν ... συνυπάρχειν δ' αὐτῷ καὶ Ἔννοιαν, ἣν δὴ καὶ Χάριν καὶ Σιγὴν ὀνομάζουσι, Iren. Haer., I, 1, 1 (I, 8 f.). In the Valentinian comm. on the Prologue to Jn.'s Gospel, 1:14 is expounded as follows: ἀκριβῶς οὖν καὶ τὴν πρώτην ἐμήνυσε τετράδα· Πατέρα εἰπών, καὶ Χάριν, καὶ τὸν Μονογενῆ, καὶ Ἀλήθειαν, Iren. Haer., I, 1, 18 (I, 80). [260] There is wild speculation in the Coptic-Gnost. works. Pist. Soph. 60 (p. 76, 33 ff.) quotes ψ 84:11 f. with the terms grace, truth, righteousness and peace, and comments: "Grace is the power of light which has come forth through the first mystery." In the Wisdom of Jesus Christ (→ n. 257) 87 f. the Redeemer praises the wealth in existent Spirit. "Because of his goodness and love (ἀγάπη) he wanted to bring forth fruit of himself that he should not enjoy his goodness alone ... Glory, incorruptibility and his boundless grace (χάρις) ..., 88:2 ff. From the light, i.e., Christ, appear four gt. lights, χάρις, σύνεσις, αἴσθησις and φρόνησις. χάρις belongs to the first light, Harmozêl, the angel (ἄγγελος) of light in the first aeon (αἰών), with which are three aeons (αἰών), χάρις, truth and μορφή, Apocr. Jn. (→ n. 257) 33:6-11. In Anon. Ancient Gnostic Work [261] 7 we read: "Thou art, thou art the μονογενής, light and life and χάρις."

χάρισμα.

A. Usage. [1]

χάρισμα, a verbal noun of χαρίζομαι, is a rare and late word, [2] one of the favourite

---

[258] Ed. W. C. Till, *Patrist. Texte u. Stud.*, 2 (1963). The perfect are Gnostics, though cf. J. Leipoldt - H. M. Schenke, "Kpt.-gnost. Schr. aus d. Pap.-Cod. v. Nag Hamadi," *Theol. Forschung*, 20 (1960), 43, n. 7: the aeons. Cf. also Saying 106 (124, 22 ff.); 114 (127, 15 ff.).
[259] Ed. M. Malinine *et al.* (1961). On its debated Valentinian character *v.* Jonas Gnosis, I³, 408-418.
[260] Λόγος, Ζωή, Ἄνθρωπος and Ἐκκλησία complete the ogdoad.
[261] Cf. C. Schmidt - W. C. Till, *Kpt.-gnost. Schriften*, I, GCS, 45³ (1959), 344, 11 ff.

χ ά ρ ι σ μ α . Bibl.: → χαίρω κτλ., χάρις κτλ. On A.: On the phenomenon: F. Taeger, *Charisma. Stud. z. Gesch. d. antiken Herrscherkultes*, I (1957), II (1960). On C.: H. Weinel, *Die Wirkungen d. Geistes u. der Geister im nachapost. Zeitalter bis auf Iren.* (1899); F. J. A. Hort, *The Christian Ecclesia* (1900), 153-170; H. Gunkel, *Die Wirkungen d. hl. Geistes*³ (1909); F. Grau, *Der nt.liche Begriff Charisma*, Diss. Tübingen (1947); T. N. Sterrett, *New Testament Charismata*, Diss. Dallas (1952); J. Brosch, *Charismen u. Ämter in d. Urkirche* (1951); G. Friedrich, "Geist u. Amt," *Wort u. Dienst*, NF, 3 (1952), 61-85; E. Kohlmeyer, "Charisma oder Recht?" *Zschr. d. Savigny-Stiftung, Kanonistische Abteilung*, 38 (1952), 1-36; H. D. Wendland, "Das Wirken d. Hl. Geistes in den Gläubigen nach Pls.," *ThLZ*, 77 (1952), 457-470; O. Perels, "Apostolat u. Amt im NT," *Schr. d. Theol. Konvents Augsburgischen Bekenntnisses*, 5 (1953), 24-39; H. Greeven, "Die Geistesgaben bei Pls.," *Wort u. Dienst*, NF, 6 (1959), 111-120; W. Schrage, *Die konkreten Einzelgebote in d. paul. Paränese* (1961), 141-6; I. Hermann, "Kyrios u. Pneuma," *Stud. z. AT u. NT*, 2 (1961), 69-85; G. Hasenhüttl, "Charisma, Ordnungsprinzip d. Kirche," *Ökumenische Forschungen*, I, 5 (1969); H. Schürmann, *Die geistlichen Gnadengaben in d. paul. Gemeinden, Ursprung u. Gestalt* (1970), 236-267.
[1] We shall not be discussing general charismatic phenomena here. On these *v.* Taeger, *passim*; G. van der Leeuw, *Phänomenologie d. Religion*² (1956), Index *s.v.* "Charismata."
[2] Cf. Liddell-Scott, Preisigke Wört., Pr.-Bauer, *s.v.*

koine [3] constructs in -μα. In Philo it occurs in Leg. All., III, 78 [4] and a fr., [5] and cf. BGU, IV, 1044, 5 (4th cent. A.D.); II, 551, 3 (Arab period); Preisigke Sammelbuch, I, 4789, 7 (Byzant.); P. Lond., I, 77, 24 (8th cent. A.D.), and also Alciphr. Ep., III, 17, 4. It denotes the result [6] of χάρις viewed as an action with no sharp distinction from this term: [7] "proof of favour," "benefit," "gift." Since the material outside the NT tells us almost nothing, the context must decide in each case.

B. Septuagint and Judaism.

חֶסֶד is transl. χάρισμα "mercy" at ψ 30:22 Θ (LXX ἔλεος). Sir. has the word twice, but the textual tradition is not secure. Sir. 7:33: One should not deny the final χάρις (Cod. S χάρισμα) to a dead man, i.e., one should grant him the practice of mercy by burial. [8] Sir. 38:30 Cod. B uses the term for a "lovely work." Philo hardly makes any distinction from χάρις, cf. Leg. All., III, 78 → n. 4. Sib., 2, 54: πᾶσά τε γὰρ ψυχὴ μερόπων θεοῦ ἐστι χάρισμα. [9]

C. New Testament.

1. General Aspects.

The word occurs only in the Pauline corpus with an echo in 1 Pt. In Paul it is restricted to R. and 1 and 2 C. (and the Past.), and the context is always soteriological. [10] χάρισμα is linked with χάρις on the one side and πνεῦμα on the other to the degree that spiritual manifestations are called χαρίσματα. [11] Apart from specific contexts the general tenor of the three epistles is to be noted. In all three χάρισμα is used already in the preface → 412, 11 ff. In 1 C. 1:7, a typical ὥστε clause, it corresponds to χάρις in v. 4 → 412, 19 f. This takes concrete shape in specific gifts (R. 12:6; 1 C. 12:11), capabilities of which two are mentioned as particularly characteristic of the church at Corinth, λόγος and γνῶσις, cf. 1 C. 12:8. This is an anticipation of the express discussion of χαρίσματα in 1 C. 12-14. [12] Also to be noted is the relation to εὐχαριστέω (→ 412, 22 ff.) and the eschatological orientation. [13] This will later prove to be a criterion in respect of the enthusiastic

---

[3] Schwyzer, I, 128: "The preponderance of constructs in -μα as compared with -σις in the koine seems to be Ionic."

[4] Cf. L. Cohn, "Philo von Alex.," NJbch. Kl. Alt., 1 (1898), 539, n. 1, who cuts out χάρισμα in the first instance and replaces it with χάρις in the second.

[5] Ed. J. R. Harris, Fragments of Philo Judaeus (1886), 84.

[6] Schwyzer, I, 522: "Later fundamentally nomina rei actae (in contrast to -μός and -σις), they (sc. neuters in -μα) were already at an early stage terms for objects as well." Acc. to Bl.-Debr. § 109, 2 also derivates in -μα usually denote the result of an action. But care is needed in the NT in spite of Bl.-Debr. § 109, 2, where it is stated that baptism is βαπτισμός while βάπτισμα includes the result as well; this is too schematic.

[7] G. P. Wetter, "Charis," UNT, 5 (1913), 174: "As χάρισμα overlaps the field of χάρις, so does χάρις that of χάρισμα," R. 15:15.

[8] Cf. V. Ryssel, Kautzsch Apkr. u. Pseudepigr. on Sir. 7:33; Grau, 16-19.

[9] χάρισμα does not occur in Joseph. [Rengstorf].

[10] The starting-pt. for understanding is illuminated by R. 11:29: χαρίσματα καὶ κλῆσις. This is formulated as a gen. sentence but with ref. to Israel. The gifts are more precisely listed in R. 9:4 f.

[11] One cannot say whether it was Paul himself who brought χαρίσματα into use as a term for πνευματικά → VI, 436, 30 ff.

[12] Even if one does not accept the unity of 1 C. the preface and c. 12-14 belong together, v. W. Schmithals, "Die Gnosis in Korinth," FRL, 66² (1965), 85 and 89.

[13] The prefaces of 2 C., Phil. and 1 Th. are eschatologically orientated.

estimation of gifts by the Corinthians. [14] In this regard the future is not just understood apocalyptically as the age that is still to come. Rather the present is eschatologically determined by χάρις as the time of the Spirit. Dialectic rules: The gift is present, but its possession is only provisional. This aspect may be seen in the ὅς καὶ βεβαιώσει of 1 C. 1:8, which is addressed to those who think they are firmly established as pneumatics. [15] The totality of the conferred gift of salvation is χάρισμα in 2 C. 1:11. [16] This is also the sense in R. 5:15 f. in the context of the Adam-Christ typology, [17] which is broken in order to bring out the supremacy of grace. χάρισμα is the result of this, or the saving act with all its effects, [18] cf. the heaping up of descriptions: ἡ χάρις... καὶ ἡ δωρεὰ ἐν χάριτι, δώρημα, δικαίωμα. [19] The sense is more formal, "gift," in R. 6:23 [20] and the preface (R. 1:11), where it is qualified by πνευματικόν: As an apostle Paul has a χάρισμα πνευματικόν to offer, though he at once corrects himself and says that it is a matter of mutual giving and receiving, cf. R. 14:19. Here χάρισμα is very generally what is given with πίστις, namely, his preaching, cf. the context. [21] There is an individualising element in 1 C. 7:7. Each has his own gift from God. [22] In the context this qualifies the demand for celibacy, which Paul regards as the ideal but does not impose as a law. [23]

2. χαρίσματα.

a. In 1 C. 12-14 and R. 12 Paul describes as χαρίσματα the ecstatic phenomena at divine worship which are regarded as operations of the Spirit, notably speaking

---

[14] Heinr. 1 K., ad loc. takes χάρισμα in 1 C. 1:7 in a broader sense than in c. 12-14 for all "supernatural powers and blessings," but Joh. W., 1 K. gives it the special sense of πνευματικά. The alternative is posed too sharply. Paul does generalise χάρισμα, but from the standpt. of grace, not the phenomena.

[15] ὑστερέομαι in v. 7 can mean "to lack," but then one would expect the gen. The sense "to lag behind" is suggested by the ἐν, cf. Schl. K., ad loc. with a ref. to 2 C. 11:5; cf. Plat. Resp., VI, 484d: μηδ' ἐν ἄλλῳ μηδενὶ μέρει ἀρετῆς ὑστεροῦντας. Yet we should accept the first meaning → VIII, 597, 22 ff. There is no comparison here but a positive ref. to the wealth of the Corinthians.

[16] Others construe more narrowly as the "gracious gift of deliverance from danger of death," Pr.-Bauer, s.v. But cf. Wnd. 2 K., ad loc.: As I see it there is no attestation for the sense of "gracious intervention."

[17] E. Brandenburger, "Adam u. Christus," Wissenschaftliche Monographien z. AT u. NT, 7 (1962), 219-231.

[18] If one understands χάρισμα as "gracious gift," one must accept the lack of any exact logical parallelism, Brandenburger, op. cit., 219 f. To get this many exegetes construe it as "gracious act," v. G. Bornkamm, "Paul. Anakoluthe im R.," Das Ende d. Gesetzes⁵ (1966), 85; C. K. Barrett, A Comm. on the Epistle to the Romans, Black's NT Comm. (1957) on 5:15. In this case it has the same content as δικαίωμα. But these statements do not demand exact parallelism and παράπτωμα is the totality, the act of Adam and its effect. χάρισμα is to be taken similarly.

[19] On the opp. side are παράπτωμα, κρίμα, κατάκριμα. On the style cf. Bl.-Debr. § 488, 3: Constructs in -μα are "among the deliciae of Hellenistic stylists."

[20] In contrast to ὀψώνιον: Death is the appropriate penalty for sin. On the other hand life is a "gift."

[21] But cf. Mi. R.¹⁴, ad loc.: Paul comes as a pneumatic. He wants to enter into dialogue with the Roman pneumatics but also to assert his authority over them.

[22] In context the emphasis is not on the fact that every Christian has a gift, though Paul assumes this, but on the fact that God assigns the gifts.

[23] Marriage is not called a χάρισμα here, v. Ltzm. K. on 1 C. 7:7. On the historical presupposition — ἐγκράτεια as a divine gift — cf. Wis. 8:21; Ep. Ar., 237, v. Joh. W. 1 K. on 7:7.

in tongues and prophecy. [24] According to the Corinthian measuring of the ecstatic life, glossolalia comes first as heavenly speech. Paul recognises that this phenomenon is the work of the Spirit but he subjects it to the criterion of χάρις. [25] He first points out the ambivalence of ecstasy as such, 1 C. 12:1-3. Then he establishes confession of the κύριος as a norm, since this is the work of the Spirit. There then follows an explication in which understanding of the phenomena is referred back to the concept of God and that of the Church, vv. 4 ff. God does not give general manfestations; He gives to each his own; in this way the Church is built up as the body of Christ. The result of this interpretation is that πνευματικά are not the eternal already present to-day. They rather represent our future possession in provisional form. All that serves to edify is χάρισμα, including everyday secular service as well as ecstatic operations. [26] An exegetical problem is posed by the triadic structure adopted by Paul, 1 C. 12:4-6. He divides the gifts into χαρίσματα, διακονίαι (→ II, 87, 16 ff.) and ἐνεργήματα (→ II, 653, 27 ff.) and relates them to the Spirit, the Lord and God. It is doubtful whether there is a strict correspondence between χαρίσματα (mediated by πνευματικά) and the Spirit, διακονίαι and the Lord, and ἐνεργήματα and God. [27] If the rhetorical element is noted one will avoid schematisation. On God's side there is a crescendo, but not on the side of the gifts or operations. [28] The rhetorical triadic presentation constitutes the multiplicity of phenomena a unity of divine manifestation and also shows that each has a gift, his own gift. The triad has theological relevance for the self-understanding of the Church. The relation between the unity of the Spirit's operation and the plurality of expressions may be seen in the fact that the χαρίσματα, διακονίαι and ἐνεργήματα are not three different groups of operations. They are simply different descriptions. They are all the operation of the one Spirit, v. 11. [29] The operations are supernatural but not magical or mechanical, for one can cultivate (ζηλόω) these gifts, cf. 12:31 and 14:1. [30] Only to a certain degree can the specific gifts mentioned be defined and distinguished.

---

[24] The change in the understanding of χαρίσματα may be seen by comparing F. C. Baur, *Pls.* (1845), Gunkel, Weinel, Wetter, *op. cit.* (→ n. 7) and modern exegesis. Baur, 559: The charismata are "in themselves... only the gifts and talents that each brings to Christianity." They become charismata only as out of them *quasi* material "Christian consciousness and life is shaped in its various individual forms" through the work of the Spirit. Baur's idealistic interpretation of the Spirit has been outdated by the study of motifs in comparative religion. This has shown that the Spirit is not understood as an enhancement of the natural but as a supernatural potency. The works of the Spirit are "unspiritual" in the idealistic sense, for they involve ecstasy.

[25] The link with χάρις is not expressly made in 1 C. 12. It is thus debated whether χάρισμα is more closely related to χάρις in Paul. But the ref. is there in R. 12. The close relation between 1 C. and R. should be noted. The concept of faith is adopted in R. 12:3; this leads to an individualising of gifts acc. to the μέτρον πίστεως, cf. Bultmann Theol.[6], 326: This "corresponds to the share in the χαρίσματα... For as πίστις individualises itself into specific attitudes, so divine χάρις individualises itself into specific gifts of grace."

[26] This is a radical secularisation, not just a transposing of the understanding of grace into terms of the world. The religious itself is seen as secular. Opposed is the objectifying of the Spirit, the autonomy of the pneumatic.

[27] Joh. W. 1 K. on 12:4 advocates correspondence, Ltzm. K. on 1 C. 12:4 f. denies it.

[28] But cf. Hermann, 71-6, who see a crescendo on both sides.

[29] διαιρέω does not stress distinction but means "to assign."

[30] There is, of course, a critical problem which is also a theological problem: Does 1 C. 13 originally belong here? Is, then, the division into higher and lower gifts originally Pauline? What is the relation of the complex superordination of the triad faith-hope-love to their inner ranking, to the superordination of love? Even if the literary question be left an open one, the

The inclusion of acts of ministry in the Church among the charismata initiated a momentous development and posed one of the most difficult problems in the early history of the Church, namely, that of Spirit and office. One cannot accept the well-known distinction between charismatics and office-bearers, [31] or at least not in terms of the way that the early Church viewed itself. [32] This distinction rests on an antithesis between office/law on the one side and Spirit on the other. [33] But the Spirit Himself posits law. [34]

b. The Pastorals develop the concept of charisma of office. This is conferred in ordination, 1 Tm. 4:14; 2 Tm. 1:6; → VI, 451, 20 ff.; 666, n. 92. No reference is made to the χάρισμα of ordinary Christians. [35] According to 1 Pt. 4:10 (→ IV, 138, 31 ff.; V, 151, 8 ff.) [36] any act of service in keeping the commandment of love is χάρισμα. Basically endowment with the Spirit has become a Christian quality. [37]

D. The Early Church.

In the post-apost. fathers [38] there is little worthy of note. Formalising may be seen in Did., 1, 5. [39] 1 Cl., 38, 1 includes the benefits of the Creator. [40] Justin uses the charismata as an argument against the Jews, Dial., 88, 1, cf. 82, 1: [41] The great gifts have passed from Judaism to Christianity. Iren. Haer., V, 6, 1 (II, 334) enlists their aid to show the divine power of the Church. [42]

---

material context is Pauline. The manifestations the Corinthians think are eternal are in reality transitory, as may be seen from the things that abide, which are not manifestations in the same sense. 1 C. 13:8-11 is in antithesis to the Corinthian assessment of the manifestations. 13:13 has a polemical edge, v. G. Bornkamm, "Der köstlichere Weg," Das Ende d. Gesetzes[5] (1966), 93-112; also "Die Erbauung d. Gemeinde als Leib Christi," ibid., 117: "The charismata bear the mark of corruptibility in contrast to love, which does not fail, and they are nothing without love."

[31] Ltzm. K. on 1 C.12:28 on ἀντιλήμψεις and κυβερνήσεις: These terms denote the technical officers, the διάκονοι and ἐπίσκοποι. "They are not among the charismatic officers in the narrower sense ... and hence they are left out again in v. 29 f." → n. 32.

[32] The same applies to the thesis that there was a twofold organisation, congregational ministers on the one side and roving charismatics with a general position in the Church on the other, v. H. Greeven, "Propheten, Lehrer, Vorsteher bei Pls.," ZNW, 44 (1952/53), 1-43: Prophets and teachers are linked to individual churches, cf. H. v. Campenhausen, "Kirchliches Amt u. geistliche Vollmacht in d. ersten drei Jhdt.," Beiträge z. hist. Theol., 14[2] (1963), 65 f. There is no antithesis between Spirit and law.

[33] R. Sohm, Kirchenrecht, I (1892), passim.

[34] v. Campenhausen, op. cit., 62: The Spirit is "the organising principle of the Chr. community." Cf. E. Käsemann, "Sätze hl. Rechtes im NT," Exeget. Versuche u. Besinnungen, II[3] (1968), 248-260; Bultmann Theol.[6], 456 f.

[35] Grau, 80-89 sees a trend towards materialising the χάρισμα as a force put in men rather than a gift. On the grace of office v. v. Campenhausen, 125 f.

[36] Grau, 90-94.

[37] v. Campenhausen, 89.

[38] G. Bardy, "La théol. de l'église de S. Clément de Rome à S. Irénée," Unam Sanctam, 13 (1945), 128-156.

[39] On the Did. ibid., 134-8 and Grau, 95-7.

[40] Cf. also Ign. Sm. Inscr.; Eph., 17, 2; Pol., 2, 2; Bardy, op. cit., 138-143.

[41] On Just. and Iren. Wetter, op. cit. (→ n. 7), 182-7.

[42] Wetter, 184: Grace detaches itself from those who bear it and becomes an autonomous force.

εὐχαριστέω, εὐχαριστία, εὐχάριστος.

Contents: A. Profane Greek: 1. Usage; 2. Meaning. B. Judaism. C. New Testament: 1. Gospels, Acts and Revelation; 2. Paul; 3. Deutero-Paulines. D. Early Church.

A. Profane Greek.

1. Usage.

a. The word group is not Attic, cf. Phryn. Ecl., 11.[1] Εὐχάριστος "pleasant" occurs for the first time in Hdt., I, 32, 9 and Xenoph. Oec., 5, 10, "grateful" for the first time in Xenoph. Cyrop., 8, 3, 49. Most of the instances are post-classical. The verb εὐχαριστέω means "to show someone a favour" καὶ τὸ εὐχαριστεῖν ἐπὶ τοῦ διδόναι χάριν, οὐκ ἐπὶ τοῦ εἰδέναι, Poll. Onom., V, 141, cf. φιλόδωρος δὲ καὶ εὐχάριστος, ἐπὶ γὰρ τούτῳ τάττεται τοὔνομα, 140. It is used with dat. of pers.: τῶι δήμωι τῶι Δηλίων, IG², XI, 4, 665, 24 f. (3rd cent. B.C.). A favour imposes the obligation of thanks εὐχαριστήσεις μοι, Witkowski, 12, 6, τοῦτο δὲ ποιήσας εὐχαριστήσεις ἡμῖν, P. Petr., II, 15, 3, 6 f. (both 3rd cent. B.C.). Hence the meaning arises "to be thankful," "to give thanks," Polyb., 16, 25, 1 etc.; τοῖς ὄχλοις, Diod. S., 20, 34, 5. Recipients are gods ἐπὶ μὲν τῶι ἐρρῶσθα[ί] σε εὐθέως τοῖς θεοῖς εὐχαρίστουν, Wilcken Ptol., 59, 9 f. (168 B.C.) and men τὴν πρὸς Ἀλέξανδρον εὐχαριστίαν, Diod. S., 17, 59, 7. The reason for thanks can be indicated by prep. ἐπί τινος, Ditt. Syll.³, II, 798, 16 f. (37 A.D.); Ditt. Or., II, 456, 63 f. (1st cent. B.C.),[2] ἐπί τινι, Wilcken Ptol., 59, 9 f. (→ 408, 28 f.); περί τινος, Ditt. Or., II, 456, 54; Philo Spec. Leg., I, 211; 1 Th. 1:2; 1 C. 1:4, ὑπέρ τινος, Philo Mut. Nom., 222; Epict. Diss., IV, 1, 105, ἐν, Philo Spec. Leg., II, 175;[3] Aristid. Apol., 15, 10,[4] or by ὅτι, Epict. Diss., I, 4, 32.[5] The pass. is unusual, Hippocr. Ep., 17 (Littré, IX, 372 → n. 65). The element of thanks can yield to the formal sense "to pray," e.g., τοῖς θεοῖς, P. Tebt., I, 56, 9 f. (2nd cent. B.C.).

b. The noun εὐχαριστία is common in inscr.,[6] esp. decrees of honour, and it can mean "gratitude," Ditt. Or., I, 227, 6 (3rd cent. B.C.); Demosth. Or., 18, 91 (→ 408, 7 ff.) or "giving thanks," Ditt. Syll.³, II, 798, 5 (37 A.D.): εἰς εὐχαριστίαν θεοῦ, Ditt. Or., I, 199, 31 (6th cent. A.D.); Wis. 16:28; Corp. Herm., 1, 29. Ps.-Andronicus Rhodius De passionibus, II, 7 [7] offers a def. of εὐχαριστία: εὐχαριστία δὲ ἐπιστήμη τοῦ τίσι καὶ πότε παρεκτέον χάριν καὶ πῶς καὶ παρὰ τίνων ληπτέον.

c. εὐχάριστος opp. ἀχάριστος, Hdt., I, 90, 4 means "pleasant," of a happy death, Hdt., I, 32, 9. It often means "grateful" in inscr. with the schema γενόμενος ὁ δῆμος εὐχάριστος (→ 408, 5 ff.), "beneficent" in the epithet of Ptolemaeus II Euergetes, P.

ε ὐ χ α ρ ι σ τ έ ω κτλ. Bibl.: T. Schermann, "εὐχαριστία u. εὐχαριστεῖν in ihrem Bedeutungswandel bis 200 n. Chr.," Philol., 69 (1910) 375-410; H. Greeven, "Gebet u. Eschatologie im NT," Nt.liche Forschungen, III, 1 (1931); G. Harder, "Pls. u. d. Gebet," ibid, I, 10 (1936); J. M. Nielen, Gebet u. Gottesdienst im NT (1937); P. Schubert, "Form and Function of the Pauline Thanksgivings," ZNW Beih., 20 (1939); P. Joüon, "Reconnaissance et action de grâces dans le NT," Recherches de science relig., 29 (1939), 112-4. E. Mócsy, "De gratiarum actione in epistolis paulinis," Verbum Domini, 21 (1941), 193-201, 225-232; G. Delling, Der Gottesdienst im NT (1952), 99-118.

1 Other compounds are also Attic, e.g., εὔχαρις, ἀχάριστος and ἀχαριστέω cf. Liddell-Scott, s.v.
2 As against Schubert, 150 f.
3 Cf. ibid., 129.
4 Ibid., 106 f.
5 In Ps.-Callisth., II, 22, 11 the ὅτι clause gives the explanation rather than the reason.
6 The noun is rare in the pap.
7 Ed. C. Schuchhardt, Diss. Heidelberg (1883), 25, 16 f., cf. v. Arnim, III, 67, 12 f.

Lond., III, 879, 11 (123 B.C.): Πτολεμαίου θεοῦ Εὐεργέτου καὶ Σωτῆρος ἑαυτῶν Εὐχαρίστου. [8] τὸ εὐχάριστον is a "grateful mind," Epict. Diss., I, 6, 1.

2. Meaning.

a. The attitude denoted by the group corresponds to the ideal of μεγαλοψυχία: εὐχάριστον καὶ μεγαλόψυχον of Alexander the Gt., Diod. S., 18, 28, 5. With the popular estimation of gratitude one finds the public secular use, the religious use in a group of inscr., and the private use in letters. The first occurs in inscr. of honours. [9] For the average style cf. Ditt. Syll.[3], II, 709, 14 (c. 107 B.C.): ἐφ' οἷς ὁ δᾶμος εὐχαριστῶν ἐτίμασε ταῖς καθηκούσαις αὐτὸν τιμαῖς. We have here the basic thought of appropriate action and counteraction, cf. Ditt. Or., II, 458, 16 f. (c. 9 B.C.): It is hard κατ' ἴσον ε[ὐχαριστ]εῖν for these beneficent acts εὐεργετήματα of the emperor → 407, 25 ff. The noun is used similarly, Ditt. Syll.[3], II, 800, 33 ff. (42 A.D.): ὅπως ἦι πᾶσιν ἀνθρώποις γνωστὰ ἅ τε τῶν ἀγαθῶν ἀνδρῶν εὐεργεσία ἅ τε τᾶς πόλιος εἰς τοὺς ἀξίους εὐχαριστία, cf. ibid., II, 731, 40 ff. (1st cent. B.C.). The adj. occurs in the formal expression ἵνα οὖν ὁ ἡμέτερος δῆμος εὐχάριστος ὤμ φαίνηται, ibid., II, 587, 15 f. (c. 196 B.C.). The movement into the religious sphere may be seen in the ruler cult: εἰς εὐχαριστίαν τηλικούτου θεοῦ (sc. the emperor, the new Helios), ibid., II, 798, 5 (37 A.D.); note the heaping up of χάρις (→ 375, 19 ff.) in the same context, line 8 f. The polis makes a resolve δι' οὗ εὐχαριστήσουσι μὲν ἐπ' αὐτῶν τῆι μητρὶ αὐτῶν, ibid., II, 798, 16 f. (37 A.D.). Typically religious is the use in a group of thanksgivings for healings, [10] ibid., III, 1173, 9 f. (2nd cent. A.D.): [11] καὶ ἐσώθη καὶ δημοσίᾳ ηὐχαρίστησεν τῷ θεῷ καὶ ὁ δῆμος συνεχάρη αὐτῷ, [12] Corp. Herm., 13, 18: εὐχαριστῶ σοι, πάτερ, . . . ὁ σὸς Λόγος δι' ἐμοῦ ὑμνεῖ σέ. δι' ἐμοῦ δέξαι τὸ πᾶν λόγῳ, λογικὴν θυσίαν, presents the thanksgiving prayer as a rational sacrifice with which the petitioner brings the all to God. [13]

Thanks to deity is a constituent part of the private [14] letter. Instructive is the letter of Isias to her brother Hephaestion, since the εὐχαριστῶ clause introduces the real subject of the missive: [15] ἐπὶ μὲν τῶι ἐρρῶσθα[ί] σε εὐθέως τοῖς θεοῖς εὐχαρίστουν, Wilcken Ptol., 59, 9 f. (168 B.C.). The famous Epistle of Apion shows that thanks are a constituent part of epistolary style: Ἀπίων Ἐπιμάχῳ τῶι πατρὶ καὶ κυρίῳ πλεῖστα χαίρειν. πρὸ μὲν πάντων εὔχομαί σε ὑγιαίνειν καὶ διὰ παντὸς ἐρ(ρ)ωμένον εὐτυχεῖν μετὰ τῆς ἀδελφῆς μου καὶ τῆς θυγατρὸς αὐτῆς καὶ τοῦ ἀδελφοῦ μου. εὐχαριστῶ τῷ κυρίῳ Σεράπιδι, ὅτι μου κινδυνεύσαντος εἰς θάλασσαν ἔσωσε

---

[8] This sense is also found in Wilcken Ptol., 41, 13 (c. 160 B.C.): δι' ὑμᾶς τοὺς εὐχαρίστους θεούς. Wilcken transl. "rich in grace"; but cf. Schubert, 165: First comes πρὸς τὸ θεῖον εὐσέβειαν καὶ πρὸς πάντας ἀνθρώπους εὐγνωμοσύνην. For this the gods are grateful.

[9] Schubert, 143-158.

[10] Weinreich AH, passim.

[11] Ibid., 108 f., 115, n. 3.

[12] Cf. also the accounts in line 13 f. and line 17 f.

[13] [Bertram].

[14] Thanksgiving to deity is not a part of the public letter, Schubert, 170. ἔντευξις is a certain exception in BGU, I, 327, 10 ff. (166 A.D.); Schubert, 177 f. Cf. χάριν ἔχω θεοῖς πᾶσιν, P. Oxy., I, 113, 13 (2nd cent. A.D.) and other expressions in Preisigke Wört. s.v. χάρις. Schubert, 159 distinguishes a threefold use in epistles: thanks to the gods, thanks to others, and showing favour. In each case the pt. is to introduce the main theme of the epistle, 180, cf. 176 and 178. Little is to be gleaned from the schematic classification of epistolary forms in later rhetoric, cf. the def. in Ps.-Procl. Περὶ ἐπιστολιμαίου χαρακτῆρος, 6 (Epistolographi, 8): εὐχαριστικὴ ἐστι δι' ἧς χάριν γινώσκομέν τινι διά τι. On the epistolary formula in gen. cf. Wendland Hell. Kult., 411-7, on thanksgiving O. Roller, "Das Formular d. paul. Br.," BWANT, 58 (1933), 62-5.

[15] Schubert, 161 f.

εὐθέως, BGU, II, 423, 1-8 (2nd cent. A.D.).[16] The wishes that follow the preface are part of the context; they are not so tightly knit as the formula.[17]

b. Compounds in εὐ- are slow and late to appear → 407, 6 ff. In the Fr. of older Stoicism we find εὐχαριστία (→ 407, 28 ff.) only once. Epict. offers a typical ethical evaluation of gratitude; his material closeness to Plato should also be noted.[18] τὸ εὐχάριστον is presented in Diss., I, 6, 1 ff. as a basic ethical attitude; without it even δύναμις ὁρατική is worthless, I, 6, 4. There is a little summary of ethics with a final stress on the duty of thanks to God in IV, 4, 14 f. and 18, cf. the religious accent in IV, 4, 29-32; I, 16, 15 ff.; IV, 1, 105. With I, 19, 25 cf. Did., 9 f.; Aristid. Apol., 15, 10 → 415, 12 f. In assessing the religious components note that the addition τῷ θεῷ has become a mere phrase, cf. I, 10, 3.

B. Judaism.

a. Hbr. has no equivalent for the group, or the group is not used for Hbr. originals.[19] Religious thanks are expressed in the thankoffering תּוֹדָה[20] and the song of thanksgiving,[21] both collective, e.g., Ps. 136,[22] and individual, e.g., Ps. 116.[23] The group εὐχαρ-, apart from εὐχάριστος in Prv. 11:16, occurs only in the apocr. and denotes the giving of thanks.[24] This might be to men, 2 Macc. 12:31; 'Εσθ. 8:12d; Wis. 18:2, but esp. to God, 2 Macc. 10:7: ὕμνους ἀνέφερον, vl. εὐχαρίστουν etc.; Jdt. 8:25; 3 Macc. 7:16. We find wisdom style at Wis. 16:28; Sir. 37:11, epistolary style at 2 Macc. 1:10 f., in the letter of the people of Jerusalem to Aristobulus: ... χαίρειν καὶ ὑγιαίνειν. ἐκ μεγάλων κινδύνων ὑπὸ τοῦ θεοῦ σεσῳσμένοι μεγάλως εὐχαριστοῦμεν αὐτῷ.[25] 2 Macc. 1:11 ff. is the prototype of Paul's salutations;[26] the sentence with εὐχαριστοῦμεν comes just after the opening formula, and introduces the main theme of the letter. Thanks are directed to God, and two reasons are indicated, the one by part.[27] and the other by γάρ.[28]

In 'Α εὐχαριστία is used for תּוֹדָה at Lv. 7:12; ψ 41:5; 49:14; 68:31; 106:22; 146:7; Am. 4:5.[29]

---

[16] Deissmann LO, 145-150.

[17] Roller, op. cit., 62-5, 459-467 reconstructs the development of epistolary style as follows. At first a wish for health is customary. This dies out in the true Gk. letter from the 2nd cent. B.C., or it is shortened and combined with the salutation. Then a new form crops up in the 2nd cent. A.D.: πρὸ μὲν πάντων and a wish for health. It seems to arise without intervening links; in Paul's day his version of the introduction is old-fashioned. Since extant material is restricted to Egypt, Roller's view is to be adopted only with caution.

[18] Schubert, 132-142.

[19] Joüon, 112-4.

[20] On the change in usage and the rise of the group -χαρ- cf. θυσία σωτηρίου in Lv. 3:1 with the rendering χαριστηρίους θυσίας in Jos. Ant., 3, 228.

[21] G. v. Rad, Theol. d. AT, I⁶ (1969), 370: The community rather than Yahweh is addressed in the first instance. C. Westermann, Das Loben Gottes in d. Ps.³ (1963), criticises the designation "songs of thanksgiving" in gen.

[22] O. Eissfeldt, Einl. in d. AT³ (1964), 162 f.

[23] Ibid., 163-6. LXX transl. terms for praise by αἴνεσις, so θυσία αἰνέσεως, ψ 49:14, and ἐξομολογέομαι, ψ 105:1; 106:1, 8 etc., cf. 104:1.

[24] Joüon, 112-4 thinks the only sense in the LXX and the NT is "to give thanks," not "to be grateful."

[25] F. M. Abel, Les livres d. Macc. (1949), 289 f.; J. P. Audet, La Didachè (1958), 386 f.

[26] Schubert, 117-9.

[27] Cf. Phlm. 4; 1 Th. 1:2; R. 1:10; Phil. 1:4; Eph. 1:16; Col. 1:3 f.

[28] Cf. the ὅτι clauses in 1 C. 1:4 f.; R. 1:8; 1 Th. 2:13; 2 Th. 1:3; 2:13.

[29] Other compounds of -χαρ- are εὔχαρις in Wis. 14:20, ἄχαρις in Sir. 20:19 and ἀχάριστος in Wis. 16:29; Sir. 29:16, 25; 18:18; 4 Macc. 9:10.

b. The material equivalent in Jewish non-Gk. works is בָּרֵךְ, normally transl. εὐλογητός → II, 764, 1 ff. [30] Among objects of thanks the most important in relation to the
NT are food and drink: "It is forbidden man to enjoy anything of this world without
benediction," bBer., 35a. "At good news one says: Blessed be He who is good and who
does good. But at bad news one says: Blessed be the judge of truth ... Man has a duty
to pronounce a blessing on the bad as he pronounces a blessing on the good," 54a. Thanks
are for ever: "In the future all sacrifices will cease, but the offering of thanks will not
cease to all eternity. Similarly all confessions will cease, but the confession of thanks will
not cease to all eternity," Pesikt., 9 (79a). The Sh. E. is the classical expression of thanks.

c. The data in Philo are significant → 414, n. 75; 415, 10 ff. [31] Whereas he uses
εὐλογέω only under the influence of biblical usage, [32] the εὐχαρ-group is common. [33]
The central theme is thanks to God: τίνι γὰρ εὐχαριστητέον ἄλλῳ πλὴν θεῷ; Deus
Imm., 7. Thanks are given for God's gifts, cf. the list in Mut. Nom., 222 f. [34] This
thanksgiving is inward veneration, [35] not material offering, [36] cf. Rer. Div. Her., 199:
τὸν κόσμον, ὃν διὰ συμβόλου τοῦ θυμιάματος οἴεται δεῖν εὐχαριστεῖν τῷ πεποιη-
κότι, cf. 200 and 226: τὸ μὲν θυμιατήριον εἰς τὴν ὑπὲρ (→ n. 34) τῶν στοιχείων
εὐχαριστίαν ἀνάγεται... ἡ δὲ τράπεζα εἰς τὴν ὑπὲρ τῶν θνητῶν ἀποτελεσμάτων
εὐχαριστίαν... ἡ δὲ λυχνία εἰς τὴν ὑπὲρ τῶν κατ' οὐρανὸν ἁπάντων... One rather
gives thanks by prayer, Plant., 126; ἑκάστη μέν γε τῶν ἀρετῶν ἐστι χρῆμα ἅγιον,
εὐχαριστία δὲ ὑπερβαλλόντως· θεῷ δὲ οὐκ ἔνεστι γνησίως εὐχαριστῆσαι δι'
ὧν νομίζουσιν οἱ πολλοὶ κατασκευῶν ἀναθημάτων θυσιῶν... rather δι' ἐπαίνων
καὶ ὕμνων (sc. of the νοῦς). [37] This thanksgiving is an obligation for gifts received:
ὅτι οἰκειότατόν ἐστιν ἔργον θεῷ μὲν εὐεργετεῖν, γενέσει δὲ εὐχαριστεῖν μηδὲν
ἔξω τούτου πλέον τῶν εἰς ἀμοιβὴν ἀντιπαρασχεῖν δυναμένη, Plant., 130, [38] cf. Spec.
Leg., I, 224: ὕμνοις τε καὶ εὐδαιμονισμοῖς καὶ εὐχαῖς θυσίαις τε καὶ ταῖς ἄλλαις
εὐχαριστίαις... ἀμείβεσθαι. [39] But it is not a human achievement, Leg. All., I, 82.
These two thoughts belong together; their unity is understandable in the totality of Philo's

---

[30] On εὐχαριστέω and εὐλογέω as synon. cf. Audet, op. cit., 386-394; Harder, 4-129.
[31] E. Bréhier, Les idées philos. et rel. de Philon d'Alex.³ (1950), 227-230; H. Windisch, Die
Frömmigkeit Philos (1909), 66-8; H. A. Wolfson, Philo, II² (1948), 237-252; Schubert,
122-131.
[32] Schl. Theol. d. Judt., 109, n. 1: εὐλογέω does not belong to Philo's own vocabulary.
Wolfson, op. cit., 241 modifies the synonymity of εὐχαριστέω and εὐλογέω in Philo.
εὐλογέω is also biblical in Jos., cf. Schl. Theol. d. Judt., 108 f. It is synon. with εὐχαριστέω
in Jos. Ant., 8, 111, but cf. 6, 145: After the victory over the Amalekites Saul greets Samuel
τῷ θεῷ... εὐχαριστῶ δόντι μοι τὴν νίκην with 1 Βασ. 15:13: εὐλογητὸς σὺ τῷ κυρίῳ.
[33] Philo also has εὐχαριστικός (3 times), εὐχαριστητικός (4), and εὐχαριστήριος (3).
[34] The constr. here is with ὑπέρ, cf. 2 C. 1:11; acc. to Schubert, 124 f. this means "in
place of" (→ VIII, 512, 23 ff.). He explains 2 C. 1:11 similarly → 413, 4 f.
[35] Bréhier, op. cit., 227-230. The material element in sacrifice is worthless; only the
disposition gives value to sacrifices, and then all are equal, Quaest. in Ex., II, 99. Morality
alone is not enough; it must have a sense of its divine origin and hence must be obedience,
Congr., 80. It thus becomes inner worship, cf. esp. Sacr. AC, 74 f., 80-86, 97, 101-4, and
materially Jos. Ant., 8, 111.
[36] Outward sacrifice is not rejected. For the sense in which it can remain → n. 35 and
cf. also H. Wenschkewitz, "Die Spiritualisierung d. Kultusbegriffe Tempel, Priester u. Opfer
im NT," Angelos Beih. 4 (1932), 76-79.
[37] The integration of virtues into worship is Stoic in impulse but Philo does it by construing
virtues as commands and viewing prayer too as commanded, v. Wolfson, op. cit., 238.
[38] ἀντιχαρίσασθαι is a variation on εὐχαριστεῖν. It contains the familiar thought of
the response of thanksgiving, which is much stressed in Philo → 408, 8 ff. The relation of
thanks is an appropriate one.
[39] This is then the leading term. Everything is summed up in αἴνεσις.

mysticism. Prayer has no goal beyond itself: τῷ γὰρ εὐχαρίστῳ μισθὸς αὐτὸ τὸ εὐχαριστεῖν αὐταρκέστατος, Plant., 136. [40]

C. New Testament.

1. Gospels, Acts and Revelation.

a. The use of the verb is secular at Lk. 17:16 and of the noun at Ac. 24:3. [41]

b. According to the Jewish-Hellenistic model εὐχαριστέω denotes the prayer of thanksgiving in general at Jn. 11:41; Ac. 28:15; Rev. 11:17 and specifically giving thanks at meals in Mk. 8:6; Mt. 15:36; Jn. 6:11, 23; Ac. 27:35; [42] on Paul → 412, 8 ff. εὐχαριστέω and εὐλογέω (→ II, 761, 12 ff.) can be used as synonyms. This may be seen from a comparison of Mk. 8:6 with 6:41. [43] The alternation of εὐχαριστήσας in 8:6 and εὐλογήσας in 8:7 is to be judged similarly, → II, 762, 34 ff. [44] There is no gradation in the manner or degree of thanksgiving. The repetition simply corresponds to the Jewish rule that a blessing should be pronounced on each food, → 410, 1 ff. [45] Thus the two terms are not to be viewed as a symbolical allusion to the eucharist, [46] though they could easily be viewed that way later. The same applies in Jn. 6:11, 23. [47]

c. Jewish practice explains the use of εὐχαριστέω in the account of the Lord's Supper → VI, 153, 17 ff.; III, 730, 28 ff. [48] Mk. 14:22 f. and Mt. 26:26 f. have both terms of blessing: λαβὼν ἄρτον εὐλογήσας ἔκλασεν—λαβὼν ποτήριον εὐχαριστήσας ἔδωκεν. Paul has only εὐχαριστήσας at the bread (1 C. 11:24). Luke first has καὶ δεξάμενος ποτήριον εὐχαριστήσας εἶπεν (22:17) [49] and then in

---

[40] Philo offers an etym. of names. Judah is ὁ εὐλογῶν, Plant., 135. Issachar, whose name means "reward" (Gn. 30:18), was born μετὰ τὸν εὐχάριστον Ἰούδαν, 136, cf. Som., II, 34.

[41] This is a topos of profane speech, the opening *captatio benevolentiae, v.* H. Conzelmann, *Die Apostelgesch., Hndbch. NT,* 7 (1963), *ad loc.* Cf. Philo Leg. Gaj., 284: ὅπως διὰ πάντων τῶν τῆς οἰκουμένης μερῶν ᾄδηταί σου τὸ κλέος καὶ οἱ μετ' εὐχαριστίας ἔπαινοι συνηχῶνται, cf. also Flacc., 98 f. The expression μετὰ (πάσης) εὐχαριστίας, cf. Ac. 4:29; 2 Macc. 3:22; Jos. Bell., 3, 398, corresponds to the style on inscr. of honour, Ditt. Syll.[3], I, 532, 7; II, 547, 30 (both 3rd cent. B.C.). It passed from these into historical writing, cf. E. Skard, "Epigraphische Formeln bei Dion. Hal.," *Symb. Osl.,* 11 (1932), 57.

[42] To see in Ac. 27:35 a prefiguration of the eucharist, so B. Reicke, "Die Mahlzeit mit Pls. auf d. Wellen d. Mittelmeers Ag. 27:33-38," ThZ, 4 (1948), 401-410 is an exercise in fantasy.

[43] On the synonymity → n. 30, 32, cf. 1 C. 14:16. Mt. in both cases follows Mk., and cf. Lk. 9:16, also Rev. 4:9 with 7:12.

[44] Kl. Mk., *ad loc.* prefers the reading εὐχαριστήσας (D q) in v. 7.

[45] Mt. viewed εὐλογέω and εὐχαριστέω as synon., using the former for the blessing of the bread and fishes in 14:16 and the latter in 15:36. Cf. on Mt. H. J. Held, "Mt. als Interpret d. Wundergeschichten," in G. Bornkamm, G. Barth and H. J. Held, *Überlieferung u. Auslegung im Mt., Wissenschaftliche Monographien z. AT u. NT,* 1[5] (1968), 171-7.

[46] G. H. Boobyer, "The Eucharistic Interpretation of the Miracles of the Loaves in St. Mark's Gospel," JThSt, NS, 3 (1952), 161-171: Mk. understands the miracle symbolically but not eucharistically.

[47] Bultmann J., 157, n. 5.

[48] Cf. J. Jeremias, *Die Abendmahlsworte Jesu*[4] (1967), 106 f., 167; J. Betz, *Die Eucharistie in d. Zeit d. griech. Väter,* I, 1 (1955), 157-162; H. Schürmann, "Der Paschamahlbericht Lk. 22:(7-14) 15-18," NTAbh, 19, 5 (1953), 28-30; also "Der Einsetzungsbericht Lk. 22:19-20," NTAbh, 20, 4 (1955), 45-47; T. Schaefer, "Eucharistia, Erbe u. Auftrag," *Benediktinische Monatsschr.,* NF, 36 (1960), 251-8.

[49] The longer text is to be preferred as the original.

v. 19 he replaces Mk.'s εὐλογέω with εὐχαριστέω at the bread [50] and leaves out Mk's εὐχαριστέω at the cup, cf. Paul. The use of εὐχαριστέω and εὐλογέω sheds no light on the disputed question whether the Pauline or the Marcan account is older. [51] For even if in itself εὐλογέω is closer to the Jewish blessing, εὐχαριστέω is a synonym in Greek speaking Judaism → 410, 10 ff. It is pure chance whether one or the other term is selected in translation, [52] as their presence alongside one another in Mk. demonstrates. [53] One cannot as yet speak of a technical use. [54]

2. Paul.

a. The most prominent feature here is the epistolary use in the prefaces. [55] These are solid components of the letters. [56] They are usually introduced by εὐχαριστῶ. [57] Paul is in the Hellenistic tradition → 360, 27 f.; 394, 6 ff. [58] It is important to show that the epistolary thanksgiving is already part of the context and can even serve to usher in the main theme. Thus in Paul it can melt into the body of the letter (1 Th., cf. 2 Th.), though usually it is formally separated quite clearly. The data in relation to private letters cannot just be transferred to Paul. It is true that the prefaces relate to the particular situations in the churches and are put in the appropriate key. Yet for the most part they constitute sections of their own, as the constant structure shows. [59] There are two main forms, εὐχαριστῶ with two to three participles, 1 Th. 1:2 ff.; Phil. 1:3 ff.; Phlm. 4 ff., cf. Eph. 1:15 ff., and εὐχαριστῶ... ὅτι, 1 C. 1:4 f.; R. 1:8, cf. 2 Th. 1:3. The prefaces to 1 Th. and R. contain a mixed type. [60]

b. Apart from the prefaces εὐχαριστῶ is used formally in 1 C. 1:14, [61] in thanks to fellow-workers at R. 16:4, [62] for grace at meals in 1 C. 10:30, cf. 31; [63] R. 14:6.

---

[50] Although he uses εὐλογέω several times, cf. the infancy stories and then Lk. 9:16 (Mk. 6:41); 24:30, 50 f., 53; Ac. 3:26.

[51] As against Jeremias, op. cit. (→ n. 48), 106 and 167.

[52] Schürmann Paschamahlbericht, 28-30 makes untenable deductions from the choice of εὐχαριστέω by Lk.

[53] Schürmann Paschamahlbericht, 29 notes that Mk. is not trying to make any clear distinction, though cf. Jeremias, op. cit., 170.

[54] In spite of Schürmann Paschamahlbericht, 55, who thinks εὐχαριστέω was very early on a eucharistic term; he ref. to its use without obj. and to Col. 4:2.

[55] Schubert, 4-39; Wendland Hell. Kult., 413 f.; Dib. Th. Exc. on 1 Th. 1:2; G. H. Boobyer, "Thanksgiving" and the "Glory of God" in Paul, Diss. Heidelberg (1929).

[56] Apart from Gl., where there is reason for the exception, since Paul in this situation cannot give thanks for the community.

[57] An exception is 2 C. 1:3, where the preface is opened by the analogous εὐλογητός, and cf. Eph. 1:3, though a synthesis is achieved here by adding a eucharistia in 1:15. N. A. Dahl, "Adresse u. Proömium d. Eph.," ThZ, 7 (1951), 241-264 would assign the two catchwords to two different genres; this is too schematic → 412, 9 ff. Cf. J. Cambier, "La bénédiction d'Eph. 1:3-14," ZNW, 54 (1963), 58-104.

[58] Elements of Jewish style, however, may be noted in the execution.

[59] For analysis cf. Schubert, 10-39.

[60] In analogy to the private Hell. letter Schubert, 183 finds in Paul, too, the rule that the preface is formally better worked out in the more intimate letters, Phlm., 1 Th., Phil., and Col. as distinct from R., 1 C., 2 Th.

[61] C D G it 𝔎 etc. add τῷ θεῷ. The dat. is fixed, 1 C. 14:18. It occurs also with the verbal noun at 2 C. 9:11f., the one NT instance, cf. class. usage and that of the pap., v. Bl.-Debr. § 187, 8; Mayser, II, 2, 146.

[62] With a ref. to the Church, this being indicated in context by the ecclesiological ἐν formula.

[63] E. Lohse, "Zu 1 K. 10:26, 31," ZNW, 47 (1956), 277-280: Paul adopts the Jewish rule about blessing each food (→ 410, 1 f.) but does not apply it legalistically. On 1 Tm. 4:3 f. → 414, 12 ff.

The systematic background is that of the thanks due the Creator, R. 1:21 → 409, 17 ff. The setting in worship may be seen in 1 C. 14:16 f. [64] The prominence of praise and thanksgiving as opposed to prayer is given its particular nuance by the fact that prayer is the work of the Spirit → lines 20 ff. Hence it is not only owed; it is made possible by God. Its purpose is to glorify God, 2 C. 1:11. [65] One can associate this v. with 1 Th. 3:9; 2 C. 4:15; 9:11 f. and find the concept of *oratio infusa* by which the grace given by God flows back to Him. [66] His δόξα is increased thereby, → VI, 265, 21 ff. [67] Less probable is the explanation of the saying in terms of the Jewish understanding of the cultus and prayer: These serve to augment God's glory and have to be made possible by God Himself. [68] God's prevenient act is the presupposition of the summons to εὐχαριστία, whether in general exhortation (1 Th. 5:18 [69] → III, 58, 39 ff.) or in a special sense, e.g., the collection among the Gentile Christian churches as a *eucharistia* (2 C. 9:11). [70] Here again the thought of increasing God's glory is also suggested, v. 12 f.

In prayer distinction is made between God and Jesus. Private petitions may be addressed to Jesus (2 C. 12:8) but not official prayer. [71] The prayer of thanksgiving is reserved for God. Christ is the mediator of this, not the recipient: εὐχαριστῶ τῷ θεῷ μου διὰ Ἰησοῦ Χριστοῦ, R. 1:8. [72]

3. Deutero-Paulines.

The Deutero-Paulines show no essential change, since the characteristic Pauline features are not found in the use of εὐχαριστέω but in the understanding of prayer as the work of the Spirit, R. 8:26 → VI, 430, 23 ff. The combination of thanksgiving, joy and confession occurs at Col. 1:12. [73] εὐχαριστέω is not to be taken technically

---

[64] Synonymity with εὐλογέω is plain the context. The vl. εὐχαριστῶ... λαλῶν at 14:18 is wrong, v. Bl.-Debr. § 415: The part. to supplement verbs of emotion is hardly found any more in the NT.

[65] Note the play on χάρισμα and εὐχαριστέω. The pass. is surprising → 407, 21 f. Hippocr. Ep., 17 (Littré, IX, 272) and Philo Rer. Div. Her., 174 are adduced as par. but the former has εὐχαριστεῖταί τις (not τι): a pers. receives thanks: ὁ σὸς πρόγονος Ἀσκληπιὸς νουθεσίη σοι γινέσθω, σώζων ἀνθρώπους κεραυνοῖσιν ηὐχαρίστηται "in thanks therefor was slain by lightning," and similarly Philo, Schubert, 46-8.

[66] Dib. Th. on 1 Th. 3:9.

[67] Cf. Herm. m., 10, 3, 2 f., v. Dib. Herm., ad loc.; Herm. s., 2, 7; Philo Plant., 126 (→ 410, 18 ff.). On ἐκ πολλῶν προσώπων Wnd. 2 K., 50 compares Δα. 3:51-90; Philo Rer. Div. Her., 226.

[68] 1 Ch. 29:14, cf. Harder, 132, 138-151.

[69] On εὐχαριστέω ἐν cf. Schubert, 106 f., 129, 141 → 407, 20 f.

[70] On the literary and historical question cf. W. Schmithals, "Die Gnosis in Korinth," FRL, 66² (1965), 90 f., 93; G. Bornkamm, "Die Vorgeschichte d. sog. 2 K.," SAH, 1961, 2² (1965), 31 f.

[71] On this ground alone the vl. at Phil. 1:3, which redirects thanks to the κύριος, is shown to be secondary.

[72] Harder, 175-182 thinks "to give thanks by Christ" is a formula. He constructs it not in terms of Christ's mediation but along the lines of 1 Βασ. 22:13, 15; 2 Βασ. 5:19; Philo Deus Imm., 7; Plant., 126 and 131; Spec. Leg., I, 275; Jos. Ant., 8, 112. He pts. to the nature and manner, the new Chr. style of praying. But he misses here the function of Christ in the salvation event. Through Him we have access to God and hence the possibility of prayer, R. 5:2. He represents us, R. 8:34. The connection between Lord, Spirit and prayer should be noted, cf. also Col. 3:17.

[73] Cf. χάρις in the preface, 1:6. E. Käsemann, "Eine urchr. Taufliturgie," Exeget. Versuche u. Besinnungen, I⁴ (1965), 34-51 finds three redactional stages: 1. Confession, v. 13 f. and hymn, vv. 15-20; v. 12 is also tradition; 2. Liturgy; 3. Col. 1:13 f. may well be tradition but the ref. to baptism is by no means certain, cf. Dib. Gefbr.³, ad loc., and it is very doubtful whether v. 13 f. was linked to vv. 15 ff. before the composition of the letter, ibid., 11.

here as a term for the confession of the community. [74] We are rather to think in terms of the liturgical tradition of Judaism. [75] The technical sense is in fact suggested neither by general NT usage nor by the context. In Col. 2:7 the summons to thanksgiving is given a christological basis, cf. 1 Th. 5:18. [76] Thanksgiving is the content of general exhortation in Col. 3:15. [77] The demand is linked with divine worship by v. 16 f. in the comprehensive phrase: εὐχαριστοῦντες τῷ θεῷ — δι' αὐτοῦ. This may be compared with Eph. 5:20. [78] Prayer — a potiori defined as prayer of thanksgiving — is the proper mode of eschatological vigilance, Col. 4:2, cf. Phil. 4:6. [79]

No clear-cut conceptual differentiation can be made among the words for prayer listed in 1 Tm. 2:1 → 411, 9 ff. But they do plainly bring out the two streams of thanksgiving and petition. The close connection between these explains the notable expression "thanksgiving for all men." [80] 1 Tm.4:3 f. (→ n. 63) attacks the Gnostically based demand for asceticism in meats by pointing to the custom of grace at meals, which is here connected with faith in God as the Creator. No laws can be set up in terms of foods. The norm is the attitude towards God. In this sense thanksgiving is the condition of enjoyment.

D. Early Church. [81]

a. In an epistolary context we find εὐχαριστῶ in Ign. Phld., 6, 3; 11, 1; Sm., 10, 1; Eph., 21, 1. Individual prayer is ref. to in Herm. s., 5, 1, 1; 7, 5; 9, 14, 3; v., 4, 1, 4. There is a call to prayer in Herm. s., 7, 5; 1 Cl., 38, 2. 4; 2 Cl., 18, 1, cf. Barn., 7, 1.

b. Of special interest is the eucharistic use, Did., 9 f.; Ign. Eph., 13, 1; Phld., 4; Sm., 7, 1; 8, 1; Just. Apol., I, 65, 3 - 66, 3. The ref. of the group is first to the prayer of thanksgiving, which is a constitutive part of the administration of the Lord's Supper, Did., 9, 1-3; Just. Dial., 41, 1, 3; 70, 4; 117, 2; Apol., I, 65, 3 and 5; 66, 2; 67, 5. Then the elements are denoted, Did., 9, 1 and 5; Ign. (→ 415, 4-9); Iren. Haer., IV, 31, 4; V, 2, 3. Finally there is ref. to the whole action, Did., 9, 1 and 5; Ign. (→ 415, 4-9); Iren. in Eus. Hist.

---

[74] Käsemann, op. cit. (→ n. 73), 43; Dib. Gefbr.[3], ad loc. finds here the motif of oratio infusa, though this is unlikely. G. Bornkamm, "Das Bekenntnis im Hb.," Stud. z. Antike u. Christentum[2] (1963), 196: Confession is εὐχαριστία in Hb. 13:15, v. H. Lietzmann, "Die Anfänge d. Glaubensbekenntnisses," Festschr. A. Harnack (1921), 241 f.

[75] Cf. ידה and the usual introd. to the Ps. of Qumran אודכה אדוני, 1 QH 2:20 etc.; ידה is normally transl. ἐξομολογέομαι in LXX, but εὐχαριστέω is used for it in Hell. Judaism, e.g., Jdt. 8:25; Philo (→ 410, 10 ff.); Jos. (→ n. 32); Orig. Orat., 14, 5: τὸ "ἐξομολογοῦμαι" ἴσον ἐστὶ τῷ "εὐχαριστῶ." J. M. Robinson, "Die Hodajot-Formel in Gebet u. Hymnus d. Frühchristentums," Festschr. E. Haenchen, ZNW Beih., 30 (1964), 194-235; E. Lohse, Die Br. an die Kol. u. an Philemon, Kritisch-exeg. Komm. über d. NT, 9, 2[14] (1968), 68-70.

[76] Formally Col. 2:7 suggests teaching tradition, but the teaching is christological.

[77] The demand seems to arise spontaneously, but this is in keeping with normal hortatory style. We find it again in Eph. 5:4, where one might ask whether there is not parechesis with εὐτραπελία. From Orig. in Cramer Cat., VI, 190 εὐχαριστία has been understood as εὐχαριτία "grace of speech," v. O. Casel, "Εὐχαριστία-εὐχαριτία," BZ, 18 (1929), 84 f.

[78] Col. 3:16: ἄδοντες... τῷ θεῷ, Eph. 5:19: ...τῷ κυρίῳ, Col. 3:17: εὐχαριστοῦντες τῷ θεῷ... δι' αὐτοῦ (sc. the Lord Jesus), Eph. 5:20: εὐχαριστοῦντες... ὑπὲρ πάντων, ἐν ὀνόματι τοῦ κυρίου ἡμῶν Ἰησοῦ Χριστοῦ, i.e., Eph. has related the πάντα ἐν ὀνόματι κυρίου Ἰησοῦ of Col. 3:17 to εὐχαριστοῦντες, v. C. L. Mitton, The Epistle to the Eph. (1951), 62 f., 80 f. It is artificial to subordinate εὐχαριστοῦντες to the preceding part.: "Sing... as you utter thanks," and to relate εὐχαριστέω to the thanksgiving at the Lord's Supper. What we have rather is a hortatory sequence, cf. 1 Th. 5:18; πάντοτε in Eph. 5:20 is to be taken in the same way as ἐν παντί in 1 Th. 5:18.

[79] Eph. 6:18 did not adopt the catchword εὐχαριστία.

[80] Cf. Dib. Past.[4], ad loc.

[81] Schubert, 100-165; Betz, op. cit., (→ n. 48), 157-162.

Eccl., V, 24, 17. Basic is Did., 9 f., where one may already see the beginnings of a technical use: περὶ δὲ τῆς εὐχαριστίας, οὕτως εὐχαριστήσατε. The concept of the thankoffering occurs, cf. 14, 1 f. To be sure, the thanksgiving is the utterance of the prayer, 9, 2; 10, 1 f., but it is then also what is blessed thereby, the eucharistic food, 9, 5. [82] Ign. Eph., 13, 1 demands coming together εἰς εὐχαριστίαν θεοῦ καὶ εἰς δόξαν, either "for thanksgiving" or "for the Lord's Supper of God." [83] σπουδάσατε οὖν μιᾷ εὐχαριστίᾳ χρῆσθαι in Phld., 4 is either to be understood in terms of Eph., 13, 1 [84] or is to be referred to the elements, [85] cf. Sm., 7, 1; εὐχαριστίας καὶ προσευχῆς ἀπέχονται, διὰ τὸ μὴ ὁμολογεῖν τὴν εὐχαριστίαν σάρκα εἶναι τοῦ σωτῆρος ἡμῶν Ἰησοῦ Χριστοῦ. In the 2nd and 3rd cent. [86] and under Philo's influence (→ 410, 10 ff.) theologians came to use εὐχαριστεῖν and εὐχαριστία almost exclusively for the sacrifice of εὐχαριστία, cf. Aristid. Apol., 15, 10: εὐχαριστοῦντες αὐτῷ κατὰ πᾶσαν ὥραν ἐν παντὶ βρώματι καὶ ποτῷ καὶ τοῖς λοιποῖς ἀγαθοῖς, Just. Apol., I, 13, 1 f.: ... λόγῳ εὐχῆς καὶ εὐχαριστίας ἐφ᾽ οἷς προσφερόμεθα πᾶσιν, ὅση δύναμις, αἰνοῦντες ... ἐκείνῳ δὲ εὐχαρίστους ὄντας διὰ λόγου πομπὰς καὶ ὕμνους πέμπειν ὑπέρ τε τοῦ γεγονέναι καὶ τῶν εἰς εὐρωστίαν πόρων πάντων ... καὶ τοῦ πάλιν ἐν ἀφθαρσίᾳ γενέσθαι διὰ πίστιν τὴν ἐν αὐτῷ ..., Just. Dial., 117, 2: ὅτι μὲν οὖν καὶ εὐχαὶ καὶ εὐχαριστίαι, ὑπὸ τῶν ἀξίων γινόμεναι, τέλειαι μόναι καὶ εὐάρεστοί εἰσι τῷ θεῷ θυσίαι, καὶ αὐτός φημι (sc. in agreement with Hell. Judaism), cf. also Dial., 41; 70, 1 and 4.

Conzelmann

---

[82] Kn. Did., ad loc. Cf. Just. Apol., I, 66, 1: καὶ ἡ τροφὴ αὕτη καλεῖται παρ᾽ ἡμῖν εὐχαριστία. On the prayers in the Did. cf. M. Dibelius, "Die Mahl-Gebete d. Did.," *Botschaft u Gesch.*, II (1956), 117-127, who ref. to their Jewish origin. Audet, op. cit. (→ n. 25), 389 and 399 stresses the connection between εὐχαριστέω and εὐλογέω. The meaning, then, is "we praise thee" rather than "we thank thee."
[83] Bau. Ign., ad loc. transl. along these lines.
[84] Bau Ign., ad loc.
[85] J. A. Fischer, *Die Apost. Väter, Schr. d. Urchr.,* I⁵ (1966), 197, n. 13.
[86] On the early Apologists cf. Schubert, 106-114. For a gen. survey cf. Schermann, *passim.*

---

† χάραγμα

A. In the Greek World.

1. χάραγμα is an engraved, etched, branded, or inscribed "mark" or "sign." Closest to the original sense of χαράσσω (→ line 17 f.; 418, 3 ff.) is the earliest example in Soph. Phil., 267, where χάραγμα denotes the bite of a snake. Elsewhere the term means an "inscription," e.g., Anth. Graec., 7, 220, 2, or anything written διὰ χαραγμάτων εὔχο-[μαι], P. Lond., V, 1658, 8 (4th cent. A.D.), also the individual character τὰ χαράγματα χειρός, Anth. Graec., 9, 401, 3, and esp. the impressed or imprinted "stamp," e.g., a brand to mark camels, Pap. Grenfell, II, 50a, 5 (142 B.C.),[1] or often an official stamp on writings, e.g., attested copies of documents, Preisigke Sammelbuch, I, 5231, 11; 5275, 11 (both 11 A.D.); 5247, 34 (47 A.D.),[2] esp. the imperial stamp to attest the validity of decrees etc.[3] χάραγμα (→ 418, 17 f.) can also mean the impress on coins, e.g., in Plut. Ages., 15 (I, 604c); De Lysandro, 16 (I, 442b); Apophth. Lac. Agesilaus, 40 (II, 211b) etc.; P. Oxy., I, 144, 6 (580 A.D.). Then it can mean "money" in gen.: ἦν μὲν γὰρ τὸ χάραγμα φέρῃς, φίλος· οὔτε θυρωρὸς ἐν ποσὶν οὔτε κύων· ἐν προθύροις δέδεται, Anth. Graec., 5, 30, 3 f.

2. χάραγμα does not occur in the LXX. χαράσσω is used at Sir. 50:27 in the sense "to inscribe," and at Ez. 4:1 Σ it is the transl. of HT חקק, cf. also in Is. 49:16 Θ (LXX διαγράφω or ζωγράφω in both instances). Cf. ἐντολὰς . . . κεχαραγμένας, Aristid. Apol., 15, 3.

3. Rev. 13:11-18 describes the appearance of the second beast, which comes as the pseudo-prophet of the first beast (→ III, 135, 18 ff.), demanding religious recognition of its cultic image. The incident gains in dramatic force as this image itself comes to life and begins to speak (v. 15). It demands of all men without exception ἵνα δῶσιν αὐτοῖς χάραγμα ἐπὶ τῆς χειρὸς αὐτῶν τῆς δεξιᾶς ἢ ἐπὶ τὸ μέτωπον αὐτῶν, καὶ ἵνα μή τις δύνηται ἀγοράσαι ἢ πωλῆσαι εἰ μὴ ὁ ἔχων τὸ χάραγμα τὸ ὄνομα τοῦ θηρίου ἢ τὸν ἀριθμὸν τοῦ ὀνόματος αὐτοῦ, v. 16 f. That the religious totalitarianism of emperor worship is indicated here is evident. Probably the choice of the word χάραγμα points to this if the reference is to the imperial stamp → line 11 f.[4] Materially, however, the required acceptance of the χάραγμα means religious signing with the mark of the beast, which is branded on the right hand or the forehead → IV, 635, 19 ff. This marking as stigmatisation[5] was common

---

χ ά ρ α γ μ α . [1] Ed. B. P. Grenfell-A. S.Hunt, *New Classical Fr. and Other Gk. and Lat. Pap.* (1897). Cf. χαρακτήρ (→ 418, 17 f.). BGU, I, 88, 6 (147 A.D.).

[2] On χάραγμα and πτῶμα in Pap. documents cf. J. C. Naber, "Observatiunculae ad papyros iuridicae," APF, 1 (1901), 316-320.

[3] These bear the year and the name of the reigning emperor, cf. Deissmann NB, 68-75; Deissmann LO, 289 f.

[4] So Deissmann LO, 289 f., followed by Loh. Apk., E. Lohse, *Die Offenbarung d. Joh.,* NT Deutsch, 11⁹ (1971), ad loc. etc.

[5] The usual term for this is σφραγίς (→ VII, 939, 1 ff.) or στίγμα (→ VII, 657, 32 ff.), and χάραγμα does not occur outside Rev., though cf. χαράσσω for the marking of the Jews with the ivy leaf of Dionysus by Ptolemy IV Philopator, 3 Macc. 2:29.

in antiquity → VII, 659, 25 ff. As slaves were shown to be their master's property by στίγματα, so many people had the marks of deities branded on them in temples → VII, 661, 33 ff. [6] In Rev. 13:18 the mark of the beast is described as the name of the beast (→ V, 280, 9 ff.) concealed in the number 666 (→ I, 462, 16 ff.). If Nero is in view, [7] the meaning of the number fits the context best, for in this case there is confrontation between the claim of the emperor and that of the Christ, whose seal (→ VII, 951, 1 ff.) is borne by the 144,000 servants of God who belong to Him, Rev. 7:1-8. The fact that this politico-religious clash is meant may be seen from other passages in Rev. which refer back to 13:16 f. The angel in 14:9, 11 threatens with eschatological wrath all those who have accepted the χάραγμα of the beast. The execution of this threat is described in 16:2 and judgment on the beast and his false prophet in 19:20, while in 20:4 all those who have not worshipped the beast or his image, nor accepted his marks on the hand or forehead, are exalted as eschatological judges.

In Ac. 17:19 we read in Paul's address on the Areopagas (→ V, 188, 5 ff.): οὐκ ὀφείλομεν νομίζειν, χρυσῷ ἢ ἀργύρῳ ἢ λίθῳ, χαράγματι τέχνης καὶ ἐνθυμήσεως ἀνθρώπου, τὸ θεῖον εἶναι ὅμοιον. χάραγμα is used here in the sense of "handiwork." What men have made cannot be like the divine, [8] but men as the creatures of God are "his offspring" (v. 28) and are thus close to Him, v. 27.

Wilckens

---

[6] Cf., e.g., Philo Spec. Leg., I, 58. There is basic material in F. J. Dölger, "Sphragis," *Stud. z. Gesch. u. Kultur d. Altertums*, 5, 3/4 (1911), 39-44; H. Lilliebjörn, *Über religiöse Signierung in d. Antike*, Diss. Uppsala (1933); bibl. in Schlier Gl.13 on 6:17; Oe. Gl., 164.

[7] On the riddle of the no. 666, which the author meant to be a riddle for the non-initiated, cf. Loh. Apk., ad loc. His proposal to explain the number as triangular and thus to reduce it to the no. 8 is not so convincing as that finally put forward by Lohse, *op. cit., ad loc.,* namely, to take 666 as gematria and with the numerical values of the Hbr. alphabet as a basis to arrive at Nero Qesar, θηρίον itself yielding the same number 666, cf. also H. B. Rosén, "Palestinian κοινή in Rabbinic Illustration," *Journ. of Semitic Stud.*, 8 (1963), 65, who thinks θηρίον is transcribed in the Hbr. תריון.

[8] This topos of early Chr. missionary preaching, cf. R. 1:23 and later apologetic, esp. Aristid. Apol., 13, 1; Just. Apol., I, 9, 1, is in the same tradition as the propaganda of Dispersion Judaism, cf. Wis. 13:10. On the whole subj. cf. P. Dalbert, "Die Theol. d. hell.-jüd. Missionsliteratur unter Ausschluss v. Philo u. Jos.," *Theol. Forschung*, 4 (1954), 129 and esp. W. Nauck, "Die Tradition u. Komposition d. Areopagrede," ZThK, 53 (1956), 11-52.

---

† χαρακτήρ

A. In the Greek World.

χαρακτήρ is orig. a nomen agentis: "one who χαράσσει." The verb, derived from the noun χάραξ, means "to cut to a point," "to sharpen," Hes. Op., 387, 573, and then later it takes on the technical sense "to inscribe" on wood, stone, or brass. Anth. Graec., 7, 710, 8; in part. it is a tt. in minting coins, Aristot. Pol., I, 9, p. 1257a, 35-41; Fr., 485, p. 1557a, 36; Fr., 551, p. 1569a, 30. [1] Since, at the time minting began, nomina agentis in Ionic and Attic were usually formed with -της, and the ancient suffix -τηρ was used only in relation to tools and vessels, [2] one may assume that χαρακτήρ first denoted an object, "die," [3] IG², II/III, 2 No. 1408, 11 f., cf. 1409, 5 (both c. 385 B.C.), [4] then "impression," "image," "impress," Plat. Polit., 289b; Aristot. Pol., I, 9, p. 1257a, 41. More gen. χαρακτήρ can then denote "coinage type," ἦν δ' ὁ ἀρχαῖος χαρακτήρ δίδραχμον, Aristot. Atheniensium Res publica, 10, 2, [5] and finally the "coin" itself. [6] In the plur. it can simply mean "money," "income," P. Flor., I, 61, 21 f. (1st cent. A.D.). [7] Similarly "stamps," e.g., the branding marks on camels (→ VII, 658, 4 ff.), BGU, I, 88, 7 (147 A.D.) and "seals," BGU, III, 763, 7 (3rd cent. A.D.) can be called χαρακτῆρες. [8] If an official, authoritative mark is meant here, χαρακτήρ can also be a "sign" in gen., esp. a "letter," and particularly when this does not express a gen. known sense, e.g., on a medical prescription, Gal. De compositione medicamentorum per genera, II, 22 (Kühn, 13, 995), cf. also the group of χαρακτῆρες at the end of the report on a sick person in Hippocr. Epid., III, 1, 1, Cod. V (Kühlewein, I, 215) and on this Gal. Comm. on Hippocr. Epid., III, 1, 4 (Kühn, 17, 1, p. 524-8); 2, 5 (p. 619), cf. also magic texts (→ n. 39), e.g., Preis. Zaub., I, 5, 311, cf. Jul. Or., 7, 216c; Iambl. Myst., III, 13 (p. 129, 16 [9]; 131, 4 ff.); also Luc. Hermot., 44: εἰ μηδὲ γράμματα γράφοιμεν ἐπὶ τῶν κλήρων, ἀλλά τινα σημεῖα καὶ χαρακτῆρας (i.e., hieroglyphics as distinct from γράμματα). If the sign element in such a χαρακτήρ may be completely hidden from the uninitiated, it is integral to the term that χαρακτήρ should be the "impress" of something, a "sign" of what is significatory, the "form" in which this is imprinted or engraved. Hence the "copy" of a book can be called χαρακτήρ: ἑώρακα γὰρ ἐγὼ ἐν χαρακτῆρι γραφῆς Ἐνώχ, Test. S. 5:4.

The sense "impression," "image on a coin," explains why the earliest examples [10] denote the "typical features" of a man or people. Astyages recognises the young Cyrus by the χαρακτήρ τοῦ προσώπου, Hdt., I,, 116, 1. This is also the meaning in the

---

χ α ρ α κ τ ή ρ .   Bibl.: Liddell-Scott, Pr.-Bauer, Preisigke Wört., s.v.; J. Geffcken, "Charakter," Exp. T., 21 (1910), 426 f.; F. J. Dölger, "Sphragis," Stud. z. Gesch. u. Kultur d. Altertums, 5, 3/4 (1911); A. Körte, "ΧΑΡΑΚΤΗΡ," Herm., 64 (1929), 69-86; F. W. Eltester, "Eikon im NT," ZNW Beih., 23 (1958), 52-4; R. Williamson, "Philo and the Epistle to the Hb.," Arbeiten z. Lit. u. Gesch. d. hell. Judt., 4 (1970), 74-80.

[1] Cf. on this Körte, 70 f.
[2] E.g., λαμπτήρ "lamp-stand," κρατήρ "mixing jug."
[3] [Lines 7-11 by Risch.]
[4] Cf. Körte, 72 f.
[5] Ed. F. G. Kenyon (1920).
[6] Examples in Körte, 75.
[7] Examples in Preisigke Wört,, s.v.
[8] Toll receipts bear at the end the note χωρὶς χαρακτῆρος, Preisigke Wört., s.v.
[9] Cf. Jamblique, Les mystères d'Égypte, ed. E. des Places (1966), 116, n. 1.
[10] χαρακτήρ does not occur in the pre-Socratics, Thuc., Xenoph. and the Attic orators. We find it once in Aristoph. and twice in Plato. In all Körte, 74, n. 1 counts only 15 instances before Aristot.

Κύπριος χαρακτήρ of Aesch. Suppl., 282.[11] Euripides' Medea bemoans the fact that there are no χαρακτῆρες on the human body whereby one can tell the bad from the good, Med., 519. Theophr. was the first to build up a kind of moral typology in his Ἠθικοὶ χαρακτῆρες (319 B.C.). We have here 30 sketches of human types, the total conduct in each case being shaped by some outstanding bad quality. This is first described in a def. and then worked out in a portrait of moral character which is very pregnantly drawn. In these character sketches there is no psychological interest in human individuality. The concern of the book is completely moral and hortatory.[12] The same applies to Menander's comedies, cf. his maxim ἀνδρὸς χαρακτὴρ ἐκ λόγου γνωρίζεται, Fr., 66 (Körte).[13] These sketches had a strong influence on later Hell. lit., cf. the characterisation of Socrates in Cic. De fato, 5, 10.[14] But antiquity did not everywhere adopt this special sense of χαρακτήρ;[15] this was reserved for modern usage.[16]

Very early on χαρακτήρ can also denote the "distinctiveness" of a language or manner of speaking. In relation to the various Ionic dialects Hdt., I, 142, 4 says: οὗτοι χαρακτῆρες γλώσσης τέσσερες γίνονται, cf. I, 57, 3; Diod. S., 1, 8, 4 (cf. Diels, II, 136, 2); Soph. Fr., 178 (TGF, 171). In Aristoph. Pax, 217-220 the ref. is more to "style." Later rhetoric follows this use; in it χαρακτήρ is a tt. for "style" χαρακτὴρ λέξεως.[17] Possibly Theophr. developed this specialised sense in rhetoric.[18] The individual "style" of a poet, orator, or philosopher is called χαρακτήρ.[19] The various ways of philosophising are also described as χαρακτῆρες.[20] Finally χαρακτήρ can be "distinctiveness" in gen. The speech of the wise, says Plat. Phaedr., 263b, must express the individuality of

---

[11] χαρακτήρ also means "feature" in inscr., e.g., Ditt. Or., II, 508, 13 (2nd cent. A.D.). Soranus De gynaecis (CMG, IV), I, 33, 5 speaks of the appearance of embryos.

[12] In goal and method Theophr. is in the Peripatetic tradition. We read of χαρακτῆρες by the Peripatetic Ariston of Keos — on him cf. W. Knögel, "Der Peripatetiker Ariston v. Keos bei Philodem," Klass.-philolog. Stud., ed. E. Bickel and C. Jensen, 5 (1933); F. Wehrli, Die Schule d. Aristot. Lykon u. Ariston v. Keos (1952), 27-67 — and by Satyros in Athen., 4, 66 (168c). Pos., too, probably drew from this tradition when in the hortatory part of his ethics he gave illustrations of good and bad types of conduct, for which others used the term χαρακτηρισμός, Sen. Ep., 15, 95, 65 [Dihle].

[13] Körte, 78, n. 1 thinks Menander was a pupil of Theophr., but cf. O. Regenbogen, Art. "Theophrastos," Pauly-W., Suppl., VII, 1358.

[14] Cf. Regenbogen, op. cit., 1506 f.

[15] Cf., e.g., Philodem. Philos. Περὶ κακιῶν, X, Col. 6, 34. Epict. Diss., III, 22, 80 also calls exemplary the "character" of Diogenes in dealing with a pupil. Cf. in gen. the admonition τάξον τινὰ ἤδη χαρακτῆρα σαυτῷ καὶ τύπον, ὃν φυλάξεις ἐπί τε σεαυτοῦ ὢν καὶ ἀνθρώποις ἐντυγχάνων, Ench., 33, 1, cf. ἰδιώτου στάσις καὶ χαρακτήρ· οὐδέποτε ἐξ ἑαυτοῦ προσδοκᾷ ὠφέλειαν ἢ βλάβην, ἀλλ' ἀπὸ τῶν ἔξω. φιλοσόφου στάσις καὶ χαρακτήρ· πᾶσαν ὠφέλειαν καὶ βλάβην ἐξ ἑαυτοῦ προσδοκᾷ, 48, 1.

[16] Cf. on this Körte, 85 f.

[17] So, e.g., Dion. Hal. De Lysia, 11 (ed. H. Usener-L. Radermacher, I [1899], 19, 22). We are probably to understand in the same way the χαρακτῆρες of Heraclides Ponticus, cf. F. Wehrli, Die Schule d. Aristot. Herakleïdes Pontikos (1953), 13.

[18] Cf. J. Stroux, De Theophr. virtutibus dicendi (1912); J. Lücke, Beitr. z. Gesch. d. genera dicendi u. genera compositionis, Diss. Hamburg (1952). The first Lat. instance is in the author of ad Herennium, IV, 11, 16 (ed. C. L. Kayser [1854]) and cf. Cic. Orator, 11, 36, cf. 39, 134, and also Gellius Noctes Atticae, 6, 14 (ed. C. Hosius [1903]); Ps.-Demetr., 36; Dion. Hal. (→ n. 17) De Demosthene, 33 (p. 203, 9).

[19] Examples in Körte, 82. In the anon. ὑπόθεσις on Eur. Rhes. a drama is taken from Eur. on stylistic grounds and conjecturally ascribed to Soph. Similarly Dion. Hal. De Dinarcho, 1 (p. 297, 1 ff.) does not ascribe to the orator Dinarchus an individual style such as Lys. and Isoc. had, cf. also De Lysia, 15 (p. 25, 9); De Demosthene, 9 (p. 144, 13; 148, 10); Ep. ad Pompeium, 1, 5 (ed. H. Usener-L. Radermacher, II, 1 [1929]); Cic. Ep. ad Quintum fratrem, II, 16, 5; Epict. Diss., II, 17, 35.

[20] Cf., e.g., Epict. Diss., III, 23, 33 ff., who seeks to show that epideictic, as it has developed as the χαρακτήρ of rhetoric, cannot be classed with the three traditional χαρακτῆρες of philosophy προτρεπτικός, ἐλεγκτικός, διδασκαλικός. On this whole subject cf. E. G. Schmidt, "Die drei Arten des Philosophierens. Zur Gesch. einer antiken Stil- u. Methodenscheidung," Philol., 106 (1962), 14-28.

things exactly: εἰληφέναι τινὰ χαρακτῆρα ἑκατέρου τοῦ εἴδους, ἐν ᾧ τε ἀνάγκη τὸ πλῆθος πλανᾶσθαι καὶ ἐν ᾧ μή. Simpl. Comm. in Aristot. Cat., 7 21 uses the term similarly in logic to denote the category of the πρός τι: καθ᾽ αὐτὰ μὲν οὐκ ἔστιν, οὐ γάρ ἐστιν ἀπόλυτα, κατὰ διαφορὰν δὲ πάντως ἔσται· μετὰ γάρ τινος χαρακτῆρος θεωρεῖται... πρός τι μὲν λέγουσιν, ὅσα κατ᾽ οἰκεῖον χαρακτῆρα διακείμενά πως ἀπονεύει πρὸς ἕτερον.

B. In Judaism.

1. χαρακτήρ occurs only three times in the LXX. 22 Lv. 13:28 ref. to the "scar" that results from burning as χαρακτὴρ τοῦ κατακαύματος. 4 Macc. 15:4 calls the likeness between parents and children a χαρακτήρ the former have impressed ἐναποσφραγίζομεν on the latter. 2 Macc. 4:10 uses Ἑλληνικὸν χαρακτῆρα for characteristic features of Hell. culture, the abolishing of the laws of the fathers and the introducing of customs contrary to the Law (4:11) such as the building of a gymnasium etc. by Jason. 23

2. The usage in Jos. covers much the same field. χαρακτήρ means "feature" in Ant., 2, 97; 13, 322, cf. also 10, 191. It can also mean "individuality" in Bell., 2, 106 and "letter," "writing" in Ant., 12, 14 f. 36, cf. Test. S. 5:4.

3. Philo often uses the fig. of the seal (→ VII, 946, 17 ff.) or the impress of a coin. By it he elucidates primarily the Stoic doctrine of perception, Deus Imm., 43: φαντασία δέ ἐστι τύπωσις ἐν ψυχῇ. 24 The soul is like a wax tablet which lets perceptions make their impress on it ὥσπερ δακτύλιός τις ἢ σφραγὶς ἐναπεμάξατο τὸν οἰκεῖον χαρακτῆρα, and it keeps these until forgetfulness expunges them, cf. Rer. Div. Her., 180 f. This Stoic doctrine with the concept of the process of impression is the basis of Philo's anthropology. The soul, when like soft wax it receives τὸν τῆς τελείας ἀρετῆς χαρακτῆρα, is the tree of life, but it is the tree of knowledge of good and evil when it receives τὸν τῆς κακίας, Leg. All., I, 61. καλοκἀγαθία, which is incorruptible in essence, impressed itself as such on the soul of Moses χαρακτῆρι θείῳ τυπωθείσῃ, Virt., 52. This impression is the εἰκών (→ II, 394, 12 ff.) that man received when created by God (Gn. 1:26 f.) and by it he is more like God than all other living creatures. The similarity does not extend to a physical impress σώματος χαρακτῆρι (→ 419, 1 ff.) but to the νοῦς, which is fashioned after the archetype of the divine Spirit and is thus like this, Op. Mund., 69. Hence the protoplast is like the cosmos in body and like God in spirit καὶ τῆς ἑκατέρου φύσεως ἐναπεμάττετο τῇ ψυχῇ τοὺς χαρακτῆρας, 151. 25 As the soul of man knows about God, whom it resembles, δέξηται χαρακτῆρας ἐξουσίας τε καὶ εὐεργεσίας αὐτοῦ καὶ τῶν τελείων μύστις γενομένη τελετῶν, Sacr. AC, 60. What this χαρακτήρ is Philo Leg. All., III, 95-104 shows in an allegory on the name Bezaleel: This name means ἐν σκιᾷ θεοῦ. This shadow of God is the logos by which God made the world. It is the archetype ἀρχέτυπον which as such is again ἀπεικόνισμα ἑτέρων.

---

21 Ed. K. Kalbfleisch, Comm. in Aristot. Graeca, 8 (1907), 166, 14 ff.

22 Apart from ψ 48:15 'Α, where χαρακτήρ seems to be used for צוּר "rock," so the qᵉre of the HT, or for צִיר "figure," so the kᵉtib. The HT is corrupt and is to be emended to וְיִצְרָם "their forms" [Bertram].

23 Cf. on this Polyb., 18, 34, 7: χαρακτήρ as "custom," "practice," in the negative sense with ref. to corruptibility.

24 A doctrine of the Stoic school, cf. Chrysipp. in Alex. Aphr. An., 135v (Bruns, 68, 11). The idea of the seal goes back to Plat. Tim., 50c, cf. Dölger, 65-9; cf. also Plut. Is. et Os., 54 (II, 373a) and on this Eltester, 59-68.

25 Cf. on this Op. Mund., 146: πᾶς ἄνθρωπος κατὰ μὲν τὴν διάνοιαν ᾠκείωται λόγῳ θείῳ, τῆς μακαρίας φύσεως ἐκμαγεῖον ἢ ἀπόσπασμα ἢ ἀπαύγασμα γεγονώς, κατὰ δὲ τὴν τοῦ σώματος κατασκευὴν ἅπαντι τῷ κόσμῳ. Eltester, 53 correctly observes that "here the motif of the impress stands alongside the thought of emanation." Cf. Mut. Nom., 223: The λογισμός is τελειότατον δὲ καὶ θειότατον ἔργον, τῆς τοῦ παντὸς ψυχῆς ἀπόσπασμα ἤ, ὅπερ ὁσιώτερον εἰπεῖν τοῖς κατὰ Μωυσῆν φιλοσοφοῦσιν, εἰκόνος θείας ἐκμαγεῖον ἐμφερές. This passage shows that Philo prefers εἰκών terminology to emanation terminology.

The *logos* is the image of God, so that there is a sequence of images: ὥσπερ γὰρ ὁ θεὸς παράδειγμα τῆς εἰκόνος, ἣν σκιὰν νυνὶ κέκληκεν, οὕτως ἡ εἰκὼν ἄλλων γίνεται παράδειγμα. These others are men, for acc. to Gn. 1:26 f. man was created after the image of God, i.e., τῆς μὲν εἰκόνος κατὰ τὸν θεὸν ἀπεικονισθείσης, τοῦ δὲ ἀνθρώπου κατὰ τὴν εἰκόνα λαβοῦσαν δύναμιν παραδείγματος, 96. Thus the soul of man has received its divine impress ὁ ἐπιγινόμενος χαρακτήρ, 97, namely, in its implanted ability to know God, 97-101. In keeping is the preceding discussion of man's creation (96), where with ref. to the double process of imaging the stress is on the likeness of the image to the imaged original as participation thereby in the original and not on the element of unlikeness or non-correspondence contained in the character as an image. The pt., then, of the difference between "archetype" παράδειγμα, ἀρχέτυπον, or with ref. to the *logos* εἰκών, and "image" ἀπεικόνισμα, χαρακτήρ, is that in the process of imaging the prototype inserts itself into the image so that it is accessible in this. This explains why in Philo's usage εἰκών statements can merge into χαρακτήρ statements. The εἰκών in the function of self-impartation — God to *logos* and *logos* to man — is like the die impressing its stamp on wax (→ 418, 10 f.), cf. Ebr., 133 and 137; Rer. Div. Her., 38. Man is linked with God through the *logos*. As λογικὴ ψυχή God has given man alone among living creatures an upright walk as an indication of the immediacy to God set in him by creation: εἶπεν αὐτὴν τοῦ θείου καὶ ἀοράτου πνεύματος ἐκείνου δόκιμον εἶναι νόμισμα σημειωθὲν καὶ τυπωθὲν σφραγῖδι θεοῦ, ἧς ὁ χαρακτήρ ἐστιν ὁ ἀΐδιος λόγος, Plant., 18, cf. Det. Pot. Ins., 83: τύπον τινὰ καὶ χαρακτῆρα θείας δυνάμεως, ἣν ὀνόματι κυρίῳ Μωυσῆς εἰκόνα καλεῖ. [26]

C. In the New Testament.

In the NT χαρακτήρ occurs only at Hb. 1:3 (→ VIII, 585, 16 ff.): [27] ὃς ὢν ἀπαύγασμα τῆς δόξης καὶ χαρακτὴρ τῆς ὑποστάσεως αὐτοῦ, φέρων τε τὰ πάντα τῷ ῥήματι τῆς δυνάμεως αὐτοῦ. The two statements correspond to the two preceding statements in v. 2b c. Viewing Christ's exaltation and pre-existence together, [28] they sing in hymnal style the eternal (or eternalised) nature of the Son → IV, 339, n. 5. The two members of the first statement (v. 3a) are in parallelism. They thus intentionally say the same thing. As δόξα (→ II, 233, 35 ff.) and ὑπόστασις (→ VIII, 572, 1 ff.) [29] are synonymous to the degree that God's glory is His nature, so the same function of the Son is expressed by ἀπαύγασμα (→ I, 508, 13 ff.) and χαρακτήρ. Since God's glory has impressed itself on Him as the One exalted by God, He is its reflection and image. The meaning of the two terms can best be explained from Wisdom [30] and Philo (→ 420, 17 ff.) in so far as one simply

---

26 Philo's teaching underwent a striking change in Gnosticism (→ 423, 8 ff.), for in the Naassene work in Hipp. Ref., V, 8, 13-15 the heavenly anthropos is by nature ἀχαρακτήριστος while the earthly Adam is κεχαρακτηρισμένος.

27 On Hb. 1:3 cf. Mi. Hb.[12]; C. Spicq, *L'Ép. aux Hb.*, II, Études Bibl. (1953), ad loc.; G. Bornkamm, "Das Bekenntnis im Hb.," *Stud. zu Antike u. Urchr.*[2] (1963), 197-200; E. Käsemann, "Das wandernde Gottesvolk," FRL, 55[2] (1957), 61-71; Eltester, 149-151.

28 In this regard Hb. 1:2-4 corresponds to the hymn in Col. 1:15-20.

29 On ὑπόστασις cf. esp. H. Dörrie, "Ὑπόστασις. Wort- u. Bedeutungsgesch.," NGG, 1955, 3 (1955); also "Zu Hb. 11:1," ZNW, 46 (1955), 196-202.

30 In Wis. 7:25 f. the relation of wisdom to God is described in a way terminologically similar to Hb. 1:3: ἀτμὶς γάρ ἐστιν τῆς τοῦ θεοῦ δυνάμεως καὶ ἀπόρροια τῆς τοῦ παντοκράτορος δόξης εἰλικρινής ... ἀπαύγασμα γάρ ἐστιν φωτὸς ἀϊδίου καὶ ἔσοπτρον ἀκηλίδωτον τῆς τοῦ θεοῦ ἐνεργείας καὶ εἰκὼν τῆς ἀγαθότητος αὐτοῦ. In interpretation cf. U. Wilckens, "Weisheit u. Torheit," *Beitr. z. hist. Theol.*, 26 (1959), 188-190. This leads on at once to Philo, whose language reminds us of Hb. 1:3, cf. esp. Som., I, 188. On the connection between Philo's doctrine of the *logos* and the tradition of Hell. Jewish wisdom → VII, 501, 6 ff., cf. H. A. Wolfson, *Philo*, I[3] (1962), 253-261. On Philonic σοφία as εἰκών cf. esp. Leg. All., I, 43 with III, 96 and Conf. Ling., 146, v. Eltester, 34; J. Jervell, "Imago Dei," FRL, 76 (1960), 136-140.

takes note of the complex of tradition to which all three belong. [31] As Philo's *logos* and the wisdom of Wis. 7 are the image of God inasmuch as God's nature, his radiant light and glory, is impressed on them, so Christ as the Son of God is the impress of God's nature, cf. Col. 1:15. But again, as the *logos* and wisdom fully represent God and allow Him to operate, so does the Son according to Hb. 1:3. His being as image and impress not only contains God's glory within it but also discloses this to the cosmos. For as Ruler of the cosmos He sustains all things by the Word of divine omnipotence, especially in relation to men, since by His humiliation and exaltation He has become for them the "cause of eternal salvation," Hb. 5:9, and by the way of discipleship God leads those who belong to Him, as sons, to glory, 2:10. [32] In the character of the Son as image there thus lies the essential presupposition of all Christ's saving work. In this respect especially Hb. differs from Philo. Whereas Philo develops his *logos* doctrine as anthropology, and thus works out the soteriological significance of the εἰκών concept in terms of the knowledge of God, Hb. expounds the humiliated and exalted Christ as the impress of God and thus develops the meaning of salvation with reference to the relation of Christians to Christ in homology. [33]

D. In the Post-Apostolic Fathers.

1 Cl., 33, 4 offers a unique exposition of Gn. 1:26 f.: ταῖς ἱεραῖς καὶ ἀμώμοις χερσὶν ἔπλασεν (sc. ὁ θεὸς τὸν ἄνθρωπον) τῆς ἑαυτοῦ εἰκόνος χαρακτῆρα. This is unique inasmuch as the κατ' εἰκόνα ἄνθρωπος is not understood as himself the image of God but rather as the impress of God's image. εἰκών here is the original whose image was impressed on man at creation. The εἰκών itself is God's own image τῆς ἑαυτοῦ εἰκόνος, [34] i.e., He Himself in His essential form. Possibly the hymnal tradition of Hb. 1:3 has influenced the usage here.

Ign. Mg., 5, 2 uses the coin metaphor to express the distinction between those who belong to Christ and the children of the world: ὥσπερ γάρ ἐστιν νομίσματα δύο, ὃ μὲν θεοῦ, ὃ δὲ κόσμου, καὶ ἕκαστον αὐτῶν ἴδιον χαρακτῆρα ἐπικείμενον ἔχει, οἱ ἄπιστοι τοῦ κόσμου τούτου, οἱ δὲ πιστοὶ ἐν ἀγάπῃ χαρακτῆρα θεοῦ πατρὸς

---

[31] Wis. 7:25 f., Philo's doctrine of the *logos* as image and of the κατ' εἰκόνα ἄνθρωπος, Hb. 1:3 and Col. 1:15 ff. (→ II, 389, 3 ff.), are different developments of a concept of image which in the Hell. age was widespread in oriental religions, as first noted by E. Käsemann, "Leib u. Leib Christi," *Beitr. z. hist. Theol.*, 9 (1933), 81-7; also "Eine urchr. Taufliturgie," *Exeget. Versuche u. Besinnungen*, I⁴ (1965), 39-43 and then fully presented by Jervell, *op. cit.*, cf. also Eltester on εἰκών in the Gk.-speaking sphere. If from an early period in the ancient Orient what is imaged is regarded as itself present in the image, Jervell, 125, then the self-declaration of the divine in a revealer-figure can be presented in this concept. The Revealer as the image of God imparts God Himself to man. In the Jewish world, in which one may see this first, the creation and constitution of Adam as primal man are depicted along these lines. The *locus classicus* for this is Gn. 1:26 f., which plays a vital role both in Philo and also in almost all the Gnostic anthropos systems, whereas in all the sophia systems the image functions are transferred to wisdom, cf. Jervell, 122-170, esp. 136-140.

[32] To this degree there is an act. element in the pass. sense of χαρακτήρ and ἀπαύγασμα, cf. Käsemann, *op. cit.* (→ n. 27 f.), 61 f. As χαρακτήρ means "impressed image," so ἀπαύγασμα also has the root meaning of "reflection" rather than "emanation" (→ I, 508, 15 ff.), cf. Wnd. Hb., Mi. Hb.¹², *ad loc.*

[33] On this soteriologically essential sense of holding fast to the confession of Christ cf. esp. Bornkamm, *op. cit.* (→ n. 27), 200-203.

[34] The ref. is not to Christ as εἰκών θεοῦ along the lines of Col. 1:15, though J. A. Fischer, *Die Apost. Vät., Schr. d. Urchr.*, I⁵ (1966), 65, n. 186 considers this possibility. Cf. correctly Pr.-Bauer, *s.v.* χαρακτήρ. On the usage cf. Ditt. Or., I, 383, 60; 404, 25 (both 1st cent. A.D.). Similarly Herm. s., 9, 9, 5 speaks of the "extraordinary beautiful figure" εὐειδέσταται τῷ χαρακτῆρι of women.

διὰ Ἰησοῦ Χριστοῦ. [35] As the continuation shows, the "character" of God which Christians have received through Jesus Christ is participation in His suffering as the presupposition of participation in His life, which "characterises" Christians as such. In Ign. Tr. Inscr.: ἀσπάζομαι... ἐν ἀποστολικῷ χαρακτῆρι, χαρακτήρ has a very weak sense: "I greet you in the manner (or: after the model) of the apostles." This formulation expresses his sense of difference from the apostles, [36] cf. in contrast 1 C. 9:2.

Wilckens

E. In Gnosticism.

In the prophetic consecration of Corp. Herm., Tat at the beginning of his ecstasy says to Herm. Trism.: τὸ γὰρ μέγεθος βλέπω τὸ σὸν τὸ αὐτό, ὦ πάτερ, σὺν τῷ χαρακτῆρι, 13, 5. In what follows, however, he is taught that his vision of the form is an illusion and that the true vision of God takes place only when ecstasy has left behind the last remnants of corporeality, to which μέγεθος, χαρακτήρ etc. belong. [37] Similarly in Anon. Ancient Gnostic Work, [38] 2 (p. 337, 19 f.) the twelfth depth is described as "unknowable," "featureless" (χαρακτήρ-) ... "inconceivable," "ineffable," though we then read paradoxically: "in which are all the marks (χαρακτῆρες)," cf. also 9 (p. 346, 3 ff.). The first-born has come forth from that which is "without mark (χαρακτήρ-) or form (σχῆμα-), 7 (p. 343, 11 ff.). The αὐτοπάτωρ is presented in the type (τύπος) of character-less (χαρακτήρ-) nineness, 12 (p. 351, 27 f.). In contrast the First Book of Jeû (→ n. 38) makes definite statements about the form (τύπος or χαρακτήρ) of the emanations of primal being; Cod. Brucianus even offers accounts of these χαρακτῆρες, e.g., I Book Jeû, 6 (p. 262, 32; 263, 11); 8 (p. 265); 12 (p. 269, 1); 14 (p. 271) etc. The closeness to magical [39] ideas and practices is unmistakable, as also in the Ophite magical saying of the soul: σύ... Ἰαλδαβαὼθ... ἔργον τέλειον υἱῷ καὶ πατρί, χαρακτῆρι τύπου ζωῆς σύμβολον ἐπιφέρων, "through the form of the image [40] bearing the sign of life," Orig. Cels., VI, 31 (p. 101, 7-8).

χαρακτήρ also occurs where there is ref. to intrinsically formless matter taking form through the operation of the upper world, → n. 26. Thus acc. to the teaching of the Peratae the Son transfers the πατρικοὶ χαρακτῆρες to ὕλη, which obviously assumes form as a result, Hipp. Ref., V, 17, 5. 7 f. But these χαρακτῆρες fall into the hands of the demiurge, ὃς ἀναλαβὼν τοὺς διαδοθέντας ἀπὸ τοῦ υἱοῦ χαρακτῆρας ἐγέννησεν ἐνθάδε, [41] V, 17, 7. When a man becomes aware of being a πατρικὸς χαρακτὴρ ἄνωθεν μετενηνεγμένος ἐνθάδε σωματοποιηθείς, he is sure of redemption, V, 17, 6. Hence Gnostics can be called ἐξυπνισμένους καὶ γεγονότας πατρικοὺς χαρακτῆρας, V, 17, 8. Much the same is reported of the Gnostic sect of the Docetae. The demiurge mocks the αἰώνιοι χαρακτῆρες which are here held fast below, VIII, 10, 1. But the third aeon establishes a firmament between heaven and earth to prevent further χαρακτῆρες from being dragged down from the upper world into darkness, VIII, 9, 4 f.; X, 16, 4.

Kelber

χαρίζομαι	→ 372, 14 ff.
χάρις	→ 372, 14 ff.
χάρισμα	→ 402, 27 ff.
χαριτόω	→ 372, 14 ff.

---

35 Bau. Ign., *ad loc.* notes par. in Cl. Al. Strom., I, 28, 176, 3; VII, 15, 90, 5 and Exc. Theod., 86, 2.

36 Cf. Bau. Ign., *ad loc.*

37 Cf. Reitzenstein Poim., 217; Nock-Fest., II, 211, n. 29.

38 Cf. C. Schmidt-W. C. Till, *Kpt.-gnost. Schr.*, I, GCS, 45³ (1959).

39 On χαρακτήρ in magic and theurgy cf. Audollent Def. Tab., p. LXXIII; C. Bonner, "Magical Amulets," HThR, 39 (1946), 40 f., 45; E. R. Dodds, *The Greeks and the Irrational* (1966), 150 f.

40 W. Foerster, *Die Gnosis*, I, (1969), 128 transl. "with the impress of the blow bearing the sign of life," but "blow" for τύπος is rare → VIII, 246, 13 f.

41 H. Leisegang, *Die Gnosis*⁴ (1955), 146 has the fine paraphrase: "and created the world here below."

> χείρ, χειραγωγέω, χειραγωγός, χειρόγραφον, χειροποίητος, ἀχειροποίητος, χειροτονέω
>
> βραχίων   (→ I, 639, 27 ff.)
> δάκτυλος   (→ II, 20, 19 ff.)
> δεξιός   (→ II, 37, 16 ff.)

† χείρ.

Contents: A. χείρ in Greek Usage: 1. χείρ to Denote Man's Hand; 2. χείρ in a Transferred Sense. B. χείρ/יָד in the Old Testament and Post-Biblical Judaism: 1. χείρ/יָד to Denote Man's Hand; 2. χείρ/יָד in a Transferred Sense; 3. The Hand of God; 4. The Laying On of Hands. C. χείρ in the New Testament: 1. χείρ to Denote Man's Hand; 2. χείρ in a Transferred Sense; 3. The Hand of God; 4. The Laying On of Hands. D. χείρ in the Post-Apostolic Fathers.

A. χείρ in Greek Usage.

1. χείρ to Denote Man's Hand.

a. The hand of man [1] is called the ὄργανον ὀργάνων by Aristot. An., III, 8, p. 432a, 1 f. As man's ψυχή determines the movement of the hands, so the hands set in motion the implements man wants to use, Aristot. Gen. An., I, 22, p. 730b, 9-19. [2] By means of his hands and feet a man accomplishes movement and action. [3] Since the power of the arm is exerted through the hand χείρ can also denote a man's arm: ἐν χερσὶ γυναικῶν... πεσέειν, Hom. Il., 6, 81 f.; ἀποταμόντα ἐν τῷ ὤμῳ τὴν χεῖρα, Hdt., II, 121 ε, 4; χεῖρες εἰς ὤμους γυμναί, Longus, I, 4, 2; ἐν τῇσι χερσὶ τῇς' ἐμῇσι, Herond. Mim., 5, 83. The acts performed by the hand are described in several expressions: οὐκ ἐχρήσατο τῇ χειρί, Hdt., IX, 72, 2; εἴρετο ὅ τι οὐ χρᾶται τῇ χειρί, III, 78, 5; ταῖς ἰδίαις χερσίν "with one's own hand," Diog. L., II, 13; Diod. S., 16, 33, 1; 17, 17, 7; ἄγομαί τι ἐς χεῖρας, "to take something in hand," e.g., μέλλοντι δέ οἱ ἐς χεῖρας ἄγεσθαι τὴν τελετὴν ἐγένετο φάσμα μέγιστον, Hdt., IV, 79, 1, cf. also I, 126, 6; VII, 8. "To have something in hand" means "to be at work on it," e.g., ἔχοντος δέ οἱ ἐν χερσὶ τοῦ παιδὸς τὸν γάμον, Hdt., I, 35, 1; τά τε τῶν ξυμμάχων διὰ χειρὸς ἔχειν, Thuc., II,

---

χείρ. Bibl.: Köhler-Baumg., s.v. יָד; Liddell-Scott, Pr.-Bauer, s.v.; Weinreich, AH, 1-75; J. Behm, Die Handauflegung im NT (1911); C. H. Turner, "χειροτονία, χειροθεσία, ἐπίθεσις χειρῶν," JThSt, 24 (1923), 496-504; J. Coppens, L'imposition des mains et les rites connexes dans le NT et dans l'église ancienne (1925); P. Galtier, Art. "Imposition des mains," Dict. de Théol. Catholique, 7 (1927), 1302-1425; G. Révész, Die menschliche Hand (1944); G. W. H. Lampe, The Seal of the Spirit (1951), 223-231; E. Lohse, Die Ordination im Spätjudt. u. im NT (1951); D. Daube, The NT and Rabbinic Judaism (1956), 224-246; U. Luck, Hand u. Hand Gottes. Ein Beitrag z. Grundlage u. Gesch. d. bibl. Gottesverständnisses, Münster (1959); S. Morenz, H. D. Wendland, W. Jannasch, Art. "Handauflegung," RGG³, III, 52-5; J. Ysebaert, "Greek Baptismal Terminology," Graecitas Christian. Primaeva, I (1962), Index, s.v. χείρ; J. K. Parratt, "The Laying on of Hands in the NT," Exp. T., 80 (1969), 210-214; K. Grayston, "The Significance of the Word Hand in the NT," Festschr. B. Rigaux (1970), 479-487.

[1] χείρ, gen. χειρός, plur. χεῖρες, dat. plur. χερσίν; Ionic and poetic also χερός, χέρες etc.

[2] On the preference of the right hand over the left → II, 38, 3 ff.

[3] Man's hands and feet are often mentioned together, e.g., οὐ χερός, οὐ ποδός, οὗ τινος ἄρχων, Soph. Phil., 859; χειρὶ καὶ ποδί, Philo Post. C., 151; χερσὶ καὶ ποσί, Agric., 22.

13, 2; ἃ εἶχον ἐν ταῖς χερσίν, P. Petr., II, 9, 2, 4 (3rd cent. B.C.). A man takes another by the hand: χειρὸς ἔχων Μενέλαον, Hom. Il., 4, 154, cf. also 1, 323; 24, 361; Od., 1, 121. A handshake is given in greeting: ἔν τ' ἄρα οἱ φῦ χειρί, Hom. Il., 6, 253 etc. The hand is raised in greeting: χερσίν τ' ἠσπάζοντο, Od., 3, 35, or in supplication to heaven: χεῖρ' ὀρέγων εἰς οὐρανὸν ἀστερόεντα, Il., 15, 371, cf. 3, 275; 7, 130: Od., 11, 423, or to mark assent; ὅτῳ δοκεῖ ... ταῦτα, ἀράτω τὴν χεῖρα, Xenoph. An., V, 6, 33. If on the one side liking or relationship is shown by the hand, 4 on the other side the hand is active also on meeting enemies. It is raised in attack or defence: οὔ τις ... σοὶ κοίλης παρὰ νηυσὶ βαρείας χεῖρας ἐποίσει, Hom. Il., 1, 88 f.; ἐς χειρῶν τε νόμον ἀπικέσθαι, Hdt., IX, 48, 2; ἄνδρας ... χεῖρας ἀνταιρομένους, Thuc., III, 32, 2. The following expressions are used for close combat or hand-to-hand fighting: ἐπειδὴ γὰρ ἐν χερσὶν ἐγίγνοντο τοῖς ἐναντίοις, Thuc., V, 72, 3; καὶ ἦν ἡ μάχη καρτερὰ καὶ ἐν χερσὶ πᾶσα, IV, 43, 2; βουλόμενοι ἐς χεῖρας ἐλθεῖν, IV, 33, 1; ἐς χεῖρας ᾖσαν, IV, 72, 3, cf. IV, 126, 5.

b. The gods also act with the hand, holding it protectively over individuals, Hom. Il., 9, 420, or directly intervening with it in earthly events, 15, 694 f. By contact or laying on the hand they transfer salvation and blessing to men. 5 Thus there is repeated praise that the god Aesculapius has healed by touching the sick with his hand φανεὶς ὁ θεὸς χεῖρα ὤρεξεν, Ael. Arist. Or., 42, 10 (Keil), cf. Ael. Fr., 99; Ditt. Syll.³, III, 1170, 23 (2nd cent. A.D.) etc. Human wonder-workers mediate healing powers by laying hands on the sick. 6 Thus it is said of Apollonius of Tyana that he raised a dead girl by touching her when she lay on the bier and speaking softly to her: οὐδὲν ἀλλ' ἢ προσαψάμενος αὐτῆς καὶ τι ἀφανῶς ἐπειπὼν ἀφύπνισε τὴν κόρην τοῦ δοκοῦντος θανάτου, Philostr. Vit. Ap., IV, 45.

2. χείρ in a Transferred Sense.

From the basic sense of "hand" extended use can develop in various ways. a. Hand can be used for the right side or the left: ἐπ' ἀριστερὰ χειρός, Hom. Od., 5, 277, cf. δεξιὰ χείρ → II, 37, 18 ff. b. The man who is active with his hands often tries to get power over others, so that χείρ frequently means "power": καὶ γὰρ δύναμις ὑπὲρ ἄνθρωπον ἡ βασιλέος ἐστὶ καὶ χεὶρ ὑπερμήκης, Hdt., VIII, 140 β, 2; πολλοὶ δὲ διέφευγον πελτασταὶ ὄντες ὁπλίτας ἐξ αὐτῶν τῶν χειρῶν, Xenoph. An., VI, 3, 4; τὰς τοῦ Σελεύκου χεῖρας διαφυγών, Diod. S., 18, 73, 4; ἐν χειρί τινα δίκην ἔχοντα, Plat. Theaet., 172e. When a thing is in one's hand, control is exercised over it: διὰ χειρῶν ἔχουσι μᾶλλον τὴν πολιτείαν, Aristot. Pol., V, 8, p. 1308a, 27. c. Work is done with the hand, and so χείρ can mean "work," e.g., in contrast to words: ἔπεσιν καὶ χερσὶν ἀρήξειν, Hom. Il., 1, 77; εἰ δέ τις ὑπέροπτα χερσὶν ἢ λόγῳ πορεύεται, Soph. Oed. Tyr., 883 f.; ταῖς τῶν γυναικῶν χερσί, Diod. S., 3, 65, 3. d. Since one writes with the hand, χείρ can mean "handwriting": κατὰ τὴν [χ]εῖρα [κα]ὶ [τὴν] πραγματε[ί]αν τοῦ [ποιητο]ῦ, Philodem. Philos. Περὶ ποιημάτων, 7 V, Col. 4, 33 f.; τοῖς φρουράρχοις ἐπιστέλλειν τῇ ἑαυτοῦ χειρί "to write the commanding officers with one's own hand," Jos. Ant., 14, 52. 8 e. Finally χείρ can also mean a "handful," "troop": πολλῇ χειρὶ ἐπεβοήθουν, Thuc., III, 96, 3; ἐστρατηλάτεε χειρὶ μεγάλῃ πλήθεος, Hdt., VII, 20, 1.

---

4 Stroking with the hand χειρί τέ μιν κατέρεξεν, Hom. Il., 1, 361; stretching out the hands or arms as a sign of loving relationship ἄμφω χεῖρε φίλοις ἑτάροισι πετάσσας, 4, 523; 13, 549.

5 Cf. for many examples Weinreich AH, passim, and also K. Sudhoff, "Die Handanlegung d. Heilgottes," Archiv f. Gesch. d. Medizin, 18 (1926), 235-250.

6 Examples in Weinreich AH, 45-48.

7 Ed. C. Jensen (1923).

8 On signature in one's own hand in ancient letters cf. Deissmann LO, 132 f., 137 f. → 430, 24 f.

B. χείρ/יְד in the Old Testament and Post-Biblical Judaism.

In almost all the instances of χείρ in the LXX the Hbr. original is יְד. Occasionally we also find the following equivalents: 1. כַּף "inner surface of the hand," e.g., Ju. 6:13 f.; 2. חֹפֶן or the dual חָפְנַיִם "hollow hands," e.g., Ez. 10:2 Cod. A; 3. שֹׁעַל "hollow of the hand," Is. 40:12; 4. תָּו "hand-sign," Job 31:35; יָמִין "right hand," e.g., Gn. 48:14. [9] Since the ref. in all these cases is to man's hand, in what follows we may basically take the equation of χείρ and יְד as a starting-pt.

1. χείρ/יְד to Denote Man's Hand.

a. Man uses hands in his acts, [10] so that what he makes can be called the work of his hands, Dt. 28:12; 31:29; Ps. 90:17 etc. In many passages the hand can stand for the man himself, e.g., "no hand (i.e., no man) shall touch him," Ex. 19:13. As in all antiquity, so in the OT greater value is attached to the right hand than the left → II, 38, 3 ff.. [11] The right hand can impart the stronger blessing, Gn. 48:14; the place at the right hand is the place of honour, Ps. 110:1. What is done by the hand is described by numerous verbs: Giving and receiving are done with the hand, a bargain is sealed with a handshake, 2 K. 10:15; Ex. 17:16. To put a hand on the mouth expresses silence, Job 21:5; Prv. 30:32. Clapping the hands is a sign of joy, Ez. 25:6. Hands are lifted up for prayer, Ps. 28:2; [12] 63:4, or an oath, Ex. 6:8; Nu. 14:30; Dt. 32:40 etc. A stretched forth hand can denote resolution even to the point of wilful and wicked defiance of God's command, Nu. 15:30, cf. Damasc. 8:8 (9:19); 10:3 (10:16); 19:21 (9:19); ·1 QS 5:12; 8:17, 22; 9:1. "Filling the hands" denotes investiture with an office, esp. the priesthood, Ex. 28:41; 29:9 etc.

b. A special pt. in the usage of post-biblical Judaism is that the laws of cleanness apply esp. to the hands and thus necessitate careful observance of rules for washing the hands. [13] The cleanness or uncleanness of objects that touch the hands can be transferred by contact. Among books that defile the hands are the canonical scriptures in virtue of the holiness attaching to them, Yad., 4, 6, [14] so that the hands must be washed after using them → III, 982, 31 ff. Hands are stretched out for prayer. [15]

2. χείρ/יְד in a Transferred Sense.

The meaning of the Hbr. יְד can be extended as follows. a. יְד is often a term of direction, indicating the right side or the left. Jonathan will come beside his father לְיַד־אָבִי, 1 S. 19:3. Absalom says that Joab has a field near his own אֶל־יָדִי, 2 S. 14:30. In the sense of "side" יְד is also used in topographical notes: עַל־יַד הַיְאֹר "on the bank of the river," Ex. 2:5, עַל יַד הַיַּרְדֵּן Nu. 13:29. b. יְד often expresses the "power" a man exercises through the hand and can thus mean "strength," "might": "The Lord hath delivered into our hands, i.e., power, all the land," Jos. 2:24, cf. also 6:2; 8:1; 10:8, 19; Ju. 3:28; 4:7, 14; 7:9, 15 etc. Israel is given up into the hands of foreign peoples, Ju. 4:2; 6:1; 10:7; 15:12 etc., but Yahweh saves His people from the hands of their enemies, Ju. 2:18; 8:22, 34 etc. Edom comes against Israel בְּעַם כָּבֵד וּבְיָד חֲזָקָה, Nu. 20:20. The hand of Israel rests ever more heavily on Jabin, Ju. 4:24. [16] c. יְד plur. יָדוֹת, can also denote objects that project

---

[9] At Nu. 14:27 Cod. A renders Hbr. מָה by χείρ, Cod. B by ἰσχύς.
[10] On what follows cf. Luck, 18-31.
[11] Lohse, 14.
[12] Cf. the impressive depiction of hands lifted up in invocation on the one tablet of the Rheneia vengeance prayers in Deissmann LO, 352 [Bertram].
[13] Examples and express presentation in Str.-B., I, 698-704.
[14] Cf. Str.-B., IV, 348.
[15] Cf. Jos. Ap., 1, 209 and further examples in Str.-B., II, 261.
[16] For Jewish examples of the sense "power" cf. Schl. Mt. on 17:22.

like hands, e.g., the sockets on the boards of the tabernacle, Ex. 26:17, 19; 36:22, 24, or the axle-trees of the wheels of the chariot for the cherubim, 1 K. 7:32 f., or the signpost, Ez. 21:24. d. יָד is very often used with prep., though in this case it loses its own sense and largely serves to strengthen the prep.: "By the hand of someone," one can send something, 1 K. 2:25, or order, Jer. 39:11, or even speak, Jer. 37:2. God speaks "by the hand of the prophets," 1 S. 28:15; Ez. 38:17 etc., cf. also 1 QS 1:3; 8:15; Damasc. 4:13 (6:9); 5:21 (8:2).

3. The Hand of God.

a. In more than 200 places the OT speaks of the hand of Yahweh. [17] The reference is always to God's activity by which He shows Himself mighty in creation and work.

Yahweh lays His hand on someone, Ex. 7:4; He stretches out His hand, Ez. 6:14; He turns, Is. 1:25, and swings His hand, Is. 11:15. His hand has established the earth and stretched out the heavens, Is. 45:11 f.; 48:13. Heaven and earth are the work of God's hands, Ps. 8:6; 102:25; Job 34:19; Is. 66:1 f. As God's hand and arm accomplished creation, so they initiate redemption, Is. 51:5, 9; 52:10. Above all Israel can say of the historical acts of Yahweh, which it has itself experienced, that His hand has brought them to pass. In the tradition of the exodus from Egypt it is stressed by constant repetition that Yahweh delivered His people from bondage and led them to freedom with a strong hand and a stretched out arm, Ex. 13:3, 14, 16; Dt. 3:24; 4:34; 5:15; 6:21; 7:8; 9:26; 11:2; 26:8 etc. Pharaoh experienced the strong hand of Yahweh when He stretched it forth against the Egyptians, Ex. 3:19 f. Israel saw the great hand which Yahweh manifested upon the Egyptians, Ex. 14:31. [18] Because Israel constantly experienced the working of the hand of God in history, it extols in worship and confession and praise the acts of salvation which the hand of Yahweh has accomplished, Ps. 89:10 f., 13; 98:1 etc. God's action in history can be called the work of His hands as creation can, Is. 5:12; Ps. 111:7. As God helped once, so in the future He will stretch forth His hand in miraculous deed and aid, Jer. 6:12; 15:6; 16:21; 51:25; Is. 25:9 f.; 26:11. His hand is not too short to liberate and help, Is. 50:2; 59:1. The hand of Yahweh comes into the life of individuals who are to be taken into His service. It empowers the prophet Elijah to run from Carmel to Jezreel in front of Ahab's chariot, 1 K. 18:46. Enablement to speak God's Word is effected through the hand of Yahweh according to 2 K. 3:15. This hand comes upon Isaiah (Is. 8:11), seizes the prophet Jeremiah (Jer. 15:17) and commandeers Ezekiel for the prophetic task he is ordered to fulfil (Ez. 1:3; 3:14, 22; 8:1; 33:22; 37:1; 40:1). Indissolubly linked to the Word of Yahweh is the mighty work in history which comes to pass through His hand.

b. The Dead Sea Scrolls adopt in various ways this practice of speaking about the hand of God. In the War Scroll the tradition of the holy war (→ VI, 511, 34 ff.) is often followed and victory over enemies, the hosts of Belial, is ascribed to the hand of God, 1 QM 11:1, 7 f., 11, or prayer is made that God will set His hand on the necks of His foes, 12:11; 19:3. On the trumpets of the fallen (→ VII, 82, 13 ff.) there is to be inscribed "hand of the power of God in battle to fell all the fallen of unfaithfulness," 3:8, and on the banners "the right hand of God" is to be written along with other names, 4:7. The thought of God's hand gives comfort in prayer, 1 QH 4:35 f., for a perfect walk comes from it, 1 QS 11:10 f., cf. 11:2.

---

[17] Cf. W. Zimmerli, *Ez., Bibl. Komm. AT*, 13 (1969), 47-50; Luck, *passim*. Cf. the passages which speak of God's right hand → II, 37, 20 ff.

[18] The problem of the origin of the idea of the hand of Yahweh is thoroughly discussed by Luck. He thinks that Israel's experience of Yahweh's mighty intervention in the holy war (→ VI, 507, 36 ff.) found expression in the ref. to God's hand, 61-76. For hist. material on the ancient oriental idea of the hand of God, *ibid.*, 42-54.

c. In Hell. Judaism, however, there are few ref. to God's hand, e.g., Sib., 3, 672 and 795. Usually attempts were made to avoid the phrase or it was given another sense by reinterpretation. Aristobulus in Eus. Praep. Ev., 8, 10, 8 offers an allegorical explanation of bibl. ref. to God's members and says that His hand represents His might. Philo, too, deduces from God's transcendence that anthropomorphic expressions are unsuitable: οὔτε ποσὶν οὔτε χερσὶν οὔτε ἄλλῳ τῶν ἐν γενέσει κεχρημένος μέρει τὸ παράπαν οὐδενί, Conf., Ling., 98. Though Philo does sometimes speak of God's hand, he means by it His effective power: τὸ ἡτοιμάσθαι ὑπὸ χειρῶν θεοῦ, τῶν κοσμοποιῶν αὐτοῦ δυνάμεων, Plant., 50. Similarly Jos. tries to steer clear of anthropomorphisms and ref. to God's hand only when directly quoting the OT, e.g., πολὺ κρεῖττον εἰς τὰς τοῦ θεοῦ χεῖρας ἐμπεσεῖν ἢ τὰς τῶν πολεμίων, Ant., 7, 323 quoting 2 S. 14:14. [19]

d. The Rabb., too, exercise gt. restraint in ref. to God's members. In the Tg. there is a noticeable tendency to replace יַד יְהוָה with other terms. [20] Whereas Ex. 14:8 says the Israelites were taken out of Egypt by God's hand, Tg. J. I renders the v. as follows: "The Israelites went out with lifted hand." M. Ex. בְּשַׁלַּח 1 on 14:8 (p. 90, 12) says: "And the Israelites went out with lifted hand, i.e., with a free head." [21]

4. The Laying On of Hands.

a. The laying on of hands [22] occurs in various contexts in the OT and post-biblical Judaism. Hands are raised in blessing; through the laying on of hands the blessing passes to the other, Gn. 48:14, so that it cannot be withdrawn, Gn. 27:35. The laying on of hands can also transfer power in the symbolical acts of the prophets, 2 K. 13:16. But never in the OT or the Rabb. tradition is the laying on of hands associated with miraculous healings. [23] bBer., 5b simply says that R. Jochanan (d. 279) came to the sick R. Chiyye bAbba (c. 280) and said to him: "Give me thy hand." In the Gn. Apocr., however, there is ref. to the laying on of hands in a story of healing. Abraham prayed for the sick Pharaoh and laid hands on him "and the plague retreated from him and the evil [spirit] removed itself [from him] and he lived," 1 Q Gn. Apocr. 20:28 f. [24]

b. The OT-Jewish concept of the resting of the hands, Hbr. סָמַךְ, סְמִיכָה, סְמִיכוּת is rendered in Gk. by ἐπιτίθημι τὴν χεῖρα or τὰς χεῖρας or ἐπίθεσις τῶν χειρῶν. This is ordered for the burnt offering, Lv. 1:4; 8:18; Ex. 29:15; Nu. 8:12, the meal offering, Lv. 3:2, 8, 13, the guilt offering, Lv. 8:22; Ex. 29:19 and the sin offering, Lv. 4:4, 15, 24, 29, 33; 8:14; Ex. 29:10; Nu. 8:12; 2 Ch. 29:23. [25] On the Day of Atonement the high-priest lays his hands on the scapegoat which is laden with the sins of Israel and sent into the wilderness, Lv. 16:21. If in the latter rite one may see clearly the idea of transfer, another idea seems to be linked with the resting of the hands on sacrifices. Probably a

---

[19] In Ant., 3, 101 χείρ is the handwriting on the tablets of the law.

[20] Cf. Luck, 116-8: יָד is mostly replaced by גְּבוּרָה or רוּחַ, cf. also Str.-B., II, 723 f.

[21] God's hand is sometimes depicted in Jewish art. Thus in the synagogue of Dura-Europos there are pictures describing how the promises of Ez. 37 are fulfilled and how God's hand awakens the dead, cf. H. Riesenfeld, "The Resurrection in Ez. 37 and in the Dura Europos Paintings," Uppsala Univ. Ársskrift, 1948, 11 (1948), 32-34, 36 f.; C. H. Kraeling, The Synagogue, The Excavations at Dura-Europos, Final Report, VIII, 1 (1956), Plates 69, 71; there is a similar depiction of God's hand at the Red Sea crossing, Plate 53.

[22] For comparative material from religious history cf. Lohse, 15.

[23] וְהֵנִיף יָדוֹ in 2 K. 5:11, however, is transl. καὶ ἐπιθήσει τὴν χεῖρα in 4 Βασ. 5:11.

[24] Ed. N. Avigad-Y. Yadin (1956), ad loc., cf. J. A. Fitzmyer, "Some Observations on the Gn. Apocryphon," The Catholic Bibl. Quarterly, 22 (1960), 284; D. Flusser, "Healing through Laying-on of Hands in a Dead Sea Scroll," Israel Exploration Journal, 7 (1957), 107 f.; H. Braun, Qumran u. d. NT, I (1966), 89 f.

[25] In connection with the laws of sacrifice one should also mention the consecration of the Levites by laying on of hands, Nu. 8:10.

relation is thereby set up between the offering and the one who makes it, so that it may be accepted in his favour. [26]

c. Institution into office is also accomplished by the laying on of hands. [27] One reads in P that Moses laid hands on Joshua and thus appointed him his successor. The laying on of hands is here a rite of transfer, since Joshua is thereby endued with the power he would need to discharge the office. According to Dt. 34:9 he was filled with the spirit of wisdom, while according to Nu. 27:18-20 he already had רוּחַ and now received the majesty הוֹד of Moses. The transferring of this gift took place before the assembled congregation in order to ratify publicly the legitimacy of the succession, Nu. 27:21-23.

After the model of the institution of Joshua, and with express appeal to it, [28] the Rabbis developed their own practice of ordination. When a fixed body of scribes came into being in the 2nd and 1st centuries B.C., it was customary to vouch for it in a public act that a candidate was worthy to receive the rights and duties of a rabbi → IV, 432, 36 ff.; VI, 962, 19 ff. It is true that only from the second half of the 1st century A.D. do we have evidence of ordinations with the names of the ordained rabbis. [29] But one may confidently assume that Rabbinic ordination goes back earlier and that it must have arisen with the development of the scribes as a specific group. [30] When after many years of work a student had achieved the required proficiency in the exposition of Scripture and the understanding of tradition, he was ordained by his teacher with the co-operation of two assistants, Sanh., 1, 3; T. Sanh., 1, 1 (Zuckermandel, 414). By the laying on of hands, which took place in the presence of witnesses, it was openly indicated that the chain of tradition reaching back to Moses would be lengthened by the addition of another link, the gift of wisdom being imparted to the authorised scholar by his teacher. [31] Only on the soil of Palestine could this act of once-for-all and non-repeatable ordination be performed. [32] In virtue of this authorisation the ordained scholar could now make his own academic and legal judgments, bear the title of rabbi (→ VI, 962, 9 ff.), and receive the honour and respect due to him. [33]

C. χείρ in the New Testament.

1. χείρ to Denote Man's Hand.

a. There are many ref. to the human hand in the NT books. [34] Man works with his hand, 1 Th. 4:11; 1 C. 4:12; Eph. 4:28; Ac. 20:34. On occasion the human members [35]

---

[26] Cf. Lohse, 23-25. Cf. the custom whereby a witness lays his hand on a condemned man, Lv. 24:14. He is forced in this way to acknowledge that the condemnation is on the basis of the witness he has given.

[27] Cf. J. Newman, Semikhah (1950); Lohse, 19-66.

[28] Cf. the Rabb. exposition of Nu. 27:15-23 and Dt. 34:9, esp. in S. Nu., 140 on 27:18 and S. Dt., 357 on 34:9; further examples in Str.-B., II, 647 f. and Lohse, 25-27.

[29] R. Jochanan bZakkai (d. c. 80) ordained his pupils R. Eliezer and R. Joshua, jSanh., 1, 3 (19a, 49 f.).

[30] On the age of Rabb. ordination cf. Lohse, 29-35.

[31] Cf. the examples assembled in Str.-B., II, 647-661.

[32] bSanh., 14a; further examples in Lohse, 48.

[33] On the further history of ordination and the later developments of סְמִיכָה cf. Lohse, 35-41; Daube, 232 f.

[34] On the declension cf. → n. 1. At Jn. 20:25 AB one finds the acc. χείραν, which occurs at times in the pap.; examples in Bau. J., ad loc., cf. Bl.-Debr. § 46, 1.

[35] Hands and feet, Mt. 22:13; Lk. 24:39; Jn. 11:44; Ac. 21:11: καὶ τὰς χείρας καὶ τὴν κεφαλήν, Jn. 13:9.

may indeed be introduced as independently acting subj.: ἐὰν σκανδαλίσῃ σε ἡ χείρ σου, Mk. 9:43 and par.; Mt. 5:30; δ . . . αἱ χεῖρες ἡμῶν ἐψηλάφησαν, 1 Jn. 1:1, cf. also 1 C. 12:15, 21. But usually the hand is mentioned as the instrument through which man fulfils his will. The ears of wheat are plucked with the hand, Lk. 6:1. The hand is set to the plough, Lk. 9:62. There is a fan in it, Mt. 3:12 and par., or a cup, Rev. 17:4. A pair of balances is carried in the hand in Rev. 6:5. Palm branches are held in the hand, Rev. 7:9. One beckons with it, Ac. 12:17; 13:16; 19:33; 21:40. The hand is stretched out, Mk. 3:5 and par.; Mt. 8:3; 12:49; 14:31; 26:51; Jn. 21:18; Ac. 26:1. It is reached, Jn. 20:20, 25, 27. One man gives another his hand, or takes him by the hand, Mk. 1:31 and par.; 5:41 and par.; 8:23; 9:27; Ac. 3:7; 9:41; 23:19. It is said of God that at the exodus from Egypt He took the Israelites by the hand, Hb. 8:9 (based on Ἰερ. 38[31]:32). Hands are laid on another violently, Mk. 14:46 and par; Lk. 20:19; 21:12; 22:53; Jn. 7:30, 44; Ac. 4:3; 5:18; 12:1; 21:27. A ring is set on the hand, i.e., the finger, Lk. 15:22. The hand can wither through sickness, Mk. 3:1, 3, 5 and par. An impressive miracle is recounted in Ac. 28:3 f.: A poisonous snake fastens itself on Paul's hand but does not hurt him. A χάραγμα is made on the hand (→ 416, 21 ff.) as a sign of ownership, Rev. 13:16; 14:9; 20:4. Hands can hang down slackly, Hb. 12:12. They are lifted up in blessing, Lk. 24:50, for prayer, 1 Tm. 2:8 (→ 426, 27 f.), or for an oath, Rev. 10:5 f. Idols are θεοὶ οἱ διὰ χειρῶν γινόμενοι, Ac. 19:26, cf. 7:41; Rev. 9:20. But God does not let Himself be worshipped ὑπὸ χειρῶν ἀνθρωπίνων, Ac. 17:25. The rules of cleanness in the Jewish Law prescribe the washing of hands, Mk. 7:2, 3, 5 and par → 426, 22 ff. With no ref. to the ritual statute Mt. 27:24 mentions washing the hands to emphasise innocence. Jm. 4:8 gives the admonition: καθαρίσατε χεῖρας, ἁμαρτωλοί, thereby demanding moral purity. With the hand one dips in the dish at the common meal, Mt. 26:23; Lk. 22:21. [36] Among the letters that the apostle dictated, cf. R. 16:22, ὁ ἀσπασμὸς τῇ ἐμῇ χειρὶ Παύλου occurs in 1 C. at 16:21; 2 Th. at 3:17; Col. at 4:18 and cf. Gl. 6:11; Phlm. 19. [37]

b. Angels as well as men have hands: ἐπὶ χειρῶν ἀροῦσίν σε, "They will bear thee in their arms," Mt. 4:6 and par. quoting Ps. 91:12 and cf. Ac. 7:35; Rev. 8:4; 10:2, 5, 8, 10; 20:1. The Risen Lord shows His disciples His hands, Lk. 24:39, 40 vl. and the divine sees the Son of Man holding seven stars (Rev. 1:16) or a sickle (14:14) in His hands.

2. χείρ in a Transferred Sense.

a. χείρ often means the "power" a man exercises through his hand. The Son of Man is given up (→ II, 169, 27 ff.) εἰς χεῖρας ἀνθρώπων, Mk. 9:31 and par.; 14:41 and par.; Lk. 24:7, cf. Jn. 10:39. God saves ἐκ χειρὸς πάντων τῶν μισούντων ἡμᾶς, Lk. 1:71, ἐκ χειρὸς ἐχθρῶν, 1:74. Paul escapes τὰς χεῖρας of Aretas, 2 C. 11:33 and Peter ἐκ χειρὸς Ἡρῴδου, Ac. 12:11, cf. also Ac. 21:11; 24:7 vl.; 28:17. Jn. ref. to the keeping power exercised by the hand of Christ: ὁ πατὴρ . . . πάντα δέδωκεν ἐν τῇ χειρὶ αὐτοῦ, Jn. 3:35; πάντα ἔδωκεν αὐτῷ ὁ πατὴρ εἰς τὰς χεῖρας, Jn. 13:3 (→ V, 895, 5 ff.), cf. also 10:28 f.

b. As in OT usage χείρ after a prep. serves to strengthen the prep. and to a large extent loses its own sense; [38] thus διὰ χειρός, Hbr. בְּיַד, means "through": [39] αἱ δυνάμεις τοιαῦται διὰ τῶν χειρῶν αὐτοῦ γινόμεναι, Mk. 6:2; the Law was given ἐν χειρὶ

---

[36] Mk. 14:20 reads: ὁ ἐμβαπτόμενος μετ᾽ ἐμοῦ, Mt. 26:23: ὁ ἐμβάψας μετ᾽ ἐμοῦ τὴν χεῖρα and in Lk. 22:21 the hand is the subj.: ἰδοὺ ἡ χεὶρ τοῦ παραδιδόντος με μετ᾽ ἐμοῦ ἐπὶ τῆς τραπέζης.

[37] On endings to letters in one's own hand cf. Deissmann LO, 137 f.; O. Roller, "Das Formular d. paul. Briefe," BWANT, 58 (1933), 181-191 etc. → 425, n. 8.

[38] Cf. Bl.-Debr. § 217, 2.

[39] In such constructions χείρ is usually in the sing., though cf. Ac. 14:3: διὰ τῶν χειρῶν αὐτῶν. Cf. Bl.-Debr. § 140.

μεσίτου, Gl. 3:19, cf. also Ac. 5:12; 14:3; 19:11; ἀποστείλαντες πρὸς τοὺς πρεσβυτέρους διὰ χειρὸς Βαρναβᾶ καὶ Σαύλου, Ac. 11:30, cf. also Ac. 15:23; 2:23; 7:25. [40]

3. The Hand of God.

In the NT reference is made to God's hand only where OT sayings are adduced or OT usage is adopted. We find quotations at Lk. 23:46 (Ps. 31:5) and R. 10:21 (Is. 65:2). Only in Lk. and Ac. is there common mention of the hand of God, and here there can be little doubt but that OT expressions are deliberately adopted, Lk. 1:66; Ac. 4:28, 30; 7:50; 11:21; 13:11. In the other NT writings the "hand of God" occurs only at Jn. 10:29; Hb. 1:10; 10:31 and 1 Pt. 5:6. [41]

The hand of God executed creation, Ac. 7:50 cf. Is. 66:2. It also acts in history, intervening to protect and help (Lk. 1:66; Ac. 11:21), but also to punish (Ac. 13:11). It is pointed out in warning: φοβερὸν τὸ ἐμπεσεῖν εἰς χεῖρας θεοῦ ζῶντος, Hb. 10:31 → 428, 10 f. Nowhere does the significance of this comparatively rare expression go beyond the content of OT statements about the hand of God → 427, 8 ff. [42]

4. The Laying On of Hands → VIII, 160, 35 ff.

a. As in the miracle stories of antiquity (→ 425, 15 ff.), there is frequent reference to the laying on of hands in the NT accounts of the healing of the sick. [43] Jesus touches the sick with His hand and they are cured. Thus Jairus asks Jesus to come and lay His hand on his very sick daughter so that she may get well again. He is convinced that through touch healing power will flow upon the child, Mk. 5:23 and par., cf. also 5:41 and par. A deaf mute is brought to Jesus so that He may heal him by the laying on of hands, Mk. 7:32. Jesus lays His hand on the eyes of the blind man at Bethesda and restores his sight, Mk. 8:23, 25. Jesus takes an epileptic boy by the hand, makes him stand up, and cures him, Mk. 9:27 and par. A crooked woman asks Jesus to save her from her affliction. By the touch of His hands she is made straight and she praises God for His act, Lk. 13:13. The sick past whom Jesus goes desire only to touch the Saviour in order that healing power may flow upon them, Mk. 3:10 and par.; 6:56 and par.; Lk. 6:19 etc. Jesus takes the mother-in-law of Peter by the hand and sets her free from the fever, Mk. 1:31 and par. He stretches out His hand, touches the leper, and makes him clean, Mk. 1:41 and par. On a Sabbath He heals the man with dropsy through touch with His hand, Lk. 14:4. In the summaries in Mk. 6:5 and Lk. 4:40 we read that Jesus performed His mighty works by the laying on of hands. The saving ministry is continued by the hands of the apostles acting with the authority of Jesus, Mk. 16:18; Ac. 5:12, 15. Peter heals the lame beggar before the temple when he takes him by the hand, Ac. 3:7. Tabitha is raised from the dead by Peter; he takes her hand and raises her up, Ac. 9:41. Paul, blinded

---

[40] ἐκ χειρὸς αὐτῆς, "from her," Rev. 19:2.

[41] Luck, 6, 130-132.

[42] To complete the picture we should note the use of δεξιά (sc. χείρ), esp. the frequent use of Ps. 110:1 as a christological proof from Scripture (→ II, 39, 5 ff.). On the depiction of God's hand in art cf. H. Jursch, Art. "Hand Gottes in d. Kunst," RGG³, III, 52 and the bibl. given there.

[43] Cf. Behm, 102-116; Lohse, 69 f.; Wendland, 53 f. On the laying on of hands or the function of the hand at the anointing of the sick cf. G. Bertram, "Die Krankensalbung im NT," *Evangelische Krankenpflege*, 11 (1962), 121-9.

on the Damascus road, receives his sight again when Ananias lays hands upon him, Ac. 9:12, 17. Mighty acts are also performed by the hands of Paul, Ac. 19:11. On the island of Malta he cures the sick father of Publius by laying hands upon him, Ac. 28:8. [44]

The common reference to touching with the hand or to the laying on of hands is thus a typical feature in the miracle stories. [45] Jesus is depicted as the Healer who enjoys divine power → III, 211, 25 ff. By contact this power is transferred to the sick and afflicted so that they are made well, Lk. 5:17; 6:19. In distinction from the miracle stories of antiquity however (→ III, 209, 27 ff.) there is no magical practice of healing in the NT records. The decisive elements are the mighty Word of Jesus and the faith that is put in Him. The healing power of Jesus is not bound up with any means or mode of transfer. His Word can operate even from afar, Mt. 8:8, 13 par. Lk. 7:7, 10; Jn. 4:50-52. [46]

b. Hands are also imposed in blessing and impartation. Children are brought to Jesus ἵνα αὐτῶν ἅψηται (Mk. 10:13), or ἵνα τὰς χεῖρας ἐπιθῇ αὐτοῖς καὶ προσεύξηται (Mt. 19:13 cf. Lk. 18:15), [47] καὶ ἐναγκαλισάμενος αὐτὰ κατευλόγει τιθεὶς τὰς χεῖρας ἐπ' αὐτά (Mk. 10:16 and par.). [48] In Ac. 8:17 and Hb. 6:2 the laying on of hands is mentioned in connection with baptism: ἐπετίθεσαν τὰς χεῖρας ἐπ' αὐτούς, καὶ ἐλάμβανον πνεῦμα ἅγιον (Ac. 8:17), καὶ ἐπιθέντος αὐτοῖς τοῦ Παύλου χεῖρας ἦλθε τὸ πνεῦμα τὸ ἅγιον ἐπ' αὐτούς Ac. 19:6. [49] The laying on of hands (→ VI, 414, 16 ff.) performed at baptism is understood as a means whereby the Spirit (→ VI, 413, 6 ff.) comes on the candidate [50] and as the visible sign that God keeps His promise and pours forth the gift of the Spirit. [51] The author of Ac. thinks it especially important to emphasise in c. 8 that only with their acceptance by the Jerusalem apostles did the Samaritan Christians become members of the one Church in the full sense, and that the way indicated in salvation history was

---

[44] Cf. also Rev. 1:17: The exalted Son of Man lays His right hand on John, who has sunk to the ground like a dead man, and grants Him life-giving force.

[45] Cf. Bultmann Trad., 237 f. For a later period cf. Ev. Veritatis (ed. M. Malinine et al. 1956), 30:19-21: "When he (sc. Jesus) had given his hand to him that was stretched out on the ground, he (sc. the Spirit) set him firmly on his feet," Cf. H. M. Schenke, Die Herkunft d. sog. Ev. Veritatis (1959), 46.

[46] That in miracles the laying on of hands is not for the narrators the unconditionally necessary means of imparting power may be seen also from the fact that it is sometimes missing in one Evangelist when mentioned in par. accounts by the others. Thus Mt. 20:34 mentions touching the eyes of the blind men but acc. to Mk. 10:52 and Lk. 18:42 f. the cure is effected by the Word of Jesus.

[47] Cf. Str.-B., I, 807 f.: The father blesses his children, the teacher his pupils. Soph., 18, 5 (Str.-B., II, 138) tells us that in Jerusalem parents had their children fast on the Day of Atonement and in the evening brought them to the scribes that these might bless them and pray for them, cf. Lohse, 51. G. Friedrich, "Beobachtungen z. messian. Hohepriestererwartung in den Synpt.," ZThK, 53 (1956), 294-7 considers whether Jesus' action is not to be regarded as priestly.

[48] Since the pericope was soon adduced as a basis for the practice of infant baptism, cf. J. Jeremias, Die Kindertaufe in d. ersten vier Jhdt. (1958), 61-8, the laying on of hands also came to be understood in relation to the practice customary at baptism.

[49] Cf. also Ac. 9:17, where, with the laying on of hands, Saul receives his sight back and is filled with the Holy Spirit.

[50] The freedom of the Spirit is safeguarded, for elsewhere we read of the coming of the Spirit without laying on of hands, Ac. 2:1-13; 10:44-48. The main pt. in Ac. is that baptism and reception of the Spirit necessarily belong together.

[51] Cf. N. Adler, "Taufe u. Handauflegung," NTAbh, 19, 3 (1951); Lampe, 223-231.

followed thereby. [52] Union with the one Church whose messengers go forth from Jerusalem was also granted to the disciples of John when they were baptised by Paul and hands were laid on them for the reception of the Spirit, Ac. 19:6.

c. At institution to office hands are laid on the office-bearer to equip him with divine power. [53] In Ac. 13:1-3 we read of a commission being given to Barnabas and Saul. After they have been separated under the direction of the Spirit, the community fasts, prays, καὶ ἐπιθέντες τὰς χεῖρας αὐτοῖς ἀπέλυσαν. [54] The transfer of an office by ordination is referred to in Ac. 6:1-6 → VIII, 161, 6 ff. The seven Hellenists (→ II, 511, 23 ff.) upon whom the apostles lay their hands with prayer are instituted in their office and confirmed by the highest authority in the Church, Ac. 6:6. [55] If as a result of the emphasis on this concept, which is so important for the author of Ac., the historical background of the tradition of the institution of the Seven can no longer be established for certain, it may be assumed with a high degree of probability that Jewish Christianity in Palestine had already adopted Rabbinic סְמִיכָה (→ 429, 11 ff.) and was using the laying on of hands for institution to office. The difference between Rabbinic ordination and the institution to office practised in the Christian community is that the Spirit plays a crucial role in deciding who are to be selected as ministers of the Word and that their installation takes place not only with the laying on of hands but also and above all with prayer.

The Pastorals offer a clear picture of Christian ordination as it was adopted by the Pauline churches from the Jewish Christian church in Palestine. [56] Charisma and office are closely interrelated here. When prophetic voices pointed to Timothy as the selected office-bearer (1 Tm. 1:18; 4:14) the divinely granted charisma (→ 406, 8 ff.) which he needed to discharge his office was imparted to him by laying on of hands. Hence the ἐπίθεσις τῶν χειρῶν is not presented merely as an accompanying sign. It also serves to pass on the gift with which God equips the office-bearer. If 2 Tm. 1:6 recalls the χάρισμα τοῦ θεοῦ, ὅ ἐστιν ἐν σοὶ διὰ τῆς ἐπιθέσεως τῶν χειρῶν μου, 1 Tm. 4:14 (→ VI, 666, n. 92) refers to the χάρισμα, ὅ ἐδόθη σοι διὰ προφητείας μετὰ ἐπιθέσεως τῶν χειρῶν τοῦ πρεσβυτερίου. If the apostle is said to have ordained on the one side and the presbytery on the other, one may

---

[52] This rather than the significance of laying on of hands is the central concern, cf. Haench. Ag.[14], *ad loc.* The example of Simon Magus in Ac. 8:18 f. shows that the laying on of hands is not to be misused as magic.

[53] Daube, 233-246 has impressively stressed the fact that the laying on of hands at the institution of office-bearers, which is based on Rabb. סְמִיכָה, must be clearly distinguished from the laying on of hands in healing the sick.

[54] Hence Ac. 13:1-3 cannot be described as ordination. What we have here is the commissioning and sending forth of two missionaries appointed by the Spirit, cf. Lohse, 71-4.

[55] Note the unmistakable allusions to Nu. 27:15-23: a. ἐπισκέψασθε in Ac. 6:3 and ἐπισκεψάσθω κύριος ὁ θεός in Nu. 27:16; b. Yahweh calls Joshua an ἄνθρωπον, ὃς ἔχει πνεῦμα ἐν ἑαυτῷ, Nu. 27:18, cf. Ac. 6:3: ἄνδρας ... πλήρεις πνεύματος καὶ σοφίας, and also v. 5; c. Joshua is installed by the priest Eleazar, Nu. 27:19, while the Seven are set before the apostles, Ac. 6:6; d. Hands are laid on, Nu. 27:18, 23 and Ac. 6:6. Since Nu. 27:15-23 serves as a basis of ordination for the Rabb., the intentional borrowing from Nu. 27 in Ac. 6:1-6 is designed to show that the institution of the Seven is meant as Chr. ordination, cf. Haench. Ag.[14] on 6:3; Lohse, 77.

[56] Cf. H. Schlier, "Die Ordnung d. Kirche nach d. Past.," *Die Zeit d. Kirche*[4] (1966), 129-147; Lohse, 80-87; also Art. "Ordination," RGG[3], IV, 1672 f.; E. Schweizer, "Gemeinde u. Gemeindeordnung im NT," AbhThANT, 35[2] (1962), 187-192; L. Goppelt, "Die ap. u. nachap. Zeit," *Die Kirche in ihrer Gesch.*, I, 1[2] (1966), 136 f.; E. Käsemann, "Das Formular einer nt.lichen Ordinationsparänese," *Exeget. Versuche u. Besinnungen*, I[5] (1967), 101-108; C. Spicq, *Les Ép. Pastorales*, II[4] (1969), 722-730.

conclude that in the Christian transfer of office, as in Rabbinic ordination (→ 429, 19 ff.), the one who ordained laid on his hands along with assistants.[57] 2 Tm., which is much more personal, recalls only the laying on of the apostle's hands, whereas 1 Tm., which has more of the character of a church order, refers expressly to the ἐπίθεσις τῶν χειρῶν by the πρεσβυτέριον. There is no mention of a power of consecration restricted only to certain individuals. God's will to call and to send determines the content of the ordination by which the office-bearer is publicly authorised before the congregation, equipped with the charisma of office, and instituted into the office of proclaiming the Word. His task is to lead the community. Hence there is set before him the particular responsibility which he must discharge in the laying on of hands: χεῖρας ταχέως μηδενὶ ἐπιτίθει, 1 Tm. 5:22. This short admonition is either to be understood as a warning not to undertake ordination too quickly or else the reference is to the reception of penitent sinners whom the office-bearer must accept only after careful testing lest he should contract joint responsibility for the sins of others.[58]

D. χείρ in the Post-Apostolic Fathers.

There is nothing essentially distinctive in the writings of the post-apost. fathers.

1. Several passages ref. to the human hand. Man works with his hands, Did., 4, 6. The hand is shaken as a threat, Mart. Pol., 9, 2. It is stretched out, Did., 4, 5; Barn., 19, 9. It is held up to God, 1 Cl., 2, 3: 29, 1. The potter takes the clay in his hand and shapes the vessel, 2 Cl., 8, 2. Barn., 16, 7 says critically of the temple that it is οἰκοδομητὸς ... διὰ χειρός.

2. In a transf. sense χείρ often means "power." Holofernes was given up by God ἐν χειρὶ θηλείας, 1 Cl., 55, 5. With Job 5:20 1 Cl., 56, 9 says: ἐν πολέμῳ δὲ ἐκ χειρὸς σιδήρου λύσει (sc. God) σε, cf. also Did., 16, 4; Barn., 5, 5. One has ἐν χειρί that with which one is occupied: ἐν χερσὶν ὁ ἀγών "the contest is our present task," 2 Cl., 7, 1. ὑπὸ χεῖρα occurs in Herm. v., 3, 10, 7; 5, 5; m., 4, 3, 6 in the sense of "on every occasion," "persistently."[59]

3. There is ref. to God's hand in OT quotations or with the adoption of OT expressions. Creation is the work of God's hands, Barn., 15, 3, cf. Gn. 2:2; 1 Cl., 27, 7, cf. ψ 18:2; Barn., 5, 10. He created man ταῖς ἱεραῖς καὶ ἀμώμοις χερσὶν ἔπλασεν τῆς ἑαυτοῦ εἰκόνος χαρακτῆρα, 1 Cl., 33, 4. The tablets of the Law which Moses received at Sinai were written τῷ δακτύλῳ τῆς χειρὸς τοῦ κυρίου, Barn., 4, 7; 14, 2, cf. Ex. 31:18; 34:28. God's hand intervenes in the life of man to punish, 1 Cl., 28, 2, to heal, 1 Cl., 56, 7 (cf. Job 5:18), and to protect, 1 Cl., 60, 3, cf. Is. 51:16; Wis. 5:16.

4. The only ref. to the laying on of hands in the post-apost. fathers is at Barn., 13, 5 (Gn. 48:14), where Jacob crosses his hands, lays his right hand on the head of Ephraim, and imparts the blessing to the younger son of Joseph.

---

[57] Daube, 244 f. tries to explain 1 Tm. 4:14 differently by construing ἐπίθεσις τῶν χειρῶν τοῦ πρεσβυτερίου Hbr. זְקֵנִים סְמִיכַת as "the leaning on of hands on persons in order to make elders, Rabbis of them," cf. also D. Daube, "Evangelisten u. Rabb.," ZNW, 48 (1957), 124 f. J. Jeremias, "ΠΡΕΣΒΥΤΕΡΙΟΝ ausserchr. bezeugt," ZNW, 48 (1957), 130, agrees: "Laying on of hands which confers presbyteral dignity," cf. also his "Zur Datierung d. Past.," Abba (1966), 314-6. The objections against this view are listed by G. Bornkamm (→ VI, 666, n. 92) and cf. also Schweizer, op. cit., 190, n. 812.

[58] Cf. N. Adler, "Die Handauflegung im NT bereits ein Bussritus? Zur Auslegung v. 1 Tm. 5:22," Festschr. J. Schmid (1963), 1-6.

[59] Cf. Bl.-Debr. § 232, 1; Pr.-Bauer, s.v. χείρ.

† χειραγωγέω, χειραγωγός.

1. The verb χειραγωγέω "to lead by the hand" is common in Gk., e.g., τρέμοντα δ' αὐτὸν ἤδη "Ἔρως ἐχειραγώγει, Carmina anacreontea,[1] 1, 9 f., ποῖ τοῦτον ἀπάγεις, ὦ 'Αργειφόντα, χειραγωγῶν, Luc. Tim., 32, cf. also Diod. S., 13, 20, 4. In the LXX the verb occurs only at Ju. 16:26 Cod. A: τὸ παιδάριον τὸν χειραγωγοῦντα αὐτόν, cf. Jos. Ant., 5, 315, Tob. 11:16 vl. The LXX does not have the noun ὁ χειραγωγός, which means "one who leads another by the hand," e.g., οὐ γὰρ ἂν ἐχρῶντο συμβούλοις καὶ στρατηγοῖς καὶ νομοθέταις ὥσπερ τυφλοῖς χειραγωγοῖς, Plut. Comm. Not., 10 (II, 1063b), cf. also An seni sit gerenda res publica, 21 (II, 794d); ζητήσατε χειραγωγὸν τὸν ὁδηγήσοντα ὑμᾶς ἐπὶ τὰς τῆς γνώσεως θύρας, Corp. Herm., 7, 2.

2. In the NT both verb and noun are used to bring out the helplessness of the blind. When Saul is blinded outside Damascus his companions take him by the hand and lead him into the city, Ac. 9:8; 22:11. The sorcerer Bar-Jesus suddenly becomes blind καὶ περιάγων ἐζήτει χειραγωγούς, Ac. 13:11.

† χειρόγραφον.

1. A document, esp. a note of indebtness, is written in one's own hand as a proof of obligation: ἐλεγχόμενοι γὰρ κατὰ πρόσωπον ὑπὸ τῶν ἰδίων χειρογράφων, Polyb., 30, 8, 4, καὶ οἱ δεδανεικότες τὰ συμβόλαια τά τε ναυτικὰ καὶ κατὰ χειρόγραφα καὶ κατὰ παραθήκας Ditt. Syll.³, II, 742, 50 f. (c. 85 B.C.). In the LXX the word occurs only in Tob.: καὶ ἔδωκεν αὐτῷ τὸ χειρόγραφον, 5:3; 9:5.

2. In the one instance of the word χειρόγραφον in the NT it has the sense of "promissory note": ἐξαλείψας τὸ καθ' ἡμῶν χειρόγραφον Col. 2:14 (→ II, 231, 25 ff.). The reference is to God's pronouncement that the note which testifies against us is cancelled (→ VII, 576, 25 ff.). The phrase is obviously based on a thought which is common in Judaism, namely, that God keeps an account of man's debt, that according to the account He calls in the debt through angels, and that He imposes the penalty.[1] Col. 2:14 adopts the metaphor[2] and works it into the context, which deals with the new life of those who have been buried and raised again with Christ.[3] There is no thought of the myth which the fathers later introduced into exposition of the passage,[4] namely, that the document written in one's own hand is a compact with the devil by which man has engaged to give

χειραγωγέω κτλ.   [1] Ed. K. Preisendanz (1912).

γειρόγραφον. Bibl.: Deissmann LO, 281-4; G. Megas, "Das χειρόγραφον Adams. Ein Beitrag zu Col. 2:13-15," ZNW, 27 (1928), 305-320; H. Burnickel, Das χειρόγραφον im ptolemäischen Recht, Diss. Erlangen (1950); A. Blanchette, "Does the cheirographon of Col. 2:14 represent Christ Himself?" The Catholic Bibl. Quarterly, 23 (1961), 306-312.
   [1] Ab., 3, 16 (R. Aqiba); further examples in Str.-B., III, 628.
   [2] The heavenly book of debts is called χειρόγραφον in Anon. Apoc. (of Jewish origin, preserved in Cpt., cf. G. Steindorff, Die Apok. d. Elias, eine unbekantte Apok. u. Bruchstücke d. Sophonias-Apok., TU, 17, 3 [1899]): Angels of the Lord write the good works of the righteous in the χειρόγραφον, 3:13 ff. (Steindorff, 39) and the angels of the accuser write all the sins of men, 4:3 ff. (41). Cf. Slav. En. B. 53:3 and Apoc. Pl. 17: Et venit angelus anime peccatricis habens in manibus cirographum (ed. M. R. James, Apocr. anecdota, I, TSt, II, 3 [1893], 20), cf., ad loc. H. Duensing, Hennecke³, II, 538 [Kelber].
   [3] Cf. Dib. Gefbr., ad loc.
   [4] Examples in Megas, 314 f. 317 and Loh. Kol., ad loc.

up his life to sin and death in return for the services that Satan will render him. [5] The point of the metaphor of the note of indebtedness is rather to underline the preceding statement χαρισάμενος ἡμῖν πάντα τὰ παραπτώματα. God has forgiven sins. He has cancelled the note of indebtedness [6] by taking it and fixing it to the cross of Christ. [7]

† χειροποίητος, ἀχειροποίητος.

1. The adj. χειροποίητος "made by hands" is found from Hdt. and brings out the difference between what man has done and what has come into being naturally λίμνη ... χειροποίητός ἐστι καὶ ὀρυκτή, Hdt., II, 149, 1 f., cf. also I, 195, 2; Thuc., II, 77, 4; Plat. Critias, 118c; Xenoph. An., IV, 3, 5; πῦρ ... χειροποίητον, Jos. Ant., 4, 55; λίμνη ... χειροποίητος, Diod. S., 13, 82, 5 and 15, 93, 4; 17, 71, 7; Jos. Bell., 1, 419; 7, 294; Ant., 15, 324; Philo Vit. Mos., II, 51. 88. 168 etc. In the LXX χειροποίητος almost always stands for Hbr. אֱלִיל [1] and it describes the gods as made with men's hands: οὐ ποιήσετε ὑμῖν αὐτοῖς χειροποίητα, Lv. 26:1; ἐποίησαν χειροποίητα, Is. 46:6, cf. also Sib., 3, 606: χειροποίητα (sc. εἴδωλα) σέβοντες, ibid., 618: ἔργα δὲ χειροποίητα πυρὸς φλογὶ πάντα πεσεῖται.

2. In the NT χειροποίητος in every passage in which it is used sets forth the antithesis of what is made with men's hands to the work of God. The saying in Mk. 14:58 opposes the ναὸν τοῦτον τὸν χειροποίητον to the temple not made with hands (→ IV, 883, 5 ff.; V, 139, 17 ff.) which will be built in the shortest possible space of time. In Ac. 7:48 and 17:24 it is expressly underlined that God οὐκ ἐν χειροποιήτοις ναοῖς (→ IV, 885, 14 ff.) κατοικεῖ (→ V, 154, 10 ff.). In Hb. 9:11, 24 the incomparability of the heavenly sanctuary into which Christ has entered is brought out by contrasting it with the earthly temple. Eph. 2:11 says that the Gentiles are called the uncircumcision ὑπὸ τῆς λεγομένης περιτομῆς ἐν σαρκὶ χειροποιήτου. Since fleshly circumcision is done by the hand of man, the reference is to the contrast to God's act and hence only relative validity attaches to the judgment that the circumcised pass on the Gentiles. Col. 2:11 sets in antithesis circumcision with hands and the περιτομὴ ἀχειροποίητος with which Christians are circumcised → VI, 83, 4 ff. By the περιτομὴ τοῦ Χριστοῦ they are those who have been buried and raised again with Christ in baptism, so that they are free from the dominion of forces and powers. In distinction from everything earthly, the heavenly house of which Paul speaks in 2 C. 5:1 (→ V, 146, 33 ff.) is not made with hands. After death God will not leave us naked. When earthly life ends, He will have ready for us a new dwelling with which we shall be clothed → II, 319, 40 ff.

---

[5] Loh. Kol., ad loc. tries to get this sense out of Col. 2:14 but merely succeeds in violently wresting the text, which contains no hint of a compact with the devil. In criticism cf. Dib. Gefbr., ad loc.

[6] Cf. "Mayest thou cancel my χειρόγραφον," Anon. Apoc. 12:7 f. (Steindorff, 55) and "expunge ... all our debts," Prayer Abinu Malkenu, line 14 (ed. W. Staerk, "Altjüd. liturg. Gebete," KIT, 58² [1930], 28), cf. Str.-B., III, 628 [Kelber].

[7] Deissmann LO, 282 f. thinks that the part. προσηλώσας which follows pts. to an unknown practice to the effect that a note of indebtness (or other document) was cancelled by crossing it through with the Gk. letter Chi (χ). But there is no mention of crossing through the χειρόγραφον. The pt. is the cancelling of the note and its fixing to the cross. The metaphor of the χειρόγραφον, which is taken from the law of debt, is dropped at once, so that neither τοῖς δόγμασιν nor προσηλώσας need be explained in the light of it.

χ ε ι ρ ο π ο ί η τ ο ς , ἀ χ ε ι ρ ο π ο ί η τ ο ς .   Bibl.: A. W. Argyle, " 'Outward' and 'Inward' in Biblical Thought," Exp. T., 68 (1956/57), 196-9.

[1] τὰ χειροποίητα, Hbr. מִקְדָּשׁ in Is. 16:12 means "pagan sanctuary."

† χειροτονέω.

1. Raising the hand to express agreement in a vote is called χειροτονέω: ὑμεῖς δὲ πάντα λογισάμενοι ταῦτα χειροτονεῖθ' ὅ τι ἂν ὑμῖν δοκῇ μάλιστα συμφέρειν τῇ πόλει, Isoc. Or., 7, 84; τὰς ἐμὰς γνώμας ἐχειροτόνει, "he voted for my views," Demosth. Or., 18, 248, cf. also Plat. Leg., VI, 755e, 756a. Philo Spec. Leg., I, 78 ref. to selection for the discharge of a specific task; highly regarded men are chosen from every town as messengers to bring in the sacred monies that have been gathered. But χειροτονέω can also mean "to nominate," [1] e.g. τὸν ὑπὸ τοῦ θεοῦ κεχειροτονημένον βασιλέα, Jos. Ant., 6, 312, cf. also 13, 45; βασιλεὺς ... ὑπὸ θεοῦ χειροτονηθείς, Philo Praem. Poen., 54; Joseph βασιλέως ὕπαρχος ἐχειροτονεῖτο, Philo Jos., 248. The term does not occur in the LXX, only the noun χειροτονία at Is. 58:9 for "stretching out the hand" in the sense "pointing with the finger," Hbr. אֶצְבַּע שְׁלֹחַ. This noun does not occur, how-ever, in the NT and Barn., 3, 5 is the only instance in the post-apost. fathers.

2. In the sense "to select" χειροτονέω occurs in 2 C. 8:19. [2] A representative chosen by the church is to accompany the apostle on his journey with the collection. [3] In Ac. 14:23 the reference is not to election by the congregation. The presbyters are nominated by Paul and Barnabas and then with prayer and fasting they are in-stituted into their offices, which they are to exercise in the churches of Pisidia and Lycaonia. [4]

Lohse

χ ε ι ρ ο τ ο ν έ ω . Bibl.: C. H. Turner, "χειροτονία, χειροθεσία, ἐπίθεσις χειρῶν," JThSt, 24 (1923), 496-504; M. A. Siotis, "Die klass. u. chr. Cheirotonie in ihrem Verhältnis," Θεολογία, 20 (1949), 314-334.

[1] χειροτονέω can already mean "to select" in the 5th cent. B.C., for acc. to Attic legal custom decisions about laws and in judicial and financial matters were not made by raising the hand but by casting stones ψῆφοι or beans or metal discs etc., cf. Aristoph. Ach., 607; Av., 1571 etc. [Dihle].

[2] Cf. Wnd. 2 K., *ad loc.*

[3] Selection by the community is also indicated by χειροτονέω in Ign. Pol., 7, 2; Phld., 10, 1; Sm., 11, 2 and Did., 15, 1.

[4] The meaning is also "to institute" in Tt. 1:9 vl. (Minusc. 460: μὴ χειροτονεῖν διγά-μους) and in the subscription later added to Tt. and 2 Tm.

┌─────────────────┐
│ † Χερουβίν   │
└─────────────────┘

1. In the OT the כְּרוּבִים [1] are mentioned as mythical angelic beings which guard Gan Eden, Gn. 3:24, on which Yahweh rides forth, Ps. 18:10, which are to be found on the mount of God, Ez. 28:14-16, which carry the throne-chariot of God, Ez. 10:1-22, and on which Yahweh is enthroned, 1 S. 4:4, 2 S. 6:2; 2 K. 19:15; Is. 37:16; Ps. 80:1; 99:1; 1 Ch. 13:6. Yahweh speaks מִבֵּין שְׁנֵי הַכְּרֻבִים, Ex. 25:22; Nu. 7:89 etc. Often the cherubim are referred to along with the ark. 1 S. 4:4 speaks of the ark of Yahweh enthroned on the cherubim. In the description of the cultic vessels in the holy of holies we find representations of the cherubim concealing the cover of the ark with their wings, Ex. 25:18-20; 37:7-9; 1 K. 6:23-32; 8:6 f. etc. The figures of the two cherubim, made of gold (Ex. 25:18; 37:7; 1 Ch. 28:18) or of wood and overlaid with gold (1 K. 6:23, 28), stand at both ends of the כַּפֹּרֶת with their faces towards one another, Ex. 25:19. [2]

2. In post-bibl. Judaism [3] the cherubim, which the seer describes as fiery in Eth. En. 14:11, are introduced as a class in the angelic hosts (Eth. En. 61:10; 71:1) which stand around the throne of God (Slav. En. 21:1; A 20:1) [4] with the archangel Gabriel as their head (Eth. En. 20:7). OT expressions are adopted when it is said that God is enthroned on the cherubim (Sib., 3, 1) or when there is ref. to the chariot of the cherubim (Sir. 49:8; Apc. Mos. 22). [5] From the name כְּרוּבִים the Rabb. deduce that they are shaped like boys. R. Abbahu (c. 300) construes כְּרוּב, Aram. כְּרַבְיָא, as כְּ "like" and רוֹבֶה, Aram. רַבְיָא, "youth," bChag., 13b. Philo, however, has another explanation when he notes concerning the name: ἃ πατρίῳ μὲν γλώττῃ προσαγορεύεται Χερουβίμ, ὡς δ᾿ ἂν Ἕλληνες εἴποιεν, ἐπίγνωσις καὶ ἐπιστήμη πολλή, Vit Mos., II, 97. Behind the allegorical ἐπίγνωσις καὶ ἐπιστήμη πολλή there probably stands an explanation of כְּרוּבִין in terms of הַכָּרָה "knowledge," רוֹב "multitude" and בִּינָה "insight." [6] In Cher., 28 Philo explains: ἀρχῆς μὲν οὖν καὶ ἀγαθότητος τῶν δυεῖν δυνάμεων τὰ Χερουβὶμ εἶναι σύμβολα. Special interest attaches to the two cherubim which stood in the holiest of all in the first temple. Jos. describes them on the basis of the OT account and he notes: τὰς δὲ Χερουβεῖς οὐδεὶς ὁποῖαί τινές εἰσιν εἰπεῖν οὐδ᾿ εἰκάσαι δύναται, Ant., 8, 73.

Χ ε ρ ο υ β ί ν . Bibl.: Pr.-Bauer, s.v.; A. Jacoby, "Zur Erklärung d. Kerube," ARW, 22 (1924), 257-265; P. Dhorme-L. H. Vincent, "Les Chérubins," Rev. Bibl., 35 (1926), 328-358, 481-495; W. F. Albright, "What were the Cherubim?" The Bibl. Archaeologist, 1 (1938), 1-3; Str.-B., III, 168 f.; J. Michl. Art. "Engel, II," RAC, V, 62 f.; T. Klauser, Art. "Engel, X," ibid., 288.
   [1] For the etym. of the name cf. Köhler-Baumg., s.v.
   [2] For OT instances cf. also H. Schmidt, "Kerubenthron u. Lade," Festschr. H. Gunkel, FRL, 36 (1923), 120-144; Eichr. Theol. d. AT,II⁵, 136-8; L. Köhler, Theol. d. AT⁴ (1966), 146.
   [3] In the LXX the Hbr. word is rendered χερουβ, plur. variously χερουβειμ, χερουβειν, χερουβιμ, χερουβιν. Jos. Ant., 7, 378 has plur. τοὺς Χερουβεῖς and 8, 72 τὰς Χερουβεῖς. The gender is mostly neut., sometimes masc., so Ex. 25:19; 38:6 f. LXX (HT 37:7 ff.); Jos. Ant., 7, 378; fem. Jos. Ant., 8, 72 f. Philo always has the neut. τὰ Χερουβίμ, Cher., 1, 11, 20 f., 23, 25, 28 f.; Fug., 100.
   [4] Cf. Str.-B., III, 582.
   [5] In Qumran texts published thus far כְּרוּבִים occurs only once: מברכים הכרובים... הכרובים 4 QSl 40, 24, 3, ed. J. Strugnell, "The Angelic Liturgy at Qumran — 4 Q Serek Šîrôt ʿôlat Haššabāt, Congress Volume, Oxford 1959," VT Suppl., 7 (1960), 336.
   [6] Cf. Str.-B., III, 168.

Whereas the Rabb. depicted the cherubim as boys or youths, bChag., 13b; bSukka, 5b, [7] Jos. Ant., 3, 137 speaks of ζῷα πετεινά and Philo Vit. Mos., II, 97 ref. to two winged creatures πτηνῶν δυοῖν. [8]

The mysterious name Χερουβίν is also frequently mentioned in magic pap. to achieve a magical effect through its power. Thus we find the formula ἐγώ εἰμι ὁ ἐπὶ τῶν δύο χερουβείν, Preis. Zaub., II, 13, 255 and 334 (346 A.D.) or there is invocation of the ἐπὶ τὰ Χερο[υ]βὶν καθήμενος, II, 7, 634 (3rd cent. A.D.), cf. also I, 4, 3061 (3rd/4th cent. A.D.): ὃν ὑμνοῦσι τὰ πτερυγώματα τοῦ χερουβίν "the winged beings of the cherubin," and II, 7, 265: ἐπὶ χερουβὶν καθήμενον.

3. In the NT the only reference to the Χερουβίν [9] is at Hb. 9:5. In the description there given of the earthly sanctuary, the cultic objects are mentioned and among them the author singles out especially τὴν κιβωτὸν τῆς διαθήκης in the holy of holies (v. 4); he then continues: ὑπεράνω δὲ αὐτῆς Χερουβὶν δόξης κατασκιάζοντα τὸ ἱλαστήριον (v. 5). [10] Bearing the divine glory, the Χερουβίν [11] stand over the mercy-seat [12] and shade it with their outspread wings. [13]

Lohse

---

[7] Further examples, *loc. cit.*

[8] For Rabbinic statements on the relation of the cherubim to one another cf. *ibid.*, 169.

[9] The word is variously written in the MSS: Χερουβίν Cod. ℵ D, Χερουβείν Cod. B. Later MSS show greater assimilation to the Hbr. word: Χερουβείμ Cod. AP, Χερουβίμ Cod. KL.

[10] In explanation cf. O. Moe, "Das irdische u. d. himmlische Heiligtum. Zur Auslegung v. Hb. 9:4 f.," ThZ, 9 (1953), 23-9.

[11] Since the author of Hb. has Χερουβίν in the neut. he is thinking of winged creatures rather than boys or youths, cf. Mi. Hb.[12], *ad loc.*

[12] On the later Antiochene tradition, acc. to which the cherubim were moved from Jeru salem to Antioch cf. W. J. Dulière, "Les Chérubins du troisième temple à Antioche," *Zschr. f Religions- u. Geistesgesch.*, 13 (1961), 201-219.

[13] In early Chr. lit. outside the NT the word Χερουβίν does not occur. The Σεραφιν to whose Trishagion Rev. 4:8 alludes, cf. Is. 6:2 f., are not mentioned in the NT. The cherubim and seraphim are frequently associated in later Chr. lit. and iconography.

† χήρα   ὀρφανός → V, 487, 22 ff.

Contents: A. Common Greek Usage. B. The Widow outside the New Testament: I. The Widow in the Pagan World around the Bible. II. The Widow in the Old Testament: 1. The Use of χήρα in the Septuagint; 2. The Plight of the Widow in the Old Testament; 3. Benevolence to the Widow in the Old Testament. III. The Widow in Ancient Judaism. C. χήρα in the New Testament: 1. Mark; 2. Luke; 3. Paul; 4. Pastorals: a. The Widow in the Family Unit; b. Younger Widowed Women; c. "True" Widows; d. Ministry in the Community; 5. James; 6. The Widow Figuratively. D. The Widow in the Early Church: 1. Allusions to Biblical Statements; 2. Organisation of Care for Widows; 3. Household Tables for Widows; 4. Widows as an Institution in the Community.

A. Common Greek Usage.

χήρα, "widow," found from Hom., e.g., Il., 6, 408 f.; 22, 484 [1] derives from the Indo-Eur. root ghē- "forsaken," "left empty" (cf. Old High German "gān," "gehen"). In Gk. cf. χῶρος, χώρα "empty space," "district," "land." [2] The orig. meaning of χήρα is thus a "woman left without husband." [3] Hence χήρα can mean not only a "widow" but also a "woman living without a husband." Hesych., s.v. expressly gives both meanings: ἡ τὸν ἄνδρα στερηθεῖσα γυνή and ἡ μετὰ γάμον μὴ συνοικοῦσα ἀνδρί. [4] The masc. χῆρος "widower" is later than the fem., e.g., Callim. Epigr., 15, 4, and much rarer, only once in the NT as a conjecture → n. 112. But the adj. χῆρος "desolate," "left," "widowed" occurs already in Hom., e.g., μήτηρ χήρη, Il., 22, 499 and then often in the poets, e.g., χῆρος πόσις "widower," Anth. Graec., 7, 522, 4. χῆρα μέλαθρα "abandoned

χ ή ρ α . Bibl.: Moult-Mill., Preisigke Wört, s.v. M. Beth, Art. "Witwe," Handwörterbuch d. Deutschen Aberglaubens, 9 (1938/41), 668-680; J. Blinzler, Art. "Witwe," LexThK², 10, 1204 f.; A. van den Born, Art. "Witwe," Bibel-Lex., ed. H. Haag² (1968), 1892 f.; H. Leclercq, Art. "Veuvage, veuve," DACL, 15, 2, 3007-3026; J. Leipoldt, Die Frau in d. antiken Welt u. im Urchr. (1962), 205-210; J. Müller-Bardorff, Art. "Witwe," Bibl.-Hist. Handwörterbuch, ed. B. Reicke and L. Rost, III (1966), 2177 f.; S. Solle, Art. χήρα, Theol. Begriffslex. z. NT, ed. L. Coenen et al., I (1967), 358-360; R. Thurnwald, Art. "Witwe," RLV, 14, 436-440. Cf. also → n. 3, 11, 13, 16, 22, 40, 41, 73, 84, 101, 115, 167, 174.
    [1] In class. lit. after Hom. χήρα is comparatively rare. It occurs in Aesch. Fr., 474, Col. 2, 30 (ed. H. J. Mette, Die Fr. d. Tragödien d. Aesch. [1959]); Soph. Ai., 653; Eur. Tro., 380, but not in, e.g., Hes., Hdt., Xenoph., Aristoph., Demosth.
    [2] Cf. also χωρέω "to give, make room," χωρίς "without." Probably χαίνω, χάσκω "to yawn," "gape," and χάος "cleft," "empty space," "chaos," belong to the same basic stem, Hofmann, 417; Prellwitz Etym. Wört., 506 f. In Mycen. Gk. the root is perhaps preserved in the perf. part. mid. ke-ke-me-na (κεχεμένα?) which is used to define the legal position of some parcels of land. The orig. meaning is perhaps "unbuilt," or "left without owner," v. C. J. Ruijgh, Études sur la grammaire et le vocabulaire du grec mycénien (1967), 365 f. [Risch].
    [3] Cf. O. Schrader, A Nehring, Art. "Witwe," Reallex. d. idg. Altertumskunde, II² (1929), 661, and the χηρωσταί of Hom. Il., 5, 158, relatives who take over an inheritance that is left without owner (χηρο-), cf. Hes. Theog., 606 f. Closely related in form and sense is heres, he who receives an orphaned possession, "heir," v. Walde-Hofmann, s.v. Later χηρωστής, in analogy to ὀρφανιστής, came to mean "representative of the interests of widows," v. Liddell-Scott, s.v. χηρωσταί, also on the linguistic derivation of the word.
    [4] This use is not common in lit. but cf. already Eur. Andr., 347 f.: ἢ σφ' ἄνανδρον ἐν δόμοις χήραν καθέξεις πολιόν; The addition of ἄνανδρον stresses this meaning. Perhaps χήρα for Hera in Paus., VIII, 22, 2, after παῖς and τελεία, means "grown woman," here orig. "old woman" [Risch]. But if Hera received the name at a time when she was separated

chambers," Eur. Alc., 862 f. [5] Synon. with χήρα from Hom., e.g., Il., 2, 289 to the later period is γυνὴ [6] χήρα, [7] e.g., Aesop. Fab., 55, 58; [8] Plut. Apophth. Antigonus, 5 (II, 182b), cf. also P. Oxy., VIII, 1120, 12 (3rd cent. A.D.): γυνὴ χήρα καὶ ἀσθενής, BGU, II, 522, 7 (2nd cent. A.D.): γυνὴ χήρα καὶ ἀβοήθητος (→ 443, 8 f.) → 444, 21 f. The derived verbs χηρόω "to make a widow," and χηρεύω "to become, to make a widow," also used in a transf. sense, occur from Hom., e.g., χήρωσας γυναῖκα, "thou hast widowed," Il., 17, 36; χήρωσε δ' ἀγυιάς "he depopulated the streets," 5, 642, [9] cf. Eur. Cyc., 304: χηρεύσῃ λέχος; "shall thy marriage-bed be widowed, be made desolate?" Eur. Alc., 1089; cf. also Hom. Od., 9, 124; Soph. Oed. Tyr., 479; Demosth. Or., 30, 11; Achill. Tat., IV, 1, 2 → n. 4. The derived noun χηρεία "widowhood" first appears in Thuc., II, 45, 2: ἐν χηρείᾳ ἔσονται → 445, 3; 447, 19 f. χήρευσις is pre-Hell. only in the law of Gortyn, [10] but is found several times in LXX → 445, 6 ff.

B. The Widow outside the New Testament.

I. The Widow in the Pagan World Around the Bible. [11]

1. From early times the fate most feared and bewailed by a woman [12] was that

---

from Zeus, the sense of ἄνανδρος is at least included for Paus. Acc. to Ps.-Clem. Hom., 2, 20, 1 Justa, the Canaanite woman of Mt. 15:22, remained χήρα when thrust out by her pagan husband. Cf. also Philo Det. Pot. Ins., 147 (→ 447, 14 ff.) and 1 Tm. 5:5 (→ 456, 2 ff.). Similarly χηρεύω can mean "to live without husband" (→ 445, 4 f.), μίαν ἡμέραν οὐκ ἐχήρευσεν, ... ἵνα μὴ χηρεύσειεν παρ' ἀνδρὸς ὡς ἄνδρ' ἐβάδιζεν, Demosth. Or., 30, 33, cf. Soph. Oed. Tyr., 479. This meaning is more commonly attested for the Lat. equivalent *vidua*, namely a. "without spouse," "unmarried," e.g., Liv., I, 46, 7; Mart., 7, 73, cf. also Digesta Iustiniani, 50, 26, 242, 3 (ed. T. Mommsen-P. Krüger, Corpus Iuris Civilis, I[19] [1966] 920): *"Viduam" non solum eam, quae aliquando nupta fuisset, sed eam quoque mulierem, quae virum non habuisset, appellari ait Labeo*, with an added etym. explanation: *viduam dictam esse sine duitate*, the prefix *ve-* signifying "lack," cf. constructs like *vecors* "infamous," and *vesanus* "mad"; b. "not living in marriage," e.g., Plaut. Miles Gloriosus, 965 f. Acc. to Tert. Ad uxorem, I, 6 (CSEL, 70) the priestesses of the African Ceres are such *viduae*, who *manentibus in vita viris ... toro decedunt*," also *viduitas* in the same sense here. In the same connection one finds *viduari* in Tert. De monogamia, 17, 4 (CSEL, 76). The whole range of meaning is covered by the attempt at popular etym. in Macrob. Sat., I, 15, 17: *vidua, id est a viro divisa.*

[5] In contrast to ὀρφανός (→ V, 487, 36 ff.; 488, 25 ff.) the transf. use of the adj. χῆρος and the verbs χηρόω and χηρεύω (→ lines 5 ff.; 447, 22 ff.) is fairly common, cf. also → n. 9.

[6] γυνή alone can also mean "widow," cf. Pap. Bruxelles, E 7616 (ed. M. Hombert-C. Préaux, "Recherches sur le recensement dans l'Egypte Romaine," Papyrologica Lugduno-Batava, 5 [1952]), Col. 4, 16; 14, 18; 15, 17.

[7] Similarly we find with the noun ὀρφανός ὀρφανὰ τέκνα, Hes. Op., 330, ὀρφανὸς παῖς, e.g., Philo Spec. Leg., II, 108, both together Jos. Ant., 4, 240: γυναιξί τε χήραις καὶ παισὶν ὀρφανοῖς Cf. also γυνὰ κερεύουσα (i.e., γυνὴ χηρεύουσα) in the law of Gortyn (ed. E. Schwyzer, Dialectorum Graec. exempla epigraphica potiora [1923], No. 179, Col. 3, 44 f., cf. line 53 [5th cent. B.C.]).

[8] Ed. B. E. Perry, Aesopica, I (1952), 342 f., 344.

[9] In the background here is the idea of the "widowed city" → 458, 28 f., cf. also Ἄργος δὲ ἀνδρῶν ἐχηρώθη, Hdt., VI, 83, 1; πολλῶν ἂν ἀνδρῶν ἤδ' ἐχηρώθη πόλις, Solon, 24, 25 (Diehl[3], I, 45); Δύμην ... χηρεύουσαν ἀνδρῶν τότε, Plut. Pomp., 28 (I, 633e).

[10] Schwyzer, op. cit. (→ n. 7), No. 179, Col. 2, 53 f.

[11] Cf. F. C. Fensham, "Widow, Orphan, and the Poor in Ancient Near Eastern Legal and Wisdom Literature," *Journ. of Near Eastern Studies*, 21 (1962), 129-139; L. Leleux, "De la condition légale de la veuve," *Thèse Caen* 1886/87 (1887); T. Mayer-Maly, Art. "vidua (viduus)," Pauly-W., 8a (1958), 2098-2107; Schrader, op. cit. (→ n. 3), 661 f.

[12] Cf. the fate of the orphaned child, as in Andromache to Hector: μὴ παῖδ' ὀρφανικὸν θῆς χήρην τε γυναῖκα, Hom. Il., 6, 432; αὐτούς (sc. the fallen heroes) μὲν ἀπεστέρησαν βίου, χήρας δὲ γυναῖκας ἐποίησαν, ὀρφανοὺς δὲ τοὺς αὐτῶν παῖδας ἀπέλιπον, Lys. Or., 2, 71; cf. also Cpt. Cod., 32, 9, 20-22: "They have laid themselves down in their graves ... their wives became widows (χήρα) their sons became orphans (ὀρφανός)," *Ägypt. Urkunden aus d. königlichen Museen zu Berlin: Kpt. Urkunden*, I (1904), p. 53.

she should become a widow. [13] When her husband died she could return to her own family if the purchase price was paid back to the husband's heirs or the dowry to the wife's family. Otherwise she had to remain in the husband's family, where she took an even more subordinate and often humiliating position. In many cases she was not allowed to remarry → lines 7 ff. This is why many widows preferred death at the burial of their husbands (→ n. 204) to further life without them. [14]

In many places the remarriage of a widow was frowned on in the ancient world and abstinence therefrom was lauded, [15] CIG, II, 2471; CIL, III, 3572; [16] Paus., II, 21, 7. Tert., who uses the pagan practice of the widow's refraining from remarriage as an argument in his battle for *monogamia* or "one marriage," De monogamia, 17, 5 (CSEL, 76) interprets the resolve to live as μόνανδρος *univir(i)a* [17] as a sacrifice for the dead husband, Ad uxorem, I, 6 (CSEL, 70); De monogamia, 17, 3 (CSEL, 76), cf. also De exhortatione castitatis, 13, 3 (CCh, 2). Above all the widow who has married only once is preferred in cultic connections, Paus., VII, 25, 13; Tert. De monog., 17, 4 f. (CSEL, 76); De exhort. castitatis, 13, 1 f. (CCh, 2); Ad uxorem, I, 6 (CSEL, 70). The high estimation of the *univira* may be seen in the fact that in the Roman Empire the widow who married again forfeited certain rights and a woman enjoyed the less respect the more marriages she contracted, Cic. Att., 13, 29, 1. [18] In express contradiction, however, is the legislation of Augustus who in carrying out his repopulation policy commanded widows between 20 and 50 yrs. of age to marry, Lex Julia et Papia Poppaea. [19] There were not lacking critics of this law, cf. Tert. Apol., 4, 8; De monog., 16, 6 ff. (CSEL, 76). Roman Judaism displays in burial inscr. the same high estimation of the μόνανδρος as the world around; a mark of piety to the dead husband is discerned here, [20] CIJ, I, 81 and 392. Elsewhere in bibl. [21] and extra-bibl. Judaism, however, widows remarry once or even twice, e.g., Ket., 1, 1 f. [22] as a gen. custom, [23] though there are warnings against three or four remarriages, bYeb., 64b; bKet., 43b. For the rest it seems that quite early in the Indo-Eur. world (Rig-Veda, 10, 40, 2) [24] as well as the Semitic sphere (→ 447, 6 ff.) Levirate marriage was practised when the husband died without male issue.

In any case in a patriarchal society the woman who had lost her spouse and children who had lost their father were in many respects disadvantaged and even oppressed from the social, economic, legal and religious standpoint. The common feature is that they have

---

[13] Cf. C. Spicq, "La parabole de la veuve obstinée et du juge inerte, aux décisions impromptues," *Rev. Bibl.*, 68 (1961), 73: The widow "est le type de l'être faible et sans appui, qui socialement n'existe pas."

[14] Cf. H. Hirt, *Die Indogermanen*, II (1907), 443 f.; Beth, 669 f.; V. Hehn, *Kulturpflanzen u. Haustiere*[8] (1911), 540.

[15] Cf. J. Leipoldt, *Jesus u die Frauen* (1921), 141, n. 426.

[16] There are further inscr. in W. Kunkel, *Röm. Privatrecht*[3] (1949), 275, n. 4; H. Preisker, *Christentum u. Ehe in d. ersten drei Jhdt.* (1927), 62, n. 319-321; G. Delling, "Pls. Stellung z. Frau u. Ehe," BWANT, 56 (1931), 137, n. 40. Cf. also Tac. De origine et situ Germanorum, 19, 2.

[17] Cf. J. B. Frey, "La signification des termes Μόνανδρος et Univira," *Recherches de Science Religieuse*, 20 (1930), 48-60.

[18] Cf. W. A. Becker-H. Göll, *Gallus*, II (1881), 57.

[19] Ed. C. G. Bruns, Fontes iuris Romani antiqui[7] (1909), 115 f.; cf. Mayer-Maly, *op. cit.* (→ n. 11), 2104 f.; Kunkel, *op. cit.* (→ n. 16), 274 f.; M. Kaser, "Röm. Privatrecht," *Hndbch. AR*, X, 3, 3 [5] (1966), 221 f.

[20] Cf. H. J. Leon, *The Jews of Ancient Rome* (1960), 129 f.

[21] Cf. the quick remarriage of Abigail, 1 S. 25:39-42.

[22] S. Krauss, *Talmud. Archäol.*, II (1912), 515; L. N. Dembitz, Art. "Widow," Jew. Enc., 12, 515.

[23] It was simply laid down that remarriage — and Levirate marriage, Jeb., 4, 10 — should take place only after the lapse of three months from the death of the husband, cf. K. H. Rengstorf, "Jebamoth," *Die Mischna*, III, 1 (1929), 49.

[24] Cf. K. F. Geldner, "Der Rig-Veda, III," *Harvard Orient. Series*, 35 (1951).

all lost their sustainer and protector. 25 Thus from ancient times widows and orphans are
often associated and even linked together as a pair → 447, 26 ff.; 448, 27 ff. n. 12).
In the writings of antiquity, esp. in oriental legal and wisdom literature, we constantly
find complaint at the lack of protection or help which the widow shares with orphans,
the poor, and strangers, and esp. at the injustice to which she is subjected by the socially
more powerful. Accusation is made against those who oppress the widow. The ancient
oppression of widows at law 26 may be seen in their frequent sale as slaves for debt. 27
In the Gk. world ἀβόηθος and ἀσθενής are more or less synon. with χήρα. 28 Part of
the existence of the widow is lamentation at the violence she suffers (P. Oxy. VIII, 1120,
12 [3rd cent. A.D.]) and at her low esteem. 29 It is true that Pericles in Thuc., II, 45, 2
lavishes some praise on war widows, and after the achievement of feminine emancipation
in early Hell. there were widows, namely, of princely families, who controlled property
and power. 30 Again, the ancient Roman law that widows (and orphans, Cic. Rep., II, 20,
36) should make regular contributions to compensate Roman knights for their expenses
on behalf of the state (Liv., I, 43, 9) presupposes well-to-do widows.

2. No less ancient than lamentation and complaint at the plight of widows is
the appeal that widows and orphans must be helped — an appeal directed especially
to rulers. The "mirrors of the prince" found in the Orient from early times to a later
period bear witness to this. 31 Of special significance here is the belief found already
in the ancient Orient that certain gods are concerned about the plight of widows

---

25 Poetically χήρα / vidua and ὀρφανός / orbus (→ V, 487, 24 ff.) can even be used
as synon. Catullus Carmina, 66, 21 (ed. W. Kroll⁵ [1968]) with his orbum cubile means
the same as Ovid Amores, II, 10, 17 and Statius Silvae, III, 5, 60 (ed. A. Marastoni [1961])
with cubile viduum.
26 Cf. Fensham, op. cit., 139.
27 Cf. Lam. 1:1: "to become a widow" par. "to become a tributary."
28 Cf. the petitions BGU, II, 522, 7 (2nd cent. A.D.), P. Oxy., VIII, 1120, 12 (3rd cent.
A.D.). where one can also catch a moral appeal for help. A result of the widow's oppression
is her notorious frugality, Aesop. Fab., 55 and 58 and cf. Philo Spec. Leg., IV, 176: ἀσθενὲς
δὲ καὶ ταπεινὸν χήρα καὶ ὀρφανὸς καὶ ἐπήλυτος "proselyte" and also as an example
the description of her situation as a widow given by the mother of Chrys., Chrys. Sacerdot.,
I, 2, 11-22.
29 Perhaps the reading χηρεύουσα in Test. Jud. 12:2 pts. to a Semitic custom whereby
a new widow should for seven days offer herself publicly for sale, cf. a related Bab. custom
in Hdt., I, 199, 4 f. For the Rom. and presumably also the Hell. world cf. Terent. Heauton
Timorumenos (ed. R. Kauer-W. M. Lindsay [1926]), 953 f.: "He dare not do to any widow
what he did to me." The widow's shame is also reflected in the comedies of later antiquity,
cf. Sostrata in Terent. Adelphoe, e.g., 932: No man pays regard to the desolate.
30 E.g., Tomyris, Queen of the Massagetae, the gt. opponent of Cyrus, Hdt., I, 205 f.;
212, 3; 214, 1. 4, or Cratesipolis, ruler of Sikyon, Diod. S., 19, 67, 1 f. and the Roman Melita
in Achill. Tat., V, 11, 5 f.
31 Cf. the reform texts of Urukaginas of Lagash (c. 2375 B.C.; v. W. Röllig, Art. "Uru-
kagina," Lex. d. Alten Welt, ed. C. Andresen et al. [1965], 3171) in A. Scharff-A. Moortgat,
Ägypten u. Vorderasien im Altertum (1950), 243: "The strong must do no hurt to the orphan
and widow." This is not just courtly style, cf. L. Dürr, Ursprung u. Ausbau d. isr.-jüd.
Heilandserwartung (1925), 19-21. Hammurapi in his famous code, Col. 24, 61 f. (AOT, 407)
boasts that he has seen to it that the orphan and widow should have their rights. For their
sakes esp. he limits slavery for debt to three yrs., e.g., Col. 3, 61 ff. (AOT, 392), cf. Fensham,
op. cit., 131. In Ugaritic lit. cf. the Aqhat poem 2 Aqht (II D), Col. 5, 7: "He (sc. Dani-il,
father of Aqhat) assessed the right of widows, he gave judgment to orphans," cf. J. Aistleitner,
Die mytholog. u. kultischen Texte aus Ras Schamra, Biblioth. Orientalis Hungarica, 8² (1964),
70, 3, also G. R. Driver, Canaanite Myths and Legends (1956), 52 f.; C. H. Gordon,
Ugaritic Literature, Scripta Pontifici Inst. Bibl., 98 (1949), 88; A. Jirku, Kanaan. Mythen u.
Epen aus Ras Schamra-Ugarit (1962), 120, cf. Fensham, op. cit., 134. Delay in fulfilling the
royal duty to widows and orphans is a subj. of complaint here, cf. Keret-Legend, II K, Col., 6,
45-50. Aistleitner, 104: Driver, 47 and J. Gray, The KRT Text in the Lit. of Ras Shamra²
(1964), 29. For ancient Egypt cf. the doctrine of King Meri-ka-re (c. 2025 B.C.) in A. Erman,
Die Lit. d. Ägypter (1923), 111 f., cf. Fensham, 132 f.; Dürr, 26. Similarly Prince Ameni under

and are their helpers (→ VI, 891, 15 f. with n. 49), e.g., the sun-god Amon-Re and also Ptah [32] in Egypt or the sun-god Shamash among the Semites. [33] One may compare with this the OT belief in Yahweh → 446, 14 ff.

We learn little [34] from the Gk. world regarding legal protection or provision for widows. Ps.-Demosth. Or., 43, 75 ref. to an Athenian law to the effect that the archon must care for orphans ... and for women who remain in the houses of their dead husbands on account of pregnancy. Thus a widow expecting a child, like one with children, could remain in the house of her dead husband with a right to support from his estate. If she had no children she was to return to her parents' house, though the dowry had to be repaid. [35] It is important that in the West the idea that the gods protect the poor, including widows, was hardly developed at all. [36] Only the stranger is under divine custody, esp. that of Zeus; the poor and those who seek protection are mentioned only occasionally → V, 17, 12 ff. On these presuppositions little care could be developed for needy widows. This applies even to the many war widows. In the military world there was indeed a welfare fund for invalids, orphans and parents, but widows were not included. [37] On the other hand the Romans had laws governing care for widows. [38] Yet their rights were largely restricted by other concepts in the law of inheritance. The *vidua inops et indotata* had now to receive a quarter of the estate of a well-to-do husband. [39]

II. The Widow in the Old Testament. [40]

1. The Use of χήρα in the Septuagint.

In the LXX χήρα is almost always used for Hbr. אַלְמָנָה [41] (אִשָּׁה). [42] We often find the form γυνὴ χήρα → 441, 1 ff.; n. 90, e.g., 2 Βασ. 14:5; 3 Βασ. 17:9 f.; 4 Macc. 16:10. Some-

---

Sesostris I (1971-1925 B.C.) asserts that "there was no widow whom I oppressed ... I gave to the widow as to her that had a husband," A. Erman-H. Ranke, *Ägypten u. ägypt. Leben im Altertum²* (1923), 105, cf. Fensham, 132, who also has a text from Egypt. wisdom lit. in which a governor is praised as "father of the orphan and husband of the widow" → 448, 12. The ancient oriental "mirrors of the prince" with their benevolence to widows had an extended influence. Thus the wise woman of Tekoah appeals to David's sense of duty in the story of the widow. As king he must receive the oppressed widow, 2 S. 14:5-7, and cf. → 461, 23 ff.; Prv. 29:14; Philo Spec. Leg., IV, 176; Decal., 42; P. Ryl., II, 114, 5 (c. 280 A.D., cf. also Moult.-Mill., *s.v.* χήρα and also Hier. Comm. in Jer. (CSEL, 59, IV, 35, 4 on 22:1-5 → 461, 25 f.

[32] Cf. the statement of account by Rameses III (d. 1168 B.C.) to Ptah in G. Roeder, *Die Ägypt. Götterwelt* (1959), 55; Fensham, 133.

[33] Cf. F. M. T. de Liagre-Böhl, "De Zonnegod als de Beschermer d. Nooddruftigen," *Opera Minora* (1953), 188-206; Fensham, 130.

[34] χήρα is very rare in inscr. The ref. in Ditt. Syll.³, I, 531, 17 (3rd cent. B.C.) is to questions as to the rights of a χήρα ἐλευθέρα καὶ ἐξ ἐλευθέρων.

[35] Cf. J. H. Lipsius, *Das Attische Recht u. Rechtsverfahren* (1905-1915), 495; H. Bolkestein, *Wohltätigkeit u. Armenpflege im vorchr. Altertum* (1939), 281 f.

[36] Cf. Bolkestein, 423-5.

[37] Cf. G. Busolt-H. Swoboda, *Gr. Staatskunde*, II, *Hndbch. AW*, IV, 1, 1³ (1926), 1045, n. 1; 1094 with n. 1; 1220.

[38] Acc. to Dion. Hal. Ant. Rom., 2, 25, 5 a law traced back to Romulus laid down that the widow of a husband who died without issue or will should be the sole heiress; otherwise she and the children would have equal shares, cf. Leleux, *op. cit.*, 19 f.

[39] Cf. Mayer-Maly, *op. cit.*, 2102-4.

[40] Cf. I. Benzinger, Art. "Familie u. Ehe bei d. Hebräern," RE³, 5, 745-7; F. Nötscher, *Bibl. Altertumskunde, Die hl. Schrift d. AT*, Suppl. Vol. 3 (1940), 88 f.

[41] On the derivation cf. H. Bauer, "Das Originalwort f. 'Witwe' im Semitischen," ZDMG, 67 (1913), 342-4. He derives אלמנה from אל and מרא "master," "husband," i.e., the "woman who has no husband," but cf. Ges.-Buhl, *s.v.*

[42] It is doubtful whether vl. ἄνανδρος is the original in 4 Macc. 16:14, as A. Deissmann thinks, Kautzsch Apkr. u. Pseudepigr., *ad loc.* (synon. χήρα as in, e.g., Eur. Cyc., 306), for elsewhere in 4 Macc. 5:31; 6:21; 8:16 ἄνανδρος means "unmanly." The two meanings are found close together in Eur. Andr., 341 and 347.

times in the LXX χήρα can also mean a "woman without a husband or separated from her husband" (→ 440, 15 ff.), e.g., 2 Βασ. 20:3: χῆραι ζῶσαι "living without a husband" [43] The LXX has some derivates not found in the NT: χηρεία "widowhood," Is. 54:4 (HT אַלְמְנוּת); 47:9 (HT אַלְמוֹן); Mi. 1:16; χηρεύω "to live as a widow, in the misery of a widow," Jdt. 8:4; ᾽Ιερ. 28(51):5 (HT אַלְמָן "widowed") (→ 447, 20 ff.); 2 Βασ. 13:20, [44] χήρευσις "widowhood," apart from Jdt. 8:6: ἡμέραι τῆς χηρεύσεως αὐτῆς, always with ref. to a widow's weeds (→ 445, 32 ff.) ἱμάτια τῆς χηρεύσεως, Gn. 38:14, 19 (HT בִּגְדֵי אַלְמְנוּת); Jdt. 8:5; 10:3; σάκκος, 10:3 vl.; στολή, 16:7.

2. The Plight of the Widow in the Old Testament.

In the OT, too, the plight of the poor widow [45] (→ 442, 29 ff.) is prominent. A woman who has been widowed is to be lamented and princes who make widows are condemned, Ex. 22:25. The fate of a widow can also be a divine punishment, hence the threat: "Ye shall not afflict any widow, or fatherless child. If thou afflict them in any wise ... I will kill you with the sword; and your wives shall be widows, and your children fatherless," Ex. 22:22 ff.; hence also the prayer against those who oppose the prophet that "their wives be bereaved of their children, and be widows," Jer. 18:21, cf. ψ 108:9.

In the OT, too, widows are associated in almost stereotyped fashion with similar disadvantaged and oppressed groups, orphans (→ V, 487, 31 ff.), e.g., Is. 1:23; Jer. 5:28; Job 22:9; 24:3, also Lam. 5:3, aliens (→ V, 9, 19 ff.), e.g., Ex. 22:21 f.; Dt. 10:18; 24:17, the poor, e.g., Is. 10:2; Zech. 7:10; Wis. 2:10, the day-labourer, Mal. 3:5. There is constant complaint at the wrongs done to widows, e.g., Is. 10:2; Ez. 22:7; Job 24:3, cf. 22:9 and esp. Ps. 94:6, and also at the rights withheld from them, Is. 1:23; Jer. 5:28. Warnings are often issued against injustice to widows, Ex. 22:22; Dt. 24:17; 27:19; Jer. 22:3; Zech. 7:10. There is also a demand that they be helped to their rights, Is. 1:17. These and other passages make it plain that the main plight of widows was in the legal sphere. It was hard for them to get their rights (→ 449, 7 ff.) and they were often deprived of them (→ 449, 1 ff.). To the sorry legal and social state of widows corresponds their low esteem (→ 443, 10) among men, cf. the expression "shame of widowhood" in Is. 54:4, the proud saying: "I shall not sit as a widow, neither shall I become childless," Is. 47:8, and the corresponding threat of widowhood and the equally despised childlessness, v. 9. [46] Possibly this low regard for widows is also expressed in the special clothes (→ 445, 6 f.; n. 81) they had to wear, Gn. 38:14, 19; Jdt. 8:5; 10:3; 16:7, including σάκκος, cf. Jdt. 9:1 (→ VII, 59, 1 f. and n. 25) [47] but not the veil, cf. Gn. 38:14, 19, which outside the house was a respectful and protective mark of both the not yet married and also the married woman; elsewhere, however, the veil is part of the clothing of the widow. [48] In particular

---

[43] χῆραι ζῶσαι is an inadequate rendering of אַלְמְנוּת חַיּוּת "widowhood while the husband is alive," cf. Ges.-Buhl, s.v. חַיּוּת.

[44] Cf. also Test. Jud. 12:1; χηρεύουσα in v. 2 (→ n. 29) is not the original reading.

[45] The widow of 2 K. 4:1-7 is a paradigm. She has nothing in the house but a cruse of oil and the debts which her husband has left and for which the creditors claim her two sons. Naturally in OT times there were also wealthy widows (→ 443, 10 ff.) who inherited all the property on the death of their husbands, e.g., Abigail, 1 S. 25:39-42, cf. v. 18, and Judith, cf. Jdt. 8:1-7.

[46] "Childlessness is a disgrace; the worst fate to befall a woman is to be sent back to her father's house a childless widow," H. Gunkel, Genesis, Handkomm. AT, 1, 1³ (1910) on 38:11, though the judgments of antiquity on this possibility are not uniform → 441, 15 ff. Cf. also Jer. 18:21 and Is. 49:21 LXX: ἐγὼ ἄτεκνος καὶ χήρα.

[47] Primarily the widow's clothing is worn in mourning, but this was worn for the whole of life and not just for a period in acc. with the ancient principle (→ n. 204) that marriage is not dissolved by death, cf. 2 S. 14:2, 5 and Gunkel, op. cit. (→ n. 46) on Gn. 38:14. On the widow's garb outside the Bible cf. Beth, 678 f.

[48] Cf. O. Böcher, "Dämonenfurcht u. Dämonenabwehr," BWANT, 90 (1870), 301 f.; B. Rehfeldt, Art. "Schleier," RGG³, V, 1422.

the low esteem of the widow may be seen in the so-called Holiness Code. The widow, and the betrothed whose bridegroom has died, is not worthy to marry the high-priest, Lv. 21:14; in this regard she is like a divorcee or a harlot. [49] In the programme for the cultus of the future in Ez. 44:22 not even an ordinary priest may marry a widow unless she is the widow of a priest.

3. Benevolence to the Widow in the Old Testament.

Although widows are little regarded in general, the authors of the OT also depict some great widows who are worthy of admiration for different reasons: Tamar in Gn. 38 → n. 131, the widow of Zarephath in 1 K. 17, and Judith, especially in Jdt. 8:4-8; 16:1-25. Furthermore the whole of the OT [50] (though → lines 24 ff.) is kindly disposed to widows like the ancient oriental "mirrors of the prince" → 443, 18 ff.; [51] the essential difference is that in the OT admonitions to treat widows benevolently are addressed to all the righteous.

The basis here is also the same. [52] God is a refuge and helper for widows, Ps. 146:9. He is the Judge who helps them to their rights, Dt. 10:18; Ps. 68:5. He sets wrongs done to them under the *ius talionis*, Ex. 22:21-23, cf. Ps. 109:9, and under the curse, Dt. 27:19. Conversely, care for widows is set under the promise of His blessing, Jer. 7:6. He Himself is a witness in favour of widows, 3 Βασ. 17:20 [53] and against those who oppress them, Mal. 3:5. Here again one should note the legal terminology which is based in part on the legal plight of widows (→ 442, 29 ff.; 445, 25 ff.) and in part on the metaphor of God's judgment. [54] In view of statements of this kind the supreme disaster that is foretold is when God Himself no longer has mercy on orphans and widows in His own people, Is. 9:16.

As the examples show, the main champions of these themes are the prophets and Dt. They are followed by the Wisdom lit., cf. the confession in Prv. 15:25: "God guarantees the border of the widow," with the command of Prv. 23:10: "Remove not the border of the widow," [55] and cf. the way in which law and wisdom overlap in this matter in lit. outside the Bible. [56] Benevolence to widows in the OT law is expressed in a series of detailed provisions esp. in Dt. The vow of a widow is valid without restriction (Nu.

---

[49] Normative here is the principle of "holiness" acc. to which the high-priest must marry one who has not been touched. Cf. Jos. Ant., 3, 277, though χήρα is avoided here and the more precise τεθηκότος ἀνδρός is used, and also Yeb., 6, 4, where an exception is made if a priest has married a widow before being appointed high-priest. Occasionally there are other instances of marriages between high-priests and widows, cf. J. Jeremias, *Jerusalem z. Zeit Jesu*³ (1962), 174-7.

[50] Cf. Dib. Herm. on m., 8, 10.

[51] In mirrors of the prince in the OT, esp. Ps. 101; 2 S. 23:3 f., the widow is not mentioned. Job's self-vindication (Job 31:16; 29:12 f.) against the unjust accusations of his friend Eliphaz in 22:9 reminds us of these at pts., cf. also → n. 31.

[52] That similar claims of the heathen for their gods were known to the OT may be seen from Ps. 82:3 f., cf. Fensham, 134 f.; but they were contested: χήραν οὐ μὴ ἐλεήσωσιν οὔτε ὀρφανὸν εὖ ποιήσουσιν (sc. false gods), Ep. Jer. 37.

[53] μάρτυς τῆς χήρας means "witness of her innocence" (cf. the ref. to her guilt in 3 Βασ.17:18), as in 1 S. 12:5 f.; Job 16:19; 1 Macc. 2:37 → IV, 483, 21 ff. Another possibility is that Elijah calls on God as guarantor of the widow's rights (→ n. 100) as elsewhere of the obligations of a pact, Gn. 31:44; 1 Βασ. 20:23, 42, also ψ 88:38; Hb. 7:22 (→ II, 329, 14 ff.) [Bertram].

[54] Cf. also Jer. 49:11 (the meaning is debated); Prv. 15:25 (→ 447, 32); Σιρ. 35:14 (32:17 HT ed. R. Smend [1906]).

[55] At Prv. 23:10 אַלְמָנָה should be read for עוֹלָם, cf. BHK; C. Steuernagel in Kautzsch, *ad loc*. A striking par. is in the Egypt. wisdom book of Amenemope, 6 (AOT, 40): "Do not violate the borders (of the field) of a widow." Cf. also H. Ringgren, *Sprüche, AT Deutsch*, 16, 1 (1962) on Prv. 23:10 f.

[56] Cf. Fensham, 129-139.

30:10), unlike that of a virgin or wife. The widow shares the tithe along with the Levite, the alien and the orphan, Dt. 14:29; 26:12 f. [57] Gleanings of the field, the olive-tree and the vineyard belong to the alien, the orphan and the widow, 24:19-21, [58] cf. also Rt. 2:2 f. With slaves, Levites, aliens and orphans, the widow can take part in harvest feasting, including the banquets of the Feast of Weeks and the Feast of Tabernacles, Dt. 16:11, 14; 14:29; 26:12. The widow's garb cannot be pledged, 24:17. [59] Some protection for the childless widow is also achieved by Levirate marriage, [60] though this is not expressly stated in the legislation in 25:5-10, since the true aim of Levirate marriage is to raise up male issue for the man who died without such and hence to maintain his name and property.

III. The Widow in Ancient Judaism. [61]

In Jos. and Philo we sometimes find γυνὴ χήρα (→ 444, 21 f.) as well as χήρα, cf. Jos. Ant., 4, 240; 8, 320; Philo Deus Imm., 136. Once χήρα can mean a "woman living apart from her husband" (→ 440, 15 ff.); only thus can one construe the striking χήρα θεοῦ at Philo Det. Pot. Ins., 147, since in Philo's allegory what is in view is a human soul that does not have the *logos* as its husband. Elsewhere, however, Philo prefers χηρεύουσα for the "woman alone," e.g., Spec. Leg., II, 30 f., [62] or the adj. χήρα, Deus Imm., 138: πᾶσα διάνοια χήρα καὶ ἐρήμη κακῶν. [63] One also finds the adj. χῆρος, e.g., Mut. Nom., 149: τὰ . . . ἔρημα καὶ φρονήσεως, and the derivates χηρεία, e.g., διὰ χηρείαν ἐπιστήμης, Ebr., 5, cf. Vit. Mos., II, 240 (→ 441, 10 f.) and χηρεύω in the sense "to be widowed," Deus Imm., 137 or "to live without husband," Spec. Leg., III, 27, but mostly in a transf. sense (→ 448, 14 ff.; 441, 15 ff.), so Det. Pot. Ins., 149: χηρεύσει . . . ἐπιστήμης "to live separated from knowledge," cf. Ps.-Plat. Alc., II, 147a (→ V, 487, 36 f.) and also Orig. Princ., IV, 2, 4 (p. 313, 16 f.).

Materially Judaism takes up OT motifs. It often combines the widow and orphans, e.g., childless old women in Philo Decal., 42. Widows are often victims of the wicked, who say in Wis. 2:10: μὴ φεισώμεθα χήρας, cf. Philo Vit. Mos., II, 240: παρ' οἷς χηρεία . . . γυναικῶν γέλως. [64] But God is the defence of widows; with Him they are not accounted despised or of low esteem, 241. In particular God hears their prayers οὐ μὴ ὑπερίδῃ ἱκετείαν ὀρφανοῦ καὶ χήραν, ἐὰν ἐκχέῃ λαλιάν "when she causes the stream of words (of complaint before Him) to flow," Σιρ. 35:14 (17) and He is their protector against injustice, cf. already Prv. 15:25: ἐστήρισεν . . . ὅριον χήρας → 446, 24 ff. God adopts orphans and widows because they have lost those who cared for them, i.e., parents or husband, and for the bereaved there is no help with men, Philo Spec. Leg., I, 310.

---

[57] Cf. Jos. Ant., 4, 240. Tob. acts acc. to this rule: ἐδίδουν αὐτὰ τοῖς ὀρφανοῖς καὶ ταῖς χήραις καὶ προσηλύτοις, Tob. 1:8 Cod. S.

[58] Only the poor and the stranger are mentioned in Lv. 23:22.

[59] But cf. Dt. 24:12 f.: The cloak of a poor man may be accepted as a pledge but must be returned overnight, and Job's complaint in Job 24:3: "They (sc. wicked-doers) drive away the ass of the fatherless, they take away the widow's ox for a pledge."

[60] If Levirate marriage was not possible the childless widow had to return to her own home (→ 444, 9 f.; 448, 6 ff.; n. 46), Lv. 22:13. On Levirate marriage in the OT cf. F. Horst, Art. "Leviratsehe," RGG³, IV, 338 f. (Bibl.); E. Lövestam, Art. "Schwagerehe," *Bibl.-Hist. Handwörterbuch*, III, ed. B. Reicke and L. Rost (1966), 1746 f. (Bibl.); C. H. Peisker, Art. "Schwagerehe," *Evang. Kirchenlex.*, III, ed. H. Brunotte et al. (1959), 874; Benzinger, op. cit. (→ n. 40), 745-7; R. Zehnpfund, Art. "Trauergebräuche bei d. Hebräern," RE³, 20, 87; I. Scheftelowitz, "Die Leviratsehe," ARW, 18 (1915), 250-256; O. Eissfeldt, Einl. in d. AT³ (1964), 653, n. 1 (Bibl.); Jeremias, op. cit. (→ n. 49), 408 with n. 114. On Levirate marriage outside the Bible cf. Beth, 675 f.; Scheftelowitz, 250-254; Thurnwald, 437-440; also Art. "Levirat," RLV, 7, 286-9; Fensham, op. cit., 136 f.

[61] Dembitz, op. cit., 514 f.; Krauss, op. cit., 53 f.

[62] Cf. I. Heinemann in *Die Werke Philos v. Alex.*, ed. L. Cohn et al., II (1910), 186, n. 3.

[63] H. Leisegang, ibid., III (1919), 323, n. 1.

[64] Cf. Apc. Elias Hbr., p. 17, 1 (3, 2 in Riessler): "They . . . slew widows and orphans on the street," and cf. Ps. 94:6.

Hence He is not ashamed to be an impartial judge for προσήλυτοι ἤ χῆραι. He honours them with His care in their lowliness, slighting kings and others in positions of power, 308, cf. IV, 177 f.: God pronounces justice for the widow because her husband, who gave her care and protection in place of her parents, has been taken from her.

In keeping is the exposition of the Torah [65] and its supplementing by other statutes and practices favourable to the widow. As long as she remains such the widow may live in the house and on the estate of her husband, Ket., 4, 12. [66] She need not return to her father's *potestas*, 4, 2. She has the right to keep her money [67] in the temple, 2 Macc. 3:10; 4 Macc. 4:7; Jos. Bell., 6, 282. [68] With orphans she is to have a share in tithes, the harvest of the Sabbatical year, and also war booty, 2 Macc. 8:28. The admonitions of the prophets and Dt. are continued, as in Sir. 4:10: γίνου ὀρφανοῖς [69] ὡς πατὴρ καὶ ἀντὶ ἀνδρὸς τῇ μητρὶ αὐτῶν, and Slav. En. 42:9 in one of nine beatitudes: "Blessed is he who judges right judgment for the orphan and widow and helps the sick." [70]

On the one side Philo represents the OT and Jewish attitude to the widow (→ 446, 10 ff.) while on the other he includes the widow in his allegorical interpretation, as in Som., II, 273: The widows and orphans of Dt. 26:13 are οἱ ... ἀπωρφανισμένοι καὶ κεχηρευκότες γενέσεως ("created world"), θεὸν δὲ τὸν τῆς ψυχῆς θεραπευτρίδος ἄνδρα [71] καὶ πατέρα γνήσιον ἐπιγεγραμμένοι, cf. the widow in Deus Imm., 136: She is a χήρα ... τῷ χηρεύειν τῶν ... παθῶν. In contrast is the χήρα θεοῦ in Det. Pot. Ins., 147, the "soul living apart from God," which χηρεύσει ἐπιστήμης (→ 447, 22 ff.), so that, thrown back on itself, it incurs the guilt resulting from sin. [72]

C. χήρα in the New Testament. [73]

Only in two of the sources of the Synoptic tradition about Jesus do widows play any role, namely, in Mk. and the special Lucan material, not in Q or the material peculiar to Mt.

1. Mark. [74]

In Mk. 12:40 and par. Jesus takes up the prophetic accusation of the injustice done to widows and orphans [75] (→ 445, 18 ff.) and directs it in sharper form against

---

[65] Philo Spec. Leg., II, 108 relates the Sabbatical year specifically to widows and orphans.

[66] Cf. Jeremias, op. cit. (→ n. 49), 150.

[67] The Rabb., too, recall some rich widows (→ n. 45), e.g., the daughter-in-law of Nicomedon b. Gorion, bKet., 65a; AbRNat, A 6 (Schechter, p. 31, 24-27).

[68] Liv., 24, 18, 13 f. tells of a similar right of Roman widows.

[69] ὀρφανός here means "semi-orphan," as often when used with χήρα.

[70] The same beatitude includes the one who clothes the naked and gives bread to the hungry. Here, then, giving legal aid to widows and orphans is among works of mercy; on these cf. Str.-B., IV, 559-610.

[71] Philo is already using in an individual sense the metaphor of the divine marriage, which is only collective in the OT, cf. on 1 Tm. 5:12 → n. 137.

[72] Cf. Leisegang, op. cit. (→ n. 63), 323, n. 1.

[73] B. Reicke, "Glauben u. Leben d. Urgemeinde," AbhThANT, 32 (1957), 117 f.; H. W. Surkau, Art. "Armenpflege, IV," RGG³, I, 620; G. Uhlhorn, Die chr. Liebestätigkeit² (1895), 49, 54 f., and cf. → n. 84, 88, 101, 115, 167.

[74] Among the attempts to explain the striking designation of Jesus as ὁ υἱὸς τῆς Μαρίας in Mk. 6:3 we find the suggestion that Jesus is hereby styled the son of a widow, cf. already E. Renan, Les évangiles et la seconde génération chrétienne (1877), 542, and then J. Blinzler, "Die Brüder u. Schwestern Jesu," Stuttgarter Bibelstud., 21 (1967), 72: "Mk. has selected the expression 'son of Mary,' or adopted it as fitting, because in his view Mary was a widow in 6:3, and Jesus was her only son." Cf. E. Schweizer, Das Ev. nach Mk., NT Deutsch, 1² (1968), ad loc.: "One must at least assume that the father has already been dead for some time," and v. also E. Haenchen, Der Weg Jesu² (1968), ad loc.; E. Stauffer, "Jeschu bMirjam," Festschr. M. Black (1969), 121.

[75] At Mk. 12:40 (not Lk. 20:47) important texts add καὶ ὀρφανῶν (DW φ it) → V, 488, n. 3. The only other instance of this common combination in the NT is at Jm. 1:27 → 458, 6 ff.

certain scribes. [76] While seeming to follow the prophetic injunction (→ 445, 23 ff.) to help widows to their rights, these charge so highly for their services that the widows lose their possessions (→ V, 131, 27 ff.) to their legal representatives. Perhaps [77] the μακρὰ προσεύχεσθαι may also be interpreted as a highly charged plea for the cause of the widow. [78] In any case the saying shows how Jesus stepped forward as the true advocate of the oppressed and exploited. [79] Linked with Mk. 12:40 by the term χήρα, and to be understood as an antithesis, is Mk. 12:41-44 and par. [80] The widow [81] whom Jesus opposes to the avaricious scribes and the rich who love to make offerings gives ὅλον τὸν βίον αὐτῆς "her whole sustenance" → VIII, 598, 21 ff. [82] Such total giving presupposes total trust in God and His provision, especially for widows. [83]

2. Luke.

To the two passages from the Marcan tradition (Lk. 20:47; 21:1-4) Lk. adds from his own tradition three further passages on the theme of Jesus and widows. The conduct of the widow in the parable of Lk. 18:2-5 (→ IV, 380, 40 ff.) [84] is an illustration of the prayer that will not be turned aside or silenced by anything and is thus confident that it will certainly be answered. The issue is a financial one in which the widow cannot get justice against a powerful opponent without a judicial

---

[76] In Mt. 23 also many texts introduce the saying in the 2nd person either before or after v. 13. I. Abrahams, "Widows' Houses," Stud. in Pharisaism and the Gospels, I (1917), 79 rightly pts. out that the charge could not be made against all scribes; he cites Rabb. sayings such as Ex. r., 30, 8 on 31:2 (Wünsche, 220): "To rob widows and orphans is to rob God." Cf. the positive form of the same thought in Mt. 25:40; Jm. 1:27. Abrahams, 80 takes Jesus' accusation to mean that wealthy widows were reduced to beggary by the much too generous gifts suggested to them by Pharisees or priests.

[77] This interpretation would be possible if καί were left out with the Western tradition at Mk. 12:40 and Lk. 20:47. If it is original, the intolerable antithesis of inhumane hypocrisy and a show of piety is scourged.

[78] Grundm. Mk., ad loc., who ref. to Ass. Mos. 7:6 as a par.

[79] Jesus is not, then, a social revolutionary, cf. M. Hengel, War Jesus Revolutionär? (1970).

[80] Acc. to A. Drews, Das Markusev. (1928), 284 the story is an illustration of 2 C. 8:2, 12, 14 invented by the evangelist Mk. In Mt. the story falls victim to the Evangelist's constructional technique.

[81] As in Lk. 7:12 the story presupposes that the widow was recognisable by her clothing → 445, 32 ff.

[82] Cf. Julian of Egypt, Anth. Graec., 6, 25, 6: The simple gift, the fishing net, that the old fisherman Kinyres consecrates to the nymphs, ὅλος ἔσκε βίος. On Jesus' statement (v. 43 f.) that the widow's gift is comparatively much greater than that of the wealthy cf., e.g., Sen. Ben., I, 8, 1 f.; other examples are given in Wettstein on Mk. 12:43; Bultmann Trad., 32 f.; Kl. Mk., ad loc.; Abrahams, op. cit., 81.

[83] This decisive element is not present in the Buddhist par. constantly adduced (text in J. B. Aufhauser, "Buddha u. Jesus in ihren Paralleltexten," KIT, 157 [1926], 13-16), though there is one striking feature in common, namely, the two copper coins that are the only gift of the poor woman. On the other hand the fact that the woman was a widow is not common to the two traditions, since she is simply a poor girl in the Buddhist story, cf. G. A. van den Bergh van Eysinga, "Indische Einflüsse auf evang. Erzählungen," FRL, 4² (1909), 50-52; G. Faber, Buddhistische u. nt.liche Erzählungen, Diss. Bonn (1913), 55-7; R. Garbe, Indien u. d. Christentum (1914), 33 f.; A. Espey, Deutscher Glaube. Die wichtigsten buddhistischen Par. zu nt.lichen Erzählungen u. ihre ethische Würdigung (1915), 40-43; H. Haas, "Das Scherflein d. Witwe" u. seine Entsprechung im Tripitaka (1922), 12 f.; H. W. Schomerus, Ist die Bibel von Indien abhängig? (1932), 120 f.; Clemen, 251-3.

[84] Cf. Jülicher Gl. J., II, 276-290; Jeremias Gl.⁷, 153-7; E. Linnemann, Gleichnisse Jesu³ (1964), 125-130 and 178-181; Spicq, op. cit., 68-90; G. Delling, "Das Gleichnis vom gottlosen Richter," ZNW, 53 (1962), 1-25.

decision. [85] With the opponent in view, the judge would seem to have kept on deferring the case, [86] not daring [87] to decide in the widow's favour. But she does not give in, cf. διά γε τὸ παρέχειν μοι κόπον (v. 5, cf. 11:7). She induces in the judge the fear ἵνα μὴ εἰς τέλος ἐρχομένη ὑπωπιάζῃ με, [88] and finally she reaches her goal. [89] In Lk. 4:25 f. the example of the widow of Sarepta, [90] one of the elect widows [91] (→ 446, 6 ff.; 459, 23 ff.) of the Bible, shows how God [92] releases his messengers from their human ties, especially those to their own people, and grants them access to the Gentiles. In the case of the widow of Nain, whose son Jesus raises from the dead in Lk. 7:11-17, [93] the accent, in distinction from Lk. 4:26 (→ n. 90), is on χήρα, the woman who with the death of her μονογενὴς υἱός (7:12) has been deprived for the second time of her provider and protector. Jesus' compassion on the weeping [94] widow [95] is perhaps to be regarded as a Messianic trait.

Luke's interest in widows is part of his broader interest in the oppressed and despised, especially the poor and women. At the very beginning of his Gospel he associates with the elect and humble virgin (1:26-38) and believing mother (2:19), and also with the prophet Simeon (2:25 ff.), the exemplary and indeed charismatic widow, the prophetess (→ VI, 836, 5 ff.) Anna (2:36-38). In the note that after a short marriage [96] Anna had been a widow for over 80 years one may discern certain

---

[85] Cf. the pap. in which widows are petitioners → n. 28.

[86] He thus acts contrary to Jewish legal practice acc. to which the complaints of orphans and widows are to be given precedence, cf. Dembitz, op. cit. (→ n. 22), 514.

[87] Cf. Jeremias Gl.[7], 134, 123, n. 2; Spicq, op. cit. (→ n. 13), 74, n. 2.

[88] Two transl. (→ VIII, 590, 27 ff.) are possible: a. "so that she does not finally come and strike me in the face with her fist," or, more freely but idiomatically, "and scratch my eyes out," → II, 426, 25 with n. 25; W. Michaelis, Die Gleichnisse Jesu[3] (1956), 234; Spicq, op. cit., 75 f. with 75, n. 6; Delling, op. cit. (→ n. 84), 12 f. with n. 45-47, or b. "so that she does not keep on coming and thus wear me out," cf. Bl.-Debr. § 207, 3; W. Grundmann, Das Ev. nach Lk., Theol. Handkomm. z. NT, 3 (1961), ad loc.; Jeremias Gl.[7], 153. Linguistically the former is the more probable, cf. Delling, 12 with n. 48.

[89] The added interpretation in v. 7 f. gives an eschatological meaning to the request and its fulfilment (cf. → 458, 15 ff. and esp. Spicq, op. cit., 88-90) which the par. parable in Lk. 11:5-8 does not have.

[90] γυνὴ χήρα occurs here in the NT → 441, 1 ff. Wellh. Lk., ad loc. suggests the original Aram. might be ארמיא "Syrian" rather than ארמלא "widow," in which case one should read Σύρα, not χήρα, cf. Mk. 7:26 B 𝔎: Σύρα Φοινίκισσα, though here sy[s] reads χήρα (for Ἑλληνίς) Τυροφοινίκισσα. Wellh.'s hypothesis has at least in its favour the fact that in context the stress is not on the woman's being a widow but rather on her being a foreigner like Naaman ὁ Σύρος in v. 27.

[91] This widow was esp. honoured in Rabb. lit. too. Acc. to Midr. Ps., 26, 7 on 26:9 (Str.-B., IV, 1134) her son was the prophet Jonah whose later fate was understood as a resurrection from the dead, cf. Mt. 12:40. Acc. to Seder Eliyyahu Rabba, 18 (Friedmann, p. 97 f.; cf. Str.-B., IV, 782 with n. 1) the son of this widow will return as Messiah bJoseph (→ χρίω, C, VI, 7).

[92] ἐπέμφθη in Lk. 4:26 is a pass. divinum like ἐκλείσθη in v. 25 and ἐκαθαρίσθη in v. 27.

[93] Lk. 7:15 has verbal allusions to the story of the widow of Zarephath in 3 Βασ. 17:23. A Palestinian reader would also catch a connection with the par. Elisha story in 2 K. 4:8-37, since Nain is near Shunem, cf. H. J. Holtzmann, Die Synpt., Hand-Comm. z. NT, I, 1[3] (1901), ad loc.

[94] Tears are almost a stock attribute of the widow, Job 31:16; Lam. 1:2; Σιρ. 35:15 (32:18 HT, ed. R. Smend [1906]), cf. also 4 Macc. 16:10, where, of course, πολύθρηνος can mean "worth bewailing" as well as "full of tears," so Riessler, 725; cf. also Ac. 9:39. On the other hand it is a special affliction when widows refuse to bewail the dead, cf. Job 27:15 (→ n. 108) or are unable to do so, cf. Ps. 78:64, where LXX puts the statement in the pass: αἱ χῆραι αὐτῶν οὐ κλαυσθήσονται.

[95] It is worth noting that nothing is said about the widow's faith, in contrast to Lk. 8:50, cf. also Mk. 5:36; Jn. 11:21 f., 26 f., 40; Ac. 9:38.

[96] Acc. to an ancient Syr. tradition the marriage lasted only 7 days, Lk. 2:36 sy[s] Ephr.

ascetic motifs, especially that of high regard for the *univira*, cf. 1 Tm. 5:9 → 442, 7 ff. The other qualities of Anna seem to be related to her abstinence from a second marriage and the corresponding fasting (v. 37). [97, 98] She is a prophet and is thus granted to see the child Jesus (v. 38). She is a witness, and is as such a model of the full-scale witness of the woman in the Christian community. [99] She is unwearying in prayer [100] (cf. Lk. 18:3 ff. → 449, 15 ff.). And in virtue of her witness and prayer she stays continually in the temple, cf. v. 49. In this regard, too, this prophetess is a model for the first community of disciples, Lk. 24:53; Ac. 2:46.

In Ac. Lk. offers two examples of the care for widows in primitive Christianity According to Ac. 6:1 [101] a διακονία καθημερινή was set up in the first Jerusalem congregation. By this the needy in the church were fed daily (cf. v. 2) and these were primarily widows. The reason for making special mention of widows is perhaps that the community was openly trying to practise the statutes of Dt. in favour of widows, → 446, 27 ff. [102] Various Jews of the *diaspora* came to live in Jerusalem in their old age, and in many cases these placed their possessions at the disposal of the congregation, Ac. 2:45; 4:32, 34 f. [103] When they died many of them left widows behind and there would have been no provision for these without the organised care of the church, since they had no relatives there. If the complaint of the Hellenists (→ II, 511, 23 ff.) [104] that their widows were neglected was justified, this was perhaps related to the fact that care for widows in the primitive community was in the hands of the Palestinians, [105] who, as tension developed between the Palestinian group (→ III, 389, 24 ff.) and the *diaspora* element in the church, looked after Hellenistic widows more negligently than Palestinian widows. [106] An example of the care of individuals for widows is Tabitha [107] (Ac. 9:36-41), who clothed widows with garments that she herself made, v. 39. It is possible, of course, that she was

---

[97] There is often ref. to widows fasting, though elsewhere in connection with offerings for the dead husband, cf. Thurnwald, 439.

[98] Cf. Ac. 21:9 and on this G. Stählin, *Die Apostelgesch., NT Deutsch*, 5³ (1968), *ad loc.*

[99] Cf. the note at the end of the Gospel in 24:9 f. and on this M. Hengel, "Maria Magdalena u. d. Frauen als Zeugen," *Festschr. O. Michel* (1963), 243-256.

[100] Widows and prayer are correlative like widows and tears (→ n. 94). If the widow is often a petitioner before men, cf. → n. 28; 2 S. 14:5; Lk. 18:3, she is so esp. before God, cf. Σιρ. 35:14 (32:17 HT, ed. R. Smend [1906]); Jdt. 9:4 (here the emphatic ἐμοῦ τῆς χήρας perhaps expresses a claim to special hearing); 1 Tm. 5:5, the helper of the widow κατ' ἐξοχήν. Although this motif (→ 449, 10 f.; n. 53) is not expressly mentioned in the NT, it stands behind the widow's total offering in Mk. 12:42-44 and the equating of care for widows and serving God in Jm. 1:27 → 458, 7 ff.

[101] Cf. J. Viteau, "L'institution des diacres et des veuves," *Revue d'Histoire Ecclés.*, 22 (1926), 513-8.

[102] So Reicke, *op. cit.* (→ n. 73), 118; on similar schemes for widows in the post-NT period → 461, 11 ff.

[103] Stählin, *op. cit.* (→ n. 98) on 4:36 f., cf. Haench. Ag.¹⁴ on 6:1, who pts. out that independent care for widows on the part of the primitive community shows progressive detachment from Jewish community life with its organised provision for the poor.

[104] Cf. Haench. Ag.¹⁴ on 6:1, esp. 214, n. 1.

[105] Cod. d and h read *a ministris Hebraeicorum* at Ac. 6:1.

[106] Haench. Ag.¹⁴, 221 f.

[107] It may be conjectured that Tabitha herself was a widow, since one would expect her husband to be mentioned in vv. 39-41 if she had been married. The same seems to be true of Lydia in Ac. 16:14 f., Mary the mother of Mark in Ac. 12:12, the Mary of R. 16:6, Phoebe in R. 16:1 f., who is called διάκονος τῆς ἐκκλησίας and προστάτις (provider → VI, 703, 1 ff.) πολλῶν, Chloe in 1 C. 1:11, and Tryphena, Tryphosa and Persis (R. 16:12), whose κοπιᾶν is extolled. In view of their special services these women might be regarded as forerunners of the congregational widows of 1 Tm. 5:3 ff. → 456, 19 ff. All those named must have been well-to-do, → 443, 10 ff.; n. 45, 67.

commissioned to do this by the church at Joppa (→ 460, 19 ff.) and that this explains the unusual concern of the church at her death, v. 38. From v. 41, which mentions the χῆραι specifically along with ἅγιοι, one might also conclude that the widows were already a special class there → n. 144.[108] The raising of Tabitha thus took place in the interest of widows like the raisings at Zarephath (→ 450, 5 ff.) and Nain (→ 450, 8 ff.).

3. Paul.

In the epistles of Paul[109] widows are mentioned in his treatment of marital questions in 1 C. 7. Between directions to the married (vv. 2-7, 10-16) Paul places some counsel to the unmarried[110] and to widows, v. 8 f. He will return to both groups later in the c., to παρθένοι[111] and ἄγαμοι in vv. 25-38 and to widows in v. 39 f. In both sections on widows the main issue is that of remarriage → 457, 3 ff. Paul leaves it up to the free decision of those concerned: ἐλευθέρα ἐστὶν ᾧ θέλει γαμηθῆναι, v. 39. In his own view, of course, they should remarry only if their sexual drive, which is especially strong in younger widows (cf. 1 Tm. 5:6, 11, 14 f.),[112] makes it impossible for them to remain unmarried without hurt. The person who can achieve this has a χάρισμα (1 C. 7:7) like Paul himself. The one who in virtue of this χάρισμα can remain unmarried has chosen the better part, cf. v. 8.[113] Indeed, Paul pronounces a beatitude on such a person in v. 40.[114]

---

[108] Cf. J. Wellhausen, "Kritische Analyse d. Ag.," AGG, 15, 2 (1914), 18. But one may question his hypothesis that the widows in v. 39 are a "corona of wailing women"; cf. also Haench. Ag.14, ad loc. That widows should bewail the dead is natural, though cf. Job 27:15: "Their widows (i.e., those of the wicked and tyrants) do not bewail them (i.e., their wicked husbands)."

[109] Various answers have been given to the question whether Paul was a widower. J. Jeremias, "War Pls. Witwer?", ZNW, 25 (1926), 310-312 thinks he was in view of the obligation of Rabb. scholars to marry: "He was a widower when he wrote 1 C. and probably already when the call of Christ reached him," 312. The objections of E. Fascher, "Zur Witwerschaft d. Pls. u. der Auslegung v. 1 K. 7," ZNW, 28 (1929), 62-9 are met by Jeremias in "Nochmals: War Pls. Witwer?", ibid., 321-3. Like Fascher, M. Dibelius-W. G. Kümmel, Pls.3 (1964), 33 do not agree, largely on account of his ambivalent attitude in 1 C. 7: "The one for whom this question presents such difficulties has no personal experience of marriage: Paul was a bachelor, not a widower." Cf. also → I, 652, n. 25. Cl. Al. Strom., III, 6, 53, 1, quoted also in Eus. Hist. Eccl., III, 30, 1, concludes from Phil. 4:3, where he takes σύζυγος to mean "wife," and from 1 C. 9:5 that Paul was married; cf. also Ps.-Ign. Phld., 4, 5 (ed. F. X. Funk, Opera Patrum Apostolicorum, II [1881]).

[110] From the use of ἄγαμος in 1 C. 7 one might conclude that the primary ref. is to divorcees (cf. v. 11); in v. 34 ἡ γυνὴ ἡ ἄγαμος is distinguished from παρθένος. Cf. Jeremias, op. cit. (→ n. 109), 310, n. 2; Joh. W. 1 K. on 7:8.

[111] J. M. Ford, "Levirate Marriage in St. Paul (1 C. 7)," NTSt, 10 (1963/64), 362 thinks the παρθένοι here are widows who were married only once. But this interpretation, like that of other passages, e.g., virginitas and continentia interchangeable in Tert. De monogamia, 3, 1 (CSEL, 76), Ford, 363, n. 5, is not a likely one.

[112] Many expositors, e.g., P. Schmiedel, Die Br. an d. Thessal. u. an d. Korinther, Hand-Commentar z. NT, II, 12 (1892) and Joh. W. 1 K. on 7:8 f. are inclined to relate v. 8 f. generally to the unmarried and preferably to men, for v. 8b has αὐτοῖς rather than αὐταῖς, the act. of γαμέω is used esp. with ref. to men (though cf. v. 28, 34), and v. 39 speaks expressly of widowed women. On this view it is tempting to read τοῖς χήροις instead of ταῖς χήραις (Schmiedel) or to leave it out (Weiss).

[113] The rendering of καλὸν αὐτοῖς by "divine gift" in Schlatter K., ad loc. fails get the point.

[114] p46 and Cl. Al. Strom., III, 12, 80, 1 have the more impressive positive μακαρία rather than the comparative μακαριωτέρα.

4. Pastorals. [115]

The most comprehensive NT passage dealing with widows is in 1 Tm. 5:3-16 within a varied series of directions as to the way in which congregational leaders should discharge their office. This passage might be called the earliest Christian order for widows → n. 144. [116] Its climax is the institution of congregational widows, ὄντως χῆραι, from whom two other groups of widows (in the broader sense) are distinguished.

a. The Widow in the Family Unit. This type of widow is mentioned only to show why she does not qualify as a widow in the technical sense (→ 455, 13 ff.) for service in the congregation nor why she cannot be accepted as a recipient of congregational care → 451, 10 ff. This widow has other tasks and if need be she should be provided for by others: "If a widow has children or grandchildren [117] they should learn first to honour God at home and to fulfil their obligation of gratitude to their parents," 1 Tm. 5:4.

From the days of the early Church [118] there have been two opposing lines of exposition here. The first relates μανθανέτωσαν to the children and grandchildren → IV, 410, 21 ff. It is supported by the change from the sing. to the plur. In this case the πρόγονοι are the widowed mothers and grandmothers [119] and εὐσεβέω means "to act piously," "to practise respect in one's own house." [120, 121] The second takes it that the subj. of μανθανέτωσαν is widows who have children and grandchildren to care for. An argument for this it that it avoids the difficult and not very clear change of subj., while for the equally difficult change from the sing. to the plur. [122] cf. the similar change in 2:15. In this case πρῶτον means that "first," i.e., before they seek office as widows, they should serve in their own home, [123] service there being training for ministry in the house of God. εὐσεβέω τι, which occurs only here in the Past., is then to be construed acc. to the common use of εὐσέβεια (→ VII, 183, 24 f.) and εὐσεβῶς ζῆν in the Past.: "to show one's piety to something." [124] By acting thus towards her children and grandchildren, the widow repays what she has received from her own forefathers. [125] Another possibility is to ref. the statement to the whole household, i.e., both the widow and her children. A similar

---

[115] Cf. J. C. K. v. Hofmann, Die hl. Schr. NT, 6 (1874), 153-170; Wbg. Past., 170-186; W. Lock, A Crit. and Exeg. Comm. on the Pastoral Epistles, ICC (1924), 56-61; Schl. Past., 136-145; Dib. Past.⁴, 57-60; J. Jeremias, Die Br. an Tm. u. Tt., NT Deutsch, 9⁹ (1968), 31-4; G. Holtz, Die Past., Theol. Handkomm. z. NT, 13 (1965), 114-123; N. Brox, Die Past., Regensburger NT, 7, 2 (1969), 184-198; J. Müller-Bardorff, "Zur Exegese v. 1 Tm. 5:3-16," Festschr. E. Fascher (1958), 113-133; H. W. Bartsch, "Die Anfänge urchr. Rechtsbildungen," Theol. Forschung, 34 (1965), 112-143; → I, 788, 15 ff., 28 ff. For further bibl. cf. Pr.-Bauer, s.v. χήρα.
[116] There is no mention of any order of widows in non-Chr. tables of duties, cf. K. Weidinger, "Die Haustafeln," UNT, 14 (1928), 71. On Pol., 4, 3 → 464, 23 ff.
[117] ἔκγονα is to be taken in juxtaposition to πρόγονοι: The ministry of πρόγονοι by which everyone lives imposes a duty of ministry to ἔκγονοι → line 27 f.
[118] Cf. Wbg. Past., ad loc.
[119] Jeremias, op. cit. (→ n. 115) transl. "aged relatives."
[120] W. Foerster, "Εὐσέβεια in d. Past.," NTSt, 5 (1958/59), 216.
[121] This is the view of Dib. Past.⁴, Jeremias, op. cit. (→ n. 115), Holtz, op. cit. (→ n. 115), Lock, op. cit. (→ n. 115), ad loc.
[122] On account of this C. F. D. Moule (in a letter) regards this interpretation as "inconceivable." For the same reason later textual authorities substituted μανθανέτω or discat for the plur., regarding the other view as improbable.
[123] The emphatic ἴδιον makes more sense in relation to widows than on the other view.
[124] Cr.-Kö., s.v. εὐσεβέω transl. "to fulfil one's duty" to someone "in the fear of God."
[125] Cf. Jos. Ap., 2, 206. This view founders on εὐσεβέω only if this is an alternative for τιμάω, Dib. Past.⁴, ad loc., but → lines 25 ff. and n. 124.

question arises in v. 8 whether τις ref. to a widow, her relatives, or both. [126] On any view v. 8 would come better directly after v. 4, when its sense could be determined by this v. [127] It would then mean that faith and active love, esp. towards members of the family living in the same house, [128] are inseparable. This might well be addressed to widows who were neglecting their immediate duty so as to be accepted for duty and care in the congregation. [129]

b. Younger Widowed Women. Among widows in the broader sense are also younger widowed women who still have much of life before them. They, too, have other tasks [130] and hence they should not be entrusted with ministry in the community. When a contrast is drawn between the ὄντως χήρα (1 Tm. 5:5) and the σπαταλῶσα (v. 6), the widow who is frivolous and who lives in pleasure, [131] the point is that σπαταλάω, as ζῶσα τέθνηκεν shows, includes inner separation from God. Surrender to sensual desire kills, i.e., separates from God, [132] and rules out acceptance by Him at the Last Judgment (v. 7). [133] When such younger widows (→ I, 788, 33 ff.), who have been wrongly entrusted with the widow's office in the congregation, [134] inwardly break free from Christ in their sensuality, they will marry again, v. 11. [135] This involves a denial of the obligation of their office, for connected herewith was an express renunciation of second marriage, ratified by a vow (?). [136] The continuation suggests that entry into the widow's office was regarded as betrothal to Christ: [137] "They thus bring down on themselves the condemnation that they have broken their first (→ VI, 866, 26 ff.) loyalty (i.e., to

---

[126] Cf. Schl. Past. on 1 Tm. 5:4, 6, 8, who relates τις to both, Wbg. Past., ad loc., who relates it to the father who should provide in good time for wife and children, with a ref. to Xenoph. Cyrop., VIII, 1, 1.

[127] τὴν πίστιν ἤρνηται in v. 8 is then the opp. of ἀπόδεκτον ἐνώπιον τοῦ θεοῦ in v. 4.

[128] οἰκεῖοι "those who live in the same household" is a narrower expression than ἴδιοι "relatives" → V, 134, 42 ff.; Schl. Past., ad loc.

[129] Possibly many widows had come with claims rather than humble requests; with Schl. Past., 137 we perhaps get a hint of this in v. 4, 11, 16.

[130] Cf. Schl. Past. on 1 Tm. 5:13.

[131] On σπαταλάω cf. Sir. 21:15; Jm. 5:5. The theme of the flighty widow (→ n. 140) who overquickly moves on from sorrow for the dead husband to new joys and carelessly sacrifices the dead for new love is an old and mobile one like many other themes in sagas and stories that travelled from India to the East and then to the West. The oldest known version in the West, the story of the matron of Ephesus, may be found in Petronius Satyricon, 111, 1 - 112, 8 (ed. K. Müller [1961]), cf. Phaedrus Fabulae, 543 (Perry, op. cit. [→ n. 8], 598 f.), though cf. Vita Aesopi, 129 (Perry, 74 f., 105), cf. E. Rohde, "Zum griech. Roman," Rhein. Mus., NF, 48 (1893), 126, n. 1; E. Grisebach, Die treulose Witwe u. ihre Wanderung durch d. Weltliteratur² (1877); T. Benfey, Pantschatantra, I (1859), 460 who sets the theme in a broad context of related stories, 436-461; Beth, 675. A notorious example is the supposed widow Melita in the story Achill. Tat., V, 11, 5 - VIII, 14, 5, cf. esp. V, 12, 3; 15, 5 (→ 443, 10 ff. with n. 30). Opposites are the young widow Ismenodora in Plut. Amat., 2 (II, 749d e), 10 (754e - 755b) and esp. the faithful widow who avenges her murdered husband, e.g., Cratesipolis, Diod. S., 19, 67, 1 f. (→ 443, 10 ff. with n. 30), the Galatian Camma, Plut. Mulier. Virtutes, 20 (II, 257e - 258c); Amat., 22 (II 768b-d); Polyaen. Strat., VIII, 39, and Charite in the story Apul. Met., VIII, 1-14; cf. E. Rohde, Der gr. Roman u. seine Vorläufer³ (1914), 590 with n. 1. Tamar is also a faithful widow who will stop at nothing to raise up male seed to her husband who has died childless, Gn. 38.

[132] Cf. Rev. 3:1 f. and esp. R. 7:8-11; Rabb. examples in Str.-B., III, 652; I, 489.

[133] ἀνεπίλημπτος in v. 7 can ref. to judgment still to come, cf. 6:14, so Schl. Past., ad loc., though also to later eligibility as a congregational widow, cf. 3:2.

[134] Cf. Schl. Past., ad loc.

[135] Ps.-Ign. Ad Antiochenses, 11, 1 (→ n. 109) combines the thoughts of v. 6 and v. 11: αἱ χῆραι μὴ σπαταλάτωσαν, ἵνα μὴ καταστρηνιάσωσι τοῦ λόγου.

[136] The Zurich Bible renders ἡ πρώτη πίστις in v. 12 by "the earlier vow," with the note that "what is meant is the promise to remain a widow."

[137] Jeremias, op. cit. (→ n. 115) on 1 Tm. 5:11 J. Moffatt, Love in the NT (1930), 220 f.

Christ)," v. 12. [138] A further fault on the part of widows who are thus unfaithful to their promise is (→ IV, 410, 13 ff.) that they misuse their duty as congregational widows to do house visitation in the community (→ I, 788, 20 ff.), [139] pandering to their curiosity, to tattling, and to even worse desires as they move from house to house (cf. 2 Tm. 3:6 f.). [140, 141] In view of these dangers the author with full apostolic authority lays down that younger widows, instead of seeking the widow's office, should marry again, since otherwise there is the threat of evil reports and a gate of entry (→ V, 473, 25 ff.) will be offered to the ever-vigilant adversary. [142] Already many widows have fallen victim to the supreme peril of abandoning the discipleship of Christ (cf. v. 8, 11 f.) for that of Satan (v. 15; → V, 473, 25 ff.). [143] The duties which the young widow will assume with a second marriage (v. 14) should leave no place for dangerous idleness, v. 13.

c. "True" Widows. For the author all that has been said about widows thus far simply constitutes the background for "true" widows who are the real concern in the order presented [144] (→ I, 788, 6 ff.). At the outset we have in 1 Tm. 5:3 what is perhaps a traditional rule: [145] χήρας τίμα, which strikes a new note, strengthened by the allusion to the fifth commandment (Ex. 20:12), as compared with the common disparagement of widows (→ 443, 10). Especially in relation to widows, however,

---

takes the same line but goes further when he says that πρώτη πίστις signifies "the marriage bond between Christ and the widow who took service in the Church, a bond to which she pledged fidelity." He adds that 1 Tm. 5:12 is the first instance of marriage between Christ and an individual, the source of *nubere deo* in the later Church; but cf. → n. 71.

[138] πρώτη πίστις cannot ref. to the pledge to the deceased husband, so Pr.-Bauer, *s.v.* πίστις, 1b; *s.v.* ἀθετέω, but only to fidelity to Christ in so far as there is a desire to live only to Him in the widowed state (→ I, 789, 36 ff.). But one may question the interpretation in Schl. Past., *ad loc.* and W. Michaelis (→ VI, 866, 26 ff.) that πίστιν ἀθετέω means "to renounce the faith" (with a ref. back to v. 8).

[139] Cf. Dib. Past.⁴, *ad loc.*

[140] The idea of the widow who wanders about seems to be a common one, cf. bSota, 22a; jSota, 3, 4 (19a, 45 in Str.-B., III, 653) → 461, 33 f.

[141] On these faults of the young widow cf. Jeremias, *op. cit.* (→ n. 115)), *ad loc.*; Schl. Past., *ad loc.*

[142] ὁ ἀντικείμενος is a collective sing. for the world that is inimical to Christ and the Church; the Past. often ref. to this, cf. 1 Tm. 3:7, where being on guard against the devil is also advised, and 5:15.

[143] We are not told how this turning aside from Christ to Satan took place, but it might be connected with the dangers noted in v. 13.

[144] Doubts have been raised as to whether we really have in 1 Tm. 5:3-16 the beginnings of the early Church order of widows. Thus F. Blanke, "Die Frau als Wortverkündigerin in der alten Kirche," F. J. Leenhardt-F. Blanke, *Die Stellung d. Frau im NT u. in d. alten Kirche* (1949), 64, thinks the ref. is only to the widow as a recipient of support. The use of καταλέγω in v. 9 and παραιτέομαι in v. 11 virtually as tt. and the conditions listed in v. 9 f. seem to pt., however, to a specific organisation, at least in germinal form. Hence 1 Tm. 5:3-16 may rightly be seen as the first witness to a Chr. order of widows, cf. also Ign. Sm., 13, 1; Ign. Pol., 4, 1 and Pol., 4, 3 so Dib. Past.⁴, 58, → I, 788, 23 ff. etc. Cl. Al. Paed., III, 12, 97, 2 associated widows with elders, bishops and deacons as groups for which directions are given in Scripture. In fact χήρα gradually becomes more technical, like πρεσβύτερος. Acc. to Leipoldt, 133 f. there are two types of congregational polity in the Past., the one with the offices of bishop (1 Tm. 3:1-7; Tt. 1:7-9), deacon (1 Tm. 3:8-13 and deaconess (1 Tm. 3:11), the other under a leader without title (Timothy and Titus) along with elders (1 Tm. 5:17-22; Tt. 1:5 f.) and widows (1 Tm. 5:3-16). Funk on Const. Ap., III, 1, 1 thinks that we have directions for widows only in 1 Tm. 5:3-8 and then for deaconesses in vv. 9-13, but in this regard he anticipates later development → 464, 5 ff.

[145] Jeremias, *op. cit.* (→ n. 115), *ad loc.*

it is important that τιμάω (→ VIII, 179, 3 ff.) like ἐπισκέπτομαι (→ II, 604, 4 ff.) also includes active care, v. 17 → VIII, 177, 1 ff.; 179, 2 ff. The rule χήρας τίμα is at once restricted to ὄντως χῆραι. The added καὶ μεμονωμένη (v. 5) is to be understood as an interpretation [146] of ἡ ὄντως χήρα, the widow who really stands alone, [147] who has no relatives to whom she is under obligation. The concept of the ὄντως χήρα καὶ μεμονωμένη obviously includes, however, another feature, namely, that she is determined not to engage in a fresh marriage. The decisive thing here is not whether she is, or feels, too old for this. What counts is the resolve μεμονῶσθαι and therewith, as implied in v. 12, to enter into a special bond with Christ → 454, 17 ff. This resolve seems to be [148] the presupposition of the statement that follows: She has put her (only) hope in God, [149] the Guardian of widows. Hence this widow in the proper sense is particularly faithful in prayer like Anna → 450, 16 ff. What is meant is not constant prayer as in 1 Th. 5:17 but the kind of prayer corresponding to the νυκτὸς καὶ ἡμέρας ὑπερεκπερισσοῦ δεῖσθαι of Paul (1 Th. 3:10), who also worked νυκτὸς καὶ ἡμέρας (1 Th. 2:9; 2 Th. 3:8). The congregational widow also has other tasks (→ 457, 19 ff.) and not just that of prayer, [150] but an attitude of constant readiness for prayer corresponds to the trust in God and the avowed fidelity of the ὄντως χήρα who has been engaged by the church.

d. Ministry in the Community. These characteristics of the ὄντως χήρα are also the inner presuppositions for election to service in the congregation. We read of the outer qualifications for this in v. 9: χήρα καταλεγέσθω. This does not have to mean that there was already a list on which those widows called to minister to the community had to be inscribed. Here and elsewhere [151] καταλέγω means "to be adopted into a fellowship by election." The term itself makes it likely that congregational widows already formed a "semi-clerical" (→ I, 788, 26 ff.) corporation. [152] The antonym is παραιτέομαί (→ I, 195, 15 ff.) τινα, "to vote down someone." We see from v. 11 that this negative decision was made by the church leader, who made a choice among available candidates, while the pass. καταλέγομαι in v. 9 denotes selection by the congregation. The qualifications for selection (cf. 1 Tm. 3:1-13; Tt. 1:6-9) as a congregational widow are as follows. The candidate must have no family (v. 5) to care for → 456, 2 ff. She must have given proof of good works (v. 10). [153] She must not be less than sixty (→ 463, 14 ff.) years old (v. 9), which should be enough to guarantee ripe experience of life and a sure immunity

---

[146] The καί is explicative, cf. Pr.-Bauer, s.v. I, 3.
[147] Probably there is an echo here of the meaning of χήρα dealt with → 450, 4 ff.: "woman living alone, esp. without a husband."
[148] Naturally the idea might be simply that a pious Christian woman who lives alone after the death of her husband turns her thoughts only to God. But probably from v. 3 on, with its ref. to ὄντως χῆραι, the author already has congregational widows in view.
[149] Cf. 6:17: ἠλπικέναι . . . ἐπὶ θεῷ τῷ παρέχοντι ἡμῖν πάντα πλουσίως εἰς ἀπόλαυσιν. Yet the widow should not just cherish this general Chr. hope but should have the special confidence in God that the Bible says she may have.
[150] So Schl. Past. on 1 Tm. 5:10; Jeremias, op. cit. (→ n. 115) on 1 Tm. 5:3 (→ 451, 5).
[151] Examples in Liddell-Scott, Pr.-Bauer, s.v.
[152] Hence one can hardly agree with Dib. Past.⁴ on 1 Tm. 5:9 that Tert.'s transl. in Ad uxorem, I, 7 (CSEL, 70): adlegi in ordinem, is far too clerical.
[153] Lists such as that here (cf. 6:18 and also R. 12:13) suggest development, cf. H. Preisker, Das Ethos d. Urchr.² (1949), 200 with n. 2; Jeremias, op. cit. (→ n. 115), ad loc. τεκνοτροφέω need not relate to the bringing up of orphans; it is more natural to think of the widow's own children (cf. v. 4, 8). On ξενοδοχέω → V, 20, 11 ff., on ἁγίων πόδας νίπτω → V, 25, n. 177; VI, 631, 29 ff.; Str.-B., III, 653; Holtz, op. cit (→ n. 115), ad loc.

from sexual perils, cf. vv. 11-15.[154] She must have been married only once (→ 450, 16 ff.) and must have refrained from a second marriage, v. 9.

The meaning of ἐνὸς ἀνδρὸς γυνή is contested. Many commentators[155] find in it only a rejection of those who in marriage or in their marriages have lived a loose life.[156] Others[157] relate the rule to the exclusion of women who have married again after divorce,[158] since in that period the remarriage of divorcees, esp. with repeated divorce, often amounted to successive polyandry → I, 788, 28 ff. Expositors who take this view usually ref. as well to the judgment of Jesus in Mt. 5:32 and Mk. 10:11 and par.[159] This interpretation of the pass. ἐνὸς ἀνδρὸς γυνή is possible. But one may ask whether in view of the time and situation in terms of which the Past. are to be understood a ref. to one marriage in the absolute is not more probable.[160] In relation to the question of Levirate marriage (→ 442, 27 ff.) in Mk. 12:24-27 and par. Jesus, with Judaism as a whole, seems not to have objected to the remarriage of a widow (→ 442, 23 ff.), although He sharply repudiated remarriage after divorce, Mk. 10:12 and par. Paul also leaves remarriage open in principle to the widow, R. 7:2 f., cf. 1 C. 7:39, 9 (→ 452, 13 ff.). In Lk., however, the widow who has been married only once is openly extolled, Lk. 2:36 f. (→ 450, 6 ff.). The relevant rules in the Past. possibly belong to this tradition, cf. 1 Tm. 5:5, 9, 11 f. (→ 456, 4 ff.).

The question of the tasks of congregational widows[161] receives no express answer in the widow's order of 1 Tm. 5. What first distinguishes the ὄντως χήρα is undoubtedly prayer and intercession, v. 5. The supreme service of the wife, as also of the husband (1 Tm. 2:8), is thought of as representative service for the community in the case of the widow in particular. One may also think of what is enjoined on the πρεσβύτιδες in Tt. 2:3-5, namely, to lead younger women to proper marriage and family life → I, 788, 25 f.[162] If the conduct of widows who are inwardly backsliders (v. 13) is in fact a caricature of right conduct (→ 455, 3 ff.), then congregational widows should also engage in charitable and pastoral visitation. It is also possible that qualified and in some circumstances wealthy widows might take charge of house churches,[163] although whether this would include the proclamation of the Word is doubtful (→ 465, 10 ff.).[164]

---

154 But χήρα cannot on this account be given the sense of "old woman" (→ n. 4) here, for πρεσβύτεραι are mentioned earlier in v. 2. Rather the χῆραι are par. to the καλῶς προεστῶτες πρεσβύτεροι in v. 17.

155 E.g., Dib. Past.⁴, ad loc.

156 The corresponding rule μιᾶς γυναικὸς ἀνήρ for bishops in 1 Tm. 3:2, deacons in 1 Tm. 3:12, and elders in Tt. 1:6 is taken similarly.

157 Schl. Past., ad loc.; Str.-B., III, 648; Jeremias, op. cit. (→ n. 115), 20 f., 33; → I, 788, 28 ff.

158 This interpretation is based on the fact that remarriage was recommended for younger widows, v. 14 (→ 455, 5 ff.), so Schl. Past., 99; Jeremias, op. cit. (→ n. 115), ad loc.

159 Cf. Schl. Past. on 1 Tm. 3:2 and 5:9. Acc. to the verdict of Jesus the woman who dissolved an earlier marriage and contracted a second has only one husband, exactly like the woman who lives with a man licentiously. Marriage is indissoluble and persists, cf. → n. 47; → 462, 12 f. with n. 204.

160 So, e.g., Delling, op. cit. (→ n. 16), 136-8; Preisker, op. cit. (→ n. 16), 148.

161 Duties are hardly set forth in v. 10 (so Dib. Past.⁴, ad loc.) since the point here is the testing of life before selection, as Dibelius himself actually says.

162 G. Blum, "Das Amt d. Frau im NT," Nov. Test., 7 (1964/65), 159, n. 1 calls this the main task of widows.

163 Apart from those mentioned → n. 107 one might recall Nympha in Col. 4:15, though much of the tradition attests to the man's name Nymphas.

164 In Tt. 2:3 older women are to be καλοδιδάσκαλοι and cf. Priscilla in Ac. 18:26, Euodia and Syntyche in Phil. 4:2: ἐν τῷ εὐαγγελίῳ συνήθλησάν μοι, unless the ref. here is to the suffering of the missionaries, cf. L. Zscharnack, Der Dienst der Frau in d. ersten Jhdt. d. chr. Kirche (1902), 47-50, 79 f.

At the conclusion of the widow's order (v. 16) there is a return (→ 455, 18 ff.) to the idea of provision for widows (→ 451, 9 ff. etc.). [165] This is in the first instance an obligation of the widow's relatives, especially the daughter if she is already a Christian housewife. [166] Then it is an obligation of the congregation whose gifts, where possible, should be only for ὄντως χῆραι.

5. James. [167]

The duty of caring for widows also finds a place in the exhortation in Jm., where ἐπισκέπτεσθαι ὀρφανοὺς καὶ χήρας [168] ἐν τῇ θλίψει αὐτῶν (1:27) [169] is equated with θρησκεία καθαρὰ καὶ ἀμίαντος παρὰ τῷ θεῷ καὶ πατρί. ἐπισκέπτομαι does not denote only visitation but active concern out of a sense of responsibility → II, 604, 4 ff. The saying may thus be listed with OT admonitions to help and protect widows (→ V, 488, 1 ff.). But it goes beyond these when it equates such assistance with serving God. [170]

6. The Widow Figuratively.

The explanation of the parable (→ IV, 187, 28 ff.; VIII, 435, 4 ff.) [171] of the unjust judge and the suppliant widow (Lk. 18:2-5; → 449, 15 ff.) sees in the widow a figure of the ἐκλεκτοὶ τοῦ θεοῦ (v. 7 f.), i.e., the eschatological people of God which in its believing (v. 8) supplication for final ἐκδίκησις (→ II, 444, 12 ff.) may be certain of an answer (→ 449, 15 ff. n. 100). John the divine depicts the opposite in the harlot Babylon that says in her heart: κάθημαι βασίλισσα καὶ χήρα οὐκ εἰμὶ καὶ πένθος οὐ μὴ ἴδω (Rev. 18:7). The author here gives us a statement which is partly a quotation and partly an allusion to the words of the OT Babylon (Is. 47:5-9; → 445, 28 ff.). The queen and the widow represent the two extremes of a woman's destiny. Whereas Jesus compares the eschatological people of God to a widow, Babylon, a code-word for the world power of Rome, declares itself to be a queen. But soon destiny will reverse the roles. She who resembles an oppressed widow will become a royal bride (21:2; → IV, 1105, 25 ff.) and haughty Babylon will become a widow (cf. 18:17, 19 ἠρημώθη), the victim of many diseases, whose ultimate lot is to be burned with fire, 18:8.

[165] Cf. Dib. Herm. on m., 8, 10 and Bau. Ign. on Sm., 6, 2.

[166] So Schl. Past., ad loc. A considerable proportion of the Western and Imperial textual tradition, however, reads εἴ τις πιστὸς ἢ πιστή.

[167] Cf. Hck. Jk., Dib. Jk.[11], Schl. Jk., J. Schneider, Die Kirchenbriefe, NT Deutsch, 10[10] (1967); F. Mussner, Der Jk., Herders Theol. Komm. NT, 13, 1[2] (1967) on 1:27.

[168] On the common pairing of widows and orphans → n. 12; 443, 1 ff. etc.

[169] M. Black, "Crit. and Exeg. Notes on Three NT Texts Hb. 11:11; Jd. 5; Jm. 1:27," Festschr. E. Haenchen, ZNW, Beih. 30 (1964), 45 directs attention to an interesting variant in the newly discovered p[74]: ἐπισκέπτεσθαι ὀρφανοὺς καὶ χήρας ἐν τῇ θλίψει αὐτῶν ὑπερασπίζειν (for ἄσπιλον ἑαυτὸν τηρεῖν) ἀπὸ τοῦ κόσμου "to care for orphans and to protect widows in their affliction at the hands of the world." One must admit that this reading has advantages, esp. as it omits the equation of keeping oneself unspotted from the world with pure and undefiled service of God. ὑπερασπίζω is a common term in the LXX; it is usually construed with gen. or ὑπέρ and gen. but twice, at Prv. 2:7 and Zech. 9:15 (vl.) with the acc. One must wait for corroboration of the reading, meantime viewing it with Black as a particularly happy corruption of the traditional text.

[170] The spirit of the prophets and of Jesus lives on here, cf. Hos. 6:6; Mt. 9:13; 12:7 and esp. 25:40.

[171] Acc. to Jülicher Gl. J., II, 284; Bultmann Trad., 189 et al. the interpretation is secondary. But the language and thought support authenticity, cf. Delling, op. cit. (→ n. 84), 13-25; Jeremias Gl.[7], 155 with n. 2 et al. In any case the collective understanding of the widow as the eschatological people of God comes from primitive Christianity.

These metaphors are part of the general biblical imagery which embraces the individual symbols of the bride and bridegroom, marriage and the marriage feast, fidelity and infidelity, the dissolution of marriage and widowhood. Both OT and NT use these images to describe the relation of God to His people (→ I, 653, 26 ff.; IV, 1104, 32 ff.; VI, 532, 13 ff.; 587, 1 ff.; 594, 16 ff.). When the people is unfaithful to God, its marriage with God breaks up and it becomes a χήρα. In this context χήρα obviously does not mean a widow but "a desolate woman abandoned by her husband" → 440, 14 ff. [172] This is how the prophets of the exile describe the self-incurred plight of Israel, Jer. 51:5; Lam. 1:1; Is. 49:21. At the same time, however, there already rings forth the promise of a new (marriage-) covenant, Is. 54:4-6, cf. also Hos. 2:21 f. What the OT prophets proclaimed for God's ancient people the NT proclaims for His eschatological people. It is now in the hopeless position of Israel during the exile, apparently forsaken by God. But it will become the bride that goes to meet her heavenly Bridegroom at the *parousia*, Rev. 22:17, 20.

In this use of the metaphor of the widow two motifs combine (cf. 4 Esr. 10:25-27): the people of God as wife and the ancient description of cities as women, which was common in the non-biblical world. [173] Jerusalem and Babylon represent the two peoples of which mankind is composed according to the biblical view. The one is the people with God (the bride) and the other is the people without God (the widow).

D. The Widow in the Early Church. [174]

1. Allusions to Biblical Statements.

In early Chr. lit. one may see many allusions to biblical sayings about widows. There are many quotations, esp. of Is. 1:17, e.g., 1 Cl., 8, 4; Just. Apol., 44, 3; 61, 7; Didasc., II, 42, 1; 51, 1, or Is. 1:23, e.g., Just. Dial., 27, 2; Const. Ap., II, 17, 2. We also find ref. to examples of true widowhood, esp. the widow of Zarephath, Judith, Anna and the widow at the treasury, usually in pairs, cf. Didasc., III, 1, 3; Const. Ap., III, 7, 6. 8; VIII, 25, 2. The ancient theme of the distress of widowhood (→ 441, 14 ff.; 444, 19 ff.; 447, 26 ff.) finds expression in the combination (→ 443, 1 ff.) χῆραι καὶ ὀρφανοί, e.g., Barn., 20, 2; Apc. Pt., 15, 30; Herm. s., 9, 26, 2, [175] cf. Sib., 2, 76; ὀρφανικοῖς χήραις, and

---

[172] The transl. "widow" is not, of course, impossible, for the Bible does not hesitate to think of God's "death," e.g., when it speaks of His testament, Gl. 3:15, 17; cf. Hb. 9:16 f. → II, 129, 19 ff.; 131, 6 ff.

[173] Cf. H. Steuding, Art. "Lokalpersonifikationen," Roscher, II, 2, 2092 f.; J. M. C. Toynbee, "Roma and Constantinopolis in Late-Antique Art from 312 to 365," JRS, 37 (1947), 135-144; S. Zimmer, *Zion als Tochter, Frau u. Mutter. Personifikation von Land, Stadt u. Volk in weiblicher Gestalt*, Diss. Munich (1959), cf. Gl. 4:22-31; Mt. 23:37; 21:5; Jn. 12:15. Cf. also Sib., 5, 169 f. on Rome: χήρη καθεδοῖο παρ' ὄχθας, καὶ ποταμὸς Τίβερίς σε κλαύσεται ἦν παράκοιτιν "as a widow thou mayest sit on the bank and the Tiber will bewail thee as his spouse." For a distinctive counterpart esp. to Rev. 18:7 cf. Sib., 3, 77: ἔνθ' ὁπόταν κόσμου παντὸς χήρη βασιλεύσῃ, sc. Cleopatra, whose reign is seen here as a sign of the end of the world.

[174] H. Achelis, Art. "Diakonissen," RE³, 4, 616-620; Blanke, *op. cit.* (→ n. 144), 64-8; L. Bopp, *Das Witwentum als organische Gliedschaft im Gemeinschaftsleben d. alten Kirche* (1950); R. H. Connolly, *Didascalia Apostolorum. The Syriac Version Transl.* (1929); R. Frick, Art. "Weibliche Diakonie," *Evangel. Kirchenlex.*, ed. H. Brunotte-O. Weber, I (1956), 922; A. Harnack, "Die Lehre d. zwölf Apostel," TU, 2, 1-2 (1884), 235; Hennecke², 566-583; A. Kalsbach, "Die altkirchl. Einrichtung d. Diakonissen bis zu ihrem Erlöschen," *Röm. Quartalsschrift*, Suppl. 22 (1926); J. Mayer, *Monumenta de viduis, diaconissis virginibusque tractantia* (1938); P. Philippi, "Thesen z. theol. Erfassung d. altkirchl. Diakonissenamts," *Die Innere Mission*, 55 (1965), 370 f.; *Testamentum Domini Nostri Jesu Christi*, ed. I. E. Rahmani (1899); W. Riedel, *Die Kirchenrechtsquellen d. Patriarchats Alexandrien* (1900); Uhlhorn, *op. cit.* (→ n. 73), 97-101; Viteau, *op. cit.* (→ n. 101), 513-536; Zscharnack, *op. cit.* (→ n. 164), 100-144.

[175] Cf. Aristid. Apol., 15, 7 (on this J. Geffcken, "Zwei gr. Apologeten," *Sammlung wissensch. Komm. zu gr. u. röm. Schriftstellern*, 5 [1907], 90); Just. Apol., 67, 6. It is worth noting that in Didasc. and Const. Ap. Book III on χηρῶν is followed by IV on ὀρφανῶν.

also in the common reckoning of widows among the poor (→ 445, 21), e.g., Pol., 6, 1; Herm. m., 8, 10; Act. Verc. 17 (p. 65, 22); Ps. Cl. Recg., III, 66, 8, [176] the ὑστερούμενοι "those in need," e.g., Herm. m., 8, 10; [177] s., 5, 3, 7; 9, 27, 2, the θλιβόμενοι [178] "oppressed," e.g., Ign. Sm., 6, 2; [179] Herm. s., 1, 8; Const. Ap., II, 25, 2; Eus. Hist. Eccl., VI, 43, 11, and strangers, e.g., Didasc., II, 4, 1; Const. Ap., II, 25, 2. In keeping again (→ 443, 12 ff.; 445, 21 ff.; 448, 27 ff.) is complaint at the despising and maltreatment of widows, e.g., Barn., 20, 2; Ign. Sm., 6, 2, and the admonition to intercede, e.g., Const. Ap., VIII, 10, 10 and to care for them, e.g., Herm. s., 5, 3, 7: δώσεις αὐτὸ (sc. what is saved by fasting) χήρᾳ ἤ ὀρφανῷ ἤ ὑστερουμένῳ, cf. Ps. Cl. Recg., III, 66, 8 (→ n. 176), common in either positive or negative form, Herm. s., 1, 8; m., 8,10, or only negative with ref. to oppressors, e.g., Didasc., IV, 3, 1: μακάριός ἐστιν, ὃς ἂν ... μὴ θλίβῃ τόπον [180] ὀρφανοῦ ξένου τε καὶ χήρας. The decisive motivation for this acc. to Const. Ap., IV, 1, 2 (based on Ps. 68:5) is that God is ὁ πατὴρ τῶν ὀρφανῶν καὶ κριτὴς τῶν χηρῶν (→ 443, 9 ff.; 446, 14 ff.; 447, 28 ff.; 449, 10 f.; n. 100). Helping widows is one of the works of Chr. charity that are pleasing to God. [181] To bear witness to our thanks to God we should be generous to widows. [182] In contrast is the depiction of the torments the rich will have to suffer in hell μὴ ἐλεήσαντες ὀρφανοὺς καὶ χήρας, Apc. Pt. 15:30. [183]

2. Organisation of Care for Widows.

The NT is followed in the organisation of care for widows (→ 451, 9 ff.; 458, 1 ff., 7 ff.) and in detailed rules in the church orders. Acc. to Hipp., 24 [184] widows and the sick should receive a share of the oblations [185] of the church members. Acc. to Cornelius of Rome writing to Fabius of Antioch there were over 1500 widows and needy in the Roman church οὓς πάντας ἡ τοῦ δεσπότου χάρις καὶ φιλανθρωπία (i.e., by the gifts of the congregation) διατρέφει, Eus. Hist. Eccl., VI, 43, 11. In Antioch in the time of Chrysostom the κατάλογος had the names of as many as 3000 widows and virgins receiving daily support, in addition to countless others who were helped, Hom. in Mt., 66, 3 on 20:29 f. (MPG, 58 [1862], 630). Missionary churches at once set out to care for widows too, cf. Act. Thom. 59: εἶχεν (sc. Thomas) γὰρ ἐν ταῖς πόλεσιν (sc. of India) συνηθροισμένας (sc. widows). Eleusius of Cyzikus (between 350 and 360) not only attacked pagan shrines but also set up homes for the church's widows χηροτροφεῖα and virgins παρθενῶνες, Sozomenus Hist. Eccl., V, 15, 5. [186]

The bishops bear primary responsibility for caring for widows, Ign. Pol., 4, 1; Didasc., II, 4, 1. They have to keep lists καταλέγειν and to enter the names of widows needing

---

[176] Ed. B. Rehm-F. Paschke, GCS, 51 (1965).

[177] Cf. Dib. Herm., ad loc.

[178] This is also a loan word in Lat.: sive viduae sive thlibomeni, Cyprianus ep. 8, 3 (ed. G. Hartel, CSEL, 3, 2 [1871]).

[179] Cf. Bau. Ign., ad loc.

[180] Cf. Apost. Church Order, 1. 23 (Harnack, op. cit. [→ n. 174], 225 and 236), also Const. Ap., III, 19, 2, cf. Pr.-Bauer, s.v. τόπος, 2b; W. Nauck, "Probleme des frühchr. Amtsverständnisses," ZNW, 48 (1957), 213 ff.; → VIII, 207, 14 ff.

[181] As we find χήρᾳ καὶ ὀρφανῷ οὐ προσέχοντες in the list of vices, Barn., 20, 2, so we find χήραις ὑπηρετεῖν in the list of virtues, Herm. m., 8, 10.

[182] So, e.g., Act. Pl. (Cpt.) 34:2 f. (p. 57) in Hennecke³, II, 253; Act. Verc. 17 (p. 65, 22); Act. Thom. 59.

[183] One may note also the blessings for gifts to widows, e.g., possessions in heaven, Herm. s., 1, 8 f., and protection through their prayers, Cl. Al. Quis Div. Salv., 34, 2 f., and esp. an altar, e.g., Pol., 4, 3; Ps.-Ign. Ad Tarsenses, 9, 1 (→ n. 109; in Ign. Eph., 5, 2; Tr., 7, 2; Phld., 4 the Church is the θυσιαστήριον θεοῦ); Tert. Ad Uxorem, I, 7 (CSEL, 70); Didasc., III, 10, 7; IV, 5, 1; Const. Ap., II, 26, 8; III, 6, 3; 14, 1, cf. Funk on Didasc., II, 26, 8; Testamentum Domini, I, 40 (Rahmani, op. cit. [→ n. 174] 97).

[184] Ed. B. Botte, "La tradition apost. de S. Hippolyte," Liturgiewissensch. Quellen u. Forschungen, 39² (1963), cf. Hennecke², 581.

[185] Cf. Hennecke², 570 with n. 1.

[186] Ed. J. Bidez-G. C. Hansen, GCS, 50 (1960).

support on them ἐγγράφεσθαι, Chrys. Sacerdot., III, 16, 296 f. Didasc., III, 4, 2, cf. II, 27, 3, lays down expressly that donors must not make gifts to widows directly. The bishop must receive them and dispense them as a prudent master of the house, Const. Ap., II, 25, 2, cf. Didasc., II, 25, 2; Const. Ap., III, 3, 2. Direction προστασία of care for widows ἡ τῶν χηρῶν θεραπεία is, with supervision of virgins and making judgments, one of the most onerous tasks of the bishop, Chrys. Sacerdot., III, 16, 295 f. In practice the presbyters and deacons help, Const. Ap., VIII, 47, 41. In Pol., 6, 1 the direction: μὴ ἀμελοῦντες χήρας ἢ ὀρφανοῦ ἢ πένητος, is addressed to the presbyters. The ref. is to the bishops and deacons in Didasc., IV, 5, 3. In the main the job was entrusted to the deacons in acc. with the usual interpretation of Ac. 6:1 ff. This is presupposed in Herm. s., 9, 26, 2, cf. Act. Thom. 59. Quite early women are mentioned along with the deacons → 451, 23 ff. Thus Grapte in Herm. v., 2, 4, 3 was probably a deaconess [187] who cared for widows and orphans spiritually as well as physically: νουθετήσει (→ IV, 1021, n. 14; 1022, 14 ff.) τὰς χήρας καὶ τοὺς ὀρφανούς. Meals donated by wealthy laymen are a special form of care based on ancient models (→ 447, 4 ff.; 451, 11 ff.). [188] Finally the deacons were to give widows special places at divine service alongside matrons, Didasc., II, 57, 8, cf. Const. Ap., II, 57, 12 → n. 213; 465, 20 ff.

The rules about caring for widows also contain provisions against abuse. Deacons are not to use this ministry as a means of self-enrichment, Herm. s., 9, 26, 2, cf. Mk. 12:40 (→ 449, 1 ff.). Gifts are not to be accepted from evil-doers, Const. Ap., IV, 6, 6; οἱ ἐκθλίβοντες χήραν καὶ ὀρφανὸν καταδυναστεύοντες and their gifts must be rejected, IV, 6, 4. Limits are also set on the support given. An older married woman must be given preference over a widow who can provide for herself, Didasc., II, 4, 2. There is a new turn, not without ancient precedent (→ 443, 18 f.), with the gt. change under Constantine, for now caring for widows and orphans (→ V, 487, 28 ff.) is undertaken by the state, Hier. Comm. in Jer., IV, 35, 4 on 22:1-5 (CSEL, 59). Constantine also passed laws to help widows, e.g., tax concessions and legal aid. [189]

3. Household Tables for Widows.

As regards the household tables now necessary for widows the Church orders could again build on the NT, 1 Tm. 5:4 ff. → 453, 4 ff.; 455, 13 ff. Didasc., III, 5, 1-11, 5 [190] and par. deal fairly fully with this, but even more so Const. Ap. Here an ideal Chr. widow is portrayed, 5, 1 f. Then the directions focus on what a true widow must not do. She must not teach, any more than other laymen or women, [191] 5, 3 - 6, 2. She must not go about from house to house (→ 455, 3 ff.) for gossip [192] or for gain, 6, 3 - 7, 5. 6, 4 has a play on words in this connection. Widows out for gain are not χῆραι but πῆραι, [193] travel pouches, beggars' sacks. [194] In contrast the model widow stays at home and prays, her prayers being answered on account of her devotion and good conduct, 7, 6-8 (→ n. 100). She is subject to the bishop, 8, 1-5. False widows are then described, 10, 1 f., with warnings against envy, giving the names of donors, 10, 3-11, and backbiting, 10, 12 - 11, 5. If the picture here and in Chrys. Sacerdot., III, 16, 297 is not flattering, it is true to life.

The life expected of widows in the early Church has many ascetic features. As in Jewish piety and primitive Christianity (→ 450, 6 ff.) fasting and prayer are integral

---

[187] Dib. Herm., ad loc.; cf. Zscharnack, op. cit. (→ n. 164), 80 f.

[188] Hipp. Ch. Order, 30, v. also Hennecke², 582, and on this 570; Canones Hipp., 35 (Riedel, op. cit. [→ n. 174], 223); also Didasc., II, 28, 1; Can. Hipp., 32 (Riedel, 221).

[189] Mayer-Maly, op. cit. (→ n. 11), 2106.

[190] Cf. Connolly, op. cit. (→ n. 174), XLII-XLV.

[191] At an earlier charismatic stage widows might have revelations during prayer (→ 450, 15 ff.); Ap. Ch. Order, 21 (Harnack, op. cit. [→ n. 174], 235).

[192] Tert. Ad Uxorem, I, 8 (CSEL, 70).

[193] So already Didasc., III, 6, 4; the Syr. transl. reads πηρούς ("blind"), not πήρας.

[194] Cf. Pr.-Bauer, s.v. πήρα, Deissmann LO, 87 f.; S. Krauss, "Die Instruktion Jesu an d. Ap.," Angelos, 1 (1925), 99 f.

to it, e.g., Hipp. Ch. Order, 23 (→ n. 184); [195] Can. Hipp., 32; [196] Can. Bas., 36. [197] Widows are also told not to drink much wine, [198] Ap. Ch. Order, 21, [199] nor to laugh too much, Can. Bas., 36. [200] They are to use any property on behalf of poor believers, Test. Domini, I, 40. [201] They are esp. admonished to live a quiet life, [202] cf. Didasc., III, 6, 3; 7, 6 and above all Test. Domini, I, 42. [203] μονογαμία, i.e., renunciation of remarriage, is also demanded → 442, 7 ff.; 452, 14 ff.; 457, 3 ff.

Opinions on this question vary. The Ebionites acc. to Epiph. Haer., 30, 18, 2 allow remarriage without restriction, ἄχρι καὶ δευτέρου καὶ τρίτου καὶ ἑβδόμου γάμου. Tert., however, even rejects Paul and his permitting of widows to remarry in R. 7:2 f. (→ 452, 14 ff.), De monogamia, 10, 1 (CSEL, 76). In De exhort. castitatis, 9, 1 (CCh, 2) he argues that Paul really regarded *secundum matrimonium* as a *species stupri*, a form of harlotry. Acc. to Tert. Chr. marriage persists beyond the grave, [204] De monog., 10, 2 (CSEL, 76). Given by God, widowhood is an opportunity for the continence that is pleasing to Him, Ad uxorem, I, 7 (CSEL, 70). In De exhort. castitatis, 12, 2 (CCh, 2); De monog., 16, 4 (CSEL, 76) he recommends that widowers take widows as spiritual wives to keep house as in an even more innocent counterpart to *virgines subintroductae*. Orig. takes what is basically the same line in Hom. in Lk., 17 on 2:36 (GCS, 49, 109 f.). The normal practice was somewhere between the two extremes. Younger widows were usually allowed to remarry, although they might be supported so as not to be driven into a second marriage, Didasc., III, 2, 1. The Can. Bas. accept a second marriage (11), [205] but will not let a clergyman pray over it (72). [206] Further marriages are fornication, Const. Ap., III, 2, 2; Can. Bas., 11. [207] Strong ascetic trends finally led the Chr. emperors, in contrast to Augustus (→ 442, 18 ff.), to lay down *poenas secundarum nuptiarum*, cf. Cod. Theodosianus, 3, 8 f. [208]

4. Widows as an Institution in the Community.

As institution of widows developed in the community → 455, 13 ff. [209] Many aspects

---

[195] Cf. Hennecke[2], 581.

[196] Riedel, *op. cit.* (→ n. 174), 220, cf. also Can., 9 (205).

[197] Riedel, 225.

[198] The rule for deacons in 1 Tm. 3:8 is almost word for word the same; the reason given is so that they can minister by night, but cf. Hipp. Ch. Order, 30 (→ n. 184), *v.* also Hennecke[2], 582.

[199] Harnack, *op. cit.* (→ n. 174), 235.

[200] Riedel, *op. cit.*, 254.

[201] Rahmani, *op. cit.*, 97.

[202] Hence in distinction from 1 Tm. 5:4 community widows are to hand over their children to the church as *pueri oblati* to be trained as priests, Test. Domini, I, 40 (Rahmani, *op. cit.*, 97).

[203] Rahmani, 101.

[204] One finds here a motif that elsewhere led to the voluntary death or burning of the widow. Since death cannot end marriage, the widow has basically no existence. Originally continuation of marriage after death was expected, cf. Leipoldt, *op. cit.* (→ n. 15), 81 f. with n. 562-8; Delling, *op. cit.* (→ n. 16), 137 with n. 41. For the Gk. and Thracian practice of slaying widows cf. Paus., IV, 2, 7; Hdt., V, 5; for India, cf. Diod. S., 19, 33, 3 - 34, 6; Cic. Tusc., V, 78; cf. Hehn, *op. cit.* (→ n. 14), 540; Hirt, *op. cit.* (→ n. 14), 444. 494. 715; Beth, 669-673; G. Wilke, Art. "Witwentötung," RLV, 14, 440-442; E. Rohde, *Der gr. Roman u. seine Vorläufer*[3] (1914), 119 with n. 1; R. Garbe, "Die Witwenverbrennung," *Beitr. z. indischen Kulturgeschichte* (1903), 141-182; H. v. Glasenapp, Art. "Witwenverbrennung," RGG[3], VI, 1787.

[205] Riedel, *op. cit.*, 240.

[206] *Ibid.*, 267.

[207] *Ibid.*, 240.

[208] Ed. T. Mommsen-P. M. Meyer, I, 2[2] (1954); cf. Mayer-Maly, *op. cit.* (→ n. 11), 2105.

[209] Ps. Cl. Hom., 11, 36, 2 ascribes the institution of the widow's office χηρικὰ συστησάμενος to Peter, but the parts of Ps. Cl. dealing with church order are in the later section, cf. C. Schmidt, "Stud. zu d. Ps. Cl.," TU, 46, 1 (1929), 58 with n. 1, 309.

of this development are obscure and controversial, e.g., whether widows were reckoned among the clergy → lines 22 ff. In the Church Orders, which mostly have special sections on widows, [210] there is often no clear-cut distinction between those living in χηρεία [211] widowhood, and those active in χηρικόν, [212] the office of widows, [213] so that in a given case it is hard to say whether the ref. is to the one or the other → n. 114. There are certain conditions for reception into the ranks of church widows; these partly adopt, partly change, and partly expand the rules of 1 Tm. 5 → 456, 19 ff. A specific time must elapse after the husband's death to give the widow a chance to test herself, Hipp. (→ n. 184), 10; [214] Test. Domini, I, 40; [215] Const. Ap., VIII, 25, 2; cf. also Epitome, 16, 2 of Const. Ap. [216] She must have been only once married, Orig. Hom. in Lk., 17 on 2:36 ff. (GCS, 49, 110, 5), cf. Tert. De exhort. castitatis, 11, 2 (CCh, 2). She must have led a blameless life as a widow, Const. Ap., VIII, 25, 2; Epitome, 16, 2, [216] and must have proved herself in care for her family and upbringing of the children, Const. Ap., VIII, 25, 2; Test. Dom., I, 40. [217] As regards canonical age for acceptance the rule of 1 Tm. 5:9 (at least 60 → 456, 32 ff.) is not usually followed. [218] Acc. to Didasc., III, 1, 1 she should be not less than 50 yrs. old, but this was later reduced for practical reasons. [219] Installation was not by ordination but by benediction and prayer, [220] Hipp. Ch. Order, 10; [221] Can. Hipp., 9. [222] When appointed a church widow, the woman takes a vow to remain a widow → 454, 17 ff. If she breaks this she will be accountable to God, cf. Didasc., III, 1, 2. No fixed no. is laid down at first. Only with Ap. Ch. Order, 21 [223] and Test. Dom., I, 34. [224] do we read of the no. three.

The relation of widows to the clergy varies. On the one hand they seem to be reckoned with them. Thus Cl. Al. Paed., III, 12, 97, 2 speaks of them along with the presbyters, bishops, and deacons, cf. Orig. Hom. in Lk., 17 on 2:36 ff. (GCS, 49, 110, 4 f.); Tert. De monogamia, 11, 1 (CSEL, 76); Didasc., III, 11, 5; the par. Const. Ap., III, 15, 5,

---

[210] Hipp. Ch. Order, 10, cf. also Hennecke[2], 577; Didasc., III (on widows here cf. H. Achelis, "Die Didask.," TU, 25, 2 [1904], 247 f.); Const. Ap., III; Ap. Ch. Order, 21 (Harnack, op. cit. [→ n. 174], 235, cf. also Hennecke[2], 568); Testamentum Domini, I, 40-43 (Rahmani, 95-105); Canones Bas., 36 (Riedel, op. cit. [→ n. 174], 254-7).

[211] For χηρεία, current already in LXX → 445, 3, cf. Const. Ap., III, 1, 2: μὴ φέρουσα τὴν ἐν νεότητι χηρείαν, and cf. III, 1, 4: δῶρον ἔχουσα χηρείας, the charisma of voluntarily maintained widowhood.

[212] Like χήρα (→ 440, 19 ff.), χηρικόν is an adj. used as noun: the institution of widows, cf. Ps. Cl. Hom., 11, 36, 2; Const. Ap., III, 1, 2; 2, 1; VIII, 25, 2, the ordo viduarum, cf. Ps. Cl. Recg., VI, 15, 5 (→ n. 176); τὸ τάγμα τῶν χηρῶν has the same sense in Ps.-Ign. Ad Philippenses, 15, 1 (→ n. 109). On these and other terms for the order cf. Kalsbach, op. cit. (→ n. 174), 95 f.

[213] In Test. Domini these widows are called "canonical widows" or those "with priority in seating," cf. Rahmani, op. cit., 163.

[214] Cf. Hennecke[2], 577. There is a probationary period for those recently widowed but seeking the office, Const. Ap., VIII, 25, 3; Epitome, 16, 3 (Funk, II, 82). Ascetic trends in evaluating widows are undeniable from the NT period (→ 442, 7 ff.; 450, 16 ff.; 452, 14 ff.; 457, 1 ff.) but these become dominant only from the 2nd century when continence is the one real qualification; thus in Asia Minor and Syria the order of widows becomes an organisation of widowed and virgin ascetics, cf. Kalsbach, op. cit., 95.

[215] Rahmani, 95.

[216] Funk, II, 82.

[217] Rahmani, 95.

[218] But cf. Const. Ap., III, 1, 1; Can. Bas., 30 (Riedel, 254).

[219] Cf. Funk, ad loc. No rule about age is given in Test. Domini.

[220] The same applies to lectors, sub-deacons, and virgins. Test. Domini, I, 41 (Rahmani, 99) has a prayer of consecration for widows to be spoken by the bishop.

[221] Cf. also Hennecke[2], 577.

[222] Riedel, 205.

[223] Harnack, op. cit. (→ n. 174), 235; cf. also Hennecke[2], 568.

[224] Rahmani, 83.

after mentioning the bishop, presbyter, and deacon, continues μήτε ἄλλος τις ἐκ τοῦ καταλόγου τοῦ ἱερατικοῦ. [225] Esp. in Test. Domini, I, 23, [226] cf. Didasc., 38, 21, [227] the widows are a cultic unity with the other office-bearers. Tert. Praescr. Haer., 3 (p. 4, 2) and Ps. Cl. Hom., 3, 71, 5 are ambiguous.

This ambiguous ranking of widows corresponds to their no less ambiguous relation to virgins and deaconesses (→ II, 91, 23 ff.). Acc. to Ign. Sm., 13, 1 there were virgins who were called widows. Hence virgins could be received into the order of widows, e.g., when there were not enough real widows. [228] Such a case, if extreme, seems to be in view in Tert. Virg. Vel., 9, 2. Often widows are closely associated with virgins, e.g., Tert. Praescr. Haer., 3 (p. 4, 2); Hipp. Ch. Order, 23. [229] In the days when widows were no longer ranked as clergy both church widows and *virgines sacratae* seem to have had semi-clerical status → 456, 24 ff. [230]

Equally indeterminate is the relation of widows to women deacons, who were called deaconesses from the 4th cent. on. [231] Since in this office the functions of guidance and supervision went along with spiritual and physical care (→ 461, 10 ff.) → VI, 700, 14 ff., deaconesses had some priority over widows, [232] who had no tasks of leadership. This explains the specific relating of deaconesses to the Holy Spirit [233] and the use of the image of the altar (→ n. 183) for widows and orphans, Didasc., II, 26, 8. [234] Probably deaconesses, later at least, were chosen primarily from the circle of virgins and only secondarily from that of widows, Const. Ap., VI, 17, 4. [235] In this sense Arab. Didasc., 38, 21 [236] can ref. to widows who are deaconesses. Even later, however, the two groups do not seem to be identical, cf. Test. Domini, I, 23. [237]

In contrast to the sparse ref. in 1 Tm. 5 we learn much more about the tasks of congregational widows (→ 457, 19 ff.) in the post-NT period. First, as in 1 Tm. 5:5, we read of prayer [238] and intercession, Pol., 4, 3; Hipp. Ch. Order, 23; [239] Didasc., III, 7, 6 f. Test. Domini, I, 42 f. [240] is esp. explicit on this. Widows should pray alone, or, better,

---

[225] On traces of five offices, bishop, presbyter, deacon, lector, and widow, cf. C. Schmidt, *op. cit.* (→ n. 209), 305 f. One can hardly see so sharp a distinction between the work of widows and that of clergy after 1 Tm. 5 as Kalsbach, *op. cit.,* 97 seems to do; → 463, 2 ff.

[226] Rahmani, 35, 37.

[227] Funk, II, 132.

[228] Bau. Ign., *ad loc.*

[229] Cf. Funk on Didasc., III, 1, 1.

[230] Cf. F. H. Kettler, Art. "Virgines sacratae," RGG³, VI, 1407.

[231] The word διακόνισσα occurs for the first time in Can., 19 of Nicaea (ed. J. D. Mansi, Sacrorum conciliorum nova et amplissima collectio, 2 [1759], 677). Possibly the first traces of the office may be seen in R. 16:1 and 1 Tm. 3:11 (→ II, 91, 13 ff.; VI, 703, 1 ff.). If so, the διάκονος would be the oldest female office-bearer in the Church, cf. Leipoldt, 133 with n. 30.

[232] Cf. Const. Ap., VIII, 19; 20, 2 with 25, 2: The deaconess is ordained by laying on of hands by the bishop, but not the widow → 463, 16 ff., though cf. Rahmani, 165.

[233] This suggests origin in a Semitic language, where the Spirit is fem., cf. Ev. Hebr. Fr., 5. But cf. Const. Ap., II, 26, 6.

[234] Cf. Connolly, *op. cit.* (→ n. 174); Funk, *ad loc.*

[235] Cf. Connolly, XLII.

[236] Funk, II, 132.

[237] Rahmani, 37, 163-6.

[238] How far this was institutionalised may be seen from Act. Verc. 19, where each widow can even be given a gold piece for praying. With *viduae* we read here of *seniores,* who are not male elders (as F. Ficker in Hennecke², 240 believes) but elder women as in Tt. 2:3. Cf. M. R. James, *The Apocryphal NT* (1924), 321: "I have bidden the widows and old women to assemble ... in my house." W. Schneemelcher in Hennecke³, II, 207 leaves this an open question.

[239] Cf. Hennecke², 581.

[240] Rahmani, 100-105. But this later order shows, as against Kalsbach, *op. cit.,* 95, that prayer is not the only remaining mark of a good widow.

with virgins, at home or in church, [241] preferably at daybreak and around midnight. [242] With prayer the job of caring for the sick is emphasised. Acc. to Ap. Ch. Order, 21 [243] one of the 3 appointed widows is charged with looking after women who are visited by illness. Acc. to Test. Domini, I, 40 cf. also Can. Hipp., 9, [244] a widow should visit the sick on Sunday with one or two deacons. One may conclude from Luc. Pergr. Mort., 12 that visiting prisoners was also one of the tasks of widows. Acc. to Ps.-Clement De virginitate, 2, 4, 3 f. [245] one of the congregational widows, a *matrona, quae et senili aetate et morum gravitate omnes antecellit,* is responsible for hospitality (cf. 1 Tm. 5:10 → n. 153) to travelling preachers. Hence Chr. widows are in equal measure the instruments as well as the recipients of congregational care. Individual ref. suggests that while widows are not granted any true teaching office, cf. Didasc., III, 5, 6 (→ 461, 32 ff.), nevertheless, they are entrusted with the instruction of women catechumens and Chr. girls, Orig. Hom. in Is., 6, 3 on 6:9 (GCS, 33, 273); Test. Domini, I, 40. [246]

The work of congregational widows is the reason they are so honoured, as frequently in early Chr. writings. The admonition at the head of the NT order (→ 455, 15 ff.) is thus passed on from generation to generation, cf. Ps. Cl. Hom., 3, 71, 5; Can. Hipp., 9. [247] Tert. Ad uxorem, I, 8 (CSEL, 70) ranks widows above virgins and Chrys. Hom. de viduis, 2 (MPG, 51 [1862], 323) can still say: [248] προστάτις ἡμῶν ἐστιν ἡ ὄντως χήρα. In practice the honouring of widows means that they form a special conclave along with the (other) clergy, Test. Domini, I, 23; [249] Arab. Didasc., 38, 21, [250] that they have special places at worship, on the left side behind the presbyters, par. to the deacons on the right side behind the bishop, Test. Domini, I, 23, [251] and that they receive communion after the deacons and before the lectors, sub-deacons, exorcists etc., I, 23. [252] Eschatological honour is also held out as a prospect for the faithful widow. She "will be honoured on earth by men and she will receive eternal glory from God in heaven," Didasc., III, 1, 3. Widows "who have served uprightly will be magnified by the archangels," Test. Domini, I, 40, [253] cf. I, 42. [254]

At the end of the early period the order of widows is no longer in existence. It was unknown even in the age of Chrys., who says in his Hom. de viduis, 3 (MPG, 51 [1862], 323): καθάπερ γάρ εἰσι παρθένων χοροί, οὕτω καὶ χηρῶν τὸ παλαιὸν ἦσαν χοροί. Possibly this ancient institution found a new form in the increasing nunneries and the service rendered by nuns to the Church.

Stählin

---

241 Anna (Lk. 2:37) is a model when Test. Domini, I, 40 (Rahmani, 95) says that the church widow should remain day and night (cf. 1 Tm. 5:5) at the altar. It may be gathered from what follows, however, that the directions in this c. are not meant as laws which are to be carried out pedantically.

242 Formularies of prayer for the period may be found in Test. Domini, I, 43 (Rahmani, 100-105). For the *laus nocturna viduarum* cf. Blanke, *op. cit.* (→ n. 144), 67 f.

243 Harnack, *op. cit.* (→ n. 174), 235.

244 Rahmani, 97; Riedel, 205.

245 Ed. F. X. Funk-F. Diekamp, Patres Apostolici, II (1913).

246 Rahmani, 97.

247 Riedel, 205.

248 In his age, of course, the order of widows no longer existed → line 28 ff.

249 Rahmani, 35-37.

250 Funk, II, 132.

251 Rahmani, 37.

252 *Ibid.,* 47.

253 *Ibid.,* 97.

254 *Ibid.,* 101.

χιλιάς, χίλιοι

A. χιλιάς/χίλιοι in Greek Usage.

The numerical term χίλιοι[1] occurs in Gk. from Hom. (only neut.): χίλια μέτρα, Il., 7, 741; χίλι' ἄρ' ἐν πεδίῳ πυρὰ καίετο, 8, 562; χίλι' (sc. πρόβατα) ὑπέστη, 11, 244; αἰχμοφόροι Περσέων οἱ ἄριστοί τε καὶ γενναιότατοι χίλιοι, Hdt., VII, 41, 1. Thuc., II, 80, 4-7 ref. to χίλιοι ὁπλῖται... χίλιοι Πελοποννησίων, βάρβαροι δὲ Χάονες χίλιοι ἀβασίλευτοι... 'Ορέσται δὲ χίλιοι... χιλίους Μακεδόνων. Diog. L., IV, 37 mentions χιλίας (sc. δραχμάς). In combinations the no. with 1000 can precede or follow: διακόσια καὶ χίλια στάδια, Isoc. Or., 4, 87; τριήρων διακοσίων καὶ χιλίων, Isoc. Or., 4, 93, but: χιλίους καὶ πεντακοσίους τῶν πολιτῶν, Aeschin. Or., II, 77. With 1000, collective words are often sing.: χιλίην... ἵππον, Hdt., V, 63, 3; ἵππος ἄλλη χιλίη ἐκ Περσέων ἀπολελεγμένη, VII, 41. 1; ἵππον ἔχω εἰς χιλίαν, Xenoph. Cyrop., IV, 6, 2; χιλίαν ὁλοκαύτωσιν, 3 Βασ. 3:4.

χιλι- is often used as a prefix. Thus χιλιέτης or χιλιετής denotes the period of 1000 yrs. during which the soul of man journeys acc. to Plat. Resp., X, 615a; 621d. The χιλιάρχης (from Hdt., VII, 81) or χιλίαρχος (from Aesch. Pers., 304) is the leader of 1000 men.[2] Since this is the only word with χιλι- as a prefix in the NT, other terms in this category may be ignored for present purposes.

Multiples of 1000 have the appropriate adv. of no. in front, δισχίλιοι, τρισχίλιοι etc.: δισχιλίην ἵππον καὶ δισχιλίους τοξότας καὶ δισχιλίους σφενδονήτας καὶ δισχιλίους ἱπποδρόμους ψιλούς, Hdt., VII, 158, 4; τρισχίλιαι ἵπποι, Hom. Il., 20, 221; στάδιοι δὲ τῆς ὁδοῦ ἑξήκοντα καὶ ὀκτακόσιοι καὶ τετρακισχίλιοι, Hdt., II, 9, 1.

χ ι λ ι ά ς, χ ί λ ι ο ι. Bibl.: Liddell-Scott, Pr.-Bauer, s.v.; J. W. Bailey, "The Temporary Messianic Reign in the Lit. of Early Judaism," JBL, 53 (1934), 170-187; W. Bauer, Art. "Chiliasmus," RAC, II, 1073-78; H. Bietenhard, "The Millennial Hope in the Early Church," The Scottish Journ. of Theology, 6 (1953), 12-30; also Das tausendjährige Reich² (1955); J. Daniélou, "La typologie millénariste de la semaine dans le christianisme primitif," Vigiliae Christ., 2 (1948), 1-16; A. Gelin, Art. "Millénarisme," Dict. de la Bible, Suppl., 5 (1957), 1289-1294; L. Gry, Le millénarisme dans ses origines et son développement (1904); H. Kraft, Art. "Chiliasmus," RGG³, I, 1651-3; W. Metzger, "Das Zwischenreich. Ein Beitrag z. exeget. Gespräch d. Kirche über den Chiliasmus," Festschr. T. Wurm (1949), 100-118; J. Sickenberger, "Das tausendjährige Reich in d. Apk.," Festschr. S. Merkle (1922), 300-316; J. F. Walvoord, "A-Millennialism in the Ancient Church," Bibliotheca Sacra, 106 (1949), 291-302; A. Wikenhauser, "Das Problem d. tausendjährigen Reiches in d. Apk.," Röm. Quartalschr., 40 (1932), 13-25; also "Die Herkunft d. Idee d. tausendjährigen Reiches in d. Apk.," ibid., 45 (1937), 1-24; also "Weltwoche u. tausendjähriges Reich," Theol. Quart., 127 (1947), 399-417.

[1] Strictly χείλιοι, so, e.g., in Ionic, related to Sanscr. sa-hásra-m "thousand," v. Boisacq, Hofmann, Frisk, s.v. On the ι in Attic χίλιοι cf. Schwyzer, I, 193 [Risch].

[2] χιλίαρχος, cf. also Jos. Ant., 7, 368; 12, 301; 17, 215, is in NT days the Roman tribunus militum, commander of a cohort. χιλίαρχος was also adopted and used as a loan word by the Rabb., cf. Krauss Lehnw., II, 285 f., 546. The word is common for the tribune in the NT, Jn. 18:12; Ac. 21:31-33, 37; 22:24, 26-29; 23:10, 15, 17-19, 22; 24:7 (vl.), 22; 25:23, but cf. Mk. 6:21; Rev. 6:15; 19:18 for higher officers in gen.

The word χιλιάς, [3] gen. χιλιάδος, denotes 1000: πολλέων ... χιλιάδων ὀργυιέων, Hdt., II, 28, 4; πολλὰς χιλιάδας ταλάντων, II, 96, 5; Ξέρξῃ δὲ ... χιλιὰς μὲν ἦν ὧν (sc. τῶν νεῶν) ἦγε πλῆθος, Aesch. Pers., 341 f.; ἐννέα χιλιάδας ἐτῶν, "9 (periods) of 1000 yrs. each," Plat. Phaedr., 256e/257a. The plur. χιλιάδες is also used for a gt. no. beyond computation: αἱ δ' ἀνάριθμοι μήλων χιλιάδες, Theocr., 16, 90 f. ἑκατοντάδας καὶ χιλιάδας βιβλίων, "books in hundreds and thousands," Luc. Hermot., 56.

χιλιάς is manifestly absent from pap. of the Hell. and Rom. period., the only instance being P. Oxy., XVI, 1909 (7th cent. A.D.). For multiples of 1000 we find δισχίλιοι in P. Greci e Latini, 8, 987, 4 (2nd cent. B.C.); Wilcken Ptol., II, 176, 7 (140 B.C.); BGU, VI, 1391, 6 (112 B.C.); τρισχίλιοι BGU, VI, 1345, 4 (100 B.C.); 1353, 4 (3rd/2nd cent. B.C.); τετρακισχίλιοι *ibid.*, 1386, 7 (112 B.C.) etc. [4]

B. χιλιάς/χίλιοι in the Old Testament and Judaism.

1. As regards OT usage the first pt. is that χιλιάς for 1000 occurs more than 250 times in the LXX and when there is a HT original corresponds always to אֶלֶף. χίλιοι is less common and like אֶלֶף means the no. 1000, e.g., χίλια δίδραχμα כֶּסֶף אֶלֶף, Gn. 20:16; χίλιοι ἑπτακόσιοι ἑβδομήκοντα πέντε σίκλοι (shekels), Ex. 39:2 (HT 38:25); ἡ πόλις, ἐξ ἧς ἐξεπορεύοντο χίλιοι, Amos 5:3; τόπος, οὗ ἐὰν ὦσιν χίλιαι ἄμπελοι χιλίων σίκλων, Is. 7:23; χίλια ἔτη ἐν ὀφθαλμοῖς σου (sc. God's) ὡς ἡ ἡμέρα ἡ ἐχθές, ἥτις διῆλθεν, καὶ φυλακὴ ἐν νυκτί, ψ 89:4. χιλιάς is common in lists with numbers: ἡ ἐπίσκεψις αὐτῶν ἐκ τῆς φυλῆς Ρουβην ἓξ καὶ τεσσαράκοντα χιλιάδες καὶ πεντακόσιοι, Nu. 1:21; ἐκ τῆς φυλῆς Συμεων ἐννέα καὶ πεντήκοντα χιλιάδες καὶ τριακόσιοι, Nu. 1:23, cf. 1:25, 27, 29, 31, 33, 35, 37, 39, 41, 43, 46; Ez. 45:1, 3, 5, 6; 48:8-10, 13, 16 (twice), 18, 20 f., 35. The plur. χιλιάδες is often used for very large numbers beyond computation. It is said of God that He shows ἔλεος εἰς χιλιάδας, Ex. 20:6; 34:7; Dt. 5:10; 'Ιερ. 39(32):18. The Psalmist extols the fact that τὸ ἅρμα τοῦ θεοῦ are μυριοπλάσιον, χιλιάδες εὐθηνούντων (blessed), ψ 67:18, and confesses: κρείσσων ἡμέρα μία ἐν ταῖς αὐλαῖς σου (God's) ὑπὲρ χιλιάδας, ψ 83:11. The hosts of ministering angels around God's throne cannot be counted: χίλιαι χιλιάδες ἐθεράπευον αὐτὸν καὶ μύριαι μυριάδες παρειστήκεισαν αὐτῷ, Δα. 7:10. [5]

2. The innumerable angelic hosts are often mentioned in Jewish apocalyptic. Eth. En. 14:22 ref. to ten thousand times ten thousand standing around the throne of God, and in 40:1 the seer reports that he saw thousands of thousands and ten thousand times ten thousand, an innumerable throng, standing before the Lord of spirits. [6] In 10:17 it is said

---

[3] Acc. to Schwyzer, I, 596 f. χιλιάς is a collective and it never lost this sense in antiquity, as may be seen by comparing δισχίλιοι, τρισχίλιοι κτλ. with δύο, τρεῖς κτλ. χιλιάδες for multiples of 1000, the former being 10 times as common as the latter except in Hdt., who has δύο κτλ. χιλιάδες fairly frequently (11 times) and δισχίλιοι κτλ. 60 times. This non-Attic usage stands alone, however, for it does not occur at all in ten Attic orators or Thuc., Aristot., Xenoph., and only once each in Plat. (→ 466, 14 f.), Luc. (→ 467, 5 f.), Plut., De Agesilao, 16 (I, 603c), and Dio C., 68, 2, 1 [Kelber].

[4] On μυριάς in the Roman period cf. P. Tebt., II, 308, 8 (174 A.D.); Pap. Panopolis (ed. T. C. Skeat [1964]), 2, 30 etc. (2nd/3rd cent. A.D.). It was already current in the age of the Ptolemies, cf. P. Greci e Lat., 4, 393, 6 (242 B.C.); Pap. Cairo Zeno, III, 59480, 7 (c. 250 B.C., ed. C. C. Edgar, *Catal. Gén. d. Antiquités Égypt. du Musée du Caire*, 58 [1928]). For multiples of 10,000 we find δύο μυριάδες, Pap. Panopolis, 2, 30, etc., τρεῖς μυριάδες, P. Greci e Lat., 4, 393, 6 (242 B.C.) etc. [Kelber].

[5] The frequency of χιλιάς in the LXX as compared with its paucity among the Gks. is due to the influence of Hbr. Yet LXX expresses thousands from 2000 to 7000 only 27 times by δύο κτλ. χιλιάδες and 117 times by δισχίλιοι κτλ. [Kelber].

[6] Cf. also Sophonias Apc. 1:27 ff. (ed. G. Steindorff, "Die Apk. d. Elias, eine unbekannte Apokal. u. Bruchstücke der Sophonias-Apok.," TU, NF, 17, 3 [1899] 113) and Anon. Apc. 13:2 f. (Steindorff, 57), and cf. the angels of punishment, *ibid.* 4:15 ff. (Steindorff, 41); other ref. in Loh. Apk. on 5:11. In Test. Jud. 4:1 Judah says that with his brothers he pursued 1000 men in battle and slew 200 of them and 4 kings.

to the righteous that they will escape approaching destruction and will live until they bring forth thousands of children. In those days vines will produce wine in superabundance and a measure will bear a thousandfold, 10:19.[7] S. Bar. 29:5 promises that in the Messianic age each vine will have a thousand shoots, each shoot a thousand clusters, each cluster a thousand grapes and each grape will produce a kor of wine. The no. 1000 plays a special role in speculations about the duration of this aeon as it hastens to its close and about the coming age of salvation. Obviously the idea of a cosmic week (→ VII, 19, 22 ff.) lies behind many theories; on this view the world will last for 7000 yrs. all told.[8] Test. Abr. B 7 (p. 112, 2 f.) speaks of 7000 times αἰῶνες that must be fulfilled, and in Ps.-Philo Antiquitates bibl.,[9] 28, 2 we read: *Haec fundamenta erunt hominibus habitantibus in eis annis VII*, the no. 7 denoting seven millennia acc. to Ps. 90:4.[10] In Slav. En. 33:1 the coming 8th millennium is obviously the beginning of the new aeon, while the 7000 yrs. of the cosmic week correspond to the 7 days of the week of creation.[11] PREl, 19 (p. 141) says that God created 7 aeons, six for man's coming and going, the seventh to be completely Sabbath and rest in eternal life.[12] Elsewhere the world is to last 6000 yrs. Thus acc. to bSanh., 97a-b Bar. it was taught in the school of Elias that the world would last 6000 yrs., 2000 without the Torah, 2000 with the Torah, and 2000 as the age of the Messiah.[13] Samaritan eschatology also taught that the world would last 6000 yrs.[14] The length of the future age of the Messiah was also computed differently. Many scribes said 1000 yrs., others 2000, and some 7000 (on the basis of Is. 62:5).[15] If the idea of a Messianic age of 1000 yrs. is found only from the 1st century A.D., it very probably derives from an older tradition[16] acc. to which it was already taught in the pre-Chr. era that the Messianic age would last 1000 yrs.[17]

3. In the Dead Sea Scrolls the no. 1000 is important in the military organisation of the community.[18] This is divided into לאלפית ומאות וחמישים ועשרות, 1 QS 2:21 f., cf. Damasc. 13:1 f. (15:4). Each 1000 has a commander to lead it into battle, 1 QM 4:2; 1 QSa 1:14, 29. The hosts of the elect of God are to be mustered לאלפיהם ולרבואותם with the saints and angels, 1 QM 12:4. The cultic community acc. to Dt. 7:9 is given the promise that those who keep God's commandments will live a thousand generations, Damasc. 7:6 (8:21); 19:1 f. (8:21 f.); 20:22 (9:45).[19]

4. The usage of Jos.[20] corresponds exactly to that in the Gk. world. Ventidius on the instructions of Antonius sent Herod χιλίους ἱππεῖς, Bell., 1, 317. John of Gischala sent τῶν περὶ αὐτὸν ὁπλιτῶν ἐπιλέξας τοὺς πιστοτάτους ἐκ τῶν χιλίων, Vit., 95. 1 Βασ. 18:7 is rendered in Ant., 6, 193 as follows: ὡς πολλὰς Σαοῦλος ἀπώλεσε Παλαιστίνων χιλιάδας ... ὡς μυριάδας Δαυίδης ἀφανίσειε. Multiples are denoted

---

[7] In both instances the Gk. text has χιλιάς.

[8] On the idea of the cosmic week cf. Wikenhauser Weltwoche, *passim;* Str.-B., III, 826 f.; IV, 989-994; Bousset-Gressm., 246 f.; Volz Esch., 143 f.

[9] Ed. G. Kisch, *Publications in Mediaeval Studies,* 10 (1949).

[10] Cf. Wikenhauser Weltwoche, 400 f.

[11] On this difficult passage cf. Volz Esch., 35 and 339; Str.-B., IV, 990; on Barn., 15, 4 → 471, 2 ff. and 15 f.

[12] Cf. Str.-B., III, 687; Volz Esch., 144.

[13] Cf. Str.-B., III, 826; IV, 990; cf. also bAZ, 9a (Str.-B., IV, 991 f.). Further examples from a later time may be found in Str.-B., IV, 991 f.

[14] Cf. Volz Esch., 35 and 143 f.

[15] Examples in Str.-B., III, 824-7.

[16] Cf. Str.-B., III, 827 and Test. Isaac 8:20 (Riessler, 1146): These who have pity on the needy "may participate in the thousand-year banquet from the first hour," cf. Wikenhauser Weltwoche, 400.

[17] χίλιοι and χιλιάς occur as loan words in the Rab., cf. Krauss Lehnw., II, 285.

[18] Cf. K. G. Kuhn, *Konkordanz zu d. Qumrantexten* (1960), *s.v.*

[19] It may be noted that Damasc. 10:21 (13:7) limits a Sabbath's journey to 1000 cubits, but Damasc. 11:5 f. (13:15) allows 2000 to drive a cow outside the city (→ VII, 11, 21 ff.).

[20] Philo has χίλιοι and χιλιάς only in quotations from the OT.

by putting an adv. of no. before χίλιοι: περὶ δὲ δισχιλίους, Bell., 1, 172: δισχιλίους ἐπιλέκτους... δισχιλίους ἱππεῖς, 2, 500; τρισχιλίους τοξότας, loc. cit.; τρισχιλίους... στρατιώτας, Vit., 213; μετὰ τρισχιλίων ὁπλιτῶν, 233; μετὰ τετρακισχιλίων, Bell., 2, 501; τετρακισχίλιοι τὸν ἀριθμὸν ὄντες, Vit., 371; πίπτουσι μὲν πεντακισχίλιοι, Bell., 1, 172; δραχμὰς εἴκοσιν καὶ μυριάδας καὶ πεντακισχιλίας πεντακοσίας, Ant., 11, 16; πεντακισχιλίους ἐξ αὐτῶν ὁπλίτας, Vit., 212; εἰς ἑξακισχιλίους, Bell., 4, 115; περὶ ἑξακισχιλίους τῶν πολεμίων, Ant., 14, 33; τοὺς ὡπλισμένους ὄντας εἰς ὀκτακισχιλίους, Bell., 1, 172.

C. χιλιάς/χίλιοι in the New Testament.

1. In the NT one finds several references to numbers containing χίλιοι and χιλιάς. [21] 2 Pt. 3:8, on the basis of Ps. 90:4, says ὅτι μία ἡμέρα παρὰ κυρίῳ ὡς χίλια ἔτη καὶ χίλια ἔτη ὡς ἡμέρα μία. The size of the herd of swine into which the unclean spirits went was ὡς δισχίλιοι according to Mk. 5:13. [22] In Ac. 2:41 we read that on the day of Pentecost "about three thousand souls" ψυχαὶ ὡσεὶ τρισχίλιαι were added to the community, and then in Ac. 4:4 that ἐγενήθη ἀριθμὸς τῶν ἀνδρῶν ὡς χιλιάδες πέντε. [23] In connection with the miracles of feeding in which Jesus gave food to vast numbers it is said that πεντακισχίλιοι ἄνδρες were satisfied in Mk. 6:44; Lk. 9:14; Mt. 14:21; [24] Jn. 16:10, and cf. Mk. 8:19; Mt. 16:9, and τετρακισχίλιοι in Mk. 8:9, 20 and par. Ac. 21:38 mentions the revolt of the Egyptian who led τοὺς τετρακισχιλίους ἄνδρας τῶν σικαρίων (→ VII, 281, 2 ff.) into the desert. Paul in R. 11:4 refers to the example in the days of Elijah when a remnant of Israel remained faithful and 7000 men would not bow the knee to Baal (1 K. 19:18). The history of Israel also supplies a warning from the fate of the wilderness generation, which provoked God's judgment, so that ἔπεσαν μιᾷ ἡμέρᾳ εἴκοσι τρεῖς χιλιάδες [25] (1 C. 10:8). Lk. 14:31 (→ VI, 514, n. 93) puts the question whether a king planning war against another king will not have to consider first εἰ δυνατός ἐστιν ἐν δέκα χιλιάσιν ὑπαντῆσαι τῷ μετὰ εἴκοσι χιλιάδων ἐρχομένῳ ἐπ' αὐτόν.

2. In Rev. the numbers mentioned in various places have a mysterious significance. This is derived in part from the apocalyptic tradition and in part from the meaning the divine gives traditional materials in the contexts in which he uses them. [26] Rev. 5:11, following Da. 7:10, speaks of μυριάδες μυριάδων καὶ χιλιάδες χιλιάδων who join in praising God → 467, 28 ff. with n. 6. 7:4 gives the number of the sealed as ἑκατὸν τεσσεράκοντα τέσσαρες χιλιάδες → II, 323, 24 ff. This is made up of 12,000 from each of the 12 tribes of Israel (7:5-8) and thus shows that the whole people belongs to God and will be kept under His protection. The Church of both Jews and Gentiles is the possession of God that has this sign and it will be kept safe through all terror and oppression. In 11:3 and 12:6 the divine mentions ἡμέρας χιλίας διακοσίας ἑξήκοντα corresponding to 42 months (cf. 11:2; 13:5) or 3½ years (cf. 12:14). According to Da. 7:25; 12:7 this period,

---

[21] For multiples of 1000 the NT twice has χιλιάς and eight times δισχίλιοι κτλ. [Kelber].

[22] The par. in Mt. and Lk. do not give the number.

[23] On the historicity of these figures cf. Haench. Ag.[14], ad loc.

[24] Mt. 14:21 offers a bigger total when he notes: πεντακισχίλιοι χωρὶς γυναικῶν καὶ παιδίων.

[25] Nu. 25:9 has 24,000, not 23,000.

[26] In relation to the passages mentioned the commentaries should be consulted, esp. Bss., Loh. Apk. and E. Lohse, Die Offenbarung des Joh., NT Deutsch, 11[3] (1971).

which is half of seven, comprises the period of severest affliction which continues and moves to its end according to God's established plan. In the earthquake that will strike the city (→ VII, 336, 19 ff.), ἥτις καλεῖται πνευματικῶς Σόδομα καὶ Αἴγυπτος, ὅπου καὶ ὁ κύριος αὐτῶν ἐσταυρώθη (11:8), ὀνόματα ἀνθρώπων χιλιάδες ἑπτά will be slain (11:13). John sees the Lamb standing on Zion καὶ μετ' αὐτοῦ ἑκατὸν τεσσεράκοντα τέσσαρες χιλιάδες who bear the sign of belonging to the Lamb and His Father (14:1, 3), which distinguishes them from followers of the beast. Here, as in 7:1-8, the reference is to the people of God which will be kept in the place of eschatological preservation (→ VII, 336, 12 ff.) through the terrors of the last time, and will finally be delivered. But the judgment that will come upon the earth will be so terrible that blood from the winepress will rise to the horses' bridles ἀπὸ σταδίων χιλίων ἑξακοσίων (14:20). The heavenly city, new Jerusalem, is of wondrous proportions. It will stretch ἐπὶ σταδίων δώδεκα χιλιάδων and its length, breadth, and height will be equal, 21:16 → III, 344, 1 ff.

3. In Rev. 20 the divine describes how the dragon will be bound for a thousand years (v. 2) ἵνα μὴ πλανήσῃ ἔτι τὰ ἔθνη, ἄχρι τελεσθῇ τὰ χίλια ἔτη (v. 3). But the faithful who are Christ's possession and who have given their lives in testimony to Him will be raised again and will reign μετὰ τοῦ Χριστοῦ χίλια ἔτη (v. 4). Whereas οἱ λοιποὶ τῶν νεκρῶν οὐκ ἔζησαν ἄχρι τελεσθῇ τὰ χίλια ἔτη (v. 5), they are rescued from the second death and will rule with Christ for a thousand years (v. 6). But when τελεσθῇ τὰ χίλια ἔτη, λυθήσεται ὁ σατανᾶς ἐκ τῆς φυλακῆς αὐτοῦ (v. 7). After a final and fearful attack by Satanic forces these will be definitively defeated (8-10) so that after the Last Judgment (11-15) the new world of God can begin (21:1 - 22:5).

The idea of the millennium which the divine works out here is to be understood against the background of the Jewish apoc. traditions that he adopts and uses. In the expectation of an intermediate Messianic kingdom which shall precede the end and the coming reign of God, Eth. En. 91:12 f.; 93:1-14; Sib., 3, 652-660; 4 Esr. 7:28 f.; S. Bar. 29:3; 30:1-5; 40:3, two forms of eschatological hope are combined. [27] Acc. to the older view the Messiah will be the end-time king restoring the Davidic monarchy and raising it to new heights. In apoc., however, a very different concept of the future age of salvation develops. On this view God's envoy will appear from heaven, the dead will rise again at his coming, and all men must come before his judgment-seat. Later an attempt was made to fuse the older national concept with the universal eschatology by putting the reign of the Messiah-King before the end of the world and the beginning of the new aeon. The earthly Messianic age will be for a limited term and it will be followed by a last assault of the powers of chaos prior to the commencement of the future world.

This Jewish idea of an intermediate kingdom found its way into Rev. in Christianised form. For Christian proclamation Jesus is Messiah-King as well as Son of Man; and hence all eschatological expectation is linked to His name. In the intermediate Messianic kingdom the perfected witnesses will reign with Christ and hence they will share His royal rule even before the end.

The suggested duration of the intermediate kingdom varied in Jewish apoc. Acc. to 4 Esr. 7:28 f. the Messiah will reign 400 yrs.; then he will die, and with him all that draw human breath; the dead will then rise again and the Last Judgment will take place. The no. 1000 is probably connected with the idea of the cosmic week, [28] acc. to which world

---

[27] Cf. Volz Esch., 71-77.
[28] Cf. Bietenhard Reich, 44-51.

history will last 6000 yrs. and the cosmic Sabbath will then make up the final 1000 yrs. → VII, 20, 1 ff. This thought is most clearly expressed in Barn., 15, 4, which, on the basis of Gn. 2:2, says that God does everything in 6 days, God's day lasting 1000 yrs. acc. to Ps. 90:4. It thus follows that everything will be fulfilled in 6 days and then God's Sabbath will follow as the 7th day when the Son of God will appear to execute judgment and to initiate the new world, Barn., 15. 5.

John the divine is interested only in the end, in the final 1000 years which constitute the divine measure of the intermediate kingdom, and he addresses to the suffering Church the consoling word that the witnesses who have suffered death will rise again for the millennium. [29]

D. χιλιάς/χίλιοι in the Post-Apostolic Fathers.

In the post-apost. fathers the no. 1000 occurs only in 1 Cl. and Barn. 1 Cl., 34, 6 adduces Da. 7:10 Θ: μύριαι μυριάδες παρειστήκεισαν αὐτῷ, καὶ χίλιαι χιλιάδες ἐλειτούργουν αὐτῷ. 1 Cl., 43, 5 mentions τὰς ἑξακοσίας χιλιάδας τῶν ἀνδρῶν from all Israel. Barn., 15, 4 (→ lines 2 ff.; 468, 11 ff.) quotes ψ 89:4 to prove ὅτι ἐν ἑξακισχιλίοις ἔτεσιν συντελέσει κύριος τὰ σύμπαντα. [30]

Lohse

---

[29] On the further development of the idea of the millennium in the early Church cf. Bauer, 1075-1078; Kraft, 1651-1653.

[30] χιλίαρχοι occurs in 1 Cl., 37, 3 with ref. to military organisation.

χλιαρός → II, 876, 22 ff.

---

† χοϊκός

A. The Greek World.

The word first becomes important, in connection with Gn. 2:7, in Paul, the Chr. Sib., and Gnosticism. Outside this Jewish-Chr. theologoumenon it is attested only in the lexicographers Hesych. and Suid., *s.v.* (Adler, IV, 813, 19) and an anon. Chr. rhetorician, Progymnasmata, 6. [1] We thus have a newly coined term (by Paul?) that is only possible on the basis of the LXX transl. of Gn. 2:7. To be sure, heroes of the primal age of myth, Aesch. Suppl., 250 f.; Hdt. VIII, 55, and those of the seed of the dragons' teeth, Fr. adespotum, 84 (TGF, 855) are called "earthborn" γηγενής. But they existed only in the primal age, [2] whereas now men and animals are begotten and born of one another, Plat. Polit., 269b; Aristot. Gen. An., III, 11, p. 762b, 29 ff. To be distinguished from this is formation from the earth, usually πηλός, as reported of Pandora in Hes. Op., 70 ff., cf. Theog., 571 ff. and of man in gen. in Aristoph. Av., 686. [3] Acc. to Plat. Leg., V, 727e the soul is to be valued more highly than the body, "for nothing earthborn is to be rated more highly than the Olympian."

B. The Old Testament.

1. The creation account in Gn. 2:7 says that Yahweh made man of dust and earth and blew into him the breath of life. Psalms, Job and Qoheleth take up the thought. The word עָפָר "dust" is most commonly used. Man has been raised up out of dust, Gn. 2:7; Job 8:19; Qoh. 3:20. Hence he is dust his whole life long, Gn. 3:19; Ps. 103:14; Qoh. 12:7. [4] Dust is the basis of his life, Job 4:19. He will return to dust, Ps. 22:29; Qoh. 3:20; Job 7:21; 17:16; 20:11; 21:26, cf. 19:25. He will himself become dust again, Gn. 3:19; Job 10:9; 34:15. Once Yahweh withdraws His Spirit, men are only dust, Ps. 104:29. [5] Dust can thus be used as a term for the dead, Ps. 30:9. The fact that man is dust or flesh (cf. Ps. 103:14 with 78:39) shows his frailty and evokes Yahweh's pity.

That אֲדָמָה "earth" should also be adopted from Gn. 2:7 is to be expected. Taken from the earth, man returns to it, Gn. 3:19. When his spirit רוּחַ leaves him, he goes back to the earth, Ps. 146:4 and sleeps in the dust of the earth, Da. 12:2. We also read that man is made of clay חֹמֶר, Job 33:6. Is. 64:7 and Jer. 16:8 carry a rather different stress when the metaphor of the potter and the clay is used to bring out God's absolute sovereignty over man, cf. Job 10:9.

χ ο ϊ κ ό ς . Bibl.: Cr.-Kö., Liddell-Scott, Pass., Pr.-Bauer, Thes. Steph., *s.v.*; E. Brandenburger, "Fleisch u. Geist," *Wissenschaftl. Monographien z. AT u. NT,* 29 (1968); H. M. Schenke, *Der Gott "Mensch" in der Gnosis* (1962).

[1] Ed. C. Walz, Rhetores Graeci, I (1832), 613, 4 f.: Body as χοϊκὸν βάρος.

[2] Cf. also Eur. Ion, 20, 267, 1466, and for Pos. M. Pohlenz, *Die Stoa,* I⁴ (1970), 234.

[3] Cf. also Hes. Fr., 268. But the thought is Orphic, cf., e.g., Orph. Fr., 233 (Kern) [Dihle]. On πηλός → VII, 1036, n. 160.

[4] עָפָר וָאֵפֶר "dust and ashes," Gn. 18:27, cf. Job 30:19; 42:6; Sir. 10:9; 17:32.

[5] In LXX at ψ 103:29 and Qoh. 12:7 we find πνεῦμα with χοῦς, not as that which survives, but as that which slips away back to God, Brandenburger, 61.

2. χοϊκός does not occur in the LXX. To express the fact that man is formed of dust, is dust, and will return to dust, πηλός is sometimes used (→ 472, 13. 31; HT חֹמֶר), but mostly χοῦς Gn. 2:7 (HT עָפָר) and also χῶμα, Job 17:16 (HT עָפָר) or γῆ (→ 472, 19 ff.; HT עָפָר); (→ 472, 28 ff.; HT אֲדָמָה), frequently with the addition καὶ σποδός (→ n. 4). πλάσμα for יֵצֶר (→ lines 24, 28; 475, 31 ff.) occurs only in Ps. 103:14; Isa. 29:16; 45:10 vl. in the sense at issue, but it is used abs. and not yet linked to χοῦς. [6] γηγενεῖς describes all men ψ 48:3 (par. υἱοὶ τῶν ἀνθρώπων), esp. as mortal, Prv. 2:18; 9:18. [7] 'Ιερ. 39(32):20 is worth nothing. Here only non-Israelites are decribed thus. Wis. 7:1 f. goes a step further when it uses the word for Adam as the father of mortals who are formed of flesh in coition and lust. [8] Expressly dualistic is Wis. 9:15: The earthly γεώδης tent weighs down the νοῦς. [9]

C. Judaism.

1. In apoc. the spheres called spirit and flesh from Is. 31:3 are increasingly differentiated as heavenly and earthly → VII, 109, 9 ff. The earthly is corruptible, S. Bar. 48:50; 4 Esr. 7:31; 8:53, [10] and will one day be changed, S. Bar. 49:3. Dwellers on earth can know only what is earthly, the heavenly only what is heavenly, 4 Esr. 4:21. Yet the dust of which Adam was made is itself God's creation, [11] and sin is due to Adam's fall, not to his being made of dust, 4 Esr. 3:4 - 7:21; S. Bar. 48:42-50; 54:19. Nor is the anthropological antithesis of flesh and spirit an essential one here. [12]

2. That man is made of dust עָפָר underscores his limitation in the Qumran texts, 1 QS 11:21; 1 QS Fr [13] 2:4, and even his impurity, 1 QH 12:24-27, cf. 1:21f. He is dust, 1 QH 11:3; 12:25, 27; 18:4, 12, 24, 27, dust and ashes, 1 QH 10:5; 1 QH Fr. 2:7, cf. 3:6, a building of dust (→ VII, 113, n. 125) or a work of dust, 1 QH 18:31; 1 QH Fr. 3:5, 14 (→ line 5 ff.). [14] The word is par. to flesh, 1 QH 15:21 → VII, 111, 23 ff. But God's Spirit has conjoined itself to this dust, 1 QH Fr. 2:9. Hence it can be stressed that God has an eternal goal for his work of dust, I QH 3:20 f. Man, however, will return to (his) dust, 1 QH 10:4, 12; 12:26, 31; 1 QH Fr. 1:4; 4:11, cf. 1 QS 11:22. The term אֲדָמָה "earth" occurs only in 1 QH 10:3 par. to dust and clay. [15] Far more important, however. is חֹמֶר "clay," always in the combination work of clay, [16] 1 QH 1:21b; 3:23 f. etc. (→ VII, 111, 22 ff.) and often par. to dust, 1 QH 12:26; 18:12. It can also be said that God shows His power in dust and what is made of clay, lifting up the worm of the dead from the dust into the community, 1 QH 11:3, 12. More significant is the fact that as flesh or dust and sometimes even as spirit or spirit of flesh (→ VII, 111, 26 ff.; 113, 27 ff.) man has fallen victim

---

[6] The verb πλάσσω occurs in Gn. 2:7.

[7] Test. Jos. 2:5 has γηγενής par. ἄνθρωπος and υἱὸς ἀνθρώπου as the opp. of God, Aristobulus Fr., 4 in Eus. Praep. Ev., 13, 12, 5 (p. 194, 5) calls Moses ὑλογενής; perhaps we should read ὑδογενής. γήϊνος has a different sense in Job 4:19 Σ.

[8] Brandenburger, 106 f.

[9] Cf. Vit. Ad., 27 where ref. to the filth of earth moves God to pity → 472, 25 f.; possibly the ref. to endowment with reason already stands in antithesis, cf. ad loc., C. Fuchs, Kautzsch Apkr. u. Pseudepigr., II, 516 Ab.

[10] All are dwellers on earth, just and unjust, 4 Esr. 6:18. Earth or dust is simply the perishing world in which the dead lie, 7:32.

[11] πλάσμα τῶν χειρῶν αὐτοῦ, Apc. Mos. 37, cf. the same phrase in 4 Esr. 3:5 (→ n. 16) as the earthen vessel from which the righteous will some day be parted, 7:88; 14:14.

[12] There are spirits of heaven and spirits of earth, Eth.En. 15:10, spirits in the soul of flesh, 16:1. We find no pre-existence of soul or spirit, Brandenburger, 78 and on the whole question 60-85.

[13] Ed. A. M. Habermann, Megilloth Midbar Yehudah (1959).

[14] "Work" alone occurs in 1 QH 18:11, 13, perhaps 1 QH Fr. 3:11; 52:3.

[15] If with J. Maier, D. Texte v. Toten Meer (1960), ad loc. we supply חמר [רק] at the end of line 3.

[16] 1 QS 11:22 interpreting in parallelism to "handiwork" → n. 11.

to sin (→ VII, 11, 21 ff.); in this regard spirit usually denotes the man who decides for God but who is not good in himself [17] → VI, 390, 22 ff. One can hardly speak of an antithesis of spirit to flesh and dust in the anthropological sense → VII, 114, 5 ff. [18]

3. χοϊκός does not occur in Philo but we find its full range of meaning in his use of χοῦς.

a. Man is made of dust, Migr. Abr., 3; he is fashioned πεπλασμένος dust, Rer. Div. Her., 58, ashes, 29. In all three passages γῆ is also used. Men and animals are thus earth-born γηγενής, Op. Mund., 69, 82, 156; Spec. Leg., II, 124. 160; Leg. All., I, 79; II, 16; Som., I, 68; Praem. Poen., 9. As already in the OT the earthly is the fleshly, Quaest. in Gn., II, 46 [19] and the bodily, Leg. All., I, 1 etc. With these the earthbound νοῦς, Leg. All., I, 88. 90. 95 [20] can stand in contrast to the πνεῦμα θεῖον → VII, 1052, 22 ff., being given a fleshly nature by the children of earth, Gig., 65. [21] On an OT basis Philo can associate νοῦς, e.g., Leg. All., I, 32 f. [22] or αἴσθησις and λόγος with σῶμα, e.g., 103 → VII, 1052, 22 ff., and ψυχή with σάρξ, e.g., Deus Imm., 2 → VII, 122, 10 ff., [23] though the soul, deriving from the spiritual, is always regarded as relatively superior, cf. Deus Imm., 2 → VII, 1053, 1 ff.; 122, 20 ff. Philo can even say expressly that to the earthly site of the image of God, the body, no soul is given that might see God of itself; only the descending breath of God's deity makes this possible, Det. Pot. Ins., 86. This theory of inspiration acc. to which αἴσθησις and νοῦς, for Philo the ψυχή, yield before the divine logos, is pre-Philonic, Som., I, 118 f., cf. Rer. Div. Her., 265 f. [24] Thus God's πνεῦμα or λόγος stands over against both body and soul → VII, 1052, 17 ff. [25]

The soul's foot, sensuality, is on the ground and its head, purest spirit, reaches up to heaven, Som., I, 146. [26] If the race of those who see is opposed to the earthly νοῦς, the μέσος νοῦς is characteristic of the whole world whose forces tend in both directions, Plant., 45 f. The soul can attach itself to God's enemies, Gig., 66. Yet, called by the logos, it can also freeze everything earthly, bodily, and sensory, and fill itself with heavenly knowledge, Leg. All., III, 168, 172, cf. Som., I, 86. Hence dust and ashes, Conf. Ling., 79, or earth, Leg. All., III, 161, like the body → VII, 122, 20 ff.; 1053, 14 ff., can be set over against the soul, which in this case is equated with the πνεῦμα θεῖον, Op. Mund., 134 f. If we should also give thanks for the physical and sensory life of the earthly body, the νοῦς is the true man in man, the immortal in the mortal, Congr., 96 f. It comes down from above to the soul, which is enslaved in its earthly dwelling, Rer. Div.

[17] Only 1 QH 4:29-31 can ask whether the opposite of flesh, work of clay and sin is God's Spirit, so Maier, op. cit., ad loc., or the spirit created by God for man, so S. Schulz, "Zur Rechtfertigung aus Gnaden in Qumran u. bei Pls.," ZThK, 56 (1959), 164; Brandenburger, 92.

[18] Brandenburger, 86-96 goes a little further, though cf. 96: The flesh, and perverted spirit, 1 QH 3:21, can be purified, and God's power at work in the spirit can aid the flesh. Admittedly a Hell. Jew could take the statements differently, Brandenburger, 95. The two spirits teaching in 1 QS 3:13 ff. is quite different, ibid., 96-99; → VI, 389, 30 ff.

[19] Further texts in Brandenburger, 115.

[20] Cf. ὁ . . . ἐκ τῆς ὕλης (sc. νοῦς), Leg. All., I, 42 and on this Brandenburger, 150 f.

[21] Plut. Gen. Socr., 22 (II, 591d) can say this of some souls but not the νοῦς → VII, 1041, 6 ff.; Brandenburger, 144, n. 4.

[22] Cf. 4 Esr. 7:62; H. A. Wolfson, Philo, I³ (1962), 387 on Leg. All., I, 32.

[23] Cf. Cher., 113: Man is σῶμα and ψυχή and possesses νοῦς, λόγος, αἴσθησις.

[24] Brandenburger, 130-132. 135.

[25] With Brandenburger, 132 f., 141-4 one might regard dualistically orientated Wisdom lit. as a preliminary stage, esp. as πνεῦμα θεῖον and σοφία can be equated, Gig., 22-27. Here anthropological Gk. dualism and the Jewish distinction of God and man as distinct spheres (→ 473, 13 ff.) are already fused, cf. 4 Esr. 5:22: The spirit of understanding enters the soul, linked with the body in 5:14.

[26] Cf. Det. Pot. Ins., 84 f.: The soul's roots are in heaven, so that only man, who walks upright (→ VII, 1036, 22 f.), can be called a heavenly plant, cf. C. Spicq, L'Ép. aux Hb., I, Études Bibl.² (1952), 52 f. On the metaphor cf. Wis. 18:16 (logos); Ps.-Philo Antiquitates Bibl., 12, 8 (ed. G. Kisch, Publications in Mediaeval Stud., 10 [1949]) (Israel).

Her., 268, 274.[27] Thus as σύνθετος χοῦς, flesh, and fashioned statue, man is only a house, burden, and corpse for the soul, Agric., 25; Deus Imm., 150, cf. → VII, 1053, 41 ff.

An important pt. is that the earthly and fleshly is not just corruptible and limited; it is plainly opposed to the heavenly. This νοῦς, the incorporeal, and the soul are equated with heaven, sensuality and the bodily with earth, Leg. All., I, 1; III, 161 f. → n. 61. Only the soul of the wicked is concerned about the earthly (Cain is a labourer, not a farmer), Agric., 22, cf. Migr. Abr., 9; Som., I, 177; Mut. Nom., 34. Vices and passions are at home in what is mean, earthly, and corruptible, Leg. All., II, 89. Cain dwells on earth, Det. Pot. Ins., 163. The ungodly, Edom, is earthly, Poster. C., 101; Migr. Abr., 146; Deus Imm., 144, 148, 159, 166, 180. Thus everything earthly and mortal, the body, is abroad, in Egypt, Conf. Ling., 79-81; Congr., 20; Agric., 64 f. In it dwell the senses and passions that harm the soul, Det. Pot. Ins., 109 f., cf. Plant., 43 f. Because men are flesh, the divine pneuma cannot dwell in them, Gig., 19, 29. Hence everything fleshly must be cut out of the soul, Ebr., 69, and the spirit of the sage, when it returns from the divine, from enthusiasm, to the corporeal and fleshly, becomes man again, Som., II, 232 f.[28] In keeping is the fact that the royal way from everything earthly does not lead aside but upwards to heaven, Deus Imm., 151, 159; Rer. Div. Her., 78 f.; Leg. All., II, 89. Purified souls can mount up from the earthly body to heaven and immortality, while the rest sink back to earth, Rer. Div. Her., 239. This is not limited to the time after death. Some wise men live in heaven, other men are at home in Hades, others again rise and fall between the two, Som., I, 151 f., cf. Rer. Div. Her., 78.[29]

b. Most interesting is the exposition of Gn. 1 f. Philo is primarily concerned with the inbreathed divine πνεῦμα of Gn. 2:7. In Leg. All., III, 161 this is simply related to man's two parts, the body of earth and the soul of aether, the divine particle ἀπόσπασμα. Det. Pot. Ins., 80-84 regards πνεῦμα, the image of God's power, as the substance of the ψυχή, not the soul of flesh but that of mind from νοῦς and λόγος. In Rer. Div. Her., 55 f. the soul of the soul, i.e., the divine πνεῦμα, is contrasted with the fleshly soul.[30] A similar view appears in Op. Mund., 69 (based on Gn. 1:26 f.): The earthly man is God's image, but only in his νοῦς.[31] In ibid., 25, however, he is only a copy of the image. The higher λόγος is the image, the human λόγος, the νοῦς, is the copy, Rer. Div. Her., 230 f.

Acc. to Op. Mund., 134-6 it is not the man who has come into being in God's image (γεγονώς) but only the second and fashioned ([δια]πλασθείς) man of Gn. 2:7 who is a mixture of the earthly and the divine. His body is χοῦς but his ψυχή is πνεῦμα θεῖον.[32] He thus shares both a mortal and an immortal nature. The γηγενής[33] is more

---

[27] Cf. Brandenburger, 155 f. Similar is Ebr., 101, cf. E. R. Goodenough, An Introduction to Philo Judaeus[2] (1962), 151-5.

[28] Cf. Brandenburger, 136 and 142.

[29] The historical background is clearest in Plut. Fac. Lun., 28-30 (II, 943a-945e): Souls loosed from the body rise up to the moon, where demons dwell, and then sink back, or, purified as sheer νοῦς, they rise up to the sun. The νοῦς is as far above the ψυχή as this is above the σῶμα, 28 (II, 943a). The underlying idea of successive stages as the elements become increasingly immaterial is still to be found in Philo. Thus birds are less subject to weakness than land or sea creatures, Cher., 89. Air is between earth/water on the one side and aether on the other, Som., I, 144 f., where we also find Plut.'s theory about the moon, Plut. Fac. Lun., 5 (II, 921 f.). On this whole subj. cf. E. Schweizer, "Die Elemente der Welt Gl. 4:3, 9; Kol. 2:8, 20," Beiträge z. Theol. d. NT (1970), 155-161.

[30] Gn. r., 14, 8 on 2:7 contrasts the spirit of life חיים נשמת and God's resurrecting spirit in Ez. 37:14, cf. B. Schneider, "The Corporate Meaning and Background of 1 C. 15:45b," The Catholic Bibl. Quart., 29 (1967), 463. Perhaps the texts collected by W. C. van Unnik in his "Three Notes on the 'Gospel of Philip,'" NTSt, 10 (1963/64), 467 f. reflect similar Jewish exposition.

[31] The mortal and inferior part of man is made by powers, the λογικόν and ἡγεμονεῦον, the true man, νοῦς, is made by God Himself, Fug., 69-71.

[32] Cf. Jos. Ant., 1, 34.

[33] Of Adam cf. also Abr., 12, 56; Virt., 199, 203 → 472, 7 ff.

glorious in body and soul, however, than all his progeny. [34] As first parent he can also be called πρῶτος ἄνθρωπος, Abr., 56 → 477, 27 ff. Two men are also distinguished in Leg. All., I, 31, 42, 53-55, 88-90; II, 4 f.; the one is heavenly, stamped, brought into being, or made in God's image, while the other is earthly γήϊνον πλάσμα, [35] being formed of χοῦς or γῆ, i.e., what is dispersed, Leg. All., I, 31, or not one, cf. Som., II, 70. [36] Even the latter, however, is not earthly man but his earthly νοῦς made of ὕλη which becomes the true vital ψυχή by inbreathed power, Leg. All., I, 32 f. [37] Only by inbreathed πνεῦμα can the νοῦς or ψυχή know God, I, 37 f. [38] The antithesis of the first, earth-created and bodily man and the second non-bodily man, the type of the new born, is even sharper in Quaest. in Ex., II, 46, cf. Leg. All., I, 5 and → n. 52.

To combine the various statements one might say that the λόγος, i.e., the higher λόγος or idea, is God's image, and the human νοῦς, the man made κατ' εἰκόνα, is its copy, Rer. Div. Her., 231, which is to be equated with the first heavenly man of Leg. All., I, 31; II, 4, [39] earthly man being again the copy. On one side the λόγος itself is ὁ κατ' εἰκόνα ἄνθρωπος, Conf. Ling., 146, while on the other sensorily perceptible man and cosmos is εἰκών of the εἰκών, Op. Mund., 25, namely, of God's λόγος, so that in fact Philo sees only two levels. The upper is λόγος = God's image, or λόγος = heavenly man created in God's image, the lower is earthly νοῦς created in God's image, or sensorily perceptible man. [40]

c. This leads to the idea of two classes of men. Members of the first class live by λογισμός in virtue of the divine Spirit, members of the other by blood and carnal desire, Rer. Div. Her., 57, cf. Leg. All., II, 4 f. etc. (→ 473, 13 ff.; 475, 3 ff.). [41] Or there might be three classes if one considers the middle position of the soul and its possibilities for good or evil → 474, 22 ff. [42] The former view derives from the dualism of the OT and apoc., and esp. that of Wisdom lit. and the Dead Sea Scrolls, while the latter corresponds to the middle position of the ψυχή (→ n. 29) and works in with Philo's ethical interest → line 28 f.

Acc. to Quaest. in Gn., I, 8 the two men were even before Philo interpreted Platonically as invisible idea and sensory concretion. But Philo espouses an ethical view which stresses the mixed character of concrete man as capable of both good and evil. [43] For Philo, then, the idea of man is identical with the εἰκών of God, Leg. All., I, 33, 42, 53 f., 92. Long

---

[34] Cf. Sir. 49:16. The cosmic Adam is of gigantic size, Philo Quaest. in Gn., I, 32, and is assembled from the four quarters, Sib., 3, 25 f., cf. Zosimus, Fr., 49, 6 (Berthelot, II, 231, 1 ff.), cf. Schenke, 52. On the whole subj. cf. E. Schweizer, "Die Kirche als Leib Christi in d. paul. Homologumena," Neotestamentica (1963), 274 f.; Schenke, 127-129.

[35] The first man is made by the πνεῦμα, hence the tree of life that produces everlasting life, the second shares a mixed, earthly body, not ἄπλαστος and ἀπλῆ φύσις, Plant., 44. On the change from ontic to ethical ideas cf. E. Brandenburger, "Adam u. Christus," Wissenschaftl. Monographien z. AT u. NT, 7 (1962), 124-7.

[36] Cf. χοϊκὸς πλασθείς, Sib., 8, 445.

[37] Leg. All., I, 33, 37 speaks of the πνεῦμα, but I, 42 distinguishes the πνοή from it and grants the πνεῦμα only to the νοῦς created in Gn. 1:27.

[38] In Rer. Div. Her., 57 f. the πλάσμα γῆς, πεπλασμένος χοῦς, needs divine help. The different views of Philo, which all use mythical material to describe man's dual character, are well presented in L. Schottroff, "Der Glaubende u. die feindliche Welt," Wissenschaftl. Monographien z. AT u. NT, 37 (1970), 127-130.

[39] Leg. All., II, 4 says plainly that God's image, for which the first man longs, is the original → 420, 27 ff. Cf. Det. Pot. Ins., 87: Even the copy of the original, the soul, is still invisible.

[40] Cf. Brandenburger, op. cit. (→ n. 35), 118 f.

[41] Cf. J. Pascher, "Η ΒΑΣΙΛΙΚΗ ΟΔΟΣ, Der Königsweg z. Wiedergeburt u. Vergottung bei Philo v. Alex.," Stud. z. Gesch. u. Kultur des Altertums, 17, 3/4 (1931), 127-131; E. Bréhier, "Les idées philos et relig. de Philon d'Alex.," Études de philosophie médiévale, 8 (1925), 121 f.

[42] Cf. the earthly, heavenly and divine in Gig., 60 and cf. 12 f.: Souls that descend into the body and immerse themselves in it, or rise up again, or have never descended.

[43] Brandenburger, op. cit. (→ n. 35), 126 f. Cf. H. Conzelmann, Der erste Br. an d. Korinther, Kritisch-exeget. Komm. über d. NT, 5¹¹ (1969), 340.

before Philo wisdom, for him identical with λόγος, [44] was viewed as "God's image," [45] Leg. All., I, 43; Rer. Div. Her., 112; Op. Mund., 25. [46] If Gen. 1:27 is taken to mean "as εἰκών," this supports the idea of the creating of wisdom or *logos* as the original of man, the idea of man, Leg. All., I, 43; Conf. Ling., 146. [47] But the OT had long since understood σοφία as God's πνεῦμα → VI, 371, 3 ff. For Philo this opened the door to an ethical understanding. Hence the origin of the mythology of two men, and the reason for difficulties in Philo's terminology, is not a primal-man myth, but the Platonic tradition and esp. the dualistically influenced σοφία tradition. [48] This produces the harsh differentiation of two classes → V, 537, 23 ff. The first man of Gn. 1:26 f. is then, in Platonic terms, the idea of man, or, in Jewish terms, wisdom or *logos* or God's Spirit, or the spiritual man fashioned thereby. [49] The second man of Gn. 2:7 is the earthly man who has become ψυχή. [50]

4. The development in Judaism is of interest. In some parts of the OT man's origin and end are found in the dust, and this affects his life between. It denotes limitation, weakness, and mortality, but not sin. Man must admit that he is dust, for this moves God to pity. The fact that he was formed thus by God is self-evident and need not be stressed. In Qumran "flesh" is a par. and the idea of sin is present, at least in the context → VII, 112, 13 ff. Also common here is the term "work," which underlines man's fragility in relation to God. In Philo it also proves that the earthly man is of lesser worth than the heavenly man → 475, 31 ff. Now dust is that which man must flee and forsake as enticing and evil. Both Qumran and Philo seem to have their roots in a dualistic Wisdom tradition, and Platonic influences may also be detected in Philo.

D. The New Testament.

In 1 C. 15:47-49 (→ II, 396, 21 ff.; VIII, 471, 13 ff.) the first man Adam is called χοϊκός on the basis of Gn. 2:7. The adjective is not found elsewhere in Greek (→ 472, 4 ff.). Contrasted with the first man is the second man from heaven, [51] Christ (→ V, 528, 25 ff.). Each man founds a race of men, earthly on the one side and heavenly on the other. There is similarity to Philo here → 475, 31 f. The difference is that the heavenly man is now the second man and is thought of christologically → VIII, 470, 24 ff. [52] The opposite of the earthly man is not to be found in man or

---

[44] Leg. All., I, 43 par. Conf. Ling., 146; cf. Pascher, *op. cit.,* 115-7; Wolfson, I, *op. cit.* (→ n. 22), 253-261.

[45] Cf. esp. Wis. 7:25 f.: "Spirit of the power of God, clear effulgence of the glory . . . , reflection . . . , flawless mirror . . . , εἰκών of his goodness." Cf. 2 C. 3:18 - 4:6.

[46] The *logos* is the ideal cosmos, the εἰκών, acc. to which the man of Gn. 1:27 and the whole perceptible cosmos was made. Cf. also Agric., 51 with Deus Imm., 31 f. and also Spec. Leg., III, 83 and 207. Acc. to Som., II, 45 the *logos* is the image and idea acc. to which the cosmos was made, or acc. to Op. Mund., 20 it is the place where all ideas dwell.

[47] In Conf. Ling., 146 the *logos* and in Op. Mund., 134 the idea man is ὁ κατ' εἰκόνα ἄνθρωπος.

[48] Cf. Schenke, 121-4; Brandenburger, 225-7, but not Brandenburger, *op. cit.* (→ n. 35), 122-4.

[49] The πνεῦμα comes only to the first man → 475, 22 ff.

[50] Although Philo does not view ψυχή negatively in this connection, he can relate the psychic that is always open to evil with the fleshly → 474, 19 ff.; cf. Conzelmann, *op. cit.* (→ n. 43), 340 f.

[51] The adj. does not occur in v. 47b, J. Héring, *La première ép. de S. Paul aux Corinthiens, Comm. du NT,* 7 (1949), *ad loc.* If ἐξ οὐρανοῦ ref. to the incarnation, not the *parousia* (but cf. → n. 58), it might denote resistance to a threatening Docetic christology in Corinth. But the word is used without restriction from v. 48b on.

[52] H. D. Wendland, *Die Br. an d. Korinther, NT Deutsch,* 7¹² (1968), on 15:45. Yet one might compare Philo Quaest. in Gn., II, 56, where Noah starts a new humanity like heavenly beings and is a type of the born again → 476, 7 ff. Acc. to Schottroff, *op. cit.,* 142 f., cf. 167-9 the decisive distinction is that Gn. 2:7 is taken negatively, for which there are no par. For Paul unredeemed man is identical with the world. Hence he contends not merely against

his original but comes from without as the gift of Christ. [53] This is still linked with the idea of spheres and corresponding substances, [54] Phil. 3:21 (→ 473, 13 ff.), but Paul's concern is with the filling of being with the Lord, [55] which can be lived out uncontested only in heavenly being. Unlike Philo (→ 475, 31 f.), Paul does not adopt ἔπλασεν from Gn. 2:7; hence he does not emphasise the distinction between created man and uncreated man. This also shows that myths of primal man play no part, nor does the pre-existence of Christ. [56] What counts is an Adam-Christ theology which perhaps has its roots before Paul in a Son of Man christology (cf. also → n. 7). [57] The man from heaven is thus the Christ of the *parousia,* cf. also πνεῦμα ζωοποιοῦν (v. 45). The reference in context is simply to the resurrection. This qualifies Him as the man from heaven → V, 541, 29 ff. [58] As χοϊκός man is differentiated from what the risen Christ already is and what man will one day be through Him. Hence the Pauline thought is close to the Rabbinic juxtaposition of the resurrecting Spirit of Ez. 37:14 and the Spirit of Gn. 2:7 → n. 30.

E. Gnosticism.

In Simon Magus (?) the world-creating εἰκών is equated with the Spirit of God, the seventh power, that hovers over the waters. But it is part of man's twofold being, Hipp. Ref., VI, 14, 3-6. With the two Gn. passages we also find here the duality of κατ' εἰκόνα as Spirit and of what is created καθ' ὁμοίωσιν. Acc. to Iren. Haer., I, 1, 10 (I, 49), cf Cl. Al. Exc. Theod., 50, 1-3 this is ref. in the Ptolemaeans to the material and psychic-divine part of man, while in the Valentinians acc. to Cl. Al. Strom., IV, 13, 90, 3 f. it is ref. to man's psychic and intellectual nature. [59] In the Naassenes we read of πλάσμα along with χοϊκόν or πήλινον, Hipp. Ref., V, 7, 36, this being opposed to the εἶδος or ἄνωθεν ἄνθρωπος from above, V, 7, 30. 36; 8, 13; this leads to the distinction

a purely temporal "pre" but also against the idea of man's twofold nature already comprising divine elements. If in Gnosticism there are par. to the figure of Christ that might even include man's historical freedom of decision, Adam plays no part, *ibid.,* 133-135; conversely there is no Christ figure in Philo, 130.

[53] This concern is found in part in the Wisdom tradition, where, as in Philo, the OT view of *pneuma* is adopted in place of Plato's concept of the ideas → 476, 27 ff.

[54] W. Bousset, *Der erste Br. an d. Korinther, Schr. NT,* II[3] on 15:47, lays one-sided stress on the element of substance.

[55] This adequately denotes the final state in 1 Th. 4:17, cf. Phil. 3:9-11.

[56] E. Schweizer, "Erniedrigung u. Erhöhung bei Jesus u. seinen Nachfolgern," AbhThANT, 28[2] (1962), 67-9; also "Aufnahme u. Korrektur jüd. Sophia-Theol. im NT," *Neotestamentica* (1963), 110-121; Conzelmann, *op. cit.* (→ n. 43), 338-341.

[57] Schweizer Erniedrigung, 112 f.; also Kirche, *op. cit.* (→ n. 34), 272-292; C. K. Barrett, *The First Ep. to the Corinthians, Black's NT Comm.* (1968), 373-7; cautiously also → VIII, 410, 6 ff.; 470, 30 ff. esp. 472, 17 ff.; Schottroff, *op. cit.* (→ n. 38), 133 f. remains sceptical.

[58] Cf. also the qualifications in v. 50, 53 f. Cf. O. Cullmann, *Die Christologie d. NT*[4] (1966), 171-4 (E. T. [1959], 167-170); O. Moe, "Der Menschensohn u. der Urmensch," *Stud. Theol.,* 14 (1960), 123, n. 1; these both relate v. 47b neither to pre-existence nor the *parousia* but take it generally. It is taken to denote eternal deity by E. B. Allo, *Première Ép. aux Corinthiens, Études Bibl.*[2] (1956) on 15:47. The basic question as to the meaning of these apoc. utterances is discussed by W. Grundmann, "Überlieferung u. Eigenaussage im eschatologischen Denken d. Ap. Pls.," NTSt, 8 (1961/2), 16 f. Joh. W. 1 K. on 15:45 thinks both v. 45b and v. 45a must ref. to the creation story, but the ref. is simply to the birth or appearing of the last Adam in the end-time. Thus in R. 11:8 the "this day" of Dt. 29:3 means Paul's own day even though, in v. 3 f., 1 K. 19:10-18 plainly ref. to the time of Elijah, with which that of Paul is simply compared in v. 5a. Conzelmann, *op. cit.* (→ n. 43), *ad loc.* would also take ἐξ οὐρανοῦ as par. to ἐκ γῆς, but it cannot mean "of heavenly substance" and the adj. is first used only in v. 48 f.

[59] Schenke, 120 f. Cf. also Conzelmann, *op. cit.,* Exc. ψυχή on 2:14. The various Gnostic myths about Adam's creation, which describe his dualistic nature and esp. his relative differentiation from the world, may be found in Schottroff, *op. cit.,* 4-41.

of ὑλικοί [60] καὶ χοϊκοί and πνευματικοί, 8, 22 (→ VII, 1086, 19 ff.). Heaven and earth acc. to the Gnostic Justin are to be equated with πνεῦμα and ψυχή, 26, 36. [61] With the concept of the earthy we also find in Of the Nature of the Archons, [62] 135, 17-27 a sharp distinction between above and below, soul and mind. We may compare also the linking of the χοϊκά μέρη (→ 475, 13), which must be cut away, with the lower creation in contrast to the ἄνω οὐσία, or new creation, in the Naassene Sermon, Hipp. Ref., V, 7, 15; cf. Apocr. of Joh. Cod. II, 14, 13 ff. [63] and Satornilus acc. to Iren. Haer., I, 18. [64] In Hipp. Ref., VI, 37, 7 f., [65] however, Valentinus takes a tripartite view (→ n. 29; VII, 1050, 23 ff.), so that in his school the ψυχικοί come between the χοϊκοί and πνευματικοί, Heracleon Fr., 46 [66] in Orig. Comm. on Jn., 20, 24 on 8:44 (p. 359), cf. Fr., 15, ibid., 10, 37 on 2:19 (p. 212). [67] The work The Thought of the Great Power from Cod. VI of Nag Hammadi also has the sequence of the fleshly aeon of Noah, the NT aeon of the soul, and the new and coming aeon. [68] The Coptic Gnostic Apoc. of Paul [69] 20:8 ff; 21:15 ff.; 22:9 f. speaks of the judgment of souls that casts them back into bodies, whereas the apostles as elect spirits are redeemed. [70] The Apoc. of Adam [71] ref. to souls that can know God (83:11-14) or do evil and die (84:2 f., 12-14), but the πνεῦμα of the Gnostic is redeemed from this (76:24-27, cf. 66:21-23; 75:5 ff.). In non-chr. Gnosticism χοϊκός does not occur in Corp. Herm., 1 but we find ὑλικὸν σῶμα in 24, man in God's image in 12, or acc. to the εἶδος of the Ἄνθρωπος in 17, cf. 24, man as twofold, ψυχή and νοῦς, consisting of earth, water, and fire on the one side and aether on the other, 15. 17, [72] also the γηγενεῖς in drunkenness and sleep, 27.

Schweizer

---

[60] The system of the Gnostic Justin uses ψυχικοί for this, Hipp. Ref., V, 26, 32; 27, 3.
[61] Cf. the exposition of Ps. 50:4 in bSanh., 91a b (Str.-B., I, 581): soul and body.
[62] Ed. R. A. Bullard, *Patristische Texte u. Stud.*, 10 (1970). Cf. J. Leipoldt-H. M. Schenke, "Kpt.-gnost. Schr. aus d. Pap.-Cod. v. Nag-Hamadi," *Theol. Forschung*, 20 (1960), 72. Cf. Schenke, 61; Brandenburger, op. cit. (→ n. 35), 95.
[63] Ed. M. Krause-P. Labib, "Die drei Versionen d. Apokr. d. Joh.," *Abh. d. Deutschen Archäol. Instituts Kairo, Kpt. Reihe*, 1 (1962), 14, 28; ὕλη, 15, 9. 25: ψυχικός, 15, 17: σάρξ, cf. Cod., III, 21, 16 ff.
[64] Cf. Schenke, 57 f., 35 f., 96; Brandenburger, op. cit. (→ n. 35), 83-93. In the Gnostic the ψυχή or νοῦς ceases to be earthy χοϊκός and becomes νοερός or ἐπουράνιος, First Book of Jeû, 2 f. (C. Schmidt-W. C. Till, *Kpt.-gnost. Schr.*, I, GCS, 45³ [1959], 258, 12 f.; 259, 16 ff.), cf. becoming earthy as par. to perishing, ibid. 4 (p. 260, 12 ff.) [Kelber]. On the idea of earthly members cf. Col. 3:5 and E. Schweizer, "Die Sünde in den Gliedern," *Festschr. O. Michel* (1963) 437-9.
[65] But this is a comm. of Hipp. on an ambivalent if authentic Fr. If Valentinus wrote the letter to Rheginos this supports a division into Spirit, soul, and body. De resurrectione, 45, 40 - 46, 2 (ed. M. Malinine et al. [1963]).
[66] Ed. W. Völker, "Quellen z. Gesch. d. chr. Gnosis," *Sammlung ausgewählter kirchen- u. dogmengesch. Quellenschr.*, NF, 5 (1932), 83 f. and 70.
[67] ὑλικοί is mostly used, e.g., Cl. Al. Exc. Theod., 56, 3, but χοϊκός occurs in Iren. Haer., I, 1, 10 (I, 49), 14 and probably Cl. Al. Exc. Theod., 54, 2. In Hipp. Ref., VI, 34, 5 f. χοϊκός is synon. with ὑλικός. But χοῦς and ὕλη are distinguished, the body being made of χοῦς and flesh of ὕλη, Iren. Haer., I, 1, 10 (I, 51).
[68] Cf. M. Krause, "Der Stand d. Veröffentlichung d. Nag Hammadi Texte" in *Le origini dello Gnosticismo*, ed. U. Bianchi, *Numen Suppl.*, 12 (1967), 73. For the Nag Hammadi texts, esp. on the soul, cf. Gnosis u. NT, ed. K. W. Tröger (1971), Chapter 1.
[69] Ed. A. Böhlig-P. Labib, "Kpt.-gnost. Apok. aus Cod. V von Nag Hammadi," *Wissensch. Zschr. d. Martin-Luther Univ. Halle-Wittenberg*, Special Vol. (1963).
[70] Cf. First Apoc. of James (→ n. 69), 33:10 f.; 34:23 f.
[71] Ed. Böhlig-Labib, op. cit.
[72] Cf. the γήϊνον σῶμα into which the wicked soul comes, Corp. Herm., 1, 10. 19, the antithesis of γήϊνος Ἀδάμ and φωτεινὸς ἄνθρωπος, Zosimus Fr., 49, 10 (Berthelot, II, 232, 20 f.) and the different view in Syrian Treasure Cave, 3, 2 (Riessler, 945), acc. to which Satan, who will not worship the dust, i.e., the cosmic Adam, is an immaterial being "fire and spirit" and thus belongs to the highest element. Par. for a positive regard for the soul (related to the πνεῦμα) are Corp. Herm., 13, 12 in Cod. VI, 54, 25 ff. of Nag Hammadi, cf. K. W. Tröger, "Mysterienglaube u. Gnosis in Corp. Herm. XIII," TU, 110 (1971), 90 and 101 f. For different views of the soul in Gnosticism cf. Schottroff, op. cit., 17 f., 25-27, 77.

χρῆμα, χρηματίζω, χρηματισμός

---

† χρῆμα.

1. Related to χρή "necessity," "it is inevitable,"[1] the abstr. χρῆμα "something necessary" does not have a neutral sense "thing," as one might think, but rather a factitive "affair," τὴν τελευτὴν παντὸς χρήματος ὁρᾶν "to see the outcome of the matter," Hdt., I, 33, or a quantitative "amount," ὑὸς[2] χρῆμα... μέγα "a huge specimen of a boar," I, 36, 1. It is common in financial contexts, sometimes sing. for "sum of money," ἐπὶ κόσῳ... χρήματι "for how much money," III, 38, 3, and formally in the plur. for "objects of value," πρόβατα καὶ ἄλλα χρήματα "sheep and other goods," Xenoph. An., V, 2, 4, also collectively "wealth," "capital," οἱ τὰ χρήματα ἔχοντες, Xenoph. Mem., I, 2, 45.

2. In the LXX χρῆμα corresponds to various Hbr. words, including כֶּסֶף "money," נְכָסִים "riches," רְכוּשׁ "what is gathered." Jos. 22:8 shows simple pleasure in booty during the Conquest, while Hell. Wisdom lit. displays some aloofness to material wealth, Sir. 5:8; 10:8; 14:3, 5; 21:8 etc.

3. In the NT we once find the singular for "sum of money": Barnabas πωλήσας ἤνεγκεν τὸ χρῆμα, "sold" the field and "brought the money from the sale," Ac. 4:37. The plural is common for "wealth" or "capital." The young ruler who comes to Jesus has many κτήματα "possessions," Mt. 19:22 par. Mk. 10:22; vl. χρήματα. Jesus notes in this regard with what difficulty οἱ τὰ χρήματα ἔχοντες "men of capital" (→ line 10) enter into the kingdom, Mk. 10:23 and par. According to an addition in some MSS he is referring to τοὺς πεποιθότας ἐπὶ χρήμασιν, "those who trust in riches," Mk. 10:24.[3] Simon Magus προσήνεγκεν... χρήματα "brought" the apostles "money" (Ac. 8:18) in the belief that God's gift of the πνεῦμα could be acquired by money, 8:20. Felix expects ὅτι χρήματα δοθήσεται αὐτῷ "that money would be given to him" by Paul, 24:26. The word thus sheds light on the attitude of Jesus and the apostles to wealth → VI, 327, 16 ff. Not money itself, but personal dependence on it and all unworthy use of it are rejected.

4. In early Chr. writings outside the NT χρῆμα occurs only once in a similitude designed to throw light on the joint operation of the goods of the wealthy and the prayers of the poor, Herm. s., 2, 5.

† χρηματίζω.

1. From χρῆμα in the sense of "affair," "business" (→ line 5), χρηματίζω means "to handle a matter" in some way. Class. authors often use it in relation to public author-

---

χ ρ ῆ μ α. Bibl.: G. Redard, "Recherches sur χρή, χρῆσθαι," *Bibliothèque de l'École des Hautes Études, Sciences Historiques et Philol.*, 303 (1953), 82-91; L. Bergson, "Zum periphrastischen χρῆμα," *Eranos*, 65 (1967), 79-117.
[1] Ref. is also made to the epic comparatives χερείων, χέρηες "lesser," Walde-Pok., I, 604; Pokorny, I, 443, but Redard, 11 and Frisk, 1119 reject such etym.
[2] On the character of this gen. cf. Bergson, 110-115; Schwyzer, II, 122.
[3] Cf. Job 6:20 LXX.

χ ρ η μ α τ ί ζ ω. Bibl.: G. Redard, "Recherches sur χρή, χρῆσθαι," *Bibliothèque de l'École des Hautes Ét., Sciences Histor. et Philolog.*, 303 (1953), 91; L. Robert, *Hellenica*, 11 f. (1960), 454-6; J. and L. Robert, "Bulletin épigraphique," *Revue des Études Grecques*, 74 (1961), 214, No. 501; 229, No. 602; 241, No. 725; 75 (1962), 205, No. 307; 211, No. 336.

ities, ἀπεχώρησαν... οἱ 'Αθηναίων πρέσβεις ὕστερον ἐφ' ἅπερ ἦλθον χρηματίσαντες, "after they had ruled on the matters for which they had gathered," Thuc., I, 87, 5.

a. In its vocabulary of government and commerce Hellenism then made of this a gen. expression for official action, "to take up a matter," "to deal with something," "to answer," e.g., ἐ]πέδωκα ἔντευξιν... τῶι στρατηγῶι, ἣν χρηματίσας ἀπέσ[τειλε, "I handed the strategos a petition which he dealt with and forwarded," Pap. Enteuxeis,[1] 75, 9 f. (3rd cent. B.C.). Often the deity is the answering authority, περὶ δὲ τῶν χρησμῶν ἔφησε μὴ χρηματίζειν τὸν θεὸν καθόλου περὶ θανάτου, "in relation to the oracle he said that the deity does not answer any questions about death," Diod. S. 15, 10, 2. A passive can be used for the recipient of instructions, cf. Moses, εἰς τὴν σκηνὴν εἰσιὼν ἐχρηματίζετο περὶ ὧν ἐδεῖτο, "when he went into the tent he was instructed regarding what he needed," Jos. Ant., 3, 212. Linguistic similarity to χράω "to give an oracle," e.g., Hdt., I, 55, 2, and χρησμός "oracle," helped to promote this religious use of the term.

b. The word also denotes public action "to be active under this or that title," i.e., "to appear publicly as something," "to be called officially," e.g., χρηματίζω βασιλεύς "to appear officially as king," Polyb., 5, 57, 2; 30, 2, 4; Μάρκος 'Αντώνιος Δεῖος καὶ ὡς χρηματίζω, "and whatever I am called," P. Oxy., I, 100, 1 (2nd cent. A.D.).[2]

2. In the LXX χρηματίζω in Jer. corresponds to Hbr. דִּבֶּר "to speak," στῆθι... καὶ χρηματιεῖς... ἅπαντας τοὺς λόγους, οὓς συνέταξά σοι αὐτοῖς χρηματίσαι, "stand... and speak... all the words that I command thee to speak unto them," 'Ιερ. 33(26):2; λόγον ἐχρημάτισαν ἐν τῷ ὀνόματί μου, "they have declared a revelation in my name," 36(29):23; γράψον πάντας τοὺς λόγους, οὓς ἐχρημάτισα πρός σέ, "that I have revealed to thee," 37(30):2. The very concrete שָׁאַג "to roar" is twice rendered by χρηματίζω when used of Yahweh in 32(25):30.

3. In the NT we find two Hellenistic developments of χρηματίζω.

a In the infancy stories, the story of Cornelius, and Hb. χρηματίζω expresses the fact that God instructs someone by revelations. We usually find passive forms with a personal subject, the recipient of revelation being an instrument of divine rule. The impartation is often imperative. Thus we read of the wise men χρηματισθέντες κατ' ὄναρ, they were "instructed by a dream" to make a specific journey, Mt. 2:12, cf. Joseph in Mt. 2:22. Then of Cornelius we read ἐχρηματίσθη ὑπὸ ἀγγέλου ἁγίου, he "was instructed by a holy angel" to fetch Peter, Ac. 10:22. Similarly we read of Moses in connection with the institution of OT worship: καθὼς κεχρημάτισται Μωϋσῆς μέλλων ἐπιτελεῖν τὴν σκηνήν, "as Moses was instructed when he was about to make the tent," Hb. 8:5 → line 10. Again, we read of Noah in connection with the building of the ark: χρηματισθεὶς Νῶε περὶ τῶν μηδέπω βλεπομένων, "he was instructed about things as yet invisible" when he made this means of salvation, 11:7. When the impartation is simply designed to enlighten an impersonal construction is used: ἦν αὐτῷ (Simeon in the temple) κεχρηματισμένον ὑπὸ τοῦ πνεύματος, "it was shown to him by the Spirit" (in answer to his prayers), Lk. 2:26.[3] Once χρηματίζω has this sense of revealing in the active, since God's activity is the point and stress is being laid on the obduracy of the Israelites as the recipients: οὐκ ἐξέφυγον ἐπὶ γῆς παραιτησάμενοι τὸν χρηματίζοντα, "they could not escape when on earth they rejected the one (Moses)

---

[1] Ed. O. Guéraud, ΕΝΤΕΥΞΕΙΣ, Publications de la Société Royale Égypt. de Papyrologie, Textes et Documents, I (1931).
[2] Later used like "to be," "to become," Sophocles Lex., s.v.
[3] But D it prefer the personal construction.

who gave instruction" (Hb. 12:25a), or according to another reading: τὸν ἐπὶ γῆς παραιτησάμενοι χρηματίζοντα, "when they rejected the one who gave instruction on earth." [4] The ensuing thought is that this will be the more true of Christians οἱ τὸν ἀπ' οὐρανῶν ἀποστρεφόμενοι, "who reject the one that has come from heaven" (Jesus), 12:25b. In this instance χρηματίζω presents the OT Law as the decree of a sovereign.

b. In two cases χρηματίζω is used of men in the sense of "appearing as something." Around 40 A.D. it came about χρηματίσαι... πρώτως ἐν 'Αντιοχείᾳ τοὺς μαθητὰς Χριστιανούς, "that for the first time in Antioch the disciples were publicly known as Christans," Ac. 11:26 (→ 481, 15; III, 516, 8 ff.). [5] When a married woman, not yet widowed, gives herself to another man, μοιχαλὶς χρηματίσει, "she will be publicly reckoned an adulteress," R. 7:3.

† χρηματισμός.

1. The word is found from Plato but in the sense of "money-making," ἰάτρευσις τε καὶ ὁ ἄλλος χρηματισμός "practice of the healing art and other means of making money," Resp., II, 357c. As a gen. Hell. term for an official or legal act χρηματισμός can mean "official answer or instruction or decree," e.g., τῆς ἐντε[ύ]ξεως καὶ τῆς (!) πρὸς αὐτὴν χρηματισμοῦ τὸ ἀντίγραφον, "the copy of the petition and the answer to it," Ditt. Or., II, 736, 21-23 (2nd/1st cent. B.C.). Religiously it is used for a "divine answer or direction," τῷ δὲ ὀνείρῳ ὅραμα τε καὶ χρηματισμός, "visions and oracular sayings are part of dreams," Artemid. Onirocr., I, 2 (p. 5, 19 f.).

2. In the LXX we find the secular meaning "dispatch," ἐπιδόντες τὸν ὑπογεγραμμένον χρηματισμόν, "when they had delivered the signed dispatch," 2 Macc. 11:17, and also the religious sense of "oracle," for Hbr. אֵשֶׂמ (Prv. 31:1), which means "oracle," in Is. 13:1 but is the name of a people in Gn. 25:14. Once at 2 Macc. 2:4 there is no Hbr. original: χρηματισμοῦ γενηθέντος, "on the basis of a divine direction."

3. In the NT χρηματισμός occurs only once in Paul. Holy Scripture had described (1 K. 19:10, 14) how Elijah ἐντυγχάνει τῷ θεῷ (→ VIII, 243, 31 ff.) "invokes God" against Israel, R. 11:2. Paul goes on to ask: ἀλλὰ τί λέγει αὐτῷ ὁ χρηματισμός; "but what does God's answer tell him?" (11:4a). There then follows the saying about the remnant of Israel (1 K. 19:18) as the content of this χρηματισμός, 11:4b. [1] In spite of the linguistic link between ἐντυγχάνω and χρηματισμός Elijah is thought of, not as an attorney submitting written petitions, nor as a mantic practising incubation, but as a man of God receiving revelations.

4. In the post-apost. fathers God's utterance from the burning bush is called a χρηματισμός "a divine instruction" in 1 Cl., 17, 5. The ref. is to the task that Moses is given.

Reicke

---

[4] p⁴⁶* KLP et al. Mi.Hb.¹², 472, n. 1.
[5] E. Peterson, "Christianus," *Frühkirche, Judt. u. Gnosis* (1959), 64-69; E. J. Bickermann, "The Name of Christians," HThR, 42 (1949), 108-124; C. Spicq, "Ce que signifie le titre de chrétien," *Studia Theologica*, 15 (1961), 69-72 (Bibl.).

χ ρ η μ α τ ι σ μ ό ς. Bibl.: G. Redard, "Recherches sur χρή, χρῆσθαι," *Bibliothèque de l'École des Hautes Études, Sciences Histor. et Philolog.*, 303 (1953), 91; J. and L. Robert, "Bulletin épigraphique," *Revue des Études Grecques*, 75 (1962), 205, No. 307.
[1] Mi.R.¹³, ad loc.

χρηστός, χρηστότης χρηστεύομαι, χρηστολογία	ἔλεος	→	II, 477, 1 ff.
	ἐπιείκεια	→	II, 588, 19 ff.
	μακροθυμία	→	IV, 374, 18 ff.
	φιλανθρωπία	→	107, 1 ff.

† χρηστός.

A. Greek Usage.

1. χρηστός, found from Hdt., I, 41, 2; 42, 2; III, 78, 2 etc.; Aesch. Pers., 228, and origin. a verbal adj. of χρῆσθαι "to take into use," [1] has the basic sense "excellent," "serviceable," "useful," "adapted to its purpose," "good of its kind." [2] The term thus expresses a relation in which the person or thing designated stands to others or to its purpose. This is an essential pt. of difference from ἀγαθός (→ I, 10, 15 ff.). ἀγαθός can also mean "useful" and express a relation, but, as distinct from the chief meaning of ἀγαθός, χρηστός does not denote the good as such in an ideal or formal sense or with ref. to material or immaterial goods. As a relational term χρηστός can have very different meanings. ἡ χρηστὴ μέλιττα in Aristot. Hist. An., IX, 40, p. 624b, 23 is the "worker bee" as opp. to the drone. An οἰκία χρηστή, Plat. Gorg., 504a, is an orderly house as opp. to one that is in disarray μοχθηρά. With foods χρηστός denotes "healthy" or "tasty," e.g., ποτόν, σῖτος, Plat. Resp., IV, 438a. [3] It is told of Phryne: πέμψαντος δέ τινος αὐτῇ τῶν γνωρίμων οἶνον χρηστὸν μέν, ὀλίγον δέ, καὶ λέγοντος ὅτι δεκαέτης ἐστίν, 'μικρὸς ὡς πολλῶν ἐτῶν' ἔφη, Athen., 13, 49 (585e). σφάγια χρηστά in Hdt., IX, 61, 3; 62, 1 are "propitious offerings"; a τελευτὴ χρηστή in VII, 157, 3 is the "favourable outcome of a matter." Bad things can also be described by χρηστός, e.g., a τραῦμα as a "serious wound," Luc. Symposium, 44, or a δῆγμα as a "serious bite," Alex., 55. Often χρηστός and its opp. shed mutual light on the special sense, e.g., χρηστός and πονηρός, Plut. Phoc., 10 (I, 746e); Plat. Prot., 313d, τὸ χρηστόν and τὸ αἰσχρόν, Soph. Phil., 476, χρηστά and λυπρά, Eur. Med., 601. The adj. as noun, usually plur., can have the special sense of "benefit(s)," Hdt., I, 41, 2; 42, 2, "good experiences," Aesch. Pers., 228, "success," "fortune," Eur. Hec., 1227 etc. These examples show that the relation of serviceability or usefulness presupposes or includes a corresponding quality, so that χρηστός can denote the good quality of a thing as such. [4]

2. This explains why, when used of persons, the word can mean "worthy," "decent," "honest," "upright," in a moral sense. Soph. Oed. Tyr., 609 f. says it is not right to regard the κακοί as χρηστοί or vice versa, and Eubulus Fr., 117, 6 ff. (FAC, II, 136) contrasts as κακαί and χρησταί the types of wicked and noble women in epic poetry. One finds the same antithesis in the phrase ἤθη χρηστά, which is first attested for certain in the v. from Menander Fr., 187 (Körte) that Paul quotes in 1 C. 15:33: φθείρουσιν ἤθη χρήσθ' ὁμιλίαι κακαί. ἤθη χρηστά are "good manners," "a good character" in the full sense of moral integrity. Aristot. Poet., 15, p. 1454a, 16 ff. explains it with ref. to the striving for ἤθη as the first goal, ὅπως χρηστὰ ᾖ. In Hell. texts the phrase in the sing. or plur. is a current expression for a "moral way of life" and a "humane disposition,"

χρηστός. Bibl.: J. Ziegler, "Dulcedo Dei," At.liche Abh., 13, 2 (1937); C. Spicq, "Bénignité, mansuétude, douceur, clémence," Rev. Bibl., 54 (1947), 321-339; L. R. Stachowiak, "Chrestotes. Ihre bibl.-theol. Entwicklung u. Eigenart," Studia Friburgensia, NF, 17 (1957).
[1] On χράομαι cf. G. Redard, "Recherches sur χρή, χρῆσθαι," Bibliothèque de l'École des Hautes Ét., Sciences Hist. et Philol., 303 (1953), 11-47.
[2] On χρηστός cf. Redard, op. cit., 98-100.
[3] Cf. Stachowiak, 31, n. 1.
[4] Stachowiak, 24 f. conjectures a pre-literary development of the word from a term of quality to one of relation.

i.e., "a good character" in the full sense, Ep. Ar., 290; P. Oxy., III, 642 (2nd cent. A.D.); XIV, 1663, 11 (2nd/3rd cent. A.D.). As a relational term χρηστός describes a person as "excellent" for a specific function or task. When the Ionians in Hdt., V, 109, 3 swear they will fulfil the military command given to them as χρηστοί they want to show that they are "reliable" and "brave," cf. VI, 13, 2. Xenoph. Oec., 9, 5 says of οἰκέται χρηστοί that they are εὖνοι. A χρηστὸς περὶ τὴν πόλιν is a "worthy" man, Lys., 14, 31. The sycophant who in Aristoph. Pl., 900 claims to be a χρηστός ... καὶ φιλόπολις would be so if he would till the land or learn a respectable trade. With respect to their achievements and significance for the common good the Optimates in Ps.-Xenoph. Ath., I, 4, 6 are called οἱ χρηστοί par. οἱ πλούσιοι, I, 4, and Menander Fr., 534 (Körte) describes τὰ χρηστὰ πράττειν as ἔργον ἐλευθέρου. Sexually the χρηστός is one who makes good use of sex, while eunuchs are οὐ χρηστοί, Hippocr. De genitura, 2 (Littré, VII, 472). When someone is called χρηστός in relation to others, the word has the special sense of "kind," "gentle," "friendly," as in the master-slave relation, Antiph. Fr., 265 (FAC, II, 296); Menand. Mon. 858, 5 or any dealings between men, Menand. Fr., 179b (Körte); Demosth. Or., 59, 2. Plut. Phoc., 10 (I, 746c d) contrasts the χρηστός, described as εὐμενής ("well-disposed") πᾶσι καὶ κοινὸς καὶ φιλάνθρωπος and typified by examples of helpfulness, with the τραχύς ("rough") ... καὶ σκυθρωπός ("surly"). Yet the word does not denote superiority, as may be seen from its more critical and even contemptuous use for "good-hearted," "simple," and even "foolish," Plat. Phaedr., 264b; Theaet., 161a, and also from the ironical address χρηστέ "my dear fellow," Demosth. Or., 18, 318 etc. As early as Soph. Oed. Col., 1014 the word is used of rulers, esp. for their "clemency," "mildness," or "magnanimity," Stob. Ecl., IV, 268, 15-17; Dio. Chrys. Or., 1, 11 ff. 6 Other highly placed persons are also extolled as χρηστοί, esp. chief captains, Soph. Oed. Col., 1430; Aristoph. Thes., 832; Plut. Phoc., 6 (I, 744b). 7 Naturally this was increasingly stylised into a title with no particular ref. to the ἦθος χρηστόν of the one concerned. The same applies to the stereotyped address χρηστέ to the dead on funerary inscr., 8 which is probably to be explained in terms of the commonly related πασίφιλε in the sense of "dear." In gen. τρόπος χρηστός is seen as the result of a man's natural disposition: κακοὺς ἢ χρηστοὺς ποιεῖ ... ἡ φύσις, Aeschin. Or., II, 152. Dio. C., 44, 47, 1 speaks of ἔμφυτος χρηστότης. This disposition enhances the value and effect of other virtues in the one concerned and makes him lovable: φιλεῖ γὰρ πρὸς τὰ χρηστὰ πᾶς ὁρᾶν, Soph. El., 972; ὅταν φύσει τὸ κάλλος ἐπικοσμῇ τρόπος χρηστός, διπλασίως ὁ προσιὼν ἁλίσκεται, Menand. Fr., 570, cf. Fr., 531 (Körte).

3. Χρηστός is also common as a proper name. 9 Thus it is used in Pap. Grenfell, I, 49, 11 (220/1 A.D.) 10 for a ἡγεμών and in an inscr. of Panticapaion, CIJ, I, 683, 5 (1st cent. A.D.) we find Χρηστή for a Jewess. A bishop of Syracuse in the time of Constantine is also called Χρηστός acc. to Eus. Hist. Eccl., X, 5, 21. The name Chrestus for Christ, attested in Suet. Caes. Claudius, 25, may be mentioned in this connection, and also the derived Chrestiani, Tac. Ann., 15, 44, 2. 11 Obviously these are not itacisms (cf.

---

5 Ed. S. Jaekel, Menandri Sententiae (1964).
6 Further examples in Stachowiak, 27, n. 1, 2.
7 Ibid., 28, n. 2. 3. 5.
8 Cf. the mostly Augustan burial inscr. in H. Lietzmann, "Jüd.-gr. Inschr. aus Tell-el-Yehudieh," ZNW, 22 (1923), 280-286, and cf. Gk. funerary poems, ed. W. Peek, Schr. u. Quellen d. Alten Welt, 7 (1960), Index, s.v. χρηστός, also IG, 9, 2; 12, 3. 7, Index, s.v. χαῖρε; IG, 12, 8. 9, Index, s.v. χρηστός.
9 On what follows cf. F. Blass, "ΧΡΗΣΤΙΑΝΟΙ-ΧΡΙΣΤΙΑΝΟΙ," Herm., 30 (1895), 465-470; Bl.-Debr. § 24; Meyer Ursprung, III, 307, n. 1.
10 Ed. B. P. Grenfell, An Alex. Erotic Fr. and Other Gk. Pap. chiefly Ptolemaic (1896).
11 S. Benko, "The Edict of Claudius of A.D. 49 and the Instigator Chrestus," ThZ, 25 (1969), 406-418 rejects the ref. of Suet.'s impulsore Chresto to Christ; he thinks Chrestus was an extremist Jewish leader, a Zealot, in Rome. Cf. also E. Koestermann, "Ein folgenschwerer Irrtum d. Tac.?" Historia, 16 (1967), 460. On Tac. Ann., 15, 44, 2 cf. A. Wlosok, Rom u. d. Christen (1970), 8-12. Wlosok opts for the reading Chrestiani as a well-attested popular name for Christians, 9. Tac. makes a bitter play on this form of the name, 10.

→ 579, n. 546); we have rather a version of Christ's name which Greeks could better understand than the one derived from χρίω. [12]

4. Only in exceptional cases is χρηστός used of the gods. M. Ant., IX, 11 says of them: συνεργοῦσιν, εἰς ὑγίειαν, εἰς πλοῦτον, εἰς δόξαν· οὕτως εἰσὶ χρηστοί. But obviously transferring of the underlying moral virtue of goodness or friendliness to the gods was avoided because of the easily suspicious nature of the virtue, which might be regarded with contempt (→ 484, 18 ff.) and was thus felt to be inappropriate to divine majesty. Plut. Superst., 6 (II, 167e) knows some who resist it with disdain. Only later, then, do we finds statements like Ar. Did. Fr., 29, 5 (→ 109, 12 f.): θεόν, εὐεργετικὸν ὄντα καὶ χρηστὸν καὶ φιλάνθρωπον δίκαιόν τε καὶ πάσας ἔχοντα τὰς ἀρετάς. Cf. the El Kab inscr. in Preisigke Sammelb., I, 158: Ἀνδρόμαχος Μακεδὼν ἀφίκετο πρὸς Ἀμενώθην χρηστὸν θεόν... καὶ ἐμαλακίσθη καὶ ὁ θεὸς αὐτῶι ἐβοήθησε αὐθημερί.

B. The Septuagint and Jewish Literature.

1. The Septuagint.

a. The LXX used χρηστός for various Hbr. words to describe things as "excellent," "genuine," "costly," e.g., figs טוֹב in Jer. 24:2, 3, 5, precious stones יְקָר in Ez. 27:22; 28:13, metal in 1 Εσδρ. 8:56, gold טָב in Da. 2:32. The personal expression ἐγενόμεθα χρηστοί in Ἰερ. 51(44):17, which is based on the Hbr. וְנִהְיֶה טוֹבִים, has in reality an impers. sense "it went well with us" [13] and describes the favourable conditions of the people's life.

b. Mostly the word is used with ref. to persons. Except at Prv. 2:21, where it is used for יְשָׁרִים par. ἄκακοι (HT תְּמִימִים), it is in this sense a transl. of טוֹב, and primarily it takes on the meaning of this word, "serviceable," "useful," corresponding to its purpose," "good." But the relation to personal conduct for which the way had been prepared in class. usage (→ 483, 29 ff.), the ethical sense, esp. "kind" in social ethics, is now predominant. If when Antiochus calls the Jews χρηστοὶ Ἰουδαῖοι in 2 Macc. 9:19 this is largely a matter of courtesy, he obviously wishes to describe the "mildness" and "goodness" of his regime when he calls himself χρηστὸς καὶ ἀγαπώμενος ἤμην ἐν τῇ ἐξουσίᾳ μου in 1 Macc. 6:11. Again, when Evil-merodach shows favour to Jehoiachin in Jer. 52:32, the ref. of ἐλάλησεν χρηστά is to "gracious, friendly words." In ψ 111:5 the οἰκτίρμων (HT חַנּוּן) and κιχρῶν (HT מַלְוֶה) is called an ἀνὴρ χρηστός (HT אִישׁ טוֹב). The χρηστός is thus a man who makes "benevolent" use of the superior position he enjoys in virtue of rank, standing, power, wealth etc.

c. Since in biblical thinking there is not the same sense as among the Gks. of a hiatus between aristocratic superiority and kindly condescension (→ 484, 18 ff.), one may readily see why χρηστός finds its most characteristic use here in worship and praise of God. [14] The cry ἐξομολογεῖσθε τῷ κυρίῳ, ὅτι χρηστός, ὅτι εἰς τὸν αἰῶνα τὸ ἔλεος αὐτοῦ is common in the Psalms and prophets, ψ 105:1; 135:1; Δα. 3:89, cf. ψ 99:4 f.; Ἰερ. 40(33):11, [15] In ψ 51:11 God's ὄνομα is called χρηστόν, and there is also an appeal to His ἔλεος once again (HT חֶסֶד). Even this is χρηστόν in ψ 68:17; 108:21. In these phrases χρηστός (HT טוֹב) and ἔλεος (HT חֶסֶד) mutually explain one another. When in ἔλεος God acts with faithfulness to His covenant promises and to His own nature as

---

[12] We owe this paragraph to Bertram.

[13] Ziegler considers the concrete meaning "we became fat."

[14] χρηστὸς ὑπάρχει interspersed in the depiction of the Creator and World-Ruler has the character of a doxology (Berachah), Sib., 1, 159. It presents Him as the One who stoops graciously to the supplications of sinful creatures.

[15] ψ 117:1 transl. טוֹב in the expression by ἀγαθός.

the covenant God (→ II, 479, 1 ff.) He shows Himself to be χρηστός thereby. Hence one can trust and hope in the κύριος χρηστός, ψ 33:9; Na. 1:7. The individual elements comprised in χρηστός are developed in series such as χρηστὸς καὶ εὐθὴς ὁ κύριος (HT טוֹב־וְיָשָׁר יְהוָה) in ψ 24:8, cf. Dt. 32:4, where God is יָשָׁר (here transl. ὅσιος) and δίκαιος (HT צַדִּיק). ψ 85:5 calls God χρηστὸς καὶ ἐπιεικῆς (→ II, 589, 2 f.) καὶ πολυέλεος, and ψ 144:7-9 adds οἰκτίρμων, ἐλεήμων, μακρόθυμος, but also speaks of His δικαιοσύνη. Later cf. Wis. 15:1: χρηστὸς καὶ ἀληθής, μακρόθυμος καὶ ἐλέει διοικῶν, and 2 Macc. 1:24: φοβερὸς καὶ ἰσχυρὸς καὶ δίκαιος καὶ ἐλεήμων ὁ μόνος βασιλεὺς καὶ χρηστός. [16] But these texts show that the severity which humbles by the Law and which exercises judgment and righteousness is the background and presupposition of χρηστότης, and is indeed contained in it, as stated in ψ 118:39-41, 65-68 and clearly expressed in the phrase τὰ κρίματά σου χρηστά. [17]

2. Philo.

Philo uses χρηστός in the phrase τὰ παρόντα ἀγαθὰ καὶ χρηστά, Spec. Leg., I, 284 in the gen. sense of "good," serviceable." In the common phrase ἐλπὶς χρηστή (also plur.) in Som., II, 94 etc. [18] the special sense of "helpful," "friendly," is already echoed. This is the assured sense when χρηστός is used with φιλάνθρωπος, e.g., Fug., 96 of the διάταξις of Scripture or κοινωνικός, e.g., Spec. Leg., II, 104 of the ἤθη contained in Scripture. In relation to persons χρηστός naturally denotes a prominent virtue and it is commonly explained by other terms like φιλάνθρωπος and ἤμερος, Virt., 182 etc. We read of the man of ἤθη χρηστά "good habits" in Det. Pot. Ins., 38 (opp. ἤθη πονηρά, Virt., 196). If this is said of a proselyte after his conversion, Virt., 182, or if only the χρηστός can be sure of being answered when he calls upon God, Leg. All., III, 215, it is evident that the word has a theological and not just a philosophical thrust for Philo, and is to be viewed in relation to the goodness and friendliness of God, which the righteous seek to emulate. A special expression of the virtue acc. to Spec. Leg., III, 116 is the adoption of exposed children (an ἔργον χρηστόν), while the parents responsible are cynically called χρηστοὶ καὶ περιμάχητοι "highly-esteemed" in Virt., 131. With ref. to rulers and their acts (→ 484, 22 ff.) the word has the more lofty sense of "gracious," as in the phrases χρηστὸς αὐτοκράτωρ in Flacc., 83 and ἀποκρίσεις χρηστότεραι in Leg. Gaj., 333. The ironical aspect and the arbitrary character are not present at all when Philo speaks rather formally of the χρηστὸς θεός. This indicates that God acts in acc. with His name and nature, Leg. All., III, 73; Det. Pot. Ins., 46, and the idea of "kind" or "friendly" is included, or is indeed, as in Mut. Nom., 253, the true meaning, or is established by synon. like φιλάνθρωπος, Abr., 203, or κολάζων δὲ ἐπιεικῶς τε καὶ πρᾴως, Det. Pot. Ins., 146.

3. Josephus.

Jos. uses χρηστός in the gen. sense of "morally good" (opp. πονηρός), as in Ant., 2, 149 for Jacob and 9, 133 for the one who delights in slaying the wicked. He also uses it in the special sense of "kind," "gentle," "benevolent." In 6, 92 the Hebrews beseech Samuel ὡς πατέρα χρηστὸν καὶ ἐπιεικῆ to intercede with God, and in 7, 270 David is certified as having shown himself μέτριος καὶ χρηστός "considerate and friendly" to the house of Saul. Like the Gks. (→ 484, 29 ff.) Jos. regards such conduct as a natural disposition, for he calls Samuel δίκαιος and χρηστὸς τὴν φύσιν in Ant., 6, 294, Ptolemy χρηστὸς δὲ ὢν φύσει καὶ δίκαιος in 13, 114, and David a χρηστὸς καὶ ἥμερος τὴν

---

[16] Stachowiak, 8-18 tries to differentiate more precisely the nuances in the use of χρηστός with ref. to God in the Ps., prophets, and later canonical writings.

[17] Stachowiak, 32 f. thinks the relation of God's goodness to His righteousness, and its basis in His omnipotence and majesty, are further developed and strengthened in Ps. Sol.

[18] Cf. Leisegang, s.v. χρηστός.

φύσιν in 7, 43. But often the word can denote the resultant qualities and effects. Thus Artaxerxes, when he calls Aman a χρηστὸς σύμβουλος, regards him as a good and useful as well as a well-disposed counsellor, Ant., 11, 255. Jacob declares his friendly mind towards Esau through his company χρηστοῖς λόγοις, 1, 330. When Jonathan promises David χρηστὰ καὶ σωτήρια τὰ παρὰ τοῦ πατρός in 6, 212, the ref. is to Saul's friendly disposition and to the favourable destiny which will follow from it. Conversely περὶ αὐτῶν οὐδὲν ἔτι χρηστὸν προσδεχομένων in 14, 354 means that no friendly disposition or happy fate can be expected for Hyrcanus and Phasael, who have been treacherously captured by the Parthians.

C. The New Testament.

1. Lk. 5:39, using a secular proverb with Jewish and Hellenistic parallels, [19] says of the wine (→ V, 163, 12 ff.): ὁ παλαιὸς χρηστός ἐστιν. Paul also introduces the secular use into the NT at 1 C. 15:33 with his quotation of ἤθη χρηστά from Menander (→ 483, 33 ff.). The context shows that what he has in view is a disciplined life which avoids excess → VII, 590, 7 ff.

2. The important and decisive texts for NT usage are those in which God Himself is called χρηστός, "mild," "kind," or "helpful," in His attitude and acts towards men. In this regard the NT follows LXX usage → 485, 34 ff. If it is not without significance that what is praise and veneration in the LXX now has the form of teaching in proclamation or exhortation, [20] the main distinction from the OT is in content. The saying of Jesus that God χρηστός ἐστιν ἐπὶ τοὺς ἀχαρίστους καὶ πονηρούς (Lk. 6:35) has parallels, [21] but in the context of the proclamation of Jesus it has a free and unrestricted sense. For the statement is to be interpreted in the light of the parables of the God who seeks and saves that which is lost (Lk. 15). In the Saviour's call (→ 85, 30 ff.) ὁ ζυγός μου χρηστός in Mt. 11:30 Jesus by His use of this term contrasts His message with that of Judaism and χρηστός contains the fulness of the kindness and friendliness of God manifested in His person and work, [22] → II, 899, 34 ff.

Paul in R. 2:4 uses the neuter of the adjective as a noun, τὸ χρηστόν. [23] Along with the substantive χρηστότης (→ 490, 47 ff.), this describes the ἀνοχὴ καὶ μακροθυμία of God which ἄγει the sinner εἰς μετάνοιαν. ὀργή (→ V, 425, 24 ff.; 432, 24 ff.) for impenitent sinners on the Day of Judgment is the alternative when they despise the χρηστὸν τοῦ θεοῦ. Since in R. 3:26 ἀνοχή (→ I, 359, 31 ff.) denotes

---

[19] In Rabb. lit. one finds the proverbial equation of חמר עתיק and חמרא טבא in Qoh. r., 3 on 3:2 (Wünsche, 41). This also lies behind the teaching in Ab., 4, 20 that one who learns from the aged instead of from children is like a שׁותה יין ישׁן, cf. also Sir. 9:10; S. Lv. בחוקותי, 3 on 26:10 and bBer., 51a. Cf. also the many examples from Gk. and Lat. lit. in Wettstein, ad loc.

[20] Cf. esp. the quotation of ψ 33:9: γεύσασθε ... ὅτι χρηστὸς ὁ κύριος, in 1 Pt. 2:3: ἐγεύσασθε ὅτι χρηστὸς ὁ κύριος.

[21] For Rabb. material cf. Str.-B., I, 374-7. For Hell. lit. cf. Sen. Ben., IV, 26, 1: Si deos, inquit, imitaris, da et ingratis beneficia: nam et sceleratis sol oritur et piratis patent maria.

[22] H. D. Betz, "The Logion of the Easy Yoke and of Rest (Mt. 11:28-30)," JBL, 86 (1967), 10-24, in a critical examination, explains the saying in terms of an origin in Wisdom lit., against the background of its use in Pist. Soph., 95 (p. 140, 19-22) and the Gospel of Thomas 90 (ed. A. Guillaumont et al. [1959]), and acc. to the par. in Mt. 28:18-20 and the Beatitudes.

[23] The ref. may be to the attitude or disposition of kindness and friendliness as an abstract noun, or to concrete action, and even a specific act, in which this finds expression, cf. Bl.-Debr. § 263, 2. As will be seen, both senses are implied in τὸ χρηστόν here.

the time of God's patience or forbearance before the expiation wrought by Christ, one might define the χρηστὸν τοῦ θεοῦ, which has ἀνοχή as its content, as God's gracious restraint in face of the sins of His people in the time prior to Christ. [24] χρηστότης, which is used interchangeably with τὸ χρηστόν in 2:4, occurs again in 11:22. It denotes here salvation for the Gentiles as this is accomplished by Paul's apostolic commission. It has a special reference, then, to God's act of grace effected in and through Christ. A survey of these texts thus yields the result that for Paul the χρηστὸν τοῦ θεοῦ is the gracious action in which God has been constantly engaged, but which He has completed in a special way and a special act, and made universal, in and through Christ. One might almost speak of a particularising in salvation history of what Jesus is talking about in His sayings about the χρηστὸς ζυγός and the χρηστὸς θεός.

The full identity of God's gracious action in the time of the fathers and in Christ is most simply expressed in the quotation (→ n. 20) ἐγεύσασθε (→ I, 676, 25 ff.) ὅτι χρηστὸς ὁ κύριος (1 Pt. 2:3), for here the divine name of κύριος, which is extolled as χρηστός in ψ 33:9, is applied to Christ (→ VI, 559, n. 83). [25]

3. Eph. 4:32, as the context shows, makes God's gracious action towards men in Christ fruitful for the mutual relations of Christians with the admonition γίνεσθε δὲ εἰς ἀλλήλους χρηστοί. [26] Too much stress should not be laid here on the limitations which are to be imposed from the standpoint of primitive Christian christology and soteriology. For the thought does not go beyond the great saying with which Jesus Himself closes His reference to the ὕψιστος χρηστός (Lk. 6:35 f.): γίνεσθε οἰκτίρμονες, καθὼς ὁ πατὴρ ὑμῶν οἰκτίρμων ἐστίν.

D. Early Christian Literature.

1. With an appeal to the promise χρηστοὶ ἔσονται οἰκήτορες γῆς in Prv. 2:21, 1 Cl., 14, 3 f. demands mutual χρηστεύεσθαι → 492, 5 ff. The context shows that imitation of the εὐσπλαγχνία καὶ γλυκύτης of the Creator is in view. In the hymnic words of Wis. 13:1, 60, 1 extols God Himself as χρηστός to them that trust in Him, so that God is generally characterised as One who acts faithfully and reliably, not disappointing or repulsing believers. In Dg., 8, 8 however, predication of God as χρηστός has in view His saving work in Christ, as the Pauline ref. clearly show.

2. From Just. Apol., 4, 1 [27] we find the understanding of Christ as χρηστός and Christians as χρηστοί which the names Christ and Christians suggested to the Greeks: ἐκ τοῦ κατηγορουμένου ἡμῶν ὀνόματος χρηστότατοι ὑπάρχομεν, cf., 4, 5: Χριστιανοὶ γὰρ εἶναι κατηγορούμεθα· τὸ δὲ χρηστὸν μισεῖσθαι οὐ δίκαιον, and Tert. Apol., 3, 5; Nat., I, 3 (p. 63:4-7); Lact. Inst., IV, 7, 4 f. The same applies to the scribe of Sinaiticus, who consistently has Χρηστιανοί at Ac. 11:26; 26:28; 1 Pt. 4:16. One may assume that in this usage the idea of a reflection of the gracious work of God in the life

---

[24] Cf. Zn. R., Ltzm. R., Mi. R.[13], ad loc.
[25] Cf. the discussion in Ziegler, 20 f.
[26] In elucidation cf. Schl. Erl., ad loc., who alludes to Col. 3:12; 2 C. 6:6; Gl. 5:22 → 491, 23 ff. Stachowiak speaks in this regard of a "special obligation to imitate the Father" (92, cf. 98), of a "living reflection of the great act of salvation fulfilled in every Christian," of an "echoing of the goodness of the Father in His adopted children," of the "fruit of consecration in the Holy Spirit," and of "actualisation in apostolic life," 89.
[27] Cf. Blass, op. cit., 468-470.

and nature of Christians (→ 488, 17 ff.) is still active. The Marcionite inscr. in Lebaba south of Damascus (318/319 A.D.) bears witness to a material alteration of Christ to Χρηστός. Conscious rejection of the OT/Jewish χριστός and choice of the divine predicate χρηστός for the Redeemer God explain the action. [28] Another example of the change is an inscr. from Refâdeh in Syria. [29] The referring of LXX quotations in which God is called χρηστός to Christ (→ 488, 13 ff.) is another influence in the interpretation of Christ's name as Χρηστός. This applies esp. to ψ 33:9: γεύσασθε καὶ ἴδετε ὅτι χρηστὸς ὁ κύριος, which in Cyr. Cat. Myst., 5, 20 is an invitation of the eucharistic Christ to the liturgy of the Lord's Supper, and which 1 Pt. 2:3 might possibly have related already to the sacramental gift of Christ. The οἶνον χρηστόν in the Abercios inscr. from Hierapolis in Phrygia, line 16 also points to the eucharistic Christ along the lines of a liturgical use of ψ 33:9. [30] In the Lat. Bible, [31] which often uses *dulcis* and *suavis* for χρηστός, and in Tert., acc. to whom the name *Chrestiani de suavitate vel bonitate modulatum est,* Nat., I, 3 (p. 63, 5 f.), the bibl. concept of the *dulcedo dei* merges into the picture of Christ and Christians. [32]

† χρηστότης.

1. Profane Greek.

In profane Gk. the noun, found from Eur. Suppl., 872, is used only to characterise persons, and, along the lines of the adj., it means a. "honesty," "respectability," "worthiness." With the understanding, it is in Menand. Fr., 535 (Körte) μέγιστον ἀγαθόν, cf. also Ps.-Plat. Def., 412e: χρηστότης ἤθους ἀπλαστία μετ' εὐλογιστίας· ἤθους σπουδαιότης. With ἐπιείκεια, εὐγνωμοσύνη etc. it pursues ἀρετή acc. to Ps.-Aristot. De Virtutibus et vitiis, 8, p. 1251b, 33 f. The formula χρηστότητος οὕνεκα in Aristophon Fr., 14, 4 (FAC, II, 528), cf. Timocles Fr., 8, 17 (*ibid.,* 608) is obviously part of the style of public proclamations of honour. The address ἡ σὴ χρηστότης in P. Giess., 7, 15 (2nd cent. A.D.) is to be taken similarly, cf. P. Lond., II, 411, 16 f. (4th cent. A.D.). It then means b. "kindness," "friendliness," "mildness," whether publicly or privately. The ruler's mildness (→ 484, 22 ff.) is χρηστότης, often paired with φιλανθρωπία and πρόνοια τοῦ κοινοῦ, Dio. C., 73, 5, 2, with σώφρων καὶ ἐπιεικὴς ἐξουσία, Herodian Hist., II, 9, 9. In private life it denotes marital love when used with φιλοστοργία in Plut. De Agide, 17 (I, 802d). Cicero's χρηστότης καὶ φιλανθρωπία acc. to Plut. Comparatio Demosth. cum Cicerone, 3 (I, 887d) was marked by his purity from the vice of avarice. [1] But χρηστότης can also be judged adversely (→ 484, 18 ff.) as false pliability or lack of severity against evil, Menand. Fr., 548 (Körte), or when on closer inspection χρηστότης... καὶ φιλανθρωπία καὶ ὁ πρὸς τοὺς δεομένους ἅπαντας οἶκτος is seen to be ἄνοια καὶ εὐήθεια καὶ ἀκρισία περὶ τῶν φίλων, Luc. Tim., 8 (→ VI, 646, 14 ff.). Hence the sage of older Stoicism is not ἐπιεικής to the culpable, Stob. Ecl., II, 96, 4-9 and rejects χρηστότης in relation to the ἐκ νόμου ἐπιβαλλούσας κολάσεις, Diog. L., VII, 123. [2]

28 Cf. A. v. Harnack, "Die älteste Kircheninschr.," *Aus der Friedens- u. Kriegsarbeit* (1916), 36 f.; also "Marcion. Das Ev. v. fremden Gott," TU, 45² (1924), 343*.
29 Ed. L. Jalabert/R. Mouterde, *Inscr. grecques et lat. de la Syrie,* I (1929), 428; cf. F. J. Dölger, ΙΧΘΥΣ I: *Das Fischsymbol in frühchr. Zeit²* (1928), 250 and II: *Der hl. Fisch in den antiken Religionen u. im Christentum* (1922), 261, n. 4.
30 H. Strathmann-T. Klauser, Art. "Aberkios," RAC, I, 12-17. On line 16 cf. Dölger, ΙΧΘΥΣ, II, 493 as against A. v. Harnack, "Zur Abercius-Inschr.." TU, 12, 4b (1895), 16.
31 Ziegler, 16-45, 63-80.
32 This paragraph is by Bertram.

χ ρ η σ τ ό τ η ς. 1 Further examples in Pr.-Bauer, *s.v.*
2 Cf. Aristot. Eth. Nic., IV, 11, p. 1126a, 1-5 on πρᾶος: ἁμαρτάνειν δὲ δοκεῖ μᾶλλον ἐπὶ τὴν ἔλλειψιν· οὐ γὰρ τιμωρητικὸς ὁ πρᾶος, ἀλλὰ μᾶλλον συγγνωμονικός. ἡ δ' ἔλλειψις, εἴτ' ἀοργησία τίς ἐστιν εἴθ' ὅ τι δή ποτε, ψέγεται. οἱ γὰρ μὴ ὀργιζόμενοι ἐφ' οἷς δεῖ ἠλίθιοι δοκοῦσιν εἶναι...

2. The Septuagint and Jewish Literature.

a. The LXX has χρηστότης with ref. to men only in the complaint of ψ 13:1, 3; 52:4 א: οὐκ ἔστιν ποιῶν χρηστότητα, where it means "piety," "righteousness," and in Est. 8:12c, where it denotes the "mildness" of Ahasuerus as a ruler, → 484, 22 ff. Elsewhere it always occurs in praise of God and apart from 1 Ἐσδρ. 5:58 ἡ χρηστότης αὐτοῦ καὶ ἡ δόξα εἰς τοὺς αἰῶνας παντὶ Ισραηλ exclusively in the Ps. But like the Hbr. originals טוֹב, טוֹבָה, טוּב and טוּב hi the word is equivocal, since it can denote God's "kindly disposition or mode of action" on the one side and the "benefits" or "prosperity" He gives on the other. The latter is the meaning when it is used par. to καρπὸς γῆς, ψ 84:13, τροφή, ψ 103:28, πιότης, ψ 64:12, [3] and also when we read of the χρηστότης τῶν ἐκλεκτῶν as a par. to the εὐφροσύνη τοῦ ἔθνους, ψ 105:5. But when in the par. member God's ἔλεος ψ 24:7; 118:65, δικαιοσύνη, ψ 144:7, or δικαιώματα, ψ 118:68 are praised, we are probably to think in terms of God's gracious disposition and attitude, although the second meaning cannot be completely ruled out. The same applies to εὐλογίαι χρηστότητος in ψ 20:4 and πλῆθος χρηστότητος in ψ 30:20. Again when the χρηστότης θεοῦ is extolled in ψ 67:11 the ref. seems to be to the good things given by Him to the poor.

b. Ps. Sol. makes ample use of the word χρηστότης (as also of χρηστός). It distinguishes sharply between the niggardly and seldom practised goodness of men and the χρηστότης of God, 5:13 f., which finds expression in the plenitude of gifts that God's mercy showers on the earth, and esp. on the righteous (the poor) of Israel, 18:1 f., cf. 2:36. It comes to penitent sinners in the form of forgiveness, 9:7, and God shows Himself χρηστός to those who have been brought to amendment of life by His chastisements, 10:1 f.

c. In Philo we find χρηστότης in lists of virtues alongside εὐθυμία and ἡμερότης, Sacr. AC, 27, or ἡμερότης, κοινωνία, μεγαλόνοια, εὐφημία, Virt., 84, or interchangeably with φιλανθρωπία (→ 110, 29 ff.) in Vit. Mos., I, 249; it forms a hendiadys with this in Leg. Gaj., 73; Spec. Leg., II, 141, here in the sense of "good citizenship." Yet Philo can censure χρηστότης in Agric., 47 when it takes the form of ἐπιείκεια "indulgence," "weakness." In such cases it is βλαβερός for both ruler and subject. If Philo follws Gk. models in this regard (→ 489, 33 ff.), he is on solid LXX ground when he affirms without qualification the χρηστότης θεοῦ → lines 4 ff.

God's dealings with men acc. to Leg. All., III, 73 are motivated by χρηστότης par. ἀγαθότης as distinct from a δυναστείᾳ κράτους αὐτεξουσίῳ χρώμενος. χρηστότης here is an attitude of "goodness and mildness" shown esp. to men, while ἀγαθότης in Vit. Mos., II, 132 characterises the manner of His world-government. God's ἐπιείκεια καὶ χρηστότης (→ II, 589, 20 ff.) imply that He prefers forgiveness to punishment, Exsecr., 166.

d. In Jos. Ant., 11, 144 χρηστότης, which is seldom used of God, means that God in "grace and magnanimity" remits the merited penalty of death. The term is more common in Jos. as an epithet for outstanding figures in history, e.g., those spared in the flood διὰ χρηστότητα "on account of their piety," 1, 96, Abraham, esp. with ref. to his "hospitality," 1, 200, David, who showed pity τῇ χρηστότητι, 7, 184, or Gedaliah and his "benevolent" governorship in Jerusalem, 10, 164.

3. The New Testament.

a. The word is used as a human attribute in R. 3:12 quoting ψ 13:3 → line 2 f.

b. It is used of God only in the Pauline corpus. Here it means the same as the adj., and like it denotes God's gracious attitude and acts toward sinners, both

---

[3] Cod. A reads χρηστότης for πιότης at ψ 103:28.

before Christ in R. 2:4 (→ 487, 29 ff.), where the πλοῦτος τῆς χρηστότητος (θεοῦ) is extolled, and also in and through Christ in R. 11:22 → 488, 4 ff.; VIII, 108, 31 ff. In Tt. 3:4 ff., too, the expression ἡ χρηστότης καὶ ἡ φιλανθρωπία (→ 111, 11 ff.) ἐπεφάνη τοῦ σωτῆρος (→ VII, 1003, 29 ff.) ἡμῶν θεοῦ is elucidated by the description of the fulness of the salvation that has come in Christ, including the eschatological consummation. The latter, depicted as rising again and ruling with Christ in the heavenly world, is also the content of the ὑπερβάλλον πλοῦτος τῆς χάριτος αὐτοῦ ἐν χρηστότητι ἐφ᾽ ἡμᾶς, Eph. 2:7. In the apostolic age, then, the word χρηστότης expressed the comprehensive fulness of Christian salvation and was a full if not very common equivalent of such terms as χάρις (→ 372, 14 ff.), δικαιοσύνη (→ II, 192, 1 ff.) and the like. This is a true development of the LXX use of χρηστός (→ 486, 2 ff.), a use which for its part derives logically from the basic sense of appropriateness → 483, 7 ff. Finally, then, the designation of God's saving work in Christ as χρηστότης implies that this work is appropriate to God. In Christ God acts as the One He is by nature, or, conversely, by His work in and through Christ God is manifested according to His true nature.

c. When Paul commends χρηστότης to Christians in the lists of virtues in his epistles, we do not interpret either this word or the related virtues enumerated with it (→ IV, 383, 14 ff.) correctly if we simply regard them as formulae taken from the Cynic-Stoic tradition and having a general humanitarian content.[4] In them the apostle is in fact expressing the great experience that God's love which is revealed in Christ and shed abroad in the hearts of His people by the Spirit (R. 5:6) works itself out in them as χρηστότης towards their neighbours. In Gl. 5:22 it is thus said to be the καρπὸς τοῦ πνεύματος, in 2 C. 6:6 it is found directly alongside the πνεῦμα ἅγιον, and in Col. 3:12 it is compared with, and based upon, the similar attitude of the κύριος.

4. The Post-Apostolic Fathers.

Dg., 9, 1 f. 6; 10, 4 speaks of the χρηστότης of God in order to give, with the clear help of Pauline ref., a full and comprehensive account of His saving work in Christ. In 10, 4 it is extended to take in also His fatherly acts as Creator, Sustainer, Redeemer, and Consummator. Other writers relate the word to God's kindness in the more general sense of the OT texts → 490, 6 ff., or to individual demonstrations and gifts of grace through Christ. Thus 1 Cl., 9, 1 demands that we submit to the χρηστότης of God which in Christ brought to all the world the grace of repentance promised by the prophets. 2 Cl., 15, 5 relates the χρηστότης θεοῦ to the promise of Is. 58:9 that God is ready to answer prayer, while in 19, 1 it is the goal of Chr. striving and therefore the gen. gift of salvation in Christ in which the Christian longs to share. Ign. again, when he speaks of the χρηστότης of God or Christ, has in mind specifically the salvation accomplished by the resurrection of Christ from the dead, namely, the raising up of those who believe in Him, Mg., 10, 1, or the force of the sacramental σάρξ of Christ achieved thereby, Sm., 7, 1.

† χρηστεύομαι.

1. This word, not found in profane Gk., is first used in Ps. Sol. 9:6: τίνι χρηστεύσῃ, ὁ θεός; where the ref. is to God and what is denoted is His proofs of grace to those who call upon Him.

---

[4] Cf. on this L. R. Stachowiak, "Chrestotes. Ihre bibl.-theol. Entwicklung u. Eigenart," *Stud. Friburgensia*, NF, 17 (1957), 93-8.

2. Paul in 1 C. 13:4 describes Christ's work as χρηστός (→ 488, 17 ff.) and uses the verb χρηστεύεσθαι to express the actualisation of χρηστότης (→ 491, 17 ff.). It is characterised here as a work of love. The use of the term in this setting shows what rank the group occupies in Paul's vocabulary of salvation.

3. In 1 Cl., 13, 2 and Cl. Al. Strom., II, 18, 91, 2 the word occurs in a demand and promise quoted as a saying of the Lord: [1] ὡς χρηστεύεσθε, οὕτως χρηστευθήσεται ὑμῖν, interpreted as ἐπιείκεια and μακροθυμία in 1 Cl., 13, 1. Like the fifth petition of the Lord's Prayer and the sayings in Lk. 6:37 f. the word derives "kind and friendly conduct" to one's neighbour from the goodness and mildness of God. 1 Cl., 14, 3 finds an express basis here for the demand χρηστευσώμεθα ἑαυτοῖς → 488, 25 ff.

† χρηστολογία.

This word is found only in R. 16:18. [1] Paul is here showing that the "friendly speeches and fine words" by which the recipients of the letter are deceitfully wooed are simply a mask for fraudulent purposes.

K. Weiss

χρηστεύομαι. [1] On the relation of this dominical saying to canonical par. from Q in Mt. and Lk. cf. Kn. Cl., *ad loc.*, where it is suggested that a lost apocr. collection is the source, though cf. also W. Michaelis, *Die apokr. Schriften zum NT*[2] (1958), 14, who thinks that we have a free rendering of the sayings in Lk. 6:36-38 and par., which are easily open to variation, rather than the original version of these sayings.

χρηστολογία. [1] The statement *christologum* (vl. *chrest-) eum appellantes, qui bene loqueretur et male faceret* in Script. Hist. Aug. Pertinax, 13, 5 (I, 125) transl. a Gk. χρηστολόγος.

χρίω, χριστός, ἀντίχριστος, χρῖσμα, χριστιανός	→ ἀλείφω, I, 229, 20 ff. → μύρον, IV, 800, 1 ff.

Contents: A. General Usage. B. מָשַׁח and מָשִׁיחַ in the Old Testament: I. General Data. II. The Act of Anointing in the Old Testament: 1. The Verb מָשַׁח and Its Occurrence; 2. Royal Anointing: a. Survey of the Occurrence in the Old Testament; b. Characteristics of Royal Anointing in Israel; 3. Anointing of Other Office-Bearers: a. The High-Priest; b. The Priests; c. Prophetic Office-Bearers; 4. Anointing of Objects. III. מָשִׁיחַ in the Old Testament: 1. Occurrence of the Noun מָשִׁיחַ in the Old Testament; 2. The King as מְשִׁיחַ יְהוָה: a. Survey; b. Saul as מְשִׁיחַ יְהוָה; c. David as מְשִׁיחַ יְהוָה; d. The Davidic King as מְשִׁיחַ יְהוָה; e. Cyrus as מְשִׁיחַ יְהוָה; f. The Fathers as Anointed Ones; 4. The Anointed High-Priest. IV. The Development of Messianic Ideas in Israel: 1. Royal Psalms; 2. Isaiah 9:5 f.; 3. Jeremiah and Ezekiel; 4. Post-Exilic Period: a. Haggai; b. Zechariah; c. Additions to Older Prophets; d. Difficult Passages; 5. Problems of Messianism. C. Messianic Ideas in Later Judaism: I. Linguistic Aspects. II. The Septuagint. III. Apocrypha and Pseudepigrapha: 1. Sirach; 2. Testaments of the Twelve Patriarchs; 3. Psalms of Solomon; 4. Ethiopian Enoch; 5. Syrian Baruch and 4 Esdras; 6. Oracula Sibyllina; 7. Pseudo-Philo; 8. Apocalypse of Abraham. IV. Qumran: 1. References to Two Messianic Figures; 2. The Kingly Messiah; 3. The Eschatological High-Priest; 4. The Two Messiahs; 5. The Teacher of Righteousness; 6. Precedence of the High-Priest. V. Philo and Josephus: 1. Philo; 2. Josephus. VI. Rabbinic Writings: 1. Prayers; 2. The Mishnah; 3. Simon bar Koseba; 4. Justin's Dialogue; 5. Targums; 6. Talmudic Literature and Midrashim; 7. The Messiah ben Joseph. D. The Christ-Statements of the New Testament: I. Occurrence of χριστός in the New Testament. II. χριστός in the Synoptic Gospels and Acts: 1. χριστός in Mark; 2. χριστός in Matthew; 3. χριστός in Luke; 4. χριστός in Acts; 5. The Gospel Titles in Mark and Matthew; 6. The Question of the Messiah in the History of Jesus and the Synoptic Tradition. III. Χριστός in Paul's Epistles: 1. Pauline Usage; 2. The Significance of ὁ Χριστός and Χριστός in Paul's Chief Epistles; 3. Jesus Christ and Christ Jesus in Paul's Chief Epistles; 4. Ἰησοῦς Χριστὸς κύριος and ὁ κύριος (ἡμῶν) Ἰησοῦς Χριστός in Paul; 5. Christ's Significance for Mankind; 6. χρίω in 2 C. 1:21 f.; 7. Χριστός in Colossians and Ephesians; 8. Χριστός in the Pastorals. IV. Χριστός in the Epistles of Peter, James and Jude and in Hebrews: 1. Χριστός in 1 Peter; 2. Χριστός in Hebrews; 3. Ἰησοῦς Χριστός in James, Jude and 2 Peter. V. The Understanding of Christ in the Johannine Writings: 1. The Gospel; 2. The Epistles: a. Christ; b. Antichrist; c. χρῖσμα; 3. Revelation. E. The Christ-Statements in the Writings of the Early Church outside the New Testament: 1. Ignatius of Antioch; 2. Polycarp and the Martyrdom of Polycarp: 3. The Didache; 4. Barnabas; 5. 1 Clement; 6. 2 Clement; 7. Diognetus; 8. Summary.

A. General Usage.

1. χρίω, found from Hom., does not occur in the Attic orators. In Plato we find only a form of ἐγχρίω "to prick" (par. κεντέω) in Phaedr., 251d, which might pt. to a basic sense "to quarrel" → n. 1. The word does not occur either in authentic Aristot. or the

χρίω κτλ. Bibl. Gen.: A. Bentzen, "Messias-Moses Redivivus-Menschensohn," AbhThANT, 17 (1948); L. Cerfaux et al., "L'Attente du Messie," Recherches bibl., 1 (1958); G. Friedrich, "Beobachtungen z. messianischen Hohepriestererwartung in d. Synpt.," ZThK, 53 (1956), 265-311; H. Gressmann, "Der Messias," FRL, 43 (1929); F. Hahn, "Christologische Hoheitstitel," FRL, 83³ (1966); U. Kellermann, "Die politische Messias-Hoffnung

(continued on p. 494, 495 and 496)

comedians apart from Aristoph. Fr., 581 (FAC, I, 730): ὁ δ' αὖ Σοφοκλέους τοῦ μέλιτι κεχριμένου ... But we find it in the tragedians, Hdt., and Xenoph., and also in post-class. prose and non-literary texts. It occurs in several pre-class. and class. dialects and in post-class. usage it is attested in pap. and inscr. as a normal koine word of non-Attic derivation. Ref. might also be made to the LXX, while in the NT it is used only of Jesus and once of His community, 2 C. 1:21. Elsewhere the NT has ἀλείφω (→ I, 229, 30 ff.) and μυρίζω (→ IV, 801, 1 ff.).

χρίω means act. "to rub the body or parts of it," "to stroke it," mid. "to rub or stroke one-self."[1] When used with oils or fats (→ II, 470, 28; IV, 800, 2) it means "to smear," "to anoint," "to anoint oneself." Poison from the robe of Deianira for Hercules χρίει δολοποιὸς ἀνάγκα πλευρὰ προστακέντος ἰοῦ, Soph. Trach., 832 f.; it was rubbed into Hercules' body by the garment. Camels were curried ἐχρίσθησαν, P. Flor., III, 364, 23 (3rd cent. A.D.). Of anointing the body after bathing we read: καὶ ἔχρισεν λίπ' ἐλαίῳ, Hom. Od., 3, 466; 10, 364, λοῦσαν καὶ χρῖσαν ἐλαίῳ, 4, 49, cf. also 6, 96 and 19, 320; 6, 220. For anointing by a deity cf. Od., 18, 193 f., and λοῦσθαι μὲν ὑπὸ τοῦ Διός, χρίεσθαι δὲ ὑπὸ τοῦ Ἡλίου, Hdt., III, 124, 1. It is said of a sick person: καὶ τρίψας μεθ' ὄξους χρῖσον, P. Masp., II, 67141, 2, recto 24 (6th cent. A.D.), and of the anointing of the dead: χρῖσόν τ' ἀμβροσίῃ, Hom. Il., 16, 670, also 680. Aphrodite ῥοδόεντι δὲ χρῖεν ἐλαίῳ ἀμβροσίῳ the dead Hector, Hom. Il., 23, 186 f. Weapons were rubbed with grease or oil, Hom. Od., 21, 179 (ἐπιχρίω); Xenoph. Cyrop., VII, 1, 2, arrows with poison, Hom. Od., 1, 262. Medea says of the robe which she has sent to Jason's bride: τοιοῖσδε χρίσω φαρμάκοις δωρήματα, Eur. Med., 789. The robe of Deianira for Hercules is rubbed with lamb's wool, Soph. Trach., 675 and 689, and birds' wings are rubbed with pitch, Hdt., IV, 195, 2. Transf. we read in Eur. Med., 632 f.: μήποτ', ὦ δέσποιν', ἐπ' ἐμοὶ χρυσέων τόξων ἐφείης ἱμέρῳ χρίσασ' ἄφυκτον οἰστόν, cf. also Plut. Vit. Dec. Orat., 7 (II, 841e); οὐ μέλανι, ἀλλὰ θανάτῳ χρίοντα τὸν κάλαμον, P. Oxy., XII, 1413, 19 f. 24 and XIV, 1665, 5 f. (both 3rd cent. A.D.) use χρίω for "to supply anointing oil." From the basic sense "to rub over" we get such meanings as "to colour," "to white-wash," "to paint," e.g., matted, red-coloured goatskins αἰγέας... ψιλὰς περὶ τὴν ἐσθῆτα θυσανωτάς ... κεχρισμένας ἐρευθεδάνῳ, Hdt., IV, 189, 2.

zwischen d. Test.," Pastoraltheol., 56 (1967), 362-377, 436-448; J. Klausner, The Messianic Idea in Israel (1956); S. Mowinckel, He That Cometh (1956). On B.: K. Baltzer, "Das Ende d. Staates Juda u. d. Messias-Frage," Festschr. G. v. Rad (1961), 33-43; A. Bentzen, Det sakrale Kongedømme (1945); K. H. Bernhardt, "Das Problem d. altorient. Königsideologie im AT," VT Suppl., 8 (1961); P. A. H. de Boer, "De Zoon van God in het OT," Leidse Voor-drachten, 29 (1958); M. Buber, Königtum Gottes³ (1956); H. L. Ellison, The Centrality of the Messianic Idea for the OT (1953); G. Fohrer, "Messiasfrage u. Bibelverständnis," Sammlung gemeinverständlicher Vorträge u. Schr., 213 f. (1957); A. R. Johnson, Sacral Kingship in Ancient Israel² (1967); R. Knierim, "Die Messianologie d. ersten Buches Samuel," Ev. Theol., 30 (1970), 113-133; E. Kutsch, "Salbung als Rechtsakt im AT u. im Alten Orient," ZAW Beih., 87 (1963); D. Lys, "L'onction dans la Bible," Les Études Théol. et Religieuses, 29, 3 (1954), 3-54; M. Noth, "Amt u. Berufung im AT," Gesammelte Stud. z. AT³ (1966), 309-333; H. Ringgren, "König u. Messias," ZAW, 64 (1952), 120-147; also "The Messiah in the OT," Stud. in Bibl. Theology, 18 (1956); W. R. Smith, The Religion of the Semites (ed. 1969), 233, 383 ff.; R. de Vaux, Ancient Israel: its Life and Institutions (1961), pp. 100-114, 372-386; H. Weinel, "משח u. seine Derivate," ZAW, 18 (1898), 1-82; G. Widengren, Sakrales Königtum im AT u. im Judt. (1955). On C.: P. Bogaert, Apoc. de Baruch, I, SCh, 144 (1969), 413-425; J. Brierre-Narbonne, Le Messie souffrant dans la litt. rabb. (1940); also Les prophéties messian. de l'AT dans la litt. juive en accord avec le NT (1933); R. E. Brown, "The Messianism of Qumran," The Catholic Bibl. Quart., 13 (1957), 53-82; also J. Starcky's Theory of Qumran Messianic Development," ibid., 28 (1966), 51-7; M. Burrows, The Dead

---

[1] Hofmann, Frisk, s.v.; this basic sense also made possible development of the sense "to sting," cf. the sting of the bee in Aesch. Prom., 566, 597, 675, 880 and Plat. Phaedr., 251d. χρίω is probably related to Lithuanian grièti "to skim the cream." Throughout section A, I am indebted to E. Risch, A. Dihle and H. Kramer.

2. χριστός, χριστή, χριστόν is a verbal adj. and means "spreadable," "smeared on," "anointed," as noun τὸ χριστόν "ointment," cf. πότερα δὲ χριστὸν ἢ ποτὸν τὸ φάρμακον; Eur. Hipp., 516; Aesch. Prom., 480. ἀρτίχριστον means "fresh ointment" Soph. Trach., 687. χριστός is never related to persons outside the LXX, the NT, and dependent writings.

3. χρῖσμα, also χρῖμα, means "what is spread on, rubbed on," "ointment," used also in medicine "healing ointment," Diosc. Mat. Med., I, 8, 3; 21; 66, 3, also "means of rubbing on," "colour," "whitewash." The word is uncommon, e.g., τοῦτο τὸ χρῖμα, Xenoph. Symp., 2, 4; πῦρ ἔκαιον καὶ ἐχρίοντο· πολὺ γὰρ ἐνταῦθα ηὑρίσκετο χρῖμα

Sea Scrolls (1955), 264 f.; also More Light on the Dead Sea Scrolls (1958), 297-323; A. Caquot, "Ben Sira et le Messianisme," Semitica, 16 (1966), 43-68; J. Carmignac, La règle de la guerre des fils de lumière contre les fils de ténèbres (1958); J. Carmignac-P. Guilbert, Les textes de Qumran, I (1961), passim; M. A. Chevallier, "L'Esprit et le Messie dans le Bas-Judaïsme et le NT," Étud. d'Histoire et de Philos. Religieuses, 49 (1958); J. Coppens, Le Messianisme royal (1968); G. Dalman, Der leidende u. sterbende Messias der Synagoge im ersten nachchr. Jhdt. (1888); R. Deichgräber, "Zur Messiaserwartung der Damask.," ZAW, 78 (1966), 333-343; J. W. Doeve, "Jodendom en koningschap bij het begin onzer jaartelling," Vox Theol., 32 (1961/62), 69-83; A. Dupont-Sommer, The Essene Writings from Qumran (1961), 358-378; I. Elbogen, Der jüd. Gottesdienst in seiner geschichtlichen Entwicklung⁴ (1962), 27-98; K. Elliger, "Stud. z. Habakukkomm. vom Toten Meer," Beitr. z. hist. Theol., 15 (1953), passim; J. A. Fitzmyer, "The Aram. 'Elect of God' Text from Qumran Cave IV," The Catholic Bibl. Quart., 27 (1965), 348-372; C. T. Fritsch, "The So-Called 'Priestly Messiah' of the Essenes," Jaarbericht van het vooraziatisch-egypt. genootschap Ex Oriente Lux, 17 (1963), 242-8; J. Gnilka, "Die Erwartung des messian. Hohenpriesters in d. Schriften v. Qumran u. im NT," Revue de Qumran, 2 (1959/60), 395-426; P. Grelot, "Le Messie dans les Apocr. de l'AT," La Venue du Messie, Recherches bibl., 6 (1962), 19-50; A. Harnack, "Judt. u. Judenchristentum in Justins Dial. mit Trypho," TU, 39, 1 (1913), 73-8; A. J. B. Higgins, "The Priestly Messiah," NTSt, 13 (1966/67), 211-239; S. Hurwitz, "Die Gestalt d. sterbenden Messias," Stud. aus dem C. G. Jung-Institut Zürich, 8 (1958); G. Jeremias, "Der Lehrer d. Gerechtigkeit," Stud. z. Umwelt d. NT, 2 (1963), 268-307; M. de Jonge, The Testaments of the Twelve Patriarchs (1953), 83-96; also "Christian Influence in the Test. of the Twelve Patriarchs," Nov. Test., 4 (1960), 182-235; also "Once More: Christian Influence in the Test. of the Twelve Patriarchs," ibid., 5 (1962), 311-319; also "The Word 'Anointed' in the Time of Jesus," ibid., 8 (1966), 132-148; also "The Role of Intermediaries in God's Final Intervention in the Future acc. to the Qumran Scrolls," Studies in the Jewish Background of the NT, ed. O. Michel et al. (1969), 44-63; B. Jongeling, Le rouleau de la guerre des manuscrits de Qumran (1962), 142-4; K. G. Kuhn, "Die beiden Messias Aarons u. Israels," NTSt, I (1954/55), 168-179; also "Achtzehngebet u. Vaterunser u. der Reim," Wissenschaftl. Untersuchungen z. NT, 1 (1950), 10 f.; 22 f., 41 f.; W. S. LaSor, "The Messianic Idea in Qumran," Festschr. A. Neumann (1962), 343-364; R. B. Laurin, "The Problem of the Two Messiahs in the Qumran Scrolls," Revue de Qumran, 4 (1963/64), 39-52; J. Liver, "The Doctrine of the Two Messiahs in Sectarian Literature in the Time of the Second Commonwealth," HThR, 52 (1959), 149-185 A. Merx, "Der Messias oder Ta'eb der Samaritaner," ZAW Beih., 17 (1909); J. T. Milik, Ten Years of Discovery in the Wilderness of Judea² (1963), 123-8; Moore, II², 323-376; M. Philonenko, "Les interpolations chr. des Testaments des Douze Patriarches et les Manuscrits de Qumran," Cahiers de la RevHPhR, 35 (1960); K. Schubert, "Die Messiaslehre in d. Texten v. Chirbet Qumran," BZ, NF, 1 (1957), 177-197; also "Die Messiaslehre in d. Test. XII im Lichte d. Texte v. Chirbet Quman," Akten d. 24. internation. Orientalisten-Kongresses, München, 1957 (1959), 197 f.; E. Sjöberg, "Der Menschensohn im äth. Henochbuch," Acta Regiae Societatis Humaniorum Litterarum Lundensis, 41 (1946), 140-146; also "Der verborgene Menschensohn in d. Ev.," ibid., 53 (1955), 41-98, 247-273; J. Starcky, "Les quatre étapes du messianisme à Qumrân," Rev. Bibl., 70 (1963), 481-505; also "Un texte messian. aram. de la grotte 4 de Qumran," Mémorial du cinquantenaire 1914-1964, Travaux de l'institut Cathol. de Paris, 10 (1964), 51-66; E. A. Wcela, "The Messiah(s) of Qumrân," The Cath. Bibl. Quart. 26 (1964), 340-349; K. Weiss, "Messianismus in Qumran u. im NT," Qumran-Probleme, ed. H. Bardtke, Deutsche Akad. d. Wissenschaften zu Berlin, Schr. d. Sektion f. Altertumswissensch., 42 (1963), 353-368; A. S. van der Woude, "Die messian. Vorstellungen d. Gemeinde v. Qumran," Stud. Semitica Neerlandica, 3 (1957); M. Zobel, Gottes Gesalbter (1938). On D.: O. Bauernfeind, "Die Worte d. Dämonen im ("fat") ᾧ ἐχρῶντο ἀντ' ἐλαίου, An., IV, 12 f., in magic, P. Lond., I, 121, 873 f. (3rd cent. A.D.): τῷ σεληνιακῷ χρίσματι, cf. 879; χρῖμα occurs, e.g., in P. Oxy., III, 529, 3 (2nd cent. A.D.).

Grundmann

B. מִשַׁח and מָשִׁיחַ in the Old Testament.

I. General Data.

Anointing means the oiling of the body or parts of it by rubbing with grease or oil → 494, 9 f. [2] Anointing that is meant to restore or to enhance physical well-being [3] is to

---

Mk.," BWANT, 44 (1927), 67-109; G. Bertram, "Die Leidensgesch. Jesu u. d. Christuskult," FRL, 32 (1922); alsò "Die Himmelfahrt Jesu v. Kreuz aus und d. Glaube an seine Auferstehung," Festschr. A. Deissmann (1927), 187-217; O. Betz, "Die Frage nach dem messian. Bewusstsein Jesu," Nov. Test., 6 (1963), 20-48; G. Bornkamm, "Christus u. d. Welt in d. urchr. Botschaft," Das Ende d. Gesetzes⁵ (1966), 157-172; W. Bousset, "Kyrios Christos," FRL, 21² (1921); M. Bouttier, "En Christ," Étud. d'Histoire et de Philosophie Relig., 54 (1962); H. Braun, "Der Sinn d. nt.lichen Christologie," Gesamm. Stud. z. NT und seiner Umwelt (1962), 243-282; W. H. Brownlee, "Messianic Motifs of Qumran and the NT," NTSt, 3 (1956/57), 12-30, 195-210; F. Büchsel, "Die Christologie d. Hb.," BFTh, 27, 2 (1922); R. Bultmann, "Die Frage nach d. messian. Bewusstsein Jesu u. das Petrusbekenntnis," Exegetica (1967), 1-9; also "Zur Frage d. Christologie," Glauben u. Verstehen, I⁶ (1966), 85-113; also "Die Christologie d. NT," ibid., 245-267; L. Cerfaux, Christus in d. paul. Theol. (1964); O. Cullmann, Die Christologie d. NT⁴ (1966), 111-137 (E. T. [1959], 111-136); N. A. Dahl, "Der gekreuzigte Messias," Der histor. Jesus u. der kerygmatische Christus, ed. H. Ristow-K. Matthiae (1960), 149-169; also "Die Messianität Jesu bei Pls.," Festschr. J. de Zwaan (1953) 83-95; E. Dinkler, "Petrusbekenntnis u. Satansvort," Signum Crucis (1967), 283-312; J. B. Frey, "Le conflit entre le Messianisme de Jésus et le Messianisme des Juifs de son temps," Biblica, 14 (1933), 133-149, 269-293; G. Friedrich, "Christus, Einheit u. Norm d. Christen," Kerygma u. Dogma, 9 (1963), 235-258; J. R. Geiselmann, Jesus der Christus (1951); J. Héring, "Messie Juif et Messie Chrétien," RevHPhR, 18 (1938), 419-431; E. E. Jensen, "The First Century Controversy over Jesus as a Revolutionary Figure," JBL, 60 (1941), 261-272; H. P. Kingdon, "Messiahship and the Crucifixion," Stud. Evangelica, 3, TU, 88 (1964), 67-86; G. Kittel, "Jesu Worte über sein Sterben," DTh, 3 (1936), 166-189; W. Kramer, "Christos Kyrios Gottessohn," AbhThANT, 44 (1963), 15-59, 131-153, 203-219; E. Lohse, "Märtyrer u. Gottesknecht," FRL, 64² (1963), 113-199, 220-224; H. van der Loos, Jezus Messias-Koning (1942); W. Manson, Jesus the Messiah (1943); T. W. Manson, The Servant Messiah (1953); O. Moe, "Das Priestertum Christi im NT ausserhalb d. Hb.," ThLZ, 71 (1947), 335-8; F. Neugebauer, In Christus (1961), 44-130, 150-181; I. de la Potterie, "L'onction du Christ," Nouvelle Revue Théol., 80 (1958), 225-252; also "L'onction du chrétien par la foi," Biblica, 40 (1959), 12-69; A. E. J. Rawlinson, Christ in the Gospels (1944); also The New Testament Doctrine of the Christ (1926); E. Schweizer, "Erniedrigung u. Erhöhung bei Jesus u. seinen Nachfolgern," AbhThANT, 28² (1962); G. Sevenster, De Christologie van het NT (1946); also Art. "Christologie, I," RGG³, I, 1745-1762; E. Stauffer, "Messias oder Menschensohn," Nov. Test., 1 (1956), 81-102; V. Taylor, The Names of Jesus (1953), 18-23; also The Person of Christ in the NT Teaching (1958); P. Vielhauer, "Ein Weg z. nt.lichen Christologie?" Aufsätze z. NT, Theol. Bücherei, 31 (1965), 141-198; also "Zur Frage d. christolog. Hoheitstitel," ThLZ, 90 (1965), 569-588; also "Erwägungen z. Christologie d. Mk," Aufs. z. NT, Theol. Bücherei, 39 (1965), 199-214; A. Vögtle, "Messiasbekenntnis u. Petrusverheissung," Das Ev. u. die Evangelien (1971), 137-170; H. Windisch, "Z. Christologie d. Past.," ZNW, 34 (1935), 213-238; W. Wrede, Das Messiasgeheimnis in d. Ev. (1901).

[2] In connection with anointing the OT always uses שֶׁמֶן for the oil, avoiding יִצְהָר.

[3] The oil prevents inflammation and thus has a healing effect, so that it is used by doctors both prophylactically and also therapeutically, Dalman Arbeit, IV, 262; Jos. Ant., 17, 172; B. Meissner, Babylonien u. Assyrien, II, Kulturgesch. Bibliothek, I, 4 (1925), 312; H. Grapow, Von den medizinischen Texten (1955), 51 f. It shows its healing power esp. on the dead by giving them new life, H. Bonnet, Art. "Salben," Reallex. d. ägypt. Religionsgesch. (1952), 647 f. The gen. power of oil is also realised, B. Meissner, Bab. u. Assyr., I, Kulturgesch. Bibliothek, I, 3 (1920), 243. Oil is also used to cleanse, Dalman Arbeit, IV, 265, n. 3. It promotes well-being; for Israel cf. Is. 1:6; 2 Ch. 28:15; Lk. 10:34; for the high value set on it Dt. 28:40; Mi. 6:15. In greater detail → II, 470, 29 ff., esp. 472, 38 ff.; Kutsch, 1-6.

be distinguished from anointing understood as a legal action. Acc. to the witness of the OT the latter involves pouring oil over the head of the one concerned. [4] An act of anointing is thus linked with the cleansing purpose. [5] The aim is to give to the one anointed כָּבוֹד power, strength, or majesty.

Among the Hittites one of the rites at the king's enthronement is his anointing. [6] This confers on him the ability to rule. [7] Sometimes there is ref. to the anointing of the king as priest; its basic significance is the same. [8] The rite is performed by the people, i.e., by its representatives, the nobility and the levy. [9] The oil of crowning which the new ruler can expect as a gift of homage on his accession is probably not itself used for the anointing. [10] The Assyrians and Babylonians seem not to have been acquainted with the rite of royal anointing. [11] Nor do we hear of any anointing of the Egypt. king at his enthronement, [12] though he himself anoints high officials at their institution into office. The vassal princes of Syria and Canaan were similarly anointed, [13] and the anointing has amongst other things validity for heirs to the throne. [14] The rite of anointing seems to have been practised, too, in some of the city states of Canaan, including Jebusite Jerusalem. [15] Not so certain is whether the rite was also known in the Aramaean state of Damascus. [16]

II. The Act of Anointing in the Old Testament.

1. The Verb מָשַׁח and Its Occurrence. [17]

The verb מָשַׁח occurs in the Masoretic text some 69 times, chiefly in the q (64 times), and only 5 times in ni forms. The root מָשַׁח seems not to be original at 2 S. 3:39. Both text and meaning are uncertain at Is. 21:5. One should perhaps read מָשׁוּחַ at 2 S. 1:21. For the difficult יְשַׂמְּחוּ־מֶלֶךְ at Hos. 7:3 יִמְשְׁחוּ מְלָכִים has been proposed. [18] If the longer LXX and Vg. text is original at 1 S. 10:1, מָשַׁח occurs twice here. The sense of מָשַׁח q is trans.; only at Am. 6:6 is יִמְשְׁחוּ to be taken as a refl. לְ with inf. [19] denotes the meaning, result, or effect of the action. The office into which anointing institutes can also be added with לְ. [20] Instead of לְ with noun or inf. וְ with finite verb is also found. [21] When the inf.

---

[4] Hbr. distinguishes the uses of anointing linguistically, reserving מָשַׁח for the legal act except at Amos 6:6; Ps. 45:7, where it is connected with care of the body, and the textually difficult 2 S. 1:21 and Is. 21:5 where it is connected with the oiling (anointing?) of a shield; on the latter → n. 48.

[5] For examples and their interpretation cf. Kutsch, 16-33.

[6] Cf. A. Goetze, Kulturgesch. d. Alten Orients, III, 1: Kleinasien, Hndbch. AW, III, 1, 3 (1957), 90, n. 3 with ref. to, and partial transl. of, the cuneiform tablets of Boghazköi, 24, ed. A. Walther (1930), No. 5, 19 ff.; 9, ed. H. Ehelolf (1923), No. 13, 7 ff.

[7] Kutsch, 37 for examples and interpretation.

[8] Ibid., 36 f.

[9] Ibid., 38 f.

[10] Ibid., 66-69.

[11] Ibid., 40 f.

[12] Ibid., 41-52 for a discussion of the problem.

[13] Ibid., 34 f.

[14] Ibid., 35.

[15] But cf. de Vaux, 104 and 347.

[16] One might deduce this from 1 K. 19:15, but this is doubtful in view of 2 K. 8:7-15 and is also historically improbable.

[17] Cf. the survey in Weinel, 1-5.

[18] Cf. J. Wellhausen, Die kleinen Propheten⁴ (1963), ad loc., but in opposition cf. H. W. Wolff, Dodekapropheten 1, Hosea, Bibl. Komm. AT, 14, 1² (1965) and W. Rudolph, Hosea, Komm. AT, 13, 1 (1966), ad loc.

[19] לְקָדְּשׁוֹ Ex. 29:36; Lv. 8:11 f.; לְהַכְרִית 2 Ch. 22:7; לְכַהֵן Ex. 30:30; Lv. 16:32.

[20] לְכֹהֵן 1 Ch. 29:22; לְנָגִיד 1 S. 9:16; 10:1 (twice?); 1 Ch. 29:22; לְמֶלֶךְ Ju. 9:15; 1 S. 15:1, 17; 2 S. 2:4, 7; 12:7; 1 K. 1:34, 45; 5:15; 19:15 f.; 2 K. 9:3, 6, 12; 1 Ch. 11:3; 14:8.

[21] וְקִדַּשְׁתָּ . . . וּמָשַׁחְתָּ Ex. 30:26, 29; 40:11; Lv. 8:10; Nu. 7:1; וַיַּמְלִיכוּ . . . וַיִּמְשְׁחוּ 2 K. 23:30. וְכִהֲנוּ . . . וּמָשַׁחְתָּ Ex. 40:15; וְכִהֲנוּ . . . וְקִדַּשְׁתָּ . . . וּמָשַׁחְתָּ Ex. 28:41, cf. 40:13.

constructus ni of מָשַׁח occurs, we regularly find constructions with the obj. acc. [22] As a derivate of מָשַׁח, apart from מָשִׁיחַ, the OT has 21 times the fem. of the form qatl or qitl מִשְׁחָה, always linked by שֶׁמֶן to the group שֶׁמֶן הַמִּשְׁחָה "anointing oil," Ex. 25:6; 29:7, 21; 31:11; 35:8, 15, 28; 37:29; 39:38; 40:9; Lv. 8:2, 10, 12, 30; 21:10; Nu. 4:16. Expansions are שֶׁמֶן מִשְׁחַת־קֹדֶשׁ Ex. 30:25 (twice); 30:31, שֶׁמֶן מִשְׁחַת יְהוָה Lv. 10:7 or שֶׁמֶן מִשְׁחַת אֱלֹהִים Lv. 21:12. Only twice do we find the qutl fem. מָשְׁחָה "anointing," Ex. 29:29; [23] 40:15.

2. Royal Anointing.

a. Survey of the Occurrence in the Old Testament. [24]

Easily the most common reference in the OT is to the anointing of the king. This royal anointing is part of the more comprehensive act of enthronement which seems to have been based on a whole ritual with various parts. In the OT anointing is the most important or the most distinctive of the individual acts.

Of the kings whose anointing is specifically mentioned David takes precedence, 1 S. 16:3, 12 f.; 2 S. 2:4, 7; [25] 5:3, 17; 12:7; Ps. 89:20; 1 Ch. 11:3; 14:8. There are quite a few ref. to Saul's anointing too, 1 S. 9:16; 10:1; [26] 15:1, 17. Later few but the descendants of David are said to have been anointed: Solomon in 1 K. 1:34, 39, 45; 5:15; 1 Ch. 29:22, Joash in 2 K. 11:12; 2 Ch. 23:11, and Jehoahaz in 2 K. 23:30, cf. Absalom in 2 S. 19:11. Jehu king of North Israel was anointed, 1 K. 19:16; [27] 2 K. 9:3, 6, 12; 2 Ch. 22:7, and so was Hazael, the Aramaean king, 1 K. 19:15. The fable of Jotham in Ju. 9:7-15 [28] ref. to the anointing of kings in gen. Yahweh does the anointing at the marriage of an unnamed king in Ps. 45:7. [29]

b. Characteristics of Royal Anointing in Israel. [30]

When there is ref. to anointing by the people or its representatives, various facts are disclosed. 2 S. 2:4, 7 and 5:3, 17 seem to be the earliest witnesses. The men of Judah, representing the house of Judah (2:7), anoint David and thereby raise him up to be king of Judah. Later the elders of Israel come to Hebron to make a covenant with David and then to anoint him, so that he becomes king of Israel too. The anointing by the elders of Israel is a valid act performed by the official representatives of the whole people organised in tribes and clans, whereas its counterpart in Judah is more a political play on the part of certain men who have attained to influence and esteem. [31] The act of anointing confers כָּבוֹד; it is thus to be regarded as an act of enablement.

In contrast it is David who authorises the anointing in the case of his successor Solomon. At David's command Zadok and Nathan perform the ceremony. The text is not

---

[22] בְּיוֹם הִמָּשַׁח אֹתוֹ Lv. 6:13; Nu. 7:10, 84 and אַחֲרֵי הִמָּשַׁח אֹתוֹ Nu. 7:88. In spite of Weinel, 4 f. there can be no argument against the combination.

[23] Here more of an inf. constructus q.

[24] To complete the survey cf. ref. which have the title מָשִׁיחַ for the ruling king → 502, 15 ff.

[25] 2 S. 3:39 is left out on textual grounds.

[26] In these two texts the more gen. and solemn נָגִיד replaces מֶלֶךְ.

[27] In this difficult text there is ref. also to the anointing of the Aramaean king Hazael by the prophet Elijah.

[28] The fable of Jotham, an extension of the story of Abimelech, might come from the age of the monarchy, i.e., from circles who disliked the institution. Exact dating is hardly possible.

[29] Hos. 7:3 might also be ref. to the anointing of a king if the conjecture יִמְשְׁחוּ for יִשְׂמְחוּ is right, but cf. → n. 18.

[30] On this section cf Kutsch, 52-60.

[31] Ch. does not mention the anointing of David as king of Judah but only as king of Israel. Israel is the total cultic community, of which Judah is a part. The elders simply do what Yahweh promised through Samuel.

quite clear here, for both men do it in 1 K. 1:34, 45 but only Zadok in 1:39. Perhaps Zadok bears chief responsibility for the performance of the rite. [32]

When Absalom is instituted king we are not told who anointed him and there is only incidental ref. to the ceremony in 2 S. 19:11. Nor are we told who did the anointing in the case of Joash in 2 K. 11:12. [33] Acc. to 2 K. 23:30 Jehoahaz was anointed by the עַם הָאָרֶץ, i.e., the free people of the land of Judah.

These accounts stand up to historical investigation. Anointing is strongly attested only in relation to the Southern Kingdom of Judah and with ref. to David and his successors. The initiators of the action are the people acting through accredited representatives. The people gives the king his power. In this connection one may recall Hittite anointing (→ 497, 5 ff.). Only among the Hittites do we find solid witness to royal anointing in the ancient Orient and here again it is the people (nobility, army) that acts as subj. If the Judaeans borrow from the Hittites in respect of anointing, one may conjecture that they did so through the Canaanites, who were influenced by the Hittites in other matters too. Jebusite Jerusalem, or even earlier Canaanite Hebron, might have played some part here. If the elders of Israel adopted the rite in the case of David, this might have been because they learned to associate it with enthronement from David and his supporters in the negotiations. But there are objections to this thesis. Thus the fable of Jotham (Ju.9:7-15), which was handed down in the North, refers to the rite of anointing.

The action was performed as follows. Oil was poured from a horn (1 S. 16:13; 1 K. 1:39) or vessel (1 S. 10:1; 2 K. 9:3, 6) on the head of the person to be anointed. [34]

In contrast to the passages cited those which mention the anointing of the king by Yahweh himself have been contested on historical grounds. We find such anointing by Yahweh or at His direct command in 1 S. 9:16; 10:1; 15:1, 17 (Saul), 1 S. 16:3, 12 f.; 2 S. 12:7; Ps. 89:20 (David), 1 K. 19:15 f. (Hazael and Jehu), 2 K. 9:3, 6, 12; 2 Ch. 22:7 (Jehu). The saying of the messenger in 2 K. 9:3, 6 makes it plain the Yahweh uses a delegate to perform the rite. Saul, of course, was anointed by the people. The point of the story that he was anointed by Samuel at Yahweh's command is that what the Israelites did was planned and accomplished long before by Yahweh. In this way the legitimacy of Saul's monarchy in the eyes of God is established. Both Saul and David are anointed by Yahweh prior to their institution as king by men. LXX is true to the same thought when it changes "and they made Saul king" to "and Samuel anointed Saul king" in 1 S. 11:15. The statement of Nathan, in Yahweh's name, at 2 S. 12:7: "I anointed thee king," is to the same effect. [35] Elijah did not in fact anoint either Hazael of Damascus or Jehu of Israel as charged in 1 K. 19:15 f.; nor did Elisha. The prophecy is designed to show that Yahweh directs the destinies of neighbouring peoples too. A historical core can be discerned in 2 K. 9, [36] though we are not told that any other king of the Northern Kingdom was actually anointed. [37]

Anointing by Yahweh Himself is a conferring of כָּבוֹד, and is thus authorisation by Him. When, however, Yahweh grants the king כָּבוֹד by anointing, the people becomes an indirect obj. instead of subj., since the king now represents the people. A specific commission is given to the king with his anointing.

---

[32] Since Ch. ignores the court intrigues that led to the accession of Solomon, the anointing of Solomon is attributed to the whole people, the קָהָל. It may be noted that Zadok is anointed as well, 1 Ch. 29:22.

[33] There is no anointing by the high-priest, as Kutsch rightly stresses, 54 f. The LXX first ascribes the anointing to Jehoiada (cf. 2 K. 11:12 HT), though cf. 2 Ch. 23:11 (Jehoiada and his sons).

[34] It makes no difference if there are secondary elements since the rite is described here as it was then performed.

[35] Cf. L. Rost, "Die Überlieferung von d. Thronnachfolge Davids," BWANT, 42 (1926), 93-6.

[36] M. Noth, Geschichte Israels⁷ (1969), 210 accepts the authenticity of this without question.

[37] Hos. 7:3 might be cited here, though the text is uncertain.

One may question whether anointing was known and practised in the Northern Kingdom. In the South we have only a few special instances, e.g., David, the first king, whom
the men of Judah chose, Absalom who set himself up as a rival king, Solomon, whose
right to the succession was tenuous, Joash, whose enthronement would shatter the tyranny
of Athaliah, and Jehoahaz, at a time when the continued existence of the kingdom could
not be taken for granted in view of the international situation (and when there was perhaps also a struggle for power between court party and עַם הָאָרֶץ). But this is hardly
enough to bring the matter into clear focus.

3. Anointing of Other Office-Bearers.

a. The High-Priest.

The rite of anointing was performed on the high-priest in the post-exilic community in Judah. But only a few passages in the OT give us information in this
regard.

We may ref. primarily to P and related texts and apart from that only to 1 Ch. 29:22
and Sir. 45:15. Texts in which the high-priest is called "the anointed" (Lv. 4:3, 5, 16; 6:15;
Da. 9:25 f.) [38] might also be adduced. [39]
The meaning of high-priestly anointing is disputed. The common view to-day is that
it is to be taken as a rite of cleansing and consecration rather than empowering. [40] But
this tends to break down on the fact that the high-priest was regarded by some as the
legitimate successor of the Davidic king. The vesture of the high-priest is described in
kingly terms in Ex. 28; 39. [41] This is not true, however, of that of the priest, and no deductions are made from the royal attire. All the same, the high-priest is regarded as the lawful
successor of the Davidic dynasty and his anointing confers כָּבוֹד on him like the royal
anointing. Later in the P texts this interpretation yields to the more appropriate one that
the anointing denotes separation and sanctification. Zech. 4:14, which calls both Zerubbabel, the "commissioner of repatriation," [42] and Joshua, the high-priest, sons of oil, [43]
does not contradict this, for the prophet is describing here, not the existing situation; [44] but
the future ideal which he longingly sees in a vision. Along with the traditional picture
of the anointed king of David's race which is common in the prophets, we have here the
new concept of an equally authorised and empowered high-priest who possesses כָּבוֹד
like the descendant of David and who is thus anointed in order to have a share in it. [45]

---

[38] To the degree that the ref. here is to the high-priest → 505, 8 ff.

[39] If P describes the anointing of Aaron rather than the high-priest, this is because the
person of Aaron is the ground and root of the high-priesthood, Ex. 29:7; 40:13; Lv. 6:13;
8:12. Once at Ex. 29:29 the ref. is to Aaron's sons who will succeed him in the office, v. 30.
When Ch. speaks of the anointing of Zadok along with Solomon (1 Ch. 29:22), the anointing
of the high-priest is put in the pre-exilic period.

[40] Kutsch, 22-27. Acc. to Kutsch, 24 f., 27 the anointing serves to sanctify the high-priest,
to make him cultically clean and hence to separate him from the people for the service of
Yahweh. The anointed high-priest is removed from the profane world around him by anointing.

[41] At any rate the items מִצְנֶפֶת, נֵזֶר and אֵפוֹד are most easily explained as parts of the
royal habit. In the synagogue of Dura-Europos Aaron is depicted in the royal attire of Iran.
For details cf. Mowinckel, 6 and Noth, 317-9.

[42] This is the precise meaning of the Hbr. title פֶּחָה (Hos. 1:1) acc. to A. Alt, "Die Rolle
Samarias bei d. Entstehung des Judt.," Kleine Schr. z. Gesch. des Volkes Israel, II (1953),
333-5.

[43] בְּנֵי־הַיִּצְהָר. Since we have here a vision in which olive-trees occur one may understand
why יִצְהָר is used even though it does not occur elsewhere in connection with anointing → n. 2.
In any case יִצְהָר has rather the sense of ointment here.

[44] Kutsch, 25 f. sees a contemporary ref. and he thus rejects the interpretation offered here.

[45] One need not suppose that Zerubbabel had been anointed, which is most unlikely, nor
that in the days of Zech. the anointing of the high-priest could be taken for granted.

When the prophet calls both representatives of the people sons of oil, the element of holiness, of separation for the sphere of Yahweh, is of considerable importance. [46]

b. The Priests.

Some passages, esp. in P, speak of the anointing of all priests. The ref. is to Aaron and his sons in Ex. 28:41; 30:30; Lv. 7:36, or to the sons of Aaron, Ex. 40:15; Nu. 3:3.

A later age, although perhaps only in theory, [47] thus extended anointing to the whole priesthood. The understanding of anointing as a rite of cleansing and consecration had now established itself. Hence it was hard to see why it should be restricted to the high-priest. Anointing became more and more an act of priestly dedication. Yet the trend in this direction never reached its final goal.

c. Prophetic Office-Bearers.

In spite of 1 K. 19:16 anointing never became a rite of initiation into the prophetic office. This is not the meaning of Is. 61:1, where the prophet says of himself that he had been given the Spirit and anointed by Yahweh. This saying is close to those that attribute the anointing of the king to Yahweh Himself → 499, 22 ff. The prophet is to discharge a specific task assigned to him by Yahweh. He is anointed for this. Thus the act of anointing confers power. Perhaps the Spirit of Yahweh is regarded as the "matter" of anointing. If so, the gift of the Spirit and the anointing are one and the same. Possession of the Spirit is permanent; hence the rite confers a *character indelebilis*.

4. Anointing of Objects.

Gn. 28:18; 31:13 tell of the anointing of a pillar, מָשַׁח being used in 31:13. Jacob in 28:18 pours oil on the pillar, so that it is taken out of the profane sphere, consecrated to God, and made a sanctuary. Possibly an older notion lies behind the practice, namely, that of increasing the power that indwells the pillar. In P altars are anointed, Ex. 29:36; Lv. 8:11; Nu. 7:1, 10, 84, 88, esp. the altar of burnt offering, Ex. 40:10, and also the tent of meeting, Ex. 30:26, the ark, Ex. 30:26, the "dwelling" מִשְׁכָּן and its contents, Ex. 40:9; Lv. 8:10; Nu. 7:1, the laver and its stand, Ex. 40:11, and all the objects relating to the altar, Ex. 40:10. [48]

III. מָשִׁיחַ in the Old Testament.

1. The Occurrence of the Noun מָשִׁיחַ in the Old Testament.

The noun מָשִׁיחַ, which means the same as the part. pass. q מָשׁוּחַ "anointed," is felt to be stronger than the part. when used as an independent noun "the anointed." It occurs

---

[46] This account follows in the main that given by F. Horst in T. H. Robinson-F. Horst, *Die Zwölf Kleinen Propheten*, Hndbch. AT, I, 14³ (1964), *ad loc.*

[47] Kutsch, 23 is right when he points out the difficulties in the assumption that all priests were anointed when taking office. This requirement was perhaps purely theoretical. It did not have to be practised, esp. as anointing of the earliest priests would be valid for all the generations that followed. But cf. Kutsch, 24 f.

[48] If shields were anointed in Israel — and the relevant texts at 2 S. 1:21 and Is. 21:5 are too insecure to base too much upon them — the ref. is probably not to ritual "anointing" but to practical "oiling," which the shield of a dead warrior no longer needs, 2 S. 1:21 [Bertram].

in the OT 38 times, always with ref. to a person, [49] whereas the part. can be used of both persons, Nu. 3:3 [50] and also things, Ex. 29:2; Lv. 2:4; 7:12; Nu. 6:15. [51]

In the first instance kings are "the anointed," in all 30 (29) times. The high-priest is 6 times given the title of מָשִׁיחַ. In two other passages the fathers are "the anointed."

The abs. use is rare, being found only in the late Da. 9:25 f.; in both vv. here מָשִׁיחַ is indefinite and in v. 25 we find נָגִיד in clarifying apposition. [52] Mostly we have מְשִׁיחַ יְהוָה 1 S. 24:7 (twice), 11; 26:9, 11, 16, 23; 2 S. 1:14, 16; 19:22; Lam. 4:20. In 2 S. 23:1 the archaic poetic expression מְשִׁיחַ אֱלֹהֵי יַעֲקֹב corresponds to this. We might also mention in this connection the many instances of מָשִׁיחַ with suffix, 1 S. 2:10, 35; 12:3, 5; 16:6; 2 S. 22:51 = Ps. 18:50; Is. 45:1; Hab. 3:13; Ps. 2:2; 20:6; 28:8; 84:9; 89:38, 51; 105:15 = 1 Ch. 16:22; Ps. 132:10 = 2 Ch. 6:42; Ps. 132:17; the suffix always ref. to Yahweh. The use of מָשִׁיחַ seems to have developed first in the sense of מְשִׁיחַ יְהוָה. Only then did the abs. use follow. There is an attributive use in Lv. 4:3, 5, 16; 6:15; one might just as well have expected the part. pass. מָשׁוּחַ here.

2. The King as מְשִׁיחַ יְהוָה.

a. Survey.

Saul is most commonly called מְשִׁיחַ יְהוָה, 1 S. 12:3, 5; 24:7, 11; 26:9, 11, 16, 23; 2 S. 1:14, 16. Apart from this the phrase is used only of the Davidic kings of Judah with the important exception of Is. 45:1. David is individually given the title indirectly in 1 S. 16:6 and directly in 2 S. 19:22; 23:1. The ref. is to David and his house in 2 S. 22:51 = Ps. 18:50 and Ps. 132:17. Lam. 4:20 seems fairly certainly to be ref. to Zedekiah, the last Davidic king. In the other texts, 1 S. 2:10, 35; Ps. 2:2; 20:6; 28:8; 84:9; 89:38, 51; 132:10 = 2 Ch. 6:42; Hab. 3:13 there can be no saying which particular king is in view.

b. Saul as מְשִׁיחַ יְהוָה.

If anointing in Israel first developed in the kingdom of Judah with the elevation of David as king (→ 198, 21 ff.), it is surprising that David's predecessor (→ 198, 14 f.), who was of a different house and tribe, should be given the title מְשִׁיחַ יְהוָה with comparatively the greatest frequency. One might explain this by conjecturing that the author of the account of David's ascent is responsible for most of the relevant passages in 1 S. 24:7, 11; 26:9, 11, 16, 23; 2 S. 1:14, 16. The true hero is thus David, not Saul. Knowing that David was anointed, the author says the same of Saul, even though there might be doubt whether or not the rite was actually performed in his case.

But this is hardly an adequate explanation. Saul's title is never מָשִׁיחַ alone; it is always מְשִׁיחַ יְהוָה. Hence the title does not have in view the anointing of the one called מָשִׁיחַ by the people or its representatives. The basis of the title is the theological principle of royal anointing, namely, that Yahweh has anointed the king and thus granted him authorisation and protection. This is given concrete expression in anointing by a mediator, e.g., Samuel in the case of Saul, 1 S. 9:16; 10:1; 15:1, 17, but the main point is the anointing by Yahweh which can be maintained whether or not there is any such act, cf. Is. 45:1. [53]

---

[49] We have left out 2 S. 1:21 on textual grounds. Probably מָשׁוּחַ is to be read, with a ref. to the shield.

[50] 2 S. 3:39, which has מָשׁוּחַ in a saying of David about himself, is probably a slip, so that we have not listed it.

[51] Probably 2 S. 1:21 belongs here → n. 49.

[52] In my view this exposition is better than relating נָגִיד to another figure, cf. O. Plöger, *Das Buch Daniel, Komm. AT*, 18 (1965); A. Bentzen, *Daniel, Hndbch. AT*, I, 19² (1952); N. W. Porteous, *Das Danielbuch, AT Deutsch*, 23² (1968), ad loc.

[53] Cf. on this Kutsch, 60-63.

The title מְשִׁיחַ יְהוָה, when used of Saul, reflects the distinctive position of the king as one who is under Yahweh's protection. Acc. to the story of the rise of David, Saul is continually called the anointed of Yahweh by David when the issue is the inviolability of his person. Because he is in a special relation to Yahweh, the person of the מְשִׁיחַ יְהוָה must not be touched.

Things are rather different in 1 S. 12:3, 5. The author calls Saul — who is meant even though he is not named — a מְשִׁיחַ יְהוָה because it is known from the existing story in 1 S. 9 f. that Samuel had anointed Saul. In pre-exilic and exilic times the title מְשִׁיחַ יְהוָה was a familiar one for Davidic kings. The author thus sees in Saul a legitimate predecessor of David who merits the same title.

c. David as מְשִׁיחַ יְהוָה.

The David ref. are closely related to those already discussed under b. 2 S. 19:22 again has in view the inviolability of the person of the anointed. The story in 1 S. 16:1-13 confirms that the title was already developed. We have a ref. to the anointed of Yahweh in v. 6 even though the anointing has not yet taken place. Par. to מְשִׁיחַ יְהוָה is the statement in vv. 8-10 that Yahweh has not chosen the elder brothers of David. Election to the royal office by Yahweh means the same as anointing. With the anointing the Spirit of Yahweh comes on David. As in Is. 61:1 there is a close relation between anointing by Yahweh and the endowment of the Spirit. Indeed, the two are probably identical. Acc. to the so-called last words of David in 2 S. 23 the king is the anointed of the God of Jacob, v. 1. David's close position to Yahweh is denoted thereby. This poetic variation of the more usual מְשִׁיחַ יְהוָה employs a term for God which belongs to a sphere with which David had little to do by birth.

Ps. which call a later king of Judah מְשִׁיחַ יְהוָה, not without express ref. to David, form a transition to the next section (d.). Ps. 89 contrasts the present plight of Israel and its anointed king with the promise given to David. Ref. is made to the anointing of David by Yahweh in v. 20, and the ruling Davidic king is also called the anointed in v. 38. Obviously David's anointing has great significance for all his successors. In Ps. 132 prayer is made that Yahweh will not abandon His anointed "for David's sake," v. 10. Ch., which adds some vv. of this psalm to the prayer of Solomon at the dedication of the temple, interprets "for David's sake" in Solomon's petition to Yahweh: "Make present (זָכְרָה) the graces of David, thy servant," 2 Ch. 6:42. These sayings all relate to the promise given by Nathan to David (→ VIII, 349, 17 ff.) whose core may be found in 2 S. 7:11b, 16, which speaks of the permanence of David's dynasty.

d. The Davidic king as מְשִׁיחַ יְהוָה.

The title מְשִׁיחַ יְהוָה is used emphatically for the king of Davidic descent when people and king are in sorry straits. The title is an urgent if indirect appeal to Yahweh to come and help. For the anointed is under His protection. The concealed petition can be strengthened by a reference to David and the promises made to him → 503, 11 ff. We find such an appeal in Lam. 4:20, and Hab. 3:13 might also be put in this group, although here the petitioner lives by the assurance that Yahweh is already on the way as his helper.

We also find the title, however, when in a style which is surprisingly rich for the the Israelites the reference is to the king himself and his acts and destiny. It is now hoped and expected that in the very near future there will be accomplished that which the present strangely does not offer in terms of the כָּבוֹד of the מְשִׁיחַ יְהוָה. Ps. 2 is an example. All the peoples are in rebellion against Yahweh's anointed in Jerusalem. But the poet is certain that Yahweh will intervene to liberate the king whom He has adopted. Passages like 1 S. 2:10; Hab. 3:13; Ps. 84:9; 132:17; Lam.

4:20 are also convinced of the all-embracing power and majesty of the anointed. Whatever part of this is not yet a full reality, Yahweh must and will bring into operation in the immediate future. [54]

> Yahweh and His anointed can be related as in Ps. 2:2, but the people and the anointed can also be associated in poetic parallelism, Hab. 3:13; Ps. 28:8. On the one side, then, the מְשִׁיחַ יְהוָה belongs wholly to the sphere of Yahweh; he is Yahweh's servant and confidant and stands under His protection. To touch him is to sin against Yahweh. On the other side, however, he belongs with the people. He thus occupies a middle position analogous to that of the man of God, the prophet, or the priest.

A definitely Messianic or eschatological understanding cannot be presupposed when the king is called מְשִׁיחַ יְהוָה. All the references are to the present king or a past king. Epigrammatically, one might say that none of the Messianic passages in the OT can be exegeted Messianically. Nevertheless, the so-called Messianic understanding is implied in many of the passages, although this is more evident in texts in which the term מָשִׁיחַ is not used → 505, 27 ff.

e. Cyrus as מְשִׁיחַ יְהוָה.

More clearly than in the case of Saul (→ 502, 24 ff.) and the kings of Judah (→ 503, 11 ff.) the use of the title מְשִׁיחַ יְהוָה for the Persian king Cyrus in Is. 45:1 shows that the title could be employed independently of the rite of anointing. Here a prophet of Israel strangely describes as מְשִׁיחַ יְהוָה an alien ruler who is of another religion and does not believe in Yahweh. He puts the title in a saying of Yahweh to Cyrus even though elsewhere in Israel any direct relating of Yahweh to non-Israelites was largely avoided. Dt. Is., however, ref. to a specific commission that Yahweh gives to Cyrus; Yahweh charges him to do something that will be to Israel's salvation. To emphasise this mission Cyrus is given the title מְשִׁיחַ יְהוָה. Furthermore, since Cyrus achieves salvation for Israel by political and military means he is not just an instrument of Yahweh; he replaces the Davidic dynasty, which is now condemned to impotence. Hence the title as applied to Cyrus is to be understood in terms of the Davidic monarchy. As salvation was expected from the kingly rule of the anointed one of the house of David, so hope now focuses on the Persian king, who steps in the breach for the line of David now that it is hampered from deploying its power. Notwithstanding these possible explanations, however, the expression, which is ventured only this one time, is an extremely bold one.

f. The Fathers as Anointed Ones.

מָשִׁיחַ occurs only once in plur. suffix form, [55] namely, at Ps. 105:15 with ref. to the fathers. [56] In this probably exilic psalm the singer describes the age of the fathers (vv. 12-15) in which the promise spoken of in 7-11 was fulfilled. By his use of מָשִׁיחַ the author is showing that the fathers were inviolable and that Yahweh saw to this by His own intervention. Here again then, as with Saul (→ 502, 24 ff.), the element of inviolability is to the fore. It is not clear how the author came to apply the title to the fathers when it had

---

[54] Historically many of these features derive from the court style of Egypt. But the derivation is not an explanation why ideas so alien to the relations in Judah should have gained a footing in Jerusalem. The probable explanation is that Yahweh's כָּבוֹד demands visible expression in an earthly representative as well as in Israel as a whole. Since the present often fails to offer this, there is the greater certainty that it will be manifested in the near future. This seems to be the root of what we call Messianic expectations → 505, 27 ff.

[55] The plur. מְשִׁיחֶיךָ in 2 Ch. 6:42 is not in the original Ps. 132:10 and hence is very probably a textual error. LXX A reads the sing. and there is no equivalent in LXX B [Bertram].

[56] With Ps. 96 and 106, Ps. 105:1-15 is quoted in 1 Ch. 16:8 ff. as a song of praise which David first taught the temple singers.

thus far been exclusively a royal title. Perhaps the line of Davidic kings was extended back into the early period and the forefathers thus came to be regarded as initial kingly figures. Possibly the description of Abraham as a נָבִיא in Gn. 20:7 also played a part. The two passages which speak of the anointing of prophets (1 K. 19:16; Is. 61:1) show that the prophetic fathers could also be regarded as anointed ones. Thus a title previously reserved for kings could be conferred on outstanding men at a later stage. This is done very rarely, however, for no other examples are to hand.

4. The Anointed High-Priest.

In four passages (Lv. 4:3, 5, 16; 6:15) which use מָשִׁיחַ for the high-priest the term is not as elsewhere meant as a noun or title but is used attributively. Nevertheless, there is no doubt but that the title מָשִׁיחַ, which was previously reserved for the Davidic king, is now intentionally adopted. In the kingless age in which the priestly author lives, the anointed priest (→ 500, 11 ff.) plays the part of the king of Judah.[57] Although the reference is only to an anointed priest, the high-priest is undoubtedly meant; the adjective גָּדוֹל is here replaced by מָשִׁיחַ.

In Da. 9:25 f. מָשִׁיחַ is an indefinite noun. The usage rests on the assumption that it will be recognised who is meant by the intentionally veiled expression "an anointed one." Interpretation is more difficult for us than for the author's contemporaries. Acc. to v. 25 the first 7 weeks of the 70 yrs. of Jer.'s prophecy in Jer. 25:11 f.; 29:10 (which is being expounded here) begin with the prophecy of Jer. and they end with the coming of an anointed one, namely, a נָגִיד. Since the 7 weeks equal 49 yrs., only a figure at the end of the exile can be intended. It is most unlikely that the ref. is to Cyrus, as in Is. → 504, 16 ff. Zerubbabel (→ 507, 21 ff.) is possible but is much less likely than the high-priest Joshua, since the anointed one of v. 26 is the high-priest. After 62 weeks (years) an anointed one is removed. This could be a ref. to the execution of the high-priest Onias III by Antiochus IV Epiphanes in 171 B.C.

IV. The Development of Messianic Ideas in Israel.

We are in a very debatable area when we discuss the development in Israel of Messianic ideas which express the hope that a time of salvation will come with the accession of a king of David's line — a time that is often regarded also as a last time. It could well be that this form of Messianic belief arose already in the South in the pre-exilic period. The main evidence for this is to be found in some of the so-called Royal Psalms[58] and in the message of the prophet Isaiah.

1. Royal Psalms.

A most important constituent element in the Royal Psalms is the oracle addressed to the reigning king, perhaps by cultic prophets, cf. Ps. 2:6 ff.; 21:9-13; 110:1, 3 f.; 89:19 ff.; 132:11 f.

This oracle promises the ruler salvation, and a divine saying which is the basis of the dynasty is quoted.[59] The prophecy of Nathan to David, which in the name of Yahweh promises that his house will last for ever (→ VIII, 349, 17 ff.), is the foundation of the

---

[57] Cf. K. Koch, "Die P von Ex. 25 bis Lv. 16," FRL, 71 (1959), 58.

[58] Fohrer, 13 oversimplifies when he says of Ps. 2; 110; 72; 101; 132 that they all have in view the reigning king. On this view there would be no Messianic psalms. The reigning or acceding king is certainly meant, but such high expectations are linked with his rule that he can never possibly satisfy them. To that degree there is a core of Messianic hope in the psalms.

[59] Cf. H. J. Kraus, Psalmen, Bibl. Komm. AT, 15 (1960), LIII.

promised salvation. [60] This promise of salvation often adopts ideas taken from the surrounding world of religion. Often these do not fit in with the situation in Judah. The most striking are the promise of world-dominion to the king of Judah and the assertion that with the change of ruler in Jerusalem the subject nations rise up in revolt, Ps. 2:1 f. The discrepancy between the actual situation in the puny kingdom of Judah-Jerusalem and the claim to world-dominion advanced in the Royal Ps. cannot be explained merely in terms of dependence on contemporary notions nor in terms of the fulsomeness of courtly style. Such a clash of claim and reality would be astonishing in Judah-Jerusalem. Israel's unique belief in God plays a decisive role here. The Israelite is permeated by the concept that God is the mightiest of all gods. But it is not enough to believe this. This power of Yahweh has to be manifested. This can happen only in the sphere of political events. Yahweh's demonstration of strength takes place in a political structure whose representative has a political office. Hence the poet of the Royal Ps. calls the king of Judah a world-ruler because he has to be this by right; only thus can Yahweh display His deity to the whole world. At the time, however, there is no world rule by the king of Judah. What is not there as yet must come into being very soon. The manifestation of the glory of Yahweh which attains visibility in the glory of the king of Judah cannot wait much longer. It will not do so.

In the grandiose statements of the Royal Psalms we thus have a prolepsis of what ought to have been for a long time but incomprehensibly has not yet come to pass. With the accession of the new king it will surely come. It must come, for only thus can one remain certain of Yahweh and His universal power. The future of which there is certainty will in some sense become the present. There is imminent expectation of the salvation which finds expression in the all-embracing dominion of the Davidic king. [61]

2. Isaiah 9:5 f.

The point here is not so much the birth as the accession of a new ruler of David's house. The prophet regards this as adoption by Yahweh. [62] If v. 5 can still be applied to the accession of a ruler of the Davidic dynasty, a more strongly eschatological expectation seems to be implied in v. 6. The new son of David will be a final and perfect ruler. Under his rule, which will be for an indefinite period, there will be salvation without end. This final Davidic ruler will be Yahweh's representative on earth. Is. 9:5 f. is thus the oldest passage to set forth clearly what is called Messianic expectation. More patently here than in the Royal Psalms (→ 505, 34 ff.) the reference is not just to a Davidic king in the course of empirical history, with whose accession the beginning of a rule of salvation is expected in the full sense, but rather to an outstanding saviour of the house of David who represents the last thing in history.

---

[60] On this cf. Rost, op. cit. (→ n. 35), 59.

[61] This view is close to Mowinckel's theory (155-9) regarding the rise of the Messianic idea. In Mowinckel the enthronement festival of Yahweh plays an important part, but the very existence of this has been hotly contested in recent research. It might be better, then, to refer to the ritual of accession rather than a hypothetical enthronement festival, since this is well supported in the Royal Psalms. Mowinckel is surely right, however, when he argues that the Messianic hope, and eschatology in gen., derives essentially from disillusionment at the present state of affairs. Individual features in the portrayal of the Messiah are taken from the religions of surrounding nations, but not the idea itself, as one must say in opposition esp. to Gressmann, 230-232. The pan-orientalism of the Uppsala school is to be completely rejected, esp. when it confers the predicate "Messianic" on a non-eschatological ideology of monarchy.

[62] In this regard it does not much matter whether the bold exegesis of A. Alt, "Js. 8:23 - 9:6. Befreiungsnacht u. Krönungstag," Kleine Schr. z. Gesch. d. Volkes Israel, II³ (1964), 206-225 is right in every detail or whether it should be treated with caution. Either way Is. 9:5 f. plainly has in view a Davidic ruler mounting the throne in Jerusalem.

3. Jeremiah and Ezekiel.

The Messianic hope of some psalms and Is., which is characterised by imminent expectation, is less prominent in the later prophets, although we still find it. The only secure example of Messianic expectation in Jer. is at 23:5 f. [63] Here the prophet awaits the ideal of a wise and righteous ruler of David's line with the programmatic name of "Yahweh our righteouness." But there is no depiction marking the reign of this king as a magnificent and even miraculous one of universal dominion. Nor it is certain whether Messianic expectation in Jer. is eschatological or not, i.e., whether or not a last time is thought to be ushered in with the accession of this king. Ezekiel's expectation is definitely not eschatological. A second David equal to the first will soon become ruler and he will be the first in a succession of similar kings, Ez. 34:23 f.; 37:22 ff. Perhaps Ez. had first expected a restoration of Jehoiachin (21:32) but was disappointed in this hope. [64]

4. Post-Exilic Period.

In the immediate post-exilic period when the returned exiles were beginning to settle again in Jerusalem and Judah, the Messianic hope was undoubtedly strong and began to put forth new shoots. Evidence of this may be found perhaps in a series of utterances thought to be added to the pre-exilic prophets, though it is impossible to date these satisfactorily. We are on more solid chronological ground when we turn to those passages in the prophets Haggai and Zechariah which express the Messianic idea.

a. Haggai. In Hag. 2:20-23 the prophet addresses the governor Zerubbabel, grandson of Jehoiachin, king of Judah, and hence a descendant of David. Following ancient tradition and prophesying disasters like the earlier prophets, Haggai proclaims that Yahweh will shake heaven and earth, will divest alien peoples of their power, and will look on the ruler that remains, namely, Zerubbabel, as a signet ring. Zerubbabel's work is thus a guarantee of Yahweh's mighty and saving presence and an accreditation of the divine promises. This Zerubbabel, the elect of Yahweh, will still be a mortal member of David's dynasty. He will only be a representative of Yahweh, the true ruler. But in the tribulations of the last time, when the thrones of foreign nations will be shattered, the Messianic age of salvation will dawn, and Zerubbabel will be the Messiah of Yahweh, who stands in a uniquely close relation to his God.

b. Zechariah. In Zech. we find the notion of two anointed ones alive and at work → 500, 25 ff. The olive-trees which the prophet sees in a night-vision (4:1-6, 10-14) represent the "sons of oil," Zerubbabel and Joshua. As the authorised representatives of the community of Yahweh they both have a right to stand before Him. In Zech. 6:9-15 the prophet is told to perform a symbolic act. In analogy to the act relating to the high-priest Joshua, the handing over of a stone (3:8-10), it is now demanded that a crown be given to the governor. [65] Thereby Zerubbabel is again designated the Messianic king of the end-time which is now dawning. He is

---

[63] Jer. 33:15 ff. is sometimes regarded as an apocalyptic pamphlet (not by Jer.) which emphasises that one can rely on Yahweh's Word of salvation, cf. W. Rudolph, *Jeremia, Hndbch. AT,* I, 12³ (1968), *ad loc.*

[64] For more detailed exegesis cf. G. Fohrer, *Ezechiel, Hndbch. AT,* I, 13 (1955) and W. Zimmerli, *Ezechiel, Bibl. Komm. AT,* 13 (1969), *ad loc.*

[65] The present text of 6:11 tells us that the high-priest Joshua was crowned, but it is commonly held that Zech. really had Zerubbabel in view, cf. Robinson-Horst, *op. cit.* (→ n. 46); K. Elliger, *Das Buch d. Zwölf Kleinen Proph.,* II, *AT Deutsch,* 25³ (1956), *ad loc.* Acc. to this theory the text was altered after Zerubbabel disappeared from the political scene for some unknown reason.

called a "branch" in 6:12, cf. Jer. 23:5 f. → 507, 3 ff. During his reign everything will bud again. In particular the temple of Yahweh will be finished. An important point here is the relation of the Messiah to the high-priest. The latter will take the place of honour at the right hand of the former. There will be no more rivalry between the political dignitary and the cultic dignitary. Yet the priest is plainly subordinate to the Messiah; he has the place of honour, but only at the right hand of one who is greater than he, cf. Ps. 110:1.

> Later some changes were made. Zerubbabel did not accomplish what was expected of him. Hence the high-priest Joshua was exalted to the crown and the fulfilment of the prophecy was expected only in a more distant future. An interpolation in 6:13, which is not in the LXX, finds in the Messiah both a priest and a king along the lines of Ps 110.

c. Additions to Older Prophets. Passages often regarded as additions to the older prophets describe the Messianic king as follows. His glory is set in stark contrast to the contemporary inadequacy of the house of David in Is. 11:1. The latter is comparable to a root out of which a new shoot will come. The same is true of Ez. 17:22-24. Here the Davidic dynasty is like a cedar. But if a sprout from this is planted on Zion, the mount of God, it will grow into an immense tree. The act of adoption at enthronement is not so prominent now. The birth of the Messianic son of David takes its place (Mi. 5:1-3). Possibly Is. 9:5 is the basis of this. If Bethlehem is mentioned as the birthplace, this may well be with a view to stressing the equality of the Messianic son of David with David himself.

The Messiah is characterised by permanent possession of the Spirit. Three pairs of concepts are used to describe this in Is. 11:1 ff. Messiahship and possession of the Spirit are now very closely related. Endowment with the Spirit makes it possible for the Messianic ruler to reign with piety, wisdom and righteousness. This reign is not marked by the common fallibility of human jurisdiction, Is. 11:3-5. It will combine power, dignity and greatness. The power of Yahweh will be manifested in it, Ez. 17:24. Its greatness will extend to the ends of the earth, Mi. 5:3. In some tension with this is the statement in Zech. 9:9 f. that the Messiah is poor and has to be helped to his position. He is characterised by humility. In everything he depends on Yahweh. A typical feature is his love of peace. He destroys all weapons throughout the world, and does away especially with horses and chariots. A figure that had previously been more martial is distinctively changed to suit a period when the Jews have no military power. The dominion of the Messiah extends beyond Judah and Jerusalem to embrace the nations. All peoples will come to him for instruction and direction, Is. 11:10. They will all see the power of Yahweh in the growth of the "cutting" into a mighty tree, Ez. 17:22-24. In particular Moab will acknowledge the Messiah, Is. 16:5. Apocalyptic features now help to fashion the idea of the Messianic end-time. When the Messiah begins his reign, the whole world achieves the state that God originally planned for it. Paradise is regained, Is. 11:6-9. Jerusalem becomes a particularly glorious dwelling-place, Is. 11:10. The affliction of the last time will be overcome with the accession of the Messiah, Is. 16:4 f.

> Various details are given only in isolated references. Acc. to Jer. 33:15 ff., an interpretation of 23:5 f. (→ 507, 3 ff.), we do not have a single Davidic ruler but a succession of Davidic kings. The priesthood is associated with the monarchy as a second pillar of the state. Ez. 17 links Messianic expectation with the descendants of king Jehoiachin, not the last king, Zedekiah. A similar view may be found in Deuteronomic writings and in Jer. 52. [66]

---

[66] Cf. Baltzer, 33-43 for the various ideas on the last legitimate king of Judah.

d. Difficult Passages. Some passages are so terse in wording and hence so hard to interpret that we can only mention them here with reservations. They do at least seem to indicate that restoration of the Davidic dynasty was expected in the near future. Am. 9:11 f.; Hos. 3:5b; Mi. 4:8; Is 32:1; Jer. 30:9 belong to this group. [67]

5. Problems of Messianism.

It is very difficult, if not impossible, to reconstruct a history of the Messianic movement in Israel and post-exilic Judaism from these scanty passages, many of which cannot be dated with any certainty. There undoubtedly must have been such a movement. This is shown by the examples given and it may also be concluded from the fact that Messianism emerges into the clear light of history in later centuries, not merely as a trend that has just arisen in Judaism, but as a movement with hundreds of years of history behind it. But many questions remain: What was the course of its history? Did a Josiah help to promote Messianism in the pre-exilic period? Is Nehemiah to be understood in the light of the movement after the exile? [68] Does the movement affect all Jews or is it restricted to a few? Does it stand in opposition to other trends or was it able to transcend them? Did it find adherents in every age or was it more or less extinguished at times? To these question no assured answers can as yet be given. [69]

Hesse

C. Messianic Ideas in Later Judaism.

I. Linguistic Aspects.

In later Jewish sources, apart from an uncertain reference in 1 QSa 2:12 (→ n. 146), the term "the anointed" with definite article and in the absolute occurs first in S. Baruch and 4 Esdras → 515, 1 ff. "My Messiah" is also found in S. Baruch. Very close to the absolute use is the expression "Messiah of righteousness." [70] Also in NT days and later we find משיח without article in the sense of an eschatological functional name, which is virtually the same as a proper name. [71] As in the OT "the Lord's anointed" or "my, his anointed" is used only for a royal figure → 502, 6.

---

[67] Cf. Fohrer, 14. Jer. 30:21 is also discussed by Fohrer in this connection, but there can be no certainty that it is ref. to the Davidic dynasty.

[68] A thesis advanced by U. Kellermann, "Nehemia," ZAW Beih., 102 (1967), esp. 179-191.

[69] On these questions cf. Kellermann, op. cit. Many verses often adduced in discussion of the Messiah have been intentionally left out here, since in our view they do not belong to this context.

[70] 4 Q patriarchal blessing 3, cf. also מורה הצדק or יורה הצדק, "teacher of righteousness," 1 QpHab 1:13; 5:10; Damasc. 1:11 (1:7); 6:11 (8:10) etc. and כוהן צדק for the eschatological high-priest, AbRNat, A 34 (Schechter, p. 100, 4); bSukka, 52b.

[71] In texts of Palestinian provenance the abs. of משיח for a proper name is attested only by Nu. r., 13, 11 on 7:13; bBB, 75b; bSanh., 93b etc., cf. Jn. 4:25: οἶδα ὅτι Μεσσίας ἔρχεται, v. J. Jeremias, "Nochmals: Artikelloses Χριστός in 1 K. 15:3," ZNW, 60 (1969), 215-7, and by the interpretative formula זה משיח "that is the Messiah" in Nu. r., 14, 2 on 7:48; 18, 21 on 16:35 etc., cf. Jeremias, 217 f. We might also ref. to בר דויד משיח and משיח בר אפרים, Tg. on Cant. 4:5; 7:4, which are not to be understood epexegetically, cf. Jeremias, 218 as against E. Güttgemanns, "Χριστός in 1 K. 15:3b — Titel oder Eigenname," Ev. Theol., 28 (1968), 538-542; cf. on this I. Plein, Ev. Theol., 29 (1969), 222 f.; E. Güttgemanns, "Artikelloses māšiaḥ? Antwort an Ina Plein," Ev. Theol., 29 (1969), 675 f., as one might expect from the alternating expressions משיחא בר דויד, Tg. Pro. on Hos. 3:5 and משיחא בר אפרים, Tg. J. I on Ex. 40:11. A def. use without art. seems to lie behind Damasc. 20:1 (9:29). On the basis of the similar Damasc. 12:23 - 13:1 (15:4); 14:19 (18:8); 19:10 f. (9:10) and the genealogical sense of מן ("of"), the ref. seems to be to "the anointed of Aaron and Israel" as "an" anointed, cf. Jeremias, 219 as against Güttgemanns, 543 f. → 541, 1 ff.

In the later Jewish period not only the eschatological king is described as anointed but also at Qumran the eschatological high-priest (→ 517, 15 ff.; 518, 25 ff.) and prophet (11 Q Melchizedek 18, cf. Sir. 48:8) and the OT prophets too → 517, 14 f.

If in what follows the reference is to a future redeemer, a divinely commissioned individual is in view who will play a part in accomplishing the awaited salvation. If, however, the reference is to a Messiah, then what we have is a future saviour or redeemer who is expressly described as "anointed one" in the texts.

II. The Septuagint.

χρίω is mostly in the LXX a transl. of מָשַׁח, 61 times in all. [72] Only once is it used for יסך at Ex. 30:32 and twice for סוך at Dt. 28:40; Ez. 16:9. χρῖσις always corresponds to Hbr. מִשְׁחָה, Ex. 29:21 etc. This is 6 times transl. by χρῖσμα, always in Ex., e.g., 29:7. Ex. 40:15 has χρῖσμα for מָשְׁחָה. The well-known Da. 9:26 has χρῖσμα for מָשִׁיחַ in both LXX and Θ. This is elsewhere rendered χριστός except at Lv. 4:3, which has κεχρισμένος for the anointed high-priest, and 2 S. 1:21, where ἐχρίσθη (A ἐχρήθη) is used of shields. The high-priest is ὁ ἱερεὺς ὁ χριστός in Lv. 4:5, 16; 6:15 (22) and ὁ ἀρχιερεὺς ὁ κεχρισμένος in Lv. 4:3, but never ὁ χριστός or χριστός or χριστὸς κυρίου, μου, σου, αὐτοῦ. [73] In the LXX these expressions always denote a royal figure, cf. the Hbr. מְשִׁיחַ יהוה, מְשִׁיחוֹ, מְשִׁיחוֹ etc. → 502, 5 ff. In the abs., i.e., without κυρίου or θεοῦ or a possess. suffix, (ὁ) χριστός is not very securely attested in the LXX. [74]

In definite deviations from the Hbr. original the LXX proclaim the Messianic hope in Hell. Judaism. When it renders Nu. 24:7 by ἐξελεύσεται ἄνθρωπος ἐκ τοῦ σπέρματος αὐτοῦ καὶ κυριεύσει ἐθνῶν πολλῶν, καὶ ὑψωθήσεται ἢ Γωγ βασιλεία αὐτοῦ, καὶ αὐξηθήσεται ἡ βασιλεία αὐτοῦ, and Nu. 24:17 by ἀνατελεῖ ἄστρον ἐξ Ιακωβ, καὶ ἀναστήσεται ἄνθρωπος ἐξ Ισραηλ, it plainly has in view an eschatological king. Similarly, by putting αὐτός instead of αὐτό after ἀνὰ μέσον τοῦ σπέρματος αὐτῆς in Gn. 3:15 it interprets this v. too in terms of a future redeemer. Sometimes LXX introduces χρίω and derivates independently, cf. τὸν χριστὸν αὐτοῦ for מַה־שֵּׂחוֹ at Am. 4:13, and καθεσταμένος for מָשׁוּחַ at 2 Βασ. 3:39, where ᾿ΑΣ read κεχρισμένος, vl. κεχαρισμένος; the text and meaning are uncertain. [75] The LXX puts in χρίω at 2 Ch. 36:1, so that the basic מלך hi is transl. twice and special stress is laid on the act of consecration. χρίω is used by Σ for מלך hi at 1 Βασ. 15:11 and נסך at Ps. 2:6. LXX read מָשַׁח for מָשַׁב at Hos. 8:10 and hence by using χρίω related the text to Messianic expectation. Again it read מָשַׁח for שָׁחַת at Ez. 43:3, and thus employed χρίω. Whereas the HT is speaking of Yahweh's future forsaking of the temple, LXX refers the v. to His return to the sanctuary which is to be dedicated afresh.   *van der Woude*

---

[72] Acc. to Hatch-Redpath 54 times for q, 5 for ni and 2 for מָשִׁיחַ. On Lv. 4:3; 2 S. 1:21 → lines 13 ff.

[73] χριστὸς θεοῦ Ιακωβ occurs only once at 2 Βασ. 23:1. At Lv. 21:12 τὸ ἅγιον ἔλαιον τὸ χριστὸν τοῦ θεοῦ is to be taken together and hence does not ref. to the anointed of God.

[74] 2 Βασ. 23:3 seems to be an exception but here χριστοῦ (only B; A reads κυρίου, other MSS θεοῦ) does not correspond to Hbr. אלהים and hence can hardly be original. Similarly only S adds πρὸς τὸν νυμφίον χριστόν at Cant. 1:7, and this seems to be late and secondary, based on Messianic interpretation. The original at Sir. 46:19 is מְשִׁיחוֹ, so that χριστοῦ αὐτοῦ seems to be the right reading (B, S*, A pl only χριστοῦ). At Sir. 47:11 B² has χριστός for κύριος but the Hbr. has Yahweh. Nor can Da. 9:26 be quoted for an abs. use of (ὁ) χριστός. מָשִׁיחַ here is transl. χρῖσμα, and it is doubtful whether a pers. or obj. is meant in the transl. φθερεῖ... τὸ ἅγιον μετὰ τοῦ χριστοῦ. At Da. 9:25 Θ has ἕως χριστοῦ ἡγουμένου for Hbr. עַד־מָשִׁיחַ נָגִיר, but the words are not in the LXX. Here again, then, the abs. use is attested only in the Chr. era. Similarly at 2 Macc. 3:30 the χριστοῦ of A for κυρίου is definitely not original.

[75] Cf. W. Hertzberg, *Die Samuelbücher, AT Deutsch,* 10² (1960), *ad loc.*

III. Apocrypha and Pseudepigrapha.

1. Sirach. In Gk. Sirach χρίω is used for the institution to office of the high-priest, the king, and once a prophet. Moses anoints Aaron with holy oil in 45:15. The prophet Samuel anoints princes over the people of God: κατέστησεν βασιλείαν καὶ ἔχρισεν ἄρχοντας ἐπὶ τὸν λαὸν αὐτοῦ, 46:13. In 48:8 it is said of the prophet Elijah: ὁ χρίων βασιλεῖς[76] (Hazael and Jehu, 1 K. 19:15 f.) εἰς ἀνταπόδομα, and later in the same v.: καὶ προφήτας (HT[77] sing.) διαδόχους μετ᾽ αὐτόν, cf. 1 K. 19:16b, 19-21. Sir. 46:19 recalls 1 S. 12:5 if χριστοῦ αὐτοῦ (sc. κυρίου) is used for the king.[78]

In Sir., then, the use of χρίω and χριστός does not relate directly to future expectation or expectation of a Messiah. The eternal character of the high-priesthood and the monarchy is, of course, emphasised. In connection with Aaron's anointing Sir. 45:15 appends the following note: ἐγενήθη αὐτῷ εἰς διαθήκην αἰῶνος καὶ τῷ σπέρματι αὐτοῦ ἐν ἡμέραις οὐρανοῦ λειτουργεῖν αὐτῷ ἅμα καὶ ἱερατεύειν καὶ εὐλογεῖν τὸν λαὸν αὐτοῦ ἐν τῷ ὀνόματι (HT בשמו).[79] The expression "eternal covenant" (cf. also 45:7) relates to Nu. 25:12 f., where the covenant of eternal priesthood is promised to Phinehas and his descendants on account of his zeal for God. A song in praise of Phinehas (Sir. 45:23-26) thus follows a longer section in which Aaron is extolled (45:6-22).[80] V. 24 and v. 25 are esp. important in this connection. After the ref. to the covenant with Phinehas in v. 24, we read of the covenant with David, son of Jesse, of the tribe of Judah, in v. 25.[81] There is a par. in the thanksgiving (only Hbr.) in 51:12 (1-16),[82] where we read in v. 12 (8):[83] "Praise him who causes a horn to come forth for the house of David," cf. Ps. 132:17, and then in v. 12 (9): "Praise him who has elected the sons of Zadok as priests." Also of interest is the close of the song in praise of the priest Simeon in Sir. 50:24, where the HT,[84] in clear reminiscence of 45:23, 15, reads: "And may he make with him the covenant of Phinehas, which will always endure for him and his posterity as the days of heaven." In this connection we need not ask whether the portions of the c. that are extant only in Hbr. belong to the original. In content at least[85] the vv. correspond to those preserved in Gk. too.[86] The ref. to Ps. 132:17 in Sir. 51:12 (8) does not have to imply expectation

---

[76] מלא in the HT (ed. R. Smend, *Die Weisheit d. Jesus Sirach* [1906]) is corrupt; read מלך or (מלכי)ם; V. Ryssel in Kautzsch Apkr. u. Pseudepigr., *ad loc.* chooses the sing. in acc. with v. 8b.

[77] Smend, *op. cit.*

[78] The use of χρῖσμα in 38:30, and χρίομαι in Jdt. 10:3, has no theological significance.

[79] Smend, *op. cit.*

[80] Sir. 45:23 LXX — there is a lacuna in HT here — calls Phinehas τρίτος εἰς δόξαν after Moses and Aaron.

[81] Neither wording nor sense of the second half of the v. is quite clear. LXX has κληρονομία βασιλέως υἱοῦ ἐξ υἱοῦ μόνου· κληρονομία ᾿Ααρον καὶ τῷ σπέρματι αὐτοῦ, HT (Smend, *op. cit.*): נחלת אש לפני כבודו נחלת אהרן לו ולזרעו. I. Lévi, *The Hebrew Text of the Book of Ecclesiasticus, Semitic Study Series*, 3 (1904), *ad loc.* conjectures an orig. נחלת מלך לבנו לבדו. Did the author want to stress the agreement or the distinction between David and Aaron? If the latter, the pt. is that the royal power and privileges are handed down from father to son, but the promise to Aaron embraces at once all his successors, cf. G. H. Box and W. O. E. Oesterley in R. H. Charles, *The Apocr. and Pseudepigr.*, I (1913), *ad loc.* Caquot, 58-64 conjectures an orig. נחלת אש לבנו בכורו and relates the Davidic covenant only to David and Solomon, cf. also J. F. Priest, "Ben Sira 45:25 in the Light of the Qumran Literature," *Rev. de Qumran*, 5 (1964-1966), 111-118.

[82] Smend, *op. cit.*

[83] Ref. has often been made to the agreement of this with Sch. E. → 521, 29 ff.

[84] Smend, *op. cit.*

[85] A. A. di Lella, "The Hebrew Text of Sir.," *Stud. in Class. Literature*, 1 (1966), 101-5 (with bibl.) thinks the song of praise, even if not authentic, is as old as Hbr. Sir. Caquot, 50, n. 1 thinks it is a sectarian addition.

[86] It is not clear why Sir. altered 50:24, did not accept 51:12 (1-16) if authentic, and yet kept 45:24.

of a Davidic Messiah. All that is said is that God gives (royal) power to David's house, 47:11 (→ 505, 35 ff.), just as He sees to it that priests of the house of Zadok officiate in the temple. [87] Hence Sir. appeals to God's promise for the priesthood in Nu. 25:12 f. and for the monarchy in 2 S. 7:12 f. The author develops Zech. 4:14, cf. the extolling of Zerubbabel and Joshua in Sir. 49:11 f. In the description of the activities of these figures their concern for the temple is particularly emphasised. [88] In gen. the author puts the priesthood above the monarchy. [89]

2. Testaments of the Twelve Patriarchs. In Test. XII [90] Jud. 21:1-5 is esp. important. It emphatically teaches the subjection of the monarchy to the priesthood for the following reason: ἐμοὶ ἔδωκε τὰ ἐπὶ τῆς γῆς, ἐκείνῳ τὰ ἐν οὐρανοῖς. Ὡς ὑπερέχει οὐρανὸς τῆς γῆς, οὕτως ὑπερέχει Θεοῦ ἱερατεία τῆς ἐπὶ γῆς βασιλείας, 21:3 f. MS b. [91] The Levi-Judah passages shows several signs of Chr. editing. Their orig. aim was probably to magnify both the priesthood of Levi and also the monarchy of Judah and also to stress that the salvation of Israel is indissolubly bound up with both. [92] Test. R. 6:8 MS b is the only v. to use χριστός: [93] διὰ τοῦτο ἐντέλλομαι ὑμῖν ἀκούειν τοῦ Λευί, ὅτι αὐτὸς γνώσεται νόμον Κυρίου, καὶ διαστέλλει (vl. διαστελεῖ and διατελεῖ) εἰς κρίσιν καὶ θυσίας ὑπὲρ παντὸς Ἰσραήλ, μέχρι τελειώσεως χρόνων ἀρχιερέως χριστοῦ, ὃν εἶπε Κύριος. The meaning of the last line is much disputed. But a Chr. explanation seems to offer fewest difficulties. [94] Spiritual leadership and the priesthood of Levi will last to the fulfilment of the times when the high-priest Christ comes of whom the Lord

---

[87] Zadok belongs to the family of Phinehas, cf. 1 Ch. 5:30, 34, cf. the magnifying of the priesthood of the sons of Zadok in, e.g., Ez. 40:46; 43:19; 44:15 f.; 48:11, and cf. Ps. 132:16.

[88] οἳ ἐν ἡμέραις αὐτῶν ᾠκοδόμησαν οἶκον καὶ ἀνύψωσαν ναὸν ἅγιον κυρίῳ ἡτοιμασμένον εἰς δόξαν αἰῶνος, Sir. 49:12 acc. to the corrupt HT (Smend, op. cit.).

[89] David is extolled in 47:1-11 and his kingdom is esp. mentioned. The section devoted to Solomon (47:12-22) contains both praise and blame. These passages plainly show that fut. expectation in Sir. is grounded in trust in God's constant care and past promises. Sir. 47:22 — the HT (Smend, op. cit.) is corrupt — reads: καὶ τῷ Ιακωβ ἔδωκεν κατάλειμμα καὶ τῷ Δαυιδ ἐξ αὐτοῦ ῥίζαν, cf. Is. 11:1, 10; 1 K. 11:39. Sir. knows only few righteous sons of David: "Apart from David, Hezekiah and Josiah they all acted wickedly and forgot the law of the Most High, the kings of Judah, all of them to the very last," 49:4. "Hence they (HT sing.) had to give their horn to another and their glory to a strange people," 49:5. Nevertheless, each king of David's line is a sign of God's faithfulness. When after the time of Elijah and Elisha the people was not converted and had to live dispersed on earth, we read in Sir. 48:16 "a small remnant of Judah remained and a prince of the house of David," though it is added at once that many acted righteously and others sinned. In the prayer for Israel's redemption in 36:1-17 David does not appear, but Aaron does; v. 16 f. LXX: "Hear, O Lord, the prayer of those who pray to thee, according to the blessing of Aaron on thy people. And all the dwellers on earth shall know that thou art the Lord, the eternal God." From what we have seen above it is no surprise that no special redeemer is ref. to in this prayer.

[90] Estimation of Test. XII is made difficult by its complicated history. Chr. redaction has to be taken into account as well as the various strata of Jewish tradition. For a good survey cf. Grelot, 32-41. It is as well to make a sharp distinction between Gk. Test. L. and the Aram. Fr. found in the Geniza of Cairo (Charles, 245-256) and in Qumran (DJD, I, 87-91; J. T. Milik, "Le Test. de Lévi en aram.," Rev. Bibl., 62 [1955], 398-406). In the Gk., traditions found in the Aram. have been worked over but in such a way that we have to speak of two different writings.

[91] Ed. M. de Jonge, Test. XII Patr., Pseudepigr. Veteris Testamenti Graece, I² (1970).

[92] For a specific analysis of the relevant passages and a survey of the views of different expositors cf. de Jonge Testaments, 86-89 and de Jonge Christian Influence, 208-218. J. Becker, "Untersuchungen zur Entstehungsgesch. d. Test. XII," Arbeiten z. Gesch. d. antiken Judt. u. d. Urchr., 8 (1970), 179 does not regard the core of Levi-Judah passages as Messianic.

[93] In Test. L. 10:2 the word occurs only in MS c, where it is plainly an addition. In various places in the MSS (e.g., b c k) Χριστός occurs in the margin in texts the author ref. to Jesus Christ. We may omit these here.

[94] Cf. de Jonge Christian Influence, 211.

has spoken. Even if χριστός is not a proper name here and we have thus to transl. "the anointed high-priest," it is evident that this priesthood is of a different order from that of Levi; the passage has to be understood against a Chr. background. 95 Test. L. 17:2 f. twice has χριστός used in context for priestly figures. 96 There are no other derivates of χρίω. Passages which predict the future in terms of the "sin-exile-return" schema may be disregarded here. If an eschatological figure is mentioned, it is always Jesus Christ. 97

Test. L. 18 and Jud. 24 are often quoted and merit special treatment. 98 It is possible that an older version of Test. Jud. contains an interpretation of Nu. 24:17a HT and that the ref. of vv. 1-4 is orig. to Levi or an eschatological figure of his tribe, and of vv. 5-6 to Judah or an eschatological figure of his tribe. 99 In the present version of Test. Jud. 24:1, however, Nu. 24:17a LXX is quoted: ἀναστήσεται ἄνθρωπος ἐκ τοῦ σπέρματός μου. Verses 2 and 3 are clearly par. to the story of the baptism of Jesus in the Jordan, cf. L. 18:6-9. The section in its present form is from a Chr. hand, esp. as the sent one of God not only receives His Spirit but it is also said of him: ἐκχεεῖ πνεῦμα χάριτος ἐφ' ὑμᾶς, v. 2. 100 The pre-Chr. version cannot be restored with any certainty. Test. L. 18 agrees in many ways with Jud. 24. The prediction is restricted here to a priestly figure. After the punishing of the priesthood the Lord raises up a new priest: τότε ἐγερεῖ κύριος ἱερέα καινόν, 18:2. 101 This ideal figure is also called a king, v. 3. His official work transcends human ideas and points plainly to Chr. influence. 102 In its present form L. 18 speaks of Jesus Christ, who is glorified here as the new high-priest and king. Nevertheless, it is possible that an older version 103 ref. only to the ideal priest of the house of Levi. 104

3. Psalms of Solomon. Ps. Sol. uses χριστός four times, but never without addition. In the title of Ps. 18 we have τοῦ χριστοῦ κυρίου. 18:5b reads: εἰς ἡμέραν ἐκλογῆς ἐν ἀνάξει 105 χριστοῦ αὐτοῦ, cf. 18:5a: εἰς ἡμέραν ἐλέους ἐν εὐλογίᾳ. This anointed of the Lord acts on the commission and in the power of God. 18:7 tells how the Lord's anointed bears the rod and is full of wisdom, righteousness and power, cf. Is. 11:2. c. 17 makes it clear that he is a king of David's house: 106 καὶ αὐτὸς βασιλεὺς δίκαιος διδακτὸς ὑπὸ θεοῦ ἐπ' αὐτούς, καὶ οὐκ ἔστιν ἀδικία ἐν ταῖς ἡμέραις αὐτοῦ ἐν

---

95 We probably have here an allusion to Ps. 110:4, as in Hb. 7:11. For Christ's high-priesthood cf. also Test. S. 7:1 f. MS b: ὅτι ἐξ αὐτῶν ἀνατελεῖ ὑμῖν τὸ σωτήριον τοῦ Θεοῦ. Ἀναστήσει γὰρ Κύριος ἐκ τοῦ Λευὶ ὡς ἀρχιερέα, καὶ ἐκ τοῦ Ἰούδα ὡς βασιλέα, Θεὸν καὶ ἄνθρωπον. Test. L. 8:11-15 corresponds to R. 6:8, de Jonge Christian Influence, 211.

96 This c. seems to be part of a longer apocalypse, de Jonge Testaments, 41.

97 For details, ibid., 83-6.

98 Ibid., 89-91 and de Jonge Christian Influence, 199-208. On the related Test. Zeb. 9:8 and D. 5:10-13 cf. de Jonge Testaments, 91-94.

99 So, e.g., van der Woude, 215 f., v. also K. Schubert, "Test. Jud. 24 im Lichte d. Texte v. Chirbet Qumran," WZKM, 53 (1957), 227-236.

100 Cf. esp. Chevallier, 125-130.

101 It is not said expressly that the new priest is of the tribe of Levi.

102 v. ἕως ἀναλήψεως αὐτοῦ, v. 3β. On. vv. 6-9 → lines 12 ff. Cf. also 9b, which is very anti-Jewish.

103 Becker, op. cit., 299 f. sees in the Jewish core of 18:1-9 a poem on the Messiah of Levi.

104 It is also possible that Jewish elements are used in this depiction. On Qumran par. cf. van der Woude, 210-214. Cf. also the prayer of Levi in the addition to Test. L. 2:3 in MS e, esp. the lines: εἰσάκουσον δὲ καὶ τῆς φωνῆς τοῦ παιδός σου Λευὶ γενέσθαι σοι ἐγγύς, καὶ μέτοχον ποίησον τοῖς λόγοις σου ποιεῖν κρίσιν ἀληθινὴν εἰς πάντα τὸν αἰῶνα, ἐμὲ καὶ τοὺς υἱούς μου εἰς πάσας τὰς γενεὰς τῶν αἰώνων. καὶ μὴ ἀποστήσῃς τὸν υἱὸν τοῦ παιδός σου ἀπὸ τοῦ προσώπου σου πάσας τὰς ἡμέρας τοῦ αἰῶνος. Cf. the Aram. Fr. in Milik, op. cit. (→ n. 90), 398-406.

105 It is not clear whether ἄναξις means bringing back or in. Cod Vossianus miscellaneus, 15 has αἰνέσει, v. W. Baars, "A New Fr. of the Gk. Version of the Ps. of Solomon," VT, 11 (1961), 441-4; cf. also T. W. Manson, "Miscellanea Apocalyptica," JThSt, 46 (1945), 41-5, who proposes ἀναδείξει. But the current text is to be preferred.

106 As in Sir. 46:19 and the OT → 502, 17 ff.

μέσῳ αὐτῶν, ὅτι πάντες ἅγιοι, καὶ βασιλεὺς αὐτῶν χριστὸς κυρίου, v. 32. [107] God's intervention is sought. Appeal is made to His faithfulness and promise. There is longing for the institution of the legitimate Lord's anointed on David's throne, who as an ideal king will do God's will in Israel and achieve victory on earth. It would be out of place to speak here — as is often done — of a national, political, earthly Messiah. This would be to mistake the emphasis in this future expectation. [108] It should be noted that the Ps. Sol. do not ref. to the anointed high-priest and that Messiah is not used in the abs. The Lord's anointed implies the special relation between the king and God. The thing that distinguishes this anointed one from others of David's line is that he will not disappoint either God or man.

4. Ethiopian Enoch. Here "anointed one" [109] occurs only twice, both times in Similitudes: 48:10: "In the days of their [110] distress there will be rest on earth; they will fall down before him (vl. them) [111] and no longer stand upright. There will be none there to take them in his hands and raise them up, for they have hated the Lord of spirits and rejected his anointed," and 52:4: "All this that thou hast seen [112] serves (to show) the lordship of his anointed, that he will be mighty and strong on earth." In context, however, other terms are used for the fut. redeemer: "son of man" in 48:2, "the elect (of God)" in 49:2; 51:3, 5; 52:6, 9. 48:10 is plainly alluding to Ps. 2:2, and in Eth. En. 48 f. we also find reminiscences of Is. 11; 42; 49. [113] These ref. are not so clear in Eth. En. as elsewhere since the author uses apoc. language. There is no allusion to Da. 7. [114] In this connection three ideas are often mentioned, that of the Son of Man (→ VIII, 423, 22 ff.), that of a Davidic Messiah, and that of God's Servant. [115] But it may be questioned whether these complexes have been fully developed as yet. [116] As regards "Messiah" present sources do not permit us to speak too confidently, but it may at least be said that the term "the Lord's Messiah" or "his Messiah" [117] occurs both here and in Ps. Sol. with specific OT ref. and denotes an ideal and righteous ruler of the future. The fact that in the apoc. framework of Eth. En. — which differs markedly in its ideas from Ps. Sol. — the designation occurs only twice, and once in direct quotation from the OT, can hardly support the thesis that here and elsewhere the content of the expression "the Lord's anointed" is fixed merely by the depiction of the Messiah in Ps. Sol. 17 and 18. [118]

---

[107] So rightly Rahlfs on the basis of Ps. Sol. 18:5, 7, cf. also K. G. Kuhn, "Die älteste Textgestalt d. Ps. Sol.," BWANT, 73 (1937), 73 f. All MSS have χριστὸς κύριος, obviously a Chr. emendation; HT משיח יהוה, cf. Lam. 4:20; Sir. 47:11 (→ n. 74), where a vl. has χριστός for κύριος, and 2 Macc. 3:30, where A has χριστοῦ for κυρίου → n. 74. Cf. Is. 11:3, 9a; 54:13 and Ps. Sol. 17 → VIII, 480, 14 ff.; M. de Jonge, De toekomstverwachting in de Ps. v. Salomo (1965), 14-24 and de Jonge The Word "Anointed" 134-7.

[108] The awaited prince does not fight only with military and political weapons. Thus ἐν ῥάβδῳ σιδηρᾷ Ps. Sol. 17:24, cf. Ps. 2:9 corresponds to ἐν λόγῳ στόματος αὐτοῦ, cf. Is. 11:4. This king is God's king; he fights for God's cause and that of Israel. Ps. Sol. 17:32-34 stresses the spiritual aspects of the reign of this king by God's grace, cf. Ps. 72; 110.

[109] Eth. En., too, presents scholars with many difficulties as regards its history and composition, cf. Grelot, 42-50. No cogent arguments have yet been adduced for Chr. redaction or interpolation in the Similitudes.

[110] The ref. is to the kings of the earth.

[111] The Son of Man (vl. the elect) previously mentioned is in view.

[112] The ref. is to all the hidden things of heaven, i.e., an iron mountain, one of copper, one of silver, one of gold, one of soft metal and one of clay, 52:2.

[113] Chevallier, 17-26, cf. also c. 46; 62.

[114] Cf. c. 46 and passim.

[115] The question of the Suffering Servant of the Lord in Eth. En. (Grelot, 49 → V, 687, 5 ff.) need not detain us here, since this aspect does not occur in 48:10 and 52:4.

[116] So Grelot, 49. Sjöberg Menschensohn Äth. Hen., 140-146 thinks that apart from the title several elements of national Messianic expectation are adopted, cf. 50; 56:5-8; 57, cf. Hahn, 158 but in opposition de Jonge the Word "Anointed," 142-144.

[117] In Eth. En., too, "the anointed" is not used in the abs.

[118] In the second vision we find an end-time redeemer in the form of a white bullock, 90:37 f. On "my son" in the Eth. text (not the Gk.) at 105:2 → VIII, 361, 2 ff.

5. Syrian Baruch and 4 Esdras. These works belong to the 1st cent. A.D. and were composed after 70 A.D. The term "the anointed" is used in the abs. here [119] with ref. to a royal figure of the end-time. In this time distinction is made between a period of salvation with which the anointed is connected and a more important era in which he plays no part. In the interpretation of the vision of the cloud rising from the sea (S. Bar. 53), with dark and bright waters that do not relate fully to what is seen, [120] one reads of various plagues in 70:8: war, earthquake, fire and hunger, and it is then added in v. 9: "And everyone who is spared and escapes all these, who have conquered and been conquered, will be delivered into the hands of my servant the Messiah." In 72-74 there then comes a section on the time of "my Messiah" (72:2). The peoples will be put to confusion (Ps. 2:1) and of all the nations called by the Messiah those that have oppressed Israel will be destroyed. Then begins the reign of peace: "Once he has humbled everything that is in the world, and is seated in peace for ever on the throne of his royal dominion, then bliss will be manifested and blessedness will come," 73:1. [121] The age of perfect salvation begins with the reign of the Messiah, for "this age is the end of what is corruptible and the beginning of what is incorruptible," 74:2. In the interpretation of the vision of the vine and the cedar (S. Bar. 36 f.) we read that the kingdom of my Messiah [122] will begin when the fourth empire comes to an end, 39:7. Evildoers will then be rooted out (39:7), esp. their "final ruler," who will have to give an account for his wicked deeds to the Messiah on Mt. Zion and who will then be slain by him, 40:1 f. The remnant of God's people will live under his protection and his dominion will last for ever until the world of corruptibility ends and the predicted times are fulfilled, 40:3. S. Bar. 29:3 - 30:1 describes the time of the Messiah in paradisial colours. Once the Messiah has begun to manifest himself (29:3) the two sea-monsters Behemoth and Leviathan will serve as food for those who survive (29:4) and the earth will yield fruit ten thousandfold, 29:5. [123] In this time manna will again fall down on the earth from above, 29:8. In 30:1 the fulfilment of the age of the Messiah, who seems to play a purely passive role in all this, is expressed as follows: "When the time of the advent of the Messiah is fulfilled and he returns in glory, then all who fell asleep in hope of him will be raised again." A return to God seems to be in view; [124] the Messianic period merges into the time of general resurrection. The transition from the kingdom of the Messiah to the time of perfected salvation is thus plainly indicated here, cf. 4 Esr. 7:29 f.

4 Esr. 12:32 relates the lion of the eagle vision of c. 11 to the anointed: *Hic est unctus, quem reservavit Altissimus in finem.* The Syr., Eth., Arab. and Arm. transl. add that the anointed is of David's seed. [125] He will judge and destroy his enemies but redeem the remnant of the people and cause them to live in joy to the day of judgment. Here again, then, the Messianic period is limited. The same applies to the contested passage in 4 Esr. 7:26-29. After the appearing of the invisible city and the hidden land the Messiah will be manifested with his companions and he will grant joy for a period to those who remain. Then the Messiah and all who have breath will die, 7:28 f. After the world has been seven

---

[119] *Hic est unctus, quem reservavit Altissimus in finem,* 4 Esr. 12:32, cf. S. Bar. 29:3; 30:1. We find "my Messiah" in S. Bar. 39:7; 40:1; 72:2 and "my servant the Messiah" in 70:9. The original of 4 Esr. is very hard to restore on account of the different versions, cf. B. Violet (GCS, 32) and L. Gry, *Les Dires prophét. d'Esdras,* I-II (1938). For S. Bar. cf. Bogaert, I, 413-425.

[120] It is noteworthy that the description of the time of David and Solomon in c. 61 bears features of the fut. time of salvation.

[121] The prophecy of Is. 11:6-8 is interwoven into the description of this kingdom of peace. The curse of Gn. 3:16-19 is removed in 73:6 - 74:1.

[122] ἀρχή is transl. "beginning" rather than "dominion" in the Syr.

[123] In the description of the fruitfulness of the vine we are strongly reminded of the Papias Fr. in Iren. Haer., V, 33, 3 f.

[124] It is not necessary to regard this passage as a Chr. addition. Orig. the words ref. to a return of the Messiah to heaven, cf. the rapture of Elijah. Perhaps later, in the Syr. transl., the text was connected with the Chr. expectation of the *parousia,* Sjöberg Menschensohn Ev., 50, n. 3, *v.* also the difficult "those who fell asleep in hope of him."

[125] Not an addition to the original acc. to B. Violet (GCS, 18) and Gry, *op. cit., ad loc.*

days in primal silence, the dead will rise again and world judgment will begin. [126]

4 Esr. 13 also demands special attention. This is the vision of the man that comes up out of the heart of the sea and flies with the clouds of heaven → VIII, 427, 16 ff. "The anointed" is not used here but this man is "my servant" → n. 126. Of him it is said that the Almighty has kept him for a long period, 13:26 cf. 12:32. He has many features that remind us of the Messiah in passages already discussed → VIII, 427, n. 211 and 428, 2 ff. There are also in 4 Esr. 13 allusions to Da., e.g., the ascent out of the sea, 13:2, 25, 51 (Da. 7:2 ff.), the expression "like unto a man," 13:3 (Da. 7:13), [127] and the mountain not hewn with human hands, 13:6, 36 (Da. 2:45). This corresponds to Eth. En. (→ 514, 16 ff.), where apoc. ideas (also from Da.) are linked with an anointed one and with concepts of the Davidic king such as one finds in Ps. Sol. → 513, 10 ff. [128]

Worth noting in these works is the use of the word "revelation."[129] In some passages, e.g., S. Bar. 29:3; 39:7; 73:1f. the term simply means that the Messiah or Messianic blessings will be manifested with no ref. to pre-existence → VIII, 428, n. 215. But when we hear of the descent of manna or the revelation of the monsters Leviathan and Behemoth or the return of the Messiah in glory (S. Bar. 30:1), pre-existence has to be presupposed even though nothing is said regarding its nature. Acc. to 4 Esr. 7:28; 13:26, 32, 52; 14:9 the author assumes that "my servant" already has now a share in a heavenly existence with God. The Messiah is thus said to be "kept" with God, 4 Esr. 12:32. Between the national redeemer and the liberator who comes from heaven there is thus no fundamental distinction here. Since interest focuses, not on ontological or metaphysical speculations, but on God's acts in salvation history, the various complexes of ideas can be the more easily used together. [130]

6. Oracula Sibyllina. Here the term "the anointed" does not occur but in the description of the coming of the divinely sent ἀπ' ἠελίοιο ... βασιλῆα in Sib., 3, 652-808 various features from the prophetic expectation of the OT may be discerned, cf. esp. 788-795 (based on Is. 11:6-9).

---

[126] The Lat. text of 7:28 f. has undergone Chr. revision. Attempts to restore the original with the help of other versions have not led to agreement. Probably the *filius meus* of 7:28 and 13:32, 37, 52; 14:9 is based on Gk. παῖς μου Hbr. עַבְדִּי, cf. the Eth. text of 7:29 (→ V, 681, n. 196; VIII, 361, 4 ff. and n. 167) and S. Bar. 70:9. If "son" is accepted one must assume that it is meant as in Ps. 2:7, cf. also 2 S. 7:14, cf. Klausner, 354, n. 19. The Messianic era lasts 400 yrs. acc. to the Lat., 30 acc. to the Syr., which is probably basing it on the yrs. of Jesus' life. The figure 1000 also occurs. Although 400 is best attested, the original cannot be fixed for certain. Some scholars think the death of the anointed one is a Jewish idea; the Messianic era ends with the death of the Messiah, cf. S. Bar. 30:1, cf. Klausner, 354 and J. Bloch, "Some Christological Interpolations in the Ezra-Apocalypse," HThR, 51 (1958), 87-94. Others perceive Chr. influence, cf. Grelot, 20 and the notes on the history of the text in Gry, *op. cit.*, 146-9 and also Gry's "La 'mort du Messie' en 4 Esr. 7:29," *Mémorial Lagrange* (1940), 133-9. This is unlikely in context; in any case a Chr. editor would have mentioned the resurrection.

[127] It is surprising that this figure in 4 Esr. comes up out of the sea and flies with the clouds of heaven like the beasts of Da. 7.

[128] N. Messel, "Die Einheitlichkeit d. jüd. Eschatologie," ZAW Beih., 30 (1915), 101-120 rightly emphasises that the Messianic kingdom and the age of perfect salvation are not clearly separated in S. Bar. and 4 Esr. and even if with some exaggeration he stresses the unity of Jewish eschatology. The current view "that 4 Esr. and S. Bar. ... accord to the Messianic kingdom the character of an intermediate kingdom between this and the coming aeon, thus trying to come to terms with traditional eschatology in the sense of a provisional and a definitive time of salvation" (cf. Hahn, 158), is based on too schematic a view of Jewish expectation of the future.

[129] On what follows cf. Sjöberg Menschensohn Ev., 46-51.

[130] The same applies *mutatis mutandis* to the pre-existence of the Son of Man in Eth. En., who is sometimes called Messiah, 48:2, 6; 62:7, cf. Sjöberg Menschensohn Ev., 44-6.

7. Pseudo-Philo. Ps.-Philo Antiquitates Bibl. [131] mentions the anointing of Phinehas as priest by God at Shiloh, 48, 2, and the anointing of David by Samuel, 59, 3, cf. also the saying of the Song of David: *Quando nominatus est christus obliti sunt me*, 59, 4. In c. 51 Samuel is esp. honoured. The people anoints him and says: *Vivat propheta in plebe, et in longo tempore sit lumen genti huic*, v. 7. With an allusion to 1 S. 2:10 it is said: *et haec sit manent quousque dent cornu christo suo, et adherit potentia throni regis eius*, v. 6. A royal figure is undoubtedly meant, cf. also 59, 3 and perhaps 62, 9.

8. Apocalypse of Abraham. The redeemer of Apc. Abr. 31 is called "mine elect," cf. Eth. En. 49:2; 55:4 etc. and Is. 42:1; 49:7. The coming of this elect one is an essential part of God's future and final action.

de Jonge

IV. Qumran.

1. References to Two Messianic Figures. With few exceptions [132] the known works from Qumran have derivates of the root מָשַׁח "to anoint" only in certain forms of the noun מָשִׁיחַ. [133] The plur. מְשִׁיחִים ref. 3 times to the OT prophets, Damasc. 2:12 (2:10); 6:1 (8:2); 1 QM 11:7, [134] cf. Ps. 105:15. Apart from 11 Q Melchizedek 18, [135] where the joyful messenger (מְבַשֵּׂר) of the end-time, who is called מְשִׁיחַ הָרוּחַ (the anointed with the Spirit) is perhaps a prophet, מָשִׁיחַ sing. or plur. ref. to the priestly or kingly anointed one of the future. The priestly sect of Qumran [136] expected "at the end of the days" (1 QSa 1:1) two Messianic figures, 1 QS 9:11; Damasc. 12:23 f. (15:4); 14:19 (18:8); 20:1 (9:29); 19:10 f. (9:10), cf. also 7:18 ff. (9:8 ff.); 4 Q Testimonia 9-13, 14-20; 4 Q Florilegium 1:11, the one a high-priest of the house of Levi, 4 Q Testimonia 14, the son of Aaron, 1 QS 9:11;

---

[131] Ed. G. Kisch, *Publications in Mediaeval Studies*, 10 (1949).

[132] 1 QM 9:8 speaks of the שֶׁמֶן מְשִׁיחַת כְּהוּנְתָם, the anointing oil of their priesthood, which in battle the priests are not to desecrate with the blood of smitten foes. In the copper roll from cave 3 מְשִׁחוֹתֵיהֶם in 12:12 (DJD, III, 298) and מָשׁוּחַ in 7:6 (291); 9:1 (293) relate to מָשַׁח "to measure," cf. also the Aram. examples in DJD, III, Index, s.v. Aram. מְשַׁחָה. Because the fr. are too small 1 Q 21 Fr. 37:2 (DJD, I, 90) and 1 Q 32 Fr. 2:3 (134) — the reading is doubtful here — are unclear in meaning.

[133] At 1 Q 30 Fr. 1:2 (DJD, I, 132) one should read רוּחַ for מָשִׁיחַ cf. van der Woude, 165.

[134] At Damasc. 2:12 (2:10) one should read מְשִׁיחֵי v. J. Maier, *Die Texte v. Toten Meer*, II (1960), 44; Y. Yadin, "Three Notes on the Dead Sea Scrolls," *Israel Exploration Journ.*, 6 (1956), 158-162; C. Rabin, "On a Puzzling Passage in the Damascus Fr.," *Journal of Jewish Stud.*, 6 (1955), 53 f.; van der Woude, 18-20. It should also be linked with רוּחַ קָדְשׁוֹ, which is not an obj. of וַיּוֹדִיעֵם (as against Hahn, 365, n. 1), since otherwise חוֹזֵי אֱמֶת — to be read for וְהוּא אֱמֶת with *The Zadokite Documents*, ed. C. Rabin² (1958) against Rost — would be left in the air. On Damasc. 6:1 (8:2) cf. DJD, III, 130; Maier, 49; van der Woude, 25-27; we are to read מְשִׁיחֵי and no other alteration is then needed. For retaining מְשִׁיחוֹ, so W. S. LaSor, "The Messiahs of Aaron and Israel," VT, 6 (1956), 429 one cannot adduce 1 Q 30 Fr. 1:2 (DJD, I, 132) → n. 133. On 1 QM 11:7 cf. Carmignac-Guilbert, 110; Jongeling, 263; Maier, 137 and esp. van der Woude, 116-124. In view of the added חוֹזֵי תְעוּדוֹת, מְשִׁיחֶיכָה does not ref. here to all who have received anointing as against J. van der Ploeg, "Le Rouleau de la Guerre," *Stud. on the Texts of the Desert of Judah*, II (1959), 141.

[135] Main ed. by A. S. van der Woude, "Melchisedek als himmlische Erlösergestalt in d. neugefundenen eschatol. Midr. aus Qumran Höhle 11," *Oudtest. Studiën*, 14 (1965), 354-373; emended text in M. de Jonge-A. S. van der Woude, "11 Q Melchizedek and the NT," NTSt, 12 (1966), 301-326; cf. also J. A. Fitzmyer, "Further Light on Melchizedek from Qumran Cave 11," JBL, 86 (1967), 25-41; M. P. Miller, "The Function of Is. 61:1-2 in 11 Q Melchizedek," JBL, 88 (1969), 467-9. The anointed one who is a joyful messenger (v. P. Stuhlmacher, "Das paul. Ev.," I, FRL, 95 [1968], 144-6) is perhaps to be equated with the prophet mentioned in 1 QS 9:11.

[136] That the primary ref. is to the priest may be seen from the precedence accorded to the priests in 1 QS 5:9; 9:7; Damasc. 14:3 f. (17:1 f.), cf. van der Woude, 217-249.

Damasc. 12:23 f. (15:4); 14:19 (18:8); 20:1 (9:29); 19:10 f. (9:10) and the other a king of the house of Judah, 4 Q Patriarchal Blessing 1, the son of David of the end-time, 4 Q Patr. Blessing 2 ff.; 4 Q Florilegium 1:11; 1 QSb 5:20-29. [137] These are mostly called "the Messiah of Aaron" and the "Messiah of Israel," nearly always together as משיחי אהרן וישראל, 1 QS 9:11 or משיח אהרן וישראל, Damasc. 12:23 f. (15:4); 14:19 (18:8); 19:10 f. (9:10) or מאהרן ומישראל (for משיח(משוח), Damasc. 20:1 (9:29). The debatable question whether משיח אהרן וישראל in Damasc. is the intentional alteration of a mediaeval (or earlier) scribe for ימשיחי אהרן וישראל[138] or whether it is original [139] cannot finally be settled. [140] This does not mean that Damasc. knew only one Messiah, sc. of Aaron and Israel. [141] For linguistically משיח אהרן וישראל might mean "the Messiah of Aaron and (the Messiah) of Israel," [142] and elsewhere in Damasc. there is expectation of two Messiahs. Thus the priestly Messiah is once separated as יורה הצדק, 6:11 (8:10) [143] and then as an eschatological figure he is set alongside the "prince of the whole community," i.e., the kingly Messiah, 7:18-20 (9:8 f.). [144] Here the priest is the דורש התורה "student of the law" as in 4 Q Florilegium 1:11, which ref. esp. to his coming with the shoot of David. כוהן הראש is also used sometimes for the priestly Messiah, 1 QSa 2:12; 1 QM 2:1; 15:4; 16:13; 18:5; 19:11, but apparently not הכוהן, not even in 1 QM 10:2; 15:6 and 1 QSa 2:19. [145]

2. The Kingly Messiah. The kingly Messiah is possibly called המשיח once at 1 QSa 2:12. [146] If so this is the oldest instance of the abs. use of Messiah as a name. משיח הצדק "true Messiah" in 4 Q Patr. Blessing 3 is already tending in this direction. Elsewhere we find for the Davidic king only נשיא (כל) העדה "prince of the community (or the whole community)," Damasc. 7:20 (9:9); 1 QSb 5:20; 1 QM 5:1; 4 Qp Isa Fr. 5 - 6:2 (DJD, V, 12) and צמח דויד "shoot of David," 4 Q Patr. Blessing 3 f.; 4 Q Florilegium 1:11, cf. 4 Qp Isa Fr. 8 - 10:17 (DJD, V, 14).

3. The Eschatological High-Priest. The eschatological high-priest is ranked above the kingly Messiah. He is mentioned first, cf. 1 QS 9:11 and Damasc. 12:23 f. (15:4) etc., the only exception being 4 Q Testimonia 9-20. [147] In the Messianic era the high-priest and his train take precedence of all others in the council, being then followed by the Messiah and his train, 1 QSa 2:11-16. [148] In the eschatological war, which is conducted as a holy war, the high-priest again plays a far more dominant role than the prince of the community, for it is he who draws up the ranks, 1 QM 15:5 f., and nearly always pronounces the blessings, 1 QM 15:5; 16:13 f., cf. 18:5 f.; 19:11-13. Whereas the high-priest figures no less

---

[137] For two figures cf. also, apart from Ez. 40-48 and Zech. 4:14, Jub. 31:12-23 and Test. Jud. 21:1-5 etc.

[138] So many scholars on the basis of 1 QS 9:11 and following Kuhn Messias, 173, cf. Liver, 152 and Jeremias, 282, n. 1.

[139] So those who either try to link the Messiah with the Teacher of Righteousness, e.g., Dupont-Sommer, 171, or speak of only one Messiah, e.g., Higgins, 215-9. M. Black, The Scrolls and Chr. Origins (1961), 157 considers whether 1 QS 9:11 might not be a scribal error.

[140] On the basis of the reading משיח attested in 4 Q Damasc. 14:19 (18:8), cf. Milik, 125, n. 3.

[141] Deichgräber, 338-342; van der Woude, 74, but cf. de Jonge Intermediaries, 57 f.

[142] Deichgräber, 341 f.; van der Woude, 29. Cf. also 1 QS 3:18 f., where the ref. of the grammatically analogous expression רוחות האמת והעול is to the spirits of truth and error and two categories are obviously meant, Burrows More Light, 299.

[143] On this debated passage cf. Jeremias, 268-289.

[144] On the text cf. Jeremias, 289-295 and van der Woude, 43-61.

[145] On the individual passages cf. van der Woude, 129 and 106.

[146] Since the text is badly preserved the reading is uncertain. On the various proposals for supplementing it cf. the survey in Maier, op. cit. (→ n. 134), 158 f.

[147] van der Woude, 182-5.

[148] On the text cf. J. F. Priest, "The Messiah and the Meal in 1 QSa," JBL, 82 (1963), 95-100 and van der Woude, 96-106.

than 5 times in the extant part of the war-scroll, 1 QM 2:1; 15:4; 16:13; 18:5; 19:11, the prince is mentioned only incidentally at 5:1, [149] though he is also in view in the quotation in 1 QM 11:6 f. The teaching function of the eschatological high-priest is expressed in the titles Teacher of Righteousness in Damasc. 6:11 (8:10) and Student of the Law in 7:18 (9:8); 4 Q Florilegium 1:11. Acc. to Damasc. 6:8-11 (8:9 f.) he gives new directions "at the end of the days." Hence some identify him as the returning Elijah, [150] though others doubt this. [151]

4. The Two Messiahs. In any case the high-priest appears along with the eschatological son of David, 4 Q Florilegium 1:11, cf. Damasc. 7:18-20 (9, 8-10); 1 QSa 2:11-14. The two Messiahs are God's instruments in the end-time. Their coming is obviously expected on the basis of the covenant which God made eternally with the priestly line of Phinehas (Nu. 25:12 f.) and the royal line of David (2 S. 7:11-16). [152] This expectation derives from older post-exilic traditions → 507, 32 ff. No superhuman features occur for certain in relation to either the Messianic high-priest or the eschatological prince. [153] Both figures embody the ideal future as seen by the community in an ungodly era. In this future the true and legitimate priesthood and monarchy will be restored acc. to God's promise. The predominantly priestly interest of Qumran comes out esp. in 1 QM 16:13 ff. etc., [154] in the superiority of the priestly Messiah of the end-time (→ 518, 25 ff.), and in the fact that the kingly Messiah has to be taught by priests, 4 Qp Isa Fr. 8-10, 23 (DJD, V, 14). Yet expectation of a Davidic king manifests a strong political interest along the lines of a new theocratic order and the annihilation of the enemies of Israel, including Magog, ibid., Fr. 8-10, 20 f. (V, 14). Both Messiahs are subordinate to God. [155] The community's expectation is orientated primarily to God and to the time of salvation which He will inaugurate at the appointed date, when righteousness will reign and there will be no more evil, 1 Qp Hab 7:13 and 1 QS 4:18-23. Hence the Messiahs are not sharply sketched as individuals. [156]

5. The Teacher of Righteousness. There is no evidence for the view that the historical Teacher of Righteousness who consolidated if he did not found the community [157] is regarded as a Messianic figure. [158] Damasc. 19:35 f. (9:20) is against such an identification since it plainly distinguishes between the teacher and the Messiah of Aaron and Israel. [159]

---

[149] Probably one should supply מגן "shield" rather than מט, from מטה "staff," which creates difficulties, as against Dupont-Sommer, 193; Jongeling, 142.

[150] So van der Woude, 55, 228 f., cf. N. Wieder, *The Judaean Scrolls and Karaism* (1962), 4 f. and Jeremias, 289.

[151] So, e.g., Maier, *op. cit.*, 50.

[152] This is not stated expressly in the Scrolls, but cf. Sir. 45:23-26 and 4 Q Patr. Blessing 2-4.

[153] Starcky Un texte messian., 51-66 finds such traits in the text from 4 Q edited by him, but Fitzmyer and Brown J. Starcky's Theory, 51 contest the Mess. significance of this text.

[154] Cf. esp. the fact that the high-priest rather than the prince draws up the battle array, 1 QM 15:5 f.

[155] Thus there are no Messian. figures in the section on the two spirits, 1 QS 3:13 - 4:26, which speaks of the new age of salvation, *v.* Y. Yadin, "A Note on DSD IV, 20," JBL, 74 (1955), 40-43.

[156] Hence some scholars find no Messiah in the Scrolls at all; T. H. Gaster, *The Dead Sea Scriptures* (1956), 19 f. sees only a priest or king "at any future epoch." It should be noted, however, that 1 QSa 1:1; 2:12 speak of an eschatological high-priest and prince and the era of salvation begins with their coming after the battle of the nations, 1 QM.

[157] With Jeremias, 161 f. one may say that the Chasidim were forerunners of the community but that God made a new beginning with the coming of the Teacher of Righteousness, so that a community arose in accordance with His will.

[158] Cf. on this Jeremias, 268-307.

[159] The text runs: "From the day of the ingathering of the teacher of righteousness to the coming of the Messiah of Aaron and Israel," cf. Jeremias, 283 f. as against Dupont-Sommer, 154, n. 2 who thinks the Messiah of Aaron and Israel in the sing. is the returning teacher.

Similarly, the thesis that the sect awaited the return of the teacher at the end of the days is without foundation; it rests on erroneous exegesis of Damasc. 6:9-11 (8:9 f.) [160] and 1 Qp Hab. 11:6-8. [161] Since בחירו in 1 Qp Hab. 5:4; 9:12 is a defective form of בחיריו "his elect" any Messianic designation of the Teacher of Righteousness is excluded here too. [162] Nor does 1 QH 3:5-18 ref. to him, [163] since the theme of this section is the Messianic woes to which the community is exposed prior to the end. [164] The righteous of the Qumran community certainly hold the teacher in the highest esteem and have every faith in him, 1 Qp Hab. 8:2 f., but they never regard him as the Messiah. It is not certain whether they saw in him the prophet like Moses of Dt. 18:15, 18. [165]

6. Precedence of the High-Priest. The idea that the Messianic views of the Qumran community changed during the yrs. or that different views are found in the sect at the same time does not find adequate support in the texts. [166] Expectation that two Messiahs would come never seems to have given ground to the hope for one Messiah nor does it seem to have arisen out of this. When one considers that the Messianology of the Dead Sea Scrolls is related to that of Zech., where we find Joshua alongside Zerubbabel in 4:14 (507, 32 ff.), and also that Sir. (→ 511, 10 ff.), Jub. 31:12-23 and Test. XII (→ 512, 8 ff.) all have both priesthood and monarchy in view, it is apparent that the Messianic ideas of Qumran do not diverge as much from traditional expectations as they might seem to do. The unequivocal precedence accorded the high-priest is in keeping with priestly Zadok traditions. It need occasion no surprise that to denote the eschatological ruler מלך is never used along with "messiah of Israel" and "shoot of David," but always נשיא, cf. P and Ez. 40-48. [167]

van der Woude

V. Philo and Josephus.

1. Philo. In Philo's depiction of the future in Praem. Poen., 79 ff. we find a redeemer in 95 but with no very distinct features. Philo adduces the first part of Nu. 24:7 LXX and paraphrases the second with a discussion of the martial acts of this ἄνθρωπος against the nations. As the context shows, the man of 95 is strictly no more than a representative of the saints, who triumph in God's strength.

2. Josephus. It is noteworthy that Jos. does not describe or allow to be described as messiahs Judas b Hiskiah, Simon and Athronges, who claimed the throne after the death of Herod, Bell., 2, 56-65; Ant., 17, 271-284. Nor does he accord the title to the many Messianic prophets who appeared in Palestine in the 1st cent. A.D. → VI, 826, 28 ff. The same applies to the leaders in the Jewish War of 66-70 A.D. Of Menahem he simply says that he was slain by his opponents when he came to pray adorned in kingly apparel, Bell., 2, 442-8 (444).

We can get some idea of Jos.' own views in other passages. Bell., 3, 351 f. tells how he had dreams in which God showed him the strokes of destiny that would fall on the Jews and the future fortunes of the Roman emperors, 351. After the fall of Jotapata he went over to the Romans and told Vespasian that he and his son Titus would be emperor, 3, 400-402. Of the various signs presaging the destruction of the temple he says in 6, 312 f.

---

[160] Cf. Jeremias, 275-289 for details. Cf. also J. Carmignac, "Le retour du Docteur de Justice à la fin des jours?" *Revue de Qumran*, 1 (1958/59), 235-248.

[161] Cf. van der Woude, 162-5 and esp. Elliger, *ad loc.*

[162] van der Woude, 156-8.

[163] Maier, *op. cit.* (→ n. 134), 72 f., 75 f.

[164] van der Woude, 144-156; de Jonge Intermediaries, 58 f.

[165] Jeremias, 295-8.

[166] Brown J. Starcky's Theory, 51-7 as against Starcky Les quatre étapes, 481-505.

[167] Perhaps there is an attack here on the royal title adopted by the later Hasmoneans, cf. van der Woude, 58 and 225.

that what incited them most to war was a twofold oracle (χρησμός) found also in Holy Scripture to the effect that at this time one from their land would rule the world. Many thought that this would be a compatriot of theirs but Jos. recognised that the saying was a prophecy of Vespasian's rule. What prophecy he had in mind is not known for certain, but this much at least is plain, that for Jos. Vespasian is the central figure in his biblically inspired expectation for the future. This hope, and the fact that he heartily detested the radicalism of the Zealots (→ II, 884, 24 ff.) and of related groups that had such unhappy consequences, believing instead that salvation would come through co-operation with the Romans, made it impossible for Jos. to present and evaluate fairly the expectations of others, esp. those of his contemporaries. [168]

de Jonge

VI. Rabbinic Writings.

1. Prayers. In the 14th benediction of the Palestinian recension of the Prayer of Eighteen Benedictions, which derives from the tradition of Shᵉmuel the Less, [169] the following petition is made to God: "In thy great mercy O Yahweh our God, have pity on Israel thy people, and on Jerusalem thy city, and on Zion the habitation of thy glory, and on thy temple, and on thy dwelling, and on the monarchy of the house of David, the Messiah of thy righteousness." Scholars are not agreed as to the age of either the prayer as a whole or of its constituent parts. [170] It is worth noting that the prayer relates more to the Davidic dynasty than, expressly, to a Messiah. This is true in the 15th Benediction of bSh. E., which is not in pSh. E. and is obviously from a later period: "Let the shoot of David sprout quickly and raise up his horn with thy help. Blessed be thou, Yahweh, that thou dost cause a horn of help to grow." In Sh. E. the Messiah is also far less important than God and seems to be only a last gift of Yahweh to his people. [171] Nothing is said about his functions in the end-time.

The prayer Habinenu, [172] an abbreviation of Sh. E. by Mar Samuel (d. 254 A.D.) of Babylon, in which the thirteen middle petitions of Sh. E. are compressed into one, [173] contains in the Palest. recension a prayer for צמח דוד עבדך, "the shoot of David thy servant," which in the Bab. recension is expanded into a prayer for "the sprouting of a horn for David thy servant and the setting up of a light for the son of Jesse thine anointed."

---

[168] In the hotly contested Testimonium Flavianum in Ant., 18, 63 f. (cf. L. H. Feldman, *Josephus*, Vol. 9, The Loeb Class. Library [1965], 49 and S. G. F. Brandon, *Jesus and the Zealots* [1967], 116, 118-121, 359-368) it is said of Jesus: ὁ χριστὸς οὗτος ἦν. James is the brother of Jesus τοῦ λεγομένου Χριστοῦ in Ant., 20, 200 → n. 546.

[169] On the history of Sh. E. cf. Elbogen, 27-41; Str.-B., IV, 208-249; Kuhn Achtzehngebet, 10 f.; E. J. Bickermann, "The Civic Prayer for Jerusalem," HThR, 55 (1962), 163-185.

[170] Thus some think the prayer for a restoration of the Davidic monarchy is a later addition, e.g., Bickermann, *op. cit.*, 166, n. 17. Others think the whole of the 14th Benediction arose only after the destruction of the temple in 70 A.D., e.g., Str.-B., IV, 208 and H. J. Schoeps, Art. "Achtzehngebet," *Bibl. Hist. Handwörterbuch*, I, ed. B. Reicke/L. Rost (1962), 22. A different view is that the origins of Sh. E. are to be sought among the Chasidim of the 2nd cent. B.C., v. K. Kohler, "The Origin and Composition of the Eighteen Benedictions," HUCA, 1 (1924), 387 f. While there is debate as to how far back the Benedictions go, esp. the prayer for the restoration of the Davidic monarchy, it must at least be conceded that the text does not presuppose the destruction of the temple but makes good sense if it is still standing, Kuhn Achtzehngebet, 22 f. The same may be said of the prayer for a Davidic restoration, though it seems doubtful whether this could be used as an official temple prayer during the Roman occupation. Thus the prayer might belong to the period prior to 63 B.C., esp in view of its agreements with the Hbr. thanksgiving in Sir. (Smend, *op. cit.* [→ n. 76]) 51:12 (1-16), Elbogen, 516.

[171] Cf. Volz Esch., 175.

[172] Ed. W. Staerk, "Altjüd. liturgische Gebete," KlT, 58² (1930), 20 and Dalman WJ, I¹ (1898), 304.

[173] Elbogen, 60.

In the Aram. Kaddish, [174] whose core seems to go back to the time before the destruction of the temple, [175] there is prayer to God for the redemption of his people and the coming of his Messiah. [176] In the Kaddish de-Rabbanan, [177] a form of the above prayer offered by mourners acc. to Talmudic statements, [178] we read: "Let the time of the kingship of thy Messiah burst forth, and redeem thy people." But in both prayers the petition for the Messiah and the redemption of the people might be later additions, since they are completely missing from one MS. [179]

The Musaph Prayer [180] for New Year's Day, whose character is shaped by the concept of God's kingdom, [181] has a petition for "the sprouting of a horn for David thy servant and the setting up of a light for the son of Jesse thine anointed."

All these prayers adopt expectations expressed, e.g., in Ps. Sol. 17 f. (→ 513, 27 ff.), but they are primarily governed by the hope of a new independent state. They thus give voice to the popular Messianic expectations that seem to have been held in many circles of the Jewish people at the time of Jesus, cf. Ac. 1:6.

2. The Mishnah. From the period prior to the destruction of the temple in 70 A.D. we do not have a single saying about the Messiah on the part of Tannaitic scholars. [182] The Mishnah incidentally mentions the name of the Messiah only once when in Soṭa, 9, 15 the collapse of order, the dissolution of norms and rules, war, pestilence and famine are all expected "directly before the coming of the Messiah." [183] But this passage is suspected of being a later addition to the Mishnah. [184] So far there has been no convincing explanation of the absence of any reference to the Messiah in the earliest Tannaitic writings. The paucity of Rabbinic source material for the period can hardly be the reason. [185] Nor is the polemic against primitive Christianity an adequate solution. It may well be that rejection of Zealot intrigues, opposition to the imminent eschatological expectation of some apocalyptic groups at the time, political considerations, the bad experiences suffered under the rule of the Hasmoneans, [186] and the fact that the leading rabbis were primarily interested in the exposition and observance of the law, [187] all contributed to a situation in which the theme of Messianic expectation was little discussed, if at all, among the older Tannaites so long as Judaea maintained some sort of independence. The view that expectation of a Messianic king died out with the end of ancient prophecy and revived only with the Christian movement has now been shown to be untenable. [188] This assumption can hardly explain how it was that Messianic expectation gained new force in Rabbinic circles after the destruction of Jerusalem.

---

[174] Ed. Dalman WJ, I¹ (1898), 305 and Staerk, *op. cit.*, 30 f.

[175] Elbogen, 93 f.

[176] Only a vl. in Staerk, *op. cit.*, 30.

[177] Ed. Dalman WJ, I¹ (1898), 305 f.; cf. Staerk, *op. cit.*, 31 f.

[178] Elbogen, 96.

[179] MS B, cf. Dalman WJ, I¹ (1898), 305, who also gives the Aram. text.

[180] Ed. Staerk, *op. cit.*, 21-25.

[181] Elbogen, 141 f. For the HT cf. Dalman WJ, I¹ (1898), 306 and Staerk, *op. cit.*, 23.

[182] Chevallier, 42; Volz Esch., 175; Klausner, 392 f.

[183] Cf. H. Bietenhard, *Die Mischna*, III, 6, Soṭa (1956), 179. Lit. בְּעִקְּבוֹת הַמָּשִׁיחַ means "on the heels of the Messiah."

[184] For the Aram. cf. Volz Esch., 175 and Bietenhard, *op. cit.*, *ad loc.*

[185] Cf. Str.-B., IV, 815.

[186] Doeve, 69-83.

[187] Klausner, 393.

[188] On this 19th cent. view cf. Schürer, II, 589 f.

3. Simon bar Koseba. Although the leader of the second war of Jewish independence, Simon bar Koseba, [189] was not of David's house, the famous scholar R. Akiba hailed him as the promised Messiah on the basis of Nu. 24:17. Acc. to jTaan., 4, 8 (68d, 48-51) R. Shim'on bYochai said: "Akiba my teacher publicly stated: 'A star (כוכב) has arisen out of Jacob,' (meaning that) Koseba has come forth out of Jacob. When my teacher Akiba saw bar Koseba he said: דין הוא מלכא משיחא 'This is the king, the Messiah.' R. Jochanan bTorta answered him: 'Akiba, grass will grow out of thy jaw-bone, and still the Son of David will not have come.'" This tradition shows plainly that not all scribes in the days of the Jewish revolt followed Akiba in his momentous interpretation of Nu. 24:17. But his authority among both scholars and people was so great that most of them hailed bar Koseba as the promised one. Thus, as coin inscr. show, a new calendar was introduced under the guiding thought of the חרות "freedom" of Jerusalem. [190] On the coins Simon bar Koseba is שמעון נשיא ישראל, [191] "Simon the prince of Israel," while in the early period of the war a certain El'azar is mentioned along with him as the high-priest. [192] In distinction from the Qumran community the prince obviously takes precedence here. If in spite of his non-Davidic descent Simon was still hailed as the Messiah, this may best be explained by the current political situation in Palestine, by his gigantic strength, and by his obedience to the Law, [193] esp. as it is doubtful whether the Davidic descent of the Messiah was as it were a dogmatic part of eschatological expectation in Israel. [194] The bar Koseba incident offers confirmation that even in the 2nd cent. A.D. Messianic ideas were not fixed, and esp. of the fact that expectation of the Messianic kingdom determined expectation of the redeemer and not *vice versa*. As one viewed the coming kingdom, so one viewed God's Messiah.

4. Justin's Dialogue. In Dial., which belongs to the 2nd cent. A.D., Just. offers several important ref. to Jewish Messianic ideas after the war of independence under bar Koseba

---

[189] Discoveries in the Wadi Murabba'at and caves in the South Judaean desert have established that the true name of this leader was שמעון בן כוסבא Pap., 24, col. 2, 2 f. (DJD, II, 124 [133 A.D.]). Probably בן כוסבא is his patronymic, DJD, II, 126. In the Talmud we find only בר/בן כוזי[בא] when after the failure of the revolt some at least called him "son of falsehood," cf. jTaan., 4, 8 (68d, 49) in Eka r., 2, 2 on 2:1 (Wünsche, 100). Early Chr. writers are familiar only with the honorary bar Kochba given him on the basis of Nu. 24:17, Just. Apol., 31, 6 (Βαρχωχέβας), cf. Eus. Hist. Eccl., IV, 6, 2 and Schürer, I, 682.

[190] In the Wadi Murabba'at letters לחרות ישראל occurs at most only in one corrupt passage, Pap., 23, 5 (DJD, II, 122 [132 A.D.]); otherwise we always find לגאלת ישראל e.g., Pap., 24, Col. 2, 2 (DJD, II, 124); 4, 2 (130); 5, 1 f. (131). Coins of the first yr. of the revolt bear the inscr. לגאולת ישראל, those of the second and third חרות ישראל, those of the fourth לגאלת ציון. But in the letters לגאלת ישראל is not restricted to the first yr., cf. DJD, II, 120, Pap., 22, recto 1, 1 (118 [131 A.D.]).

[191] Cf. A. Reifenberg, *Ancient Jewish Coins*[2] (1947), 60-66 and DJD, II, 126, Pap., 24, Col. 2, 3 (124). In the desert letters too we find שמעון בן כוסבא נסיא ישראל, e.g., Pap., 24, Col. 2, 2 f. (124); 3, 2 f. (128), cf. 2, 9 f. (124), or שמעון בן כוסבא נשי ישראל Pap., 24, Col. 4, 2 f. (130); 6, 2 f. (132); 7, 2 f. (133).

[192] Identification of this high-priest with the R. El'azar of Modeïn slain by bar Koseba in Beth-Ter is very uncertain, cf. H. Bietenhard, "Die Freiheitskriege der Juden unter den Kaisern Trajan u. Hadrian und der messianische Tempelbau," *Judaica*, 4 (1948), 163, n. 138.

[193] Eka r., 2, 2 on 2:1 (Wünsche, 100) tells how at the siege of the fortress of Beth-Ter bar Koseba caught stones hurled by the enemy on his knee and flung them back, killing many men with them, cf. Str.-B., I, 13; Bietenhard, *op. cit.*, 173. When R. El'azar of Modeïn was suspected of treachery he killed him with a kick and it was thought that only God could have smitten him, Bietenhard, 174. Cf. on the political situation and bar Koseba's obedience to the Law, *ibid.*, 167 f.

[194] Cf. Str.-B., I, 11 f. If Davidic descent had been a fixed element in Jewish expectation, Akiba's action would be hard to explain, as against Hahn, 157, n. 1.

(132-5). Acc. to Trypho [195] the whole Jewish people was expecting the Messiah, 89, 1, although as a man born of men, 48, 1; 49, 1; 67, 2. Trypho charges Christians with accepting a second God alongside the Creator of the world, 55, 1 ff.; 68, 3; 74, 1, and with putting their final hope, not in God, but in a man, the Messiah, 8, 3. The Messiah might be there already, but if so, it would be in concealment and without his knowing himself to be the Messiah, 8, 4; 49, 1; 110, 1. Elijah will anoint and manifest him, 49, 1. He will then come forth in glory, 110, 1, distinguish himself by perfect observance of the Law, 67, 2, and vindicate himself as the Messiah. Surprisingly Trypho ref. to the suffering of the Messiah, 36, 1; 39, 7; 89, 2; 90, 1. He resolutely rejects crucifixion, however, as contrary to the Law, 89, 2; 90, 1.

5. Targums. Acc. to the view of the Targums [196] the Messianic kingdom precedes the resurrection and the Last Judgment and is thus distinct from the coming aeon.

Hope is set in the Messiah, Tg. Pro. on Is. 52:14, but he will remain hidden for a long time because of Israel's unrighteousness, *ibid.*, on Mi. 4:8, cf. Just. Dial., 8, 4; 49, 1; 110, 1. Yet God has established his future from of old and named him in primal time, *ibid.*, on Mi. 5:1; Zech. 4:7. God Himself is the author of the new time, on Is. 9:6, which begins with Messiah's reign, J. I and J. II on Gn. 3:15. The Messiah is a pious descendant of David, born in Bethlehem, Tg. Pro. on M. 5:1, of the race of Jesse, on Is. 11:1; 14:29, cf. on Jer. 23:5; 33:15. Gripped by God's power, on Is. 11:2; Mi. 5:3, he arms for war, J. I and J. II on Gn. 49:11, destroys Israel's foes — Gog also acc. to J. I on Nu. 24:17 ff. — esp. the antichrist, with his lips, Pro. on Is. 11:4, so that all nations will be fully vanquished, on Is. 10:27; 11:4; 14:29; 42:1; 52:15; 53:7, 11 f.; Jer. 23:6; Zech. 4:7; 10:4. He will distribute rich spoil to the victorious Jews, on Is. 53:11 f. and restore peace, 28:6. In his time Israel will receive forgiveness, 53:4, 5, 6, 12. Its sins will fall on the Gentiles, 53:8. The Messiah will rule all kingdoms, on Is. 53:3; 16:1; Am. 9:11; Zech. 4:7. Because God is with him, he will be everywhere triumphant, on Is. 42:6; Mi. 5:3; Is. 28:16; 41:25. Freed by the Messiah, on Is. 53:8; 42:7, the Dispersion will return, 11:11 f.; 42:7; 53:8; Hos. 14:8; Mi. 4:6 f. 5:3, including the ten tribes, cf. Tg. Pro. on Zech. 10:6; Hos. 2:2.

The Messiah is a prophet and teacher of the Law as well as king. He makes a new and living reality of the covenant between God and the people, Tg. Pro. on Is. 42:6. Led by fear of God, 11:3, he does not transgress any commandments of the Law, 9:5, for he has received prophetic gifts, 11:2, and the Holy Spirit rests upon him, 42:1. He has the task of establishing right, 42:4. Hence he causes all to hearken to the Law, 53:11 f.; 42:7, and sinners will be hurled by him into Gehenna, 53:9. Apart from an incidental ref. in 42:6 there is nothing about enlightening the Gentiles. The Messiah rules thus in the cleansed land, on Zech. 6:13. There is peace and prosperity, on Is. 9:5 f.; 11:6-9; 16:5; 53:2, 5; Hos. 3:5; 14:8; Jer. 23:6; 33:16 ff. All unrighteousness will cease, on Jer. 23:5; 33:15; for the Messiah will rule righteously, on Is. 9:6; 11:3 f.; 16:5; 28:6; Jer. 23:5; 33:15. He will rebuild the temple, on Is. 53:5; Zech. 6:12 f. In his days there will be resurrections, on Hos. 14:8, and other miracles, on Is. 53:8; Hab. 3:18, and men will live long, on Is. 53:10. There is nothing about the later fate of the Messiah, for the focus is on the dawning of the new age. Since the Messiah will inaugurate this as God's instrument, the Tg. frequently document the longing of an enslaved people for his coming.

6. Talmudic Literature and Midrashim. In the Talmudic lit. and the Midrashim there is frequent mention of the Messiah and his functions and qualities. As might be expected the material is very like that in the Tg. We find basically the same ideas, though these have been embellished and combined with other traditions in the course of time. Apart from one tradition acc. to which R. Hillel (4th cent.) thought the Messiah had come in the days of Hezekiah (bSanh., 98b), there is agreement that he belongs to the

---

[195] For an evaluation of the ref. in Just. Dial, cf. Harnack, 47-53.
[196] On Tg. Pro. cf. P. Humbert, "Le Messie dans le Tg. des prophètes," RevThPh, 43 (1910), 420-447; 44 (1911), 5-46.

future. Acc. to Pesikt., 4 (54a), cf. Pesikt. r., 33 (153a), the name of the Messiah was created before the world along with the Torah, conversion, the garden of Eden, Gehenna, the throne of grace and the temple. The gen. view is that his coming on earth will be preceded by a time of severe distress and tribulation. These woes of the Messiah חֶבְלוֹ שֶׁלְּמָשִׁיחַ cf. Hos. 13:13; Mt. 24:8; Mk. 13:8 (→ ὠδίνω) are characterised by war, famine, pestilence, bad crops, apostasy, the overthrow of moral ordinances and even the breakdown of natural laws, bSanh., 97a; 98a. [197]

In Talmudic literature the Messianic era is often distinguished from this aeon. Yet as an era prior to the resurrection and final judgment it is also distinct from the coming aeon. [108] As in the Talmud one cannot always harmonise the various rabbis in this regard → I, 207, 4 ff. Some after the model of R. Akiba teach that the Messianic period is part of this wretched aeon, cf. Gn. r., 44, 22 f. on 15:18, [199] while others from the 3rd century on are of the opinion that Israel's dead will already be raised again in the days of the Messiah, Pesikt. r., 1 (4b). [200] In general the Messianic age is regarded as an intermediate one with different views as to its length. [201] Since it is a new aeon as compared with this aeon the Messianic time can sometimes be called עוֹלָם הַבָּא, bBB, 122a etc.

The Rabb. do not agree about the name of the Messiah or the details of his appearance on earth. Some equate him with David, jBer., 2, 4 (5a, 11 f.), cf. Tg. Pro. on Hos. 3:5, but the prevailing view is that he is David's son. His names [202] are Shiloh, bSanh., 98b, [203] Yinnon, loc. cit., [204] Chaninah, loc. cit., [205] Menachem bHezekiah, loc. cit., [206] David, jBer., 2, 4 (5a, 11 f.), bar Naphle, bSanh., 96b/97a on the basis of Am. 9:11, Semach, jBer., 2, 4 (5a, 13), cf. Zech. 6:12 etc., the titles of Is. 9:5, Midr. Maase Torah, [207] and the leper of the house of instruction, bSanh., 98b. [208]

His coming will be prepared for by conversion and obedience to the Law, since sins delay Israel's redemption. Another view is that God will send the Messiah when there are many traitors in Israel and few pupils in the houses of instruction, bSanh., 97a. [209] Many attempts are made to fix the time — usually imminent — of his appearing, but most Rabb. decisively reject calculations of this type. [210] The coming of the Messiah, [211] who acc. to one tradition is to be found first among the lepers and other sick in Rome, bSanh., 98a, will be announced by Elijah. Elijah will show himself in Israel on the pinnacles of the temple and he will light up the peoples to the ends of the earth with his raiment, Pesikt., 22 (149a b). Once the nations hear of this coming they will assemble under the leadership of the Roman Empire to fight against Jerusalem, Pesikt. r., 15 (75b). The Messiah will then either be thrown into prison by hostile Israelites and Gentiles, Pesikt. r., 37 (163a) or he

---

[197] Cf. Str.-B., IV, 981-6.
[198] Ibid., 816-844; Klausner, 408-419.
[199] Cf. Str.-B., IV, 817, 825.
[200] Ibid., III, 828-830; IV, 819.
[201] Ibid., III, 824-7; A. Cohen, Le Talmud (1933), 424; Klausner, 420-426.
[202] On what follows cf. Str.-B., I, 64-66.
[203] So in the school of R. Shilah on the basis of Gn. 49:10; cf. Gn. r., 99, 8 on 49:10.
[204] So in the school of R. Yannai (Ps. 72:17).
[205] So in the school of R. Chaninah (Jer. 16:13).
[206] Cf. Eka r., 1, 16 on 1:16 (Wünsche, 88) and jBer., 2, 4 (5a, 19 f.). The link with Hezekiah is based on the prophecies of Is., cf. Klausner, 463-5, cf. the saying of Rabban Jochanan bZakkai: "Prepare a throne for Hezekiah, the king of Judah, who will come," bBer., 28b, cf. jSota, 9, 17 (24c, 31), jAZ, 3, 1 (42c, 44).
[207] Ed. A. Jellinek, Bet ha-Midrasch, II⁸ (1967), 100.
[208] So acc. to the Rabbanan on the basis of the 30 year suffering of R. Jehuda Ha-Nasi, cf. Str.-B., I, 66.
[209] Cf. Klausner, 434 f.
[210] Cf. Str.-B., IV, 977-1015 for details.
[211] On what follows, ibid., 872-880.

will flee with his followers to the wilderness, Pesikt., 5 (49b). [212] After a certain time, i.e., forty-five days, he will destroy his enemies with the breath of his mouth, Pesikt. r., 37 (163a). Acc. to another tradition he will blunt the teeth of all opposing peoples, Gn. r., 98, 8 on 49:10; 99, 8 on 49:10. Only the nations that have not enslaved Israel will remain alive, Pesikt. r., 1 (2a), cf. Nu. r., 2, 13 on 2:32 (Wünsche, 24); 10, 2 on 6:2 (205) and they will be subject to him and his people. As a ninth empire the kingdom of the Messiah will encompass all peoples and will precede the tenth empire, the kingdom of God alone, PREl, 11 (p. 83). [213] In the Messianic age Israel will have the frontiers promised in Gn. 15:19-21, bBB, 56a; Gn. r., 44 on 15:18; Nu. r., 14, 1 on 7:48 (Wünsche, 346), cf. Gn. r., 64, 3 on 26:3. [214] Every Israelite will have his own property, cf. bBB, 122a, and the dispersed will return to the Holy Land, Midr. Qoh., 1, 7 on 1:7 (Wünsche, 12). [215] God, Midr. Ps., 147, 3 on 147:2, or the Messiah, Gn. r., 98, 9 on 49:11 will gather them, or the nations will give them to the latter as a gift, Midr. Ps., 87, 6 on 87:5.

The Messiah is a king who reigns in peace and whose sceptre is right and righteousness, bSanh., 93b. He is also a teacher of the Law, cf. Gn. r., 98, 11 on 49:11; 99, 11 on 49:11. [216] Concern for the Torah brings him the blessings of God promised therein. In his time the Holy Spirit will be poured out on all flesh, Midr. Ps., 14, 6 on 14:7 [217] and the Israelites will obey God's Law, Midr. Ps., 73, 4 on 73:10. The fruitfulness of the land, S. Lv. בחוקותי 1, 3 on 26:4 f. (Winter, 646) and its inhabitants, ibid., 2, 5 on 26:9 will reach unprecedented proportions, [218] and peace, joy, and happiness will reign, cf. Midr. Ps. 147, 3 on 147:3. [219] Acc. to a tradition found in Gn. r., 12, 4 on 2:4 (Wünsche, 53) the Messiah will restore the lost radiance of Adam, the length of human life, the gigantic size of man, the fruitfulness of vegetation and of the inhabitants of the Holy Land, and the brightness of the heavenly bodies. [220] Jerusalem will be rebuilt more beautifully than ever, Ex. r., 52, 5 on 39:32 (Wünsche, 348), [221] and so will the temple, Pesikt., 21 (145a). [222] Acc. to most Rabb. sacrifices will cease at this time apart from thankofferings and thanksgivings, Pesikt., 9 (79a), [223] since sin itself will cease. The boundary between the Messianic time and the coming aeon is not strictly fixed and so many of these notions cover both. Yet it seems that the idea of Paradise regained in the time of the Messiah came to be accepted only slowly and later. [224] Acc. to most Rabb. the Messianic time will end with the onslaught on Israel under Gog and Magog (→ I, 790, 6 ff.), bAZ, 3b. [225] The Messiah is never a divine figure. Although endowed with special gifts, he is the human king and teacher of the Law in the end-time preceding the עולם הבא. The author of the salvation manifested in this time is God. The focus of interest is obviously the redemption and glorifying of the enslaved people of God.

7. The Messiah ben Joseph. The Messiah ben Joseph [226] or bEphraim or more rarely bManasseh [227] is first attested in literature in the 2nd cent. A.D. [228] Ref. to this remark-

---

[212] Str.-B., II, 285.
[213] *Ibid.*, III, 472.
[214] *Ibid.*, IV, 899.
[215] *Ibid.*, 903-913.
[216] *Ibid.*, 883, 918.
[217] *Ibid.*, II, 615-617.
[218] *Ibid.*, IV, 888-891, 948-958.
[219] *Ibid.*, 892, 965 f.
[220] *Ibid.*, I, 19.
[221] *Ibid.*, IV, 883, 919 f.
[222] *Ibid.*, I, 1003 f.; IV, 884, 929 f.
[223] *Ibid.*, IV, 885, 936 f.
[224] *Ibid.*, 892 f.
[225] *Ibid.*, 893, 967.
[226] Hurwitz, 41-163; Dalman, 2-26; Str.-B., II, 292-9; Klausner, 483-501.
[227] Hurwitz, 41.
[228] bSukka, 52a b. The Messiah ben Joseph is not mentioned by either the Tg., the Mishnah, or Just. Dial.

able figure are few, esp. in the Tannaitic period. In contrast to the Messiah bDavid, who is anointed for kingly rule, the Messiah bJoseph is anointed for military action and is thus called משוח מלחמה, Pesikt. r., 8 (30a); Gn. r., 99, 2 on 48:26; Nu. r., 14, 1 on 7:48 (Wünsche, 341). [229] There is a tradition in Seder Eliyyahu Rabba, 18 (97 f.) [230] that he is the son of the widow of Zarephath whom Elijah raised again. After his manifestation he will lead his armies from Upper Galilee to Jerusalem where he will rebuild the temple and defeat the peoples surrounding Israel. After forty years of peace he will be killed in battle against his enemies, later identified as Gog. The people will lift up a lament for him, cf. Zech. 12:10. The Messiah bDavid, whose coming is contemporary with or just after that of the Messiah bJoseph, will finally conquer the enemies of Israel, Lêqach tob בלק on Nu. 24:17 (129b, 130a). [231] In no sense does the death of the Messiah bJoseph have expiatory significance. [232] If it is not possible to fix the origin of the Messiah bJoseph with any certainty, [233] this figure is not a product of the imagination on the basis of certain texts. [234] It goes back to an older Messianic concept which the Synagogue neither could nor would suppress altogether. It is perhaps a proof that Messianic ideas were much more complicated in the time of Jesus than we can show from the written sources at our disposal.

van der Woude

D. The Christ-Statements of the New Testament.

I. Occurrence of χριστός in the New Testament.

The NT witnesses bring Messianic expectation with them from their history and origins. In them the complex of Messianic ideas is given a real content which is provided by the story of Jesus and which refashions the whole concept of the Messiah. One may see from the Gospels that Messianic expectation was attached to Jesus and yet is neither plain nor indisputable that Jesus called Himself the Messiah. After Easter He obviously bears the title in a new form fashioned by the Easter event.

The OT-Jewish χριστὸς κυρίου or αὐτοῦ occurs in the NT only in the Lucan writings. We often find the absolute ὁ χριστός, which is very insecurely attested in the pre-Christian era and which occurs in older Jewish apocalypse only after Christ's own time → 509, 21 ff. In Paul we also find quite often χριστός without article, especially in the mostly Pauline formulae ἐν Χριστῷ (→ II, 541, 6 ff.), διὰ Χριστοῦ (→ II, 68, 27 ff.) and σὺν Χριστῷ (→ VII, 781, 15 ff.). The absolute

---

229 Str.-B., II, 292.
230 Ed. M. Friedmann (1902), 97 f. Cf. Str.-B., II, 297.
231 Ed. S. Buber (1880). Cf. Str.-B., II, 297.
232 The same may be said of the suffering of the Messiah bDavid, cf. Str.-B., II, 285.
233 Some scholars think the Messiah bJoseph is an invention of scribes on the basis of passages like Dt. 33:17 and Zech. 12:10 ff. Acc. to Str.-B., II, 294 the unsuccessful revolt of Simon bar Koseba (→ 523, 1 ff.) might have given rise to such a figure. Others suggest a Zealot Messiah, esp. as he is expected to appear first in Galilee, cf. Gressmann, 461. Others again relate him to the Samaritan Ta'eb, e.g., Merx, 46-9, or see in the two Messiahs figures corresponding to Saul, who acc. to later tradition was of Ephraim, and David, v. A. Spiro, "Pseudo-Philo's Saul and the Rabbis' Messiah ben Ephraim," *Proceedings of the American Academy for Jewish Research,* 21 (1952), 137. Klausner, 493 espouses the view that after the defeat of bar Koseba the political and spiritual functions of the one Messiah were divided between two figures. Finally, the thesis that the Synagogue set up the slain Messiah bJoseph as a counterpart to the crucified Christ of the Church is most improbable, cf. Str.-B., II, 294.
234 This thesis is rightly rejected by Klausner, 485 for the following reason: " . . . a passage of Scripture (unless it indicates a certain fact with complete clarity) does not create a new idea; but the new idea, which is already emerging, finds proof and support in the Scriptural passage."

ὁ χριστός is put with the name Jesus to give us ὁ Χριστὸς 'Ιησοῦς. Intelligible as a title only in the world of Judaism, ὁ χριστός quickly became a name for Jesus outside Jewish Christian congregations, and is found in the form 'Ιησοῦς Χριστός, which is common throughout the NT and which can often be reversed as Χριστὸς 'Ιησοῦς, especially in the dative. With it ὁ κύριος is also used, so that we have the complete title ὁ κύριος ἡμῶν 'Ιησοῦς Χριστός.

In various forms χριστός occurs 529 times altogether in the NT, [235] 379 of these being in Paul alone, 22 in 1 Pt., 37 in Luke's writings (Lk. 12 and Ac. 25), 19 in the Johannine material, the others distributed among the rest of the books. It is striking how small a share of the total use is to be found in the Synpt. Gospels, 7 instances in Mk., 12 in Lk. and 17 in Mt., cf. 19 in Jn. From χριστός also comes the term Χριστιανοί "Christians" for believers in Christ (→ 536, 35 ff.) and in the post-apost. period we also find Χριστιανισμός to denote their faith and fellowship → 576, 7 ff.; 577, 15 ff.

II. χριστός in the Synoptic Gospels and Acts.

1. χριστός in Mark.

a. In Mk. 15:32 ὁ χριστὸς ὁ βασιλεὺς 'Ισραήλ occurs in the mocking demand that Jesus should come down from the cross → III, 384, 25 ff. The appositional association "the Messiah, the king (→ I, 577, 38 ff.) of Israel" is interpretative. [236] Pilate adopts the title "king of the Jews" in his questions at the hearing (15:2, 9, 12). Jesus is derided as the king of the Jews (15:18) and this is also the superscription on the cross, 15:26. What is in view is always the Messiah (→ I, 574, 2 ff.), for this lies behind the title "king of the Jews." King of Israel in 15:32 is the more exact designation, cf. also Jn. 1:49. The superscription on the cross [237] has historical significance; it shows that Jesus was crucified as a Messianic pretender. The question of His Messiaship is thus at issue. In the passion story a climax is reached when the high-priest puts the question (→ VII, 869, 15 ff.): [238] σὺ εἶ ὁ χριστός, ὁ υἱὸς τοῦ εὐλογητοῦ; (14:61). [239] In this form the question is shaped by the Christian confession of Jesus as Messiah and Son of God, cf. Mt. 16:16; Jn. 1:49; 20:31. Hence Jesus has to reply in the affirmative. He thus describes Himself as the Son of Man and expounds His Messiahship, which includes divine sonship, in terms of Son of Man christology. In the question and answer of Mk. 14:61 f. the essential christological predicates are united in Jesus: Messiah, Son of God (→ VIII, 379, 5 ff.), and Son of Man (→ VIII, 453, 19 ff.). These expound one another. Jesus is the Messiah as the Son of God, and as such He is the Son of Man. New precision is

---

[235] Acc. to R. Morgenthaler, *Statistik d. nt.lichen Wortschatzes* (1958), 156.

[236] In Mk. the Messian. kingship of Jesus comes to the fore with the entry into Jerusalem. It is related here to the peaceful kingdom of the poor in Zech. 9:9 (→ 508, 28 ff.). Mt. 21:5; Lk. 19:38; Jn. 12:15 develop the theme further. The cleansing of the temple is also important in this regard, for building and reforming the temple are the king's prerogative, cf. A. Schalit, *König Herodes* (1969), 313; Betz., 35 f.

[237] Cf. on this Dahl Messias, 159-163; Hahn, 176-9, though Bultmann Trad., 307 sees a dogmatic motif in the superscription. Probably it had a derisive note.

[238] This is true whether or not the Messianic question is implicit in the temple saying of Jesus quoted by the witnesses. On this saying, if unequivocal, a charge of witchcraft and temple desecration might have been brought, and this carried the death penalty acc. to Jewish law. Betz thinks the purpose of building a new temple implies a Messianic claim, 35 f.

[239] ὁ χριστός does not occur in D. This would mean that the divine sonship is at issue, which is affirmed in Jn. 5:18; 19:7, cf. 10:31-33, and vehemently opposed by the Jews and described as a blasphemy, the ground of Jesus' execution → VIII, 386, 16 ff.

thus given to the meaning of the Messiah by the history of Jesus. [240] The concentration of christological titles on Jesus gives evidence of the theological interest of the Evangelist at a decisive point in the hearing, the historical basis (→ VIII, 453, 30 ff.) [241] being that Jesus is sent by the Sanhedrin to Pilate on the charge of being a Messianic pretender. [242]

b. According to Mk. 8:27-33 and par. (→ VIII, 444, 29 ff.; 454, 11 ff.), in which various elements have been discerned, [243] Simon Peter calls Jesus the Messiah [244] in contrast to the people, who, impressed by His works, describe Him as a prophet (→ VI, 841, 27 ff.). [245] Jesus' attitude to the designation is one of reserve, and He replies with teaching about the Son of Man who must suffer many things and be rejected. Mk. thus believes that the Messiah is the Son of Man and this equation is traced back to Jesus Himself, [246] cf. Mk. 14:61 f. → V, 989, n. 278. According to the saying of Jesus Peter's opposition to Jesus' announcement of His passion is based on human ideas; men are unable to associate the concept of the Messiah and the necessity of suffering. [247] Jesus, however, has to think the thoughts of God, cf.

---

[240] Note in this connection that the ideas of Servant of the Lord and prophet are combined in Mk. 14:65, for the deriding of Jesus recalls Is. 50:4-9 and He is mocked as a prophet. Cf. on this C. Maurer, "Knecht Gottes u. Sohn Gottes im Passionsbericht d. Mk.," ZThK, 50 (1953). 1-38, esp. 26 f.; Grundm. Mk., ad loc.

[241] On the debated historical basis cf. H. Lietzmann, "Der Prozess Jesu," Kleine Schr., II, TU, 68 (1958), 251-263; J. Jeremias, "Zur Geschichtlichkeit des Verhörs vor dem Hohen Rat," Abba (1966), 139-144 (Bibl.); J. Blinzler, Der Prozess Jesu⁴ (1970), 87-186; P. Winter, "On the Trial of Jesus," Studia Judaica, I (1961), 20-30 and 160-166; Bultmann Trad., 290-292 and 448 f. Cf. also M. E. Thrall, "Gk. Particles in the NT," NT Tools and Studies, 3 (1962), 70-78. A moot pt. is whether a regular hearing before the Sanhedrin was held (cf. Mk. and Mt.) or only a preliminary investigation to formulate an accusation (cf. Lk. and Jn.).

[242] A survey of the individual texts Mk. 15:2, 9, 12, 18, 26, 32; Mt. 26:68; 27:11, 17, 22, 40, 42 f.; Lk. 23:2, 3, 35, 39 suggests that the Evangelists independently expound the accusation that Jesus is the king of the Jews along the lines of a Messianic claim and thus confirm the Messianic character of the charge.

[243] Cf. Bultmann Trad., 275-8: E. Percy, Die Botschaft Jesu (1953), 227-231; K. L. Schmidt, Der Rahmen d. Gesch. Jesu (1919), 215-220; Hahn, 174 f., 226-230; Dinkler, 284-300; v. also Grundm. Mk., ad loc. for detailed exegesis. Hahn thinks Mk. 8:27a, 29b, 33 is the basis of the pericope, which preserves an incident from Jesus' life in the form of a biographical apophthegm, and he theorises that the saying of v. 33 with its rebuke of Peter, which could not be passed on independently, cannot have arisen in the post-Easter period, 174. Basically Dinkler, 310 f. is of the same view.

[244] Only Mk. has ὁ χριστός abs. in the reply of Peter. Lk. in Jewish fashion adds τοῦ θεοῦ, 9:20; Mt. has a christianised form: "the Christ, the son of the living God," 16:16.

[245] Transition from recognition of Jesus as a prophet to expectation of His Messiahship also underlies Jn. 6:14 f.; Lk. 24:19-21. He who as a prophet reconstitutes the people of God by His teaching and works will be its king and liberator. There is thus a close connection between prophetic and royal activity, cf. in Israel the interpretation of John Hyrcanus (→ VI, 825, 26 ff.) and also prophetic Messianic claimants (→ VI, 826, 20 ff.).

[246] As regards the exposition of the Son of Man concept in Mk. cf. also 9:2-29. The whole complex, enframed by two passion predictions, tells us what the designation Son of Man implies. Cf. on this K. Weiss, "Ekklesiologie, Tradition u. Gesch. in d. Jüngerunterweisung Mk. 8:27 - 10:52," Der historische Jesus u. der kerygmatische Christus, ed. H. Ristow-K. Matthiae (1960), 429-437.

[247] On the understanding of δεῖ (→ II, 23, 10 ff.) cf. H. E. Tödt, Der Menschensohn in d. synpt. Überlieferung² (1963), 174-9 and the review by W. Grundmann in ThLZ, 86 (1961), 427-433. Tödt thinks the necessity of the passion is grounded in the will of God as revealed in Scripture (177) and he thus objects to exposition of the δεῖ formula as eschatological-apocalyptic. But there seems to be here a material connection rather than a contradiction since it is God's will revealed in Scripture that sets the eschatological-apocal. events in train and is fulfilled in them.

Is. 55:8 f. From this passage it is apparent that Jesus' Messianic consciousness is not shaped in content merely by the Messianic expectation of Israel. [248] A very different understanding of His eschatological mission is developed and accepted, and He believes that this comes from God's own thinking. [249]

c. In Mk. 12:35 and par. Jesus Himself raises the Messianic question, not in order to affirm or contest His own Messiahship, but in order to draw attention to the difficulty which arises in Scripture itself when the Davidic sonship of the Messiah is brought face to face with Ps. 110:1, → VIII, 484, 17 ff. This part of the tradition comes at the end of the debates in Jerusalem and it shows afresh that Jesus' Messiahship was a key issue in the last days there. Jesus' question runs: πῶς λέγουσιν οἱ γραμματεῖς ὅτι ὁ χριστὸς υἱὸς Δαυὶδ ἐστιν; on the basis of Ps. 110:1 it then takes the form: αὐτὸς Δαυὶδ λέγει αὐτὸν κύριον, καὶ πόθεν αὐτοῦ ἐστιν υἱός; v. 37. [250] Scholars are divided as to whether the question comes from community theology, possibly that of Hellenistic Jewish Christian circles, [251] or whether it is authentically dominical; [252] community theology finds an answer in the combination of χριστός and κύριος. [253] At all events, the tradition shows that the history of Jesus gives rise to a new form of Messianic teaching. What is decisive is not earthly descent, [254] but the thought and act of God.

d. The apocalyptic discourse in Mk. 13:21 f. gives a warning against being deceived by the appearance of alleged Messiahs. The term ψευδόχριστοι, [255] which occurs only in Mk. 13:22 (→ II, 353, 2 ff.) and Mt. 24:24, gives evidence, like ψευδοπροφῆται (→ VI, 855, 16 ff.), that it was coined in the troubled period before and during the Jewish War, when Messianic claimants and self-proclaimed prophets came on the scene and expectation of the *parousia* reached a climax in the Christian community. [256] The warning presupposes acceptance of Jesus' Messiahship in the Palestinian community, which awaited His *parousia* from heaven as the Son of Man. [257]

e. The formulation ὅτι Χριστοῦ ἐστε occurs only in Mk. at 9:41 in a saying which Mt. also has at 10:42 → IV, 652, 7 ff. [258] χριστός is here used without art. and in the abs., as often in Paul. The reference is to Jesus as the Messiah who gives the disciples a special significance and position. They belong to Christ as in 1 C.

---

[248] On this issue cf. G. Vos, *The Self-Disclosure of Jesus* (1954).

[249] On the problems involved cf. W. Grundmann, "Das Problem d. nt.lichen Christologie," ThLZ, 65 (1940), 69 f.

[250] Mt. and Lk. offer only stylistic, not material, alterations. Cf. also Grundm. Mk. on 12:35-37; also *Das Ev. nach Mt., Theol. Handkomm. z. NT*, 1² (1971) on 22:41f.; also *Das Ev. nach Lk., ibid.*, 3⁶ (1971) on 20:41ff.

[251] Bultmann Trad., 144-6, 429; Hahn, 112-5, 190 f. and 259-262. Acc. to C. Burger, "Jesus als Davidssohn," FRL, 98 (1970), 71 the tradition does not come from Jesus Himself and Mk. misunderstands it when he sees a transcending rather than a rejection of Davidic sonship, 168 f.

[252] Even if formulated in Hellenistic Jewish Christian circles, the question could originate in Messianic expectation linked to Jesus.

[253] Friedrich Hohepriestererwartung, 286-9 thinks the question is rejecting a mistaken son of David eschatology in favour of a correct institution as Messianic high-priest.

[254] Cullmann, 133 f. ref. to Mk. 3:31-35 and par., where earthly relationship is secondary to what God does for men who do his will.

[255] Only at Mt. 24:24 is ψευδόχριστοι textually assured. At. Mk. 13:22 it is not found in D i k and might be supplied with v. 21. Deceptive signs and wonders are more a mark of false prophets than Messiahs.

[256] Cf. Bousset-Gressm., 223 f.

[257] Hahn, 181 f.

[258] *Ibid.*, 223 f.; Grundm. Mk. on 9:41; Kl. Mk., *ad loc.*; Bultmann Trad., 152 f.

15:23. χριστός is also used without art. in Mk. 1:34. [259] Here we read of the demons: ἤδεισαν αὐτὸν χριστὸν εἶναι. [260] Mk. 1:24; 3:11 and 5:7 are therewith expounded in a Messianic sense, the high-priestly Messiah rather than the kingly → 518, 25 ff. [261]

2. χριστός in Matthew.

a. The Evangelist Matthew adopts the χριστός passages of Mk. (Mt. 16:16; 22:42; 24:23 f.; 26:23) and augments them by further development. Thus in 16:20 the disciples are expressly forbidden to tell anyone ὅτι αὐτός ἐστιν ὁ χριστός. Mt. maintains, then, something that is left open in Mk., namely, that Jesus accepted the confession of Peter and that He is the Messiah. [262] In the warning against false teachers (24:5) he expands the statement of those who come in the name of Jesus from ἐγώ εἰμι to ἐγώ εἰμι ὁ χριστός. In so doing He establishes self-revelation by the title and assimilates it to Mt. 24:23 par. Mk. 13:21 → 530, 19 ff. Similarly the confession before the Sanhedrin (Mt. 26:64) [263] is adopted by the scoffers (26:68) with the use of χριστέ, which is not found in Mk. Pilate (→ III, 376, 3 ff.) makes use of the Jewish accusation when he refers to Ἰησοῦν τὸν λεγόμενον χριστόν in 27:17, 22. [264]

b. The statement Ἰησοῦς ὁ λεγόμενος χριστός [265] occurs in 1:16 at the end of the genealogy. Its point is that Jesus is the Messiah as the son of David and offshoot of Abraham, that he belongs to Israel, and that by virtue of his royal descent He is the kingly Messiah who comes at the end of the world period which extends ἕως τοῦ Χριστοῦ 1:17. [266] With the probably correct reading τοῦ δὲ Χριστοῦ ἡ γένεσις οὕτως ἦν (1:18) [267] a smooth transition is then made to the

---

259 In MSS BW Θ.

260 Perhaps taken from Lk. 4:41.

261 Friedrich Hohepriestererwartung, 275-280, but not Hahn, 235-241, who contests the influence of the idea of the high-priestly Messiah on the Gospels. Yet it can hardly be ruled out as an element that shaped certain traditions. One may see it esp. at the beginning of Mk., cf. Grundm. Mk. on cc. 1-3.

262 This is the reason for the basic reconstruction of the Markan original with the addition of the sayings of Jesus to Simon in 16:17-19, cf. Grundmann Mt., op. cit. (→ n. 250), ad loc. and → VI, 104, 23 ff.

263 R. Hummel, Die Auseinandersetzung zwischen Kirche u. Judt. im Mt.² (1966), 142 thinks the changes in Mt. as compared to Mk. are due to Mt.'s total understanding. The Messiahship of Jesus is related to His mission to Israel and is a period of lowliness. It is ended by the exaltation and opens the way to the Gentile mission. But in Mt. the works and teaching of the earthly Jesus have paradigmatic significance for the work of the exalted Lord, cf. H. J. Held, "Mt. als Interpret der Wundergeschichten," G. Bornkamm / G. Barth / H. J. Held, Überlieferung u. Auslegung im Mt.⁴ (1965), 155-287. Even if the mission to Israel is limited in time, the nature of the work in Israel is not, cf. Grundmann Mt., 10-15.

264 In both passages Mk. has "king of the Jews." In Mk's passion there are 6 "king" passages as compared to 4 in Mt., while in Matthew's passion there are 4 "Christ" passages as compared to 2 in Mk.

265 The meaning of this phrase is clarified by Σίμωνα τὸν λεγόμενον Πέτρον in 4:18, cf. 10:2. λεγόμενος gives the nickname the significance of a title and thus reminds us of its true meaning. Simon, who confesses Jesus as the Christ, is instituted by him as "Peter." Jesus is similarly instituted as the Messiah by God. Hence Mt. resists the downgrading of Christ to a mere name, as against G. Strecker, "Der Weg der Gerechtigkeit," FRL, 82² (1966), 126.

266 On the structure of the genealogy with its apoc. ten-week series cf. Grundmann Mt., op. cit. on 1:1-17. The Messiah comes at the end of the ninth and the beginning of the tenth cosmic week.

267 The reading τοῦ δὲ Χριστοῦ without the name of Jesus is to be preferred on the basis of latt sy^sc 71 Ir. The ref. is to the birth of the Messiah and its special features. The upshot is that the Messiah is Jesus, 1:21.

account which shows how the virgin-born is a member of David's house and is thus the son of David who is ordained to be the Saviour from sins and hence Immanuel → VII, 776, 10 ff. [268] The circle is completed with the biblically foretold birth at Bethlehem: Jesus is the legitimate Messiah. The question of the birth of the king of the Jews is also put again when it is asked in 2:2-6 where the Messiah should be born: ποῦ ὁ χριστὸς γεννᾶται;

The works of Jesus to which the Baptist is referred in 11:4-6 and par. are called τὰ ἔργα τοῦ Χριστοῦ in an editorial note by Matthew at 11:2. Jesus' healings, which were not regarded as Messianic signs in the older tradition in Mk. 3:22-30; 8:11 f.; Lk. 11:14-23, cf. Mt. 12:22-25 and 16:1-4, have here the significance of Messianic works. [269] For Mt. the miracles and the Scripture proofs bear witness to the hidden Messiahship of Jesus, 16:20. [270] In the attack on the ambition of the scribes we read: καθηγητὴς ὑμῶν ἐστιν εἷς ὁ Χριστός, 23:10. [271] For Mt. part of the Messiahship of Jesus is also His teaching (→ II, 140, 9 ff.) and His power (7:28 f.; 9:33), by which He exercises His royal dominion. [272] Under the influence of the concept of the Messianic prophet (→ VI, 826, 20 ff.; 845, 16 ff.) [273] Mt.'s reconstruction of the concept of the Messiah in terms of the history of Jesus is brought to completion.

3. χριστός in Luke.

a. Luke, who differs plainly from Mt. in his treatment of the question of the Messiah, takes over three Christ passages from Mk. (9:20; 20:41; 22:67), two with the abs. ὁ χριστός (20:41; 22:67), the other in the phrase τὸν χριστὸν τοῦ θεοῦ (9:20). This usage, which follows that of the OT, is peculiar to Lk in the NT. The *gen. auctoris* shows from whom the anointing of the anointed one derived and to whom he belongs. The Messiah is subject to God and is charged by Him to execute His saving work. In his passion narrative Lk. reproduces the question of the high-priest in twofold form. First the high-priest asks Jesus about His Messiahship: εἰ σὺ εἶ ὁ χριστός, εἰπὸν ἡμῖν (22:67), and Jesus replies that those who ask lack the

---

[268] In 1:16 with its many textual emendations and esp. in the link between the genealogy and the narrative of 1:18-25 one may see how hard Mt. is trying to combine two different christological understandings, namely, that of the Davidic sonship of the Messiah with its two-stage christology, and that of conception by the Spirit and birth of the virgin, which mean that Jesus is the Son of God, although Mt. does not say this directly in connection with the nativity.

[269] The reply to the Baptist with its warning against taking offence at Jesus shows plainly that the works mentioned in the answer were not regarded unequivocally as Messianic works; they were the works of the prophetic Messiah rather than the kingly Messiah → VI, 847, 4 ff. Not the works themselves, but their plenitude proclaims the restoration of paradisial conditions. Jn. in his own way follows the same path as Mt.; for him the acts of Jesus are σημεῖα, Messianic signs → VII, 243, 14 ff.

[270] The healings are also understood Messianically in Mt. 12:23 and 21:14-16, as shown by the use of "Son of David," which is esp. important for Mt. (→ VIII, 485, 29 ff.), cf. the bibl. → VIII, 478, to which may be added G. Ruggieri, "Il Figlio di Dio davidico," *Analecta Gregoriana*, 166 (1968); Burger, *op. cit.* (→ n. 251).

[271] Mt. 23:10 looks like a doublet of 23:8, where some MSS like 𝔎 read καθηγητής for διδάσκαλος; 𝔎 syᶜ also supply ὁ χριστός. Cf. Pr.-Bauer, *s.v.* καθηγητής and Dalman WJ, I, 276 and 279, *v.* also Grundmann Mt., *loc. cit.*

[272] Cf. Grundmann Mt., 281-3.

[273] Cf. K. Bornhäuser, "Das Wirken d. Christus in Worten u. Taten," BFTh, 2, 2² (1924); R. Meyer, *Der Prophet aus Galiläa* (1940); Hahn, 351-404; R. Schnackenburg, "Die Erwartung d. 'Propheten' nach dem NT u. d. Qumrantexten," *Stud. Evangelica*, I, TU, 73 (1959), 622-639. The expectation discernible in Mk. 8:27-29; Lk. 24:19-21; Jn. 6:14 f. helps to promote a link between the Messianic prophet and the Messianic king → n. 245.

presupposition for a discussion of the question. [274] The appended question about His sonship Jesus answers in the affirmative. [275] Again in the passion narrative we find χριστὸν βασιλέα in the accusation before Pilate (23:2) and ὁ χριστὸς τοῦ θεοῦ in the mocking of Jesus (23:35), this time with the implication that God has forsaken the One who calls Himself God's Anointed. Finally an absolute ὁ χριστός (23:39) is uttered by the impenitent thief; this is made more precise by the ὁ χριστὸς τοῦ θεοῦ which comes a little earlier in 23:35 → IV, 189, 10 ff.

b. The question of the Messiah occupies a decisive position in the Lucan infancy stories. To the shepherds the angel hails the new-born child in Bethlehem as σωτήρ (→ VII, 1015, 20 ff.), ὅς ἐστιν χριστὸς κύριος, ἐν πόλει Δαυίδ, 2:11. [276] Lk. elucidates what is a problem in the question as to the son of David; [277] the Messiah is the Kurios, cf. Lk. 1:43. He thus combines the Jewish Christian confession of Jesus as the Messiah with the Gentile Christian confession of Jesus as the Lord. This is an ecumenically important statement in both Lk. and Ac. Lk. also makes it plain that the eternal King announced by Gabriel to Mary (1:31-33) is the Messiah, the royal Messiah of David's house, as in Mt. (→ 531, 17 ff.). [278] The proclamation of the angel to the shepherds is supported by the witness of Simeon, to whom the Holy Spirit has given a promise μὴ ἰδεῖν θάνατον πρὶν ἢ ἂν ἴδῃ τὸν χριστὸν κυρίου,

---

[274] The point of Jesus' answer seems to be that even if He replied to their question He would not find faith among them. This means that He does not fit the idea of the Messiah held by members of the Sanhedrin. In a question and answer discussion they would not share the presuppositions from which He starts in His understanding of the Messiah. The annexed Son of Man confession seems to be taken from Mk. and worked into the slightly different account in the special Lucan material, the chronological note (ἀπὸ τοῦ νῦν) being added. Like Jn., Lk. seems to present this as an unofficial hearing (unlike Mt. and Mk.) to clarify matters by interrogation → n. 241. Cf. G. Schneider, "Verleugnung, Verspottung und Verhör Jesu nach Lk. 22:54-71," Studien z. AT u. NT, 22 (1969), 105-132, 172-174.

[275] Cf. on this Lucan passage → n. 239.

[276] There is here a textual question whether we should read χριστὸς κύριος with most MSS or χριστὸς κυρίου with sy^pal r^l and in line with 2:26. If the latter is preferred, the proclaimed deliverer is the Lord's Messiah — מישׁח יהוה — as in ψ 88:52 (lit. "thine anointed"). But there is good reason to stay with the more gen. attested and more difficult reading in which κύριος is in apposition to χριστός. In this case the angel's proclamation is like that of Peter in Ac. 2:36, which confirms the former as God's act in relation to Jesus. It is true that in Ac. 2:36 κύριος and χριστός are not asyndetically linked but are connected by καί - καί. P. Winter, "Lk. Miszellen," ZNW, 49 (1958), 65-77 thinks χριστὸς κυρίου is original because he postulates a Hbr. basis in which κύριος would mean God and ὁ κύριος Jesus, cf. O. Sol. 29:6: "I believed in the Lord's anointed and it seemed to me that he is the Lord." From a study of Lk.'s usage Winter does not think it likely that he himself would have χριστὸς κύριος; his main interest is in the postulated source. He is followed to a large extent by U. Wilckens, "Die Missionsreden d. Äg.," Wissenschaftl. Monographien z. AT u. NT, 5^2 (1963), 161, n. 5; 162, n. 1; on the meaning of χριστὸς κυρίου cf. 159-161. Schl. Lk.^2 (1960), ad loc. strongly favours a χριστὸς κυρίου. In opposition H. Sahlin, "Der Messias u. das Gottesvolk," Acta Seminarii Neotest. Upsaliensis, 12 (1945), 217-220 defends the reading χριστὸς κύριος. He too discerns משׁיח יהוה behind it but thinks it is the highest conceivable and most lofty designation of Christ, 217; he relates ἐν πόλει Δαυίδ to κύριος and not to ἐτέχθη, 219, construing it as Zion, cf. Is. 24:23 and Tg. Pro. on Is. 16:15: "Then will the Messiah establish his throne in goodness and sit on it in truth in the city of David." On χριστὸς κύριος in Ps. Sol. 17:32 as distinct from χριστὸς κυρίου in 18:5, 7 (→ 513, 23 ff.) cf. H. Braun, "Vom Erbarmen Gottes über den Gerechten," Gesamm. Stud. z. NT u. seiner Umwelt (1962), 60, n. 461; R. Kittel in Kautzsch Apkr. u. Pseudepigr., ad loc.; → n. 107.

[277] Ps. 110:1 is quoted in Ac. 2:34 f. before the proclamation in 2:36.

[278] Lk. 1:31-35 is based on Nathan's promise that David's house will continue, expounding it in terms of the eternal rule of the announced υἱὸς ὑψίστου. On the significance of Nathan's promise in the theology of Qumran and the Synoptic Gospels cf. Betz, 24-28.

2:26. Here χριστὸς κυρίου is important, for this is the one who is expected by the righteous in Israel; He will establish the full salvation denoted by εἰρήνη (→ II, 412, 28 ff.). In contrast, when the disciples of John wish to attribute Messiahship to him, he rejects it: μήποτε αὐτὸς εἴη ὁ χριστός, 3:15 f. In addition to linking Messiah and Lord, Lk. also establishes a relation between Messiah and Son of God. This is what the angel calls Him in 1:32, and the demon-possessed cry out to Him as such in 4:41. Here Lk. adds by way of elucidation: καὶ ἐπιτιμῶν οὐκ εἴα αὐτὰ λαλεῖν, ὅτι ἤδεισαν τὸν χριστὸν αὐτὸν εἶναι, 4:41. Finally Lk. puts the question how far Jesus is χριστός, and he lets Jesus Himself give the answer from Is. 61:1 at His first appearance (→ VII, 923, 12 ff.): πνεῦμα κυρίου ἐπ' ἐμέ, οὗ εἵνεκεν ἔχρισέν με (4:18). He is χριστός as the recipient of the Spirit of God by whom He is conceived and who is given to Him personally in baptism. [279]

c. Jesus, proclaimed the Messiah from His birth, says to the disciples on the way to Emmaus: οὐχὶ ταῦτα ἔδει παθεῖν (→ V, 913, n. 64) τὸν χριστὸν καὶ εἰσελθεῖν εἰς τὴν δόξαν αὐτοῦ; Lk. 24:26, and He then explains this necessity to them from the Scriptures. It had not been envisaged in any previous form of Messianic expectation. Yet this is the primitive Christian understanding of the Messiah on which Luke builds, and for primitive Christianity it opened up the Scriptures in a new way (→ I, 758, 26 ff.). For Luke this disclosure was understood and accepted as a gift of the risen Lord. As distinct from Mt., Lk. presents the story of Jesus between His birth and His crucifixion and resurrection as prophetic rather than Messianic action (→ VI, 841, 14 ff.). [280] Only the way through the cross to glory actualises the Messiahship proclaimed at the outset. Hence Lk.'s picture of the Messiah is decisively shaped by the crucifixion and the resurrection of Jesus. The reconstruction of the concept of the Messiah in terms of the history of Jesus may again be descried.

4. χριστός in Acts.

a. In Ac. Lk. continues what he began in the Gospel. As in Lk. 4:18, Jesus, the holy Servant of God (→ I, 102, 21 ff.), is designated the one ὃν ἔχρισας, Ac. 4:27. In the house of Cornelius Simon Peter says of Him: ἔχρισεν αὐτὸν ὁ θεὸς πνεύματι ἁγίῳ καὶ δυνάμει, 10:38, cf. Lk. 4:14. [281] The material transition from the Gospel to Acts may be found in Lk. 24:25-27, which is established and developed by Peter in his sermon at Pentecost. [282] If in this sermon we read about the ἀνάστασις

---

[279] On the threefold linking of the reception of the Spirit and christology in Lk. cf. Grundmann Lk., op. cit. (→ n. 250), 27; O. Betz, "Die Geburt der Gemeinde durch den Lehrer," NTSt, 3 (1956/57), 324-6.

[280] Cf. 7:16, 39; 24:19. Through Jesus' prophetic work the kingdom of God is perceptible and visible, 16:16; 17:21; 10:23 f.; 11:20. Acc. to Lk. Jesus' concept of the kingdom of God and the Messiah differs from that of His contemporaries, 17:20 f.; 19:10; 22:67 f.; 24:21a, 25-27.

[281] Lk. expressly puts the question as to the meaning of χριστός and he goes back to the original sense. Whereas for most Jews Messiah was now a fixed term and there was little sense of the relation to "anointing," "to anoint," Lk., who is introducing the concept to Hellen. churches in which it would be unintelligible, is forced to elucidate the term.

[282] Cf. the Scripture ref., Ps. 16:8-11; 110:1 and Is. 52:13 for the resurrection (2:22-35 and 3:13), and Ps. 2:1 f. for the passion (Lk. 4:25-27). The one in whom these prophesies are fulfilled is the Messiah. Cf. H. Conzelmann, "Die Mitte d. Zeit," Beiträge z. histor. Theol., 17⁴ (1962), 159, n. 2, who argues that materially the title does not so much signify the relation between God and Jesus as the connection between promise and fulfilment. Nevertheless, Lk.'s trick of providing χριστός with the gen. τοῦ θεοῦ or αὐτοῦ has also the relation to God in view.

τοῦ Χριστοῦ in 2:31, in the next address we read about His passion: ὁ δὲ θεὸς ἃ προκατήγγειλεν διὰ στόματος πάντων τῶν προφητῶν, παθεῖν τὸν χριστὸν αὐτοῦ, ἐπλήρωσεν οὕτως, 3:18. Between the two is the basic proclamation to the whole house of Israel with which the Pentecost kerygma closes: ἀσφαλῶς οὖν γινωσκέτω πᾶς οἶκος Ἰσραὴλ ὅτι καὶ κύριον αὐτὸν καὶ χριστὸν ἐποίησεν ὁ θεός, τοῦτον τὸν Ἰησοῦν ὃν ὑμεῖς ἐσταυρώσατε, 2:36. [283] Since from the very first Jesus is for Luke καὶ κύριος καὶ χριστός (→ 533, 10 ff.) the statement cannot be taken to imply adoptionist christology; [284] instead the final saying relates to all the work of God in relation to His Christ, 2:22-24, 32 f. [285] His resurrection and exaltation have manifested His ordination as κύριος and χριστός; this takes place by way of His rejection by the house of Israel. [286] But the *parousia* is also part of the total picture. Peter speaks of this in a second address to the people. Having mentioned the sufferings of Christ (3:18), he calls for conversion to this Christ so that the sins committed with His rejection may be blotted out, 3:19. This conversion to Christ is a presupposition of the actualisation of the eschatological salvation which will be set up with the return of Christ. The Messiah is Jesus. God already appointed Him Messiah — καὶ ἀποστείλῃ τὸν προκεχειρισμένον ὑμῖν χριστὸν Ἰησοῦν, 3:20. Heaven must receive Him until He comes again to effect the eschatological consummation. This ancient, pre-Lucan tradition [287] uses expressions about Jesus which describe Him as the eschatological prophet (→ VI, 826, 19 ff.), as expressly shown by the proof from Scripture which follows. It is thus evident that the eschatological prophet is divinely instituted as the royal Messiah, although the manifestation of His rule will come only with the *parousia*. [288]

The whole Christ event is probably in view when it is said comprehensively of the apostles: οὐκ ἐπαύοντο διδάσκοντες καὶ εὐαγγελιζόμενοι τὸν χριστὸν Ἰησοῦν, 5:42. Similarly we read concerning Philip's Samaritan mission: ἐκήρυσσεν αὐτοῖς τὸν Χριστόν, 8:5. This is developed in 8:12. The Samaritans believe Philip εὐαγγελιζομένῳ περὶ τῆς βασιλείας τοῦ θεοῦ καὶ τοῦ ὀνόματος Ἰησοῦ Χριστοῦ. [289] Here we find the primitive Christian form Ἰησοῦς Χριστός, linked with ὄνομα. The direct proximity of this name to the title of 8:5 shows that in Ac. Χριστός is not part of the proper name but a sobriquet expressing the realisation that He who

---

[283] The construction should be noted, for the final accusation makes it clear that Israel has incurred guilt. By crucifying Jesus it has sinned against God, who has made Him Messiah and Lord. The effect of this accusation determines the continuation of the story in 2:37 ff.

[284] It is subject to debate whether the statement is Luke's or whether it contains an ancient christological formula of adoptionist character, cf. Wilckens, *op. cit.* (→ n. 276). 170-174, who thinks it is Luke's and Hahn, 116, n. 2 and Cullmann, 222 f., who support a pre-Lucan tradition.

[285] So Wilckens, *op. cit.*, 170-174, as against Hahn, 116, n. 3. Lk. might well be using a formulation that derives from adoptionist christology and relates to Jesus' resurrection and exaltation. But he reconstructs it as a statement about all God's work in relation to Jesus Christ.

[286] The ἐποίησεν corresponds to what Lk. says about God's acts, cf. Grundmann Lk., *op. cit.*, 1-6.

[287] Cf. on this Bau. Ag., 66-8; Hahn, 184-6; Wilckens, *op. cit.*, 153-5, 157 f.

[288] Wilckens, *op. cit.*, 157 f. is surely wrong when he robs this saying of its future ref. and relates it to an already enacted fulfilment, 158. Lk. does not eliminate the *parousia* but in his interpretation of salvation history distinguishes between what has been fulfilled and what is still to be fulfilled.

[289] In noteworthy fashion Lk. both here and at the end of Ac. (28:31) sums up the content of the message of Jesus presented in the Gospel and of the teaching of the apostles developed in Ac.: the kingdom of God and the name of Jesus Christ.

bears it brings salvation, and that His name is thus charged with power. God has sent His word to Israel εὐαγγελιζόμενος εἰρήνην (→ II, 412, 28 ff.) διὰ 'Ιησοῦ Χριστοῦ, 10:36. This should be borne in mind when there is reference to baptism ἐπὶ τῷ ὀνόματι 'Ιησοῦ Χριστοῦ (2:38) as the saving event of a transfer of possession to this Jesus Christ. [290] On this ground Christians can be described as those who call on the name of the Lord (Ac. 2:21; 9:14, 21, cf. also 1 C. 1:2) and πιστεύσαντες ἐπὶ τὸν κύριον 'Ιησοῦν Χριστόν (Ac. 11:17). Here the full form κύριος 'Ιησοῦς Χριστός is used, cf. Lk. 2:11; Ac. 2:36. The Philippian gaoler is told: πίστευσον ἐπὶ τὸν κύριον 'Ιησοῦν Χριστόν, καὶ σωθήσῃ σὺ καὶ ὁ οἶκός σου, 16:31, though Χριστόν is not textually secure in this v. [291] Paul speaks similarly to the Ephesian elders. He testifies to both Jews and Greeks τὴν εἰς θεὸν μετάνοιαν καὶ πίστιν εἰς τὸν κύριον ἡμῶν 'Ιησοῦν Χριστόν, 20:21. [292] On the other hand, in Paul's address to the governor Felix and Drusilla περὶ τῆς εἰς Χριστὸν 'Ιησοῦν πίστεως (24:24) the name of Jesus is textually uncertain. [293] Its absence might be due to the use of Christ as a title: εἰς Χριστόν. Ac. concludes with the significant statement concerning Paul's work in Rome: κηρύσσων τὴν βασιλείαν τοῦ θεοῦ καὶ διδάσκων τὰ περὶ τοῦ κυρίου 'Ιησοῦ Χριστοῦ μετὰ πάσης παρρησίας ἀκωλύτως, 28:31, [294] cf. 8:12. Jesus Christ and His name (→ V, 277, 25 ff.) and person are not only the content of the message and the doctrine of faith; they are also the power of healing, 4:10; 9:34.

b. A special aspect of the testimony to Jesus in Ac. may be seen in relation to Paul. When Paul visits Thessalonica we are told that for three sabbaths he reasoned with the synagogue congregation ἀπὸ τῶν γραφῶν (→ I, 752, 19 ff.), διανοίγων καὶ παρατιθέμενος ὅτι τὸν χριστὸν ἔδει παθεῖν καὶ ἀναστῆναι ἐκ νεκρῶν, καὶ ὅτι οὗτός ἐστιν ὁ χριστός, ὁ 'Ιησοῦς, ὃν ἐγὼ καταγγέλλω ὑμῖν, 17:2 f. This statement shows that Paul presented a new Messianic doctrine in the synagogue and that he supported it from Scripture. At the end of his presentation, which was based on the facts about Jesus, he said that this Messiah whom Scripture expects is Jesus, whom I proclaim. The witness of Scripture is fulfilled. Here Ac. preserves an essential methodological element in Paul's missionary witness which makes it clear, as Luke never tires of showing, that the reality of Jesus has produced a new understanding of what the Messiah is, and hence of what Scripture says about Him. [295] The same form of witness to Christ may also be seen in 17:10 f.; 18:4 f.; 26:22 f.

c. Ac. 11:26 contains a note that the disciples — obviously the term which the original believers used for themselves (→ IV, 442, 33 ff.; 446, 37 ff.; 457, 21 ff.) [296] — were first called Χριστιανοί in Antioch (→ III, 516, 9 ff.). Χριστιανός is formed

[290] But cf. G. Delling, Die Zueignung des Heils in der Taufe (1961), 89.
[291] C D 𝕽 read Χριστόν.
[292] 𝕳 E p⁷⁴ read Χριστόν.
[293] א c A Cvid 𝕽 do not have it.
[294] א* 614 syʰ do not have Χριστοῦ. At 4:33, which is the first of this group in Ac., 28:31 being the climax, א A and vg have τῆς ἀναστάσεως 'Ιησοῦ Χριστοῦ τοῦ κυρίου, whereas most texts read τοῦ κυρίου 'Ιησοῦ τῆς ἀναστάσεως. Cf. on Ac. 28:31 Haench. Ag.¹⁴, 653-5; Bau. Ag., ad loc.
[295] Possibly Paul used florilegia, like those of Qumran, in which Chr. scholars gathered passages from Scripture showing the necessity of the passion and resurrection of Jesus. If so, these would be the basis of the proof from scripture in primitive Christianity, and as such they would find a place in the writings of the apost. and post-apost. age.
[296] Cf. also Haench. Ag.¹⁴, 213, n. 2.

from Christ in analogy to Ἡρῳδιανοί and Καισαριανοί. It denotes Christ's adherents, those who belong to Him. [297] It seems most likely that the term was first used by non-Christians, though this does not have to imply that it was meant derisively → 484, 38 ff. Since such designations are usually based on names, [298] it is possible that in Antioch Χριστός was taken to be a proper name outside the Christian community, probably the name of a god. A reason for coining the term Χριστιανοί is that the Christians in Antioch were now viewed as a separate society rather than as a section of the Jewish synagogue (on this cf. Ac. 11:19-26a); [299] possibly they were regarded as a kind of mystery fellowship. It is also worth noting that the term Χριστιανοί (Ac. 11:26) is connected with Paul's work in Antioch. He spent a full year there and attracted a large following. Paul speaks very pointedly of Jesus as Χριστός (→ 540, 6 ff.) — a pre-Pauline formula which he is quick to adopt. Thus the designation Χριστός was perhaps the dominant one for Jesus in Antioch, and Paul played a decisive part in promoting it. This leads to the use of Χριστιανοί for the μαθηταί, and the term spreads rapidly to other places → 576, 7 ff.; 577, 15 ff. [300]

5. The Gospel Titles in Mark and Matthew.

In the titles at the beginning of their Gospels Mk. and Mt. use the common Chr. designation Ἰησοῦς Χριστός, Mk. 1:1; Mt. 1:1, 18 (→ 531, 21 ff.), whereas Luke in the introductions to Lk. and Ac. speaks more generally and links the term χριστός and the name of Jesus only in the course of his presentation. [301] Mk. and Mt. have the twofold name Jesus Christ at the very outset and the title has now become a second name attached to the common personal name Jesus. Both Evangelists can still use χριστός as a title.

6. The Question of the Messiah in the History of Jesus and the Synoptic Tradition.

The Gospel witness does not offer incontestable proof of the Messianic consciousness of Jesus. This observation is supported by the fact that the sayings source does not contain an unequivocal Messianic designation. The earliest tradition seems to present Jesus as an exorcist and healer, a prophet and a teacher of wisdom, although with an authority which far surpasses that of any past prophets or teachers, Mt. 12:41 f. par. and which grants Him liberating power in face of the might of evil, Mk. 3:27; → III, 399, 39 ff. His authority is eschatological in nature; the final destiny

---

[297] Cf. Pr.-Bauer, s.v., with older bibl.; also Haench. Ag.[14], 311, n. 3; Hahn, 222, n. 1. The thesis of E. Peterson, "Christianus," Frühkirche, Judt. u. Gnosis (1959), 64-87 that the word is used for a supposed political group within Judaism can hardly be true in the days when Lk. was writing and it is very doubtful for the time when the expression originated.

[298] Such names come from the Lat. and are then put into Gk. They are common for groups from the 1st cent. B.C., e.g., Marianus, Sullianus etc. Cf. P. Chantraine, "La formation des noms en grec ancien," Collection linguistique, 38 (1933), 197 [Risch].

[299] The development triggered by the term brought with it two problems. First, Χριστιανοί ceased to enjoy the protection as a religio licita which they had enjoyed as a Jewish sect. Secondly, they had to face the question how they related their knowledge of the Messiah to the Messianic promise given to Israel, cf. Haench. Ag.[14], 308-316.

[300] Cf. the use of Χριστιανοί in Ac. 26:28 for the greater Palestinian area, in Tac. Ann., 15, 44, 2 and Suet. Caes., VI, 16, 2 for Rome, in Ign. (→ 576, 7 ff.) for Antioch and Syria, and in 1 Pt. 4:16 and Plin. ep., X, 96, 1-3 for Asia Minor, all in the 1st cent. or the first half of the 2nd cent. A.D. → 579, n. 546. On Χρηστιανοί → 484, 38 ff.

[301] Cf. W. Marxsen, "Bemerkungen zur 'Form' d. sog. synpt. Ev.," ThLZ, 81 (1956), 345-8; J. Klausner, Jesus of Nazareth (1929), 317-320; 398-407; cf. also → n. 267.

of man is decided in relation to Him, [302] since it is grounded in His position *vis-à-vis* God. [303] The Gospels accept the fact that Jesus is the Messiah. They thus relate the confession of His Messiahship to His history. Mark does this with his concept of the Messianic secret. The history of Jesus is shaped by His intentionally concealed Messiahship, which He discloses only at the trial (14:61 f.) and which is manifested only after the resurrection. [304] Nevertheless, in Mk. the secret is more that of the Son of Man than the Messiah. [305] This is perhaps due to the derivation of the concept from the idea of an apocalyptic-eschatological secret, [306] with some contributions from the actual history of Jesus. [307] The Messianic secret does not imply that Jesus' work was inadequate to support the application of the Messianic title to Him. It implies that the title as then understood was inadequate to express His authoritative work. It has thus to be related to the history of Jesus and re-interpreted accordingly. Luke adopts the passages found in Mk. and concentrates his Messianic statements in the infancy and resurrection narratives. Mt. in some editorial sections uses the title in relation to the work of Jesus even outside the infancy material. For Mt. the work of Jesus comes under the rubric of the new Messianic understanding. It may thus be seen from the Evangelists that the oldest tradition exercised great restraint in its use of the Messianic title. Only the history of Jesus can explain this. His disciples and the people who heard him linked Messianic expectation with His person. His work and its influence on wide sectors of the people strengthened His disciples and adherents in their Messianic hope concerning Him. This brought Him close to the political Zealot Messianic claimants. [308] He was accused of being such a claimant before Pilate, and he was executed on this ground. Jesus Himself did not correspond to the hoped for Messiah of Israel. He did not regard political power as the adversary in His message about the imminent kingdom of God. The Satanic power of evil played this part. He did not seek power or authority; He understood His work in terms of service. If rule is for Him a constitutive part of Messiahship, He actualized it in ministry. The way of the Messiah is to dominion through battle and victory;

---

[302] Cf. Lk. 12:8 f. and par.; Mk. 8:38 and par., and also Tödt, *op. cit.* (→ n. 247), 50-56 (37-42), and the conclusion of the Sermon on the Mount in Q, Mt. 7:24-27 and par.

[303] In this basic question the word abba calls for notice → I. 5, 1 ff.; J. Jeremias, *Abba* (1966), 15-66; also *Nt.liche Theologie*, I (1971), 68-73, 175-180; W. Grundmann, "Die Frage nach der Gottessohnschaft d. Messias im Lichte v. Qumran," *Festschr. H. Bardtke* (1968), 86-111; J. C. G. Greig, "Abba and Amen: Their Relevance to Christology," *Stud. Evangelica*, V, TU, 103 (1968), 2-13; → VIII, 372, 23 ff. Son, Son of God, and Son of Man also call for discussion in this connection.

[304] Cf. Wrede; Bauernfeind, 67-104; E. Bickermann, "Das Messiasgeheimnis u. d. Komposition d. Mk.," ZNW, 22 (1923), 122-140; H. J. Ebeling, "Das Messiasgeheimnis u. die Botschaft d. Mk.," ZNW Beih., 19 (1939); Percy, *op. cit.* (→ n. 243), 271-299; G. H. Boobyer, "The Secrecy Motif in St. Mark's Gospel," NTSt, 6 (1959/60), 225-235. Cf. also J. Roloff, "Das Mk. als Geschichtsdarstellung," *Ev. Theol.*, 27 (1969), 84-93.

[305] Loh. Mk., 1-7; T. W. Manson, "The Son of Man in Daniel, Enoch and the Gospels," *Stud. in the Gospels and the Epistles* (1962), 123-145; Sjöberg Menschensohn Ev., 100-132, 150-175; T. A. Burkill, "The Hidden Son of Man in St. Mark's Gospel," ZNW, 52 (1961), 189-213; also *Mysterious Revelation* (1963); Grundm. Mk., 185-7.

[306] Cf. esp. Sjöberg Menschensohn Ev., 1-40.

[307] Cf. the metaphor of the thief for the coming of Jesus, Mk. 3:27, cf. 1 Th. 5:2; Mt. 24:43 and par.; Rev. 3:3; 16:15; 2 Pt. 3:10, and also the hiddenness of the βασιλεία in Mk. 4:26-29; Mt. 13:31-33 and par.; Mk. 4:30-32; Mt. 13:44-46, and the tension between Jesus' task as a messenger and the danger of His being misunderstood as a thaumaturgist, Mk. 1:32-45; cf. Grundm. Mk., *ad loc.*

[308] Cf. Hahn, 161-179; O. Cullmann, *Der Staat im NT²* (1961), 1-35 (E. T. [1955], 1-49); also *Jesus and the Revolutionaries* (1970).

that of Jesus is marked by suffering and defeat, Mk. 8:27-33; 10:35-45; Lk. 22:24-28;
→ II, 84, 1 ff.; 85, 29 ff. In the ministering lordship which includes suffering, and
which is based on the thinking of God's thoughts (→ IV, 343, 38 ff.), Mk. 8:33
(→ VIII, 444, 29 ff.), there dawns a new concept of Messiahship. This prevents Jesus
from letting Himself be called the Messiah, since if He were it could only promote
misunderstanding of His mission. On the other hand, Messianic expectation was so
firmly linked with the prophetic promise and the people's hope (→ 505, 28 ff.) that it
necessarily came to be related to Him in the new form impressed upon it by His
history. Primitive Christianity was brought face to face with this necessity by the
condemnation and execution of Jesus as a Messianic claimant. Its answer was to
the effect that Jesus is the Messiah as the crucified and risen One whose speedy
return is expected and whose exaltation as the Kurios is believed and confessed. [309]
On the basis of the history of Jesus the charismatic nature of His appearing has a
hand in this; [310] it is explained by His endowment with the Spirit. [311] This is important, for already in the OT (→ 508, 28 ff.) and older Jewish expectation (→ VI,
384, 11 ff.) the Messiah is anointed by God's Spirit. This is the basis of His special
relation to God [312] and of the lordship of service which results from His authority.
All the Evangelists, and Luke especially (→ VI, 404, 25 ff.), refer to His endowment
and anointing with the Spirit. Decisive for the new understanding of the Messiah
is the confession that the Messiah has become the Lord over the power of evil in
sin and death. He frees His followers from its dominion and brings them under His
own lordship. This is a primary statement of apostolic witness. If the Messiah in
Israel is an earthly man, on whom religious, national and political hopes are set,
for Christians He is the Conqueror of the death which He suffered for those who
confess Him. He frees them from their guilt and He Himself has entered into God's
eternity. The development of this view is influenced by the Son of Man concept,
which transcends that of the Messiah, and also by the predicate of divine sonship.
The connecting of Messiahship to the resurrection and exaltation gives new expression to what is conferred by anointing in the OT; it imparts strength and glory. The
person of the anointed is invincible because He is commended to God's protection
as one who is commissioned and sent by Him, and He is equipped for His task by
anointing with the Spirit of God.

The historical uniqueness of Jesus which recasts the whole concept of the Messiah helps to explain why the characteristics not only of the Messianic King (→

---

[309] Hahn traces the detailed stages of development through His work. We can hardly
follow him, however, in separating the *parousia* and exaltation and assigning them to different
communities. In the *parousia* expectation, which awaits Jesus as the coming Son of Man,
the exaltation is implied, and both are based on the resurrection. This is more than a transitional
stage; it is the dawn of the eschatological event. If stress is laid on the exaltation implicit in
the resurrection, this is explained by the thinking of both Jewish and Gentile Christian congregations and by the experience of delay. If it is a development of *parousia* expectation, it
is not a new thing in relation to it. They are connected by the resurrection.

[310] Cf. R. Otto, *Reich Gottes und Menschensohn*[3] (1954), 267-309; W. Grundmann, *Die
Gesch. Jesu Christi*[3] (1961), 265-270, 289-292.

[311] The importance of the endowment with the Spirit for the confession of Jesus in His
community is esp. emphasised by W. C. van Unnik, "Jesus the Christ," NTSt, 8 (1961/62),
101-116, cf. Hahn, 220, n. 5. It is related to the baptism of Jesus and also, in the infancy stories
in Mt. and Lk., to Jesus' conception by the Spirit.

[312] On the question of the abs. "the son" (corresponding to "abba") to express the relation
to God cf. W. Grundmann, "Mt. 11:27 und die joh. 'Der Vater — der Sohn' — St.," NTSt,
12 (1965/66), 42-49, where a critical position is adopted towards Hahn, 323-9; cf. also
Jeremias, *Abba* (→ n. 303), 47-54.

506, 26 ff.) but also of the Messianic High-priest (→ 517, 15 ff.) [313] and the Prophet like unto Moses (→ VI, 845, 18 ff.) were all transferred to Him, so that what Josephus found in Hyrcanus (→ VI, 825, 26 ff.) was fulfilled in Jesus.

III. Χριστός in Paul's Epistles. [314]

1. Pauline Usage.

a. Paul's usage stands under a basic presupposition. The Easter event has plainly related Israel's Messianic expectation to Jesus. Jesus of Nazareth is the promised and expected Messiah. If he does not conform to the ordinary concept of the Messiah, God Himself has accredited Him as the Messiah at Easter. A decisive reconstruction of the term is thus accomplished in combination with the history of Jesus. Along these lines the Messianic designation χριστός becomes a name, for χριστός is Jesus. In the non-Palestinian world, where the word χριστός was not understood, it became a sobriquet attached to the name of Jesus or doing duty for it. By means of this commonly used name the unmistakable uniqueness of Jesus is emphasised.

b. Χριστός occurs in Paul in the abs., sometimes with art. ὁ Χριστός sometimes without art. Χριστός. In genitive constructions, which are common with Christ, the article of the related term carries with it the article of the genitive: τοῦ Χριστοῦ, whereas absence of the preceding article means absence of the article: Χριστοῦ, [315] e.g., οὐκ οἴδατε ὅτι τὰ σώματα ὑμῶν μέλη Χριστοῦ ἐστιν; ἄρας οὖν τὰ μέλη τοῦ Χριστοῦ ποιήσω πόρνης μέλη; (1 C. 6:15; → IV, 564, 29 ff.). One may conclude from this that Χριστός means the same whether with the article or without it. Since proper names are used with the article (e.g., Mk. 15:43-45; Lk. 23:25), Χριστός with the article can have the same sense as Χριστός without it. In the vocabulary of older Greek speaking Christianity Χριστός is one of those words which can be used both with and without the article. [316] Use of the article does not help us to decide when Χριστός is a title and when it is a name. The uniqueness of the One of whom it is used is in any case expressed. [317] Whether Paul says ὁ Χριστός or Χριστός he has this uniqueness in view. Whereas his non-Jewish readers would take it as a proper name, Paul himself is fully acquainted with the title originally meant by the term.

---

[313] Cf. Friedrich Hohepriestererwartung; Grundm. Mk., 30-59 etc. Hahn, 231-241 tries to deprive the passages assembled by Friedrich of their force, but he overlooks the fact that they are just as scattered as those he himself adduces for the eschatological prophet, 351-404. They have considerable force for Mk.

[314] Kramer, 199-222; Neugebauer, 44-56; E. v. Dobschütz, "ΚΥΡΙΟΣ ΙΗΣΟΥΣ," ZNW, 30 (1931), 97-123; Dob. Th., 61; Dahl Messianität; S. V. McCasland, "Christ Jesus," JBL, 65 (1946), 377-383.

[315] Bl.-Debr. § 259, v. also § 253 f.

[316] Schwyzer, II, 24 f.; Bl.-Debr. § 253 f.

[317] A being *sui generis*, Bl.-Debr. § 254. Such designations without art. are often very close to proper names. Cf. Cerfaux, 294: "Christ is the key word in Paul's epistles. It is repeated more than 400 times, while Jesus occurs only some 200 times. Even if Christ were only a proper name, as is often maintained, it would be worth while investigating what aspect of Jesus is denoted... But does not the word Christ, originally the term for a class, often remind us of its original sense in Paul's usage? Is not this the reason why it is combined with certain fixed formulae?", 296: "If Χριστός were merely a proper name, why does he never say ὁ κύριος Χριστός instead of ὁ κύριος Ἰησοῦς?"

ὁ Χριστός occurs in 1 C. 1:13; 10:4; 11:3; 12:12; R. 9:5; 15:3, 7. Χριστός without art. is far more common. The abs. מְשִׁיחָ occurs both in the Rabb. of the Babyl. Talmud [318] and also in Palestinian usage → 509, 21 ff. [319] It probably arose through shunning of the name of God. Paul follows Palestinian usage and that of pre-Pauline Christianity. ὁ Χριστός and Χριστός occur in a series of Pauline passages with no distinction of sense, R. 14:15 Χριστός and v. 18 τῷ Χριστῷ, 15:7 ὁ Χριστός and v. 8 Χριστὸν διάκονον, 1 C. 1:12 ἐγὼ δὲ Χριστοῦ and v. 13 ὁ Χριστός, [320] v. 17 Χριστός and ὁ σταυρὸς τοῦ Χριστοῦ. One should also adduce the materially related 1 C. 3:23: ὑμεῖς δὲ Χριστοῦ, Χριστὸς δὲ θεοῦ, and 1 C. 11:3: παντὸς ἀνδρὸς ἡ κεφαλὴ ὁ Χριστός ἐστιν, ... κεφαλὴ δὲ τοῦ Χριστοῦ ὁ θεός.

Thus ὁ Χριστός and Χριστός mean the same. The titular significance is brought out by Paul in ... εἰς Χριστὸν καὶ χρίσας, 2 C. 1:21.

c. We also find in Paul the expressions Χριστὸς Ἰησοῦς and Ἰησοῦς Χριστός. Only in two thirds of the instances is the textual witness unequivocal. In one third there is vacillation between the two, so that reversal or supplementation by another hand has to be considered. The importance of the Χριστός occurrences would be enhanced thereby. [321] This is strengthened by the observable tendency to use the double form at significant points, e.g., in opening salutations, in the conclusions to individual sections, and in vital statements when the even more important designation ὁ κύριος (ἡμῶν) Ἰησοῦς Χριστός (R. 5:1, 11; 15:6, 30; 1 C. 1:7 f., 10; 15:57; 2 C. 1:3; 8:9; Gl. 6:14; 1 Th. 1:3; 2:19; 5:23; 2 Th. 1:12; 2:1, 14, 16; 1 C. 6:11; 8:6; 16:23; [322]

---

[318] Dalman WJ, I, 238-240; I. Abrahams, "The Personal Use of the Term 'Messiah,'" *Stud. in Pharisaism and the Gospels*, I (1917), 136-8.

[319] K. H. Rengstorf, *Die Auferstehung Jesu*⁵ (1967), 129-131; C. C. Torrey, "Χριστός," *Festschr. K. Lake* (1937), 317-324; Hahn, 208 f., n. 6; B. Otzen, "Die neugefundenen hbr. Sektenschr. u. d. Test. XII," *Stud. Theologica*, 7 (1953/54), 147 f.; Vielhauer Weg, 180-182; J. Jeremias, "Artikelloses Χριστός," ZNW, 57 (1966), 211-5; also "Nochmals: Artikelloses Χριστός," *op. cit.* (→ n. 71); Güttgemanns, *op. cit.* (→ n. 71); also "Der leidende Ap. u. sein Herr," FRL, 90 (1966), 66, n. 70; E. Lohse, "Die at.lichen Bezüge im nt.lichen Zeugnis vom Tode Jesu," *Zur Bdtg. des Todes Jesu*, ed. F. Viering (1967), 105; H. Conzelmann, *Grundriss d. Theol. d. NT*² (1968), 91 f., 222. Jeremias, "Nochmals: Artikelloses Χριστός," 219 concludes that "מְשִׁיחָ is thus widely used without art. like a proper name not only in Mesopotamian but also in Palestinian Judaism, although there is full awareness of its derivation from מָשַׁח and of its titular sense." Cf. further K. Schubert, Review of K. Lehmann, "Auferweckt am dritten Tag nach der Schrift," *Quaestiones disputatae*, 38 (1968) in *Kairos*, 11 (1969), 232.

[320] Friedrich Christus, 241 thinks the ὁ Χριστός of 1 C. 1:13 is an abbreviation for τὸ σῶμα τοῦ Χριστοῦ.

[321] Dobschütz's thesis is widely accepted that "Jesus Christ" is original and that determination of the case by Χριστός (Jesus being the same in the gen. and dat.) brings about the change, but cf. the critical question of McCasland, *op. cit.* (→ n. 314), who is usually inclined to agree with Dobschütz: "I am unable to say why 48 of the 91 examples of 'Christ Jesus' are in the dative and why 102 of the 127 instances of 'Jesus Christ' are in the genitive," 383. It seems to me that the thesis is building more on the situation of a translator than that of the author, who knows what case follows what prep. — ἐν! — and when the gen. is called for. Cerfaux, 310 attempts, though he cannot document it in detail, a theological differentiation: "Paul senses a distinction between Jesus Christ and Christ Jesus. When he uses the former the original thought is that of the man Jesus whom God raises up and to whom He accords the dignity and position of the Christ, the Messianic deliverer. Conversely, when he uses the latter the original thought is that of the pre-existent Christ who has revealed Himself in a man, in Jesus of Nazareth... A stylist and theologian like Paul, a man who knew what words like Χριστός or κύριος mean, used with full deliberation these expressions that we casually treat as interchangeable."

[322] א B and other MSS do not have Χριστοῦ.

Phil. 4:23; 2 Th. 3:6) [323] or Ἰησοῦς Χριστὸς ὁ κύριος ἡμῶν (R. 5:21; 6:23; 7:25; 8:39; 1 C. 1:9; 15:31) is not used. In these fuller expression κύριος is a title expressing worth, whereas Χριστός is to some degree a proper name.

The question arises whether in Paul's writings Χριστός is really a second proper name or whether its character as a title of dignity is still maintained. The question is not very well phrased when put in this either / or form. As a second proper name Χριστός guarantees the particularity and integrity of the name "Jesus." Hence the element of dignity is imported into the proper name by it. This is particularly clear when Χριστός comes first. It retains its full force for Paul even though its content is largely unfamiliar to the non-Jewish world. Paul stands within the history of the living Messianic hope. The primitive community which he fought against prior to his conversion differs from the Jewish world around it by reason of the fact that it knows the Messiah whom the latter expected. This Messiah is Jesus of Nazareth. Paul was offended at the idea (→ VII, 354, 3 ff.) that someone who had been crucified should be the promised Messiah of Israel. This made him a persecutor of the community; Χριστὸς ἐσταυρωμένος is Ἰουδαίοις μὲν σκάνδαλον, 1 C. 1:23. Paul saw and experienced the fact that this Χριστὸς ἐσταυρωμένος is θεοῦ δύναμις καὶ θεοῦ σοφία, 1 C. 1:24, so that he says: οὐ γὰρ ἔκρινά τι εἰδέναι ἐν ὑμῖν εἰ μὴ Ἰησοῦν Χριστὸν καὶ τοῦτον ἐσταυρωμένον, 1 C. 2:2 → VII, 582, 6 ff. The Gentile churches formed as a result of Paul's ministry, however, do not take this in the same way as the apostle. For them the Messiah-Christ is not related to the divine promise which makes Him God's supreme proxy. When Χριστός is used with the name Jesus they regard it as a double name. Caesar Augustus is a parallel. [324] He styled himself Imperator Caesar Augustus. Κύριος Ἰησοῦς Χριστός has a similar ring. Since one should not underestimate the Jewish Christian influence on the Gentile Christian churches, or their knowledge of the Septuagint, in their use of Ἰησοῦς Χριστός they probably caught something of the titular significance of the second name as well. Χριστός is thus a second name which can replace the real proper name and which may to some indeterminable degree bear also the suggestion of worth, function and title. This is supported by the fact that Paul avoids using κύριος and Χριστός together without the name Jesus (→ 533, n. 276; 540, n. 317), [325] since this would merely combine two titles. In the full form Jesus comes between κύριος and Χριστός or κύριος is added to Ἰησοῦς Χριστός in apposition.

That Χριστός still suggests dignity is supported also by the fact that in a series of passages the terms are interchangeable with no distinction of sense, e.g., R. 15:16-20: λειτουργὸν Χριστοῦ Ἰησοῦ, v. 16; ἐν Χριστῷ Ἰησοῦ, v. 17; Χριστός, v. 18; τὸ εὐαγγέλιον τοῦ Χριστοῦ, v. 19; οὐχ ὅπου ὠνομάσθη Χριστός, v. 20, or 2 C. 4:4-6: τὸ εὐαγγέλιον τῆς δόξης τοῦ Χριστοῦ, v. 4; κηρύσσομεν... Χριστὸν Ἰησοῦν κύριον, v. 5; ἐν προσώπῳ Χριστοῦ, v. 6, cf. also Gl. 2:16 - 3:1: διὰ πίστεως Ἰησοῦ Χριστοῦ... εἰς Χριστὸν Ἰησοῦν ἐπιστεύσαμεν... ἐκ πίστεως Χριστοῦ, v. 16; ἐν Χριστῷ and Χριστός, v. 17; Χριστῷ συνεσταύρωμαι... ζῇ δὲ ἐν ἐμοὶ Χριστός, v. 19 f., Ἰησοῦς Χριστὸς προεγράφη ἐσταυρωμένος, v. 1, Gl. 6:12, 14, where we find σταυρὸς τοῦ Χριστοῦ and σταυρὸς τοῦ κυρίου ἡμῶν Ἰησοῦ Χριστοῦ close together, Phil. 1:15-26: τὸν Χριστὸν κηρύσσομεν, v. 15; τὸν Χριστὸν καταγγέλλουσιν, v. 17; Χριστὸς καταγγέλλεται, v. 18; ἐπιχορηγίας τοῦ πνεύματος Ἰησοῦ Χριστοῦ, v. 19; μεγαλυνθήσεται Χριστός, v. 20; ἐμοὶ γὰρ τὸ ζῆν Χριστός, v. 21; σὺν Χριστῷ

---

[323] Kramer, 217 f.; Neugebauer, 45 and 60.

[324] [Risch] Octavian, of the gens Octavia, took the name Caesar when adopted by Caesar. The conferred honorary title Augustus (Σεβαστός) was taken up into the name as a cognomen.

[325] R. 16:18 is the only exception and its authenticity is challenged, Kramer, 213 f.

εἶναι, v. 23; ἐν Χριστῷ 'Ιησοῦ, v. 26, and finally Phil. 3:7-14: διὰ τὸν Χριστόν, v. 7; γνώσεως Χριστοῦ 'Ιησοῦ τοῦ κυρίου μου, v. 8; ἵνα Χριστὸν κερδήσω ... διὰ πίστεως Χριστοῦ, v. 8 f.; κατελήμφθην ὑπὸ Χριστοῦ 'Ιησοῦ, v. 12; ἐν Χριστῷ 'Ιησοῦ, v. 14. [326] In much the same way as he uses Χριστός and ὁ Χριστός Paul uses νόμος, which in R. 10:4 is clearly contrasted with Christ: τέλος γὰρ νόμου Χριστός (→ IV, 1075, 37 ff.). [327] The use is analogous to that of Χριστός. In both cases the use without art. is esp. typical of Paul and in both there is no distinction of sense as between the use with art. and that without it, → IV, 1070, 9 ff. Νόμος is the proper name of the Law. The Law and the Christ, or Law and Christ, are thought of as two powers. The one brings down perdition and the curse on man because of his sin; it is called Law. The other brings salvation to man in the midst of perdition; it is a person and bears the name of Jesus the Saviour. The power of Jesus as Saviour, in contrast to the power of perdition called Law, is given the name of Χριστός or ὁ Χριστός.

Jesus Christ, or Christ Jesus, means Jesus the Saviour.

2. The Significance of ὁ Χριστός and Χριστός in Paul's Chief Epistles.

a. Throughout Paul's epistles we find the formula τὸ εὐαγγέλιον τοῦ Χριστοῦ, → II, 731, 3 ff. What is meant is the good news which has Christ as its content and source, R. 1:16; [328] 15:19; 1 C. 9:12; 2 C. 2:12; 9:13; 10:14; Gl. 1:7; Phil. 1:27; 1 Th. 3:2. Paul can also refer to the εὐαγγέλιον τῆς δόξης τοῦ Χριστοῦ (2 C. 4:4), the μαρτύριον τοῦ Χριστοῦ (1 C. 1:6), τὸ εὐαγγέλιον τοῦ θεοῦ (1 Th. 2:9) and the εὐαγγέλιον θεοῦ (R. 1:1), [329] which makes it clear that the good news which has Christ as its content and source is God's own good news, Christ being God's proxy. From the basic formula we then get such phrases as those in Phil. 1:15-18: τὸν Χριστὸν κηρύσσουσιν (v. 15), τὸν Χριστὸν καταγγέλλουσιν (v. 17), [330] and Χριστὸς καταγγέλλεται (v. 18). Proclamation of the good news, called ῥῆμα Χριστοῦ in R. 10:17, [331] leads to hearing, and this to saving faith.

Paul took over the content of the Gospel of God or Christ from the churches which were already there before him, 1 C. 15:3-5. [332] This tradition is introduced

---

[326] For Paul's use of a sobriquet interchangeably with the proper name cf. his employment of Cephas without Simon, without art. 1 C. 1:12, 9:5; 15:5; Gl. 1:18; 2:9, 11, with art. Gl. 2:14. He avoids the Gk. Πέτρος, which has been put for Κηφᾶς in some of these passages. Πέτρος came into use outside the Pauline corpus, and like other names it was often given an art., Mk. 14:48, 54 f., 62, 66 etc.; 15:2, 4 etc., cf. Bl.-Debr. § 260. Being bilingual Paul knows exactly what Κηφᾶς means, and we must assume the same in the case of Χριστός.

[327] Paul uses ὁ νόμος in the nomin. R. 3:19; 7:1; Gl. 3:12, 19, 21, 24; 1 C. 9:8, in dependent cases R. 2:14 f., 18, 26 f.; 3:19; Gl. 3:13, and νόμος without art. in the nomin. R. 2:14, Gl. 3:21; 5:23, in dependent cases R. 2:14, 17, 27; 3:20 f.; 4:14; 9:31; Gl. 2:16, 19; 3:10, 18; R. 7:1. He has ἐν τῷ νόμῳ in R. 2:20; 1 C. 9:9 and ἐν νόμῳ in R. 2:12, 23; Gl. 3:11; 5:4; διὰ νόμου occurs in R. 4:13; Gl. 2:19, 21 and ὑπὸ νόμον in Gl. 4:4 f.; 5:18; 1 C. 9:20.

[328] τοῦ Χριστοῦ is not textually secure in R. 1:16, being found only in 𝔎.

[329] Comparison of 1 Th. 2:9 and R. 1:1 confirms what is said in → lines 6 ff.

[330] No. art. in B G 1739. Since Χριστός without art. occurs in Da. 1:18 it may be seen again that there is no distinction between the two forms.

[331] 𝔎 A sy have θεοῦ for Χριστοῦ, while G has no gen. Has an abs. ῥῆμα been supplemented in different ways?

[332] Kramer, 46-51; Stuhlmacher, op. cit. (→ n. 135), 266-282. Cf. also E. Lichtenstein, "Die älteste chr. Glaubensformel," ZKG, 63 (1950/51), 1-74; H. Conzelmann, "Zur Analyse d. Bekenntnisformel 1 Kor. 15:2-5," Ev. Theol., 25 (1965), 1-11; U. Wilckens, "Der Ursprung d. Überlieferung der Erscheinungen des Auferstandenen," Festschr. E. Schlink (1963), 56-95; B. Klappert, "Zur Frage d. semitischen oder griech. Urtextes v. 1 Kor. 15:3-5," NTSt, 13 (1966/67), 168-173; H. W. Bartsch, "Die Argumentation d. Pls. in 1 K. 15:3-11," ZNW, 55 (1964), 261-274. Cf. also the Bibl. → n. 319. Hahn, 199-211 and Wilckens, 80 f. think two different and originally independent formulae have perhaps been fused in 1 C. 15:3-5, cf. also

by Χριστός without article. The same is true even in the more developed passage adopted in R. 8:34. [333] From both testimonies we gather that the content of the Gospel is Christ dead, raised again and exalted for us, Christ representing us. Both formulae avoid mention of the crucifixion, since the shameful and accursed death on the cross was a problem for the very first Christians. Paul, who had taken offence at the idea of a crucified Messiah and regarded it as a σκάνδαλον (→ VII, 354, 4 ff.), stated clearly what was avoided in the confessions adopted by him. He thus put in words the event that could not be expected by any man: Χριστὸς ἡμᾶς ἐξηγόρασεν ἐκ τῆς κατάρας τοῦ νόμου γενόμενος ὑπὲρ ἡμῶν κατάρα, ὅτι γέγραπται· ἐπικατάρατος πᾶς ὁ κρεμάμενος ἐπὶ ξύλου, Gl. 3:13. Paul accepts the fact that Christ is accursed on the cross (→ VII, 575, 6 ff.); this is the σκάνδαλον. But He is accursed on our account, not His own. This is Paul's new insight and this is what demands confession of the crucified Christ. Instead of the death of Christ Paul speaks emphatically of the σταυρὸς τοῦ Χριστοῦ, 1 C. 1:17, 23; 2:2; Gl. 6:12; Phil. 3:18. The crucifixion of Christ is for him a declaration of the love of God fulfilled in the love of Christ, R. 5:5 f., 8; 8:35. [334] For Christ died at a time when those who now believe in Him were still weak as sinners and enemies, R. 5:6, 8, 10. [335] Hence Paul himself has been able διὰ τὸν Χριστόν to forswear his own past boasting of descent and achievement, ἵνα Χριστὸν κερδήσω, Phil. 3:8, cf. 7. Christ has become the centre of his life, moulding it by the love which was perfected in sacrifice ζῶ δὲ οὐκέτι ἐγώ, ζῇ δὲ ἐν ἐμοὶ Χριστός, Gl. 2:20.

Just as the crucifixion, as a saving event, is linked with Χριστός, so, too, is the resurrection: ἠγέρθη Χριστὸς ἐκ νεκρῶν διὰ τῆς δόξης τοῦ πατρός, R. 6:4, cf. v. 9. He is proclaimed as the risen Lord by the witnesses: ... Χριστὸς κηρύσσεται ὅτι ἐκ νεκρῶν ἐγήγερται, 1 C. 15:12. As the risen Lord He guides eschatological occurrence to its consummation: ἀπαρχὴ Χριστός, v. 23. [336]

The saving events of the crucifixion and the resurrection that are linked with the name of Χριστός lay upon the believer an obligation regarding his manner of life. Through His death and resurrection Christ is the Lord of the living and the dead: εἰς τοῦτο γὰρ Χριστός ἀπέθανεν καὶ ἔζησεν, ἵνα καὶ νεκρῶν καὶ ζώντων κυριεύσῃ, R. 14:9. He is the paschal offering which opens up a new way of life for man, 1 C. 5:7. He is the purchase price of man's redemption, 1 C. 6:20; 7:23; Gl. 3:13; 4:5. Thus the conduct of Christ's community is determined by the freedom

---

Wilckens, op. cit. (→ n. 276), 73-80. The postulated short formulae, e.g., R. 10:9, L. Goppelt, "Das Osterkerygma heute," Christologie u. Ethik (1968), 86 calls formulae of confession in response to the Gospel rather than formulae which are themselves proclamation. 1 C. 15:3-5 belongs to the latter group.

[333] In context the confessional formula says that since God is for us, there can be no judge or accuser but only the advocate, R. 8:31-34. R. 8:34 goes beyond 1 C. 15:3-5 by speaking of Christ's exaltation and intercession for His people. R. 8:31-34 belongs to the same group as Lk. 10:18; 22:31 f.; Jn. 12:31 f. and Rev. 12:7-18; the group has its source in Job 1 and 2.

[334] At R. 8:35 the texts vacillate between "love of Christ," "love of God," and "love of God in Christ Jesus," the last being an assimilation to 8:39.

[335] The basic statement of 1 C. 15:3-5 is adopted and developed in 1 Pt. 3:18, 22 → 543, 27 f.; n. 332.

[336] ἀπαρχή is the firstfruits (→ I, 485, 9 ff.) which the corruptible world offers to the eternal God. By it the whole is sanctified, R. 11:16. In exposition cf. W. Grundmann, "Die Übermacht der Gnade," Nov. Test., 2 (1957), 50-72; also "Überlieferung u. Eigenaussage im eschatologischen Denken des Ap. Pls.," NTSt, 8 (1961/62), 12-26; P. Hoffmann, "Die Toten in Christus," NTAbh, NF, 2 (1966); A. H. Wilcke, "Das Problem eines messianischen Zwischenreiches bei Pls.," AbhThANT, 51 (1965), 76-85; Güttgemanns, op. cit. (→ n. 319), 73-81.

which must be granted to the brother if Χριστὸς is not to be the ἀμαρτίας διάκονος, Gl. 2:17. Paul warns against surrendering the freedom for which Christ has made us free, Gl. 5:1. But he also warns against misusing it in such a way that the brother perishes δι' ὃν Χριστὸς ἀπέθανεν. To those who offend against their brother he says: εἰς Χριστὸν ἁμαρτάνετε, 1 C. 8:11 f. The whole event of salvation may be seen in the sacrifice of life: ὁ Χριστὸς οὐχ ἑαυτῷ ἤρεσεν, R. 15:3, and in the continuation of this statement witness is borne to Christ: ὁ Χριστὸς προσελάβετο ἡμᾶς, R. 15:7. The point of both sayings is that Christians' dealings with one another should be shaped by Christ's dealings with men.

Christ, who accepted the curse of the Law for us (Gl. 3:13 → I, 450, 2 ff.) and who is thus the end of the Law (R. 10:4 → VIII, 56, 13 ff.), liberates from the Law. But this freedom (→ II, 496, 31 ff.) from sin (→ I, 309, 14 ff.) and death (→ II, 498, 7 ff.) as freedom from the power and operation of the condemnatory Law (1 C. 15:56; R. 6:23 → IV, 1073, 25 ff.), does not mean that there is now no obligation. Christ takes the place of the Law. [337] Hence Paul says about his freedom from the Law that he is not ἄνομος θεοῦ ἀλλ' ἔννομος Χριστοῦ, 1 C. 9:21. To be ἔννομος Χριστοῦ is to fulfil τὸν νόμον τοῦ Χριστοῦ, which consists in the demand ἀλλήλων τὰ βάρη βαστάζετε, Gl. 6:2. The life-moulding position of Christ is threatened when the Gospel of Christ is supplemented and burdened by additional requirements, e.g., circumcision. These negate Christ's saving and liberating act, Gl. 5:1-6, cf. 2:21.

Paul is anxious for the Galatians μέχρις οὗ μορφωθῇ Χριστὸς ἐν ὑμῖν, Gl. 4:19, i.e., that Christ should fashion them according to His own image [338] (→ IV, 753, 33 ff.), cf. also πάντες γὰρ υἱοὶ θεοῦ ἐστε διὰ τῆς πίστεως ἐν Χριστῷ Ἰησοῦ· ὅσοι γὰρ εἰς Χριστὸν ἐβαπτίσθητε, Χριστὸν ἐνεδύσασθε, Gl. 3:26 f. → II, 320, 16 ff. [339] Christ is for Paul the εἰκὼν τοῦ θεοῦ, 2 C. 4:4 → II, 395, 26 ff. In Him — ἐν προσώπῳ Χριστοῦ — there shines the glory of God (→ II, 247, 27 ff.) which illumines the hearts of men in a new creation, 2 C. 4:6; 5:17. If Christ is God's image, man attains by Him to the divine likeness for which he was created. [340] This takes place through the δύναμις τοῦ Χριστοῦ which Paul desires, so that he will gladly boast of his own weakness and infirmity ἵνα ἐπισκηνώσῃ ἐπ' ἐμὲ ἡ δύναμις τοῦ Χριστοῦ, 2 C. 12:9 → II, 316, 23 ff. In the apostle who thus follows Christ's will and clings to Him in his own weakness Christ is manifested. [341]

2 C. 5:14-21 is a kind of summary of Paul's Christ theology. He speaks here about the ἀγάπη τοῦ Χριστοῦ (v. 14) which controls and unites those who belong to Him, so that their lives no longer belong to themselves but to Him who died and rose again for them, v. 15, [342] cf. R. 14:7-9. This is a new knowledge (2 C. 5:16) about

---

[337] This is in plain antithesis to the Rabb. concept of the Messiah as an expositor of the Torah, cf. Str.-B., IV, 1-3.

[338] But cf. R. Hermann, "Über den Sinn d. Μορφοῦσθαι Χριστὸν ἐν ὑμῖν in Gl. 4:19," ThLZ, 80 (1955), 713-726.

[339] But cf. J. Leipoldt, Von den Mysterien zur Kirche (1961), 34, 40, 74. The putting on has to do with becoming like Christ or Christ's manifestation in believers.

[340] This statement is developed esp. in Col. and Eph., cf. on this J. Jervell, "Imago dei," FRL, 76 (1960), 231-256.

[341] Cf. on this Güttgemanns, op. cit. (→ n. 319), 11-30.

[342] Here Χριστός becomes κύριος. The one who has attained to salvation through Christ receives and actualises it under the lordship of Jesus Christ which controls and shapes the new life, cf. Kramer, 168: With the title κύριος the focus is not on the past salvation event but on the connection between present concrete acts and the Kurios. The Kurios is not just the authority to which an account must be given for all deeds. He is also the One who has power to give revelations, duties, success etc. Cf. also Neugebauer, 58: κύριος is a relational term designed to express the position of Jesus vis à vis His community and His apostle.

man and about Christ. The prior knowledge κατὰ σάρκα (→ VII, 131, 5 ff.) [343] saw Christ as a man accursed, Gl. 3:13 f. This is how Paul regarded Him and why he persecuted Him. [344] But this knowledge belongs to the old things that have passed away. He now knows Christ as the One who in love was accursed for our sake, who died and rose again for us, and who is thus the Reconciler, 2 C. 5:15, 18. Thus Paul, determined by His love, is, ἐν Χριστῷ, a new creation (→ III, 449, 16 ff.), for which the former things have passed away and all things have become new, v. 17. This new creation is grounded in the reconciliation (→ I, 255, 12 ff.) which God has effected διὰ Χριστοῦ (→ II, 67, 14 ff.), vv. 18-20. It is entirely God's act, for God was ἐν Χριστῷ, so that Christ is in the full sense God's envoy, the mediator of salvation, who represents God among men. [345] The apostles continue His work; they represent Him among men as messengers ὑπὲρ Χριστοῦ who beseech men ὑπὲρ Χριστοῦ (→ VIII, 513, 15 ff.): Be reconciled to God. This task entails their suffering ὑπὲρ Χριστοῦ, Phil. 1:29; 2 C. 12:10, cf. also 2 C. 1:5. [346]

By focusing on the Christ event and Christ's rule, Paul, like primitive Christianity in general, [347] tackles the Messianic question as it was posed by history and in principle and he, too, gives a wholly new form to Messianic expectation. Christ is for him the One who came to victory through the disaster and defeat of the cross. Hence Paul trusts Him in his very weaknesses. He sees in these the manifestation of Christ at work. With primitive Christianity Paul adopts the proof from Scripture (κατὰ τὰς γραφάς, 1 C. 15:3-5), works it out in his own way (1 C. 5:7; 10:4; Gl. 3:16), and speaks of the ἡμέρα Χριστοῦ (Phil. 1:10; 2:16) which is the day of judgment (2 C. 5:10). In the foreground, however, is Paul's boasting of the ἀγάπη τοῦ Χριστοῦ (Gl. 2:20; 2 C. 5:14; R. 8:35), calling by God ἐν χάριτι Χριστοῦ (Gl. 1:6), the πραΰτης καὶ ἐπιείκεια τοῦ Χριστοῦ (2 C. 10:1 → VI, 650, 1 ff.), the ὑπομονὴ τοῦ Χριστοῦ (2 Th. 3:5), and the ἀλήθεια Χριστοῦ (2 C. 11:10), expressions which are all shaped in part by the impression made on Paul by the historical Jesus, even though he refers to Him very little in his epistles. Christ or the Christ is for Paul God's agent of salvation who accomplishes salvation for mankind by His cross and resurrection.

---

[343] In view of v. 16a κατὰ σάρκα goes with ἐγνώκαμεν and not Χριστόν. The obj. of this knowledge is man (v. 16) and the Christ, but the latter not as the historical Jesus. Paul refers to Jesus in R. 9:5: ὁ Χριστὸς τὸ κατὰ σάρκα, where κατὰ σάρκα comes after and is related to the Christ by the art. The earthly Christ is of David's seed (1:3) and is thus of Israel (9:5). In 2 C. 5:16, however, the stress is on knowing κατὰ σάρκα and the content of this knowledge is Christ as one accursed. This is replaced with knowledge of Christ ὑπὲρ ἡμῶν, i.e., Christ as Reconciler, v. 17 f. Cf. also J. Roloff, Das Kerygma u. der irdische Jesus (1970), 182, n. 265; J. W. Fraser, "Paul's Knowledge of Jesus: 2 C. 5:16 once more," NTSt, 17 (1970/71), 293-313.

[344] It is plain that in context Paul's statement is not disparaging the pre-Easter Christ but that the ref. is to the old and the new knowledge of Christ, cf. 1 C. 1:23 f.; 12:3; Gl. 3:13, etc. 2 C. 5:16 is not speaking about the significance of the pre-Easter Jesus for Paul.

[345] If it is true that in His historical manifestation up to the resurrection Jesus represents God to men, it is also true that in His historical manifestation and esp. as the ascended Lord He represents men to God, R. 8:34; Gl. 3:13. Christ is thus the Mediator as God's Representative to men and men's Representative to God.

[346] The basis of this life is the saving work of Christ (2 C. 5:21) which claims the apostle for the divinely instituted διακονία or λόγος τῆς καταλλαγῆς.

[347] The church at Antioch played a decisive role for Paul, esp. as it was there that the predicate Christ became so significant, cf. the probable origin there of the use of Χριστιανοί for believers → 536, 34 ff. The tie between Antioch and Jerusalem allows of the assumption that the tradition may be traced back to Jerusalem.

b. To Christ belongs the people of Christ, οἱ τοῦ Χριστοῦ, who follow Him, the ἀπαρχή, in the resurrection, 1 C. 15:23. They become Christ's folk in baptism, in which they are appropriated to Him: ὅσοι γὰρ εἰς Χριστὸν ἐβαπτίσθητε, Χριστὸν ἐνεδύσασθε, Gl. 3:27. Baptism is the death of the old man with Christ — Χριστῷ συνεσταύρωμαι, Gl. 2:19 — and the beginning of a new man determined by Christ (Gl. 2:20) and also separated from sin. Otherwise Christ would become the ἁμαρτίας διάκονος (Gl. 2:17) and His death would also be in vain if men let themselves be bound to the Law as well (Gl. 2:21 → 545, 18 ff.); for ὑμεῖς ἐθανατώθητε τῷ νόμῳ διὰ τοῦ σώματος τοῦ Χριστοῦ, εἰς τὸ γενέσθαι ὑμᾶς ἑτέρῳ, τῷ ἐκ νεκρῶν ἐγερθέντι, R. 7:4. All life and hope is grounded in Christ. In acute danger of death Paul says that the whole aim of his work is to magnify Christ (→ IV, 543, 31 ff.): ἐν πάσῃ παρρησίᾳ ὡς πάντοτε καὶ νῦν μεγαλυνθήσεται Χριστὸς ἐν τῷ σώματί μου, εἴτε διὰ ζωῆς εἴτε διὰ θανάτου, Phil. 1:20. He confesses: ἐμοὶ γὰρ τὸ ζῆν Χριστὸς καὶ τὸ ἀποθανεῖν κέρδος, Phil. 1:21. For Paul to live is Christ, [348] and this is a life which by death will be set in full communion with the One who lives in him, Gl. 2:20. Hence Paul has within him the desire εἰς τὸ ἀναλῦσαι καὶ σὺν Χριστῷ εἶναι, Phil. 1:23 → VII, 783, 15 ff. [349] In virtue of this commitment to Christ, Paul's reply to the Corinthians who contest it is the testimony concerning himself and his fellow-workers: ἡμεῖς δὲ νοῦν Χριστοῦ ἔχομεν (1 C. 2:16), i.e., the thinking of Christ controls him. This is what he has in mind when he speaks of the Χριστὸς ἐν ὑμῖν, R. 8:10; cf. vv. 5-9 and Gl. 2:20. He can use πνεῦμα Χριστοῦ (→ VI, 433, 1 ff.) to express the same thing, so that he can say: εἰ δέ τις πνεῦμα Χριστοῦ οὐκ ἔχει, οὗτος οὐκ ἔστιν αὐτοῦ, R. 8:9. πνεῦμα Χριστοῦ, however, means πνεῦμα θεοῦ (R. 8:9), for Christ is God's proxy. God acts through Him and in Him, for God's Spirit, which is also πνεῦμα Χριστοῦ, is τὸ πνεῦμα τοῦ ἐγείραντος τὸν Ἰησοῦν ἐκ νεκρῶν, R. 8:11. [350] Membership of Christ is an effective event, since it takes place through the Spirit of Him who has raised up Christ from the dead and who makes man new. To have a part in Christ is to receive from Him His Spirit who sets us in the sonship by which those who belong to Him are συγκληρονόμοι Χριστοῦ, R. 8:17. Paul calls himself μιμητὴς Χριστοῦ (1 C. 11:1 → IV, 668, 37 ff.), [351] and the churches for their part are to follow him. This controls his and their conduct in forgiveness ἐν προσώπῳ Χριστοῦ (2 C. 2:10), in renunciation of self-pleasing (R. 15:3), and in the receiving of the weak in the community (R. 15:7).

Those who belong to Christ, His people, are one σῶμα, which is called σῶμα Χριστοῦ in 1 C. 12:12, 27, → VII, 1068, 20 ff. This statement is very surprising, since Paul has consistently spoken before this of the κύριος who is the giver of

---

[348] Cerfaux, 197-214.

[349] In view of this passage and also Gl. 2:19 f. and Phil. 3:8-14 Neugebauer's (55) statement is surely exaggerated when he says: "Christ is indeed a person, but this person is interpreted by Paul as God's act of eschatological salvation. This view can hardly be grouped with the christology of mysticism with its idea of spiritual personality. If Christ is the event of salvation, fellowship with Christ can never be fellowship with a spiritual personality." For Paul Christ as the bringer of salvation is God's saving act, but one participates in this act through the ascended Lord who establishes fellowship with Himself by the gift of the Spirit.

[350] From these and other passages it is plain that Christ is for Paul God's Mediator. The aim of Christ's work is to unite believers to God, cf. on this W. Thüsing, "Per Christum in Deum," NTAbh, NF, 1 (1965).

[351] Cf. W. Grundmann, "Pls., aus dem Volke Israel, Ap. der Völker," Nov. Test., 4 (1960), 288-290; O. Betz, "Nachahmen u. Nachfolgen," Beiträge z. Histor. Theol., 37 (1967), 137-189.

charismata and the recipient of worship (1 C. 12:3). Now, however, we are told that the many who call on the Lord and receive His gifts of grace are members; πάντα δὲ τὰ μέλη (→ VI, 562, 31 ff.) τοῦ σώματος πολλὰ ὄντα ἕν ἐστιν σῶμα, οὕτως καὶ ὁ Χριστός (1 C. 12:12); Christ is the body and the individual is a member of the body because he is ἐν Χριστῷ and Christ is in him. Christians can thus be told: ὑμεῖς δέ ἐστε σῶμα Χριστοῦ καὶ μέλη ἐκ μέρους, 1 C. 12:27. Because Christ's people belong to Him, and He is present in them, Χριστός is used here. As μέλη Χριστοῦ they can no longer belong to a harlot (1 C. 6:15) or to Βελιάρ, Christ's adversary (2 C. 6:15). The determinative basis of their membership of Christ is that His body was given and His blood was shed for them; they partake of this body and blood of Christ in the Lord's Supper: τὸ ποτήριον τῆς εὐλογίας ὃ εὐλογοῦμεν, οὐχὶ κοινωνία ἐστὶν τοῦ αἵματος τοῦ Χριστοῦ; τὸν ἄρτον, ὃν κλῶμεν, οὐχὶ κοινωνία τοῦ σώματος τοῦ Χριστοῦ ἐστιν; 1 C. 10:16. Being bound to Christ, they are liberated from all powers and forces and with Him they are bound to God, by whom they are given freedom through their bondage to Christ. Paul describes this in the words: πάντα γὰρ ὑμῶν ἐστιν ... πάντα ὑμῶν, ὑμεῖς δὲ Χριστοῦ, Χριστὸς δὲ θεοῦ, 1 C. 3:21-23, cf. also Gl. 3:29. Binding to Christ is binding to God, for Christ is Christ only because He is God's. Paul makes a similar statement in 1 C. 11:3 (→ III, 679, 8 ff.), where, speaking about the relation of man and woman, he says: παντὸς ἀνδρὸς ἡ κεφαλὴ ὁ Χριστός ἐστιν, κεφαλὴ δὲ γυναικὸς ὁ ἀνήρ, κεφαλὴ δὲ τοῦ Χριστοῦ ὁ θεός. In distinction from the statement that Christ is the σῶμα, He is here called the Head. If σῶμα expresses Christ's manifestation and work in His people, κεφαλή expresses the supremacy of Christ, although He for His part is subject to God. If Christ is supreme as the Head, His people are under obligation to Him, αἰχμαλωτίζοντες πᾶν νόημα εἰς τὴν ὑπακοὴν τοῦ Χριστοῦ, 2 C. 10:5. In relation to the social distinction between free men and slaves, for Paul the slave, even though he remains in the same estate, is as ἐν κυρίῳ κληθείς an ἀπελεύθερος κυρίου, while the socially free man δοῦλός ἐστιν Χριστοῦ, 1 C. 7:22. [352]

The churches in their mutual greetings are αἱ ἐκκλησίαι πᾶσαι τοῦ Χριστοῦ, R. 16:16. They are the bride which the apostle is concerned ἑνὶ ἀνδρὶ παρθένον ἁγνὴν παραστῆσαι τῷ Χριστῷ, 2 C. 11:2 → V, 837, 1 ff. Because the bride belongs to Christ, through whose saving work she has become παρθένος ἁγνή, τῷ Χριστῷ is used here rather than τῷ κυρίῳ. [353] The same point of belonging to Christ is made when Paul calls the community ἐπιστολὴ Χριστοῦ διακονηθεῖσα ὑφ᾽ ἡμῶν, → VII, 594, 17 ff. It is also ἡ ἐπιστολὴ ἡμῶν (2 C. 3:2 f.), namely, through Paul's ministry on the commission of Christ. Through his apostolic work Paul has a part in the triumphant procession of God which is in Christ ἐν τῷ Χριστῷ and in which we are carried along as the spoils, → III, 160, 5 ff. This takes place as through the apostles He manifests τὴν ὀσμὴν τῆς γνώσεως αὐτοῦ in all places. The apostles thus become Χριστοῦ εὐωδία (→ II, 809, 38 ff.), the smell of the sacrifices offered in the triumph, 2 C. 2:14 f. Through their ministry Christ [354] fills the places where He is proclaimed

---

[352] If δοῦλος Χριστοῦ is used here instead of δοῦλος κυρίου, this may be due to the fact that Paul is making use of an earlier formula, even though it is he who above all develops its content → II, 274, 14 ff.

[353] Cf. Kramer, 208. Kramer suggests that the title of dignity is downgraded to a proper name on the ground that the idea of the bride of the Messiah is not found in Jewish Messianic expectation. He overlooks the fact that Paul is developing a new concept of the Messiah on the basis of the actual events. Cf. the OT and Jewish material → V, 832, 28 ff.

[354] Χριστοῦ in 2 C. 2:15 is a gen. auct.

with the savour which means life for some and death for others, 2 C. 2:15 f.; hence they themselves are εὐωδία in the world.

The apostles, who are members of the body of Christ (1 C. 12:27 f.), proclaim as His envoys the good news which has Him as its content, 1 C. 1:17; 2 C. 5:19 f. [355] In view of the fact that false apostles try to change themselves into ἀπόστολοι Χριστοῦ (2 C. 11:13), [356] Paul in his ministry knows what is the necessary accreditation (→ II, 258, 5 ff.), δοκιμὴ τοῦ ἐν ἐμοὶ λαλοῦντος Χριστοῦ (2 C. 13:3). Christ Himself speaks through the apostle. The ἀπόστολοι ἐκκλησιῶν are to be regarded as the δόξα Χριστοῦ, 2 C. 8:23. Paul as ἀπόστολος Χριστοῦ is δοῦλος Χριστοῦ, Gl. 1:10 → II, 276, 23 ff. He belongs to Christ like a slave. [357] If his opponents call themselves διάκονοι Χριστοῦ, Paul himself is more so. He shows this by his sufferings for Christ, 2 C. 11:23, 24-33. His visions and revelations also show him to be an ἄνθρωπον ἐν Χριστῷ, 2 C. 12:1 f. He and his fellow-workers are ὑπηρέται Χριστοῦ καὶ οἰκονόμοι μυστηρίων θεοῦ, 1 C. 4:1 → VIII, 542, 11 ff. Again the service rendered to Christ is service of God. For Christ's ministers are those who faithfully handle the mysteries of God, which are entrusted to them in the διακονία τῆς καταλλαγῆς. The servant-lordship of Christ is continued in the work of the ἀπόστολοι Χριστοῦ. Of Epaphroditus, the loyal envoy of the Philippian church who came to visit him in his imprisonment, Paul says, ὅτι διὰ τὸ ἔργον (τοῦ) Χριστοῦ μέχρι θανάτου ἤγγισεν, Phil. 2:30. His concern for the apostle and his ministering to him Paul described as an ἔργον Χριστοῦ, cf. Mt. 11:2. Through him Christ Himself works on His apostle's behalf. It is generally true that if God's kingdom consists in righteousness, peace and joy in the Holy Spirit, ὁ ... ἐν τούτῳ δουλεύων τῷ Χριστῷ εὐάρεστος τῷ θεῷ καὶ δόκιμος τοῖς ἀνθρώποις, R. 14:18. For this kingdom of God is the saving work of Christ. Paul, who gives up all things ἵνα Χριστὸν κερδήσω (Phil. 3:8), is ready, for Israel, ἀνάθεμα εἶναι αὐτὸς ἐγὼ ἀπὸ τοῦ Χριστοῦ, R. 9:3, i.e., to offer himself as a sin-offering, to be accursed from Christ, and hence to be separated from him → I, 354, 31 ff. [358]

In Corinth a group formed which fought Paul's proclamation of the Gospel under the slogan ἐγὼ δὲ Χριστοῦ. [359] His question to them is: μεμέρισται ὁ Χριστός; Christ was crucified for all, and all are baptised into Him, 1 C. 1:12 f. To all parties

---

[355] Neugebauer, 126 f. differentiates the relation of Christ to the community from that to the apostle on the ground that the community is a function of the apostle, but he sees definite parallelism. Since Christ is related to His saving work on the one side and to the people which arises out of it on the other, the apostles as His commissioned servants for God's people also belong to this people. Treating their relation to Christ separately is a purely methodological matter, for Neugebauer, 127 says: "Just as a specific congregation is also the eschatological ecclesia, so Paul as a specific ἀπόστολος is also a member of the eschatological people of God."

[356] On the question of a pre-Pauline formula cf. Kramer, 51-9, who concludes that all the evidence points to Paul himself having related the term "apostle" to Christ, 56, cf. 57, n. 177. G. Klein, "Die zwölf Ap.," FRL, 77 (1961), 54-9 suggests that the phrase came from Paul's opponents. W. Schmithals, "Das kirchliche Apostelamt," FRL, 79 (1961), traces the concept of the apostle to Gnosticism.

[357] Cf. on this G. Friedrich, "Die Gegner d. Pls. im 2 K.," Festschr. O. Michel (1963), 185-8.

[358] Cf. Mi. R.[13] (1966), 226: "ἀπὸ τοῦ Χριστοῦ means here expulsion from fellowship with the Messiah (note the art.) and therefore eschatological judgment ... The phrase is not accidental; as the opposite of ἐν Χριστῷ in R. 9:1 it is a form of excommunication of particular solemnity." Cf. also 226.

[359] W. Schmithals, "Die Gnosis in Korinth," FRL, 66[3] (1969), 106-9 adopts the thesis of F. C. Baur that Paul is facing a solid front in Corinth rather than different parties. Its distinctive mark is separation of the earthly Jesus from the heavenly Christ, which Paul disputes, 117-133.

Paul also speaks of the freedom conferred by allegiance to Christ, 1 C. 3:21-23 → 548, 13 ff. To the Christ group, which also seems to be in view in 2 C. and which was perhaps given a strong fillip by wandering apostles with their appeal to Christ,[360] Paul declares εἴ τις πέποιθεν ἑαυτῷ Χριστοῦ εἶναι, τοῦτο λογιζέσθω πάλιν ἐφ' ἑαυτοῦ, ὅτι καθὼς αὐτὸς Χριστοῦ, οὕτως καὶ ἡμεῖς, 2 C. 10:7. Membership in Christ is transferred in baptism.

c. ὁ Χριστός and Χριστός are combined with a whole series of prepositions in Paul. Christ is for Paul the bringer of salvation whose crucifixion and resurrection are the salvation event. This establishes a time and space of salvation after the manner of a spiritual field of force which has Christ, the bringer of salvation, at its centre.[361] Relation to this field of force is expressed by prepositions. A man enters it by baptism, which is εἰς Χριστόν → I, 539, 25 ff.; II, 433, 7 ff., cf. Gl. 3:27; R. 6:3.[362] Epaenetus is called the ἀπαρχὴ τῆς 'Ασίας εἰς Χριστόν (R. 16:5), i.e., the first to become Christ's by baptism and hence the firstfruits offered by the province to Christ.[363] Paul speaks of God as βεβαιῶν ἡμᾶς σὺν ὑμῖν εἰς Χριστόν (2 C. 1:21),[364] i.e., He upholds and confirms us in the assignment to Christ effected by baptism. The wish for Philemon in Phlm. 6 is along the same lines. The preposition εἰς denotes entry into Christ's field of force. Transfer to Christ links with Him σὺν Χριστῷ (→ VII, 781, 15 ff.), brings on to His path, and is consummated in union with Him, which is the eschatological goal of life, Phil. 1:23. In this field of force the operation is always that of God through Christ: διὰ τοῦ Χριστοῦ (→ II, 67, 30 ff.; 68, 27 ff.) is used to express this.[365] From him comes the consolation which Paul finds in prison and which he can pass on: ... διὰ τοῦ Χριστοῦ περισσεύει καὶ ἡ παράκλησις ἡμῶν, 2 C. 1:5. From Him comes Paul's confidence towards God: πεποίθησιν δὲ τοιαύτην ἔχομεν διὰ τοῦ Χριστοῦ πρὸς τὸν θεόν, namely, that his apostolic work will bear fruit in Corinth in spite of every obstacle (2 C. 3:4), a confidence which he has gained through Christ because God called the crucified Lord back to life again, R. 4:17, 24. Through Christ God has made reconciliation θεὸς καταλλάξας ἡμᾶς ἑαυτῷ διὰ Χριστοῦ, 2 C. 5:18. The ἐν expresses the fact that salvation is operative in the field of force of Christ, → II, 541, 6 ff.[366]

---

[360] So G. Bornkamm, "Die Vorgeschichte d. sog. 2 K.," Gesch. u. Glaube, II (1971), 163-171; G. Friedrich, op. cit. (→ n. 357), 181-215, and D. Georgi, "Die Gegner d. Pls. im 2 K.," Wissenschaftl. Monographien z. AT u. NT, 11 (1964) as against Schmithals, who thinks Paul is fighting the same foes as in 1 C. Whatever our view of this matter may be, there can be no doubt but that these adversaries with their claims and their disparagement of Paul caused Paul to clarify and express his apostolic consciousness. The same applies to the adversaries in Gl., whom Schmithals thinks to be akin to those in 1 and 2 C., cf. W. Schmithals, "Pls. u. d. Gnosis," Theol. Forschung, 35 (1965), 9-46.

[361] Neugebauer, 41 draws attention to the fact that often, if not always, Paul in key passages follows the basically dynamic, temporal and historical structure of Hbr. thought. The spatial ref. of the prep. has led to neglect of this aspect. By adopting the concept of a field of force we shall try to do justice to the dynamic element in a space-time continuum.

[362] So B Marcion; the other MSS add 'Ιησοῦν.

[363] Cf. Grundmann, op. cit. (→ n. 351), 278-283.

[364] Cf. E. Dinkler, "Die Taufterminologie in 2 K. 1:21 f.," Signum Crucis (1967), 99-117.

[365] Cf. on this Thüsing, op. cit. (→ n. 350), 164-237.

[366] Neugebauer, 39, n. 27 thinks the decisive aspect of the ἐν construction is that it denotes general circumstance, i.e., that which is around a thing or event. Here it is Christ who is around all things and events, or, to put it rather differently, Christ is the centre of the spiritual field of force. For a discussion of ἐν Χριστῷ cf. also Thüsing, op. cit. (→ n. 350), 61-114; Bouttier; E. Brandenburger, "Fleisch u. Geist," Wissenschaftl. Monographien z. AT u. NT, 29 (1968), 54-7.

The event and reception of salvation are spoken of in Gl. 2:17; 1 C. 15:19, 22; 2 C. 3:14; 5:17, 19, [367] 21, the work of salvation in 1 C. 4:15; 2 C. 2:14, 17; [368] 12:19; R. 9:1; 16:9 f.; Phil. 1:13; Phlm. 8, 20, the saved community in Gl. 1:22; 1 C. 3:1; [369] 4:10; R. 12:5; Phil. 2:1; 1 Th. 4:16; 1 C. 15:18, [370] its individual members in 2 C. 12:2; R. 16:7-10. Paul has in mind a field of force in which all events are spiritually caused and ordained by God through Christ.

3. Jesus Christ and Christ Jesus in Paul's Chief Epistles.

a. Along with Χριστός and ὁ Χριστός Paul uses Jesus Christ and also Christ Jesus. The common Χριστὸς Ἰησοῦς implies knowledge of Christ as the bringer of salvation who is called Jesus. How strongly related Χριστός or ὁ Χριστός and Χριστὸς Ἰησοῦς or Ἰησοῦς Χριστός are for Paul may be seen first from the passages in which they are accompanied by prepositions → 550, 7 ff.

We find εἰς Χριστὸν ἐβαπτίσθητε in Gl. 3:27 and ἐβαπτίσθημεν εἰς Χριστὸν Ἰησοῦν in R. 6:3. διὰ Ἰησοῦ Χριστοῦ is often found as well as διὰ τοῦ Χριστοῦ (→ 550, 20 ff.). Jesus Christ is the author of thanksgiving to God (R. 1:8; 16:27), of the lordship of life in which those are set who have received the gift of grace of the one Jesus Christ (R. 5:15, 17), of the fruit of righteousness which, like righteousness itself, is produced by Jesus Christ (Phil. 1:11). [371] Coming judgment takes place διὰ Χριστοῦ Ἰησοῦ (R. 2:16); [372] that is, Christ has been appointed judge, cf. also Ac. 17:31. Finally Paul's apostleship comes from Him: ἀπόστολος, οὐκ ἀπ' ἀνθρώπων οὐδὲ δι' ἀνθρώπου ἀλλὰ διὰ Ἰησοῦ Χριστοῦ καὶ θεοῦ πατρὸς τοῦ ἐγείραντος αὐτὸν ἐκ νεκρῶν, Gl. 1:1. What Paul is saying here is that he has not received his office from a man οὔτε ἐδιδάχθην, ἀλλὰ δι' ἀποκαλύψεως Ἰησοῦ Χριστοῦ, Gl. 1:12. The expression describes Jesus Christ as the One who has revealed Himself and made him His apostle, this revelation being an act of God's grace, Gl. 1:15 f. Jesus Christ is the One through whom God acts. The fact that he is the apostle of Jesus Christ Paul works out and emphasises in his debate with those who fight him [373] → 549, 3 ff.

ἐν Χριστῷ Ἰησοῦ has the same meaning as ἐν Χριστῷ (→ 550, 29 ff.), at any rate in relation to the event, the reception, and the work of salvation, and also the saved community, Gl. 2:4, 17; 3:14, 26; 5:6; [374] 1 C. 1:4 f.; 2 C. 1:19 f.; [375] R. 3:24; 8:1; Phil.

---

367 Neugebauer transl. here: "God reconciled in Christ the world with Himself," 66, cf. also 86, he thus sees another ἐν Χριστῷ statement in this v. But why in this case did not Paul use an aor. or other preterite form of καταλλάσσω? Why does he have θεὸς ἦν ἐν Χριστῷ κόσμον καταλλάσσων ἑαυτῷ? He surely means that God is active and present in Christ as the Reconciler. The expression has a durative sense.

368 Worth noting is ὡς ἐκ θεοῦ κατέναντι θεοῦ ἐν Χριστῷ λαλοῦμεν. God is the source of the speech which is made in answer to Him in the field of force of Christ, cf. also 2 C. 12:19, a significant statement of the apostolic consciousness.

369 The phrase ὡς νηπίοις ἐν Χριστῷ for the Corinthians shows that there is development and increase ἐν Χριστῷ, cf. W. Grundmann, "Die ΝΗΠΙΟΙ in d. urchr. Paränese," NTSt, 5 (1958/59), 188-205.

370 The community ἐν Χριστῷ includes the dead, since death cannot snatch them away from Christ's field of force.

371 The continuation again shows clearly that all the events accomplished by Christ are done to God: εἰς δόξαν καὶ ἔπαινον θεοῦ → n. 350.

372 The MSS vacillate between διὰ Χριστοῦ Ἰησοῦ and διὰ Ἰησοῦ Χριστοῦ.

373 It should not be overlooked that after the break with Barnabas, which disturbed his relations with the church at Antioch (Ac. 15:39 f.), Paul undertook the work in Greece and then in Ephesus independently with fellow-workers who joined him, and was only to a small extent supported by a church. This gave his opponents the chance to dispute his apostleship and forced him to lay express emphasis on its derivation from commissioning by Christ Jesus.

374 This stresses the fact that in the sphere of salvation in Jesus Christ only πίστις δι' ἀγάπης ἐνεργουμένη matters, not cultic or ritual matters such as circumcision or uncircumcision → n. 377.

375 The ἐν αὐτῷ in 2 C. 1:20 relates to ὁ τοῦ θεοῦ... υἱὸς Χριστὸς Ἰησοῦς ὁ ἐν ὑμῖν δι' ἡμῶν κηρυχθείς, v. 19.

3:14; [376] 4:7, 19. There are ref. to the saved community in 1 Th. 2:14; Gl. 3:28; [377] 1 C. 1:30; [378] its members are ἡγιασμένοι ἐν Χριστῷ ᾿Ιησοῦ, 1 C. 1:2, cf. Phil. 1:1; 4:21; in it one's boasting is ἐν Χριστῷ ᾿Ιησοῦ, Phil. 1:26; 3:3; 1 C. 15:31; R. 15:17; Jesus Christ is the norm of its thinking and action, Phil. 2:5; 1 Th. 5:18. The work of salvation is spoken of in 1 C. 4:15, 17, where Paul stresses his fatherly activity in relation to the church and speaks of his ways (→ V, 88, 13 ff.) [379] which are in Christ Jesus, cf. also R. 16:3; Phlm. 23.

b. The kinship of (ὁ) Χριστός and Χριστὸς ᾿Ιησοῦς or ᾿Ιησοῦς Χριστός is also shown by verses in which these are used in various formulations.

As Paul speaks of the cross of Christ or the crucified Christ (1 C. 1:17, 23 → 544, 10 ff.), he also speaks of Jesus Christ the crucified (Gl. 3:1; 1 C. 2:2). He speaks similarly of the resurrection of Christ (R. 6:4, 9; 1 C. 15 *passim*) and also of that of Jesus Christ (R. 8:11, 34; [380] Gl. 1:1). Alongside τὸ εὐαγγέλιον τοῦ Χριστοῦ (Gl. 1:7) we find τὸ κήρυγμα ᾿Ιησοῦ Χριστοῦ (R. 16:25). Paul also says in relation to His work: θεμέλιον γὰρ ἄλλον οὐδεὶς δύναται θεῖναι παρὰ τὸν κείμενον, ὅς ἐστιν ᾿Ιησοῦς Χριστός, 1 C. 3:11. [381] He speaks of the grace of Christ (Gl. 1:6) and of the χάρις ... τοῦ ἑνὸς ἀνθρώπου ᾿Ιησοῦ Χριστοῦ (R. 5:15). Christ is revealed (Gl. 1:16), and so, too, is Jesus Christ (1:12). Paul stresses the importance of πίστις and ref. to the πίστις Χριστοῦ (Gl. 2:16; Phil. 3:9), the πίστις ᾿Ιησοῦ (R. 3:26), though this is less secure textually, and often the πίστις Χριστοῦ ᾿Ιησοῦ. The basic formulation runs: οὐ δικαιοῦται ἄνθρωπος ἐξ ἔργων νόμου ἐὰν μὴ διὰ πίστεως Χριστοῦ ᾿Ιησοῦ, καὶ ἡμεῖς εἰς Χριστὸν ᾿Ιησοῦν ἐπιστεύσαμεν, ἵνα δικαιωθῶμεν ἐκ πίστεως Χριστοῦ καὶ οὐκ ἐξ ἔργων νόμου, Gl. 2:16, cf. also 3:22; R. 3:22. A crucial question is how we are to construe the gen. Χριστοῦ ᾿Ιησοῦ (→ VI, 210, n. 267) [382] and why "Jesus Christ" is predominant in statements about faith. εἰς Χριστὸν ᾿Ιησοῦν ἐπιστεύσαμεν makes it clear that faith is directed to Jesus Christ who effects pardon and salvation for guilty man. Yet He is also the author of this faith, which does not exist without Him. This is why the designation Christ, the bringer of salvation, is accompanied by the name of Jesus, from whom faith comes. [383]

---

[376] In the κατελήμφθην ὑπὸ Χριστοῦ ᾿Ιησοῦ of Phil. 3:12 the ἄνω κλῆσις τοῦ θεοῦ ἐν Χριστῷ ᾿Ιησοῦ reaches Paul, v. 14.

[377] In face of sexual, national and social distinctions the community of Jesus finds its unity in orientation to Jesus Christ as ἐν Χριστῷ ᾿Ιησοῦ it is brought into His field of force, πάντες γὰρ ὑμεῖς εἷς ἐστε ἐν Χριστῷ ᾿Ιησοῦ → n. 374.

[378] Here again the relation to God is emphasised: ἐξ αὐτοῦ (sc. τοῦ θεοῦ) δὲ ὑμεῖς ἐστε ἐν Χριστῷ ᾿Ιησοῦ → n. 371.

[379] In 1 C. 4:15 ἐν Χριστῷ is primarily related to μυρίους παιδαγωγούς. On the basis of some MSS, including p46, it is possible that the true reading in 4:15b and 17 as well is simply ἐν Χριστῷ.

[380] B D sy 𝔐 do not have ᾿Ιησοῦς, p46 Ir read ἅμα δὲ Χριστός → n. 390.

[381] Possibly ᾿Ιησοῦς Χριστός has a special sense here. If the Corinthian Gnostics reject the earthly historical Jesus and even curse Him in favour of the heavenly Christ, 1 C. 12:3, cf. Schmithals, *op. cit.* (→ n. 359), 117-124, Paul is emphasising that Jesus is the bringer of salvation and not a heavenly being only loosely connected with the historical Jesus. For ὅς ἐστιν ᾿Ιησοῦς Χριστός cf. Gl. 3:16.

[382] The MSS vacillate between Χριστοῦ ᾿Ιησοῦ and ᾿Ιησοῦ Χριστοῦ.

[383] Since the time of J. Haussleiter, *Der Glaube Jesu Christi u. der chr. Glaube* (1891), the question has been put whether the gen. with πίστις is a subj. gen. H. W. Schmidt, *Der Brief d. Pls. an d. Römer, Theol. Handkomm. z. NT,* 6 (1962), 71 f. considers this possibility with Haussleiter. Since Paul speaks of faith in the way he speaks of God's righteousness or of Christ, and finds the whole of being a Christian in it, it is probable that faith in Jesus has its basis in the faith of Jesus, just as Paul can speak of the obedience of Jesus, Phil. 2:8; R. 5:19, cf. 1:5. The relation of Son, God's sons and divine sonship might also be adduced in this connection, cf. W. Grundmann, "Der Geist d. Sohnschaft," *Disciplina Domini, Thüringer Kirchl. Stud.,* 1 (1963), 172-192. Schmidt, 72 speaks of a polarity of meaning between faith

As the saved community is called οἱ τοῦ Χριστοῦ in 1 C. 15:23, cf. also 3:23 and the group designation in 1:12; 2 C. 10:7, it can also be styled: οἱ δὲ τοῦ Χριστοῦ Ἰησοῦ τὴν σάρκα ἐσταύρωσαν, Gl. 5:24, [384] cf. Χριστῷ συνεσταύρωμαι of Paul himself, Gl. 2:19. The members of the saved community are asked if they do not know ὅτι Ἰησοῦς Χριστὸς ἐν ὑμῖν, 2 C. 13:5, [385] cf. Χριστὸς ἐν ὑμῖν in R. 8:10, cf. also Gl. 2:20. They are called κλητοὶ Ἰησοῦ Χριστοῦ in R. 1:6. Paul pts. the community to the ἡμέρα Χριστοῦ in Phil. 1:10; 2:16 and to perfecting ἄχρι ἡμέρας Χριστοῦ Ἰησοῦ, Phil. 1:6. [386] He writes about himself: κατελήμφθην ὑπὸ Χριστοῦ Ἰησοῦ, Phil. 3:12, [387] and he calls himself ἀπόστολος Χριστοῦ Ἰησοῦ, 1 C. 1:1; 2 C. 1:1, cf. Gl. 1:1. But he can also speak about the ἀπόστολοι Χριστοῦ, 2 C. 11:13. He calls himself δοῦλος Χριστοῦ Ἰησοῦ [388] in R. 1:1 and λειτουργὸς Χριστοῦ Ἰησοῦ in R. 15:16. He bears witness to the Galatians, ὡς ἄγγελον θεοῦ ἐδέξασθέ με, ὡς Χριστὸν Ἰησοῦν, 4:14. He hopes that his trial will turn out for salvation διὰ τῆς ὑμῶν δεήσεως καὶ ἐπιχορηγίας τοῦ πνεύματος Ἰησοῦ Χριστοῦ, Phil. 1:19, cf. πνεῦμα Χριστοῦ in R. 8:9. Paul prays for the Romans, to whom he has presented Christ in His saving acts, that God may grant them τὸ αὐτὸ φρονεῖν ἐν ἀλλήλοις κατὰ Χριστὸν Ἰησοῦν, R. 15:5. [389] He testifies that Timothy, in contrast to the selfishness of others who τὰ ἑαυτῶν ζητοῦσιν, οὐ τὰ Χριστοῦ Ἰησοῦ, [390] is likeminded with himself, Phil. 2:21.

It is clear from the contexts in which they are used that Χριστός, ὁ Χριστός, Χριστὸς Ἰησοῦς and Ἰησοῦς Χριστός all mean the same thing. The bringer of salvation — Χριστός — is Jesus. Jesus then is also known as Χριστός. This is the witness of Paul.

4. Ἰησοῦς Χριστὸς κύριος and ὁ κύριος (ἡμῶν) Ἰησοῦς Χριστός in Paul.

The frequently attested pre-Pauline κύριος Ἰησοῦς (1 C. 12:3; R. 10:9) becomes κύριος Ἰησοῦς Χριστός in the hymn which Paul adopts in Phil. 2:6-11. Septuagint echoes suggest that the hymn comes from a Hellenistic-Jewish church [391] so that if Χριστός is not woven into the hymn by Paul himself it is used in its Christian Messianic sense for the One who brings salvation through His death and exaltation and whose name which is above every name is κύριος Ἰησοῦς Χριστός. Paul describes as the content of His work: οὐ γὰρ ἑαυτοὺς κηρύσσομεν (→ III, 710, 12 ff.) ἀλλὰ Χριστὸν Ἰησοῦν κύριον, ἑαυτοὺς δὲ δούλους ὑμῶν διὰ Ἰησοῦν, 2 C. 4:5. [392]

---

in Jesus and the faith of Jesus and concludes that Paul so clearly stresses the full humanity of Jesus that he undoubtedly locates the relation of the earthly Jesus to God, like that of other men, in faith, cf. also 64. But cf. Neugebauer, 168, n. 69 with bibl. On this whole question cf. also T. F. Torrance, "One Aspect of the Biblical Conception of Faith," Exp. T., 68 (1956/57), 111-114, who thinks this is a gen. auct.

[384] Ἰησοῦ does not occur in p⁴⁶ D G 𝔐 lat syᵖ Marcion Cl.

[385] It should be considered whether ἐν ὑμῖν here means "among you" rather than "in you," i.e., "in your hearts," cf. Bouttier, 80.

[386] Some MSS read Ἰησοῦ Χριστοῦ.

[387] Some important MSS read only Χριστοῦ.

[388] Some MSS read Ἰησοῦ Χριστοῦ.

[389] Some MSS reverse the order here: Ἰησοῦν Χριστόν.

[390] Some MSS reverse the order here: Ἰησοῦ Χριστοῦ. It is thus possible that in most of the textually uncertain passages (→ n. 382, 384, 386-390) an original Χριστός has been supplemented by a Ἰησοῦς put either before it or after it. If so this would increase the no. of Χριστός ref.

[391] For this thesis cf. D. Georgi, "Der vorpaul. Hymnus Phil. 2:6-11," Festschr. R. Bultmann (1964), 263-293 with bibl. For a more Gentile Chr. origin cf. J. Gnilka, Der Phil., Herders Theol. Komm. NT, 10, 3 (1968), 147. Cerfaux, 233-245 makes a fresh attempt to show that Paul himself composed the hymn.

[392] Behind Paul's statement stands a passage like Mk. 10:41-45 and par.; there is allusion to this in the διὰ Ἰησοῦν at 2 C. 4:5.

The content of his preaching is the saving event which is Christ Jesus,[393] who is Lord of all who accept the preaching, cf. R. 14:7-9. Believers are put in a relation to Christ Jesus [394] in which He is Lord. This is Paul's testimony when he speaks about the overwhelming significance τῆς γνώσεως Χριστοῦ Ἰησοῦ τοῦ κυρίου μου, Phil. 3:8. Christ Jesus is the One ὃς ἐγενήθη σοφία ἡμῖν ἀπὸ θεοῦ, δικαιοσύνη τε καὶ ἁγιασμὸς καὶ ἀπολύτρωσις, 1 C. 1:30. [395] It is thus evident once again that Christ is all this as the One who is commissioned by God — ἀπὸ θεοῦ. The Ἰησοῦ Χριστοῦ τοῦ κυρίου ἡμῶν of Paul in R. 1:3 f. sums up the traditional confession of Jesus as the Son of God. For Paul sonship (→ VIII, 366, 22 ff.; 384, 22 ff.) and lordship embrace the earthly and the eternal modes of Christ Jesus. In the confessional formula which rejects many gods (→ III, 101, 5 ff.; 108, 25 ff.) and lords we read: ἡμῖν εἷς θεὸς ὁ πατήρ (→ V, 1012, 2 ff.), ἐξ οὗ τὰ πάντα καὶ ἡμεῖς εἰς αὐτόν, καὶ εἷς κύριος (→ III, 1091, 13 ff.) Ἰησοῦς Χριστός, δι' οὗ τὰ πάντα καὶ ἡμεῖς δι' αὐτοῦ, 1 C. 8:6.

This formulation develops what is said in the salutations: χάρις ὑμῖν καὶ εἰρήνη ἀπὸ θεοῦ πατρὸς ἡμῶν καὶ κυρίου Ἰησοῦ Χριστοῦ, R. 1:7; 1 C. 1:3; 2 C. 1:2; Gl. 1:3; [396] Phil. 1:2; Phlm. 3, cf. also Col. 1:2; [397] Eph. 1:2; 2 Th. 1:2. [398] No matter whether this statement was taken over by Paul or formulated by him, [399] it displays a balanced structure which leads to the full designation κύριος Ἰησοῦς Χριστός. [400] Its origin is to be sought in Septuagint formulations like κύριος ὁ θεός or θεὸς κύριος. Under homological influence this was transformed in Christian worship [401] into θεὸς πατήρ and the co-ordinated κύριος Ἰησοῦς Χριστός, the point being that he who has Jesus Christ as his Lord has God as his Father. The threefold κύριος Ἰησοῦς Χριστός occupies an important place in salutations. When used elsewhere, its position also gives it considerable significance. One may see this in the use on three occasions of ἐν Χριστῷ Ἰησοῦ τῷ κυρίῳ ἡμῶν (R. 6:23; 8:39; [402] 1 C. 15:31) and also in διὰ Ἰησοῦ Χριστοῦ τοῦ κυρίου ἡμῶν (R. 5:21; 7:25) and διὰ τοῦ κυρίου ἡμῶν Ἰησοῦ Χριστοῦ (R. 5:1, 11; 15:30; 1 C. 15:57). From the area of baptismal formulae one may adduce τὸ ὄνομα τοῦ κυρίου ἡμῶν Ἰησοῦ Χριστοῦ (1 C. 1:2, 10; 6:11; 2 Th. 1:12; 3:6), while confession of the God who reveals Himself to men in Jesus Christ yields the statement θεὸς καὶ πατὴρ τοῦ κυρίου ἡμῶν Ἰησοῦ Χριστοῦ, R. 15:6; 2 C. 1:3. Worth noting is the number of expressions

---

[393] Some MSS, p46 ℵ A C D lat, read instead Ἰησοῦν Χριστὸν κύριον. In this case the titles clash → 542, 24 ff.

[394] Cf. Neugebauer, 55-64; Kramer, 61-64.

[395] Cerfaux, 128-214 expounds wisdom, righteousness etc. as applied to Christ. If we put them in direct speech, we get a possible step to the "I am" sayings in Jn.

[396] Here p46, 51 B D G 𝔐 put ἡμῶν after κυρίου, not πατρός; this reading is to be preferred; it gives evidence of development → n. 398.

[397] The salutation in B D it vg sy and Orig does not have καὶ κυρίου Ἰησοῦ Χριστοῦ; perhaps there is later assimilation in most MSS.

[398] The development ref. to in → n. 396 is clear in 1 Th. 1:1: τῇ ἐκκλησίᾳ Θεσσαλονικέων ἐν θεῷ πατρὶ καὶ κυρίῳ Ἰησοῦ Χριστῷ· χάρις ὑμῖν καὶ εἰρήνη. This is perhaps its starting-point, cf. Kramer, 149-153.

[399] The pre-Pauline origin of the formulation maintained by E. Lohmeyer, "Probleme paul. Theol., I," ZNW, 26 (1927), 158-161 is challenged on weighty grounds by G. Friedrich, "Lohmeyers These über 'Das paul. Briefpräskript' kritisch beleuchtet," ZNW, 46 (1955), 272-4.

[400] Cf. on this Kramer, 152. He regards the formula χάρις ὑμῖν καὶ εἰρήνη ἀπὸ θεοῦ πατρὸς ἡμῶν καὶ κυρίου Ἰησοῦ Χριστοῦ as a structured one.

[401] Cf. Kramer, 151.

[402] We should perhaps add R. 6:11, where some MSS have the full form.

at the beginning of 1 C.,[403] where along with Χριστὸς ᾽Ιησοῦς (1 C. 1:1 f., 4) and Χριστός (v. 6) we also find the form ὁ κύριος ἡμῶν ᾽Ιησοῦς Χριστός or ᾽Ιησοῦς Χριστὸς ὁ κύριος ἡμῶν (1:2, 7-10). There are perhaps two reasons for this accumulation. First, the Corinthian church is orientated to men and it needs to be pointed to the sole basis and reference point of its faith, to its salvation in Christ and its control by the Kurios. Secondly, there is need to make it clear that this Christ and Kurios is Jesus, whom the Corinthian Gnostics were trying to sunder from a heavenly being called Christ. At various points, especially in concluding greetings, Paul refers to the χάρις τοῦ κυρίου ἡμῶν ᾽Ιησοῦ Χριστοῦ, 2 C. 8:9; 1 C. 16:23; Phil. 4:23 → VII, 777, 39 ff. ἐλπὶς τοῦ κυρίου ἡμῶν ᾽Ιησοῦ Χριστοῦ occurs in 1 Th. 1:3: "the hope which is directed to and based upon our Lord Jesus Christ." The παρουσία τοῦ κυρίου ἡμῶν ᾽Ιησοῦ Χριστοῦ is mentioned in both 1 Th. 5:23 and 2 Th. 2:1.[404]

5. Christ's Significance for Mankind.

Paul not only relates Christ to David (R. 1:3), as the pre-Pauline community had done. He also relates Him to Adam and sees in Christ Jesus the second or last Adam (→ I, 142, 26 ff.). As the bringer of salvation He is the author of a new humanity (1 C. 15:47 f.). Paul's preaching includes Χριστὸν διάκονον γεγενῆσθαι περιτομῆς ὑπὲρ ἀληθείας θεοῦ in R. 15:8 and κατειργάσατο Χριστὸς δι᾽ ἐμοῦ εἰς ὑπακοὴν ἐθνῶν in R. 15:18. The understanding of the Messiah loses its national political and religious significance and the significance of the Messiah in human history is attested and expounded. This is the distinctive theological achievement of Paul.

6. χρίω in 2 C. 1:21 f.

Only once in the Pauline corpus do we find the verb χρίω. In distinction from Lk. 4:18; Ac. 4:27; 10:38 and Hb. 1:9 it is related to ἡμᾶς rather than to Jesus as Messiah. The context contains baptismal terminology:[405] ὁ δὲ βεβαιῶν ἡμᾶς σὺν ὑμῖν εἰς Χριστὸν καὶ χρίσας ἡμᾶς θεός, ὁ καὶ σφραγισάμενος ἡμᾶς καὶ δοὺς τὸν ἀρραβῶνα τοῦ πνεύματος ἐν ταῖς καρδίαις ἡμῶν, 2 C. 1:21 f. In contrast to βεβαιῶν (→ I, 603, 21 ff.) ἡμᾶς σὺν ὑμῖν εἰς Χριστόν, which proclaims God's ongoing work in the baptised, the three expressions which follow, χρίσας, σφραγισάμενος (→ VII, 940, 24 ff.), δοὺς τὸν ἀρραβῶνα are in the aorist and have in view the act of God which establishes the new existence and aims at βεβαιῶν᾽... εἰς Χριστόν. Are these three aorist participles co-ordinated?[406] Or does χρίσας have comprehensive significance? This is suggested by its co-ordination with βεβαιῶν and its relation to the ὁ δὲ ... θεός which embraces both. If so, its meaning is worked out in the ὁ καὶ σφραγισάμενος ἡμᾶς καὶ δοὺς τὸν ἀρραβῶνα τοῦ πνεύματος ἐν ταῖς καρδίαις ἡμῶν, which is attached by the textually insecure ὁ[407] and the comprehensive καί... καί. Since the use of oil at baptism is attested only for the end

---

[403] Cf. Friedrich Christus, 238-240.

[404] Cf. also 2 Th. 2:14: δόξα τοῦ κυρίου ἡμῶν ᾽Ιησοῦ Χριστοῦ, and v. 16: αὐτὸς δὲ ὁ κύριος ἡμῶν ᾽Ιησοῦς Χριστὸς καὶ ὁ θεὸς πατὴρ ἡμῶν, ὁ ἀγαπήσας ἡμᾶς καὶ δοὺς παράκλησιν αἰωνίαν καὶ ἐλπίδα ἀγαθὴν ἐν χάριτι.

[405] Cf. Dinkler, op. cit. (→ n. 364), who correctly notes the legal character of the terms used in this whole section, and also the connection with 2 C. 1:15-24.

[406] So Dinkler, op. cit., 103 and cf. also W. Nauck, "Die Tradition und der Charakter d. 1 J.," Wissenschaftl. Untersuchungen z. NT, 3 (1957), 165-7.

[407] It is not in 𝔓 K or 69.

of the 2nd century A.D. and not for primitive Christianity, [408] one must assume that the sense is transferred. χρίσας denotes the appropriation to Christ accomplished at baptism by the God who is at work in all things. [409] This is sealed in the act of baptism and efficacious in the gift of the Holy Spirit (→ I, 475, 1 ff.) who refashions the baptised into the likeness of Christ, cf. 2 C. 3:18; R. 8:29; Gl. 4:19. God Himself confirms the baptised in his membership of Christ until he is perfected, cf. 1 C. 1:8; Phil. 1:6. The one who is appropriated to Christ is a Χριστιανός → 536, 35 ff. This is indicated by the participle χρίσας even though the term is not used. As ὁ τοῦ Χριστοῦ he belongs to the σῶμα Χριστοῦ → 547, 35 ff.

7. Χριστός in Colossians and Ephesians.

In Colossians and Ephesians [410] the new Messianic understanding worked out in primitive Christianity and by Paul is brought to completion. This is done in controversy with Gnostic doctrines of redemption. Χριστός is now a leading concept [411] and apocalyptic ideas of the *parousia* are pushed in the background. Χριστός is a historical and not a mythical figure. The μυστήριον τοῦ Χριστοῦ is the essential theme of the letters → IV, 819, 11 ff. What is meant is the mystery of God which is disclosed in the Christ event and preached to the community in the Gospel. This mystery of Christ is for the community Χριστὸς ἐν ὑμῖν, at work as ἡ ἐλπὶς τῆς δόξης, Col. 1:27, cf. R. 3:23. The formulation guards against any ecstatic overleaping of time by the Gnostics. Relation to Christ does not come about in ecstatic enthusiasm. It is in faith that the presence of Christ is enacted and the hope of His glory is kindled. Ephesians goes further to the extent that the mystery of Christ is also the mystery of the Church: τὸ μυστήριον τοῦτο μέγα ἐστίν, ἐγὼ δὲ λέγω εἰς Χριστὸν καὶ εἰς τὴν ἐκκλησίαν, Eph. 5:32; in Ephesians Christology and soteriology are sustained by ecclesiology → III, 509, 20 ff. [412] Christ is the mystery

---

[408] Cf. Dinkler, *op. cit.*, 105-7.

[409] Dinkler, *op. cit.*, 107 relates χρίω to the baptismal act as an "infusion with water . . . which effects the incorporation of those anointed into fellowship with the Anointed and brings about the sanctification of those anointed by God Himself." It must be asked, however, whether χρίσας does not denote appropriation to the Anointed and whether the baptismal act is not first referred to with σφραγισάμενος ἡμᾶς: the sealing in baptism together with the gift of the Spirit which expresses the reception of the one appropriated by the Christ and Lord; but cf. → VII, 949, 24 ff. with no ref. to baptism.

[410] I regard it as probable that Paul is the author of Col. (→ VII, 785, n. 92). The linguistic and theological peculiarities of Col. can be explained by its treatment of the Colossian error, the delay in the *parousia,* and esp. the use of hymnal passages taken over by Paul, cf. also Neugebauer, 175-9. If not written by Paul himself it must have been written by one of his assistants who after his imprisonment or death worked in his place in Ephesus and wrote in his name. Eph. — ἐν Ἐφέσῳ in 1:1 is uncertain since it is not in p46 א* B* Marcion Orig *et al.* — is in my view written by a disciple of Paul around 70 A.D. when many Jewish Christians were leaving Palestine for Asia Minor. This would explain the interest in uniting Jews and Gentiles in the one Church. On the authorship of G. Schille, "Der Autor d. Eph.," ThLZ, 82 (1957), 325-334, who contends for Pauline authorship; on the hymns used in Eph. cf. also Schille's *Frühchr. Hymnen* (1962), 24-30, 53-60, 65-73, 95 f.; on Qumran influences → VII, 652, n. 40. On the authorship of Col. cf. E. Lohse, *Die Briefe an d. Kol. u. an Philemon, Krit.-exeg. Komm. über d. NT,* 9, 2¹⁴ (1968), 249-257.

[411] As in 1 C. → 555, 1 ff. On the Colossian error cf. G. Bornkamm, "Die Haeresie d. Kol.," *Das Ende d. Gesetzes*⁵ (1966), 139-156; E. Haenchen, Art. "Gnosis, II," RGG³, II, 1654; H. Hegermann, "Die Vorstellung vom Schöpfungsmittler im hell. Judt. u. Urchr.," TU, 82 (1961), 161-199.

[412] Cf. on this Hegermann, *op. cit.* (→ n. 411), 184 f.; E. Käsemann, "Das Interpretationsproblem d. Eph.," ThLZ, 86 (1961), 1-7 in debate with H. Schlier, *Der Brief an die Eph.*⁶ (1968); H. Chadwick, "Die Absicht d. Eph.," ZNW, 51 (1960), 145-153.

of God because all the treasures of wisdom and knowledge are hidden in Him (Col. 2:2 f.), all the fulness of the Godhead dwells in Him bodily (2:9), and He is the Head (→ III, 680, 40 ff.) of all dominion and power (2:10). The Gnostic teachers in Colossae are in error in cleaving to the elemental powers of the universe as well as Christ (→ VII, 685, 17 ff.) on the ground that, while Christ grants forgiveness of sin, human existence in its materiality is dependent on these powers and is not set aside by Christ. Paul's reply is that what separates man from God is his sin, not his materiality, and that the forgiveness of sin through Christ means full salvation (Col. 1:12-14). In worshipping the elemental powers the false teachers fall victim to a deceptive human teaching οὐ κατὰ Χριστόν (2:8). Here again, as in Mk. 8:33 and 1 C. 1:23-31, human tradition and secular thought are distinguished from the way and work of God. The proclamation which has this mystery as its content has as its goal ἵνα παραστήσωμεν πάντα ἄνθρωπον τέλειον ἐν Χριστῷ (Col. 1:28). [413] Since Christ is the mystery of God, man finds fulfilment in the sphere of Christ. In Eph. with its ecclesiological orientation Jesus Christ is the ἀκρογωνιαῖος (→ I, 792, 22 ff.) of the spiritual building of the community (Eph. 2:20-22). The understanding of the Church is governed by the mystery of Christ (3:4) in the fulfilment of which the nations are fellow-heirs, members of the same body, and participants in the promise given in Jesus Christ; herein is τὸ ἀνεξιχνίαστον πλοῦτος τοῦ Χριστοῦ which Paul proclaims (3:6-8). Both epistles agree that the eternal and hidden mystery of God is revealed and accessible at the present moment in Christ, Col. 1:26 f.; Eph. 3:5, 10 f.

Adopting an ancient confessional formula, Eph. describes Christ as the one who grants confidence and access to God to both Jews and Gentiles (Eph. 2:18; 3:12; → I, 134, 5 ff.); [414] these were not available to the Gentiles χωρὶς Χριστοῦ (2:12), but νυνὶ δὲ ἐν Χριστῷ Ἰησοῦ (2:13) [415] is set in antithesis to χωρὶς Χριστοῦ. The ref. to Christ involves, not timeless gnosis, but a historical and eschatological event of revelation and salvation. Christ has become our peace (2:14) inasmuch as he brings divided men together by His work, Eph. 2:14, 17. This work, by bringing men to God and making peace between them (→ II, 415, 12 ff.), constitutes Him the Saviour (→ VII, 1016, 3 ff.) and the Head of the community which is His body, Eph. 5:23, cf. also 1:22; 4:15 f. → VII, 1077, 17 ff. [416] The community is subject to the Head (→ III, 680, 8 ff.), 5:24. His relation to the community is like that of the husband (→ I, 656, 6 ff.) to the wife; the two relations elucidate one another. All love is focused on the Church, 5:2, 25, 29. In this regard there is emphatic reference

---

413 𝕽 and vg add Ἰησοῦ.

414 Traces of this confession may be seen in R. 5:2; 1 Pt. 3:18; Hb. 7:25a; 10:19 f.

415 On the problem of ἐν Χριστῷ or ἐν κυρίῳ sayings in Eph. cf. J. A. Allan, "The 'In Christ' Formula in Eph.," NTSt, 5 (1958/59), 54-62. Allan pts. out that the formula is more common but less intensive than in the main Pauline epistles. "'In Christ' is no longer for this Writer the formula of incorporation into Christ, but has become the formula of God's activity through Christ." Is it used instrumentally and often has the same sense as the adj. "Christian." Allan, 55 can also ref. to "profound personal identification with Christ," but in the sense, not of identity mysticism, but of fashioning in the likeness of Christ on the basis of incorporation, → VII, 787, 34 ff. If there is thus a shift of accent compared with the main epistles, here as in the Past. (→ n. 445) we are still in the sphere of what we have called the field of force of Jesus Christ. P. Pokorny, Der Eph. u. d. Gnosis (1965), 56 draws attention to the connection with κεφαλή - σῶμα.

416 In distinction from 1 C. 12:12 Christ and the body are not equated. Christ is now the Head and believers are the body. In 1 C. 12:14-27 membership of the body is emphasised. This is mentioned but not worked out in Eph. 4:25; 5:30. The Head (Christ) has in the first instance cosmological significance in Col. but the main significance in Eph. is ecclesiological.

to ὁ Χριστός who exercises His ministering lordship to the Church by caring for it, nourishing it, and giving Himself for it, as all primitive Christianity confesses. Awareness of the new significance of ὁ Χριστός thus moves forward into the post-apostolic period. [417] In Col., too, the community belongs to Christ as His people; Paul speaks of the σῶμα (→ VII, 1074, 28 ff.) αὐτοῦ (= τοῦ Χριστοῦ) and offers the definition: ὅ ἐστιν ἡ ἐκκλησία, Col. 1:24. The reality of God, which projects its shadows σκιὰ τῶν μελλόντων in the religions, has become present in the community τὸ δὲ σῶμα τοῦ Χριστοῦ, 2:17; for the λόγος τοῦ Χριστοῦ is to be richly attested and the εἰρήνη τοῦ Χριστοῦ is to win the prize of conflict in their hearts, 3:15. In Christ the things that separate men are overcome, the rule now being: πάντα καὶ ἐν πᾶσιν Χριστός, 3:11, cf. Gl. 3:28. The community is addressed as τοῖς ἐν Κολοσσαῖς ἁγίοις καὶ πιστοῖς ἀδελφοῖς ἐν Χριστῷ, Col. 1:2, cf. Eph. 1:1. [418] As in the chief epistles Paul is ἀπόστολος Χριστοῦ Ἰησοῦ (Col. 1:1; Eph. 1:1); he is ὁ δέσμιος τοῦ Χριστοῦ Ἰησοῦ ὑπὲρ ὑμῶν (Eph. 3:1) and he fills up τὰ ὑστερήματα (→ VIII, 599, 30 ff.) τῶν θλίψεων τοῦ Χριστοῦ, Col. 1:24. Epaphras is called a πιστὸς ... διάκονος τοῦ Χριστοῦ, Col. 1:7. God is "the Father of our Lord Jesus Christ," Col. 1:3; Eph. 1:3. [419] Christians confess the God who is conjoined to the person of Jesus Christ and who has become their God. [420] If peace and love with faith are desired for the community from God the Father and the Lord Jesus Christ, the grace which gives these things is imparted to those who love our Lord Jesus Christ in sincerity, Eph. 6:23 f. The love of Christ for His community and the responsive love of the members of the community plainly surpasses all knowledge, cf. also 3:19. The personal structure of faith in Christ clearly differs from the *gnosis* of the divine self in man as the accomplishment of redemption.

In Eph., in which the Church is the salvation event, the individual member of the body is caught up in this event and brought to fulfilment. This is accomplished by the δωρεὰ τοῦ Χριστοῦ (4:7), who has effected it by His descent to earth and ascent to heaven (4:8-10 → III, 642, 11 ff.), [421] so that He is the One who fulfils all things. His gifts are conferred through the ministry of those whom He takes up into His service, 4:11. All their work aims πρὸς τὸν καταρτισμὸν τῶν ἁγίων εἰς ἔργον διακονίας, εἰς οἰκοδομὴν τοῦ σώματος τοῦ Χριστοῦ, 4:12. This is accomplished as all come to the unity of faith through the knowledge of God and hence εἰς ἄνδρα τέλειον, εἰς μέτρον ἡλικίας τοῦ πληρώματος τοῦ Χριστοῦ, 4:13. The ἀνὴρ τέλειος who grows up into Christ is marked by steadfastness (→ VII, 652, 10 ff.), resoluteness, truth and love as the work of Christ. Christ initiates a process of growth of which He Himself is the goal [422] and in which He Himself sets us, 4:15 f. [423] Col. states emphatically that the knowledge of Christ leads to τὴν τάξιν καὶ τὸ στερέωμα τῆς εἰς Χριστὸν πίστεως ὑμῶν which Paul rejoices to find among

---

[417] It might well be that the encounter of Gentile and Jewish Christians in Ephesus (→ n. 410) led to a strengthening of the Messianic element in the understanding of Christ for the sake of the Jewish Christians.

[418] On ἐν Ἐφέσῳ → n. 410.

[419] Χριστοῦ does not occur in Col. 1:3 B. Several MSS do not have καὶ κυρίου Ἰησοῦ Χριστοῦ in the salutation at Col. 1:2.

[420] We find this first in Paul's later letters, 2 C. 1:3; 11:31; R. 15:16 and then in Col. 1:3; Eph. 1:3 and also 1 Pt. 1:3, cf. Rev. 1:6. It is modelled on the OT formula "the God of Abraham ... " This is the God who has bound Himself to historical persons.

[421] There is a similar proof from Scripture in R. 10:6 f. The idea of a descending and ascending Redeemer is Gnostic. The author adopts it, but relates it to the historical Jesus in death and resurrection.

[422] Cf. on this Grundmann, *op. cit.* (→ n. 369), 194-6.

[423] In some MSS, e.g., D G 𝔊 , we find the art. ὁ before Χριστός.

the Colossians, 2:5, → VII, 614, 1 ff. and cf. also 1:4.[424] Faith in Christ necessarily works itself out in a way of life which is shaped by it, Col. 2:6. Christians forgive one another and fashion their lives by Christ's prior forgiveness of them, Eph. 4:32; 5:2. They do everything in the name of the Lord Jesus Christ, Col. 3:17,[425] and they serve the Lord Christ[426] (3:24). This takes place by following the path κατὰ Χριστόν (2:8) through περιτομῇ ἀχειροποιήτῳ... τοῦ Χριστοῦ (2:11), which is trodden in dying and rising again with Christ, 2:20; 3:1, 4, cf. Eph. 2:4-7 → VII, 792, 19 ff. In Col., as in Phil. 1:21, Christ is called "our life"; our life which is hidden in Christ is revealed along with Christ Himself, 3:4. Believers are to set their minds on Him who is exalted at the right hand of God, 3:1. In His death, resurrection and ascension God has triumphed over principalities and powers, so that there can be no question of worshipping them as well as Christ, 2:15.[427] The term "Christ" is again linked to Christ's cross and resurrection. Believers are taken up into this event by baptism.

In relation to the salvation connected with it, the designation "Christ" occurs in the hymnal passages which are adopted and expounded especially in Eph. (1:3-14; 2:4-7, 10, 14-18; 3:14-21; 5:14)'. The first of these (1:3-14) begins by praising the Father of our Lord Jesus Christ who has conferred on us the spiritual blessing which is at work among the heavenly ones (1:3) by placing us among them with Him (2:6).[428] Christ, who is elect from all eternity, is the beloved (1:6), so that the salvation foreordained for men, and the fulfilment of this salvation, can be called υἱοθεσία διὰ 'Ιησοῦ Χριστοῦ εἰς αὐτόν, 1:5. It is "redemption... according to the riches of his grace" on the basis of His death and resurrection, 1:7, cf. 2:4, 7. Christ is both the foundation and also the goal of the salvation event κατὰ τὴν εὐδοκίαν αὐτοῦ, ἣν προέθετο ἐν αὐτῷ εἰς οἰκονομίαν τοῦ πληρώματος τῶν καιρῶν (1:9 f.), which embraces all men in their lost relation to God and the world ἀνακεφαλαιώσασθαι τὰ πάντα ἐν τῷ Χριστῷ τὰ ἐπὶ τοῖς οὐρανοῖς καὶ τὰ ἐπὶ τῆς γῆς ἐν αὐτῷ (1:10). Worth noting in this connection is ἐν τῷ Χριστῷ, which occurs twice more in Eph.[429] In Him the actualisation of salvation is foreordained and hope is grounded, 1:11-14.[430] The author takes up the hymnal statements into his own thanksgiving (1:15)[431] and prays that the community may have knowledge of the

---

[424] Faith is drawn as by a magnet into the field of force of Christ. The "in Christ" has a dynamic aspect.

[425] Χριστοῦ is added in ℵ* vgcl; A C D* G do not have κυρίου, nor p46 B 𝔖 Χριστοῦ.

[426] As at Lk. 2:11 and R. 16:18 some MSS have κυρίῳ Χριστῷ together here. G it have a different text: (ἀπο)λήμψεσθε τὴν ἀνταπόδοσιν τῆς κληρονομίας τοῦ κυρίου ἡμῶν 'Ιησοῦ Χριστοῦ, ᾧ δουλεύετε.

[427] ἐν αὐτῷ in Col. 2:15 relates to τοῦ Χριστοῦ in 2:11; the v. is part of the hymn which probably begins in v. 13b.

[428] An argument for a hymn in Eph. 1:3-14 is that the introductory thanksgiving comes only in 1:15. The more meditative style of the stanza is like that of the Qumran hymns. Schille Hymnen (→ n. 410), 65-73 thinks that v. 12b and v. 13 are epistolary additions, but cf. H. Krämer, "Zur sprachlichen Form der Eulogie Eph. 1:3-14," Wort u. Dienst, NF, 9 (1967), 44 f. H. Conzelmann, Der Brief an d. Eph., NT Deutsch, 8¹⁰ (1965), 59 calls it a meditation on the theme of God — in Christ. The ἐν Χριστῷ is often repeated in the forms ἐν αὐτῷ or ἐν ᾧ.

[429] In the main Pauline epistles we find this formula only at 1 C. 15:22 to balance ἐν τῷ 'Αδάμ, and at 2 C. 2:14, which again seems to be a hymnal passage → n. 415.

[430] Here we again have ἐν τῷ Χριστῷ at v. 12. Those who hope in Him in their earthly existence are ordained εἰς ἔπαινον δόξης αὐτοῦ. The προ- in προηλπικότας is to be construed in terms of this eschatological foreordination. Cf. Schille Hymnen, 104-7.

[431] πίστιν ἐν τῷ κυρίῳ 'Ιησοῦ in 1:15 seems not to be Pauline, Neugebauer, 179-181. Cf. also Col. 1:4 and Allan, op. cit. (→ n. 415).

might and power of God ἦν ἐνήργηκεν ἐν τῷ Χριστῷ ἐγείρας αὐτὸν ἐκ νεκρῶν, καὶ καθίσας ἐν δεξιᾷ αὐτοῦ ἐν τοῖς ἐπουρανίοις, 1:20. [432] The omnipotence of God which brings about the resurrection and exaltation of Christ gives the community protection against alien forces and assurance of the eschatological consummation. [433]

In the middle of the letter, at the end of the predominantly didactic section, there stands a prayer to the Father which in a series of expressions asks for the indwelling of Christ in the heart (3:17) and knowledge of the love of Christ which surpasses all knowledge (3:19) and which is the love of God in Jesus Christ (cf. 2:4; 5:2, 25). In the paraenetic section we find part of a baptismal hymn which promises illumination through Christ: ἔγειρε, ὁ καθεύδων, καὶ ἀνάστα ἐκ τῶν νεκρῶν, καὶ ἐπιφαύσει σοι ὁ Χριστός, 5:14. [434] This illumination consists in what is at issue in the prayer of 3:14-19. Throughout the one who brings salvation is ὁ Χριστός. In distinction from the Gnosticism which both epistles reject, He is not sent by a strange God into a world which is strange to Him. He comes from the God who is the Creator of this world. He is one with Him. He shares in His work of creation. He now reveals the hitherto mysterious purpose of the Creator for His creation. He leads creation back to Him, Col. 1:15-23.

8. Χριστός in the Pastoral Epistles.

a. The Pastoral Epistles contain a series of firmly formulated confessional sections which come from the Hellenistic community and are adopted and either adapted or developed by the author. In most of them we find Χριστὸς Ἰησοῦς. 1 Tm. 1:15 reads: Χριστὸς Ἰησοῦς ἦλθεν εἰς τὸν κόσμον ἁμαρτωλοὺς σῶσαι. The putting of Χριστός before the name Jesus shows awareness of its material significance. Since remission of sins takes place through the cross and resurrection of Christ, this statement [435] may be grouped with those that link Χριστός to this event, cf. also 1 Tm. 2:5 f. (→ IV, 619, 8 ff.), which uses Mk. 10:45 (→ VI, 544, 6 ff.) in a way that betrays the influence of the Hellenistic community: [436] εἷς γὰρ θεός, εἷς καὶ μεσίτης θεοῦ καὶ ἀνθρώπων, ἄνθρωπος Χριστὸς Ἰησοῦς, ὁ δοὺς ἑαυτὸν ἀντίλυτρον ὑπὲρ πάντων. [437] 1 Tm. 6:13 refers directly to the passion. Be-

---

[432] Here, as in Eph. 5:2, 25, a confession is quoted in a context which is itself hymnal; this explains the third ἐν τῷ Χριστῷ, v. 10 and 12.

[433] Eph. 2:1-10 and 2:11-18, esp. vv. 4-7, 10, with their frequent ἐν Χριστῷ Ἰησοῦ, are also hymnal in character. The chief statement is that ἐν Χριστῷ Ἰησοῦ believers are set among the heavenly ones, v. 6. ἐν Χριστῷ Ἰησοῦ the overwhelming riches of the grace of God in His kindness toward us are displayed to the insurgent powers of the aeon, v. 7. ἐν Χριστῷ Ἰησοῦ the possibility of good works before God is opened up, 2:10. Acc. to Schille Hymnen, 24-31, 2:14-18 is hymnal; the primary ref. was to the breaking down of the wall between God and men but the author expounds it in terms of the antithesis between Jews and Gentiles, cf. also Ac. 10:36. God in Christ reconciles those who are strangers to the covenant by His atoning act (2:13), so that Christ is our peace (2:14). He unites Jews and Gentiles in one body, fashions out of them one new man, and leads both in the one Spirit to God, 2:14-18.

[434] Cl. Al. Prot., IX, 84, 2 has the continuation: " . . . the Lord, the Son of the resurrection, born before the morning-star, who gives life through His own beams." This is an appositional statement of what Χριστός means for the author of Eph. 5:14.

[435] It is introduced by the solemn πιστὸς ὁ λόγος καὶ πάσης ἀποδοχῆς ἄξιος, 1 Tm. 1:15 → II, 55, 39 ff.

[436] Cf. J. Jeremias, "Das Lösegeld für Viele (Mk. 10:45)," Abba (1966), 216-229. On the Christology of the Past. cf. Windisch.

[437] It is an open question how far ἄνθρωπος denotes here Christ's humanity or how far it takes its sense from the Gnostic primal man or the apocalyptic Son of Man.

hind it is a confessional piece which probably ran: Χριστὸς Ἰησοῦς ὁ μαρτυρήσας ἐπὶ Ποντίου Πιλάτου τὴν καλὴν ὁμολογίαν. [438] 2 Tm. 1:9 f. speaks of χάρις. God has granted it to us ἐν Χριστῷ Ἰησοῦ πρὸ χρόνων αἰωνίων. Hidden from eternity, but actual in God's purpose, it is manifest νῦν διὰ τῆς ἐπιφανείας τοῦ σωτῆρος ἡμῶν Χριστοῦ Ἰησοῦ, καταργήσαντος μὲν τὸν θάνατον φωτίσαντος δὲ ζωὴν καὶ ἀφθαρσίαν διὰ τοῦ εὐαγγελίου. [439] Here Χριστὸς Ἰησοῦς [440] is connected with the resurrection of Jesus. How far καταργήσαντος ... τὸν θάνατον is also related to the death of Christ Jesus is an open question, but it is likely enough in view of the μέν - δέ. 2 Tm. 2:8 also contains a confessional statement which in the form of two-stage Christology speaks of the earthly manifestation of Christ and then of His state of exaltation: μνημόνευε Ἰησοῦν Χριστὸν ἐγηγερμένον ἐκ νεκρῶν, ἐκ σπέρματος Δαυίδ, cf. R. 1:3 f. In both the great epiphany passages in Tt. [441] Χριστὸς Ἰησοῦς occurs. Tt. 2:11-14 speaks of waiting for τὴν μακαρίαν ἐλπίδα καὶ ἐπιφάνειαν τῆς δόξης τοῦ μεγάλου θεοῦ καὶ σωτῆρος ἡμῶν Χριστοῦ Ἰησοῦ, ὃς ἔδωκεν ἑαυτὸν ὑπὲρ ἡμῶν ἵνα λυτρώσηται ἡμᾶς, 2:13. [442] The statement about redemptive self-sacrifice is linked to Χριστὸς Ἰησοῦς. Tt. 3:6 refers to the baptismal outpouring of the renewing and justifying Spirit διὰ Ἰησοῦ Χριστοῦ τοῦ σωτῆρος ἡμῶν, → VII, 1017, 36 ff. These confessional fragments confirm the close connection between Χριστός and the cross and resurrection of Jesus and also His redemptive work in baptism.

b. In the Past. we find a few Pauline salutations with ἀπὸ θεοῦ πατρὸς καὶ Χριστοῦ Ἰησοῦ τοῦ κυρίου ἡμῶν, 1 Tm. 1:2; 2 Tm. 1:2, cf. Tt. 1:4 [443] and also Paul's self-designation as ἀπόστολος Χριστοῦ Ἰησοῦ in 1 Tm. 1:1 with the extension κατ' ἐπιταγὴν θεοῦ σωτῆρος ἡμῶν καὶ Χριστοῦ Ἰησοῦ τῆς ἐλπίδος ἡμῶν. 2 Tm. 1:1 adds: διὰ θελήματος θεοῦ κατ' ἐπαγγελίαν ζωῆς τῆς ἐν Χριστῷ Ἰησοῦ. In both cases the apostolate is grounded in the overruling will of God and the salvation event in Christ Jesus. [444] Timothy is called διάκονος Χριστοῦ Ἰησοῦ in 1 Tm. 4:6 and καλὸς στρατιώτης Χριστοῦ Ἰησοῦ in 2 Tm. 2:3. 1 Tm. 6:3 speaks of the ὑγιαίνουσιν λόγοις τοῖς τοῦ κυρίου ἡμῶν Ἰησοῦ Χριστοῦ. There is a striking ref. to the πίστις καὶ ἀγάπη ἡ ἐν Χριστῷ Ἰησοῦ in 1 Tm. 1:14; 2 Tm. 1:13. The author speaks of the σωτηρία... ἡ ἐν Χριστῷ Ἰησοῦ μετὰ δόξης αἰωνίου (2 Tm. 2:10), which is developed in a hymn (→ VII, 793, 20 ff.), of the χάρις ἡ ἐν Χριστῷ Ἰησοῦ (2 Tm. 2:1), and of the ζῆν εὐσεβῶς ἐν Χριστῷ Ἰησοῦ (2 Tm. 3:12). [445] The witness-formula διαμαρτύρομαι

---

[438] In the confession μαρτυρήσας probably means active witness through suffering. The addition of the author (τὴν καλὴν ὁμολογίαν) gives it the sense of "giving testimony," i.e., by confession → IV, 499, 19 ff.

[439] On σωτήρ (→ VII, 1016, 29 ff.) and ἐπιφάνεια (→ 10, 1 ff.) cf. Dib. Past.⁴, 74-8.

[440] C G 𝔐 have Ἰησοῦ Χριστοῦ.

[441] On the terminology of these sections cf. Dib. Past.⁴, 108-110.

[442] A C D 𝔐 have Ἰησοῦ Χριστοῦ. On ἐπιφάνεια... σωτῆρος ἡμῶν Ἰησοῦ Χριστοῦ for the *parousia* cf. also 1 Tm. 6:14; 2 Tm. 4:1. On the relation of sayings about God to sayings about Christ → IV, 538, 22 ff.

[443] 1 Tm. 1:2 and 2 Tm. 1:2 have an ἔλεος instead of ὑμῖν καί between χάρις and εἰρήνη, and instead of the simple κυρίου Ἰησοῦ Χριστοῦ we find Χριστοῦ Ἰησοῦ τοῦ κυρίου ἡμῶν, with assimilation at 2 Tm. 1:2 in some MSS. Tt. 1:4 has χάρις καὶ εἰρήνη and a τοῦ σωτῆρος ἡμῶν with Χριστοῦ Ἰησοῦ.

[444] In Tt. 1:1-3 Paul's apostleship is based on a concept of the economy of salvation.

[445] Cf. on this J. A. Allan, "The 'In Christ' Formula in the Pastoral Epistles," NTSt, 10 (1963/64), 115-121. In the Past. the formula is less common than in the chief Pauline epistles and esp. Eph. (→ n. 415). A distinction of use is seen. "There seems no compelling reason to regard the formula in the Pastorals as doing more than indicate Christ as the source of faith, love, godly living etc.," 117. It is used "in eight places in connexion with abstract nouns and in one in connexion with a verb," 116. For a comparison of 2 Tm. 1:9 with 1 C. 1:4 cf. Allan, 120.

ἐνώπιον τοῦ θεοῦ καὶ Χριστοῦ 'Ιησοῦ is peculiar to the Past., 1 Tm. 5:21; 2 Tm. 4:1 [446] → IV, 511, 31 ff. In 1 and 2 Tm. Paul is a model appointed by Christ. He gives thanks τῷ ἐνδυναμώσαντί με Χριστῷ 'Ιησοῦ τῷ κυρίῳ ἡμῶν, 1 Tm. 1:12 → II, 313, 6 ff., cf. 2 Tm. 4:17; 2:1. He bears witness: διὰ τοῦτο ἠλεήθην, ἵνα ἐν ἐμοὶ πρώτῳ ἐνδείξηται 'Ιησοῦς Χριστὸς τὴν ἅπασαν μακροθυμίαν, πρὸς ὑποτύπωσιν τῶν μελλόντων πιστεύειν ἐπ' αὐτῷ εἰς ζωὴν αἰώνιον, 1 Tm. 1:16. It may be seen quite clearly in this passage how a term for God's work — μακροθυμία — can be transferred to Christ.

In all these passages Χριστός is linked with the name "Jesus." The absolute Χριστός, which is typical of Paul, does not occur. Only 1 Tm. 5:11 says regarding widows: ὅταν γὰρ καταστρηνιάσωσιν τοῦ Χριστοῦ, γαμεῖν θέλουσιν... Sensual impulses can lead to conduct which is against Christ. In the Pastorals God and Christ Jesus are often co-ordinated but it is always maintained that Jesus Christ is God's proxy and that God acts in Him. [447] υἱὸς τοῦ θεοῦ does not occur. How far the idea of pre-existence is implied by ἐπιφάνεια Χριστοῦ 'Ιησοῦ is not clear. The usage and Christology are more generally Christian rather than specifically Pauline.

IV. Χριστός in the Epistles of Peter, James and Jude and in Hebrews.

1. Χριστός in 1 Peter.

In distinction from other later epistles, 1 Peter, like Paul, uses Χριστός (1:11, 19; 2:21; 3:16, 18; 4:1, 14; 5:10), ὁ Χριστός (3:15; 4:13; 5:1) and 'Ιησοῦς Χριστός alongside one another in the same sense. At the heart of the epistle we find primitive Christian confession with commentary which, like 1 C. 15:3 and R. 8:34, begins with Χριστός and then runs: Χριστὸς ἅπαξ περὶ ἁμαρτιῶν ἀπέθανεν, δίκαιος ὑπὲρ ἀδίκων, ἵνα ὑμᾶς προσαγάγῃ τῷ θεῷ, θανατωθεὶς μὲν σαρκί (→ VII, 144, n. 346) ζωοποιηθεὶς δέ πνεύματι·... ὅς ἐστιν ἐν δεξιᾷ θεοῦ, πορευθεὶς εἰς οὐρανόν, ὑποταγέντων αὐτῷ ἀγγέλων καὶ ἐξουσιῶν καὶ δυνάμεως, 3:18, 22. [448] The beginning is a variation on 1 C. 15:3. In 1 Pt., too, Χριστός is the bringer of salvation. Salvation consists in the access to God which is accomplished by Him (→ 557, 21 ff.) and which is made possible by His death, resurrection and exaltation and by the subjection of the powers to His dominion. The introduction to the letter develops this confession. The ῥαντισμὸς αἵματος 'Ιησοῦ Χριστοῦ (1:2) is His saving death, the price which consists in τιμίῳ αἵματι ὡς ἀμνοῦ ἀμώμου καὶ ἀσπίλου Χριστοῦ (1:19). [449] The ἀνάστασις 'Ιησοῦ Χριστοῦ is the ground of regeneration in the interpretation of the confession (1:3, cf. also 3:21). There is reference to the revelation of Christ, who manifests His invisible glory (1:7). Χριστός links promise and fulfilment, for τὸ ἐν αὐτοῖς πνεῦμα Χριστοῦ revealed to the prophets τὰ εἰς Χριστὸν παθήματα καὶ τὰς μετὰ ταῦτα δόξας (1:11). Believers are to set their hope in the grace which comes to them therewith: τελείως

---

[446] In 2 Tm. 4:1 τοῦ μέλλοντος κρίνειν ζῶντας καὶ νεκρούς, καὶ τὴν ἐπιφάνειαν αὐτοῦ καὶ τὴν βασιλείαν αὐτοῦ is added to Χριστοῦ 'Ιησοῦ.

[447] Cf. Dib. Past.⁴, 8 f.

[448] Bultmann Theol., 505 attempts a reconstruction of the conclusion of the confession: πορευθεὶς (δὲ) εἰς οὐρανὸν ἐκάθισεν ἐν δεξιᾷ θεοῦ ὑποταγέντων αὐτῷ ἀγγέλων καὶ ἐξουσιῶν καὶ δυνάμεως, cf. also his "Bekenntnis- u. Liedfragmente im 1 Pt.," Exegetica (1967), 285-297, and cf. also C. H. Hunzinger, "Zur Struktur der Christus-Hymnen in Phil. 2 u. 1 Pt. 3," Festschr. J. Jeremias (1970), 142-5.

[449] The familiar statement of Eph. and Col. that what was hidden from primal ages is now revealed occurs also in 1 Pt. 1:9 f. It characterises the salvation event.

ἐλπίσατε ἐπὶ τὴν φερομένην ὑμῖν χάριν ἐν ἀποκαλύψει Ἰησοῦ Χριστοῦ (1:13). [450]
A peculiarity in 1 Pt., however, is that Christ in His passion and glorification is seen as an active model. He is this for slaves in their situation and also for the whole community in persecution. The confessional formula is adopted in the saying to slaves: Χριστὸς ἔπαθεν ὑπὲρ ὑμῶν, ὑμῖν ὑπολιμπάνων ὑπογραμμὸν ἵνα ἐπακολουθήσητε τοῖς ἴχνεσιν αὐτοῦ (2:21), which is then expounded in 2:22-25. [451] The preceding confession (3:18, 22) is also adopted in the summons to the community in 4:1: Χριστοῦ οὖν παθόντος σαρκὶ καὶ ὑμεῖς τὴν αὐτὴν ἔννοιαν ὁπλίσασθε. If the believer is a follower of Christ's sufferings, this is a reason for joy; for καθὸ κοινωνεῖτε τοῖς τοῦ Χριστοῦ παθήμασιν (→ V, 934, 23 ff.) χαίρετε, ἵνα καὶ ἐν τῇ ἀποκαλύψει τῆς δόξης αὐτοῦ χαρῆτε ἀγαλλιώμενοι, 4:13. This applies to the suffering which overtakes a man ὡς Χριστιανός, 4:15. Χριστιανός (→ 536, 35 ff.) here is one who shows his allegiance to Christ by letting Himself be fashioned by the image of Christ in his afflictions. The suffering of Christ, who died δίκαιος ὑπὲρ ἀδίκων (3:18), finds expression in the fact that it can fall on τὴν ἀγαθὴν ἐν Χριστῷ ἀναστροφήν, 3:16. To walk well, to renounce sin (4:1 f.) and to accept suffering is to sanctify κύριον δὲ τὸν Χριστόν [452] in the heart (3:15). [453] He who suffers thus ὡς Χριστιανός, μὴ αἰσχυνέσθω, δοξαζέτω δὲ τὸν θεὸν ἐν τῷ ὀνόματι τούτῳ (4:16). Trust in the salvation event which is summed up in the word Χριστός as the bringer of salvation means ὥστε τὴν πίστιν ὑμῶν καὶ ἐλπίδα εἶναι εἰς θεόν (1:21). In this faith and hope there is access to God through Christ who is the Word of God (→ 104, 8 ff.; IV, 116, 31 ff.) which begets man anew, 1:23. Spiritual sacrifices are brought to God διὰ Ἰησοῦ Χριστοῦ (2:5), for to Him belong glory and power to eternity, which the community extols in every regard διὰ Ἰησοῦ Χριστοῦ, since everything that it receives comes through Him (4:10 f.). He is ὁ... θεὸς πάσης χάριτος, ὁ καλέσας ὑμᾶς εἰς τὴν αἰώνιον αὐτοῦ δόξαν ἐν Χριστῷ, ὀλίγον παθόντας, 5:10. The author styles himself ἀπόστολος Ἰησοῦ Χριστοῦ (1:1), and in keeping with his understanding of the exemplary nature of the salvation event he also calls himself συμπρεσβύτερος καὶ μάρτυς τῶν τοῦ Χριστοῦ παθημάτων, ὁ καὶ τῆς μελλούσης ἀποκαλύπτεσθαι δόξης κοινωνός, 5:1. But of believers he says with reference to their relation to Christ, ὃν οὐκ ἰδόντες ἀγαπᾶτε, εἰς ὃν ἄρτι μὴ ὁρῶντες πιστεύοντες δὲ ἀγαλλιᾶσθε χαρᾷ ἀνεκλαλήτῳ καὶ δεδοξασμένῃ, κομιζόμενοι τὸ τέλος τῆς πίστεως σωτηρίαν ψυχῶν, 1:8 f. [454] At the end of the letter his salutation runs: εἰρήνη ὑμῖν πᾶσιν τοῖς ἐν Χριστῷ, 5:14.

2. Χριστός in Hebrews.

In Hb. Jesus Christ is the Son who receives the eternal high-priesthood because He offers Himself as a sacrifice, 5:8-10. As High-priest He leads the sons who have

---

[450] The fact that 1 Pt., like Col., uses revelation for the parousia shows that what is in mind is the hidden lordship and activity of the exalted Lord which will be made manifest at the parousia.

[451] Sin is borne by Christ on the cross, 1:2, 19; 2:24. This commits us to the setting aside of sin (2:1 f.) and the control of the new life by the example of Christ, to whom believers have turned, 2:25.

[452] As in R. 16:18 and Col. 3:24 κύριος and Χριστός are used together here without the name Jesus between them, although the text is uncertain, since ℵ and P have θεόν instead.

[453] Part of this sanctification is readiness to reply to anyone who asks for λόγον περὶ τῆς ἐν ὑμῖν ἐλπίδος, 3:15.

[454] Here again we see how strongly the saving event of the crucifixion, resurrection and exaltation stamps and shapes the existence of the believer. This seems to be characteristic of the Peter tradition, cf. Jn. 21:15-19 and 1 Pt. 1:8; 5:1-4 (→ VIII, 23, n. 75).

attained to sonship through Him, as their ἀρχηγός and πρόδρομος (2:10; 12:2; 6:20), [455] into the sanctuary. The term Χριστός is less prominent. We find Χριστός between 3:6 and 9:28 (cf. also 11:26) and 'Ιησοῦς Χριστός from 10:10 to 13:21, but there is no discernible distinction between the two forms. Χριστός is related to the high-priesthood of the ascended Lord (9:11), which is a royal priesthood after the order of Melchisedec, 5:10; 6:20; 7:1-10. Here, then, the link between Messiah-ship and high-priesthood, which is suggested in many other NT passages, although without actual use of Χριστός (→ n. 313), is finally made. [456]

Hb. 1:8 f. contains a quotation of ψ 44:7 f., which is taken by the author to be a saying of God to His Son: ἔχρισέν σε, ὁ θεός, ὁ θεός σου ἔλαιον ἀγαλλιάσεως. He is Χριστός by reason of what God does in relation to Him: ὁ Χριστὸς οὐχ ἑαυτὸν ἐδόξασεν γενηθῆναι ἀρχιερέα, ἀλλ' ὁ λαλήσας πρὸς αὐτόν..., 5:5. [457] Christ Himself is explained to be the High-priest → III, 278, 38 ff. His people, called οἶκος, is set under Him, Χριστὸς δὲ ὡς υἱὸς ἐπὶ τὸν οἶκον αὐτοῦ· οὖ οἶκός ἐσμεν ἡμεῖς, 3:6. He has won this people for Himself: Χριστὸς... διὰ... τοῦ ἰδίου αἵματος εἰσῆλθεν ἐφάπαξ εἰς τὰ ἅγια, αἰωνίαν λύτρωσιν εὑράμενος as a παραγενόμενος ἀρχιερεὺς τῶν γενομένων ἀγαθῶν, 9:11 f. ὁ Χριστός also occurs in this connection. In the case of τὸ αἷμα τοῦ Χριστοῦ in 9:14 the article is used in view of τὸ αἷμα. Those who confess: ὃς διὰ πνεύματος αἰωνίου ἑαυτὸν προσήνεγκεν ἄμωμον τῷ θεῷ, καθαριεῖ τὴν συνείδησιν ἡμῶν ἀπὸ νεκρῶν ἔργων, have become μέτοχοι τοῦ Χριστοῦ (3:14) on the condition that they hold fast the confidence to which they have thus attained (3:6, 14), this being a constant summons of the author to his readers. In 9:14-28 there is successive reference to the saving significance of Christ, to His passion, under the concept τὸ αἷμα τοῦ Χριστοῦ (9:14), [458] then to His exaltation οὐ γὰρ εἰς χειροποίητα εἰσῆλθεν ἅγια Χριστός... ἀλλ' εἰς αὐτὸν τὸν οὐρανόν, νῦν ἐμφανισθῆναι τῷ προσώπῳ τοῦ θεοῦ ὑπὲρ ἡμῶν (9:24), and finally to His *parousia* οὕτως καὶ ὁ Χριστός, ἅπαξ προσενεχθεὶς εἰς τὸ πολλῶν ἀνενεγκεῖν ἁμαρτίας, ἐκ δευτέρου χωρὶς ἁμαρτίας ὀφθήσεται τοῖς αὐτὸν ἀπεκδεχομένοις εἰς σωτηρίαν, 9:28. We thus have a development of the primitive Christian confession of Christ which seems to be referred to as ὁ τῆς ἀρχῆς τοῦ Χριστοῦ λόγος in 6:1. Christ as a term for the bringer of salvation has become a sobriquet which needs elucidation. This is accomplished by an exposition of salvation and by the use of terms which characterise the bringer of salvation as such in a way that Χριστός no longer does. It is worth noting, however, that Χριστός is still connected with the passion and exaltation of Jesus and also with the Church as the people of Christ. The fading of awareness of what Χριστός was meant to express is clear in Hb. in passages which speak of Jesus Christ. [459] The reference is

---

[455] Cf. on this and on the religious background of the idea E. Käsemann, "Das wandernde Gottesvolk," FRL, 55⁴ (1961); E. Grässer, "Der Glaube im Hb.," *Marburger Theol. Stud.,* 2 (1965).

[456] Cf. the discussion in Hahn, 231-341.

[457] This statement is followed by a song, cf. G. Friedrich, "Das Lied vom Hohenpriester im Zshg, v. Hb. 4:14 - 5:10," ThZ, 18 (1962), 95-115. Christ is High-Priest on the basis of His passion and in the state of His exaltation. Witness is borne to this by Ps. 2 and 110 Messianically interpreted and the reasons are given in the high-priestly song and its exposition.

[458] Cf. the symbolical expression τὸν ὀνειδισμὸν τοῦ Χριστοῦ in 11:26 and also 13:10-13, which relates to Jesus' humiliation even to the slave-death of the cross. The μισθαποδοσία of 11:26 relates the humiliation and exaltation.

[459] Cf. also the ref. to Jesus: ἐν τῷ αἵματι 'Ιησοῦ, 10:19, εἰς τὸν τῆς πίστεως ἀρχηγὸν καὶ τελειωτὴν 'Ιησοῦν, 12:2, with a ref. to the passion and exaltation διαθήκης νέας μεσίτῃ 'Ιησοῦ, 12:24, καὶ 'Ιησοῦς, ἵνα ἁγιάσῃ διὰ τοῦ ἰδίου αἵματος τὸν λαόν...

to the sanctifying sacrifice of Jesus Christ ἡγιασμένοι ... διὰ τῆς προσφορᾶς τοῦ σώματος 'Ιησοῦ Χριστοῦ ἐφάπαξ (10:10) and to His exaltation (10:13 f.). Hb uses the formula διὰ 'Ιησοῦ Χριστοῦ (13:21). The central Pauline formula ἐν Χριστῷ does not occur. The presentation of the Christ event is linked to earlier and contemporary Christianity by the basic affirmation which sets the readers in fellowship with their teachers who have now been perfected: "Jesus Christ, the same yesterday and today and to all aeons" (13:8). [460]

3. 'Ιησοῦς Χριστός in James, Jude and 2 Peter.

In James, Jude and 2 Pt. 'Ιησοῦς Χριστός is common and it is often combined with the title κύριος. Χριστός has now become in the full sense the second name of Jesus and its original sense of bringer of salvation is much weakened.

a. In Jm. 'Ιησοῦς Χριστός occurs twice. At 1:1 the writer calls himself θεοῦ καὶ κυρίου 'Ιησοῦ Χριστοῦ δοῦλος and at 2:1 there is ref. to the πίστις τοῦ κυρίου ἡμῶν 'Ιησοῦ Χριστοῦ τῆς δόξης, the τοῦ κυρίου being here an obj. gen. and τῆς δόξης a gen. qual.: "faith in our Lord Jesus Christ in his glory." In both instances one has to consider the possibility that 'Ιησοῦς Χριστός was added to an original. [461]

b. Jude calls himself 'Ιησοῦ Χριστοῦ δοῦλος and he sends greetings τοῖς ἐν θεῷ πατρὶ ἠγαπημένοις καὶ 'Ιησοῦ Χριστῷ τετηρημένοις κλητοῖς, v. 1. [462] He speaks of the ἀπόστολοι τοῦ κυρίου ἡμῶν 'Ιησοῦ Χριστοῦ in v. 17 and of those who by their conduct are τὸν μόνον δεσπότην καὶ κύριον ἡμῶν 'Ιησοῦν Χριστὸν ἀρνούμενοι (v. 4). He contrasts the community with them as προσδεχόμενοι τὸ ἔλεος τοῦ κυρίου ἡμῶν 'Ιησοῦ Χριστοῦ εἰς ζωὴν αἰώνιον, v. 21. He sings praise μόνῳ θεῷ σωτῆρι ἡμῶν διὰ 'Ιησοῦ Χριστοῦ τοῦ κυρίου ἡμῶν, v. 25. [463]

c. The author of 2 Pt. calls himself δοῦλος καὶ ἀπόστολος 'Ιησοῦ Χριστοῦ and he greets those who have obtained πίστιν ἐν δικαιοσύνῃ τοῦ θεοῦ ἡμῶν καὶ σωτῆρος 'Ιησοῦ Χριστοῦ, 1:1, [464] praying that they may be filled with grace and peace ἐν ἐπιγνώσει τοῦ θεοῦ καὶ 'Ιησοῦ Χριστοῦ τοῦ κυρίου ἡμῶν, 1:2, cf. Jn. 17:3. [465] The accent is on this ἐπίγνωσις 'Ιησοῦ Χριστοῦ, 1:8; 2:20; 3:18. It has as its content: ... ἐγνωρίσαμεν ὑμῖν τὴν τοῦ κυρίου ἡμῶν 'Ιησοῦ Χριστοῦ δύναμιν καὶ παρουσίαν, 1:16, but not that which is contained in the word Χριστός. Χριστός has become part of the proper name of the One through whom salvation has been accomplished; it does not characterise Him as the bringer of salvation. The author refers to the revelation that he has received: ὁ κύριος ἡμῶν 'Ιησοῦς Χριστὸς ἐδήλωσέν μοι, 1:14. His wish for the community is that ἡ εἴσοδος εἰς τὴν αἰώνιον βασιλείαν τοῦ κυρίου ἡμῶν καὶ σωτῆρος 'Ιησοῦ Χριστοῦ (1:11) may be granted to it.

ἔπαθεν, 13:12, ὁ ἀναγαγὼν ἐκ νεκρῶν τὸν ποιμένα τῶν προβάτων τὸν μέγαν ἐν αἵματι διαθήκης αἰωνίου, τὸν κύριον ἡμῶν 'Ιησοῦν, 13:20, though MSS Ψ D* 33 it vg^cl supply Χριστόν here.

[460] It is worth noting how strong is the ref. back to the "yesterday," i.e., to the pre-Easter Jeus, whose earthly history led Him through learning to the perfection which is necessary for His saving significance and which He attains through God's dwelling with Him, cf. 2:10 f., 14 f., 17; 5:4-10; 12:1 f.; 13:12 etc. The influence of the Jesus tradition which leads to the Gospels is unmistakable in Hb.

[461] Cf. on this Dib. Jk.¹¹, 37, 94, 158-161.

[462] syh and 1611 read only τοῖς ἐν θεῷ πατρὶ ἠγαπημένοις κλητοῖς.

[463] διὰ 'Ιησοῦ Χριστοῦ καὶ κυρίου ἡμῶν is not in 𝔄.

[464] It is not certain, but probable, that the σωτὴρ 'Ιησοῦς Χριστός, cf. also 1:11; 3:18, is also called ὁ θεὸς ἡμῶν here, as in Ign. and probably Tt. 2:13.

[465] ℵ A L and a series of other MSS have Χριστοῦ, but not B C 𝔄 p⁷² P Ψ and some vg cod read only ἐν ἐπιγνώσει τοῦ κυρίου ἡμῶν.

Although Χριστός is now for the most part used unemphatically as a proper
name, this is not a uniform development at the end of the primitive period and the
beginning of the age of the early Church. The Johannine writings and some early
fathers show that awareness of the questions posed by Χριστός is still very alive.

V. The Understanding of Christ in the Johannine Writings.

1. The Gospel.

a. The Gospel proclaims Jesus as the only Revealer of God. The man who believes
in Him as the One sent by God, [466] in whom God may be seen and heard (cf. esp. 12:44-
50), receives life in this faith in Jesus which is faith in God (12:44; 14:1). All the predicates
of the Revealer and the bringer of salvation in the Jewish and Hell. world are employed in
the service of this witness and so are all the metaphors which convey the thought of
salvation. [467] Among these is the OT and Jewish concept of the Messiah (1:41, 45, 49)
and also the Samaritan expectation of the Ta'eb Messiah (Jn. 4:25) [468] → I, 388, 22 ff.

b. In two verses we find the name Jesus Christ and their position in the Gospel
gives it special significance. [469] In the Prologue the incarnate Logos who has come
into the world is Jesus Christ, 1:17. [470] He is set over against Moses as the giver
of the Law (cf. also 5:45-47 and 9:28) and His gift is described as ἡ χάρις καὶ ἡ
ἀλήθεια, which have been enacted in Him. In the high-priestly prayer it is said of
life — openly and without a figure — that knowledge of the only true God and of
Jesus Christ whom He has sent is eternal life (17:3), for knowledge carries with it
dedication to what is known. Since the Evangelist is aware of the meaning of ὁ
Χριστός as a predicate of the bringer of salvation, the formulation "Jesus Christ,"
by the secondary name "Christ," characterises Jesus as the Revealer who is as such
the bringer of salvation.

c. The use of χριστός as a title or predicate of the Revealer makes it apparent
that the Evangelist is engaged in various debates. In the connecting of the Messiah
with the Son and in the "I am" sayings his relation to the Jewish and Christian tradition and his reinterpretation may be clearly seen.

One debate is with followers of the Baptist who see in John the Baptist the Messiah. [471] The first statement that the Baptist makes is a contesting of his own Mes-

---

[466] Cf. E. Haenchen, "'Der Vater der mich gesandt hat,'" NTSt, 7 (1962/63), 208-216.

[467] Cf. Bau. J. on 1:41.

[468] Merx rev. P. Kahle, ThLZ, 36 (1911), 198-200; G. Bornkamm, "Der Paraklet im Joh.,"
Gesch. u. Glaube, I (1968), 79 f.; Hahn, 362; J. MacDonald, The Theology of the Samaritans
(1964).

[469] On the well thought out structure cf. W. Grundmann, "Zeugnis und Gestalt des Joh.,"
Arbeiten z. Theol., 7 (1961).

[470] Bultmann J., 4, 378 thinks that 1:17 and 17:3 are glosses that the Evangelist added to
his source. This may be so, but it does not affect their significance in the total conception.
Acc. to Schille Hymnen, op. cit. (→ n. 410), 125, 1:17 is part of the original of the Prologue,
since it has "Jesus Christ" in very "non-Johannine fashion." But surely 17:3 and other ref.
in the Epistles do not permit us to say "non-Johannine fashion." We have here a common
Chr. expression which is used in the Johannine writings too; the specific use of Χριστός
in each writer decides whether Χριστός has a weaker or more significant sense when combined with Jesus.

[471] The debate with followers of John the Baptist controls the depiction of John in 1:6-8,
15, 19-37; 3:22-36; 5:31-36; 10:40-42. The idea that John, not Jesus, is the Messiah is attested
in Ps. Clem. Recg., I, 54, 8 f.; 60, 1-3 (GCS, 51). Cf. also Ephr. Expositio evangelii con-
cordantis App., 2, 1: et discipuli Iohannis de eo gloriantur, et maiorem esse eum quam Iesum
dicunt, ut et ipse, aiunt, testatus est: Non est in natis mulierum maior quam Iohannes (cf. L.
Leloir, Corp. Script. Christ. Or., 145 [1954]).

siahship (1:20, repeated in 3:28). [472] Andrew, who comes from this group, confesses to his own brother Simon concerning Jesus: εὑρήκαμεν τὸν Μεσσίαν ὅ ἐστιν μεθερμηνευόμενον χριστός, 1:41. The absolute form of this statement is noteworthy (→ 540, 16 ff.) and it is given greater precision in the witness of Philip to Nathanael: "We have found him, of whom Moses in the Law, and the prophets, did write," 1:45. For Jn. the Messiah is the one who was promised by Moses and the prophets and whom the disciples found in Jesus. Nathanael Himself characterises this Messiah in the words: "Master, thou art the Son of God, thou art the king (→ I, 577, 38 ff.) of Israel," 1:49. [473] Jesus Himself catches up this statement in His saying about the Son of Man in 1:51. [474] The Messiah is thus the kingly Messiah. He is the Son of God and Son of Man. He is the Messiah because He receives the Spirit of God, 1:33. To lead to faith in Him and to eternal life in this faith is the aim of the Gospel, which is written ἵνα πιστεύητε ὅτι Ἰησοῦς ἐστιν ὁ χριστὸς ὁ υἱὸς τοῦ θεοῦ, καὶ ἵνα πιστεύοντες ζωὴν ἔχητε ἐν τῷ ὀνόματι αὐτοῦ, 20:31. The term "Son" makes it plain what ὁ χριστός means. He is the One who acts in unity with the Father → VIII, 386, 32 ff. ὁ χριστός is not adequate alone. It needs exposition. Martha confesses faith in Jesus, Messiah and Son of God. When Jesus shows His mastery over death she replies: ἐγὼ πεπίστευκα ὅτι σὺ εἶ ὁ χριστὸς ὁ υἱὸς τοῦ θεοῦ ὁ εἰς τὸν κόσμον ἐρχόμενος, 11:27. In the addition ὁ εἰς τὸν κόσμον ἐρχόμενος we may perhaps detect again the combining of Messiah and Son of Man which is intimated in 1:49, 51 → VIII, 468, 25 ff., for the Son of Man is the One who comes into the world from God and who is endowed with fulness of life. Since confession of the Messiah and the granting of life are connected, the new understanding of the Messiah in John comes to light. The Messiah, as the Son, is the One who gives life, 5:21, 26.

Those who share Jewish Messianic expectation are not the only ones to see in Jesus the Messiah according to the accounts in Jn. The Samaritan woman does the same. She says to the inhabitants of Sychar: δεῦτε ἴδετε ἄνθρωπον ὃς εἶπέν μοι πάντα ἃ ἐποίησα· μήτι οὗτός ἐστιν ὁ χριστός; 4:29. She bases this judgment on her encounter with Jesus. He has made Himself known to her as the Messiah, 4:25 f. His teaching about the true worship of the Father led her to say that the Messiah would tell all things when He came. [475] Behind this statement stood Samaritan ex-

---

[472] In Jn. 1:20 f. John first denies that he is the royal Messiah and then he does not let himself be regarded as the Messianic high-priest or the Messianic prophet of Dt. 18:15. The Messianic prophet and the high-priestly and kingly Messiah are mentioned together here as in 1 QS 9:11 → 518, 25 ff.

[473] The combining of king (= Messiah) and Son of God does not occur again in Jn. until the passion story, which clarifies it. Cf. M. de Jonge, "The Use of the Word χριστός in the Johannine Epistles," Festschr. J. N. Sevenster, Nov. Test. Suppl., 24 (1970), 66-74.

[474] The combining of Messiah and Son of Man continues and develops a similar combination pioneered in the Apoc. of Enoch and adopted in the primitive Chr. tradition (→ 539, 26 ff.), cf. Sjöberg Menschensohn Äth. Hen. 140-146; Hahn, 157 f. In Jn. cf. 12:34 and 9:22, 35 as well as 1:51. Jn. 9 illustrates what we find in the dominical saying in Lk. 12:8. The man born blind confesses Jesus before his neighbours and the Pharisees, and the Son of Man confesses him when he is cast out, 9:35. Jesus and the Son of Man are thus equated.

[475] The Samaritan woman does not base her judgment (v. 29) on the teaching of Jesus which leads to His self-attestation as the Messiah, 4:25 f. This has given rise to the conjecture that v. 25 is an editorial interpolation by the Evangelist into his source. Cf. Bau. J., ad loc.: v. 25 f. is part of the material with which the Evangelist himself enriches the tradition of Jesus' work in Samaria. If this is correct, the purpose of the Evangelist is clear. The woman of Samaria has viewed Jesus as a Jew (4:9), as a magus comparable to the magi of Samaria (4:12, 15), and as a prophet (4:19). Jesus now reveals Himself as the Messiah (v. 25 f.), whereas, if this is an interpolation, it is she who comes to this insight in the original. Cf. the

pectation of the Ta'eb → n. 468; → VII, 89, 20 ff. [476] The Evangelist stresses the fact that the Messiah can be known only when He reveals Himself. This is why Jesus replies to her statements: ἐγώ εἰμι, ὁ λαλῶν σοι, 4:26. This is unique in Jn. We see here once again that the question of the Messiah is put to Jesus and that it is His history that gives the Messianic understanding the new form which is traced back to Him.

Jn. brings Jesus into the discussion of His Messiahship which is going on among the Jews. [477] Reflected here are the debates between Jews and Christians at the time when the Gospel was written. The Jews object to His birth at Nazareth and they champion the view that the origin of the Messiah will be a secret, 7:26 f., cf. 1:46; 6:41 f. [478] If the leaders can be brought to recognition ὅτι οὗτός ἐστιν ὁ χριστός (7:26), those who are under their spiritual direction (7:11-13, 45-51) and who dare not arrive at a clear decision about Jesus will get a new chance. In answer to the claim that the Messiah is concealed before His manifestation [479] Jesus appeals to His sending by the Father, whom the Jews do not know, 7:28 f. He is in fact the hidden Messiah (cf. 2:24) [480] since His true origin is concealed in His earthly descent. This true origin is the basis of His power and it characterises His Messiahship.

Jesus' descent not only does not conflict with the doctrine of the hidden origin of the Messiah; it is also in keeping with what is promised concerning His earthly origins. When some confess Him as the Messiah, the Jews object on scriptural grounds [481] to the fact that He comes from Galilee: μὴ γὰρ ἐκ τῆς Γαλιλαίας ὁ χριστὸς ἔρχεται; they are also not aware of His Davidic lineage and His birth at Bethlehem, 7:41 f., cf. also 1:45 f., 6:42. [482] Their dogmatic conviction is a hindrance to their recognition of Jesus. But this is a further indication that confession of Jesus gives a basically new shape to the concept of Messiahship. What brings about confession of the Messiahship of Jesus is the power and content of His sayings, 7:40, 46. Finally the cross becomes the main focus of objection to His Messiahship. When He speaks of His crucifixion as His exaltation (→ VIII, 610, 4 ff.) He is confronted with the argument: ἡμεῖς ἠκούσαμεν ἐκ τοῦ νόμου ὅτι ὁ χριστὸς μένει εἰς τὸν αἰῶνα, καὶ πῶς λέγεις σὺ ὅτι δεῖ ὑψωθῆναι τὸν υἱὸν τοῦ ἀνθρώπου (12:34) —

---

development in the story of the man born blind, Grundmann, op. cit. (→ n. 469), 53. Cf. also G. Friedrich, Wer ist Jesus? Die Verkündigung d. vierten Evangelisten, dargestellt an Joh. 4: 4-42 (1967).

[476] The Ta'eb, "he who returns," is expected as an eschatological prophet and teacher on the basis of Dt. 18:15, 18. As such he will be able to see right through men as is the experience of the Samaritan woman, cf. also 2:24 f.

[477] Cf. C. H. Dodd, The Interpretation of the Fourth Gospel (1953), 228-240.

[478] There is confirmation of this doctrine of the hidden Messiah in Trypho, Just. Dial., 8, 4; 110, 1 → 524, 4 ff.

[479] The doctrine of the hiddenness of the Messiah or Son of Man is apoc. in origin, as may be seen from 4 Esr. 13:52, cf. Str.-B., II, 488 f. Gnosticism adopted and developed it in relation of the Gnostic Redeemer, cf. W. Bousset, "Hauptprobleme d. Gnosis," FRL, 10 (1907), 238 f. This dogma undoubtedly influenced Jn. John the Baptist describes Jesus as "not known" in 1:26. He is not known even to the Baptist. What happens at baptism is what makes Jesus known to him, 1:31-34. After this he can proclaim Him as the one that should come, 1:29, 34, 36 and cf. 1:15, 27. He thus fulfils the role that is ascribed to Elijah in Just. → II, 934, 14 ff. The disciples of Jesus know who He is only by means of His revelation (6:66-69) and glorification (2:22; 7:39; 13:7 etc.).

[480] Cf. E. Stauffer, "Agnostos Christos: Jn. 2:24 und d. Eschatologie des vierten Ev.," Festschr. C. H. Dodd (1956), 281-299.

[481] Cf. sayings like 2 S. 7:12 f.; Mi. 5:1; Jer. 23:5; ψ 88:5 etc.

[482] It has been conjectured that we might have here a tradition which is unfamiliar with, or rejects, the view of the Messiah which underlies the infancy stories in Mt. and Lk.

a saying which for its part connects the Messiah and the Son of Man (→ VIII, 467, 13 ff.). According to John, Jesus replies by pointing to the limited duration of His earthly work, which must be exploited to the full (cf. 12:35 f. and also 9:4 f.; 11:9 f.). He also bears witness to the eternal work (→ IV, 575, 34 ff.) of the glorified Lord (12:31 f.; 14:12-14; 15:1-17; 17:24-26; 18:36-38). [483]

d. The fact that Jesus does not openly tell the Jews that He is the Messiah and that this causes constant debate about His Messiahship leads to the urgent demand: ἕως πότε τὴν ψυχὴν ἡμῶν αἴρεις; εἰ σὺ εἶ ὁ χριστός, εἰπὸν ἡμῖν παρρησίᾳ, 10:24. In the reply it is plain how the Evangelist forms and understands confession of the Messiahship of Jesus. The question shows that the Jews want a clear answer to the question whether Jesus is the promised one or not, and for them this hinges on the term Messiah. [484] He ought to make an open confession and no longer keep them in tension and suspense. [485] They want to know where they are with Him. Jesus refers to His Word, which only faith perceives and which is concealed from unbelief, 10:25. Being the Messiah means that Jesus leads His own, who receive life by listening to His Word in faith and who are united to Him as His community. His Messiahship is set forth under the metaphor of the Shepherd (→ VI, 494, 17 ff.) whose power [486] is superior to the destructive force of death and of the ruler of this world (12:31 f.), being grounded in His unity with God. This Messiahship is linked with His death and His exaltation (summed up in the word δοξάζω) and He expresses it in the "I am" sayings (→ II, 249, 24 ff.). As the Messiah Jesus is the Revealer of God who in revealing grants life, 17:3. It belongs to His Messiahship that He is God's Son (1:49; 11:27; 20:31) and the Jews take offence at this unique union with God, 5:18; 10:31-33; 19:7. [487] The precedence of divine sonship (→ VIII, 386, 32 ff.) over Messiahship makes it clear that Jesus is the Messiah because He is God's Son. Through Him there takes place what is commonly confessed, namely, access to the Father → n. 414; 562, 27 ff. [488] Confession of the Messiahship of Jesus is punished by the Jews with excommunication → VII, 852, 1 ff. [489]

---

[483] In Lk. 1:32 f. the OT promise of the eternal rule of the house of David is related to the eternal rule of the Messiah. The basis of this expectation is to be found in passages like 2 S. 7:12, 16; Is. 9:6; Ps. 110:4; Da. 7:14, 18 (the Son of Man); Ps. Sol. 17:4; Sib., 3, 49 f., 766; Eth. En. 49:1; 64:14 (the Son of Man).

[484] Cf. Schl. J. on 10:24: "No proclamation of the divine work and rule, however powerful, no statement about the sending of Jesus, however rich in content, could replace for the Jews what the formula "the anointed one" means for them. Only with this was the prophetic promise unequivocally brought to present fulfilment. The decision depended on this name. If Jesus pronounced it, He would be demanding from the Jews and all mankind the unlimited obedience with which all things would be put in His hands."

[485] Cf. Bau. J. on 10:24.

[486] Cf. on this Grundmann, op. cit. (→ n. 469), 54-57; on the comprehensive significance of the metaphor of the shepherd cf. I. Seibert, "Hirt-Herde-König," Deutsche Akad. d. Wissenschaften zu Berlin, Schriften d. Sektion für Altertumswissenschaft, 53 (1969).

[487] Here is the sharpest antithesis to Jewish Messianic expectation. "We all ... await ... in the Messiah a man of men whom Elijah will anoint after his coming. Even when he is manifested as Christ he must still be explained as a man of men," Just. Dial., 49, 1.

[488] Cf. also W. Grundmann, "Zur Rede Jesu vom Vater im Joh.-Ev.," ZNW, 52 (1961), 213-230.

[489] Excommunication is pronounced on the man born blind, Jn. 9:34, and this leads on to the discourse on the Good Shepherd (10:1-21) which establishes the autonomy of the community of Jesus over against the Jewish Synagogue and which again raises the question of the Messiah (10:22-39).

2. The Epistles.

a. Christ.

In the Johannine Epistles, too, the divine sonship of Jesus takes precedence of His Messiahship, → VIII, 387, 13 ff. When the name Ἰησοῦς Χριστός is used here it is usually connected with the predicate Son of God or referred to it, 1 Jn. 1:3; 3:23; 5:5 f., 20; 2 Jn. 3. Exceptions are 1 Jn. 2:1; 4:2; 2 Jn. 7. The last two of these are developed confessional formulae, and the same may well be true of the first, cf. R. 8:34. [490] As in the Gospel we also find the titular use of χριστός, 1 Jn. 2:22; 5:1; 2 Jn. 9. In the Epistles the close relation of the name and predication shows that awareness of Christ as a predicate of salvation is a factor in the name-combinations, particularly when we note that here alone in the NT there is an extension of usage in the terms ἀντίχριστος (→ 571, 11 ff.) and χρῖσμα (→ 572, 9 ff.).

Jesus is the Christ because He is the Son of God. This means that in the Epistles, too, a new exposition of the Messiah may be discerned. He is from the beginning, 1 Jn. 1:1, cf. Jn. 1:1. He is the Word of life, 1 Jn. 1:1 f.; 5:20. He has also appeared in history as a man, 1 Jn. 1:1-3. Through Him the witnesses who stand behind 1 Jn. have fellowship with the Father and with His Son Jesus Christ, and they pass this on to those who pay heed to their witness, 1 Jn. 1:3. This statement confirms the insight that through Christ there is access to the Father, which is life through the Word that the Son speaks, 1 Jn. 2:22 f.; 4:15; 5:9-12; 5:20; [491] 2 Jn. 9. Jesus Christ is an advocate with the Father for him who sins, 1 Jn. 2:1. What He wants of man, what His commandment is, 1 Jn. sums up as follows: καὶ αὕτη ἐστὶν ἡ ἐντολὴ αὐτοῦ, ἵνα πιστεύσωμεν τῷ ὀνόματι τοῦ υἱοῦ αὐτοῦ Ἰησοῦ Χριστοῦ καὶ ἀγαπῶμεν ἀλλήλους καθὼς ἔδωκεν ἐντολὴν ἡμῖν, 3:23, cf. Jn. 13:34 f.; 15:10-12, 17. Faith and love are the issue in the διδαχὴ τοῦ Χριστοῦ, 2 Jn. 9. Because Christ redeems man from subjection to sin, evil, the power of the devil and the world, and unites him with God, He Himself must be God, 1 Jn. 1:7 f.; [492] 2:1; 3:8; 4:9; 5:18-20. His Messianic work is God's own work and not that of a man. From God and from Jesus Christ come χάρις, ἔλεος, εἰρήνη ... ἐν ἀληθείᾳ καὶ ἀγάπῃ, 2 Jn. 3. The later doctrine of the work of salvation in the early Church, namely, that God became man in order that man might be participant in God, has its roots in the Johannine writings.

This helps us to understand the bitter fight against false teachers who deny the Messiahship of Jesus understood in terms of deity. 1 Jn. speaks of those who say ὅτι Ἰησοῦς οὐκ ἔστιν ὁ χριστός, 1 Jn. 2:22. They have left the community and broken away from it, 2:19. As in the Gospel this denial may be Jewish contesting of the Messiahship of Jesus → 568, 7 ff. It may imply Ebionite Christology which acknowledges Jesus as a prophet but not as the Messiah and Son of God. More probably, however, the opponents in 1 Jn. are docetic Gnostics who teach the tempo-

---

[490] In the Gospel this is developed in Jn. 17.

[491] 1 Jn. 5:20 raises the question how ἵνα γινώσκωμεν τὸν ἀληθινόν· καὶ ἐσμὲν ἐν τῷ ἀληθινῷ is to be understood, whether with ref. to the Father or to Jesus Christ, to whom it is related in what follows. The textual variations on ἐν τῷ υἱῷ αὐτοῦ Ἰησοῦ Χριστῷ and the adding of θεόν to τὸν ἀληθινόν (→ I, 249, 25 ff.) show that early exegetes were already exercised about this question. On the basis of Jn. 17:3 it is best to relate τὸν ἀληθινόν to the Father and to see in ἐν τῷ υἱῷ αὐτοῦ Ἰησοῦ Χριστῷ and the def. οὗτός ἐστιν ὁ ἀληθινὸς θεός the apposition which makes it clear what is the point in 1 Jn., namely, that in the Son we have the Father, and in the Son we know Him, cf. Jn. 1:18; 20:31.

[492] A 𝔐 vg syh have τὸ αἷμα Ἰησοῦ Χριστοῦ τοῦ υἱοῦ αὐτοῦ.

rary union of the heavenly being Christ with the man Jesus. [493] This is how 1 Jn. 5:6 is to be construed when it says of Jesus Christ: οὗτός ἐστιν ὁ ἐλθὼν δι᾽ ὕδατος καὶ αἵματος, ᾽Ιησοῦς Χριστός· οὐκ ἐν τῷ ὕδατι μόνον, ἀλλ᾽ ἐν τῷ ὕδατι καὶ ἐν τῷ αἵματι. [494] Jesus Christ, the Son of God (5:5), was the one Jesus Christ when He received baptism and He remained this when He passed through the death which cleanses from all sin. [495] The formulation οὗτός ἐστιν ὁ ἐλθὼν δι᾽ ὕδατος καὶ αἵματος, ᾽Ιησοῦς Χριστός (5:6) makes it clear that Jesus Christ is not just a double name. Christ is to be regarded as a sobriquet qualifying Jesus. Only thus does the expression have any special meaning in reply to false teaching → VIII, 329, 36 ff.

b. Antichrist.

Confession of the sonship of Jesus (1 Jn. 4:15; 5:5) and of His Messiahship and His coming in the flesh (2:22; 4:2; 5:1; 2 Jn. 7) is all of a piece. Those who confess the Messiahship of Jesus are said to be born of God (1 Jn. 4:2; 5:1) and their confession is attributed to the Spirit (4:2). But those who contest it are ἀντίχριστοι (2:22; 4:1-3; 2 Jn. 7). They are governed by the spirit τοῦ ἀντιχρίστου, ὃ λύει τὸν ᾽Ιησοῦν [496] (4:2 f.; → IV, 336, 16 ff.).

The term ἀντίχριστος occurs in the NT only in John's Epistles and is very rare in the first teachers of the early Church. [497] The author of 1 Jn. can speak of the awareness of the community that antichrist will come, 2:18; 4:3. [498] Antichrist is here a coming apocalyptic figure. This figure is connected with the opponent of God in Jewish apocalyptic, which for its part is found elsewhere in the history of religion. [499] The opponent of God increases his power and dominion on earth just before the apocalyptic end; he is then judged and destroyed. In primitive Christian apocalyptic, confession of Jesus as the Messiah gives antichrist the features of a counter-christ (cf. Rev. 13 etc.; 2 Th. 2:3-10; Mk. 13:14-27), though the term ἀντίχριστος is not used until we come to John's Epistles. [500] These give actuality to the apocalyptic

---

[493] Cf. on this Wnd. J. on 4:3; Bü. J., 65 f.; H. Braun, "Literar-Analyse u. theol. Schichtung im 1 J.," Gesammelte Stud. z. NT und seiner Umwelt (1962), 237-242. The question of sources in 1 Jn., which was raised by E. v. Dobschütz, "Joh. Studien, I," ZNW, 8 (1907), 1-8 and R. Bultmann, "Analyse d. 1 J.," Exegetica (1967), 105-123, and which is taken up again by Braun, seems to have no bearing on the question of Χριστός in 1 and 2 Jn. The statements in 1 Jn. form a unity. On the whole problem cf. Nauck, op. cit. (→ n. 406); K. Weiss, "Orthodoxie u. Heterodoxie im 1 J.," ZNW, 58 (1967), 247-255.

[494] This is confirmed by the teaching of Cerinthus, in whom F. Neugebauer, "Die Entstehung d. Joh.-Ev.," Arbeiten z. Theol., 36 (1968), 28-39 sees the adversary against whom the Johannine writings are aimed. On Cerinthus cf. Iren. Haer., I, 21 and cf. on this Schnckbg. J.⁴, 15-23.

[495] A sacramental understanding of this passage in terms of a ref. to baptism and the Lord's Supper does not commend itself, since the contested Christology of the opponents is obviously in view and there is no clear discussion of the sacraments. Cf. also Schnckbg. J. ⁴, 258 f. Acc. to de Jonge, op. cit. (→ n. 473) the central problem in 1 Jn. is the relation of the unity of Father and Son to the concrete humanity of Jesus which is essential for the connection between the Son of God and the children of God. On the basis of the exposition of χριστός in John's Gospel, χριστός and. υἱός are interchangeable in 1 Jn., cf. 5:1 and 5:5.

[496] So acc. to the earliest reading, cf. Bü. J. on 1 Jn. 4:3.

[497] It occurs only in Pol., 7, 1 quoting 1 Jn. 4:2 f. and 2 Jn. 7.

[498] Schnckbg. J.⁴, 145-9.

[499] Cf. Bü. J. on 1 Jn. 2:18; Str.-B., III, 637-640; W. Bousset, Der Antichrist (1895); Bousset-Gressm., 254-6; B. Rigaux, L'Antéchrist (1932).

[500] The formation of the term causes difficulty. It follows the pattern of words like "antigeneral," i.e., the enemy general. These are found from class. times and many more instances arose during the Roman civil wars. Caesar wrote two works Anticato. Cf. on this E. Risch, "Griech. Determinativkomposita," Idg. Forschung, 59 (1949), 249. ἀντίχριστος denotes the

figure by saying that it is already at work in false prophets who lead Christians astray by contesting their confession of Christ and thereby undermining their allegiance to the Father. The ἀντίχριστοι come from the community itself. They threaten it from within. Their coming shows that the last hour is dawning → VI, 246, 26 ff.: παιδία, ἐσχάτη ὥρα ἐστίν, καὶ καθὼς ἠκούσατε ὅτι ἀντίχριστος ἔρχεται, καὶ νῦν ἀντίχριστοι πολλοὶ γεγόνασιν· ὅθεν γινώσκομεν ὅτι ἐσχάτη ὥρα ἐστίν, 1 Jn. 2:18, cf. 4:3; 2 Jn. 7.

c. χρῖσμα.

When the community assaulted by antichrists it can resist only in the power of the Spirit, the χρῖσμα, 2:20, 27. The use of this term, which means "anointing oil," implies that the community is anointed with the Spirit, this being the basis of the fact that it belongs to Christ. χρῖσμα imparts to the community its comprehensive knowledge — οἴδατε πάντα (2:20) [501] — which confers on it the clarity of faith and judgment and the assurance in life and decision that come from its relationship to God. This statement about the χρῖσμα of the community is directly connected with what Christ says about the παράκλητος (→ V, 813, 1 ff.) in Jn. 16:8-10, 13 f. The community has received the χρῖσμα as a power which remains in it and gives it comprehensive and reliable instruction, 2:27. [502] A notable feature in the ecclesiastical situation in which the Johannine Epistles were written is that the author does not refer the community to an authoritative teaching office but reminds it of its reception of the χρῖσμα which is itself the teacher (→ II, 143, 19 ff.) and which makes the community independent of a teaching office: τὸ αὐτοῦ χρῖσμα διδάσκει ὑμᾶς περὶ πάντων, 2:27. [503] This shows how strongly in John the understanding of the Messiah is determined by the anointing of the Spirit and how the relation between the Son and sons, which is based on reception of the Spirit, finds an echo in the connection between the anointed One and the anointed.

3. Revelation.

a. ἀποκάλυψις Ἰησοῦ Χριστοῦ, ἣν ἔδωκεν αὐτῷ ὁ θεός (1:1) is what John (1:4, 9) calls his work and he calls Jesus Christ the One who is commissioned by God, who reveals through Him ἃ δεῖ γενέσθαι ἐν τάχει, 1:1. To the author this revelation is made known διὰ τοῦ ἀγγέλου αὐτοῦ so that ἐμαρτύρησεν τὸν λόγον τοῦ θεοῦ καὶ τὴν μαρτυρίαν Ἰησοῦ Χριστοῦ, ὅσα εἶδεν, 1:2 → IV, 500, 32 ff. In the salutation to the churches this Ἰησοῦς Χριστός is presented as ὁ μάρτυς ὁ πιστός (→ IV, 495, 32 ff.), as ὁ πρωτότοκος τῶν νεκρῶν (→ VI, 878, 9 ff.; VIII, 369, n. 248) καὶ ὁ ἄρχων τῶν βασιλέων τῆς γῆς, 1:5. He is this through His work. The

opposing apoc. being and can also be the man who is against Christ Jesus. Both senses are suggested in 1 Jn. 2:18, 22 [Risch].

[501] We accept the reading οἴδατε πάντα A C 𝕬 lat syh and not πάντες B ℵ, since the latter is a softening of the all-embracing πάντα.

[502] The grammatical structure of this difficult statement is probably as follows: "And you! The chrism which you have received from him remains in you and you have no need that any should teach you. But as his chrism teaches you about all things, it is reliable and without any lie, and, as it has taught you, abide in it." Cf. Jn. 14:17: τὸ πνεῦμα τῆς ἀληθείας, ὃ ὁ κόσμος οὐ δύναται λαβεῖν, and 14:26: ἐκεῖνος ὑμᾶς διδάξει πάντα καὶ ὑπομνήσει ὑμᾶς πάντα ἃ εἶπον ὑμῖν ἐγώ. C. H. Dodd, The Johannine Epistles, MNTC (1946), 63 describes χρῖσμα as "knowledge . . . against the poison of false teaching." Cf. Schnckbg. J.⁴ on 1 Jn. 2:20.

[503] The question whether αὐτοῦ relates to the Father or the Son does not allow of any clear-cut answer. As in Jn. 14:16, 26; 15:26 it may relate to either. The ambivalence reflects the unity of the Father and the Son, though cf. Schnckbg. J.⁴, 161.

basis of this is His love for us which is demonstrated in His redeeming self-sacrifice and which makes His community a priestly kingdom, 1:5 f. [504] This means that Jesus Christ is the bringer of salvation; in this regard His death and resurrection are the decisive salvation event. Thus Revelation belongs to the structure of apostolic witness. A distinctive point is that in it Ἰησοῦς Χριστός occurs only in these three verses in the introduction. Since we find four other passages in which ὁ χριστός is used in an obviously titular sense, Ἰησοῦς Χριστός denotes awareness that Jesus is the bringer of salvation. [505]

b. The four passages in which ὁ χριστός has a titular sense may be found in two sections in the structure of Revelation. The first two references are in 11:15 and 12:10 in connection with the assuming of dominion by Christ at God's side. [506] In the song of the heavenly choirs which introduces this we read in 11:15: ἐγένετο ἡ βασιλεία τοῦ κόσμου τοῦ κυρίου ἡμῶν καὶ τοῦ χριστοῦ αὐτοῦ, καὶ βασιλεύσει εἰς τοὺς αἰῶνας τῶν αἰώνων. 12:10 comes at the conclusion: ἄρτι ἐγένετο... ἡ βασιλεία τοῦ θεοῦ ἡμῶν καὶ ἡ ἐξουσία τοῦ χριστοῦ αὐτοῦ. The result of the event is the banishing of Satan, 12:9 f. The place of the κατήγωρ τῶν ἀδελφῶν ἡμῶν (12:10 → III, 636, 4 ff.) is taken by Christ, who intercedes for them, cf. R. 8:34 and Jn. 12:31 f. An essential part of the primitive Christian confession is thus presented. [507] The other references are in 20:4, 6 in connection with the co-dominion of overcomers in the millennium → 470, 15 ff. [508] This is described as a royal priest-hood (cf. 1:6) corresponding to the rule of the χριστός, which is a priestly kingdom in 1:12-20. [509] Revelation in its use of the term Christ resolutely clings to the fact that Christ is Ruler. He is the Lord who protects and cares for His community and He is the Lord who governs every dominion on earth, 1:5; 19:16. [510] According to Revelation this dominion of His was won by His death and conferred by God. It is a priestly dominion which is now concealed and will be manifested only in the millennium. [511] This will be followed by the coming aeon when God is all in all and His own lordship is displayed, 21:1-7, 22 f.; 22:1-5, cf. 1 C. 15:23-28.

E. The Christ-Statements in the Writings of the Early Church outside the New Testament.

In early Christian writings outside the NT two strands may be clearly seen. First, Christ is part of the name of Jesus as in James, Jude and 2 Peter → 562, 16 ff.

---

[504] Cf. T. Holtz, "Die Christologie d. Apok. d. Joh.," TU, 85² (1971); these basic ref. are discussed here, 55-70.

[505] Ibid., 22-26 on Ἰησοῦς, 5-9 on χριστός.

[506] Ibid., 95-109.

[507] These ideas are taken up in various other passages → n. 333. They are based on Job 1:2.

[508] On the millennium cf. Holtz, op. cit., 181-3 with bibl. Cf. also E. Lohse, Offenbarung d. Joh., NT Deutsch, 11¹⁰ (1971), 104 f.; Wilcke, op. cit. (→ n. 336), 13-49.

[509] The correspondence between the priestly kingdom of the overcomers (12:11) and that of the Overcomer (5:5), like the correspondence between 1:5; 3:14 and 2:13: Ἀντιπᾶς ὁ μάρτυς μου ὁ πιστός, shows that in Rev. too Christ fashions His people in His own image.

[510] From these two angles Holtz, op. cit. finely develops the Christology of Rev. under the heads: "Christ as the Exalted Lord, I: Lord of the Community" (c. 6) and "Christ as the Exalted Lord, II: Lord of the Cosmos" (c. 7).

[511] The divine's picture of Christ is influenced by the Christian interpretation of the Messiah but the pre-Christian, older Jewish tradition comes to expression in his depiction of the millennium and in the preceding section 19:11-21. Cf. also the idea of the co-rule of God's people, though with the modification that there are no contrasted subjects.

Secondly there is continuing awareness of the saving significance of the term Christ as in the Johannine writings → 566, 5 ff. Justin's Dialogue with Trypho (→ 523, 24 ff.) gives evidence of this when there has to be debate with Judaism.

1. Ignatius of Antioch. [512]

a. Christ and Jesus Christ.

With few exceptions Ign. uses the full form of the name Ἰησοῦς Χριστός. Eph., 14, 2 ref. to οἱ ἐπαγγελλόμενοι Χριστοῦ εἶναι who may be known by their deeds. This expression shows awareness of the special nature of the term Christ. In R., 4, 1 Ign. expresses the wish that in his martyrdom he may be found pure bread τοῦ Χριστοῦ, and in 4, 2 he demands: λιτανεύσατε τὸν Χριστὸν ὑπὲρ ἐμοῦ. Sm., 1, 1 has ἐν τῷ αἵματι Χριστοῦ, cf. 6, 1. These are cultic passages influenced by the Lord's Supper, cf. 1 C. 10:16. Ἰησοῦς Χριστός occurs in the nominative, Eph., 4, 1; 20, 1; Phld., 3, 1; Sm., 9, 2; 10, 2, and in the dependent case, Eph., 2, 2; 5, 1; 9, 1 f.; Tr., 12, 2 etc., κύριος Ἰησοῦς Χριστός, Phld. prooem.; 1, 1; 11, 2; Sm., 1, 1; Pol. prooem. ὁ κύριος ἡμῶν Ἰησοῦς Χριστός is found only at Eph., 7, 2; Phld., 4, 1; 9, 2 and is thus much rarer than in Paul. Ἰησοῦς Χριστός is combined with υἱός in R. prooem. (twice) and with ἠγαπημένος in Sm. prooem. πατὴρ Ἰησοῦ Χριστοῦ for God occurs in Eph., 2, 1; Mg., 3, 1; Tr. prooem. διὰ Ἰησοῦ Χριστοῦ may be found in Eph., 4, 2; Mg., 5, 2.

In distinction from other works outside the NT Ign. often has the ἐν formula, ἐν Χριστῷ Ἰησοῦ as in Paul (→ 551, 28 ff.) at Tr., 1, 1; Eph., 1, 1; 11, 1; 12, 2; Mg. prooem.; R., 1, 1; 2, 2; [513] Phld., 10, 1; 11, 2, but more frequently ἐν Ἰησοῦ Χριστῷ, Eph. prooem.; 3, 1; 8, 2; 10, 3; 20, 2 (twice); Mg. prooem.; 6, 2; Tr., 13, 2 f.; Phld., 10, 2. We also find expressions like ἐν δυνάμει Ἰησοῦ Χριστοῦ, Eph., 11, 2, ἐν πίστει Ἰησοῦ Χριστοῦ, Mg., 1, 1, ἐν τιμῇ Ἰησοῦ Χριστοῦ, Mg., 15, 1, ἐν ὑπομονῇ Ἰησοῦ Χριστοῦ, R., 10, 3, ἐν γνώμῃ Ἰησοῦ Χριστοῦ Phld. prooem., ἐν τῇ χάριτι τοῦ Ἰησοῦ Χριστοῦ, Phld., 11, 1, ἐν ἑνότητι Ἰησοῦ Χριστοῦ, Phld., 5, 2, ἐν ὀνόματι Ἰησοῦ Χριστοῦ, Sm., 4, 2; 12, 2; Pol., 5, 1, ἐν ἀγάπῃ θεοῦ πατρὸς καὶ κυρίου Ἰησοῦ Χριστοῦ, Phld., 1, 1, and ἐν θεῷ ἡμῶν Ἰησοῦ Χριστῷ, Pol., 8, 3. This shows that the ἐν formula needs interpretation. It is related to what believers acquire from Jesus Christ.

One may still see plainly in Ign. the link between Jesus Christ and the mystery of the cross and resurrection which is understood as the salvation event. Statements about Christ's love are also made in Ign. We read of the ἀγάπη Ἰησοῦ Χριστοῦ in Tr., 6, 1; R. prooem. There is ref. to His cross, blood and death in Eph., 9, 1; [514] 16, 2; Tr., 2, 1; Sm., 1, 1; 6, 1; Phld. prooem., and to His passion and resurrection in R., 6, 1; Phld., 8, 2; 9, 2; Sm., 7, 1; 12, 2; Tr. prooem.

The co-ordination of God and Jesus Christ and the transferring of the term God to Christ push into the background the idea of Christ as the divine proxy, which is implicit in the word "Christ." Jesus Christ is ὁ θεὸς ἡμῶν and He is co-ordinated with God as such, Eph. prooem. Eph., 1, 1 says of the Ephesians who have won a good name for themselves κατὰ πίστιν καὶ ἀγάπην ἐν Χριστῷ Ἰησοῦ, [515] ... μιμηταὶ ὄντες θεοῦ, ἀναζωπυρήσαντες ἐν αἵματι θεοῦ. The name God is also used for Jesus Christ in Eph., 18, 2; Tr., 7,

---

[512] On the fundamental question of the relation of Ign. to the earlier community cf. R. Bultmann, "Ign. u. Pls.," *Exegetica* (1967), 400-411; C. Maurer, *Ign. v. Antiochien u. d. Joh.-Ev.* (1949); T. Preiss, "La mystique de l'imitation du Christ et de l'unité chez Ignace d'Antioche," RevHPhR, 18 (1938), 197-241; H. Schlier, "Religionsgeschichtliche Untersuchungen zu den Ignatiusbriefen," ZNW Beih., 8 (1929); H. Rathke, "Ign. v. Antiochien u. die Paulusbriefe," TU, 99 (1967).

[513] Some MSS read ἐν Ἰησοῦ Χριστῷ here.

[514] Determinative here is the singular image of the spiritual building of God's house in which the cross is the crane and the Holy Spirit is the rope with which believers are lifted up like stones. In deviation from the use in Paul, 19, 1 speaks of the θάνατος τοῦ κυρίου.

[515] πίστις and ἀγάπη are the life-style of those who belong to Jesus Christ; they are linked to Him, so Eph., 9, 1 (→ n. 514), expounded in 9, 2. Cf. also 14, 1; Mg., 1, 2; 5, 2.

1; R. prooem.; 6, 3; Sm., 1, 1; 10, 1; Pol., 8, 3; God and Jesus Christ are co-ordinated, Tr., 1, 1; Phld., 3, 2. The significance of Jesus Christ is also brought out by the use of ὁ σωτὴρ ἡμῶν in Mg. prooem.; Phld., 9, 2, and ἡ ἐλπὶς ἡμῶν in Mg., 11, 1; Tr. prooem.; 2, 2. Jesus Christ is τὸ διὰ παντὸς ἡμῶν ζῆν, Mg., 1, 2, τὸ ἀληθινὸν ἡμῶν ζῆν, Sm., 4, 1, τὸ ἀδιάκριτον ἡμῶν ζῆν, τοῦ πατρὸς ἡ γνώμη, Eph., 3, 2. With the formula ὅς or ὅ ἐστιν Ἰησοῦς Χριστός we also find gen. concepts in relation to Jesus Christ, θεοῦ γνῶσις in Eph., 17, 2, ἡ χαρὰ ἡ ἄμωμος in Mg., 7, 1, νέα ζύμη in Mg., 10, 2, ἀδιά-κριτον πνεῦμα in Mg., 15, ἡ τελεία ἐλπίς in Sm., 10, 2. [516] From these passages it is plain that for Ign. himself and for the churches to which he writes Χριστός has largely lost its true sense and is no longer enough to express the Christian interpretation of the primitive Church. New ways have to be found to say who Jesus Christ is.

b. Confessional Formulae and New Confessional Statements.

Ign. adopts several confessional formulae and either develops them or forms similar confessional statements which unfold the significance of the name of Jesus Christ. An adopted formula of this kind occurs in Eph., 7, 2; εἷς ἰατρός ἐστιν, σαρκικός τε καὶ πνευματικός, γεννητὸς καὶ ἀγέννητος, ἐν σαρκὶ γενόμενος θεός, ἐν θανάτῳ ζωὴ ἀληθινή, καὶ ἐκ Μαρίας καὶ ἐκ θεοῦ, πρῶτον παθητὸς καὶ τότε ἀπαθής, Ἰησοῦς Χριστὸς ὁ κύριος ἡμῶν. [517] The core of this is the passion and resurrection. The incarnation is mentioned in an anti-docetic sense. There is also confession of the deity of Jesus Christ. Another formulation, obviously taken from a baptismal confession, may be found in Eph., 18, 2; this begins with Ἰησοῦς ὁ Χριστός, which does not occur elsewhere in Ign. [518] Jesus Christ πρὸ αἰώνων παρὰ πατρὶ ἦν καὶ ἐν τέλει ἐφάνη in Mg., 6, 1 also seems to be a statement that Ign. has adopted. An anti-docetic confession, similar in the first half to 1 Pt. 3:18, 22, lies behind the exposition given by Ign. in Tr., 9, 1 f. Sm., 1, 1 f. also contains an expounded and developed confession. [519] Mg., 8, 2 seems to be modelled on a εἷς θεός statement like that in 1 Tm. 2:5 f.: ὁ φανερώσας ἑαυτὸν διὰ Ἰησοῦ Χριστοῦ τοῦ υἱοῦ αὐτοῦ, ὅς ἐστιν αὐτοῦ λόγος ἀπὸ σιγῆς προελθών. R., 8, 2 is similar: Ἰησοῦς δὲ Χριστός . . . τὸ ἀψευδὲς στόμα, ἐν ᾧ ὁ πατὴρ ἀληθῶς ἐλάλησεν. Both statements follow the linking of λόγος and Ἰησοῦς Χριστός in Jn. 1:1 ff. and they offer a fresh formulation of the meaning of Christ.

c. Christ and the Church.

The close connection between Christ and His people, which Paul expresses in the term τὸ σῶμα τοῦ Χριστοῦ (→ VII, 1068, 19 ff.), is strongly emphasised in Ign. The Church, however, is now an institutional body which is episcopally rather than charismatically [520] constituted and which is represented by its office-bearers. Christ's presence is linked with it ὅπου ἂν ᾖ Ἰησοῦς Χριστός, ἐκεῖ ἡ καθολικὴ ἐκκλησία, Sm., 8, 2. [521] There is a par. between its relation to Christ and His to the Father, ὡς ἡ ἐκκλησία Ἰησοῦ Χριστῷ

---

[516] 1 C. 1:30 and these Ign. ref. confirm the fact that the "I am" sayings in Jn. are to be understood as Christ sayings.

[517] Whereas Ign. calls Jesus Christ the life and has the infin., we find ζωή here, which suggests an adopted formula. On Ign. Eph., 7, 2 cf. Schille Hymnen, op. cit. (→ n. 410), 39. A. Grillmeier, "Die theol. u. sprachliche Vorbereitung d. christologischen Formel v. Chalcedon," Das Konzil v. Chalcedon, I, ed. A. Grillmeier-H. Bracht (1951), 30 discusses the problems of the reading ἐν σαρκὶ γενόμενος θεός.

[518] ὁ θεὸς ἡμῶν is probably from the pen of Ign.; on Ign. Eph., 18, 2 cf. Schille Hymnen, 119. Eph., 20, 2 contains part of a confessional formula.

[519] Cf. Schille Hymnen, 39 f.

[520] Cf. on this E. Käsemann, "Amt u. Gemeinde im NT," Exeget. Versuche u. Besin-nungen, I⁵ (1965), 109-134; also "Pls. u. der Frühkatholizismus," ibid., II³ (1968), 239-252.

[521] So acc. to Bihlmeyer-Schneemelcher. F. X. Funk, Die Apost. Väter., Sammlung aus-gewählter kirchen- u. dogmengesch. Quellenschr., II, 1² (1906) and T. Zahn, Patr. Apostolic. Opera, II (1876), have here Χριστὸς Ἰησοῦς, which is rarer in Ign., but which perhaps brings out more strongly the connection between Christ and His people.

καὶ ὡς Ἰησοῦς Χριστὸς τῷ πατρί, Eph., 5, 1. This is variously expressed, e.g., Tr., 3, 1; Mg., 13, 2, where, as in Eph., 20, 2; Mg., 2; Tr., 2, 1; Sm., 8, 1, obedience to the ministers is regarded as necessary to salvation. Ign. warns the Trallians not to be puffed up nor to let themselves be separated from θεοῦ Ἰησοῦ Χριστοῦ καὶ τοῦ ἐπισκόπου καὶ τῶν διαταγμάτων τῶν ἀποστόλων, 7, 1. Jesus Christ, the bishop's office and the apostolic witness are inter-related and seen as par.

d. Χριστιανός and Χριστιανισμός.

Χριστιανός is common in Ign. for a member of the community. He wants the Eph. to pray ἵνα ἐν κλήρῳ Ἐφεσίων εὑρεθῶ τῶν Χριστιανῶν, οἳ καὶ τοῖς ἀποστόλοις πάντοτε συνήνεσαν ἐν δυνάμει Ἰησοῦ Χριστοῦ, Eph., 11, 2. If agreement with the apostles is decisive, Χριστιανός must not be just a name; it must express a being, μὴ μόνον καλεῖσθαι Χριστιανούς, ἀλλὰ καὶ εἶναι, Mg., 4, cf. also R., 3, 2, where Ign. applies this to himself. The decisive thing for a Christian is: Χριστιανὸς ἑαυτοῦ ἐξουσίαν οὐκ ἔχει, ἀλλὰ θεῷ σχολάζει, Pol., 7, 3, cf. Paul in R. 14:7-9. Ign. uses Χριστιανός as an adj.: μόνῃ τῇ χριστιανῇ τροφῇ χρῆσθε, Tr., 6, 1.

In Ign. we also find the noun Χριστιανισμός, being a Christian as expressed in life-style and in opp. to Ἰουδαϊσμός, → III, 383, 15 ff. Ign. describes it as ἄτοπόν ἐστιν Ἰησοῦν Χριστὸν λαλεῖν καὶ ἰουδαΐζειν, cf. Gl. 2:11-14 and he offers the reason: ὁ γὰρ Χριστιανισμὸς οὐκ εἰς Ἰουδαϊσμὸν ἐπίστευσεν, ἀλλὰ Ἰουδαϊσμὸς εἰς Χριστιανισ-μόν, Mg., 10, 3, cf. also Phld., 6, 1.[522] In Mg., 10, 1 it is being a disciple in Jesus: μαθηταὶ αὐτοῦ γενόμενοι, μάθωμεν κατὰ Χριστιανισμὸν ζῆν. ὃς γὰρ ἄλλῳ ὀνόματι καλεῖται πλέον τούτου, οὐκ ἔστιν τοῦ θεοῦ.[523] This def. makes it plain that Χρισ-τιανισμός simply means discipleship. Acc. to Ac. 11:26 the original οἱ μαθηταί came to be called Χριστιανοί in Antioch → 536, 35 ff. Ign. shows that the two are related and as bishop of Antioch he confirms the observation in Ac. 11:26 that the rise of the term Χριστιανός, now extended to Χριστιανισμός, is of particular importance in Antioch.

We also find in Ign. other terms like χριστοφόρος (Eph., 9, 2) in the series σύνο-δοι..., θεοφόροι καὶ ναοφόροι, χριστοφόροι, ἁγιοφόροι, κατὰ πάντα κεκο-σμημένοι ἐν ταῖς ἐντολαῖς Ἰησοῦ Χριστοῦ.[524] A similar word is χριστόνομος in R. prooem. One may also compare χριστομαθία in Phld., 8, 2; Ign. is warning the church μηδὲν κατ' ἐρίθειαν πράσσειν, ἀλλὰ κατὰ χριστομαθίαν, i.e., as they have learned as disciples of Christ.

2. Polycarp and the Martyrdom of Polycarp.

a. In the introduction and at the end of his letter Polycarp uses the full form ὁ κύριος ἡμῶν Ἰησοῦς Χριστός along with formulations which confess the cross and resurrection of Jesus as the salvation event, 1, 1 f.; 2, 1; 12, 2, cf. 14.[525] In the prooem., the name Ἰησοῦς Χριστός is found alongside ὁ σωτὴρ ἡμῶν and it is co-ordinated with the name of God. διὰ Ἰησοῦ Χριστοῦ as the author of salvation θελήματι θεοῦ occurs in 1, 3, and in a way familiar to us from Ign. (→ 575, 5 ff.) it is said of ἡ ἐλπὶς ἡμῶν καὶ

---

[522] This is God's purpose: εἰς ὃν (sc. Χριστιανισμόν) πᾶσα γλῶσσα πιστεύσασα εἰς θεὸν συνήχθη, Mg., 10, 3.

[523] Cf. Mg., 9, 1: ἵνα εὑρεθῶμεν μαθηταὶ Ἰησοῦ Χριστοῦ τοῦ μόνου διδασκάλου ἡμῶν. The prophets are disciples in 9, 2. The idea of discipleship is taken up in 10, 1 and leads to the conclusion: ... μάθωμεν κατὰ Χριστιανισμὸν ζῆν.

[524] Ign. says of himself in R. prooem: ὁ καὶ Θεοφόρος. His wish in R., 4, 1 is ἵνα καθαρὸς ἄρτος εὑρεθῶ τοῦ Χριστοῦ. In 4, 2 he wants to be μαθητὴς ἀληθῶς Ἰησοῦ Χριστοῦ and hopes that ἀπελεύθερος γενήσομαι Ἰησοῦ Χριστοῦ καὶ ἀναστήσομαι ἐν αὐτῷ ἐλεύθερος, 4, 3. He desires ἵνα Ἰησοῦ Χριστοῦ ἐπιτύχω, R., 5, 3 (twice). Thus χριστοφόρος, formed after the analogy of θεοφόρος, expresses his personal attachment to Christ.

[525] ὁ κύριος ἡμῶν occurs in 6, 3; 13, 2 and ὁ κύριος for the historical and exalted Jesus in 2, 3; 4, 1; 5, 2; 6, 2; 7, 1 f.; 9, 2.

ὁ ἀρραβὼν τῆς δικαιοσύνης ἡμῶν, ὅς ἐστι Χριστὸς Ἰησοῦς, 8, 1. Χριστός occurs in 3, 3: ἀγάπη... εἰς θεὸν καὶ Χριστὸν καὶ εἰς τὸν πλησίον. Similarly θεὸς καὶ Χριστός are co-ordinated ὡς θεοῦ καὶ Χριστοῦ διάκονοι, 5, 2. ὑποτασσομένους τοῖς πρεσβυτέροις καὶ διακόνοις ὡς θεῷ καὶ Χριστῷ, 5, 3. 526

b. As in the epistle, so in the introduction and at the end of the Mart. Pol. we find the full form ὁ κύριος ἡμῶν Ἰησοῦς Χριστός, prooem.; 19, 2; 527 21; 22, 3. Χριστός without art. is used in 6, 2: Polycarp Χριστοῦ κοινωνὸς γενόμενος, and 19, 1: κατὰ τὸ εὐαγγέλιον Χριστοῦ. ὁ Χριστός occurs in 2, 2 f.; 14, 2; 17, 2. 528 It is plain from 9, 3 that the term Χριστός is linked to awareness of the Messiahship of Jesus. One may see this in the explanation contained in the reply of Polycarp to the demand λοιδόρησον τὸν Χριστόν: πῶς δύναμαι βλασφημῆσαι τὸν βασιλέα μου τὸν σώσαντά με; Christ is the bringer of salvation. Polycarp knows the significance of Χριστός but he has to explain it to the pagans, since they cannot understand it. Ἰησοῦς Χριστός occurs in 14, 1 and 3; 529 20, 2; 22, 1.

c. Polycarp calls himself Χριστιανός in 10, 1; 12, 1. He is called by his enemies ὁ τῆς Ἀσίας διδάσκαλος, ὁ πατὴρ τῶν Χριστιανῶν, 12, 2, and he himself confesses: εἰ δὲ θέλεις τὸν τοῦ Χριστιανισμοῦ μαθεῖν λόγον, δὸς ἡμέραν καὶ ἄκουσον, 10, 1. The author of Mart. Pol. speaks of the γενναιότης τοῦ θεοφιλοῦς καὶ θεοσεβοῦς γένους τῶν Χριστιανῶν, 3, 2.

3. The Didache.

The name Ἰησοῦς Χριστός occurs only once in Did. in the formula διὰ Ἰησοῦ Χριστοῦ, 9, 4. Χριστιανός occurs once at 12, 4. 530 The consistent term for Jesus Christ is κύριος, 6, 2; 9, 5 etc.

4. Barnabas.

In Barn. one finds ὁ καινὸς νόμος τοῦ κυρίου ἡμῶν Ἰησοῦ Χριστοῦ, 2, 6. The statement ὁ Χριστὸς υἱός ἐστιν Δαυίδ occurs in 12, 10 on the basis of Ps. 110:1, but He is then described as Son of God and Lord with a ref. to Is. 45:1. In both cases ὁ Χριστός is understood as Messiah. 14, 9 quotes Is. 61:1: οὗ εἵνεκεν ἔχρισέν με. It is the more surprising, then, that in Barn. we do not find Χριστός with Jesus except at 2, 6, although we do not find κύριος, 531 υἱὸς τοῦ θεοῦ, 532 and the name Ἰησοῦς. 533 All three designations are connected with the salvation event of the cross and resurrection, 5, 9 and 11; 7, 2; 12, 5; 14, 5; 15, 9, where we usually have the simple Χριστός.

---

526 Cf. also the quotations from 2 C. 5:10 in 6, 2 and 1 Jn. 4:2 f. in 7, 1.

527 Note the threefold characterisation: τὸν σωτῆρα τῶν ψυχῶν ἡμῶν καὶ κυβερνήτην τῶν σωμάτων ἡμῶν καὶ ποιμένα τῆς κατὰ τὴν οἰκουμένην καθολικῆς ἐκκλησίας, Mart. Pol., 19, 2.

528 Note the significant formulation: ἀγνοοῦντες, ὅτι οὔτε τὸν Χριστόν ποτε καταλιπεῖν δυνησόμεθα, τὸν ὑπὲρ τῆς τοῦ παντὸς κόσμου τῶν σωζομένων σωτηρίας παθόντα ἄμωμον ὑπὲρ ἁμαρτωλῶν, οὔτε ἕτερόν τινα σέβεσθαι. τοῦτον μὲν γὰρ υἱὸν ὄντα τοῦ θεοῦ προσκυνοῦμεν, Mart. Pol., 17, 2 f.

529 In Polycarp's prayer God is addressed as ὁ τοῦ ἀγαπητοῦ καὶ εὐλογητοῦ παιδός σου Ἰησοῦ Χριστοῦ πατήρ, δι' οὗ τὴν περὶ σοῦ ἐπίγνωσιν εἰλήφαμεν, Mart. Pol., 14, 1. Christ is called διὰ τοῦ αἰωνίου καὶ ἐπουρανίου ἀρχιερέως Ἰησοῦ Χριστοῦ, ἀγαπητοῦ σου παιδός, Mart. Pol., 14, 3. On παῖς in prayers cf. Ac. 4:27; Did., 9, 2 f.; 10, 2; Mart. Pol., 20, 2; 1 Cl., 59, 2-4.

530 The one who wants to be an idle guest cared for by the community is χριστέμπορος, 12, 5, i.e., one who peddles Christ, Pr.-Bauer, s.v.

531 Since κύριος also ref. to God, both God and Jesus are called κύριος, 1, 3 f. and 6; 2, 3; 4, 13 etc.

532 E.g., 7, 2 and 9; 12, 10; 15, 5.

533 So 4, 8: ἡ διαθήκη... ἡ τοῦ ἠγαπημένου Ἰησοῦ, cf. 14, 15 and also 6, 9; 7, 7 and 10 f.; 8, 2 and 4; 9, 7 f.; 11:11; 12, 5-8 and 10; 15, 9.

5. 1 Clement.

Here we find the statement οἱ ἀπόστολοι ἡμῖν εὐηγγελίσθησαν ἀπὸ τοῦ κυρίου Ἰησοῦ Χριστοῦ, Ἰησοῦς ὁ Χριστὸς ἀπὸ τοῦ θεοῦ ἐξεπέμφθη. ὁ Χριστὸς οὖν ἀπὸ τοῦ θεοῦ καὶ οἱ ἀπόστολοι ἀπὸ τοῦ Χριστοῦ, 42, 1 f. This shows awareness of the Messianic significance of ὁ Χριστός and its fusion into the comprehensive ὁ κύριος ἡμῶν Ἰησοῦς Χριστός, cf. also 1 Cl. prooem.; 16, 2 vl.; 20, 11; 42, 3; 44, 1; 50, 7 and 65, 2. At 49, 6, in a statement that comes from a confessional formula about the redemptive significance of suffering, we read: Ἰησοῦς Χριστὸς ὁ κύριος ἡμῶν, and cf. ὁ Χριστός in 7, 4; [534] 21, 6, with ref. to the resurrection of Jesus Ἰησοῦς Χριστός, 24, 1, cf. also 42, 3. The community is τὸ ποίμνιον τοῦ Χριστοῦ in 44, 3; 54, 2; 57, 2. ὁ Χριστός also occurs in the expressions τοῖς ἐφοδίοις τοῦ Χριστοῦ, 2, 1, τὸ καθῆκον τῷ Χριστῷ, 3, 4, κηρύσσοντες τὴν ἔλευσιν τοῦ Χριστοῦ, 17, 1, cf. also 46, 7; 49, 1; 50, 3, ταπεινοφρονούντων γάρ ἐστιν ὁ Χριστός, 16, 1, of whom it is said in what follows: τὸ σκῆπτρον τῆς μεγαλωσύνης τοῦ θεοῦ, ὁ κύριος Ἰησοῦς Χριστός, οὐκ ἦλθεν ἐν κόμπῳ ἀλαζονείας οὐδὲ ὑπερηφανίας, καίπερ δυνάμενος, ἀλλὰ ταπεινοφρονῶν, 16, 2. 46, 6 should also be noted here: ἡ οὐχὶ ἕνα θεὸν ἔχομεν καὶ ἕνα Χριστὸν καὶ ἓν πνεῦμα τῆς χάριτος. Ἰησοῦς Χριστός occurs in 36, 1; [535] 58, 2; 59, 2-4; [536] 61, 3; [537] 64. ἐν Χριστῷ is used in 1, 2; 21, 8; 22, 1; 43, 1; 46, 6; 47, 6; 48, 4; 49, 1; 54, 3, ἐν Χριστῷ Ἰησοῦ in 32, 4; 38, 1. Except at 43, 1; 32, 4 and 38, 1 the ἐν formulae are always combined with nouns that express a style of life and conduct which is shaped by Christ and grounded in Him, εὐσέβεια, 1, 2, παιδεία, 21, 8, πίστις, 22, 1, κλῆσις, 46, 6, ἀγωγή, 47, 6. δικαιοσύνη, 48, 4, ἀγάπη, 49, 1, κλέος, 54, 3. [538] The influence of the usage of esp. the Past. is unmistakable.

6. 2 Clement.

The early Chr. sermon found in 2 Cl. is governed in its Χριστός statements by the witness Χριστὸς ὁ κύριος ὁ σώσας ἡμᾶς, 9, 5, for ὁ Χριστὸς ἠθέλησεν σῶσαι τὰ ἀπολλύμενα, καὶ ἔσωσεν πολλούς, ἐλθὼν καὶ καλέσας ἡμᾶς ἤδη ἀπολλυμένους, 2, 7. Testimony is thus given: ἡ δὲ ἐπαγγελία τοῦ Χριστοῦ μεγάλη καὶ θαυμαστή ἐστιν, 5, 5. [539] For, as we read in the introduction, οὕτως δεῖ ἡμᾶς φρονεῖν περὶ Ἰησοῦ Χριστοῦ, ὡς περὶ θεοῦ, ὡς περὶ κριτοῦ ζώντων καὶ νεκρῶν· καὶ ... περὶ τῆς σωτηρίας ἡμῶν, 1, 1. Salvation is based on His passion, 1, 2. Χριστός or ὁ Χριστός — both are used — is the Saviour. Those whose lives are shaped by him are the ἐκκλησία ζῶσα which is the σῶμα Χριστοῦ, 14, 2. τὸ ἄρσεν ... ὁ Χριστός, τὸ θῆλυ ἡ ἐκκλησία is understood [540] as the conjunction of the male and female, 14, 2. In the union of flesh

---

[534] 12, 7 reads: διὰ τοῦ αἵματος τοῦ κυρίου. ὁ Χριστός and ὁ κύριος are interchangeable.

[535] The name is explained: τὸ σωτήριον ἡμῶν... τὸν ἀρχιερέα τῶν προσφορῶν ἡμῶν, τὸν προστάτην καὶ βοηθὸν τῆς ἀσθενείας ἡμῶν.

[536] Note the conclusion of the Christianised Jewish prayer: σὺ εἶ ὁ θεὸς μόνος καὶ Ἰησοῦς Χριστὸς ὁ παῖς σου καὶ ἡμεῖς λαός σου καὶ πρόβατα τῆς νομῆς σου, 59, 4. On the common παῖς θεοῦ → n. 529; on τὰ πρόβατα τῆς νομῆς σου cf. τὸ ποίμνιον τοῦ Χριστοῦ, 44, 3; 54, 2; 57, 2.

[537] Cf. διὰ τοῦ ἀρχιερέως καὶ προστάτου τῶν ψυχῶν ἡμῶν in 61, 3 and 64 (→ n. 535).

[538] We find Jesus without Χριστός but with κύριος in 13, 1; 32, 2; 46, 7.

[539] τὸ θέλημα τοῦ Χριστοῦ occurs at 6, 7. 17, 6 ref. to the ἐντολαὶ Ἰησοῦ Χριστοῦ. ὁ Χριστός, Χριστός and Ἰησοῦς Χριστός are used without discernible distinction. The art. in front of Χριστός shows that the author is aware of its redemptive significance.

[540] This question is discussed in 2 Cl., 12, 2 and cf. Gospel of Thomas Logion 22 (ed. A. Guillaumont et al. [1959]), cf. R. M. Grant/D. N. Freedman, Secret Sayings of Jesus (1960), 136 f. It is odd that the end of the teaching on the Church in 2 Cl., 14, 5 should have a connection with the Gospel of Thomas Logion 17 (cf. 1 C. 2:9), v. Grant/Freedman, 132 with other examples.

and spirit we call the Church the flesh καὶ τὸ πνεῦμα Χριστόν, 14, 4; it appears ἐν τῇ σαρκὶ Χριστοῦ, [541] 14, 3. He who sins against the flesh, οὐ μεταλήψεται τοῦ πνεύματος, ὅ ἐστιν ὁ Χριστός, 14, 4. [542] Christ as Saviour and the Church which is united and corresponds to Him are closely related. The full formula "our Lord Jesus Christ" does not occur in 2 Cl. The simple name Jesus is used and the designation κύριος. [543]

7. Diognetus.

Dg. does not have Χριστός in any form or combination, but Χριστιανός is common, since the author aims to depict τὴν θεοσέβειαν τῶν Χριστιανῶν, 1, 1. Christians are hated by the world, 2, 6, for they will not submit to the gods, 2, 10. Yet they love those by whom they are hated, 6, 6. They are for the world what the ψυχή is for the σῶμα: ὅπερ ἐστὶν ἐν σώματι ψυχή, τοῦτ' εἰσὶν ἐν κόσμῳ Χριστιανοί, 6, 1. The author thus deduces Χριστιανοὶ κατέχονται μὲν ὡς ἐν φρουρᾷ τῷ κόσμῳ, αὐτοὶ δὲ συνέχουσι τὸν κόσμον... Χριστιανοὶ παροικοῦσιν ἐν φθαρτοῖς, τὴν ἐν οὐρανοῖς ἀφθαρσίαν προσδεχόμενοι, 6, 7 f. [544] What Jesus Christ is, the author of Dg. describes in a new way of his own, cf. esp. 7, 4 f.; [545] the designation Son is adopted, 9, 2 and 4; 10, 2.

8. Summary.

Our review of early Christian writings outside the NT has shown that there is still some awareness that Χριστός denotes the Messiahship of Jesus. The understanding of His crucifixion and resurrection as the salvation event is also linked to the term, often in the broader form ἔλευσις τοῦ Χριστοῦ. Χριστός is the bringer of salvation. It is also obvious, however, that in circles which do not know what Χριστός means and which take the term to be a name, [546] the content of the word as the bringer of salvation has to be continually translated in new ways; σωτήρ especially (→ VII, 1020, 39 ff.) becomes very important in this regard. The writings

---

[541] Surprisingly the art. is not used here although demanded by ἐν τῇ σαρκί. This shows that Χριστός and ὁ Χριστός are used interchangeably.

[542] Thus both Χριστός and ὁ Χριστός are used for τὸ πνεῦμα in 14, 4.

[543] ὁ Ἰησοῦς occurs in 5, 4; 14, 2. ἐν τῷ Ἰησοῦ, 17, 5, τὸν Ἰησοῦν, 17, 7, ὁ κύριος, e.g., 5, 2; 8, 5; 12, 2; 13, 2; 17, 4. Cf. the concluding christological statement: τὸν σωτῆρα καὶ ἀρχηγὸν τῆς ἀφθαρσίας, δι' οὗ καὶ ἐφανέρωσεν ἡμῖν τὴν ἀλήθειαν καὶ τὴν ἐπουράνιον ζωήν, 20, 5.

[544] The main use of Χριστιανός is in 6, 1-9. Another instance is 5, 1.

[545] ἐν ἐπιεικείᾳ καὶ πραΰτητι ὡς βασιλεὺς πέμπων υἱὸν βασιλέα ἔπεμψεν, ὡς θεὸν ἔπεμψεν, ὡς ἄνθρωπον πρὸς ἀνθρώπους ἔπεμψεν, ὡς σῴζων ἔπεμψεν, ὡς πείθων, οὐ βιαζόμενος· βία γὰρ οὐ πρόσεστι τῷ θεῷ. ἔπεμψεν ὡς καλῶν, οὐ διώκων· ἔπεμψεν ὡς ἀγαπῶν, οὐ κρίνων, 7, 4 f.

[546] As in the few non-chr. ref. in the 1st and early 2nd cent. Suet. Caes., V, 25, 11 seems to relate Christus and the slave name Chrestus. As compared to the unfamiliar Christus the latter was a common name for slaves and freedmen → 484, 35 ff., cf. Pr.-Bauer, s.v. Χριστός, 2. Suet. Caes., VI, 16, 3 speaks of Christiani as genus hominum superstitionis novae ac maleficae. Tac. is aware that Christiani comes from Christus, Ann., 15, 44, 3. Plin. often ref. to Christiani and connects them with Christus, whom they cannot be forced to revile but to whom they sing songs quasi deo; he has Christus like Tac., Plin. ep., X, 96, 5-7. Cf. for the texts J. B. Aufhauser, "Antike Jesuszeugnisse," KIT, 126 (1913); for discussion K. L. Schmidt, Art. "Jesus Christus," RGG², III, 122 f.; H. Conzelmann, Art. "Jesus Christus," RGG³, III, 622. In so far as Ant., 20, 200 is genuine Jos. is aware of the Messianic significance of Christ. He speaks of Ἰησοῦ τοῦ λεγομένου Χριστοῦ like Mt. 1:16; 27:17, 22. In the interpolated or christianised Ant., 18, 63 f. we read ὁ χριστὸς οὗτος (sc. Jesus) ἦν → n. 168. On Slav. Jos. cf. E. Barnikol, Das Leben Jesu der Heilsgeschichte (1958), 246-251; W. Bienert, Der älteste nichtchr. Jesusbericht unter bes. Berücksichtigung d. altrussischen Jos. (1936).

of the early Church outside the NT contain a series of notable attempts to express what Χριστός means. Early Christianity [547] is particularly concerned to say in different ways who Χριστός is for it. [548]

Grundmann

---

[547] ψ 44:8, first ref. to Christ in Hb. 1:9, becomes in Just. Dial., 38, 4 etc., along with other OT texts, a basis for developing the idea of the anointing of Christ and believers. Thus Just. Dial., 40, 1, with ref. to the smearing of the doorposts with the blood of the passover lamb, has χρίω at Ex. 12:7 for the weaker τιθέναι/ נתן, with an obvious christological ref. Men are anointed as abodes of the divine Spirit, Dial., 40, 1; 11, 3 (cf. 1 C. 3:16). Dial., 86, 2 f. links the anointing of the stone at Bethel in Gn. 28:18; 31:13 to Ps. 45:7. The symbolism and sacrament of anointing, as well as many Chr. and Gnostic speculations, rest on this. God the Father anointed Christ with the Spirit, Lk. 4:18. Christ anoints the world and the Church, Iren. Epid., 47. This stress on anointing retains the true content of the title or name of Christ in the sense of active or passive unction. The sacrament of anointing or baptising with oil is described in Act. Thom. 27, 157. The cross is constitutive for the sacrament of oil. This is derived from the cross, and as the cross is the tree of life, so oil comes from the tree of life in Paradise, or the olive-tree is there with the tree of life, cf. Slav. En. B 8:5. Acc. to Slav. En. 22:8 f. the anointing imparted to the recipient of revelation is identical with investiture with the garment of light. Cf. G. Bertram, "Die Krankensalbung im NT," in *Die evangelische Krankenpflege* (1962), 121-9; A. Orbe, "La unción del Verbo," *Estudios Valentinianos*, 3, Analecta Gregoriana, 113 (1961), 629-656 and Index, *s.v.* χρῖσμα, χριστός; Review by G. Bertram, ThLZ, 91 (1966), 907-915 [Bertram]. Cf. also A. Wlosok, "Laktanz u. die philosophische Gnosis," AAHdbg, 1960, 2 (1960), 247 f.

[548] K. Berger, NTSt, 17 (1970/71), 391-425 could not be considered further.

<table>
<tr><td rowspan="4">† χρόνος</td><td>αἰών → I, 197 14 ff.</td></tr>
<tr><td>νῦν   → IV, 1106, 5 ff. → ὥρα</td></tr>
<tr><td>καιρός → III, 455, 1 ff.</td></tr>
<tr><td>→ ὥρα</td></tr>
</table>

Contents: A. χρόνος in the Greek World: I. Lexical Data; II. The Problem of Time in Greek Philosophy. B. Time in Judaism: I. The Septuagint: 1. Hebrew Equivalents; 2. Works with No Hebrew Text. II. Non-Biblical Judaism: 1. The Testaments of the Twelve Patriarchs; 2. Qumran. III. The Understanding of Time in Judaism. C. χρόνος in the New Testament: I. Lexical Data. II. Specific Sayings. D. The Post-Apostolic Fathers.

A. χρόνος in the Greek World.

I. Lexical Data.

1. χρόνος outside philosophical discussions can mean "time" in general, "time in its course" (→ n. 41), [1] χρόνωι πίστευε, Ditt. Syll.[3], III, 1268, col. 2, 18 (3rd cent. B.C.), time which brings forth many strange and wonderful things, Menand. Fr., 466 (Körte), which takes all else from man but makes φρονεῖν, understanding, more certain, Fr., 643 (Körte), which teaches man, Aesch. Prom., 981; Xenoph. An., VII, 7, 47, which proves a doctor, Menand. Fr., 652 (Körte), [2] which like a comb unravels what is matted and rectifies

---

χρόνος. Bibl.: J. Barr, *Biblical Words for Time*[2] (1969); R. Bijlsma, A. D. R. Polman, J. N. Sevenster, "Chronos en kairos. Het tijdsprobleem in het NT," *Vox Theologica Beih.*, 2 (1952); H. Blauert, *Die Bedeutung d. Zeit in d. joh. Theol.*, Diss. Tübingen (1953); T. Boman, *Das hbr. Denken im Vergleich mit dem griech.*[5] (1968), 104-133; 140-142; A. L. Burns, "Two Words for 'Time' in the NT," *Australian Biblical Review*, 3 (1953), 7-22; P. F. Conen, "Die Zeittheorie d. Aristot.," *Zetemata*, 35 (1964); O. Cullmann, *Christus u. d. Zeit*[3] (1962), E. T. *Christ and Time* (1950); R. E. Cushman, "Greek and Christian Views of Time," *Journ. of Religion*, 33 (1953), 254-265; G. Delling "Zeit und Endzeit," *Bibl. Stud.*, 58 (1970); E. v. Dobschütz, "Zeit u. Raum im Denken des Urchr.," *JBL*, 41 (1922), 212-223; W. Eichrodt, "Heilserfahrung u. Zeitverständnis im AT," *ThZ*, 12 (1956), 103-125; H. Fränkel, "Die Zeitauffassung in d. frühgriech. Lit.," *Wege u. Formen frühgriech. Denkens*[2] (1960), 1-22; E. Fuchs, *Das Zeitverständnis Jesu, Zur Frage nach d. historischen Jesus*[2] (1965), 304-376, esp. 335-349; V. Goldschmidt, *Le système stoïcien et l'idée de temps* (1953); J. van Goudoever, *Biblical Calendars*[2] (1961); J. Guitton, *Le temps et l'éternité chez Plotin et S. Augustin* (1933); T. Holtz, "Die Christologie d. Apok. d. Joh.," *TU*, 85[2] (1971), 216-221; W. G. Kümmel, "Verheissung u. Erfüllung," *AbhThANT*, 6[3] (1956), esp. 133-140; H. Leisegang, *Die Begriffe d. Zeit u. Ewigkeit im späteren Platonismus* (1913); A. Levi, *Il concetto del tempo nei suoi rapporti coi problemi del divenire e dell'essere nella filosofia greca sino a Platone* (1919); also *Il concetto del tempo nei suoi rapporti coi problemi del divenire e dell'essere nella filosofia greca di Platone* (1920); J. Mánek, "The Biblical Concept of Time and our Gospels," *NTSt*, 6 (1959/60), 45-51; J. Marsh, *The Fulness of Time* (1952); P. Neuenzeit, "Als die Fülle d. Zeit gekommen war... (Gl. 4:4)," *Bibel u. Leben*, 4 (1963), 223-239; C. v. Orelli, *Die hbr. Synonyma d. Zeit u Ewigkeit* (1871); G. v. Rad, *Theol. d. AT*, I[6] (1969), 119-124; II[5] (1968), 108-121, 321-3; M. Rissi, "Was ist u. was geschehen soll danach. Die Zeit- u. Geschichtsauffassung d. Offenbarung d. Joh.," *AbhThANT*, 46 (1965); M. Sekine, "Erwägungen z. hbr. Zeitauffassung," *VT Suppl.*, 9 (1963), 66-82; P. Vidal-Naquet, "Temps des dieux et temps des hommes," *RHR*, 157 (1960), 55-80; W. Vollborn, *Stud. z. Zeitverständnis d. AT*, Diss. Göttingen (1951), cf. *ThLZ*, 77 (1952), 702-4; J. R. Wilch, *Time and Event. An Exeg. Study of the Use of 'eth in the OT in Comparison to Other Temporal Expressions in Clarification of the Concept of Time* (1969); further bibl. → IV, 1110, n. 35.

[1] In Hom. χρόνος occurs only for duration of time with the acc. in such expressions as πολὺν χρόνον or ἐπὶ χρόνον "for a time" [Risch]. For details cf. Fränkel, 1 f., 15 f.; for Homer's view of time in gen. 2-7.

[2] For a collection of sayings about time from the poets cf. Stob. Ecl., I, 93, 15 ff.

all things, Artemid. Onirocr., II, 6; "passing time," a house is ruined χρόνωι, Ditt. Syll.³, II, 837, 13 f. (127 A.D.). The plur. too can mean time in gen. ἐκ παλαιῶν... χρόνων, *ibid.,* II, 559, 23 (207/6 B.C.), ἐκ... τῶν ἔμπροσθε χρόνων within the span of a man's rule, I, 371, 13 (289/8 B.C.), μέχρι τῶν νῦν χρόνων, II, 742, 41 (c. 85 B.C.), προϊόντων... τῶν χρόνων, "in the course of the years," II, 888, 63 (238 A.D.), πολλοῖς ἤδη χρόνοις "who has already dwelled many years among us," 836, 6 f. (125 A.D.), though perhaps the meaning here is the one which follows.

2. χρόνος is then a. a "section of time," τοῦ ἔτους χρόνον, "a part of a year," Xenoph. Mem., I, 4, 12, τὸν τᾶς ζωᾶς χρόνον, "for life," Ditt. Syll.³, III, 1209, 25 f. (at the latest 15/16 A.D.), διὰ τὸν χρόνον, "in virtue of the length of time," III, 1023, 12 (c. 200 B.C.), II, 725, 4 (99 B.C.); τὸν ἀΐδιον χρόνον "for ever," I, 169, 6 (before 351 B.C.), εἰς τὸν ἀεὶ χρόνον, "for eternal times," I, 151, 1 f. (375/4 B.C.), 184, 4 (361/0 B.C.); b. "measure of time," completed at the end of a specific period, μέχρι τοῦ τὸν χρόνον πληρωθῆναι, P. Oxy., II, 275, 23 f. (66 A.D.), etc. "span," πρὸς χρόνον access is barred "for a limited time," Ditt. Syll.³, III, 1109, 89 (before 178 B.C.); c. "delay," αἰτεῖσθαι χρόνον, Preisigke Sammelbuch, I, 5239, 8; 5954, 8 (c. 14 and 15 A.D.), cf. χρόνους ἐμποιεῖν "to postpone for a long while," Demosth. Or., 23, 93, χρόνοι "delays," Artemid. Onirocr., II, 24 (p. 117, 19).

3. χρόνος also means a "point of time." Sacrifices are made ἐν τοῖς καθήκουσιν χρόνοις, Ditt. Syll.³, I, 466, 15 (c. 245 B.C.), cf. ἐν τοῖς ὡρισμένοις χρόνοις, 495, 171 (c. 230 B.C.), τὸν χρόνον ἐν ᾧ ὑβρίσθη "the time of day when he was roughly treated," P. Hal., I, 212 (middle of the 3rd cent. B.C.), "within two months ἀπὸ τοῦ χρόνου, "of the date of the agreement," Ditt. Syll.³, II, 588, 53 (196 B.C.), χρό(νος ὁ α(ὐτός), "the same date," P. Oxy., I, 101, 60 (142 A.D.). The plur. χρόνοι means "indications of time," "dates" etc., Thuc., I, 97, 2; Isoc. Or., 11, 36; Demosth. Or., 18, 225 → 587, 20 f.

II. The Problem of Time in Greek Philosophy.

When Suid., *s.v.* χρόνος (Adler, IV, 827) says: οἱ φιλόσοφοι ἀσώματον αὐτὸν εἶναί φασι, διάστημα ("interval") ὄντα τῆς τοῦ κόσμου κινήσεως. τούτου δὲ τὸν μὲν παρῳχηκότα ("past") καὶ τὸν μέλλοντα ἀπείρους, τὸν δὲ ἐνεστῶτα πεπερασμένον. ἀρέσκει δ' αὐτοῖς καὶ φθαρτὸν εἶναι τὸν κόσμον..., at least some important insights from the discussion of time in Greek philosophy are suggested. The underlying questions are whether time is unending or limited, whether the corruptibility of the universe means the finitude of time, whether the reality of time is bound up with the movement of the cosmos, whether time is in fact a reality.

1. The first discussions of time arise out of the question of the origin of the world → I, 480, 1 ff. In the Orphics Χρόνος is the first cause of all things, Orph. Fr. (Kern), 68, the originator of the cosmic egg, Fr., 70, ³ cf. 57. For Emped. time is that which gives order in the eternal flux of cosmic events, Fr., 30 (Diels, I, 325), cf. 17, 27-29 (317), and also Heracl. → VI, 294, 32 ff. The Sophist Antiphon calls time a mere term of measure νόημα ἢ μέτρον with no real significance, Fr., 9 (Diels, II, 339). Critias, however, says that unwearying time gives birth to itself in a constant flow, so that it is infinite and uncreated, Fr., 18, 1-3 (Diels, II, 384). The cosmos or starry heaven is the work of a wise builder, time, 25, 33 f. (II, 388), not of the gods. For the Eleatics being is uncreated and imperishable; it cannot even be spoken of in the past or future, since it is a connected

---

³ With Chronos as originator of the cosmic egg is Aether, whose father was Chronos acc. to Orph. Fr. (Kern), 54, 66a. In Fr., 54 Chronos, a mixed figure as in 57, is a third principle (→ I, 480, 6) with water and earth: Ἀνάγκη is linked to Chronos. On the religious background of this depiction → I, 198, 30 ff.

whole in the now, Parmen. Fr. 8, 3-6. 19 f. (Diels, I, 235 f.). Hence "that which man has posited in the belief that it is true: becoming and perishing, being and non-being, is a mere name," 38-40 (238). What is, always was and will be; it is ἄπειρον, Melissus Fr., 1 f. (Diels, I, 268 f.); it cannot alter, 7, 2 f. (270 f.). What alters is not real, 8, 5 f. 10 (275). Implicitly the idea of time is also called a purely human ὄνομα here. Zeno, the disciple of Parmenides, tries to show that it is nonsensical through the fourth of his proofs that there is no real movement; acc. to this half time is like double time and hence it does not exist, Aristot. Phys., VI, 9, p. 239b, 33-240b, 7. [4] Here again time is related to movement and viewed as dependent on it.

2. Acc. to Plato time is just a moved image of eternity, Tim., 37d. It arose with the οὐρανός, the sun, moon and planets; the stars are ὄργανα χρόνων, 41e, or χρόνου, 42d. Time will perish with the heavens, 38b-c. Like others before him, Plato thus links time with cosmic movement; being numerically measurable it moves in a circle, 38a. The past and fut. do not relate to eternal being; hence being does not belong to time, 37e, 38a. The original is eternal (πάντα αἰῶνά ἐστιν ὄν), while the copy continually (διὰ τέλους τὸν ἅπαντα χρόνον) was and is and is to come, 38c. Only the former has true being. The specific pt. in Plato is that eternity is outside time, which, having come into being, [5] is only an approximate (εἰς δύναμιν, 37d) reflection of it.

3. Aristot., who deals with time esp. in Phys., IV, 10-14, p. 217b, 29-224a, 17 (→ IV, 1110, n. 35), [6] parts company with Plato when he stresses that the all (οὐρανός) is eternal and hence incorruptible and uncreated, Cael., I, 9, p. 227b, 28 f. Outside heaven is neither space, emptiness, nor time, 279a, 11 f. Aristot. can speak of time only in terms of movement, change, an earlier and a later, Phys., IV, 11, p. 218b, 21-219b, 1. He thus offers the def.: τοῦτο γάρ ἐστιν ὁ χρόνος, ἀριθμὸς κινήσεως κατὰ τὸ πρότερον καὶ ὕστερον, a measure of time, a numerical definition of movement acc. to the relation of earlier and later, 219b, 1 f., cf. also 220a, 24 f. The peripatetic Strato [7] rejects this def. acc. to Simpl., Fr., 75 (25, 25 f.). There is before and after in rest as well as movement, 76 and 77 (26, 11-13, 28-30). [8] To be in time is not to be encircled by it, 80 (27, 8 f.). Time measures duration in action or inaction, 76 (26, 13 f.). Day, night, month and year are not time or parts of it; time is τὸ πόσον in which are fulfilled brightening (day), darkening (night), and the courses of the moon and the sun, 76 (26, 24-26). For Strato time is an accident, as it is also for Epic. acc. to Sext. Emp. Math., X, 219. In Epic. time is σύμπτωμα συμπτωμάτων; it simply accompanies days and nights, movement and permanence, Fr., 294 (Usener).

4. Stoicism firmly relates time to movement; in a much quoted formula it is defined as διάστημα κινήσεως "an interval of movement," Zeno in Stob. Ecl., I, 104, 7 f.; Philo Op. Mund., 26; Aet. Mund., 4, 52; Sext. Emp. Math., X, 170. Nothing happens or is outside time, Zeno in Stob. Ecl., I, 104, 9-11. With ref. to both past and fut. time is infinite. Yet it can also be said that it does not exist, Chrysippus in Stob. Ecl., I, 106, 12-14. The present exists, but one side of it still belongs to the past and another side already belongs to the fut. Plut. Comm. Not., 41 (II, 1081 f.). Time is only a notion καθ' αὑτό τι νοούμενον πρᾶγμα, Sext. Emp. Math., X, 218.

5. Sext. Emp. Math., X, 169-247 and more briefly Pyrrh. Hyp., III, 136-150 sum up the discussion of time by the Sceptics. The upshot is that no objectively valid insight can be gained through the concept of time, so that here too [9] no certainty can be ex-

---

[4] Aristot. can easily refute this.

[5] ἵνα γεννηθῇ χρόνος, Tim., 38c. This is how Plato is understood by Aristot. τὸν . . . χρόνον . . . Πλάτων δ' αὐτὸν γεννᾷ μόνος, Phys., VIII, 1, p. 251b, 17 f. and others.

[6] Cushman compares Plat. and Aristot. with Aug.

[7] Ed. F. Wehrli, *Die Schule d. Aristot., Straton v. Lampsakos* (1950).

[8] Aristot. says this in Phys., IV, 12, p. 221b, 7-23, ὁ δὲ χρόνος κινήσεως καὶ ἠρεμίας μέτρον, line 22 f.

[9] The Sceptics champion the principle: "We define nothing," Diog. L., IX, 74 and 104.

pected. [10] Time is neither limited nor endless, Math., X, 189-192. It is neither indivisible nor divisible, 193-202. It is neither created and corruptible nor uncreated and incorruptible, 203-214. If, e.g., it were limited, we should have to say: ἦν ποτὲ χρόνος, ὅτε χρόνος οὐκ ἦν, and there would once have been a time when there was no time, 189. Sext. Emp. does not conclude from this that the idea of time is a necessary construct of thought. He infers dialectically from the contradictoriness of ordinary statements and possible discussions that the concept is unserviceable.

6. In what he says about time Philo follows his normal practice of combining statements of different origin. As regards the Jewish belief in God the created nature of time is important. God, who is above space and time ὑπεράνω καὶ τόπου καὶ χρόνου, Poster. C., 14, in his work too — ἄχρονον θεοῦ δύναμιν, Sacr. AC, 76 — is the Creator of time. His own existence is eternity, not time. Eternity is the original of time (→ 583, 14 ff.) and in it is only continuance, not past or future, Deus Imm., 31 f. Time was not there before the cosmos, Op. Mund., 26. [11] Using the Stoic def. as the basis of a Platonic thought, Philo calls time an interval of cosmic movement. Movement, however, cannot precede what is moved, Op. Mund., 26. Philo relates what he says in Op. Mund., 26-29 to Gn. 1:1, which he ref. to the creation of an incorporeal heaven and invisible earth, the idea of the air and empty space etc., so that this takes place outside time. As the seventh thing God created the idea of light, the incorporeal original (νοητὸν ... παράδειγμα) of the sun and stars of the visible cosmos, Op. Mund., 29. Only with movement is time possible, and there can be nothing outside it, Decal., 30 f., apart, of course, from God, the ideas etc. The world did not come into being in time (Philo ref. here to Gn. 2:2). Time came into being through the universe, [12] through the movement of the sun over and under the earth. The movement of the heavens brought the nature φύσιν of time to light, Leg. All., I, 2. Days, months etc. arose through the ordered courses of the sun and moon etc., Op. Mund., 60, cf. 55; Spec. Leg., I, 90, and with these came number too, Op. Mund., 60. [13]

7. Plut. follows Plat. [14] when he suggests that time arose with the cosmos, Quaest. Plat., 8, 4 (II, 1007c.). For Plut., too, only the eternal, uncreated and incorruptible has true being, Delph., 19 (II, 392e). Only to God (Apollo here) can one say: εἶ "thou art," 20 (393b); for he does not exist acc. to the measure of time κατ' οὐδένα χρόνον but according to timeless and unchangeable eternity, 20 (393a). Time is something moved and it is considered together with moved matter, being fleeting and impermanent, 19 (392e).

8. Plot. devotes Enn., III, 7, 7, 1-13, 69 to the problem of time. Like Plat. he thinks the relation between eternity and time, with which III, 7 deals, is that of original παράδειγμα and copy εἰκών, III, 7, 1, 18-20. He shows the difficulties involved in the traditional def. of time as an "interval" διάστημα of movement, 8, 23-69, or as a measure of movement, 9, 1-84. For Plot. time did not at first exist. It rested in being without existing. It then originated with the rise of the world and the springing into activity of the world soul. The world soul made itself temporal by creating the perceptible world. It subjected this to time ἔδωκε δουλεύειν χρόνῳ. Hence one cannot conceive of time apart from the world soul. It rests in this as eternity is in being and not outside it. Time is the life of the world soul in a movement which moves on from one form of life to another, 11, 35-45. The world soul brought it forth ἐγέννησεν with the universe and it will end when this activity of

[10] This sentence is by Dihle.

[11] The idea of the infinity of time, it is argued, contradicts the idea of its creation, De providentia, II, 53 (ed. M. C. E. Richter, VIII [1830]).

[12] How fixed these lines of thought are may be seen from Corp. Herm., 11, 2: The cosmos makes time; the nature of time is change.

[13] But Philo can also say that months and years and other divisions of time are simply human δόγματα, Fug., 57 → 582, 40 f. and 583, 5 f.

[14] For the discussion of time in Middle Platonism cf. C. Andresen, "Logos und Nomos," Arbeiten zur Kirchengeschichte, 30 (1955), 276-291.

the world soul ceases. It is measured by the courses of the heavenly bodies, being indicated rather than originated by these, 12, 22-54. Time is everywhere because the world soul is not separated from any part of the world. It is in all individual souls, which are in concert a single soul, 13, 47-49. The cosmos is in constant movement in its striving for real being, οὐσία, ἀεὶ εἶναι, eternity, in which time ceases to be, 4, 28-43. From the standpoint of eternity, or God, man has a share in this and hence he is raised above time, 5, 7-22.

It is evident that thought about the problem of time in the Greek world is very largely determined — least of all in Plotinus → 584, 34 ff. — by the physical and cosmological approach. Nevertheless we also find statements to the effect that time is a human concept of order → 582, 40 f.; 583, 5 f. At any rate the Greek can to no small degree detach himself from the reality of time. This may also be seen in symbolical statements in older Greek poetry in which time is personified. All-seeing time judges, Soph. Oed. Tyr., 1213 f. [15] In the philosophers dependence on time seems to be unavoidable when time is viewed as unending and only the visible world is taken into account as in Aristot. → 583, 19 ff. This bondage to time can be overcome only when eternity as the epitome of true being is given precedence over perishable time.

B. Time in Judaism.

I. The Septuagint.

1. Hebrew Equivalents.

In works of which we have the HT — all ref. are given [16] — χρόνος is not very common as distinct from καιρός → III, 458, 3 ff. It is most often used for יָמִים [17] in a rendering chosen in distinction from the lit. ἡμέραι → II, 947, 25 ff. χρόνος is a period of time in Jos. 24:29 LXX (Jos. 24:31 HT obviously has a different sense), the time of a ruler's reign or life ὡς χρόνος βασιλέως, or that of a man's life ὡς χρόνος ἀνθρώπου (LXX gloss), Is. 23:15, "lifetime," 38:5, ὃς οὐκ ἐμπλήσει τὸν χρόνον αὐτοῦ, 65:20, "years of life," νεώτερος τῷ χρόνῳ, Job 32:6, "age" as compared to youth ὁ χρόνος ἐστὶν ὁ λαλῶν, 32:7, ἐν τῷ χρόνῳ τινός "in the age of someone" as a relative chronological note, Gn. 26:15, v. v. 1, ἐν παντὶ χρόνῳ, Jos.. 4:24, and πάντα τὸν χρόνον (HT different), "at all times," Prv. 15:15, τὸν ἅπαντα χρόνον, "lifelong," Dt. 22:19, 29, cf. ὅσον χρόνον ἔζη (HT "all the days of his life"), Jos. 4:14. יָמִים for "lifetime" can also be transl. χρόνος but with the addition of ζάω, Dt. 12:19; Prv. 9:11; 28:16, βιόω, Job 29:18, βίος 10:20 (but v. BHK). At Ἰερ. 45(38):28 ἕως χρόνου οὗ is used for "up to the day." At Ezr. 4:15; Da. 2:44 the plur. of Aram. יוֹם is transl. χρόνοι. In contrast to the HT χρόνος is used pleonastically in the expression εἰς τὸν αἰῶνα χρόνον, which occurs for עַד־עוֹלָם in Ex. 14:13; Is. 9:6; 34:17, לְעוֹלָם in Is. 14:20; 30:10a, לָנֶצַח in Is. 13:20; 33:20, הָלְאָה in Is. 18:7. χρόνος is used for זְמָן "delay" in Da. 2:16, but cf. 2:21; 7:12bβ, τοῖς πᾶσιν χρόνος, "there is a time for everything," Qoh. 3:1, ἀπὸ χρόνων for מִזְמַנִּים,

---

[15] The statement that "time is the wisest of all things since it discovers all things" is attributed to Thales, Diog. L., I, 35, cf. Plut. Sept. Sap. Conv., 9 (II, 153d); on this cf. O. Brendel, "Symbolik der Kugel," Röm. Mitt., 51 (1936), 36-39.

[16] J. C. v. Kölichen did the spadework for this section.

[17] Derivates of χρόνος are also used for statements with יָמִים, cf. μακροχρόνιος Ex. 20:12; Dt. 5:16; 4:40 vl.; 17:20 vl., μακροχρονίζω 17:20, πολυχρόνιος Gn. 26:8 etc. Often "my" or "thy days" etc. in Job are transl. by βίος μου etc. 7:6, 16 etc., ζωὴ αὐτοῦ only 7:1. "Length of days" in Prv. 3:2, 16 is transl. by μῆκος βίου, "many days" in Is. 24:22 by πολλαὶ γενεαί (only here), "days" in Job 38:21 by ἔτη. Other terms are deliberately selected in these cases.

2 Ἐσδρ. 20:35 or מְזִמֻּנוֹת 23:31.[18] χρόνος is used for עֵת only (→ III, 458, 4) at Ἰερ. 30:2[19] (49:8); 37(30):7; 38(31):1 with ref to a specific future time, cf. the HT. χρόνος is a transl. of עֵת in the sense of "time." Sir. 43:6 LXX reads as opp. to HT: The moon is set εἰς... ἀνάδειξιν χρόνων. The content of time seems to be in view in Job 6:11. χρόνος for פֹּה in Job 14:13 means a "set time," cf. 14:5. The double פַּעַם of Prv. 7:12 is rendered by χρόνον... τινά... χρόνον "a while"... "a while." Two constructs of רָחֹק for "from afar" are given a temporal sense in Is. 30:27; 49:1 (with expansion). For תּוֹר "turn" we find χρόνος in Est. 2:15: ἐν... τῷ ἀναπληροῦσθαι τὸν χρόνον Εσθηρ. For עֲלוּמִים "youth of the king" (hence θρόνου for χρόνου in Β) LXX[20] has "life" in ψ 88:46, while עֵשׁ is transl. χρόνος in Is. 51:8 (a garment is eaten away by time), but cf. 50:9, χρόνον μικρόν for רֶגַע קָטֹן, Is. 54:7, χρόνος ζωῆς for אֲרֻכָה "length of life," Da. 7:12bα. Under the influence of לְ, without regard for the suffix, אַחֲרִית "outcome," "end," is taken in a fut. sense εἰς τὸν ἐπιόντα χρόνον, Dt. 32:29. Prv. 1:22 has ὅσον... χρόνον, for עַד־מָתַי, Is. 34:10b εἰς χρόνον πολύν for לְנֵצַח נְצָחִים, Job 12:12 ἐν πολλῷ χρόνῳ "in old age" for בִּישִׁישִׁים "among the aged."[21] "Numbered, numbered, has God thy reign" in Da. 5:26 is freely transl. by LXX as ἠρίθμηται ὁ χρόνος σου τῆς βασιλείας. The relation between HT and LXX[22] is not clear in Is. 27:10 f.; 54:9;[23] Job 12:5; 14:11; Est. 9:28. The text is expanded with the use of χρόνος in Δα. 4:27 (→ VI, 284, 31); 4:33b, 34, cf. also 4:37: God ἀλλοιοῖ καιροὺς καὶ χρόνους (→ n. 57); Job 2:9; Prv. 9:18d; Est. 3:13g; 8:12x; Sir. prooem. 32 (→ line 27). We do not have the HT of Sir. 29:5: ἐν καιρῷ ἀποδόσεως παρελκύσει χρόνον. Comparatively χρόνος is less common in the LXX (132 times) than the NT (54 times).

2. Works with No Hebrew Text.

Time as such is hardly an object of special reflection in the Septuagint. Yet in the writings composed in the Hellenistic *diaspora*[24] we find some contacts with popular concepts or ideas even though only in a general sense.

More striking than διάστημα τοῦ χρόνου in Sir. prooem. 32; 3 Macc. 4:17 is ἀμερὴς χρόνος in 5:25; 6:29. ἀμερής occurs only here in the LXX.[25] Acc. to Wis. 7:17-19 God or wisdom (v. 21) has given Solomon knowledge about the σύστασις κόσμου "construction of the world," cf. Plat. Tim., 32c, the ἐνέργεια στοιχείων (→ VII, 676, 23 ff.), the beginning, end, and middle of times, the alternation of the suns and the year, the yearly cycle, and the positions of stars. In context ἀρχὴν καὶ τέλος καὶ μεσότητα χρόνων in v. 18a does not mean the division of time[26] but the rise ἀρχή of time (the

---

[18] In the OT the verb occurs only at Ezr. 10:14 in the same form as Neh. 10:35, 2 Ἐσδρ. 10:14 has ἀπὸ συνταγῶν.

[19] 29:9 in the ed. of J. Ziegler, *Jeremias, Vetus Test. Graec. auctoritate Societatis Litter. Gottingensis ed.*, 15 (1957).

[20] At Is. 54:4 LXX has αἰώνιος for the same noun.

[21] The Hbr. word is transl. more literally at Job 15:10; 29:8; 32:6; in LXX 12:12a α is formally par. to v. 12b α.

[22] The texts mentioned in → line 17 are sometimes transl. very freely.

[23] Did the translators read בִּימֵי נֹחַ here?

[24] Wis. and 3 Macc. seem to have been written in Alexandria, cf. O. Eissfeldt, *Einl. in das AT*³ (1964), 815 and 789.

[25] ἀμερής is obviously not in popular use, cf. the instances in Liddell-Scott, *s.v.*

[26] Thus Aristobul Fr., 5 in Eus. Praep. Ev., 13, 12, 12: ἵνα τοὺς χρόνους δηλώσῃ (with a ref. here to Gn. 1:1 - 2:4). The three-membered Gk. formula (cf. Plat. Leg., IV, 715e) in Wis. 7:18 supports the interpretation given above. Αἰών is described as ἀρχὴν μεσότητα τέλος οὐκ ἔχων in Ditt. Syll.³, III, 1125, 10 f. (time of Augustus); Wis. 7:18: Time has a beginning, end, and middle. J. Fichtner, *Die Weisheit Salomos, Hndbch. AT*, 2, 6 (1938), 30 f. stresses the special interest of the passage in the calendar.

plur. denotes its totality) with creation, its cessation, and between these the extension which is of the essence of time. The ref. is to the Hell. view of the world which the author sees in relation to the bibl. story of creation → 584, 8 ff. In 8:8, however, the ref. is obviously to knowledge of fut. events in history which represent decisive processes ἐκβάσεις καιρῶν καὶ χρόνων "periods of time"; wisdom knows them in advance.

In works with no Hbr. text — not all ref. are given (→ 586, 19 f.) — χρόνος means "passing time" (→ 582, 1 f. 4 f.) ὡς... χρόνος διῆλθεν "when a certain time had elapsed," 2 Macc. 1:22, ἐν χρόνῳ "in the course of time" our name will be forgotten, Wis. 2:4, or custom will become law, 14:16. Then χρόνος is a "span of time" with specific ref. to the no. of months, Wis. 7:2, or yrs., 2 Macc. 4:23; 10:3; 14:1 "for all time," εἰς τὸν ἅπαντα χρόνον, 1 Macc. 10:30; 11:36; 15:8, εἰς τὸν ἀεὶ χρόνον (→ 582, 13) 3 Macc. 3:29 (plur. 7:23), εἰς τὸν αἰῶνα χρόνον (→ 585, 36 f.) Bar. 3:32, ἀπ' αἰῶνος χρόνου "from of old," 3 Macc. 5:11. The word can denote an "epoch," in the time of someone, e.g., Joshua, 2 Macc. 12:15, plur. 1 Ἐσδρ. 1:18; 2:12, in gen. "the times of our fathers," 1 Ἐσδρ. 8:73, also shorter spaces of time, ἐκ τῶν παλαιῶν χρόνων, 2 Macc. 6:21, or, to denote content, τῆς ἐρημώσεως, 1 Ἐσδρ. 1:55, παροικίας, 3 Macc. 7:19, ἀκμῆς "of maturity," 4 Macc. 18:9, ἀμειξίας, 2 Macc. 14:3, 38 (both times plur.). χρόνος is a "span," 1 Ἐσδρ. 9:12; Wis. 12:20 (plur.), ἐν αὐτῷ τῷ χρόνῳ "at this time," 1 Ἐσδρ. 6:3, μέχρι χρόνου "to the time," i.e., a specific time, Tob. 14:4, υ. ἕως τοῦ χρόνου, οὗ, 14:5 S. βίβλος τῶν χρόνων τῶν βασιλέων in 1 Ἐσδρ. 1:40 means a book with the (relative) dating of specific events → 593, 20 f.

II. Non-Biblical Judaism.

1. The Testaments of the Twelve Patriarchs.

In Test. XII — all ref. are given — χρόνος means a "period of time," that to which a specific event belongs ἐν τῷ τότε χρόνῳ, Iss. 2:5, of a fixed length which is not given but presupposed, the year, [27] S. 1:1, χρόνων εἴκοσι "twenty yrs. old," Jud. 7:10, or month G. 5:11, more generally χρόνους πολλούς... τοῦ ζῆν "to live a long time," Iss. 4:3, καθ' ὧν χρόνων "as long as," G. 5:11, ἕως χρόνου a "certain time," Jos. 3:8, ἐν ἑτέρῳ χρόνῳ "at another pt. in time," Jos. 5:1. The context and meaning are uncertain in the case of μέχρι τελειώσεως χρόνων in R. 6:8, "to the end of the times" (→ VIII, 85, 2 ff.), or to the times of the anointed high-priest.

2. Qumran.

a. In the Qumran writings עת [28] means first a "period of time." Declarations of God's will were made for different "epochs," 1 QS 9:13a. Each time has its order acc. to 9:12, cf. משפט עת ועת, Damasc. 12:21 (15:2), cf. 1 QS 8:15; 9:13b (plur.). "This time" is that of the separation of the community, 1 QS 9:5, cf. 9:20, cf. also 9:19 (→ 588, 3), and the plur. (→ 588, 29 ff.; 589, 12 f.) "in these times" for the present time of the community, 9:21; 10:26. "The law of the time" is that which is valid for the epoch of the community, 9:14a, [29] cf. "order of the time," 8:4; 9:18. "The elect of the time" are the sect, 9:14b. Damasc. 16:3 (20:1) ref. to a book of the divisions of time. Often constructions with עת are used to characterise a time as, e.g., that of affliction, 1 QM 1:11 f.; 15:1, salvation,

---

[27] The meaning "year," as modern Gk. shows, developed in post-class. popular speech [Dihle]. Cf. P. Oxy., I, 35 verso line 1 (3rd cent. A.D.): βασειλέων χρόνοι "years of rule" → 587, 20 f.

[28] All the ref. given by K. G. Kuhn, Konkordanz zu d. Qumrantexten (1960), s.v. are given here.

[29] Cf. perhaps 1 QS 9:23. 1 QM 15:5 ref. to a עת סרך. Y. Yadin, The Scroll of the War of the Sons of Light against the Sons of Darkness (1962), 330 f., 17 regards עתו as the title of a book. The two ref. are the only ones with עת and suffix.

1:5, visitation, 4 QPIsᵇ, Col. 2:2 (DJD, V, 15), purification and sifting, 4 QpPs 37, Col. 2:18 (V, 44); 4 Q Floril. 2:1. Cf. also the "time of summer heat," 1 QH 8:23, also with following inf. "time to prepare the way," 1 QS 9:19, cf. Is. 30:3, or with relative clause, Damasc. 1:13 (1:9) (on 10:15 [13:1] → line 7 f.); 4 Q Test. 21. עולם לעת is quantitative "for ever," 1 QSb 4:26, cf. perhaps 5:18. We find עת with gen. in 1 QH Fr. 45:2; [30] לפי העת is gen. in Damasc. 10:5 (11:2) "at any time." עת seems to be a calendar time in 1 QH 12:8. [31] עת is a "period of time" in Damasc. 10:15 (13:1), cf. "at this time," 1 QM 18:3, "feast-time," 1 QS 1:14 (plur.) par. מועד line 15, cf. 1 QM 14:13 = 4 QMa 11. [32] In the main, then, עת is used to denote a specific time, [33] though קץ can also be used in this sense → lines 16 ff.

b. קץ, which is more common than עת, mostly denotes a "period of time" → VIII, 53, n. 28; only rarely does it mean "end" in a spatial sense. For this we find קצה in 1 QH 6:31 and קצת in 1 QM 1:8, cf. באחרית הקץ "at the end of the time," 4 QpNa 3:3. The sense "point of time" or "fixed time" is uncommon, though cf. the "times of the day" fixed by God, 1 QS 10:1, the "time" of the cessation of night, 1 QH 12:6, from one time, e.g., hour, of praise to another, 12, 4, the time of the feast-day מועד ... 1 QpHab 11:6. Added gen. often characterise a time in the past, pres., or fut., [34] cf. time of wrath קץ חרון for an earlier epoch in Israel's history, Damasc. 1:5 (1:5), also 1 QH 3:28, plur. 1 QH Fr 1:5; [35] 1 QpHosᵃ, Col. 1:12 (DJD, V, 31), the time of Israel's unfaithfulness, Damasc. 20:23 (9:47); 4 QpHosᵃ, Col. 1:9 (V, 31), of the devastation of the land of Palestine, Damasc. 5:20 (8:1), of transgression, 6:10 (8:9), 14 (8:12); 12:23 (15:4); 15:7 (19:7); 1 QpHab 5:7 f., of the wars of God, 1 QM 11:8 (plur.), of judgment, 1 QH 6:29; Fr. 58:5 (→ n. 30), of visitation, Damasc. 7:21 (9:10); 19:10 f. (9:10 f.), of witness, 1 QH Fr 5:11, [36] of God's good-pleasure or gracious will , ibid. 9:8, [37] v. 1 Q 34 Fr. 3, Col. 2:5 (DJD, I, 154), of the manifestation of God's aid, 1 QH 5:11 f., of the glory of God, 12:22, salvation, 1 QS 3:15, dominion for the men of God's lot, 1 QM 1:5, peace, 1 QH 18:30 (plur.), the ministry of the sons of Ṣadok, Damasc. 4:5 (6:3). In the plur., too, the word mostly denotes a span of time. [38] We read of the "epochs" of Israel's blindness in Damasc. 16:2 f. (20:1). In different connections the plur. means "all times" with נצח in 1 QSb 4:26, "for all eternal times" before God, 1 QH 1:24, with עולמים in 1 QS 4:16a, perhaps 4:25b; 1 QH Fr. 20:4; [39] 1 QM 1:8, with עד 1 QSb 5:18, "eternal times," 1 QM 10:15 f.: "all God's epochs come in their regulated measure," 1 QpHab 7:13. "Thy times" are God's appointed times in 1 QH 13:20, "his time" is the time set by God for a specific event, 1 QM 1:4, cf. 1 QS 3:23, while "their times" are those of sinners, Damasc. 2:9 f. (2:8), cf. 1 QS 4:13. קץ can also denote the ages of different generations, 1 QH 1:16. Calendar times are obviously meant in 1 QS 1:14. The context of Damasc. 4:9 (6:5), 10 (6:7); 20:15 (9:40) shows that parts of the year are in view. God sets a time for wickedness, 1 QS 4:18, cf. "to the appointed time

---

[30] Ed. A. M. Habermann, מגלות מדבר יהודה (1959), 144.

[31] M. Weise, "Kultzeiten u. kultischer Bundesschluss in d. 'Ordensregel' vom Toten Meer," Studia Post-Biblica, 3 (1961), 17.

[32] Ed. C. H. Hunzinger, "Fr. einer ältern Fassung d. Buches Milḥamā aus Höhle 4 von Qumran," ZAW, 69 (1957), 135.

[33] Acc. to Vollborn, 25 עת in the OT is above all "the specific point of time when something happens," the point or period of time determined by or for something.

[34] Cf. on this קץ משיח in bMeg., 3a.

[35] Habermann, op. cit., 134.

[36] Ibid., 137.

[37] Ibid., 139.

[38] לקצים 1 QH 5:27; 8:31, perhaps "time by time," cf. "God helps from one time to another" in 9:7 f.

[39] Habermann, op. cit., p. 143.

and the making of what is new," 4:25a. God made known to the prophet the events of the last generation but not the completion of the time, 1 QpHab 7:2. In the use of קץ it is plain that time is largely seen as having a specific content and also as ordained by God. [40]

c. The meaning "specific point of time" applies esp. to מוֹעֵד, which in the Scrolls denotes a set time, mostly a feast-day or festival, then assembly (5 times), and elsewhere time (of a battle, the war), 1 QM 15:5, 12. It can often be broader e.g., time of night, 1 QH 12:6, even of the sabbatical year, 1 QM 2:6; it can also be used in the expression "eternal times," 12:3; 13:8. It then means the time fixed by a common or special event, "time" of harvest or sowing, 1 QS 10:7, "time" of visitation, 4:18 f., of good-pleasure (→ 588, 23 f.), 1 QH 15:15, of judgment (→ loc. cit.), 1 QS 4:20, set time of penitence, 4 QpPs 37:1, 9, plur. "times" of their afflictions, 1 QS 3:23, of darkness, 1 QM 1:8, of testimonies, 1 QS 1:9; 3:10. 1 QM speaks of the "set time" of God, e.g., his intervention, 3:7 f.; 4:7, cf. also 11:11. "Today is his time" we read in 17:5 (→ 588, 32 f.; 590, 22 f.). God's time is contrasted with the times of darkness, 1:8. The features common to the three terms should not be overlooked.

III. The Understanding of Time in Judaism.

Jewish history, including that of Palestinian Judaism, does not differ from Greek-Hellenistic history in its fixing of events in time. To this extent a certain linear concept of time seems to be presupposed in it. [41]

1 Macc. 1:10 dates acc. to the βασιλεία Ἑλλήνων, i.e., the Seleucid era. More dates acc. to the same reckoning are given in v. 20. 13:42 signals the introduction of the national era after the high-priest Simon, cf. also 14:27. There is already a similar co-ordination of events in historical sequence in the OT, [42] cf. the years of Solomon's reign in 1 K. 6:1, v. 15:1 etc.; Is. 36:1; Jer. 1:2 f. Later the reckoning is acc. to foreign rulers, Ezr. 1:1; 4:24; Da. 2:1; 7:1; 9:1 etc. 1 K. 6:1 tries to establish an epoch from the exodus, which was the decisive event for the self-understanding of Israel as God's people. [43] Jos. dates the flood (Ant., 1, 82), the beginning of the building of the temple (8, 62), and its destruction (10, 148) from Adam. He synchronises his ref. with the number of years from the exodus, the migration of Abraham and the flood, 8, 61. [44] Jub. has a system of dating from creation, cf. the special dating of the flood in 3:17. The division of time after the manner of Jub. is regarded here as the only legitimate one. It is sanctioned by the fact that it was revealed to Moses on Sinai, 1:4, 29. The exact dating in Jub. is connected with the fixing of the religious calendar advocated in the book. [45] One may ref. to the similar concerns in 1 Macc.

---

[40] Cf. Yadin, op. cit. (→ n. 29), 258: קץ "preordained period or moment of history," and v. B. J. Roberts, "Some Observations on the Damascus Document and the Dead Sea Scrolls," The Bulletin of the John Rylands Library, 34 (1951/52), 380 f.

[41] Yet not in the sense of the par. between time and a line as in Aristot. Phys., IV, 11, p. 220a, 9-21, or in that of the course of time as in Emped. Fr., 17, 29 (Diels, I, 317); Hdt., II, 121, 2α, cf. Aristot. Phys., IV, 14, p. 223b, 28-34.

[42] Cf. A. Jepsen-R. Hanhart, Untersuchungen z. isr.-jüd. Chronologie (1964); Barr, 28-33.

[43] The no. 480 assumes 12 generations.

[44] Diaspora Judaism offers a first attempt at relative chronology in the Fr. of Demetrius (end of the 3rd cent. B.C.), cf. Eus. Praep. Ev., 9, 19, 4; 21, 1-19; 29, 1-3, 15, 16c, cf. also Cl. Al. Strom., I, 21, 141, 1 f., v. N. Walter, Untersuchungen z. d. Fr. d. jüd.-hell. Historiker, Halle (1967), 17-36. On Rabb. reckonings cf. B. Z. Wacholder, "How Long did Abram Stay in Egypt?" HUCA, 35 (1964), 43-56.

[45] Cf. J. Morgenstern, "The Calendar of the Book of Jubilees," VT, 5 (1955), 34-76; van Goudoever, 62-70.

1:54; 4:52. Religious calendars were much developed in the Greek-Hell. sphere, [46] but the religious festivals were grounded in myth and no attempt was made, even fictionally, to find for them a historical or chronological basis. In contrast cf. the day of atonement in Jub. 34:12-19; in the OT the Passover esp. is linked to a historical event, cf. Jos. Ant., 2, 317; 3, 248; [47] Bell., 4, 402; 5, 99.

In 1 QM 10:12, 15 f. time is ordered according to a yearly calendar, which is important at Qumran as in Gn. 1:14. Epochs of time are also viewed as established by God → 588, 31 ff. God fixes the times for powers and events. The march of time or the times is determined by him. In at least a general sense the determination of time in terms of its content (→ 587, 40 ff.; 588, 16 ff.; 589, 9 ff.) is already characteristic of the OT → II, 947, 26 ff.; III, 458, 18 ff. [48] In Judaism this is particularly plain in the scheme of the two aeons (→ I, 206, 7 ff.) and also in other divisions, [49] e.g., the scheme of the 14 waters (S. Bar. 56:1 - 74:4), which is called an order of the times (56:2), and in which an epoch that is judged negatively in terms of its decisive event leads on to one that is judged positively. At the beginning of this history of epochs is the fall of Adam and at the end is the age of the Messiah, which still belongs to this aeon, 74:2, 4 Esr. 7:28 f. [50] Almost always the relation between God and the Jewish people is decisive in the assessment of the times. The ages of Abraham, Moses, David/Solomon, Hezekiah, Josiah, and the rebuilding of Zion after the exile are regarded positively. [51] If the order of the times — the expression is used in S. Bar. 14:1; 20:6 — is fixed by God, this means that they assuredly come, 20:6. Their duration is established in advance [52] by God. [53] The delay of judgment is not primarily due to God's longsuffering but to His foreordination of the times (4 Esr. 7:74), which He has measured out (4:37). [54] The times may thus be called His times, 11:39, 44 → 588, 17 f.; 589, 15 f. The distinction between the OT and Jewish view of time on the one side, and the non-biblical view on the other, may be seen [55] especially in the fact that God is in the full sense the Lord of time, [56] for

---

[46] Cf. M. P. Nilsson, "Die Entstehung u. religiöse Bdtg. d. griech. Kalenders," Lunds Univ. Årsskrift, NF Avdelning, 1, 14, No. 21 (1918).

[47] Jos. Ant., 3, 248 illustrates the relation of worship in Jos. day to the exodus: "The sacrifice that we ... offered at the exodus from Egypt."

[48] Outside the Bible a specific ref. to content can be made very gen. in the simple use of words for time, cf. the use of καιρός (→ III, 455, 29 ff.). The idea of a span or point of time is esp. linked with χρόνος in the non-biblical sphere, → 582, 8 ff. 19 ff.

[49] There is no par. to this in Hes. Op., 109-201. Vergil Ecl., 4, 4-9 presents a cyclic view when it speaks of the return of the golden age after the age of iron.

[50] For another scheme cf. Da. 7, v. also 4 Esr. 12:11. On the theme in gen. cf. J. Licht, "Time and Eschatology in Apocalyptic Literature and in Qumran," The Journal of Jewish Studies, 16 (1965), 177-182. On Rabb. reckonings cf. Str.-B., IV, 989-993.

[51] The scheme of ten weeks in Eth. En. 93:1-10; 91:12-17 is less clear. Noah and Abraham are decisive figures, while decisive events are the exodus, the receiving of the Torah, the building of the temple, apostasy under the kings, the exile, apostasy to Hellenism, and the age of the Maccabees.

[52] The immutability of their ordination finds expression in the fact that they are inscribed on heavenly tables or in books, Eth. En. 93:1 f.

[53] Cf. on this W. Harnisch, "Verhängnis u. Verheissung d. Gesch.," FRL, 97 (1969), 281-3.

[54] God does not intervene until the allotted measure has been fulfilled, 4 Esr. 4:37.

[55] The god Chronos (→ 582, 36 ff.) is a symbolical figure. Above all, however, the Gk. sense of dependence on time is very different from the Jewish sense of the ordaining of time by God. Philo Sacr. AC, 76 emphasises that the worship of time overlooks the timeless power of God.

[56] A. Strobel, "Untersuchungen z. eschatol. Verzögerungsproblem," Nov. Test. Suppl., 2 (1961), 28 etc. speaks of a theocentric view of time.

He is the Lord of history. [57] This is made plain in other ways in the OT, cf. Is. 41:2-4; 45:1-7; Ezr. 1:1 f. In the great survey of history from Abraham to the conquest the exodus occupies a special place, Ps. 105.

If God is the Lord of time, He for His part is not dependent on it. In the OT this may be seen in creation sayings which speak of God creating through the Word, Ps. 33:9, cf. 148:5. This is expressly stressed by Philo in Op. Mund., 13. God the Creator does not need time. He acts by command and even by thought. Six days are mentioned in Gn. 1 to show the orderliness of the world, 28, cf. Decal., 99 and 101. Whether Palestinian Judaism also toyed at least with the idea that the Lord of time exists outside time (→ 584, 10 ff.) is uncertain → I, 202, 2 ff. Timelessness is not necessarily meant when in relation to the enumeration of ten weekly periods (→ n. 51) eternity is denoted by expressions like "many weeks without number," Eth. En. 91:17. [58] At any rate eternity must have been normally understood as unlimited time. [59]

C. χρόνος in the New Testament.

I. Lexical Data.

χρόνος mostly means "span of time," e.g., the time of the work of Jesus in Ac. 1:21; ἐφ' ὅσον χρόνον "as long as," R. 7:1; 1 C. 7:39; Gl. 4:1. The span may be undetermined, χρόνον τινά, 1 C. 16:7, ἐπὶ χρόνον, "a while," Lk. 18:4, ὅσον χρόνον, "as long as," Mk. 2:19, ἐπὶ πλείονα χρόνον, "longer," Ac. 18:20, or it may be fixed, 40 years, Ac. 7:23; 13:18, what is felt to be a short time μικρός, Rev. 6:11; 20:3; Jn. 7:33; 12:35, ἐν στιγμῇ χρόνου "in a moment," Lk. 4:5, [60] what is felt to be long, ἱκανός, Ac. 8:11; 14:3; 27:9, οὐκ ὀλίγος, 14:28, τοσοῦτος, Jn. 14:9. In acounts of exorcisms the difficulty is sometimes stressed by mentioning the length of the possession, πόσος χρόνος, Mk. 9:21, χρόνῳ ἱκανῷ, Lk. 8:27, πολλοῖς χρόνοις, v. 29, cf. πολὺν ... χρόνον in the healing in Jn. 5:6. Abs. χρόνον means a "time," Ac. 19:22, τὸν πάντα χρόνον "the whole time," 20:18, cf. ποιεῖν χρόνον (τινά) "to spend some time," [61] 15:33; 18:23. "Span of time" is probably meant in Mt. 2:7,16 as well, while in Hb. 5:12 διὰ τὸν χρόνον means the length of time that has passed since becoming a Christian → 582, 10 f. χρόνος can then mean the time available as in the rhetorical expression in Hb. 11:32. It is a "set time" in Ac. 1:7, or more narrowly the "delay" that is granted to allow time for conversion, Rev. 2:21, or "postponement" in Rev. 10:6 → 582, 15 ff. When the plur. is used the ref. may be to larger segments of times, the whole pre-Chr. age in Ac. 1:7 in contrast to τὰ νῦν, cf. R. 3:26. On 1 Pt. 1:20 → 592, 17 f., on χρόνοι αἰώνιοι → 592, 26 ff. Yet the plur. can also be used more weakly (→ 582, 16 f.), cf. Lk. 8:29; 20:9 (→ 592, 12); 23:8; Ac. 3:21 (though cf. → I, 391, 39). In Ac. 7:23 (→ VI, 294, 20 ff.) we read very gen. of the "maturing" (ἐπληροῦτο) of a span of time (→ 582, 13 f.; 586, 7 f.; 593, 12 f.), while Lk. 1:57 is connected with the idea of the end of a fixed period (→ VI, 130, 25 ff.) and the reaching of a term. Typical gen. are used with χρόνος in Ac. 17:30 (→ 590, 9 ff.; I, 118, 5 f.); 1 Pt. 1:17 (→ 592, 21 ff.; V, 852, 4 ff.). Ac. 7:17 ref. to the time when the promise of v. 5, 7 was fulfilled. χρόνος has more of the sense of a "point of time" in Ac. 1:6. χρόνος is relatively most common in 1 Pt. (4 times) and Ac. (17 times), but

---

[57] This combination comes to expression in, e.g., Da. 2:21: God changes times and seasons (→ 586, 19), deposing kings and setting them up. This verse is not referring specifically to the events of the last time.

[58] "End of the times" means end of the cosmic time(s) that God has ordained, 4 Esr. 3:14; 12:9, cf. 14:5, not the end of time as such.

[59] For the NT cf. Delling, 50-54 with bibl.

[60] The time (duration) of human life is a στιγμή, M. Ant., II, 17, 1.

[61] Cf. ὅλον τὸν χρόνον ὃν ἐποιήσαμεν ἐνταῦθα, Paral. Jerem. 7:29.

different conclusions may be drawn in evaluation of the statistical findings. The use of χρόνος in Ac. often shows that within certain limits the author is trying to present a connected historical narrative.

II. Specific Sayings.

In the formal sense the NT, too, makes no basic statements about time, [62] Rev. 10:6 does not mean that time itself comes to an end → IV, 824, 7 f. [63] All that is meant is that the judgment of God will not be delayed any longer, → VIII, 59, 21 ff., cf. οὐ χρονίσει in Hb. 10:37 quoting Hab. 2:3. [64] Behind Rev. 6:11 ἔτι χρόνον μικρόν, as behind 10:6, there stands the Christian expectation that the eschatological events of judgment and salvation will be fulfilled as proclaimed. That Christians must await this is indicated in various parables: μετὰ ... πολὺν χρόνον (Mt. 25:19), χρόνους ἱκανούς (Lk. 20:9); the bridegroom or the Lord delays χρονίζει (Mt. 25:5; 24:48 and par.). [65] God in His ἐξουσία has established the times [66] of the events before the end (Ac. 1:7, cf. Mk. 13:32 and par. → ὥρα) and no detailed information can be given about them (Ac. 1:7; 1 Th. 5:1 [67] → 590, 7 ff.). In this connection Paul issues the warning that the day of the Lord (→ II, 952, 7 ff.) will come suddenly, 1 Th. 5:2-4. It can be said emphatically that Jesus has been manifested at the end of the times, 1 Pt. 1:20. [68] The point here is that the time of God's eschatological action has come in Christ. Gl. 4:4 is to the same effect. Time reaches its fulness with the coming of the Son → VI, 305, 17 ff. In Jd. 18 the last time is the time immediately before the end in the strict sense; we are conscious of being in this time. The time which still remains to Christians in the earthly body τὸν ἐπίλοιπον ἐν σαρκὶ ... χρόνον (1 Pt. 4:2 f.) is paraenetically set in juxtaposition with the παρεληλυθὼς χρόνος and is thus a time of alienation, 1 Pt. 1:17.

At three points in the Pauline corpus the expression χρόνοι αἰώνιοι denotes the distance in time between the present (emphatic νῦν in 2 Tm. 1:10; R. 16:26 → IV, 1113, 16 ff.) revelation (→ 4, 23 ff.) of salvation history in Christ and the plan of this salvation history as it was conceived or expressed by God. In 2 Tm. 1:9 f. (→ VIII, 166, 11 ff.; 167, 15 ff.) the gracious work of God that was actualised in Jesus Christ was already given to us "before eternal times," while the promise of eternal life that is given before unimaginable times is manifested in [69] the word of apostolic proclamation (Tt. 1:2 f.), the possibility of fulfilment first coming in Christ. R. 16:25 (→ VII, 524, n. 403) says that the mystery of salvation was not uttered

---

[62] Cf. Cullmann, 59 E. T., 60.

[63] μακάριος ... χρόνος awaits him who suffers for his obedience in the present times. 2 Cl., 19, 4. On God's eternity in Rev. → II, 398, 14 ff.

[64] On χρονίζω in Hab. 2:3 and elsewhere cf. Strobel, op. cit. (→ n. 56), 161-170. Cf. בהמשך עליהם הקץ האחרון "when the last time comes upon them" in 1 QpHab 7:12 and ταχὺ ἔρχεται καὶ οὐ χρονιεῖ in Is. 13:22 LXX.

[65] Bibl. E. Grässer, "Das Problem d. Parusieverzögerung in d. synpt. Ev. u. in d. Ag.," ZNW Beih., 22² (1960); for a different view cf. Kümmel, 47-57 and Strobel, op. cit. (→ n. 56), on Mt. 24 f. v. 207-222, 233-254.

[66] This is the sense of χρόνοι with καιροί in Ac. 1:7; 1 Th. 5:1; on καιροί → III, 461, 16 ff. καιροί, too, can mean spans of time in apoc. (→ III, 459, 19 ff.), which can use the two terms synon.

[67] 1 Th. 5:1 seems to be the answer to a question raised in the Thessalonian church; on περί → VI, 54, 12 ff.

[68] Phrases from Jewish apoc. are adopted here, 4 Esr. 3:14; 12:9, cf. 9:5 f. (→ n. 58).

[69] This relation is in view even though it is not expressed syntactically.

(in) [70] eternal times, which means that the plan of salvation was conceived before unimaginable times, cf. Col. 1:26. [71] The spacing of time within the word of OT revelation — the word given through David in Ps. 95:7 f. comes "so long a time" after Nu. 14:22 f. [72] — is noted in Hb. 4:7.

D. The Post-Apostolic Fathers.

Here χρόνος means esp. a "stretch of time" (→ 582, 13 ff.), the time of the Lord's absence up to the *parousia*, Herm. s., 5, 5, 3. The duration of a life of pleasure is short whereas that of punishment is long, 6, 4, 4, ὀλίγον χρόνον, "a short time," 2 Cl., 19, 3, ἐν μικρῷ χρόνῳ, "in a short time," Ign. Eph., 5, 1, μετὰ χρόνον τινά, e.g., Herm. s., 5, 2, 5, χρόνον τινά "a certain length of time," 7, 2. τῷ χρόνῳ (with the) "length of time," 9, 26, 4, ἐκ τοῦ χρόνου, Mart. Pol., 22, 3. The whole time of faith is nothing worth without perseverance to the end, Did., 16, 2; Barn., 4, 9. χρόνος is the "set time" in 1 Cl., 25, 2; Herm. s., 6, 5, 2, both times with πληρόομαι. More general is the use in expressions like ἐν... τῷ πρόσθεν χρόνῳ, Dg., 9, 6, cf. 9, 1 or ἐν παντὶ... χρόνῳ, "in every time," Did., 14, 3. The plur. (→ 582, 2 ff.) may also ref. to "stretches of time," Herm. s., 6, 5, 1 or "dates" (→ 582, 19 ff.). But we also read more gen. of "earlier times," τοῖς προτέροις χρόνοις, Herm. s., 9, 20, 4, ἐξ ἀρχαίων... χρόνων, i.e., of the founding of the community, Pol., 1, 2, v. "in our times," Mart. Pol., 16, 2, cf. 2 Cl., 19, 4. The πολλοὶ χρόνοι of 1 Cl., 44, 3 embrace only a few decades but those of 42, 5 are the time from the writing of Is. 60:17. The τὰς ἀναγραφὰς τῶν χρόνων of 1 Cl., 25, 5 are the "chronicle(s)" of pagan priests → 587, 20 f.

Delling

ψάλλω	→ VIII, 490, 36 ff.
ψαλμός	→ VIII, 491, 4 ff.
ψευδάδελφος	→ I, 144, 1 ff.
ψευδαπόστολος	→ I, 445, 18 ff.
ψευδοδιδάσκαλος	→ II 160, 3 ff.
ψευδόμαρτυς	→ IV, 513, 1 ff.
ψευδομαρτυρέω	→ IV, 514, 11 ff.
ψευδομαρτυρία	→ IV, 514, 17 ff.
ψευδοπροφήτης	→ VI, 781, 2 ff.

---

[70] Acc. to Bl.-Debr. § 200 the temporal dat. in the NT usually denotes a point of time, not a space of time, but → 582, 6 f. and Wis. 7:2 (Job 14:11? on Job 32:6 → 585, 27). We find 19 instances of ἐν χρόνῳ or ἐν χρόνοις in the LXX, usually as a note of time. Perhaps, then, we should see here a dat. of participation.

[71] Cf. also Eph. 3:5; 1 Pt. 1:20; 1 C. 2:7. We have here a common contrast which is perhaps pre-Pauline → 4, 28 ff.

[72] Cf. Wnd. Hb., *ad loc.*: "from Moses to David."

ψεῦδος, ψεύδομαι, ψευδής,
ψεῦσμα, ψεύστης, ἀψευδής,
ἄψευστος

A. Profane Greek.

1. Usage.

The derivation of the root is uncertain. [1] The primary meaning is "false" in the broad sense, Hom. Il., 2, 349, breach of an agreement, 4, 235, obj. false assertion, 5, 635, error, 10, 534, a deliberately false statement, 23, 576. [2] a. The act. verb (Attic, rare in prose) means "to deceive," with acc. ψεύδει γὰρ ἡ 'πίνοια τὴν γνώμην, Soph. Ant., 389, cf. Oed. Col., 628, with gen. "to deceive" about something μὴ ψεῦσον, [3] ὦ Ζεῦ, τῆς ἐπιούσης ἐλπίδος, Aristoph. Thes., 870, pass. "to be deceived," "to deceive oneself," par. ἀμαθῆ εἶναι, Plat. Resp., II, 382b, with acc. Xenoph. An., 8, 11, with dat. γνώμῃ, Hdt., VII,

ψεῦδος κτλ. Bibl.: General → I, 233 (Bibl. A.); A. Kern, *Die Lüge* (1930); H. v. Soden, "Was ist Wahrheit?" *Urchr. u. Gesch.*, I (1951), 1-24; M. Heidegger, *Plat. Lehre v. der Wahrheit*[2] (1954); H. Blumenberg, "Licht als Metapher d. Wahrheit," *Stud. Generale*, 10 (1957), 432-447; O. F. Bollnow, *Wesen u. Wandel d. Tugenden* (1958), 135-154; E. Fuchs/G. Gawlick, Art. "Wahrheit," in RGG[3], VI, 1515-1525; W. Kamlah, "Der moderne Wahrheitsbegriff," *Festschr. G. Krüger* (1962), 107-130; H. G. Gadamer, *Wahrheit u. Methode*[2] (1965); J. Barr, *The Semantics of Biblical Language* (1961). On A.: L. Schmidt, *Die Ethik der Alten Griechen*, II (1882), 403-414; R. Hirzel, "Was war die Wahrheit f. d. Griechen?" *Rede zur Feier d. akad. Preisverteilung am 24. 6. 1905* (1905); M. Wittmann, *Die Ethik d. Aristot.* (1920), 205; R. Schottlaender, "Die Lüge in d. Ethik d. griech.-röm. Philosophie" in O. Lipmann/P. Plaut, *Die Lüge in psychologischer, philosophischer, juristischer, pädagogischer, historischer, soziologischer, sprach- u. literaturwissenschaftlicher u. entwicklungsgeschichtlicher Betrachtung* (1927), 98-121; W. S. Maćkowiak, *Die ethische Beurteilung d. Notlüge in d. altheidnischen, patristischen, scholastischen u. neueren Zeit*, Diss. Fribourg (1933); J. Stelzenberger, *Die Beziehung d. frühchr. Sittenlehre z. Ethik d. Stoa* (1933), 297-300; W. Luther, *"Wahrheit" u. "Lüge" im ältesten Griechentum*, Diss. Göttingen (1935); P. Wilpert, "Zum aristot. Wahrheitsbegriff," *Philosophisches Jbch.*, 53 (1940), 3-16; also "Die Wahrhaftigkeit in d. aristot. Ethik," ibid., 324-338; E. Wolf, *Griech. Rechtsdenken*, I (1950), 240 and 293; II (1952), 240, 288 and 294; K. Deichgräber, *Der listensinnende Trug d. Gottes* (1952), 108-141; J. Kätzler, ψεῦδος, δόλος, μηχάνημα in d. griech. Tragödie, Diss. Tübingen (1959); E. Heitsch, "Die nichtphilosophische ἀλήθεια," *Herm.*, 90 (1962), 24-33; G. Müller, "Die Wahrhaftigkeitspflicht u. d. Problematik d. Lüge," *Freiburger Theol. Stud.*, 78 (1962), 321-330; H. Frisk, "'Wahrheit' u. 'Lüge' in d. idg. Sprachen," *Kleine Schriften z. Indogermanistik u. griech. Wortkunde, Stud. Graeca et Lat. Gothoburgensia*, 21 (1966), 1-33. On B.: M. Wiener, "Wahrhaftigkeit u. Lüge in d. isr.-jüd. Religion" in O. Lipmann/P. Plaut, op. cit. (under A.), 15-31; M. A. Klopfenstein, *Die Lüge nach d. AT* (1964). On D.: F. Büchsel, *Der Begriff d. Wahrheit in d. Ev. u. den Briefen d. Joh.* (1911); F. M. Schindler, "Die Lüge in d. patristischen Lit.," *Festschr. A. Ehrhard* (1922), 421-433; H. Mulert, "Die Bewertung d. Lüge in d. Ethik d. NT u. des evangelischen Christentums" in O. Lipmann/P. Plaut, op. cit. (under A.), 32-52; C. H. Dodd, *The Interpretation of the Fourth Gospel* (1953), passim; also *The Bible and the Greeks*[2] (1954), Index s.v: ψευδής, ψεῦδος; A. Böhlig, "Mysterion u. Wahrheit," *Arbeiten z. Gesch. d. späteren Judt. u. d. Urchr.*, 6 (1968), 3-40; J. Blank, "Der joh. Wahrheitsbegriff," BZ, NF, 7 (1963), 163-173; S. Aalen, "'Truth,' a Key Word in St. John's Gospel," *Studia Evangelica*, II, TU, 87 (1964), 3-24; R. Bultmann, "Untersuchungen z. Joh.-Ev.," *Exegetica* (1967), 124-197; K. H. Schelkle, *Theol. d. NT*, III (1970), 266-283.

[1] Hofmann, s.v. Frisk, s.v. ref. to Arm. *sut* "lie," "lying" and Slavic cognates. Other forms are ψυδρός "lying" and ψύθος "lie."

[2] Luther, 80 f.

[3] These words are a parody of Soph. Fr., 453 (TGF, 240), v. Schwyzer, II, 343.

9 γ, with gen. [4] ἐψεῦσθαι τῆς ἀληθείας, Plat. Resp., III, 413a, ἐψευσμένοι γνώμης, "to be deceived in their opinion," Hdt., VIII, 40, 1, ἐψεῦσθαι ἑαυτῶν opp. εἰδέναι ἑαυτούς, Xenoph. Mem., IV, 2, 26, cf. Plat. Ap., 22d, mostly mid. [5] "to speak falsely," "to play" τοῖς λόγοις καὶ τοῖς ἔργοις, Plut. Apophth. Philippus, 7 (II, 177e), [6] though only the context and not the term itself shows whether this is intentional or not, cf. Xenoph. Mem., IV, 2, 19 f., with part. in the sense "to say what is false," Hes. Op., 283, intr. "to lie" ψεύσομαι, ἦ ἔτυμον ἐρέω; "Do I err or do I say the truth?" Hom. Il., 10, 534, cf. Aesch. Ag., 1208, trans. "to lie to," "to deceive," [7] Xenoph. Hist. Graec., III, 1, 25; An., I, 3, 10 (with double acc.), cf. ὅρκια ψεύσασθαι, "to break treaties," Hom. Il., 7, 351 f., τὴν ξυμμαχίαν Thuc., V, 83, 4. γάμους ψεύσασθαι, Eur. Ba., 31 and 245. ψεῦσμα ἐψευσμένους, Plat. Men., 71d, with inf. "to feign," Plut. De garrulitate, 9 (II, 506d), with prep. to denote the pers. πρός τινα, Xenoph. An., I, 3, 5, κατά τινος, Plat. Euthyd., 284a, to denote the content ἀμφί, Pind. Olymp., 13, 52, περί, Plat. Prot., 347a. b. The noun ψεῦδος [8] means "what is untrue," "deceit," "falsehood," "lying," "lie," Hom. Od., 3, 20; Soph. El., 1220; whether in the obj. or the subj. sense is open as in the case of the verb. [9] This leads on to the use in logic on the one side and in ethics on the other → lines 32 ff. c. The adj. ψευδής [10] means trans. "deceiving," of persons in Thuc., IV, 27, 4, dreams in Eur. Iph. Taur., 569, oracles in Luc. Alex., 43, and in the pass. "deceived," Eur. Iph. Aul., 852, intr. "untrue," "false," "fabricated," τρέπεται ἐπὶ ψευδέα ὁδόν, Hdt., I, 117, 2. [11] The adv. also means "falsely," Eur. Iph. Taur., 1309 vl., Plat. Phileb., 40d, "mistakenly," Polyb., 5, 110, 7. d. ἀψευδής, common in Plat., means "without deception," "true," of the gods: Apollo is μάντις ἀψευδής, Aesch. Choeph., 559; Plat. Resp., II, 382e, of men: he who is not deceived, Plat. Theaet., 160d, or does not deceive, Plat. Hi., II, 369c. e. A late and synon. word is ἄψευστος, of the νόμος, Plut. De Artaxerxe, 28 (I, 1025e). f. ψεύστης is the "liar," Hom. Il., 24, 261, also adj., Hdt., VII, 209, 5, [12] with gen.: ὧν... ψεῦσται φανούμεθα, Soph. Ant., 1194 f. g. ψεῦσμα means "untruth," "deception," "lie," Plat. Men., 71d; Luc. Tim., 55; Philops., 240.

2. Meaning.

Lying cannot be viewed merely as the opposite of truth. [13] Basic to the general and philosophical use of the word group is the twofold sense, namely, objective and subjective appearance, untruth as non-being and error as a false judgment of reality. [14] The norm of the ethical assessment of lying is the firm bond between ἀλήθεια and δίκη. [15] At issue is the divinely protected order of the world.

---

[4] Schwyzer, II, 93.

[5] This is perhaps an intensive mid., *ibid.*, II, 232.

[6] On the constr. with the dat. cf. Job 34:6; Jer. 5:12; Ac. 5:4, also with acc. 5:3, cf. Bl.-Debr. § 187, 4.

[7] Cf. also Is. 57:11; Job 8:18.

[8] Acc. to Frisk, 19 the noun ψεῦδος, not the adj. ψευδής, is often found with ἀληθής and other adj., cf. Plat. Ap., 34e; Crat., 385c, but → n. 11.

[9] ψεῦδος λέγειν is not synon. with ψεύδεσθαι, cf. Philo Det. Pot. Ins., 58: It is possible ψεῦδος λέγειν... μὴ ψευδόμενον, Sext. Emp. Math., VII, 44.

[10] The sing. neut. is not found in early writings.

[11] Opp. ἀληθής, Plat. Crat., 385b, cf. ὀρθὴ ἢ ψευδής, Theaet., 161d, for logic cf. Aristot. Topica, VIII, 12, p. 162b, 3-30.

[12] Cf. also Anth. Pal., 7, 275: Κρῆτες ὅπου ψεῦσται καὶ Διὸς ἔστι τάφος "Where the Cretans are liars and Zeus has a tomb among them."

[13] "The terms truth and lie are usually taken to be logically contradictory but in relation to linguistic modes of expression (in the Indo-Eur. languages) they are by no means par. A secondary abstract noun serves to express truth while a primary verbal noun usually expresses falsehood. A lie is an activity or the result of an activity but truth is always present as an abstraction denoting something independent of any activity," Frisk, 30 f.

[14] Naturally one may ask whether and how the twofoldness is related to the Greek understanding of the world.

[15] Hirzel, 7. On the legal aspects cf. Luther, 137 f.

Hence the worst lie is perjury, Heracl. Fr., 28 (Diels, I, 157); Plat. Leg., XI, 937b c; Aristot. Eth. Nic., V, 5, p. 1131a, 7. Subj. values enter in here. [16] Lying, esp. direct lying against others, [17] i.e., "calumniation" διαβολή, is alien to the good man, Chaeremon Fr., 27 (TGF, 789), cf. Theogn., 1, 607 ff. (Diehl[3], II, 39). [18] It deprives of honour and is an assault on human dignity, Plat. Gorg., 525a; Resp., VII, 535e; III, 414c; Leg., V, 730c; Aristot. Eth. Nic., IV, 13, p. 1127a, 28 f. The aristocratic order demands esp. that one should not deceive those to whom one owes respect, Plat. Leg., XI, 917a. On the other hand the gods deceive (δόλος) men, Hom. Il., 15, 14 f., cf. 22, 15. [19] Naturally popular reasons are given for not lying: "No one believes the man who once lies," Diog. L., V, 17 (attributed to Aristot.).

These norms leave scope for deception, as in the affirmation of one who is intellectually superior, cf. Hom. Od., 9, 19 and Il., 9, 313. Thus Odysseus is no swindler, Od., 11, 363 ff. Lies for social or political reasons are also permissible (friendship or the state) when some aim or need requires, Plat. Resp., I, 331b, 334b; Xenoph. Cyrop., I, 6, 28-35; Thuc., III, 43, 2, cf. Aesch. Fr., 302 (TGF, 94): ψευδῶν δὲ καιρὸν ἔσθ' ὅπου τιμᾷ θεός. [20] The Sophists justify purposeful lying theoretically. [21] Deception is also allowed in art. [22] Hes. Theog., 27 f. first discussed the problem of the poet or the muse narrating what is true and false. In tragedy deceit and cunning are a way of effecting just punishment, cf., e.g., Aesch. Choeph., 554-564 and Soph. El., 56-61. This is not an ethical problem. The situation is different in Soph. Phil., where the magnanimous nature of the son of Achilles can no longer tolerate the deceit which Odysseus practises to change the fate of the army in the siege of Troy, cf., e.g., 902 f. [23]

Historians contrast the truth of their accounts with the fictions of the poets, [24] Ephorus of Kyme Fr., 8 (FGrHist, II, A 38, 31-39). They defend themselves against lying colleagues, Jos. Ap., 1, 3 or against emotional distortion. History is to be presented *sine ira et studio*, cf. Jos. Bell., 1, 2; Ant., 20, 154-7; Dion. Hal., 1, 6, 5; Luc. Quomodo historia conscribenda sit, 38 f., cf. 7 and 9. Assurances of truth and reliability are offered in the prooem. of historians, Diod. S., 1, 2, 7; 1, 4, 4 f.; Jos. Ant., 1, 4; Bell., 1, 2; Lk. 1:1-4. [25]

3. The Word Group in Philosophy.

The meaning of ψευδ- opens up two themes: a. the determining of what is true and false in logic, and b. the determining of what is (1) truth and falsehood [26] and (2) truth-

---

[16] Obj. and subj. norms intersect. Lying is hated by both gods and men, Hom. Il., 9, 312 f.; Plat. Resp., II, 382; Schmidt, 405.

[17] On the usage of Hes. cf. Luther, 135; cf. also Aristot. Eth. Nic., IV, 7, 13, p. 1127b, 5.

[18] Schmidt, 405; on Hom. cf. Müller, 329 f.

[19] Cf. Luther, 85 f.

[20] On Socrates cf. Xenoph. Mem., IV, 2, 14-18; Müller, 330-4; Schottlaender, 116.

[21] On the doctrine of δικαία ἀπάτη cf. Gorg. Fr., 23 (Diels, II, 305 f.); Dialexeis, 3, 2 f. (II, 410, 8 ff.), cf. W. Nestle, *Vom Mythos zum Logos* (1940), 318-326. On the lie of necessity cf. Maćkowiak, 47-58. A charming speech of Darius under Sophist influence permits this, Hdt., III, 72, 2-5. cf. I, 138, 1: αἴσχιστον δὲ αὐτοῖσι (sc. the Persians) τὸ ψεύδεσθαι νενόμισται, cf. 136, 2.

[22] On the question of poetic truth cf. Plat. Resp., II, 377a-378e; III, 390a-392c; Aristot. Poet., 24, p. 1460a, 5-36. Luc.'s true histories are a climax. On the background — the connection between lying and fate and the insight into universal order in deceptive speech — cf. K. Reinhardt, *Sophokles*[3] (1947), Index *s.v.* "Trugreden," "Verhüllung."

[23] On this whole subject cf. Kätzler, 74-83.

[24] Schottlaender, 106-8.

[25] Cf. esp. Luc. Quomodo historia conscribenda sit, 7, 9 and 38, and on the history of this theme, which came into historical writing from the time of Hecataeus of Miletus Fr., 1a (FGrHist, IA, 7 f.), cf. G. Avenarius, *Luc. Schrift z. Geschichtsschreibung* (1956), 16-22, 40-46.

[26] Familiar is the "liar" of Eubulides in Diog. L., II, 108, who offers a supposedly logical proof that lying is not possible, cf. A. Rüstow, *Der Lügner*, Diss. Erlangen (1910), 40.

fulness and falsehood in ethics. [27] Gorgias deals with the twofold problem in his doctrine of δικαία ἀπάτη, cf. Dialexeis, 3, 2 (Diels, II, 410, 8 f.); Plat. Resp., I, 334a-335e. The discovery that sense perceptions may deceive is normative in epistemology. [28] But this does not stand up to logical analysis → lines 10 ff. In Plat., esp. in Hi. II περὶ τοῦ ψεύδους, the ethical question becomes important in the criticism of the Sophists, [29] esp. as regards the matter of a new theoretical foundation. Basic is the understanding of truth in equation with reality and being, Plat. Soph., 240b, cf. the argument in 263a-264b. Speech is true when it says of things what they are, Crat., 385b. [30]

In Aristot. the logical question of untruth takes precedence of the ontological question. [31] Perception is true; thinking may be wrong. The source of error is the synthesis which forms judgments and concepts out of ideas, An., III, 6. p. 430a, 27-430b, 1. [32] In ethics lying is defined in terms of truthfulness. Within the ideal of μεγαλοψυχία [33] this is the mean between the self-inflation of the ἀλαζών and the self-deflation of the εἴρων "hypocrite." [34] Important is the introduction of a new standpoint, purpose. A δόξα is true or false but not good or bad, for προαίρεσις is ordered to the good and the bad, Eth. Nic., III, 4, p. 1111b, 4 ff. A decisive step is thus taken in ethical analysis. Truthfulness becomes an autonomous ἀρετή and not a mere ἕξις. [35]

B. The Old Testament.

1. Hebrew Usage.

Hbr. equivalents to the group in the LXX [36] are a. כּזב [37] which is first a verbal lie. The verb means q "to lie," Ps. 116:11, ni "to be a liar," Prv. 30:6, "to deceive," Job 41:1, here intr. of hope, hi "to give the lie to," Job 24:25, mostly pi "to lie," Nu. 23:19. [38] The noun כָּזָב means "deception," "lie," דִּבֶּר כָזָב Ju. 16:10, 13, also "that which deceives," Ps. 5:6, the "vanity" of man, Ps. 62:9. [39] b. כחשׁ as a verb means "not to say that..." and "to say that... not...," [40] cf. Jos. 7:11 with Gn. 18:15 and ni "to belie oneself," "to

---

[27] The first def. of lying come incidentally in the discussion of untruth. The question of the nature of the true and the false is brought into prominence with the debate between the Sophists and Socrates, Schottlaender, 102.

[28] Πυθαγόρας Ἐμπεδοκλῆς Ξενοφάνης Παρμενίδης... Ἀναξαγόρας Δημόκριτος... (sc. "teach") ψευδεῖς εἶναι τὰς αἰσθήσεις, Aetius De placitis reliquiae, IV, 9, 1 (ed. H. Diels, Doxographi Graeci [1879], 396), cf. Democr. in Sext. Emp. Math, VIII, 6. On Parm. Schottlaender, 99 f. notes that logical theory takes on an ethical tone.

[29] Socrates defends himself against false accusers in Plat. Ap., 17 f. On the intentional and non-intentional lie cf. Hi. II, 370e. Plat. Euthyd., 283e-284b attempts a def. in answer to the false view of contemporaries that there can be no lie, Schottlaender, 102.

[30] Error can arise when a δόξα connects images and originals wrongly, Theaet., 194a-195a. Sensations can be true or false, Phileb., 36c-38a. On Aristot. → lines 9-17.

[31] Cf. Wilpert Wahrheitsbegriff, 6 f. Aristot. Metaph., 3, 7, p. 1011b, 26 f. gives a def.

[32] On the problems of Metaph., 5, 4, p. 1027b, 17-1028a, 6 and 8, p. 1045b, 27-1052a, 11 cf. Wilpert Wahrheitsbegriff, 7-13; W. Jaeger, Aristoteles² (1955), 211-7.

[33] Wittmann, 196-206; W. Jaeger, "Der Grossgesinnte," Die Antike, 7 (1931), 97-105.

[34] On the systematic ranking of truth under natural virtues cf. Eth. Nic., IV, 7 f., esp. p. 1127a, 13-1127b, 32; Wilpert Wahrhaftigkeit, 325 and 336.

[35] Wilpert Wahrhaftigkeit, 333.

[36] In frequency the order is ψευδής, ψεῦδος, ψεύδομαι.

[37] Klopfenstein, 176-254. The verb and noun are usually transl. by forms of ψευδ- in the LXX, but we sometimes find forms of μαται- and other terms.

[38] A special instance is the stream that does not deceive in Is. 58:11, cf. אַכְזָב "deceitful," Mi. 1:14; Jer. 15:18, also Job 6:15; the metaphor is used again in 1 QSb 1:4; Klopfenstein, 243-252.

[39] The LXX moralises, cf. also Is. 28:15.

[40] Klopfenstein, 254-297, although he links the group too closely to sacral and secular penal law.

feign surrender," Dt. 33:29, [41] cf. hitp 2 S. 22:45, pi "to lie," "to deny," Gn. 18:15; Job 8:18; Lv. 5:21 f. Jer. 5:12; Jos. 24:27 speak of denying God. The noun means "leanness" in Job 16:8, "deceit," "lie" in Hos. 7:3; 10:13; 12:1, cf. also the prophetic accusation in Na. 3:1. c. קֶשׁ is rare as a verb. The noun שֶׁקֶר, esp. in Jer. and Ps., means "false witness," as in the Decalogue, Ex. 20:16, unfaithfulness to God or neighbour, cf. the expression "deceitful right hand" in Ps. 144:8, 11. [42] In the Ps. the term occurs mostly in individual songs of complaint or thanksgiving, as an interjection in Jer. 37:14; 2 K. 9:12. d. כחד "to hide" is transl. ψεύδομαι in Job 6:10; 27:11, cf. ברא in Neh. 6:8. Materially, in view of the Qumran findings, we may compare עוֹלָה, [43] מרמה, שׁוא, Aram. the group רגל.

2. Meaning. [44]

Three spheres may be differentiated. Legally the worst offence against truth is perjury, Ex. 20:16 par. Dt. 5:20. [45] Slander (Ps. 15:3) is also a legal matter, and so is lying in relation to that which is committed to one's keeping, Lv. 6:2 f. כחשׁ. Lying is a transgression because Yahweh is the protector of the right. Prv. 6:16-19 lists six or seven things that Yahweh hates, and these include: "He who scatters lies as false witness," v. 19. Perjury is a particularly heinous offence because the lie is in Yahweh's name. A curse thus rests on the man who commits it, Zech. 5:3 f.

In wisdom [46] and everyday morality (Prv. 30:8) lying and liars are generally condemned (Ps. 4:2; 62:4). Wisdom, however, works out refined distinctions between calumniation, action, and silence, Prv. 6:12-15; 20:17 f.; 26:23-28; Sir. 5:14; 7:12 f. [47] On the margin is recognition of the lie of necessity, Gn. 12:13; Jer. 38:24-27. [48] A typical argument of wisdom is that lying is folly (Prv. 17:7). It is futile to try to heap up treasures by means of a false tongue, Prv. 21:6. Wisdom saves the suffering righteous and convicts opponents, Wis. 10:14; Sus. 45-64. Yahweh and fear of Him are the guarantee. The connection between ethics and the concept of God is not just external. There are lies against God Himself, Ps. 78:36. His law must be kept pure, Prv. 30:5-10. The charge against lying attains prophetic intensity in Hos. 7:1, 3, 13; 10:13; Mi. 6:12. [49]

Along with the legal sphere and that of wisdom, in which Yahweh is the protector of right and truth, we also find a specifically religious sphere with many themes of its own, e.g., unfaithfulness against God, or apostasy to lying gods, or false prophecy. The three spheres are united by the common presupposition that God does not

---

[41] LXX transl. ψεύσονταί σε οἱ ἐχθροί σου.

[42] Klopfenstein, 2-176. The group is a tt. for breaking agreements, 8 etc.; LXX uses forms of ψευδ-, ἀδικ- and ἀνομ- for it, cf. Gn. 21:23; Lv. 19:11; Ps. 44:17; 89:34. There is ref. to conduct here as well as the verbal lie.

[43] In Zeph. 3:13 עוֹלָה is transl. by ἀδικία, כָּזָב by μάταια, and לְשׁוֹן תַּרְמִית by γλῶσσα δολία, cf. Job 6:29 f.; 13:7; 1 QS 4:17-25.

[44] Klopfenstein, 321 attempts a clear distinction, assigning שֶׁקֶר to contract law, כחש to sacral and secular penal law, and כזב to everyday life. But the terms merge into one another.

[45] οὐ ψευδομαρτυρήσεις κατὰ τοῦ πλησίον σου μαρτυρίαν ψευδῆ, Dt. 5:20.

[46] Cf. Egypt. stories about truth and falsehood, S. Schott, Altägypt. Liebeslieder[2] (1950), 205-8; G. Roeder, "Mythen u. Legenden um ägypt. Gottheiten u. Pharaonen," Die ägypt. Religion in Texten u. Bildern, II (1960), 74-84.

[47] Cf. Eichr. Theol. AT, II/III, 235.

[48] On discussion cf. G. v. Rad, Das erste Buch Mose, AT Deutsch, 2/4[7] (1964), ad loc.; J. Hempel, "Das Ethos d. AT," ZAW Beih., 67[2] (1964), 36; A. Weiser, Das Buch d. Propheten Jer., AT Deutsch, 20/21[6] (1969), ad loc.

[49] Cf. on the other hand the prophecy in Zeph. 3:13.

deceive, Ps. 89. Unfaithfulness against God recurs repeatedly, cf. Am. 2:4; [50] Ps. 40:4. The prophet complains that lies are spoken about God, Hos. 7:13. He is denied by idol worship, Job 31:28. The denial is not just a negative thing; it is an active attitude: "Because thou hast denied me, and trusted in falsehood...," Jer. 13:25, cf. Is. 59:13. Idols are deceitful, Is. 44:20. This thought is more broadly developed in the polemical works of Hellenistic Judaism. It is the basic concept in the attack on images, which are dead and therefore vain and deceitful. Images can be directly described as ψευδεῖς, 2 Ch. 30:14 LXX. Their powerlessness is compared with the might of Yahweh, Jer. 16:19. Deceit and deception are connected with idolatry, Is. 57:4 ff.; Jer. 3:23; 13:25.

Prophetic literature is full of the fight against false prophecy → VI, 809, 13 ff. [51] This prophecy is especially reprehensible because it appeals to Yahweh, Ez. 13:6 f. Yahweh Himself, however, can send a lying spirit into the prophets in order to cause blindness, 1 K. 22:22 f. [52] In practice the appeal to Yahweh is an appeal to inspiration, Jer. 23:32. In the age of salvation the deception of false prophets will end, Zech. 13:2-6. The inner relation between false prophecy and apostasy is brought to light in Ez. 13:19. [53] The criteria of differentiation, especially that of the alien word, are worked out most sharply, and with the greatest personal intensity, in Jer., cf. 14:14 f.; 20:6; 23:17 ff. etc.

C. Judaism.

1. Qumran. [54]

בדא does not occur. We find כחד once and כחש twice, as noun in a list in 1 QS 4:9; 10:22; כזב occurs twice as verb and is more common as noun, as is also שׁקר. [55] Various answers have been given to the question of foreign (Persian) influence. [56] The linking of ethical dualism to two spirits is at least common to Parseeism and one layer of the Qumran texts, 1 QS 3:17 - 4:14 and Yasna, 30, 3-6, [57] and it cannot be traced back to the OT or to internal development within Judaism. The sphere qualifies man or his acts abs., with no psychological or ethical gradations. In the religion of Zoroaster lying expresses the negative side of ethical dualism. [58] Truth and lying may be equated with salvation and perdition, Yasna, 33, 2; 46, 6. [59] In Parseeism as in the Scrolls eschatology

---

[50] Acc. to A. Weiser, *Das Buch d. zwölf kl. Propheten*, I, *AT Deutsch*, 245 (1967), ad loc. the saying is close to Deuteronomistic piety. LXX: καὶ ἐπλάνησεν αὐτοὺς τὰ μάταια (related then to idols) αὐτῶν.

[51] E. Osswald, "Falsche Prophetie im AT," *Sammlung gemeinverständlicher Vorträge u. Schriften aus dem Gebiet d. Theol. u. Religionsgesch.*, 237 (1962).

[52] Mi. 2:11: "He who practises lying and deception (שֶׁקֶר, כָּזָב), shall be the prophet of this people."

[53] On the attack on lying oracles and images cf. Hab. 2:18 and on this 1 QpHab 12:10 - 13:4.

[54] F. Nötscher, "Zur theol. Terminologie d. Qumran-Texte," *Bonner Bibl. Beiträge*, 10 (1956), 95 f.; H. Braun, "Spätjüd.-häret. u. frühchr. Radikalismus," I, *Beiträge z. histor. Theol.*, 24 (1957), Index, *s.v.* שׁקר, אמן, אמת, כזב, עולה.

[55] For a survey cf. S. Wibbing, "Die Tugend- u. Lasterkataloge im NT," ZNW Beih. 25 (1959), 92.

[56] Acc. to K. Elliger, "Stud. z. Hab.-Komm. vom Toten Meer," *Beiträge z. histor. Theol.*, 15 (1953), 285 it is "hard to say" whether we have foreign influence here; Nötscher, *op. cit.*, 86-92.

[57] Cf. W. Hinz, *Zarathustra* (1961), 169 f. → 317, n. 44; cf. K. G. Kuhn, "Die Sektenschr. u. d. iranische Religion," ZThK, 49 (1952), 296-316.

[58] H. Lommel, *Die Religion Zarathustras* (1930), 43, and more gen. 40-52.

[59] Cf. Hinz, *op. cit.*, 177 and 191.

is combined with decision, Yasna, 34, 4; [60] 1 QS 4:11-14. Undoubtedly, then, there seems to be a connection. But the precise wording of the Persian texts is lost in the Scrolls. [61] Different expressions are now used for the two opposing attitudes, 1 QS 4:9; 10:22. [62] The Test. XII also have a dualistic concept of decision, Test. A. 5:3. But here the thought is much more individual and psychological than in the Qumran texts, cf. the theme of Test. D. 1:3; 2:1, 4 etc., where θυμός is associated with ψεῦδος. [63] The positive ideal is ἁπλότης, Iss. 4.

2. Rabbinic Writings. [64]

There are hardly any characteristic features here. Naturally lying is condemned. Mockers, hypocrites, liars שקרים and calumniators will not see God, bSota, 42a, cf. Ps. 101:7. The common wisdom principle that "no one believes..." (→ 596, 9 f.) also occurs in the Rabb., cf. bSanh., 89b. Superstition is rejected; he who conjures up the dead is a liar, bBer., 59a. God has created all things in the world apart from the standard of lying שקר and falsehood שוא, cf. Pesikt. r., 24 (125b). [65]

3. Philo.

Philo often links ψευδής with δόξα. A false notion can concern God, Leg. All., I, 51, cf. manticism, Deus. Imm., 181 (Balaam), heathenism, Spec. Leg., I, 309, idolatry, Spec. Leg., I, 53, images, Gig., 59. As in the Test. XII (→ line 5 f.), the lie is connected with θυμός, Leg. All., III, 123 f., cf. 127. A specific point is the putting of ὅρασις before ἀκοή, the one being an ἀπατηλόν and the other an ἀψευδές, Fug., 208. Lying comes within the doctrine of virtue [66] and can be listed, Virt., 195 and 205. A link with the Jewish tradition is preserved when the doctrine of virtue is presented as an exposition of the Law, Spec. Leg., IV, 41 ff.; Decal., 138 f., cf. Decal., 6 with 86.

D. The New Testament.

1. The Synoptic Gospels and Acts.

The noun and adj. do not occur except at Ac. 6:13 (→ IV, 489, 34 ff.). The verb is found only at Mt. 5:11; Ac. 5:3 f.

The beatitude in Mt. 5:11 is distinguished from the other beatitudes by its compound nature and by the use of the second person (Lk. 6:22 f.). [67] ψευδόμενοι seems

---

[60] Cf. Hinz, op. cit., 180.

[61] H. Braun, Qumran u. d. NT, I (1966), 124 f., 297-300 shows what this means in assessment of the relation of the Johannine writings to Qumran, cf. Jn. 8:44; 1 Jn. 4:1-6. In the Qumran texts lying characterises the "man of lies" rather than the spirit of darkness, 1 QpHab 2:1f. etc.

[62] On the special problem of the "man of lies" in 1 QpHab 2:2 etc. cf. G. Jeremias "Der Lehrer d. Gerechtigkeit," Stud. z. Umwelt d. NT, 2 (1963), 77 f. → 30, 20 ff.

[63] Cf. the list in Test. B. 6:4 and the protestation of innocence in Iss. 7:4, and on this G. v. Rad, "Die Vorgeschichte d. Gattung v. 1 K. 13:4-7," Gesammelte Stud. z. AT³ (1965), 281-296. The spirit of lies in Test. R. 3:5 is only one of many spirits.

[64] Cf. Levy Wört., Jastrow, s.v. בדי, כרב, כרבא, כחש, כזב, דגל, דגלא, עול, שוא, שקר; Levy Chald. Wört., s.v. שקר, דגלותא.

[65] Str.-B., I, 813 f.

[66] Cf. the admonition to κάθαρσις in Mut. Nom., 240.

[67] Mt. 5:11 seems to have been revised acc. to the tradition, cf. 1 Pt. 3:14; Pol., 2, 3, v. H. T. Wrege, "Die Überlieferungsgesch. d. Bergpredigt," Wissenschaftl. Untersuchungen z. NT, 9 (1968), 267. The redactional combination of v. 10 and v. 12 means intensification in terms of the concept of the Church in Mt. Cf. also ἕνεκεν ἐμοῦ, δικαιοσύνη, v. G. Barth, "Das Gesetzesverständnis d. Evang. Mt." in G. Bornkamm / G. Barth / H. J. Held, Überlieferung u. Auslegung im Mt, Wissenschaftl. Monographien z. A u. NT, 1⁶ (1970), 131.

to be an interpretation introduced by Matthew himself. [68] The word is used in the absolute. [69] It goes with εἴπωσιν, not καθ᾽ ὑμῶν. Ac. 5:3 f. belongs to the sphere of sacral law. Offences against the Church and its sanctity are offences against the Holy Spirit and they automatically incur God's wrath.

2. The Pauline Corpus.

a. The catchword ψεύδομαι is used by Paul according to OT and secular models in the solemn protestation in R. 9:1 (cf. 2 C. 11:31; Gl. 1:20); [70] ἐν Χριστῷ brings out the character of the asseveration as witness. The reference to the conscience and the Holy Spirit is parallel. In R. 1:25 the noun ψεῦδος characterises the total conduct of sinful humanity in exchanging the truth of God (→ I, 243, 28 ff.) for a lie. Paul is not theorising on the origin of lying. One might think of the work of Satan, but according to R. 5:12 sin comes into the world through man. The dialectical concept of revelation also comes to expression in R. 3:4 (→ V, 426, 15 ff.). When the truth of God is manifested, every man becomes a liar, i.e., every man is shown to be a liar by revelation, cf. Ps. 116:11. The aim of the statement is to work out the absoluteness of grace as the act of grace, R. 5:20. When one sees that the saving event from God to man has the character of word, and is thus unilateral, and that in these respects it is irreversible, the absurdity of the objection that Paul dismisses is evident. [71]

b. In the Pauline antilegomena the group [72] occurs in connection with the predication of God as ἀψευδής in Hellenistic style, Tt. 1:2. [73] In an eschatological context it occurs also in 2 Th. 2:9, 11: The parousia of antichrist is accompanied by deceitful signs (→ VII, 260, 5 ff.). God sends the ἐνέργεια πλάνης εἰς τὸ πιστεῦσαι αὐτοὺς τῷ ψεύδει (par. ἀδικία, opp. ἀλήθεια). The group is also used in exhortation, e.g., Col. 3:9. We find it in a loose series of admonitions in Eph. 4:25 [74] and in a list of particularly serious offences in 1 Tm. 1:9 f. [75] We also find exhortation with a dualistic thrust in Jm. 3:14. [76]

---

[68] From the standpt. of textual criticism ψευδόμενοι is original, cf. J. Dupont, Les Béatitudes, I² (1958), 232-6.

[69] Pr.-Bauer, s.v. ψεύδομαι.

[70] Cf. also 1 Tm. 2:7; Job 6:28; 27:11; 4 Macc. 5:34; Plut. Comm. Not., 1 (II, 1059a); Luc. Verae Hist., I, 4. Materially cf. 1 Th. 2:5; Phil. 1:8; Luc. Philops., 271 Philo Decal., 86.

[71] Cf. also ψεῦσμα in R. 3:7.

[72] In a secular context cf. the quotation from Epimenides about the lying Cretans in Tt. 1:12, v. Dib. Past.⁴, ad loc. → n. 12.

[73] Cf. Job 36:4 Σ; Wis. 7:17; materially Hb. 6:18; 1 Cl., 27, 2; Orph. Fr., 168 (Kern); Aesch. Prom., 1032 f.; Philo Vit. Mos., I, 283, v. Dib. Past.⁴, ad loc.

[74] On the hortatory form cf. Dib. Gefbr., ad loc. and exc. on Eph. 5:14, also Dib. Jk., passim. It is worth noting that Eph. 4:25 adds a ref. to Christ's body to the quotation from Zech. 8:16. Cf. Sir. 7:12 f.; Test. R. 3:9; Test. D. 1:3; 2:4 etc.; Did., 2, 5; 5, 2.

[75] Cf. A. Vögtle, "Die Tugend- u. Lasterkataloge im NT," NTAbh, 16, 4/5 (1936), 96-106, 234-7.

[76] A. Meyer, "Das Rätsel d. Jk.," ZNW Beih., 10 (1930), 282 f. relates the passage to the name Naphthali (ζῆλος καὶ ἐριθεία). Pr.-Bauer, s.v. κατακαυχάομαι, Wnd. Jk., F. Mussner, Der Jk., Herders Theol. Komm. NT, 13, 1 (1964), ad loc. relate κατὰ τῆς ἀληθείας only to ψεύδομαι, Dib. Jk., ad loc. to κατακαυχάομαι and ψεύδομαι. The readings avoid the problem. The Jewish wisdom tradition may be discerned in the passage; on the connection between lying and folly → 598, 22 f.

3. John.

a. An antithesis of ἀλήθεια and ψεῦδος would have fitted in well with the style of John's Gospel, since ἀλήθεια is one of the leading concepts. [77] No such antithesis is found, however, until we come to Jn. 8:44 f. → V, 188, 3 ff. [78] Here the lie, like the truth, has a personal representative who again has his children. This is in analogy to Qumran → 599, 24 ff. But there is no direct historical or literary connection. [79] In accordance with the Johannine meaning of ἀλήθεια (→ I, 245, 24 ff.), the lie is not just error but an active contesting of the truth, i.e., unbelief → VI, 223, 19 ff. This much is clear, but in other respects the passage is obscure. The Jews do not descend from the devil but from the devil's father. This is obviously an *ad hoc* construction designed to work out the analogy. On the one side we find God, His Son, and the children of God, while on the other side we have the father of the devil the devil as antichrist rather than antigod, and the children. Naturally the father of the devil has no concrete function. [80] Murderer and liar go together as ζωή and ἀλήθεια do on the other side, Jn. 14:6. [81]

b. The use of the group in 1 Jn. is essentially hortatory. The demand that we do the truth and not lie is based on the statement that God is light. Doing the truth takes place in brotherhood, 1 Jn. 1:6; [82] 2:4; 4:20. Lying is also a denial of the confession, 2:21 f. [83] The liar is a historical manifestation of antichrist → 601, 20 ff. The style of protestation may be seen in 2:27 → line 18 f. The Paraclete concept of the Gospel (→ V, 803, 27 ff.; 811, 31 ff.) is now expressed in the language of 1 Jn. χρῖσμα is used instead of Paraclete or Spirit, for in 1 Jn., as distinct from Jn., the word "spirit" is equivocal. The confession includes admission of one's own sin. If we do not make this admission we oppose the truth of God and treat God as a liar, 1 Jn. 1:10; 5:10. [84]

c. Revelation polemicises against the Jews who falsely take this name to themselves (3:9) — the thought of the true people of God lies in the background — and also against false apostles (2:2 → VI, 669, n. 110). An eschatological perspective

---

[77] Blank, 163-173.

[78] Bultmann J., 226 f.

[79] The confrontation between the representatives is not worked out as such. John is closer to the average Jewish idea of the devil than to the Qumran concept of two spirits → n. 84. On the other hand the antithesis of truth and lying is not developed conceptually in Qumran → n. 61; Braun, 124 f.

[80] It hardly helps to take τοῦ πατρός in apposition in 8:44, since there seems to be a ref. to the father of the devil at the end of the v. Gnosis adopted the idea, v. Bau. J., *ad loc.*

[81] Lying is natural to the devil, Act. Thom. 143, cf. Lidz. Ginza R., 22, 22 f.: Satan is full of magic, deception, and seduction.

[82] R. Bultmann, "Analyse d. 1. J.," *Exegetica* (1967), 106 puts 1:6 in his reconstructed sayings source, but cf. W. Nauck, "Die Tradition u. d. Charakter d. 1 J.," *Wissenschaftl. Untersuchungen z. NT,* 3 (1957), 18 f.; E. Haenchen, "Neue Lit. zu d. Joh.-Br.," ThR, NF, 26 (1960), 10 f.; v. also Schnckbg. J.[4], *ad loc.*

[83] V. 22 works out v. 21 in the form of a statement. To understand the confession in 1 Jn. cf. 4:2, where it is developed in opposition to Gnosticism. We are to see this in terms of the conflict between orthodoxy and heresy at the stage of reflection on the faith.

[84] Materially one may compare the antithesis between the two spirits in 1 Jn. 4:1-6 → VI, 448, 24 ff. 1 Jn., however, speaks of the spirit of error rather than the spirit of lies. This corresponds to the linguistic bent of Gnosticism → 603, 13 f. In Jn. the Spirit is unequivocal. Distinction between the true Spirit and a false spirit corresponds to reflection on the distinction between true teaching and false teaching. χρῖσμα is introduced as an unequivocal and positive entity (→ 572, 8 ff.) corresponding to πνεῦμα in the Gospel.

prevails; no lies are found on the lips of the 144,000 elect (14:5 → VII, 700, 27 ff.). The list of things excluded from salvation in 21:27 is interesting, and so too is the list connected with the beatitude in 22:14 f. → 138, 1 ff. In both cases lying comes emphatically at the end, cf. also 21:8. [85]

E. The Early Church.

No basically new features are to be found in the post-apost. fathers. In detail one may note that truthfulness πνεῦμα ἄψευστον is a gift of God, while an attack on it is like theft, Herm. m., 3, 2. The meaning of ψευδής/ψεύδομαι is brought out in antitheses: What was earlier ψευδῆ ἐν πραγματείαις is to prove itself as πιστά, 3, 5; cf. ψεύδεσθαι "to be unfaithful" — ὁ πιστός in 1 Cl., 27, 1 f. In Herm. m., 3, 3 ψεῦδος has the sense of "hypocrisy": καὶ τὸ ψεῦδός μου ἀληθὲς ἐπέδειξα παρὰ πᾶσιν ἀνθρώποις. In Herm. s., 9, 15, 3 ψεῦδος is personified. ὅρκος ψευδής means "perjury" in Barn., 2, 8.

In Valentinian Gnosticism falsehood is less prominent than πλάνη, cf. Ev. Veritatis 17:23 ff. [86] and Heracleon's exposition of Jn. 8:44. [87] For the Mandaeans כושטא 'truth' is the epitome of their religion. but "lying" is not used a great deal. [88]

Conzelmann

---

[85] Vögtle, op. cit., 98-104; E. Kamlah, "Die Form d. katalogischen Paränese im NT," *Wissenschaftl. Untersuchungen z. NT,* 7 (1964), 23 f.

[86] Ed. M. Malinine et al. (1956).

[87] In Orig. Comm. in Joh., 20, 28 on 8:44 (p. 365, 8-15), v. W. Völker, "Quellen zur Gesch. d. chr. Gnosis," *Sammlung ausgewählter kirchen- u. dogmengesch. Quellenschr.,* NF, 5 (1932), 84.

[88] Examples are Lidz. Liturg., 97, 8; 104, 8; 198, 4; 218, 1; Lidz. Joh., 97-99; 104, 2 f.

→ ψευδόχριστος (→ 530, 19 ff.)

---

† ψῆφος, † ψηφίζω, † συμψηφίζω
† (καταψηφίζομαι) συγκαταψηφίζομαι

Contents: A. Normal Greek Usage: 1. ψῆφος; 2. ψηφίζω, συμψηφίζω, (καταψηφίζομαι) συγκαταψηφίζομαι; B. The Septuagint and Hellenistic Judaism: 1. The Septuagint; 2. Josephus; 3. Philo. C. The New Testament and Post-Apostolic Fathers.

A. Normal Greek Usage.

1. ψῆφος.

ψῆφος, [1] from Aesch., Pind. and Hdt. first means a "little stone" as distinct from bigger ones (→ IV, 268, 10 ff.), e.g., "the heads (skulls) of Persians are so weak that one can pierce them merely with a little stone ψήφῳ μούνῃ." The continuation brings out the distinction from λίθος: "Those of the Egyptians are so strong that one can hardly break them with a stone λίθῳ παίσας," Hdt., III, 12, 1. ψῆφος is used accordingly for the innumerable "pebbles" which are found on the seashore, Pind. Olymp., 13, 46. But the stress can be less on the small size than on the nature of the material, e.g., the "dressed stone" on which the list of victors is chiseled, Pind. Olymp., 7, 86 f., the "precious stone" mentioned along with gold in Philostr. Vit. Ap., III, 27 (p. 104, 27) or the "stone used in mosaics," [2] Gal. Adhort. ad artes addiscendas, 8 (Kühn, I, 19).

Small stones were used in board games, [3] Plat. Resp., VI, 487c, and in counting, e.g., Hdt., II, 36, 4, so that in texts which refer to calculations the meaning can be "number," e.g., P. Lips., I, 105, 17-19 (1st cent. A.D.) and in the plur. "account," ταῖς ταμιακαῖς ψήφοις δοῦναι "to put in the treasury account," [4] P. Lips., I, 64, 7 (4th cent. A.D.). Stones were used in astrological calculations, Vett. Val., I, 22 (p. 46, 16), [5] and also in magic, Preis. Zaub., I, 4, 1046-48 (4th cent. A.D.) and soothsaying καὶ δοὺς διδάσκεται τὴν διὰ τῶν ψήφων μαντικήν, Apollodorus Mythographicus, Bibliotheca, III, 10, 2. [6]

Above all, however, stones were used in votes: [7] "when the generals met and divided the stones τὰς ψήφους ... to determine who should be first and second, each voted for himself" ἑαυτῷ ἐτίθετο τὴν ψῆφον, Hdt., VIII, 123, 2. The passage shows that the word can mean "voice" or "vote" as well as stone. It can then have the more gen. sense

---

ψῆφος κτλ. Bibl.: Thes. Steph., Pape, Pass., Moult.-Mill., Preisigke Wört., Liddell-Scott, Pr.-Bauer, G. W. H. Lampe, A Patristic Greek Lex. (1961), s.v.; Krauss Lehnw., II, 470-472; W. M. Ramsay, "The White Stone and the 'Gladiatoral' Tessera," ET, 16 (1905), 558-561; F. Boll, "Aus d. Offenbarung Johannis," ΣΤΟΙΧΕΙΑ, 1 (1914), 28; W. Bousset, "Kyrios Christos," FRL, 21² (1921), 114; H. Lietzmann, "Notizen," ZNW, 20 (1921), 249-256.

[1] For the etym. cf. Frisk, s.v.

[2] Cf. for this the synagogue inscr. of Noarah: טימי פסיפסה (τιμή/ψῆφος), Lietzmann, 252. In Jewish lit. ψῆφος is a loan word esp. in the sense of "mosaic," cf. Krauss, 470 f., walls decorated with mosaics, Neg., 11, 7 etc., ceilings with mosaics, AbRNat, A 24 (Schechter, p. 77, 18); doors, Tamid., 1, 3 etc., pillars or partitions, Mid., 1, 6 etc. Cf. also ψηφολογεῖν "to decorate with mosaics," Tob. 13:17. For archaeological examples cf. Y. Yadin, Masada³ (1969), 119-129: ornamental Herodian flooring.

[3] As a loan word in Jewish lit. in the sense of "little stone" in Dt. r., 1, 10 on 1:1; jShab., 7, 2 (10b, 5) etc.; board games, T. Sanh., 5, 2 (Zuckermandel, 423, 3) etc.; cf. Krauss, 470.

[4] Preisigke Wört., s.v.

[5] Cf. I, 2 (p. 10, 15); I, 21 (39, 13); IV, 24 (199, 13) etc.

[6] Ed. J. G. Frazer (1921).

[7] As a loan word in Jewish lit. in the sense of a "voting stone," hence "decision," "destiny," Pesikt., 17 (131a), cf. Krauss, 470.

of "voice," "opinion," σὲ μὲν ἡγοῦνται Κόννου ψῆφον, Aristoph. Vesp., 675. Then, esp. in the legal sphere, it can mean "voting," e.g., on banishment, Xenoph. An., VII, 7, 57. Finally we find the meaning "resolve," "verdict," Soph. Ant., 60 and "court," Eur. Iph. Taur., 945.

2. ψηφίζω, συμψηφίζω, (καταψηφίζομαι) συγκαταψηφίζομαι.

a. ψηφίζω means act. "counting" or "calculating" with stones etc. ἐκεῖναί τε γὰρ κατὰ τὴν τοῦ ψηφίζοντος βούλησιν ἄρτι χαλκοῦν καὶ παραυτίκα τάλαντον ἰσχύουσιν, Polyb., 5, 26, 13, transf. "reaching a verdict," e.g., "they would never again reach such a verdict against another," οὐκ ἄν ποτε δίκην κατ' ἄλλου φωτὸς ὧδ' ἐψήφισαν, Soph. Ai., 448 f. More common is the mid. use. ψηφίζομαι means first "giving one's vote by casting a little stone into an urn," Xenoph. Hist. Graec., I, 7, 9; Plat. Ap., 32b, then more gen. "to vote," with no necessary use of a stone καὶ γὰρ νῦν εἰσιν ἐψηφισμένοι Παγασὰς ἀπαιτεῖν, Demosth. Or., 2, 11. We then have the meaning "to resolve," [8] "to reach a decision," quite apart from voting, as, e.g., in Hdt., VII, 207. In the pass. the meaning "to be condemned" is found in Eur. Heracl., 141 f.

b. συμψηφίζω is not very common and means "to reckon up," "to add," Preis. Zaub., II, 13, 348 (3rd/4th cent. A.D.), "to agree on," Preisigke Sammelbuch, III, 7378, 9 f. (103 A.D.), συμψηφίζομαί τινι, "to give the same vote as someone," Aristoph. Lys., 142.

c. καταψηφίζομαι means "to pronounce guilty," e.g., Plat. Ap., 36a, 41d, pass. "to be condemned," e.g., Plat. Resp., VIII, 558a. We also find the meaning "to resolve" in the positive sense, e.g., Aristot. Pol., IV, 14, p. 1298b, 39 f. συγκαταψηφίζομαι is attested only in Plut. Them., 21 (I, 122e). It means here the co-condemnation of Themistocles.

B. The Septuagint and Hellenistic Judaism.

1. The Septuagint.

a. ψῆφος occurs in Lam. 3:16 for צְץ "little stone," "pebble," while in Ex. 4:25 it is the transl. of צֹר, the sharp stone with which the foreskin is cut. At Qoh. 7:25 it is the equivalent of חֶשְׁבּוֹן and is used alongside σοφία. [9] At Sir. 18:10 ψῆφοι are little stones in the sand; with drops of water these are a simile for the years in comparison with the day of eternity. The sense of "voting stone" is present in 4 Macc. 15:26. The mother holds in her hand two stones for her children; the one brings death and the other deliverance. In Orig. 4 Βασ. 12:5 runs ἀργύριον παρερχόμενον ἀνὴρ ψήφῳ ψυχῶν and ref. to calculation of the money brought into the temple.

b. ψηφίζω in 3 Βασ. 3:8; 8:5 Orig. is as a vl. a synon. of ספר ni. It denotes the reckoning or counting of the people or the sheep and cattle. [10]

c. συμψηφίζω occurs in 'Ιερ. 30:14 (49:20) Cod AQ and ref. to the counting of sheep. Neither καταψηφίζομαι nor συγκαταψηφίζομαι is found in the LXX.

2. Josephus.

a Jos. [11] uses ψῆφος 15 times, esp. in the sense of "resolve," Bell., 2, 205, "to make a resolve" ψῆφον ἐνεγκεῖν, Ant., 2, 163; 10, 60 and 91, "to give votes" (for the accused),

---

[8] Cf. also Ditt. Or., 666, 15 (1st cent. A.D.); P. Oxy., I, 41, 15 (3rd/4th cent. A.D.); P. Lond., V, 1707, 7 (6th cent. A.D.); v. Preisigke Wört., s.v.

[9] On Qoh. 7:25 cf. G. Bertram, "Hbr. u. griech. Qoh. Ein Beitrag z. Theol. d. hell. Bibel," ZAW, 64 (1952), 41 f. σοφίαν καὶ ψῆφον means "wise decision."

[10] ψηφίζω and cognates are more common in the Hexapla, e.g., Ex. 4:25 Σ; Prv. 20:17 Θ; 30:27 Σ etc.

[11] K. H. Rengstorf kindly placed at our disposal the Josephus Concordance which is being prepared in the Institutum Judaicum Delitzschianum at Münster.

Bell., 4, 341. God's counsel is at issue in Bell., 7, 359; Ant., 3, 44; 4, 225, and His judgment in Ant., 5, 168. The vote needed to reach a verdict is the same in Ap., 2, 265: θάνατον αὐτοῦ παρ' ὀλίγας ψήφους κατέγνωσαν.

b. ψηφίζομαι occurs 29 times and means esp. "to resolve,"[12] Bell., 2, 205. The people is the subj. in Bell., 4, 251 and the senate in Ant., 14, 217 and 18, 54. A triumph is resolved on in Bell., 7, 121 and honours in Ant., 19, 183 and 231. The ref. is to God's counsel in Ant., 17, 43 and Caesar's resolve in Ant., 17, 319. The sense "to reckon" occurs in Ap., 1, 121.

c. συμψηφίζω and συγκαταψηφίζομαι do not occur in Jos. καταψηφίζομαι is attested 15 times in the sense "to condemn," e.g., Bell., 2, 414; 6, 250; Ant., 1, 96, "to condemn to death," Ant., 15, 229.

3. Philo.

a. Philo uses ψῆφος esp. in the sense "pronouncement," "verdict," "judicial verdict." The ref. in Spec. Leg., IV, 57 is to insight in reaching a verdict. Decal., 140 speaks of "unjust and illegal pronouncements" on the one hand and "just and legal" ones on the other. Deus Imm., 75 mentions a judgment of condemnation τὴν καταδικάζουσαν ψῆφον, cf. Migr. Abr., 115. Verdict is the meaning in Decal., 141 καὶ τοὺς κυρίους τῆς ψήφου συνεξαμαρτάνειν ἀναπείθοντες "the judges who have to reach a verdict" so that they have a part in the offence. Som., II, 104 ref. to the voices of the majority that always prevail.

b. ψηφίζομαι means "to decree," "to resolve." Flacc., 97 reads: πάσας (sc. τιμὰς) Γαΐῳ ψηφισάμενοι καὶ ἐπιτελέσαντες, cf. Leg. Gaj., 149; Ebr., 109. Det. Pot. Ins., 143 speaks of the resolve to flee, Ebr., 224 of the decreeing of banishment, Fug., 119 of the command to return home, Ebr., 8 of the resolve to move in, Op. Mund., 125 of the decree of death or deliverance.

c. συμψηφίζω and συγκαταψηφίζομαι do not occur in Philo. καταψηφίζομαι means "to condemn," e.g., Vit. Mos., I, 134; Ebr., 71; Leg. All., III, 74.

C. The New Testament and Post-Apostolic Fathers.

1. In Ac. 26:10 Luke has Paul say that he had a part in sentencing Christians to death by giving his voice (ψῆφος) against them.[13]

2. The white stone of Rev. 2:17 on which the new name is written is thought to be an amulet.[14, 15] In religious history the amulet has a place in the magical beliefs of the time → V, 250, 35 ff. Magical formulae, in this case the new name, mediate supernatural powers and offer protection against demons[16] and evil forces.[17] The

---

[12] Cf. Schl. Lk., 345.
[13] Wdt. Ag., ad loc. thinks καταφέρω ψῆφον is simply a fig. equivalent of συνευδοκέω in Ac. 8:1; 22:20. Acc. to Haench. Ag.[14], ad loc., however, Ac. 26:10 is stronger than Ac. 8:1. As Luke describes it Paul had an act. part in the voting and καταφέρω ψῆφον should not be weakened to συνευδοκέω, cf. also H. Conzelmann, Die Ag., Hndbch. NT, 7 (1963), ad loc.
[14] Cf. Pr.-Bauer, s.v.
[15] Cf. W. Heitmüller, "Im Namen Jesu," FRL, 1, 2 (1903), 128-265 and Bss. Apk., ad loc.
[16] Cf. Loh. Apk., ad loc.
[17] For older exegesis cf. F. Düsterdieck, "Krit.-Exeget. Handbuch über d. Offenbarung Johannis," Krit.-exeget. Komm. über d. NT, 16⁴ (1887), ad loc. and Bss. Apk., ad loc.

fact that the stone is described as white (→ IV, 250, 7 ff.) is an indication of the supernatural, the distinctive, and the extraordinary. [18] A new sphere is opened up → V, 281, 28 ff. [19]

3. Lk. 14:28 uses ψηφίζω in the sense "to reckon." Before work is begun on the tower the cost has to be worked out. The man who wants to be a disciple of Jesus should do the same. [20] He should examine himself [21] to see whether he has the requisite means and strength. [22] V. 33 carries the thought of v. 28 a stage further: Having reckoned up his resources, he must now renounce them all. This is how the Evangelist Luke interpreted the tradition. [23] In Ac. 19:19 the value of the magical books that are brought in is calculated (συμψηφίζω). The addition yields an unusually high sum → VIII, 178, 17 ff.

4. In Rev. 13:18 the number (→ I, 463, 1 ff.) of the beast, which is also the number of a man, is to be counted. This counting can only mean putting the number given in the corresponding Hebrew, Greek, or Latin letters and thus arriving at the mysterious name (→ V, 280, 9 ff.; IX, 417, 3 ff.). [24] But the calculation also means finding out what numbers together add up to 666. [25] The answer is 36, for 666 is the sum of the numbers 1 to 36. But 36 itself is the sum of the numbers 1 to 8. In Gnostic systems, however, the number 8, the ogdoad, is identical with sophia (→ VII, 524, 14 ff.). If this view is correct, Rev. 13:18, when combined with 17:11, tells us that sophia is meant by worship of the beast, and Gnosticism is the enemy that we must fight. [26]

5. If συγκατεψηφίσθη [27] in Ac. 1:26 is based on καταψηφίζομαι [28] "to resolve," the meaning is that thereby he was (officially) given a place along with the eleven. [29, 30].

6. Herm. v., 3, 1, 4 uses συμψηφίζω in the sense "to reckon," "to add up," "to calculate": καὶ συνώψισα (vl. συνεψήφισα) τὰς ὥρας, cf. s., 5, 3, 7.

Braumann

---

[18] Boll, 28.

[19] In Rev. "white" denotes a change of category, cf. the white clothes, Rev. 3:4 f., 18; 4:4 etc.

[20] Acc. to Bultmann Trad., 216 the original meaning has been lost.

[21] Cf. Jeremias Gl.7, 195.

[22] Cf. E. Biser, *Die Gleichnisse Jesu* (1965), 62.

[23] Cf. Ac. 4:34; Lk. 5:11, 28 and already Mk. 10:28 and par.

[24] Cf. P. Corssen, "Noch einmal die Zahl d. Tieres in d. Apok.," ZNW, 3 (1902), 238-242; also "Zur Verständigung über Apk. 13:18," ZNW, 4 (1903), 264-7. "The beast has a name x = 666, but 666 is like the name of a man, both names are, as they called it, ἰσόψηφα," ZNW, 3 (1902), 240.

[25] Cf. G. A. van den Bergh van Eysinga, "Die in d. Apok. bekämpfte Gnosis," ZNW, 13 (1912), 293-305; Loh. Apk., 117 f.

[26] Cf. van den Bergh van Eysinga, *op. cit.*, 299. E. Stauffer, "666," *Festschr. A. Fridrichsen* (1947), 237-341 arrives at the name of Domitian with the help of gematria.

[27] Since in the NT συγκαταβαίνω occurs only in Ac. 25:5 and συγκατατίθημι only in Lk. 23:51, it is possible that Lk. coined συγκατεψηφίσθη ad hoc. But cf. συγκατάθεσις in 2 C. 6:16.

[28] κατεψηφίσθη א* is to be taken in the sense "to decree or resolve something," cf. Aristot. Pol., IV, 14, p. 1298b, 39 f., not as condemnation with the eleven, e.g., Plat. Resp., VIII, 558a, Jos. Ant., 15, 229; Philo Vit. Mos., I, 134 etc.

[29] On μετά cf. Bl.-Debr. § 221 and 227.

[30] If, however, we take συμψηφίζω as the basis (cf. Ac. 19:19), cf. Wdt. Ag., ad loc., the meaning is that he was counted with the eleven, cf. v. 17, κατηριθμημένος ἦν.

```
┌─────────────────────────────────────────────┐
│   ψυχή, ψυχικός, ἀνάψυξις,                    │
│   ἀναψύχω, δίψυχος, ὀλιγόψυχος                │
└─────────────────────────────────────────────┘
```

Contents: A. ψυχή in the Greek World: 1. ψυχή in Homer; 2. ψυχή in Older and Classical Usage; 3. ψυχή in the Philosophy of Plato; 4. The Psychology of Post-Platonic Philosophy: a. Constitution of the Soul; b. Division of the Soul; 5. Popular Ideas of the Post-Classical Age. B. The Anthropology of the Old Testament: 1. נֶפֶשׁ: a. נֶפֶשׁ and Breath; b. נֶפֶשׁ and Blood; c. נֶפֶשׁ and Person; d. נֶפֶשׁ as Corpse and Tomb; e. נֶפֶשׁ as Expression of the Will; 2. Flesh and Body: a. Flesh; b. Bones; 3. Different Parts of the Body as the Seat of Life: a. The Head; b. The Face; c. The Hand; d. The Foot; e. The inner Organs; 4. The Heart as the Centre of Life and the Epitome of the Person; 5. The Spirit: a. Origin of the Concept; b. The Outworking in Man; c. The Creative Activity of the Spirit in Man; d. The Relation to נֶפֶשׁ and Heart; e. Flesh and Spirit; 6. The Relational Character of Old Testament Anthropology. C. Judaism: I. Hellenistic Judaism: 1. Septuagint Works with a Hebrew Original; 2. Apocalyptic and Pseudepigraphical Works; 3. Septuagint Works in Greek; 4. Aristeas and Josephus; 5. Philo. II. נֶפֶשׁ/ψυχή in Palestinian Judaism: 1. Qumrân; 2. The Rabbis. D. The New Testament: I. The Gospels and Acts: 1. ψυχή as Natural Physical Life: a. General; b. The Giving of Life; c. Seeking, Killing and Saving Life; 2. ψυχή as a Term for the Whole Man; 3. ψυχή as the Place of Feeling: a. Man as Influenced by Others; b. Man as He Experiences Joy, Sorrow and Love; c. ψυχή in the Sense of Heart; 4. ψυχή as True Life in Distinction from Purely Physical Life (Mk. 8:35 and par.): a. Jesus; b. Mark; c. Mt. 10:39; d. Lk. 17:33; e. Jn. 12:25; f. ψυχή as the God-given Existence which Survives Death; 5. Life as the Supreme Good (Mk. 8:35 f. and par.); 6. ψυχή in Contrast to the Body (Mt. 10:28); 7. Lucan Sayings about the ψυχή After Death: a. Lk. 12:4 f.; 9:25; Ac. 2:31; b. Lk. 12:20; c. Lk. 21:19. II. Paul Including Colossians and Ephesians: 1. ψυχή as Natural Life and as True Life; 2. ψυχή as Person; 3. μία ψυχή; 4. Colossians and Ephesians; 5. Secularity of the Usage. III. Hebrews. IV. The Catholic Epistles: 1. John; 2. James; 3. 1 Peter; 4. 2 Peter. V. Revelation: 1. ψυχή as Physical Life; 2. ψυχή as Person; 3. ψυχή as Life After Death. VI. New Testament Usage in Distinction from πνεῦμα. E. Gnosticism.

A. ψυχή in the Greek World.

1. ψυχή in Homer.

At the earliest accessible level, namely, Homer, Greek has no words for our concepts of body and soul. σῶμα (→ VII, 1025, 16 ff.) is simply the corpse; the living organism is denoted by plur. expressions like μέλεα, γυῖα, or in terms of its

ψ υ χ ή κ τ λ . Bibl.: General: Thes. Steph., Liddell-Scott, Pr.-Bauer, s.v.; G. Dautzenberg, "Sein Leben bewahren," Stud. z. AT u. NT, 14 (1966); M. Delcor, "L'immortalité de l'âme dans le Livre de la Sagesse et dans les documents de Qumrân," Nouvelle Rev. Théol., 77 (1955), 614-630; J. Fichtner, "Seele oder Leben?" ThZ, 17 (1961), 305-318; R. B. Onians, The Origins of European Thought about the Body, the Mind, the Soul, the World, Time and Fate² (1954); F. Rüsche, "Blut, Leben u. Seele," Stud. z. Gesch. u. Kultur d. Altertums, Suppl. Vol. 5 (1930), on A.: A. W. H. Adkins, Merit and Responsibility (1960); J. Böhme, Die Seele u. d. Ich im homerischen Epos (1929); W. Burkert, "Weisheit u. Wissenschaft," Erlanger Beiträge z. Sprach- u. Kunstwissenschaft, 10 (1962), 98-142; E. R. Dodds, The Greeks and the Irrational (1951); B. Meissner, Mythisches u. Rationales i. d. Psychologie der euripideischen Tragödie, Diss. Göttingen (1951); J. Moreau, L'âme du monde de Platon aux Stoiciens (1939);

(continued on p. 609 and 610)

appearance by δέμας or χρώς.[1] ψυχή, etym. related to ψύχω "to blow (to cool)" and ψῦχος "cold," is on this view the vital force which resides in the members and which comes to expression especially in the breath. The reference, then, is to the breath-soul. In battle the ψυχή (life) is hazarded, Hom. Il., 9, 322. This ψυχή leaves man at the moment of death, escaping through the mouth (9, 408 f.) or, according to another view, through the wound. This leads to the idea of the blood-soul, cf. 14, 518 f. The soul goes to the underworld (5, 654) and may sometimes show itself to a living person in a dream prior to burial of the corpse (23, 106), taking on the appearance of the living man for this purpose. In the underworld it leads a shadowy existence which has little to do with the self of man. This self has gone, having become food for the dogs and the birds (1, 3 ff.), or, in the special instance of Hercules, having been taken up to be with the gods (Od., 11, 601 ff.). Nothing is expected of the shadowy existence of the ψυχή in the underworld.[2] Neither in life nor death does the ψυχή have anything at all to do with the intellectual or spiritual functions of man.

M. Pohlenz, *Die Stoa*, I⁴ (1970), 81-93, 141-153, 196-201 etc.; II⁴ (1970), 49-53, 77-83 etc.; T. M. Robinson, "Plato's Psychology," *Phoenix Suppl.*, VIII, (1971); F. Rüsche, "Das Seelenpneuma," *Stud. z. Gesch. u. Kultur d. Altertums*, 18, 3 (1933); B. Snell, *Die Entdeckung d. Geistes*³ (1955), 17-42; Aristot., *Über d. Seele*, ed. W. Theiler in *Aristot., Werke in deutscher Übers.*, 13² (1966); Tertullian De Anima, ed. J. H. Waszink (1947). On B.: L. Adler, "Das Wesen d. Menschen in jüd. Sicht," *Kerygma u. Dogma*, 16 (1970), 188-198; P. Bratsiotis, "נֶפֶשׁ/ψυχή. Ein Beitrag z. Erforschung d. Sprache u. d. Theol. d. LXX," *Volume du Congrès Genève 1965*, VT Suppl., 15 (1966), 58-89; also Ἀνθρωπολογία τῆς Παλαιᾶς Διαθήκης 1. Ὁ ἄνθρωπος ὡς θεῖον δημιούργημα (1967); J. S. Croatto, "Nota de antropologia bibl.," *Rivista Bibl.*, 25 (1963), 29 f.; F. Delitzsch, *System d. bibl. Psychologie* (1855); E. Dhorme, *L'emploi métaphorique des noms de parties du corps en hébreu et en akkadien* (1923); A. M. Dubarle, "La conception de l'homme dans l'AT," *Sacra Pagina I, Bibliotheca Ephemeridum Theol. Lovaniensium*, 12 (1959), 522-536; R. Dussaud, "La notion d'âme chez les Israélites et les Phéniciens," *Syria*, 16 (1935), 267-277; W. Eichrodt, "Das Menschenverständnis d. AT," AbhThANT (1944); G. Fohrer, "Theol. Züge d. Menschenbildes im AT," *Stud. z. at.lichen Theol. u. Gesch.* (1949-1966), ZAW Beih., 115 (1969), 176-194; J. de Fraine, *Adam u. seine Nachkommen* (1962); K. Galling, "Das Bild vom Menschen in bibl. Sicht," *Mainzer Univ.-Reden*, 3 (1947); A. Gelin, "L'homme selon la Bible," *Foi Vivante, 75* (1968); J. Hempel, "Gott u. Mensch im AT," BWANT, 38² (1936); A. R. Johnson, *The Vitality of the Individual in the Thought of Ancient Israel* (1949); A. Kammenhuber, "Die hethischen Vorstellungen v. Seele u. Leib, Herz u. Leibesinnerem, Kopf u. Person," *Zschr. f. Assyriologie*, NF, 22 (1964), 150-212; J. Köberle, *Natur u. Geist nach d. Auffassung d. AT* (1901); L. Köhler, *Der hbr. Mensch* (1953); F. M. T. de Liagre Böhl, "Das Menschenbild in babylon. Schau," *Anthropologie religieuse*, ed. C. J. Bleeker, Suppl. to Numen, 2 (1955), 28-48; D. Lys. "Nèphèsh," *Étud. d.Hist. et de Philosophie Relig.*, 50 (1959); also "Rûach. Le Souffle dans l'AT," *ibid.*, 56 (1962); also *La Chair dans l'AT.* Bâsâr (1967); V. Maag, "At.liche Anthropogonie in

[1] The earliest instance of σῶμα for "living human body" is in Hes. Op., 540; χρήματα γὰρ ψυχὴ πέλεται δειλοῖσι βροτοῖσιν in 686 ref. to the life, not the self of man.

[2] Naturally Homeric ideas of the ψυχή are not as uniform as this brief survey might suggest. This is due in part of the different sources of different parts of the extant epics. Thus the prophetic activity of the soul of the dead Patroclus in Il., 23, 69-92 is not in keeping with ideas of the ψυχή elsewhere. The cult of heroes, which honours the dead in the tomb, does not, however, presuppose a separate and significant continuation of the life of the soul in opposition to Homeric notions. It merely assumes that the recipient of worship has a power that extends beyond death, so that he can come back to threaten or protect the living and dispense either malediction or benediction. The δαίμονες which the men of the golden age became acc. to Hes. Op., 121-126 are not to be thought of as incorporeal souls (→ 615, 12 ff.), and the same applies to the heroes who for various reasons are taken up to a place of eternal and immutable bliss, e.g., Aethiopis in Proclus Chrestomathia, 198 (ed. A. Severyns, *Recherches sur la Chrestomathie d. Proclos, IV, Bibliothèque de la Faculté de Philosophie et Lettres de l'Univ. de Liège*, 170 [1963], 88) or Hes. Op., 170, cf. A. Schnaufer, "Frühgriech. Totenglaube," *Spudasmata*, 20 (1970), 103-7.

This sphere is described by several words which either denote specific intellectual or spiritual activities (μένος, νόος etc.) or the individual organs of these activities (στῆθος, καρδία, ἦτορ, φρένες etc.) or both at once (θυμός). [3] Like other peoples the Greeks first thought that the parts of the body were agents of intellectual or spiritual functions either in specific situations (χεῖρες, πόδες) or permanently (ἦτορ, φρένες). [4] But the νόος, cf. νοέω "to perceive," "to intend" (→ IV, 948, 15 ff.), [5] which one bears in the

---

ihrem Verhältnis z. altorientalischen Mythologie," *Asiat. Stud.,* 9 (1955), 15-44; also "Alter Orient," *ibid.,* 13 (1960), 19-31; F. Michaéli, *Dieu à l'image de l'homme* (1950); A. Murtonen, "The Living Soul," *Stud. Or.,* 23, 1 (1958); G. Pidoux, "L'homme dans l'AT," *Cahiers théol.,* 32 (1953); also "L'homme dans l'AT," *Anthropologie relig.,* ed. C. J. Bleeker, *Suppl. to Numen,* 2 (1955), 155-165; H. W. Robinson, "Hebrew Psychology," *The People and the Book,* ed. A. S. Peake (1925), 353-382; J. Rothermund, "Chr. u. jüd. Menschenbild," *Kerygma u. Dogma,* 16 (1970), 199-222; A. Safran, "La conception juive de l'homme," RevThPh, 98 (1964), 193-207; J. Scharbert, "Fleisch, Geist u. Seele im Pent.," *Stuttgarter Bibelstud.,* 19 (1966); O. Schilling, "Geist u. Materie in bibl. Sicht," *Ev. Theol.,* 25 (1967); W. Schmidt, "Anthropolog. Begriffe im AT," *Ev. Theol.,* 24 (1964), 374-388; W. Zimmerli, "Das Menschenbild d. AT," *Theol. Ex.,* NF, 14 (1949). On C.: Bousset-Gressm., 399-402; H. Hübner, "Anthropolog. Dualismus in den Hodayoth?" NTSt, 18 (1972), 268-284; D. Lys, "The Israelite Soul acc. to the LXX," VT, 16 (1966), 181-228; R. Meyer, "Hellenistisches in d. rabb. Anthropologie," BWANT, 74 (1937); Moore, I, 485-9; II, 292-5; Volz Esch., 118 f., 266-272; Weber, 203-5, 217-223. On D.: F. Barth, "La notion Paulinienne de ΨΥΧΗ," RevThPh, 44 (1911), 316-336; E. Brandenburger, "Fleisch u. Geist," *Wissenschaftl. Monographien z. AT u. NT,* 29 (1968); H. v. Campenhausen, "Tod, Unsterblichkeit u. Auferstehung," *Festschr. L. Jaeger u. W. Stählin* (1963), 295-311; O. Cullmann, *Unsterblichkeit d. Seele oder Auferstehung von den Toten?*[3] (1964); J. Dupont, "Gnosis," *Univ. Cathol. Lovaniensis Diss. ad gradum magistri in Facultate Theol. consequendum conscriptae,* II, 40[2] (1960), 151-180; F. P. Fiorenza-J. B. Metz, "Der Mensch als Einheit v. Leib u. Seele," *Mysterium Salutis,* ed. J. Feiner-M. Löhrer, II (1967), 584-632; C. Guignebert, "Remarques sur quelques conceptions chrét. antiques touchant l'origine et la nature de l'âme," RevHPhR, 9 (1929), 428-450; W. Gutbrod, "Die paul. Anthropologie," BWANT, 67 (1934), 75-9; C. Masson, "L'immortalité de l'âme ou résurrection des morts?" RevThPh, NS, III, 8 (1958), 250-267; B. Reicke, "Body and Soul in the NT," *Stud. Theol.,* 19 (1965), 200-212; M. Schmaus, "Unsterblichkeit d. Geistseele oder Auferstehung v. d. Toten?" *Festschr. L. Jaeger u. W. Stählin* (1963), 311-337; J. Schmid, "Der Begriff d. Seele im NT," *Festsch. G. Söhngen*[2] (1963), 128-147; J. N. Sevenster, *Het begrip psyche en het NT* (1946); also "Die Anthropologie d. NT," *Anthropologie relig.,* ed. C. J. Bleeker, *Numen Suppl.,* 2 (1955), 166-177; W. D. Stacey, "St. Paul and the 'Soul,'" Exp. T., 66 (1954/1955), 274-7; also *The Pauline View of Man* (1956), 121-7. On E.: "Le origini dello gnosticismo," ed. U. Bianchi, *Numen Suppl.,* 12 (1967); C. Colpe, "Die religionsgeschichtl. Schule," FRL, 78 (1961), Index *s.v.* "Seele"; A. J. Festugière, "La révélation d'Hermès Trismégiste, III. Les doctrines de l'âme," *Étud. Bibl.* (1953); H. Jonas, *Gnostic Religion* (1958), 291-330.

[3] θυμός etym. related to Lat. *fumus* "smoke," primarily means in Hom. the ability to move. At death this leaves the body directly, not through the mouth (Hom. Il., 13, 671), and it does not go to the underworld. Since θυμός is not just the physiological cause of movement but also the spiritual impulse to action it can also be the inner man who in self-reflection on one's own acts and experiences is the partner in the dialogue which such reflection quite early becomes for the Gks., e.g., Il., 11, 403; Archiloch. Fr., 105 (ed. G. Tarditi, Archilochus, Lyricorum Graec. quae exstant, 2 [1968], 122). The same role can be played by the heart, in which physical traces of spiritual emotions are seen, Hom. Od., 20, 18.

[4] The Gks., like other peoples, commonly regard blood as the bearer of the life-force. Through drinking blood shades in the underworld acquire the power to converse with Odysseus, Od., 11, 98. The gods as qualitatively different beings do not have αἷμα in their veins but ἰχώρ, Il., 5, 340. Already in the 6th cent. the Pythagorean Hippo attacks the naive equation of αἷμα and ψυχή, Aristot. An., I, 2, p. 405b, 4. Like other pre-Socratics, e.g., Anaximenes Fr., 2 (Diels, I, 95) and Diogenes of Apollonia Fr., 4 (II, 60 f.) the Pythagoreans obviously found in air the sub-stratum of the power of thought, Fr., 40 (I, 462), cf. Aristot. An. I, 2, p. 404a, 16. Acc. to a common view blood was also the bearer of the emotional life, e.g., Diogenes of Apollonia in Theophr. De sensu, 39-43.

[5] If C. J. Ruijgh, *Étud. sur la grammaire et le vocabulaire du grec mycénien* (1967), 370 f. is right in associating νοέω and νέομαι "to return (from danger)," then the basic sense of νόος must be "plan" [Risch].

heart or breast or elsewhere, Il., 3, 63; Od., 14, 490, or which a god has put there, Od., 18, 136, can become a permanent and integral part of man, Il., 4, 309; 10, 122. Many combinations among these and other expressions yield a varied psychological vocabulary which is more specialised than the Hbr. because the vital force and the activity of thought are in particular linguistically differentiated. There is, however, no master-concept of the soul.

2. ψυχή in Older and Classical Usage.

Although no link can be found with the usage in Homer, ψυχή did in fact become the term for this newly found master-concept in the 6th century. [6] That it did so is connected with the belief in retribution in the hereafter, which became widespread from the 7th century onwards. [7] Naturally this retribution cannot affect a mere εἴδωλον. The ψυχή in the underworld has to guarantee the continuity of life in this world and life in the world to come. [8] In close connection herewith the doctrine of the transmigration of the soul [9] is found for the first time among the Greeks in the 6th century; it is a basic part of Pythagorean ethics. Here the ψυχή is the epitome of the individual. It can be thought of apart from the body and is indeed of greater worth than this. Already in the oldest available stratum of Orphic and Pythagorean speculation we find the idea of the σῶμα/σῆμα, i.e., the body (→ VII, 1026, 29 ff.; 1028, 32 ff.) as the tomb of the soul, Orph. Fr., 8 (Kern, 84 f.); Philolaus Fr., 14 (Diels, I, 413). The scoffing reference to Pythagoras' doctrine of transmigration in his younger contemporary Xenophanes Fr., 7 (Diels, I, 131) offers us the first instance of the new meaning of ψυχή. In the period around and after 500 B.C. ψυχή is then commonly used as an omnibus term for human thought, will and emotion and also for the essential core of man which can be separated from his body and which does not share in the body's dissolution.

Anacr. Fr., 15 (4) [10] says to the beloved: ὅτι τῆς ἐμῆς ψυχῆς ἡνιοχεύεις. Pind. Fr., 133 speaks of the ascent of the immortal soul to the sun and we find expressions like χερσὶ καὶ ψυχᾷ, Nem., 9, 39, or μορφὰν βραχύς, ψυχὰν δ' ἄκαμπτος, Isthm., 4, 53 (71) to denote the total psychophysical person. φίλα ψυχά can then be used in (self-)address (Pyth., 3, 61), and with many modifications this is an ongoing usage. Whereas up to the 6th cent. we find in Solon. Fr., 1, 46 (Diehl³, I, 24); Tyrtaeus Fr., 7, 18; 8, 5 [11] a poetic metaphorical use of the word ψυχή [12] in the sense of life or vital force, the usage of Pindar shows that a transition has now been made to the meaning "soul" in our sense, and this becomes the dominant although not the exclusive meaning.

---

[6] In Hom., of course, the ψυχή is specifically human. Only θυμός, not ψυχή, leaves the members of an animal at death, Il., 23, 880 etc.

[7] In lit. we find this first in the so-called Orphic interpolations of Nekyia, Hom. Od., 11, 576 ff. and Alcaeus Fr., 38 (ed. E. Lobel-D. L. Page, Poetarum Lesbiorum Fr. [1955], 128).

[8] How strongly religious thought was concerned about the problem of continuity may be seen from the myth of the underworld waters of Lethe and Mnemosyne, cf. Nilsson, II, 225-9; also "The Immortality of the Soul in Gk. Religion," Eranos, 39 (1941), 1-16.

[9] The origin of the idea of the transmigration of the soul has not been explained. It constantly found adherents in Greece both before and after Plato. It was debated whether the same soul can come only into human bodies or also into those of animals and plants, Emped. Fr., 117 (Diels, I, 359); Plat. Phaedr., 249b; Plut. Ser. Num. Vind., 31 (II, 567e); Oracula Chaldaica in Procl. in Rem Publ., X, 620a (II, 336, 29 f.); Philo Som., I, 139. In the same age we find the first appearance of shaman-type men in the Gk. world, Abaris, Aristeas, Zamolxis etc., who can send their souls on trips, cf. Max. Tyr. Diss., 10, 2 f.; Cl. Al. Strom., I, 21, 133, 2, cf. J. D. P. Bolton, Aristeas of Proconnesus (1962), 142-175.

[10] Ed. D. L. Page, Poetae Melici Graeci (1962), 184.

[11] Ed. C. Prato, Tyrtaeus, Lyricorum Graec. quae exstant, 3 (1968), 29 and 31.

[12] Cf. B. Snell, "Tyrtaios u. d. Sprache d. Epos," Hypomnemata, 22 (1969), 7-20.

It is presupposed in the first attempt at a philosophical psychology in Heracl. Heracl. makes a principle of the phenomenon described already in early Gk. lyric poetry, e.g., Sappho Fr., 96, [13] namely, that the life of the soul is not bound by the limits of space, Heracl. Fr., 45 (Diels, I, 161). He also formulates the insight that the soul has a self-expanding *logos,* so that the development of its life, of knowledge, memory etc., is not to be understood as the addition of quantitatively measurable entities or as the work of powers outside man, Fr., 115 (I, 176). Finally, he stresses that there is a communication between the souls of men which is independent of the factual sphere. [14] The *logos* of the soul, however, is not just common to men, among whom it finds realisation as speech. The order denoted by it extends to all being, Fr., 1 (I, 150) etc. The expression "world soul" is not yet found in Heracl.

Throughout the 5th and 4th centuries both in and outside philosophy the autonomy and higher worth of the soul are taken for granted → VII, 1026, 18 ff. They are either asserted, like the precedence of thought over action, Aesch. Sept. c. Theb., 571-596; Simonides Fr., 542, 27-30; [15] Eur. Hipp., 173; Democr. Fr., 170 f. (Diels, II, 178 f.); Isoc. Or., 15, 180 or they come out in expressions like πᾶσα πολιτεία ψυχὴ πόλεως, Isoc. Or., 12, 138 or οἷον ψυχὴ ὁ μῦθος τῆς τραγῳδίας, Aristot. Poet., 6, p. 1450a, 38 f. The causes of man's wickedness are to be sought within himself, Democr. Fr., 159 (Diels, II, 175 f.), and moral instruction is a training of the soul for the contests of virtue, as the inscr. on the statue of the orator Gorgias puts it, Epigr. Graec., 875a (4th cent. B.C.). Finally we find many new compounds at this period, e.g., μεγαλοψυχίη, Democr. Fr., 46 (Diels, II, 156), εὐψυχία, Aesch. Pers., 326, μικροψυχίη, Isoc. Or., 5, 79, which all presuppose the dominant meaning "soul." Medicine in the 5th cent. and later also presupposes the division of man into body and soul, Hippocr. De aere aquis locis, 19, 7 (CMG, I, 1, 2, p. 68), the ψυχή being the seat of all spiritual and moral qualities, *ibid.,* 24 (p. 77 f.). The ψυχή is the self of a man, Eur. Suppl., 160; Ba., 75; Hdt., II, 123, 2; this in no way contradicts the older sense of "life," Eur. Alc., 462; Or., 1163; Hdt., I, 24, 2.

3. ψυχή in the Philosophy of Plato.

In the light of what has been said, Socrates' concentration of all moral effort on ἐπιμελεῖσθαι τῆς ψυχῆς (Plat. Ap., 30b) and his constantly repeated assertion that profit and loss are merely that which makes the soul of the individual better or worse are simply the résumé of a long development. Since man may now be judged exclusively by the state of the soul, as an individual acting morally he is independent of external events or the judgment of the world around. Plato starts with this Socratic position but also comes under other influences in his comprehensive psychology.

a. ἑκὼν ἀέκοντί γε θυμῷ, Hom. Il., 4, 43 and θυμὸς δὲ κρείσσων τῶν ἐμῶν βουλευμάτων, Eur. Med., 1079 bear witness to the early experience that resolve based on insight into the situation can come up against spontaneous impulses that have their origin in the soul too. Trichotomy is the answer to this. λογιστικόν, θυμοειδές and ἐπιθυμητικόν are to be found together in the soul, Plat. Resp., IV, 439c-441b etc.

b. The different parts of the soul have different worth acc. to ontological categories. λογιστικόν communicates most strongly with pure being that is accessible only to thought, while ἐπιθυμητικόν is bound to the sense-world which is a reflection and which does not enjoy true being. In his life-long struggle for true knowledge, then, man must ensure for λογιστικόν its due control over the other parts of the soul, cf. the comparison

---

[13] Ed. Lobel-Page, *op. cit.* (→ n. 7).
[14] On the early stages in lyric speech cf. Snell, *op. cit.,* 19 and cf. also H. Fränkel, *Dichtung u. Philosophie d. früh. Griechentums*[2] (1962), 432 f., 444-7.
[15] Ed. Page, *op. cit.* (→ n. 10), 282.

with the charioteer in Plat. Phaedr., 246a-d. This leads logically to the teaching that moral struggle is a flight from the world of sense and an approximation to intelligible being, i.e., to God, Theaet., 176b. [16]

c. Since the soul, or its pre-eminent part, belongs to transcendent being, [17] it is not bound by the finitude of the sense-world. It is pre-existent and immortal. With the help of the Pythagorean teaching about the next world and about transmigration Plato explains this view mythically, e.g., Resp., X, 614b ff. But he rejects the Pythagorean def. of the soul as the numerically understood harmony of the organism, since this contradicts the nature of the soul as being, Phaed., 92a ff.

d. Plato sees the structure of the individual soul in that of the true state as well, which is a larger model of the soul, e.g., Resp., IV, 435a; 441a. This thought, which presupposes that man's nature develops only in the *polis*, was not so fruitful later as that of the connection between the individual soul and that of the cosmos, Tim., 30b-31b. [18] This doctrine understands the world as a living and functionally ordered organism. Life, however, means movement, [19] and this is said to be of the ἴδιον of the soul, Phaedr., 245c. The older sense of "life" is thus constitutive for the concept of the world soul.

Up to later antiquity psychology underwent further development in the individual philosophical schools. Neo-Platonism was esp. original in this area. Only a few details of the later development can be dealt with here. [20]

4. The Psychology of Post-Platonic Philosophy.

a. Constitution of the Soul.

While the Platonists with few exceptions, e.g., Ptolemaeus in Stob. Ecl., I, 378, 1 ff., cling to the immortality of the soul as a part of intelligible being, and accept the difficult process of its temporary union with a material body, for the Peripatetics [21] the immaterial soul is the principle of the form, life, and activity of the total organism, since there is no separate intelligible being in Aristotelian ontology → VII, 1031, 11 ff. [22] The Epicureans and Stoics (→ VII, 1032, 16 ff.) think the soul is

---

[16] The τέλος formula ὁμοίωσις θεῷ, which became a fixed one in the academic tradition from the time of Xenocrates, can thus be construed in terms of an asceticism that is hostile to the body as well as in the more reasonable sense that we must think of God's nature intellectually and imitate His goodness, cf. H. Merki, "Ὁμοίωσις Θεῷ," *Paradosis,* 7 (1952).

[17] For Plato, then, only the λογιστικόν of the soul is immortal. Xenocrates Fr., 75 (ed. R. Heinze, *Xenocrates* [1892], 188) extends immortality to the whole of the soul. Albinus and Atticus return to Plato's view here, while Iamblichus and Porphyrius follow Xenocrates, cf. Procl. in Tim. on 41c d (III, 234, 7 ff.).

[18] For Plato and the Academy the individual soul is not part of the cosmic soul, as in Stoicism, but it has the same οὐσία even if created later by the demiurge, cf. F. M. Cornford, *Plato's Cosmology* (1937), 57 f. Plut. De Virtute Morali, 3 (II, 441 f.) calls the individual soul a μίμημα of the world soul.

[19] Self-movement as a special feature of the soul remains an important principle in psychology, cf. Aristot. An., II, 1, p. 412b, 16 f.; M. Ant., V, 19.

[20] Cf. the rich doxography in Stob. Ecl., I, 362, 23 - 383, 14 (from Iambl.) and Eus. Praep. Ev., 15, 60 f. (Ps.-Plut. Plac. Phil., IV [II, 898c-899b], cf. H. Diels, Doxographi Graeci [1879], 389-392).

[21] The Peripatetics always shunned both the materialistic psychology of the Stoics and Epicureans and also the spiritual psychology of the Academy. Thus Dicaearchus Fr., 8 (F. Wehrli, *Die Schule d. Aristot. Dikaiarchos²* [1967], 14 f.) disputes the theory that the soul has its own οὐσία, while Alex. Aphr. An., I, 126r (I, 19, 6-20); II, 145v (I, 114, 36) contests its description as σῶμα λεπτομερές (Epicurean) or πνεῦμα (Stoic).

[22] Aristot. Metaph., VII, 6, p. 1045b, 7 ff. etc.

material like all being, whether it be made up of especially small and mobile atoms [23] or whether it be like πνεῦμα, fire, a stream of the finest material which flows through the coarser body and is more compressed in the head and the heart, in the centres of vital force and in the power of thought. [24] This finest matter is the force which gives form and order and life to the whole cosmos. It may be seen in purity in the fiery stars which move in mathematically-rational courses. The individual soul is simply a broken off part of the world soul with which it will be reunited at death. In the Stoics there is a narrower correspondence between the individual soul and the world soul than in the Academics, who followed Plato's Timaeus (→ n. 18). The otherworldly home of the soul in the Platonic myth, the ὑπερουράνιος τόπος, corresponds to the starry world, which is immanent but which is still outside true experience. Apart from the fact that the materialistic psychology of the soul can easily become spiritual, both doctrines lead to the view that the soul and the cosmos are closely related. Psychology has much in common with astronomy or astrology. [25]

b. Division of the Soul.

Platonic trichotomy (→ VI, 395, 9 ff.) is the starting-point of all later divisions. Aristot. An., III, 10, p. 433b, 1 ff. etc. has in the strict sense only a division into δυνάμεις and not μέρη. He expressly ascribes all vegetative and animal functions to the soul, and thus adds these to its structure along with the forces known from Plato. The rational sphere of the soul is specifically human, the irrational and impulsive sphere man shares with animals, and the vegetative sphere he shares with both animals and plants, Gen. An., I, 4, p. 741a, 1 etc. [26] All understandings agree [27] that the power of thought has the highest worth. [28] Stoicism goes so far as to say that all affections of the soul, even those that are called irrational, are to be regarded as judgments of the understanding or resultant impulses, [29] while Panaetius and Pos., following the ideas of the Academy and the Peripa-

---

[23] Epic. Ep., I, 63 (Usener): ἡ ψυχὴ σῶμά ἐστι λεπτομερὲς παρ' ὅλον τὸ ἄθροισμα παρεσπαρμένον, προσεμφερέστατον δὲ πνεύματι θερμοῦ τινα κρᾶσιν ἔχοντι καὶ πῇ μὲν τούτῳ προσεμφερές, πῇ δὲ τούτῳ.

[24] Cf. Fr., 773-911 (v. Arnim, II, 217-263). With its view that the soul-pneuma is nourished by blood Stoicism follows the old idea of the blood-soul, Zeno, Cleanthes and Chrysipp. acc. to Diogenes Babylonius Fr., 30 (v. Arnim, III, 216).

[25] For the idea that σῶμα and ψυχή are constitutionally dependent on climate and other environmental influences cf. Hippocr. De aere aquis locis, 19, 7 (CMG, I, 1, 2, p. 68); 23, 5 (p. 76); 24, 3 (p. 78) etc.; Emped. Fr., 106 (Diels, I, 350); Plat. and the Platonists, Ps.-Plat. Epin., 987d e, esp. Plot., cf. K. Reinhardt, Art. "Poseidonios," Pauly-W., 22 (1954), 678 f. In astrology we then have a determination of the soul by the different constellations acc. to geographical location, Ptolemaeus Tetrabiblos, II, 2 (ed. F. Boll-A. Boer, Apotelesmatica [1940], 58-61).

[26] There are comparable differentiations already among the pre-Socratics. Thus the Pythagorean Philolaus Fr., 13 (Diels, I, 413) locates the power of thought νοῦς in the brain, emotion ψυχὴ καὶ αἴσθησις in the heart, the power of nourishment and growth in the lower body and that of reproduction in the genitalia. The word νοῦς (→ IV, 954, 12 ff), which is here a fixed one in distinction from ψυχή, can be more or less fixed also in many pre-Socratics, esp. Anaxag., e.g., Fr., 12 (Diels, II, 38, 4 f.). Thus the way is prepared early for the differentiation of νοῦς and ψυχή, which is found in part in Plat. Phileb., 30c; Tim., 30b.

[27] Cf. the material on Tert. De Anima, 14, 2 in Waszink, 210-215.

[28] For the leading organ of the soul, which in almost all schools is the power of pure thought, the originally Stoic term ἡγεμονικόν came to be used. This can be called the God or daemon which acc. to an ancient religious view, e.g., Hes. Op., 121 ff., watches over man's way. Cf. Xenocrates Fr., 81 (ed. Heinze, op. cit. [→ n. 17]), 191; Pos. in Gal. De Placit. Hippocratis et Platonis, V (ed. I. Müller [1874], 448, 15 f.); Diog. L., VII, 88 and the comm. of W. Theiler, Kaiser Marc. Aurel. Wege zu sich selbst (1951), 309 f. on M. Ant., II, 13, 1.

[29] In orthodox Stoic teaching human action is explained psychologically as follows. From sense impressions reason forms an idea φαντασία and from this, in its own act of knowledge, it reaches a συγκατάθεσις whether it applies to the subject as the morally

tetics, recognise the autonomy of the alogical sphere and postulate its control by the understanding, cf. the relevant polemic against Chrysipp. in Gal., De Placitis Hippocratis et Platonis, V, p. 463 f. [30] The psychology of Middle Platonism uses the distinction between νοῦς and ψυχή, which is clear in Aristot. but not yet so in Plato, [31] to characterise the ladder of descent from transcendence to immanence. The soul has a part in νοῦς, from which it has proceeded, and it thus belongs primarily to intelligible being. On entering the world of sense, however, it assumes powers which enable it to work on matter. Thus the νοῦς affects the ψυχή at a higher level and the ψυχή affects the σῶμα at a lower level, Plut. De Animae Procreatione in Timaeo, 27 ff. (II, 1026c ff.); Albinus, Didascalius, 4, 5 ff. [32] Thus the innermost core of man is the νοῦς, Plut. Fac. Lun., 30 (II, 944 f.). [33] If only the first stage of the descent is traversed, we have demons, which are ψυχαί without bodies but not purely noetic beings. Something of the same can happen to the human soul when it ascends after death, Sext. Emp. Math., IX, 74. A psychological basis is thus found for a widespread popular belief.

Integration of the ψυχή into a hierarchy of being is also found in Pos., though with no antithesis of matter and spirit. [34] The πνεῦμα, in Stoicism the substance of the ψυχή (→ 613, 27 ff.), becomes in Pos. [35] the substratum of the ἄλογος ψυχή, which is distinct from the νοῦς, and which M. Ant., V, 33, 4; VII, 16, 3; XII, 26 2 disparagingly calls ψυχάριον, cf. also Ascl., 18 (→ VI, 356). The scale σῶμα, ψυχή, νοῦς in M. Ant., III, 16, 1, cf. XII, 3, 1 etc., ultimately goes back to Pos., and with the separation of the νοερόν from the four elements, M. Ant., IV, 4, 3 it is a spiritualising of the concept of the soul that is fundamentally alien to Stoic psychology. [36] Later Peripatetics for their

---

acting individual (ἐφ' ἡμῖν) and hence whether it has worth or not. There follows an irresistible urge to act, since the individual tries to do what is of worth and to avoid what is not. The impulse is a ὁρμὴ πλεονάζουσα on the basis of a wrongly conceived or wrongly evaluated idea. As an impulse it exceeds all measure, since the aim it seeks does not exist in reality but is wrongly assumed.

[30] Ed. I. Müller (1874). In the orthodox view apathy, or freedom from all affections, is the goal of moral striving. This is the power of right judgment unaffected by errors and the like. In contrast Platonists and Peripatetics teach metriopathy, the control and direction of intrinsically legitimate affections by reason. God as pure νοῦς or λόγος is without affections, cf. M. Pohlenz, "Vom Zorne Gottes," FRL, 12 (1909). In the imperial period these differences are less important and the Platonist Plut. can commend apathy in De Curiositate, 1 (II, 515c).

[31] For Aristot. An., I, 4, p. 408b, 18 only the divine νοῦς and not the individual soul is immortal.

[32] Ed. P. Louis, Albinos, Epitomé (1945). Cf. Xenocrates acc. to Heinze, op. cit. (→ n. 17), IX.

[33] In the allegorical interpretation of myth in Plut. Is. et. Os., 49 (II, 371a b) the νοῦς corresponds to the good Osiris and the ἄλογος ψυχή and σῶμα to the wicked Typhon-Seth. For details cf. W. Theiler, "Gott u. Seele im kaiserzeitl. Denken. Forschungen z. Neuplatonismus," Quellen u. Stud. z. Gesch. d. Philosophie, 10 (1966), 104-123.

[34] It is open to question whether Plat. and the Platonists derived evil directly from the antithesis of body and soul or matter and spirit, cf. Festugière, 1-32. In Phaedr., 246a-c Plat. has a kind of fall of the soul or deviation from its destiny in the fulfilment of ἐνσωμάτωσις. Acc. to Tim., 30a matter is in chaotic and hence evil movement prior to its fashioning into the cosmos by the world soul created by the demiurge, and in virtue of its proclivity to disorder one can in fact regard it as the source of evil. Middle Platonism, however, was influenced by Aristot.'s view of ὕλη, which is without quality and hence cannot be the cause of evil. Plut. De Animae Procreatione in Timaeo, 7 (II, 1015c) traces back evil to the ψυχή, which has a share in many stages of being, and not to the νοῦς. On the history of the problem cf. E. Schröder, Plotins Abhandlung ΠΟΘΕΝ ΤΑ ΚΑΚΑ, Diss. Rostock (1916). For Pos. cf. Reinhardt, op. cit. (→ n. 25), 752. Pos. has to take into account the Stoic view that in truth there is no κακά.

[35] Cf. Theiler, op. cit. (→ n. 28), 320 and 326.

[36] For a full doctrine of hierarchical being cf. Neo-Platonism. Under the influence of Neo-Pythagorean speculation on numbers the Neo-Platonists view the transition from being to non-being as a transition from unity to plurality. We thus have the scale ἕν, νοῦς, ψυχή, σῶμα, for with νοῦς comes the cleavage of original unity into subj. and obj. in the act of thought.

part modified their teaching under the influence of the psychology of Stoicism. Ptolemaeus De Iudicandi Facultate, 15 [37] distinguishes two ἡγεμονικά → n. 28. Alex. Aphrod. An., II, 143v (I, 106, 19 ff.) offers the doctrine of the threefold νοῦς: ὑλικός, ἐπίκτητος (attained by learning, cf. I, 138r [I, 82, 1]) and ποιητικός. Only the last is divine and it is an accident rather than a constituent part of the soul, which does not have immortality acc. to the Peripatetic view. [38] In Neo-Pythagoreanism the attempt to emphasise the spiritual leads to the doctrine of two souls, the first of which, the λογικὴ ψυχή which is equated with νοῦς, comes from the intelligible world. The ἄλογος ψυχή is again πνεῦμα (→ 615, 16), the material garment of the λογικὴ ψυχή, which is put on by this in its descent through the astral spheres, Numenius in Stob. Ecl., I, 350, 25 ff.; Oracula Chaldaica, p. 63, 61. [39]

The total picture shows that in the philosophical language of the Hellenistic-Roman period ψυχή denotes the totality of the functions of mind and soul but that in virtue of its distinction from νοῦς, ψυχή undergoes a certain devaluation, since is can no longer denote pure spirituality.

The wealth of psychological theories in post-class. medicine is connected at all pts. with philosophy and naturally a special interest is shown in the organic relation of intellectual functions. Opinions about the corporeality of the ψυχή differ sharply, cf. the polemic in Gal. De Naturalibus Facultatibus, I, 12 (Kühn, II, 26-30) against the so-called methodical school. The fact that a corpse seems heavier than a living body is claimed as an argument both for and against the corporeality of the soul. [40]

5. Popular Ideas of the Post-Classical Age.

Popular ideas correspond in large part to what we now mean by soul. The ψυχή is the impalpable essential core of man, the bearer of thought, will and emotion, the quintessence of human life.

The stylist Ps.-Demetr. De Elocutione, 227 says that a letter ought to be the εἰκὼν τῆς ψυχῆς, i.e., the nature of the sender. A good Ethiopian has a black body but a white soul acc. to a burial inscr. [41] and the faithful wife is a ψυχὴ φιλανδροτάτη, Epigr. Graec., 547, 14 (1st/2nd cent. A.D.). One must have a rich ψυχή, says the comic writer Antiph. Fr., 327 (CAF, II, 134); χρήματα are only the wings of life, which corresponds to the ἔξω χορηγία of Peripatetic ethics. One can sacrifice to the gods ἁπλῇ τῇ ψυχῇ,

---

[37] Ed. F. Lammert (1952).
[38] Acc. to Alex. Aphr. An., I, 139v (I, 89, 16 ff.) only the divine νοῦς ποιητικός is immortal. Every other νοῦς dies with the related soul.
[39] Ed. W. Kroll, "De oraculis Chaldaicis," Breslauer philolog. Abh., 7, 1 (1894), cf. O. Geudtner, "Die Seelenlehre d. chald. Orakel, 1," Beiträge z. klass. Philologie, 35 (1971), 16-24. Perhaps in Numenius, as in many Gnostics (→ 656, 23 ff.), the story of the ascent and descent of the soul through the starry spheres is to be taken lit. and not as the mythical explanation of a speculatively understood process in the soul, cf. E. A. Leemans, Stud. over den wijsgeer Numenius van Apamea met uitgave d. fragmenten (1936), 43-9. This can hardly be true of the myth (deriving from Pos.) in Plut. Fac. Lun., 28 f. (II, 943a-f) which underlies the relation νοῦς/ἥλιος, cf. Vett. Val., I, 1 (p. 1 f.), ψυχή/σελήνη and σῶμα/γῆ. Plat. Phaed., 65c-69d and Plot. Enn., VI, 9, 9 show that myths are told to illustrate processes in the soul. Naturally philosophical mythopoeia uses current religious notions so that an unskilled reader can understand them religiously as the impartation of supernatural knowledge. Philosophical systematising, too, often takes into account prevailing religious views. Thus the immortality of the individual soul does not fit in with Stoic physics and yet Cleanthes teaches that all ψυχαί, and Chrysipp. that those of the σοφοί, will have individual existence after death up to the next ἐκπύρωσις that closes an epoch, Diog. L., VII, 157.
[40] Cf. Waszink, 157-9 on Tert. De Anima, 8, 3.
[41] Ed. W. Peek, "Griech. Grabgedichte," Schr. u. Quellen d. Alten Welt, 7 (1960), 420 (3rd cent. A.D.).

Ditt. Syll.³, III, 1042, 12 (2nd cent. A.D.), or do something ὅλῃ τῇ ψυχῇ, so already Xenoph. Mem., III, 11, 10, cf. ἐκ πάσης ψυχῆς, Epict. Diss., III, 22, 18, or be bound to others μιᾷ ψυχῇ, Dio Chrys. Or., 36, 30. Marital fellowship extends to outward goods βίος, to σῶμα and ψυχή, ⁴² Ditt. Syll.³, II, 783, 33 (1st cent. B.C.). A magical defixion embraces χεῖρες, πόδες, γλῶσσα, ψυχή, ibid., III, 1175 (3rd cent. B.C.). σὴ ψυχὴ ἐπίσταται means "you know very well," BGU, IV, 1141, 23 f. (1st cent. B.C.). καθαρὰ ψυχή is a pure conscience or good disposition, BGU, IV, 1040, 21 (2nd cent. A.D.), and ἔχω κατὰ ψυχήν means "to have in view," Pap. Societ. Archaeol. Atheniensis, 62, 17 f. (1st/2nd cent. A.D.). ⁴³ Artemidor.'s book of dreams, which circulated widely, distinguishes ἴδια σώματος like eating and sleeping from ἴδια ψυχῆς like joy and sorrow, Onirocr., I, 1 (p. 3), and assumes that ideas like the relation of the soul to the cosmos, II, 60 (p. 155), its ascent to heaven, II, 68 (p. 160) and its trips during physical sleep, V, 43 (p. 262) are well known. That souls after death go to the hereafter, to heaven, the aether or the like, to a place of punishment or bliss, is an ancient, Eur. Suppl., 533, and widespread, Epigr. Graec., 433 (2nd cent. A.D.); Gr., VI, 1031 (2nd/3rd cent. A.D.), ⁴⁴ but not undisputed view, Callim. Epigr., 13; IG, IX, 2, 640. ⁴⁵ The satires on the underworld in Luc. presuppose a cleavage here. That moral significance attaches only to the state of the soul is taught not merely by philosophy. Astrology promises that it can free the soul, and hence man as such, by setting forth the rules determining physical events, Vett. Val., V, 9 (p. 220, 21). Human freedom is freedom of the soul and its consciousness and decisions. The ψυχή is the most worthwhile thing in man, Menand. Mon., 843. ⁴⁶ ψυχή can still mean "life." ⁴⁷ σῶσαι πολλὰς ψυχάς means "to save many human lives," P. Tebt., I, 56, 11 (2nd cent. A.D.) or P. Oxy., VII, 1033, 11 (4th cent. A.D.). The expression ἐπιβουλευθεὶς μὲν εἰς τὴν ψυχήν denotes an attempt on the life, Achill. Tat. VIII, 3, 1. Whether πᾶσα ψυχή "everyone" adopts this sense or is a term for man acc. to his most important element it is hard to say, for the ideas overlap. παραβάλλομαι τῇ ψυχῇ in Diod. S., 3, 36 means "to hazard one's life," cf. the honorary inscr. ψυχῇ καὶ σώματι παραβαλλόμενος καὶ δαπάναις χρώμενος ταῖς τοῦ ἐκ βίου, Ditt. Syll.³, II, 762, 39 f. (1st cent. B.C.). Later combinations with ψυχή in the post-class. age are all based on the meaning "soul," cf. μακρόψυχος "patient," Preis. Zaub., I, 4, 2902 (4th/5th cent. A.D.) alongside the older μακρόθυμος and μακροψυχέω, P. Greci e Lat., IV, 299, 11 (3rd cent. A.D.).

Dihle

B. The Anthropology of the Old Testament.

1. נֶפֶשׁ.

The Hbr. term for ψυχή is נֶפֶשׁ; ψυχή is also used twice for רוּחַ at Gn. 41:8; Ex. 35:21, once for חַיִּים ψ 63 (64):2, and 25 times for לֵב 2 K. 6:11; 1 Ch. 12:39; 15:29; 17:2; 2 Ch. 7:11; 9:1; 15:15; 31:21; ψ 20 (21):3; 36 (37):15 vl.; 68:20, 32; Qoh. 7:21; Prv. 6:21; 15:32; 26:25; Is. 7:2, 4; 10:7; 13:7; 24:7; 33:18; 42:25; 44:19; Jer. 4:19. In the trend toward uniformity one may see an attempt at systematisation and also evidence that the three Hbr.

---

⁴² This division corresponds to the Peripatetic teaching on goods which was adopted by Middle Platonism, Cic. De Orat. II, 342 (cf. Stob. Ecl., II, 130, 15 ff.).
⁴³ Ed. G. A. Petropulos, ΠΡΑΓΜΑΤΕΙΑΙ ΤΗΣ ΑΚΑΔΗΜΙΑΣ ΑΘΗΝΩΝ, I (1939).
⁴⁴ R. Lattimore, Themes in Gk. and Lat. Epitaphs² (1962), 44-54.
⁴⁵ Ibid., 74-8.
⁴⁶ Ed. S. Jaekel, Menandri Sententiae (1964).
⁴⁷ Cf. the use of the words ἔμψυχος/ἄψυχος in non-philosophical speech. The beast is ἔμψυχον as a living being, P. Giess., 40, II, 22 (2nd/3rd cent. A.D.), cf. Thuc. VII, 29, 4, and the slave is def. as ὄργανον ἔμψυχον, Aristot. Eth. Nic., IX, 13, p. 1161b, 4; but the beast is also ἄλογον, an irrational being, as already Plat. Prot., 321b, later used only for the horse, P. Oxy., I, 138, 29 (7th cent. A.D.).

words were so close that they could be viewed as interchangeable. נֶפֶשׁ is as hard to define as it is to translate [48] owing to its fluid and dynamic aspect.

a. נֶפֶשׁ and Breath.

The root נפשׁ[49] means "to respire," "to breathe." This physical aspect may be seen in נפשׁ "to breathe" "to draw breath," and also in נשׁף "to breathe heavily," Ex. 15:10, נשׁב "to blow," Is. 40:7 and נשׁם "to breathe with difficulty," Is. 42:14. נפשׁ occurs only three times as a verb, once concretely "to draw breath," when physically exhausted, 2 S. 16:14, and twice in connection with the Sabbath rest, Ex. 23:12; 31:17, Yahweh being the subj. in the latter v. Since the Sabbath is the gt. regulator of time, which consists alternately of rest and activity, breathing with its similar alternation can denote the life which is constantly threatened and constantly won again in the cosmos and in man. [50] The deciding mark of the living creature is breathing, and its cessation means the end of life. Hence the root נפשׁ in the form of the noun נֶפֶשׁ, which occurs 755 times in the Hbr. Bible, denotes "life" or "living creature," the special sense of "breath" being expressed by נְשָׁמָה, although often this shares the development of נֶפֶשׁ,[51] Dt. 20:16; Jos. 10:40; 11:11, 14; 1 K. 15:29; Ps. 150:6; Is. 57:16. One might say that נֶפֶשׁ always includes נְשָׁמָה but is not limited to it. In 1 K. 17:17 lack of נְשָׁמָה causes the departure of נֶפֶשׁ, which returns when the prophet gives the child breath again, for נֶפֶשׁ alone is what makes a living creature into a living organism. The fluid form of breath opens up various possibilities of usage which sometimes stress the fluidity and sometimes try to be more concrete. Thus the meaning "neck," "throat," which נֶפֶשׁ can have in some passages (→ n. 52), is an attempt to localise at a specific and visible place the expression of life. [52] Always, however, this is a derived

---

[48] There are three recent monographs on נֶפֶשׁ. J. H. Becker, *Het begrip nefesj in het OT* (1942) analyses all the passages in which the word occurs and divides them into groups: a. נֶפֶשׁ as life, b. as goal of life, c. as individual and personal pron., d. as someone, e. as a living creature. Lys Nèphèsh in his historical section surveys the concept of the soul in antiquity and then in a chronological and statistical section offers a division acc. to literary genres. More attention should be paid to his exeg. observations than to the historical deductions from them. Murtonen starts with the sense of life in orientation to something. In our view, this study, which sticks to the linguistic data and stresses the functional aspect of נֶפֶשׁ, is the best starting-point for further investigation.

[49] How the letters in the root relate to one another may be seen in the schema in Becker, *op. cit.*, 100, which is based on Mandelkern and Ges.-Buhl.

[50] Lys Nèphèsh, 121.

[51] The root נשׁם occurs 26 times in the OT, 24 as noun, and means the "breath" which God blows into man or the breath in man (LXX πνοή) which is always viewed as God's gift to man. Animals are excluded, cf. T. C. Mitchell, "OT Usage of nešama," VT, 11 (1961), 177-187.

[52] Cf. L. Dürr, "Hbr. נֶפֶשׁ = akk. napištu = Gurgel, Kehle," ZAW, 43 (1925), 262-9. None of the instances adduced by Dürr necessitates the sense of "throat." When neck is meant we find צַוָּאר, Is. 8:8; 30:28. בָּתֵּי הַנֶּפֶשׁ in Is. 3:20 is contested but it can hardly mean "houses on the neck," as Dürr contends (268), nor little perfume flasks that sweeten the breath, for נֶפֶשׁ never means "perfume." The content suggests magical devices to protect the life from danger, cf. in Ez. 13:18-20 the magical practices of prophetesses to gain control of human lives נְפָשׁוֹת so as to give them life or death. Things are rather different in Accad. Kunuk kišadi "seal on the neck" is equivalent to kunukku napištika "seal of the throat." Ugaritic is par. to the OT. Closest to the sense "throat" is bnpsh par. bgngnh "what is inward," Baal, II, VII, 48 (G. R. Driver, "Canaanite Myths and Legends," *OT Stud.*, 3 [1956] 100 f.) = II, AB, VII, 48 (J. Aistleitner, "Die myth. u. kult. Texte aus Ras Schamra," *Biblioth. Orient. Hungarica*, 8² [1964], 45) = 51, VII, 48 (C. H. Gordon, "Ugaritic Textbook," *Analecta Orient.*, 38 [1965], 173); šat npšh "what comes from his נֶפֶשׁ," Keret, II, I, 35 (Driver, 40 f.) = II, K I-II, 35˙ (Aistl. 99) = 125, 35 (Gordon, II, 192) npšh llḥm tptḥ "he

sense and in no Hbr. text does it express the original meaning. Jon. 2:6 is not ref. to water that reaches up to the neck but to the chaotic element which threatens life, so that there is equation with בּֽה or with expressions that suggests drowning. Is. 5:14; Hab. 2:5; Qoh. 6:7; Ps. 63:5; Prv. 13:2 allude to fervent desire rather than to a part of the body. The link with breath is very plain when death is def. as a departure of the נֶפֶשׁ. Yet one should not conclude that the נֶפֶשׁ is an immaterial principle which can be abstracted away from its material sub-structure and which can lead an independent existence. The departure of the נֶפֶשׁ is a metaphor for death; a dead man is one who has ceased to breathe. The alternation of breathing corresponds to the fluid nature of the terms life and death in the OT. Life and death are two worlds which cannot be sharply differentiated. [53] When, e.g., sickness and anxiety are said to be a constriction of the נֶפֶשׁ, Nu. 21:4; Ju. 10:16, this means that they are manifestations of the world of death. The concrete sense may also be seen in the combination of נֶפֶשׁ and נפח "to breathe out," Jer. 15:9; Job 11:20; 31:39.

b. נֶפֶשׁ and Blood.

The relation between נֶפֶשׁ and blood is probably along other lines which are independent of the relation between נֶפֶשׁ and breath. Basic to both, however, is the idea of the body as a living organism. When breath and blood leave the body, then every form of life disappears. [54]

The three texts which most clearly illustrate the connection between נֶפֶשׁ and blood take us into the ritual sphere. In the prohibition בָּשָׂר בְּנַפְשׁוֹ דָמוֹ לֹא תֹאכֵלוּ in Gn. 9:4 דָמוֹ is an explanatory gloss which is designed to stress that the נֶפֶשׁ is to be sought only in the blood. Lv. 17:11 confirms that the seat of the נֶפֶשׁ is in the blood. The rather different formulation in v. 14 corresponds to the LXX. With his double statement that the נֶפֶשׁ is the blood and that it is in the blood the preacher of the Law is warning against a magical understanding of blood. Blood can work atonement only so long as the vital force נֶפֶשׁ is in it. This is also the pt. in Dt. 12:23, although here the ref. is to eating rather than to expiation. Attempts to find a connection between blood and breath, e.g., breath as the steam of fresh blood, must be abandoned. In the above texts נֶפֶשׁ has nothing whatever to do with a breath-soul or a blood-soul; [55] it simply denotes the vital force. There is

---

opened his נֶפֶשׁ to the bread" Keret II, VI, 11 (Driver, 44 f.) == II, K VI, 11 (Aistl., 103) == 127, 11 (Gordon, 194). In these texts, however, npšh and brlth, which in the last ref. is par. to npšh, mean the desire for food or sexual satisfaction rather than the throat.

[53] Modern research gen. accepts this view in relation to the thought of Israel, cf. J. Pedersen, *Israel, Its Life and Culture*, I-II (1926), 453 and C. Barth, *Die Errettung vom Tode in d. individuellen Klage- u. Dankliedern d. AT* (1947), 67.

[54] Blood plays no part in the OT creation stories. The Bab. creation myth calls the blood of the vanquished god an essential constituent of the human body, Enuma eliš, VI, 35 (J. B. Pritchard, *Ancient Near Eastern Texts rel. to the OT²* [1955], 68), but this feature does not occur in the Sumerian texts. The Islamic tradition, like that of Israel, speaks of the fashioning of man out of mud, Koran, Sura 6, 2; 15, 26; 23, 12-14. Only in Wis., which was influenced by Hellenism, do "scientific" aspects come to the fore. Here man arises out of a mixture of male sperm with female menstrual blood, 7:2. The relation of sperm to blood gave rise to speculation in Gk. philosophy, esp. among the Stoics. Because it is *spuma sanguinis*, Diog. v. Apoll., Fr., 6 (Diels, II, 62); Aristot. Gen. An., I, 19, p. 762b, 1-13, the sperm has a pneumatic element. For other ref. to the relation between blood, soul and life cf. Rüsche Blut, 57-307. In the OT blood is mentioned only in legal and cultic connections. Exceptions are Ps. 72:14 and 1 Ch. 11:19, where it is par. to נֶפֶשׁ.

[55] Rüsche Blut, 319-340 and before him M. Lichtenstein, "Das Wort נפש in d. Bibel," *Schrift d. Lehranstalt f. d. Wissenschaft d. Judt.*, IV, 5-6 (1920) find the first stage of OT anthropology in the localisation of נֶפֶשׁ in the blood. Later breath became its seat and this led to the idea of the steam of blood, which is found in the works of Hom., e.g., Il., 23, 880;

a more likely connection with blood in expressions like "to pour out" the נֶפֶשׁ in Lam. 2:12; Ps. 42:4; 1 S. 1:15; Job 30:16, though נֶפֶשׁ might be more appropriately understood as "tears." The emptying of the נֶפֶשׁ in Ps. 141:8; Is. 53:12 and the use of נֶפֶשׁ and דָם as par. in Ps. 72:14; 2 S. 23:17, cf. 1 Ch. 11:19 strongly favour a connection between נֶפֶשׁ and blood even outside the ritual sphere.

c. נֶפֶשׁ and Person.

נֶפֶשׁ is the usual term for a man's total nature, for what he is and not just what he has. This gives the term priority in the anthropological vocabulary, [56] for the same cannot be said of either spirit, heart, or flesh. The classical text in Gn. 2:7 clearly expresses this truth when it calls man in his totality a נֶפֶשׁ חַיָּה. Perhaps in view of its over-logical formulation this passage never became normative for the OT as a whole. It should be noted that it expresses the external aspect of a man rather than the modalities of his life. [57] The word נֶפֶשׁ developed in two main directions which correspond more to structures of thought than to a chronological sequence. The two directions might be defined in terms of form and movement. The נֶפֶשׁ is almost always connected with a form. It has no existence apart from the body. Hence the best translation in many instances is "person" comprised in corporeal reality. The person can be marked off and counted, Gn. 12:5; 46:18; Jos. 10:28; 11:11. Each individual is a נֶפֶשׁ, and when the texts speaks of a single נֶפֶשׁ for a totality, the totality is viewed as a single person, a "corporate personality." [58] Hence נֶפֶשׁ can denote what is most individual in human nature, namely, the ego, and it can become a synonym of the personal pronoun, Gn. 27:25: "that my נֶפֶשׁ (I) may bless thee," and Jer. 3:11: "Unfaithful Israel has justified its נֶפֶשׁ, i.e., has shown itself to be righteous."

d. נֶפֶשׁ as Corpse and Tomb.

The accent on the person allowed the term to be retained even with reference to the person in its least mobile state and under what is naturally its least vital aspect. The lifeless corpse is either a נֶפֶשׁ מֵת (Nu. 6:6; 19:13) or simply a נֶפֶשׁ (Lv. 19:28; 22:4; Nu. 5:2; 9:6, 10; Hag. 2:13).

Od., 10, 163 but does not actually occur in the Bible. Lichtenstein's rendering of Dt. 12:23: "For the blood is what we to-day call soul" (25) imports into the OT an idea that is more attractive than convincing. Cf. also C. F. Jean, "Tentatives d'explication du 'moi' chez les anciens peuples de l'Orient méditerranéen," RHR, 121 (1940), 109-127.

[56] Murtonen, 11, cf. 76 offers the following def. of נֶפֶשׁ which is applicable both here and in all periods: "the living and active being of its possessor." Yet he seems to overstress the collective sense of נֶפֶשׁ. If the people has a נֶפֶשׁ this is not because the totality is greater than the individual, true though this is in part, but rather because the people is viewed as an individual. The נֶפֶשׁ is always seen in its individual manifestation and physical restriction. That the Bible speaks of בֶּן־אָדָם but never בֶּן־נֶפֶשׁ is perhaps a pointer in this direction.

[57] The two main definitions of bibl. anthropology, נֶפֶשׁ חַיָּה and צֶלֶם אֱלֹהִים have this in common, namely, that they view man in his being rather than his having. Again, they both see man in his autonomy and also his dependence. They denote a person, but the terms חַיָּה and אֱלֹהִים bring out the theonomous aspect of OT anthropology as well.

[58] This is the expression used by H. W. Robinson, "The Hebrew Concept of Corporate Personality" in J. Hempel, Werden u. Wesen d. AT, ZAW Beih., 66 (1936), 49-61.

That the ref is to the נֶפֶשׁ of a dead man and not to a dead נֶפֶשׁ may be seen from the
full statement in Nu. 19:13: נֹגֵעַ בְּמֵת בְּנֶפֶשׁ הָאָדָם אֲשֶׁר יָמוּת, "Wosoever toucheth a dead
man, i.e., the body of any man that is dead." In the Bible נֶפֶשׁ ref. only to the corpse
prior to its final dissolution and while it still has distinguishing features. When at a later
date outside the Bible נֶפֶשׁ is used for "tomb" the point is that the individual is in some
way present after death. [59] Acc. to the OT the נֶפֶשׁ has no existence apart from the
individual who possesses it, or, better, who is it. It never leaves him to pursue an independent life of its own. Even less is it a force outside the individual that works variously in
life and death. The inhabitants of sheol are never called נֶפֶשׁ. [60] Belief in the survival of
the dead in the underworld where they may be either in peril or in bliss is not to be
explained by animistic notions but by the attempt to do justice to the mystery of death
and the presence of a resting-place for the dead. [61]

e. נֶפֶשׁ as Expression of the Will.

The aspect of movement triumphed over that of form. This is certainly more in
keeping with the original sense of the term. The נֶפֶשׁ is manifest in orientation to an
object, whether this be the elemental realities of hunger and thirst on the one side
(Dt. 12:15, 20 ff.; 1 S. 2:16; Mi. 7:1; Ps. 107:9; Prv. 6:30; 10:3; 12:10; 23:2; 25:25)
or the lofty aspiration of yearning for God on the other. When it is restricted to
movement, the נֶפֶשׁ is never located in a single organ but can dwell in various parts
of the organism, and these can sometimes be used as synon. for it.

We find נֶפֶשׁ with ref. to the sex drive in Gn. 34:3, 8; Jer. 2:24, the hatred that fills
an enemy in Ps. 27:12; 41:2; Prv. 13:2, pain and sorrow, 1 S. 1:10; 30:6; Ez. 27:31; Job

---

[59] The use of נֶפֶשׁ in this sense expands in post-bibl. Hbr., as in Talmudic texts like bErub.,
53a; 55b; bSheq., II, 5. We also find the expression outside Israel in Syria, Canaan, Palmyra
and Nabatea, v. M. Lidzbarski, Ephemeris f. semitische Epigraphik, I (1902), 91a D. 4
(p. 215) and C. F. Jean-J. Hoftijzer, Dict. des Inscr. sémitiques de l'Ouest (1965), s.v. נבשׁ;
H. Donner-W. Röllig, Kanaan. u. aram. Inschr., I² (1966), 128 and 136, cf. II² (1968), 132 f.,
135 f. (here נאשׁ). In most cases the use of נֶפֶשׁ in this sense can be explained from the development of the Semitic word. In some instances one might ask whether נֶפֶשׁ might not be the
transl. of an original ψυχή in the sense of "butterfly," for in view of the latter's transformation the Gks. often depicted it on tombs as a symbol of life and immortality, cf. B. Lifschitz,
"Der Ausdruck ψυχή in d. griech. Grabinschr.," ZDPV, 76 (1960), 159. At any rate we
find this meaning for נֶפֶשׁ only at a later time and it is to be associated with the development
of more precise ideas about the survival of the individual after death. The supposed Ugaritic
par. (→ n. 52) are better explained in terms of "need," "appetite." At most in ard bnpšny
Baal III* C 20 (Driver, op. cit., 78 f.) = III AB C 20 (Aistleitner, op. cit., 48) = 129, 20
(Gordon, op. cit., 196) there might be an allusion to the grave of Mot.

[60] Murtonen, 3, 12 etc. takes a critical view of M. Seligson. "The meaning of npš mt in the
OT," Stud. Or., 16, 2 (1951). For Seligson נֶפֶשׁ is a "mysterious potency" which influences
man from without. It works in life but more mysteriously in death. In the attempt to explain
the OT concept along other lines than that of the modern soul this thesis pays too little regard
to the Semitic usage which connects נֶפֶשׁ generally with the breath or breathing.

[61] A view that differs from that of Israel may be found in the inscr. of King Panammuwa
of Sam'al from the middle of the 8th cent. B.C., Donner-Röllig, op. cit. (→ n. 5), 214, cf.
ibid., II, 214-223. This Aram. king, who put up a statue to Hadad, expresses the wish: "May
the נֶפֶשׁ of Panammuwa eat and drink with Hadad," line 17, 22. The ref. here is not to the
tomb but a possibility of survival is expressed. In contrast cf. Nu. 23:10; Ju. 16:30, which ref.
to the death of the נֶפֶשׁ. It should not be forgotten that in the Panammuwa inscr. what is at
issue is the survival of a king who already in life, and then also in death, has an unusual
life-potency.

27:2, the will, Gn. 23:8. It is not surprising that the נֶפֶשׁ reaches its full expression in supreme striving after God, so that man is נֶפֶשׁ esp. in the relation to God, [62] Is. 26:9; Ps. 63:1; 84:2; 119:20, 28; 130:5; 143:6, 8. The vocative form נַפְשִׁי in Ps. 42:5, 11; 43:5; 62:5; 103:1 f., 22; 104:1, 35; 116:7; 146:1 is a kind of question that the petitioner addresses to himself, to his vital force which is now to come to its full intensity, or to his responsibility before God, which means that religiously the individual attachment is no less strong than is the collective. [63] Man does not turn to his conscience. Before God, who is the only true source of life, he gathers up all his strength, and before the divine One he finds his own oneness. When the goal is reached, the tension between yearning and having relaxes, cf. Ps. 131:2: "I have brought my נֶפֶשׁ to silence, it has become like a weaned child." [64]

2. Flesh and Body (→ VII, 105, 14 ff.; 1044, 13 ff.).

The significance which is given to the body in נֶפֶשׁ carries with it a certain antithesis to the flesh. Hence בָּשָׂר can sometimes denote the whole man as well as נֶפֶשׁ.

a. Flesh.

In some texts בָּשָׂר has a very material sense, e.g., "edible flesh" in Lv. 7:19; Nu. 11:4, 13; Dt. 32:42; Is. 22:13; Prv. 23:20; Da. 10:3; Job 31:31. בָּשָׂר is used 104 times with ref. to animals and 169 times with ref. to men; later texts contain more ref. בָּשָׂר means the whole body and may have at times what is perhaps the original sense of "skin." [65] We naturally find it in proximity to נֶפֶשׁ, although the individual aspect is stronger in the latter. Thus כָּל-נֶפֶשׁ means "all individuals that can be counted" and כָּל-בָּשָׂר "every living thing." Like נֶפֶשׁ, בָּשָׂר is connected with the blood, Ps. 50:13; Dt. 12:23; Lv. 17:11. But we find the pairing "flesh and blood" for the first time only in Sir. 14:18. [66] Later it means "human" as distinct from God, Gr. En. 15:4; T Ber., 7, 18 (Zuckermandel, 16), or it is used to denote relationship, which is in the OT is expressed by בָּשָׂר alone, Gn. 29:14; 37:27; Ju. 9:2, perhaps also Gn. 2:23 f. In what is still a material sense בָּשָׂר can then mean the "male member," Ez. 23:20; 16:26; Ex. 28:42; Lv. 15:2 f. When we read of the circumcision of the flesh in Gn. 17:11; Ez. 44:7 it is not immediately evident whether we again

---

[62] Murtonen, 50.

[63] The Gk. transl. of the OT tried to do justice to the many senses of נֶפֶשׁ. Thus we often find the personal pronoun for it, Am. 6:8; Ps. 105:22; Est. 4:13, or ἀνήρ in Gn. 14:21; Prv. 16:26; 28:25, ἐμπνέον in Jos. 10:28, 30, 35, 37, 39; 11:11, "hands" in Ps. 41:2; Prv. 13:4, the "arm" in 'Ιερ. 28:14 (51:14), the "head" in Is. 43:4, cf. the basic study Lys Soul LXX.

[64] As H. A. Brongers, "Das Wort 'NPŠ' in d. Qumranschr.," Rev. de Q., 4 (1963), 407-415 has shown, Qumran has the same mutiple use of נֶפֶשׁ as the OT. Only הֵקִים עַל נֶפֶשׁ "to pledge oneself by oath to something," Damasc. 16:4, 7 (20:2, 4 f.); 1 QH 14:17 seems to be new, but the way is prepared for it in Est. 9:31 and Nu. 30:2-15.

[65] That this might be the original sense is suggested by the Arab. bashara. Ps. 102:6: "My bones cleave to my בָּשָׂר "is surely ref. to the skin. If בָּשָׂר is the flesh covered by the skin, this might explain the use of the same root in the sense "to proclaim good tidings," the common denominator being that of outward manifestation, so W. Gesenius, Thesaurus philolog. criticus Linguae Hebr. et Chaldaeae Veteris Test., I (1835), s.v. בָּשָׂר : בָּשָׂר caro, in qua cernitur hominis pulchritudo, and E. Dhorme "L'emploi métaph. des noms de parties du corps en hébr. et en akkad.," Rev. Bibl., 29 (1920), 475 and 481, and finally R. W. Fischer, A Study of the Semitic Root BSR "to bring (good) tidings," Diss. Columbia (1966). But one must be careful about drawing semantic conclusions from etym.

[66] The expression "flesh and blood" has not yet been found in the Dead Sea Scrolls. But we find it a few times in Mandaean writings, cf. Lidz. Ginza R., 10, 30; 193, 35; 247, 19; L., 437, 39.

have this restricted sense. When used for the whole man בָּשָׂר is often synon. with נֶפֶשׁ,[67] Ps. 84:2; 119:120; Job 4:15; 21:6; Prv. 4:22, and it can denote concentration on a goal.[68]

When בָּשָׂר is not associated with נֶפֶשׁ, however, it is used for man in his weakness and corruptibility. That man is flesh means that he must perish like a plant. Is. 40:6. Limited to flesh, he sees that his days are few, Gn. 6:3, for the purely vegetative element prevails. Confidence reposed in the flesh is thus of no help. If the flesh does not stand in relation to God it is merely weakness and corruptibility, Jer. 17:5; Is. 31:3. The final result of this tendency is that the flesh becomes the evil principle which is in opposition to God and which overcomes man's better inclinations. This kind of dualism, however, is never found in the OT [69] and would deny the very foundations of OT anthropology. So long as the flesh is an organism which receives life from the spirit, it is connected with longing for God and the praise of God, Ps. 145:21. It is important, then, that man should direct the way of the בָּשָׂר in such a manner that he is not brought to destruction, Gn. 6:12. A dualistic view is found for the first time in Wis. 8:19; 9:15, where under Greek influence the flesh is the antithesis of the soul and spirit.

b. Bones.

We should not fail to note that in death the flesh undergoes complete destruction, whereas it is possible to think of נֶפֶשׁ and especially רוּחַ as having another existence apart from that in the body. For the Israelite, then, special importance attaches to that part of the body which withstands decay the longest, i.e., the bones. The bones עֲצָמִים are the solid part of the body which supports the other parts of the building like a framework. The special care with which they are treated after death might express a hope of restoration to life again, 2 K. 13:20; Da. 12:2; Is. 66:14 and esp. Sir. 46:12; 49:10. The bones rather than the soul sleep in the grave. The concept of resurrection that lies behind Ez. 37 accords a special place to them. They are often given a function that is very similar to that of the נֶפֶשׁ and the בָּשָׂר: "My נֶפֶשׁ shall be joyful in Yahweh, and all my bones shall say, Yahweh, who is like unto thee?" (Ps. 35:9 f.). The image of the bones is also used to show how very violent emotions can shake even that which is usually the most solid part of the human body, and how they can thus threaten life itself, Is. 38:13; 58:11; Jer. 23:9; Ps. 6:2; 31:10; 32:3; 51:8;

---

[67] Another word for flesh is שְׁאֵר. Like the Arab. ta'r it means "blood," or "bloody flesh," Ex. 21:10; Ps. 78:20, 27. It is used for relationship, denoting a specific relative, whereas בָּשָׂר is more gen., Lv. 18:6 (שְׁאֵר בְּשָׂרוֹ), 12; 20:19; 25 : 49. It is also used for man in gen. along with בָּשָׂר, Prv. 5:11, לֵב Ps. 73:26, נֶפֶשׁ Prv. 11:17. It is hard to detect any distinction between שְׁאֵר and בָּשָׂר in the OT.

[68] כָּל־בָּשָׂר never means Israel alone but always Israel along with other peoples. The expression is most common in P, which connects it with sin in Gn. 6:12 f., v. A. R. Hulst, "Kol basar in d. priesterl. Fluterzählung," Oudtest. Stud., 12 (1958), 28-68.

[69] Is. 10:18: מִנֶּפֶשׁ וְעַד־בָּשָׂר, hardly intends a dualism of soul and body. The two words are related synthetically rather than antithetically. That is, they are basically synon. and both denote the vitai force that seeks external manifestation. If, as O. Sander, "Leib-Seele-Dualismus im AT," ZAW, 77 (1965), 329-332, tries to show, נֶפֶשׁ means here the soul-organ of nourishment and בָּשָׂר that of reproduction, this has little bearing on our present study.

102:4; Job 4:14; 30:17 etc. Finally עֶצֶם, like נֶפֶשׁ (→ 620, 21 ff.), can denote the ego, man's true being, or the substance of inorganic things, Ex. 24:10; Gn. 7:13; Ez. 24:2.

The same development takes place in regard to גֶּרֶם, which is rare in bibl. Hbr. (it is used in a transf. sense in 2 K. 9:13), but which took on the sense of "ego" or "self" in Aram., Syr., and later Hbr.

3. Different Parts of the Body as the Seat of Life.

While the flesh, blood and bones, in virtue of their presence throughout the organism, provide the material sub-stratum for a description of the person in its totality, other parts of the human body, even though they are obviously localised, have a significance which extends beyond their exact position in the body. For according to Hebrew anthropology man is not the sum of the elements that form the body. The totality can be concentrated in a part. For this reason some writers speak of a scattering of consciousness, [70] though this is undoubtedly exaggerated, for it would mean that the Israelites were unable to think of human reality except in a very empirical way. It is beyond question, however, that on the basis of the fluid transition from the collective to the individual, and in a desire to see human life in its dynamism, the Israelites contemplated life in its manifestation, and viewed the body in its movement rather than its form. The part of the body which displays the greatest potency at a given moment is often regarded as the seat of life in the absolute.

a. The Head (→ III, 675, 1ff.).

One part in which life is concentrated is the head רֹאשׁ. This is why hands are laid on it in blessing, Gn. 48:14; Dt. 33:16; Prv. 10:6; 11:26. Punishing someone for a transgression is called bringing his blood upon his head, Jos. 2:19; 2 S. 1:16; 3:29; Ez. 33:4; 1 K. 2:44. When Achish wants to convey to David his trust in him he says: "I will make thee keeper of my head" (1 S. 28:2), i.e., the guardian of my life and person. The expression "the white hairs of someone will go down into sheol," Gn. 42:38; 44:29; 1 K. 2:6, 9, is based on the idea that the life of an individual is concentrated in the head. In Da. 2:28; 4:2, 7, 10; 7:1, 15 the head is the seat of knowledge, though everywhere else in the OT knowledge is related to the heart.

b. The Face (→ VI, 771, 1ff.).

On the principle that the expression is more important than the form, Hebrew psychology attaches great significance to the face. The exclusive use of the plur. פָּנִים brings out the multiple role of the face. The difference in nuances and possibilities of expression reflects exactly the total life attitude, Jer. 30:6; Is. 13:8; Jl. 2:6; Na. 2:11.

---

[70] Cf. H. W. Robinson, "Human Nature and Its Divine Control," *Inspiration and Revelation* (1946), 72, and for justifiable criticism Johnson, 83. The Israelites had a much more definite view of the unity of consciousness than the imagery suggests. The common use of the personal pronoun אֲנִי אָנֹכִי from the earliest texts onwards is a proof of this.

The face can express the whole range of emotions from severity, Dt. 28:50; Is. 50:7 to mildness and approval, Prv. 15:3; Qoh. 7:3. This polarity of the face led men to think that they could influence it to bring about a change of disposition, cf. the expression חִלָּה פָנִים "to soften the face." Construed with the prep. בְּ and לְ, פָּנִים is identical with the personal pronoun, esp. in statements about God, Ex. 20:3; Dt. 5:7, so that the face of Yahweh has almost a hypostatic character, Dt. 4:37; Is. 63:9. The face itself changes acc. to the different organs which animate it. Clarity of the eyes (→ V, 376, 8 ff.) is a sign of enhanced vital force, e.g., after eating, 1 S. 14:27. Less material influences, like God's Law, can also cause it, Ps. 19:8. The eyes can express envy, Prv. 23:6; 28:22, pride, Ps. 18:27; Prv. 6:17, and force, Ezr. 9:8. The eye is then synon. with נֶפֶשׁ, esp. when viewed in relation to another, Job 24:15; Jer. 32:4; 34:3. [71] The forehead usually expresses arrogance and strength, Jer. 3:3; Ez. 3:7. The neck עֹרֶף is the seat of pride, Ex. 32:9; 33:3, 5; 34:9; Dt. 9:6, 13; 31:27. These forms of expression are determined in part by observation of bodily postures, but they all take on a metaphorical sense. The nose אַף, dual אַפַּים, is the sign and seat of wickedness, Ps. 10:4, and esp. of anger, which is represented as strong blowing, Ez. 38:18, before it becomes an emotion, Prv. 14:17; 16:32. The verb חָרָה "to glow," which often characterises anger, expresses vividly the dynamism of the emotion, which as long as it lasts pushes other aspects of being into the background.

c. The Hand (→ IX, 426, 9 ff.).

The hand יָד, often also the palm כַּף or finger אֶצְבַּע, is the seat of power. The comparable expression יֶשׁ־לְאֵל יָדִי, Gn. 31:29; Dt. 28:32; Neh. 5:5; Prv. 3:27; Mi. 2:1, is not, however, the reminiscence of a divine spirit אֵל which animates the hand. The strength of the right hand (→ II, 37, 20 ff.) is greater than that of the left, Gn. 48:8-22; Qoh. 10:2. Hands are laid on to convey blessing, Nu. 27:18-20. The hand is the organ which takes up a matter and executes it. To give power to someone is to "strengthen the hands," Ju. 9:24; 1 S. 23:16; Ezr. 6:22; Is. 35:3. In man hand expresses the will and the means to carry it out. In God it is the means by which He works in creation and history.

d. The Foot (→ VI, 626, 5 ff.).

The foot רֶגֶל can also express power, although less so than the hand, cf. 1 S. 23:22 where Saul tries to find out where the feet of his opponent David are. The foot that is planted on the neck of the enemy, Jos. 10:24; cf. 2 S. 22:39, is also evidence of the power of this part of the body. A man with normal strength stands on his feet, and he can do this esp. when he is on solid ground, e.g., a rock, Ps. 31:8; 40:2; 1 S. 2:9. But often the foot is to be construed in a purely fig. sense, as when the feet slip, Ps. 94:18, stumble, Job 12:5; Ps. 73:2, do evil, Prv. 1:16; Is. 59:7, or are caught in a net, Ps. 9:15; Lam. 1:13; Jer. 18:22.

e. The Inner Organs.

The inner organs which are not seen but whose significance is fairly well understood also serve to express certain qualities of human nature. The high estimation of the entrails רַחֲמִים מֵעֶה rests primarily on physical sensation. Violent grief or great joy can affect certain organs, the bowels, liver, reins, and heart, so that the results can be viewed as the cause, such organs being regarded as the seat of the emotions.

Sympathy dwells in the bowels. Since בֶּטֶן and רֶחֶם the "womb" is where life begins, it can naturally be used for life as a whole. In Ps. 44:26 נֶפֶשׁ and בֶּטֶן are par. In Prv. 18:20

---

[71] In Ps. 31:9 עַיִן, נֶפֶשׁ and בֶּטֶן occur together. The two last words are an amplification which is designed to show that everything connected with the origin and force of life can be concentrated in the eyes.

בֶּטֶן is similar to the personal pron. and in Prv. 2:18 the words of the wise are kept in it. The word קֶרֶב denotes the inward parts as the gen. centre. It does not ref. so much then to a specific place but is used for all the inner processes within man, often in contrast to those that are external, Jer. 31:33; Ps. 64:6. The deepest emotions and impulses have their dwelling in the reins כְּלָיוֹת. They are so strongly anchored there that the reins can play the part of conscience and instruct man about God, Ps. 16:7. The loins חֲלָצִים, מָתְנַיִם denote the power that dispenses life, Gn. 35:11; 1 K. 8:19 and they can sometimes be used for the whole person, Job 31:20. There is undoubtedly a connection between the reins and the girdle which covers them and which as the chief article of clothing can express the whole person. In Israel the reins seem to play a more important role than the liver כָּבֵד,[72] although this is the centre of life for the Assyrians and Arabs. Expressions like Lam. 2:11: "My liver is poured upon the earth," show, however, that the term can sometimes be used for נֶפֶשׁ.

4. The Heart as the Centre of Life and the Epitome of the Person.

The heart לֵב, לֵבָב (→ III, 609, 31 ff.) is often mentioned along with the inner organs, Jer. 11:20; 17:10; Ps. 26:2. Nevertheless it holds a special place, for it is the most common of all anthropological terms (850 instances).[73] In contrast to נֶפֶשׁ and בָּשָׂר whose physical relations are vague, the heart is localised exactly. It is the more important because it can represent life in its totality. The relation between it and נֶפֶשׁ might be stated as follows. The נֶפֶשׁ is the soul in the sum of its totality in its manifestation, whereas the heart is the soul in its inner worth.[74] Although the Israelites had only a rudimentary knowledge of physiology,[75] they had a fairly accurate idea of the important role of the heart in the human organism. The heart, like breathing, can denote the ebb and flow of life. But the death of the heart need not mean the end of life, as may be seen from the story in 1 S. 25, where Nabal's death comes only 10 days after his heart died. A purely physical use of the term is fairly rare, Ex. 28:29 f.; 1 S. 25:37; 2 S. 18:14; 2 K. 9:24; Hos. 13:8; Na. 2:8; Ps. 37:15; 38:10; 45:5; Cant. 8:6. One may add to this list those passages which speak of the heart as the centre of vital force in a biological sense, Gn. 18:5; Ju. 19:5, 8, or in which the heart is strengthened by nourishment, Ps. 22:26; 102:4; 104:15. The twofold aspect of the heart as an active and yet concealed part of the body makes it a psychological organ in

---

[72] One may assume that the Hbr. כָּבוֹד often replaces an original כָּבֵד; textual criticism does not rule this out. A fairly sure instance is Gn. 49:6, where it is par. to נֶפֶשׁ. In the Ps., where כָּבוֹד is a theologically pregnant term, the Masoretic reading may be retained, cf. 7:5; 16:9; 30:12; 57:7; 108:1. כָּבוֹד is here what gives man his importance, which is usually denoted by heart. We have, then, an estimation of man that does not rest on the correspondence between spiritual experiences and parts of the body, though cf. F. Nötscher, "Heisst kabod auch 'Seele'?" VT, 2 (1952), 358-362.

[73] F. H. v. Meyenfeldt, Het hart (leb, lebab) in het OT (1950), takes up the question of etym. and comes to the conclusion that gt. caution is needed in def. לֵב. Derivation from a root "to be firm," "to be fat," "to move," seems to be importing what is said about the heart into etym.

[74] Pedersen, op. cit. (n. 53), I-II, 104.

[75] H. Kornfeld, "Herz u Gehirn in altbibl. Auffassung," Jahrbücher f. jüd. Gesch. u. Lit., 12 (1909), ascribes too much knowledge to the Israelites when he writes: "OT teaching is based on the fact that everything spiritual is mediated through the blood and that this works primarily on the heart and vessels. The heart acquires ability to react through an accession of blood, and this shows itself in an inexplicable pulsation of the heart not caused by the nerves." As is well known, the brain has no part in OT physiology and psychology. The word מֹחַ, which is the later term for the brain, occurs in the OT only once at Job 21:24, where it denotes the marrow of the bones; the bones are the important thing here and they have no connection with the brain.

which all life can concentrate and can also remain. It is the place where the נֶפֶשׁ is at home. [76] The heart is the point where all impressions from outside meet, pain, 1 S. 1:8; Ps. 13:2, and joy, 1 S. 2:1; Ps. 16:9; Prv. 15:13. What man sees and esp. what he hears enters the heart. In the OT, then, לֵב is closest to what we call conscience, [77] e.g., 1 S. 25:31 (→ VII, 908, 21 ff.). The act. role of the heart is even greater, however, than its receptive role. The heart is a spring, Prv. 4:23. The ways of life have their origin there, and it is the task of life to guide them aright. The heart must first keep what it has received. Memories, and esp. the divine commandments, are written on the tablets of the heart. Since these commandments make a man pious and intelligent, piety and understanding reside in the heart. This is the most common use. An intelligent man is a man with a heart, Job 34:10. When Job wants to show that he is not inferior to his friends in understanding, he cries out: "I have a heart as well as you," Job 12:3. The insane man has no heart. To make someone harmless, one takes from him his intelligence and ability to act, i.e., one steals his heart, Gn. 31:20; 2 S. 15:6. Wine and whoredom take away the heart, i.e., affect the judgment, Hos. 4:11; Prv. 6:32. For the heart as the seat of understanding there are many analogies in Egypt. The role of the heart in the historical novel and wisdom lit. might well be traced to Egypt. influences. [78] The idea of the heart as a kind of other soul or external soul probably comes from Egypt too. [79] In the OT we find this idea in Ju. 16:17: "He (Samson) told her all his heart," and 1 S. 9:19, where Samuel tells Saul that he will disclose the secret of his heart. The heart is a specifically human organ that differentiates man from animals. The heart of animals, which is mentioned in 2 S. 17:10; Job 41:16, is purely physical and is not intelligence. That the animal does not have intelligence is shown by the way in which Da. 4:13, cf. 7:4, says that the heart of Nebuchadnezzar was changed into that of a beast and then by the behaviour of Nebuchadnezzar. The heart, however, does not merely record and keep impressions which it receives. It also forges plans [80] by which the impressions are changed into acts. The verb חָשַׁב, of which the heart is often the subj., denotes act. thinking which is translated into action at once. The creative function of the heart is plain in the expression יֵצֶר in the classical passage Gn. 6:5: יֵצֶר מַחְשְׁבֹת לִבּוֹ. But these inventions of the heart lead to no lasting result. To speak out of one's own heart is to deviate from the truth, as in the case of false prophets, Nu. 16:28; 24:13; 1 K. 12:33; Neh. 6:8; Ez. 13:2, 17. The heart can fulfil its function only when God enables it to do so. By nature the heart of man is not absolutely pure, Ps. 101:4; Prv. 11:20; 17:20. It inclines to falsehood, is divided, בְּלֵב וָלֵב, Ps. 12:2; 1 Ch. 12:34, and proud, Ps. 131:1; Prv. 16:5; 18:12; Ez. 28:2; Prv. 22:15. The heart can cover itself with a layer of fat, Is. 6:10; Ps. 119:70 and become as hard as a stone, Ez. 11:19; Zech. 7:12. But God is concerned about the heart. He examines it and tests it, Ps. 17:3; Jer. 12:3; 1 Ch. 29:17. He weighs it, Prv. 21:2; 24:12. He knows it as it really is, 1 K. 8:39; Ps. 33:15; Prv. 15:11. He makes it pure and firm and causes it to be one with Him, 1 K. 8:61; 11:4, or to be one אֶחָד as God is one, Ps. 86:11; Jer. 32:39; 1 Ch. 12:39. The heart is not just the organ that is indispensable to life. By God's action it can become the principle of a new life. The

---

[76] G. F. Oehler, Art. "Herz," RE[1], 6 (1854-68), 16.

[77] The LXX never transl. לֵב by συνείδησις (→ n. 94). The only instance of this in Qoh. 10:20 corresponds to Hbr. מַדָּע "knowledge."

[78] In many Egypt. texts the heart is the organ with which man can receive and grasp divine inspirations, for it is always open to the divine will. For details cf. S. Morenz, Ägypt. Religion, Die Religionen d. Menschheit, 8 (1960), 66-9, 134-142; A. Piankoff, Le "coeur" dans les textes égypt. depuis l'Ancien jusqu'à la fin du Nouvel Empire (1930); H. Brunner, "Das Herz als Sitz des Lebensgeheimnisses," Archiv f. Orientforschung, 17 (1954/56), 140 f. The Book of the Dead, esp. c. 125, adds to the texts illustrations in which the heart, the quintessence of body, soul and will, is set on the scales of Osiris and Maat.

[79] The heart is a kind of alter ego in the familiar story of Elisha and Gehazi. Elisha's heart goes with Gehazi when the latter is at a distance, 2 K. 5:26. But it might be that the expression is ironical and does not reflect any precise notion.

[80] Meyenfeldt, op. cit. (→ n. 73), 146.

circumcision of the heart, Lv. 26:41; Dt. 10:16; 30:6; Jer. 4:4; 9:25 → VI, 77, 17 ff., and the changing of a heart of stone into a heart of flesh and blood, Ez. 11:19; 36:26; Ps. 51:10, express the fact that the new creation begins with the heart.[81] The movement towards God שׁוּב, which the prophets continually ask from the human will, also begins in the heart, Jer. 3:10; 29:13 etc.

The description of man as נֶפֶשׁ and concentration on the heart do not correspond to two different anthropologies. They are two tendencies within one and the same picture of man. The first views man from the standpoint of his vegetative life and his exterior. The second views him in terms of his inner worth. The dynamism of the anthropology demands a centre, a conscience, which allows man to find himself and to grow beyond himself.

5. The Spirit (→ VI, 359, 37 ff.).

The life of the organs and of their corresponding psychological functions is effected by the spirit רוּחַ.

a. Origin of the Concept.

Without רוּחַ there is no life and the source of life is outside man. These two principles lie behind all biblical statements about the רוּחַ. The expression suggests that the origin of the concept is to be found in the physical world. The stem רוח is perhaps an onomatopoeic word[82] which represents the rushing of the wind just as נֶפֶשׁ suggests breath, and it might be interpreted as a particular instance of the general life-force.

In many passages the only possible transl. of רוּחַ is "wind" or "breath of wind," esp. in Jer., Ez., Job and Ps. (→ VI, 360, 12 ff.). Wind has twofold significance. Being fleeting and inconstant, it can be a symbol of vanity, Job 16:3; Jer. 5:13; Hos. 8:7; Qoh. 1:17; 2:26; 4:4 etc. But it is also a life-giving power since it brings rain-bearing clouds. God uses this power in His revelation, 2 S. 22:11; Gn. 8:1; Ex. 10:13; 14:21; 15:8, 10, perhaps also Gn. 1:2, where the transl. "mighty wind" is often preferred to the rendering "Spirit of Elohim." In texts like Hos. 13:15; Is. 40.7; 59:19 wind is both a natural phenomenon and also the breath of God. When the word is used in Is. 31:3 to express the uniqueness of the divine nature, the physical aspect disappears and a transf. use emerges. In this case רוּחַ means power and invisibility. The concept moved into anthropology from cosmology and theology and it never lost contact with its material origin.

b. The Outworking in Man.

In the oldest passages in which רוּחַ is used with reference to man it denotes a power which comes down from God on specific individuals, not to give them life, but to give them a life-force which is beyond the ordinary and which enables them to do especially mighty deeds, Ju. 13:25; 14:6; 15:14. In 1 S. 10:6, 10; 19:20 the Spirit impels to prophecy. The great prophets, however, seldom ascribe their calling

---

[81] In the demand for love of God the heart takes precedence of נֶפֶשׁ. This shows that love comes from within and that it is not an impulse but something considered, Dt. 4:9, 29; 6:5; 10:12; 11:13; 13:4; 26:16; 30:2, 6, 10; Jos. 22:5; 23:14; 1 K. 2:4; 8:48. Jer. 32:41 speaks of the love which comes from God and which manifests the same structure.

[82] Gesenius, *op. cit.* (→ n. 65), III (1842), *s.v.* רוּחַ finds an element of breathing in רוּחַ as in פוּחַ and נוּחַ, and esp. rustling in רוּחַ, cf. Lys Ruach, 20.

to the Spirit, Hos. 9:7; Mi. 3:7. The Messiah is distinguished from ordinary mortals by the fact that he has a superabundant measure of the Spirit, Is. 11. From outside, but not from God, comes the spirit which is a kind of demonic being, which God can use, but which can also oppose Him, 1 S. 16:14; 18:10; 1 K. 22:21ff. Perhaps we have even here a reminiscence of the heavenly spirits which are all united in Yahweh. Even when the Spirit is referred to as a power that works within man, this work is still spoken of as if there were possession by a demon. Even more strongly than נֶפֶשׁ, רוּחַ is characterised by dynamism. One might say that רוּחַ is the condition of נֶפֶשׁ and that it regulates its force. Without נֶפֶשׁ an individual dies, but without רוּחַ a נֶפֶשׁ is no longer an authentic נֶפֶשׁ.

When Samson is dying of thirst, the spirit returns when he has drunk and he revives, Ju. 15:19. The same applies to a man who has fasted for three days, 1 S. 30:12. Faced by the magnificence displayed by Solomon, the Queen of Sheba has no more רוּחַ, 1 K. 10:5. She is not dying of weakness but she has been shaken in spirit. רוּחַ is vital force esp. in passages which have an anthropological emphasis. God breathes the רוּחַ into man's nostrils when He creates him, Gn. 2:7; 6:3, 17; 7:22, where we find the fuller expression which combines J and P: נִשְׁמַת־רוּחַ חַיִּים.

c. The Creative Activity of the Spirit in Man.

The רוּחַ is the breath of life without which there can be no life in any sphere of creation, Ps. 104:29; Nu. 16:22; 27:16. In the last two ref. אֱלֹהֵי הָרוּחֹת לְכָל־בָּשָׂר [83] means that the flesh can exist only through the vivifying spirit. The Spirit is no longer the extraordinary power which is reserved for a privileged few. It is the indispensable creative power of life, as the combination with נְשָׁמָה shows, Is. 42:5; Job 4:9; 27:3; 33:4; 34:14. When רוּחַ is used for specific feelings, these are always feelings which express extreme intensity or extraordinary weakness, e.g., grief, 1 S. 1:15; impatience, Ex. 6:9. The spirit of fornication in Hos. 4:12; 5:4, of falsehood in Mi. 2:11, of jealousy in Nu. 5:14, and of sleep in Is. 29:10 all denote an irresistible feeling by which man is controlled and which takes his will captive. The stimulating role of the spirit comes out in the expression "to awaken the רוּחַ," Hag. 1:14; 1 Ch. 5:26; 2 Ch. 21:16; 36:22; Jer. 51:1. Man has רוּחַ and the נֶפֶשׁ has him, is a succinct formulation of the matter. [84] רוּחַ with ref. to man is never used for the personal pronoun, not even in the later texts in which it takes the place of נֶפֶשׁ, Is. 26:9; Job 7:11; Zech. 12:1; Qoh. 3:21; 11:5. Nor is רוּחַ ever related to a specific physical organ. As its nature demands, it is always spiritual.

d. The Relation to נֶפֶשׁ and Heart.

The fact that רוּחַ takes over the functions of נֶפֶשׁ does not involve a shift in anthropological orientation along the lines of spiritualising or dualism. [85] In many passages we find נֶפֶשׁ where one would normally expect heart, Is. 29:24. This is esp. clear in Is. 40:13, where LXX transl. νοῦς, the common equivalent of לֵב. Heart and spirit occur together in Ex.

---

[83] This very difficult expression seems orig. to be expressing the fact that the vital elements which come from God are multiple. LXX offers a different explanation: κύριος ὁ θεὸς τῶν πνευμάτων καὶ πάσης σαρκός. It probably sees in πνεύματα the heavenly spirits.

[84] Köberle, 210.

[85] In many passages נֶפֶשׁ and רוּחַ are simply interchangeable. The same qualities have their seat partly in the one and partly in the other. Thus impatience is shortness of נֶפֶשׁ in Nu. 21:4; Ju. 16:16 and רוּחַ in Ex. 6:9; Job 21:4. Patience is length of נֶפֶשׁ in Job 6:11 and רוּחַ in Qoh. 7:8. Bitterness has its seat in נֶפֶשׁ in 1 S. 1:10; 22:2; 30:6; Job 3:20; 27:2, רוּחַ in Gn. 26:35.

35:21; Ps. 34:18; 51:17; 78:8, but here the parallelism does not efface the special nuances of the two terms, for the heart expresses inwardness and the spirit motivating power. Nevertheless the distinction has almost been obliterated when there is ref. to the thought which rises up to the spirit in Ez. 11:5; 20:32 and to that which enters the heart in Jer. 3:17; 7:31; 44:21; Is. 65:17.

In later texts one may discern a tendency to psychologise the רוּחַ. It is hard to say at what point in history this shift took place. Some have found a decisive turning-pt. in Dt. 2:30, [86] where רוּחַ is an independent reality which Yahweh hardens. A more promising theory is that the development takes place in wisdom circles as these are reflected in Qoh. Yet there can be no question of a separate anthropology. The nature of man can never be traced back to רוּחַ. Nor can it be maintained that man becomes a spirit when his body decays. The use of spirit for the dead lies outside the OT field, cf. Lk. 24:39. Even in death man remains a נֶפֶשׁ, i.e., either flesh which is given life by the רוּחַ or lifeless flesh.

e. Flesh and Spirit.

The antithesis of flesh and spirit is found occasionally in the OT, Gn. 6:1-8; Is. 31:3. It is not, however, the antithesis of two principles but of man's weakness and God's strength. [87] These two are not irreconcilable, for the God who has made man of corruptible matter also does all that is needed to transfer something of His strength to man. Flesh and spirit are incompatible only when flesh forgets to trust in the God who is Spirit and trusts in itself, Jer. 17:5 ff.; 2 Ch. 32:8. In the eschatological age all tensions will be overcome, yet not in the sense of a radical transformation of human nature which will replace the flesh by spirit and make man a spiritual being. Since spirit is common to God and man and is the element in man which is most immediate to God, one might expect that it would play the chief role in the relation between God and man. We do indeed find a specifically religious use of spirit in a few passages, Ps. 31:5; 34:18; 51:17; Is. 61:1; 66:2; Prv. 16:2; Is. 29:24, but when the reference is to the decisive manifestations of piety, such as fear of God or love of God, heart and נֶפֶשׁ have the decisive part. The passages which mention spirit show that OT anthropology views man less according to his nature and more in his relation to God as this is worked out in the given situation.

6. The Relational Character of Old Testament Anthropology. [88]

The following conclusions may be drawn from our survey.

a. In principle OT anthropology is the same as that of other Near Eastern peoples. Terms like נֶפֶשׁ and לֵב have the same meanings in Accadian, Ugaritic and

---

[86] Lys Ruach, 349 thinks Dt. 2:30 is a decisive point in development. When God hardens the spirit and heart of a man, רוּחַ is no longer a potentiality which is subject to change. It is the personal and decisive centre of the will which characterises man in contrast to lower creatures.

[87] The use of רוּחַ to epitomise all expressions of human life does not offer favourable soil for dualism. For the רוּחַ is that which is common to God and man and which thus links them together. The seeds of dualism are not to be found in man's nature. But the decision of the will can bring it about that either flesh or spirit gains the upper hand and a new orientation can be given to human nature therewith.

[88] In spite of many variations OT anthropology is basically the same throughout. The dynamism which characterises it is not opposed by the static elements which occur at points, e.g., the important role of the bones and of outward form. These must be taken into account if one is to understand how the dynamism leads to the union of body and spirit. Thus the OT speaks of resurrection and not of an eternal life in an invisible world.

Hebrew. Outside the Bible, too, the metaphorical use of parts of the body shows that man is regarded as a psycho-physical being whose life can manifest itself by extension or concentration in all parts of the body. The OT has nothing strictly new to say about human nature. No purely scientific interest may be seen in the OT or elsewhere; this first emerges under Hellenistic influence, cf. Wis. 7:1-2. The specific qualities of the God of Israel are what invest biblical anthropology with a distinctive coherence which non-biblical world anthropology does not have. The one God who is not only the Creator but also the Lord of history, directing it to a specific goal, gives to what is said about man a unity of structure and thrust. In the sight of God, who is believed in as a living person, man is a Thou who is fully free and responsible. For this reason, undoubtedly, the collectivist element could never restrict the significance of the individual in Israel, not even in the earliest period.

b. Older distinctions between dichotomy and trichotomy must be abandoned so far as OT anthropology is concerned. Israelite anthropology is monistic. Man is always seen in his totality, which is quickened by a unitary life. The unity of human nature is not expressed by the antithetical concepts of body and soul but by the complementary and inseparable concepts of body and life.

c. The OT never views man as an abstraction. He is always set in a specific situation. Hence the interest is more in the individual man than in human nature in general. Apart from the traditions about primal history and the wisdom books, where one might speak about a humanism based on the unity of the human race, man is always evaluated as an individual or as the member of a people in its historical role. The name, which is more important for OT man than features which are shared in common with other men, expresses the fact that man, and indeed each man, has his own special history.

d. The life of OT man is not simply marked by its various stages from birth by way of growth and aging to death. Life is constantly threatened and a counter-thrust is found only in contact with the source of life, i.e., with God. The common metaphor of breath and breathing (→ B1a), which is the undergirding substructure of the anthropological vocabulary, presents life as an ongoing exercise of breathing in which both the manner of breathing and also the quality of the air breathed in are both important. Above all human breathing is dependent on the breath of God, Job 34:14 f. If God ceases to breathe into man, which can happen any moment, life stops, Ps. 104:29. It would be wrong to deduce from this that OT anthropology is pessimistic, for the end is viewed as completion and hence as a victory for life in its supreme potency. [89]

e. The relational aspect of anthropology may be seen in the expression "image of God" (→ II, 390, 10 ff.). For the representative function which this implies can be discharged by man only through constant relationship to his divine original. Imago dei and נֶפֶשׁ חַיָּה are very close together, since both rest on the connection with God and with a divine task. There finally stands behind all that the OT says about man the assertion and the belief that man is really alive only in the situation of choice in which he fulfils what he is.

Jacob

---

[89] Life in its supreme potency is naturally the life of God. In face of God's victory, whether this be denoted by preservation of the chosen people or by re-creation of the world, the limitation of human life can hardly be a problem, and when it is, it finds its solution in a new emphasis on the life of God, Ps. 73:26; Job 19:25; → II, 843, 8 - 849, 2.

C. Judaism.

I. Hellenistic Judaism.

1. Septuagint Works with a Hebrew Original.

In the transl. Gk. of the LXX ψυχή corresponds mostly, although not exclusively, to נֶפֶשׁ.[90] Only in individual cases can one decide whether the choice of the word is due primarily to its association with vital force or with soul as the seat of the spirit or mind. In Nu. 35:11; ψ 22:3 and the prayer of Elijah to the Lord that He would take his soul from him in 3 Βασ. 19:4 the former applies, but in Dt. 11:18; 18:6; Prv. 19:15 f. the latter. Both can be correctly expressed by נֶפֶשׁ or ψυχή. But there is the following distinction. In class. and post-class. Gk. (→ 616, 22 ff.) both meanings are connected with the common idea of the soul as an immaterial or at least invisible essential core of man that can be thought of as distinct from the body. It gives worth and duration to the human self beyond the limits of physical existence. This idea is in every way alien to the OT. If נֶפֶשׁ (→ 618, 12 ff.), the most common term for man's vitality, can denote spiritual passion and action of every type, this is only a particularly broad understanding of the life principle and there need be no idea of an antithesis of body and soul.[91] This distinction is blurred by the lexically incontestable equation of נֶפֶשׁ and ψυχή, although it comes out in many passages. In Is. 10:18 and ψ 62:2 the total man is denoted by the double expression ψυχή/σάρξ, but in Gk. this undoubtedly suggests that the two are in juxtaposition The Hbr. has נֶפֶשׁ/בָּשָׂר, and as a later text like Qoh. 5:5 shows, these words indicate only a slight distinction of meaning and not one that embraces the antithesis of body and soul. The comparable expresion καρδία/σάρξ, Hbr. בְּשָׂרִי/לֵב. in ψ 83:3 corresponds exactly to a simple נֶפֶשׁ in the same verse. Cf. also ψ 72:26: σάρξ/καρδία = שְׁאֵר/לְבָב Hbr. ψ 15:10 is simply saying in the Hbr. that God will keep the life of the psalmist and not deliver him up to the realm of the dead. In the Gk. the ψυχή will not stay in Hades. It is thus presupposed that the ψυχή will be separate from the body and will spend some time in the underworld. Something of the same applies in Job 7:15 and Ἰερ. 38(31):12, where the Gk. can be more easily understood than the Hbr. in terms of the beliefs in the soul and the resurrection current in later Judaism (→ 637, 5 ff.). A similar difference in ideas is indicated when a λω in Gk. script is wrongly interpreted as "my soul shall live to him" (לוֹ) instead of "he hath not sustained my soul, i.e., me, in life" (לֹא).[92] When used to denote the bearer of intellect and intention ψυχή naturally does not correspond to the Hbr. נֶפֶשׁ, e.g., ψ 103:1, nor to several other words[93] in the psychological vocabulary of Hbr., which is rich if undifferentiated (→ B 5d) as compared with Gk., cf. לֵב, רוּחַ.[94] On the other hand ψυχή and καρδία are transl. variants for נֶפֶשׁ in Dt. 12:20 A. ψυχή, following genuinely Gk. and idiomatically fixed usage (→ 617, 25 ff.), can also denote living creatures, e.g., ἀριθμὸς ψυχῶν "census" in Ex. 16:16 or πᾶσα ψυχή "everybody," cf. ψυχαὶ δὲ πολλαί ... ἔθανον, Aristoph. Thes., 864 f. In such cases we are always to think of the no. of living people rather than moral individualities. The Israelites as well as the Gks. were acquainted with the ancient idea that the blood is the carrier of the life-force (→ B 1b). One may see this from the Gk. text of the OT, e.g., Gn. 9:5; Lv. 17:11.

---

[90] Hatch-Redp., s.v. ψυχή.
[91] Sander, op. cit. (→ n. 69) with bibl. [Bertram].
[92] [Bertram].
[93] Hatch-Redp., s.v. νοῦς, καρδία, πνεῦμα.
[94] Thus the reins are called in to help describe the phenomenon of conscience in ψ 15:7 (→ n. 77; VII, 908, 11 ff.) and the heart in ψ 4:5.

2. Apocalyptic and Pseudepigraphical Works.

The conceptual differentiation of body and soul as we find it in Gk. thought, and as it sometimes crops up in the LXX in deviation from the Hbr. (→ C I 1), is very common in the non-canonical writings whether these were composed in Gk. or are by chance preserved in a Gk. version. Naturally we first find expressions which correspond to customary OT usage, e.g., ἡ ψυχή μου, "I" etc. in Apc. Abr. 11 (p. 23, 11); 17 (p. 28, 6); Jub. 17:18; 26:13, or "my soul is anxious," Test. Sol. 1:4, or "to do something with all one's soul and heart," Jub. 1:15; S. Bar. 66:1, cf. Dt. 4:29, or the equation of soul and life in 1 Macc. 9:2; 2 Macc. 14:38; Jdt. 10:15; S. Bar. 51:15 etc. Here and in what follows ψυχή is either attested for a Gk. version or is to be presupposed for one that is not extant. Other passages show better what ideas are associated with the word. When the soul is scandalised by non-observance of circumcision it means the inner man, 1 Macc. 1:48; in this book the psychological meaning predominates by far. [95] Vit. Ad. 27 distinguishes between the soul as the moral and spiritual self of man and his breath as the vital force. "The soul lives on after death," Ps.-Phocylides, 105 ff., [96] whether it returns to God, Apc. Esr. 7:3 (p. 32); 6:4 f. (p. 31), directed or received by angels, Test. A. 6:5 f.; Test. Iobi 52 f., [97] or whether it must go to hell or the underworld, S. Bar. 21:23; Apc. Esr. 4:12 (p. 28); Sophonias Apc. [98] 1:1 ff. (p. 111). At any rate it parts from the body and the ascent of the latter is a special distinction for the patriarch Abraham, Test. Abr. B 8 (p. 112, 15 f.). After death judgment awaits souls with either reward or punishment, ibid., 9 (p. 113, 22 ff.). This applies only to the souls of men, for those of animals stay in a special place and will be witnesses for the prosecution at the judgment, Slav. En. A 58:4-6. We also find the idea that body and soul will be reunited for the judgment, Apocr. Ez. (→ n. 96) Fr., 1 (p. 121, 5, cf. 122, 9 f.). In a conjuration of the dead, in contrast to the story of the witch of Endor in 1 S. 28:14 ff., cf. Is. 14:9, the soul of the dead appears, Jannes and Mambres 1 (Riessler, 496). Magicians can steal human souls, Slav. En. 10:5, and the soul can leave the body for a time, Paral. Jerem. 9:11 ff.

Religious and moral qualities, and hence human responsibility, belong to the sphere of the soul, Jud. 18:4; Ps.-Phocylides (→ n. 96), 50, 228. The soul is white or black, Test. Isaac [99] Folio 17, and like the body it can be castigated in penitence. Test. Jud. 19:2 f. How widespread is the idea that the body and soul are twofold may be seen from the fact that, directly or indirectly under the influence of philosophical anthropology, thought is given to the distribution of the functions of the soul to members of the body, Apc. Sedrach 9 ff., [100] as also to the ensouling of the embryo, Apc. Esr. 5:13 (p. 30). That the psychologising of religious and moral ideas comes almost naturally in later Judaism with the formulation of thinking in Gk. may be seen from a comparison of 1 QS 3:13 ff., Test. Jud. 20:1 f. and Test. A. 1:3 ff. To the two spirits or angels which stand by man and influence his deeds correspond two πνεύματα in his soul or even two διαβούλια of the soul. As things now stand we cannot say for certain what is the origin of the common separation of body and soul in Judaism.

3. Septuagint Works in Greek.

a. In Wis. the ideas connected with ψυχή are wholly Gk. The body/soul antithesis dominates religious and moral thinking (→ VII, 1047, 1 ff.). The body is a burden for

---

[95] Cf. the expression "circumcision of the heart" or "spirit" in Jer. 4:4; Col. 2:11; Thomas Ev. Logion 53, ed. A. Guillaumont et al. (1959).

[96] Ed. A. M. Denis, Fr. Pseudepigr. Graeca, Pseudepigr. Veteris Test. Graece, 3 (1970).

[97] Ed. S. P. Brock, Test. Iobi, Pseudepigr. Veteris Test. Graece, 2 (1967).

[98] Ed. G. Steindorff, "Die Apk. Eliae, eine unbekannte Apok. u. Bruchstücke d. Sophonias-Apok.," TU, 17, 3 (1899).

[99] Trans. W. E. Barnes, TSt, II, 2 (1892), 150, 21 f.

[100] Ed. M. R. James, TSt, II, 3 (1893), 133-5.

the soul or for its noblest part, the νοῦς or λογισμός, 9:15. [101] Well-being of soul is more important than that of the body. Unfruitfulness and childlessness, which in the OT are punishments from God, are μετ' ἀρετῆς better than the reverse, 3:13 f.; 4:1. This is esp. true in relation to the hereafter in which the soul lives on and reaps reward or punishment, 3:1. Only ignorant sinners think that death ends all, 2:1 ff. An ascetic motivation is thus clear, 8:21. Yet unlike Gnostic texts (→ 656, 17 ff.), Wis. never says that the soul is or contains a truly divine constituent. The whole man is God's creature, even though he is destined for immortality as the image of his Creator, 2:23. Thus Solomon, who proclaims this teaching, can say of himself that God has given him a ψυχὴ ἀγαθή and a σῶμα ἀμίαντον, 8:19 f., but that in answer to his prayer a divine σοφία or πνεῦμα — on the identity of the two cf. 1:6 — has come into his soul as a supernatural gift, 9:4; 10:16. Such a gift cannot come into a bad ψυχή, 1:4. The πνεῦμα, whose nature and work are expressly described in 7:24 ff., is not, then, an original part of man's being as it is in Gnosticism. It comes into the souls of some ὅσιοι as an emanation ἀπαύγασμα, ἀπόρροια of God; this is how we have prophets and friends of God (→ 167, 12 ff.). [102] The hierarchy πνεῦμα/ψυχή/σῶμα rests on a purely theological base, unlike the par. series νοῦς/ψυχή/σῶμα of philosophical anthropology, which rests on a distinction of the ontic qualities of parts or forces of the soul. The hierarchy is common in Jewish lit. even earlier, Apc. Abr. 10 (p. 21, 14 f.); Eliae 36:17 ff. (p. 97). On Philo → 635, 11 ff. νοῦς or λόγος, however, can replace πνεῦμα. This shows the proximity of philosophical terminology and gives rise to difficulties in the exact interpretation of some passages. [103]

b. 4 Macc. reproduces popular philosophical psychology which cannot be restricted to a single school → VII, 1047, 12 ff. Along with ψυχή in the familiar sense of "life" we find the psychological doctrine of the πάθη with which the λογισμός has to deal, 1:20 ff. We also find the Platonic trichotomy (→ A 3a), 3:2 ff. In 14:6 the ψυχή is in the organism the centre of consciousness and feeling, while in 15:25 it is the vehicle of intellectual functions and in 15:4 of what we call character: Brothers are like one another in μορφή and ψυχή.

4. Aristeas and Josephus.

The works thus far mentioned cannot all be dated nor assigned to specific groups in Judaism. Nor can we be sure of their original wording nor completely purge them of Chr. additions. Yet it may be said that on the whole they express a uniform picture of the nature and destiny of the soul whose preciseness increases the closer the text is to authentically Gk. modes af expression. The same applies to Ep. Ar. (→ VII, 1050, 7 ff.) and Jos. (→ VII, 1056, 21 ff.) Both authors have a modest philosophical training and both write for Jews and non-Jews, although their periods are two centuries apart. Jos. Ant., 3, 260 uses the equation of blood with ψυχή and πνεῦμα in Moses to explain the Jewish ritual of slaughtering. We find here a differentiated psychological terminology in which πνεῦμα means what Posidonius understood by it → 615, 16 ff. [104] In

---

[101] Aristob. Fr. 4 acc. to Eus. Praep. Ev., 13, 12, 5 (p. 192, 9 f.) has changed the allegedly Orphic v. οὐδέ τις αὐτὸν/εἰσοράει θνητῶν, αὐτὸς δέ γε πάντας ὁρᾶται, Fr. (Kern), 247, 11 f. (vl.) into οὐδέ τις αὐτὸν εἰσορᾷ ψυχῶν (vl.) θνητῶν, νῷ δ' εἰσοράαται.

[102] On the idea of the friend of God cf. È. Dirlmeier, "ΘΕΟΦΙΛΙΑ — ΦΙΛΟΘΕΙΑ," Philol., 90 (1935), 57-77.

[103] The use of this hierarchical series in Wis., which runs counter to Gnostic ideas, shows how carefully we must handle the label Gnostic even when there is an obvious kinship of themes. But cf. A. Adam, "Die Ps. d. Thomas u. das Perlenlied als Zeugnisse vorchr. Gnosis," ZNW Beih., 24 (1959), 31-3, who thinks that the Wis. insertions are evidence of pre-Chr. Gnosticism.

[104] It may be noted that there are two ref. to the transmigration of souls in Jos. in Bell., 3, 362 f.; 6, 34 ff. But this is a distinction rather than a fatal bondage to the mortal body, since the souls of the brave first go up to heaven and then come back into the bodies of worthy men. Both passages reflect the tradition of military addresses and hence they cannot be used as evidence of the views of the author.

Aristeas we find the common σῴζω τὴν ψυχήν "to save the life," 292, cf. also ψυχῆς καθαρὰ διάθεσις, virtue in philosophical def. In such an expression purity as a matter of the mind is attributed to the soul in distinction from the body. The same emphasis on the disposition as opposed to cultic or other achievements may naturally be found in the OT prophets, but not on the basis of an intellectual antithesis between body and soul.

5. Philo.

Philo (→ VII, 1051, 31 ff.) [105] deserves a special place as the only known author in Hell. Judaism with extensive philosophical training. His use of ψυχή is to be explained by his use of the vocabulary of various philosophical schools. If this is inconsistent, it is based on wide reading.

He is acquainted with the Platonic division of the soul into 3 parts (→ VII, 1052, 18 ff.), Spec. Leg., IV, 92, with Aristot.'s division into 8 parts, Agric., 30 f., and also with the simple division into a superior rational part and a subordinate irrational part, Leg. All., I, 24; Fug., 69. [106] In a popularisation of Stoic ideas, but also in acc. with contemporary medical theories, he identifies the lower part with the blood, Det. Pot. Ins., 79-85 and the upper with the νοῦς, which he calls ψυχή τις ψυχῆς, Op. Mund., 66, cf. Rer. Div. Her., 54 ff., and which he compares to the eye of the body, Op. Mund., 66. The οὐσία of the soul or its νοῦς or λογισμός is the divine πνεῦμα. Philo uses this term from the basically materialistic psychology of Stoicism both spiritually after the manner of the Platonic-Stoic syncretism of his day and also theologically. He has in mind the immaterial, Deus. Imm., 46, fiery, Fug., 133, ἀπόσπασμα θεῖον which is made up of αἰθήρ, Leg. All., III, 161 ff., cf. Rer. Div. Her., 283, and which is the divine spirit itself taking up its dwelling in the ψυχή as λογικόν, Virt., 218, to cure it of the passions, Som., I, 12. Whereas in the passages thus far mentioned the words νοῦς-πνεῦμα-λογικὸν ψυχῆς-λόγος-λογισμός-ἡγεμονικόν mean essentially the same thing after the manner of philosophical syncretism, Philo can also rank λόγος and νοῦς as the Gnostics did, Migr. Abr., 3 f., the λόγος being the receptacle of the νοῦς.

Philo agrees with philosophical speculations that only through the highest part of the soul can man have union with God, Poster. C., 27, cf. Aristobul. (→ n. 101). On the other hand Philo stresses that all parts of the soul share in the rise of sin, Conf. Ling., 22. Here the philosophical and Gnostic idea of the kinship of the soul to God gives place to the OT idea of an unbridgeable gulf between them which is manifested in sin. It is worth noting that in Leg. All., I, 82 ff. ecstatic union with the Most High is not an ἔργον τῆς ψυχῆς but a gift of grace.

That angels and demons are ψυχαί, Gig., 16 was an idea common to both Gks. and Jews at this time (→ 475, n. 29; 615, 11 ff.). Philo agrees with philosophical cosmology when he speaks of the ψυχή of the world as a living organism governed by rational laws, Aet. Mund., 50 etc. (→ VII, 1054, 16 ff.).

Dihle

II. נֶפֶשׁ/ψυχή in Palestinian Judaism.

In the Hbr. works of post-bibl. Judaism, as in the OT, נֶפֶשׁ denotes the vital element in man, his breath, his life-force, his ego.

1. This Jewish usage, which was influenced by the OT, may be seen in the Qumran texts. כל נפש אדם is "each living man," Damasc. 11:16 (13:26), כל נפש חיה "every living creature," 12:12 f. (14:12 f.). As נֶפֶשׁ man experiences sorrow and persecution. The נֶפֶשׁ comes into need, 1 QH 5:12, and is smitten by bitterness: מרורי נפשי 1 QH 5:12, cf. 5:34,

---

[105] On Philo cf. Leisegang Indices, *s.v.* ψυχή and the bibl. in → VII, 1051, n. 318; 1052, n. 320, Merki, *op. cit.* (→ n. 16), XV, and H. Hegermann, "Die Vorstellung v. Schöpfungsmittler im hell. Judt. u. Urchr.," TU, 82 (1961), XI-XV.

[106] Naturally Philo knew in detail the philosophical doctrine of the emotions, as may be seen from the discussion of remote areas like the doctrine of εὐπάθεια or προπάθεια.

39; 1 QpHab 9:11. Enemies seek the נֶפֶשׁ of the righteous, Damasc. 1:20 (1:15); 1 QH 2:21, 24, 29 etc. But God saves the נֶפֶשׁ of the righteous by protecting it from the devices of the wicked, setting it in the bundle of life, and helping it, 1 QH 2:7, 20, 23, 32, 34 f.; 5:13, 18; 7:23; 9:33 etc. [107] As a vow is made in prayer to love God with the whole נֶפֶשׁ, 1 QH 15:10, so the נֶפֶשׁ belongs wholly to God. נֶפֶשׁ does not mean the soul as one part of man but the whole man living his life in responsibility. Often נֶפֶשׁ simply means the ego. Thus when God is confessed to have saved and kept the נֶפֶשׁ, this means: Thou hast redeemed, freed, and helped me, 1 QH 2:7, 20, 23, 28; 3:19; 1 QS 11:13 etc. When it is said that the נֶפֶשׁ is troubled, 8:32, or reflects, 9:7, or rejoices, 9:8; 11:7, the ref. is again to the suffering, thinking, or acting I. Often נֶפֶשׁ or נַפְשׁוֹ can simply be used for a reflexive, so יקום...עַל נפשו in 1 QS 5:10, "he should pledge his soul, i.e., himself," cf. also Damasc. 16:1 (19:14), 4 (20:2), 7 (20:5), 9 (20:6), 1 QH 14:17.

2. In Rabb. works (→ VI, 376, 28 ff.) we find on the one hand a continuation of OT usage. [108] נֶפֶשׁ denotes the living man in thought, decision, and action. The נֶפֶשׁ, which is in the blood acc. to Dt. 12:23 (→ B 1b), is the vital force, Gn. r., 14, 9 on 2:7. כל נפש ref. to "every living thing," bBer., 44b, Bar.; דיני נפשות means "capital trials" where life and death are involved, Sanh., 4, 5; bSanh., 2a. To destroy the נֶפֶשׁ is to slay the life, while to uphold the נֶפֶשׁ is to preserve the life, Sanh., 4, 5. [109] There is ref. to the נֶפֶשׁ as the seat of thought and decision in, e.g., jTaan., 3, 1 (66b, 60 f.), where it is said of the scribal college מכיון שנתנו בית דין נפשן לעשות כמי שעשוי, "as soon as the scribal college directs its thoughts to doing something, it is as though it were already done."

On the other hand, the Rabbis, under Hellenistic influence, also develop an anthropology that goes beyond what we find in the OT, contrasting the body and the soul in a way that is not found in older Judaism → VI, 377, 32 ff.; VII, 116, 31 ff. [110] If according to earlier views the soul of man was created with the body, R. Simai has the later formulation (c. 210): "All creatures which were made from heaven, whose soul and body is from heaven and his body is from earth," S. Dt., 306 on 32:3. From this it is deduced that when man keeps the Law and does the will of the Father in heaven he acts like the higher creatures, but when he does not he acts like the lower creatures. [111] The soul, which is of heavenly origin, dwells on earth like a guest in the body [112] and gives man the strength to keep the divine commandment. It receives new powers from heaven in order that man may do this. "In the hour when man sleeps it (sc. the soul) rises up and creates for him (sc. man) new life from above," says R. Me'ir (c. 150), Gn. r., 14, 9 on 2:7. [113] The influence of Greek ideas about the immortality of the soul (→ A3c), which is esp. strong in Hellen. Judaism (→ 633, 14 ff.), may be seen already in the statements of the Tannaites and is even more evident in those of the Amoraeans. Pre-existence as well as a heavenly origin is now ascribed to the soul → VI, 379, 12 ff. R. Levi (c. 300

---

[107] We nowhere read of the immortality of the soul nor is there any clear ref. to the resurrection of the dead, though cf. Delcor, passim. Jos. Bell., 2, 154 f. says that the Essenes taught that souls come from the rarest ether and return to their heavenly home after life on earth.

[108] With נֶפֶשׁ, רוּחַ and נְשָׁמָה are also used for the soul of man with no clear distinction between the terms → VI, 376, 32 ff.

[109] Cf. Str.-B., I, 749 f.

[110] Meyer, passim.

[111] Cf. Str.-B., II, 430; Meyer, 27; → VII, 118, 2 ff.

[112] Hillel (c. 20 B.C.) told his pupils he was going to do a work of love, and when asked whether he had a guest every day he said: "Is not then my poor soul a guest in the body? Today it is here and tomorrow it is not here." Lv. r., 34, 3 on 25:25. Cf. Str.-B., I, 654 f.; Meyer, 49 → VI, 380, 16 ff.

[113] Meyer, 51; → VII, 118, 16 ff.

A.D.) can thus say that souls dwelt already with God before he created the world. He deliberated with them and then did the work of creation, Gn. r., 8 on 1:26. [114]

In Rabbinic statements which thus set the soul and the body in antithesis, however, there is no disparagement of the body. According to the OT legacy man is seen as a unity → 631, 14 ff. At the moment of death the soul leaves the body (4 Esr. 7:78) [115] but at the resurrection of the dead the reawakened body is reunited with the soul. [116] It is as a whole, body and soul, that man is responsible to God. At the Last Judgment the body cannot blame on the soul sins which have been committed nor can the soul blame them on the body.

Both are responsible, as Rabbi (c. 150 A.D.) shows in a parable. When a blind man had put a lame man on his shoulders and both had taken the fruits of another's garden, the owner told the lame man to ride on the blind man and he judged both together. So God will fetch the soul and bring it into the body and will then judge them both, bSanh., 91a b. [117]

Lohse

D. The New Testament.

I. The Gospels and Acts.

1. ψυχή as Natural Physical Life.

a. General.

In Ac. 20:10 ψυχή is the life which remains in Eutyches. 27:22 says in good [118] OT style that there will be no loss of life. 27:10 refers to the danger not merely to the ship and cargo but also to the ψυχαί of the passengers. The plural shows already that ψυχή can individualise very strongly. In Mt. 6:25 ψυχή is parallel to σῶμα → VII, 1058, 13 ff. The life needs food as the body needs clothes. [119] Animals, too, have a ψυχή → 653, 32 ff.

b. The Giving of Life.

In Mk. 10:45 we read of the διδόναι of the ψυχή as a ransom for many, → I, 373, 1 ff.; IV, 341, 34 ff. [120] According to Greek and Jewish usage [121] ἑαυτόν or σῶμα

---

[114] Cf. Str.-B., II, 342.

[115] On funerary inscr. we repeatedly find the wish נוח נפש "rest to his soul." Cf. CIJ, I, 569, 611; II, 892, 900, 1096, etc. → VI, 376, 22 ff.; 378, 35 ff.

[116] Cf. Volz. Esch., 118 f., 266-272.

[117] Cf. Str.-B., I, 581; Moore, I, 487 f.; II, 384 with other parallels.

[118] Haench. Ag.15, ad loc.

[119] The parallelism is so non-Gk. that Just. Apol., 15, 14-16 omits the ref., H. T. Wrege, "D. Überlieferungsgesch. d. Bergpredigt," *Wissensch. Untersuchungen z. NT,* 9 (1968), 119. Yet the linking of the body and clothes is non-Jewish and ties in with the Gk. view of the body, Dautzenberg, 92-6.

[120] C. K. Barrett, "The Background of Mk. 10:45," *Festschr. T. W. Manson* (1959), 1-18 thinks the link with Is. 53 is insecure and understands the saying mainly in terms of Da. 7 and Jewish martyr theology: Like the Son of Man Israel is justified and exalted only by martyrdom in the Syrian persecution. The vicarious nature of martyrdom is a common idea that is obviously rooted in Is. 53, E. Schweizer, "Erniedrigung u. Erhöhung bei Jesus u. seinen Nachfolgern," AbhThANT, 28² (1962), 21-52.

[121] With ἑαυτόν in 1 Macc. 6:44 we find τὰς ψυχὰς ὑμῶν in 2:50. For other Jewish ref. → n. 123. Gk.: Eurip. Phoen., 998: ψυχήν τε δώσω τῆσδ' ὑπερθανεῖν χθονός, Dion. Hal. Ant. Rom., V, 65, 4: τὰ δέ σώματα καὶ τὰς ψυχάς ... ἐπιδιδόντες, cf. 2 Macc. 7:37; with παραδίδωμι cf. also Herm. s., 9, 28, 2; Eus. Hist. Eccl., VIII, 6, 4; with ἐπιδίδωμι Jos. Bell., 2, 201; cf. also → VII, 1058, 25 f. Eth. En. 108:8; W. Popkes, "Christus Traditus," AbhThANT, 49 (1967), 19, 38, 86-8.

may be used instead in this sense, → II, 166, 11 ff. As compared with ζωή (חַיִּים) ψυχή (נֶפֶשׁ) is more concretely the life bound up with flesh and blood. [122] It also denotes the individual ego. Yet there is no sharp differentiation in usage, → II, 849, 4 ff. John always has τιθέναι as the verb, Jn. 10:11, 15, 17; [123] 13:27 f.; 15:13; 1 Jn. 3:16 → VI, 496, 5 ff.; VIII, 155, 29 ff. This can mean "to risk" as well as "to give." [124] If Jesus' sacrifice of life leads to that of His disciples too, it is said only of Jesus that He has the power to take His life again. Here, then, "life" is close to "soul" → 650, 38 ff. [125] What is again meant is the individual life which is possible after death, and not a carrier different from the life itself. In Ac. 15:26 παραδίδωμι means expenditure of resources which does not lead to death and probably does not expressly include the risk of martyrdom. [126] Finally Rev. 12:11 speaks of those who do not love their ψυχή unto death, and in Ac. 20:24 Paul bears witness that he does not hold his life dear but will complete his course and ministry. [127] ψυχή is added at Lk. 14:26 as compared to Mt. 10:37 in order to embrace everything that can make up earthly life and that must be hated for the sake of Jesus. In these passages life is always linked to the individual; it is my life.

c. Seeking, Killing and Saving Life.

In Mt. 2:20 ψυχή is the life of the child Jesus which His enemies are seeking. In Lk. 12:20 (→ 647, 14 ff.) it is that of the rich farmer which is required by God. There is criticism here of a purely this-worldly view of the life which is loaned by God. [128] Mk. 3:4 is given a place of emphasis in the Gospel. The power of Jesus and His victory over demons have proved His lordship over sin and the Law. [129] The problem of the Law is now focused on the question of doing good or evil, of saving life or taking it. [130] The neighbour and his salvation are thus set up as the true criterion. The reply of Jesus' opponents is a decision for death (3:6). Here, too, the ψυχή is physical life (→ 637, 19 ff.), although naturally in individual terms. In accordance with OT ideas abandoning the sick means taking their lives. Because the bearer of the ψυχή is not mentioned one can hardly render it "everyman" along the lines of OT statutes. [131] But it is clear that there is no neutral zone, only life or death, good or evil. The earthly life is taken so seriously that in sickness it is not worth calling real life at all. The mere movement of the heart or drawing of breath is not enough. Life has content here as the full life which God intended at creation. It is not just a formal concept. We can easily see, then, why in the last resort life can properly be called this only when it is lived in God's service and to

---

[122] Barth, 317 f.

[123] Jewish par. in P. Fiebig, "Die Mekhilta u. d. Joh.-Ev.," Angelos, 1 (1925), 58 f.

[124] Bultmann J., on 10:11. Cf. Popkes, op. cit., 88, n. 248; on the OT, 19.

[125] Dautzenberg, 110-113.

[126] Cf. Str.-B., II, 537, 740; Dautzenberg, 99 f.

[127] The construction is difficult, but not a slip (so Pr. Ag., ad loc.); Haench. Ag.[15], ad loc.: "I do not regard my life as worth talking about," seems to be on the right track.

[128] Dautzenberg, 90.

[129] Cf. S. Schulz, "Mk. u. d. AT," ZThK, 58 (1961), 193 f.; E. Schweizer, "Die theol. Leistung d. Mk.," Beitr. z. Theol. d. NT (1970), 29.

[130] In the par. Mt. 12:11 f. the question is more concrete cf. Lk. 14:5: Who will not rescue an animal that has fallen into a well on the Sabbath? Here, too, curing sickness is compared to the saving of physical life from death. Much weaker is the comparison to watering cattle on the Sabbath in Lk. 13:15 f.

[131] So Dautzenberg, 154-6, who takes Mk. 3:4 like Ac. 2:43 → 639, 22 ff.

God's praise, so that the question of greater or smaller physical powers or the degree of health is a subsidiary one. It might be asked whether Mk. 3:4 does not have in view the whole existence of man and not just his physical life, although this is plainly the primary meaning. [132] This is certainly true in the addition to Lk. 9:56. The correction of the vengeful disciples by the Son of Man who has come to save the ψυχαί of men and not to destroy them undoubtedly has the physical life in view but the positive formulation shows that more is intended than mere protection against natural disasters. [133] This is fully brought out if Lk. 19:10 is seen as a prototype, for here seeking and saving are plainly understood as a summons to faith. Yet physical life and the life of faith cannot be sundered in the way that they so easily are in our thinking. The call to faith is a call to the true life given and intended by God. Salvation is always salvation from anything that might hamper the development of this life, whether it be death and sickness or unbelief and sin. This may be seen from a comparison of Mk. 3:4; Lk. 9:56; 19:10 and from the choice of ψυχή for the life of the I in both spheres — a life which is always thought of corporeally.

2. ψυχή as a Term for the Whole Man.

ψυχή is in the first instance the physical life. Thus there can be reference to the slaying, giving, hating, and persecuting of the ψυχή. ψυχή is limited and threatened by death. Yet the ψυχή cannot be separated from man or beast. This shows that what is at issue is not the phenomenon of life in general but the life which is always manifested in an individual man. Hence πᾶσα ψυχή is used as in the OT (→ 632, 37) for "everyman" (Ac. 2:43 → D II 2) and yet Ac. 3:23, where it is contrasted with πᾶσα σάρξ (→ VII, 106, 17 ff.; 129, 18 ff.), shows that it is to be taken in an individualising way. [134] The distinction from σάρξ and the relation to the equally individualising σῶμα also find expression in the fact that ψυχή can be used in numbers (→ 632, 38 ff.), Ac. 2:41; 7:14 (based on Gn. 46:27 LXX); [135] 27:37. [136] Mt. 11:29 promises rest to those who accept the yoke of Jesus. The expression comes from Jer. 6:16. [137] ψυχαὶ ὑμῶν is thus an OT expression (→ 620, 21 ff.) for ὑμεῖς (cf. Gosp. of Thom. 90 → n. 95) with an implication of subjection to death. One may ask, however, whether Mt. does not mean rather more by it. If one remembers the great significance of the reinterpretation of the Law and the strong orientation to coming judgment in Mt., [138] ψυχή probably means for him already the self of man which

---

[132] With Loh. Mk. against V. Taylor, *The Gospel acc. to St. Mark* (1952), ad loc., though not, of course, in such a way that the charge against his enemies that they wanted to kill Him is contained in it, but at most along the lines of 2:27 with its question whether the Sabbath and the Law were not given by God to man's salvation. This is naturally the theological point of the question, though the saying can still carry a ref. to the true I of man, since the purely physical life probably symbolises the reality which is not yet denoted by ψυχή.

[133] Since the ref. here is to the healthy man σῴζω (in contrast to Mk. 3:4) cannot ref. merely to the maintaining of this condition and so ψυχή must have the more comprehensive sense of man's existence before God → 642, 25 ff.

[134] This is a mixed quotation from Dt. 18:19 and Lv. 23:29 in which ὁ ἄνθρωπος, ὃς ἐὰν ... is equated with πᾶσα ψυχή, ἥτις. Pr. Ag. on 3:22; cf. Dautzenberg, 155 for Jewish material.

[135] The numbers also correspond to the LXX, cf. Haench. Ag.[15], ad loc.

[136] αἱ πᾶσαι ψυχαί altogether, cf. Bl.-Debr. § 275, 7.

[137] F. Christ, "Jesus Sophia," AbhThANT, 57 (1970), 106. LXX replaces מַרְגּוֹעַ "place of rest" by ἁγιασμός, but εὑρίσκω ἀνάπαυσιν is common in the LXX. Possibly Gn. 8:9 LXX had some influence, Schl. Mt., ad loc. and esp. Dautzenberg, 134.

[138] G. Strecker, "Der Weg d. Gerechtigkeit," FRL, 82[3] (1971), 158 f., 235 f.

lives before God and will one day have to give an account to Him at the Last Judgment. [139] If this is naturally implied already in the OT, it is first made explicit and given emphasis in Mt. Yet Mt. does this in a way which differs completely from what we find in the Greek world, where the soul finds rest when it is liberated from the body (→ 611, 15 f.), [140] for here the unity and totality of man are upheld. It is in his physical acts in obedience that man will find God's rest. Here, however, is the problem, for if the physical life is seen as God's gift, can it still be separated from the life with God which takes shape in, e.g., prayer, praise and obedience, and which fashions a union with God that does not come to an end with physical life?

3. ψυχή as the Place of Feeling.

a. Man as Influenced by Others.

The adversaries of Paul ἐκάκωσαν τὰς ψυχὰς [141] τῶν ἐθνῶν (Ac. 14:2). According to Ac. 15:24 the ψυχαί of the brethren in Antioch are led astray by different words. Here ψυχαὶ ὑμῶν is parallel to ὑμεῖς as ταράσσω is to ἀνασκευάζω, [142] so that the participial clause only develops more precisely what is said already with ἐτάραξαν ὑμᾶς. ψυχή is the man who can be moved inwardly. In distinction from πνεῦμα (→ VI, 392, 26 ff.; 435, 12 ff.) it is the man as such, whether pagan or disciple. The OT affinity to heart (→ 626, 29 ff.) may easily be combined with this usage. This applies in Jn. 10:24: "How long dost thou hold our ψυχή in suspense?" [143] Here there is a slight shift of sense to the degree that the ψυχή is the place where decision is made for or against Jesus. This means that the object towards which the psychical movement or decision is orientated determines the character of the ψυχή more closely. This is plainer in other passages. Man can be moved, of course, toward the good as well as the bad. Thus Paul and Barnabas strengthen the ψυχαί of the disciples to stand fast in faith, Ac. 14:22. Here, too, ψυχή can simply be the man himself as one who can be influenced or moved in thought or feeling. But each time the question arises whether the ψυχή is equally the locus of faith as it is of confusion or stimulation, of joy or sorrow. In other words, is faith to be viewed simply as a psychological matter like joy, sorrow, or perplexity?

b. Man as He Experiences Joy, Sorrow and Love.

The quotation in Mt. 12:18 speaks of the ψυχή of God which takes good-pleasure in His servant. This is probably to be understood in terms of active divine decision (→ II, 740, 13 ff.; 741, 19 ff.). In Lk. 12:19 the ψυχή is addressed in soliloquy, → 633, 5 ff. [144] It has goods, can take its ease, can eat, drink and be merry. The reference is interesting because both physical and psychical activities

---

[139] Cf. W. Michaelis, Das Ev. nach Mt., II (1949), ad loc.

[140] Cf. esp. Jos. Bell., 7, 349 (→ VII, 1057, 9 ff.); O. Bauernfeind-O. Michel, "Die beiden Eleazarreden," ZNW, 58 (1967), 270 f.

[141] Nu. 29:7; 30:14 use the same expression for self-castigation.

[142] Pr.-Bauer, s.v.; Bau. Ag., ad loc. We have here LXX speech and careful Greek.

[143] Cf. the par. Jos. Ant., 3, 48: οἱ δ᾽ ἦσαν ἐπὶ τὸν κίνδυνον τὰς ψυχὰς ἡρμένοι, "courageous," "ready for danger," but not ψ 24:1; 85:4, cf. Bultmann J., ad loc.

[144] Par. in H. Thyen, "Der Stil d. jüd.-hell. Homilie," FRL, 65 (1955), 89 f.; 97-100; also without ὦ Charito, De Chaerea et Callirhoe, III, 2, 9, ed. R. Hercher, Erotici Scriptores Graeci, II (1859); cf. τὴν ψυχὴν βαπτίζομαι fig. of the passion of love, ibid., III, 2, 6. On the OT with its address "my soul" cf. Dautzenberg, 85.

are included, [145] although with an emphasis on the property and on eating and drinking. The following verse shows that a decision is made which affects the value of the life before God, → D I 7b. We have here a negatively assessed self-satisfaction. [146] A positive assessment may be seen in the hymn in Lk. 1:46, which is heavily influenced by the OT and in which the ψυχή is a subject of praise of God. Typically ψυχή is found alongside πνεῦμα here; [147] stress is thereby laid on the fact that such activity of the ψυχή is ultimately the gift and work of God [148] → VI, 415, 13 ff.

The ψυχή is also the locus of sorrow, Mk. 14:34 = ψ 41:6. Jn. 12:27 has τετάρ-ακται for this (→ 640, 14 ff.), which shows that the καρδία is not basically differ-entiated, Jn. 14:1, 27. [149] ψυχή should not be overtranslated, since originally ψ 41:6 shaped the formulation. [150] The saying in Mk. 12:30 (quoting Dt. 6:5), [151] which demands love with all one's soul and heart, is a perfect parallel. ψυχή here is close to strength of will. This is more strongly so in Mt. 22:37 and par. (→ II, 140, 2 ff.), where the Hebrew-Rabbinic instrumental understanding dominates with ἐν, than it is in the LXX version in Mk. 12:30, where the ἐξ stresses inwardness. But the fact that Mk. can leave out ψυχή in v. 33 shows how little what is distinctive is seen in it. Ac. 4:32 is to be adjudged similarly. This says of the community that it was καρδία καὶ ψυχή μία, which corresponds to both Greek and OT usage. [152] On the other hand only ψυχή occurs in Lk. 2:35 with its metaphor of the sword of sorrow that pierces the ψυχή (→ VI, 995, 12 ff.). [153]

c. ψυχή in the Sense of Heart.

ψυχή thus denotes the man who can be influenced by others and who is exposed to joy and sorrow but who can also praise God and love Him. The last use, which brings the word very close to καρδία (→ 640, 18 ff.), is found only when OT formulations are adopted. We are thus brought back to the question whether the man who is open to emotional movements and who can be affected and swayed by

---

[145] As in Judaism, Dautzenberg, 18 f., 85.

[146] For details on the piety of poverty which is the background of this assessment, ibid., 90 f.

[147] ψ 34:9: ἡ δὲ ψυχή μου ἀγαλλιάσεται ἐπὶ τῷ κυρίῳ, is obviously identical with ἐγὼ δὲ ἐν τῷ κυρίῳ ἀγαλλιάσομαι in Hab. 3:18. For the interchanging of נֶפֶשׁ and רוּחַ cf. also 11 QPsᵃ Col. 27:4, 28:5 (DJD, IV, 48 f.; cf. 92 and 55).

[148] The distinction made by A. Plummer, The Gospel acc. to St. Luke, ICC (1896), ad loc. between the seat of the religious and the seat of the emotional life has something in its favour, but the two overlap. The catena (Kl. Lk., ad loc.) shows that πνεῦμα and ψυχή mean the same. They are not, however, immaterial parts of man in contrast to the body. The idea that the ψυχή is the total living creature and πνεῦμα = רוּחַ is the life-principle (A. R. C. Leaney, The Gospel acc. to St. Luke [1958], ad loc.) does not fit in too well with this passage.

[149] Cf. ψυχή in 12:27 and Dautzenberg, 132; cf. 16:6, 22.

[150] Cf. Gn. 41:8; ψ 30:10; 54:5; Lam. 2:11; Bultmann J. on 12:27. As against F. W. Gros-heide, Comm. on the First Ep. to the Corinthians (1953), on 1 C. 15:45 it must be stated that ψυχή is also used of Christ here. The oddness of the usage suggests that it comes from the OT but also shows how little ψυχή as such contains the character of the divine. That the context gives the term a religious turn (Dautzenberg, 132) may be granted, but this is second-ary and is not native to ψυχή as such.

[151] In Dt. heart and soul are the true centre of the person which determines a man's conduct, Haench Ag.¹⁵ on 4:32; Dautzenberg, 114-123.

[152] Acc. to Aristot. Eth. Nic., IX, 8, p. 1168b 7 f. μία ψυχή = κοινὰ τὰ φίλων. In 1 Ch. 12:39 לֵב אֶחָד is transl. by ψυχὴ μία.

[153] The fig. is realistically used of war in Sib., III, 316, cf. with ref. to Israel Ez. 14:17; cf. 2 Βασ. 12:10.

joy and sorrow is also open as such to love God and to praise Him. Is he moved by God in the same way as he is by other men? Is the praise of God an emotional movement on the same level as pleasure in eating and drinking? Is love for God an expression of the will like any other?

4. ψυχή as True Life in Distinction from Purely Physical Life (Mk. 8:35 and par.).

The saying appears in four different forms [154] at Mk. 8:36 and par., Mt. 10:39; Lk. 17:33 and Jn. 12:25. On the negative side ἀπόλλυμι "to destroy," "to lose," is always used, [155] but on the positive side there is fluctuation between σῴζω (Mk. 3:35 and par.), εὑρίσκω (Mt. 10:39), ζωογονέω and περιποιέομαι (Lk. 17:33), φυλάσσω εἰς ζωὴν αἰώνιον and φιλέω (Jn. 12:25). The two latter show that ἕνεκεν ἐμοῦ, with the addition καὶ τοῦ εὐαγγελίου in Mk., is not original.

a. Jesus.

The original form of the saying might well have been: "He who would save his ψυχή will lose it, He who loses his ψυχή will save it." [156] Both the reference to preserving the ψυχή [157] and also the positively assessed losing of the ψυχή show that primarily the reference is to what is commonly called life, i.e., physical life on earth. [158] The promise that life will be saved, however, shows that what is in view (→ 639, 5 ff.; 639, 29 ff.; 651, 2 ff.) is true and full life as God the Creator made and fashioned it. This at least leaves open the possibility that God has destined it for more than the span which is limited by death. Jesus is thus telling man that he will achieve full life only when he no longer clings to it but finds it in loss or sacrifice. The saying thus goes a step further than the logion about the fowls of the air and the lilies in Mt. 6:25-34. These are models for freedom from nervous clutching to life but they do not illustrate the offering up of life. The religious life does not differ from natural life, but it is this life as it is experienced by the man who is freed from trying to preserve it. It is thus a released and liberated and open life which God and neighbour can penetrate and yet not disrupt it but instead fulfil it. [159]

---

[154] In analysis cf. C. H. Dodd, "Some Johannine 'Herrenworte' with Par. in the Synoptic Gospels," NTSt, 2 (1955/56), 78-81; Dautzenberg, 52 f.

[155] Except in the second member of Jn. 12:25, where we find μισέω (cf. Lk. 14:26).

[156] Since εὑρίσκω fits in the second member (→ II, 769, 38) and not the first, this seems to be secondary interpolation based on the relation of losing and finding. It would be different if a Hbr. original stood behind it, so that ὁ εὑρών in Mt. 10:39 would only be a transl. variant based on reading מוֹצִיא "lead out," "deliver" in Ps. 135:7 as מֹצֵא, H. Grimme, "Stud. z. Hbr. Urmt.," BZ, 23 (1935/36), 263 f. But since this is impossible for Aram. the hypothesis is improbable unless one opts for an original Hbr. on other grounds. In textual criticism of Lk. 17:33 cf. B. Rigaux, "La petite apoc. de Luc.," Biblioth. Ephemeridum Theol. Lovaniensium, 27 (1970), 425, n. 46. Cf. also J. Jeremias, Nt.liche Theol., I (1971), 36.

[157] In Mt. 10:39 this is implied only by the preceding v. 37.

[158] It may even be said that affirmation means limitation in finding life, E. Fuchs, Zur Frage nach d. historischen Jesus² (1965), 358 f.

[159] One may say with Wellh. Mk., ad loc. that ψυχή has no adequate equivalent since it means soul, life, and self, but the word is not really ambivalent and it does not hint at the supreme value of the soul, Taylor, op. cit. (→ n. 132) on 8:35 and 36 f. The ψυχή is this creaturely life when it is lived in the freedom which God intended, Cf. P. Doncoeur, "Gagner ou perdre sa ψυχή," Recherches de Science Relig., 35 (1948), 116-9; Dautzenberg, 77, 90, 161 def. it as concrete existence reaching out to life in this world as well as in the world to come.

Hence the saying does not correspond to the Rabb. saying in bTamid., 32a: "What should man do that he may live? Let him kill himself. And what should man do that he may die? Let him enjoy life,"[160] for here the stringency of asceticism corresponds to good living. Nor can it be equated with Epict. Diss., IV, 1, 165, which with ἀποθνῄσκων σῴζεται ref. to Socrates, who kept his reputation and his character as an example, not his σωμάτιον (→ VII, 1036, 25 ff.).[161] Neither of these contains the paradoxical and liberating statement that man finds precisely what he is ready to give up and lose, not something different from it. Both involve a call to man to achieve something higher by asceticism.

b. Mark.

Mk. groups the saying with the discipleship saying in v. 34 (→ VII, 577, 21 ff.) and sets it in the immediate context of the first intimation of the passion of the Son of Man. Jn. 12:24-26 shows that this arrangement is old. It stresses the fact that this giving of life is possible only as one follows Him who gave His own life for all. He, then, is the new centre. Two impressive metaphors offer illustration in v. 34. Only he who says a basic No to his own self is able to give his life; there is no explicit or exclusive ref. to martyrdom here (→ VII, 579, 16 ff.). The grouping with the prediction of the passion and resurrection of the Son of Man shows already that the saying of Jesus will retain its validity even beyond physical death. This is not a new statement, for the original implied it to the degree that Jesus understood life as the life which is lived from the hand of God, according to the purpose of God, and therefore in the presence of God.

This means that death is not stronger than this life, for the point is that man will find his life only in giving it and it will be preserved by God even though the loss of physical life is entailed. Death is not a frontier which makes God's truth untrue. Resurrection is the final actualisation of the fact that man receives his life wholly as a gift from the hands of God. The addition "for my sake (and the gospel's)" shows that only orientation to Jesus and not to the soul can lead to this.[162]

c. Mt. 10:39.

That the paradoxical saying was found to be difficult is shown by the changing of the verb in the positive side. εὑρίσκω[163] is also put in the second member in Mt. 16:25. Mt. is hereby stressing the fact that the ψυχή which Jesus has in view is not just given to man from the outset. Only when he is ready to lose it (→ I, 395, 5 ff.) does he attain to it. ὁ εὑρών in the first member in Mt. 10:39 is hard to understand and seems to be a mechanical adjustment. At the end of the missionary address and after v. 28 (→ D I 6), Mt. in 34-7 is perhaps thinking of the martyr's death, so that the ψυχή which the victim will find is eternal life.

d. Lk. 17:33.

ζῳογονέω can denote God's act of deliverance from death but it can also have the simple meaning "to leave alive" (→ II, 873, 30 ff.).[164] περιποιέομαι (→ n. 86) occurs

---

[160] Incorrectly quoted in Kl. Mk., ad loc. Cf. Sir. 14:4: ὁ συνάγων ἀπὸ τῆς ψυχῆς αὐτοῦ, i.e., mortifying it, but this is merely a wisdom saying claiming that the avaricious man heaps up riches only for his descendants.

[161] J. B. Bauer, "'Wer sein Leben retten will'...' Mk. 8:35 par." Festschr. J. Schmid (1963), 7-10 ref. to the cohortatio in military speeches and gives several examples, but neither formerly nor materially are these very close.

[162] Dautzenberg, 61. We have here the opp. of a doctrine of the immortality of the soul in which the soul is regarded as a continuous possession of man even if on the basis of God's gift. Cf. → 655, 29 ff.

[163] A favourite word in Mt., Dautzenberg, 62.

[164] 3 Βασ. 21:31: τὰς ψυχὰς ἡμῶν.

in Gn. 12:12; Ex. 1:16 etc. as the opp. of "to kill" in the sense "to leave alive." In Gn. 36:6 it means "to win" with נַפְשׁוֹת as obj., transl. σώματα, not ψυχάς, in the LXX. In Ez. 13:19 it has ψυχάς as obj. (opp. "to kill") with a ref. to superstitious practices designed to save men from death. It might be, then, that Lk. is simply using LXX expressions without affecting the sense. Yet if we think of 1 Th. 5:9; Hb. 10:39 and esp. Lk. 21:19 (→ D I 7c) and the strongly eschatological context of Lk. 17:20 ff., it seems likely that the originally act. sense of the verb influences Lk. and that the primary sense of ψυχή, then, is eternal life. The connection with v. 32 shows that he loses his true life who looks back on life like Lot's wife and cannot detach himself from it (9:62), whereas he wins life truly who gives it up (→ 642, 21 ff.). The apoc. context carries a ref. to the time after the *parousia*.

e. Jn. 12:25.

The formulation here shows the influence of Lk. 14:26, an extension of Mt. 10:37 taken with the saying at Mt. 10:39. φιλέω (*q.v.*) and μισέω (*q.v.*) emphasise even more strongly man's total participation. In direct connection with v. 24 the saying relates primarily to Jesus Himself. This means that loss of life [165] comes to a climax in physical death. Only v. 26 makes it plain that the statement applies to the disciples too, cf. 15:13-21; 1 Jn. 3:16. The fact that either way the ref. is to both earthly and eternal life is expressly underlined by the juxtaposition of ἐν τῷ κόσμῳ τούτῳ and εἰς ζωὴν αἰώνιον. Yet the two spheres are not just distinct, for the ψυχή is kept to eternal life. It is thus the true life which is already lived in this aeon if the disciple lives where his Master is, seeking the centre of his life, not in himself, but in the One who has gone before him.

Two delimitations must be made. The awakening to eternal life is not a magical change, for the believer already has ψυχή. Again, the ψυχή is not an immortal soul, for otherwise we should not be called upon to hate it. ψυχή is the life which is given to man by God and which through man's attitude towards God receives its character as either mortal or eternal (→ 638, 4 ff.). In Jn. there can be no question of possession. Life is kept by God for eternity only in the lasting sacrifice of life and in permanently living by the gift of God. Hence we never read of the ψυχή αἰώνιος or ἀθάνατος, only of the ψυχή which is given by God and kept by Him to ζωὴ αἰώνιος.

f. ψυχή as the God-given Existence which Survives Death.

In all variants of the saying, then, ψυχή is the life which is given by God and which is no other than physical life. This life in its authenticity, however, is viewed as one that is given by God and is thus lived before Him. One might translate ψυχή by self or ego so long as it is not forgotten that this ego or self is lived only in the body. If σῶμα, in opposition to the Hellenists in Corinth, maintains the concrete corporeality of the self from which one may not escape into mere spirituality (→ VII, 1063, 17 ff.), ψυχή is a guarantee that human life is not just health or wealth, but is the life that is constantly given by God, that cannot then be limited by death, but is life as God intended it. Here, then, the Greek division into body and spirit, into a bodily and earthly life on the one side and a heavenly and spiritual life on the other, is plainly overcome.

---

[165] Cf. the pres. ψυχή is undoubtedly life in 10:11, 15, 17 too, Bultmann J., *ad loc.*

5. Life as the Supreme Good (Mk. 8:35 f. and par.).

The saying might originally have been secular: Wealth does not protect from death and life is the highest of goods. [166] This would apply only to v. 36, since v. 37 seems to be moulded by Ps. 49:7 f. [167] In the first instance, then, ψυχή means physical life. But we must realise how imprecise the expression is when no other life is known. For physical life is existence itself, the self, or being. Ps. 49, the teaching of Jesus, and even more clearly the combination with v. 35 in Mk. define the ψυχή more closely as the life which is lived before God and Ps. 49 also teaches that death cannot be a final negation of it. Of this true life which is lived before God it is then stated that man finds it, not by gaining the whole world, but by being a disciple of Jesus, v. 34. Life, then, is not just a natural phenomenon. Man lives it. If he is not aware of this, and regards life only as a natural phenomenon, he interprets it in a definite way, namely, in such sort that he misses what ought to be his life. Nor can there be any substitute for it. He has already lost his life. [168] ψυχή, then, is more than being physically alive. It is not completely different from this. As this, it is that in which the human self expresses itself. Lk. 9:25 can thus put ἑαυτόν for τὴν ψυχὴν αὐτοῦ (→ 646, 27 ff.). [169] This is already true in this world and is primarily understood with this reference. But in the faithfulness of God it also applies beyond physical death. In Mk. this is given emphasis by the connection with v. 38. [170] What happens now will one day be brought to light in the judgment. The coming of the Son of Man and His witness for or against man will make it plain that the orientation of earthly life to the κόσμος ὅλος or to God will have validity for God. Yet even here the ψυχή is not just a future, eternal life nor is it a part of man that is thought of in isolation from the body. It is life lived in the body which can lose itself or find itself, and which will be unmasked as such, and consummated by God, in the Last Judgment. Thus judgment makes it plain whether a man lives by God's gift. His ψυχή, then, is not a substance which survives death; it is life by God's action, the event of fellowship with God which will come to its fulfilment through the judgment.

6. ψυχή in Contrast to the Body (Mt. 10:28).

Mt. 10:28 presents God as the One who can destroy both body and ψυχή in Gehenna. In this regard he is contrasted with man, who can kill the body alone and not the ψυχή.

That God has power to cast into Hades and to take out of it is an OT concept. [171] Wis. 16:13-15 also says that man can only kill but has no power over the πνεῦμα that has departed or the ψυχή that has been taken away. [172] Rabbis agree that God can kill

---

[166] Hom. Il., 9, 401: οὐ γὰρ ἐμοὶ ψυχῆς ἀντάξιον. But cf. Sir. 26:14, where ψυχή denotes the person, i.e., the woman.

[167] Since S. Bar. 51:15 has a variation on v. 36b, 37 the possibility of Jewish tradition cannot be ruled out.

[168] Not "suffer harm in soul" (Luther), cf. Kl. Mk., ad loc. Gk. par. speak of care for the soul or its suffering in contrast to wealth, fame, or the body, Plat. Ap., 29d e; Isoc. Or., 2, 46. Cf. H. Hommel, "Herrenworte im Lichte sokrat. Überlieferung," ZNW, 57 (1966), 8 f.

[169] J. H. Moulton, Gram. of NT Gk., Prolegomena (1906), 87.

[170] Stressed by ἀπολέσας in Lk. 9:25 (cf. v. 24a), Dautzenberg, 81, while ζημιωθῆναι simply denotes loss, not punishment in the judgment, ibid., 75.

[171] Dt. 32:39; 1 S. 2:6; Tob. 13:2. Cf. Jm. 4:12; R. Schütz, Les idées eschatologiques du Livre de la Sagesse (1935), 189 f.

[172] There is hardly any thought of resurrection or eternal life, Schütz, op. cit., n. 171; K. Siegfried in Kautzsch Apkr. u. Pseudepigr., but cf. P. Heinisch, Das Buch d. Weisheit (1912), 306. The statement that one cannot escape God's hand (v. 15) brings us close to the idea that the πνεῦμα that has departed and the ψυχή that has been taken away are in God's hand.

both in this aeon and in that which is to come. [173] Even more precisely we find in 4 Macc. 13:13-15 a summons not to fear him who only seems to kill. God is the Giver of ψυχαί and σώματα, and there awaits evil-doers a more serious conflict of the ψυχή and the danger of eternal torment. The doctrine of the immortal soul is plainly intimated here. [174]

In Mt. 10:28, however, the reference to God's power to destroy the ψυχή and σῶμα in Hades is opposed to the idea of the immortality of the soul [175] → VII, 1058, 15. [176] For it is again apparent that man can be thought of only as a whole, both ψυχή and σῶμα. This view of man comes up against the undeniable fact that men are killed, e.g., in the persecution of the community. As Mk. 8:35 ff. (→ D I 4 f) already maintains, however, the ψυχή, i.e., the true life of man as it is lived before God and in fellowship with God, is not affected by this. Only the σῶμα (→ VII, 1058, 15 ff.) is killed here. God alone controls the whole man, ψυχή as well as σῶμα. It can hardly be contested that Greek ideas have influenced the formulation → 613, 5 ff. Nevertheless the saying is to be understood in terms of the development indicated and its point is that man can end only the life which is in some way limited by the earthly σῶμα and which is not, then, life in the true sense. As man does not really control his life, since sickness and sin already threaten it, and it is thus death rather than life, [177] so it is not in the power of man to end it. Here again ψυχή is ultimately life in the authenticity which God intended and which has still to be regarded as bodily life even in hell. Thus man can be presented only as corporeal, but what affects the body does not necessarily affect the man himself, for whom a new body has already been prepared by God, → VII, 1060, 16 ff. [178]

7. Lucan Sayings about the ψυχή after Death.

a. Lk. 12:4 f.; 9:25; Ac. 2:31.

The most striking feature is the reconstruction of Mt. 10:28. Lk. obviously wants to avoid the statement that man cannot kill the soul and he leaves out the more precise reference to the body and soul in punishment in Gehenna. [179] We find confirmation of this in 9:25, where he edits the ζημιωθῆναι τὴν ψυχὴν αὐτοῦ of Mk. 8:36, since this might be misconstrued as the punishment of the soul after death. Further confirmation may be seen in Ac. 2:31 (→ VII, 124, 32 ff.), where in distinction from ψ 15:8-11, which is quoted in Ac. 2:25-28, he avoids the ref. to the ψυχή not being left in Hades, and says instead that the σάρξ of Jesus did not see corruption. [180] Similarly

---

[173] Acc. to Dt. r., 10, 4 on 31:14 (Wünsche, 106) no being has power over the soul after death if it rests under the throne of glory in heaven. Str.-B., I, 581; Schl. Mt., ad loc.

[174] 4 Macc. 14:6. Yet the addition τῆς εὐσεβείας, which is to be taken adj., suggests that immortality is for the righteous and not self-evidently for all men. Cf. Str.-B., IV, 1036-1043.

[175] Schmaus, 321 f. P. Bratsiotis, "Das Menschenverständnis d. NT" in C. H. Dodd. Man in God's Design according to the NT (1952), 23 defends this even in Jesus.

[176] Logically one might ref. v. 28a to the intermediate state when man is without a body and 28b to the time after the resurrection, Dautzenberg, 149 f. as opp. to → VII, 1058, 17 ff. But it is very doubtful whether the dogmatic idea that God will put the soul back in the body and then judge both (→ 637, 5 ff.) is presupposed.

[177] Lk. 15:32: "He . . . was dead, and is alive again."

[178] Strictly man is thought of as necessarily living in the body, but living as a body might ref. to either the old body or the new. R. Laurin, "The Concept of Man as a Soul," Exp. T., 72 (1960), 133 warns against a dichotomous understanding.

[179] K. Köhler, "Zu Lk. 12:4, 5," ZNW, 18 (1917/18), 140 f. even thinks that v. 4b from τὸ σῶμα on is not part of the original text of Lk.

[180] Lk. interprets ψυχή in the Ps. as person and the stress on σάρξ is designed to show that this must be regarded as bodily.

Lk. 16:22 f. (→ I, 148, 8 ff.) and 23:43 presuppose that immediately after death man as a whole will either be in the torments of Hades or in Paradise. The resurrection appearances are also portrayed with great bodily realism in Lk., the risen Lord being distinguished from a shade. [181] This all points in the same direction → VI. 415, 19 ff. Lk. is obviously teaching the corporeality of the resurrection as distinct from the Hellenistic survival of the soul, although the time of the resurrection is not clear. [182] The weighty role of judgment in the summons to repentance, which demands the resurrection of both the just and the unjust (Ac. 24:15), competes with the older understanding of resurrection as a salvation blessing which leads to a life in heaven similar to that of the angels and which is granted only to believers, Lk. 20:35 f. [183] The former is obviously characteristic only of Ac., whereas in the parallel to Mt. 10:28b σῶμα as well as ψυχή is avoided in relation to the condemned in hell, as is also the idea of going into hell with hands, feet, or eyes. [184]

b. Lk. 12:20.

This saying is simply to the effect that the rich farmer must die. Yet it might be asked whether the ψυχή is not already viewed here as a loan which God demands back from him, → VI, 378, 9 ff.; 392, 7 ff. [185] Even this, of course, would mean only that man is responsible for the life that God has given him and must one day present it to God for judgment.

c. Lk. 21:19.

One might ask whether κτήσεσθε τὰς ψυχὰς ὑμῶν does not simply mean the preservation of earthly life. [186] But after v. 16b, and in replacement of Mk. 13:13: "He that endures to the end shall be saved," [187] the saying is probably to the effect that those who hold out in persecution will find true and authentic life. This goes beyond the passages already adduced (→ D I 4) to the degree that the ψυχή is now something that one only attains to. If it might be inferred from the other sayings that true life is simply given when it is orientated to God and does not seek itself, ψυχή here is plainly understood as eternal life. On the other hand this saying, too, steers clear of the idea that Lk. rejects (→ lines 5 ff.), namely, that of an immortal soul which man does not attain to only in the future.

---

[181] Only Lk. 24:39 speaks of flesh and bones, which go with the soul in the OT → 623, 26 f. Mt. 28:18 uses the typical προσελθών with the *verbum dicendi* and thus makes a heavenly appearance of the risen Lord into an earthly encounter. It is, however, the risen Lord who appears on earth and there is no further ref. to His corporeality.

[182] Apart from Lk. 16:22 f.; 23:43, Ac. 7:55 also presupposes immediate dwelling with Christ after death. On the other hand the day of judgment is a fut. event for all, Ac. 17:31; cf. Lk. 17:22 ff.; 19:11; Ac. 10:42; H. Conzelmann, "Die Mitte d. Zeit," *Beiträge z. hist. Theol.,* 17⁵ (1964), 101 f.; J. Dupont, "L'après-mort dans l'oeuvre de Luc," *Rev. Théol. de Louvain,* 3 (1972), 3-21.

[183] V. 35 alters the Marcan original and v. 36 limits the life of divine sonship (→ VIII, 390, 10 ff.) to the children of the resurrection. In itself, then, resurrection is a salvation blessing, cf. the use of the term in Jn. (apart from 5:29), Paul and Rev., although materially Paul and Rev. presuppose a resurrection to judgment.

[184] Lk. omits the whole section Mk. 9:42-50. Lk. 17:1 f. comes from a different tradition.

[185] 3 Βασ. 19:4: λαβὲ δὴ τὴν ψυχήν μου ἀπ᾽ ἐμοῦ. Cf. also Wis. 15:8; Philo Rer. Div. Her., 129. Very weak, too, is Cic. Rep., I, 3, 4, where the return of life *(vita)* to nature is simply unavoidable death.

[186] Considered as a possibility by Kl. Lk., *ad loc.*

[187] Lk. alters the wording because the τέλος is further away from the persecutions that began already prior to the Jewish War.

II. Paul Including Colossians and Ephesians.

Worth noting in Paul is the rare use of ψυχή in comparison with the OT. [188] Paul does not think in such strongly Greek terms that he can adopt the Hellenistic idea of the soul [189] nor in such strongly non-Greek terms that he can ignore the fact that in Greek culture ψυχή means something different from נֶפֶשׁ.

1. ψυχή as Natural Life and as True Life. [190]

The quotation in R. 11:3 speaks of the attempt on the ψυχή of Elijah. Paul himself bears witness in Phil. 2:30 that Epaphroditus hazarded his ψυχή for the sake of Christ's work when he was near to death. In 1 Th. 2:8 Paul says of himself and his fellow-workers that they would give not only the Gospel but their own ψυχαί for the community, → 638, 6 ff. Here the reference is not so much to the giving of physical life in death as to the giving of that which constitutes life, e.g., time, energy, and health. [191] Similarly the apostle writes concerning Prisca and Aquila in R. 16:4 that they sacrificed themselves to the uttermost for his ψυχή. Here again we are probably to think of the fuller sense of life, [192] so that the point is, not that they kept the apostle from death, but that they tried to make for him the good and healthy life that was needed for his work. According to 2 C. 12:15 Paul was ready to offer up himself for the ψυχαί of the community. Again this obviously does not mean that he wanted to preserve them from physical death but rather that he wanted to impart to them the true and authentic life which is given its fulness by God and lived in responsibility before Him. It is physical life, but this life as God intended it to be in truth. [193] In all these instances ψυχή with personal pronoun or genitive of person means little more than the pronoun or the personal indication alone. At the very most it merely indicates a specific perspective.

2. ψυχή as Person.

πᾶσα ψυχὴ ἀνθρώπου in R. 2:9 is not stressing the fact that God will judge the soul; [194] it is simply a way of referring to individuals → 617, 25 ff.; 632, 37 ff. [195]

---

[188] OT has נֶפֶשׁ 756 times, Paul has ψυχή 13 times including OT quotations: Stacey View, 121-7; Gutbrod, 75; Schmid, 134 f. The proportion, however, is much the same throughout the NT, Sevenster Begrip, 12.

[189] ψυχή does not occur in 2 C. 5:1-5, cf. J. N. Sevenster, "Some Remarks on the γυμνός in 2 C. 5:3," Festschr. J. de Zwaan (1953), 210 f.; U. Luz, "Das Geschichtsverständnis d. Pls.," Beitr. z. evang. Theol., 49 (1968), 366-9. Nor does it occur in 1 C. 5:3-5; 15:38-49; 2 C. 12:2 f.; Phil. 1:21-23; 2:6-11; 3:8-10, i.e., in all statements about Christ's pre- and post-existence, life after death, and ecstatic experiences, cf. Stacey View, 121-7, also Paul, 274, n. 1 (Bibl.); E. Hatch, Essays in Bibl. Greek (1889), 30 stresses the different usage in Philo.

[190] Cf. Bultmann Theol.[6], 204-6.

[191] Acc. to C. Masson, Les deux Ep. de S. Paul aux Thess., Comm. du NT, 11a (1957), ad loc. 1 Th. 2:8 is par. to 2 C. 12:15, while Dib. Th., ad loc. suggests the good side of the inward man and compares Col. 3:23; Eph. 6:6; Jos. Ant., 17, 177.

[192] Not, however, in the sense of the religious life that is to be saved from condemnation, nor in that of the psychological personality, nor of course with a ref. to a "part" of Paul. The sense is close to that of physical life. Cf. Mi. R.[13], ad loc.

[193] When Barth, 324 speaks of the ψυχή that is tied to the σάρξ as distinct from the originally equal πνεῦμα, and of the freeing of this ψυχή only by Christ, he is right so long as we do not think of parts of man. Yet πνεῦμα means primarily God's Spirit and only secondarily that of the man endowed with God's Spirit, while ψυχή is primarily the life which is given by the Creator, which is responsible to Him, and which will be led by Him to true freedom, so that we can never read strictly of God's ψυχή → 640, 31 ff.; n. 212.

[194] M. J. Lagrange, Saint Paul. Ep. aux Romains, Ét. Bibl. (1950), ad loc.

[195] Cf. also Lv. 4:27; Nu. 15:27; Mi. R.[13], ad loc.; O. Kuss, Der Römerbr. (1959), ad loc.

The πᾶσα ψυχή of R. 13:1 is to be taken in the same way. Both phrases come in traditional Jewish contexts.

In 2 C. 1:23, however, ψυχή almost replaces the πνεῦμα of R. 1:9 → VI, 435, 18 ff. It does, of course, correspond to the Hebrew use of וֶפֶשׁ for the reflexive pronoun → 620, 21 ff.,[196] but in context what is obviously meant is the self that is aware of being responsible to God, as in R. 1:9.

3. μία ψυχή.

Phil. 1:27 has μία ψυχή (→ 617, 2 ff.) as a parallel to ἓν πνεῦμα, → VI, 435, 3 ff. Here, in accordance with traditional usage, ψυχή is the locus of emotional movement, of the psychological life → 640, 34 ff.[197] Anthropological trichotomy can hardly lie behind this.[198] We simply have rhetorical variation in which ἓν πνεῦμα perhaps lays stronger emphasis on the unity that is given by God[199] while μία ψυχή describes the task that is to be achieved. If it is true that in Paul πνεῦμα can be parallel to ψυχή in the believer,[200] there is no thought of a soul that is regenerated through the Spirit and gradually detached from the flesh.[201] That ψυχή as such bears no intrinsic qualification may also be seen from the fact that in distinction from the Greek world[202] πνεῦμα is always the opposite of σάρξ, or νοῦς in the unbeliever, but never ψυχή[203] → VI, 428, 10 ff.; VII, 126, 22 ff.; 132, 20 - 134, 13.

In all these passages ψυχή may be neutrally man's physical life, or positively the healthy and strong physical life which is pleasing to God, or the person, or its intellectual and spiritual faculties. On the other hand, it is never assessed negatively. On 1 C. 15:45; 1 Th. 5:23 → 662, 20 ff.; VI, 435, 9 ff.[204]

4. Colossians and Ephesians.

Here we find the expression ἐκ ψυχῆς, Col. 3:23; Eph. 6:6;[205] → 641, 12 ff. ψυχή is not what is intrinsically pure and good nor does it belong to the sphere of the carnal and sinful.[206] It is to be taken in a purely neutral sense.

---

[196] J. Héring, La seconde ép. de S. Paul aux Corinth., Comm. du NT, 8 (1958), ad loc.; E. B. Allo, S. Paul. Seconde ép. aux Corinth., Ét. Bibl. (1956), ad loc. compares with Mt. 5:36 "to swear by one's head," although the ἐπί here hardly means the same as the ἐν there.

[197] Not a higher part of man, Dib. Ph., ad loc., cf. also Ltzm. R., Exc. 7:14-25.

[198] So Loh. Ph., ad loc. who explains the absence of σῶμα by the use of ἓν σῶμα only collectively for the community as Christ's body. Cf., however, τῷ αὐτῷ πνεύματι in 2 C. 12:18, where it is supplemented by τοῖς αὐτοῖς ἴχνεσιν. (μία) καρδία is par. in Ac. 4:32 → 641, 17 ff. On the Gk. background → 617, 2 f. and W. Theiler, Review of P. Merlan, Monopsychism, Mysticism, Metaconsciousness, in Gnomon, 37 (1965), 22 f.

[199] P. Bonnard, L'ép. de S. Paul aux Philipp., Comm. du NT, 10 (1950), ad loc. thinks the ref. is to the Holy Spirit.

[200] Ltzm. R. on 8:11.

[201] So Barth, 335: Janus' head, bound to the flesh yet aspiring to the spirit → VI, 436, 9 ff.

[202] The usual antithesis is σῶμα and ψυχή, but we find variations in the Gk. world too, Plut. Quaest. Conv., V (II, 672e, 673b); Cons. ad Apoll., 13 (II, 107 f.) etc. → VII, 103, 32 ff.

[203] Not because the ψυχή is quasi-material and bound to the body but because it denotes man and his existence as he lives in the body, while πνεῦμα basically suggests God's action.

[204] R. Jewett, "Paul's Anthropological Terms," Arbeiten z. Gesch. d. antiken Judt. u. d. Urchr., 10 (1971), 175-183 suggests the adoption of anthropological trichotomy by the enthusiasts who opposed him.

[205] The formulation ποιεῖν τὸ θέλημα τοῦ θεοῦ, 1 Ἐσδρ. 9:9; 4 Macc. 18:16; Mt. 7:21; 12:50; Mk. 3:35 is traditional, cf. Schlier Eph.[7], ad loc.

[206] Loh. Kol. on 3:23.

One can hate ἐκ ψυχῆς, Test. G. 2:1, and love κατὰ τὴν ψυχήν, Test. B. 4:5. One can obey and reverence God ἐν πάσῃ or ὅλῃ ψυχῇ, Sir. 6:26; 7:29, and sin ἀπὸ ψυχῆς, 19:16. ψυχή, par. δύναμις, describes man's total commitment, although with ref. to his powers of soul rather than his physical powers. 207

The absence of a doctrine of the soul is all the more astonishing in view of the fact that the Colossian heretics taught a Jewish brand of Neo-Pythagoreanism in which the purification of the soul from everything earthly and its ascent to the highest element where Christ dwells occupied a central place. 208 The author is plainly conducting the controversy wholly in terms of christology and not anthropology. Even statements about the Spirit are surprisingly sparse.

5. Secularity of the Usage.

It may be inferred that Paul's use of ψυχή is a more considered one than that of the Gospels. Paul employs ψυχή rarely. He never has it for the life which survives death, for to him it is all-important that the new life of the risen Lord should be understood wholly as a gift on the basis of a new creative act of God. Hence not even in germ is it to be found in man. It is to be viewed entirely as a divine and heavenly life which lies in the future or in heaven, 1 C. 15:38; 45-47, 49; 2 C. 5:1f.; Phil. 3:11f. etc. Nevertheless Paul's understanding of man does not differ completely from that of the Gospels. For him, too, there is continuity between the earthly life and that of the resurrection. If in their use of ψυχή the Gospels say that true life that is not threatened by death is found only by the man who orientates his life to God and not himself, so that he does not live in his own strength but by the gift of God (→ 644, 37 ff.), Paul says with greater theological sharpness that the continuity lies wholly in God and hence can no longer be denoted by ψυχή but only by πνεῦμα → VI, 420, 3 ff.

III. Hebrews.

In Hb. 12:3 the ψυχαί of the community are the place where it grows weary. 209 One may thus think of life-force, courage, or readiness for sacrifice, but it may be doubted whether the specifically spiritual life of the community is in view. This is the meaning, however, in 13:17, for the ψυχαί over whom the leaders of the community watch and for whom they must render an account are naturally the members of the community as in 2 C. 12:15 (→ 648, 17 ff.), but described now with more emphatic reference to their spiritual life. ψυχή is the man for whom an account must be given at the Last Judgment. He is not commended to the leader of the community in general, as the neighbour is. He is specifically commended; the leader must bring him to salvation and not to judgment. The only question is whether ψυχή is meant to place bigger stress on man as a whole person or on his life before God, 210 which is supported by 10:39. περιποίησις ψυχῆς in contrast to ἀπώλεια obviously means

---

207 Barth, 320 ref. to Calvin's transl. "de courage."
208 In Alexander Polyhist. (1st cent. B.C.) all the terms of Col. 2 occur in Fr., 1a of an anon. Pythagorean, Diels, I, 448, 33 ff., cf. E. Schweizer, *Die "Elemente d. Welt"* (→ n. 129), 160-163.
209 The par. in Polyb., 20, 4, 7; 29, 17, 4 support the view that ταῖς ψυχαῖς goes with ἐκλυόμενοι. The first passage contrasts ψυχαί and σώματα; there is weakening in both.
210 Acc. to Mi. Hb., *ad loc.* the ref. is to eschatological life. Reicke, 208 f. sees in Hb. 10:39, as in Jm. 1:21; 1 Pt. 1:9, a supreme religious good, a part of the person which will be saved for eternal life.

the attainment of true and authentic life → 643, 38 ff. [211] In the context this is the life that is achieved or preserved through the Last Judgment. [212] Since περιποίησις alongside ἀπώλεια means "preservation" or "attainment," we have here something of the insight that the earthly life which is lived before God reaches its consummation through God's judgment and resurrection with no complete break between this life and life after death (→ 642, 18 ff.). This is also suggested by 6:19, where hope is understood as an anchor of the ψυχή which has penetrated to the inner sanctuary where Jesus the fore-runner dwells. The spiritual existence of man before God is obviously intended here. Here, too, the ψυχή is not in itself good or divine. It is assailed and threatened and needs an anchor. Yet it lives in virtue of the fact that it has sent on its hope ahead and thus in a sense already lives where it will one day be perfected. Through the idea of a fore-runner, eschatological statements about the coming life with God can be changed into spatial statements about the location of the hope of the believer in the innermost part of the temple.

The most difficult passage is 4:12 (→ VI, 446, 4 ff.). It must be asked whether πνεῦμα and ψυχή are separated by God's Word (→ IV, 118, 17 ff.) or whether this Word pierces them both. Since the parting of the bones and marrow is hard to imagine, the text is probably saying that the Word has penetrated the πνεῦμα and ψυχή as it has the bones and marrow.

If so, these are to be explained in terms of traditional anthropology as in 1 Th. 5:23 (→ VI, 435, 9 ff.). The saying can then be understood in the light of Philo Rer. Div. Her., 130-132. Here the λόγος of God, for Philo the divine reason which can make logical distinctions, is described as the τομεύς ("the cutter") which can pierce and dissect not only corporeal things even down to atoms but even ψυχή, λόγος, and αἴσθησις, and that which is perceived with the spirit. [213]

Thus Hb. 4:12 is saying that the Word of God pierces all things even to the inwardness of physical and psychical man. There is no stress on ψυχή alongside πνεῦμα. It goes with it rather than being distinguished from it. No definite theological trichotomy is in view.

IV. The Catholic Epistles.

1. John.

On 1 Jn. 3:16 → 638, 4 ff. In 3 Jn. 2 the author expresses the wish that the recipient will be as well and healthy in all things as his ψυχή is. We thus have here a distinction between the physical and the spiritual life which has been lurking for a long time in the background but which has nowhere come out so clearly. If ψυχή means the true life before God, experience shows that this can be sound even in a man who is sick in body. Hence ψυχή is not just the whole self or life of man which embraces the physical too and experiences πάντα. It is the life which is

---

211 In the Gk. par. Xenoph. Cyrop., IV, 4, 10; Isoc. Ep., 2, 7 περιποιέομαι τὴν ψυχήν means "to preserve life," but the par. in 1 Th. 5:9: εἰς περιποίησιν σωτηρίας, cf. εἰς περιποίησιν δόξης, 2 Th. 2:14, is closer, C. Spicq, L'ép. aux Hb., II, Ét. bibl. (1953), ad loc.
212 V. 39 interprets the quotation from Hab. 2:4 in v. 38. Here, too, we have ψυχή, but God's ψυχή which takes no pleasure in the one who draws back.
213 Cf. Wis. 7:22 ff., where something similar is said about God's πνεῦμα, and O. Sol. 12:5 for something comparable about the Word. Philo Virt., 103 equates ψυχή and διάνοια.

ultimately important, i.e., which is orientated to God. Naturally ψυχή is not set in express antithesis to the bodily side here. The hope is that the two will be in harmony, not that they will be separated from one another. [214]

2. James.

Since the ἔμφυτος λόγος (1:21), in spite of Epict. Diss., II, 11, 3, is not reason, but the Word of God rooted in man (1:18, 22), [215] σῴζω embraces eschatological salvation. ψυχή is thus the life of man before God which will find its consummation in the resurrection. The same applies in 5:20, as the addition ἐκ θανάτου shows. ψυχή is again man's existence in responsibility to God; this is saved through death or through the judgment of condemnation. Whether θάνατος means the former or the latter depends on whether we see in ψυχή that of the sinner or that of the monitor. [216] Tob. 4:10; Ab., 5, 18, [217] cf. Ez. 3:18-21, [218] seem to favour the latter. Barn., 19, 10; 2 Cl., 15, 1, cf. 19, 1; Ep. Apostolorum, 51 (Copt.) [219] contain both thoughts, cf. also Pist. Soph., 104 (GCS, 171, 35 ff.). Prv. 10:12, which is possibly quoted at the end of the saying, supports the former. A multitude of sins could hardly be spoken of in relation to the monitor. For these two reasons it is perhaps better to refer both the statements of v. 20b to the sinner. [220] In this case ψυχή is here again the true life before God. This is saved through judgment, which threatens it with death.

3. 1 Peter.

3:20 seems to be just a numerical reference (→ 639, 25 f.). Since we have here the righteous who are preserved through the flood and who typify the baptised, it is just possible, however, that the author has in view the eight souls which live in God's sight and are kept by Him for salvation. In 1:9 the σωτηρία ψυχῶν is the eschatological goal of faith. Plainly, then, ψυχή is the individual life, or the person thus denoted, that stands before the judgment and is saved through it after the *parousia* of Christ (v. 7). [221] This life from God, however, is already lived and sanctified on earth in obedience to God, i.e., in love (1:22). 4:18 is to be construed

---

[214] Schnckbg. J.² (1963), ad loc. The best par. is Philo Rer. Div. Her., 285. Here we have the εὐοδοῦσθαι of τὰ ἐκτός, τὰ σώματος, and τὰ ψυχῆς, which is ethically understood. The usage shows, however, that one cannot differentiate so easily the natural life, the life of faith on its natural side, and the supernatural life (Schnckbg., *loc. cit.*). The life of faith, as the use of ψυχή shows, is the natural life which is lived before God and by His gift, and which finds its fulfilment in the resurrection.

[215] τοῦτο τὸ ἔμφυτον ἔχο[υσα], "that has passed into flesh and blood," P. Masp., I, 67006, recto 3 (6th cent. A.D.), cf. Preisigke Wört., *s.v.*

[216] If ψυχή is related to the monitor, one should consider whether the thought is not simply that he attains to life for eternity beyond physical death. If αὐτοῦ is to be cut out with 𝕽, we must certainly decide in favour of the first sense.

[217] Cf. Str.-B., III, 229 f.

[218] Also the Gk. of Act. Thom., 6, ed. M. R. James, Apocr. Anecdota, II, TSt, 5, 1 (1897), 29; cf. Hennecke², 35, no. 8.

[219] Ed. H. Duensing, KIT, 152 (1925), 33 f., cf. Hennecke³, I, 149.

[220] Logically the saying about the covering of sins certainly comes before that about the saving of the ψυχή from death, Dib. Jk., *ad loc.*, but it is added in confirmation as a bibl. quotation.

[221] G. Dautzenberg, "Σωτηρία ψυχῶν (1 Pt. 1:9)," BZ, NF, 8 (1964), 262-276 emphasises the underlying apocal. tradition; the lack of art. suggests a fixed usage influenced by the Semitic st.c. ψυχή is the centre of existence, life, but not a higher ego.

along similar lines. Intrinsically it is possible to think of those who suffer persecution commending their physical life to God. But since martyrdom has to be reckoned with as a present-day reality later (4:12 ff.; 5:9), this is unlikely. The commending is to be in the doing of good and God is expressly invoked as the Creator. Obviously, then, the reference is to the life which the Creator Himself takes into His keeping hands through death and fashions anew. Christ as the "overseer of your souls" (2:25) is indubitably the One who cares for the faith life of the community (→ 650, 29 ff.; II, 615, 25 ff.).

2:11 is the most strongly Hellenised ψυχή passage in the NT (→ VII, 144, 19 ff.). Here ψυχή is clearly a life which is given by God and lived before Him. Fleshly desires war against it. [222] It thus seems to be a part of man, the flesh being another part. The first part is not, of course, unconditionally and in all circumstances good. It is exposed to attack and conflict. Above all it is not summoned to asceticism, which will simply mortify the flesh. Instead, it is summoned to a life which, even though lived in the earthly sphere, is already at home in the heavenly sphere (→ VI, 447, 11 ff.). Nevertheless, this is the only NT passage where ψυχή plainly stands in antithesis to σάρξ. Since elsewhere in the letter ψυχή is the individual life which survives physical death, which is created afresh after it, and which attains to salvation after the parousia, ψυχή comes close here to the Greek understanding (→ 611, 15 ff.). It thus takes the place that is occupied by πνεῦμα in Paul (Gl. 5:17). On the other hand πνεῦμα here stresses that God is the subject and it is confined in the OT sense to prophets, apostles, and martyrs (→ VI, 447, 3 ff.).

4. 2 Peter.

In 2:8, 14 ψυχή is the person, but the person who lives responsibly, distinguishing between good and evil, and hence exposed to temptation. In itself, then, ψυχή is neutral, being qualified positively or negatively by δικαία or ἀστήρικτος. It is certainly not an intrinsically bad principle or one of lesser worth.

V. Revelation.

1. ψυχή as Physical Life.

Very much along OT lines is the use of πᾶσα ψυχή (→ 632, 36 ff.) in 16:3 except that the added ζωῆς emphasises the fact that the reference is to living creatures and not to plants or animals. Only here and in 8:9 is ψυχή used for animal life in the NT; in both cases marine creatures are in view. In 12:11 ψυχή means the physical life which the martyrs are not to preserve or love.

2. ψυχή as Person.

The use in 18:13 also follows the OT (→ 639, 24 ff.; Ex. 27:13). Materially the word is parallel to σώματα (→ VII, 1035, 13 ff.; 1058, 1 f.), but horror at the traffic in slaves, who are also human persons, is probably expressed in the fuller expression ψυχαὶ ἀνθρώπων, so that the word is not just a numerical term. A beginning of critical social ethics might be detected here.

---

222 Cf. also the Apoc. of Adam, 75, 4 f., ed. A. Böhlig-P. Labib, "Kpt.-gnost. Apok. aus Cod V v. Nag Hammadi," *Wissenschaftl. Zschr. d. Martin-Luther-Univ. Halle-Wittenberg,* Special Vol. (1963), 107.

3. ψυχή as Life after Death.

This sense is clearest in 6:9, which again reflects the OT (→ 634, 3 ff.). Here ψυχή is the man who survives death prior to his resurrection. He is seen as one who has self-awareness, who awaits the day of God's righteous judgment, and who is protected by God under the heavenly altar (→ VII, 934, 31 ff.). Yet the ψυχαί are not intentionally or emphatically presented as non-corporeal, since the divine can see them and they are robed in white garments. Only hereby are they marked as belonging to God (v. 11). [223] Nevertheless, it must be maintained that this intermediate state is not a true life; this will come only with the new corporeality at the resurrection. Furthermore the reference here is expressly to martyrs; it seems to be assumed in 20:13 that for non-believers at least there will be no consciously experienced intermediate state (→ D VI 5).

Finally the ψυχή in 20:4 is the person which stands before God's judgment and which is endowed with the glory of the millennium before His throne. Obviously the reference here again is to the final state after the first resurrection. It now becomes plain that ψυχή does not denote a purely provisional and definitely non-corporeal state which will become full humanity again only with the gift of the body at the resurrection. This is confirmed by the relation of the word to the relative masculine pronoun, which shows how much it embraces the whole person. ψυχή is thus adopted as a term for man as he lives in eschatological salvation. It does not carry with it any clear distinction between a non-corporeal and a corporeal state.

VI. New Testament Usage in Distinction from πνεῦμα.

1. Except in Hb., Jm. and 1 and 2 Pt. ψυχή means the physical life of man, that of animals too in Rev. (→ 653, 30 ff.). In popular use, although not in the studied theological style of Paul and John, πνεῦμα can be used for it (→ VI, 377, 16 ff.). [224] But a difference may be seen already in the fact that the soul, unlike the spirit, can be hated, persecuted, and slain. Even when there is reference to the παρατίθεσθαι of the πνεῦμα, this can be only in such a way that God is central as the recipient (→ VI, 415, 17 ff.; 452, 39 ff.), not in such a way that the cessation of life is stressed. A real antithesis develops here when ψυχή definitely describes the purely natural life which can be ended. Thus 1 C. 15:45 can adopt dualistic speculations about the contrast between the Adam who became a living ψυχή, and the Adam who became a πνεῦμα ζωοποιοῦν (→ 661, 29 ff., 662, 20 ff.).

2. On the other hand, ψυχή is always my life, never the phenomenon of life as such. Like πνεῦμα then (→ VI, 435, 3 ff.) it can denote man as a whole, a person. It can thus be used for the reflexive pronoun, or in the formula πᾶσα ψυχή, or as a purely numerical term (→ 639, 24 ff.). The fact that πνεῦμα cannot be used in these ways shows already that even when it denotes man as a totality, it presents him under a special aspect. Again ψυχή, like πνεῦμα [225] (→ VI, 357, 1 ff.; 396, 22 f.; 435, 1 ff.), can be the locus of joy and sorrow and love and hate; it can thus describe man from the standpoint of inward participation. In contrast πνεῦμα

---

[223] Cf. C. Brütsch, Die Offenbarung Jesu Christi, I² (1970), 293-7.
[224] For the OT cf. Dautzenberg, 109 f. Cf. 2 Macc. 7:22 f.
[225] Cf. Mk. 2:8 with 5:30. In Phil. 1:27 and Hb. 4:12 we have the two words together.

is never used of non-Christians or for impulses that are ethically negative, [226] since it denotes God's gift more clearly than ψυχή. Certainly ψυχή, which is closely related to καρδία with its emphasis on the will and on conscious inward participation, can be the locus of faith. On the other hand faith is of no interest as a psychological phenomenon, as Paul stresses when he takes up the matter in 1 C. 12:1 ff. The only point is that God can use man's psychological faculties. The decisive thing, however, is the proclamation of Jesus as Lord and the edification of the community, and this takes place through the πνεῦμα, → VI, 423, 16 ff.

3. A further development calls for notice here. Although ψυχή can never be sundered from the purely physical life, it is not identical with it. One may find or miss life as God intended it → 642, 14 ff. [227] Precisely when man views it as his ultimate goal and tries to win the whole world, he loses it. Only in giving it does he find it. In this sense, too, ψυχή is the natural life, but it is this as life in its authenticity as this is given by God and received from Him. This is where the problem arises. The difficulty with πνεῦμα is not to let God's Spirit working in man become an inner spiritual life that is given to man (→ VI, 415, 13 ff.; 435, 12 ff.). With ψυχή, however, the difficulty is the opposite one of not restricting the God-given life to the purely physical sphere which is threatened by death, but also embracing therein the gift of God which transcends death.

4. The OT had already shown that God's faithfulness does not come to an end with the death of man. On occasion there could even be individual expectation of life, as in Ps. 49 → 645, 6 ff. This takes on clearer outlines in Jesus' teaching about losing and finding the ψυχή → 642, 14 ff. Thus ψυχή gradually comes to be used more specifically to denote a life that is not ended by death → 643, 37 ff; 645, 31 ff. In later texts of the NT this can be expressly identified as the religious life which is to be pastorally nurtured, with an emphasis on the fact that it is a gift and that it implies responsibility → 650, 33 ff. In the context of exhortation 1 Pt. 2:11 (→ 653, 9 ff.) can present it in typical Hellenistic fashion as a life attacked by carnal desires. As in the idea of the immortality of the soul continuity is maintained between the life of faith and the resurrection life, but this continuity resides, not in an indwelling of God in man which is guaranteed by nature or sacrament, but solely in the faithfulness of God. Hence πνεῦμα too (→ VI, 435, 20 ff.; 445, 27 ff.) can denote the departed Christian. In both cases the reference is not to a part of man that has survived death, [228] but to the total existence of man as this is given by God and lived out before Him. [229] After death, then, it is bodily if not fleshly → VII, 1060, 16 ff. Continuity with the physical life of man is naturally expressed by ψυχή, so that only this and not πνεῦμα can be used in a saying like

---

[226] Unless the ref. is to an evil πνεῦμα (Mk. 9:20; Ac. 19:15; Rev. 16:13 f. etc.), which will obviously be a supernatural power.

[227] The way is prepared for this by the OT idea that the sick life is not life as God intended it and is thus more death than life, Ps. 86:13, cf. 16:10.

[228] So Bratsiotis, op. cit. (→ n. 175), 29: In Paul ψυχή and πνεῦμα are two aspects of the part of man also called νοῦς; they belong to man along with σῶμα.

[229] Cf. Cullmann, 37-41; v. Campenhausen, 303 f., 307 f. P. H. Menoud, "Le sort des trépassés d'après le NT," Cahiers théol. de l'Actualité Protestante, 9 (1945), 17-20. C. K. Barrett, "Immortality and Resurrection," The London Quart. and Holborn Review, 34 (1965), 91-102 rightly emphasises not merely these NT passages but also Gk. statements about resurrection, and he pts. out that not every Greek is a Platonist. Cf. also P. Pédesch, "Les idées relig. de Polybe," RHR, 167 (1965), 38-42.

Mk. 8:35 (→ 643, 10 ff.). John can develop this usage (→ 644, 12 ff.), whereas Paul speaks only of the πνεῦμα which is to be saved through death (→ VI, 435, 20 ff.) because this sets in relief continuity with God's activity in the early life of the believer and in the life of the resurrection. After Paul, however, ψυχή can be used to describe an existence which will reach its goal only after death. It thus becomes identical with the soul as the Greeks understood it, although this is never thought to be pre-existent (→ 653, 16 ff.).

5. ψυχή does not seem to occur as a term for life in the intermediate state (→ III, 17, 6 ff.) [230] any more than πνεῦμα does (→ VI, 415, 19 ff.), not even in Rev. 6:9 (→ 654, 2 ff.) [231] and certainly not in 2 C. 5:3 (→ VII, 1060, 26 ff.). [232] There is dispute, of course, about Mt. 10:28, → n. 176. Luke (→ D I 7c) seems to be interested in a bodily resurrection (24:39) immediately after death (16:22 ff.?; 23:43?) and he thus avoids expressions which might suggest the mere survival of the soul. Paul is wisely satisfied to know that the dead are with Christ, Phil. 1:23, though cf. 3:21 → I, 149, 16 ff.

Schweizer

E. Gnosticism.

1. Gnosticism is made up of many doctrines of salvation both inside Christianity and outside it. The relevant texts are highly varied in speech and origin. The history of the motifs is most uncertain. It is thus impossible to generalise about a Gnostic concept of the soul. Common to all Gnostic teachings is the fact that the self of redeemable man is viewed as part of the transcendent world of light which is entangled in this cosmos. The insight into its origin which is brought by an extraterrestrial bringer of salvation enables the self to free itself and to return to its home. [233] The fall and ascent of the soul are seen as part of a cosmic process. [234] If in what follows the human self is called the soul, this cannot be taken for granted in non-Gk. texts of the Gnostic tradition. Yet in Gk.-speaking Gnosticism the terminology of the popular philosophical doctrine of the soul is used in anthropology, [235] so that the pairs light/darkness, good/evil, spirit/matter and soul/body correspond to one another. [236]

2. In their use of ψυχή the Gnostics adopt the hierarchy of the non-corporeal world current from the days of Plato. But whereas in philosophy the rational power as the dominant factor in the human soul opens up the possibility of recognising the rational

---

[230] In opp. to v. Campenhausen, cf. Schmaus, 324-7, to Cullmann, Masson, 250-267. Sevenster Anthropologie, 176 thinks Paul teaches a survival of the ψυχή in the intermediate state, and materially cf. Masson, *op. cit.* (→ n. 229), 42. Guignebert, 435 even believes that man was already divided into flesh, soul and spirit in the time of Jesus and that only the last went to God, while the soul went to sheol.

[231] Rev. 20:4 should be adduced with caution, since it ref. to the state after the first resurrection, so that the ψυχή is naturally presented as a full person.

[232] For an explicit discussion of the questions involved here cf. M. J. Harris, *The Interpretation of 2 C. 5:1-10 and its Place in Pauline Eschatology,* Diss. Manchester (1970).

[233] Many Gnostic trends share an affinity to astrology with the Neo-Pythagoreans, who worked out their ideas on the ascent of the soul in dependence on Plat. Tim., 47a ff. In this pseudo-philosophy many individual philosophical principles serve as the content of revelation. Cf. Burkert, 335-347. On astrology in the mystery religions, cf. Nilsson, II, 596. On the Gnostic version of the ascent of the soul, cf. C. Colpe, "Die 'Himmelsreise d. Seele' ausserh. u. innerh. d. Gnosis," *Le origini,* 429-447.

[234] Colpe, *op. cit.* (→ n. 233), 439-445.

[235] The Gnostic systems, which claim to be the revelation of suprarational insight, use philosophical concepts and figures taken from their discursive rational context, and also the mythological ἱερὸς λόγος, which by derivation expounds a cult, esp. a difficult mystery cult.

[236] Cf. S. Pétrement, *Le dualisme chez Platon, les Gnostiques et les manichéens* (1947).

and good order of the universe, and of imitating it in moral action, on the Gnostic view the ψυχή or inward core of empirical man is subjected to a cosmos whose matter is indeed fashioned and quickened by the presence of pneumatic particles but which is still sharply separated from the good world of light, having been made by a god of lesser rank, cf. Basilides in Hipp. Ref., VII, 23, 2 f. [237] Only the πνεῦμα belongs to the world of light → χάρις F. [238] If in Stoicism the πνεῦμα was called the finest matter as the carrier of rationality, this concept was given a spiritualised turn in Stoic-Platonic syncretism, and if Pos. et al. saw in the πνεῦμα the carrier of emotional impulses, the πνεῦμα now becomes the effective counterpart of the ψυχή. The ψυχή is immaterial, but it belongs to the present cosmos [239] and is subject to matter as the essential part of man, cf. the Gnostic Justin in Hipp. Ref., V, 26, 8 f. The threefold structuring of man [240] as πνεῦμα/ψυχή/σῶμα, which is common in the Gnostics, cf. the Naassenes in ibid., V, 7, 9-15, Valentinus in VI, 37, is based on a philosophical model. In Middle Platonism, e.g., Plut. Fac. Lun., 28 (II, 943a) the most valuable part of man, the νοῦς, derives from the solar sphere. The ψυχή is formed as its annex in transition through the moon hades, and it is joined to a body on earth (→ 475, n. 29). In spite of the disparagement of matter in this and related understandings, and in spite of the hope of a return of the νοῦς to its origin, there is a difference from comparable Gnostic teachings, cf. Corp. Herm., 1, 22; 13, 7 ff. For the Platonic tradition the union of the spirit with matter and the resultant development of man and the cosmos are always an act of self-unfolding νοῦς. This and the rise of the ψυχή are a matter for regret amongst the Gnostics, since the effect is the essential alienation of the pneumatic particle. The rules by which ψυχαί live and act in this cosmos, whether they be bodiless demons, the archons of the astral sphere, or the souls of human bodies, are not the rules of the πλήρωμα, the world of light. In the Platonic tradition and even in the astrology independent of Gnosticism it is a matter of understanding the unbreakable order of the cosmos as both εἱμαρμένη and benevolent πρόνοια. The soul is able to do this as the bearer of the intellect, and this willing re-cognition confers on man the freedom which differentiates him from animals and plants. In Gnostic thought, however, "just" εἱμαρμένη [241] is the very thing that disqualifies the cosmos. A ὑπεράνω τῆς εἱμαρμένης γενέσθαι, cf. Pist. Soph., 13 (GCS, 45, p. 13, 24 ff.); 26 f. (p. 22, 17 ff.; 26, 4 ff.) [242] does not mean, as in philosophy, perceiving the agreement between the cosmos and the soul and imitating it in life; it means the extra-rational insight that natural and moral laws control the pneumatic self, withhold from it the freedom which is its due, and prevent it from entering the pleroma. Relevant here is the threefold νόμος, Ptolemaeus Ad Floram in Epiph. Haer., 33, 5, 1-2, Marcion's distinc-tion between the good God and the just God, and Epiphanes' work Περὶ δικαιοσύνης. [243] The Apocr. Joh. [244] Cod. IV, p. 40, 21 ff.; II, 26, 8 ff. explains that the ψυχή is good only to the extent that it has taken πνεῦμα into itself and lets itself be guided by it. Otherwise

---

[237] Acc. to the Gnostic Justin, Hipp. Ref., V, 26, 32 only the ψυχικὸς καὶ χοϊκὸς αν-θρωπος suffered Jesus' passion, while the πνεῦμα went back to the Father. Cf. Act. Joh. 98 ff.

[238] The metaphors for the pneumatic component of man (spark etc.) mostly come from philosophy, e.g., Synesius of Cyrene hymnus, 1 (3), 560-9, ed. N. Terzaghi, I Script. Graeci et Latini (1939), and one might ask whether sometimes the Gnostics took them lit.

[239] Acc. to Hipp. Ref., VI, 34, 1 the Valentinians call the divine σοφία πνεῦμα and the demiurge, the maker of this cosmos, ψυχή. Plotin. in Enn., II, 9, 5 f. attacks the ideas which underlie this terminology.

[240] Acc. to Iren. Haer., I, 14, 1 some Gnostics regard the baptism of Jesus as psychical and that of the Christ incarnated in Him as pneumatic; only the latter is part of the process of redemption.

[241] The Hermetics use εἱμαρμένη in this negative sense synon. with ἁρμονία, Corp. Herm., 1, 9 or 1, 15.

[242] The freedom of the Gnostic, ἀβασίλευτον εἶναι, is thus a central theme, cf. the Naassenes in Hipp. Ref., V, 8, 30.

[243] Cf. W. Völker, "Quellen z. Gesch. d. chr. Gnosis," Sammlung ausgewählter kirchen-u. dogmengeschichtl. Quellenschr., NF, 5 (1932), 34 f.

[244] Ed. M. Krause/P. Labib, "Die drei Versionen d. Apokr. d. Joh. im Kpt. Museum zu Alt-Kairo," Abh. d. Deutschen Archäolog. Instituts Kairo, Kpt. Reihe, 1 (1962).

it is the seat of the ἀντίμιμον πνεῦμα which causes it to err and do wrong. The ψυχή marks the disputed territory of redemption, while πνεῦμα (νοῦς) and σῶμα (σάρξ) are quite unequivocal. 245

3. In detail there are gt. differences in the psychological terminology of the Gnostics. For most of them ψυχή has relative value only in coordination with πνεῦμα, cf. the Gnostic Justin in Hipp. Ref., V, 26, 25, while it has a negative accent in antithesis to πνεῦμα. Valentinian Gnosticism adopts the doctrine of two souls (which is found in Numenius, → 616, 8 ff.), cf. Cl. Al. Exc. Theod., 50, 1 ff., 246 so that the ψυχή can be the pneumatic self of man, although this has no new implications. Elsewhere νοῦς/πνεῦμα/λόγος mean much the same and are contrasted with ψυχή. Corp. Herm., 10, 13 has the crescendo πνεῦμα, ψυχή, λόγος, νοῦς, πνεῦμα being here the blood-substratum of ψυχή, cf. Philo Migr. Abr., 3 ff. but also Plot. Enn., II, 9, 1, 57-63. In Corp. Herm. Fr., 23, 18 f. Ascl., 12; Corp. Herm. Fr., 18; Basilides Fr., 3 (→ n. 243) and esp. as a basis for the ethical libertinism of the Carpocratians, Hipp. Ref., VII, 32, 7 f. the transmigration of souls it taught, though cf. Corp. Herm., 10, 20. Strictly redemption can apply only to the πνεῦμα or νοῦς of man, cf. Heracleon Fr., 27 (→ n. 243), but in this connection the texts not infrequently speak of the ψυχή too, cf. Basilides in Iren., 1, 19, 3. Sometimes πνεῦμα and σάρξ are contrasted and the ψυχή is left out, cf. Hipp. Ref., V, 7, 40. Naturally most differentiations occur in systems concocted by those who went through the philosophical schools. Thus Basilides compared the ψυχή to a bird and the πνεῦμα to its wings. The bird cannot soar without wings, but wings without the bird are useless, Hipp. Ref., VII, 22, 11. Between πνεῦμα and ψυχή there is thus a reciprocal εὐεργετεῖν, cf. 22, 10. Logically, then, Basilides assigns the πνεῦμα a place between κόσμος and ὑπερκόσμια, cf. VII, 23, 2. 247 In popular Gnosticism, e.g., the magic pap. or the allegorical interpretation of myths and cults, we are not to expect an exact interrelating or use of terms, cf. the Naassene interpretation of the Attis myth in Hipp. Ref., V, 7, 11-15.

Dihle

4. The Coptic texts of Cod. 13 of Nag-Hammadi contain a wealth of new material on the trichotomy πνεῦμα-ψυχή-σῶμα/σάρξ, "spirit-soul-body (flesh)" 248 and on the Gnostic understanding of ψυχή.

a. Trichotomy. The trichotomous principle of Gnosticism is found in the Nag-Hammadi texts and is more or less broadly developed, as in Ep. Iacobi Apocr., 249 11, 35 - 12, 13; the Apocr. of Joh. (→ n. 244) Cod., II, 1, p. 25, 17 - 27, 30; the work Hypostasis of the Archons, 250 144, 17-27; the tractate Authenticos Logos 251 Cod., VI, 3 and the work Noēma (→ n. 251) Cod., VI, 4, p. 37, 23 ff. In a consistent application of the trichotomous principle not just mythology and anthropology but the Gnostic system, and esp.

---

245 For similar ideas cf. Corp. Herm., 16, 15 f.
246 Cf. Basilides' doctrine περὶ προσφυοῦς ψυχῆς acc. to Cl. Al. Strom., II, 20, 133, 3 f.
247 If in Corp. Herm., 16, 6 God is distinguished from the πνεῦμα this does not imply any disparagement of the πνεῦμα compared to its position in the structure of being in other systems.
248 On the relations cf. K. W. Tröger, "Mysterienglaube u. Gnosis in Corp. Herm., XIII," TU, 110 (1971), 94 f.; → VI, 392, 13 ff., esp. 395, 8 ff.; VII, 1085, 8 ff.
249 Ed. M. Malinine et al. (1968).
250 Ed. R. A. Bullard, Patristische Texte u. Stud., 10 (1970). The numbering corresponds to P. Labib, Coptic Gnostic Pap. in the Coptic Museum at Old Cairo, I (1956).
251 Ed. M. Krause-P. Labib, "Gnost. u. hermet. Schr. aus Cod II u. Cod VI," Abh. d. deutschen Archäol. Instituts Kairo, Kpt. Reihe, 2 (1971); cf. The Facsimile Ed. of the Nag Hammadi Cod, Cod VI (1972).

soteriology, are affected. The so-called work on the origin of the world (no title) [252] speaks of the first, second and third (pneumatic, psychical and earthly) Adam, 165, 28 - 166, 6, cf. 170, 6-9, and also of three baptisms, one of spirit, one of fire and one of water, 170, 13-16. Acc. to the Epistle to Rheginus De Resurrectione [253] there is a resurrection of spirit πνευματική which engulfs that of soul ψυχική and that of flesh σαρκική, 45, 39 - 46, 2.

b. Varied Use of ψυχή. The varied use of ψυχή, which is not uncommon in Gnosticism and calls for notice, occurs also in the Nag Hammadi texts. To discover the given meaning of the ambivalent term ψυχή the distinction between the cosmic soul and the supercosmic soul has proved helpful. The former is the ψυχή in the narrower sense as the dowry of the cosmic forces, esp. the stars, while the latter is the πνεῦμα, the inner pneumatic man. [254] The true soul, then, is not the ψυχή but the πνεῦμα, the supercosmic soul which comes into the field of force of the stars when it falls. The ψυχή is understood as the true and supercosmic soul in this sense in, e.g., the tractate Exegesis of the Soul Cod., II, 6 (→ n. 5). Opp. to it are the body, the flesh, and this life. After its fall this ψυχή, now understood as the one higher principle, stands in need of redemption, which is imparted to it by its bridegroom, the life-giving Spirit → 660, 24 ff. Mostly a cosmic soul stands in antithesis to the ψυχή which is identified with the πνεῦμα, cf. the terms pneumatic and hylic ψυχή, Authenticos Logos (→ n. 251) Cod., VI, 3, p. 23, 12 ff. Sometimes immortal and mortal souls are differentiated, e.g., in the Apoc. of Peter [255] Cod., VII, 3, p. 75, 12 - 76, 17, cf. 76, 34 — 77, 22. In most cases ψυχή, in acc. with the trichotomous principle, means the cosmic ψυχή. As such it comes between [256] πνεῦμα and σῶμα, and everything depends on which way it inclines. Acc. to the tractate The Doctrines of Silvanus (→ n. 254) Cod., VII, 4 man, i.e., the Gnostic, has three roots, the divine νοῦς, the soul, and the body, or matter, p. 92, 15-33. "God is the pneumatic one. Man has taken form from the substance of God. The divine soul has partial fellowship with him. The soul also has partial fellowship with the flesh. The bad soul turns hither and thither," i.e., vacillates, but in no case should it incline to the animal and carnal nature, p. 93, 25-32, cf. the total context p. 93, 9 - 94, 5. The middle position of the soul is very clearly taught in Ep. Iacobi Apocr. (→ n. 249): The flesh longs after the soul, without which it cannot sin. On the other hand the soul cannot be redeemed without the spirit, 11, 35 ff. "It is the spirit that makes the soul alive, but it is the body that kills it, i.e., it is itself that kills it," 12, 5-8. In most texts ψυχή and πνεῦμα (or νοῦς) and σῶμα/σάρξ are interrelated in this or a similar way. Very common is the negative evaluation of the cosmic soul. In this regard we may ref. to texts which certainly place the psychic above the hylic but regard it as far removed from the pneumatic. Thus the Hypostasis of the Archons (→ n. 250), 135, 17-20 says that the psychic cannot attain to the pneumatic. Here the man who is made by the archons is in the first instance totally χοϊκός, 135, 26 ff. → χοϊκός, E. But even the man who has become psychic is still unable to raise himself, 136, 3 ff. Only when the πνεῦμα sees the psychic man and stoops downs to him does man become a living soul and can he motivate himself, 136, 12-17. But when the archons bring the sleep of forgetfulness on Adam, take living woman out of his rib, and fill up his side with σάρξ, Adam again becomes totally psychic and the pneumatic woman must first awaken him and raise him up, 137, 3-13. To this corresponds the depiction of the creation of Adam in the work on the origin of the world (no title → n. 252), 162, 24 - 164, 5: In Adam, psychic

---

[252] Ed. A. Böhlig-P. Labib, "D. kpt.-gnost. Schrift ohne Titel aus Cod II v. Nag Hammadi," *Deutsche Akad. d. Wissensch. zu Berlin, Institut f. Orientforschung*, 58 (1962), The numbering rests on Labib (→ n. 4), although the adduced passages are not given there.

[253] Ed. M. Malinine *et al.* (1963).

[254] The distinction was proposed by H. Jonas, "Gnosis u. spätantiker Geist, I" FRL, 51³ (1964), 5.

[255] Not yet ed. Numbered acc. to the thus far accepted system of M. Krause, cf. D. M. Scholer, "Nag Hammadi Bibl. 1948-1969," *Nag Hammadi Studies*, 1 (1971), 109 f., 118-190; also "The Coptic Gnostic Library," *Nov. Test.*, 12 (1970), 83-5.

[256] On the middle place of the psychic cf. Cl. Al. Exc. Theod., 56, 3; Iren. Haer., I, 1, 11.

man, was no spirit. The chief archon let him lie 40 days "without soul." In the Apocr. of Joh. (→ n. 244) Cod., II, 1, p. 15, 9-11 the first archon copies psychically the first and perfect, i.e., pneumatic, upper man. He is then called Adam. Then the powers make 7 different kinds of soul, that of flesh etc., p. 15, 13 ff. 18, 34 f. speaks of the material hylic ψυχή. In order that man, who has a psychic and a material or hylic σῶμα, p. 19, 5 f., 12, may elevate himself, Ialdabaoth must blow πνεῦμα, the power of his mother, in his face, p. 19, 23-27, and this δύναμις comes thereby into the psychic σῶμα, lines 28-30. These are examples of a relatively close connection of ψυχή and σῶμα as compared with the qualitatively different πνεῦμα. The ψυχή is evaluated negatively in the Paraphrase of Sēem too (→ n. 254), where it is a "work of uncleanness" and a "profanation of light thought," Cod., VII, 1, p. 24 (20), 25-27.

c. The Destiny of the Soul. This is the gt. theme of Gnostic texts and it is developed in many different ways. The descent and reascent or fall and redemption of the soul are described in mythological, anthropological and soteriological categories which we can only sketch here. Acc. to Phil. Ev. [257] the soul fell among thieves who took it prisoner § 9 (101, 11 f.). "This is the situation of the soul. It is worthy, but it fell unto an unworthy body" § 22 (104, 24-26). What the σῶμα means for the ψυχή is depicted in Thomas Ev. (→ n. 95) Logion 112 (99, 10-12): "Jesus said: Woe to the flesh that clings to the soul; Woe to the soul that clings to the flesh," cf. Logion 87 (96, 4-7). The tractate Authenticos Logos (→ n. 251) Cod., VI, 3 constantly has new metaphors to depict the destiny of the soul that has fallen into the world and it ref. to its redemption. In the Apocr. of Joh. (→ n. 244) John and Jesus speak about the fate of different souls. This is decided by whether the life πνεῦμα or the ἀντίμιμον πνεῦμα has won control of the soul, Cod., II, 1, p. 25, 17 - 27, 31 par.; III, 1, p. 32, 23 - 36, 15; IV, 1, p. 39, 17 - 43, 6; Cod. Berolinensis, 8502, [258] p. 64, 14 - 71, 2. In the Exegesis of the soul Cod., II, 6 (→ n. 251) the soul after its fall into the body is oppressed by the archons and degraded as a harlot, p. 127, 25 ff. but on repentance is redeemed by the Father. He sends to it the μονογενής who unites with it in the bridal chamber, p. 132, 7 ff. From its bridegroom, the life-dispensing spirit, p. 134 1 f., the soul has good children and it brings them up. After this new birth the soul can ascend. "This is the (true) resurrection of the dead; this is redemption from imprisonment; this is the ascent to heaven; this is the way to the Father," p. 134, 11-15. In the second Logos of the great Seth (→ n. 254) Cod., VII, 2 the subject is again the origin, destiny and liberation of the soul, cf. p. 57, 27 - 58, 4: "The soul which comes from on high." In some texts the soul is judged, e.g., the Coptic-Gnostic Asclepios (→ n. 251) Cod., IV, 8, p. 72, 27-37; 76, 22 - 77, 28. The gt. demon is the judge of souls. In the First Apoc. of James (→ n. 222) three heavenly powers forcefully snatch away ascending souls, 33, 8-11; 34, 20-24. There is a purification of souls in the tractate Noēma (→ n. 251) Cod., VI, 4, p. 45, 28 f. There are pure souls and souls that are punished, p. 47, 9 ff. The Apoc. of Adam (→ n. 222), 84, 1-3, 12-14 speaks of souls that can die and those that are full of blood and filthy works. In the Apoc. of Paul (→ n. 222), 20, 8 - 21, 20, cf. 22, 9 f. the soul is scourged by angels, examined, condemned after testimony, and put back in the σῶμα. The Book of Thomas (→ n. 251) Cod., II, 7 ref. to the burning of souls, p. 140, 25-28 and the destruction of souls when men hope only in the flesh, p. 143, 10-15. Saved souls are in the ogdoad and sing "praise in silence," De Ogdoade et Enneade (→ n. 251) Cod., VI, 6, p. 58, 17-20; 59, 26 ff., cf. the saving of souls through the φωστήρ in the Apoc. of Adam (→ n. 222), 76, 15-27.

Tröger

---

[257] Ed. W. C. Till, *Patristische Texte u. Stud.,* 2 (1963).
[258] Ed. W. C. Till, "D. gnostische Schr. d. kpt. Pap. Berolinensis, 8502," TU, 60 (1955).

† ψυχικός.

1. The Greek World.

The word occurs first in the context of philosophical explication of the concept of the soul, Aristot. Hist. An., II, 3, p. 737a, 8 etc., and it is often used in philosophical and religious speech as the complement of σωματικός, ὑλικός, χοϊκός on the one side and νοερός and πνευματικός on the other, the latter also in the Gnostics → 659, 36 ff. Since a more or less distinct concept of the soul soon achieved common acceptance, nothing prevented the term entering ordinary speech as the adj. of soul. In contrast to ψυχεινός "cool," "refreshing", which occurs in early medical lit., a use of ψυχικός apart from the idea of the soul is uncertainly attested only once as a vl. in Vett. Val., I, 2 (p. 6, 27). Understandably, if oddly, ψυχικῶς means "from the heart," "very much," as a simple intensification with a verb of emotion, at 2 Macc. 4:37; 14:24, where we perhaps have a Semitism. In a similar context Gk. usually has ἐκ (ὅλης) ψυχῆς etc. → 617, 1 ff. No less singular, but possibly attesting only a less familiar idiom, is the quotation from the comedian Alexis Fr., 338 (CAF, II, 407, 4th cent. B.C.) in which ψυχικός has the sense "manly," "brave," for which εὔψυχος is normally used.

Dihle

2. Judaism.

Except in the vv. already quoted (→ line 11 f.) ψυχικός occurs in the LXX only at 4 Macc. 1:32 (→ VII, 1047, n. 286). Decisive for the NT, however, is the development discussed under χοϊκός (→ 473, 12 ff.), which in Judaism came to stress increasingly the contrast between the earthly, human, and non-spiritual and the heavenly, divine and spiritual. This may be seen in the antithesis of ψυχικός and χοϊκός in 1 C. 15:46-49, cf. ἐπίγειος and οὐράνιος or ἄνωθεν κατερχόμενος in Jm. 3:15. The alternation between ψυχικός and σαρκικός (→ VII, 144, 8 ff.) and the synon. use with a simple ἄνθρωπος is also to be understood in this light. So, too, is the sharp antithesis to πνευματικός in 1 C. 2:13 f.; 15:44, 46. [1] God's Spirit is contrasted with man as a purely psychical being, i.e., flesh → 471, n. 30. Finally Jm. 3:15 points clearly to Jewish wisdom as the locus of this usage. This suggests the development, [2] but the use is so technical and is so taken for granted that a more precise basis may be conjectured, namely, a speculation which related Gn. 1:27 to the pneumatic man and Gn. 2:7 to the merely psychical or fleshly man. [3] The influence of this may be seen in Philo (→ 477, 9 ff.) although it is probably closer to the theory that he rejected (→ 476, 27 ff.). That a basis of this type underlay the whole use in the NT is shown by its disavowal in 1 C. 15:46a in connection with Paul's very different exposition of Gn. 2:7. [4]

Philo moves closest to this in Leg. All., III 247. Here the soul is an earthly component of man. It is the "earth" cursed by God in Gn. 3:17. It rouses the man in man and

---

ψυχικός: [1] Cf. W. D. Stacey, *The Pauline View of Man* (1956), 146 ff., cf. also the equation of ψυχικός with πνεῦμα μὴ ἔχων in Jd. 19.

[2] It should be recalled that ψυχικός is more neutral than σαρκικός, which easily suggests the sinful, Joh. W. 1 K., 372.

[3] With R. Bultmann, "Gnosis," Review of J. Dupont, *Gnosis* (1949), JThSt, NS, 3 (1952), 16 one has to admit that Gn. 2:7 alone cannot be the source of this idea. But we can agree that νοῦς as the opp. of ψυχή replaced an original πνεῦμα in Corp. Herm. (*ibid.*, 15) only if we assume stronger Jewish influence on the original, since πνεῦμα (apart from → VI, 393, 9 ff.) is not found in Gk. formulations. The question arose on both Gk. and Jewish soil, but the strict juxtaposition of God's πνεῦμα and man is rooted in OT and Jewish thought or in speculation on Gn. 2:7, J. Dupont, *Gnosis*, Univ. Cath. Lovaniensis Diss. ad gradum magistri in Facultate Theol. consequendum conscriptae, II, 40² (1960) 172-180. The Eth. text at 4 Esr. 7:116 concludes from Gn. 2:7 not only that dust can produce only a dead body (4 Esr. 3:4 f.) cf. the Golem motif in Gnosticism, but also that "earth" led it to sin, cf. W. Harnisch, "Verhängnis u. Verheissung d. Gesch.," FRL, 97 (1969), 52.

[4] It is obvious that Paul is exegeti g Gn. 1 f., cf. v. 38 with Gn. 1:11, vv. 45-48 with Gn. 2:7, v. 49 with Gn.1:26 f. and 5:3. Cf. further B. Schneider, "The Corporate Meaning and Background of 1 Cor. 15:45b," *Catholic Bibl. Quart.*, 29 (1967), 149.

brings him lifelong grief. While his reason is neutral and may lean to good or evil, the irrational impulses of his soul seduce him like the serpent, 246, cf. 251. Earth and flesh are almost interchangeable, 143 f. → 474, 25 ff., so that for all the ambiguity a negative estimation of the soul may be inferred, or more likely stands behind Philo's statements.

3. The New Testament.

The term ψυχή is ambiguous. On the one side it can denote the true life which God has given, which He requires, which will last into eternity, or which is first found there (→ 655, 20 ff.). This makes possible a neutral estimation of that which belongs to the soul, or indeed its exaltation above the purely bodily, as we find this in the LXX (→ VII, 1047, n. 286) and sometimes in Gnosticism (→ 479, 8 ff.), but not in the use of the adjective in the NT. On the other hand ψυχή means the physical life which is proper to everybody (→ 637, 20 ff.; 654, 24 ff.), the decisive thing being added only by the Spirit of God. In this case God's Spirit stands in sharp antithesis to man, whose psychical nature is strictly of earth. The only question is whether this confrontation took place before time, so that God's Spirit is in some way imparted to the earthly nature of man and thus makes man a twofold being, or whether it is regarded as eschatological, in which case the psychical describes man as earthly and the pneumatic is understand only as a miracle which anticipates the coming consummation → VI, 420, 3 ff.; 422, 17 ff. On the latter view the pneumatic does not belong to man as such. It cannot, then, be read into the two expressions image and likeness in Gn. 1:26 or earth and breath in Gn. 2:7, nor into a combination of the two passages. It must be set in antithesis to the one who became ψυχή in Gn. 2:7.

a. 1 C. 15:44-49. This is Paul's view in v. 45 → VI, 437, 3 ff. In the background is the spherical thinking of Wisdom and Philo, as may be seen from Jn. 3:31 [5] → VII, 138, 25 ff. The psychical is neither sinful as such nor does it incline to the πνεῦμα → VI, 436, 8 ff. [6] But it is corruptible and finds no access into God's kingdom, v. 50 → VII, 128, 26 ff.; 129, 24 ff. [7] Paul opposes to it the risen Christ as πνεῦμα ζωοποιοῦν, just as Gn. r., 14, 8 on 2:7b opposes the Spirit of God in resurrection (Ez. 37:14) to the mortal soul of Gn. 2:7 (→ 475; n. 30). The fact that the fall is in view here [8] links Paul to the Wisdom tradition, which stresses the earthly and corruptible side of man, and it also distinguishes him from pure apocalyptic → 472, 17 ff. [9] Of a piece with this is the idea of humanity as belonging to Adam or to a new Adam → 476, 27 ff.; VI, 865, 6 ff.; VIII, 471, 13 ff. What separates Paul from his opponents, however, is the eschatological caveat that the heavenly pneumatic being is still future [10] and is not a seed hidden in the husk of the psychical (→ VI, 420, 17 ff.). [11] What is to come is given only as the promise of God

---

[5] Bultmann Theol.[6], 177 f., cf. esp. ἐκ γῆς, 1 C. 15:47.

[6] As against F. Barth, "La notion paulinienne de ψυχή," RevThPh, 44 (1911), 335, cf. 346.

[7] On the radicalising in Judaism cf. → 474, 16 ff. and E. Schweizer, "R. 1:3 f. u. d. Gegensatz v. Fleisch u. Geist," Neotest. (1963), 184.

[8] Bultmann Theol.[6], 177, cf. also H. Müller, "Der rabb. Qal-Wachomer-Schluss in paulin. Typologie," ZNW, 58 (1967), 90: Resurrection is more than restoration of the original state.

[9] Cf. A. Feuillet, "La demeure céleste et la destinée des chrétiens," Recherches de Science Relig., 44 (1956), 372 f., 376; also Barth, op. cit. (→ n. 6)), 327-331.

[10] At v. 49 we should read φορέσομεν with MS B et al.

[11] So H. Clavier, "Brèves remarques sur la notion de σῶμα πνευματικόν," Festschr. C. H. Dodd (1956), 352 f. It is correct that Paul is fighting against the idea of a mere shade as well as an apoc. parousia materialism, ibid., 361, but cf. R. Morisette, "L'antithèse entre le 'psychique' et le 'pneumatique' en 1 C. 15:44-46," Rev. d. Sciences Rel., 46 (1972), 97-143.

to faith, and continuity between the psychical and the pneumatic lies wholly outside us in the faithfulness of God, in the πνεῦμα ζωοποιοῦν which is the risen Christ. The soberness of Paul as compared with the excesses of the Corinthians is not content, however, merely to emphasise the future nature of the pneumatic. Even in the consummation man will not be identical with Christ notwithstanding v. 48b. The parallel breaks down here. If man is ψυχὴ ζῶσα like Adam, he will never be πνεῦμα ζωοποιοῦν, Creator Spirit, like Christ. He will only be a σῶμα πνευματικόν. [12]

b.. 1 C. 2:14 (→ VI, 425, 2 ff.; 424, n. 605). Here again ψυχικός means neutrally the natural man who lives without the eschatological gift of the πνεῦμα and who thus belongs to the world (v. 12) and not to God (v. 10). A striking point is that the unbeliever is ψυχικός but the believer who is making no progress is σαρκικός (→ VII, 144, 8 ff.), 3:3. This shows that on the one side ψυχικός does not stand for a higher stage than σαρκικός, and is not blameworthy as such, while on the other side σαρκικός denotes the one who is orientated to the σάρξ, and it does entail censure and admonition. Epigrammatically one might say that the ψυχικός becomes a σαρκικός when he confesses that he is a believer but is still exclusively set on what is earthly. [13]

c. Jm. 3:15. Here once more the problem of knowing God and His mysteries is under discussion. ψυχικός describes that which is earthly and which is thus closed to the world of God. Here, however, this restriction is demonic → II, 17, 30 ff. [14] The earth or lower sphere is governed by wicked demons and hence gives rise to strife, unrest, and conflict → 661, 36 ff.

d. Jd. 19. Even more plainly Jd. equates the ψυχικός who lives apart from God's πνεῦμα with the ungodly man who lives according to his own desires. Certainly what is earthly is not evil as such. But the impulses already observed (→ 477, 16 ff.) are stronger now than in Paul. Thus it presupposed that without the aid of God's Spirit man will be the victim of his own lusts and of ungodliness.

4. Gnosticism → 478, 15 ff.; 656, 16 ff.

Schweizer

† ἀναψύχω.

1. The basic sense is "to cool and refresh by a breath," Hom. Od., 4, 568 etc., or "to dry out," Hdt., VII, 59, 3 etc. Both nuances persist, as, e.g., in medicine, where ἀναψύχω denotes treatment of a wound by fresh air, Hippocr. De Fracturis, 25 (II, 81, 20, Kühlewein). Also ancient is the transf. use of the term for physical or spiritual refreshment, restoration, healing etc., e.g., Hom. Il., 13, 84: ἀνέψυχον φίλον ἦτορ. In this use there need not be any association with freshening or drying by air, since ἀναψύχω can also express cooling and refreshing by water, [1] Eur. Iph. Aul., 421. ἀναψύχω is found in

---

[12] K. Stalder, *Das Werk des Geistes in d. Heiligung bei Pls.* (1962), 59 f.

[13] This is in fact the view of Paul. That the impulses already noted → 661, 19 ff. help to influence him is undeniable. Thus the distinction is erased again by ἔτι (3:3) and esp. ἄνθρωποι (3:4 → VII, 144, 9 ff.). Nevertheless we do not find the nuance of the demonic and evil (→ 3c). ψυχικός certainly differentiates sharply the natural man who belongs to the earthly sphere from the man who is endowed with the Spirit of God and who understands heavenly wisdom, but it does not imply that this man is *eo ipso* bad.

[14] Does the Gk. identification of demons as souls (→ 475, n. 29) exert some influence here?

ἀ ν α ψ ύ χ ω . [1] ψυκτήρ is a vessel in which wine is cooled with water, Hesych., *s.v.* ψυκτήρ (IV, 314, Schmidt).

epic, poetic, Ionic and then Hell. usage, but Attic prefers the simple form ψύχω in the same sense. Of religious significance is the idea of the reviving of the soul in the underworld, Orph. Fr., 230 (Kern): ἀναψύχω κακότητος τὰς ἀνθρωπίνας ψυχάς. [2]

Whereas in older usage ἀναψύχω is always trans., and "to refresh oneself" or "to be cooled" must be expressed in the mid. pass., in the late class. period, both in literature and popular speech, we also find the act. "to refresh oneself," e.g., P. Oxy., X, 1296, 7 (3rd cent. A.D.).   *Dihle*

2. The unity of body and soul that is discernible in ψυχή may be seen here too. In the LXX "to refresh oneself" means primarily the regaining of physical strength: on the Sabbath, Ex. 23:12, after the battle which Samson fought with the jawbone of an ass, Ju. 15:19, on David's flight, 2 Βασ. 16:14, in severe sickness ψ 38:14, in the pause between conferences or battles, 2 Macc. 4:46; 13:11, though cf. also Saul's respite from affliction by an evil spirit, 1 Βασ. 16:23.

3. Whereas in the LXX the verb is always intransitive, in the one example in the NT [3] at 2 Tm. 1:16 it has the transitive sense "to refresh." One cannot say for certain whether the reference is to physical ministry in prison, i.e., attending to necessary wants, as the use of διακονέω prior to Paul's imprisonment might suggest (1:18), or whether we are to think more in terms of spiritual encouragement. This is typical; the two cannot really be separated.

                                                                              Schweizer

† ἀνάψυξις.

1. This word, like the synon. ἀναψυχή, which is attested from the time of Eur. and Plat., comes from ἀναψύχω "to cool by blowing," Hom. Od., 4, 568, "to dry," Hdt., VII, 59, 3; Strabo, 10, 2, 19, or gen. "to refresh," "to relieve," "to strengthen," Hom. Il., 13, 84; Eur. Hel., 1094. It occurs first in the early Hippocratic tractate De Fracturis, 25 (II, 83, 11 f., Kühlewein), where it denotes the drying out and healing of an open wound which the surgeon has left exposed to the air when bandaging a broken limb. Pos. has it in the sense of "cooling" in a climatological context, Fr., 78 (FGrHist, II, A 270). We also find it for "alleviation," "liberation," πόνων ἀνάψυξις, Jul. Ep. ad Themistium, 258c, relief from the plague of frogs, Ex. 8:11 LXX; Philo Abr., 152 uses it neutrally for "rest."

                                                                              Dihle

2. In the NT the term occurs only at Ac. 3:20. As the aorist of the verb and the choice of the noun καιρός in the note of time show, we are not to think of mere breaks in the end-time affliction [1] but are to construe the word along the lines of → I, 391, 35 ff. [2] The context makes sense only if the "times of refreshing" are the definitive age of salvation. The expression is undoubtedly apocalyptic in origin, [3] as is the accompanying phrase "from the face of the Lord." [4] The reference, then, is to the eschatological redemption which is promised to Israel if it repents. The

---

[2] Cf. on this A. Dieterich, *Nekyia*[2] (1913), 95-100 and A. M. Schneider, *Refrigerium,* Diss. Freiburg im Breisgau, 1926 (1928); A. Stuiber, "Refrigerium interim," *Theophaneia,* 11 (1957).

[3] Apart from R. 15:32 vl. intransitive.

ἀ ν ά ψ υ ξ ι ς .   [1] Bauernfeind Ag., *ad loc.*
[2] So Haench. Ag.[15], *ad loc.;* H. Conzelmann, *Die Apostelgesch., Hndbch. NT,* 7 (1963), *ad loc.;* G. Lohfink, "Christologie u. Geschichtsbild in Ag. 3:19-21," BZ, NF, 13 (1969), 230 f., n. 24.
[3] 4 Esr. 11:46: After liberation from the power of the eagle the whole world will breathe easily. *Refrigeret* (vl. *refrigeretur*) here corresponds to ἀναψύχει, cf. Ex. 23:12; ψ 38:14; 2 Macc. 4:46 LXX with Vg, Lohfink, *op. cit.,* 231 Ex. 8:11 (→ line 29 f.) is no help.
[4] Lohfink, *op. cit.,* 232 as against Haench. Ag.[15], *ad loc.*

Jewish idea that conversion will hasten the coming of the end can hardly be present, but simply the warning that this redemption will not come at all for Israel unless it repents now. Yet it is disputed whether we have in vv. 19-21 or (19b), 20, 21a ancient Elijah expectation which is attributed to Christ, primitive rapture christology, or purely Lucan theology. [5] Probably Luke does the composition but uses phrases which go back to Jewish traditions like that about Elijah. Since there is no mention of the conversion of all Israel as in R. 11:25 f., [6] nor of the restoration of all things [7] (→ I, 391, 29 ff.), what is said is simply that the times of refreshing and the redemption of all the promises will come only after a further space of time, so that there is still a chance for conversion. An essential point in Luke is that 3000, 5000 and indeed great numbers of Jews are converted, Ac. 2:41; 4:4; 5:14; 21:20. As a distinction is thus made between the authentic and the inauthentic Israel, [8] it is also plain that Gentiles who come to faith are adopted into Israel [9] and that in this sense the *parousia* brings the perfecting of Israel.

Schweizer

† δίψυχος.

This term does not occur prior to Jm. 1:8 (→ III, 947, 18 ff.); 4:8. Like the related word, found first in Christianity, διακρίνομαι (→ III, 947, 2 ff.) or διστάζω (→ III, 948, 31 ff.), it denotes the divided man as opposed to the "simple" man → I, 386, 1 ff. [1]

An original may be seen in בלב ולב "with divided heart," 1 QH 4:14, [2] cf. also materially Dt. 29:17; Ez. 14:3-5. Even before Jm. the Hbr. expressions must have been transl. by δίψυχος, as is shown by the quotations of unknown origin in 1 Cl., 23, 3 f.; 2 Cl., 11, 2 ff. and Herm. m., 11, 1 ff. [3] Herm. is very fond of the word and of the derived διψυχία.

Schweizer

† ὀλιγόψυχος.

1. This rare word is found in the *koine* in the sense "faint-hearted," Artemid. Oneirocr., III, 5. [1] But the related ὀλιγοψυχία can show that "short breath" may denote physical

---

[5] For a survey cf. Lohfink, *op. cit.*, 223-7.

[6] O. Bauernfeind, "Tradition u. Komposition in d. Apokatastasisspruch Ag. 3:20 f.," *Festschr. Michel, Arbeiten z. Gesch. d. Spätjudt. u. Urchr.*, 5 (1963), 15, 20-23.

[7] G. Stählin, *Die Apostelgesch., NT Deutsch,* 5³ (1968) on 3:21, but cf. A. Vögtle, *Das NT u. d. Zukunft des Kosmos* (1970), 166, n. 108a, cf. 172 and 187.

[8] Up to Ac. 28:24-28, though even here true Israelites prove to be members of the community of the real Israel.

[9] J. Jervell, "Das gespaltene Israel u. d. Heidenvölker," *Stud. Theol.*, 19 (1965), 68-96; E. Schweizer, *Jesus Christus im vielfältigen Zeugnis d. NT²* (1970), 149 f.

δίψυχος. [1] Cf. 1 QH 2:9; 1 QpHab 12:4; 1 Q 14 Fr. 6-7, 3 (DJD, I, 77); Fr. 8-10, 5 (78); J. Amstutz, "ΑΠΛΟΤΗΣ," *Theophaneia*, 19 (1968).

[2] On the alternation of heart and soul → 641, 17 ff.

[3] O. J. F. Seitz, "Antecedents and Signification of the Term ΔΙΨΥΧΟΣ," JBL, 66 (1947), 211-9; also "Afterthoughts on the Term 'Dipsychos,'" NTSt, 4 (1957-8), 327-334.

ὀλιγόψυχος. [1] In the form ὀλιόψυχος the word characterises a woman as "impatient," Preisigke Sammelbuch Beih. 2 B, No., 2, 50 (117 A.D.). In the pap. ὀλιγοψυχέω means "to lose heart," Witkowski, 16, 12 (3rd cent. B.C.); Pap. Reinach, II, 117, 10 (ed. P. Collart, *Bulletin de l'Institut Français d'Archéol. Orientale*, 39 [1940], end of the 3rd cent. A.D.), "to be despondent," Wilcken Ptol., I, 78, 10 (159 A.D.), "to be anxious," Wilcken Ptol., I, 63, 1 (158 B.C.); P. Oxy., X, 1294, 13 (2nd/3rd cent. A.D.); Preisigke Sammelb., V, 8002, 17 (2nd/3rd cent. A.D.) [Hammerich] .

weakness too, Hippocr. Epid., VII, 47 (V, 416, Littré). The word must be relatively old, for the secondary ὀλιγοψυχέω "to be cowardly," "to lose heart," occurs already in Isoc. Or., 19, 39 in a court speech, and the LXX (→ line 10 f.) and pap. (→ n. 1) show that it is an established part of ordinary Hell. usage.

2. The word is found in the Septuagint and Hexapla 6 times, and the related verb and noun 14 times. The Hbr. original seems to be קְצַר־רוּחַ, which is to be taken lit. as a sign that one has too few resources to meet the situation. The various nuances may then be defined more narrowly acc. to context. Thus ὀλιγοψυχία means "despondency," "crossness," "impatience" in Ex. 6:9 cf. Test. G. 4:7. ὀλιγοψυχέω (HT קָצַר נֶפֶשׁ) implies rejection of God in Nu. 21:4. Samson is driven to desperation in Ju. 16:16. The weakness of Jonah the prophet in Jon. 4:8 (HT עלף) is to be viewed similarly. For acc. to the saying of Yahweh that follows the condition of Jonah is one of soul rather than body. Within the set limits ὀλιγοψυχέω can also be used for other Hbr. words. Thus at Ju. 8:4, for עיף it means "exhaustion." At Hab. 2:13 for יעף it means "to break down" in the sense of the Lat. deficere. The sense "to be fainthearted," "anxious," can be considered only at Sir. 4:9. [2] Everywhere else the word means "to be despondent" in the religious sense, Sir. 7:10; Jdt. 7:19; 8:9.

At Prv. 14:29 the meaning of ὀλιγόψυχος seems to be "short-tempered" if μακρόθυμος and ὀλιγόψυχος are set in contrast as slow and quick to anger rather than as magnanimous and petty, cf. ὀξύθυμος in v. 17. Whereas Prv. 18:14 Mas. ref. to wounded spirit, the LXX contrasts the wrathful man whom a clever servant can pacify with one who is spiritually unrestrained because of his weakness of will. The transl. of Is. in all 4 instances of ὀλιγόψυχος uses it for "despondent" in a religious sense, Is. 25:5; 35:4; 54:6; 57:15. This consistent usage seems not to stick to the Hbr. too closely but rather to follow a tendency which may be seen sometimes at other pts. too, namely, that of taking the social categories of the HT psychologically. [3]

Bertram

3. Whereas ἄψυχος in 1 C. 14:7 differentiates lifeless musical instruments from living creatures that have voices, and is thus plainly connected with the purely physical aspects of ψυχή, ὀλιγόψυχος "of little faith" in 1 Th. 5:14, [4] σύμψυχος in Phil. 2:2, ἰσόψυχος in Phil. 2:20 and the verb εὐψυχῶ in Phil. 2:19 describe the sound or less sound spiritual state of man, i.e., his courage and strength. This state is always measured and evaluated, of course, in terms of the task that God has set. There is an echo here of those aspects of ψυχή that embrace the inward man and his experiences.

Schweizer

---

[2] In the HT we find קוץ "to feel loathing." But the transl. seems to have read קצר, cf. Sir. 7:10.

[3] Cf. J. Ziegler, "Untersuchungen z. LXX d. Buches Js.," *At.liche Abh.*, 12, 3 (1934), 82 f.

[4] ὀλιγόπιστος in Mt. and Lk. (→ VI, 205, 13 ff.), which is orig. Jewish like δειλόψυχος, is even more precise. δειλός in Mt. 8:26 does not mean "cowardice" in the profane sense but "poverty before God," synon. ὀλιγόπιστος, ὀλιγόψυχος [Bertram].

ψυχρός → II, 876, 22 ff.
ᾧ　　 → I, 1, 1 ff.
ᾠδή　 → I, 164, 14 ff.

† ὠδίν	λύπη → IV, 313, 1 ff.
† ὠδίνω	ὀδύνη → V, 115, 1 ff.
	πάσχω → V, 904, 4 ff.

ὠδίν, ὠδίνω has not been explained etym. The various attempts at derivation are mere conjectures. [1] For ὠδίς we find ὠδίν in the NT; this is attested too in Is. 37:3 [2] and later Hell. texts (acc. to Suidas). [3] The verb first occurs only in the pres.; later we find forms of the aor., as in LXX, where these were needed for the Hbr., cf. also Ps.-Oppian., I, 5; Jul. Or., 2, 56d.; also mid. ψ 113:7 vl. 'A and pass., ψ 89:2 'A; Prv. 8:25 'A. [4]

A. The Word Group in Secular Greek.

ὠδῖνες means "birth pangs," ὠδίνω "to suffer birth pangs." The word might orig. have denoted the cries of women at the onset of labour. The noun also means "what is born (with pain)," and transf. "(fruit of) travail." [5] We first find "travail" as a metaphor in Hom. Il., 11, 269 and 271 where the ref. is to the sudden and violent pain of wounds sustained in battle ὀδύναι (→ V, 115, 2 ff.), cf. 268 and 272. In Hom. Od., 9, 415 the verb is used directly for the cries of pain of Cyclops: στενάχων τε καὶ ὠδίνων ὀδύνηισιν. [6] The group occurs only three times in Hom. and elsewhere it is used only rarely for other pains or sorrows. [7] Here as elsewhere ὀδύνη and ὀδυνάω (Ionic ὀδυνέομαι) are both conceptually and materially close to the group [8] and can be synon, Plat. Resp., IX, 574a, or may be interchangeable as readings, Plat. Tim., 84e, 86c, or orthographically, Preis. Zaub., II, 16, 22. 58. 73. In Pind. Olymp., 6, 42 f. Eileithyia and the Moiras were present at the birth, the "sweet pangs," that produced Iamos, cf. Schol. Pind. Nem., 7, 1 (p. 117, 25 f.). [9] In Eur. Iph. Aul., 1234 f. ὠδίνω and ὠδῖνα λαμβάνω mean "to suffer maternal pains" when a child is born or is to die.

In Plat. the group takes on a technical sense within Socratic maieutics. The use is a transf. one for the coming forth of (native) knowledge from ignorance through the teacher. [10] Socrates is proud of being able to cause and cure such pains. Like his mother, the midwife Phainarete, he regards this art of midwifery as a divine gift, Plat. Theaet., 148e, 151a, 210b; ὠδῖνος ἀπολύω [11] "to remove the pains," Symp., 206e; ὠδίς "urge to give birth," Resp., VI, 490b. [12] For the pain and trouble that parents have to accept for their children ὠδίς and ἐπιμέλεια are used, Leg., IV, 717 c. The ref. is to spiri-

---

ὠδίν. Bibl.: Thes. Steph., Pape, Liddell-Scott, Frisk, s.v.; G. D. Read, Childbirth without Fear⁴ (1972); J. Scharbert, "Der Schmerz im AT," Bonner Bibl. Beiträge, 8 (1955).
[1] Walde-Pok., I, 666; Boisacq, 1079 f.; Frisk, II, 1143 f.
[2] Helbing, 49.
[3] Bl.-Debr. § 46, 4. Cf. Eustath. Thessal. Comm. in Il. on 11, 269; Etym. M., s.v. (p. 821, 5).
[4] Liddell-Scott, s.v. ὠδίνω; Helbing, 93.
[5] Frisk, s.v.
[6] Acc. to the hymn handed down in Hipp. Ref., V, 9, 9 vl. Attis is not to be worshipped with wailing οὐ ὠδίνων. But cf. F. J. Dölger, "Klingeln, Tanz u. Händeklatschen im Gottesdienst d. chr. Melitianer in Ägypten," Ant. Christ, IV (1934), 261 f.
[7] For the lines that follow we are indebted to Dihle.
[8] The Gks. often use ὠδίς and ὀδύνη together [Risch].
[9] Ed. A. B. Drachmann, III (1927).
[10] Dihle has supplied some of the details in → lines 29 ff.
[11] H. Usener, "Kallone," Kleine Schr., IV (1913), 81, n. 155.
[12] Cf. K. Vretska, Platon, Der Staat (1958).

tual sorrow in Ps.-Plat. Ep., II, 313a. A miscarriage of soul is threatened if it does
not turn to what is appropriate to it. Aristot. in a restricted use has the term only for
the natural process of birth. Pregnancy brings with it many infirmities πόνοι, Hist. An.,
VII, 9, p. 586b, 27-29. In Hist. An., VI, 2, p. 560b, 22 ὠδίς seems to mean "birth" itself
and in Fr., 66, p. 1487a, 3 it denotes the acute pain that it brings. συνωδίνω in Eur. Hel.,
727 is an isolated and in view of the rest of the usage tasteless metaphor for sympathy.
Aristot. Eth. Eud., VII, 6, p. 1240a, 36 has συνωδίνω for "fellow-suffering" in an ethical
sense alongside ἀλγοῦντι συναλγέω and φίλῳ συλλυπέομαι, though these are not
synon. Ref. is made to the relation of mothers to their children and to birds, among which
the male has a share in the hatching, which corresponds to labour in mammals, ὥσπερ...
συνωδίνοντες ὄρνιθες, loc. cit., cf. the συναγανάκτησις of the cock pigeon, Hist. An.,
IX, 7, p. 612b, 35. Plot. uses ὠδίς both cosmologically and psychologically in connection
with the emergence of the lower hypostases. There is no specific pt. in the metaphor; it is
simply an enrichment of the possibilities of linguistic expression face to face with phenomena that cannot be described with any precision. Thus the rise of creation and the
gradated emanation of the lower hypostases may be compared to a painful birth, Enn., IV,
7, 13, 6 f., to the degree that the higher stage already contains the constituents of the
lower and. esp. to the degree that the cleavage of the original unity means a loss of being;
the goal of the movement in being is ultimately the return of the lower hypostases to the
original unity. These pangs, then, have no true sexual ref.: γέννησις and γένεσις are
not differentiated clearly. [13] Souls come down willingly to earth and go where the world-
spirit calls them, Enn., IV, 3, 13, 31 f. In V, 5, 5, 26; VI, 7, 26, 6 f. the term "pangs" is
again introduced to explain the mysterious processes of life. For the rest ὠδίς does not
seem to be expressly included among painful experiences. It does not occur in Stob. Ecl.,
II, 91, 8. 9; 92, 7-17 in an enumeration of unpleasant emotions. The word denotes a physical
process, a shattering which can bring close to death or cause death, as in the pains of the
woman with child. Thus in mythology the Moiras or Parcae, the goddesses of fate, and
Ananke, are present with Eileithyia at birth. [14] They rule over the pangs, as Themist. Or.,
32 (356b) puts it. [15] In keeping is the fact that fairly often on Gk. monuments ὠδῖνες
are mentioned as the cause of death, cf. many places in the Hell. world from the 3rd cent.
B.C. Moira and Eileithyia and the pains led the dead woman to Hades, we read in
an inscr. from Smyrna, Epigr. Graec., 238, 1-2 (1st cent. B.C.), [16] cf. also one from
Alexandria, Gr., VI, 1353, 2 f. (3rd cent. B.C.). [17] In these inscr. the word is never used
for the emotion of grief or sorrow for the dead. [18]

Finally ὠδίς can be the result of the pangs, i.e., the "fruit" or "child," e.g., Pind.
Olymp., 6, 31; Aesch. Ag., 1418; Eur. Ion, 45. On the whole the group is not common.
Nor can the different meanings always be differentiated with precision.

B. The Word Group in the Hebrew and Greek Old Testament.

Many terms cover sorrow in the OT, esp. the roots כאב [19] and עצב. [20] But none of
these roots or derivates is rendered by ὠδίνω in the Gk. OT. In the decisive passage
Gn. 3:16, the divine punishment which is the ground and cause of the pains of childbirth,

---

[13] W. Rodemer, Die Lehre von d. Urzeugung bei d. Griech. u. Römern, Diss. Giessen
(1928) 5 f.
[14] A. Mayer, Moira in griech. Inschr., Diss. Giessen (1927), 20.
[15] Cf. Usener, op. cit. (→ n. 11), 85, n. 159.
[16] Cf. also the Jewish inscr. from Tell el Yehudieh (Leontopolis), Preisigke Sammelbuch,
III, 6647, 5 f. → VI, 871, 14 ff. On this inscr., which has the date 1.28.5 B.C., cf. H. Lietzmann, "Jüd.-Griech. Inschr. aus Tell el Yehudieh," ZNW, 22 (1923), 283.
[17] Cf. also Gr., VI, 548, 3; 1606, 2; 1681, 5; 1842, 2; 1871, 9; 1873, 3 etc.; inscr. 1462, 2
(3rd cent. B.C.) has ὀδύναι for "pangs."
[18] The index in W. Peek, "Griech. Grabgedichte," Schr. u. Quellen d. Alten Welt, 7
(1960) has a long list of expressions which in part even exceeds the Stoic list of unpleasant
emotions in Stob. → line 24 f.
[19] Scharbert, 41-7.
[20] Ibid., 27-32.

we find instead λύπη for עֶצֶב and עִצָּבוֹן, while הֵרוֹן, from הרה "to be pregnant," is transl. στεναγμός. Thus the Gk. transl. speaks of subj. feelings of pain whereas the Hbr. words ref. more obj. to the burden of childbearing. In Ex. 1:16, where one might expect ὠδῖνες, [21] the Hbr. אָבְנָים "birth-stones" is paraphrased πρὸς τῷ τίκτειν. ὠδίνω and ὠδῖνες are used for Hbr. words that denote pregnancy as such with no special thought of the painful experiences involved. Thus חיל/חול and derivatives are the main original, some 20 times. חול means the rhythm of the dance, not the round dance, but that of rhythmic up and down. It can also mean "to tremble," "to quake." It can then denote bodily movements in dancing, in cold, starting at psychic phenomena, anxiety, fear and terror. [22] When we find the metaphor of childbirth, as in Hom. (→ A), at ψ 47:7; Jer. 6:24; 50(27):43, cf. Jer. 4:31, the *tertium comparationis* is not the loud crying but the quivering and trembling of the mother at the physical exertion, in the contraction, pressure and stress at the beginning of labour. [23] Usually in the OT the comparison is not related to the sorrows or wounds of an individual but to public distress, anxiety and affliction in times of war or national struggles, or anxiety and fear at God's wrath and judgment, cf. also Na. 2:11. In Ps. 51(50):5 חִיל polal, like ὠδινήθων in Σ, means "to be born (in pain)," but συνελήμφθην in the LXX means "to be conceived." Thus it seems that the various stages from conception to birth can be expressed by the verb. Creation is compared to birth in ψ 89:2, where חיל is transl. ὠδίνω in ᾽ΑΣ, cf. Prv. 25:23 ᾽Α. In Dt. 32:18 God is the subj. of the saying with חיל; ᾽Α has ὠδίνω, [24] cf. the pass. statement about the birth of wisdom in Prv. 8:25 ᾽Α, but LXX has γεννᾷ με with God as subj. in ψ 28:8, 9 God is again the subj. of ὠδίνω in ᾽Α, but LXX rightly has συσσείω at v. 8 for חיל. [25] Hence ὠδίνω must mean "to cause to tremble or quake," and there is no ref. to bearing or being born, as in Job 39:1. What is meant is the terrible revelation of God at which the peoples quake, Hab. 3:10. In Is., in so far as חיל is transl. by ὠδίνω, it is used trans. for national birth or rebirth. This is so in Dt. Is. 45:10, where Yahweh Himself, Israel's Maker, stands for the father who begets and the mother who gives birth in pain. In Is. 51:1f. Abraham and Sarah are called the rock and fountain from which Israel is formed, v. 1. The images are perhaps related to primitive ideas of mother earth. [26] At the same time Abraham is the earthly father and Sarah is the mother who bore Israel, v. 2. LXX ref. v. 1 to Yahweh and calls Sarah ὠδίνουσα. [27] In Is. 54:1-6 the image of Yahweh's marriage with Israel is in the background. Yahweh takes back the young wife, who has known no travail since the separation. In Is. 66:7 חֵבֶל is the πόνος τῶν ὠδίνων. Before the pain of labour came, Zion bore a son. In the miracle of national rebirth there is repeated what is reported of the Hebrew women in Ex. 1:16. The word about Sidon in Is. 23:4 contains in some sense the counterpart to Is. 54:1 and 66:7. On the other hand the so-called apocalypse in Is. 24-27, in the lament handed down in it in 26:17 f. acc. to the HT, uses the metaphor of pregnancy and travail to depict the time of distress and affliction which will precede salvation, while v. 19 acc. to the usual but doubtful interpretation proclaims the resurrection. [28]

[21] Cf. the corresponding passages in Jos. → C 3.
[22] חיל is transl. in different ways in the LXX, σαλεύομαι in ψ 95:9; 96:4; 113:7; Sir. 43:16, ταράσσομαι, Est. 4:4 ψ 54:5; Ez. 30:16, φοβέομαι in 1 Ch. 16:30; ψ 76:17, εὐλαβέομαι in Jer. 5:22; At ψ 95:9; 113:7; 54:5 ᾽Α has ὠδίνω, so too Σ at ψ 95:9.
[23] Scharbert, 25.
[24] In Hebr. as in Gk. one would expect a fem. subj., esp. as חיל is par. to ילד.
[25] Acc. to F. Wutz, *Die Psalmen* (1925), ad loc. the LXX read אֵלוֹת "oaks." That the oaks should sway in God's revelation in the storm fits the context better than that the hinds should calve (in anxiety), as the Mas. is usually understood. Cf. H. J. Kraus, *Psalmen, Bibl. Komm. AT,* 15⁴ (1972), ad loc.
[26] G. Fohrer, *Das Buch Js.* III, *Zürcher Bibelkomm.* (1964), ad loc.
[27] Similar ideas seem to be presupposed in Nu. 11:12.
[28] LXX and Vg, then modern exegetes, cf. H. Guthe in Kautzsch, ad loc.; B. Duhm, *Das Buch Js., Handkomm. AT,* III, 1⁴ (1922), ad loc., but not G. Fohrer, *Das Buch Js.* II, *Zürcher Bibelkomm.* (1962), ad loc.

The image of birth out of death — the land bears the shades (to new life) — forms the conclusion.

In the root חבל one may see four different senses [29] whose linguistic relations are contested. The verb in the pi means "to be pregnant," "to lie in labour," lit. "to roll," "to twist in cramps or pains"; it occurs only 3 times in Cant. 8:5 (twice) and Ps. 7:14 (fig.) and is always rendered ὠδίνω. The Ps. seems to be ref. to conception, Cant. to birth. The noun חֵבֶל/חֶבֶל is 12 times transl. ὠδίς, while this is used for חֵבֶל and חִיל (vl. ὀδύνας) together at Jer. 22:23. It denotes the result of labour, i.e., young, at Is. 66:7; Job 39:3, cf. 2:9 LXX. The metaphor of bearing is common, Hos. 13:13, or of the one who gives birth, Is. 13:8; 26:17 → 669, 10 ff.; Jer. 13:21; 22:23; 49:24 'A; cf. also Jer. 48(31):41 'AΘ; 49:22 (29:23) [30] for צרר or ערה; Is. 21:3 for ציר. In Job 21:17 חֲבָלִים must mean "destruction"; [31] if LXX introduces ὠδῖνες, which is characterised by ἀπὸ ὀργῆς, it is paving the way for the eschatological use of the term. We also find changes at Ps. 18(17):4, 5; 116(114):3; 2 Sam. 22:6; in context the Mas. חֶבְלֵי־מָוֶת or חֶבְלֵי שְׁאוֹל (from חֶבֶל "cord") have to be (with מוֹקְשֵׁי מָוֶת) "snares of Hades or death." But the st.c. of חֶבֶל can be the same, and mythical concepts of the "prison" מֵצַר, lit. "affliction," of Hades [32] or of Hades as a womb have some influence. The usage in Hos. 13:13 f. is similar to that in the Ps.: חֶבְלֵי יוֹלֵדָה מִשְׁבַּר בָּנִים from מַשְׁבֵּר ("breaking forth," "orifice of the uterus"), v. 13, שְׁאוֹל, מָוֶת v. 14. Cf. also 2 Sam. 22:5, 6 מִשְׁבְּרֵי־מָוֶת (from מִשְׁבָּר), v. 5, חֶבְלֵי שְׁאוֹל v. 6, cf. also ὠδίνων 2 K. 19:3; ὠδῖν τῇ τικτούσῃ, Is. 37:3. This helps us to understand the metaphor of the ὠδῖνες which is introduced in the LXX. To this metaphor belong also the verbs περιέχω, κυκλόω, which describe how the womb of death or Hades gives up those who are kept in it, but → IV, 337, 1 ff. The pangs of death and Hades are the presupposition of birth from death and its kingdom. The judgments passed on the people are the birthpangs of a new era. Ephraim has not known his hour, the hour of his new birth Hos. 13:13. [33] The people is like an unborn child that has died in its mother's womb. [34]

Whether we have mortal pains (gen. qual., not obj. or subj.) or labour in the technical sense has always been a problem for exegetes and translators. The image of travail, which is so often used for annihilating disasters and divine judgments, Jer. 30:5 f.; 48:41; 49:22, pts. beyond itself. As maternal joy necessarily presupposes maternal pain, so the sharp experience of Yahweh's judgments stands in contrast to the hopes and expectations of new salvation, Is. 66:7 ff.; Jer. 30:7 f.; Mi. 4:9 f. [35] Yahweh Himself takes his children out of the natural womb, Ps. 22:9; 71:6 and also out of the womb of suffering and the kingdom of death; He will not finally destroy, Jer. 17:7; Jon. 4:11; Ps. 130:8. [36]

C. The Word Group in Judaism.

1. The Qumran Community, Ethiopian Enoch and 4 Esdras.

The significance of the metaphor of travail for the Qumran community is hard to estimate. The sorrows of the poet, perhaps the teacher of righteousness, are compared to

---

[29] Köhler-Baumg., s.v.; Scharbert, 18-20.

[30] Ed. J. Ziegler, Septuaginta Gotting., 15 (1957); 30, 16 (Rahlfs).

[31] Cf. G. Hölscher, Das Buch Hiob, Hndbch. AT, 17² (1952), ad loc.; Scharbert, 19 with n. 12.

[32] Cf. H. Schmidt, D. Psalmen, Hndbch. AT, 15 (1934), ad loc.; Kraus, op. cit. (→ n. 25), ad loc. The conjecture מצורי for מצורי, v. Köhler-Baumg., s.v. מצור, also presupposes a mythical understanding.

[33] Cf. H. W. Wolff, Dodekaproph., I, Hos., Bibl. Komm. AT, 14, 1² (1965), ad loc.

[34] Cf. T. H. Robinson, Die zwölf kleinen Proph., Hndbch. AT, 14² (1954), ad loc.; A. Weiser, D. Büch d. zwölf kleinen Proph., AT Deutsch, 24, 1³ (1959), ad loc.

[35] Scharbert, 99, 129, 214 f.

[36] Ibid., 222.

those of a woman in childbirth in 1 QH 5:30-32. The comparison is worked out more broadly in 3:7-12, but whom the woman represents, the poet or teacher of righteousness, the community, or the mother of the Messiah, and who the child or children are, the Messiah, or members of the community of the end-time, or the spiritual children of the teacher or the righteous, is not at all certain. There are in the passage many echoes of the OT with fig. ref. to birthpangs → 669, 13 ff. The familiar terms are also used, esp. חבלים and משברים along with צירים, but the meaning of the two former words is obscure. [37] The only sure pt. is that the afflictions of the end-time are in view. The community lives under pressures which it regards as a prelude to the Messianic age. There are many testimonies to similar ideas in the Judaism of the time. Acc. to Eth. En. 62:4 the experience of birthpangs in face of final judgment will overtake the mighty of this world. In 4 Esr. 4:42 the comparison with a woman in childbirth serves to represent new birth in the resurrection. Sheol and the chambers of souls are like the womb which after a certain time can no longer hold the child.

2. Philo.

Philo does not have the group in a strict terminological sense. The verb and noun each occur 15 times in his works. [38] He adopts OT birth stories, Gn. 16:11 in Fug., 208, Gn. 19:33 in Poster. C., 176, and 1 S. 1:20, 28 in Deus. Imm., 5 f. The stories and characters are expounded allegorically in his usual fashion. What Philo wants to bring out in this way is the destiny of the soul. The soul receives the seed of divine wisdom, falls into labour ὠδίνει, and bears a sound mind which is worthy of the Father that begot it, Poster. C., 135; Deus Imm., 137, cf. Det. Pot. Ins., 127; Cher., 42. If the soul selfishly seeks to bear without God's blessing, the result will be miscarriages or the birth of what is bad, Migr. Abr., 33, cf. Leg. All., I, 76; Cher., 57. In Conf. Ling., 21 it is anger, in Poster. C., 74 passion, in Agric., 101 lusts that in labour bring forth that which is evil. The one soul bears Abel, who loves God, and Cain, who is self-seeking, Sacr. AC, 3. A cosmological statement is that wisdom receives God's seed and in travail which promises fulfilment gives birth to the son of God, i.e., this world, Ebr., 30, cf. Op. Mund., 43. 167.

3. Josephus.

Jos. uses ὠδῖνες only on an OT basis, so Ant., 1, 49, cf. Gn. 3:16, for the labour or pregnancy which for their part bring pain, cf. 1, 343 (ὀδύνη → n. 3). In 2, 206 and 218 Jos. stresses that the pangs of Hbr. women were easy so that the midwives could not get there in time, cf. Ex. 1:19.

4. The Rabbinic Tradition.

The Rabb. tradition follows the חֶבְלֵי־מָוֶת of Ps. 18:4. Interpretation of the v. is twofold. In context the ref. is to the snares of death → 670, 13 f. But under the influence of the mythical ideas of the travail of death or Hades, to which the LXX bears witness, most Rabb. adopt the metaphor of the womb of the earth and hence of labour

---

[37] Cf. S. Holm-Nielsen, Hodayot. Psalms from Qumran (1960), 52-64. He ref. (53) to the ambiguity of the terms used at 1 QH 3:12. For O. Betz, "Offenbarung u. Schriftforschung in d. Qumransekte," Wissenschaftl. Untersuchungen z. NT, 6 (1960), 64-7, 117, 164 it is the spiritual children of the community of salvation that see the light of day in the travail of the end-time. Acc. to A. S. van der Woude, Die messian. Vorstellungen d. Gemeinde v. Qumran (1957), 144-157 the persecutions to which the teacher and his community are exposed at the hands of the ungodly priest are viewed as the Messianic woes of the end-time, 155, 188 and 242.

[38] Acc. to Leisegang, s.v.

and its pangs. Speculations about the woes of the Messiah. [39] Tg. on Ps. 18:4; Tg. Pro on 2 S. 22:5, are based on these ideas. Acc. to R. Eliezer (c. 90 A.D.) the main pt. is preservation through the sorrows and afflictions of the last time, the woes of the Mes- siah. The term is used only in the sing.: חֶבְלוֹ שֶׁל מָשִׁיחַ, Aram.: חֶבְלֵיהּ דִּמְשִׁיחַ, "the woes of the Messiah," [40] Tanch. נח, 3 on Gn. 10:1. In Midr. Ps., 18, 10 on 18:4 the afflic- tions are viewed so generally that the ref. might be the snares of death as well as the pangs of death as in Tg. on Ps. 18:4. [41] These were not just the troubles or afflictions that struck the Messiah but the birthpangs of the Messianic age. Possibilities of preserva- tion were held out for men threatened by the coming end-time. Thus bKet., 111a has traditions about those who are spared the woes of the Messiah. M. Ex., 4, 4 (p. 169) on Ex. 16:25 sets out the conditions for this. Acc. to bSanh., 98b study of the Torah and works of love are required. Acc. to bShab., 118a the three prescribed Sabbath meals must be observed; these will protect against the woes of the Messiah and the punishments of the end-time. Tg. Ps. on 18:4 says: "Affliction encompassed me as when a woman sits on the birthstool and has no strength to bear, so that she is in danger of death." At issue, then, are the afflictions or woes that announce this age, namely, unrest, war, pestilence and famine. Both in Gk. and Hbr. the senses travail and woe merge into one another (Ez. 2:10). Thus the interjection Woe, as in Rev. 9:12 f., so in the Rabb. in the form בְּיָיה, is also used as a noun alongside the interjection וָאי, Gn. r., 93, 6 on 44:18. [42] In this way the sphere of ὠδίν is detached from the metaphor of birthpangs and becomes directly an apoc. term. [43]

D. The Word Group in the New Testament.

1 Th. 5:3 adopts the metaphor of travail and the singular is either used collectively or with reference to the first pang. The *tertium comparationis* is the suddenness of the onset. At issue is not a sign but the destruction which will come ineluctably [44] on those who think they are safe. The metaphor is not designed to point to the coming age of salvation or the return of Christ, nor does it refer to the sufferings or afflictions which believers must accept at the end. Rather destruction will come like a birthpang on those who live in self-deception and false security.

Seduction, wars, [45] famines and earthquakes (→ VII, 198, 38 ff.) are the woes with which the end-time is ushered in, or the beginning of sorrows which will be followed by others that are even more severe, Mk. 13:8. [46] The parenthetical statements: "The end is not yet" (v. 7), and: "These are the beginning of sorrows" (v. 8), might be regarded as observations designed to check over-hasty expectation of the end. Delay in the *parousia* meant that eschatological statements had to be restricted in this way. [47] Mt. 24:8 relates the expression "beginning of sorrows" to all the eschat- ological happenings that he depicts. The woes precede the new birth of the world,

---

[39] Str.-B., II, 618; on the signs and calculations of the days of the Messiah cf. *ibid.*, IV, 977-1015; on the phrase "woes of the Messiah," IV, 564, 1042, 1067.

[40] Str.-B., I, 950.

[41] *Ibid.*, II, 617 f.

[42] *Ibid.*, III, 810.

[43] Volz Esch., 105, 147, 162.

[44] Wbg. Th., *ad loc.*; Dob. Th., *ad loc.*

[45] H. Conzelmann, "Die Mitte d. Zeit," *Beitr. z. histor. Theol.*, 17⁵ (1964), 118.

[46] Kl. Mk., *ad loc.*, cf. also Wellh. Mk., *ad loc.*; H. Grotius, *Annotationes in NT* (1641) on Mt. 24:8: *dolor multo gravior in partu ipso sequitur.*

[47] E. Grässer, "Das Problem der Parusieverzögerung in d. synpt. Ev. u. in d. Ag," ZNW, Beih., 22² (1960), 103 f., 157 f.

cf. Mt. 19:28. [48] They are an indication of the imminence of the time of salvation and of the birth of the new people of God in the eschatological future. [49]

In R. 8:22 the eschatological woes are a cosmic event. πᾶσα ἡ κτίσις ... συνω-δίνει. [50] All creation waits together for the rebirth, the new birth of the world, which entails the coming into being of a new heaven and a new earth. [51]

In Gl. 4:27 Paul quotes the OT saying in Is. 54:1. [52] According to this the children of mother Zion come into the world without pain. The apostle applies this to the Christian community and its members. The woman who does not bear, who is un-fruitful, and has no labour pains, now has many children through the gracious miracle of God.

In Gl. 4:19 Paul appeals to the primal father or mother relationship which arises with the birthpangs of the establishment of the community. After it has been shatter-ed in the crisis, it must be reconstituted. To underline the painful efforts that he has been willing to make on the Galatians' behalf Paul says that he has gone through the pangs of labour for them.

In Rev. 12:2 the sign of a pregnant woman is seen in heaven. She cries out in the pangs of birth and under the torment of bearing. [53] In Ac. 2:24 the ref. is to the birth of the Messiah or rather to new birth through the resurrection (→ IV, 336, 30 ff.; VI, 877, n. 40). God Himself has relieved the pangs of birth out of death. [54] The abyss can no more hold the Redeemer than a pregnant woman can hold the child in her body. Under severe labour pains the womb of the underworld must release the Redeemer. [55] God Himself helps it to end the pains.

The christological orientation of the metaphor of birthpangs [56] to the resurrection of Jesus fits into the general NT picture of birthpangs as signs of the time which are interpreted both as the end and renewing of the world and also as admonition and warning for the community. [57] In this regard the onset is always sudden in spite

---

[48] Zn. Mt., 665; Bengel, ad loc.: ὠδῖνες, qui antecedunt regenerationem.

[49] Hck. Mk., ad loc.; Scharbert, 214 f.

[50] The Gk. version of G has the simple form ὀδυνεῖ. Aug. suggests dolet, the Lat. of G parturit. This may support an original ὠδίνει for συνωδίνει, Ltzm. R., ad loc. Cf. Theod. Mops. in Staab, 139 and Grotius, op. cit. (→ n. 46), ad loc.; omnes simul mundi partes suspirant et parturiunt hactenus; Mi. R.[13], ad loc.

[51] Gennadius in Staab, 381; J. Calvin, Comm. in ep. ad Romanos (1539), ad loc.; Zn. R., ad loc.; cf. G. Bertram, "'Αποκαραδοκία," ZNW, 49 (1958), 264-270.

[52] Zn. Gl., ad loc.; Schlier Gl., ad loc. ref. to the Rabb. tradition and esp. Tg. Pro. on Is. 54:1; Oe. Gl., ad loc.; Grotius, op. cit., ad loc.; Is. 54:1 is taken up in S. Bar. 10:13 f.: In the time of the affliction of Zion women should not pray to bear children and the unfruitful and childless can be glad.

[53] The severity of the pangs is emphasised by the par. βασανιζομένη τεκεῖν. The verb is not used anywhere else in the Gk. Bible in this sense. For the noun in the sense of birth-pangs Pr.-Bauer s.v. βασανίζω ref. to Anth. Pal., 9, 311; → I, 562, 19 ff.; 563, 10 f. and n. 13.

[54] In spite of Job 39:2 Moule (in a letter) takes (ὠδῖνας) λύειν in the sense of "loose" and ref. in support to Haenchen Ag., ad loc. and G. Stählin, Die Apostelgesch., NT Deutsch, 5[12] (1968), ad loc. Cf. also Bengel, ad loc.: in resurrectione facta est solutio non dolorum, sed vinculorum, quae dolorem attulerant, dum obiret. Acc. to Grotius, op. cit. however, God liberates Christ from severe and mortal pains.

[55] Cf. O. Sol. 24:3; H. Gressmann, "Die Sage v. d. Taufe Jesu u. d. vorderorient. Tauben-göttin," ARW, 20 (1920), 27-9; J. Kroll, "Gott u. Hölle," Stud. d. Bibl. Warburg, 20 (1932), 42, n. 1; D. Plooij, "Der Descensus ad inferos in Aphrahat u. d. O. Sal.," ZNW, 14 (1913), 229 f.

[56] G. Bertram, "Die Himmelfahrt Jesu vom Kreuz aus u. der Glaube an seine Auf-erstehung," Festschr. A. Deissmann (1927), 199, n. 1.

[57] Volz Esch., 147-152. Materials on Jewish apoc. may be found throughout the pseudepigr., cf. Volz Esch., 16-51. In part Jewish apoc. works were taken over and edited by Christians, cf. Umwelt des Urchr., ed. J. Leipoldt-W. Grundmann, I (1965), Index, s.v. "Apokalyptik."

of every reference to advance signs. Actual events like the destruction of Jerusalem might have helped to shape the tradition but there is no trace of them at least in the metaphor of travail.

E. The Word Group in the Post-Apostolic Fathers and the Apologists.

The influence of OT and NT employment of the group on the early Chr. tradition is negligible. It is limited to a few bibl. quotations which are handled in stereotyped fashion. In Pol., 1, 2 the idea of relieving the pangs of Hades (Ps. 18:4) as this is related to Christ in Ac. 2:24 is adopted in a type of confessional statement. 2 Cl., 2, 1 f. quotes Is. 54:1 and adapts it, as Gl. 4:27 does. [58] The saying: "Rejoice and cry, thou that art not in labour," is reinterpreted. [59] It is made into a warning against timorousness (in prayer) as in the case of women in labour. Just. Apol., 53, 5 uses Is. 54:1 as a prophecy of missionary success which the prophetic Spirit has given. Just. Dial., 85, 8 f. ref. the promise of Is. 66:6 f. to the birth of the community with its members. In this connection Is. 66:6 seems to be saying that the birth of Christ Himself took place without the effort of labour. Acc. to Just. Dial., 111, 2 the powers cherish the desire and hope of liberation from woes as this is also attested in the Rabb. They lie in sorrows which are to be relieved by Christ, who alone has the power to do this in the past, present, or future.

Bertram

---

[58] Kn. Cl., *ad loc.*
[59] Just. Dial., 13, 8 relates Is. 54:1 to Christ or the Chr. community. The exact point of the quotation is hard to fix since Just. uses the whole section Is. 52:10 - 54:6.

---

† ὥρα	καιρός → III, 455, 1 ff. χρόνος → IX, 581, 1 ff.

A. Non-Biblical Usage. [1]

1. The word [2] means first the "right, fixed, favourable time," cf. ἄωρος "untimely," πρὸ ὥρας "premature," Epict. Diss., IV, 8, 38 f., πρὸ ὥρας ... ἀποθανεῖν, II, 5, 25; cf. πρὸ καιροῦ, Mt. 8:29; ὥρα is "the time for something." It takes the gen.: time for sowing, Jos. Bell., 2, 200, γάμων ὥρα, "the right time to marry," Philo Op. Mund., 103. cf. Jos. Ant., 12, 187, the gen. of inf. as noun πρὶν ἐλθεῖν τὴν ὥραν τὴν τοῦ τρυγᾶν "to reap," Plat. Leg., VIII, 844e, or the inf. ἐμοὶ ... ἰέναι πάλαι ὥρα, Plat. Prot., 362a. It is also the "right time" in P. Greci e Latini, VI, 624, 12 f. (3rd cent. B.C.): ἕως τοῦ ὥραν γενέσθαι "until the correct time has come ..." As the vine will naturally bear grapes ἐν τῇ ὥρᾳ at the right time, so the just man does good, M. Ant., V, 6, 4, cf. IX, 10, 1; ἐν ὥρᾳ means "timely," Xenoph. Oec., 20, 16. Along the same lines ὥρα can then be the customary time for something: περὶ ἀρίστου ὥραν, Thuc., VII, 81, 1, μέχρι ἀρότου ὥρης, "up to the time of ploughing," Ditt. Syll.³, III, 1004, 3 f. (4th cent. B.C.), ὅταν ὥρα ἥκῃ "when the time has come," Xenoph. Mem., II, 1, 2, τῆς ὥρας ἐλθούσης, "since the time has come," Epict. Diss., I, 1, 32. We then have the more gen. sense of a fixed time: ταύτην τὴν ὥραν, "at this time," that of sunrise and sunset, Aristot. Hist. An., VIII, 19, p. 602b, 7-9 τῇδε τῇ ὥρᾳ "at the time fixed," Epict. Diss., I, 12, 28, κατ' αὐτὴν ἐκείνην τὴν ὥραν, "at this moment," also in this situation, Jos. Bell., 2, 531, cf. 3, 482; cf. τῇ ὥρᾳ ταύτῃ "forthwith," Aesop. Fabul., 163, II, 4,[3] αὐτῇ τῇ ὥρᾳ "immediately," P. Oxy., III, 528, 14 (2nd cent. A.D.), "at once," 1 'Εσδρ. 8:62,[4] here at the end of a sentence, ἐν τῇ ὥρᾳ, "instantly," BGU, IV, 1208, 41 (27/26 B.C.), ὥρᾳ τεταγμένῃ, "at the set time," Epict. Diss., III, 15, 3. In Artemid. Oneirocr. ὥρα still seems to be mostly the right or usual time, esp. for an event, II, 8 (p. 109, 7-13): Whether what is seen in a dream takes place κατὰ or παρὰ τὴν ὥραν, in acc. with the appointed time or not, is important in interpretation. In fact the time of the year is mostly in view.

2. A special use of ὥρα is for the "best time" in the year → lines 5 ff.[5] "the favourable time," esp. spring or spring and autumn as the time of growth and ripening.[6] or

---

ὥ ρ α. Bibl.: G. Bilfinger, *Die antiken Stundenangaben* (1888); H. Blauert, *Die Bdtg. d. Zeit in d. johann. Theol.,* Diss. Tübingen (1953), 107-111; K. Bornhäuser, *Tage u. Stunden im NT* (1937), rev. G. Delling, ThLBl, 58 (1937), 196-8; H. J. Cadbury, "Some Lucan Expressions of Time," JBL, 82 (1963), 276-8; F. K. Ginzel, *Handbuch d. mathemat. u. technischen Chronologie,* II (1911), 163-170, 304-308; J. Jeremias, "'Εν ἐκείνῃ τῇ ὥρᾳ, (ἐν) αὐτῇ τῇ ὥρᾳ," ZNW, 42 (1949), 214-7; W. Kubitschek, "Grundriss d. antiken Zeitrechnung," Hndbch. AW, I, 7 (1928), 178-187; J. H. H. Schmidt, *Synonymik d. griech. Sprache,* II (1878), 61-70; Str.-B., I, 577; II, 401 f.; III, 300.

[1] Cf. the art. on ὥρα in Liddell-Scott.

[2] From *ἰορα, cf. old eccles. Slavic jara "spring," Germ. "Jahr," Eng. "year," v. Boisacq, Hofmann, Frisk. Cf. L. Deroy, "Prob. de phonétique grecque. A propos de l'étym. de πρῶτος et de ὥρα," *L'Antiquité Classique,* 39 (1970), 381 f.

[3] Ed. A. Hausrath, Corpus Fabularum Aesopicarum, I, 1⁴ (1970).

[4] Ezr. 8:34b is recast in 2 'Εσδρ. 8:34.

[5] We find the Horae in Il., where they watch over the clouds (rain). In Hes. Theog., 901 they are the daughters of Zeus and Themis and bear the names Dike, Eunomia and Eirene, thus embodying righteous world government. In Op., 75 they are closely related to the Charites, cf. Hom. Hymn. Ap. 194. ὡραῖος means first "acc. to the time of the year," "belonging to the right time," then simply "right," "appropriate." In popular post-class. speech it can mean "beautiful," which may be derived from "appropriate to time and occasion" and also from "bloom of youth." In modern Gk. ὡραῖος then develops into "good," cf. καλός [Dihle].

[6] Cf. the Horai in myth, A. Rapp, Art. "Horai," Roscher, I, 2712-2741.

summer as the time of harvest. Xenoph. Hist. Graec., II, 1, 1. Then ὥρα is the time of the greatest bodily fitness in human life, "the bloom of youth," Isoc. Or., 10, 58, or gen. "the time of the year," Philo Op. Mund., 58 → n. 12. In Philo "time of year" is most common but "bloom of youth" also occurs, Vit. Mos., I, 297; Spec. Leg., I, 103 etc., cf. also Jos. Ant., 1, 200; 3, 275 etc. Then ὥρα can be a specific segment of time τήνδε τὴν ὥραν τοῦ ἔτους τε καὶ τῆς ἡμέρας, "at this time of the year and day," Plat. Phaedr., 229a. πάσῃ ὥρᾳ to ride "at any time" is possible because the emperor maintains peace, Epict. Diss., III, 13, 9. The ὧραι of the day and night in Xenoph. Mem., IV, 3, 4 are generally the "times" of the day and night. [7]

3. From 1. and 2. we get the meaning "short stretch of time," esp. "hour," ὥρας δευτέρας, Ditt. Syll.[3], II, 671, 9 (162/160 B.C.); [8] μιᾷ ὥρᾳ (par. ἄφνω) "in a brief hour," Epict. Diss., I, 15, 8. The passing of the "hour" as a mere part of the day becomes a fig. of man's transitoriness, II, 5, 13. ἐννόησον τὴν ἐσχάτην ὥραν, "the hour of death," warns M. Ant., VII, 29, 6. Live so that the τελευταία ὥρα "the last moment," finds you in possession of a good conscience, VI, 30, 15. Only occasionally in Philo does ὥρα mean a twelfth part of the day or night, Fug., 184. [9] The meaning "hour" is also rare in Artemid. We catch the secondary sense "the set hour" in Oneirocr., III, 66 (p. 233, 5 f.): "Men do all things in relation to the hours," which the clock shows. It is also better in a dream to count the hours before the sixth than after it, line 8 f.

B. The Use in the Septuagint.

For the transl. of the LXX, too, ὥρα obviously means primarily "the fixed time." Hence the noun is used most often (31 times including Sir.) for עֵת: καθ' ὥραν means "at the right time," Job 5:26, ἐν ὥρᾳ "to time" in Sir. 32(35):11. [10] With the gen. ὥρα denotes the time of the evening sacrifice, Da. 9:21, the early meal, 2 Βασ. 24:15. καθ' ὥραν αὐτοῦ means "in its season" (grain) par. ἐν καιρῷ αὐτοῦ, Hos. 2:11. With the inf. ὥρα is the usual time for an event, Gn. 29:7, cf. ὥρᾳ τοῦ φαγεῖν, Rt. 2:14. The set time is also denoted by other expressions: ταύτην τὴν ὥραν αὔριον, "in the morning about this time," namely, of the day, Ex. 9:18; Jos. 11:6; 3 Βασ. 19:2; 21:6, corresponding to ὡς ἡ ὥρα αὕτη αὔριον, 4 Βασ. 7:1, 18, or even more lit. ὡς ἡ ὥρα αὔριον, 10:6, cf. εἰς ὥρας "in a year," Gn. 18:10, 14, [11] even more lit. ὡς ἡ ὥρα ζῶσα, 4 Βασ. 4:16 f. ὥρα is also used with a gen. to characterise its content, the appointed time of want, Sir. 39:33, that which is marked by the activity of the ἐχθροί, Job 38:23. Sometimes in this connection an adj. is used καθ' ὥραν πρόϊμον καὶ ὄψιμον "the time of the former and the latter rain," [12] Dt. 11:14; Zech. 10:1. ὥρα is then "the time appointed by God," Δα. 11:40 → VIII, 65, 34 ff., [13] cf. εἰς ὥραν καιροῦ, 8:17. The plur. means times fixed

---

[7] Obviously "segments of time" are meant in Ps. Sol. 18:10, cf. Gn. 1:14 and on the other hand Jos. Ant., 1, 31.

[8] This division goes back to the Babyl. model where day and night together were split into 12 rather than 24 parts, so-called double hours, cf. Hdt., II, 109, 3. In the liter. texts available this sense is much less common than it probably was in everyday usage. In Lat. hōra, which was loaned from the Gk., is found for "hour" from Plautus [Risch]. J. Palm, "Eine Bemerkung über °Ωρα == Stunde," Eranos, 57 (1959), 72 f. gives other examples which show that indicating time by numbered hours was common in lit. too in the last two centuries B.C.

[9] Leisegang, Index, s.v., lists only Flacc., 27 in addition to this.

[10] Ed. J. Ziegler, Sapientia Iesu Filii Sirach, Vetus Test. Graecum auctoritate Societ. Litter. Gottingensis ed., 12, 2 (1965).

[11] Cf. Plat. Ep., VII, 346c. Cf. O. Loretz, "k't ḥyh — 'wie jetzt ums Jahr,' Gn. 18:10 Biblica, 43 (1962), 75-8.

[12] Unless the transl. related the adj. to ὑετόν, cf. Jer. 5:24; Hos. 6:3; Jl. 2:23. Cf. ὥρα χειμερινή 1 Ἐσδρ. 9:11.

[13] Cf. Jos. Ant., 10, 142: What is indicated by God as a fut. event (ἃ ... δεῖ γενέσθαι) takes place καθ' ὥραν.

by God, 11:6, perhaps also Job 24:1.[14] The use of עֵת here as an equivalent of ὥρα corresponds in large part to that in the Dead Sea Scrolls → 587, 33 ff. ὥρα for עֵת also means more gen. "short period of time," cf. πᾶσαν ὥραν "at any time," Ex. 18:22, 26; Lv. 16:2, cf. ἐν ὥρᾳ ταχινῇ, Sir. 11:22, κάκωσις ὥρας, "sufferings of a brief hour," v. 27, cf. ὥραν "for a period," Sir. 12:15. Along the same lines is the use, fully adduced here, for Aram. שַׁעֲתָא: αὐτῇ τῇ ὥρᾳ "at once," Da. 3:6 Θ; 3:15 Θ (LXX αὐθωρί), "straight-way," Da. 4:33 Θ, ἐν αὐτῇ ὥρᾳ ἐκείνῃ, "forthwith," Δα. 5:5, cf. Θ. ὥραν μίαν means "a certain time," in fact minutes Δα. 4:19, cf Θ. ὥρα also means "moment" as a transl. of Aram. עִדָּן Da. 3:5 Θ (LXX ὅταν) "at once." In this usage ὥρα often suggests a spe-cific time, as the context of Da. 3:5, 15 shows. Finally in the sense "set time" ὥρα occurs three times for מוֹעֵד. The Passover is to be kept καθ᾽ ὥραν αὐτοῦ, "in its season," Nu. 9:2. The sayings in Δα. 8:19; 11:35, where ὧραι are obviously "terms," ref. to the end-time. The use of ὥρα for נָאוָה in Is. 52:7 goes back to the meaning "bloom or strength of youth," cf. the rendering in R. 10:15. In Dt. 33:13 f., 16 ὥρα for מֶגֶד means "what is precious" (v. 15b κορυφή) with ref. to the gifts of nature.

Only in parts of the LXX with no HT do we find ὥρα in the sense of "hour": ἐν ὥρᾳ μιᾷ τῆς ἡμέρας, "short time," Δα. 4:17a (14a), and only at 3 Macc. 5:14 is a numbered hour in view.[15] εἰς ὥραν καὶ καιρόν relates to the established time of the Day of Judgment, Est. 10:3h. ἐν τῇ ὥρᾳ ταύτῃ in the prayer of Judith stresses immediacy: "at once," Jdt. 13:4. The Jews escaped the hour set by Ptolemy, the fate of destruction, 3 Macc. 5:13. Elsewhere in Macc. we find the expressions: pressed for time, i.e., the imminent dawn of the Sabbath, 2 Macc. 8:25, to die πρὸ ὥρας "prematurely," 4 Macc. 12:4, κατὰ τὴν ὥραν ταύτην, "now" declare thy mercy, 3 Macc. 2:19. For more on the LXX → 675, 21 ff.; 678, 19; n. 7, 17 f.

C. ὥρα in the New Testament.

1. The use of ὥρα in the NT corresponds very largely to that in non-biblical texts and the LXX. First it means "the time set for something," e.g., the feast ar-ranged in Lk. 14:17, the prescribed time for the offering of incense in 1:10, the "hour" of prayer in Ac. 3:1, with a numbered hour → C 7. Here the meanings "hour" and "set time," which were both widespread at the time of the NT, combine. For-mally we have in Rev. 9:15 the hour of a specific day etc. which is set for an apoc-alyptic event, while it may be seen from the genitive of content in 14:7 and the explanatory infinitive in 14:15 that ὥρα is in general "the divinely appointed time" for the actualisation of apocalyptic happenings. ἦλθεν ἡ ὥρα means "it takes place now." The ὥρα τοῦ πειρασμοῦ is the situation which is characterised by apocalyptic temptation, Rev. 3:10. Similarly "this hour" in Jn. 12:27[16] (the Gethsemane incident) marks the situation when there takes place the required confirmation of Jesus which God has appointed and whose uniqueness is underlined by this expression. The hour is defined by the content given to it. Hence ὥρα can itself stand for this content, Mk. 14:35.[17] The Christian present is characterised by the fact that the day dawns and this demands watchfulness, R. 13:11 f. It is high time to awake and to act with

---

[14] The ref. is to set times of judgment, v. G. Fohrer, Das Buch Hiob, Komm. AT, 16 (1963), ad loc.

[15] 4 Βασ. 20:9; Is. 38:8 ref. to the βαθμοί or ἀναβαθμοί of the pointer on the sundial.

[16] Cf. X. Léon-Dufour, "'Père, fais-moi passer sain et sauf à travers cette heure!' (Jn. 12:27)," Festschr. O. Cullmann (1972), 157-165.

[17] Formally similar is 3 Macc. 5:13 → line 20 f., v. also ἐὰν ... ἡ ὥρα αὐτὸν ἐπαναγ-κάσῃ — corrected to καταλάβῃ — "if the situation requires," P. Flor., II, 248, 4. 9-11 (257 A.D.).

vigilance. The requirement of the given situation is expressed by ὥρα and the infinitive.

2. Then the time for human suffering or action, which may in certain circumstances be strictly limited, is denoted by the expression ὥρα τινός. For a pregnant woman "her hour" is that of childbirth in which her motherhood is actualised, Jn. 16:21. [18] The sayings about the hour of Jesus in Jn. find, then, a secular parallel. As elsewhere ὥρα commonly denotes in such sayings "the time which is given or appointed for something," especially now "a time which God has set" for the action of Jesus. [19] The idea of obedience to the will of God for Jesus in the "hour" is implied by the expression "my time has come or not yet come." Jesus fulfils the requirement of the hour which God has fixed for Him when He goes to the cross (Jn. 13:1) and willingly performs the act of love which the footwashing as such depicts. The fact that Jesus knows that the time for going to the cross has been set with precision is expressed by the statement that "his hour had not yet come" (Jn. 7:30; 8:20). In 2:4, [20] however, the same phrase obviously relates in context to the act of Jesus face to face with the sudden lack of wine. [21] Here again there is included the thought of obedience to God's direction within the given situation. ὥρα with genitive of person can also denote negatively the hour of the action of the adversaries of Jesus, Lk. 22:53; [22] Jn. 16:4, cf. ὥρα ἐχθρῶν, Job 38:23.

3. Alongside the phrase "my time has come" (→ II, 673, 21 ff.) we find the absolute expression "the time has come" (→ II, 673, 21 ff.), i.e., the time appointed by God, Jn. 17:1, [23] cf. 12:23 and also Mk. 14:41 and par. [24] The linguistic form of this phrase is also found outside the Bible → 675, 8 f., [25] cf. the absolute ὅτε ἐγένετο ἡ ὥρα "when the hour (of the Passover) had come," Lk. 22:14. [26]

---

[18] Cf. ἐν τῇ ὥρᾳ τοῦ τεκεῖν αὐτήν, Gr. Bar. 3:5. In Nidda, 1, 1 the term "her hour" ref. to another female experience, Str.-B., II, 402. Of the texts adduced in Str.-B., II, 401 f. only those under γ relate to this passage, not those under α and β, which unite the concept of destiny with that of the hour, cf. I, 577; III, 300. The terms in Rabb. lit. for the hour set by God are שָׁעָה and esp. זְמָן, II, 402. Neither has been found thus far in the Qumran lit. זְמָן is transl. ὅρος in 2 Ἐσδρ. 12:6: a "set time," "term." Acc. to A. Feuillet, "L'heure de la femme (Jn. 16:21) et l'heure de la Mère de Jésus (Jn. 19:25-27)," Biblica, 47 (1966), 169-184, 361-380, 557-573, the hour of Mary is in view in Jn. 16:21 (171). Mary comes into the divine plan. Feuillet ref. to what Jesus says about His hour (174). The hour is also to be taken theologically in 19:27 (179). Mary is here the mother of the Christian world (184).
[19] For the sense "time of action" cf. S. Dt., 48 on Dt. 11:22 (p. 127, Kittel): "And how? If Shaphan had not risen in his hour (2 K. 22:8-10; 2 Ch. 34:15-18) and Ezra in his hour and R. Aqiba in his hour, would not the Torah have been forgotten in Israel?" cf. Schl. J., 67.
[20] J. Hanimann, "L'heure de Jésus et les noces de Cana," Revue Thomiste, 64 (1964), 569-583. J. Michl, "Bemerkungen zu Jn. 2:4," Biblica, 36 (1955), 492-509, ref. to the similar construction of the twofold question in Mt. 8:29 (505) and with patristic and modern exegesis reads v. 2b as a question: "Has my hour, i.e., the time of my Messianic work (507), not yet come?"
[21] In this act is revealed His present glory, R. Schnackenburg, Das Johannesev., I, Herders Theol. Komm. NT, 4 (1965), 335.
[22] Here ὥρα is par. to ἐξουσία and esp. ὑμῶν τὸ σκότος → VII, 433, 1 ff.; 440, 1 ff. with n. 146.
[23] A. George, "'L'heure' de Jean XVII," Rev. Bibl., 61 (1954), 392-7 contains some general considerations.
[24] Mt. 26:45 has ἤγγικεν. On ἦλθεν... cf. also Rev. 14:7, 15.
[25] For Rabb. examples of the coming of the hour cf. Schl. J. on 2:4; 4:21.
[26] On this expression cf. H. Schürmann, "Der Paschamahlbericht Lk. 22 (7-14), 15-18," NTAbh, 19, 5 (1953), 104-106.

4. In Jn. the phrase "the time will come" is used in intimation of future events 4:21, 23; 5:25, 28; 16:2, 25 (→ V, 856, 19 ff.), 32; in the same connection ἔρχεται ὥρα καὶ νῦν ἐστιν (→ IV, 1119, 8 ff.) in 4:23; 5:25 [27] or ἔρχεται ὥρα καὶ ἐλήλυθεν in 16:32 denotes something that is just at hand. In these statements the stress is on the event whose coming is impressively indicated by ἔρχεται ὥρα... instead of the simple future. The expression ἐσχάτη ὥρα "end-time" corresponds to קץ האחרון, 1 QpHab 7:7, 12; 1 QS 4:16 f. → 589, 5 ff.

5. In the NT ὥρα can then mean more generally the "fixed or measured time," as in the phrases ἐν τῇ ὥρᾳ ἐκείνῃ "in that moment," Mt. 8:13, ἀπὸ τῆς ὥρας ἐκείνης, "from that time on," [28] 9:22; 15:28; 17:18, αὐτῇ τῇ ὥρᾳ, "instantly," Ac. 16:18; 22:13. [29] Except at Ac. 22:13 these expressions always come at the end and give emphasis to the suddenness of healing (→ 675, 20; 677, 8), esp. when Mt. wants to lay special stress on this. The expressions thus have the same meaning as εὐθέως etc. in the Synoptic healings. "At the time" of trial the disciples will be given the right words by God, Mk. 13:11; Mt. 10:19, ἐν αὐτῇ τῇ ὥρᾳ, Lk. 12:12. In Rev. 11:13 [30] ἐν ἐκείνῃ τῇ ὥρᾳ seems to mean "at once." ἐν αὐτῇ τῇ ὥρᾳ emphasises the temporal sequence of events in Lk. 20:19 ("immediately"), cf. αὐτῇ τῇ ὥρᾳ in 24:33; 2:38, ἐν ἐκείνῃ τῇ ὥρᾳ, 7:21, ἐν αὐτῇ τῇ ὥρᾳ, 10:21, and ἐν ἐκείνῃ τῇ ὥρᾳ, Mt. 26:55. In Lk. 13:31 and Mt. 18:1 we find the expression [31] ἐν αὐτῇ τῇ ὥρᾳ or ἐν ἐκείνῃ τῇ ὥρᾳ as simply a connecting link, while in Ac. 16:33 ἐν ἐκείνῃ τῇ ὥρᾳ means "at once," even in the night. One might also ref. here to ἄχρι τῆς ἄρτι ὥρας, "up to the present moment," 1 C. 4:11, and πᾶσαν ὥραν, 1 C. 15:30, cf. on this → 676, 7 f.

6. That the coming of the *parousia* has always to be reckoned with is stressed in a statement based on the parable at Mt. 24:50; Lk. 12:46: The day and hour of the *parousia* are not known, Mt. 25:13. Even the Son does not know them, Mk. 13:32 and par. ὥρα here may mean a section of the day or night (→ 676, 8 f.) and does not have to denote a twelfth part. The Son of Man comes at an unexpected time, Mt. 24:44; Lk. 12:40, cf. 12:39. ὥρα is understood figuratively here as daytime or night-time, as the sequence ἡμέρᾳ-φυλακῇ-ὥρᾳ in Mt. 24:42-44 shows. The thought of a surprising coming (→ III, 755, 30 ff.) is obviously important in these passages. The master of the house returns unexpectedly, Mt. 24:48-50 and par., by night according to Lk. 12:35-38. The bridegroom approaches at an unknown time in the night, Mt. 25:10-13. The thief also comes unexpectedly by night, Mt. 24:43 f.; Rev. 3:3. [32] This does not mean that the *parousia* will actually take place during the night. The element of surprise is especially linked to a coming by night in the parable. The

---

[27] The ref. here is to the raising of Lazarus.

[28] Cf. Jeremias, 216. Linguistically cf. Jn. 19:27 and the simple ἀφ' ἧς "from then on" in Lk. 7:45.

[29] Cf. ἐν αὐτῇ τῇ ὥρᾳ "at that very time" in the addition in Mt. 8:13 א CΘλ.

[30] Jeremias, 216 transl. "suddenly"; cf. Δα. 5:5.

[31] Schl. Lk., on 13:31 says that ἐν αὐτῇ τῇ ὥρᾳ is a Palestinian formula, cf. M. Black, *An Aramaic Approach to the Gospels and Acts*³ (1967), 108-112. On the formally similar expressions with καιρός which are discussed here → III, 461, 39 ff.; Jeremias, 215, n. 4.

[32] For the relation of these parables and statements to the delay in the *parousia* cf. E. Grässer, "Das Problem der Parusieverzögerung in d. synpt. Ev. u. d. Ag.," ZNW Beih., 22² (1960), 77-95 etc. and on this O. Cullmann, "Parusieverzögerung u. Urchr.," ThLZ, 83 (1958), 1-12. On the present passage cf. also Jeremias Gl.⁷, 45-60; A. Strobel, "Untersuchungen z. eschatolog. Verzögerungsproblem," *Nov. Test. Suppl.*, 2 (1961), 203-254. W. G. Kümmel, "Verheissung u. Erfüllung," AbhThANT, 6³ (1956), 7-52 deals with the texts under the heading of "The Urgent Imminence of the End."

admonition to watch is also in the first instance figurative, Mk. 13:33-37; Mt. 24:42 f.; 25:13; Lk. 12:37; 21:36; Rev. 3:3.

7. In the NT ὥρα can also mean a twelfth part of the day, Jn. 11:9. [33] In the Synoptic Gospels, apart from the parable in Mt. 20:3, 5 f., 9, only the events of the passion are related to specific times, Mk. 15:25, 33 f. and par.; cf. Jn. 19:14. [34] This obviously gives emphasis to these events. [35] The same applies, if perhaps in a different way, [36] to the event which is given a time in Jn. 1:39. In Jn. 4:52 f. a reference to the time shows that the healing of the sick boy took place at the word of Jesus. Jn. 4:6 gives the time as midday, cf. Ac. 10:9. [37] It is morning in Ac. 2:15, while Ac. 23:23 tells us the hour of night when Paul left with his escort. The ninth hour of 10:3, 30 is that of afternoon prayer, cf. 3:1. [38] In the general ref. in Mk. 6:35; [39] 11:11 ὥρα means daytime, cf. Mt. 14:15.

Periods of several hours are mentioned in the NT only at Ac. 5:7; 19:34, [40] cf. 19:19 D. A time of about one hour is meant in Lk. 22:59. On the other hand μιᾷ ὥρᾳ means "in a short time," "instantly," in Rev. 18:10, 17, 19, [41] πρὸς ὥραν = "for a short time" in Jn. 5:35; 2 C. 7:8; Gl. 2:5, in contrast to αἰώνιον, Phlm. 15; πρὸς καιρὸν ὥρας = "for the period of a short hour," 1 Th. 2:17. In the language of apoc., in which the measure of time has a secret meaning, [42] μίαν ὥραν means "for a short time" in Rev. 17:12. In Mk. 14:37 and par. the ref. is to a brief period, not strictly an hour, though an hour is meant in Mt. 20:12.

---

[33] We thus have the common reckoning of the hours from the beginning of daylight, cf. ἡμέρα ... ἡ ἐκ τῶν δώδεκα ὡρῶν συνεστῶσα, Sext. Emp. Math., X, 185. Division was common from the middle of the 2nd cent. B.C., Schmidt, 66; Ginzel, 308; Bilfinger argues for an earlier date, 74 f. Since the length of day and night varies (→ II, 948, 13 ff.) the same applies to the hours. Acc. to Bilfinger, 157 and 159 the average length of an hour in Alexandria from the middle of June to the middle of July was 70 minutes and from the middle of December to the middle of January 50 minutes. The variation in Rome was between 75 and 44 minutes. On Jewish reckoning cf. Str.-B., II, 442, 543 f. On primitive measurement of time → VII, 670, 8 ff.

[34] The stress on the hour in connection with the day is perhaps connected here with the fact that in Jn. Jesus died at the time when the Passover lambs were being slain, cf. C. K. Barrett, The Gospel According to St. John (1955), ad loc.; Bultmann J., 514, n. 5; Str.-B. II, 836 f.

[35] Except at Mt. 20:9; Jn. 1:39; 4:52 only the 3rd, 6th and 9th hours and πρωΐ and ὀψέ are mentioned in the NT, Bilfinger, 59, i.e., the terms that express a division into four parts. This is esp. noteworthy in the account of the passion. Cf. the prodigies in the Jewish war which were seen in the 9th or 6th hour of the night, Jos. Bell., 6, 290 and 293. Elsewhere in Jos. Bell. we have gen. indications of the hour of night in this way, 6, 68. 79. 131. 147, the day, 5, 538; 6, 58, but usually there is greater precision in relation to the day, 2, 129; 6, 79. 147. 157. 244. 248. 423.

[36] Acc. to Bultmann J., 70 the tenth hour was the hour of fulfilment, ten being the no. of perfection; for examples, including Jewish → II, 36, 3 ff.

[37] Cf. the indication of the hour in Ac. 19:19 D [Moule].

[38] πρωΐ τε καὶ περὶ ἐνάτην ὥραν sacrifice is made on the altar in Jerusalem, Jos. Ant., 14, 65. On the Jewish hours of prayer cf. Str.-B., II, 696-702; on Ac. 10:9 ibid., 698 f.; on 2:15, 697 f.; on 2:15, 697 f.; on 3:1, 698.

[39] On Mk. 6:35 cf. ἄχρι πολλῆς ὥρας ... τέως ἡ νὺξ ἐπιλαβοῦσα ..., Dion. Hal. Ant. Rom., 2, 54, 4. ὥρα is to be supplied in ref. like πρωΐας δὲ γενομένης, Mt. 27:1, cf. Jn. 21:4, ὀψίας (δὲ) γενομένης, Mk. 1:32 etc.; Mt. 8:16 etc.; we find only ὀψία at Jn. 6:16; 20:19.

[40] ἐπὶ δύο ὥρας "two hours long," Test. B. 3:7, cf. Test. Jud. 3:4, v. C. Burchard, "Fussnoten z. nt.lichen Griech.," ZNW, 61 (1970), 157-171.

[41] Cf. ἐν ... μιᾷ ὥρα will I come and punish thee, Test. Job 7:12 (ed. S. P. Brock. Test. Iobi, Pseudepigr. VT Graece, 2 [1967]); ἐπὶ μιᾶς ὥρας, Jos. Bell., 3, 228; 5, 490, ὑπὸ μίαν ὥραν, 2, 457. 561.

[42] Here long periods can be counted as hours, Apc. Abr. 28, 29 (p. 37, 20-38, 6); Ass. Mos. 7:1; Hbr. Test. N. 3:4, v. S. Aalen, "Die Begriffe 'Licht' u. 'Finsternis' im AT, im Spätjudt. u. im Rabbinismus," Skrifter utgitt av Det Norske Videnskaps-Akademi i Oslo, II. Hist.-Filos. Klasse, 1 (1951), 156 f.

D. The Word in the Post-Apostolic Fathers.

Here ὥρα means 1. "a time set for something," περὶ δείπνου ὥραν, Mart. Pol., 7, 1. The ministry of the temple is to be fulfilled ὡρισμένοις καιροῖς καὶ ὥραις, 1 Cl., 40, 2, cf. καθ᾽ ὥραν, "at the right time," 1 Cl., 56, 15 quoting Job 5:26. The time of the Lord's coming is not known, Did., 16, 1 on the basis of Mt. 24:(42)44. 2. ὥρα then means an hour filled with content, Mart. Pol., 14, 2. 3. Polycarp asks for a period of time to pray, Mart. Pol., 7, 2. 4. ὥρα can be a twelfth part of the day in indication of specific hours, e.g., Herm. v., 3, 1, 2, which can be calculated, 3, 1, 4; cf. καθ᾽ ὥραν, "by the hour," 2 Cl., 12, 1. In the plur. ὥρα is a period of several hours ἐπὶ δύο ὥρας, Mart. Pol., 7, 3, while in the sing. it can be a "short time." Thus διὰ μιᾶς ὥρας stands in contrast to eternal life, Mart. Pol., 2, 3. From the sense of hour as a measure of time ὥρα can take on the general sense of a "period of time," Herm. s., 6, 4, 4.

Delling

† ὡσαννά

1. The cry הוֹשִׁיעָה נָּא, which is addressed to Yahweh in Ps. 118:25, expresses the prayer that God will grant help and success. Similar expressions, e.g., יְהוָה הוֹשִׁיעָה occur repeatedly in the Psalms, [1] although they do not have any specific liturgical connection, Ps. 12:1; 20:9; 28:9; 60:5; 108:6. [2] The cry of Ps. 118:25 is first given a settled liturgical place only in post-biblical Judaism, in which the Hallel-Psalms (113-118) are sung on the high days of the feasts of the Passover and Tabernacles. [3]

On the seven days of Tabernacles, after the Musaph offering, the priests (cf. bSukka, 43b) took willow branches in their arms, went in solemn procession around the altar of burnt offering, and cried repeatedly: אָנָּא ויו הוֹשִׁיעָה נָּא אָנָּא וְהוֹשִׁיעָה נָּא "Oh, Lord help us; oh, help us," Sukka, 4, 5. [4] This procession was repeated seven times on the seventh day of the feast and the monotonous cry of prayer was supposed to express the urgent request for rain. [5] The prayers which were uttered during the Tabernacles procession [6] were given the name הושענות in the synagogue and the seventh day of the feast was called יום הושענא, Lv. r., 37, 2 on 27:2. [7] Since the cry Hosanna was accompanied by the rustling of the festal branches, Sukka, 3, 8, the term הוֹשַׁענָא was sometimes used, bSukka, 37b. [8] The common use of הוֹשַׁענָא shows that it had become a liturgical formula. The prayer for help has also become an expression of praise. This sense must have been acquired already in pre-chr. Judaism, for when the temple was still standing, i.e., prior to 70 A.D., hosanna was shouted out repeatedly as a fixed formula in the procession round the altar of burnt offering. [9] As Tabernacles itself became a feast of praise instead of petition, [10] the hosanna shared this movement and the cry for help became a shout of jubilation. [11]

ὡσαννά. Bibl.: Pr.-Bauer, s.v.; E. Nestle, "Hosianna," ZAW, 28 (1908), 69; J. Barth, "Zu 'Hosianna,'" ibid., 148; F. Spitta, "Der Volksruf beim Einzug Jesu in Jerusalem," ZwTh, 52 (1910), 307-320; Dalman WJ, I, 180-2; H. Bornhäuser, Sukka, Die Mischna, II, 6 (1935), 106 f.; F. D. Coggan, "Note on the Word ὡσαννά," ExpT, 52 (1940/41), 76 f.; E. F. F. Bishop, "Hosanna. The Word of the Joyful Jerusalem Crowds," ibid., 53 (1941/2), 212-4; E. Werner, "'Hosanna' in the Gospels," JBL, 65 (1946), 97-122; J. S. Kennard, "'Hosanna' and the Purpose of Jesus," JBL, 67 (1948), 171-6; J. J. Petuchowski, "'Hoshi'ah na' in Ps. 118:25 — a Prayer for Rain," VT, 5 (1955), 266-271; E. Lohse, "Hosianna," Nov. Test., 6 (1963), 113-9; B. Sandvik, "Das Kommen des Herrn beim Abendmahl im NT," AbhThANT, 58 (1970), 37-51; C. Burger, "Jesus als Davidssohn," FRLANT, 98 (1970), 47-51.

[1] The cry for help occurs as an address to the king for grace in 2 S. 14:14; 2 K. 6:26.

[2] As against Petuchowski, who begins with later Rabb. ref. and then claims that already in Ps. 118:25 the cry Hoshiana is "intimately linked both with the processions and with the shaking of the lulabh... These findings would suggest that the words anna YHWH hoschi'ah... na were the prayer for rain, offered up at the Festival of Sukkoth." In criticism cf. also H. J. Kraus, Psalmen, Bibl. Komm. AT, 15³ (1966), ad loc.

[3] Cf. Str.-B., I, 845-9.

[4] Cf. Str.-B., I, 845; II, 793 f.

[5] Cf. J. Jeremias, "Golgotha," Angelos-Beih., 1 (1926), 60-64.

[6] The imp. הוֹשִׁיעָה was often shortened to הוֹשַׁע.

[7] Cf. I. Elbogen, Der jüd. Gottesdienst in seiner geschichtl. Entwicklung³ (1931), 138 f. On the later form of the synagogue liturgy and the songs sung at the procession, cf. 219 f.

[8] Cf. Str.-B., I, 850 with more examples.

[9] Cf. J. Jeremias, "Die Muttersprache d. Evangelisten Mt.," Abba. Stud. z. nt.lichen Theol. u. Zeitgeschichte (1966), 258 f.

[10] Cf. Str.-B., II, 805-7.

[11] Cf. Jeremias, op. cit. (→ n. 9), 259.

Ps. 118 was sometimes interpreted Messianically, e.g., Midr. Ps., 118, 22 on 118:24, [12] so that the Messianic hope was probably echoed in the hosanna which the Jewish community raised in the pre-christian period. [13]

2. In the NT ὡσαννά [14] occurs only in the story of the entry of Jesus into Jerusalem. According to Mk. 11:9 f. the crowd greeted Jesus with shouts of jubilation [15] that began and ended with hosanna. The introductory ὡσαννά [16] is followed as in Ps. 118:25 by εὐλογημένος ὁ ἐρχόμενος ἐν ὀνόματι κυρίου, and then the Messianic significance of this is brought out in the next verse: εὐλογημένη ἡ ἐρχομένη βασιλεία τοῦ πατρὸς ἡμῶν Δαυίδ. Hosanna then returns in ὡσαννά ἐν τοῖς ὑψίστοις with its summons to strike up songs of praise in the heavenly heights. By adopting the ὡσαννά [17] which was familiar to every Jew the Evangelist wants to emphasise that every Messianic expectation has now been realised. [18] Whereas Luke leaves out hosanna, which would not be intelligible to Hellenistic readers, and replaces it by the hymnal ἐν οὐρανῷ εἰρήνη καὶ δόξα ἐν ὑψίστοις (Lk. 19:38, cf. Lk. 2:14), Mt. shortens and changes the Marcan original. [19] The cry ὡσαννά τῷ υἱῷ Δαυίδ now precedes the quotation from Ps. 118:25, and then ὡσαννά ἐν τοῖς ὑψίστοις follows it, Mt. 21:9. In place of the phrase about the coming dominion of our father David [20] there is now reference to the Son of David, cf. Mt. 21:15. Praise and salvation are to be ascribed to Jesus, who as the υἱὸς Δαυίδ (→ VIII, 486,

---

[12] Cf. J. Jeremias, *Die Abendmahlsworte Jesu*[4] (1967), 247-9; cf. for further examples Str.-B., I, 849 f.; Werner, 114-122.

[13] In the Chr. era the synagogue had to attempt differentiation from the Chr. use of ὡσαννά and it thus suppressed the Messianic aspect, Werner, 112-122. The cry אנא יהוה הושיעה נא was invested with a veil of mystery and אנא יהוה was replaced by אני יהוא. Cf. the variants in Sukka, 4, 5; Bornhäuser, 115-9; Werner, 121.

[14] ὡσαννά renders the Hbr. הוֹשִׁיעָה נָּא, not an Aram. term. Linguistically cf. Dalman Gr., 249; Zahn Einl., I, 14. In Gk. the rough breathing corresponds to ה, hence ὡσαννά rather than ὡσαννά. Cf. E. Nestle, "Spiritus asper u. lenis in d. Umschreibung hbr. Wörter," *Philol.*, 68 (1909), 462. Acc. to Cramer Cat. on Mt. 11:8 ὡσαννά is perhaps to be explained in terms of the Gk.: ὡς (= εἰς) ἀνά· τὴν δοξολογίαν ἀναπέμπουσιν. Cf. F. J. Dölger, "Sol Salutis," *Liturgiewissensch. Quellen u. Forschungen*, 16/17[3] (1971), 200, 208 f. on Did., 10, 6; 301-320; W. Grundmann, Art. "Aufwärts-abwärts," RAC, I, 955 f.; J. Haussleiter, "Erhebung d. Herzens," RAC, VI, 1-22; G. Bertram, "Erhöhung," RAC, VI, 22-43 [Bertram].

[15] The cry ὡσαννά has a place in the witness of the confessing community; Jesus is the Messiah. But cf. Kennard, 175, who thinks the cry is to be understood in terms of the expectations cherished by Galilean pilgrims to the feast: he assumes they wanted to "indicate their hope that he (sc. Jesus) would perform a Messianic act like that of Judas Maccabeus in cleansing the sanctuary." Burger, 47 f. objects that the cry did not have a Messian. ring in pre-chr. Judaism and agrees with Loh. Mk., 231 that it was a festal cry in the form of a prayer to God that He would bless His people and protect his way.

[16] The first ὡσαννά does not occur in D W it, cf. F. C. Burkitt, "W and Θ: Stud. in the Western Text of St. Mark," JThSt, 17 (1916), 139-149.

[17] Since הוֹשִׁיעָה נָּא occured not only at Tabernacles but also in the Hallel Psalms at Passover, it is a mistake to think that the mention of branches in Mk. 11:8 and par. is in some way an allusion to the liturgy of Tabernacles.

[18] In contemporary Jewish lit. there is no ref. to the coming reign of our father David. On "our father David" cf. Str.-B., II, 26; Loh. Mk., ad loc. But cf. "the dominion of the house of David comes," jBer., 3, 1 (6a, 58); → VIII, 481, 19 f.

[19] On Mt. 21:9, 15 cf. the comm. and also K. Stendahl, "The School of St. Matthew," *Acta Seminarii Neotest. Upsaliensis*, 20 (1954), 64 f.

[20] Mt. obviously wants to avoid equating βασιλεία τῶν οὐρανῶν, which he understands eschatologically, with the royal dominion of David. Cf. G. Bornkamm, "Enderwartung u. Kirche im Mt.," in G. Bornkamm, G. Barth, H. J. Held, *Überlieferung u. Auslegung im. Mt.*, *Wissenschaftl. Monographien z. AT u. NT*, 1[6] (1970), 31.

15 ff.) has fulfilled the promise of Israel. [21] The cry ὡσαννά τῷ υἱῷ Δαυίδ is in Mt. taken up by the children who greet Jesus with jubilation in the temple, Mt. 21:15. When the chief priests and scribes protest, Jesus justifies the conduct of the children on the basis of ψ 8:3, showing thereby that children are a model and image of true discipleship. [22] In Jn. the cry of the crowd is the same as in Mk. 11:9: ὡσαννά, εὐλογημένος ὁ ἐρχόμενος ἐν ὀνόματι κυρίου, Jn. 12:13. [23] That ἐρχόμενος (→ II, 670, 12 ff.) means the entering Messianic King is underlined by the reference to ὁ βασιλεὺς τοῦ Ἰσραήλ (→ I, 578, 5 ff.).

3. As a liturgical cry ὡσαννά was already used quite early in the worship of the Chr. community. At the beginning of the celebration of the Lord's Supper [24] acc. to Did., 10, 6 the sentences were spoken: ἐλθέτω χάρις καὶ παρελθέτω ὁ κόσμος οὗτος. Ὡσαννὰ τῷ θεῷ Δαυίδ. [25] εἴ τις ἅγιός ἐστιν, ἐρχέσθω· εἴ τις οὐκ ἔστι, μετανοείτω· μαρὰν ἀθά· ἀμήν. The ὡσαννά with which Christ is hailed as the coming Lord is not taken from one of the Gospels but from liturgical tradition, which came into the Chr. community from Judaism. [26] The eschatological character which the hosanna shares with μαρὰν ἀθά is brought out by the legend about the end of James, the Lord's brother, in Hegesipp. When James had pointed to Jesus, who is throned at the right hand of the great power in heaven and who will come on the clouds of heaven, many interrupted his witness with the joyful shout of praise: ὡσαννὰ τῷ υἱῷ Δαυίδ, Eus. Hist. Eccl., II, 23, 13 f. In the Gk. speaking Church, however, the original meaning of the Hbr. cry was no longer known, so that Cl. Al. sought to explain the term as follows: φῶς καὶ δόξα καὶ αἶνος μεθ᾽ ἱκετηρίας τῷ κυρίῳ· τουτὶ γὰρ ἐμφαίνει ἑρμηνευόμενον Ἑλλάδι φωνῇ τὸ ὡσαννά, Paed., I, 5, 12, 5. [27]

Lohse

ὠτάριον → V, 559, 1 ff.
ὠτίον → V, 558, 11 ff.

---

[21] Dalman WJ, I, 180-2 rightly sees that ὡσαννά in Mt. 21:9-15 means "praise," "salvation," since the ensuing dat. demands this interpretation. But he wrongly infers from the double ὡσαννὰ τῷ υἱῷ Δαυίδ in Mt. that the author of Mt. was "no Hebraist." The hosanna must have already changed from a cry for help to one of jubilation in pre-chr. Judaism → 682, 17 ff. As against Dalman cf. Werner, 101 f.; Jeremias, *op. cit.* (→ n. 9) 258 f.

[22] Cf. Bornkamm, *op. cit.* (→ n. 20), 31.

[23] There is no intentional quotation in Jn. 12:13, either from the OT or from a catena. Cf. B. Noack, *Zur joh. Tradition* (1954), 87.

[24] Cf. G. Bornkamm, "Das Anathema in d. urchr. Abendmahlsliturgie," *Das Ende d. Gesetzes*⁵ (1966), 123-132; Jeremias, *op. cit.* (→ n. 12), 245.

[25] The text is uncertain here; the Cpt. version reads τῷ οἴκῳ Δαυίδ; the reading in Const. Ap., VII, 16, 5: τῷ υἱῷ Δαυίδ, seems to be a correction acc. to Mt. 21:9. Cf. H. Köster, "Synpt. Überlieferung bei d. Apost. Vät.," TU, 65 (1957), 197.

[26] Cf. Köster, *op. cit.* (→ n. 25), 198, *ad loc.*, cf. also J. P. Audet, "La Didachè," *Étud. Bibl.* (1958), 420-422; Sandvik, 50: "In the eucharist the community prays for the *parousia* but also in the hosanna cry pays homage to Christ as the Lord who is present."

[27] Cf. Werner, 111, who in his study adduces other examples of the liturgical use of ὡσαννά. Cf. also E. Werner, *The Sacred Bridge. The Interdependence of Liturgy and Music in Synagogue and Church during the First Millennium* (1959), Index, *s.v.* "Hosanna."